ABC Thumb Index

With the help of the ABC Thumb Index at the edge of this page you can quickly find the letter you are looking for in the German-English or English-German section of this dictionary.

You place your thumb on the letter you want at the edge of this page, then flick through the dictionary till you come to the appropriate pages in the German-English or English-German section.

Left-handed people should use the ABC Thumb Index at the end of the book.

A
B
C
D
E
F
G
H
I
J
K
L
M
N
O
P
Q
R
S
T
U
V
W
Z

W9-CUU-056

Langenscheidt

German – English
English – German
Dictionary

Edited by the
Langenscheidt Editorial Staff

BARNES
&NOBLE
BOOKS
NEW YORK

© *2003 by Langenscheidt KG, Berlin and Munich*

This edition published by Barnes & Noble, Inc.
by arrangement with Langenscheidt Publishers Inc.

ISBN: 0-7607-4844-6

Printed in Germany

MP 9 8 7 6 5 4 3

Preface

This German – English / English – German Dictionary has been completely revised and updated.

The characteristic, and most important, feature of this dictionary is its particular lexical range. When selecting words and phrases which go beyond a broad, general vocabulary, the editors focused their attention on the fields of business, trade and travel, and of course gave due consideration to politics, technology and cultural affairs. The following examples will also make clear the specific aim of this dictionary series: *asylum seeker, backpacker, consumer protection, data protection, double taxation, emission-free, hole in the ozone layer, technology transfer, wheel clamp*; *schadstofffrei, Technologietransfer, Verbraucherschutz*. It is, then, the aim to give practical and useful help to as many people as possible when they communicate with each other in the twenty-first century.

Designed for the widest possible variety of uses, this dictionary, with its more than 50,000 references and 100,000 translations, will be of great value to students, teachers, and tourists as well as in home and office libraries.

Contents

Guide for the User 5

  German and English headwords 5

  Spelling... 6

  The different typefaces and their functions........... 7

  Pronunciation 8

  The tilde.. 11

  List of abbreviations 12

  Translations and phraseology 14

  Grammatical references 15

German-English Dictionary...................... 21

English-German Dictionary........................ 343

Appendix 647

States of Germany and Austria and the Cantons of
  Switzerland 648

German and European Currency...................... 649

Numerals 650

German Weights and Measures 652

Conversion Tables for Temperatures.................... 654

Clinical Thermometer 655

Alphabetical List of the German Irregular Verbs 656

Alphabetical List of the English Irregular Verbs 658

Examples of German Declension and Conjugation....... 660

Proper Names 667

German Abbreviations 671

Guide for the User

This dictionary endeavors to do everything it can to help you find the words and translations you are looking for as quickly and as easily as possible.

To enable you to get the most out of your dictionary, you will be shown exactly where and how to find the information that will help you choose the right translation in every situation – whether at school or at home, in your profession, when writing letters, or in everyday conversation.

1. German and English headwords

1.1 When you are looking for a particular word it is important to know that the dictionary entries are arranged in strict **alphabetical order:**

    Aal – ab
    beugen – biegen
    hay – haze

In the German-English section the umlauts *ä ö ü* are treated as *a o u. ß* is treated as *ss.*

1.2 Besides the headwords and their derivatives and compounds, the past tense and past participle of irregular German verbs are also given as individual entries in alphabetical order in the German-English section, e.g. **ging, gegangen.**

1.3 Many German and English proper names and abbreviations are included in the vocabulary.

1.4 How then do you go about finding a particular word? Take a look at the words in bold print at the top of each page. These are the so-called **catchwords** and they serve as a guide to tracing your word as quickly as possible. The catchword on the top left gives you the first headword on the left-hand page, while the one on the top right gives you the last word on the right-hand page, e.g.

Gesundheit – Glanz

1.5 What about entries comprising hyphenated expressions or two or more words, such as **D-Zug, left-handed** or **mass media?** Expressions of this kind are treated in the same way as single words and thus appear in strict alphabetical order. Should you be unable to find a compound in the dictionary, just break it down into its components and look these up separately. In this way the meaning of many compound expressions can be derived indirectly.

When using the dictionary you will notice many 'word families', or groups of words stemming from a common root, which have been collated within one article in order to save space:

> Einkaufs... – ~bummel – ~preis – ~wagen – ~zentrum
> amend – amendment – amends

2. Spelling

2.1 Where American and British spelling of a word differs, the American spelling is given first as in

> center, *Br* **centre**
> center (*Br* **centre**) **forward**
> dialog, *Br* **dialogue**
> analy|ze, *Br* **-se** etc.

or in the English-German section as a separate headword, e.g. **theater, defense** etc.

A 'u' or an 'l' in parentheses in a word also indicates variant spellings:

> colo(u)red means: American **colored**, British **coloured**
> travel(l)er means: American **traveler**, British **traveller**

2.2 Word division in a German word is possible after each syllable, e.g.

> ein-hül-len, Zu-cker, ba-cken, tes-ten

In the English-German section the centered dots within a headword indicate syllabification breaks.

3. The different typefaces and their functions

3.1 Bold type is used for the German and English headwords and for Arabic numerals separating different parts of speech (nouns, transitive and intransitive verbs, adjectives and adverbs etc.) and different grammatical forms of a word:

> **bieten 1.** *v/t* ... **2.** *v/i* ...
> **hängen 1.** *v/i* (*irr, ge-, h*) hang (***an*** *dat* on...); **2.** *v/t* (*ge-, h*) hang (***an*** *acc* on)
> **feed 1.** Futter *n* ; ... **2.** *v/t* füttern

3.2 *Italics* are used for

a) grammatical and other abbreviations: *v/t, v/i, adj, adv, appr, fig* etc.
b) gender labels (masculine, feminine and neuter): *m, f, n*
c) grammatical references in brackets in the German-English section
d) any additional information preceding or following a translation (including dative or accusative objects):

> **knacken** *v/t and v/i* ... *twig:* snap; *fire, radio:* crackle
> **Etikett** *n* ... label (*a. fig*)
> **Gedanke** *m* (*-n; -n*) ...
> **geben** (*irr, ge-, h*) ...
> **befolgen** ... follow, take (*advice*); observe (*rule etc*)
> **file** ... *Briefe etc* ablegen
> **labored** schwerfällig (*style etc*); mühsam (*breathing etc*)

3.3 *Boldface italics* are used for phraseology etc., notes on German grammar and prepositions taken by the headword:

> **Lage** *f* ... ***in der ~ sein zu*** *inf* be able to *inf*
> **BLZ** ... ABBR *of **Bankleitzahl***
> **abheben** (*irr, **heben***, *sep, -ge-, h*)
> **abfahren** ... (*irr, **fahren***, *sep, -ge-, sein*) leave, depart (*both:* ***nach*** for)
> **line** ... ***hold the ~*** TEL bleiben Sie am Apparat
> **agree** ... sich einigen (***on*** über *acc*)

3.4 Normal type is used for translations of the headwords.

4. Pronunciation

When you have found the headword you are looking for in the German-English section, you will notice that very often this word is followed by certain symbols enclosed in square brackets. This is the phonetic transcription of the word, which tells you how it is pronounced. And one phonetic alphabet has come to be used internationally, namely that of the International Phonetic Association. This phonetic system is known by the abbreviation **IPA.** The symbols used in this dictionary are listed in the following tables on page 9 and 10.

4.1 The length of vowels is indicated by [ː] following the vowel symbol.

4.1.1 Stress is indicated by ['] or [ˌ] preceding the stressed syllable. ['] stands for strong stress, [ˌ] for weak stress:

Kabel ['kaːbəl] – **Kabine** [ka'biːnə]
'nachsehen – Be'sitz – be'sprechen
Jus'tizminis,terium – Mi'nisterpräsi,dent

4.1.2 The glottal stop [ʔ] is the forced stop between one word or syllable and a following one beginning with a vowel, as in

Analphabet [anʔalfa'beːt]
beeindrucken [bəʔ'ʔaindrʊkən]

4.2 No transcription of compounds is given if the parts appear as separate entries. Each individual part should be looked up, as with

'Blumenbeet (= **Blume** and **Beet**)

4.2.1 If only part of the pronunciation changes or if a compound word consists of a new component, only the pronunciation of the changed or new part is given:

Demonstrant [demɔn'strant]
Demonstration [-straˈtsjoːn]
'Kinderhort [-hɔrt]

4.3 Guide to pronunciation for the German-English section

A. Vowels

[a] as in French *carte*: **Mann** [man]

[aː] as in *father*: **Wagen** ['vaːgən]

[e] as in *bed*: **Tenor** [te'noːɐ]

[eː] resembles the first sound in English [eɪ]: **Weg** [veːk]

[ə] unstressed e as in *ago*: **Bitte** ['bɪtə]

[ɛ] as in *fair*: **männlich** ['mɛnlɪç], **Geld** [gɛlt]

[ɛː] same sound but long: **zählen** ['tsɛːlən]

[ɪ] as in *it*: **Wind** [vɪnt]

[i] short, otherwise like [iː]: **Kapital** [kapi'taːl]

[iː] long, as in *meet*: **Vieh** [fiː]

[ɔ] as in *long*: **Ort** [ɔrt]

[o] as in *molest*: **Moral** [moˈraːl]

[oː] resembles the English sound in *go* [ɡəʊ] but without the [ʊ]: **Boot** [boːt]

[øː] as in French *feu*. The sound may be acquired by saying [e] through closely rounded lips: **schön** [ʃøːn]

[ø] same sound but short: **ökumenisch** [økuˈmeːnɪʃ]

[œ] as in French *neuf*. The sound resembles the English vowel in *her*. Lips, however, must be well rounded as for [ɒ]: **öffnen** ['œfnən]

[ʊ] as in *book*: **Mutter** ['mʊtɐ]

[u] short, otherwise like [uː]: **Musik** [muˈziːk]

[uː] long, as in *boot*: **Uhr** [uːɐ]

[ʏ] short, opener than [yː]: **Hütte** ['hʏtɐ]

[y] almost like the French u as in *sur*. It may be acquired by saying [ɪ] through fairly closely rounded lips: **Büro** [byˈroː]

[yː] same sound but long: **führen** ['fyːrən]

B. Diphthongs

[aɪ] as in *like*: **Mai** [maɪ]

[aʊ] as in *mouse*: **Maus** [maʊs]

[ɔʏ] as in *boy*: **Beute** ['bɔʏtɐ], **Läufer** ['lɔʏfɐ]

C. Consonants

[b] as in *better*: **besser** ['bɛsɐ]

[d] as in *dance*: **du** [duː]

[f] as in *find*: **finden** ['fɪndən], **Vater** ['faːtɐ], **Philosoph** [filoˈzoːf]

[g] as in *gold*: **Gold** [gɔlt]

[ʒ] as in *measure*: **Genie** [ʒeˈniː]

[h] as in *house* but not aspirated: **Haus** [haʊs]

[ç] an approximation to this sound may be acquired by assuming the mouth-configuration for [ɪ] and emitting a strong current of breath: **Licht** [lɪçt], **Mönch** [mœnç], **lustig** ['lʊstɪç]

[x] as in Scottish *loch*, Whereas [ç] is pronounced at the front of the mouth, [x] is pronounced in the throat: **Loch** [lɔx]

[j] as in *year*: **ja** [jaː]

[k] as in *kick*: **keck** [kɛk], **Tag** [taːk], **Chronik** ['kroːnɪk], **Café** [kaˈfeː]

[l] as in *lump*. Pronounced like English initial "clear l": **lassen** ['lasən]

[m] as in *mouse*: **Maus** [maʊs]

[n] as in *not*: **nein** [naɪn]

[ŋ] as in *sing, drink*: **singen** ['zɪŋən], **trinken** ['trɪŋkən]

[p] as in *pass*: **Pass** [pas], **Trieb** [triːp], **obgleich** [ɔpˈglaɪç]

[r] as in *rot*. There are two pronunciations: the frontal or lingual r: **rot** [roːt] and the uvular r [ʁ] (unknown in the

English language): **Mauer** ['mauɐ]

[s] as in *miss*. Unvoiced when final, doubled, or next a voiceless consonant: **Glas** [glaːs], **Masse** ['masə], **Mast** [mast], **nass** [nas]

[z] as in *zero*. S voiced when initial in a word or syllable: **Sohn** [zoːn], **Rose** ['roːzə]

[ʃ] as in *ship*: **Schiff** [ʃif], **Charme**

[ʃarm], **Spiel** [ʃpiːl], **Stein** [ʃtain]

[t] as in *tea*: **Tee** [teː], **Thron** [troːn], **Stadt** [ʃtat], **Bad** [baːt], **Findling** ['fintliŋ], **Wind** [vint]

[v] as in *vast*: **Vase** ['vaːze], **Winter** ['vintɐ]

[ã, ɛ̃, õ] are nasalized vowels. Examples: **Ensemble** [ã'sãːbəl], **Terrain** [tɛ'rɛ̃ː], **Bonbon** [bõ'bõː]

4.3.1 Phonetic changes in plurals

singular		plural		example
-g	[-k]	-ge	[-gə]	Flug – Flüge
-d	[-t]	-de	[-də]	Grund – Gründe, Abend – Abende
-b	[-p]	-be	[-bə]	Stab – Stäbe
-s	[-s]	-se	[-zə]	Los – Lose
-ch	[-x]	-che	[-çə]	Bach – Bäche
-iv	[-iːf]	-ive	[-iːvə]	Stativ – Stative

4.3.2 The German alphabet

a [aː], b [beː], c [tseː], d [deː], e [eː], f [ɛf], g [geː], h [haː], i [iː], j [jɔt], k [kaː], l [ɛl], m [ɛm], n [ɛn], o [oː], p [peː], q [kuː], r [ɛr], s [ɛs], t [teː], u [uː], v [fau], w [veː], x [iks], y ['ypsilɔn], z [tsɛt]

4.3.3 List of suffixes

The German suffixes are not transcribed unless they are parts of headwords.

-bar	[-baːɐ]	-isch	[-iʃ]
-chen	[-çən]	-ist	[-ist]
-d	[-t]	-keit	[-kait]
-de	[-də]	-lich	[-liç]
-ei	[-ai]	-ling	[-liŋ]
-en	[-ən]	-losigkeit	[-loːziçkait]
-end	[-ənt]	-nis	[-nis]
-er	[-ɐ]	-sal	[-zaːl]
-haft	[-haft]	-sam	[-zaːm]
-heit	[-hait]	-schaft	[-ʃaft]
-icht	[-içt]	-sieren	[-ziːrən]
-ie	[-iː]	-ste	[-stə]
-ieren	[-iːrən]	-tät	[-tɛːt]
-ig	[-iç]	-tum	[-tuːm]
-ik	[-ik]	-ung	[-uŋ]
-in	[-in]	-ungs-	[-uŋs-]
		-wärts	[-vɛrts]

5. The tilde (~)

5.1 A symbol you will repeatedly come across in the dictionary articles is the so-called tilde (~), which serves as a replacement mark. For reasons of space, related words are often combined in groups with the help of the tilde. In these cases, the tilde represents either the complete headword or that part of the word up to a vertical line (|):

> Ski ... ~fahrer(in) (= *Skifahrer, Skifahrerin*)
> Ess|löffel ... ~stäbchen (= *Essstäbchen*)
> jet ... ~ engine (= *jet engine*)
> natural| resources ... ~ science (= *natural science*)

5.2 In the case of the phrases in boldface italics, the tilde represents the headword immediately preceding, which itself may also have been formed with the help of a tilde:

> kommen ... *zu spät ~* (= *kommen*)
> ange|bracht ... ~gossen ... *wie ~* (= *angegossen*) *sitzen*
> foreign ... ~ (= *foreign*) *affairs*
> break ... *take a ~* (= *break*)

6. Abbreviations of grammatical terms and subject areas are designed to help the user choose the appropriate headword or translation of a word.

In the dictionary words which are predominantly used in British English are marked by the abbreviation *Br*:

> **Bürgersteig** *m* sidewalk, *Br* pavement
> **girl guide** *Br* Pfadfinderin *f*

12

List of abbreviations

a.	*also*, auch	GASTR	*gastronomy*, Kochkunst
ABBR	*abbreviation*, Abkürzung	*gen*	*genitive (case)*, Genitiv
acc	*accusative (case)*, Akkusativ	GEOGR	*geography*, Geografie
adj	*adjective*, Adjektiv	GEOL	*geology*, Geologie
adv	*adverb*, Adverb	*ger*	*gerund*, Gerundium
AGR	*agriculture*, Landwirtschaft	GR	*grammar*, Grammatik
Am	*American English*, amerikanisches Englisch		
		h	*haben*, have
ANAT	*anatomy*, Anatomie	HIST	*history*, Geschichte
appr	*approximately*, etwa	HUMOR	*humorous*, humorvoll
ARCH	*architecture*, Architektur		
art	*article*, Artikel	*impers*	*impersonal*, unpersönlich
ASTR	*astrology*, Astrologie; *astronomy*, Astronomie	*indef*	*indefinite*, unbestimmt
		inf	*infinitive (mood)*, Infinitiv
attr	*attributively*, attributiv	*int*	*interjection*, Interjektion
AVIAT	*aviation*, Luftfahrt	*interr*	*interrogative*, fragend
		irr	*irregular*, unregelmäßig
BIOL	*biology*, Biologie		
BOT	*botany*, Botanik	*j-m*	*jemandem, to someone*
Br	*British English*, britisches Englisch	*j-n*	*jemanden, someone*
		j-s	*jemandes, someone's*
		JUR	*jurisprudence*, Recht
CHEM	*chemistry*, Chemie		
cj	*conjunction*, Konjunktion	LING	*linguistics*, Sprachwissenschaft
coll	*collectively*, als Sammelwort	LIT	*literary*, nur in der Schriftsprache vorkommend
comp	*comparative*, Komparativ		
contp	*contemptuously*, verächtlich	*m*	*masculine*, männlich
cpds	*compounds*, Zusammensetzungen	MAR	*maritime term*, Schifffahrt
		MATH	*mathematics*, Mathematik
dat	*dative (case)*, Dativ	*m-e*	*my*, meine
		MED	*medicine*, Medizin
ECON	*economy*, Wirtschaft	METEOR	*meteorology*, Meteorologie
EDP	*electronic data processing*, Elektronische Datenverarbeitung	MIL	*military term*, militärisch
		MOT	*motoring*, Kraftfahrwesen
		m-r	*meiner, of my, to my*
e-e	*a(n)*, eine	*mst*	*mostly, usually*, meistens
e.g.	*for example*, zum Beispiel	MUS	*music*, Musik
ELECTR	*electrical engineering*, Elektrotechnik		
		n	*neuter*, sächlich
e-m	*einem, to a(n)*	*neg!*	*negative, usually considered offensive*, kann als beleidigend empfunden werden
e-n	*einen, a(n)*		
e-r	*einer, of a(n), to a(n)*		
e-s	*eines, of a(n)*	*nom*	*nominative (case)*, Nominativ
esp.	*especially*, besonders	*num*	*numeral*, Zahlwort
et., et.	*etwas, something*		
etc	*et cetera, and so on*, usw., und so weiter	OPT	*optics*, Optik
		o.s., *o.s.*	*oneself*, sich
F	*colloquial*, umgangssprachlich	PAINT	*painting*, Malerei
f	*feminine*, weiblich	PARL	*parliamentary term*, parlamentarischer Ausdruck
fig	*figuratively*, übertragen		

pass	*passive voice*, Passiv		SPORT	*sports*, Sport
PED	*pedagogy*, Schulwesen		*s-r*	*seiner*, of his, of one's, to his, to one's
pers	*personal*, persönlich			
PHARM	*pharmacy*, Pharmazie		*s-s*	*seines*, of his, of one's
PHIL	*philosophy*, Philosophie		s.th., *s.th.*	*something*, etwas
PHOT	*photography*, Fotografie		*su*	*substantive*, Substantiv
PHYS	*physics*, Physik		*subj*	*subjunctive (mood)*, Konjunktiv
pl	*plural*, Plural			
POET	*poetry*, Dichtung		*sup*	*superlative*, Superlativ
POL	*politics*, Politik			
poss	*possessive*, besitzanzeigend		TECH	*technology*, Technik
POST	*post and telecommunications*, Postwesen		TEL	*telegraphy*, Telegrafie; *telephony*, Fernsprechwesen
pp	*past participle*, Partizip Perfekt		THEA	*theater*, Theater
pred	*predicative*, prädikativ		TV	*television*, Fernsehen
pres	*present*, Präsens			
pres p	*present participle*, Partizip Präsens		u., *u.*	*und*, and
			UNIV	*university*, Hochschulwesen, Studentensprache
pret	*preterit(e)*, Präteritum			
PRINT	*printing*, Druckwesen		V	*vulgar*, vulgär, unanständig
pron	*pronoun*, Pronomen		*v/aux*	*auxiliary verb*, Hilfsverb
prp	*preposition*, Präposition		*vb*	*verb*, Verb
PSYCH	*psychology*, Psychologie		VET	*veterinary medicine*, Veterinärmedizin, Tiermedizin
RAIL	*railroad*, *railway*, Eisenbahn		*v/i*	*intransitive verb*, intransitives Verb
refl	*reflexive*, reflexiv			
REL	*religion*, Religion		*v/refl*	*reflexive verb*, reflexives Verb
RHET	*rhetoric*, Rhetorik		*v/t*	*transitive verb*, transitives Verb
s-e	*seine*, his, one's		ZO	*zoology*, Zoologie
sep	*separable*, abtrennbar			
sg	*singular*, Singular		→	*see*, *refer to*, siehe
sl	*slang*, Slang			
s-m	*seinem*, to his, to one's		®	*registered trademark*, eingetragenes Markenzeichen
s-n	*seinen*, his, one's			
s.o., *s.o.*	*someone*, jemand(en)			

7. Translations and phraseology

After the boldface headword in the German-English section, the phonetic transcription of this word, its part of speech label, and its grammar, we finally come to the most important part of the entry: **the translation(s).**

7.1 It is quite rare for a headword to be given just one translation. Usually a word will have several related translations, which are separated by a **comma.**

7.2 Different senses of a word are indicated by

a) **semicolons:**

> **Fest** ... celebration; party; REL festival
> **balance** ... Waage *f*; Gleichgewicht *n*

b) italics for **definitions:**

> **Läufer** ... runner (*a . carpet*); *chess*: bishop
> **call** ... Berufung *f* (**to** in *ein Amt*; auf *einen Lehrstuhl*)
> **cake** ... Tafel *f Schokolade*, Stück *n Seife*

c) **abbreviations** of subject areas:

> **Bug** *m* ... MAR bow; AVIAT nose
> **Gespräch** *n* talk (*a.* POL); ... TEL call
> **daisy** BOT Gänseblümchen *n*
> **duck** ... ZO Ente *f*

7.2.1 Where a word has fundamentally different meanings, it very often appears as two or more separate entries distinguished by **exponents** or raised figures:

> **betreten**[1] *v/t* ... step on; enter
> **betreten**[2] *adj* embarrassed
> **Bauer**[1] *m* ... farmer
> **Bauer**[2] *n, m* ... (bird)cage
> **chap**[1] ... Riss *m*
> **chap**[2] ... *Br* F Bursche *m*

This does not apply to senses which have directly evolved from the primary meaning of the word.

7.3 When a headword can be several different parts of speech, these are distinguished by boldface **Arabic numerals** (see also the section on p.7, paragraph 3.1 concerning the different typefaces):

geräuschlos	1. *adj* noiseless (*adjective*) 2. without a sound (*adverb*)
work	1. Arbeit *f* (*noun*) 2. *v/i* arbeiten (*verb*)
green	1. grün (*adjective*) 2. Grün *n* (*noun*)

7.3.1 In the German-English section boldface Arabic numerals are also used to distinguish between transitive, intransitive and reflexive verbs (if this affects their translation) and to show that where there is a change of meaning a verb may be differently conjugated:

> fahren (*irr, ge-*) **1.** *v/i* (*sein*) go; *bus etc*: run; ... **2.** *v/t* (*h*) drive (*car etc*) ...

If grammatical indications come before the subdivision they refer to all translations that follow:

> bauen (*ge-, h*) **1.** *v/t* build ...; **2.** *fig v/i*: ~ *auf* ...

7.3.2 Boldface Arabic numerals are also used to indicate the different meanings of nouns which can occur in more than one gender and to show that where there is a change of meaning a noun may be differently inflected:

> Halfter **1.** *m, n* (*-s; -*) halter; **2.** *n* (*-s; -*), *f* (*-; -n*) holster

7.4 Illustrative phrases in boldface italics are generally given within the respective categories of the dictionary article:

> baden **1.** *v/i* ... ~ *gehen* go swimming; **2.** *v/t* ...
> good **1.** ... *real* ~ F echt gut (= *adjective*); **2.** ... *for* ~ für immer (= *noun*)

8. Grammatical references

Knowing what to do with the grammatical information available in the dictionary will enable the user to get the most out of this dictionary.

8.1 verbs (see the list of irregular German verbs on page 656).

Verbs have been treated in the following ways:

a) **bändigen** *v/t* (*ge-, h*)

The past participle of this word is formed by means of the prefix *ge-* and the auxiliary verb *haben*: **er hat gebändigt.**

16

b) **abfassen** *v/t (sep, -ge-, h)*

In conjugation the prefix *ab* must be separated from the primary verb *fassen*: **sie fasst ab; sie hat abgefasst.**

c) **finden** *v/t (irr, ge-, h)*

irr following a verb means that it is an irregular verb. The principal parts of this particular word can be found as an individual headword in the main part of the German-English section and in the list of irregular German verbs on page 656: **sie fand; sie hat gefunden.**

d) **abfallen** *v/i (irr, **fallen**, sep, -ge-, sein)*

A reference such as *irr, **fallen*** indicates that the compound word ***abfallen*** is conjugated in exactly the same way as the primary verb ***fallen*** as given in the list of irregular German verbs on page 656: **er fiel ab; er ist abgefallen.**

e) **senden** *v/t ([irr,] ge-, h)*

The square brackets indicate that ***senden*** can be treated as a regular or an irregular verb: **sie sandte** or **sie sendete; sie hat gesandt** or **sie hat gesendet.**

8.2 nouns

The inflectional forms (*genitive singular; nominative plural*) follow immediately after the indication of gender. No forms are given for compounds if the parts appear as separate headwords.

The horizontal stroke replaces the part of the word which remains unchanged in the inflection:

> Affäre *f (-; -n)*
> Keks *m, n (-es; -e)*
> Bau *m (-[e]s; Bauten)*
> Blatt *n (-[e]s; Blätter ['blɛtə])*

The inflectional forms of German nouns ending in **-in** are given in the following ways:

> Ärztin *f (-; -nen)*
> Chemiker(in) *(-s; -/-; -nen)* = **Chemiker** *m (-s; -)* and **Chemikerin** *f (-; -nen)*

8.3 Prepositions

If, for instance, a headword (verb, adjective or noun) is governed by certain prepositions, these are given in boldface italics and in brackets together with their English or German translations and placed next to the appropriate translation. If the German or English preposition is the same for all or several translations, it is given only once before or after the first translation and then also applies to the translations which follow it:

> abrücken ... **1.** *v/t* (*h*) move away (***von*** from)
> befestigen *v/t* (*no -ge-*, *h*) fasten (***an*** *dat* to), fix (to), attach (to)
> dissent ... **2.** anderer Meinung sein (***from*** als)
> dissimilar (***to***) unähnlich (*dat*); verschieden (von)

With German prepositions which can take the dative or the accusative, the case is given in brackets:

> fürchten ... **sich ~** ... be afraid (***vor*** *dat* of)
> bauen ... **~ auf** (*acc*) rely *or* count on

We hope that this somewhat lengthy introduction has shown you that this dictionary contains a great deal more than simple one-to-one translations, and that you are now well-equipped to make the most of all it has to offer.

PART I

GERMAN-ENGLISH
DICTIONARY

A

à [a] *prp* **5 Karten ~ DM 20** 5 tickets at 20 marks each *or* a piece

Aal [aːl] *m* (-[e]s; -e) ZO eel

aalen ['aːlən] *v/refl* (ge-, h) **sich in der Sonne ~** bask in the sun

'aal·glatt *fig adj* (as) slippery as an eel

Aas [aːs] *n* (-[e]s) a) *no pl* carrion, b) F *contp pl* **Äser** beast, *sl* bastard

'Aasgeier *m* ZO vulture (*a. fig*)

ab [ap] *prp and adv:* **München ~ 13.55** departure from Munich (at) 1.55; **~ 7 Uhr** from 7 o'clock (on); **~ morgen (1. März)** starting tomorrow (March 1st); **von jetzt ~** from now on; **~ und zu** now and then; **ein Film ~ 18** an X(-rated) film; **ein Knopf ist ~** a button has come off

'abarbeiten *v/t* (sep, -ge-, h) work out *or* off (*debts*); **sich ~** wear o.s. out

Abart ['apˀaːrt] *f* (-; -en) variety

abartig ['apˀaːrtɪç] *adj* abnormal

Abb. ABBR *of* **Abbildung** fig., illustration

'Abbau *m* (-[e]s; *no pl*) mining; TECH dismantling; *fig* overcoming (*of prejudices etc*); reduction (*of expenditure, staff etc*); **'abbauen** *v/t* (sep, -ge-, h) mine; TECH dismantle; *fig* overcome (*prejudices etc*); reduce (*expenditure, staff etc*); **sich ~** BIOL break down

'abbeißen *v/t* (irr, **beißen**, sep, -ge-, h) bite off

'abbeizen *v/t* (sep, -ge-, h) remove *old paint etc* with corrosives

'abbekommen *v/t* (irr, **kommen**, sep, *no -ge-*, h) get off; **s-n Teil** *or* **et. ~** get one's share; **et. ~** *fig* get hurt, get damaged

'abberufen *v/t* (irr, **rufen**, sep, *no -ge-*, h), **'Abberufung** *f* recall

'abbestellen *v/t* (sep, *no -ge-*, h) cancel one's subscription (*or* order) for

'Abbestellung *f* cancellation

'abbiegen *v/i* (irr, **biegen**, sep, -ge-, sein) turn (off); **nach rechts (links) ~** turn right (left)

'abbilden *v/t* (sep, -ge-, h) show, depict

'Abbildung *f* (-; -en) picture, illustration

'Abbitte *f* apology; **j-m ~ leisten wegen** apologize to s.o. for

'abblasen F *v/t* (irr, **blasen**, sep, -ge-, h) call off, cancel

'abblättern *v/i* (sep, -ge-, sein) *paint etc:* flake off

'abblenden 1. *v/t* (sep, -ge-, h) dim; **2.** *v/i* MOT dim (*Br* dip) the headlights

'Abblendlicht *n* MOT dimmed (*Br* dipped) headlights *pl*, low beam

'abbrechen *v/t* (irr, **brechen**, sep, -ge-) **1.** *v/t* (h) break off (*a. fig*); pull down, demolish (*building etc*); strike (*camp, tent*); **2.** *v/i* a) (sein) break off, b) (h) *fig* stop; **'abbremsen** *v/t* (sep, -ge-, h) slow down; **'abbrennen** *v/t* (irr, **brennen**, sep, -ge-) **1.** *v/i* (sein) burn down; **2.** *v/t* (h) burn down (*building etc*); let *or* set off (*fireworks*); **'abbringen** *v/t* (irr, **bringen**, sep, -ge-, h) **j-n von e-r Sache ~** talk s.o. out of (doing) s.th.; **j-n vom Thema ~** get s.o. off a subject

'Abbruch *m* (-[e]s; *no pl*) breaking off; demolition; **'abbruchreif** *adj* derelict, due for demolition

'abbuchen *v/t* (sep, -ge-, h) debit (**von** to); **'Abbuchung** *f* debit

'abbürsten *v/t* (sep, -ge-, h) brush off (*dust etc*); brush (*coat etc*)

Abc [aːbeˈtseː] *n* (-; *no pl*) ABC, alphabet; **ABC-Waffen** *pl* MIL nuclear, biological and chemical weapons

'abdanken *v/i* (sep, -ge-, h) resign; *king etc:* abdicate; **'Abdankung** *f* (-; -en) resignation; abdication

'abdecken *v/t* (sep, -ge-, h) uncover; untile (*roof*); unroof (*house*); clear (*the table*); ECON cover (up)

'abdichten *v/t* (sep, -ge-, h) TECH seal

'abdrängen *v/t* (sep, -ge-, h) push aside

'abdrehen 1. *v/t* (sep, -ge-, h) turn *or* switch off (*light, water etc*); **2.** *v/i* (*a.* sein) ship, plane: change one's course

'Abdruck *m* print, mark

'abdrucken *v/t* (sep, -ge-, h) print

'abdrücken (sep, -ge-, h) **1.** *v/t* fire (*gun*); **2.** *v/i* pull the trigger

Abend ['aːbənt] *m* (-s; -e) evening; **am ~** in the evening, at night; **heute ~** tonight; **morgen (gestern) ~** tomorrow (last) night; → **bunt, essen**; **~brot** *n* (-[e]s; *no pl*), **~essen** *n* supper, dinner,

Br a. high tea; **~kasse** *f* THEA *etc* box office; **~kleid** *n* evening dress *or* gown; **~kurs** *m* evening classes *pl*

'**Abendland** *n* (-[e]s; *no pl*) West, Occident; **abendländisch** ['a:bəntlɛndɪʃ] *adj* Western, Occidental

'**Abendmahl** *n* (-[e]s; *no pl*) the (Holy) Communion, *the* Lord's Supper; **das ~ empfangen** receive Communion

abends ['a:bənts] *adv* in the evening, at night; **dienstags ~** (on) Tuesday evenings

'**Abendschule** *f* evening classes *pl*, night school

Abenteuer ['a:bəntɔɪɐ] *n* (-s; -) adventure (*a. in cpds* ...**ferien**, ...**spielplatz**); '**abenteuerlich** *adj* adventurous; *fig* risky; fantastic

Abenteurer ['a:bəntɔɪrɐ] *m* (-s; -) adventurer; **Abenteurerin** [~rərɪn] *f* (-; -nen) adventuress

aber ['a:bɐ] *cj and adv* but; **oder ~** or else; **~, ~!** now then!; **~ nein!** not at all!

'**Aberglaube** *m* superstition

abergläubisch ['a:bɐglɔɪbɪʃ] *adj* superstitious

'**aberkennen** *v/t* (*irr,* **kennen**, *sep, no -ge-, h*) **j-m et. ~** deprive s.o. of s.th. (*a.* JUR); '**Aberkennung** *f* (-; -en) deprivation (*a.* JUR)

abermalig ['a:bɐma:lɪç] *adj* repeated

abermals ['a:bɐma:ls] *adv* once more *or* again

aber'tausend *adj:* **tausende und ~e** thousands upon thousands

'**abfahren** (*irr,* **fahren**, *sep, -ge-*) **1.** *v/i* (*sein*) leave, depart (*both:* **nach** for); F (*voll*) **~ auf** (*acc*) really go for; **2.** *v/t* (*h*) carry *or* cart away

'**Abfahrt** *f* departure (**nach** for), start (for); *skiing:* descent

'**Abfahrts|lauf** *m* downhill skiing (*or* race); **~zeit** *f* (time of) departure

'**Abfall** *m* waste, refuse, garbage, trash, *Br a.* rubbish; **~beseitigung** *f* waste disposal; **~eimer** *m* → **Mülleimer**

'**abfallen** *v/i* (*irr,* **fallen**, *sep, -ge-, sein*) fall (off); *terrain:* slope (down); *fig* fall away (**von** from); *esp* POL secede (from); **vom Glauben ~** renounce one's faith; **~ gegen** compare badly with

'**abfällig 1.** *adj* derogatory; **2.** *adv:* **~ von**

j-m sprechen run s.o. down

'**Abfallpro|dukt** *n* waste product

'**abfälschen** *v/t* (*sep, -ge-, h*) SPORT deflect; '**abfangen** *v/t* (*irr,* **fangen**, *sep, -ge-, h*) catch, intercept; MOT, AVIAT right; '**abfärben** *v/i* (*sep, -ge-, h*) color *etc:* run, *material: a.* bleed; *fig* **~ auf** (*acc*) rub off on; '**abfassen** *v/t* (*sep, -ge-, h*) compose, word, write

'**abfertigen** *v/t* (*sep, -ge-, h*) dispatch; *customs:* clear; serve (*customers*); check in (*passengers etc*); **j-n kurz ~** be short with s.o.; '**Abfertigung** *f* dispatch; clearance; check-in

'**abfeuern** *v/t* (*sep, -ge-, h*) fire (off); launch (*rocket*)

'**abfinden** *v/t* (*irr,* **finden**, *sep, -ge-, h*) ECON pay off (*creditor*); buy out (*partner*); compensate; **sich mit e-r Sache ~** put up with s.th.; '**Abfindung** *f* (-; -en) ECON satisfaction; compensation

'**abflachen** *v/t and v/refl* (*sep, -ge-, h*) flatten; '**abflauen** *v/i* (*sep, -ge-, sein*) *wind etc:* drop (*a. fig*); '**abfliegen** *v/i* (*irr,* **fliegen**, *sep, -ge-, sein*) AVIAT leave, depart; '**abfließen** *v/i* (*irr,* **fließen**, *sep, -ge-, sein*) flow off, drain (off *or* away)

'**Abflug** *m* AVIAT departure

'**Abfluss** *m* (-es; *Abflüsse*) *a) no pl* flowing off, b) TECH drain

'**Abflussrohr** *n* wastepipe, drain(pipe)

'**abfragen** *v/t* (*sep, -ge-, h*) quiz *or* question *s.o.* (**über** *acc* about), test s.o. orally

Abfuhr ['apfu:ɐ] *f* (-; -en) removal; **j-m e-e ~ erteilen** rebuff (F SPORT lick) s.o.

'**abführen** (*sep, -ge-, h*) **1.** *v/t* lead *or* take away; ECON pay (over) (**an** *acc* to); **2.** *v/i* MED move one's bowels; act as a laxative; '**abführend** *adj*, '**Abführmittel** *n* MED laxative

'**abfüllen** *v/t* (*sep, -ge-, h*) bottle; can

'**Abgabe** *f* (-; -*n*) *a) no pl* handing in, b) SPORT pass, c) ECON rate; duty

'**abgabenfrei** *adj* tax-free

'**abgabenpflichtig** *adj* dutiable

'**Abgang** *m* (-[e]s; *Abgänge*) *a) no pl* departure; *Am* graduation; *Br* school-leaving; THEA exit (*a. fig*), b) SPORT dismount; **Abgänger** ['apgɛŋɐ] *m* (-s; -) *Am* graduate, *Br* school-leaver

'**Abgas** *n* waste gas; *pl* emission(s *pl*); MOT exhaust fumes *pl*

'**abgasfrei** *adj* emission-free

'**Abgasuntersuchung** f MOT *Am* emissions test, *Br* exhaust emission test
'**abgearbeitet** *adj* worn out
'**abgeben** v/t (*irr*, **geben**, *sep*, *-ge-*, *h*) leave (**bei** with); hand in; deposit (*one's baggage etc*); hand over (*ticket etc*) (*an acc* to); cast (*vote*); pass (*ball*); give off, emit (*heat etc*); make (*offer*, *statement etc*); *j-m et.* ~ share s.th. with s.o.; *sich* ~ *mit* concern o.s. with *s.th.*, associate with *s.o.*
'**abge**|**brannt** *adj* burnt down; F *fig* broke; ~**brüht** *fig adj* hard-boiled; ~**droschen** *adj* hackneyed; ~**fahren** *adj* tires: worn out; ~**griffen** *adj* worn; ~**hackt** *fig adj* disjointed; ~**hangen** *adj*: **gut** ~**es Fleisch** well-hung meat; ~**härtet** *adj* hardened (**gegen** to)
'**abgehen** v/i (*irr*, **gehen**, *sep*, *-ge-*, *sein*) train etc: leave; *mail*, *goods*: get off; THEA go off (stage); *button etc*: come off; *path etc*: branch off; **von der Schule** ~ leave school; ~ **von** drop (*plan etc*); **von s-r Meinung** ~ change one's mind or opinion; **ihm geht ... ab** he lacks ...; **gut** ~ end well, pass off well
'**abge**|**hetzt** *adj*, ~**kämpft** *adj* exhausted, worn out; ~**kartet** ['apgəkartət] F *adj*: ~**e Sache** put-up job; ~**legen** *adj* remote, distant; ~**macht** *adj* fixed; ~! it's a deal!; ~**magert** *adj* emaciated; ~**neigt** *adj*: ~**e-r Sache** ~ **sein** be averse to s.th.; **ich wäre nicht** ~, **et. zu tun** I wouldn't mind doing s.th.; ~**nutzt** *adj* worn out
Abgeordnete ['apgəˀɔrdnətə] m, f (*-n*; *-n*) *Am* representative, congress|man (-woman), *Br* Member of Parliament (ABBR MP); '**Abgeordnetenhaus** n *Am* House of Representatives, *Br* House of Commons
'**abgepackt** *adj* prepack(ag)ed
'**abgeschieden** *adj* secluded
'**Abgeschiedenheit** f (*-*; *no pl*) seclusion
'**abge**|**schlossen** *adj* completed; ~**e Wohnung** self-contained apartment (*Br* flat); ~**sehen** *adj*: ~ **von** aside (*Br a.* apart) from; **ganz** ~ **von** not to mention, let alone; ~**spannt** *adj* exhausted, weary; ~**standen** *adj* stale; ~**storben** *adj* dead (*tree etc*); numb (*leg etc*); ~**stumpft** *adj* insensitive, indifferent (**gegen** to); ~**tragen**, ~**wetzt** *adj* worn out; threadbare, shabby

'**abgewöhnen** v/t (*sep*, *-ge-*, *h*) *j-m et.* ~ make s.o. give up s.th.; *sich* (*dat*) **das Rauchen** ~ stop or give up smoking
'**Abgott** m idol (*a. fig*); **abgöttisch** ['apgœtɪʃ] *adv*: *j-n* ~ **lieben** idolize s.o.
'**abgrasen** v/t (*sep*, *-ge-*, *h*) graze; *fig* scour
'**abgrenzen** v/t (*sep*, *-ge-*, *h*) mark off; delimit (**gegen** from)
'**Abgrund** m abyss, chasm, gulf (*all a. fig*); **am Rande des** ~**s** *fig* on the brink of disaster; '**abgrund'tief** *adj* abysmal
'**abgucken** F v/t (*sep*, *-ge-*, *h*) *j-m et.* ~ learn s.th. from (watching) s.o.; → **abschreiben**
'**Abguss** m cast
'**abhaben** F v/t (*irr*, **haben**, *sep*, *-ge-*, *h*) **willst du et.** ~? do you want some (of it)? '**abhacken** v/t (*sep*, *-ge-*, *h*) chop or cut off; '**abhaken** v/t (*sep*, *-ge-*, *h*) check (*Br* tick) off; F forget; '**abhalten** v/t (*irr*, **halten**, *sep*, *-ge-*, *h*) hold (*meeting etc*); *j-n von der Arbeit* ~ keep s.o. from his work; *j-n davon* ~, *et. zu tun* keep s.o. from doing s.th.
'**abhandeln** v/t (*sep*, *-ge-*, *h*) treat (*subject etc*); *j-m et.* ~ make a deal with s.o. for s.th.; '**Abhandlung** f treatise (**über** *acc* on)
'**Abhang** m slope
'**abhängen**[1] v/t (*sep*, *-ge-*, *h*) take down (*picture etc*); RAIL *etc* uncouple; F shake s.o. off
'**abhängen**[2] v/i (*irr*, **hängen**, *sep*, *-ge-*, *h*) ~ **von** depend on; **das hängt davon ab** that depends
abhängig ['aphɛŋɪç] *adj*: ~ **von** dependent on; *a.* addicted to *drugs etc*
'**Abhängigkeit** f (*-*; *-en*) dependence (**von** on); addiction (to)
'**abhärten** v/t (*sep*, *-ge-*, *h*) *sich* ~ harden o.s. (**gegen** to)
'**abhauen** (*irr*, **hauen**, *sep*, *-ge-*) **1.** v/t (*h*) cut or chop off; **2.** F v/i (*sein*) make off (**mit** with), run away (with); **hau ab!** beat it!, scram!
'**abheben** (*irr*, **heben**, *sep*, *-ge-*, *h*) **1.** v/t lift or take off; pick up (*receiver*); (with)draw (*money*); cut (*cards*); *sich* ~ stand out (**von** among, from), *fig a.* contrast with; **2.** v/i cut the cards; answer the phone; *plane*: take (*esp rocket*: lift) off
'**abheften** v/t (*sep*, *-ge-*, *h*) file

'abheilen v/i (sep, -ge-, sein) heal (up)

'abhetzen v/refl (sep, -ge-, h) wear o.s. out

'Abhilfe f remedy; ~ schaffen take remedial measures

'Abholdienst m pickup service

'abholen v/t (sep, -ge-, h) pick up, collect; j-n von der Bahn ~ meet s.o. at the station; 'abholzen v/t (sep, -ge-, h) fell, cut down (trees); deforest (area); 'abhorchen v/t (sep, -ge-, h) MED auscultate, sound; 'abhören v/t (sep, -ge-, h) listen in on, tap (telephone conversation), F bug; → abfragen

'Abhörgerät n bugging device, F bug

Abitur [abi'tuːɐ] n (-s; -e) school-leaving examination (qualifying for university entrance)

'abjagen v/t (sep, -ge-, h) j-m et. ~ recover s.th. from s.o.; 'abkanzeln F v/t (sep, -ge-, h) tell s.o. off; 'abkaufen v/t (sep, -ge-, h) j-m et. ~ buy s.th. from s.o.

Abkehr ['apkeːɐ] f (-; no pl) break (von with); 'abkehren v/refl (sep, -ge-, h) sich ~ von turn away from

'abklingen v/i (irr, klingen, sep, -ge-, sein) fade away; pain etc: ease off

'abklopfen v/t (sep, -ge-, h) MED sound

'abknallen F v/t (sep, -ge-, h) pick off

'abknicken v/t (sep, -ge-, h) snap or break off; bend

'abkochen v/t (sep, -ge-, h) boil

'abkomman,dieren v/t (sep, no -ge-, h) MIL detach (zu for)

'abkommen v/i (irr, kommen, sep, -ge-, sein) ~ von get off; drop (plan etc); vom Thema ~ stray from the point; → Weg

'Abkommen n (-s; -) agreement, treaty; ein ~ schließen make an agreement

Abkömmling ['apkœmlɪŋ] m (-s; -e) descendant

'abkoppeln v/t (sep, -ge-, h) uncouple (von from); undock (spacecraft)

'abkratzen (sep, -ge-) 1. v/i h scrape off; 2. F v/i (sein) kick the bucket

'abkühlen v/t and v/refl (sep, -ge-, h) cool down (a. fig)

'Abkühlung f cooling

'abkürzen v/t (sep, -ge-, h) shorten; abbreviate; den Weg ~ take a short cut

'Abkürzung f abbreviation; short cut

'abladen v/t (irr, laden, sep, -ge-, h) unload; dump (waste etc)

'Ablage f (-; -n) a) no pl filing, b) filing tray, c) Swiss → Zweigstelle

'ablagern (sep, -ge-, h) 1. v/t season (wood); let wine age; GEOL etc deposit; sich ~ settle, be deposited; 2. v/i (a. sein) season; age; 'Ablagerung f (-; -en) CHEM, GEOL deposit, sediment

'ablassen (irr, lassen, sep, -ge-, h) 1. v/t drain off (liquid); let off (steam); drain (pond etc); 2. v/i: von et. (j-m) ~ stop doing s.th. (leave s.o. alone)

'Ablauf m (-[e]s; Abläufe) a) course; process; order of events, b) no pl expiration, Br expiry, c) → Abfluss

'ablaufen (irr, laufen, sep, -ge-) 1. v/i (sein) water etc: run off; performance etc: go, proceed; come to an end; period, passport etc: expire; time, record, tape: run out; clock: run down; gut ~ turn out well; 2. v/t (h) wear down

'ablecken v/t (sep, -ge-, h) lick (off)

'ablegen (sep, -ge-, h) 1. v/t take off (clothes); file (letters etc); give up (habit etc); take (examination, oath); abgelegte Kleider cast-offs pl; 2. v/i take off one's (hat and coat); MAR put out, sail

'Ableger m (-s; -) BOT layer; offshoot (a. fig)

'ablehnen v/t (sep, -ge-, h) refuse; turn down (application etc); PARL reject; object to; condemn; ~d adj negative

'Ablehnung f (-; -en) refusal; rejection; objection (gen to)

'ableiten v/t (sep, -ge-, h) divert; LING, MATH derive (aus dat, von from) (a. fig)

'Ableitung f diversion; LING, MATH derivation (a. fig)

'ablenken v/t (sep, -ge-, h) divert (von from); soccer: turn away (ball); deflect (rays etc); j-n von der Arbeit ~ distract s.o. from his work; er lässt sich leicht ~ he is easily diverted

'Ablenkung f diversion

'ablesen v/t (irr, lesen, sep, -ge-, h) read

'abliefern v/t (sep, -ge-, h) deliver (bei to, at); hand over (to)

'ablösbar adj detachable; 'ablösen v/t (sep, -ge-, h) detach; take off; take s.o.'s place, relieve; replace; esp MIL relieve; replace; sich ~ take turns (driving etc); 'Ablösesumme f SPORT transfer fee; 'Ablösung f relief

'abmachen v/t (sep, -ge-, h) remove,

take off; settle, arrange

'**Abmachung** f (-; -en) arrangement, agreement, deal

'**abmagern** v/i (sep, -ge-, sein) get thin

'**Abmagerung** f (-; -en) emaciation

'**Abmagerungskur** f slimming diet

'**abmähen** v/t (sep, -ge-, h) mow

'**abmalen** v/t (sep, -ge-, h) copy

'**Abmarsch** m (-[e]s; no pl) start; MIL marching off; '**abmar,schieren** v/i (sep, no -ge-, sein) start; MIL march off

'**abmelden** v/t (sep, -ge-, h) cancel the registration of (car etc); cancel s.o.'s membership (in a club etc); give notice of s.o.'s withdrawal (from school); **sich ~** give notice of change of address; report off duty; '**Abmeldung** f notice of withdrawal; notice of change of address

'**abmessen** v/t (irr, **messen**, sep, -ge-, h) measure; '**Abmessung** f measurement; pl dimensions

'**abmon,tieren** v/t (sep, no -ge-, h) take off; take down; TECH dismantle

'**abmühen** v/refl (sep, -ge-, h) work very hard; try hard (to do s.th.); struggle (**mit** with)

'**abnagen** v/t (sep, -ge-, h) gnaw (at)

Abnahme ['apna:mə] f (-; -n) reduction, decrease; loss (a. of weight); ECON purchase; TECH acceptance

'**abnehmbar** adj removable

'**abnehmen** (irr, **nehmen**, sep, -ge-, h) **1.** v/t take off (a. MED), remove; pick up (receiver); TECH accept; ECON buy; **j-m et. ~** take s.th. (away) from s.o.; **2.** v/i decrease, diminish; lose weight; answer the phone; moon: wane

'**Abnehmer** m (-s; -) buyer; customer

'**Abneigung** f (**gegen**) dislike (of, for); aversion (to)

abnorm [ap'nɔrm] adj abnormal; exceptional, unusual; **Abnormität** [apnɔrmi'tɛːt] f (-; -en) abnormality

'**abnutzen**, '**abnützen** v/t and v/refl (sep, -ge-, h) wear out

'**Abnutzung**, '**Abnützung** f (-; no pl) wear (and tear) (a. fig)

Abonnement [abɔnə'mãː] n (-s; -s) subscription (**auf** acc to); **Abonnent** [abɔ'nɛnt] m (-en; -en) subscriber; THEA season-ticket holder; **abonnieren** [abɔ'niːrən] v/t (no -ge-, h) subscribe to

Abordnung f (-; -en) delegation

Abort [a'bɔrt] m (-[e]s; -e) lavatory, toilet

'**abpassen** v/t (sep, -ge-, h) watch or wait for (s.o., s.th.); waylay s.o. (a. fig)

'**abpfeifen** v/t and v/i (irr, **pfeifen**, sep, -ge-, h) SPORT blow the final whistle; stop the game

'**abplagen** v/refl (sep, -ge-, h) struggle (**mit** with)

'**abprallen** v/i (sep, -ge-, sein) rebound, bounce (off); bullet: ricochet

'**abputzen** v/t (sep, -ge-, h) wipe off; clean

'**abraten** v/i (irr, **raten**, sep, -ge-, h) **j-m ~ von** advise or warn s.o. against

'**abräumen** v/t (sep, -ge-, h) clear away; clear (the table)

'**abrea,gieren** v/t (sep, no -ge-, h) work off (one's anger etc) (**an** dat on); **sich ~** F let off steam

'**abrechnen** (sep, -ge-, h) **1.** v/t deduct, subtract; claim (expenses); **2.** v/i: **mit j-m ~** settle accounts (fig a. get even) with s.o.; '**Abrechnung** f settlement; F fig showdown

'**abreiben** v/t (irr, **reiben**, sep, -ge-, h) rub off; rub down (body); polish

Abreise f departure (**nach** for)

'**abreisen** v/i (sep, -ge-, sein) depart, leave, start, set out (all: **nach** for)

'**abreißen** (irr, **reißen**, sep, -ge-) **1.** v/t (h) tear or pull off; pull down (building); **2.** v/i (sein) break; button etc: come off

'**Abreißka,lender** m tear-off calendar

'**abrichten** v/t (sep, -ge-, h) train (animal), a. break a horse in

'**abriegeln** v/t (sep, -ge-, h) block off, cordon off

'**Abriss** m (-es; -e) a) (no pl) demolition, b) outline, summary

'**abrollen** v/i (sep, -ge-, sein) and v/t (h) unroll (a. fig)

'**abrücken** (sep, -ge-) **1.** v/t (h) move away (**von** from); **2.** v/i (sein) draw away (**von** from); MIL march off

'**Abruf** m: **auf ~** ECON on call

'**abrufen** v/t (irr, **rufen**, sep, -ge-, h) call away; EDP recall, fetch, retrieve

'**abrunden** v/t (sep, -ge-, h) round (off)

'**abrupfen** v/t (sep, -ge-, h) pluck (off)

abrupt [ap'rʊpt] adj abrupt

'**abrüsten** v/i (sep, -ge-, h) MIL disarm

'**Abrüstung** f (-; no pl) MIL disarmament

'abrutschen v/i (sep, -ge-, sein) slide down; slip (off) (**von** from)

ABS [a:be:'ɛs] → **Antiblockiersystem**

Absage ['apza:gə] f (-; -n) refusal; cancellation; '**absagen** (sep, -ge-, h) **1.** v/t call off, cancel (event etc); **2.** v/i call off; **j-m ~** a. cancel one's appointment with s.o.; decline (the invitation)

'absägen v/t (sep, -ge-, h) saw off; F fig oust, sack s.o.

'absahnen F v/i (sep, -ge-, h) cash in

'Absatz m paragraph; ECON sales pl; shoe: heel; stairs: landing

'abschaben v/t (sep, -ge-, h) scrape off

'abschaffen v/t (sep, -ge-, h) do away with, abolish; repeal (law); put an end to (abuses etc); '**Abschaffung** f (-; no pl) abolition; repeal

'abschalten (sep, -ge-, h) **1.** v/t switch or turn off; **2.** F v/i relax, switch off

'abschätzen v/t (sep, -ge-, h) estimate; assess; size up; **abschätzig** ['apʃɛtsɪç] adj contemptuous; derogatory

Abschaum m (-s; no pl) scum (a. fig)

'Abscheu m (-s; no pl) disgust (**vor, gegen** at, for); **e-n ~ haben vor** abhor, detest; '**abscheuerregend** adj revolting, repulsive

ab'scheulich adj abominable, despicable (a. person), a. atrocious (crime)

'abschicken v/t (sep, -ge-, h) → **absenden**

'abschieben fig v/t (irr, **schieben**, sep, -ge-, h) push away; get rid of; deport; **et. auf j-n ~** shove s.th. off on (to) s.o.

Abschied ['apʃi:t] m (-[e]s; -e) parting, farewell; **~ nehmen (von)** say goodbye (to), take leave (of); **s-n ~ nehmen** resign, retire

'Abschiedsfeier f farewell party

'Abschiedskuss m goodbye kiss

'abschießen v/t (irr, **schießen**, sep, -ge-, h) shoot off (AVIAT down); launch (rocket); shoot, kill (deer); F pick s.o. off; fig oust; get rid of s.o.

'abschirmen v/t (sep, -ge-, h) shield (**gegen** from); fig protect (**gegen** against, from); '**Abschirmung** f (-; -en) shield, screen; fig protection

'abschlachten v/t (sep, -ge-, h) slaughter (a. fig)

'Abschlag m SPORT kickout; ECON down payment; '**abschlagen** v/t (irr,

schlagen, sep, -ge-, h) knock off; cut off (head); cut down (tree); refuse (request etc), turn s.th. down

'abschleifen v/t (irr, **schleifen**, sep, -ge-, h) grind off (sand)(paper), smooth

'Abschleppdienst m MOT emergency road (Br breakdown) service

'abschleppen v/t (sep, -ge-, h) MOT (give s.o. a) tow; police: tow away

'Abschlepp|seil n towrope; **~wagen** m Am tow truck, Br breakdown lorry

'abschließen (irr, **schließen**, sep, -ge-, h) **1.** v/t lock (up); close, finish; complete; take out (insurance); conclude (research etc); **e-n Handel ~** strike a bargain; **sich ~** shut o.s. off; → **Wette**; **2.** v/i close, finish; **~d 1.** adj concluding; final; **2.** adv: **~ sagte er** he concluded by saying

'Abschluss m conclusion, close; **~prüfung** f final examination, finals pl, esp Am a. graduation; **s-e ~ machen** graduate (an dat from); **~zeugnis** n Am diploma, Br school-leaving certificate

'abschmecken v/t (sep, -ge-, h) season

'abschmieren v/t (sep, -ge-, h) TECH lubricate, grease

'abschminken v/t (sep, -ge-, h) **sich ~** remove one's make-up

'abschnallen v/t (sep, -ge-, h) undo; take off (skis); **sich ~** MOT, AVIAT unfasten one's seat belt

'abschneiden (irr, **schneiden**, sep, -ge-, h) **1.** v/t cut off (a. fig); **j-m das Wort ~** cut s.o. short; **2.** v/i: **gut ~** come off well

'Abschnitt m passage, section (of book etc); paragraph; MATH, BIOL segment; period (of time), stage (of journey), phase (of development); coupon, slip, stub (of check etc)

'abschnittweise adv section by section

'abschrauben v/t (sep, -ge-, h) unscrew

'abschrecken v/t (sep, -ge-, h) deter (**von** from); GASTR douse eggs etc with cold water; **~d** adj deterrent; **~es Beispiel** warning example

'Abschreckung f (-; -en) deterrence

'abschreiben v/t (irr, **schreiben**, sep, -ge-, h) copy; PED crib; ECON write off (a. F fig); '**Abschrift** f copy, duplicate

'abschürfen v/t (sep, -ge-, h) graze

'**Abschürfung** f (-; -en) abrasion
Abschuss m launch(ing) (of rocket); AVIAT shooting down, downing; kill; **~basis** f MIL launching base
abschüssig ['apʃʏsɪç] adj sloping; steep
'**Abschussliste** F f: **auf der ~ stehen** be on the hit list
'**Abschussrampe** f MIL launching pad
'**abschütteln** v/t (sep, -ge-, h) shake off
'**abschwächen** v/t (sep, -ge-, h) lessen, diminish
'**abschweifen** fig v/i (sep, -ge-, sein) digress (**von** from)
'**Abschweifung** f (-; -en) digression
absehbar ['apzeːbaːɐ] adj foreseeable; **in ~er (auf ~e) Zeit** in the (for the) foreseeable future
'**absehen** v/t (irr, sehen, sep, -ge-, h) foresee; **es ist kein Ende abzusehen** there is no end in sight; **es abgesehen haben auf** (acc) be after; **~ von** refrain from
'**abseilen** v/refl (sep, -ge-, h) descend by a rope, Br a. abseil; F make a getaway
abseits ['apzaɪts] adv and prp away or remote from; **~ stehen** soccer: be off-side; fig be left out
'**Abseitsfalle** f soccer: offside trap
'**absenden** v/t (irr, senden, sep, -ge-, h) send (off), dispatch; mail, esp Br post (letter etc)
'**Absender** m (-s; -) sender
absetzbar ['apzɛtsbaːɐ] adj: **steuerlich ~** deductible from tax
'**absetzen** (sep, -ge-, h) **1.** v/t take off (hat, glasses etc); set or put down (bag etc); drop (passenger); dismiss (employee); THEA, film: take off; deduct (from tax); depose (king etc); ECON sell; **sich ~** CHEM, GEOL settle, be deposited; **2.** v/i: **ohne abzusetzen** without stopping
'**Absetzung** f (-; -en) dismissal; deposition; THEA, film: withdrawal
'**Absicht** f (-; -en) intention; **mit ~** on purpose; '**absichtlich 1.** adj intentional; **2.** adv on purpose
'**absitzen** (irr, sitzen, sep, -ge-) **1.** v/i (sein) dismount (**von** from); **2.** v/t (h) serve (sentence); F sit out (play etc)
absolut [apzoˈluːt] adj absolute
Absolvent [apzɔlˈvɛnt] m (-en; -en), **Absol'ventin** f (-; -nen) graduate; **absolvieren** [apzɔlˈviːrən] v/t (no -ge-, h)

attend (school); complete (studies); graduate from (college etc)
'**absondern** v/t (sep, -ge-, h) separate; MED, BIOL secrete; **sich ~** cut o.s. off (**von** from); '**Absonderung** f (-; -en) separation; MED, BIOL secretion
absorbieren [apzɔrˈbiːrən] v/t (no -ge-, h) absorb (a. fig)
'**abspeichern** v/t (sep, -ge-, h) EDP store, save
abspenstig ['apʃpɛnstɪç] adj: **j-m die Freundin ~ machen** steal s.o.'s girl-friend
absperren v/t (sep, -ge-, h) lock; turn off (water, gas etc); block off (road); cor-don off; '**Absperrung** f (-; -en) barrier; cordon
'**abspielen** v/t (sep, -ge-, h) play (record etc); SPORT pass (the ball); **sich ~** happen, take place
'**Absprache** f agreement
'**absprechen** v/t (irr, sprechen, sep, -ge-, h) agree upon; arrange; **j-m die Fähigkeit** etc **~** dispute s.o.'s ability etc
'**abspringen** v/i (irr, springen, sep, -ge-, sein) jump off; AVIAT jump, bail out; fig back out (**von** of)
'**Absprung** m jump; SPORT take-off; fig **den ~ schaffen** make it
'**abspülen** v/t (sep, -ge-, h) rinse; wash up
'**abstammen** v/i (sep, no past participle) be descended (**von** from); CHEM, LING derive; '**Abstammung** f (-; no pl) descent; derivation; '**Abstammungslehre** f theory of the origin of species
'**Abstand** m distance (a. fig); interval; **~ halten** keep one's distance; fig **mit ~** by far
abstatten ['apʃtatən] v/t (sep, -ge-, h) **j-m e-n Besuch ~** pay a visit to s.o.
'**abstauben** v/t (sep, -ge-, h) dust; F fig sponge; swipe
'**Abstauber** F m (-s; -), '**Abstaubertor** n SPORT opportunist goal
'**abstechen** (irr, stechen, sep, -ge-, h) **1.** v/t stick (pig etc); **2.** v/i contrast (**von** with); '**Abstecher** m (-s; -) side-trip, excursion (a. fig)
'**abstecken** v/t (sep, -ge-, h) mark out
'**abstehen** v/i (irr, stehen, sep, -ge-, h) stick out, protrude; → **abgestanden**
'**absteigen** v/i (irr, steigen, sep, -ge-, sein) get off (a horse etc); climb down;

'stay (**in** dat at); SPORT Am be moved down to a lower division, Br be relegated; '**Absteiger** m (-s; -) SPORT Br relegated club

'**abstellen** v/t (sep, -ge-, h) put down; leave (s.th. with s.o.); turn off (gas etc); park (car); fig put an end to s.th.

'**Abstellgleis** n RAIL siding; **j-n aufs ~ schieben** F push s.o. aside

'**Abstellraum** m storeroom

'**abstempeln** v/t (sep, -ge-, h) stamp

'**absterben** v/i (irr, **sterben**, sep, -ge-, sein) die off; limb: go numb

Abstieg ['apʃtiːk] m (-[e]s; -e) descent; fig decline; SPORT Br relegation

'**abstimmen** v/i (sep, -ge-, h) vote (**über** acc on)

'**Abstimmung** f vote; radio: tuning

Abstinenzler [apsti'nɛntslɐ] m (-s; -) teetotal(l)er

'**Abstoß** m SPORT goal-kick

'**abstoßen** v/t (irr, **stoßen**, sep, -ge-, h) repel; MED reject; push off (boat); F get rid of s.th.; **~d** fig adj repulsive

abstrakt [ap'strakt] adj abstract

'**abstreiten** v/t (irr, **streiten**, sep, -ge-, h) deny

'**Abstrich** m MED smear; pl ECON cuts; fig reservations

'**abstufen** v/t (sep, -ge-, h) graduate; gradate (colors)

'**abstumpfen** (sep, -ge-) 1. v/t (h) blunt, dull (a. fig); 2. fig v/i (sein) become unfeeling

'**Absturz** m, '**abstürzen** v/i (sep, -ge-, sein) fall; AVIAT, EDP crash

'**absuchen** v/t (sep, -ge-, h) search (**nach** for)

absurd [ap'zʊrt] adj absurd, preposterous

Abszess [aps'tsɛs] m (-es; -e) MED abscess

Abt [apt] m (-[e]s; Äbte ['ɛptə]) REL abbot

'**abtasten** v/t (sep, -ge-, h) feel (for); MED palpate; frisk; TECH, EDP scan

'**abtauen** v/t (sep, -ge-, h) defrost

Abtei [ap'taɪ] f (-; -en) REL abbey

Abteil [ap'taɪl] n (-[e]s; -e) RAIL compartment

'**abteilen** v/t (sep, -ge-, h) divide; ARCH partition off

Ab'teilung f (-; -en) department (a. ECON); ward (of hospital); MIL detach-

ment; **Ab'teilungsleiter** m head of (a) department; Am floorwalker, Br shopwalker

Äbtissin [ɛp'tɪsɪn] f (-; -nen) REL abbess

'**abtöten** v/t (sep, -ge-, h) kill (bacteria etc); fig deaden (feelings etc)

'**abtragen** v/t (irr, **tragen**, sep, -ge-, h) wear out (clothes); clear away (dishes etc); pay off (debt)

'**Abtrans,port** m transportation

'**abtreiben** (irr, **treiben**, sep, -ge-) 1. v/i MED (h) have an abortion; MAR, AVIAT (sein) be blown off course; 2. v/t (h) MED abort; '**Abtreibung** f (-; -en) abortion; **e-e ~ vornehmen** perform an abortion

'**abtrennen** v/t (sep, -ge-, h) detach; separate; MED sever

'**abtreten** (irr, **treten**, sep, -ge-) 1. v/t (h) wear down (heels); wipe (one's feet); fig give up (**an** acc to); 2. v/i (sein) resign; THEA; exit; '**Abtreter** m (-s; -) doormat

'**abtrocknen** (sep, -ge-, h) 1. v/t/i dry; **sich ~** dry o.s. off; 2. v/i dry the dishes, Br a. dry up

abtrünnig ['aptrʏnɪç] adj unfaithful, disloyal; '**Abtrünnige** [-nɪgə] m, f (-n; -n) renegade, turncoat

abtun v/t (irr, **tun**, sep, -ge-, h) dismiss (**als** as), brush s.o., s.th. aside

abwägen ['apvɛːgən] v/t (irr, **wägen**, sep, -ge-, h) weigh (**gegen** against)

'**abwählen** v/t (sep, -ge-, h) vote out

'**abwälzen** v/t (sep, -ge-, h) **et. auf j-n ~** shove s.th. off on (to) s.o.

'**abwandeln** v/t (sep, -ge-, h) vary, modify

'**abwandern** v/i (sep, -ge-, sein) migrate (**von** from; **nach** to); '**Abwanderung** f migration

'**Abwandlung** f modification, variation

'**Abwärme** f TECH waste heat

Abwart ['apvart] m (-s; -e) Swiss → **Hausmeister**

'**abwarten** (sep, -ge-, h) 1. v/t wait for, await; 2. v/i wait; **warten wir ab!** let's wait and see!; **wart nur ab!** just wait!

abwärts ['apvɛrts] adv down, downward(s)

Abwasch ['apvaʃ] m (-[e]s; no pl) **den ~ machen** do the washing-up

'**abwaschbar** adj washable

'**abwaschen** (irr, **waschen**, sep, -ge-, h)

1. *v/t* wash off; **2.** *v/i* do the dishes, *Br a.* wash up

'**Abwaschwasser** *n* dishwater

'**Abwasser** *n* TECH waste water, sewage; **~aufbereitung** *f* TECH sewage treatment

'**abwechseln** *v/i* (*sep*, *-ge-*, *h*) alternate; **sich mit j-m ~** take turns (**bei et.** at [doing] s.th.); **~d** *adv* by turns

'**Abwechslung** *f* (*-; -en*) change; **zur ~** for a change; '**abwechslungsreich** *adj* varied; colo(u)rful

'**Abweg** *m*: **auf ~e geraten** go astray

abwegig ['apveːgɪç] *adj* absurd, unrealistic

'**Abwehr** *f* (*-; no pl*) defen|se, *Br* -ce (*a.* SPORT); warding off (*of blow etc*); save (*of ball*)

'**abwehren** *v/t* (*sep*, *-ge-*, *h*) ward off (*blow etc*); beat off; SPORT block

'**Abwehr|fehler** *m* SPORT defensive error; **~kräfte** *pl* MED resistance; **~spieler** *m* SPORT defender; **~stoffe** *pl* MED antibodies

'**abweichen** *v/i* (*irr*, **weichen**, *sep*, *-ge-*, *sein*) deviate (**von** from); digress

'**Abweichung** *f* (*-; -en*) deviation

'**abweisen** *v/t* (*irr*, **weisen**, *sep*, *-ge-*, *h*) turn away; rebuff; decline, turn down (*request*, *offer etc*); **~d** *adj* unfriendly

'**abwenden** *v/t* ([*irr*, **wenden**,] *sep*, *-ge-*, *h*) turn away (*a.* **sich ~**) (**von** from); avert (*tragedy etc*)

'**abwerfen** *v/t* (*irr*, **werfen**, *sep*, *-ge-*, *h*) throw off; AVIAT drop; BOT shed (*leaves*); ECON yield (*profit*)

'**abwerten** *v/t* (*sep*, *-ge-*, *h*) ECON devalue; **~d** *fig adj* disparaging

'**Abwertung** *f* ECON devaluation

'**abwesend** *adj* absent

'**Abwesenheit** *f* (*-; no pl*) absence

abwickeln *v/t* (*sep*, *-ge-*, *h*) unwind; ECON handle; transact (*business*)

'**abwiegen** *v/t* (*irr*, **wiegen**, *sep*, *-ge-*, *h*) weigh (out)

'**abwischen** *v/t* (*sep*, *-ge-*, *h*) wipe (off)

'**Abwurf** *m* dropping; *soccer*: throw-out

'**abwürgen** F *v/t* (*sep*, *-ge-*, *h*) MOT stall; *fig* stifle; AVIAT drop

'**abzahlen** *v/t* (*sep*, *-ge-*, *h*) make *monthly etc* payments for; pay off; '**abzählen** *v/t* (*sep*, *-ge-*, *h*) count

'**Abzahlung** *f*: **et. auf ~ kaufen** *Am* buy s.th. on the instalment plan (*Br* on hire purchase)

'**abzapfen** *v/t* (*sep*, *-ge-*, *h*) tap, draw off

'**Abzeichen** *n* badge; medal

'**abzeichnen** *v/t* (*sep*, *-ge-*, *h*) copy, draw; sign, initial; **sich ~** (begin to) show; stand out (**gegen** against)

'**Abziehbild** *n* *Am* decal, *Br* transfer

'**abziehen** (*irr*, **ziehen**, *sep*, *-ge-*) **1.** *v/t* (*h*) take off, remove; MATH subtract; strip (*bed*); take out (*key*); **das Fell ~** skin; **2.** *v/i* (*sein*) go away; MIL withdraw; *smoke*: escape; *storm*, *clouds*: move off

'**Abzug** *m* ECON deduction; discount; MIL withdrawal; PRINT copy; PHOT print; *gun*: trigger; TECH vent, outlet; cooker hood

abzüglich ['aptsyːklɪç] *prp* less, minus

'**abzweigen** (*sep*, *-ge-*) **1.** *v/t* (*h*) divert (*resources etc*) (**für** to); **2.** *v/i* (*sein*) *path etc*: branch off

'**Abzweigung** *f* (*-; -en*) junction

ach [ax] *int* oh!; **~ je!** oh dear!; **~ so!** I see; **~ was!** *surprised*: really?, *annoyed*: of course not!, nonsense!

Achse ['aksə] *f* (*-; -n*) TECH axle; MATH *etc* axis; F **auf ~ sein** be on the move

Achsel ['aksəl] *f* (*-; -n*) ANAT shoulder; **die ~n zucken** shrug one's shoulders

'**Achselhöhle** *f* ANAT armpit

acht [axt] *adj* eight; **heute in ~ Tagen** a week from today, *esp Br* today week; (**heute**) **vor ~ Tagen** a week ago (today)

Acht *f*: **~ geben** be careful; pay attention (**auf** *acc* to); take care (**auf** *acc* of); **gib ~!** look *or* watch out!, be careful!; **außer ~ lassen** disregard; **sich in ~ nehmen** be careful, look *or* watch out (**vor** *dat* for)

achte ['axtə] *adj* eighth

'**achteckig** *adj* octagonal

Achtel ['axtəl] *n* (*-s; -*) eighth (part)

achten (*ge-*, *h*) **1.** *v/t* respect; **2.** *v/i*: **~ auf** (*acc*) pay attention to; keep an eye on; watch; be careful with; **darauf ~, dass** see to it that

ächten ['ɛçtən] *v/t* (*ge-*, *h*) ban; *esp* HIST outlaw

Achter ['axtɐ] *m* (*-s; -*) *rowing*: eight

'**Achterbahn** *f* roller coaster

'**achtfach** *adj and adv* eightfold

'**achtlos** *adj* careless, heedless

'**Achtung** *f* (*-; no pl*) respect (**vor** *dat* for); **~!** look out!; MIL attention!; **~!**

~! attention please!; ~! **Fertig! Los!** On your marks! Get set! Go!; ~ **Stufe!** *Am* caution: step!, *Br* mind the step!

'**achtzehn** *adj* eighteen

'**achtzehnte** *adj* eighteenth

achtzig ['axtsɪç] *adj* eighty; *die ~er Jah-re* the eighties; **~ste** *adj* eightieth

ächzen ['ɛçtsən] *v/i* (*ge-, h*) groan (*vor dat* with)

Acker ['akɐ] *m* (*-s; Äcker* ['ɛkɐ]) field; **~bau** *m* (*-[e]s; no pl*) agriculture; farming; ~ *und Viehzucht* crop and stock farming; **~land** *n* (*-[e]s; no pl*) farmland

'**ackern** *F v/i* (*ge-, h*) slog (away)

Adapter [a'daptɐ] *m* (*-s; -*) TECH adapter

addieren [a'di:rən] *v/t* (*no -ge-, h*) add (up); **Addition** [adi'tsio:n] *f* (*-; -en*) addition, adding up

Adel ['a:dəl] *m* (*-s; no pl*) aristocracy

'**adeln** *v/t* (*ge-, h*) ennoble (*a. fig*); *Br* knight

Ader ['a:dɐ] *f* (*-; -n*) ANAT blood vessel, vein

Adjektiv ['atjɛkti:f] *n* (*-s; -e*) LING adjective

Adler ['a:dlɐ] *m* (*-s; -*) ZO eagle

adlig ['a:dlɪç] *adj* noble; **Adlige** ['a:dlɪgə] *m, f* (*-n; -n*) noble|man (-woman)

Admiral [atmi'ra:l] *m* (*-s; -e*) MAR admiral

adoptieren [adɔp'ti:rən] *v/t* (*no -ge-, h*) adopt; **Adoptivkind** [adɔp'ti:f-] *n* adopted child

Adressbuch [a'drɛs-] *n* directory

Adresse [a'drɛsə] *f* (*-; -n*) address

adressieren [adrɛ'si:rən] *v/t* (*no -ge-, h*) address (*an acc* to)

Advent [at'vɛnt] *m* (*-[e]s; no pl*) REL Advent; Advent Sunday

Ad'ventszeit *f* Christmas season

Adverb [at'vɛrp] *n* (*-s; Adverbien* [at'vɛrbiən]) LING adverb

Aerobic [ɛ'ro:bɪk] *n* (*-s; no pl*) aerobics

Affäre [a'fɛ:rə] *f* (*-; -n*) affair

Affe [a'fə] *m* (*-n; -n*) ZO monkey; ape

Affekt [a'fɛkt] *m* (*-[e]s; -e*) im ~ in the heat of passion (*a. JUR*)

affektiert [afɛk'ti:rt] *adj* affected

Afrika ['a:frika] Africa; **Afrikaner** [afri'ka:nɐ] *m* (*-s; -*), **Afri'kanerin** [-nərɪn] *f* (*-; -nen*), **afri'kanisch** *adj* African

After ['aftɐ] *m* (*-s; -*) ANAT anus

AG ABBR *of Aktiengesellschaft Am* (stock) corporation, *Br* PLC, public limited company

Agent [a'gɛnt] *m* (*-en; -en*), **A'gentin** *f* (*-; -nen*) agent; POL (secret) agent

Agentur [agɛn'tu:ɐ] *f* (*-; -en*) agency

Aggression [agrɛ'sio:n] *f* (*-; -en*) aggression; **aggressiv** [agrɛ'si:f] *adj* aggressive; **Aggressivität** [agrɛsivi'tɛ:t] *f* (*-; no pl*) aggressiveness

Agitator [agi'ta:to:ɐ] *m* (*-s; -en* [-ta-'to:rən]) agitator

ah [a:] *int* ah!

äh [ɛ:] *int* er; *disgusted*: ugh!

aha [a'ha] *int* I see!, oh!

A'ha-Erlebnis *n* aha-experience

Ahn [a:n] *m* (*-[e]s; -en; -en*) ancestor, *pl a.* forefathers

ähneln ['ɛ:nəln] *v/i* (*ge-, h*) resemble, look like

ahnen ['a:nən] *v/t* (*ge-, h*) suspect; foresee, know

ähnlich ['ɛ:nlɪç] *adj* similar (*dat* to); *j-m ~ sehen* look like s.o.

'**Ähnlichkeit** *f* (*-; -en*) likeness, resemblance, similarity (*mit* to)

'**Ahnung** *f* (*-; -en*) presentiment, *a.* foreboding; notion, idea; *ich habe keine ~* I have no idea; '**ahnungslos** *adj* unsuspecting, innocent

Ahorn ['a:hɔrn] *m* (*-s; -e*) BOT maple

Ähre ['ɛ:rə] *f* (*-; -n*) BOT ear; spike

Aids [eɪdz] *n* (*-; no pl*) MED AIDS

'**Aids|-Kranke** *m, f* MED AIDS victim or sufferer; **~test** *m* MED AIDS test

Airbag ['ɛəbæg] *m* (*-s; -s*) MOT airbag

Akademie [akade'mi:] *f* (*-; -n*) academy, college; **Akademiker(in)** [aka'de:mikɐ (-kərɪn)] *(-s; -/-; -nen)* university graduate; **akademisch** [-'de:mɪʃ] *adj* academic

akklimatisieren [aklimati'zi:rən] *v/refl* (*no -ge-, h*) acclimatize (*an acc* to)

Akkord [a'kɔrt] *m* (*-[e]s; -e*) MUS chord; *im ~* ECON by the piece *or* job; **~arbeit** *f* ECON piecework; **~arbeiter(in)** ECON pieceworker

Akkordeon [a'kɔrdeɔn] *n* (*-s; -s*) MUS accordion

Ak'kordlohn *m* ECON piece wages

Akku ['aku] *F m* (*-s; -s*), **Akkumulator** [akumu'la:to:ɐ] *m* (*-s; -en* [-la'to:rən]) TECH (storage) battery, *Br a.* accumulator

Akkusativ ['akuzati:f] m (-s; -e) LING accusative (case)

Akne ['aknə] f (-; -n) MED acne

Akrobat [akro'baːt] m (-en; -en), **Akro'batin** f (-; -nen) acrobat; **akro'batisch** adj acrobatic

Akt [akt] m (-[e]s; -e) act(ion); THEA act; PAINT, PHOT nude

Akte ['aktə] f (-; -n) file; pl. files, records; **zu den ~n legen** file

'Akten|deckel m folder; **~koffer** m attaché case; **~ordner** m file; **~tasche** f briefcase; **~zeichen** n reference (number)

Aktie ['aktsiə] f (-; -n) ECON share, esp Am stock; **'Aktiengesellschaft** f Am corporation, Br joint-stock company

Aktion [ak'tsioːn] f (-; -en) campaign, drive; MIL ect operation; **in ~** in action

Aktionär [aktsio'nɛːɐ] m (-s; -e), **Aktio'närin** f (-; -nen) ECON shareholder, esp Am stockholder

aktiv [ak'tiːf] adj active

Aktiv ['aktiːf] n (-s; no pl) LING active voice; **Aktivist** [akti'vist] m (-en; -en) esp POL activist

Ak'tivurlaub m activity vacation

aktualisieren [aktu̯ali'ziːrən] v/t (no -ge-, h) update

aktuell [aktu̯'el] adj topical; current; up-to-date; TV, radio: **e-e ~e Sendung** a current affairs or news feature

Akupunktur [akupʊŋk'tuːɐ] f (-; -en) MED acupuncture

Akustik [a'kustɪk] f (-; no pl) acoustics

a'kustisch adj acoustic

akut [a'kuːt] adj urgent (problem etc); a. MED acute

Akzent [ak'tsɛnt] m (-[e]s; -e) accent; stress (a. fig)

akzeptabel [aktsɛp'taːbəl] adj acceptable; reasonable (price etc)

akzeptieren [aktsɛp'tiːrən] v/t (no -ge-, h) accept

Alarm [a'larm] m (-[e]s; -e) alarm; **~ schlagen** sound the alarm; **~anlage** f alarm system; **~bereitschaft** f: **in ~ on** standby, on the alert

alarmieren [alar'miːrən] v/t (no -ge-, h) call; alert; **~d** adj alarming

albern ['albɐn] adj silly, foolish

Album ['albʊm] n (-s; Alben ['albən]) album (a. record)

Algen ['algən] pl BOT algae; **~pest** f plague of algae, algal bloom

Algebra ['algəbra] f (-; no pl) MATH algebra

Alibi ['aːlibi] n (-s; -s) JUR alibi

Alimente [ali'mɛntə] pl JUR alimony

Alkohol ['alkohoːl] m (-s; no pl) alcohol; **'alkoholfrei** adj nonalcoholic, soft; **Alkoholiker(in)** [alko'hoːlikɐ (-kərɪn)] (-s; -/-; -nen) alcoholic; **alko'holisch** adj alcoholic; **Alkoholismus** [alkoho'lɪsmʊs] m (-; no pl) alcoholism; **alkoholsüchtig** adj addicted to alcohol; **Alkoholtest** m MOT breath test

all [al] indef pron and adj all; **~es** everything; **~es (Beliebige)** anything; **~e (Leute)** everybody; anybody; **~e beide** both of them; **wir ~e** all of us; **~es in ~em** all in all; **auf ~e Fälle** in any case; **~e drei Tage** every three days; → **Art, Gute, vor**

All n (-s; no pl) universe; (outer) space

alle ['alə] F adj: **~ sein** be all gone; **mein Geld ist ~** I'm out of money

Allee [a'leː] f (-; -n) avenue

allein [a'lain] adj and adv alone; lonely; by o.s.; **ganz ~** all alone; **er hat es ganz ~ gemacht** he did it all by himself; **~stehend** single

Al'lein|erziehende m, f (-n; -n) single parent; **~gang** m: **im ~** single-handedly, solo

alleinig [a'lainɪç] adj sole

Al'leinsein n (-s; no pl) loneliness

Allerbeste ['alɐ'bestə]: **der (die, das) ~** the best of all, the very best

allerdings ['alɐ'dɪŋs] adv however, though; **~!** certainly!, esp Am F sure!

'aller'erste adj very first

Allergie [alɛr'giː] f (-; -n) MED allergy (**gegen** to); **allergisch** [a'lɛrgɪʃ] adj allergic (**gegen** to)

aller'hand F adj a good deal (of); **das ist ja ~!** that's a bit much!

'Aller'heiligen n REL All Saints' Day

allerlei ['alɐ'lai] adj all kinds or sorts of

aller'letzte adj last of all, very last; **~'liebst 1.** adj (most) lovely; **2.** adv: **am ~en mögen** like best of all; **~'meiste** adj (by far the) most; **~'nächste** adj very next; **in ~r Zeit** in the very near future; **~'neu(e)ste** adj very latest

'Aller'seelen n REL All Souls' Day

allerseits ['alɐ'zaits] *adv* F: *Tag ~!* hi, everybody!

'aller'wenigst *adv*: *am ~en* least of all

allesamt ['alə'zamt] *adv* all together

'allge'mein **1.** *adj* general; common; universal; **2.** *adv*: *im Allgemeinen* in general, generally; *~ verständlich* intelligible (to all), popular

'Allge'meinbildung *f* general education

'Allge'meinheit *f* (-; *no pl*) (general) public

All'heilmittel *n* cure-all (*a. fig*)

Allianz [a'ljants] *f* (-; *-en*) alliance

Alligator [ali'ga:to:ɐ] *m* (-s; *-en*) alligator

Alliierte [ali'i:ɐtə]: *die ~n pl* POL the Allies

'all|'jährlich *adv* every year; *~ stattfindend* annual; *~'mächtig adj* omnipotent; Almighty (*God*)

allmählich [al'mɛ:lɪç] **1.** *adj* gradual; **2.** *adv* gradually

'Allradantrieb *m* MOT four-wheel drive

allseitig ['alzaitɪç] *adv*: *~ interessiert sein* have all-round interests

'Alltag *m* everyday life

'all|'täglich *adj* everyday; *fig a.* ordinary; *~'wissend adj* omniscient

'allzu *adv* (all) too; *~ viel* too much

Alm [alm] *f* (-; *-en*) alpine pasture, alp

Almosen ['almo:zən] *n* (-s; -) alms

'Alpdruck *m* (-[*e*]*s*; *no pl*) nightmare (*a. fig*)

Alphabet [alfa'be:t] *n* (-[*e*]*s*; -e) alphabet; *alpha'betisch adj* alphabetical

alpin [al'pi:n] *adj* alpine

'Alptraum *m* nightmare (*a. fig*)

als [als] *cj time*: when; while; *after comp*: than; *~ ich ankam* when I arrived; *~ Kind (Geschenk)* as a child (present); *älter ~* older than; *~ ob* as if, as though; *nichts ~* nothing but

also ['alzo] *cj* so, therefore; F well, you know; *~ gut!* very well (then)!, all right (then)!; *~ doch* so ... after all; *du willst ~ gehen etc?* so you want to go *etc*?

alt [alt] *adj* old; HIST ancient; classical (*language*); *ein 12 Jahre ~er Junge* a twelve-year-old boy

Alt *m* (-s; *no pl*) MUS alto

Altar [al'ta:ɐ] *m* (-s; *Altäre* [al'tɛ:rə]) REL altar

'Alte *m*, *f* (-*n*; -*n*) *der ~* the old man (*a.*

fig); the boss; *die ~* the old woman (*a. fig*); *die ~n pl* the old

'Altenheim *n* → *Altersheim*

'Altenpfleger(in) geriatric nurse

Alter ['altɐ] *n* (-s; *no pl*) age; old age; *im ~ von ...* at the age of ...; *er ist in deinem ~* he's your age

älter ['ɛltɐ] *adj* older; *mein ~er Bruder* my elder brother; *ein ~er Herr* an elderly gentleman

'altern *v/i* (*ge*-, *sein*) grow old, age

alternativ [altɐna'ti:f] *adj* alternative; POL ecological, green; *a.* counterculture (*movement etc*)

Alternative[1] [altɐna'ti:və] *f* (-; -*n*) alternative; option, choice

Alterna'tive[2] *m*, *f* (-*n*; -*n*) ecologist, member of the counterculture movement

'Alters|grenze *f* age limit; retirement age; *~heim n* old people's home; *~rente f* old-age pension; *~schwäche f* (-; *no pl*) infirmity; *an ~ sterben* die of old age; *~versorgung f* old age pension (scheme)

Altertum *n* (-s; *no pl*) antiquity

'Altglascon,tainer *m Am* glass recycling bin, *Br* bottle bank

altklug *adj* precocious

'Altlasten *pl* residual pollution

'Altme,tall *n* scrap (metal)

altmodisch *adj* old-fashioned

'Altöl *n* waste oil

'Altpa,pier *n* waste paper

'altsprachlich *adj*: *~es Gymnasium appr* classical secondary school

'Altstadt *f* old town; *~sa,nierung f* town-cent|er (*Br* -re) rehabilitation

'Altwarenhändler *m* second-hand dealer

Alt'weibersommer *m* Indian summer; gossamer

Aluminium [alu'mi:njum] *n* (-s; *no pl*) alumin(i)um

am [am] *prp* at the (*window etc*); *time*: in the (*morning etc*); at the (*weekend etc*); on (*Sunday etc*); *~ 1. Mai* on May 1st; *~ Tage* during the day; *~ Himmel* in the sky; *~ meisten* most; *~ Leben* alive

Amateur [ama'tø:ɐ] *m* (-s; -*e*) amateur; *~funker m* radio amateur, F radio ham

Amboss ['ambɔs] *m* (-es; -*e*) anvil

ambulant [ambu'lant] *adv*: *~ behandelt werden* MED get outpatient treatment

Ambulanz [ambu'lants] f (-; -en) MED outpatients' department; MOT ambulance

Ameise ['aːmaɪzə] f (-; -n) ZO ant

Ameisenhaufen m ZO anthill

Amerika [a'meːrika] America

Amerikaner [ameri'kaːnɐ] m (-s; -), **Amerikanerin** [-nərm] f (-; -nen), **amerikanisch** adj American

Amnestie [amnes'tiː] f (-; -n), **amnestieren** v/t (no -ge-; h) JUR amnesty

Amok ['amɔk] m: ~ **laufen** run amok

Ampel ['ampəl] f (-; -n) traffic light(s)

Amphibie [am'fiːbjə] f (-; -n) ZO amphibian

Ampulle [am'pʊlə] f (-; -n) ampoule

Amputation [amputa'tsjoːn] f (-; -en) MED amputation; **amputieren** [ampu'tiːrən] v/t (no -ge-; h) MED amputate

Amsel ['amzəl] f (-; -n) ZO blackbird

Amt [amt] n (-[e]s; Ämter ['ɛmtɐ]) office, department, esp Am bureau; position; duty, function; TEL exchange

amtlich adj official

Amts|arzt m medical examiner (Br officer); **~einführung** f inauguration; **~geheimnis** n official secret; **~geschäfte** pl official duties; **~zeichen** n TEL dial (Br dialling) tone; **~zeit** f term (of office)

Amulett [amu'lɛt] n (-[e]s; -e) amulet, (lucky) charm

amüsant [amy'zant] adj amusing, entertaining

amüsieren [amy'ziːrən] v/t (no -ge-; h) amuse; **sich ~** enjoy o.s., have a good time; **sich ~ über** (acc) laugh at

an [an] 1. prp: ~ **der Themse** (Küste, Wand) on the Thames (coast, wall); ~ **s-m Schreibtisch** at his desk; ~ **der Hand** by the hand; ~ **der Arbeit** at work; ~ **den Hausaufgaben sitzen** sit over one's homework; **et. schicken ~** (acc) send s.th. to; **sich lehnen ~** (acc) lean against; ~ **die Tür** etc **klopfen** knock at the door etc; ~ **e-m Sonntagmorgen** on a Sunday morning; ~ **dem Tag, ...** on the day ...; ~ **Weihnachten** etc at Christmas etc; → **Mangel, Stelle, sterben**; 2. adv on (a. light etc); **von jetzt** (da, heute) ~ from now (that time, today) on; **München** ~ **16.45** arrival Munich 4.45 p.m.

Anabolikum [ana'boːlikum] n (-s; -ka)

PHARM anabolic steroid

analog [ana'loːk] adj analogous

Analog... in cpds analog(ue) (computer etc)

Analphabet [an'ʔalfa'beːt] m (-en; -en), **Analphabetin** f (-; -nen) illiterate (person)

Analyse [ana'lyːzə] f (-; -n) analysis

analysieren [analy'ziːrən] v/t (no -ge-; h) analyze, Br -se

Ananas ['ananas] f (-; -, -se) BOT pineapple

Anarchie [anar'çiː] f (-; -n) anarchy

Anatomie [anato'miː] f (-; -n) anatomy **anatomisch** [ana'toːmɪʃ] adj anatomical

anbahnen v/t (sep, -ge-; h) pave the way for; **sich ~** be developing; be impending

Anbau m (-[e]s; -ten) a) AGR (no pl) cultivation, b) ARCH annex, extension

anbauen v/t (sep, -ge-; h) AGR cultivate, grow; ARCH add (**an** acc to), build on

anbehalten v/t (irr, halten, sep, no -ge-; h) keep on

anbei adv ECON enclosed

anbeißen (irr, beißen, sep, -ge-; h) **1.** v/t take a bite of; **2.** v/i fish: bite; fig take the bait; **anbellen** v/t (sep, -ge-; h) bark at; **anbeten** v/t (sep, -ge-; h) adore, worship (a. fig)

Anbetracht m: **in ~** (**dessen, dass**) considering (that)

anbetteln v/t (sep, -ge-; h) **j-n um et. ~** beg s.o. for s.th.; **anbiedern** [-biːdɐn] v/refl (sep, -ge-; h) curry favo(u)r (**bei** with); **anbieten** v/t (irr, bieten, sep, -ge-; h) offer; **anbinden** v/t (irr, binden, sep, -ge-; h) tie up; ~ **an** (acc or dat) tie to

Anblick m sight; **anblicken** v/t (sep, -ge-; h) look at; glance at

anbohren v/t (sep, -ge-; h) tap

anbrechen (irr, brechen, sep, -ge-; h) **1.** v/t (h) break into (supplies); open; **2.** v/i (sein) begin; day: break; night: fall

anbrennen v/i (irr, brennen, sep, -ge-; sein) burn (a. ~ lassen)

anbringen v/t (irr, bringen, sep, -ge-; h) fix (**an** dat to)

Anbruch m (-[e]s; no pl) beginning; **bei ~ der Nacht** at nightfall

anbrüllen v/t (sep, -ge-; h) roar at

Andacht ['andaxt] f (-; -en) REL a) (no

pl) devotion, b) service; prayers

andächtig ['andɛçtɪç] *adj* REL devout

andauern *v/i* (*sep*, *-ge-*, *h*) continue, go on, last; **~d** *adj and adv* → **dauernd**

'**Andenken** *n* (*-s*; *-*) keepsake; souvenir (*both*: **an** *acc* of); **zum ~ an** (*acc*) in memory of

andere ['andərə] *adj and indef pron* other; different; **mit ~n Worten** in other words; **am ~n Morgen** the next morning; **et.** (*nichts*) **~s** s.th. (nothing) else; **nichts ~s als** nothing but; **die ~n** the others; **alle ~n** everybody else

andererseits ['andərə'zaɪts] *adv* on the other hand

ändern ['ɛndɐn] *v/t* (*ge-*, *h*) change; alter (*clothes*); **ich kann es nicht ~** I can't help it; **sich ~** change

'**andern**'**falls** *adv* otherwise

anders ['andɐs] *adv* different(ly); **jemand ~** somebody else; **~ werden** change; **~ sein** (**als**) be different (from); **es geht nicht ~** there is no other way; **~herum 1.** *adv* the other way round; **2.** F *adj* queer; **~wo**(**hin**) *adv* elsewhere

anderthalb ['andɐt'halp] *adj* one and a half

'**Änderung** *f* (*-*; *-en*) change; alteration

andeuten *v/t* (*sep*, *-ge-*, *h*) hint (at); suggest; indicate; **j-m ~, dass** give s.o. a hint that

'**Andeutung** *f* (*-*; *-en*) hint, suggestion

'**Andrang** *m* (*-[e]s*; *no pl*) crush; ECON rush (**nach** for), run (**zu, nach** on)

andrehen *v/t* (*sep*, *-ge-*, *h*) turn on; F **j-m et. ~** fob s.th. off on s.o.

androhen *v/t* (*sep*, *-ge-*, *h*) **j-m et. ~** threaten s.o. with s.th.

aneignen *v/refl* (*sep*, *-ge-*, *h*) acquire; *esp* JUR appropriate

anei'**nander** *adv* tie *etc* together; **~ denken** think of each other; **~ geraten** clash (**mit** with)

'**Anekdote** [anɛk'do:tə] *f* (*-*; *-n*) anecdote

anekeln *v/t* (*sep*, *-ge-*, *h*) disgust, sicken; **es ekelt mich an** it makes me sick

anerkannt *adj* acknowledged, recognized

anerkennen *v/t* (*irr*, *kennen*, *sep*, *no* *-ge-*, *h*) acknowledge, recognize; appreciate; **~d** *adj* appreciative

'**Anerkennung** *f* (*-*; *-en*) acknowledg(e)ment, recognition; appreciation

'**anfahren** (*irr*, **fahren**, *sep*, *-ge-*) **1.** *v/i* (*sein*) start; **2.** *v/t* (*h*) deliver; MOT *etc* hit, *car etc*: *a.* run into; *fig* **j-n ~** jump on s.o.; '**Anfahrt** *f* journey, ride

'**Anfall** *m* MED fit, attack

'**anfallen** *v/t* (*irr*, **fallen**, *sep*, *-ge-*, *h*) attack, assault; *dog*: go for

'**anfällig** *adj* delicate; **~ für** susceptible to

'**Anfang** *m* beginning, start; **am ~** at the beginning; **~ Mai** early in May; **~ nächsten Jahres** early next year; **~ der neunziger Jahre** in the early nineties; **er ist ~ 20** he is in his early twenties; **von ~ an** from the beginning *or* start; '**anfangen** *v/t and v/i* (*irr*, **fangen**, *sep*, *-ge-*, *h*) begin, start; do; '**Anfänger** *m* (*-s*; *-*), '**Anfängerin** *f* (*-*; *-nen*) beginner

'**anfangs** *adv* at first

'**Anfangs**|**buchstabe** *m* initial (letter); **großer ~** capital (letter); **~stadium** *n*: **im ~** at an early stage

'**anfassen** *v/t* (*sep*, *-ge-*, *h*) touch; take (hold of); **sich ~** take each other by the hands; F **zum Anfassen** everyman's

'**anfechtbar** *adj* contestable; '**anfechten** *v/t* (*irr*, **fechten**, *sep*, *-ge-*, *h*) contest; '**Anfechtung** *f* (*-*; *-en*) contesting

'**anfertigen** *v/t* (*sep*, *-ge-*, *h*) make, manufacture

'**anfeuchten** *v/t* (*sep*, *-ge-*, *h*) moisten

'**anfeuern** *fig v/t* (*sep*, *-ge-*, *h*) cheer

'**anflehen** *v/t* (*sep*, *-ge-*, *h*) implore

'**anfliegen** *v/t* (*irr*, **fliegen**, *sep*, *-ge-*, *h*) AVIAT approach; fly (regularly) to

'**Anflug** *m* AVIAT approach; *fig* touch

'**anfordern** *v/t* (*sep*, *-ge-*, *h*) demand; request; '**Anforderung** *f* (*-*; *-en*) demand; request; *pl* requirements, qualifications

'**Anfrage** *f* (*-*; *-n*) inquiry

'**anfragen** *v/i* (*sep*, *-ge-*, *h*) inquire (**bei** *j-m* **nach et.** of s.o. about s.th.)

'**anfreunden** *v/refl* (*sep*, *-ge-*, *h*) make friends (**mit** with)

'**anfühlen** *v/refl* (*sep*, *-ge-*, *h*) feel; **es fühlt sich weich an** it feels soft

'**anführen** *v/t* (*sep*, *-ge-*, *h*) lead; state; F fool; '**Anführer**(**in**) leader

'**Anführungszeichen** *pl* quotation marks, inverted commas

'**Angabe** *f* (*-*; *-n*) statement; indication; F big talk; *tennis*: service; *pl* information, data; TECH specifications

'**angeben** (*irr*, *geben*, *sep*, -*ge*-, *h*) **1.** *v/t* give, state; *customs*: declare; indicate; quote (*price*); **2.** *v/i* F *fig* brag, show off; *tennis*: serve; '**Angeber** F *m* (-*s*; -) braggart, show-off; **Angeberei** [ange:bə'rai] F *f* (-; *no pl*) bragging, showing off

angeblich ['ange:plɪç] *adj* alleged; ~ **ist er ...** he is said to be ...

'**angeboren** *adj* innate, inborn; MED congenital

'**Angebot** *n* (-[*e*]*s*, -*e*) offer (*a.* ECON); ~ **und Nachfrage** supply and demand

'**ange|bracht** *adj* appropriate; ~**bunden** *adj*: *kurz* ~ curt; ~**gossen** F *adj*: *wie* ~ *sitzen* fit like a glove; ~**heitert** *adj* tipsy, *Br a.* (slightly) merry

'**angehen** (*irr*, *gehen*, *sep*, -*ge*-, *sein*) **1.** F *v/i* light etc: go on; **2.** *v/t* concern; *das geht dich nichts an* that is none of your business; ~**d** *adj* future; ~*er Arzt* doctor-to-be

'**angehören** *v/i* (*sep*, *no* -*ge*-, *h*) belong to; '**Angehörige** *m*, *f* (-*n*; -*n*) relative; member; *die nächsten* ~*n* the next of kin

'**Angeklagte** *m*, *f* (-*n*; -*n*) JUR defendant

Angel ['aŋəl] *f* (-; -*n*) fishing tackle; TECH hinge

'**Angelegenheit** *f* (-; -*en*) matter, affair

angelehnt *adj* door etc: ajar

'**angelernt** *adj* semi-skilled (*worker*)

'**Angelhaken** *m* fishhook

'**angeln** (-*ge*-, *h*) **1.** *v/i* (*nach* for) fish, angle (*both a.* fig); **2.** *v/t* catch, hook

'**Angelrute** *f* fishing rod

'**Angelsachse** [-zaksə] *m* (-*n*; -*n*), '**angelsächsisch** [-zɛksɪʃ] *adj* Anglo-Saxon

'**Angelschein** *m* fishing permit

'**Angelschnur** *f* fishing line

angemessen *adj* proper, suitable; just (*punishment*); reasonable (*price*)

'**angenehm** *adj* pleasant, agreeable; ~! pleased to meet you

'**ange|nommen** *cj* (let's) suppose, supposing; ~**regt** *adj* animated; lively; ~**schrieben** *adj*: *bei j-m gut* (*schlecht*) ~ *sein* be in s.o.'s good (bad) books; ~**sehen** *adj* respected

'**angesichts** *prp* (*gen*) in view of

'**Angestellte** *m*, *f* (-*n*; -*n*) employee (*bei* with), *pl* the staff

'**ange|tan** *adj*: *ganz* ~ *sein von* be taken

with; ~**trunken** *adj* (slightly) drunk; *in* ~**em Zustand** under the influence of alcohol; ~**wandt** *adj* applied; ~**wiesen** *adj*: ~ *auf* (*acc*) dependent (up)on

'**angewöhnen** *v/t* (*sep*, *no* -*ge*-, *h*) *sich* (*j-m*) ~, *et. zu tun* get (s.o.) used to doing s.th.; *sich das Rauchen* ~ take to smoking; '**Angewohnheit** *f* habit

Angina [aŋ'gi:na] *f* (-; -*nen*) MED tonsillitis

angleichen *v/t* (*irr*, *gleichen*, *sep*, -*ge*-, *h*) adjust (*an acc* to)

Angler ['aŋlɐ] *m* (-*s*; -) angler

Anglist [aŋ'glɪst] *m* (-*en*; -*en*), **An'glistin** *f* (-; -*nen*) student of (*or* graduate in) English

'**angreifen** *v/t* (*irr*, *greifen*, *sep*, -*ge*-, *h*) attack (*a.* SPORT *and* fig); affect (*health etc*); touch (*supplies*)

'**Angreifer** *m* (-*s*; -) attacker, SPORT *a.* offensive player; *esp* POL aggressor

'**angrenzend** *adj* adjacent (*an acc* to)

'**Angriff** *m* attack (*a.* SPORT *and* fig); MIL assault, charge; *in* ~ *nehmen* set about

'**angriffslustig** *adj* aggressive

Angst [aŋst] *f* (-; *Ängste* ['ɛŋstə]) fear (*vor dat* of); ~ *haben* (*vor dat*) be afraid *or* scared (of); *j-m* ~ *einjagen* frighten *or* scare s.o.; (*hab*) *keine Angst!* don't be afraid!; ~**hase** F *m* chicken

ängstigen ['ɛŋstɪgən] *v/t* (*ge*-, *h*) frighten, scare; *sich* ~ be afraid (*vor dat* of); be worried (*um* about)

ängstlich ['ɛŋstlɪç] *adj* timid, fearful; anxious

'**anhaben** F *v/t* (*irr*, *haben*, *sep*, -*ge*-, *h*) have on (*a.* light etc), *a.* wear, be wearing (*dress etc*)

'**anhalten** (*irr*, *halten*, *sep*, -*ge*-, *h*) **1.** *v/t* stop; *den Atem* ~ hold one's breath; **2.** *v/i* stop; continue; ~**d** *adj* continual

'**Anhalter** *m* (-*s*; -) hitchhiker; F *per* ~ *fahren* hitchhike

'**Anhaltspunkt** *m* clue

an'hand *prp* (*gen*) by means of

'**Anhang** *m* a) appendix, b) (*no pl*) relations; '**anhängen** *v/t* (*sep*, -*ge*-, *h*) add; hang up; RAIL, MOT couple (*an acc* to); '**Anhänger** *m* (-*s*; -) follower, supporter (*a.* SPORT); pendant; label, tag; MOT trailer; '**anhänglich** *adj* affectionate; *contp* clinging

'**anhäufen** *v/t und v/refl* (*sep*, -*ge*-, *h*)

heap up, accumulate

'**Anhäufung** f (-; -en) accumulation

'**anheben** v/t (irr, **heben**, sep, -ge-, h) lift, raise (a. price); MOT jack up

'**anheften** v/t (sep, -ge-, h) attach, tack (both: **an** acc to)

Anhieb m: **auf** ~ on the first try

'**anhimmeln** F v/t (sep, -ge-, h) idolize, worship

'**Anhöhe** f rise, hill, elevation

anhören v/t (sep, -ge-, h) listen to; **mit** ~ overhear; **es hört sich ... an** it sounds ...; '**Anhörung** f (-; -en) hearing

animieren [ani'miːrən] v/t (no -ge-, h) encourage; stimulate

'**ankämpfen** v/i (sep, -ge-, h) ~ **gegen** fight s.th.

'**Ankauf** m purchase

Anker ['aŋkɐ] m (-s; -) MAR anchor; **vor** ~ **gehen** drop anchor

'**ankern** v/i (ge-, h) MAR anchor

'**anketten** v/t (sep, -ge-, h) chain up

'**Anklage** f (-; no pl) JUR accusation, charge (a. fig); '**anklagen** v/t (sep, -ge-, h) JUR accuse (**wegen** of), charge (with) (both a. fig.)

'**anklammern** v/t (sep, -ge-, h) clip s.th. on; **sich** ~ (**an** acc) cling (to)

Anklang m: ~ **finden** meet with approval

'**ankleben** v/t (sep, -ge-, h) stick on (**an** dat or acc to)

'**anklicken** v/t (sep, -ge-, h) EDP click

'**anklopfen** v/i (sep, -ge-, h) knock (**an** dat or acc at)

'**anknipsen** v/t (sep, -ge-, h) switch on

'**anknüpfen** v/t (sep, -ge-, h) tie (**an** acc to); fig begin; **Beziehungen** ~ (**zu**) establish contacts (with)

'**ankommen** v/i (irr, **kommen**, sep, -ge-, sein) arrive; **nicht gegen j-n** ~ be no match for s.o.; **es kommt (ganz) darauf an** it (all) depends; **es kommt darauf an, dass** what matters is; **darauf kommt es nicht an** that doesn't matter; **es darauf** ~ **lassen** take a chance; **gut** ~ (**bei**) fig go down well (with)

'**ankündigen** v/t (sep, -ge-, h) announce; advertise; '**Ankündigung** f announcement; advertisement

Ankunft ['ankʊnft] f (-; no pl) arrival

'**anlächeln**, '**anlachen** v/t (sep, -ge-, h) smile at

'**Anlage** f arrangement; facility; plant; TECH system; (stereo etc) set; ECON investment; enclosure; fig gift; (car) park, gardens; **sanitäre** ~**n** sanitary facilities

Anlass ['anlas] m (-es; Anlässe ['anlɛsə]) occasion; cause

'**anlassen** v/t (irr, **lassen**, sep, -ge-, h) MOT start; F keep on, leave on (a. light etc); '**Anlasser** m (-s; -) MOT starter

anlässlich ['anlɛslɪç] prp (gen) on the occasion of

'**Anlauf** m SPORT run-up; fig start

'**anlaufen** (irr, **laufen**, sep, -ge-) **1.** v/i (sein) run up; fig start; metal: tarnish; glasses etc: steam up; **2.** v/t (h) MAR call or touch at

'**anlegen** (sep, -ge-, h) **1.** v/t put on (dress etc); lay out (garden etc); build (road etc); invest (money); found (town etc); MED apply (dressing etc); lay in (supplies); **sich mit j-m** ~ pick a quarrel with s.o.; **2.** v/i MAR land; moor; **es** ~ **auf** (acc) aim at; '**Anleger** m (-s; -) ECON investor; MAR landing stage

'**anlehnen** v/t (sep, -ge-, h) lean (**an** acc against); leave door etc ajar; **sich** ~ **an** (acc) lean against, fig lean on s.o.

Anleihe ['anlaɪə] f (-; -n) ECON loan

'**Anleitung** f (-; -en) guidance, instruction; written instructions

'**Anliegen** n (-s; -) request; message (of a film etc)

Anlieger ['anliːgɐ] m (-s; -) resident

'**anlocken** v/t (sep, -ge-, h) attract, lure

'**anmachen** v/t (sep, -ge-, h) light (fire etc); turn on (light etc); dress (salad); F chat s.o. up; turn s.o. on

'**anmalen** v/t (sep, -ge-, h) paint

'**Anmarsch** m: **im** ~ on the way

anmaßen v/t (sep, -ge-, h) **sich** ~ assume; claim (right); **sich** ~, **et. zu tun** presume to do s.th.; ~**d** adj arrogant

'**anmelden** v/t (sep, -ge-, h) announce (visitor); register (birth etc); customs: declare; **sich** ~ enrol(l) (for classes etc); register (at a hotel); **sich** ~ **bei** make an appointment with (doctor etc)

'**Anmeldung** f announcement; registration, enrol(l)ment

'**anmerken** v/t (sep, -ge-, h) **j-m et.** ~ notice s.th. in s.o.; **sich et. (nichts)** ~ **lassen** (not) let it show; '**Anmerkung** *f* (-; -en) note; annotation, footnote

Anmut ['anmuːt] *f* (-; *no pl*) grace

'**anmutig** *adj* graceful

'**annähen** *v/t* (*sep*, *-ge-*, *h*) sew on (**an** *acc* to)

'**annähernd** *adv* approximately

'**Annäherung** *f* (-; -en) approach (**an** *acc* to); **Annäherungsversuche** *pl* advances, F pass

Annahme ['annaːmə] *f* (-; -n) a) (*no pl*) acceptance (*a. fig*), b) assumption

'**annehmbar** *adj* acceptable; reasonable (*price etc*); '**annehmen** *v/t* (*irr*, *nehmen*, *sep*, *-ge-*, *h*) accept; suppose; adopt (*child*, *name*); take (*ball*); take on (*color*, *look etc*); **sich e-r Sache** *or* **j-s** ~ take care of s.th. *or* s.o.; '**Annehmlichkeiten** *pl* comforts, amenities

Annonce [a'nõːsə] *f* (-; -n) advertisement

annullieren [anʊ'liːrən] *v/t* (*no -ge-*, *h*) annul; ECON cancel

anöden ['anˀøːdən] F *v/t* (*sep*, *-ge-*, *h*) bore *s.o.* to death

anonym [anoˈnyːm] *adj* anonymous

Anonymität [anonymiˈtɛːt] *f* (-; *no pl*) anonymity

Anorak ['anorak] *m* (-*s*; -*s*) anorak

'**anordnen** *v/t* (*sep*, *-ge-*, *h*) arrange; give order(s), order; '**Anordnung** *f* (-; -en) arrangement; direction, order

'**anorganisch** *adj* CHEM inorganic

'**anpacken** F *fig* (*sep*, *-ge-*, *h*) **1.** *v/t* tackle; **2.** *v/i*: **mit** ~ lend a hand

'**anpassen** *v/t* (*sep*, *-ge-*, *h*) adapt, adjust (*both a.* **sich** ~) (*dat*, **an** *acc* to)

'**Anpassung** *f* (-; -en) adaptation, adjustment

'**anpassungsfähig** *adj* adaptable

'**Anpassungsfähigkeit** *f* adaptability

'**Anpfiff** *m* SPORT starting whistle; F *fig* dressing-down

'**anpflanzen** *v/t* (*sep*, *-ge-*, *h*) cultivate; plant; '**Anpflanzung** *f* cultivation

'**anpöbeln** *v/t* (*sep*, *-ge-*, *h*) accost; shout abuse at; **anprangern** ['anpraŋɐn] *v/t* (*sep*, *-ge-*, *h*) denounce; '**anpreisen** *v/t* (*irr*, *preisen*, *sep*, *-ge-*, *h*) push; plug; '**anpro,bieren** *v/t* (*no -ge-*, *h*) try on; '**anpumpen** F *v/t* (*sep*, *-ge-*, *h*) touch *s.o.* (**um** for); '**anraten** *v/t* (*irr*, *raten*, *sep*, *-ge-*, *h*) advise; '**anrechnen** *v/t* (*sep*, *-ge-*, *h*) charge; allow

'**Anrecht** *n*: **ein** ~ **haben auf** (*acc*) be entitled to

'**Anrede** *f* address; '**anreden** *v/t* (*sep*, *-ge-*, *h*) address (**mit Namen** by name)

'**anregen** *v/t* (*sep*, *-ge-*, *h*) stimulate; suggest; ~**d** *adj* stimulating

'**Anregung** *f* stimulation; suggestion

'**Anregungsmittel** *n* PHARM stimulant

'**Anreiz** *m* incentive

'**anrichten** *v/t* (*sep*, *-ge-*, *h*) GASTR prepare, dress; cause, do (*damage etc*)

anrüchig ['anryçıç] *adj* disreputable

'**Anruf** *m* call (*a.* TEL.); ~**beantworter** *m* TEL answering machine

'**anrufen** *v/t* (*irr*, *rufen*, *sep*, *-ge-*, *h*) TEL call *or* ring up, phone

'**anrühren** *v/t* (*sep*, *-ge-*, *h*) touch; mix

'**Ansage** *f* announcement; '**ansagen** *v/t* (*sep*, *-ge-*, *h*) announce; **Ansager** ['anzaːgɐ] *m* (-*s*; -), '**Ansagerin** [-gərɪn] *f* (-; -nen) announcer

'**ansammeln** *v/t* and *v/refl* (*sep*, *-ge-*, *h*) accumulate; '**Ansammlung** *f* collection, accumulation; crowd

'**Ansatz** *m* start (**zu** of); attempt (**zu** at); approach; TECH attachment; MATH set-up; *pl* first signs

'**anschaffen** *v/t* (*sep*, *-ge-*, *h*) get; **sich et.** ~ buy *or* get (o.s.) s.th.

'**Anschaffung** *f* (-; -en) purchase, buy

'**anschauen** *v/t* (*sep*, *-ge-*, *h*) → **ansehen**; '**anschaulich** *adj* graphic (*account etc*); '**Anschauung** *f* (-; -en) (**von**) view (of), opinion (about, of)

'**Anschauungsmateri,al** *n* PED visual aids

'**Anschein** *m* (-[*e*]*s*; *no pl*) appearance; **allem** ~ **nach** to all appearances; **den** ~ **erwecken**, **als** (**ob**) give the impression of ...; '**anscheinend** *adv* apparently

'**anschieben** *v/t* (*irr*, *schieben*, *sep*, *-ge-*, *h*) give a push (*a.* MOT)

'**Anschlag** *m* attack; poster; bill, notice; typewriter: stroke; MUS, *swimming*: touch; **e-n** ~ **auf j-n verüben** make an attempt on s.o.'s life; ~**brett** *n* bulletin (*esp Br* notice) board

'**anschlagen** (*irr*, *schlagen*, *sep*, *-ge-*, *h*) **1.** *v/t* post; MUS strike; chip (*cup etc*); **2.** *v/i* dog: bark; take (effect) (*a.* MED); *swimming*: touch the wall

'**anschließen** *v/t* (*irr*, *schließen*, *sep*, *-ge-*, *h*) ELECTR, TECH connect; **sich** ~ follow; agree with; **sich j-m** *or* **e-r**

Sache ~ join s.o. or s.th.; **~d 1.** *adj* following; **2.** *adv* then, afterwards

'**Anschluss** *m* connection; *im* ~ *an* (*acc*) following; ~ *finden* (*bei*) make contact *or* friends (with); ~ *bekommen* TEL get through

'**anschmiegen** *v/refl* (*sep*, *-ge-*, *h*) snuggle up (*an* acc to)

'**anschmiegsam** *adj* affectionate

'**anschnallen** *v/t* (*sep*, *-ge-*, *h*) strap on, put on (*a. ski*); *sich* ~ AVIAT, MOT fasten one's seat belt; '**anschnauzen** F *v/t* (*sep*, *-ge-*, *h*) tell s.o. off, *Am a.* bawl s.o. out; '**anschneiden** *v/t* (*irr*, *schneiden*, *sep*, *-ge-*, *h*) cut; *fig* bring up; '**anschrauben** *v/t* (*sep*, *-ge-*, *h*) screw on (*an* acc to); '**anschreiben** *v/t* (*irr*, *schreiben*, *sep*, *-ge-*, *h*) write on the (black)board; *j-n* ~ write to s.o.; (*et.*) ~ *lassen* buy (s.th.) on credit; → *angeschrieben*; '**anschreien** *v/t* (*irr*, *schreien*, *sep*, *-ge-*, *h*) shout at

'**Anschrift** *f* address

'**Anschuldigung** *f* (*-*; *-en*) accusation

'**anschwellen** *v/i* (*irr*, *schwellen*, *sep*, *-ge-*, *sein*) swell (*a. fig*); '**anschwemmen** *v/t* (*sep*, *-ge-*, *h*) wash ashore

'**ansehen** *v/t* (*irr*, *sehen*, *sep*, *-ge-*, *h*) look at, have *or* take a look at; watch; see (*all a.* *sich* [*dat*] ~); ~ *als* look upon as; *et. mit* ~ watch *or* witness s.th.; *man sieht ihm an, dass ...* one can see that ...; '**Ansehen** *n* (*-s*; *no pl*) reputation

ansehnlich ['anzeːnlɪç] *adj* considerable

'**anseilen** *v/t and v/refl* (*sep*, *-ge-*, *h*) rope

'**ansetzen** (*sep*, *-ge-*, *h*) **1.** *v/t* put (*an* acc to); put on, add; fix, set (*date etc*); *Fett etc* ~ put on weight *etc*; **2.** *v/i*: ~ *zu* prepare for (*landing etc*)

'**Ansicht** *f* (*-*; *-en*) view, *a.* opinion, *a.* sight; *der* ~ *sein, dass ...* be of the opinion that ...; *meiner* ~ *nach* in my opinion; *zur* ~ ECON on approval

'**Ansichts|karte** *f* picture postcard; **~sache** *f* matter of opinion

'**anspannen** *v/t* (*sep*, *-ge-*, *h*) strain

'**Anspannung** *f* (*-*; *-en*) strain, exertion

'**anspielen** *v/i* (*sep*, *-ge-*, *h*) soccer: kick off; ~ *auf* (*acc*) allude to, hint at

'**Anspielung** *f* (*-*; *-en*) allusion, hint

'**anspitzen** *v/t* (*sep*, *-ge-*, *h*) sharpen

'**Ansporn** *m* (*-[e]s*; *no pl*) incentive

'**anspornen** *v/t* (*sep*, *-ge-*, *h*) encourage, spur s.o. on

'**Ansprache** *f* address, speech; *e-e* ~ *halten* deliver an address

'**ansprechen** *v/t* (*irr*, *sprechen*, *sep*, *-ge-*, *h*) address, speak to; *fig* appeal to; **~d** *adj* attractive

'**Ansprechpartner** *m* s.o. to talk to, contact

'**anspringen** (*irr*, *springen*, *sep*, *-ge-*) **1.** *v/i* (*sein*) engine: start; **2.** *v/t* (*h*) jump (up)on

'**anspritzen** *v/t* (*sep*, *-ge-*, *h*) spatter

'**Anspruch** *m* claim (*auf* acc to) (*a.* JUR); ~ *haben auf* (*acc*) be entitled to; ~ *erheben auf* (*acc*) claim; *Zeit in* ~ *nehmen* take up time

'**anspruchslos** *adj* modest; light, undemanding (*reading etc*); *contp* trivial

'**anspruchsvoll** *adj* demanding; sophisticated, refined (*tastes etc*)

Anstalt ['anʃtalt] *f* (*-*; *-en*) establishment, institution; mental hospital; **~en machen zu** get ready for

'**Anstand** *m* (*-[e]s*; *no pl*) decency; manners; '**anständig** *adj* decent (*a. fig*)

'**anstandslos** *adv* unhesitatingly; without difficulty

'**anstarren** *v/t* (*sep*, *-ge-*, *h*) stare at

an'**statt** *prp* (*gen*) *and cj* instead of

'**anstechen** *v/t* (*irr*, *stechen*, *sep*, *-ge-*, *h*) tap (*barrel*)

'**anstecken** *v/t* (*sep*, *-ge-*, *h*) stick on; put on (*ring*); light; set fire to; MED infect; *sich bei j-m* ~ MED catch s.th. from s.o.; **~d** *adj* MED infectious, contagious, catching (*all a. fig*)

'**Anstecknadel** *f* pin, button

'**Ansteckung** *f* (*-*; *no pl*) MED infection, contagion

'**anstehen** *v/i* (*irr*, *stehen*, *sep*, *-ge-*, *h*) (*nach* for) stand in line, *Br* queue up

'**ansteigen** *v/i* (*irr*, *steigen*, *sep*, *-ge-*, *sein*) rise

'**anstellen** *v/t* (*sep*, *-ge-*, *h*) engage, employ; TV *etc*: turn on; F be up to (*s.th. illegal etc*); make (*inquiries etc*); *sich* ~ line up (*nach* for), *Br* queue up (for); F (make a) fuss

'**Anstellung** *f* job, position; *e-e* ~ *finden* find employment

Anstieg ['anʃtiːk] *m* (*-[e]s*; *no pl*) rise, increase

'anstiften *v/t* (*sep, -ge-, h*) incite
'Anstifter *m* instigator
'Anstiftung *f* incitement
'anstimmen *v/t* (*sep, -ge-, h*) MUS strike up
'Anstoß *m* soccer: kickoff; *fig* initiative, impulse; offen|se, *Br* -ce; **~ erregen** give offense (*bei* to); **~ nehmen an** take offense at; **den ~ zu et. geben** start s.th., initiate s.th.; 'anstoßen (*irr*, **stoßen**, *sep, -ge-*) **1.** *v/t* (*h*) nudge *s.o.*; **2.** *v/i* a) (*sein*) knock, bump, b) (*h*) clink glasses; **~ auf** (*acc*) drink to *s.o.* or *s.th.*
anstößig ['anʃtøːsɪç] *adj* offensive
'anstrahlen *v/t* (*sep, -ge-, h*) illuminate; beam at *s.o.*
'anstreichen *v/t* (*irr*, **streichen**, *sep, -ge-, h*) paint; PED mark (*mistakes etc*)
'Anstreicher *m* (house)painter
'anstrengen *v/refl* (*sep, -ge-, h*) try (hard), make an effort; **~d** *adj* strenuous, hard
'Anstrengung *f* (*-; -en*) exertion, strain; effort
'Ansturm *fig m* (*-[e]s; no pl*) rush (*auf acc* for)
'Anteil *m* share (*a.* ECON), portion; **~ nehmen an** (*dat*) take an interest in; sympathize with; **~nahme** [-naːmə] *f* (*-; no pl*) sympathy; interest
Antenne [an'tɛnə] *f* (*-; -n*) antenna, *Br* aerial
Anti..., anti... *in cpds* anti...
Anti|alko'holiker *m* teetotal(l)er; **~'babypille** F *f* birth control pill, F the pill; **~'biotikum** *n* MED antibiotic; **~blo-'ckiersys,tem** *n* MOT anti-lock braking system
antik [an'tiːk] *adj* antique, HIST *a.* ancient; **An'tike** *f* (*-; no pl*) ancient world
'Antikörper *m* MED antibody
Antilope [anti'loːpə] *f* (*-; -n*) zo antelope
Antipathie [antipa'tiː] *f* (*-; -n*) antipathy
Antiquariat [antikva'rjaːt] *n* (*-[e]s; -e*) second-hand bookshop
antiquarisch [anti'kvaːrɪʃ] *adj and adv* second-hand
Antiquitäten [antikvi'tɛːtən] *pl* antiques; **~laden** *m* antique shop
Antisemit [-ze'miːt] *m* (*-en; -en*) anti-Semite; **antise'mitisch** *adj* anti-Semitic; **Antisemitismus** [-zemi'tɪsmʊs] *m* (*-; no pl*) anti-Semitism
Antrag ['antraːk] *m* (*-[e]s; Anträge* ['an-

tri:gə]) application; PARL motion; proposal; **~ stellen auf** (*acc*) make an application for; PARL move for; **~steller (in)** [-ʃtɛlɐ (-lərɪn)] *m* (*-s; -/-; -nen*) applicant; PARL mover
'antreiben (*irr*, **treiben**, *sep, -ge-*) **1.** *v/t* (*h*) TECH drive; urge *s.o.* (on); **2.** *v/i* (*sein*) float ashore
'antreten (*irr*, **treten**, *sep, -ge-*) **1.** *v/t* (*h*) enter upon (*office etc*); take up (*position*); set out on (*journey*); **2.** *v/i* (*sein*) take one's place; MIL line up
'Antrieb *m* TECH drive (*a. fig*), propulsion; *fig* motive, impulse; **aus eigenem ~** of one's own accord
'antun *v/t* (*irr*, **tun**, *sep, -ge-, h*) **j-m et. ~** do s.th. to s.o.; **sich et. ~** lay hands on o.s.
Antwort ['antvɔrt] *f* (*-; -en*) answer (*auf acc* to), reply (to)
'antworten *v/i* (*-ge-, h*) answer (*j-m* s.o., *auf et.* s.th.), reply (to s.o. *or* s.th.)
'anvertrauen *v/t* (*sep, no -ge-, h*) **j-m et. ~** (en)trust s.o. with s.th.; confide s.th. to s.o.
'anwachsen *v/i* (*irr*, **wachsen**, *sep, -ge-, sein*) BOT take root; *fig* increase
Anwalt ['anvalt] *m* (*-[e]s; Anwälte* ['anvɛltə]) → **Rechtsanwalt**
'Anwärter *m* candidate (*auf acc* for)
'anweisen *v/t* (*irr*, **weisen**, *sep, -ge-, h*) instruct; direct, order
'Anweisung *f* instruction; order
'anwenden *v/t* ([*irr*, **wenden**,] *sep, -ge-, h*) use; apply (*auf acc* to)
'Anwendung *f* use; application
'anwerben *v/t* (*irr*, **werben**, *sep, -ge-, h*) recruit (*a. fig*)
'Anwesen *n* (*-s; -*) estate; property
'anwesend *adj* present
'Anwesenheit *f* (*-; no pl*) presence; PED attendance; **die ~ feststellen** call the roll; 'Anwesenheitsliste *f* attendance record (*Br* list)
'anwidern ['anviːdɐn] *v/t* (*sep, -ge-, h*) make s.o. sick
'Anzahl *f* (*-; no pl*) number, quantity
'anzahlen *v/t* (*sep, -ge-, h*) pay on account; 'Anzahlung *f* down payment
'anzapfen *v/t* (*sep, -ge-, h*) tap
'Anzeichen *n* symptom (*a.* MED), sign
Anzeige ['antsaigə] *f* (*-; -n*) advertisement; announcement; JUR information; EDP display; TECH reading

'anzeigen *v/t* (*sep, -ge-, h*) announce; report to the police; TECH indicate, show

'anziehen *v/t* (*irr, ziehen, sep, -ge-, h*) put on (*dress etc*); dress *s.o.*; *fig* attract, draw; tighten (*screw*); pull (*lever etc*); **sich ~** get dressed; dress; **~d** *adj* attractive

'Anziehung *f* (*-; no pl*), 'Anziehungskraft *f* (*-; no pl*) PHYS attraction, *fig a.* appeal

'Anzug *m* suit

anzüglich ['antsy:klɪç] *adj* suggestive (*joke*); personal, offensive (*remark etc*)

'anzünden *v/t* (*sep, -ge-, h*) light; set on fire

apart [a'part] *adj* striking

Apartment [a'partmənt] *n* (*-s; -s*) studio (apartment *or Br* flat)

apathisch [a'pa:tɪʃ] *adj* apathetic

Apfel ['apfəl] *m* (*-s; Äpfel* ['ɛpfəl]) BOT apple; **~mus** *n* GASTR apple sauce

Apfelsine [apfəl'zi:nə] *f* (*-; -n*) BOT orange

'Apfelwein *m* cider

Apostel [a'pɔstəl] *m* (*-s; -*) REL apostle

Apostroph [apo'stro:f] *m* (*-s; -e*) apostrophe

Apotheke [apo'te:kə] *f* (*-; -n*) pharmacy, drugstore, *Br* chemist's

Apotheker [apo'te:kɐ] *m* (*-s; -*), Apo'thekerin *f* (*-; -nen*) pharmacist, druggist, *Br* chemist

App. ABBR *of Apparat* TEL ext., extension

Apparat [apa'ra:t] *m* (*-[e]s; -e*) apparatus; device; (tele)phone; radio; TV set; camera; POL *etc* machine(ry); **am ~!** TEL speaking!; **am ~ bleiben** TEL hold the line

Appell [a'pɛl] *m* (*-s; -e*) appeal (**an** *acc* to); MIL roll call

appellieren [apɛ'li:rən] *v/i* (*no -ge-, h*) (make an) appeal (**an** *acc* to)

Appetit [ape'ti:t] *m* (*-[e]s; no pl*) appetite (**auf** *acc* for); **~ auf et. haben** feel like s.th.; **guten ~!** enjoy your meal!

appe'titanregend *adj* appetizing

Appe'tithappen *m* GASTR appetizer

appe'titlich *adj* appetizing, savo(u)ry, *fig a.* inviting

applaudieren [aplau'di:rən] *v/i* (*no -ge-, h*) applaud; Applaus [a'plaus] *m* (*-es; no pl*) applause

Aprikose [apri'ko:zə] *f* (*-; -n*) BOT apricot

April [a'prɪl] *m* (*-[s]; no pl*) April; **~! ~!** April fool!

Aquaplaning [akva'pla:nɪŋ] *n* (*-[s]; no pl*) MOT hydroplaning, *Br* aquaplaning

Aquarell [akva'rɛl] *n* (*-s; -e*) watercolo(u)r

Aquarium [a'kva:rjʊm] *n* (*-s; -ien*) aquarium

Äquator [ɛ'kva:to:ɐ] *m* (*-s; no pl*) equator

Ära ['ɛːra] *f* (*-; no pl*) era

Araber ['arabɐ] *m* (*-s; -*), 'Araberin [-bərɪn] *f* (*-; -nen*) Arab

arabisch [a'ra:bɪʃ] *adj* Arabian; Arabic

Arbeit ['arbait] *f* (*-; -en*) work, ECON, POL *a.* labo(u)r; employment, job; PED test; *scientific etc* paper; workmanship; **bei der ~** at work; **zur ~ gehen** *or* **fahren** go to work; **gute ~ leisten** make a good job of it; **sich an die ~ machen** set to work; 'arbeiten *v/i* (*ge-, h*) work (**an** *dat* at, on)

'Arbeiter *m* (*-s; -*), 'Arbeiterin *f* (*-; -nen*) worker

'Arbeitgeber *m* (*-s; -*) employer

'Arbeitnehmer *m* (*-s; -*) employee

'Arbeits|amt *n Am* labor office, *Br* job centre; **~blatt** *n* PED worksheet; **~erlaubnis** *f* green card, *Br* work permit

'arbeitsfähig *adj* fit for work

'Arbeits|gang *m* TECH operation; **~gemeinschaft** *f* work *or* study group; **~gericht** *n* JUR labor court, *Br* industrial tribunal; **~hose** *f* overalls; **~kleidung** *f* working clothes; **~kräfte** *pl* workers, labo(u)r

'arbeitslos *adj* unemployed, out of work; 'Arbeitslose *m, f* (*-n; -n*) **die ~n** *pl* the unemployed

'Arbeitslosengeld *n* unemployment compensation (*Br* benefit); **~ beziehen** *Br* be on the dole

'Arbeitslosigkeit *f* (*-; no pl*) unemployment

'Arbeits|markt *m* labo(u)r market; **~mi,nister** *m Am* Secretary of Labor; *Br* Minister of Labour; **~niederlegung** *f* strike, walkout; **~pause** *f* break, intermission; **~platz** *m* workplace; job

'arbeitsscheu *adj* work-shy

'Arbeits|speicher *m* EDP main memory; **~suche** *f*: **er ist auf ~** he is looking for a job; **~süchtige** *m, f* workaholic; **~tag** *m* workday

'**arbeitsunfähig** *adj* unfit for work; *permanently* disabled

'Arbeits|weise *f* method (of working); **~zeit** *f* (**gleitende** flexible) working hours; **~zeitverkürzung** *f* fewer working hours; **~zimmer** *n* study

Archäologe [arçɛo'lo:gə] *m* (-n; -n) arch(a)eologist; **Archäologie** [arçɛolo'gi:] *f* (-; *no pl*) arch(a)eology; **Archäo'login** *f* (-; -nen) arch(a)eologist

Arche ['arçə] *f* (-; -n) ark; **die ~ Noah** Noah's ark

Architekt [arçi'tɛkt] *m* (-en; -en), **Archi'tektin** *f* (-; -nen) architect; **architektonisch** [-tɛk'to:nɪʃ] *adj* architectural; **Architektur** [-tɛk'tu:ɐ] *f* (-; -en) architecture

Archiv [ar'çi:f] *n* (-s; -e) archives; record office

Arena [a're:na] *f* (-; -nen) ring

Ärger ['ɛrgə] *m* (-s; *no pl*) anger (**über** *acc* at); trouble; F **j-m ~ machen** cause s.o. trouble; '**ärgerlich** *adj* angry (**über, auf** *acc* at *s.th.*; with *s.o.*); annoying; '**ärgern** *v/t* (ge-, h) annoy; **sich ~** be annoyed (**über** *acc* at, about *s.th.*, with *s.o.*); '**Ärgernis** *n* (-ses; -se) nuisance

arglos ['arklo:s] *adj* innocent

Argwohn ['arkvo:n] *m* (-[e]s; *no pl*) suspicion (**gegen** of)

'argwöhnisch [-vø:nɪʃ] *adj* suspicious

Arie ['a:rjə] *f* (-; -n) MUS aria

Aristokratie [arɪstokra'ti:] *f* (-; -n) aristocracy

arm [arm] *adj* poor; **die Armen** the poor

Arm *m* (-[e]s; -e) ANAT arm; GEOGR branch; F **j-n auf den ~ nehmen** pull s.o.'s leg

Armaturen [arma'tu:rən] *pl* TECH instruments; (*plumbing*) fixtures; **~brett** *n* MOT dashboard

'Armband *n* bracelet

'Armbanduhr *f* wrist-watch

Armee [ar'me:] *f* (-; -n) MIL armed forces; army

Ärmel ['ɛrməl] *m* (-s; -) sleeve

ärmlich ['ɛrmlɪç] *adj* poor (*a. fig*); shabby

'Armreif(en) *m* bangle

'armselig *adj* wretched, miserable

Armut ['armu:t] *f* (-; *no pl*) poverty; **~ an** (*dat*) lack of

Aroma [a'ro:ma] *n* (-s; -men) flavo(u)r; aroma

Arrest [a'rɛst] *m* (-[e]s; -e) PED detention; **~ bekommen** be kept in

arrogant [aro'gant] *adj* arrogant, conceited

Arsch [arʃ] V *m* (-es; Ärsche ['ɛrʃə]) ass, *Br* arse; **~loch** V *n* asshole, *Br* arsehole

Art [art] *f* (-; -en) way, manner; kind, sort; BIOL species; **auf diese** (*in*) this way; **e-e ~ ...** a sort of ...; **Geräte aller ~** all kinds *or* sorts of tools

'Artenschutz *m* protection of endangered species

Arterie [ar'te:rjə] *f* (-; -n) ANAT artery

Ar'terienverkalkung *f* MED arteriosclerosis

Arthritis [ar'tri:tɪs] *f* (-; -tiden) MED arthritis

artig ['a:rtɪç] *adj* good, well-behaved; **sei ~!** be good!, be a good boy (*or* girl)!

Artikel [ar'ti:kəl] *m* (-s; -) article

Artillerie [artɪlə'ri:] *f* (-; *no pl*) MIL artillery

Artist [ar'tɪst] *m* (-en; -en), **Ar'tistin** *f* (-; -nen) acrobat, (*circus*) performer

Arznei [a:rts'nai] *f* (-; -en), **~mittel** *n* medicine, drug

Arzt [a:rtst] *m* (-es; Ärzte ['ɛ:rtstə]) doctor, physician; **Ärztin** ['ɛ:rtstɪn] *f* (-; -nen) (lady) doctor *or* physician

'ärztlich *adj* medical; **sich ~ behandeln lassen** undergo treatment

As [as] *n* (-; -) MUS A flat

Asbest [as'bɛst] *m* (-[e]s; -e) asbestos

Asche ['aʃə] *f* (-; -n) ash(es)

'Aschen|bahn *f* SPORT cinder-track; MOT dirt track; **~becher** *m* ashtray

Ascher'mittwoch *m* Ash Wednesday

äsen ['ɛ:zən] *v/i* (ge-, h) HUNT feed, browse

Asiat [a'zja:t] *m* (-en; -en), **Asi'atin** *f* (-; -nen) Asian; **asi'atisch** *adj* Asian, Asiatic; **Asien** ['a:zjən] *n* (-s; *no pl*) Asia

Asket [as'ke:t] *m* (-en; -en), **as'ketisch** *adj* ascetic

'asozial *adj* antisocial

Asphalt [as'falt] *m* (-s; -e) asphalt

asphaltieren [asfal'ti:rən] *v/t* (*no* -ge-, h) (cover with) asphalt

Ass [as] *n* (-es; -e) ace (*a. tennis and fig*)

aß [a:s] *pret of* **essen**
Assistent [asɪsˈtɛnt] *m* (-en; -en),
Assisˈtentin *f* (-; -nen) assistant
Assisˈtenzarzt *m Am* intern, *Br* house-
man
Ast [ast] *m* (-es; Äste [ˈɛstə]) BOT branch
Astronaut [astroˈnaut] *m* (-en; -en),
Astroˈnautin *f* (-; -nen) astronaut
Astronom [astroˈnoːm] *m* (-en; -en) as-
tronomer; **Astronomie** [-noˈmiː] *f* (-;
no pl) astronomy
ASU [aːˌɛsˈuː] ABBR *of* **Abgas-Sonder-
-Untersuchung** MOT *Am* emissions
test, *Br* exhaust emission test
Asyl [aˈzyːl] *n* (-s; -e) asylum; **Asylant**
[azyˈlant] *m* (-en; -en), **Asyˈlantin** *f*
(-; -nen) asylum seeker, (political) refugee
Aˈsyl|bewerber(in) asylum seeker;
~recht *n* right of (political) asylum
Atelier [ateˈljeː] *n* (-s; -s) studio
Atem [ˈaːtəm] *m* (-s; *no pl*) breath; **außer** ~ out of breath; (tief) ~ **holen** take
a (deep) breath; **'atemberaubend** *adj*
breathtaking; **'Atemgerät** *n* MED res-
pirator; **'atemlos** *adj* breathless;
'Atempause *f* F breather; **'Atemzug**
m breath
Äther [ˈɛːtə] *m* (-s; *no pl*) CHEM ether;
radio etc: air
Athlet [atˈleːt] *m* (-en; -en), **Athˈletin** *f*
(-; -nen) SPORT athlete
athˈletisch *adj* athletic
Atlas [ˈatlas] *m* (-ses; -se, Atlanten) atlas
atmen [ˈaːtmən] *v/i and v/t* (ge-, h)
breathe
Atmosphäre [atmoˈsfɛːrə] *f* (-; -n) atmosphere
'Atmung *f* (-; *no pl*) breathing, respiration
Atoll [aˈtɔl] *n* (-s; -e) atoll
Atom [aˈtoːm] *n* (-s; -e) atom
A'tom... *in cpds* -energie, -forschung,
-kraft, -krieg, -müll, -rakete, -reaktor,
-waffen *etc* nuclear ...
atomar [atoˈmaːɐ̯] *adj* atomic, nuclear
A'tombombe *f* MIL atom(ic) bomb
A'tomkern *m* PHYS (atomic) nucleus
a'tomwaffenfrei *adj* nuclear-free
Attentat [atɛntˈaːt] *n* (-[e]s; -e) assassi-
nation attempt, attempt on s.o.'s life;
Opfer e-s ~s werden be assassin-
ated
'Attentäter *m* (-s; -) assassin

Attest [aˈtɛst] *n* (-[e]s; -e) (doctor's) certificate
Attraktion [atrakˈtsjoːn] *f* (-; -en) attraction; **attraktiv** [-ˈtiːf] *adj* attractive
Attrappe [aˈtrapə] *f* (-; -n) dummy
Attribut [atriˈbuːt] *n* (-[e]s; -e) LING
attribute (*a. fig*)
ätzend [ˈɛtsənt] *adj* corrosive, caustic (*a.
fig*); F gross; *das ist echt* ~ it's the pits
au [au] *int* ouch!; ~ *fein!* oh, good!
Aubergine [oberˈʒiːnə] *f* (-; -n) BOT egg-
plant, *Br* aubergine
auch [aux] *cj* also, too, as well; *ich* ~ so
am (*or* do) I, F me too; ~ *nicht* not
either; *wenn* ~ even if; *wo* ~ *(immer)*
wherever; *ist es* ~ *wahr?* is it really
true?
Audienz [auˈdjɛnts] *f* (-; -en) audience
(*bei* with)
auf [auf] *prp (dat and acc) and adv* on; in;
at; open; up; ~ *Seite 20* on page 20; ~
der Straße on (*Br* in) the street; on the
road; ~ *der Welt* in the world; ~ *See* at
sea; ~ *dem Lande* in the country; ~
dem Bahnhof etc at the station *etc*; ~
Urlaub on vacation; *die Uhr stellen*
~ (*acc*) set the watch to; ~ *deutsch* in
German; ~ *deinen Wunsch* at your request; ~ *die Sekunde genau* to the
second; ~ *und ab* up and down
'auf|arbeiten *v/t* (*sep, -ge-, h*) catch up
on (*backlog*); refurbish; **~atmen** *v/i*
(*sep, -ge-, h*) heave a sigh of relief
'Aufbau *m* (-[e]s; *no pl*) building (up);
structure; **'aufbauen** *v/t* (*sep, -ge-, h*)
build (up) (*a. fig*); set up; construct
'auf|bauschen *v/t* (*sep, -ge-, h*) exagge-
rate; **~bekommen** *v/t* (*irr, kommen,
sep, no -ge-, h*) get *door etc* open; be
given (*a task etc*); **~bereiten** *v/t* (*sep,
no -ge-, h*) process, clean, treat; **~bes-
sern** *v/t* (*sep, -ge-, h*) raise (*salary etc*);
~bewahren *v/t* (*sep, no -ge-, h*) keep;
~bieten *v/t* (*irr, bieten, sep, -ge-, h*)
muster; **~blasen** *v/t* (*irr, blasen, sep,
-ge-, h*) blow up; **~bleiben** *v/i* (*irr, bleiben, sep, -ge-, sein*) stay up; *door etc*:
remain open; **~blenden** *v/i* (*sep, -ge-,
h*) MOT turn the headlights on; **~bli-
cken** *v/i* (*sep, -ge-, h*) look up (*zu* at)
(*a. fig*); **~blitzen** *v/i* (*sep, -ge-, h, sein*)
flash (*a. fig*)
'aufbrausen *v/i* (*sep, -ge-, sein*) fly into a
temper; **~d** *adj* irascible

'**aufbrechen** (*irr, brechen, sep, -ge-*) **1.** *v/t* (*h*) break *or* force open; *fig* leave (*nach* for) **2.** *v/i* (*sein*) burst open; *fig* leave (*nach* for)

'**aufbringen** *v/t* (*irr, bringen, sep, -ge-, h*) raise (*money*); muster (*courage etc*); start (*fashion etc*); → **aufgebracht**

'**Aufbruch** *m* (*-[e]s; no pl*) departure, start

'**auf|brühen** *v/t* (*sep, -ge-, h*) make; **~bürden** *v/t* (*sep, -ge-, h*) **j-m et. ~** burden s.o. with s.th.; **~decken** *v/t* (*sep, -ge-, h*) uncover; **~drängen** *v/t* (*sep, -ge-*) **j-m et. ~** force s.th. on s.o.; **sich j-m ~** impose on s.o.; **sich ~** *fig* suggest itself; **~drehen** F (*sep, -ge-, h*) **1.** *v/t* turn on; **2.** *v/i* MOT step on the gas

'**aufdringlich** *adj* obtrusive

'**Aufdruck** *m* imprint; *on stamps:* overprint, surcharge

aufei'nander *adv* on top of each other; one after another; **~ folgend** successive

Aufenthalt ['aufɛnthalt] *m* (*-[e]s; -e*) stay; RAIL stop

'**Aufenthalts|genehmigung** *f* residence permit; **~raum** *m* lounge, recreation room

'**auferstehen** *v/i* (*irr, stehen, sep, no -ge-, sein*) rise (from the dead)

'**Auferstehung** *f* (*-; -en*) REL resurrection

'**aufessen** *v/t* (*irr, essen, sep, -ge-, h*) eat up

'**auffahren** *v/i* (*irr, fahren, sep, -ge-, sein*) crash (*auf acc* into); *fig* start up; '**Auffahrt** *f* approach; driveway; *Br* drive; '**Auffahrunfall** *m* MOT rear-end collision; pileup

'**auffallen** *v/i* (*irr, fallen, sep, -ge-, sein*) attract attention; **j-m ~** strike s.o.

'**auffallend**, '**auffällig** *adj* striking; conspicuous; flashy (*clothes*)

'**auffangen** *v/t* (*irr, fangen, sep, -ge-, h*) catch (*a. fig*)

'**auffassen** *v/t* (*sep, -ge-, h*) understand (*als* as)

'**Auffassung** *f* view; interpretation

'**auffinden** *v/t* (*irr, finden, sep, -ge-, h*) find, discover

'**auffordern** *v/t* (*sep, -ge-, h*) **j-n ~, et. zu tun** ask (*or* tell) s.o. to do s.th.

'**Aufforderung** *f* request; demand

'**auffrischen** *v/t* (*sep, -ge-, h*) freshen up; brush up

'**aufführen** *v/t* (*sep, -ge-, h*) THEA *etc* perform, present; state; **sich ~** behave

'**Aufführung** *f* THEA *etc* performance; *film:* showing

'**Aufgabe** *f* task, job; duty; PED task, assignment; MATH problem; *fig* surrender; **es sich zur ~ machen** make it one's business

'**Aufgang** *m* staircase; AST rising

'**aufgeben** (*irr, geben, sep, -ge-, h*) **1.** *v/t* give up; mail, send, *Br* post; check (*baggage*); PED set, give, assign (*homework etc*); ECON place (*order etc*); **2.** *v/i* give up *or* in

'**aufgebracht** *adj* furious; **~dreht** F *adj* excited; **~dunsen** ['aufgədʊnzən] *adj* puffed(-up)

'**aufgehen** *v/i* (*irr, gehen, sep, -ge-, sein*) open; sun, dough etc: rise; MATH come out even; **in Flammen ~** go up in flames

'**aufge|hoben** *fig adj*: **gut ~ sein bei** be in good hands with; **~legt** *adj*: **zu et. ~ sein** feel like (doing) s.th.; **gut (schlecht) ~** in a good (bad) mood; **~regt** *adj* excited; nervous; **~schlossen** *fig adj* open-minded; **~ für** open to; **~weckt** *fig adj* bright

'**aufgreifen** *v/t* (*irr, greifen, sep, -ge-, h*) pick up

auf'grund (*gen*) because of

'**auf|haben** F *v/t* (*irr, haben, sep, -ge-, h*) have on, wear; PED have *homework etc* to do; **~halten** *v/t* (*irr, halten, sep, -ge-, h*) stop, hold up (*a. traffic, thief etc*); keep open; **sich ~** (*bei j-m*) stay (with s.o.); **~hängen** *v/t* (*sep, -ge-, h*) hang (up); **j-n ~** hang s.o.; **~heben** *v/t* (*irr, heben, sep, -ge-, h*) pick up; keep; abolish (*law etc*); break up (*meeting etc*); **sich gegenseitig ~** neutralize each other; → **aufgehoben**

'**Aufheben** *n* (*-s; no pl*) **viel ~s machen** make a fuss (*von* about)

'**auf|heitern** *v/t* (*sep, -ge-, h*) cheer up; **sich ~** *weather:* clear up; **~helfen** *v/i* (*irr, helfen, sep, -ge-, h*) help s.o. up; **~hellen** *v/t and v/refl* (*sep, -ge-, h*) brighten; **~hetzen** *v/t* (*sep, -ge-, h*) **j-n ~ gegen** set s.o. against; incite; **~horchen** *v/i* (*sep, -ge-, h*) prick (up) one's ears; **~ lassen** make *s.o.* sit up; **~hören** *v/i* (*sep, -ge-, h*) stop, end, finish, quit; *mit et.* ~ stop (doing) s.th.; *hör(t) auf!* stop it!; **~kaufen** *v/t (sep, -ge-, h)* buy up

'**aufklären** *v/t (sep, -ge-, h)* clear up, *a.* solve (*crime*); *j-n* ~ *über (acc)* inform s.o. about; *j-n (sexuell)* ~ F tell s.o. the facts of life; '**Aufklärung** *f (-; no pl)* clearing up, solution; information; sex education; PHILOS Enlightenment; MIL reconnaissance

'**aufkleben** *v/t (sep, -ge-, h)* paste *or* stick on; '**Aufkleber** *m (-s; -)* sticker

'**aufknöpfen** *v/t (sep, -ge-, h)* unbutton

'**aufkommen** *v/i (irr, kommen, sep, -ge-, sein)* come up; come into fashion *or* use; *rumo(u)r etc*: arise; ~ *für* pay (for)

'**aufladen** *v/t (irr, laden, sep, -ge-, h)* load; ELECTR charge

'**Auflage** *f* edition; circulation

'**auflassen** F *v/t (irr, lassen, sep, -ge-, h)* leave *door etc* open; keep *one's hat etc* on; **~lauern** *v/i (sep, -ge-, h) j-m* ~ waylay s.o.

'**Auflauf** *m* crowd; GASTR soufflé, pudding

'**auflaufen** *v/i (irr, laufen, sep, -ge-, sein)* MAR run aground; **~leben** *v/i (sep, -ge-, sein) a. (wieder)* ~ *lassen* revive; **~legen** *(sep, -ge-, h)* **1.** *v/t* put on, lay on; **2.** *v/i* TEL hang up

'**auflehnen** *v/t and v/refl (sep, -ge-, h)* lean *(auf acc* on); *sich* ~ rebel, revolt *(gegen* against); '**Auflehnung** *f (-; -en)* rebellion, revolt

'**auflesen** *v/t (irr, lesen, sep, -ge-, h)* pick up *(a. fig)*; **~leuchten** *v/i (sep, -ge-, h)* flash (up); **~listen** *v/t (sep, -ge-, h)* list *(a.* EDP); **~lockern** *v/t (sep, -ge-, h)* loosen up; *fig* liven up

'**auflösen** *v/t (sep, -ge-, h)* dissolve; solve *(a.* MATH); disintegrate; '**Auflösung** *f* (dis)solution; disintegration

'**aufmachen** F *v/t (sep, -ge-, h)* open; *sich* ~ set out; '**Aufmachung** *f (-; -en)* get-up

'**aufmerksam** *adj* attentive *(auf acc* to); thoughtful; *j-n* ~ *machen auf (acc)* call s.o.'s attention to

'**Aufmerksamkeit** *f (-; -en) a) (no pl)* attention, b) small present

'**aufmuntern** *v/t (sep, -ge-, h)* encourage; cheer up

Aufnahme ['aufna:mə] *f (-; -n)* taking up; reception *(a.* MED *etc)*; admission;

photo(graph); recording; *film*: shooting

'**aufnahmefähig** *adj* receptive *(für* of)

'**Aufnahme|gebühr** *f* admission fee; **~prüfung** *f* entrance exam(ination)

'**aufnehmen** *v/t (irr, nehmen, sep, -ge-, h)* take up *(a. post etc)*; pick up; take s.o. up; hold; take *s.th.* in; receive; PED *etc* admit; PHOT take a picture *of*; record; take *(the ball)*; *es* ~ *mit* be a match for

'**aufpassen** *v/i (sep, -ge-, h)* pay attention; take care; ~ *auf (acc)* take care of, look after; keep an eye on; *pass auf!* look out!

'**Aufprall** *m (-[e]s; no pl)* impact

'**aufprallen** *v/i (sep, -ge-, sein)* ~ *auf (dat or acc)* hit

'**aufpumpen** *v/t (sep, -ge-, h)* pump up

'**aufputschen** *v/t (sep, -ge-, h)* pep up

'**Aufputschmittel** *n* PHARM stimulant, pep pill

'**aufraffen** *v/refl (sep, -ge-, h) sich* ~ *zu* bring o.s. to *do s.th.*; **~räumen** *v/t (sep, -ge-, h)* tidy up; clear

'**aufrecht** *adj and adv* upright *(a. fig)*; **~erhalten** *v/t (irr, halten, sep, no -ge-, h)* maintain, keep up

'**aufregen** *v/t (sep, -ge-, h)* excite, upset; *sich* ~ get excited *or* upset *(über acc* about); **~d** *adj* exciting

'**Aufregung** *f* excitement; fuss

'**aufreiben** *fig v/t (irr, reiben, sep, -ge-, h)* wear down; **~d** *adj* stressful

'**aufreißen** *v/t (irr, reißen, sep, -ge-, h)* tear open; fling *door etc* open; open *one's eyes* wide; F pick *s.o.* up

'**aufreizend** *adj* provocative

'**aufrichten** *v/t (sep, -ge-, h)* put up, raise; *sich* ~ straighten up; sit up

'**aufrichtig** *adj* sincere; frank

'**Aufrichtigkeit** *f (-; no pl)* sincerity; frankness

'**Aufriss** *m (-es; -e)* ARCH elevation

'**aufrollen** *v/t and v/refl (sep, -ge-, h)* roll up

'**Aufruf** *m* call; appeal *(zu* for)

'**aufrufen** *v/t (irr, rufen, sep, -ge-, h)* call on

Aufruhr ['aufru:ɐ] *m (-s; no pl)* revolt; riot; turmoil; '**Aufrührer** *m (-s; -)* rebel; rioter; **aufrührerisch** ['aufry:rərɪʃ] *adj* rebellious

'**aufrunden** *v/t (sep, -ge-, h)* round off

'**aufrüsten** *v/t and v/i (sep, -ge-, h)* (re)arm; '**Aufrüstung** *f* (re)armament '**auf|rütteln** *fig vt* (*sep, -ge-, h*) shake up, rouse; **~sagen** *v/t* (*sep, -ge-, h*) say; *a.* recite (*poem*)

aufsässig ['aufzɛsɪç] *adj* rebellious

'**Aufsatz** *m* PED essay, *Am a.* theme; (*newspaper etc*) article; TECH top

'**auf|saugen** *v/t* (*sep, -ge-, h*) absorb (*a. fig*); **~scheuern** *v/t* (*sep, -ge-, h*) chafe; **~schichten** *v/t* (*sep, -ge-, h*) pile up; **~schieben** *fig v/t* (*irr, schieben, sep, -ge-, h*) put off, postpone; delay

'**Aufschlag** *m* impact; ECON extra charge; lapel; cuff, *Br* turnup; *tennis*: service; '**aufschlagen** (*irr, schlagen, sep, -ge-, h*) **1.** *v/t* open (*book, eyes etc*); pitch (*tent*); cut (*one's knee etc*); *Seite 3 ~* open at page 3; **2.** *v/i tennis*: serve; *auf dem Boden ~* hit the ground

'**auf|schließen** *v/t* (*irr, schließen, sep, -ge-, h*) unlock, open; **~schlitzen** *v/t* (*sep, -ge-, h*) slit *or* rip open

'**Aufschluss** *m* information (*über acc* on)

'**auf|schnappen** F *fig v/t* (*sep, -ge-, h*) pick up; **~schneiden** (*irr, schneiden, sep, -ge-, h*) **1.** *v/t* cut open; GASTR cut up; **2.** F *fig v/i* brag, boast, talk big

'**Aufschnitt** *m* (*-[e]s; no pl*) GASTR cold cuts, *Br* (slices of) cold meat

'**auf|schnüren** *v/t* (*sep, -ge-, h*) untie; unlace; **~schrauben** *v/t* (*sep, -ge-, h*) unscrew; **~schrecken** (*sep, -ge-*) **1.** *v/t* (*h*) startle; **2.** *v/i* (*sein*) start (up)

'**Aufschrei** *m* yell; scream, outcry (*a. fig*)

'**auf|schreiben** *v/t* (*irr, schreiben, sep, -ge-, h*) write down; **~schreien** *v/i* (*irr, schreien, sep, -ge-, h*) cry out, scream

'**Aufschrift** *f* inscription

'**Aufschub** *m* postponement; delay; adjournment; respite

'**Aufschwung** *m* SPORT swing-up; *esp* ECON recovery, upswing; boom

'**aufsehen** *n* (*-s; no pl*) **~ erregen** attract attention; cause a sensation; **~ erregend** sensational

'**Aufseher** *m* (*-s; -*), '**Aufseherin** *f* (*-; -nen*) guard

'**aufsetzen** (*sep, -ge-, h*) **1.** *v/t* put on; draw up (*letter etc*); *sich ~* sit up; **2.** *v/i* AVIAT touch down

'**Aufsetzer** *m* (*-s; -*) SPORT awkward bouncing ball

'**Aufsicht** *f* (*-; no pl*) supervision, con-

trol; **~ führen** PED *etc* be on (break) duty; proctor, *Br* invigilate

'**Aufsichts|behörde** *f* supervisory board; **~rat** *m* ECON board of directors; supervisory board

'**auf|sitzen** *v/i* (*irr, sitzen, sep, -ge-, h*) mount; **~spannen** *v/t* (*sep, -ge-, h*) stretch; put up (*umbrella*); spread; **~sparen** *v/t* (*sep, -ge-, h*) save; **~sperren** *v/t* (*sep, -ge-, h*) unlock; F open wide; **~spielen** *v/refl* (*sep, -ge-, h*) show off; *sich ~ als* play; **~spießen** *v/t* (*sep, -ge-, h*) spear, skewer; *animal*: gore; **~springen** *v/i* (*irr, springen, sep, -ge-, sein*) jump up; *door etc*: fly open; *lips etc*: chap; **~spüren** *v/t* (*sep, -ge-, h*) track down; **~stacheln** *v/t* (*sep, -ge-, h*) goad (*s.o. into doing s.th.*); **~stampfen** *v/i* (*sep, -ge-, h*) stamp (one's foot)

'**Aufstand** *m* revolt, rebellion

'**Aufständische** *m, f* (*-n; -n*) rebel

'**auf|stapeln** *v/t* (*sep, -ge-, h*) pile up; **~stechen** *v/t* (*irr, stechen, sep, -ge-, h*) puncture, prick open; MED lance; **~stecken** *v/t* (*sep, -ge-, h*) put up (*hair*); F *fig* give up; **~stehen** *v/i* (*irr, stehen, sep, -ge-, sein*) get up, rise; **~steigen** *v/i* (*irr, steigen, sep, -ge-, sein*) rise (*a. fig*); get on (*horse, bicycle*); be promoted; SPORT *Am a.* be moved up to a higher division

'**aufstellen** *v/t* (*sep, -ge-, h*) set up, put up; post (*guard*); set (*trap, record etc*); nominate *s.o.*; draw up (*table, list etc*)

'**Aufstellung** *f* putting up; nomination; list; SPORT line-up

Aufstieg ['aufʃtiːk] *m* (*-[e]s; -e*) ascent, *fig a.* rise

'**auf|stöbern** *fig v/t* (*sep, -ge-, h*) ferret out; **~stoßen** (*irr, stoßen, sep, -ge-, h*) **1.** *v/t* push open; **2.** *v/i* belch; **~stützen** *v/refl* (*sep, -ge-, h*) lean (*auf acc* or *dat* on); **~suchen** *v/t* (*sep, -ge-, h*) visit; see

'**Auftakt** *m* MUS upbeat; *fig* prelude

'**auf|tanken** *v/t* (*sep, -ge-, h*) fill up; MOT, AVIAT refuel; **~tauchen** *v/i* (*sep, -ge-, sein*) appear; MAR surface; **~tauen** *v/t* (*sep, -ge-, h*) thaw; GASTR defrost; **~teilen** *v/t* (*sep, -ge-, h*) divide (up)

Auftrag ['auftraːk] *m* (*-[e]s; Aufträge* ['auftrɛːgə]) instructions, order (*a.* ECON); MIL mission; *im~ von* on behalf of; **auftragen** v|t (irr, **tragen**, sep, -ge-, h) serve (up) (*food*); apply (*paint*); **j-m et. ~** ask (or tell) s.o. to do s.th; F **dick ~** et. ~ exaggerate; '**Auftraggeber** m (-s; -) principal; customer

'auf|treffen v|i (irr, **treffen**, sep, -ge-, sein) strike, hit; **~treiben** F v|t (irr, **treiben**, sep, -ge-, h) get hold of; raise (*money*); **~trennen** v|t (sep, -ge-, h) undo (*seam*), cut open; **~treten** v|i (irr, **treten**, sep, -ge-, sein) THEA etc appear (**als** as); behave, act; occur

'**Auftreten** n (-s; no pl) appearance; behavio(u)r; occurrence

'**Auftrieb** m (-[e]s; no pl) PHYS buoyancy (a. fig); AVIAT lift; fig impetus

'**Auftritt** m THEA entrance

'auf|tun v|refl (irr, **tun**, sep, -ge-, h) open (a. fig); abyss: yawn; **~türmen** v|t (sep, -ge-, h) pile or heap up; **sich ~** pile up; **~wachen** v|i (sep, -ge-, sein) wake up; **~wachsen** v|i (irr, **wachsen**, sep, -ge-, sein) grow up

'**Aufwand** ['aufvant] m (-[e]s; no pl) expenditure (**an** dat of), a. expense; pomp

'aufwändig ['aufvɛndɪç] adj costly; extravagant (*lifestyle*)

'aufwärmen v|t (sep, -ge-, h) warm up; F fig contp bring up

'aufwärts ['aufvɛrts] adv upward(s); **~ gehen** fig improve

'auf|wecken v|t (sep, -ge-, h) wake (up); **~weichen** v|t (sep, -ge-, h) soften; soak; **~weisen** v|t (irr, **weisen**, sep, -ge-, h) show, have; **~wenden** v|t ([irr, **wenden**,] sep, -ge-, h) spend (**für** on); **Mühe ~** take pains

aufwendig → **aufwändig**

'aufwerfen v|t (irr, **werfen**, sep, -ge-, h) raise (*question etc*)

'aufwerten v|t (sep, -ge-, h) ECON revalue; fig increase the value of

'**Aufwertung** f revaluation

'aufwickeln v|t and v|refl (sep, -ge-, h) wind up, roll up; put *hair* in curlers

'aufwiegeln ['aufvi:gəln] v|t (sep, -ge-, h) stir up, incite, instigate

'aufwiegen v|t (irr, **wiegen**, sep, -ge-, h) make up for

'**Aufwiegler** ['aufvi:glɐ] m (-s; -) agitator; instigator

'**Aufwind** m upwind; **im ~** fig on the upswing

'auf|wirbeln v|t (sep, -ge-, h) whirl up; fig (**viel**) **Staub ~** make (quite) a stir; **~wischen** v|t (sep, -ge-, h) wipe up; **~wühlen** fig v|t (sep, -ge-, h) stir, move

'aufzählen v|t (sep, -ge-, h) name (one by one), list; '**Aufzählung** f enumeration, list

'aufzeichnen v|t (sep, -ge-, h) TV, radio etc: record, tape; draw; '**Aufzeichnung** f recording; pl notes

'aufzeigen v|t (sep, -ge-, h) show; demonstrate; point out (*mistake etc*)

'aufziehen (irr, **ziehen**, sep, -ge-) **1.** v|t (h) draw or pull up; (pull) open; bring up (*child*); wind (up) (*clock*); mount (*photo etc*); **j-n ~** tease s.o.; **2.** v|i (sein) come up; '**Aufzug** m elevator, Br lift; THEA act; F contp get-up

'aufzwingen v|t (irr, **zwingen**, sep, -ge-, h) **j-m et. ~** force s.th. upon s.o.

'**Augapfel** ['auk-] m ANAT eyeball

Auge ['augə] n (-s; -n) ANAT eye; **ein blaues ~** a black eye; **mit bloßem ~** with the naked eye; **mit verbundenen ~n** blindfold; **in meinen ~n** in my view; **mit anderen ~n** in a different light; **aus den ~n verlieren** lose sight of; **ein ~ zudrücken** turn a blind eye; **unter vier ~n** in private; F **ins ~ gehen** go wrong

'**Augenarzt** m eye specialist

'**Augenblick** m moment, instant

'augenblicklich **1.** adj present; immediate; momentary; **2.** adv at present, at the moment; immediately

'**Augen|braue** f eyebrow; **~licht** n (-[e]s; no pl) eyesight; **~lid** n eyelid; **~maß** n: **ein gutes ~** a sure eye; **nach dem ~** by the eye; **~merk** n: **sein ~ richten auf** (acc) turn one's attention to, fig a. have in view; **~schein** m (-s; no pl) appearance; **in ~ nehmen** examine, inspect; **~zeuge** m eyewitness

August [au'gʊst] m (-; no pl) August

Auktion [auk'tsjo:n] f (-; -en) auction

Auktionator [auktsjo'na:to:ɐ] m (-s; -en [-na'to:rən]) auctioneer

Aula ['aula] f (-; -s, Aulen) auditorium, Br (assembly) hall

aus [aus] prp (dat) and adv mst out of, from; of (silk etc); out of (spite etc); light etc: out, off; play etc: over, finished; SPORT out; **dem Fenster** etc out of the window *etc*; ~ **München** from Munich; ~ **Holz** (made) of wood; ~ **Mitleid** out of pity; ~ **Spaß** for fun; ~ **Versehen** by mistake; ~ **diesem Grunde** for this reason; **von hier** ~ from here; F **von mir** ~! I don't care!; ~ **der Mode** out of fashion; F ~ **sein** be over; be out; ~ **sein auf** (*acc*) be out for; be after (*s.o.'s money etc*); **die Schule (das Spiel) ist** ~ school (the game) is over; **einl**~ TECH on/off

Aus *n*: **im** ~ *ball*: out of play

'**aus|arbeiten** *v/t* (*sep, -ge-, h*) work out; prepare; **~arten** *v/i* (*sep, -ge-, sein*) get out of hand; **~atmen** *v/t and v/i* (*sep, -ge-, h*) breathe out; **~baden** F *v/t* (*sep, -ge-, h*) **et. ~ müssen** take the rap for s.th.

'**Ausbau** *m* (*-[e]s; no pl*) extension; completion; removal; '**ausbauen** *v/t* (*sep, -ge-, h*) extend; complete; remove; improve; '**ausbaufähig** *adj*: **et. ist** ~ there is potential for growth *or* development

'**ausbessern** *v/t* (*sep, -ge-, h*) mend, repair, F *a.* fix; '**Ausbesserung** *f* (*-; -en*) repair(ing)

'**Ausbeute** *f* (*-; no pl*) gain, profit; yield; '**ausbeuten** *v/t* (*sep, -ge-, h*) exploit (*a. contp*); '**Ausbeutung** *f* (*-; no pl*) exploitation

'**ausbilden** *v/t* (*sep, -ge-, h*) train, instruct; **j-n ~ zu** train s.o. to be

'**Ausbilder** *m* (*-s; -*) instructor

'**Ausbildung** *f* (*-; -en*) training, instruction

'**ausbleiben** *v/i* (*irr, bleiben, sep, -ge-, sein*) stay out; fail to come; **es konnte nicht ~** it was inevitable

'**Ausblick** *m* view (**auf** *acc* of); *fig* outlook (*for*)

'**ausbrechen** *v/i* (*irr, brechen, sep, -ge-, sein*) break out (*a. fig*); **in Tränen** ~ burst into tears; '**Ausbrecher** *m* (*-s; -*) escaped prisoner

'**ausbreiten** *v/t* (*sep, -ge-, h*) spread (out); **sich** ~ spread; '**Ausbreitung** *f* (*-; no pl*) spreading

'**ausbrennen** *v/t* (*irr, brennen, sep, -ge-, sein*) burn out

'**Ausbruch** *m* escape, breakout; outbreak (*of fire etc*); eruption (*of volcano*); (out)burst (*of resentment etc*)

'**ausbrüten** *v/t* (*sep, -ge-, h*) hatch (*a. fig*)

'**Ausdauer** *f* perseverance, stamina, *esp* SPORT *a.* staying power; '**ausdauernd** *adj* persevering; SPORT tireless

'**ausdehnen** *v/t and v/refl* (*sep, -ge-, h*) stretch; *fig* expand, extend

'**Ausdehnung** *f* expansion; extension

'**ausdenken** *v/t* (*irr, denken, sep, -ge-, h*) think s.th. up; invent (*a. fig*)

'**Ausdruck** *m* expression, term; EDP print-out; '**ausdrucken** *v/t* (*sep, -ge-, h*) EDP print out

'**ausdrücken** *v/t* (*sep, -ge-, h*) stub out (*cigarette etc*); *fig* express

ausdrücklich ['ausdryklɪç] *adj* express, explicit

'**ausdrucks|los** *adj* expressionless, blank; **~voll** *adj* expressive

'**Ausdrucksweise** *f* language, style

'**Ausdünstung** *f* (*-; -en*) exhalation; perspiration; odo(u)r

auseinander [aus²ai'nandɐ] *adv* apart; separate(d); ~ **bringen** separate, ~ **gehen** part; *meeting etc*: break up; *opinions etc*: differ; *married couple*: separate; ~ **halten** tell apart; ~ **nehmen** take apart (*a. fig*); ~ **setzen** explain; **sich ~ setzen mit** deal with; argue with s.o.

Ausei'nandersetzung *f* (*-; -en*) argument

'**auserlesen** *adj* choice, exquisite

'**ausfahren** (*irr, fahren, sep, -ge-*) **1.** *v/i* (*sein*) go for a drive *or* ride; **2.** *v/t* (*h*) take s.o. out; AVIAT extend (*landing gear*); '**Ausfahrt** *f* drive, ride; MOT exit

'**Ausfall** *m* TECH, MOT, SPORT failure; loss

'**ausfallen** *v/i* (*irr, fallen, sep, -ge-, sein*) fall out; not take place, be cancelled; TECH, MOT break down, fail; **gut etc** ~ turn out well *etc*; ~ **lassen** cancel; **die Schule fällt aus** there is no school

'**ausfertigen** *v/t* (*sep, -ge-, h*) draw up (*contract etc*); make out (*check etc*)

'**Ausfertigung** *f* drawing up; copy; **in doppelter** ~ in duplicate

'**ausfindig** *adj*: ~ **machen** find

ausflippen ['ausflɪpən] F *v/i* (*sep, -ge-, sein*) freak out

Ausflüchte ['ausflʏçtə] *pl* excuses

'**Ausflug** *m* trip, excursion, outing

Ausflügler ['ausflyːklɐ] *m* (*-s; -*) daytripper

'**Ausfluss** m TECH outlet; MED discharge

'**aus|fragen** v/t (sep, -ge-, h) question (*über* acc about); sound out; **~fransen** v/i (sep, -ge-, sein) fray; **~fressen** F v/t (irr, *fressen*, sep, -ge-, h) *et.* **~** be up to no good

Ausfuhr ['ausfuːɐ] f (-; -en) ECON export (ation); '**ausführbar** adj practicable; '**ausführen** v/t (sep, -ge-, h) take *s.o.* out; carry out (*task etc*); ECON export; explain

ausführlich ['ausfyːɐlɪç] **1.** adj detailed; comprehensive; **2.** adv in detail; '**Ausführlichkeit** f: *in aller* **~** in great detail

'**Ausführung** f execution, performance; type, model, design

'**ausfüllen** v/t (sep, -ge-, h) fill out (Br in) (*form*)

'**Ausgabe** f distribution; edition; expense; issue; EDP output

'**Ausgang** m exit, way out; end; result, outcome; TECH, ELECTR power, outlet

'**Ausgangs|punkt** m starting point; **~sperre** f POL curfew

'**ausgeben** v/t (irr, *geben*, sep, -ge-, h) give out; spend; F *j-m e-n* **~** buy *s.o.* a drink; *sich* **~** *als* pass o.s. off as

'**ausge|beult** adj baggy; **~bildet** adj trained, skilled; **~bucht** adj booked up; **~dehnt** adj extensive; **~dient** adj: **~** *haben* fig have had its day; **~fallen** adj odd, unusual; **~glichen** adj (well-)balanced

'**ausgehen** v/i (irr, *gehen*, sep, -ge-, sein) go out; end; hair: fall out; money, supplies: run out; *leer* **~** get nothing; **~** *von* start from or at; come from; *davon* **~**, *dass* assume that; *ihm ging das Geld aus* he ran out of money

'**ausge|kocht** fig adj cunning; out-and-out (*villain etc*); **~lassen** fig adj cheerful; hilarious; **~** *sein* be in high spirits; **~macht** adj agreed(-on); downright (*nonsense*); **~prägt** adj marked, pronounced; **~rechnet** adv: **~** *er* of all people; **~** *heute* today of all days; **~schlossen** adj out of the question; **~storben** adj extinct; **~sucht** adj select, choice; **~wachsen** adj fullgrown; **~wogen** adj (well-)balanced; **~zeichnet** adj excellent

ausgiebig ['ausgiːbɪç] adj extensive, thorough; substantial (*meal*)

'**ausgießen** v/t (irr, *gießen*, sep, -ge-, h) pour out

'**Ausgleich** m (-[e]s; no pl) compensation; SPORT even score, Br equalization; *tennis:* deuce; '**ausgleichen** v/t and v/i (irr, *gleichen*, sep, -ge-, h) compensate; equalize (Br a. SPORT); ECON balance; SPORT make the score even

'**Ausgleichs|sport** m remedial exercises; **~tor** n, **~treffer** m SPORT tying point, Br equalizer

'**ausgraben** v/t (irr, *graben*, sep, -ge-, h) dig out or up (a. fig)

'**Ausgrabungen** pl excavations

'**ausgrenzen** v/t (sep, -ge-, h) isolate

'**Ausguss** m (kitchen) sink

'**aushalten** (irr, *halten*, sep, -ge-, h) **1.** v/t bear, stand; keep (*mistress etc*); *nicht auszuhalten sein* be unbearable; **2.** v/i hold out

'**aushändigen** ['aushɛndɪgən] v/t (sep, -ge-, h) hand over

'**Aushang** m notice; bulletin

'**aushängen** v/t (sep, -ge-, h) hang out, put up; unhinge (*door*)

'**aus|heben** v/t (irr, *heben*, sep, -ge-, h) dig (*trench*); raid (*place etc*); **~helfen** v/i (irr, *helfen*, sep, -ge-, h) help out

'**Aushilfe** f (temporary) help

'**Aushilfs...** *in cpds* -kellner etc: temporary

'**aus|holen** v/i (sep, -ge-, h) *zum Schlag* **~** swing (to strike); fig *weit* **~** go far back; **~horchen** v/t (sep, -ge-, h) sound (*über* acc on); **~hungern** v/t (sep, -ge-, h) starve out; **~kennen** v/refl (irr, *kennen*, sep, -ge-, h) *sich* **~** (*in* dat) know one's way (about); fig know a lot (about); **~klingen** v/i (irr, *klingen*, sep, -ge-, sein) draw to a close; **~klopfen** v/t (sep, -ge-, h) knock out; **~kommen** v/i (irr, *kommen*, sep, -ge-, sein) get by; **~** *mit* manage with s.th.; get along with *s.o.*

Auskunft ['auskʊnft] f (-; *Auskünfte* ['auskʏnftə]) a) information, b) (no pl) information desk; TEL inquiries

'**aus|lachen** v/t (sep, -ge-, h) laugh at (*wegen* for); **~laden** v/t (irr, *laden*, sep, -ge-, h) unload

'**Auslage** f window display; pl expenses

'**Ausland** n (-[e]s; no pl) *das* **~** foreign countries; *ins* **~**, *im* **~** abroad

Ausländer ['auslɛndɐ] m (-s; -) foreigner; ~**feindlichkeit** f hostility to foreigners, xenophobia

Ausländerin ['aʊslɛndərɪn] f (-; -nen) foreigner

'**ausländisch** [-lɛndɪʃ] adj foreign

'**Auslands|gespräch** n international call; ~**korrespondent(in)** foreign correspondent

'**auslassen** v/t (irr, lassen, sep, -ge-, h) leave out; melt (butter etc); let out (seam); **s-n Zorn an j-m** ~ take it out on s.o.; **sich** ~ **über** (acc) express o.s. on

'**Auslassung** f (-; -en) omission

'**Auslassungszeichen** n LING apostrophe

'**Auslauf** m room to move about; dog: exercise; '**auslaufen** v/i (irr, laufen, sep, -ge-, sein) MAR leave port; pot etc: leak; liquid etc: run out; '**Ausläufer** m METEOR ridge, trough; pl GEOGR foothills; '**Auslaufmo,dell** n ECON close-out (Br phase-out) model

'**auslegen** v/t (sep, -ge-, h) lay out; carpet; line (with paper etc); display (goods); interpret (text etc); advance (money)

'**Auslegung** f (-; -en) interpretation

'**aus|leihen** v/t (irr, leihen, sep, -ge-, h) lend (out), loan; **sich** (dat) **et.** ~ borrow s.th.; ~**lernen** v/i (sep, -ge-, h) complete one's training; **man lernt nie aus** we live and learn

'**Auslese** f choice, selection; fig pick

'**auslesen** v/t (irr, lesen, sep, -ge-, h) pick out, select; finish (book etc)

'**ausliefern** v/t (sep, -ge-, h) hand or turn over, deliver (up); POL extradite; '**Auslieferung** f delivery; extradition

'**aus|liegen** v/i (irr, liegen, sep, -ge-, h) be laid out; ~**löschen** v/t (sep, -ge-, h) put out; fig wipe out; ~**losen** v/t (sep, -ge-, h) draw (lots) for

'**auslösen** v/t (sep, -ge-, h) TECH release; ransom, redeem; cause, start, trigger s.th. off; '**Auslöser** m (PHOT shutter) release; trigger

'**ausmachen** v/t (sep, -ge-, h) put out (fire); turn off (light etc); arrange (date etc); agree on (price etc); make up; amount to; settle (dispute); sight, spot; **macht es Ihnen et. aus (, wenn...)?** do you mind (if ...)?; **es macht mir nichts aus** I don't mind; **das macht (gar**

nichts aus that doesn't matter (at all)

'**ausmalen** v/t (sep, -ge-, h) paint; **sich et.** ~ imagine s.th.

'**Ausmaß** n extent; pl proportions

aus|merzen ['aʊsmɛrtsən] v/t (sep, -ge-, h) eliminate; ~**messen** v/t (irr, messen, sep, -ge-, h) measure

Ausnahme f ['aʊsnaːmə] f (-; -n) exception; ~**zustand** m POL state of emergency

'**ausnahmslos** adv without exception

'**ausnahmsweise** adv by way of exception; just this once

'**ausnehmen** v/t (irr, nehmen, sep, -ge-, h) clean (chicken etc); except; F contp fleece s.o.; ~**d** adv exceptionally

'**aus|nutzen** v/t (sep, -ge-, h) use; take advantage of (a. contp); exploit; ~**packen** (sep, -ge-, h) **1.** v/t unpack; **2.** F v/i talk; ~**pfeifen** v/t (irr, pfeifen, sep, -ge-, h) boo, hiss; ~**plaudern** (sep, -ge-, h) blab out; ~**plündern** v/t (sep, -ge-, h) plunder, rob; ~**pro,bieren** v/t (sep, no -ge-, h) try (out), test

'**Auspuff** m MOT exhaust; ~**gase** pl MOT exhaust fumes; ~**rohr** n MOT exhaust pipe; ~**topf** m MOT muffler, Br silencer

'**aus|quar,tieren** v/t (sep, no -ge-, h) move out; ~**ra,dieren** v/t (sep, no -ge-, h) erase; fig wipe out; ~**ran,gieren** v/t (sep, no -ge-, h) discard; ~**rauben** v/t (sep, -ge-, h) rob; ~**räumen** v/t (sep, -ge-, h) empty; clear out (room etc); fig clear up (doubt etc); ~**rechnen** v/t (sep, -ge-, h) work out

'**Ausrede** f excuse

'**ausreden** (sep, -ge-, h) **1.** v/i finish speaking; **j-n** ~ **lassen** hear s.o. out; **2.** v/t: **j-m et.** ~ talk s.o. out of s.th.

'**ausreichen** v/t (sep, -ge-, h) be enough; ~**d** adj sufficient, enough; grade: (barely) passing, only average, weak, D

'**Ausreise** f departure; '**ausreisen** v/i (sep, -ge-, sein) leave (a or one's country); '**Ausreisevisum** n exit visa

'**ausreißen** (irr, reißen, sep, -ge-, h) **1.** v/t (h) pull or tear out; **2.** F v/i (sein) run away; '**Ausreißer** m (-s; -) runaway

'**aus|renken** v/t (sep, -ge-, h) MED dislocate; ~**richten** v/t (sep, -ge-, h) tell s.o. s.th.; deliver (message); accomplish; arrange (party etc); **richte ihr e-n Gruß von mir aus!** give her my regards;

kann ich et. ~? can I take a message

'**ausrotten** v/t (*sep, -ge-, h*) exterminate

'**Ausrottung** f (-; *-en*) extermination

'**ausrücken** v/i (*sep, -ge-, sein*) F run away; MIL march out

'**Ausruf** m cry, shout; '**ausrufen** v/t (*irr, **rufen**, sep, -ge-, h*) cry, shout, exclaim; call out (*name*); POL proclaim; '**Ausrufung** f (-; *-en*) POL proclamation; '**Ausrufungszeichen** n LING exclamation mark

'**ausruhen** v/i, v/t and v/refl (*sep, -ge-, h*) rest

'**ausrüsten** v/t (*sep, -ge-, h*) equip; '**Ausrüstung** f equipment

'**ausrutschen** v/i (*sep, -ge-, sein*) slip

'**Aussage** f statement; JUR evidence

'**aussagen** v/i (*sep, -ge-, h*) state, declare; JUR testify

'**ausschalten** v/t (*sep, -ge-, h*) switch off; *fig* eliminate

'**Ausschau** f: *~ **halten** nach →* '**ausschauen** v/i (*sep, -ge-, h*) *~ **nach*** look out for, watch out for

'**ausscheiden** (*irr, **scheiden**, sep, -ge-*) **1.** v/i (*sein*) be ruled out; SPORT *etc* drop out (*aus dat of*); retire (*aus dat* from office *etc*); *~ **aus*** (*dat*) leave (*a firm etc*); **2.** v/t (*h*) eliminate; MED *etc* secrete, exude; '**Ausscheidung** f elimination (*a.* SPORT); MED secretion

'**Ausscheidungs...** *in cpds ...spiel etc*: SPORT qualifying...

'**ausschlachten** *fig* v/t (*sep, -ge-, h*) salvage, B *a.* cannibalize; *contp* exploit;

'**ausschlafen** (*irr, **schlafen**, sep, -ge-, h*) **1.** v/i sleep in; **2.** v/t sleep off

'**Ausschlag** m MED rash; TECH deflection; *den ~ **geben*** decide it

'**ausschlagen** (*irr, **schlagen**, sep, -ge-, h*) **1.** v/t knock out (*tooth etc*); *fig* refuse, decline (*offer etc*); **2.** v/i horse: kick; BOT bud; TECH deflect

'**ausschlaggebend** *adj* decisive

'**ausschließen** v/t (*irr, **schließen**, sep, -ge-, h*) lock out; *fig* exclude; expel; SPORT disqualify

'**ausschließlich** *adj* exclusive

'**Ausschluss** m exclusion; expulsion; SPORT disqualification; *unter ~ **der Öffentlichkeit*** in closed session

'**ausschmücken** v/t (*sep, -ge-, h*) decorate; *fig* embellish; *~**schneiden*** v/t (*irr, **schneiden**, sep, -ge-, h*) cut out

'**Ausschnitt** m *clothing*: neck; (*press*) clipping (*Br* cutting); *fig* part; extract; *mit tiefem ~* low-necked

'**ausschreiben** v/t (*irr, **schreiben**, sep, -ge-, h*) write out (*a.* check *etc*); advertise (*post etc*); '**Ausschreibung** f advertisement

'**Ausschreitungen** *pl* violence, riots

'**Ausschuss** m committee, board; TECH (*no pl*) refuse, waste, rejects

'**ausschütteln** v/t (*sep, -ge-, h*) shake out; *~**schütten*** v/t (*sep, -ge-, h*) pour out (*a. fig*); spill; ECON pay; *sich vor Lachen ~* split one's sides

'**ausschweifend** *adj* dissolute

'**Ausschweifung** f (-; *-en*) debauchery, excess

'**aussehen** v/i (*irr, **sehen**, sep, -ge-, h*) look; *krank* (*traurig*) *~* look ill (sad); *~ wie ...* look like ...; *wie sieht er aus?* what does he look like? '**Aussehen** n (-s; *no pl*) look(s), appearance

außen ['ausən] *adv* outside; *nach ~* (*hin*) outward(s); *fig* outwardly

'**Außenbordmotor** m outboard motor

'**aussenden** v/t ([*irr, **senden**,*] *sep, -ge-, h*) send out

'**Außen|dienst** m field service; *~**handel*** m foreign trade; *~**mi,nister*** m *Am* Secretary of State, *Br* Foreign Secretary; *~**minis,terium*** n *Am* State Department, *Br* Foreign Office; *~**poli,tik*** f foreign affairs; foreign policy

'**außenpo,litisch** *adj* foreign-policy

'**Außenseite** f outside

'**Außenseiter** [-zaitɐ] m (-s; -) outsider

'**Außen|spiegel** m MOT rearview mirror; *~**stände*** *pl* ECON receivables; *~**stelle*** f branch; *~**stürmer*** m SPORT winger; *~**welt*** f outside world

außer ['ausɐ] **1.** *prp* (*dat*) out of; aside from, *Br* beside(s); except; *~ **sich sein*** be beside o.s. (*vor Freude* with joy); *alle ~ **e-m*** all but one; → *Betrieb, Gefahr*, **2.** *cj:* *~ **dass*** except that; *~ **wenn*** unless

'**außerdem** *cj* besides, moreover

äußere ['ɔysərə] *adj* exterior, outer, outward; '**Äußere** n (-n; *no pl*) exterior, outside; (outward) appearance

'**außergewöhnlich** *adj* unusual

'**außerhalb** *prp* (*gen*) and *adv* outside; out of; beyond

'**außerirdisch** *adj* extraterrestrial

'**äußerlich** adj external, outward

'**Äußerlichkeit** f (-; -en) formality; minor detail

äußern ['ɔysɐn] v/t (ge-, h) utter, express; **sich ~** say s.th.; **sich ~ zu** or **über** (acc) express o.s. on

'**außer'ordentlich** adj extraordinary

'**außerplanmäßig** adj unscheduled

äußerst ['ɔystɛst] **1.** adj outermost; fig extreme; **im ~en Fall** at (the) worst; at (the) most **2.** adv extremely

außer'stande adj.: **~ sein** be unable

'**Äußerung** f (-; -en) utterance, remark

'**aussetzen** (sep, -ge-, h) **1.** v/t abandon; expose (dat to); **et. auszusetzen haben an** (dat) find fault with; **2.** v/i stop, break off; MOT, TECH fail

'**Aussicht** f view (**auf** acc of); fig prospect (of), chance (**auf Erfolg** of success); '**aussichtslos** adj hopeless, desperate; '**Aussichtspunkt** m vantage point; '**aussichtsreich** adj promising; '**Aussichtsturm** m lookout tower

'**Aussiedler** m resettler, evacuee

'**aussitzen** v/t (irr, **sitzen**, sep, -ge-, h) sit s.th. out

aussöhnen ['ʔauszø:nən] v/refl (sep, -ge-, h) **sich ~ (mit)** become reconciled (with), F make it up (with)

'**Aussöhnung** f (-; -en) reconciliation

'**aus|sor,tieren** v/t (sep, no -ge-, h) sort out; **~spannen** (sep, -ge-, h) **1.** v/t unharness; **2.** fig v/i (take a) rest, relax

'**aussperren** v/t (sep, -ge-, h) lock out (a. ECON); '**Aussperrung** f (-; -en) ECON lock-out

'**aus|spielen** (sep, -ge-, h) **1.** v/t play; **j-n gegen j-n ~** play s.o. off against s.o.; **2.** v/i card game: lead; **er hat ausgespielt** fig he is done for; **~spio,nieren** v/t (sep, no -ge-, h) spy out

'**Aussprache** f pronunciation; discussion; private heart-to-heart (talk)

'**aussprechen** v/t (irr, **sprechen**, sep, -ge-, h) pronounce; express; **sich ~ für (gegen)** speak for (against); **sich mit j-m gründlich ~** have a heart-to-heart talk with s.o.

'**Ausspruch** m saying; remark

'**aus|spucken** v/i and v/t (sep, -ge-, h) spit out; **~spülen** v/t (sep, -ge-, h) rinse

'**Ausstand** m strike, F walkout

'**ausstatten** v/t (sep, -ge-, h) fit out,

equip, furnish; '**Ausstatung** f (-; -en) equipment, furnishings; design

'**aus|stechen** v/t (irr, **stechen**, sep, -ge-, h) GASTR cut out (a. fig); put out (eyes); **~stehen** (irr, **stehen**, sep, -ge-, h) **1.** v/t stand, endure; F **ich kann ihn (es) nicht ~** I can't stand him (it); **2.** v/i: **(noch) ~** be outstanding or overdue

'**aussteigen** v/i (irr, **steigen**, sep, -ge-, sien) get out (**aus** dat of); (a. **~ aus** dat) get off a bus, train; F fig drop out; '**Aussteiger** F m (-s; -) drop-out

'**ausstellen** v/t (sep, -ge-, h) exhibit, display, show; make out (check etc); issue (passport); '**Aussteller** m (-s; -) exhibitor; issuer; drawer (of check)

'**Ausstellung** f exhibition, show

'**aussterben** v/i (irr, **sterben**, sep, -ge-, sein) die out, become extinct (both a. fig)

'**Aussteuer** f trousseau; dowry

'**aussteuern** v/t (sep, -ge-, h) ELECTR modulate; '**Aussteuerung** f ELECTR modulation; level control

Ausstieg ['ausʃti:k] m (-[e]s; -e) exit; fig withdrawal (**aus** dat from)

'**ausstopfen** v/t (sep, -ge-, h) stuff; pad

'**Ausstoß** m TECH, PHYS discharge, ejection; ECON output

'**ausstoßen** v/t (irr, **stoßen**, sep, -ge-, h) TECH, PHYS give off, eject, emit; ECON turn out; give (cry, sigh); expel

'**aus|strahlen** v/t (sep, -ge-, h) radiate (happiness etc); TV, radio: broadcast, transmit; '**Ausstrahlung** f radiation; broadcast; fig magnetism, charisma

'**aus|strecken** v/t (sep, -ge-, h) stretch (out); **~streichen** v/t (irr, **streichen**, sep, -ge-, h) strike out; **~strömen** v/i (sep, -ge-, sein) escape (**aus** dat from); **~suchen** v/t (sep, -ge-, h) choose, pick

'**Austausch** m (-[e]s; no pl) exchange

'**austauschbar** adj exchangeable

'**austauschen** v/t (sep, -ge-, h) exchange (**gegen** for)

'**Austauschschüler(in)** exchange student

'**austeilen** v/t (sep, -ge-, h) distribute, hand out; deal (out) (cards, blows)

Auster ['austɐ] f (-; -n) ZO oyster

'**austragen** v/t (irr, **tragen**, sep, -ge-, h) deliver (mail); settle (dispute etc); hold (contest etc); **das Kind ~** have the baby

'**Austragungsort** m SPORT venue

Australien [aus'tra:ljən] Australia
Australier [aus'tra:ljə] *m* (-s; -), **Aust-'ralierin** [-ljərɪn] *f* (-; -nen), **aust'ra-lisch** *adj* Australian
'aus|treiben *v/t* (*irr*, **treiben**, *sep*, -*ge*-, *h*) exorcise; F *j-m et.* ~ cure s.o. of s.th.; ~**treten** (*irr*, **treten**, *sep*, -*ge*-) **1.** *v/t* (*h*) tread *or* stamp out (*fire*); wear out (*shoes*); **2.** *v/i* (*sein*) escape (*aus dat* from); F go to the bathroom (*Br* toilet); ~ *aus* (*dat*) leave (*a club etc*); resign from; ~**trinken** *v/t* (*irr*, **trinken**, *sep*, -*ge*-, *h*) drink up; empty
'Austritt *m* leaving; resignation; escape
'austrocknen *v/t* (*sep*, -*ge*-, *h*) and *v/i* (*sein*) dry up
'ausüben *v/t* (*sep*, -*ge*-, *h*) practi|ce, *Br* -se; hold (*office*); exercise (*power etc*); exert (*pressure etc*); **'Ausübung** *f* (-; *no pl*) practice; exercise
'Ausverkauf *m* ECON (clearance) sale
'ausverkauft *adj* ECON, THEA sold out; *vor ~em Haus spielen* play to a full house
'Auswahl *f* choice, selection (*both a.* ECON); SPORT representative team
'auswählen *v/t* (*sep*, -*ge*-, *h*) choose, select
'Auswanderer *m* emigrant
'auswandern *v/i* (*sep*, -*ge*-, *sein*) emigrate; **'Auswanderung** *f* emigration
auswärtig ['ausvɛrtɪç] *adj* out-of-town; POL foreign
'auswärts *adv* out of town
'Auswärts|sieg *m* SPORT away victory; ~**spiel** *n* SPORT away game
'auswechseln *v/t* (*sep*, -*ge*-, *h*) exchange (*gegen* for); change (*tire*); replace; *A gegen B* ~ SPORT substitute B for A; *wie ausgewechselt* (like) a different person; **'Auswechselspieler** *m* SPORT substitute
'Ausweg *m* way out; **'auswegelos** *adj* hopeless; **'Ausweglosigkeit** *f* (-; *no pl*) hopelessness
'ausweichen *v/i* (*irr*, **weichen**, *sep*, -*ge*-, *sein*) make way (*dat* for); *fig* avoid *s.o.*; evade (*question*); ~**d** *adj* evasive
'ausweinen *v/refl* (*sep*, -*ge*-, *h*) have a good cry
Ausweis ['ausvais] *m* (-es; -e) identification (card); card
'ausweisen *v/t* (*irr*, **weisen**, *sep*, -*ge*-, *h*) expel; *sich* ~ identify o.s.

'Ausweispa,piere *pl* documents
'Ausweisung *f* (-; -*en*) expulsion
'ausweiten *fig v/t* (*sep*, -*ge*-, *h*) expand
'auswendig *adv* by heart; *et.* ~ *können* know s.th. by heart; ~ *lernen* memorize; learn by heart
'auswerfen *v/t* (*irr*, **werfen**, *sep*, -*ge*-, *h*) throw out; cast (*anchor*); TECH eject
'auswerten *v/t* (*sep*, -*ge*-, *h*) evaluate, analyze, interpret; utilize, exploit; **'Auswertung** *f* evaluation; utilization
'auswickeln *v/t* (*sep*, -*ge*-, *h*) unwrap
'auswirken *v/refl* (*sep*, -*ge*-, *h*) *sich* ~ *auf* (*acc*) affect; *sich positiv* ~ have a favo(u)rable effect; **'Auswirkung** *f* effect
'auswischen *v/t* (*sep*, -*ge*-, *h*) wipe out
'auswringen *v/t* (*irr*, **wringen**, *sep*, -*ge*-, *h*) wring out
'Auswuchs *m* (-*es*; *Auswüchse* ['aus-vy:ksə]) excrescence; *fig pl* excesses
'aus|wuchten *v/t* (*sep*, -*ge*-, *h*) TECH balance: ~**zahlen** *v/t* (*sep*, -*ge*-, *h*) pay (out); pay *s.o.* off; *sich* ~ pay; ~**zählen** *v/t* (*sep*, -*ge*-, *h*) count; *boxing:* count out
'Auszahlung *f* payment; paying off
'auszeichnen *v/t* (*sep*, -*ge*-, *h*) price, mark (out) (*goods*); *sich* ~ distinguish o.s.; *j-n mit et.* ~ award s.th. to s.o.; **'Auszeichnung** *f* marking; *fig* distinction, hono(u)r; award; decoration
'ausziehen (*irr*, **ziehen**, *sep*, -*ge*-) **1.** *v/t* (*h*) take off (*coat etc*); pull out (*table etc*); *sich* ~ undress; **2.** *v/i* (*sein*) move out
'Auszubildende *m*, *f* (-*n*; -*n*) apprentice, trainee
'Auszug *m* move, removal; extract, excerpt; statement of account)
authentisch [au'tɛntɪʃ] *adj* authentic, genuine
Autismus [au'tɪsmus] *m* PSYCH autism
autistisch [au'tɪstɪʃ] *adj* PSYCH autistic
Auto ['auto] *n* (-s; -s) car, auto(mobile); (*mit dem*) ~ *fahren* drive, go by car
'Autobahn *f Am* expressway, *Br* motorway; ~**dreieck** *n* interchange; ~**gebühr** *f* toll; ~**kreuz** *n* interchange
Autobiogra'phie *f* autobiography
'Auto|bombe *f* car bomb; ~**bus** *m* → *Bus*; ~**fähre** *f* car ferry; ~**fahrer(in)** motorist, driver; ~**fahrt** *f* drive; ~**fried-**

hof F *m* car dump, auto junkyard

Autogramm [auto'gram] *n* autograph; **~jäger** *m* autograph hunter

'**Auto|karte** *f* road map; **~kino** *n* drive-in theater (*Br* cinema)

Automat [auto'ma:t] *m* (*-en*; *-en*) vending (*Br a.* slot) machine; TECH robot; → **Spielautomat**; **Automatik** [auto'ma:tɪk] *f* (*-; no pl*) automatic (system *or* control); MOT automatic transmission; automatic; **Automation** [automa'tsjo:n] *f* (*-; no pl*) automation; **au-to'matisch** *adj* automatic

'**Autome,chaniker** *m* car mechanic

autonom [auto'no:m] *adj* autonomous

'**Autonummer** *f* license (*Br* licence) number

Autor ['auto:ɐ] *m* (*-s*; *-en* [au'to:rən]) author

'**Autorepara,turwerkstatt** *f* garage, car repair shop

Autorin [au'to:rɪn] *f* (*-; -nen*) author(ess)

autorisieren [autori'zi:rən] *v/t* (*no -ge-, h*) authorize; **autoritär** [autori'te:ɐ] *adj* authoritarian; **Autorität** [autori'te:t] *f* (*-; -en*) authority

'**Auto|tele,fon** *n* car phone; **~vermie-tung** *f* car rental (*Br* hire) service; **~waschanlage** *f* car wash

Axt [akst] *f* (*-; Äxte* ['ɛkstə]) ax(e)

Bach [bax] *m* (*-[e]s*; *Bäche* ['bɛçə]) brook, stream, *Am a.* creek

'**Backblech** *n* baking sheet

'**Backbord** *n* (*-s; no pl*) MAR port

Backe ['bakə] *f* (*-; -n*) ANAT cheek

backen *v/t and v/i* ([*irr*, **backen**,] *-ge-, h*) bake

'**Backenzahn** *m* ANAT molar (tooth)

Bäcker ['bɛkɐ] *m* (*-s; -*) baker; **beim ~** at the baker's; **Bäckerei** [bɛkə'rai] *f* (*-; -en*) bakery, baker's (shop)

'**Back|form** *f* baking tin; **~hendl** ['bak-hendl] *Austrian n* (*-s; -n*) fried chicken; **~obst** *n* dried fruit; **~ofen** *m* oven; **~pflaume** *f* prune; **~pulver** *n* baking powder; **~stein** *m* brick

backte ['baktə] *pret of* **backen**

'**Backwaren** *pl* breads and pastries

Bad [ba:t] *n* (*-[e]*; *Bäder* ['bɛːdɐ]) bath; swim; bathroom; → **Badeort; ein ~ nehmen** → **baden** 1

'**Bade|anstalt** *f* swimming pool, public baths; **~anzug** *m* swimsuit; **~hose** *f* bathing trunks; **~kappe** *f* bathing cap; **~mantel** *m* bathrobe; **~meister** *m* pool *or* bath attendant

baden ['ba:dən] (*-ge-, h*) **1.** *v/i* bathe, take *or* have a bath; swim; **~ gehen** go swimming; **2.** *v/t* bathe (*a.* MED); *Br a.* bath

'**Bade|ort** *m* seaside (*or* health) resort; **~tuch** *n* bath towel; **~wanne** *f* bath-tub; **~zimmer** *n* bathroom

baff [baf] *adj*: F **~ sein** be flabbergasted

Bagatelle [baga'tɛlə] *f* (*-; -n*) trifle

Baga'tellschaden *m* superficial damage

Bagger ['bagɐ] *m* (*-s; -*) TECH excavator; dredge(r); '**baggern** *v/i* (*ge-, h*) TECH excavate; dredge

Bahn [ba:n] *f* (*-; -en*) railroad, *Br* railway; train; way, path, course; SPORT track; **mit der ~** by rail; **~ frei!** make way!; *cpds* → *a.* **Eisenbahn**

'**bahnbrechend** *adj* epoch-making

'**Bahndamm** *m* railroad (*Br* railway) embankment

'**bahnen** *v/t* (*ge-, h*) **den Weg ~** clear the way (*dat* for *s.o. or s.th.*); **sich e-n Weg ~** force *or* work one's way

'**Bahn|hof** *m* (railroad, *Br* railway) station; **~linie** *f* railroad (*Br* railway) line; **~steig** [-ʃtaik] *m* (*-[e]s; -e*) platform; **~übergang** *m* grade (*Br* level) crossing

Bahre ['ba:rə] *f* (*-; -n*) stretcher; bier

Baisse ['bɛːsə] *f* (*-; -n*) ECON fall, slump

Bakterien [bak'te:rjən] *pl* MED bacteria, germs

balancieren [balã'si:rən] *v/t and v/i* (*no -ge-, h*) balance

bald [balt] *adv* soon; F almost, nearly; **so ~ wie möglich** as soon as possible

baldig ['baldɪç] *adj* speedy; **~e Antwort**

B

ECON early reply; *auf (ein)* ~*es Wiedersehen!* see you again soon!

balgen ['balgən] *v/refl* (*ge-*, *h*) scuffle (*um* for)

Balken ['balkən] *m* (*-s*; *-*) beam

Balkon [bal'kɔŋ] *m* (*-s*; *-s*, *-e* [-'ko:nə]) balcony; ~*tür* *f* French window

Ball [bal] *m* (*-[e]s*; *Bälle* ['bɛlə]) ball; dance; *am* ~ *sein* SPORT have the ball; *am* ~ *bleiben* *fig* stick to it

Ballade [ba'la:də] *f* (*-*; *-n*) ballad

Ballast ['balast] *m* (*-[e]s*; *no pl*) ballast, *fig a.* burden; ~*stoffe pl* MED roughage, bulk

ballen ['balən] *v/t* (*ge-*, *h*) clench (*fist*)

'Ballen *m* (*-s*; *-*) bale; ANAT ball

Ballett [ba'lɛt] *n* (*-[e]s*; *-e*) ballet

Ballon [ba'lɔŋ] *m* (*-s*; *-s*) balloon

'Ballungs|raum *m*, ~*zentrum* *n* congested area, conurbation

Balsam ['balza:m] *m* (*-s*; *no pl*) balm

Bambus ['bambus] *m* (*-ses*, *-*; *-se*) BOT bamboo; ~*rohr* *n* BOT bamboo (cane)

banal [ba'na:l] *adj* banal, trite

Banane [ba'na:nə] *f* (*-*; *-n*) BOT banana

Banause [ba'nauzə] *m* (*-n*; *-n*) philistine

band [bant] *pret of* **binden**

Band[1] *n* (*-[e]s*; *Bänder* ['bɛndɐ]) ribbon; tape; (*hat*) band; ANAT ligament; *fig* tie, link; *auf* ~ *aufnehmen* tape; *am laufenden* ~ *fig* continuously

Band[2] *m* (*-[e]s*; *Bände* ['bɛndə]) volume

Bandage [ban'da:ʒə] *f* (*-*; *-n*) bandage

bandagieren [banda'ʒi:rən] *v/t* (*no -ge-*, *h*) bandage (up)

'Bandbreite *f* ELECTR bandwidth; *fig* range

Bande ['bandə] *f* (*-*; *-n*) gang; *billiards*: cushions; *ice hockey*: boards; *bowling*: gutter

'Bänderriss *m* MED torn ligament

bändigen ['bɛndigən] *v/t* (*ge-*, *h*) tame (*a. fig*); restrain, control (*children etc*)

Bandit [ban'di:t] *m* (*-en*; *-en*) bandit, outlaw

'Band|maß *n* tape measure; ~*scheibe* *f* ANAT (intervertebral) disk (*Br* disc); ~*scheibenschaden* *m*, ~*scheibenvorfall* *m* MED slipped disk; ~*wurm* *m* ZO tapeworm

bange ['baŋə] *adj* afraid; anxious

'Bange *f*: *j-m* ~ *machen* frighten or scare s.o.; *keine* ~*!* (have) no fear!

'bangen *v/i* (*ge-*, *h*) be anxious or worried (*um* about)

Bank[1] [baŋk] *f* (*-*; *Bänke* ['bɛŋkə]) bench; F *durch die* ~ without exception; *auf die lange* ~ *schieben* put off

Bank[2] *f* (*-*; *-en*) bank; *auf der* ~ in the bank

'Bankangestellte *m*, *f* bank clerk or employee

'Bankauto,mat *m* → *Geldautomat*

Bankett [baŋ'kɛt] *n* (*-[e]s*; *-e*) banquet

'Bankgeschäfte *pl* banking transactions

Bankier [baŋ'kje:] *m* (*-s*; *-s*) banker

'Bank|konto *n* bank(ing) account; ~*leitzahl* *f* A.B.A. number, *Br* bank (sorting) code; ~*note* *f* bill, *Br* (bank) note; ~*raub* *m* bank robbery

bankrott [baŋ'krɔt] *adj* ECON bankrupt

Bank'rott *m* (*-[e]s*; *-e*) ECON bankruptcy; ~ *machen* go bankrupt

'Bankverbindung *f* account(s), account details

Bann [ban] *m* (*-[e]s*; *no pl*) ban; spell

'bannen *v/t* (*ge-*, *h*) ward off; (*wie*) *gebannt* spellbound

Banner ['banə] *n* (*-s*; *-*) banner (*a. fig*)

bar [ba:ɐ] *adj* (in) cash; *gegen* ~ for cash

Bar *f* (*-*; *-s*) bar; nightclub

Bär [bɛ:ɐ] *m* (*-en*; *-en*) ZO bear

Baracke [ba'rakə] *f* (*-*; *-n*) hut; *contp* shack

Barbar [bar'ba:ɐ] *m* (*-en*; *-en*) barbarian; **barbarisch** [bar'ba:rɪʃ] *adj* barbarous, *a.* atrocious (*crime etc*)

'Bardame *f* barmaid

'barfuß *adj and adv* barefoot

barg [bark] *pret of* **bergen**

'Bargeld *n* cash

'bargeldlos *adj* noncash

'Barhocker *m* bar stool

Bariton ['ba:ritɔn] *m* (*-s*; *-e* [-'to:nə]) MUS baritone

Barkasse [bar'kasə] *f* (*-*; *-n*) MAR launch

barm'herzig *adj* merciful; charitable

Barm'herzigkeit *f* (*-*; *no pl*) mercy; charity

'Barmixer *m* barman

Barometer [baro'me:tɐ] *n* (*-s*; *-*) barometer

Baron [ba'ro:n] *m* (*-s*; *-e*) baron

Ba'ronin *f* (*-*; *-nen*) baroness

Barren ['barən] *m* (*-s*; *-*) bar, ingot, *a. gold, silver* bullion; SPORT parallel bars

Barriere [ba'rje:rə] *f* (*-*; *-n*) barrier

Barrikade [bari'kɑːdə] f (-; -n) barricade

barsch [barʃ] adj rough, gruff, brusque

Barsch m (-[e]s; -e) ZO perch

'Barscheck m (negotiable) check, Br open cheque

barst [barst] pret of **bersten**

Bart [baːɐt] m (-[e]s; Bärte ['bɛːɐtə]) beard; TECH bit; **sich e-n ~ wachsen lassen** grow a beard

bärtig ['bɛːɐtɪç] adj bearded

'Barzahlung f cash payment

Basar [ba'zaːɐ] m (-s; -e) bazaar

Base ['baːzə] f (-; -n) cousin; CHEM base

basieren [ba'ziːrən] v/i (no -ge-, h) ~ **auf** (dat) be based on

Basis ['baːzɪs] f (-; Basen) basis; MIL, ARCH base

Baskenmütze ['baskən-] f beret

Bass [bas] m (-es; Bässe ['bɛsə]) MUS bass

Bassin [ba'sɛ̃ː] n (-s; -s) basin; (swimming) pool

Bassist [ba'sɪst] m (-en; -en) MUS bass singer or player

Bast [bast] m (-[e]s; -e) bast; HUNT velvet

Bastard ['bastart] m (-s; -e) BIOL hybrid; mongrel; V bastard

basteln ['bastəln] (ge-, h) **1.** v/i make or repair things o.s.; **2.** v/t build, make

Bastler ['bastlɐ] m (-s; -) home handyman, do-it-yourselfer

bat [baːt] pret of **bitten**

Batik ['baːtɪk] m (-s; -en), f (-; -en) batik

Batist [ba'tɪst] m (-[e]s; -e) cambric

Batterie [batə'riː] f (-; -n) ELECTR, MIL battery

Bau [bau] m (-[e]s; Bauten) a) (no pl) building, construction; build, frame, b) building, c) ZO (pl Baue) hole, den; **im ~** under construction; **~arbeiten** pl construction work; road works; **~arbeiter** m construction worker; **~art** f style (of construction); type, model

Bauch [baux] m (-[e]s; Bäuche ['bɔʏçə]) belly (a. fig); ANAT abdomen; F tummy

'bauchig adj bulgy

'Bauch|landung f AVIAT belly landing; **~redner** m ventriloquist; **~schmerzen** pl stomachache; **~tanz** m belly dancing

bauen ['bauən] (ge-, h) **1.** v/t build, construct, a. make (furniture etc); **2.** fig v/i: **~ auf** (acc) rely or count on

Bauer¹ ['bauɐ] m (-n; -n) farmer; chess: pawn

'Bauer² n, m (-s; -) (bird)cage

Bäuerin ['bɔʏərɪn] f (-; -nen) farmer's wife; farmer

bäuerlich ['bɔʏɐlɪç] adj rural; rustic

'Bauern|fänger contp m trickster, conman; **~haus** n farmhouse; **~hof** m farm; **~möbel** pl rustic furniture

'baufällig adj dilapidated

'Bau|firma f builders and contractors; **~genehmigung** f building permit; **~gerüst** n scaffold(ing); **~herr** m owner; **~holz** n lumber, Br a. timber; **~ingenieur** m civil engineer; **~jahr** n year of construction; **~ 1995** 1995 model; **~kasten** m box of building blocks (Br bricks); TECH construction set; kit; **~leiter** m building supervisor

'baulich adj structural

Baum [baum] m (-[e]s; Bäume ['bɔʏmə]) BOT tree

'Baumarkt m do-it-yourself superstore

baumeln ['bauməln] v/i (ge-, h) dangle, swing; **mit den Beinen ~** dangle one's legs

'Baum|schule f nursery; **~stamm** m trunk; log; **~wolle** f cotton

'Bau|plan m architectural drawing; blueprints; **~platz** m building site

Bausch [bauʃ] m (-[e]s; -e) wad, ball; **in ~ und Bogen** lock, stock and barrel

'Bausparkasse f building and loan association, Br building society

'Bau|stein m brick; (building) block; fig element; **~stelle** f building site; MOT construction zone, Br roadworks; **~stil** m (architectural) style; **~stoff** m building material; **~techniker** m engineer; **~teil** n component (part), unit, module; **~unternehmer** m building contractor; **~vorschriften** pl building regulations; **~werk** n building; **~zaun** m hoarding; **~zeichner** m draftsman, Br draughtsman

Bayern ['baiɐn] Bavaria; **Bayer** ['baiɐ] m (-n; -n), **Bayerin** ['baiərɪn] f (-; -nen), **bay(e)risch** ['bai(ə)rɪʃ] adj Bavarian

Bazillus [ba'tsɪlʊs] m (-; -len) MED bacillus, germ

beabsichtigen [bə'ʔapzɪçtɪgən] v/t (no -ge-, h) intend, plan; **es war beabsichtigt** it was intentional

be'achten v/t (no -ge-, h) pay attention

B

to; observe, follow (*rule etc*); **~ Sie, dass ...** note that ...; **nicht ~** take no notice of; disregard; **be'achtlich** *adj* remarkable; considerable

Be'achtung *f* (-; *no pl*) attention; consideration; observance

Beamte [bə'ʔamtə] *m* (-n; -n), **Be'amtin** *f* (-; -nen) official; (*police etc*) officer; civil servant

be'ängstigend *adj* alarming

beanspruchen [bə'ʔanʃpruxən] *v/t* (*no -ge-, h*) claim; take up (*time etc*); TECH stress; **Be'anspruchung** *f* (-; -en) claim; TECH stress, strain (*a. fig*)

beanstanden [bə'ʔanʃtandən] *v/t* (*no -ge-, h*) complain about; object to

beantragen [bə'ʔantra:gən] *v/t* (*no -ge-, h*) apply for; JUR, PARL move (for); propose

be'antworten *v/t* (*no -ge-, h*) answer, reply to

be'arbeiten *v/t* (*no -ge-, h*) work; AGR till; hew (*stone*); process; be in charge of (*a case etc*); treat (*subject*); revise; THEA adapt (**nach** from); *esp* MUS arrange; **f j-n ~** work on s.o.

Be'arbeitung *f* (-; -en) working; revision; THEA adaptation; *esp* MUS arrangement; TECH processing, treatment

be'atmen *v/t* (*no -ge-, h*) MED give artificial respiration to s.o.

beaufsichtigen [bə'ʔaufzɪçtɪgən] *v/t* (*no -ge-, h*) supervise; look after; **Be'aufsichtigung** *f* (-; -en) supervision; looking after

be'auftragen *v/t* (*no -ge-, h*) commission; instruct; **~ mit** put in charge of; **Be'auftragte** [-tra:ktə] *m, f* (-n; -n) agent; representative; commissioner

be'bauen *v/t* (*no -ge-, h*) build on; AGR cultivate

beben ['be:bən] *v/i* (*ge-, h*) shake, tremble; shiver (*all: **vor** with*); *earth:* quake

bebildern [bə'bɪldɐn] *v/t* (*no -ge-, h*) illustrate

Becher ['bɛçɐ] *m* (-s; -) cup, mug

Becken ['bɛkən] *n* (-s; -) basin, bowl; pool; ANAT pelvis; MUS cymbal(s)

bedacht [bə'daxt] *adj:* **darauf ~ sein zu** *inf* be anxious to *inf*

bedächtig [bə'dɛçtɪç] *adj* deliberate; measured

bedang [bə'daŋ] *pret of* **bedingen**

be'danken *v/refl* (*no -ge-, h*) **sich bei j-m für et. ~** thank s.o. for s.th.

Bedarf [bə'darf] *m* (-[e]s; *no pl*) need (**an** *dat* of), want (of); ECON demand (for); **bei ~** if necessary

Be'darfshaltestelle *f* request stop

bedauerlich [bə'dauɐlɪç] *adj* regrettable; **be'dauerlicher'weise** *adv* unfortunately

be'dauern *v/t* (*no -ge-, h*) feel *or* be sorry for s.o., pity s.o.; regret s.th.; **Be'dauern** *n* (-s; *no pl*) regret (**über** *acc* at); **be'dauernswert** *adj* pitiable, deplorable

be'decken *v/t* (*no -ge-, h*) cover

be'deckt *adj* METEOR overcast

be'denken *v/t* (*irr, denken, no -ge-, h*) consider, think s.th. over; **Be'denken** *pl* doubts; scruples; objections

be'denkenlos *adv* unhesitatingly; without scruples

be'denklich *adj* doubtful; serious, critical; alarming

Be'denkzeit *f:* **e-e Stunde ~** one hour to think it over

be'deuten *v/t* (*no -ge-, h*) mean; **~d** *adj* important; considerable; distinguished

Be'deutung *f* (-; -en) meaning; importance; **be'deutungslos** *adj* insignificant; meaningless; **be'deutungsvoll** *adj* significant; meaningful

be'dienen (*no -ge-, h*) **1.** *v/t* serve, wait on s.o.; TECH operate, work; **sich ~** help o.s.; **~ Sie sich!** help yourself! **2.** *v/i* serve; wait (at table); *card games:* follow suit; **Be'dienung** *f* (-; -en) a) (*no pl*) service, b) waiter, waitress; shop assistant, clerk, c) TECH operation, control; **Be'dienungsanleitung** *f* operating instructions

bedingen [bə'dɪŋən] *v/t* ([*irr.*] *no -ge-, h*) require; cause; imply, involve; **be'dingt** *adj:* **~ durch** caused by, due to

Be'dingung *f* (-; -en) condition; *pl* ECON terms; requirements; conditions; **unter einer ~** on one condition

be'dingungslos *adj* unconditional

be'drängen *v/t* (*no -ge-, h*) press (hard)

be'drohen *v/t* (*no -ge-, h*) threaten, menace; **be'drohlich** *adj* threatening; **Be'drohung** *f* threat, menace (*gen* to)

be'drücken *v/t* (*no -ge-, h*) depress, sadden

bedungen [bə'dʊŋən] *pp of* **bedingen**

Bedürfnis [bə'dʏrfnɪs] *n (-ses; -se)* need, necessity (**für, nach** for); **~anstalt** *f* comfort station, *Br* public convenience (*or* toilets)

be'dürftig *adj* needy, poor

be'eilen *v/refl (no -ge-, h)* hurry (up)

beeindrucken [bə'ʔaɪndrʊkən] *v/t (no -ge-, h)* impress

beeinflussen [bə'ʔaɪnflʊsən] *v/t (no -ge-, h)* influence; affect

beeinträchtigen [bə'ʔaɪntrɛçtɪgən] *v/t (no -ge-, h)* affect, impair

be'end(ig)en *v/t (no -ge-, h)* (bring to an) end, finish, conclude, close

beengen [bə'ɛŋən] *v/t (no -ge-, h)* make s.o. (feel) uncomfortable; **be'engt** *adj:* **~ wohnen** live in cramped quarters

be'erben *v/t (no -ge-, h) j-n* **~** be s.o.'s heir

beerdigen [bə'ʔeːrdɪgən] *v/t (no -ge-, h)* bury; **Be'erdigung** *f (-; -en)* burial, funeral

Beere ['beːrə] *f (-; -n)* BOT berry; grape

Beet [beːt] *n (-[e]s; -e)* bed, patch

befähigen [bə'fɛːɪgən] *v/t (no -ge-, h)* enable; qualify (**für, zu** for); **be'fähigt** *adj (cap)able; zu et. ~* fit *or* qualified for s.th.; **Be'fähigung** *f (-; no pl)* qualification(s), (cap)ability

befahl [bə'faːl] *pret of* **befehlen**

be'fahrbar *adj* passable, practicable; MAR navigable

be'fahren *v/t (irr, fahren, no -ge-, h)* drive *or* travel on; MAR navigate

be'fallen *v/t (irr, fallen, no -ge-, h)* attack, seize (*a. fig*)

be'fangen *adj* self-conscious; prejudiced, JUR *a.* bias(s)ed

Be'fangenheit *f (-; no pl)* self-consciousness; JUR bias, prejudice

be'fassen *v/refl (no -ge-, h) sich* **~ mit** engage *or* occupy o.s. with; work on s.th.; deal with s.o., s.th.

Befehl [bə'feːl] *m (-[e]s; -e)* order; command (**über** *acc* of); **be'fehlen** *v/t (irr, no -ge-, h)* order; command

Be'fehlshaber *m (-s; -)* MIL commander

be'festigen *v/t (no -ge-, h)* fasten (**an** *dat* to), fix (to), attach (to); MIL fortify; **Be'festigung** *f (-; -en)* fixing, fastening; MIL fortification

be'feuchten *v/t (no -ge-, h)* moisten, damp

be'finden *v/refl (irr, finden, no -ge-, h)* be (situated); **Be'finden** *n (-s; no pl)* (state of) health

be'flecken *v/t (no -ge-, h)* stain; *fig a.* sully

befohlen [bə'foːlən] *pp of* **befehlen**

be'folgen *v/t (no -ge-, h)* follow, take (*advice*); observe (*rule etc*); REL keep; **Be'folgung** *f (-; no pl)* following; observance

be'fördern *v/t (no -ge-, h)* carry, transport; haul, ship; promote (**zu** to)

Be'förderung *f (-; -en)* a) (*no pl*) transport(ation); shipment, b) promotion

be'fragen *v/t (no -ge-, h)* question, interview

be'freien *v/t (no -ge-, h)* free, liberate; rescue; exempt (**von** from); **Be'freiung** *f (-; no pl)* liberation; exemption

Befremden [bə'frɛmdən] *n (-s; no pl)* irritation, displeasure; **be'fremdet** *adj* irritated, displeased

befreunden [bə'frɔʏndən] *v/refl (no -ge-, h) sich* **~ mit** make friends with; *fig* warm to; **be'freundet** *adj* friendly; **~ sein** be friends

befriedigen [bə'friːdɪgən] *v/t (no -ge-, h)* satisfy; *sich selbst* **~** masturbate; **~d** *adj* satisfactory; *grade:* fair

befriedigt [bə'friːdɪçt] *adj* satisfied, pleased

Be'friedigung *f (-; no pl)* satisfaction

be'fristet *adj* limited (**auf** *acc* to), temporary

be'fruchten *v/t (no -ge-, h)* BIOL fertilize, inseminate; **Be'fruchtung** *f (-; -en)* BIOL fertilization, insemination

Befugnis [bə'fuːknɪs] *f (-; -se)* authority; *esp* JUR competence; **befugt** [bə'fuːkt] *adj* authorized; competent

be'fühlen *v/t (no -ge-, h)* feel, touch

Be'fund *m* finding(s) (*a.* MED, JUR)

be'fürchten *v/t (no -ge-, h)* fear, be afraid of; suspect; **Be'fürchtung** *f (-; -en)* fear, suspicion

be'fürworten [bə'fyːɐvɔrtən] *v/t (no -ge-, h)* advocate, speak *or* plead for; **Be'fürworter** *m (-s; -)* advocate

begabt [bə'gaːpt] *adj* gifted, talented

Be'gabung *f (-; -en)* gift, talent(s)

begann [bə'gan] *pret of* **beginnen**

B

be'geben *v/refl* (*irr,* **geben,** *no -ge-, h*)
  sich in Gefahr ~ expose o.s. to danger
Be'gebenheit *f* (-; *-en*) incident, event
begegnen [bə'ge:gnən] *v/i* (*no -ge-, sein*)
  meet (*a. fig mit* with); **sich** ~ meet
Be'gegnung *f* (-; *-en*) meeting, encounter (*a.* SPORT)
be'gehen *v/t* (*irr,* **gehen,** *no -ge-, h*)
  walk (on); celebrate (*birthday etc*);
  commit (*crime*); make (*mistake*); **ein**
  Unrecht ~ do wrong
begehren [bə'ge:rən] *v/t* (*no -ge-, h*) desire; **be'gehrenswert** *adj* desirable
be'gehrlich *adj* desirous, covetous
begehrt [bə'ge:ɐt] *adj* (very) popular,
  (much) in demand
begeistern [bə'gaistən] *v/t* (*no -ge-, h*)
  fill with enthusiasm; carry away (*audience*); **sich** ~ **für** be enthusiastic about
be'geistert *adj* enthusiastic
Be'geisterung *f* (-; *no pl*) enthusiasm
Begierde [bə'gi:ɐdə] *f* (-; *-n*) desire
  (**nach** for), lust
be'gierig *adj* greedy; eager (**nach, auf**
  acc for; **zu** *inf* to *inf*)
be'gießen *v/t* (*irr,* **gießen,** *no -ge-, h*)
  water; GASTR baste; F *fig* celebrate
  s.th. (with a drink)
Beginn [bə'gɪn] *m* (-[*e*]*s; no pl*) beginning, start; **zu** ~ at the beginning
be'ginnen *v/t and v/i* (*irr, no -ge-, h*) begin, start
beglaubigen [bə'glaubɪgən] *v/t* (*no -ge-,
  h*) attest, certify; **Be'glaubigung** *f* (-;
  -en) attestation, certification
be'gleichen *v/t* (*irr,* **gleichen,** *no -ge-,
  h*) pay, settle
be'gleiten *v/t* (*no -ge-, h*) accompany (*a.*
  MUS **auf** *dat* on); **j-n nach Hause** ~ see
  s.o. home; **Be'gleiter(in)** (-*s; -/-; -nen*)
  companion; MUS accompanist
Be'gleit|erscheinung *f* concomitant;
  MED side effect; **~schreiben** *n* covering letter
Be'gleitung *f* (-; *-en*) company; *esp* MIL
  escort; MUS accompaniment
be'glückwünschen *v/t* (*no -ge-, h*)
  congratulate (**zu** on)
begnadigen [bə'gna:dɪgən] *v/t* (*no -ge-,
  h*), **Be'gnadigung** *f* (-; *-en*) JUR pardon; amnesty
begnügen [bə'gny:gən] *v/refl* (*no -ge-,
  h*) **sich** ~ **mit** be satisfied with; make
  do with

begonnen [bə'gɔnən] *pp of* **beginnen**
be'graben *v/t* (*irr,* **graben,** *no -ge-, h*)
  bury (*a. fig*); **Begräbnis** [bə'grɛ:pnɪs]
  n (-*ses; -se*) burial; funeral
begradigen [bə'gra:dɪgən] *v/t* (*no -ge-,
  h*) straighten
be'greifen *v/t* (*irr,* **greifen,** *no -ge-, h*)
  comprehend, understand
be'greiflich *adj* understandable
be'grenzen *v/t* (*no -ge-, h*) limit, restrict
  (**auf** *acc* to); **be'grenzt** *adj* limited
Be'griff *m* (-[*e*]*s; -e*) idea, notion; term
  (*a.* MATH); **im** ~ **sein zu** *inf* be about to
  inf; **be'griffsstutzig** *contp adj* F slow
  on the uptake
be'gründen *v/t* (*no -ge-, h*) give reasons
  for; **be'gründet** *adj* well-founded, jus-
  tified; **Be'gründung** *f* (-; *-en*) reasons,
  arguments
be'grünen *v/t* (*no -ge-, h*) landscape
be'grüßen *v/t* (*no -ge-, h*) greet,
  welcome (*a. fig*); **Be'grüßung** *f* (-;
  -en) greeting, welcome
begünstigen [bə'gynstɪgən] *v/t* (*no -ge-,
  h*) favo(u)r
be'gutachten *v/t* (*no -ge-, h*) give an
  (expert's) opinion on; examine; ~ *lassen* obtain expert opinion on
begütert [bə'gy:tɐt] *adj* wealthy
be'haart *adj* hairy
behäbig [bə'hɛ:bɪç] *adj* slow; portly
be'haftet *adj: mit Fehlern* ~ flawed
behagen [bə'ha:gən] *v/i* (*no -ge-, h*) **j-m**
  ~ please *or* suit s.o.; **Be'hagen** *n* (-*s; no
  pl*) pleasure, enjoyment; **behaglich**
  [bə'ha:klɪç] *adj* comfortable; cozy, snug
be'halten *v/t* (*irr,* **halten,** *no -ge-, h*)
  keep (*fig* **für sich** to o.s.); remember
Behälter [bə'hɛltɐ] *m* (-*s; -*) container,
  receptacle
be'handeln *v/t* (*no -ge-, h*) handle; treat
  (*a.* MED); **sich (ärztlich)** ~ **lassen**
  undergo (medical) treatment
Be'handlung *f* (-; *-en*) handling; *a.* MED
  treatment
beharren [bə'harən] *v/i* (*no -ge-, h*) insist
  (**auf** *dat* on)
be'harrlich *adj* persistent
behaupten [bə'hauptən] *v/t* (*no -ge-, h*)
  claim; pretend; **Be'hauptung** *f* (-; *-en*)
  statement, claim
be'heben *v/t* (*irr,* **heben,** *no -ge-, h*)
  repair (*damage etc*)
be'heizen *v/t* (*no -ge-, h*) heat

be'helfen *v*/*refl* (*irr*, **helfen**, *no* -*ge*-, *h*) **sich ~ mit** make do with; **sich ~ ohne** do without

Be'helfs... *in cpds mst* temporary

beherbergen [bə'hɛrbɛrgən] *v*/*t* (*no* -*ge*-, *h*) accommodate

be'herrschen *v*/*t* (*no* -*ge*-, *h*) rule (over), govern; ECON dominate, control; have a (good) command of (*language*); **sich ~** control o.s.; **Be'herrschung** *f* (-; *no pl*) command, control

beherzigen [bə'hɛrtsɪgən] *v*/*t* (*no* -*ge*-, *h*) take to heart, mind

be'hilflich *adj*: **j-m ~ sein** help s.o. (**bei** with, in)

be'hindern *v*/*t* (*no* -*ge*-, *h*) hinder; obstruct (*a.* SPORT); **be'hindert** *adj* MED handicapped; disabled

Be'hinderung *f* (-; *-en*) obstruction; MED handicap

Behörde [bə'hø:ɐdə] *f* (-; *-n*) authority, *mst the* authorities; board

be'hüten *v*/*t* (*no* -*ge*-, *h*) guard (**vor** *dat* from)

behutsam [bə'hu:tza:m] *adj* careful; gentle

bei [bai] *prp* (*dat*) near; at; with; by; *time*: during; at; **~ München** near Munich; **wohnen ~** stay (*or* live) with; **~ mir** (**ihr**) at my (her) place; **~ uns** (**zu Hause**) at home; **arbeiten ~** work for; **e-e Stelle ~** a job with; **~ der Marine in** the navy; **~ Familie Müller** at the Müllers'; **~ Müller** c/o Müller; **ich habe kein Geld ~ mir** I have no money with *or* on me; **~ e-r Tasse Tee** over a cup of tea; **wir haben Englisch ~ Herrn X** we have Mr X for English; **~ Licht** by light; **~ Tag** during the day; **~ Nacht** (**Sonnenaufgang**) at night (sunrise); **~ s-r Geburt** at his birth; **~ Regen** (**Gefahr**) in case of rain (danger); **~ 100 Grad** at a hundred degrees; → **Arbeit, beim, weit**

'beibehalten *v*/*t* (*irr*, **halten**, *sep*, *no* -*ge*-, *h*) keep up, retain

'beibringen *v*/*t* (*irr*, **bringen**, *sep*, *no* -*ge*-, *h*) teach; tell; inflict (*dat* on)

Beichte ['baiçtə] *f* (-; *-n*) REL confession

'beichten *v*/*t and v*/*i* (*ge*-, *h*) REL confess (*a. fig*)

'Beichtstuhl *m* REL confessional

beide ['baidə] *adj and pron* both; **m-e ~n**

Brüder my two brothers; **wir ~** the two of us; both of us; **keiner von ~n** neither of them; **30 ~** *tennis*: 30 all

beiei'nander *adv* together

'Beifahrer *m* front(-seat) passenger

'Beifall *m* (-[*e*]*s*; *no pl*) applause; *fig* approval

'Beifallssturm *m* (standing) ovation

'beifügen *v*/*t* (*sep*, -*ge*-, *h*) enclose (*dat* with)

beige [be:ʃ] *adj* beige

'beigeben (*irr*, **geben**, *sep*, -*ge*-, *h*) **1.** *v*/*t* add; **2.** F *v*/*i*: **klein ~** knuckle under

Bei|geschmack *m* smack (**von** of) (*a. fig*); **~hilfe** *f* aid, allowance; JUR aiding and abetting

Beil [bail] *n* (-[*e*]*s*; *-e*) hatchet; ax(e)

'Beilage *f* supplement; GASTR side dish; vegetables

'beiläufig *adj* casual

'beilegen *v*/*t* (*sep*, -*ge*-, *h*) add (*dat* to); enclose (with); settle (*dispute*)

'Beilegung *f* (-; *-en*) settlement

'Beileid *n* (-[*e*]*s*; *no pl*) condolence; **herzliches ~** my deepest sympathy

'beiliegen *v*/*i* (*irr*, **liegen**, *sep*, -*ge*-, *h*) be enclosed (*dat* with)

beim [baim] *prp*: **~ Bäcker** at the baker's; **~ Sprechen** *etc* while speaking *etc*; **~ Spielen** at play; → *a.* **bei**

'beimessen *v*/*t* (*irr*, **messen**, *sep*, -*ge*-, *h*) attach *importance etc* (*dat* to)

Bein [bain] *n* (-[*e*]*s*; *-e*) ANAT leg; bone

beinah(e) ['baina:(ə)] *adv* almost, nearly

'Beinbruch *m* MED fracture of the leg

'beipflichten *v*/*i* (*sep*, -*ge*-, *h*) agree (*dat* with)

be'irren *v*/*t* (*no* -*ge*-, *h*) confuse

beisammen [bai'zamən] *adv* together

Bei'sammensein *n*: **geselliges ~** get--together

'Beischlaf *m* JUR sexual intercourse

bei'seite *adv* aside; **~ schaffen** remove; liquidate *s.o.*

'beisetzen *v*/*t* (*sep*, -*ge*-, *h*) bury

'Beisetzung *f* (-; *-en*) funeral

'Beispiel *n* (-[*e*]*s*; *-e*) example; **zum ~** for example, for instance; **sich an j-m ein ~ nehmen** follow s.o.'s example

'beispiel|haft *adj* exemplary; **~los** *adj* unprecedented, unparalleled

'beispielsweise *adv* such as

beißen ['baisən] v/t and v/i (irr, -ge-, h) bite (a. fig); **sich ~** colors: clash; **~d** adj biting, pungent (both a. fig)

'**Beistand** m (-[e]s; no pl) assistance

'**bei**|**stehen** v/i (irr, **stehen**, sep, -ge-, h) **j-m ~** assist or help s.o.; **~steuern** v/t (sep, -ge-, h) contribute (**zu** to)

Beitrag m (-[e]s; **Beiträge** ['baitrɛːɡə]) contribution; dues, Br subscription; '**beitragen** v/t (irr, **tragen**, sep, -ge-, h) contribute (**zu** to)

'**beitreten** v/i (irr, **treten**, sep, -ge-, sein) join; '**Beitritt** m (-[e]s; -e) joining

'**Beiwagen** m MOT sidecar

bei'**zeiten** adv early, in good time

beizen ['baitsən] v/t (ge-, h) stain (wood); pickle (meat)

bejahen [bə'jaːən] v/t (no -ge-, h) answer in the affirmative, affirm; **~d** adj affirmative

be'**kämpfen** v/t (no -ge-, h) fight (against)

bekannt [bə'kant] adj (well-)known; familiar; **et. ~ geben** announce s.th.; **j-n mit j-m ~ machen** introduce s.o. to s.o.; **Be'kannte** m, f (-n; -n) acquaintance, mst friend

be'**kanntlich** adv as you know

Be'kanntmachung f (-; -en) announcement

Be'kanntschaft f (-; -en) acquaintance

be'**kehren** v/t (no -ge-, h) convert

be'**kennen** v/t (irr, **kennen**, no -ge-, h) confess (a. REL); admit; **sich schuldig ~** JUR plead guilty; **sich ~ zu** profess s.th.; claim responsibility for; **Be'kennerbrief** m letter claiming responsibility

Be'kenntnis n (-ses; -se) confession, REL a. denomination

be'**klagen** v/t (no -ge-, h) deplore; **sich ~** complain (**über** acc about)

be'**klagenswert** adj deplorable

be'**kleben** v/t (no -ge-, h) stick (or paste) on s.th.; **mit Etiketten ~** label s.th.

be'**kleckern** F v/t (no -ge-, h) stain; **sich ~** mit spill s.th. over o.s.

Be'kleidung f (-; -en) clothing, clothes

be'**kommen** (irr, **kommen**, no -ge-) **1.** v/t (h) get, receive; MED catch; be having (baby); **2.** v/i (sein) **j-m (gut) ~** agree with s.o.; **bekömmlich** [bə'kœmlɪç] adj wholesome

be'**kräftigen** v/t (no -ge-, h) confirm

be'**kreuzigen** v/refl (no -ge-, h) cross o.s.

bekümmert [bə'kʏmɐt] adj worried

be'**laden** v/t (irr, **laden**, no -ge-, h) load, fig a. burden

Belag [bə'laːk] m (-[e]s; **Beläge** [bə'lɛːɡə]) covering; TECH coat(ing); MOT lining; (road) surface; MED fur; plaque; GASTR topping; spread; (sandwich) filling

be'**lagern** v/t (no -ge-, h) MIL besiege (a. fig); **Be'lagerung** f (-; -en) MIL siege

be'**lassen** v/t (irr, **lassen**, no -ge-, h) leave; **es dabei ~** leave it at that

be'**langlos** adj irrelevant

be'**lastbar** adj resistant to strain or stress; TECH loadable; **be'lasten** v/t (no -ge-, h) load; fig burden; JUR incriminate; pollute; damage; **j-s Konto ~ mit** charge s.th. to s.o.'s account

be'**lästigen** [bə'lɛstɪɡən] v/t (no -ge-, h) molest; annoy; disturb, bother; **Be'lästigung** f (-; -en) molestation; annoyance; disturbance

Be'lastung f (-; -en) load (a. TECH); fig burden; strain; stress; JUR incrimination; pollution, contamination

Be'lastungszeuge m JUR witness for the prosecution

be'**laufen** v/refl (irr, **laufen**, no -ge-, h) **sich ~ auf** (acc) amount to

be'**lauschen** v/t (no -ge-, h) eavesdrop on

be'**leben** fig v/t (no -ge-, h) stimulate; **~d** adj stimulating

belebt [bə'leːpt] adj busy, crowded

Beleg [bə'leːk] m (-[e]s; -e) proof; receipt; document; be'**legen** v/t (no -ge-, h) cover; reserve (seat); prove; enrol(l) for, take (classes); GASTR put s.th. on; **den ersten** etc **Platz ~** SPORT take first etc place

Be'legschaft f (-; -en) staff

be'**legt** adj taken, occupied; hotel etc: full; TEL busy, Br engaged; MED coated; **~es Brot** sandwich

be'**lehren** v/t (no -ge-, h) teach, instruct, inform; **sich ~ lassen** take advice

be'**leidigen** [bə'laidɪɡən] v/t (no -ge-, h) offend (a. fig), insult; **~d** adj offensive, insulting

Be'leidigung f (-; -en) offense, Br offence, insult

be'**lesen** adj well-read

B

be'leuchten v/t (no -ge-, h) light (up), illuminate (a. fig); fig throw light on
Be'leuchtung f (-; -en) light(ing); illumination
Belgien ['bɛlgjən] Belgium; Belgier ['bɛlgjə] m (-s; -), 'Belgierin [-gjərɪn] f (-; -nen), 'belgisch adj Belgian
be'lichten v/t (no -ge-, h) PHOT expose
Be'lichtungsmesser m PHOT exposure meter
Be'lieben n: nach ~ at will
beliebig [bə'liːbɪç] adj any; optional; jeder ~e anyone
beliebt [bə'liːpt] adj popular (bei with)
Be'liebtheit f (-; no pl) popularity
be'liefern v/t (no -ge-, h) supply, furnish (mit with); Be'lieferung f supply
bellen ['bɛlən] v/i (ge-, h) bark (a. fig)
be'lohnen v/t (no -ge-, h) reward
Be'lohnung f (-; -en) reward; zur ~ as a reward
be'lügen v/t (irr, lügen, no -ge-, h) j-n ~ lie to s.o.
belustigen [bə'lʊstɪgən] v/t (no -ge-, h) amuse; be'lustigt [-tɪçt] adj amused; Be'lustigung f (-; -en) amusement
bemächtigen [bə'mɛçtɪgən] v/refl (no -ge-, h) get hold of, seize
be'malen v/t (no -ge-, h) paint
bemängeln [bə'mɛŋəln] v/t (no -ge-, h) find fault with
bemannt [bə'mant] adj manned
be'merkbar adj noticeable; sich ~ machen draw attention to o.s.; begin to show; be'merken v/t (no -ge-, h) notice; remark; be'merkenswert adj remarkable; Be'merkung f (-; -en) remark (über acc about)
be'mitleiden v/t (no -ge-, h) pity, feel sorry for; be'mitleidenswert adj pitiable
be'mühen v/refl (no -ge-, h) try (hard); sich ~ um try to get s.th.; try to help s.o.; bitte ~ Sie sich nicht! please don't bother; Be'mühung f (-; -en) effort; danke für Ihre ~en! thank you for your trouble
be'muttern v/t (no -ge-, h) mother s.o.
be'nachbart adj neighbo(u)ring
benachrichtigen [bə'naːxrɪçtɪgən] v/t (no -ge-, h) inform, notify
Be'nachrichtigung f (-; -en) information, notification
benachteiligen [bə'naːxtaɪlɪgən] v/t (no -ge-, h) place s.o. at a disadvantage; discriminate against s.o.; benachteiligt [bə'naːxtaɪlɪçt] adj disadvantaged; die Benachteiligten the underprivileged; Be'nachteiligung f (-; -en) disadvantage; discrimination
be'nehmen v/refl (irr, nehmen, no -ge-, h) behave (as s.o.); Be'nehmen n (-s; no pl) behavio(u)r; manners
be'neiden v/t (no -ge-, h) j-n um et. ~ envy s.o. s.th.
be'neidenswert adj enviable
BENELUX ['beːnelʊks] ABBR of Belgien, Niederlande, Luxemburg Belgium, the Netherlands and Luxembourg
be'nennen v/t (irr, nennen, no -ge-, h) name
Bengel ['bɛŋəl] m (-s; -) (little) rascal, urchin
benommen [bə'nɔmən] adj dazed, F dopey
be'noten v/t (no -ge-, h) grade, Br mark
be'nötigen v/t (no -ge-, h) need, want, require
be'nutzen v/t (no -ge-, h) use
Be'nutzer m (-s; -) user
be'nutzerfreundlich adj user-friendly
Be'nutzeroberfläche f EDP user interface
Be'nutzung f use
Benzin [bɛn'tsiːn] n (-s; -e) gasoline, F gas, Br petrol
beobachten [bə'ʔoːbaxtən] v/t (no -ge-, h) watch; observe
Be'obachter m (-s; -) observer
Be'obachtung f (-; -en) observation
be'pflanzen v/t (no -ge-, h) plant (mit with)
bequem [bə'kveːm] adj comfortable; easy; lazy; be'quemen v/refl (no -ge-, h) sich ~ zu inf bring o.s. to inf
Be'quemlichkeit f (-; -en) a) comfort; alle ~en all conveniences, b) (no pl) laziness
be'raten v/t (irr, raten, no -ge-, h) advise s.o.; debate, discuss s.th.; sich ~ confer (mit j-m with s.o.); über et. on s.th.); Be'rater m (-s; -) adviser, consultant; Be'ratung f (-; -en) advice (a. MED); debate; consultation, conference; Be'ratungsstelle f counsel(l)ing center (Br centre)
be'rauben v/t (no -ge-, h) rob

be'rauschend *adj* intoxicating; F *fig nicht gerade ~!* not so hot!; **be-'rauscht** *fig adj*: ~ *von* drunk with
be'rechnen *v/t* (*no -ge-, h*) calculate; ECON charge (*zu* at); ~*d adj* calculating
Be'rechnung *f* calculation (*a. fig*)
berechtigen [bə'rɛçtɪgən] *v/t*: *j-n ~ zu* entitle (*or* authorize) s.o. to; **be'rechtigt** [-tɪçt] *adj* entitled (*zu* to); authorized (to); legitimate; **Be'rechtigung** *f* (*-; no pl*) right (*zu* to); authority
Beredsamkeit [bə'reːtzaːmkaɪt] *f* (*-; no pl*) eloquence
beredt [bə'reːt] *adj* eloquent (*a. fig*)
Be'reich *m* (*-[e]s; -e*) area; range; field
bereichern [bə'raɪçɐn] *v/t* (*no -ge-, h*) enrich; *sich ~* get rich (*an dat* on); **Be'reicherung** [bə'raɪçərʊŋ] *f* (*-; no pl*) enrichment
Be'reifung *f* (*-; -en*) (set of) tires (*Br* tyres)
be'reinigen *v/t* (*no -ge-, h*) settle
be'reisen *v/t* (*no -ge-, h*) tour; cover
bereit [bə'raɪt] *adj* ready, prepared; willing; **be'reiten** *v/t* (*no -ge-, h*) prepare; cause; **be'reithalten** *v/t* (*irr, halten, sep, -ge-, h*) have s.th. ready; *sich ~* stand by; **be'reits** *adv* already; **Be'reitschaft** *f* (*-; no pl*) readiness; *in ~* on standby; **Be'reitschaftsdienst** *m*: *~ haben* doctor etc: be on call; **be'reitstellen** *v/t* (*sep, -ge-, h*) provide; **be-'reitwillig** *adj* ready, willing
be'reuen *v/t* (*no -ge-, h*) repent (of); regret
Berg [bɛrk] *m* (*-[e]s; -e*) mountain; *~e von* F loads of; *die Haare standen ihm zu ~e* his hair stood on end
berg'ab *adv* downhill (*a. fig*)
'Bergarbeiter *m* miner
berg'auf *adv* uphill
'Berg|bahn *f* mountain railroad (*Br* railway); **~bau** *m* (*-[e]s; no pl*) mining
bergen ['bɛrgən] *v/t* (*irr, ge- h*) rescue, save s.o.; salvage s.th.; recover (*body*)
'Bergführer *m* mountain guide
bergig ['bɛrgɪç] *adj* mountainous
'Berg|kette *f* mountain range; **~mann** *m* (*-[e]s; -leute*) miner; **~rutsch** *m* landslide; **~schuhe** *pl* mountain(eering) boots; **~spitze** *f* (mountain) peak; **~steigen** *n* mountaineering, (mountain) climbing; **~steiger** *m* (*-s; -*) mountaineer, (mountain) climber

'Bergung *f* (*-; -en*) recovery; rescue
'Bergungsarbeiten *pl* rescue work; salvage operations
'Bergwacht *f* alpine rescue service
'Bergwerk *n* mine
Bericht [bə'rɪçt] *m* (*-[e]s; -e*) report (*über acc* on), account (of)
be'richten *v/t and v/i* (*no -ge-, h*) report (*über acc* on); *j-m et. ~* inform s.o. of s.th.; tell s.o. about s.th.
Be'richt|erstatter *m* (*-s; -*) reporter; correspondent; **~erstattung** *f* (*-; -en*) report(ing)
berichtigen [bə'rɪçtɪgən] *v/t* (*no -ge-, h*) correct; **Be'richtigung** *f* (*-; -en*) correction
be'rieseln *v/t* (*no -ge-, h*) sprinkle
Bernstein ['bɛrnʃtaɪn] *m* (*-s; no pl*) amber
bersten ['bɛrstən] *v/i* (*irr, -ge-, sein*) burst (*fig vor dat* with)
berüchtigt [bə'rʏçtɪçt] *adj* notorious (*wegen* for)
berücksichtigen [bə'rʏkzɪçtɪgən] *v/t* (*no -ge-, h*) take into consideration; *nicht ~* disregard
Be'rücksichtigung *f*: *unter ~* (*gen*) in consideration of
Be'ruf *m* (*-[e]s; -e*) job, occupation; trade; profession; **be'rufen** *v/t* (*irr, rufen, no -ge-, h*) appoint (*zu* [as] *s.o.*; to *s.th.*); *sich ~ auf* (*acc*) refer to
be'ruflich *adj* professional; *~ unterwegs* away on business
Be'rufs... *in cpds* ...*sportler etc*: professional ...; **~ausbildung** *f* vocational (*or* professional) training; **~berater** *m* careers advisor; **~beratung** *f* careers guidance; **~bezeichnung** *f* job designation *or* title; **~kleidung** *f* work clothes; **~krankheit** *f* occupational disease; **~schule** *f* vocational school
be'rufstätig *adj*: *~ sein* (go to) work, have a job; **Be'rufstätige** *m, f* (*-n; -n*) working person, *pl* working people
Be'rufsverkehr *m* rush-hour traffic
Be'rufung *f* (*-; -en*) appointment (*zu* to); JUR appeal (*bei* to); *unter ~ auf* (*acc*) with reference to; on the grounds of
be'ruhen *v/i* (*no -ge-, h*) *~ auf* (*dat*) based on; *et. auf sich ~ lassen* let s.th. rest
beruhigen [bə'ruːɪgən] *v/t* (*no -ge-, h*)

quiet(en), calm, soothe; reassure *s.o.*;
sich ~ calm down; **~d** *adj* reassuring;
MED sedative;
Be'ruhigung *f* (-; -*en*) calming (down);
soothing; relief; **Be'ruhigungsmittel** *n*
MED sedative; tranquil(l)izer
berühmt [bə'ry:mt] *adj* famous (**wegen**
for); **Be'rühmtheit** *f* (-; -*en*) a) (*no pl*)
fame, b) celebrity, star
be'rühren *v/t* (*no -ge-*, *h*) touch (*a.* *fig*);
concern; **Be'rührung** *f* (-; -*en*) touch;
in ~ kommen come into contact
Be'rührungs|angst *f* fear of contact;
~punkt *m* point of contact
besänftigen [bə'zɛnftɪgən] *v/t* (*no -ge-*,
h) appease, calm, soothe
Be'satzung *f* (-; -*en*) AVIAT, MAR crew;
MIL occupying forces
Be'satzungs|macht *f* MIL occupying
power; **~truppen** *pl* MIL occupying
forces
be'saufen F *v/refl* (*irr*, **saufen**, *no -ge-*,
h) get drunk, get bombed
be'schädigen *v/t* (*no -ge-*, *h*) damage
Be'schädigung *f* (-; -*en*) damage
be'schaffen *v/t* (*no -ge-*, *h*) provide, get;
raise (*money*); **Be'schaffenheit** *f* (-; *no
pl*) state, condition
beschäftigen [bə'ʃɛftɪgən] *v/t* (*no -ge-*,
h) employ; keep *s.o.* busy; **sich ~** occupy o.s.; **be'schäftigt** [-tɪçt] *adj* busy,
occupied; **Be'schäftigte** *m*, *f* (-*n*; -*n*)
employed person, *pl* employed people;
Be'schäftigung *f* (-; -*en*) employment;
occupation
be'schämen *v/t* (*no -ge-*, *h*) shame *s.o.*,
make *s.o.* feel ashamed; **~d** *adj* shame-
ful; humiliating
be'schämt *adj* ashamed (**über** *acc* of)
be'schatten *fig v/t* (*no -ge-*, *h*) shadow,
F tail
Bescheid [bə'ʃait] *m* (-[*e*]*s*; -*e*) answer;
JUR decision; information (**über** *acc*
on, about); **sagen Sie mir ~** let me
know; (**gut**) **~ wissen über** (*acc*) know
all about
be'scheiden *adj* modest (*a.* *fig*); humble; **Be'scheidenheit** *f* (-; *no pl*) modesty
bescheinigen [bə'ʃainɪgən] *v/t* (*no -ge-*,
h) certify
Be'scheinigung *f* (-; -*en*) a) (*no pl*) certification, b) certificate
be'scheißen V *v/t* (*irr*, **scheißen**, *no*

-ge-, *h*) cheat; **j-n ~ um** do s.o. out of
be'schenken *v/t* (*no -ge-*, *h*) **j-n** (**reich**)
~ give s.o. (shower s.o. with) presents
Be'scherung *f* (-; -*en*) distribution of
(Christmas) presents; F *fig* mess
be'schichten *v/t* (*no -ge-*, *h*) TECH coat
Be'schichtung *f* (-; -*en*) TECH coat
be'schießen *v/t* (*irr*, **schießen**, *no -ge-*,
h) MIL fire *or* shoot at; bombard (*a.*
PHYS), shell
be'schimpfen *v/t* (*no -ge-*, *h*) abuse, insult; swear at; **Be'schimpfung** *f* (-; -*en*)
abuse, insult
be'schissen V *adj* lousy, rotten
Be'schlag *m* TECH metal fitting(s); **in ~
nehmen** *fig* monopolize *s.o.*; bag; occupy; **be'schlagen** (*irr*, **schlagen**, *no
-ge-*) **1.** *v/t* (*h*) cover; TECH fit, mount;
shoe (*horse*); **2.** *v/i* (*sein*) window *etc*:
steam up; **3.** *adj* steamed-up; *fig*
well-versed (**auf**, *in* *dat* in)
Be'schlagnahme [bə'ʃla:kna:mə] *f* (-;
-*n*) confiscation; **be'schlagnahmen**
v/t (*no -ge-*, *h*) confiscate
beschleunigen [bə'ʃlɔynɪgən] *v/t* *and
v/i* (*no -ge-*, *h*) accelerate, speed up;
Be'schleunigung *f* (-; -*en*) accelera-
tion
be'schließen *v/t* (*irr*, **schließen**, *no
-ge-*, *h*) decide (on); pass (*law*); conclude; **Be'schluss** *m* decision
be'schmieren *v/t* (*no -ge-*, *h*) smear,
soil; scrawl all over; cover *wall etc* with
graffiti; spread (*toast etc*)
be'schmutzen *v/t* (*no -ge-*, *h*) soil (*a.*
fig), dirty
be'schneiden *v/t* (*irr*, **schneiden**, *no
-ge-*, *h*) clip, cut (*a.* *fig*); prune; MED cir-
cumcise
be'schönigen [bə'ʃø:nɪgən] *v/t* (*no -ge-*,
h) gloss over
beschränken [bə'ʃrɛŋkən] *v/t* (*no -ge-*,
h) confine, limit, restrict; **sich ~ auf**
(*acc*) confine o.s. to; **be'schränkt** *adj*
limited; *contp* dense; narrow-minded
Be'schränkung *f* (-; -*en*) limitation, restriction
be'schreiben *v/t* (*irr*, **schreiben**, *no
-ge-*, *h*) describe; write on
Be'schreibung *f* (-; -*en*) description
be'schriften *v/t* (*no -ge-*, *h*) inscribe;
mark (*goods*); **Be'schriftung** *f* (-;
-*en*) inscription
beschuldigen [bə'ʃʊldɪgən] *v/t* (*no -ge-*,

B

h) blame; **j-n e-r Sache ~** accuse s.o. of s.th. (*a.* JUR); **Be'schuldigung** *f* (*-; -en*) accusation

be'schummeln F *v/t* (*no -ge-, h*) cheat

Be'schuss *m*: **unter ~** MIL under fire

be'schützen *v/t* (*no -ge-, h*) protect, shelter, guard (**vor** *dat* from)

Be'schützer *m* (*-s; -*) protector

Beschwerde [bə'ʃveːʁdə] *f* (*-; -n*) complaint (**über** *acc* about; **bei** to); *pl* MED complaints, trouble

beschweren [bə'ʃveːrən] *v/t* (*no -ge-, h*) weight s.th.; **sich ~** complain (**über** *acc* about; **bei** to)

be'schwerlich *adj* hard, arduous

beschwichtigen [bə'ʃvɪçtɪgən] *v/t* (*no -ge-, h*) appease (*a.* POL), calm

be'schwindeln *v/t* (*no -ge-, h*) tell a fib *or* lie; cheat

beschwingt [bə'ʃvɪŋt] *adj* buoyant; MUS lively, swinging

beschwipst [bə'ʃvɪpst] F *adj* tipsy

be'schwören [bə'ʃvøːrən] *v/t* (*irr,* **schwören,** *no -ge-, h*) swear to; implore; conjure up

beseitigen [bə'zaɪtɪgən] *v/t* (*no -ge-, h*) remove (*a. s.o.*), *a.* dispose of (*waste etc*); eliminate; POL liquidate

Be'seitigung *f* (*-; no pl*) removal; disposal; elimination

Besen ['beːzən] *m* (*-s; -*) broom

'**Besenstiel** *m* broomstick

besessen [bə'zɛsən] *adj* obsessed (**von** by, with); **wie ~** like mad

be'setzen *v/t* (*no -ge-, h*) occupy (*a.* MIL); fill (*post etc*); THEA cast; squat in; **be'setzt** *adj* occupied; *seat:* taken; *bus etc:* full up; TEL busy, *Br* engaged; **Be'setztzeichen** *n* TEL busy signal, *Br* engaged tone; **Be'setzung** *f* (*-; -en*) THEA cast; MIL occupation

besichtigen [bə'zɪçtɪgən] *v/t* (*no -ge-, h*) visit, see the sights of; inspect

Be'sichtigung *f* (*-; -en*) sightseeing; visit (*gen* to); inspection (of)

be'siedeln *v/t* (*no -ge-, h*) settle; colonize; populate; **be'siedelt** *adj:* **dicht** (**dünn**) **~** densely (sparsely) populated; **Be'siedlung** *f* (*-; -en*) settlement; colonization; population

be'siegeln *v/t* (*no -ge-, h*) seal

be'siegen *v/t* (*no -ge-, h*) defeat, beat; conquer (*a. fig*)

besinnen *v/refl* (*irr,* **sinnen,** *no -ge-, h*) remember; think (**auf** *acc* about); **sich**

anders ~ change one's mind

be'sinnlich *adj* contemplative

Be'sinnung *f* (*-; no pl*) MED consciousness; (**wieder**) **zur ~ kommen** MED come round; *fig* come to one's senses

be'sinnungslos *adj* MED unconscious

Be'sitz *m* (*-es; no pl*) possession; property; **~ ergreifen von** take possession of; **be'sitzanzeigend** *adj* LING possessive; **be'sitzen** *v/t* (*irr,* **sitzen,** *no -ge-, h*) possess, own; **Be'sitzer** *m* (*-s; -*) possessor, owner; **den ~ wechseln** change hands

besoffen [bə'zɔfən] F *adj* drunk, plastered, stoned

be'sohlen [bə'zoːlən] *v/t* (*no -ge-, h*) **~ lassen** have (re)soled

Be'soldung *f* (*-; -en*) pay; salary

besondere [bə'zɔndərə] *adj* special, particular; peculiar

Be'sonderheit *f* (*-; -en*) peculiarity

be'sonders *adv* especially, particularly; chiefly, mainly

be'sonnen *adj* prudent, level-headed

be'sorgen *v/t* (*no -ge-, h*) get, buy; → **erledigen**; **Besorgnis** [bə'zɔrknɪs] *f* (*-; -se*) concern, alarm, anxiety (**über** *acc* about, at); **~ erregend** alarming; **besorgt** [bə'zɔrkt] *adj* worried, concerned; **Be'sorgung** *f* (*-; -en*) **~en machen** go shopping

be'spielen *v/t* (*no -ge-, h*) make a recording on

be'spitzeln *v/t* (*no -ge-, h*) spy on s.o.

be'sprechen *v/t* (*irr,* **sprechen,** *no -ge-, h*) discuss, talk s.th. over; review (*book etc*); **Be'sprechung** *f* (*-; -en*) discussion, talk(s); meeting, conference; review

be'spritzen *v/t* (*no -ge-, h*) spatter

besser ['bɛsɐ] *adj and adv* better; **es ist ~, wir fragen ihn** we had better ask him; **immer ~** better and better; **es geht ihm ~** he is better; **oder ~ gesagt** or rather; **es ~ wissen** know better; **es ~ machen als** do better than; **~ ist ~** just to be on the safe side

'**bessern** *v/refl* (*ge-, h*) improve, get better; '**Besserung** *f* (*-; no pl*) improvement; **auf dem Wege der ~** on the way to recovery; **gute ~!** get better soon

'**Besserwisser** [-vɪsɐ] *m* (*-s; -*) F smart aleck

Be'stand *m* a) (*no pl*) (continued) existence, b) stock; **~ haben** last, be lasting

be'ständig *adj* constant, steady (*a. character*); settled; **...beständig** *in cpds* ...-resistant, ...proof

Be'standsaufnahme *f* ECON stocktaking (*a. fig*); **~ machen** take stock (*a. fig*)

Be'standteil *m* part, component

be'stärken *v/t* (*no -ge-, h*) confirm, strengthen, encourage (*in dat* in)

bestätigen [bə'ʃtɛːtɪgən] *v/t* (*no -ge-, h*) confirm; certify; acknowledge (*receipt*); **sich ~** prove (to be) true; come true; **sich bestätigt fühlen** feel affirmed; **Be'stätigung** *f* (*-; -en*) confirmation; certificate; acknowledg(e-)ment; letter of confirmation

bestatten [bə'ʃtatən] *v/t* (*no -ge-, h*) bury; **Be'stattungsinsti,tut** *n* funeral home, *Br* undertakers

be'stäuben *v/t* (*no -ge-, h*) dust; BOT pollinate

beste ['bɛstə] *adj and adv* best; **am ~n** best; **welches gefällt dir am ~n?** which one do you like best?; **am ~n nehmen Sie den Bus** it would be best to take a bus; **Beste** *m, f* (*-n; -n*), *n* (*-n; no pl*) the best; **das ~ geben** do one's best; **das ~ machen aus** make the best of; (*nur*) **zu deinem ~n** for your own good

be'stechen *v/t* (*irr, stechen, no -ge-, h*) bribe; fascinate (*durch* by)

be'stechlich *adj* corrupt

Be'stechung *f* (*-; -en*) bribery, corruption; **Be'stechungsgeld** *n* bribe

Besteck [bə'ʃtɛk] *n* (*-[e]s; -e*) (set of) knife, fork and spoon; cutlery

be'stehen (*irr, stehen, no -ge-, h*) **1.** *v/t* pass (*examination etc*); **2.** *v/i* be, exist; **~ auf** (*dat*) insist on; **~ aus** (*in*) (*dat*) consist of (in); **~ bleiben** last, survive

Be'stehen *n* (*-s; no pl*) existence

be'stehlen *v/t* (*irr, stehlen, no -ge-, h*) **j-n ~** steal s.o.'s money *etc*

be'steigen *v/t* (*irr, steigen, no -ge-, h*) climb; get on *a* bus *etc*; ascend (*the throne*)

be'stellen *v/t* (*no -ge-, h*) order; book (*room etc*); reserve (*seat etc*); call (*taxi*); give, send (*message etc*); AGR cultivate; **kann ich et. ~?** can I take a message?;

~ Sie ihm bitte, ... please tell him ...

Be'stellschein *m* ECON order form

Be'stellung *f* (*-; -en*) booking; reservation; ECON order; **auf ~** to order

'bestenfalls *adv* at best

'bestens *adv* very well

bestialisch [bɛs'tjaːlɪʃ] *adj fig* bestial

Bestie ['bɛstjə] *f* (*-; -n*) beast, *fig a.* brute

be'stimmen *v/t* (*no -ge-, h*) determine, decide; define; choose, pick; **zu ~ haben** be in charge, F be the boss; **bestimmt für** meant for; **be'stimmt 1.** *adj* determined, firm; LING definite (*article*); **~e Dinge** certain things; **2.** *adv* certainly; **ganz ~** definitely; **er ist ~ ...** he must be ...; **Be'stimmung** *f* (*-; -en*) regulation; destiny

Be'stimmungsort *m* destination

'Bestleistung *f* SPORT (personal) record

be'strafen *v/t* (*no -ge-, h*) punish

Be'strafung *f* (*-; -en*) punishment

be'strahlen *v/t* (*no -ge-, h*) irradiate (*a.* MED); **Be'strahlung** *f* (*-; -en*) irradiation; MED ray treatment, radiotherapy

be'streichen *v/t* (*irr, streichen, no -ge-, h*) spread; **be'streiten** *v/t* (*irr, streiten, no -ge-, h*) challenge; deny; pay for, finance; **be'streuen** *v/t* (*no -ge-, h*) sprinkle (*mit* with); **be'stürmen** *v/t* (*no -ge-, h*) urge; bombard

be'stürzt *adj* dismayed (*über acc* at); **Be'stürzung** *f* (*-; no pl*) consternation, dismay

Besuch [bə'zuːx] *m* (*-[e]s; -e*) visit (*gen, bei, in dat* to); call (*bei* on; *in dat* at); attendance (*gen* at); **~ haben** have company *or* guests; **be'suchen** *v/t* (*no -ge-, h*) visit; call on, (go to) see; look *s.o.* up; attend (*meeting etc*); go to (*pub etc*); **Be'sucher(in)** (*-s; -/-; -nen*) visitor, guest; **Be'suchszeit** *f* visiting hours; **be'sucht** *adj*: **gut** (**schlecht**) **~** well (poorly) attended; much (little) frequented

betagt [bə'taːkt] *adj* aged

be'tasten *v/t* (*no -ge-, h*) touch, feel

be'tätigen *v/t* (*no -ge-, h*) TECH operate; apply (*brake*); **sich ~** be active

Be'tätigung *f* (*-; -en*) activity

betäuben [bə'tɔybən] *v/t* (*no -ge-, h*) stun (*a. fig*), daze; MED an(a)esthetize

Be'täubung *f* (*-; -en*) MED an(a)esthetization; an(a)esthesia; *fig* daze, stupor

B

Be'täubungsmittel *n* MED an(a)esthetic; narcotic

Bete ['be:tə] *f* (-; -n) **rote ~** BOT beet, *Br* beetroot

beteiligen [bə'tailɪɡən] *v/t (no -ge-, h)* **j-n ~** give s.o. a share (**an** *dat* in); **sich ~** take part (**an** *dat, bei* in), participate (in) (*a.* JUR); **beteiligt** [bə'tailɪçt] *adj* concerned; **~ sein an** (*dat*) be involved in; ECON have a share in; **Be'teiligung** *f* (-; -en) participation (*a.* JUR, ECON); involvement; share (*a.* ECON)

beten ['be:tən] *v/i (ge-, h)* pray (**um** for), say one's prayers; say grace

beteuern [bə'tɔyɐn] *v/t (no -ge-, h)* protest (*one's innocence etc*)

Beton [be'tɔŋ] *m* (-s; -s, -e [be'to:nə]) concrete

betonen [bə'to:nən] *v/t (no -ge-, h)* stress, emphasize

betonieren [beto'ni:rən] *v/t (no -ge-, h)* (cover with) concrete

Be'tonung *f* (-; -en) stress; *fig* emphasis

betören [bə'tø:rən] *v/t (no -ge-, h)* infatuate, bewitch

Betr. ABBR *of* **betrifft** re

Betracht [bə'traxt] *m:* **in ~ ziehen** take into consideration; **nicht in ~ kommen** be out of the question

be'trachten *v/t (no -ge-, h)* look at, *fig a.* view; **~ als** look upon *or* regard as, consider; **Be'trachter** *m* (-s; -) viewer

beträchtlich [bə'trɛçtlɪç] *adj* considerable

Be'trachtung *f* (-; -en) view; **bei näherer ~** on closer inspection

Betrag [bə'tra:k] *m* (-[e]s; Beträge [bə'trɛ:ɡə]) amount, sum; **be'tragen** (*irr, tragen, no -ge-, h*) **1.** *v/t* amount to; **2.** *v/refl* behave (o.s.); **Be'tragen** *n* (-s; *no pl*) behavio(u)r, conduct

be'trauen *v/t (no -ge-, h)* entrust (**mit** with)

be'treffen *v/t (irr, treffen, no -ge-, h)* concern; refer to; **was ... betrifft** as for ..., as to ...; **betrifft** (ABBR **Betr.**) re; **~d** *adj* concerning; **die ~en Personen** etc the people *etc* concerned

be'treiben *v/t (irr, treiben, no -ge-, h)* operate, run; go in for (*sport etc*)

be'treten¹ *v/t (irr, treten, no -ge-, h)* step on; enter; **Betreten (des Rasens) verboten!** keep out! (keep off the grass!)

be'treten² *adj* embarrassed

betreuen [bə'trɔyən] *v/t (no -ge-, h)* look after, take care of; **Be'treuung** *f* (-; *no pl*) care (*gen* of, for)

Betrieb [bə'tri:p] *m* (-[e]s; -e) a) business, firm, company, b) (*no pl*) operation, running, c) (*no pl*) rush; **in ~ sein (setzen)** be in (put into) operation; **außer ~** out of order; **im Geschäft war viel ~** the shop was very busy

Be'triebs|anleitung *f* operating instructions; **~berater** *m* business consultant; **~ferien** *pl* company (*Br a.* works) holiday; **~fest** *n* annual company fête; **~kapi,tal** *n* working capital; **~klima** *n* working atmosphere; **~kosten** *pl* operating costs; **~leitung** *f* management; **~rat** *m* works council

be'triebssicher *adj* safe to operate

Be'triebs|störung *f* TECH breakdown; **~sys,tem** *n* EDP operating system; **~unfall** *m* industrial accident; **~wirtschaft** *f* business administration

be'trinken *v/refl (irr, trinken, no -ge-, h)* get drunk

betroffen [bə'trɔfən] *adj* affected, concerned; dismayed, shocked; **Be'troffenheit** *f* (-; *no pl*) dismay, shock

betrübt [bə'try:pt] *adj* sad, grieved (**über** *acc* at)

Betrug [bə'tru:k] *m* (-[e]s; *no pl*) cheat; JUR fraud; deceit; **be'trügen** (*irr, trügen, no -ge-, h*) deceive; cheat (**beim Kartenspiel** at cards); swindle, trick (**um et.** out of s.th.); be unfaithful to; **Be'trüger(in)** (-s; -/-; -nen) swindler, trickster

betrunken [bə'trʊŋkən] *adj* drunken; **~ sein** be drunk

Be'trunkene *m, f* (-n; -n) drunk

Bett [bɛt] *n* (-[e]s; -en) bed; **am ~** at the bedside; **ins ~ gehen (bringen)** go (put) to bed; **~bezug** *m* comforter case, *Br* duvet cover; **~decke** *f* blanket; quilt

betteln ['bɛtəln] *v/i (ge-, h)* beg (**um** for)

'Bettgestell *n* bedstead

'bettlägerig [-lɛ:ɡərɪç] *adj* bedridden

'Bettlaken *n* sheet

Bettler ['bɛtlɐ] *m* (-s; -) beggar

'Bett|nässer [-nɛsɐ] *m* (-s; -) MED bedwetter; **~ruhe** *f* bed rest; **j-m ~ verordnen** tell s.o. to stay in bed; **~vorleger** *m* bedside rug; **~wäsche** f bed linen; **~zeug** n bedding, bedclothes

beugen ['bɔygən] v/t (ge-, h) bend; LING inflect; **sich ~** (vor dat) bend, bow

Beule ['bɔylə] f (-; -n) MED bump; MOT dent

beunruhigen [bə'ʔʊnruːɪgən] v/t (no -ge-, h) alarm, worry

beurlauben [bə'ʔuːɐ̯laubən] v/t give s.o. leave or time off; suspend; **sich ~ lassen** ask for leave; **be'urlaubt** [-laupt] adj on leave

be'urteilen v/t (no -ge-, h) judge (**nach** by); rate; **Be'urteilung** f (-; -en) judg(e)ment; evaluation

Beute ['bɔytə] f (-; no pl) booty, loot; ZO prey (a. fig); HUNT bag; fig a. victim

Beutel ['bɔytəl] m (-s; -) bag; pouch

bevölkern [bə'fœlkɐn] v/t (no -ge-, h) populate; **be'völkert** adj → **besiedelt**; **Be'völkerung** f (-; -en) population

bevollmächtigen [bə'fɔlmɛçtɪgən] v/t (no -ge-, h) authorize

be'vor cj before

bevor|munden [bə'foːɐ̯mʊndən] v/t (no -ge-, h) patronize; **~stehen** v/i (irr, stehen, sep, -ge-, h) be approaching; lie ahead; be imminent; **j-m ~** be in store for s.o., await s.o.

be'vorzugen [-tsuːgən] v/t (no -ge-, h) prefer; favo(u)r; **Be'vorzugung** f (-; -en) preferential treatment

be'wachen v/t (no -ge-, h) guard, watch over; **Be'wacher** m (-s; -) guard; SPORT marker; **Be'wachung** f (-; -en) a) (no pl) guarding; SPORT marking, b) guard

bewaffnen [bə'vafnən] v/t (no -ge-, h) arm (a. fig); **Be'waffnung** f (-; -en) armament; arms

be'wahren v/t (no -ge-, h) keep; **~ vor** (dat) keep or save from

be'währen v/refl (no -ge-, h) prove successful; **sich ~ als** prove to be

bewährt [bə'vɛːɐ̯t] adj (well-)tried, reliable; experienced; **Be'währung** f (-; -en) JUR probation

Be'währungs|frist f JUR (period of) probation; **~helfer** m JUR probation officer; **~probe** f (acid) test

bewaldet [bə'valdət] adj wooded, woody

bewältigen [bə'vɛltɪgən] v/t (no -ge-, h) manage, cope with; cover (distance)

bewandert adj (well-)versed (**in** dat in)

be'wässern v/t (no -ge-, h) irrigate; **Be'wässerung** f (-; -en) irrigation

bewegen [bə'veːgən] v/t and v/refl (no -ge-, h) move (a. fig); **nicht...!** don't move!; (irr) **j-n zu et. ~** get s.o. to do s.th.

Be'weggrund m motive

beweglich [bə'veːklɪç] adj movable; agile; flexible; TECH moving (parts); **Be'weglichkeit** f (-; no pl) mobility; agility; **be'wegt** adj rough (sea); choked (voice); eventful (life); fig moved, touched; **Be'wegung** f (-; -en) movement (a. POL); motion (a. PHYS); exercise; fig emotion; **in ~ setzen** set in motion; **Be'wegungsfreiheit** f (-; no pl) freedom of movement (fig a. of action); **be'wegungslos** adj motionless

Beweis [bə'vais] m (-es; -e) proof (**für** of); **~(e)** evidence (esp JUR)

be'weisen v/t (irr, **weisen**, no -ge-, h) prove; show

Be'weismittel n JUR (piece of) evidence

Be'weisstück n (piece of) evidence, JUR exhibit

be'wenden v/i: **es dabei ~ lassen** leave it at that

be'werben v/refl (irr, **werben**, no -ge-, h) **sich ~ um** apply for; **Be'werber(in)** (-s; -/-; -nen) applicant; **Be'werbung** f (-; -en) application; **Be'werbungsschreiben** n (letter of) application

be'werten v/t (no -ge-, h) assess; judge; **Be'wertung** f (-; -en) assessment

bewilligen [bə'vɪlɪgən] v/t (no -ge-, h) grant, allow; **be'wirken** v/t (no -ge-, h) cause; **bewirten** [bə'vɪrtən] v/t (no -ge-, h) entertain

be'wirtschaften v/t (no -ge-, h) run; AGR farm; **be'wirtschaftet** adj open (to the public)

Be'wirtung f (-; -en) catering; service; hospitality

bewog [bə'voːk] pret of **bewegen**

bewogen [bə'voːgən] pp of **bewegen**

be'wohnen v/t (no -ge-, h) live in; inhabit; **Be'wohner(in)** (-s; -/-; -nen) inhabitant; occupant; **be'wohnt** adj inhabited; occupied

bewölken [bə'vœlkən] v/refl (no -ge-, h) METEOR cloud over (a. fig); **be'wölkt**

B

adj METEOR cloudy, overcast

Be'wölkung *f* (-; *no pl*) METEOR clouds

Bewunderer [bə'vʊndərɐ] *m* (-s; -) admirer; **be'wundern** *v/t* (*no* -ge-, *h*) admire (**wegen** for); **be'wundernswert** *adj* admirable; **Be'wunderung** *f* (-; *no pl*) admiration

bewusst [bə'vʊst] *adj* conscious; intentional; **sich e-r Sache ~ sein** be conscious *or* aware of s.th., realize s.th.; **j-m et. ~ machen** make s.o. realize s.th.

be'wusstlos *adj* MED unconscious

Be'wusstsein *n* (-s; *no pl*) MED consciousness; **bei ~** conscious

be'zahlen *v/t* (*no* -ge-, *h*) pay; pay for (*a. fig*); **be'zahlt** *adj*: **~er Urlaub** paid leave; **es macht sich ~** it pays; **Be'zahlung** *f* (-; *no pl*) payment; pay

be'zaubern *v/t* (*no* -ge-, *h*) charm; **~d** *adj* charming, F sweet, darling

be'zeichnen *v/t* (*no* -ge-, *h*) **~ als** call, describe as; **~d** *adj* characteristic, typical (**für** of)

Be'zeichnung *f* (-; -en) name, term

be'zeugen *v/t* (*no* -ge-, *h*) JUR testify to

be'ziehen *v/t* (*irr*, **ziehen**, *no* -ge-, *h*) cover; put clean sheets on (*bed*); move into; receive; subscribe to (*paper etc*); **~ auf** (*acc*) relate to; **sich ~** cloud over; **sich ~ auf** (*acc*) refer to; **Be'ziehung** *f* (-; -en) relation (**zu** to *s.th.*; **with** *s.o.*); connection (**zu** with); relationship; respect; **~en haben** have connections

be'ziehungsweise *cj* respectively; or; or rather

Bezirk [bə'tsɪrk] *m* (-[e]s; -e) precinct, *Br a.* district

Bezug [bə'tsu:k] *m* (-[e]s; *Bezüge* [bə'tsy:gə]) a) cover(ing); case, slip, b) (*no pl*) ECON purchase; subscription (*gen* to), c) *pl* earnings; **~ nehmen auf** (*acc*) refer to; **in ~ auf** (*acc*) → **bezüglich**

bezüglich [bə'tsy:klɪç] *prp* (*gen*) regarding, concerning

Be'zugs|per,son *f* PSYCH person to relate to, role model; **~punkt** *m* reference point; **~quelle** *f* source (of supply)

be'zwecken *v/t* (*no* -ge-, *h*) aim at, intend; **be'zweifeln** *v/t* (*no* -ge-, *h*) doubt, question; **be'zwingen** *v/t* (*irr*, **zwingen**, *no* -ge-, *h*) conquer, defeat

Bibel ['bi:bəl] *f* (-; -n) Bible

Biber ['bi:bɐ] *m* (-s; -) ZO beaver

Bibliothek [biblio'te:k] *f* (-; -en) library

Bibliothekar [bibliote'ka:ɐ] *m* (-s; -e), **Bibliothe'karin** *f* (-; -nen) librarian

biblisch ['bi:blɪʃ] *adj* biblical

bieder ['bi:dɐ] *adj* honest; square

biegen ['bi:gən] *v/t* (*irr*, ge-, *h*) and *v/i* (*sein*) bend (*a. sich ~*), road: *a.* turn; **um die Ecke ~** turn (round) the corner

biegsam ['bi:kza:m] *adj* flexible

'Biegung *f* (-; -en) curve

Biene ['bi:nə] *f* (-; -n) ZO bee

'Bienen|königin *f* ZO queen (bee); **~korb** *m*, **~stock** *m* (bee)hive; **~wachs** *n* beeswax

Bier [bi:ɐ] *n* (-[e]s; -e) beer; **~ vom Faß** draft (*Br* draught) beer; **~deckel** *m* coaster, beer mat; **~krug** *m* beer mug, stein

Biest [bi:st] F *fig n* (-[e]s; -er) beast; (**kleines**) **~** brat, little devil, pest

bieten ['bi:tən] (*irr*, ge-, *h*) **1.** *v/t* offer; **sich ~** present itself; **2.** *v/i* auction: (make a) bid

Bigamie [biga'mi:] *f* (-; -n) bigamy

Bikini [bi'ki:ni] *m* (-s; -s) bikini

Bilanz [bi'lants] *f* (-; -en) ECON balance; *fig* result; **~ ziehen aus** (*dat*) *fig* take stock of

Bild [bɪlt] *n* (-[e]s; -er ['bɪldɐ]) picture; image; **sich ein ~ machen von** get an idea of; **~ausfall** *m* TV blackout; **~bericht** *m* photo(graphic) essay (*Br* report)

bilden ['bɪldən] *v/t* (ge-, *h*) form (*a. sich ~*); shape; *fig* educate (**sich** o.s.), be, constitute

'Bilderbuch *n* picture book

'Bildfläche *f*: F **auf der ~ erscheinen** (**von der ~ verschwinden**) appear on (disappear from) the scene

'Bildhauer *m* (-s; -), **'Bildhauerin** *f* (-; -nen) sculptor

'bildlich *adj* graphic; figurative

'Bildnis *n* (-ses; -se) portrait

'Bildplatte *f* videodisk (*Br* -disc)

'Bildröhre *f* picture tube

'Bildschirm *m* TV screen, EDP *a.* display, monitor; **~arbeitsplatz** *m* workstation; **~gerät** *n* visual display unit, VDU; **~schoner** *m* (-s; -) screen saver; **~text** *m* videotext, *Br* viewdata

'bild'schön *adj* most beautiful

B

'Bildung *f* (-; *-en*) a) (*no pl*) education, b) formation

'Bildungs... *in cpds* ...**chancen**, ...**reform**, ...**urlaub** *etc*: educational ...; **~lücke** *f* gap in one's knowledge

'Bildunterschrift *f* caption

Billard ['bɪljart] *n* (-s; *-e*) billiards; pool; **~kugel** *f* billiard ball; **~stock** *m* cue

Billett [bɪl'jɛt] *n* (-[e]s; *-e*) *Swiss* ticket

billig ['bɪlɪç] *adj* cheap (*a. contp*), inexpensive

billigen ['bɪlɪgən] *v/t* (ge-, h) approve of; 'Billigung *f* (-; *no pl*) approval

Billion [bɪl'joːn] *f* (-; *-en*) trillion

bimmeln ['bɪməln] F *v/i* (ge-, h) jingle; TEL ring

binär [bi'nɛːɐ] *adj* MATH, PHYS *etc* binary

Binde ['bɪndə] *f* (-; *-n*) bandage; sling; → **Damenbinde**; **~gewebe** *n* ANAT connective tissue; **~glied** *n* (connecting) link

'Bindehaut *f* ANAT conjunctiva; **~entzündung** *f* MED conjunctivitis

binden (*irr*, ge-, h) **1.** *v/t* bind (*a. book*), tie (**an** *acc* to); make (*wreath etc*); knot (*tie*); **sich ~** bind *or* commit o.s.; **2.** *v/i* bind

'Bindestrich *m* LING hyphen

'Bindewort *n* LING conjunction

Bindfaden ['bɪnt-] *m* string

'Bindung *f* (-; *-en*) tie, link, bond; *skiing:* binding

Binnen|hafen ['bɪnən-] *m* inland port; **~handel** *m* domestic trade; **~markt** *m*: **Europäischer ~** European single market; **~schifffahrt** *f* inland navigation; **~verkehr** *m* inland traffic *or* transport

Binse ['bɪnzə] *f* (-; *-n*) BOT rush

'Binsenweisheit *f* (-; *-en*) truism

Bio..., bio... [bio-] *in cpds* ...**chemie**, ...**dynamisch**, ...**sphäre** *etc*: bio...

Biografie, Biographie [biogra'fiː] *f* (-; *-n*) biography

bio'grafisch, bio'graphisch *adj* biographic(al)

Bioladen ['biːo-] *m* health food shop *or* store

Biologe [bio'loːgə] *m* (-n; *-n*) biologist

Biologie [biolo'giː] *f* (-; *no pl*) biology

Bio'login *f* (-; *-nen*) biologist

biologisch [bio'loːgɪʃ] *adj* biological; AGR organic; **~ abbaubar** biodegradable

'Biorhythmus *m* biorhythms

'Biotechnik *f* (-; *no pl*) biotechnology

Biotop [bio'toːp] *n* (-s; *-e*) biotope

Birke ['bɪrkə] *f* (-; *-n*) BOT birch (tree)

Birne ['bɪrnə] *f* (-; *-n*) BOT pear; ELECTR (light) bulb

bis [bɪs] *prp* (*acc*) *and adv and cj time:* till, until, (up) to; *space:* (up) to, as far as; **von ... ~ ...** from ... to ...; **~ auf** (*acc*) except; **~ zu** up to; **~ später!** see you later!; **~ jetzt** up to now, so far; **~ Montag** by Monday; **zwei ~ drei** two or three; **wie weit ist es ~ ...?** how far is it to ...?

Bischof ['bɪʃɔf] *m* (-s; *Bischöfe* ['bɪʃœfə]) REL bishop

bisexuell ['bɪːzɛksuɛl] *adj* bisexual

bis'her *adv* up to now, so far; **wie ~** as before

bisherig [bɪs'heːrɪç] *adj* previous

Biskuit [bɪs'kviːt] *n* (-[e]s; *-e*) sponge cake (*mix*)

biss [bɪs] *pret of* **beißen**

Biss *m* (-es; *-e*) bite (*a. fig*)

bisschen ['bɪsçən] *adj and adv:* **ein ~** a little, a (little) bit (of); **nicht ein ~** not in the least

Bissen ['bɪsən] *m* (-s; *-*) bite; **keinen ~** not a thing

bissig ['bɪsɪç] *adj fig* cutting; **ein ~er Hund** a dog that bites; **Vorsicht, ~er Hund!** beware of the dog!

Bistum ['bɪstuːm] *n* (-s; *Bistümer* ['bɪstyːmɐ]) REL bishopric, diocese

bis'weilen *adv* at times, now and then

Bit [bɪt] *n* (-[s]; *-[s]*) EDP bit

bitte ['bɪtə] *adv* please; **~ nicht!** please don't!; **~ (schön)!** that's all right, not at all, you're welcome; here you are; (**wie ~?** pardon?; **~ sehr?** can I help you?; **'Bitte** *f* (-; *-n*) request (**um** for); **ich habe e-e ~ (an dich)** I have a favo(u)r to ask of you; **'bitten** *v/t* (*irr*, ge-, h) **j-n um et.** ask s.o. for s.th.; **darf ich ~?** may I have (the pleasure of) this dance?; → **Erlaubnis**

bitter ['bɪtɐ] *adj* bitter (*a. fig*), *a.* biting (*cold*); **~'kalt** *adj* bitterly cold

blähen ['blɛːən] *v/refl* (ge-, h) swell

'Blähungen *pl* MED flatulence, *Br a.* wind

blamabel [bla'maːbəl] *adj* embarrassing; **Blamage** [bla'maːʒə] *f* (-; *-n*) disgrace, shame; **blamieren** [bla'miːrən]

B

v/t (no -ge-, h) **j-n ~** make s.o. look like a fool; **sich ~** make a fool of o.s.

blank [blaŋk] *adj* shining, shiny, bright; polished; F broke

Blanko... ['blaŋko] *in cpds* ECON blank

Bläschen ['blɛːsçən] *n (-s; -)* MED vesicle, small blister

Blase ['blaːzə] *f (-; -n)* bubble; ANAT bladder; MED blister

'**Blasebalg** *m* (pair of) bellows

'**blasen** *v/i (irr, ge-, h)* blow (*a.* MUS)

'**Blas|instru,ment** *n* MUS wind instrument; **~ka,pelle** *f* brass band; **~rohr** *n* blowpipe

blass [blas] *adj* pale (**vor** with); **~ werden** turn pale; **Blässe** ['blɛsə] *f (-; no pl)* paleness, pallor

Blatt [blat] *n (-[e]s; Blätter* ['blɛtɐ]) BOT leaf; piece, sheet (*a.* MUS); (news)paper; *card games:* hand; **blättern** ['blɛtɐn] *v/i (ge-, h)* **~ in** *(dat)* leaf through

'**Blätterteig** *m* puff pastry

blau [blau] *adj* blue; F loaded, stoned; **~es Auge** black eye; **~er Fleck** bruise; **Fahrt ins Blaue** mystery tour

'**blau|äugig** [-ɔygɪç] *adj* blue-eyed; *fig* starry-eyed

'**Blaubeere** *f* BOT blueberry, *Br* bilberry

'**blaugrau** *adj* bluish-gray (*Br* -grey)

'**bläulich** ['blɔylɪç] *adj* bluish

'**Blaulicht** *n (-[e]s; -er)* flashing light(s)

'**Blauhelme** *pl* MIL UN soldiers

'**blaumachen** F *v/i (sep, -ge-, h)* stay away from work *or* school

'**Blausäure** *f* CHEM prussic acid

Blech [blɛç] *n (-[e]s; -e)* sheet metal; *in cpds ...dach, ...löffel etc:* tin ...; *...instrument:* MUS brass ...

'**blechen** F *v/t and v/i (ge-, h)* shell out

'**Blech|büchse**, **~dose** *f* can, *Br a.* tin; **~schaden** *m* MOT bodywork damage

Blei [blai] *n (-[e]s; -e)* lead; **aus ~** leaden

Bleibe ['blaibə] *f (-; -n)* place to stay

'**bleiben** *v/i (irr, ge-, sein)* stay, remain; **~ bei** stick to; F **et. ~ lassen** not do s.th.; **lass das ~!** stop that!; **das wirst du schön ~ lassen!** you'll do nothing of the sort!; → **Apparat, ruhig, ~d** *adj* lasting, permanent

bleich [blaiç] *adj* pale (**vor** *dat* with)

'**bleichen** *v/t ([irr,] ge-, h)* bleach

bleiern ['blaiɐn] *adj* lead(en *fig*)

'**bleifrei** *adj* MOT unleaded

'**Bleistift** *m* pencil; **~spitzer** *m* pencil sharpener

Blende ['blɛndə] *f (-; -n)* blind; PHOT aperture; **(bei) ~ 8** (at) f-8

'**blenden** *v/t (ge-, h)* blind, dazzle (*both a. fig*); **~d** *adj* dazzling (*a. fig*); brilliant; **~ aussehen** look great

'**blendfrei** *adj* OPT antiglare

blich [blɪç] *pret of* **bleichen**

Blick [blɪk] *m (-[e]s; -e)* look (**auf** *acc* at); view (of); **flüchtiger ~** glance; **auf den ersten ~** at first sight; '**blicken** *v/i (ge-, h)* look, glance (*both:* **auf** *acc,* **nach** at)

'**Blickfang** *m* eye-catcher

'**Blickfeld** *n* field of vision

blieb [bliːp] *pret of* **bleiben**

blies [bliːs] *pret of* **blasen**

blind [blɪnt] *adj* blind (*a. fig* **gegen, für** to; **vor** *dat* with); dull (*mirror etc*); **~er Alarm** false alarm; **~er Passagier** stowaway; **auf e-m Auge ~** blind in one eye; **ein Blinder** a blind man; **e-e Blinde** a blind woman; **die Blinden** the blind

'**Blinddarm** *m* ANAT appendix; **~entzündung** *f* MED appendicitis; **~operati,on** *f* MED appendectomy

'**Blinden|hund** ['blɪndən-] *m* seeing eye (*Br* guide) dog; **~schrift** *f* braille

'**Blindgänger** [-gɛŋɐ] *m (-s; -)* MIL dud

'**Blindheit** *f (-; no pl)* blindness

'**blindlings** ['blɪntlɪŋs] *adv* blindly

'**Blindschleiche** *f* ZO blindworm

blinken ['blɪŋkən] *v/i (ge-, h)* sparkle, shine; twinkle; flash (a signal); MOT indicate; **Blinker** ['blɪŋkɐ] *m (-s; -)* MOT turn signal, *Br* indicator

'**blinzeln** ['blɪntsəln] *v/i (ge-, h)* blink (one's eyes)

Blitz [blɪts] *m (-es; -e)* (flash of) lightning; PHOT flash; **~ableiter** *m (-s; -)* lightning conductor

'**blitzen** *v/i (ge-, h)* flash; **es blitzt** it's lightening

'**Blitz|gerät** *n* PHOT (electronic) flash; **~lampe** *f* PHOT flashbulb; flash cube; **~licht** *n (-[e]s; -er)* PHOT flash(light); **~schlag** *m* lightning stroke

'**blitz'schnell** *adj and adv* like a flash; *attr* split-second

Block [blɔk] *m (-[e]s; Blöcke* ['blœkə]) block; POL, ECON bloc; *(writing)* pad

Blockade [blɔ'kaːdə] *f (-; -n)* MAR, MIL blockade

'Blockflöte f recorder
'Blockhaus n log cabin
blockieren [blɔˈkiːrən] v/t and v/i (no -ge-, h) block; MOT lock
'Blockschrift f block letters
blöde ['bløːdə] F adj silly, stupid
'blödeln v/i (ge-, h) fool or clown around
'Blödheit ['bløːthait] f (-; no pl) stupidity
'Blödsinn F m (-[e]s; no pl) rubbish, nonsense
'blödsinnig F adj stupid, idiotic
blöken ['bløːkən] v/i (ge-, h) ZO bleat
blond [blɔnt] adj blond, fair
Blondine [blɔnˈdiːnə] f (-; -n) blonde
bloß [bloːs] 1. adj bare; naked (eye); mere; 2. adv only, just, merely
Blöße ['bløːsə] f (-; -n) nakedness; sich e-e ~ geben lay o.s. open to attack or criticism
'bloß|legen v/t (sep, -ge-, h) lay bare, expose; ~stellen v/t (sep, -ge-, h) expose, compromise, unmask; sich ~ compromise o.s.
blühen ['blyːən] v/i (ge-, h) (be in) bloom; (be in) blossom; fig flourish
Blume ['bluːmə] f (-; -n) flower; GASTR bouquet; head, froth
'Blumen|beet n flowerbed; ~händler m florist; ~kohl m BOT cauliflower; ~laden m flower shop, florist's; ~strauß m bunch of flowers; bouquet; ~topf m flowerpot; ~vase f vase
Bluse ['bluːzə] f (-; -n) blouse
Blut [bluːt] n (-[e]s; no pl) blood
'blutarm adj MED an(a)emic (a. fig)
'Blut|armut f MED an(a)emia; ~bad n massacre; ~bahn f ANAT bloodstream; ~bank f (-; -en) MED blood bank
'blutbefleckt adj bloodstained
'Blut|bild n MED blood count; ~blase f MED blood blister; ~druck m MED blood pressure
Blüte ['blyːtə] f (-; -n) flower; bloom (a. fig); blossom; fig height, heyday; in (voller) ~ in (full) bloom
'Blutegel m ZO leech
'bluten v/i (ge-, h) bleed (aus dat from)
'Blüten|blatt n petal; ~staub m pollen
Bluter ['bluːtɐ] m (-s; -) MED h(a)emophiliac
'Blut|erguss m bruise; MED h(a)ematoma; ~gefäß n ANAT blood vessel; ~gerinnsel n MED blood clot; ~gruppe

f MED blood group; ~hund m ZO bloodhound
'blutig adj bloody; ~er Anfänger rank beginner, F greenhorn
'Blut|körperchen n MED blood corpuscle; ~kreislauf m MED (blood) circulation; ~lache f pool of blood
'blutleer adj bloodless
'Blutprobe f MED blood test
'blutrünstig [-rynstɪç] adj bloodthirsty, gory
'Blutschande f JUR incest
'Blutspender m blood donor
'Blutsverwandte m, f blood relation
'Blutübertragung f MED blood transfusion
'Blutung f (-; -en) MED bleeding, h(a)emorrhage
'blutunterlaufen adj bloodshot
'Blut|vergießen n (-s; no pl) bloodshed; ~vergiftung f MED blood poisoning; ~wurst f black sausage (Br pudding)
BLZ [beːɛlˈtsɛt] ABBR of Bankleitzahl A.B.A. number, Br bank (sorting) code
Bö [bøː] f (-; -en) gust, squall
Bob [bɔp] m (-s; -s) bob(sled); ~bahn f bob run; ~fahrer m bobber
Bock [bɔk] m (-[e]s; Böcke ['bœkə]) ZO buck; he-goat, billy-goat; ram; SPORT buck; F e-n ~ schießen (make a) blunder; F keinen (or null) ~ auf et. haben have zero interest in s.th.
'bocken v/i (ge-, h) buck; sulk
'bockig adj obstinate; sulky
'Bockspringen n leapfrog
Boden ['boːdən] m (-s; Böden ['bøːdən]) ground; AGR soil; bottom; floor; attic
'Boden|perso,nal n AVIAT ground crew; ~re,form f land reform; ~schätze pl mineral resources; ~stati,on f AVIAT ground control; ~turnen n floor exercises
Body ['bɔdi] m (-s; -s) bodysuit
bog [boːk] pret of biegen
Bogen ['boːgən] m (-s; Bögen ['bøːgən]) bend, curve; MATH arc; ARCH arch; skiing: turn; bow; sheet; ~schießen n archery; ~schütze m archer
Bohle ['boːlə] f (-; -n) plank
Bohne ['boːnə] f (-; -n) BOT bean; grüne ~n green (Br a. French) beans
'Bohnenstange f beanpole (a. F)
bohnern ['boːnɐn] v/t (ge-, h) polish,

B

wax; '**Bohnerwachs** *n* floor polish

bohren ['bo:rən] *v/t* (*ge-, h*) bore, drill (*a. dentist*); **~d** *fig adj* piercing (*look*); insistent (*questions etc*)

Bohrer ['bo:rə] *m* (*-s; -*) TECH drill

'**Bohr|insel** *f* oil rig; **~loch** *n* borehole, well(head); **~ma,schine** *f* (electric) drill; **~turm** *m* derrick

'**Bohrung** *f* (*-; -en*) drilling; bore

Boje ['bo:jə] *f* (*-; -n*) MAR buoy

Bolzen ['bɔltsən] *m* (*-s; -*) TECH bolt

bombardieren [bɔmbar'di:rən] *v/t* (*no -ge-, h*) bomb; *fig* bombard

Bombe ['bɔmbə] *f* (*-; -n*) bomb; *fig* bombshell

'**Bomben|angriff** *m* air raid; **~anschlag** *m* bomb attack; **~erfolg** F *m* roaring success; THEA *etc* smash hit; **~geschäft** F *n* super deal

'**Bombenleger** *m* (*-s; -*) bomber

'**bombensicher** *adj* bombproof

Bomber ['bɔmbɐ] F *m* (*-s; -*) MIL bomber (*a.* SPORT)

Bon [bɔŋ] *m* (*-s; -s*) coupon, voucher

Bonbon [bɔŋ'bɔŋ] *m, n* (*-s; -s*) candy, *Br* sweet

Boot [bo:t] *n* (*-[e]s; -e*) boat

'**Bootsmann** *m* (*-[e]s; -leute*) boatswain

Bord[1] [bɔrt] *n* (*-[e]s; -e*) shelf

Bord[2] *m:* **an ~** AVIAT, MAR on board; **über ~** MAR overboard; **von ~ gehen** MAR disembark

Bordell [bɔr'dɛl] *n* (*-s; -e*) brothel, F whorehouse

'**Bordkarte** *f* AVIAT boarding pass

'**Bordstein** *m* curb, *Br* kerb

borgen ['bɔrgən] *v/t* (*ge-, h*) borrow; **sich et. von j-m ~** borrow s.th. from s.o.; *j-m et. ~* lend s.th. to s.o.

Borke ['bɔrkə] *f* (*-; -n*) BOT bark

borniert [bɔr'ni:ɐt] *adj* narrow-minded

Börse ['bœrzə] *f* (*-; -n*) ECON stock exchange

'**Börsen|bericht** *m* market report; **~kurs** *m* quotation; **~makler** *m* stockbroker; **~speku,lant** *m* stock-jobber

Borste ['bɔrstə] *f* (*-; -n*) bristle

'**borstig** *adj* bristly

Borte ['bɔrtə] *f* (*-; -n*) border; braid, lace

bösartig ['bøːsˀaːɐtɪç] *adj* vicious; MED malignant

Böschung ['bœʃʊŋ] *f* (*-; -en*) slope, bank; RAIL embankment

böse ['bøːzə] *adj* bad, evil, wicked;

angry (*über acc* about; *auf j-n* with s.o.), mad (*auf acc* at); *er meint es nicht ~* he means no harm

'**Böse** *n* (*-n; no pl*) (the) evil

'**Bösewicht** *m* (*-[e]s; -er*) villain

boshaft ['bo:shaft] *adj* malicious

Bosheit ['bo:shait] *f* (*-; no pl*) malice

'**böswillig** *adj* malicious, JUR *a.* wil(l)ful

bot [bo:t] *pret of* **bieten**

Botanik [bo'ta:nɪk] *f* (*-; no pl*) botany

Bo'taniker *m* (*-s; -*) botanist

bo'tanisch *adj* botanical

Bote ['bo:tə] *m* (*-n; -n*) messenger

'**Botengang** *m* errand; *Botengänge machen* run errands

Botschaft ['bo:tʃaft] *f* (*-; -en*) message; POL embassy

'**Botschafter** *m* (*-s; -*) POL ambassador (*in dat* to); '**Botschafterin** *f* (*-; -nen*) POL ambassadress (*in dat* to)

Bottich ['bɔtɪç] *m* (*-s; -e*) tub, vat

Bouillon [bul'jɔŋ] *f* (*-; -s*) consommé, bouillon, broth

Boulevard|blatt [bulə'vaːɐ-] *n*, **~zeitung** *f* tabloid

Bowle ['bo:lə] *f* (*-; -n*) (cold) punch; bowl

boxen ['bɔksən] (*ge-, h*) **1.** *v/i* box; **2.** *v/t* punch; '**Boxen** *n* (*-s; no pl*) boxing; '**Boxer** ['bɔksɐ] *m* (*-s; -*) boxer

'**Box|handschuh** *m* boxing glove; **~kampf** *m* boxing match, fight; **~sport** *m* boxing

Boykott [bɔy'kɔt] *m* (*-[e]s; -e*), **boykottieren** [bɔykɔ'tiːrən] *v/t* (*no -ge-, h*) boycott

brach [braːx] *pret of* **brechen**

brachliegend *adj* AGR fallow

brachte ['braxtə] *pret of* **bringen**

Branche ['brãːʃ(ə)] *f* (*-; -n*) ECON line (of business); '**Branchenverzeichnis** *n* TEL yellow pages

Brand [brant] *m* (*-[e]s; Brände* ['brɛndə]) fire; *in ~ geraten* catch fire; *in ~ stecken* set fire to; **~blase** *f* MED blister

branden ['brandən] *v/i* (*ge-, sein*) surge (*gegen* against)

'**Brand|fleck** *m* burn; **~mal** *n* brand

'**brandmarken** *fig v/t* (*ge-, h*) brand, stigmatize

'**Brand|mauer** *f* fire wall; **~stätte** *f*, **~stelle** *f* scene of fire; **~stifter** *m* arsonist; **~stiftung** *f* arson

B

'**Brandung** f (-; no pl) surf, surge, breakers

'**Brandwunde** f MED burn; scald

brannte ['brantə] pret of **brennen**

'**Branntwein** m brandy, spirits

braten ['bra:tən] v/t (irr, ge-, h) roast; grill, broil; fry; **am Spieß ~** roast on a spit, barbecue

'**Braten** m (-s; -) roast (meat); joint; **~fett** n dripping; **~soße** f gravy

'**Brat|fisch** m fried fish; **~huhn** n roast chicken; **~kar,toffeln** pl fried potatoes; **~ofen** m oven; **~pfanne** f frying pan

Bratsche ['bra:tʃə] f (-; -n) MUS viola

'**Bratwurst** f grilled sausage

Brauch [braux] m (-[e]s; Bräuche ['brɔʏçə]) custom; habit, practice

'**brauchbar** adj useful

'**brauchen** v/t (ge-, h) need; require; take (time); use; **wie lange wird er ~?** how long will it take him?; **du brauchst es nur zu sagen** just say the word; **ihr braucht es nicht zu tun** you don't have to do it; **er hätte nicht zu kommen ~** he need not have come

brauen ['brauən] v/t (ge-, h) brew

Brauerei [brauə'rai] f (-; -en) brewery

braun [braun] adj brown; (sun)tanned; **~ werden** (get a) tan

Bräune ['brɔʏnə] f (-; no pl) (sun)tan

'**bräunen** (ge-, h) **1.** v/t brown, tan; **2.** v/i (get a) tan

'**Braunkohle** f brown coal, lignite

'**bräunlich** adj brownish

Brause ['brauzə] f (-; -n) shower; → **Limonade**; '**brausen** v/i a) (ge-, h) roar, b) (sein) rush, c) (h) → **duschen**

Braut [braut] f (-; Bräute ['brɔʏtə]) bride; fiancée; **Bräutigam** ['brɔʏtɪgam] m (-s; -e) (bride)groom; fiancé

'**Braut|jungfer** f bridesmaid; **~kleid** n wedding-dress; **~paar** n bride and (bride)groom; engaged couple

brav [bra:f] adj good; honest; **sei(d) ~!** be good!

BRD [be:ʔɛr'de:] ABBR of **Bundesrepublik Deutschland** FRG, Federal Republic of Germany

brechen ['brɛçən] (irr, ge-) **1.** v/t (h) break (a. fig); MED vomit; **sich ~** OPT be refracted; **sich den Arm ~** break one's arm; **2.** v/i a) (h) MED vomit, F throw up, Br a. be sick; **mit j-m ~** break with s.o.; **~d voll** crammed, packed, b) (sein) break, get broken, fracture

'**Brechreiz** m MED nausea

'**Brechstange** f crowbar

'**Brechung** f (-; -en) OPT refraction

Brei [brai] m (-[e]s; -e) pulp, mash; pap; porridge; pudding

'**breiig** adj pulpy, mushy

breit [brait] adj wide; broad (a. fig); F **sich ~ machen** spread o.s., take up room

'**breitbeinig** adj with legs (wide) apart

Breite ['braitə] f (-; -n) width, breadth; ASTR, GEOGR latitude

'**breiten** v/t (ge-, h) spread

'**Breiten|grad** m degree of latitude; **~kreis** m parallel (of latitude)

'**Breitwand** f film: wide screen

Bremsbelag ['brɛms-] m brake lining

Bremse ['brɛmzə] f (-; -n) TECH brake; ZO gadfly; '**bremsen** (ge-, h) **1.** v/i MOT brake, put on the brake(s); slow down; **2.** v/t MOT brake; fig curb

'**Brems|licht** n (-[e]s; -er) MOT stop light; **~pe,dal** n MOT brake pedal; **~spur** f MOT skid marks; **~weg** m MOT stopping distance

'**brennbar** adj combustible; (in)flammable; **brennen** ['brɛnən] (irr, ge-, h) **1.** v/t burn; distil(l) (whisky etc); bake (bricks); **2.** v/i burn; be on fire; wound, eyes: smart, burn; F **darauf ~ zu** inf be dying to inf; **es brennt!** fire!; **Brenner** ['brɛnɐ] m (-s; -) burner

'**Brenn|holz** n firewood; **~materi,al** n fuel; **~nessel** f BOT (stinging) nettle; **~punkt** m focus, focal point; **~spiritus** m methylated spirit; **~stab** m TECH fuel rod; **~stoff** m fuel

brenzlig ['brɛntslɪç] adj burnt; fig hot

Bresche ['brɛʃə] f (-; -n) breach (a. fig), gap

Brett [brɛt] n (-[e]s; -er) board

'**Bretterzaun** m wooden fence

'**Brettspiel** n board game

Brezel ['bre:tsəl] f (-; -n) pretzel

Brief [bri:f] m (-[e]s; -e) letter; **~beschwerer** m (-s; -) paperweight; **~bogen** m sheet of (note)paper; **~freund(in)** pen pal (Br friend); **~kasten** m mailbox, Br letterbox

'**brieflich** adj and adv by letter

'**Brief|marke** f (postage) stamp; **~markensammlung** f stamp collection; **~öffner** m letter opener, Br paper

B

knife; **~pa,pier** n stationery; **~tasche** f wallet; **~taube** f ZO carrier pigeon; **~träger(in)** (-s; -/-; -nen) mailman (mailwoman), Br postman (postwoman); **~umschlag** m envelope; **~wahl** f postal vote; **~wechsel** m correspondence

briet [bri:t] pret of **braten**

Brikett [bri'kɛt] n (-s; -s) briquet(te)

brillant [brɪl'jant] adj brilliant

Brillant m (-en; -en) (cut) diamond

Brillantring m diamond ring

Brille ['brɪlə] f (-; -n) (pair of) glasses, spectacles; goggles; toilet seat

Brillen|etui n eyeglass (Br spectacle) case; **~träger(in)** (-s; -/-; -nen) ~ **sein** wear glasses

bringen ['brɪŋən] v/t (irr, ge-, h) bring; take; cause; make (sacrifice); yield (profit); **j-n nach Hause ~** see (or take) s.o. home; **in Ordnung ~** put in order; **das bringt mich auf e-e Idee** that gives me an idea; **j-n dazu ~, et. zu tun** get s.o. to do s.th.; **et. mit sich ~** involve s.th.; **j-n um et. ~** deprive s.o. of s.th.; **j-n zum Lachen ~** make s.o. laugh; **j-n wieder zu sich ~** bring s.o. round; **es zu et. (nichts) ~** go far (get nowhere); F **es ~** make it; **das bringt nichts** it's no use

Brise ['bri:zə] f (-; -n) breeze

Brite ['brɪtə] m (-n; -n), **'Britin** f (-; -nen) Briton; **die Briten** pl the British

'britisch adj British

bröckeln ['brœkəln] v/i (ge-, h, sein) crumble

Brocken ['brɔkən] m (-s; -) piece; lump; rock; GASTR chunk; morsel; **ein paar ~ Englisch** a few scraps of English; F **ein harter ~** a hard nut to crack

Brombeere ['brɔm-] f BOT blackberry

Bronchitis [brɔn'çi:tɪs] f (-; -tiden [brɔn-çi'ti:dən]) MED bronchitis

Bronze ['brõ:sə] f (-; -n) bronze; **~zeit** f (-; no pl) HIST Bronze Age

Brosche ['brɔʃə] f (-; -n) brooch, pin

broschiert [brɔ'ʃiːrt] adj paperback

Broschüre [brɔ'ʃyːrə] f (-; -n) pamphlet, brochure

Brot [broːt] n (-[e]s; -e) bread; sandwich; **ein (Laib) ~** a loaf (of bread); **e-e Scheibe ~** a slice of bread; **sein ~ verdienen** earn one's living

Brötchen ['brøːtçən] n (-s; -) roll

'Brot|rinde f crust; **~(schneide)ma,schine** f bread cutter

Bruch [brux] m (-[e]s; Brüche ['bryçə]) break; MED fracture; hernia; MATH fraction; GEOL fault; fig breach (of promise etc); JUR violation; **zu ~ gehen** be wrecked; **~bude** F f dump, hovel

brüchig ['bryçɪç] adj brittle

'Bruch|landung f AVIAT crash landing; **~rechnung** f MATH fractional arithmetic, F fractions

'bruchsicher adj breakproof

'Bruch|strich m MATH fraction bar; **~stück** n fragment; **~teil** m fraction; **im ~ e-r Sekunde** in a split second; **~zahl** f MATH fraction(al) number

Brücke ['brykə] f (-; -n) bridge (a. SPORT); rug; **'Brückenpfeiler** m pier

Bruder ['bruːdɐ] m (-s; Brüder ['bryːdɐ]) brother (a. REL); **~krieg** m civil war

brüderlich ['bryːdɐlɪç] **1.** adj brotherly; **2.** adv: ~ **teilen** share and share alike

'Brüderlichkeit f (-; no pl) brotherhood

'Brüderschaft f: ~ **trinken** agree to use the familiar 'du' form of address

Brühe ['bryːə] f (-; -n) broth; stock; F dishwater; slops; F filthy water, bilge

'Brühwürfel m beef cube

brüllen ['brylən] v/i (ge-, h) roar (**vor Lachen** with laughter); ZO bellow; F bawl; **~des Gelächter** roars of laughter

brummen ['brumən] v/i (ge-, h) growl; ZO hum, buzz (a. engine etc); head: be buzzing; **'brummig** adj grumpy

brünett [bry'nɛt] adj brunette, dark-haired

Brunnen ['brunən] m (-s; -) well, spring, fountain

Brunstzeit ['brunst-] f ZO rutting season

Brust [brust] f (-; Brüste ['brystə]) ANAT a) (no pl) chest, b) breast(s); bosom; **~bein** n ANAT breastbone; **~beutel** m neck pouch, Br money bag

brüsten ['brystən] v/refl (ge-, h) boast, brag (**mit** of)

'Brust|kasten m, **~korb** m ANAT chest, thorax; **~schwimmen** n breaststroke

'Brüstung f (-; -en) parapet

'Brustwarze f ANAT nipple

Brut [bruːt] f (-; -en) ZO brooding; brood (a. F), hatch; fry

brutal [bru'taːl] adj brutal; **Brutalität** [brutali'tɛːt] f (-; -en) brutality

'**Brutappa,rat** *m* ZO incubator
brüten ['bry:tən] *v/i* (*ge-, h*) ZO brood, sit (on eggs); **~ über** (*dat*) *fig* brood over
'**Brutkasten** *m* MED incubator
brutto ['bruto] *adv* ECON gross
'**Brutto|einkommen** *n* ECON gross earnings; **~sozi,alpro,dukt** *n* ECON gross national product
Bube ['bu:bə] *m* (*-n; -n*) boy, lad; *card game:* knave, jack
Buch [bu:x] *n* (*-[e]s; Bücher* ['by:çɐ]) book; **~binder** *m* (*-s; -*) (book)binder; **~drucker** *m* printer; **~druckerei** *f* print shop, *Br* printing office
Buche ['bu:xə] *f* (*-; -n*) BOT beech
'**buchen** *v/t* (*ge-, h*) book; ECON enter
Bücherbord ['by:çɐ-] *n* bookshelf
Bücherei [by:çə'raɪ] *f* (*-; -en*) library
'**Bücherre,gal** *n* bookshelf
'**Bücherschrank** *m* bookcase
'**Buch|fink** *m* ZO chaffinch; **~halter(in)** bookkeeper; **~haltung** *f* (*-; no pl*) bookkeeping; **~händler(in)** bookseller; **~handlung** *f* bookstore, *Br* bookshop; **~macher** *m* bookmaker
Büchse ['bʏksə] *f* (*-; -n*) can, *Br* tin; box; rifle
'**Büchsen|fleisch** *n* canned (*Br* tinned) meat; **~öffner** *m* (*-s; -*) (tin) opener
Buchstabe ['bu:xʃta:bə] *m* (*-n; -n*) letter; **großer (kleiner) ~** capital (small) letter; **buchstabieren** [bu:xʃta'bi:rən] *v/t* (*no -ge-, h*) spell; **buchstäblich** ['bu:xʃte:plɪç] *adv* literally
'**Buchstütze** *f* bookend
Bucht [bʊxt] *f* (*-; -en*) bay, creek, inlet
'**Buchung** *f* (*-; -en*) booking; ECON entry
Buckel ['bʊkəl] *m* (*-s; -*) hump, hunch; **e-n ~ machen** hump or hunch one's back
bücken ['bʏkən] *v/refl* (*ge-, h*) bend (down), stoop
bucklig ['bʊklɪç] *adj* hunchbacked
Bücklige ['bʊklɪgə] *m, f* (*-n; -n*) hunchback
Bückling ['bʏklɪŋ] *m* (*-s; -e*) smoked herring, *Br* kipper
Buddhismus [bu'dɪsmʊs] *m* (*-; no pl*) Buddhism; **Buddhist** [bu'dɪst] *m* (*-en; -en*), **bud'dhistisch** *adj* Buddhist
Bude ['bu:də] *f* (*-n; -n*) stall, booth; hut; F pad, *Br* digs; *contp* shack, dump, hole
Budget [by'dʒe:] *n* (*-s; -s*) budget
Büfett [by'fɛt] *n* (*-[e]s; -s, -e*) counter,

bar, buffet; sideboard; cupboard; **kaltes ~** GASTR cold buffet (meal)
Büffel ['bʏfəl] *m* (*-s; -*) ZO buffalo
'**büffeln** F *v/i* (*ge-, h*) grind, cram, swot
Bug [bu:k] *m* (*-[e]s; -e*) MAR bow; AVIAT nose; ZO, GASTR shoulder
Bügel ['by:gəl] *m* (*-s; -*) hanger; bow; **~brett** *n* ironing board; **~eisen** *n* iron; **~falte** *f* crease
'**bügelfrei** *adj* no(n)-iron
'**bügeln** *v/t* (*ge-, h*) iron, press
buh [bu:] *int* boo!
buhen ['bu:ən] *v/i* (*ge-, h*) boo
Bühne ['by:nə] *f* (*-; -n*) stage, *fig a.* scene
'**Bühnen|bild** *n* (stage) set(ting); **~bildner(in)** (*-s; -/-; -nen*) stage designer
'**Buhrufe** *pl* boos
Bullauge ['bʊl-] *n* MAR porthole
'**Bulldogge** *f* ZO bulldog
Bulle ['bʊlə] *m* (*-n; -n*) ZO bull (*a. fig*); F *contp* cop, *pl the* fuzz
Bummel ['bʊməl] F *m* (*-s; -*) stroll; **Bummelei** [bʊmə'laɪ] *f* (*-; no pl*) F *contp* dawdling; slackness; '**bummeln** F *v/i* a) (*ge-, sein*) stroll, saunter, b) (*ge-, h*) *contp* dawdle; ECON go slow; '**Bummelstreik** *m* ECON slowdown, *Br* go-slow (strike); **Bummler** ['bʊmlɐ] F *m* (*-s; -*) stroller; *contp* dawdler, slowpoke, *Br* slowcoach
bumsen ['bʊmzən] *v/i and v/t* (*ge-, h*) F → *krachen*; V screw
Bund¹ [bʊnt] *m* (*-[e]s; Bünde* ['bʏndə]) union, federation, alliance; association; (waist)band; *der* Federal Government; F → *Bundeswehr*
Bund² *n* (*-[e]s; -e*) bundle; bunch
Bündel ['bʏndəl] *n* (*-s; -*) bundle
'**bündeln** *v/t* (*ge-, h*) bundle (up)
Bundes... ['bʊndəs-] *in cpds* Federal ...; German ...; **~bahn** *f* Federal Railroad(s); **~genosse** *m* ally; **~kanzler** *m* Federal Chancellor; **~land** *n appr* (federal) state, Land; **~liga** *f* SPORT First Division; **~post** *f* Federal Postal Administration; **~präsi,dent** *m* Federal President; **~rat** *m* Bundesrat, Upper House of German Parliament; **~repu,blik** *f* Federal Republic; **~staat** *m* federal state; confederation; **~straße** *f* Federal Highway; **~tag** *m* (*-[e]s; no pl*) Bundestag, Lower House of German Parliament; **~trainer** *m* coach

of the (German) national team; **~verfassungsgericht** n Federal Constitutional Court, *Am appr* Supreme Court; **~wehr** f (-; *no pl*) MIL (German Federal) Armed Forces

bündig ['byndɪç] *adj* TECH flush; *kurz und* ~ terse(ly); point-blank

Bündnis ['byntnɪs] n (-ses; -se) alliance

Bunker ['bʊŋkɐ] m (-s; -) air-raid shelter, bunker

bunt [bʊnt] *adj* colo(u)red; multicolo(u)red; colo(u)rful (*a. fig*); varied; **~er Abend** evening of entertainment; F *mir wird's zu* ~ that's all I can take

'Buntstift m colo(u)red pencil, crayon

Bürde ['byrdə] f (-; -n) burden (*für j-n* to s.o.)

Burg [bʊrk] f (-; -en) castle

Bürge ['byrgə] m (-n; -n) JUR guarantor (*a. fig*); **'bürgen** v/i (ge-, h) *für j-n* JUR stand surety for s.o.; *für et.* ~ guarantee s.th.

Bürger ['byrgɐ] m (-s; -), **'Bürgerin** f (-; -nen) citizen; **~initia,tive** f (citizen's *or* local) action group; **~krieg** m civil war

'bürgerlich *adj* civil; middle-class; *esp contp* bourgeois; **~e Küche** home cooking; **'Bürgerliche** m, f (-n; -n) commoner

'Bürger|meister m mayor; **~rechte** pl civil rights; **~steig** [-ʃtaik] m (-[e]s; -e) sidewalk, *Br* pavement

'Bürgschaft f (-; -en) JUR surety; bail

Büro [by'ro:] n (-s; -s) office; **~angestellte** m, f (-n; -n) clerk, office worker; **~klammer** f (paper) clip

Bürokrat [byro'kra:t] m (-en; -en) bureaucrat; **Bürokratie** [byrokra'ti:] f (-; -n) bureaucracy; *contp* red tape

Bü'rostunden pl office hours

Bursche ['bʊrʃə] m (-n; -n) fellow, guy

burschikos [bʊrʃi'ko:s] *adj* (tom)boyish, pert

Bürste ['byrstə] f (-; -n) brush

'bürsten v/t (ge-, h) brush

'Bürstenschnitt m crew cut

Bus [bʊs] m (-ses; -se) bus; coach

Busch [bʊʃ] m (-[e]s; *Büsche* ['byʃə]) BOT bush, shrub

Büschel ['byʃəl] n (-s; -) bunch; tuft

'buschig *adj* bushy

Busen ['bu:zən] m (-s; -) ANAT bosom, breast(s)

'Busfahrer m bus driver

'Bushaltestelle f bus stop

Bussard ['bʊsart] m (-s; -e) ZO buzzard

Buße ['bu:sə] f (-; -n) REL penance; repentance; ~ *tun* do penance

büßen ['by:sən] v/t (ge-, h) pay *or* suffer for *s.th.*; REL repent

'Bußgeld n fine, penalty

'Bußtag m REL day of repentance

Büste ['by:stə] f (-; -n) bust

'Büstenhalter m bra

Butter ['bʊtɐ] f (-; *no pl*) butter; **~blume** f BOT buttercup; **~brot** n (slice *or* piece of) bread and butter; F *für ein* ~ for a song; **~brotpa,pier** n greaseproof paper; **~dose** f butter dish; **~milch** f buttermilk

b.w. ABBR *of bitte wenden* PTO, please turn over

bzw. ABBR *of beziehungsweise* resp., respectively

C

C ABBR *of Celsius* C, Celsius, centigrade

ca. ABBR *of circa* approx., approximately

Café [ka'fe:] n (-s; -s) café, coffee house

campen ['kɛmpən] v/i (ge-, h) camp

Camper ['kɛmpɐ] m (-s; -) camper

Camping- ['kɛmpɪŋ-] *in cpds* ...*bett*, ...*tisch etc* camp ...; **~bus** m camper (van *Br*); **~platz** m campground, *Br* campsite

Catcher ['kɛtʃɐ] m (-s; -) wrestler

CD [tse:'de:] f (-; -s), **C'D-Platte** f CD, compact disk (*Br* disc); **C'D-ROM** CD-ROM; **C'D-Spieler** m CD player

Cellist [tʃɛ'lɪst] m (-en; -en), **Cel'listin** f (-; -nen) MUS cellist

Cello ['tʃɛlo] n (-s; -s, *Celli*) MUS cello

Celsius ['tsɛlzjʊs] *5 Grad* ~ (ABBR *5° C*) five degrees centigrade *or* Celsius

Cembalo ['tʃɛmbalo] n (-s; -s, -li) MUS harpsichord

Champagner [ʃam'panjɐ] m (-s; -) champagne

Champignon ['ʃampɪnjɔŋ] m (-s; -s) BOT mushroom

Chance ['ʃãːsə] f (-; -n) chance; die ~n stehen gleich (3 zu 1) the odds are even (three to one); 'Chancengleichheit f equal opportunities

Chaos ['kaːɔs] n (-; no pl) chaos

Chaot [ka'oːt] m (-en; -en) chaotic person; POL anarchist, pl a. lunatic fringe

cha'otisch adj chaotic

Charakter [ka'raktɐ] m (-s; -e [-'teːrə]) character, nature; charakterisieren [-teri'ziːrən] v/t (no -ge-, h) characterize, describe (als as); charakteristisch [-te'rɪstɪʃ] adj characteristic, typical (für of); Cha'rakterzug m trait

charmant [ʃar'mant] adj charming

Charme [ʃarm] m (-s; no pl) charm

Chassis [ʃa'siː] n (-; -) TECH chassis

Chauffeur [ʃɔ'føːɐ] m (-s; -e) chauffeur, driver

Chauvi ['ʃoːvi] m (-s; -s) F male chauvinist (pig)

Chauvinismus [ʃovi'nɪsmʊs] m (-; no pl) chauvinism, POL a. jingoism

Chef [ʃɛf] m (-s; -s) head, chief, F boss; ~arzt m medical director, Br senior consultant; ~sekre,tärin f executive secretary

Chemie [çe'miː] f (-; no pl) chemistry; ~faser f synthetic fiber (Br fibre)

Chemikalien [çemi'kaːljən] chemicals; Chemiker(in) ['çeːmikɐ (-kərin)] (-s; -/-; -nen) (analytical) chemist; chemisch ['çeːmɪʃ] adj chemical; ~e Reinigung dry cleaning

Chemothera'pie [çemo-] f MED chemotherapy

Chiffre ['ʃɪfrə] f (-; -n) code, cipher; box (number); chiffrieren [ʃɪ'friːrən] v/t (no -ge-, h) (en)code

China ['çiːna] China; Chinese [çi'neːzə] m (-n; -n), Chi'nesin f (-; -nen), chi'nesisch adj Chinese

Chinin [çi'niːn] n (-s; no pl) PHARM quinine

Chip [tʃɪp] m (-s; -s) a. EDP chip; GASTR pl chips, Br crisps

Chirurg [çi'rʊrk] m (-en; -en) surgeon

Chirurgie [çirʊr'giː] f (-; -n) surgery

Chirurgin [çi'rʊrgɪn] f (-; -nen) surgeon

chirurgisch [çi'rʊrgɪʃ] adj surgical

Chlor [kloːɐ] n (-s; no pl) CHEM chlorine

chloren ['kloːrən] v/t (ge-, h) chlorinate

Cholera ['koːlera] f (-; no pl) MED cholera; cholerisch [ko'leːrɪʃ] adj choleric

Cholesterin [çoleste'riːn] n (-s; no pl) MED cholesterol

Chor [koːɐ] m (-[e]s; Chöre ['køːrə]) MUS choir (a. ARCH); im ~ in chorus

Choral [ko'raːl] m (-s; Choräle [ko'rɛːlə]) MUS, REL chorale, hymn

Christ [krɪst] m (-en; -en) REL Christian; ~baum m Christmas tree

'Christenheit: die ~ REL Christendom

'Christentum n (-s; no pl) REL Christianity

Christin ['krɪstɪn] f (-; -nen) REL Christian

'Christkind n Infant Jesus; Father Christmas, Santa Claus

'christlich adj REL Christian

Christus ['krɪstʊs] REL Christ; vor ~ B.C.; nach ~ A.D.

Chrom [kroːm] n (-s; no pl) chrome, CHEM a. chromium

Chromosom [kromo'zoːm] n (-s; -en) BIOL chromosome

Chronik ['kroːnɪk] f (-; -en) chronicle

chronisch ['kroːnɪʃ] adj MED chronic

chronologisch [krono'loːgɪʃ] adj chronological

circa → zirka

City ['sɪti] f (-; -s) downtown, (city) center, Br centre

Clique ['klɪkə] f (-; -n) F group, set; contp clique

Clou [kluː] F m (-s; -s) highlight, climax; der ~ daran the whole point of it

Compactdisc ['kɔmpæktdɪsk] f (-; -s) compact disk (Br disc)

Computer [kɔm'pjuːtɐ] m (-s; -) computer; ~ausdruck m computer printout

com'puter|gesteuert adj computer-controlled; ~gestützt adj computer-aided

Com'putergrafik f computer graphics

computerisieren [kɔmpjutəri'ziːrən] v/t (no -ge-, h) computerize

Com'puter|spiel n computer game; ~virus m EDP computer virus

Conférencier [kõferã'sje:] *m* (*-s*; *-s*) master of ceremonies, F emcee, MC, *Br* compère

Cord *etc* → **Kord** *etc*

Couch [kautʃ] *f* (*-*; *-s*) couch

Coupé [ku'pe:] *n* (*-s*; *-s*) MOT coupé

Coupon → **Kupon**

Cousin [ku'zɛ̃:] *m* (*-s*; *-s*), **Cousine** [ku'zi:nə] *f* (*-*; *-n*) cousin

Creme [kre:m] *f* (*-*; *-s*) cream (*a. fig*)

Curry ['kari] *m* (*-s*; *-s*) curry powder

Cursor ['kɔ:sə] *m* (*-s*; *-s*) EDP cursor

D

da [da:] **1.** *adv space*: there; here; *time*: then, at that time; **~ drüben (draußen, hinten)** over (out, back) there; **von ~ aus** from there; **das ... ~** that ... (over there); **~ kommt er** here he comes; **~ bin ich** here I am; **~ sein** be there; exist; **ist noch ... ~?** is any ... left?; **noch nie ~ gewesen** unprecedented; **er ist gleich wieder ~** he'll be right back; **von ~ an** or **ab** from then on; **2.** *cj* as, since, because

'**dabehalten** *v/t* (*irr, halten, sep, no -ge-, h*) keep; **j-n ~** keep s.o. in

dabei [da'bai] *adv* there, present; near or close by; at the same time; included with it; **~ sein** be there; take part; be in on it; **~ kommt er ...!** count me in!; **er ist gerade ~ zu gehen** he's just leaving; **es ist nichts ~** there's nothing to it; there's no harm in it; **was ist schon ~?** (so) what of it?; **lassen wir es ~!** let's leave it at that!; **~bleiben** *v/i* (*irr, bleiben, sep, -ge-, sein*) stick to it; **~haben** F *v/t* (*irr, haben, sep, -ge-, h*) have with (or on) one

'**dableiben** *v/i* (*irr, bleiben, sep, -ge-, sein*) stay

Dach [dax] *n* (*-[e]s*; *Dächer* ['dɛçɐ]) roof

'**Dach|boden** *m* attic; **~decker** [-dekɐ] *m* (*-s*; *-*) roofer; **~fenster** *n* dormer window; **~gepäckträger** *m* MOT roof-rack

'**Dachgeschoss** *n*, '**Dachgeschoß** *Austrian n* attic; **~wohnung** *f* loft apartment, *Br* attic flat

'**Dach|kammer** *f* garret; **~luke** *f* skylight; **~pappe** *f* roofing felt; **~rinne** *f* gutter

Dachs [daks] *m* (*-es*; *-e*) ZO badger

'**Dachstuhl** *m* roof framework

dachte ['daxtə] *pret of* **denken**

'**Dachter,rasse** *f* roof terrace

'**Dachverband** *m* ECON *etc* umbrella organization

Dackel ['dakəl] *m* (*-s*; *-*) ZO dachshund

'**dadurch** *adv and cj* this or that way; for this reason, so; **~, dass** due to the fact that

dafür [da'fy:ɐ] *adv* for it, for that; instead; in return, in exchange; **~ sein** be in favo(u)r of it; **er kann nichts ~** it is not his fault; **~ sorgen, dass** see to it that

dagegen [da'ge:gən] *adv and cj* against it; however, on the other hand; **~ sein** be against (or opposed to) it; **haben Sie et. ~, dass ich ...?** do you mind if I ...?; **wenn Sie nichts ~ haben** if you don't mind; **... ist nichts ~** ... can't compare

daheim *adv* at home

'**daher** *adv and cj* from there; that's why

dahin *adv* there, to that place; gone, past; **bis ~** till then; up to there

dahinten *adv* back there

dahinter *adv* behind it; **es steckt nichts ~** there is nothing to it; F **~ kommen** find out (about it)

'**dalassen** F *v/t* (*irr, lassen, sep, -ge-, h*) leave behind

damalig ['da:ma:lıç] *adj* then

damals ['da:ma:ls] *adv* then, at that time

Dame ['da:mə] *f* (*-*; *-n*) lady; partner; *cards, chess*: queen; checkers, *Br* draughts

'**Damen...** *in cpds* ladies' ...; SPORT women's ...; **~binde** *f* sanitary napkin (*Br* towel)

'**damenhaft** *adj* ladylike

'**Damen|toi,lette** *f* ladies' room (*Br* toilet), *the* ladies; **~wahl** *f* ladies' choice

damit 1. ['da:mɪt] *adv* with it or that; by

it, with it; **was will er ~ sagen?** what's
he trying to say?; **wie steht es ~?**
how about it?; **~ einverstanden sein**
have no objections; **2.** [da'mɪt] *cj* so
that; in order to *inf*; **~ nicht** so as not
to *inf*

Damm [dam] *m* (-[e]s; *Dämme* ['dɛmə])
dam; embankment

dämmerig ['dɛmərɪç] *adj* dim

'**Dämmerlicht** *n* (-[e]s; *no pl*) twilight

'**dämmern** ['dɛmɐn] *v/i* (*ge*-, *h*) dawn (a. F
j-m to s.o.); get dark *or* dusky

'**Dämmerung** *f* (-; -en) dusk; dawn

Dämon ['dɛ:mɔn] *m* (-s; -en [dɛ'mo:nən])
demon; **dämonisch** [dɛ'mo:nɪʃ] *adj*
demoniac(al)

Dampf [dampf] *m* (-[e]s; *Dämpfe*
['dɛmpfə]) steam; PHYS vapo(u)r

'**dampfen** *v/i* (*ge*-, *h and sein*) steam

'**dämpfen** ['dɛmpfən] *v/t* (*ge*-, *h*) deaden;
muffle (*voice*); soften (*light, sound,
blow*); GASTR steam, stew; steam-iron;
fig put a damper on; curb (a. ECON)

'**Dampfer** ['dampfɐ] *m* (-s; -) steamer,
steamship

'**Dampf**|**kochtopf** *m* pressure cooker;
~ma,schine *f* steam engine; **~schiff**
n steamer, steamship

da'nach *adv* after it *or* that; afterwards;
for it; according to it; **ich fragte ihn ~** I
asked him about it; F **mir ist nicht ~** I
don't feel like it

Däne ['dɛ:nə] *m* (-n; -n) Dane

da'neben *adv* next to it, beside it; besides, as well, at the same time; beside
the mark; **~benehmen** F *v/refl* (*irr,
nehmen, sep, no ge*-, *h*) step out of
line; **~gehen** F *v/i* (*irr, gehen, sep,
-ge*-, *sien*) miss (the target); F misfire

'**Dänemark** Denmark

Dänin ['dɛ:nɪn] *f* (-; -nen) Danish woman
or girl; '**dänisch** *adj* Danish

dank [daŋk] *prp* (*gen*) thanks to

Dank *m* (-[e]s; *no pl*) thanks; **Gott sei ~!**
thank God!; **vielen ~!** many thanks!

'**dankbar** *adj* grateful (*j-m* to s.o.);
rewarding (*task etc*)

'**Dankbarkeit** *f* (-; *no pl*) gratitude

'**danken** *v/i* (*ge*-, *h*) thank (*j-m für et.*
s.o. for s.th.); **danke** (**schön**) thank
you (very much); (**nein,**) **danke** no,
thank you; **nichts zu ~** not at all

dann [dan] *adv* then; **~ und wann**
(every) now and then

daran [da'ran] *adv* on it; *die,* think *etc* of
it; *believe etc* in it; *suffer etc* from it; →
liegen

darauf [da'rauf] *adv* on (top of) it; after
(that); *listen, drink etc* to it; *proud etc* of
it; *wait etc* for it; **am Tage ~** the day
after; **zwei Jahre ~** two years later; **~
kommt es an** that's what matters

darauf'hin *adv* after that; as a result

daraus [da'raus] *adv* from (*or* out of) it;
was ist ~ geworden? what has be-
come of it?; **~ wird nichts!** F nothing
doing!

Darbietung ['da:ɐbi:tʊŋ] *f* (-; -en) presentation; performance

darin [da'rɪn] *adv* in it; ['da:rɪn] in that

darlegen ['da:ɐ-] *v/t* (*sep, -ge*-, *h*) explain, set out

Darlehen ['da:ɐle:ən] *n* (-s; -) loan; **ein ~
geben** grant a loan

Darm [darm] *m* (-[e]s; *Därme* ['dɛrmə])
ANAT bowel(s), intestine(s); GASTR skin;
~grippe *f* MED intestinal flu

darstellen ['da:ɐ-] *v/t* (*sep, -ge*-, *h*) represent, show, depict; describe; THEA play,
do; trace, graph; '**Darsteller(in)** (-s; -/-;
-nen) THEA performer, actor (actress);
'**Darstellung** *f* (-; -en) representation;
description; account; portrayal

darüber [da'ry:bɐ] *adv* over *or* above it;
across it; in the meantime; *write, talk
etc* about it; **~ und ~ ...** and more; **~
werden Jahre vergehen** that will take
years

darum [da'rʊm] *adv and cj* (a)round it;
because of it, that's why; **~ bitten** ask
for it; → *gehen*

darunter [da'rʊntɐ] *adv* under *or* below
it, underneath; among them; including;
... und ~ ... and less; **was verstehst du
~?** what do you understand by it?

das [das] → *der*

'**Dasein** *n* (-s; *no pl*) life, existence

dass [das] *cj* that; so (that); **es sei denn,
~** unless; **nicht ~ ich wüsste** not that I
know of

'**dastehen** *v/i* (*irr, stehen, sep, -ge*-, *h*)
stand (there)

Datei [da'tai] *f* (-; -en) EDP file; **~verwal-
tung** *f* EDP file management

Daten ['da:tən] *pl* data (a. EDP), facts;
particulars; **~bank** *f* (-; -en) EDP data-
base, data bank; **~schutz** *m* JUR data
protection; **~speicher** *m* data memory

or storage; **~träger** *m* data medium *or* carrier; **~übertragung** *f* data transfer; **~verarbeitung** *f* data processing

datieren [da'ti:rən] *v/t and v/i (no -ge-, h)* date

Dativ ['da:ti:f] *m (-s; -e)* dative (case)

Dattel ['datəl] *f (-; -n)* BOT date

Datum ['da:tum] *n (-s; Daten* ['da:tən]) date; **welches ~ haben wir heute?** what's the date today?

Dauer ['dauɐ] *f (-; no pl)* duration; continuance; **auf die ~** in the long run; **für die ~ von** for a period *or* term of; **von ~ sein** last; **~arbeitslosigkeit** *f* long-term unemployment; **~auftrag** *m* ECON standing order; **~geschwindigkeit** *f* MOT *etc* cruising speed

dauerhaft *adj* lasting; durable

'Dauer|karte *f* season ticket; **~lauf** *m* SPORT jogging; **im ~** at a jog; **~lutscher** *m* lollipop

dauern *v/i (ge-, h)* last, take; → **lange**

'Dauerwelle *f* permanent, *Br* perm

Daumen ['daumən] *m (-s; -)* ANAT thumb; F **j-m den ~ halten** keep one's fingers crossed (for s.o.); **am ~ lutschen** suck one's thumb

Daunen ['daunən] *pl* down

'Daunendecke *f* eiderdown

da'von *adv* (away) from it; by it; about it; away; of it *or* them; **et. ~ haben** get s.th. out of it; **das kommt ~!** there you are!, that will teach you!; **~kommen** *v/i (irr, kommen, sep, -ge-, sein)* escape, get away; **~laufen** *v/i (irr, laufen, sep, -ge-, sein)* run away

da'vor *adv* before it; in front of it; *be afraid,* warn *s.o. etc* of it

da'zu *adv* for it, for that purpose; in addition; **noch ~** into the bargain; **~ ist es da** that's what it's there for; **Salat ~?** a salad with it?; → **kommen, Lust, ~gehören** *v/i (sep, no -ge-, h)* belong to it, be part of it; **~gehörig** *adj* belonging to it; **~kommen** *v/i (irr, kommen, sep, -ge-, sein)* join *s.o.*; be added

da'zwischen *adv* between (them); in between; among them; **~kommen** *v/i (irr, kommen, sep, -ge-, sein)* intervene, happen; **wenn nichts dazwischenkommt** if all goes well

DB [de:'be:] *ABBR of* **Deutsche Bahn** German Rail

dealen ['di:lən] *v/i (ge-, h)* F push drugs

Dealer ['di:lɐ] *m (-s; -)* drug dealer, F pusher

Debatte [de'batə] *f (-; -n)* debate

debattieren [deba'ti:rən] *v/i (no -ge-, h)* debate (**über** *acc* on)

Debüt [de'by:] *n (-s; -s)* debut; **sein ~ geben** make your debut

dechiffrieren [deʃi'fri:rən] *v/t (no -ge-, h)* decipher, decode

Deck [dɛk] *n (-[e]s; -s)* MAR deck

Decke ['dɛkə] *f (-; -n)* blanket; quilt; ARCH ceiling

Deckel ['dɛkəl] *m (-s; -)* lid, cover, top

'decken *v/t and v/i (ge-, h)* roof (*a.* zo), SPORT *a.* mark; **sich ~ (mit)** coincide (with); → **Tisch**

'Deckung *f (-; no pl)* cover; *boxing:* guard; **in ~ gehen** take cover

defekt [de'fɛkt] *adj* defective, faulty; TECH out of order; **De'fekt** *m (-[e]s; -e)* defect, fault

defensiv [defen'si:f] *adj,* **Defensive** [-'zi:və] *f (-; no pl)* defensive

definieren [defi'ni:rən] *v/t (no -ge-, h)* define; **Definition** [defini'tsjo:n] *f (-; -en)* definition

Defizit ['de:fitsit] *n (-s; -e)* deficit; deficiency

Degen ['de:gən] *m (-s; -)* sword; *fencing:* épée

degradieren [degra'di:rən] *v/t (no -ge-, h)* degrade (*a. fig*)

dehnbar ['de:nba:ɐ] *adj* flexible, elastic (*a. fig*); **dehnen** ['de:nən] *v/t (ge-, h)* stretch (*a. fig*)

Deich [daiç] *m (-[e]s; -e)* dike

Deichsel ['daiksəl] *f (-; -n)* pole, shaft

dein [dain] *poss pron* your; **~er, ~e, ~(e)s** yours; **deinerseits** ['dainɐ'zaits] *adv* on your part; **deines'gleichen** ['dainəs-] *pron contp* the likes of you

deinetwegen ['dainət've:gən] *adv* for your sake; because of you

Dekan [de'ka:n] *m (-s; -e)*, **De'kanin** *f (-; -nen)* REL, UNIV dean

Deklination [deklina'tsjo:n] *f (-; -en)* LING declension; **deklinieren** [dekli'ni:rən] *v/t (no -ge-, h)* decline

Dekolleté [dekɔl'te:] *n (-s; -s)* low neckline

Dekorateur [dekora'tø:ɐ] *m (-s; -e)*, **Dekora'teurin** *f (-; -nen)* decorator; window dresser; **Dekoration** [-'tsjo:n] *f (-; -en)* decoration; (window) display;

deuten

THEA scenery; **dekorativ** [-'ti:f] *adj* decorative; **dekorieren** [deko'ri:rən] *v/t (no -ge-, h)* decorate; dress

Delfin → **Delphin**

delikat [deli'ka:t] *adj* delicious, exquisite; *fig* delicate, ticklish

Delikatesse [delika'tɛsə] *f (-; -n)* delicacy; **Delika'tessenladen** *m* delicatessen, F deli

Delphin [dɛl'fi:n] *m (-s; -e)* ZO dolphin

Dementi [de'mɛnti] *n (-s; -s)* (official) denial; **dementieren** [demɛn'ti:rən] *v/t (no -ge-, h)* deny (officially)

dementsprechend, **demgemäß** ['de:m-] *adv* according to that

'**demnach** *adv* according to that

'**demnächst** *adv* shortly, before long

Demo ['de:mo] F *f (-; -s)* demo

Demokrat [demo'kra:t] *m (-en; -en)* democrat; **Demokratie** [demokra'ti:] *f (-; -n)* democracy; **Demo'kratin** *f (-; -nen)* democrat; **demo'kratisch** *adj* democratic

demolieren [demo'li:rən] *v/t (no -ge-, h)* demolish, wreck

Demonstrant [demɔn'strant] *m (-en; -en),* **Demon'strantin** *f (-; -nen)* demonstrator; **Demonstration** [-stra'tsjoːn] *f (-; -en)* demonstration; **demonstrieren** [-'stri:rən] *v/t and v/i (no -ge-, h)* demonstrate

demontieren [demɔn'ti:rən] *v/t (no -ge-, h)* dismantle

demoralisieren [demorali'zi:rən] *v/t (no -ge-, h)* demoralize

Demoskopie [demosko'pi:] *f (-; -n)* public opinion research

Demut ['de:mu:t] *f (-; no pl)* humility, humbleness; **demütig** ['de:my:tɪç] *adj* humble; **demütigen** ['de:my:tɪgən] *v/t (ge-, h)* humiliate; '**Demütigung** *f (-; -en)* humiliation

denkbar ['dɛŋkba:ɐ] **1.** *adj* conceivable; **2.** *adv:* ~ **einfach** most simple

denken ['dɛŋkən] *v/t and v/i (irr, ge-, h)* think (*an acc, über acc* of, about); **da-ran ~ (zu inf)** remember (to inf)

'**Denkfa,brik** *f* think tank

'**Denkmal** *n* monument; memorial

'**denkwürdig** *adj* memorable

denn [dɛn] *cj and adv* for, because; **es sei ~, dass** unless; **mehr ~ je** more than ever; **dennoch** ['dɛnnɔx] *cj* yet, still, nevertheless

Denunziant [denʊn'tsjant] *m (-en; -en)* informer; **denunzieren** [-'tsi:rən] *v/t (no -ge-, h)* inform on *or* against

Deodorant [de'ʔodo'rant] *n (-s; -e, -s)* deodorant

Deponie [depo'ni:] *f (-; -n)* dump, waste disposal site

deponieren [depo'ni:rən] *v/t (no -ge-, h)* deposit, leave

Depot [de'po:] *n (-s; -s)* depot (*a.* MIL); *Swiss:* deposit

Depression [deprɛ'sjoːn] *f (-; -en)* depression (*a.* ECON)

depressiv [deprɛ'si:f] *adj* depressive

deprimieren [depri'mi:rən] *v/t (no -ge-, h)* depress; **~d** *adj* depressing

deprimiert [depri'mi:ɐt] *adj* depressed

der [de:ɐ], **die** [di:], **das** [das] **1.** *art* the; **2.** *dem pron* that, this; he, she, it; *die pl* these, those, they; **3.** *rel pron* who, which, that; **derartig 1.** *adv* so (much); like that; **2.** *adj* such (as this)

derb [dɛrp] *adj* coarse; tough, sturdy

'**der'gleichen** *dem pron: nichts ~* nothing of the kind

'**der**', '**die**-', '**dasjenige** [-je:nigə] *dem pron* the one; *diejenigen pl* the ones, those

dermaßen ['de:ɐ'ma:sən] *adv* so (much), like that

Dermatologe [dɛrmato'lo:gə] *m (-n; -n),* **Dermato'login** *f (-; -nen)* dermatologist **der-, die-, dasselbe** [-'zɛlbə] *dem pron* the same

Deserteur [dezɛr'tø:ɐ] *m (-s; -e)* MIL deserter; **desertieren** [dezɛr'ti:rən] *v/i (no -ge-, sein)* MIL desert

deshalb ['dɛs'halp] *cj and adv* therefore, for that reason, that is why, so

Desinfektionsmittel [dɛs'ʔmfɛk'tsjoːns-] *n* MED disinfectant

desinfizieren [dɛs'ʔɪnfi'tsi:rən] *v/t (no -ge-, h)* MED disinfect

'**Desinteresse** *n (-s; no pl)* indifference

'**desinteres,siert** *adj* uninterested, indifferent

destillieren [dɛstɪ'li:rən] *v/t (no -ge-, h)* distil(l)

desto ['dɛsto] *cj and adv* → **je**

'**des'wegen** *cj and adv* → **deshalb**

Detail [de'tai] *n (-s; -s)* detail

detailliert [deta'ji:ɐt] *adj* detailed

Detektiv [detɛk'ti:f] *m (-s; -e)* detective

deuten ['dɔytən] *(ge-, h)* **1.** *v/t* interpret;

2. v/i: **~ auf** (acc) point at

'**deutlich** adj clear, distinct, plain

deutsch [dɔʏtʃ] adj German; **auf Deutsch** in German

'**Deutsche** m, f (-n; -n) German

'**Deutschland** Germany

Devise [de'vi:zə] f (-; -n) motto

De'visen pl ECON foreign currency

Dezember [de'tsɛmbɐ] m (-[s]; -) December

dezent [de'tsɛnt] adj discreet, unobtrusive; conservative (clothes etc); soft (music etc)

Dezimal... [detsi'ma:l-] MATH in cpds ...**bruch**, ...**system** etc: decimal ...; **~stelle** f MATH decimal (place)

DGB [de:ge:'be:] ABBR of **Deutscher Gewerkschaftsbund** Federation of German Trade Unions

d.h. ABBR of **das heißt** i.e., that is

Dia ['di:a] n (-s; -s) PHOT slide

Diagnose [dia'gno:zə] f (-; -n) diagnosis

diagonal [diago'na:l] adj, **Diago'nale** f (-; -n) diagonal

Dialekt [dia'lɛkt] m (-[e]s; -e) dialect

Dialog [dia'lo:k] m (-[e]s; -e) dialog, Br dialogue

Diamant [dia'mant] m (-en; -en) diamond

'**Diapro,jektor** m slide projector

Diät [di'ɛ:t] f (-; -en) diet; **e-e ~ machen** (**Diät halten**) be on (keep to) a diet

Di'äten pl PARL allowance

dich [dɪç] pers pron you; **~ (selbst)** yourself

dicht [dɪçt] **1.** adj dense, a. thick (fog); heavy (traffic); F closed, shut; **2.** adv: **~ an** (dat) or **bei** close to

'**dichten** v/t and v/i (ge-, h) write (poetry); **Dichter(in)** ['dɪçtɐ (-tərɪn)] (-s; -/-; -nen) poet; writer; **dichterisch** ['dɪçtərɪʃ] adj poetic; **~e Freiheit** poetic licen|se, Br -ce

'**dichthalten** F v/i (irr, **halten**, sep, -ge-, h) keep mum

'**Dichtung**[1] f (-; -en) TECH seal(ing)

'**Dichtung**[2] f (-; -en) poetry

dick [dɪk] adj thick; fat; **es macht ~** it's fattening

'**Dicke** f (-; -n) thickness; fatness;

'**dickfellig** F adj thick-skinned

'**dickflüssig** adj thick; TECH viscous

Dickicht ['dɪkɪçt] n (-[e]s; -e) thicket

'**Dick|kopf** m stubborn or pig-headed person; **~milch** f soured milk

Dieb [di:p] m (-[e]s; -e ['di:bə]), **Diebin** ['di:bɪn] f (-; -nen) thief

diebisch ['di:bɪʃ] adj thievish; fig malicious (glee etc)

Diebstahl ['di:pʃta:l] m (-[e]s; -stähle [-ʃtɛ:lə]) theft; JUR mst larceny

Diele ['di:lə] f (-; -n) board, plank; hallway, Br a. hall

dienen ['di:nən] v/i (ge-, h) serve (**j-m** s.o.; **als** as); **Diener** ['di:nɐ] m (-s; -) servant; fig bow (**vor** dat to)

Dienst [di:nst] m (-[e]s; -e) service; work; **~ haben** be on duty; **im** (**außer**) **~** on (off) duty; **~ tuend** on duty; **~...** in cpds ...**wagen**, ...**wohnung** etc: official ..., company ..., business ...

'**Dienstag** m (-[e]s; -e) Tuesday

'**Dienstalter** n seniority, length of service

'**dienstbereit** adj on duty

diensteifrig adj (contp over-)eager

'**Dienstgrad** m grade, rank (a. MIL)

'**Dienstleistung** f service

'**dienstlich** adj official

'**Dienstreise** f business trip

'**Dienststunden** pl office hours

'**Dienstweg** m official channels

dies [di:s], **dieser** ['di:zɐ], **diese** ['di:zə], **dieses** ['di:zəs] dem pron this; this one; **diese** pl these

diesig ['di:zɪç] adj hazy, misty

'**diesjährig** [-jɛ:rɪç] adj this year's

'**diesmal** adv this time

diesseits [-zaits] prp (gen) on this side of; '**Diesseits** n (-; no pl) this life or world

Dietrich ['di:trɪç] m (-s; -e) TECH picklock, skeleton key

Differenz [dɪfə'rɛnts] f (-; -en) difference; disagreement

differenzieren [dɪfərɛn'tsi:rən] v/i (no -ge-, h) distinguish

Digital... [digi'ta:l] in cpds ...**anzeige**, ...**uhr** etc: digital ...

Diktat [dɪk'ta:t] n (-[e]s; -e) dictation; **Diktator** [dɪk'ta:to:ɐ] m (-s; -en [dɪkta'to:rən]) dictator; **diktatorisch** [dɪkta'to:rɪʃ] adj dictatorial; **Diktatur** [dɪkta'tu:ɐ] f (-; -en) dictatorship; **diktieren** [dɪk'ti:rən] v/t and v/i (no -ge-, h) dictate

Dik'tiergerät n Dictaphone®

Dilettant [dile'tant] m (-en; -en) amateur

teur; **dilet'tantisch** *adj* amateurish

DIN [diːn] ABBR *of Deutsches Institut für Normung* German Institute for Standardization

Ding [dɪŋ] *n* (-[e]s; -e) thing; *vor allen ~en* above all; F *ein ~ drehen* pull a job

'Dings(bums) *m, f, n*, **Dingsda** *m, f, n* F thingamajig, whatchamacallit

Dinosaurier [dino'zauriɐ] *m* (-s; -) ZO dinosaur

Dioxid [di'ʔɔksyːt] *n* (-s; -e) CHEM dioxide

Dioxin [diɔ'ksiːn] *n* (-s; -e) CHEM dioxin

Diphtherie [dɪfte'riː] *f* (-; -n) MED diphtheria

Diplom [di'ploːm] *n* (-s; -e) diploma, degree; *~... in cpds ...ingenieur etc:* qualified ..., graduate ...

Diplomat [diplo'maːt] *m* (-en; -en) diplomat; **Diplomatie** [diploma'tiː] *f* (-; *no pl*) diplomacy; **Diplo'matin** *f* (-; -nen) diplomat; **diplo'matisch** *adj* diplomatic (*a. fig*)

dir [diːɐ] *pers pron* (to) you; *~ (selbst)* yourself

direkt [di'rɛkt] **1.** *adj* direct; TV live; **2.** *adv* direct; *fig* directly, right; TV live; *~ gegenüber (von)* right across

Direktion [dirɛk'tsjoːn] *f* (-; -en) management

Direktor [di'rɛktoːɐ] *m* (-s; -en [dirɛk'toːrən]) director, manager; PED principal, *Br* headmaster; **Direktorin** [dirɛk'toːrɪn] (-; -nen) director, manager; PED principal, *Br* headmistress

Di'rektübertragung *f* TV live transmission or broadcast

Dirigent [diri'gɛnt] *m* (-en; -en) conductor; **dirigieren** [diri'giːrən] *v/t and v/i* (*no -ge-, h*) MUS conduct; *fig* direct

Dirne ['dɪrnə] *f* (-; -n) prostitute, whore

Disharmonie [dɪs-] *f* MUS dissonance (*a. fig*); **dishar'monisch** *adj* MUS discordant

Diskette [dɪs'kɛtə] *f* (-; -n) EDP diskette, floppy (disk); **Dis'kettenlaufwerk** *n* EDP disk drive

Disko ['dɪsko] *f* (-; -s) disco

Diskont [dɪs'kɔnt] *m* (-s; -e) ECON discount

Diskothek [dɪsko'teːk] (-; -en) disco, discotheque

diskret [dɪs'kreːt] *adj* discreet; **Diskretion** [dɪskre'tsjoːn] *f* (-; *no pl*) discretion

diskriminieren [dɪskrimi'niːrən] *v/t* (*no -ge-, h*) discriminate against

Diskrimi'nierung *f* (-; -en) discrimination (*von* against)

Diskussion [dɪsku'sjoːn] *f* (-; -en) discussion, debate

Diskussi'onsleiter *m* (panel) chairman; *~runde* f, *~teilnehmer* *pl* panel

Diskuswerfen ['dɪskus-] *n* (-s; *no pl*) SPORT discus throwing

diskutieren [dɪsku'tiːrən] *v/t and v/i* (*no -ge-, h*) discuss

Disqualifikation *f* SPORT disqualification (*wegen* for); **disqualifi'zieren** *v/t* (*no -ge-, h*) SPORT disqualify

Dissident [dɪsi'dɛnt] *m* (-en; -en), **Dissi'dentin** *f* (-; -nen) POL dissident

Distanz [dɪs'tants] *f* (-; -en) distance

distanzieren [dɪstan'tsiːrən] *v/refl* (*no -ge-, h*) distance o.s. (*von* from)

Distel ['dɪstəl] *f* (-; -n) BOT thistle

Distrikt [dɪs'trɪkt] *m* (-[e]s; -e) district

Disziplin [dɪstsi'pliːn] *f* (-; -en) a) (*no pl*) discipline, b) SPORT event; **diszipliniert** [dɪstsipli'niːrt] *adj* disciplined

divers [di'vɛrs] *adj* various; several

Dividende [divi'dɛndə] *f* (-; -n) ECON dividend

dividieren [divi'diːrən] *v/t* (*no -ge-, h*) MATH divide (*durch* by)

Division [divi'zjoːn] *f* (-; -en) MATH, MIL division

DJH [deːjɔt'haː] ABBR *of Deutsches Jugendherbergswerk* German Youth Hostel Association

DM [deː'ɛm] ABBR *of Deutsche Mark* German mark(s)

doch [dɔx] *cj and adv* but, however; yet; *kommst du nicht (mit)? - ~!* aren't you coming? - (oh) yes, I am!; *ich war es nicht~ !* I didn't do it - yes, you did!; *er kam also ~?* so he did come after all?; *du kommst ~?* you're coming, aren't you?; *kommen Sie ~ herein!* do come in!; *wenn ~ ...!* if only ...!

Docht [dɔxt] *m* (-[e]s; -e) wick

Dock [dɔk] *n* (-s; -s) MAR dock

Dogge ['dɔgə] *f* (-; -n) ZO mastiff; Great Dane

Dogma ['dɔgma] *n* (-s; *Dogmen* ['dɔgmən]) dogma; **dogmatisch** [dɔg'maːtɪʃ] *adj* dogmatic

Dohle ['doːlə] *f* (-; -n) ZO (jack)daw

Doktor ['dɔktoːɐ] *m* (-s; -en [dɔk'toːrən]) doctor; UNIV doctor's degree; **~arbeit** *f* UNIV (doctoral *or* PhD) thesis

Dokument [doku'mɛnt] *n* (-[e]s; -e) document

Dokumentar... [dokumɛn'taːɐ-] *in cpds* ...**spiel** *etc*: documentary ...; **~film** *m* documentary (film)

Dolch [dɔlç] *m* (-[e]s; -e) dagger

Dollar ['dɔlar] *m* (-[s]; -s) dollar

dolmetschen ['dɔlmɛtʃən] *v/i* (ge-, h) interpret; **'Dolmetscher(in)** (-s; -/-; -nen) interpreter

Dom [doːm] *m* (-[e]s; -e) cathedral

dominierend [domi'niːrənt] *adj* (pre-)dominant

Dompteur [dɔmp'tøːɐ] *m* (-s; -e), **Dompteuse** [dɔmp'tøːzə] *f* (-; -n) animal tamer *or* trainer

Donner ['dɔnɐ] *m* (-s; *no pl*) thunder

'donnern *v/i* (ge-, h) thunder (*a. fig*)

'Donnerstag *m* (-[e]s; -e) Thursday

'Donnerwetter F *n* (-s; -) dressing-down; **~!** wow!

doof [doːf] F *adj* stupid, dumb

Doppel ['dɔpəl] *n* (-s; -) duplicate; *tennis etc*: doubles; **~... ** *in cpds* **...bett,** **...zimmer** *etc*: double ...

'Doppeldecker [-dɛkɐ] *m* (-s; -) AVIAT biplane; MOT double-decker (bus)

'Doppelgänger [-gɛŋɐ] *m* (-s; -) double, look-alike

'Doppelhaus *n* duplex, *Br* pair of semis; **~hälfte** *f* semidetached (house)

'Doppel|pass *m* soccer: wall pass; **~punkt** *m* LING colon; **~stecker** *m* ELECTR two-way adapter

doppelt *adj* double; **~ so viel (wie)** twice as much (as)

'Doppelverdiener *pl* two-income family

Dorf [dɔrf] *n* (-[e]s; *Dörfer* ['dœrfɐ]) village; **~bewohner** *m* villager

Dorn [dɔrn] *m* (-[e]s; -en) BOT thorn (*a. fig*); TECH tongue; spike

'dornig *adj* thorny (*a. fig*)

Dorsch [dɔrʃ] *m* (-[e]s; -e) ZO cod(fish)

dort [dɔrt] *adv* there

'dorther *adv* from there

'dorthin *adv* there

Dose ['doːzə] *f* (-; -n) can, *Br a.* tin

'Dosen... *in cpds* canned, *Br a.* tinned

dösen ['døːzən] F *v/i* (ge-, h) doze

'Dosenöffner *m* can (*Br* tin) opener

Dosis ['doːzɪs] *f* (-; *Dosen*) MED dose

Dotter ['dɔtɐ] *m, n* (-s; -) yolk

Double [du'baːl] *n* (-s; -s) *film*: stunt man (*or* woman)

Dozent [do'tsɛnt] *m* (-en; -en), **Do'zentin** *f* (-; -nen) (university) lecturer, assistant professor

Dr. ABBR *of* **Doktor** Dr., Doctor

Drache ['draxə] *m* (-n; -n) dragon

'Drachen *m* (-s; -) kite; SPORT hang glider; **e-n ~ steigen lassen** fly a kite; **~fliegen** *n* SPORT hang gliding

Draht [draːt] *m* (-[e]s; *Drähte* ['drɛːtə]) wire; F **auf ~ sein** be on the ball

'drahtig ['draːtɪç] *fig adj* wiry

'drahtlos *adj* wireless

'Drahtseil *n* TECH cable; *circus*: tightrope; **~bahn** *f* cable railway

'Drahtzieher *fig m* (-s; -) wirepuller

drall [dral] *adj* buxom, strapping

Drall *m* (-[e]s; *no pl*) twist, spin

Drama ['draːma] *n* (-s; *Dramen*) drama

Dramatiker [dra'maːtikɐ] *m* (-s; -) dramatist, playwright

dra'matisch *adj* dramatic

dran [dran] F *adv* → **daran**; **du bist ~** it's your turn; *fig* you're in for it

Drang [draŋ] *m* (-[e]s; *no pl*) urge, drive (**nach** for)

drängeln ['drɛŋəln] F *v/t and v/i* (ge-, h) push, shove

drängen ['drɛŋən] *v/t and v/i* (ge-, h) push, shove; *j-n zu et.* **~** press *or* urge s.o. to do s.th.; *sich* **~** press; force one's way; **~d** *adj* pressing

'drankommen F *v/i* (*irr, kommen, sep, -ge-, sein*) have one's turn; **als erster ~** be first

drastisch ['drastɪʃ] *adj* drastic

drauf [drauf] F *adv* → **darauf**; **~ und dran sein, et. zu tun** be just about to do s.th.; **'Draufgänger** [-gɛŋɐ] *m* (-s; -) daredevil

draus [draus] F *adv* → **daraus**

draußen ['drausən] *adv* outside; outdoors; **da ~** out there; **bleib(t) ~!** keep out!

drechseln ['drɛksəln] *v/t* (ge-, h) turn (on a lathe)

Drechsler ['drɛkslɐ] *m* (-s; -) turner

Dreck [drɛk] F *m* (-[e]s; *no pl*) dirt; filth (*a. fig*); mud; *fig* trash; **dreckig** ['drɛkɪç] F *adj* dirty; filthy (*both a. fig*)

Dreh|arbeiten ['dre:-] *pl film*: shooting; **~bank** *f* (-; *-bänke*) TECH lathe

'**drehbar** *adj* revolving, rotating

'**Drehbuch** *n film*: script

drehen ['dre:ən] *v/t* (*ge-*, *h*) turn; *film*: shoot; roll; **sich ~** turn, rotate; spin; **sich ~ um** *fig* be about; → **Ding**

Dreher ['dre:ɐ] *m* (*-s*; *-*) TECH turner

'**Dreh|kreuz** *n* turnstile; **~orgel** *f* barrel-organ; **~ort** *m film*: location; **~strom** *m* ELECTR three-phase current; **~stuhl** *m* swivel chair; **~tür** *f* revolving door

'**Drehung** *f* (-; *-en*) turn; rotation

'**Drehzahl** *f* TECH (number of) revolutions; **~messer** *m* MOT rev(olution) counter

drei [drai] *adj* three

Drei *f* (-; *-en*) three; *grade*: fair, C

'**drei|beinig** *adj* three-legged; **~dimensio,nal** *adj* three-dimensional

'**Dreieck** *n* (*-[e]s*; *-e*) triangle

'**dreieckig** *adj* triangular

dreierlei ['draiɐ'lai] *adj* three kinds of

'**dreifach** *adj* threefold, triple

'**Drei|gang...** TECH *in cpds* three-speed ...; **~kampf** *m* SPORT triathlon; **~rad** *n* tricycle; **~satz** *m* (*-es*; *no pl*) MATH rule of three; **~sprung** *m* (*-[e]s*; *no pl*) SPORT triple jump

dreißig ['draisıç] *adj* thirty

'**dreißigste** *adj* thirtieth

dreist [draist] *adj* brazen, impertinent

'**dreistufig** [-ʃtu:fıç] *adj* three-stage

dreizehn(te) *adj* thirteen(th)

Dresche ['drɛʃə] *f* (-; *no pl*) thrashing

'**dreschen** *v/t and v/i* (*irr*, *ge-*, *h*) AGR thresh; thrash; '**Dreschma,schine** *f* AGR threshing machine

dressieren [drɛ'si:rən] *v/t* (*no -ge-*, *h*) train

Dressman ['drɛsmən] *m* (*-s*; *-men*) male model

Dressur [drɛ'su:ɐ] *f* (-; *-en*) training; act; **~reiten** *n* dressage

dribbeln ['drıbəln] *v/i* (*ge-*, *h*), **Dribbling** *n* (*-s*; *-s*) SPORT dribble

drillen ['drılən] *v/t* (*ge-*, *h*) MIL drill (*a. fig*)

Drillinge ['drılıŋə] *pl* triplets

drin [drın] F *adv* → **darin**; **das ist nicht ~!** no way!

dringen ['drıŋən] *v/i* (*irr*, *ge-*, *h*) **~ auf** (*acc*) insist on; **~ aus** come from; **~ durch** force one's way through, penetrate, pierce; **~ in** (*acc*) penetrate into; **darauf ~, dass** urge that; **~d** *adj* urgent, pressing; strong (*suspicion etc*)

drinnen ['drınən] F *adv* inside; indoors

dritte ['drıtə] *adj* third; **wir sind zu dritt** there are three of us; **die Dritte Welt** the Third World; '**Drittel** *n* (*-s*; *-*) third; '**drittens** *adv* thirdly; '**Dritte-Welt-Laden** *m* third world shop

Droge ['dro:gə] *f* (-; *-n*) drug

'**drogenabhängig** *adj* addicted to drugs; **~ sein** be a drug addict

'**Drogen|abhängige** *m, f* (*-n*; *-n*) drug addict; **~missbrauch** *m* drug abuse

'**drogensüchtig** → **drogenabhängig**

'**Drogentote** *m, f* drug victim

Drogerie [drogə'ri:] *f* (-; *-n*) drugstore, *Br* chemist's (shop)

Drogist [dro'gıst] *m* (*-en*; *-en*), **Dro'gistin** *f* (-; *-nen*) chemist

drohen ['dro:ən] *v/i* (*ge-*, *h*) threaten, menace

dröhnen ['drø:nən] *v/i* (*ge-*, *h*) roar

'**Drohung** *f* (-; *-en*) threat (*gegen* to)

drollig ['drɔlıç] *adj* funny, droll

Dromedar [dromə'da:ɐ] *n* (*-s*; *-e*) ZO dromedary

drosch [drɔʃ] *pret of* **dreschen**

Drossel ['drɔsəl] *f* (-; *-n*) ZO thrush

'**drosseln** *v/t* (*ge-*, *h*) TECH throttle

drüben ['dry:bən] *adv* over there (*a. fig*)

drüber ['dry:bɐ] F *adv* → **darüber, drunter**

Druck [drʊk] *m* (*-[e]s*; *-e*) pressure; printing; print

'**Druckbuchstabe** *m* block letter

Drückeberger ['drʏkəbɛrgɐ] F *m* (*-s*; *-*) shirker

'**drucken** *v/t* (*ge-*, *h*) print; **et. ~ lassen** have s.th. printed *or* published

drücken ['drʏkən] (*ge-*, *h*) **1.** *v/t* press; push; *fig* force down; **j-m die Hand ~** shake hands with s.o.; **2.** *v/i* pinch; **3.** F *v/refl*: **sich vor et. ~** shirk (doing) s.th.; **~d** *adj* heavy, oppressive

Drucker ['drʊkɐ] *m* (*-s*; *-*) printer (*a. EDP*)

Drücker ['drʏkɐ] *m* (*-s*; *-*) latch; trigger; F hawker

Druckerei [drʊkə'rai] *f* (-; *-en*) printers

'**Druck|fehler** *m* misprint; **~kammer** *f* pressurized cabin; **~knopf** *m* snap fastener, *Br* press stud; TECH (push) button; **~luft** *f* TECH compressed air; **~sa-**

D

che f printed (or second-class) matter; **~schrift** f block letters; **~taste** f TECH push button

drunter ['drʊntɐ] F adv → **darunter, es ging ~ und drüber** it was absolutely chaotic

Drüse ['dry:zə] f (-; -n) ANAT gland

Dschungel ['dʒʊŋəl] m (-s; -) jungle (a. fig)

Dschunke ['dʒʊŋkə] f (-; -n) MAR junk

du [du:] pers pron you

Dübel ['dy:bəl] m (-s; -), **'dübeln** v/t (ge-, h) TECH dowel

ducken ['dʊkən] v/refl (ge-, h) duck; fig cringe (**vor** dat before); crouch

Duckmäuser ['dʊkmɔyzɐ] m (-s; -) coward; yes-man

Dudelsack ['du:dəlzak] m MUS bagpipes

Duell [du'ɛl] n (-s; -e) duel; **duellieren** [due'li:rən] v/refl (no -ge-, h) fight a duel

Duett [du'ɛt] n (-[e]s; -e) MUS duet

Duft [dʊft] m (-[e]s; Düfte ['dyftə]) scent, fragrance, smell (**nach** of); **'duften** v/i (ge-, h) smell (**nach** of); **'duftend** adj fragrant; **'duftig** adj dainty

dulden ['dʊldən] v/t (ge-, h) tolerate, put up with; suffer

duldsam ['dʊltza:m] adj tolerant

dumm [dʊm] adj stupid, F dumb

'Dummheit f (-; -en) a) (no pl) stupidity, ignorance, b) stupid or foolish thing

'Dummkopf m contp fool, blockhead

dumpf [dʊmpf] adj dull; fig vague

Düne ['dy:nə] f (-; -n) (sand) dune

Dung [dʊŋ] m (-[e]s; no pl) dung, manure

düngen ['dyŋən] v/t (ge-, h) fertilize; manure; **Dünger** ['dyŋɐ] m (-s; -) fertilizer; manure

dunkel ['dʊŋkəl] adj dark (a. fig)

'Dunkelheit f (-; no pl) dark(ness)

'Dunkelkammer f PHOT darkroom; **~ziffer** f number of unreported cases

dünn [dyn] adj thin; weak (coffee etc)

Dunst [dʊnst] m (-[e]s; Dünste ['dynstə]) haze, mist; CHEM vapo(u)r; **dünsten** ['dynstən] v/t (ge-, h) GASTR stew, braise; **'dunstig** adj hazy, misty

Duplikat [dupli'ka:t] n (-[e]s; -e) duplicate; copy

Dur [du:ɐ] n (-; no pl) MUS major (key)

durch [dʊrç] prp (acc) and adv through;

across; MATH divided by; GASTR (well) done; **~ j-n (et.)** through by s.o. (s.th.); **~ und ~** through and through

'durcharbeiten (sep, -ge-, h) **1.** v/t study thoroughly; **sich ~ durch** work (one's way) through a text etc; **2.** v/i work without a break

durch'aus adv absolutely, quite; **~ nicht** by no means

'durchblättern v/t (sep, -ge-, h) leaf or thumb through

'Durchblick m grasp of s.th.

'durchblicken v/i (sep, -ge-, h) look through; **~ lassen** give to understand; **ich blicke (da) nicht durch** I don't get it

durch'bohren v/t (no -ge-, h) pierce; perforate

'durchbraten v/t (irr, braten, sep, -ge-, h) roast thoroughly

'durchbrechen¹ (irr, brechen, sep, -ge-) **1.** v/t (h) break (in two); **2.** v/i (sein) break through or apart

durch'brechen² v/t (irr, brechen, no -ge-, h) break through

'durchbrennen v/i (irr, brennen, sep, -ge-, sein) ELECTR blow; reactor: melt down; F run away

'durchbringen v/t (irr, bringen, sep, -ge-, h) get (MED pull) s.o. through; go through one's money; support (family)

'Durchbruch m breakthrough (a. fig)

durch'dacht adj (well) thought-out

'durchdrehen (sep, -ge-, h) **1.** v/i wheels: spin; F fig crack up, flip; **2.** v/t GASTR grind, Br mince

'durchdringend adj piercing

durchei'nander adv confused; (in) a mess; **~ bringen** confuse, mix up; mess up; **Durchei'nander** n (-s; no pl) confusion, mess

durch'fahren¹ v/t (irr, fahren, no -ge-, h) go (or pass, drive) through

'durchfahren² v/i (irr, fahren, sep, -ge-, sein) go (or pass, drive) through

'Durchfahrt f passage; **~ verboten** no thoroughfare

'Durchfall m MED diarrh(o)ea

'durchfallen v/i (irr, fallen, sep, -ge-, sein) fall through; fail, F flunk (test etc); F be a flop; **j-n ~ lassen** fail (F flunk) s.o.; **~fragen** v/refl (sep, -ge-, h) ask one's way (**nach, zu** to)

'durchführbar adj practicable, feasible

'**durchführen** v/t (sep, -ge-, h) carry out, do

'**Durchgang** m passage

'**Durchgangs...** in cpds ...verkehr etc: through ...; ...lager etc: transit ...

'**durchgebraten** adj well done

'**durchgehen** (irr, **gehen**, sep, -ge-, sein) **1.** v/i go through (a. RAIL and PARL); fig run away (**mit** with); horse: bolt; **2.** v/t go or look through; **~ lassen** tolerate; **~d** adj continuous; **~er Zug** through train; **~ geöffnet** open all day

'**durchgreifen** fig v/i (irr, **greifen**, sep, -ge-, h) take drastic measures; **~d** adj drastic; radical

'**durchhalten** (irr, **halten**, sep, -ge-, h) **1.** v/t keep up; **2.** v/i hold out

'**durchhängen** v/i (irr, **hängen**, sep, -ge-, h) sag; F have a low

'**durchkämpfen** v/t (sep, -ge-, h) fight out; **sich ~** fight one's way through

'**durchkommen** v/i (irr, **kommen**, sep, -ge-, sein) come through (a. MED): get through; get along; get away (**mit e-r Lüge** etc with a lie etc)

durch'**kreuzen** v/t (no -ge-, h) cross, thwart

'**durchlassen** v/t (irr, **lassen**, sep, -ge-, h) let pass, let through

'**durchlässig** adj permeable (**für** to)

'**durchlaufen**[1] (irr, **laufen**, sep, -ge-) **1.** v/i (sein) run through; **2.** v/t (h) wear through

durch'**laufen**[2] v/t (irr, **laufen**, no -ge-, h) pass through

'**Durchlauferhitzer** m (-s; -) (instant) water heater, Br a. geyser

'**durchlesen** v/t (irr, **lesen**, sep, -ge-, h) read through

durch'**leuchten** v/t (no -ge-, h) MED X-ray; fig screen; **~löchern** [-'lœçən] v/t (no -ge-, h) perforate, make holes in

'**durchmachen** F v/t (sep, -ge-, h) go through; **viel ~** suffer a lot; **die Nacht ~** make a night of it

'**Durchmesser** m (-s; -) diameter

durch'**nässen** v/t (no -ge-, h) soak

'**durchnehmen** v/t (irr, **nehmen**, sep, -ge-, h) PED do, deal with

'**durchpausen** v/t (sep, -ge-, h) trace

durch'**queren** v/t (no -ge-, h) cross

'**Durchreiche** f (-; -n) hatch

'**Durchreise** f: **ich bin nur auf der ~** I'm only passing through; '**durchreisen** v/i

(sep, -ge-, sein) travel through

'**Durchreisevisum** n transit visa

'**durchreißen** (irr, **reißen**, sep, -ge-) **1.** v/t (h) tear (in two); **2.** v/i (sein) tear, break; **~ringen** v/refl (irr, **ringen**, sep, -ge-, h) **sich ~, et. zu tun** bring o.s. to do s.th.

'**Durchsage** f announcement

durch'**schauen** v/t (no -ge-, h) see through s.o. or s.th.

'**durchscheinen** v/i (irr, **scheinen**, sep, -ge-, h) shine through; **~d** adj transparent

'**durchscheuern** v/t (sep, -ge-, h) chafe; wear through

'**durchschlafen** v/i (irr, **schlafen**, sep, -ge-, h) sleep through

'**Durchschlag** m (carbon) copy

durch'**schlagen**[1] v/t (irr, **schlagen**, no -ge-, h) cut in two; bullet etc: go through, pierce

'**durchschlagen**[2] (irr, **schlagen**, sep, -ge-) **1.** v/refl (h): **sich ~ nach** make one's way to; **2.** v/i (sein) come through (a. fig); **~d** adj sweeping; effective

'**Durchschlagpapier** n carbon paper; **~schlagskraft** fig f force, impact

'**durchschneiden** v/t (irr, **schneiden**, sep, -ge-, h) cut (through)

'**Durchschnitt** m average; **im** (**über, unter dem**) **~** on an (above, below) average; **im ~ betragen** (**verdienen** etc) average

'**durchschnittlich 1.** adj average; ordinary; **2.** adv on an average

'**Durchschnitts...** in cpds average ...

'**Durchschrift** f (carbon) copy

'**durchsehen** v/t (irr, **sehen**, sep, -ge-, h) look or go through; check; **~setzen** v/t (sep, -ge-, h) put (or push) s.th. through; **s-n Kopf ~** have one's way; **sich ~** get one's way; be successful; **sich ~ können** have authority (**bei** over)

durch'**setzt** adj: **~ mit** interspersed with

'**durchsichtig** adj transparent (a. fig); clear; see-through

'**durchsickern** v/i (sep, -ge-, sein) seep through; fig leak out

'**durchstarten** v/i (sep, -ge-, sein) AVIAT climb and reaccelerate

durch'**stechen** v/t (irr, **stechen**, no -ge-, h) pierce

'**durch**|**stecken** v/t (sep, -ge-, h) stick through; **~stehen** v/t (irr, **stehen**, sep, -ge-, h) go through
durch'stoßen v/t (irr, **stoßen**, no -ge-, h) break through
durch'streichen v/t (irr, **streichen**, sep, -ge-, h) cross out
durch'suchen v/t (no -ge-, h) search, F frisk; **Durch'suchung** f (-; -en) search; **Durch'suchungsbefehl** m search warrant
durch|**trieben** [-'tri:bən] adj cunning, sly; **~'wachsen** adj GASTR streaky
'**Durchwahl** f (-; no pl) TEL direct dial(l)ing; '**durchwählen** v/i (sep, -ge-, h) TEL dial direct
'**durchweg** [-vɛk] adv without exception
durch'weicht adj soaked, drenched
durch'wühlen v/t (no -ge-, h) rummage through
'**durch**|**zählen** v/t (sep, -ge-, h) count off (Br up); '**durchziehen** (irr, **ziehen**, sep, -ge-) **1.** v/i (sein) pass through; **2.** v/t (h) pull s.th. through; fig carry s.th. through (to the end)
durch'zucken v/t (no -ge-, h) flash through
'**Durchzug** m (-[e]s; no pl) draft, Br draught
dürfen ['dʏrfən] **1.** v/aux (irr, no -ge-, h) be allowed or permitted to inf; **darf ich gehen?** may I go?; **ja**(, **du darfst**) yes, you may; **du darfst nicht** you must not, you aren't allowed to; **dürfte ich ...?** could I ...?; **das dürfte genügen**

that should be enough; **2.** v/i (irr, ge-, h) **er darf** (**nicht**) he is (not) allowed to inf
durfte ['dʊrftə] pret of **dürfen**
dürftig ['dʏrftɪç] adj poor; scanty
dürr [dʏr] adj dry; barren, arid; skinny
Dürre ['dʏrə] f (-; -n) a) drought, b) (no pl) barrenness
Durst [dʊrst] m (-[e]s; no pl) thirst (**auf** acc for); **~ haben** be thirsty
durstig adj thirsty
Dusche ['dʊʃə] f (-; -n) shower
'**duschen** v/refl and v/i (ge-, h) have or take a shower
Düse ['dy:zə] f (-; -n) TECH nozzle; jet
'**düsen** F v/i (ge-, sein) jet
'**Düsen**|**antrieb** m jet propulsion; **mit ~** jet-propelled; **~flugzeug** n jet (plane); **~jäger** m MIL jet fighter; **~triebwerk** n jet engine
düster ['dy:stɐ] adj dark, gloomy (both a. fig); dim (light); fig dismal
Dutzend ['dʊtsənt] n (-s; -e) dozen
'**dutzendweise** adv by the dozen
duzen ['du:tsən] v/t (ge-, h) use the familiar 'du' with s.o.; **sich ~** be on 'du' terms
Dynamik [dy'na:mɪk] f (-; no pl) PHYS dynamics; fig dynamism
dy'namisch adj dynamic
Dynamit [dyna'mi:t] n (-s; no pl) dynamite
Dynamo [dy'an:mo] m (-s; -s) ELECTR dynamo, generator
D-Zug ['de:-] m express train

Ebbe ['ɛbə] f (-; -n) ebb, low tide
eben ['e:bən] **1.** adj even; flat; MATH plane; **zu ~er Erde** on the first (Br ground) floor; **2.** adv just; **an ~ dem Tag** on that very day; **so ist es ~** that's the way it is; **gerade ~ so** or **noch** just barely
'**Ebenbild** n image
'**ebenbürtig** [-bʏrtɪç] adj: **j-m ~ sein** be a match for s.o., be s.o.'s equal
Ebene ['e:bənə] f (-; -n) GEOGR plain;

MATH plane; fig level
'**ebenerdig** adj and adv at street level; on the first (Br ground) floor
'**ebenfalls** adv as well, too
'**Ebenholz** n ebony
'**Ebenmaß** n (-es; no pl) symmetry; harmony; regularity; '**ebenmäßig** adj symmetrical; harmonious; regular
'**ebenso** adv and cj just as; as well; **~ wie** in the same way as; **~ gern**, **~ gut** just as well; **~ sehr**, **~ viel** just as much; **~**

wenig just as little *or* few

Eber ['e:bɐ] *m* (-s; -) zo boar

ebnen ['e:bnən] *v/t* (*ge-*, *h*) even, level; *fig* smooth

Echo ['ɛço] *n* (-s; -s) echo; *fig* response

echt [ɛçt] *adj* genuine (*a. fig*), real; true; pure; fast (*color*); authentic; F ~ **gut** real good; **Echtheit** *f* (-; *no pl*) genuineness; authenticity

Eckball ['ɛk-] *m* SPORT corner (kick)

Ecke ['ɛkə] *f* (-; -n) corner; edge; SPORT *lange* (*kurze*) ~ far (near) corner; → **Eckball**; **eckig** ['ɛkɪç] *adj* square, angular; *fig* awkward

'Eckzahn *m* canine tooth

edel ['e:dəl] *adj* noble; MIN precious

'Edelme,tall *n* precious metal

'Edelstahl *m* stainless steel

'Edelstein *m* precious stone; gem

EDV [e:de:'fau] ABBR *of* **Elektronische Datenverarbeitung** EDP, electronic data processing

Efeu ['e:fɔy] *m* (-s; *no pl*) BOT ivy

Effekt [ɛ'fɛkt] *m* (-[e]s; -e) effect

effektiv [ɛfɛk'ti:f] **1.** *adj* effective; **2.** *adv* actually; **Effektivität** [ɛfɛktivi'tɛ:t] *f* (-; *no pl*) effectiveness

ef'fektvoll *adj* effective, striking

Effet [ɛ'fe:] *m* (-s; -s) SPORT spin

EG [e:'ge:] HIST ABBR *of* **Europäische Gemeinschaft** EC, European Community

egal [e'ga:l] F *adj*: ~ *ob* (*warum, wer etc*) no matter if (why, who, etc); *das ist* ~ it doesn't matter; *das ist mir* ~ I don't care, it's all the same to me

Egge ['ɛgə] *f* (-; -n), **'eggen** *v/t* (*ge-*, *h*) AGR harrow

Egoismus [ego'ɪsmʊs] *m* (-; *no pl*) ego(t)ism; **Egoist(in)** [ego'ɪst(ɪn)] (-en; -en/-; -nen) ego(t)ist; **ego'istisch** *adj* selfish, ego(t)istic(al)

ehe ['e:ə] *cj* before; *nicht* ~ not until

Ehe ['e:ə] *f* (-; -n) marriage (*mit* to); ~**beratung** *f* marriage counseling (*Br* guidance); ~**brecher** *m* (-s; -) adulterer; ~**brecherin** *f* (-; -nen) adulteress

'ehebrecherisch *adj* adulterous

'Ehe|bruch *m* adultery; ~**frau** *f* wife; ~**leute** *pl* married couple

'ehelich *adj* conjugal; JUR legitimate

ehemalig ['e:əma:lɪç] *adj* former, ex-...

ehemals ['e:əma:ls] *adv* formerly

'Ehemann *m* husband

'Ehepaar *n* (married) couple

eher ['e:ɐ] *adv* earlier, sooner; *je* ~, *desto lieber* the sooner the better; *nicht* ~ *als* not until *or* before

'Ehering *m* wedding ring

ehrbar ['e:ɐba:ɐ] *adj* respectable

Ehre ['e:ɐə] *f* (-; -n) hono(u)r; *zu* ~*n* (*von*) in hono(u)r of

'ehren *v/t* (*ge-*, *h*) hono(u)r; respect

'ehrenamtlich *adj* honorary

'Ehren|bürger *m* honorary citizen; ~**doktor** *m* UNIV honorary doctor; ~**gast** *m* guest of hono(u)r; ~**kodex** *m* code of hono(u)r; ~**mann** *m* man of hono(u)r; ~**mitglied** *n* honorary member; ~**platz** *m* place of hono(u)r; ~**rechte** *pl* civil rights; ~**rettung** *f* rehabilitation

'ehrenrührig *adj* defamatory

'Ehren|runde *f esp* SPORT lap of hono(u)r; ~**sache** *f* point of hono(u)r; ~**tor** *n*, ~**treffer** *m* SPORT consolation goal

'ehrenwert *adj* hono(u)rable

'Ehrenwort *n* (-[e]s; -e) word of hono(u)r; F ~! cross my heart!

ehrerbietig ['e:ɐʔɐbi:tɪç] *adj* respectful

Ehrfurcht ['e:ɐ-] *f* (-; *no pl*) respect (*vor dat* for); awe (of); ~ *gebietend* awe-inspiring, awesome; **'ehrfürchtig** [-fʏrçtɪç] *adj* respectful

'Ehrgefühl *n* (-[e]s; *no pl*) sense of hono(u)r

'Ehrgeiz *m* ambition; **'ehrgeizig** *adj* ambitious

'ehrlich *adj* honest; frank; fair; **'Ehrlichkeit** *f* (-; *no pl*) honesty; fairness

'Ehrung *f* (-; -en) hono(u)r(ing)

'ehrwürdig *adj* venerable

Ei [ai] *n* (-[e]s; -er) egg; V *pl* balls

Eiche ['aiçə] *f* (-; -n) oak(-tree)

Eichel ['aiçəl] *f* (-; -n) BOT acorn; *card games*: club(s); ANAT glans (penis)

eichen ['aiçən] *v/t* (*ge-*, *h*) ga(u)ge

Eichhörnchen ['aiçhœrnçən] *n* (-s; -) zo squirrel

Eid [ait] *m* (-[e]s; -e) oath; *e-n* ~ *ablegen* take an oath

Eidechse ['aidɛksə] *f* (-; -n) zo lizard

eidesstattlich ['aidəs-] *adj*: ~*e Erklärung* JUR statutory declaration

'Eidotter *m*, *n* (egg) yolk

'Eier|becher *m* eggcup; ~**kuchen** *m*

pancake; **~li,kör** m eggnog; **~schale** f eggshell; **~stock** m ANAT ovary; **~uhr** f egg timer

Eifer ['aifə] m (-s; no pl) zeal, eagerness; **glühender ~** ardo(u)r

'**Eifersucht** f (-; no pl) jealousy

'**eifersüchtig** adj jealous (**auf** acc of)

eifrig adj eager, zealous; ardent

'**Eigelb** n (-[e]s, -e) (egg) yolk

eigen ['aigən] adj own, of one's own; peculiar; particular, F fussy; **...eigen** in cpds staats **etc:** ...-owned

'**Eigenart** f peculiarity

'**eigenartig** adj peculiar; strange

'**Eigenbedarf** m personal needs

'**Eigengewicht** n dead weight

'**eigenhändig** [-hɛndɪç] **1.** adj personal; **2.** adv personally, with one's own hands

'**Eigen|heim** n home (of one's own); **~liebe** f self-love; **~lob** n self-praise

'**eigenmächtig** adj arbitrary

'**Eigenname** m proper noun

'**Eigennutz** m (-es; no pl) self-interest

'**eigennützig** [-nʏtsɪç] adj selfish

'**eigens** adv (e)specially, expressly

'**Eigenschaft** f (-; -en) quality; TECH, PHYS, CHEM property; **in s-r ~ als** in his capacity as; '**Eigenschaftswort** n (-[e]s; -wörter) LING adjective

'**Eigensinn** m (-[e]s; no pl) stubbornness; '**eigensinnig** adj stubborn, obstinate

eigentlich ['aigəntlɪç] **1.** adj actual, true, real; exact; **2.** adv actually, really; originally

'**Eigentor** n SPORT own goal (a. fig)

Eigentum n (-[e]s; no pl) property

Eigentümer ['aigəntyːmɐ] m (-s; -), '**Eigentümerin** f (-; -nen) owner, proprietor (proprietress)

'**eigentümlich** [-tyːmlɪç] adj peculiar; strange, odd; '**Eigentümlichkeit** f (-; -en) peculiarity

'**Eigentumswohnung** f condominium, F condo, Br owner-occupied flat

'**eigenwillig** adj wil(l)ful; individual, original (style etc)

eignen ['aignən] v/refl (ge-, h) **sich ~ für** be suited or fit for; '**Eignung** f (-; no pl) suitability; aptitude, qualification

'**Eignungs|prüfung** f, **~test** m aptitude test

Eil|bote ['ail-] m: **durch ~n** by special

delivery; **~brief** m special delivery (Br express) letter

Eile ['ailə] f (-; no pl) haste, hurry; '**eilen** v/i a) (ge-, sein) hurry, hasten, rush, b) (ge-, h) be urgent; '**eilig** adj hurried, hasty; urgent; **es ~ haben** be in a hurry

Eimer ['aimɐ] m (-s; -) bucket, pail

ein [ain] **1.** adj one; **2.** indef art a, an; **3.** adv: **„einIaus"** "on/off"; **~ und aus gehen** come and go; **nicht mehr ~ noch aus wissen** be at one's wits' end

einander [ai'nandɐ] pron each other, one another

'**einarbeiten** v/t (sep, -ge-, h) train, acquaint s.o. with his work, F break s.o. in; **sich ~** work o.s. in

'**einarmig** [-armɪç] adj one-armed

'**einäschern** ['ain'ɛʃɐn] v/t (sep, -ge-, h) cremate; **Einäscherung** ['ain'ɛʃərʊŋ] f (-; -en) cremation

'**einatmen** v/t (sep, -ge-, h) inhale, breathe

'**einäugig** [-ɔygɪç] adj one-eyed

'**Einbahnstraße** f one-way street

einbalsamieren ['ainbalzamiːrən] v/t (no -ge-, h) embalm

'**Einband** m (-[e]s; -bände) binding, cover

'**Einbau** m (-[e]s; -bauten) installation, fitting, **~...** in cpds ...möbel etc: built-in ...; '**einbauen** v/t (sep, -ge-, h) build in, instal(l), fit

'**einberufen** v/t (irr, **rufen**, sep, no -ge-, h) MIL draft, Br call up; call (meeting etc); '**Einberufung** f (-; -en) MIL draft, Br call-up

'**ein|beziehen** v/t (irr, **ziehen**, sep, no -ge-, h) include; **~biegen** v/i (irr, **biegen**, sep, -ge-, sein) turn (**in** acc into)

'**einbilden** v/refl (sep, -ge-, h) imagine; **sich et. ~ auf** (acc) be conceited about

'**Einbildung** f (-; no pl) imagination, fancy; conceit

'**einblenden** v/t (sep, -ge-, h) TV fade in

'**Einblick** m insight (**in** acc into)

'**einbrechen** v/i (irr, **brechen**, sep, -ge-, sein) collapse; winter: set in; **~ in** (acc) break into, burgle; fall through (the ice); '**Einbrecher** m (-s; -) burglar

'**einbringen** v/t (irr, **bringen**, sep, -ge-, h) bring in; yield (profit etc)

'**Einbruch** m burglary; **bei ~ der Nacht** at nightfall

'**einbürgern** [-bʏrgɐn] v/t (sep, -ge-, h)

naturalize; **sich ~** fig come into use
'Ein|bürgerung f (-; -en) naturalization
'Einbuße f (-; -n) loss
'einbüßen v/t (sep, -ge-, h) lose
'eindämmen [-dɛmən] v/t (sep, -ge-, h)
dam (up), fig a. get under control
'eindecken fig v/t (sep, -ge-, h) provide
(**mit** with)
'eindeutig [-dɔytɪç] adj clear
'eindrehen v/t (sep, -ge-, h) put hair in
curlers
'eindringen v/i (irr, **dringen**, sep, -ge-,
sein) ~ **in** (acc) enter (a. fig); force one's
way into; MIL invade; '**eindringlich** adj
urgent; '**Eindringling** m (-s; -e) intruder; MIL invader
'Eindruck m impression; '**eindrücken**
v/t (sep, -ge-, h) break or push in
'eindrucksvoll adj impressive
'eineiig ['aɪnʔaɪɪç] adj identical (twins)
'einein'halb adj one and a half
'einengen ['aɪnʔɛŋən] v/t (sep, -ge-, h)
confine, restrict
einer ['aɪnə], eine ['aɪnə], ein(e)s ['aɪn
(-ə)s] indef pron one
'Einer m (-s; -) MATH unit; rowing: single
sculls
einerlei ['aɪnə'laɪ] adj: **ganz ~** all the
same; ~ **ob** no matter if; '**Einer'lei** n:
das tägliche ~ the daily grind or rut
'einer'seits adv on the one hand
'einfach adj simple; easy; plain;
one-way (Br single) (ticket)
'Einfachheit f (-; no pl) simplicity
'einfädeln [-fɛːdəln] v/t (sep, -ge-, h)
thread; F start, set afoot; MOT merge
'einfahren (irr, **fahren**, sep, -ge-) **1.** v/t
(h) MOT run in; bring in (harvest); **2.**
v/i (sein) come in, RAIL a. pull in
'Einfahrt f entrance, way in
'Einfall m idea; MIL invasion
'einfallen v/i (irr, **fallen**, sep, -ge-, sein)
fall in; collapse; MUS join in; ~ **in** (acc)
MIL invade; **ihm fiel ein, dass** it came
to his mind that; **mir fällt nichts ein** I
have no ideas; **es fällt mir nicht ein** I
can't think of it; **dabei fällt mir ein** that
reminds me; **was fällt dir ein?** what's
the idea?
einfältig ['aɪnfɛltɪç] adj simple-minded;
stupid
Einfa'milienhaus n detached house
'einfarbig adj solid-colored, Br self-col-
oured

'ein|fassen v/t (sep, -ge-, h) border; ~**fet-
ten** v/t (sep, -ge-, h) grease; ~**finden**
v/refl (irr, **finden**, sep, -ge-, h) appear,
arrive; ~**flechten** fig v/t (irr, **flechten**,
sep, -ge-, h) work in; ~**fliegen** v/t (irr,
fliegen, sep, -ge-, h) fly in; ~**fließen**
v/i (irr, **fließen**, sep, -ge-, sein) fig et.
~ **lassen** slip s.th. in; ~**flößen** v/t (sep,
-ge-, h) pour (**j-m** into s.o.'s mouth); fig
fill with (awe etc)
'Einfluss m influence
'einflussreich adj influential
'einförmig [-fœrmɪç] adj uniform
'einfrieren (irr, **frieren**, sep, -ge-) **1.** v/i
(sein) freeze (in); **2.** v/t (h) freeze (a. fig)
'einfügen v/t (sep, -ge-, h) put in; fig insert; **sich ~** fit in; adjust (o.s.) (**in** acc
to); '**Einfügetaste** f EDP insert key
einfühlsam ['aɪnfyːlzaːm] adj sympathetic; '**Einfühlungsvermögen** n (-s;
no pl) empathy
Einfuhr ['aɪnfuːɐ] f (-; -en) ECON a) (no
pl) importation, b) import
'einführen v/t (sep, -ge-, h) introduce;
instal(l) s.t.: insert; ECON import
'Einfuhrstopp m ECON import ban
'Einführung f (-; -en) introduction
'Einführungs... in cpds ...kurs, ...preis
etc: introductory ...
'Eingabe f petition; EDP input; ~**taste** f
EDP enter or return key
'Eingang m entrance; ECON arrival; receipt; '**eingängig** adj catchy (tune etc)
'eingangs adv at the beginning
'eingeben v/t (irr, **geben**, sep, -ge-, h)
MED administer (dat to); EDP feed, enter
'eingebildet adj imaginary; conceited
(**auf** acc of)
'Eingeborene m, f (-n; -n) native
'Eingebung f (-; -en) inspiration; impulse
'eingefallen adj sunken, hollow
'eingefleischt adj confirmed
'eingehen (irr, **gehen**, sep, -ge-, sein) **1.**
v/i ECON come in, arrive; BOT, ZO die;
fabric: shrink; ~ **auf** (acc) agree to; go
into (detail); listen to s.o.; **2.** v/t enter
into (a contract etc); make (a bet);
take (a risk etc); ~**d** adj thorough; detailed
'eingemacht adj preserved
eingemeinden ['aɪngəmaɪndən] v/t (sep,
no -ge-, h) incorporate (**in** acc into)

E

'einge|nommen *adj* partial (**für** to); prejudiced (**gegen** against); **von sich ~** full of o.s.; **~schlossen** *adj* locked in; trapped; ECON included; **~schnappt** F *adj* in a huff; **~schrieben** *adj* registered; **~spielt** *adj*: (**gut**) *aufeinander ~ sein* work well together, be a good team; **~stellt** *adj*: **~ auf** (*acc*) prepared for; **~ gegen** opposed to

Eingeweide ['aingəvaidə] *pl* ANAT intestines, guts

'Eingeweihte *m, f* (-*n*; -*n*) insider

'eingewöhnen *v*|*refl* (*sep, no -ge-, h*) **sich ~ in** (*acc*) get used to, settle in

'eingießen *v*|*t* (*irr, gießen, sep, -ge-, h*) pour

'eingleisig [-glaizıç] *adj* single-track

'eingliedern *v*|*t* (*sep, -ge-, h*) integrate

'Eingliederung *f* integration

'ein|graben *v*|*t* (*irr, graben, sep, -ge-, h*) bury; **~gra,vieren** *v*|*t* (*sep, no -ge-, h*) engrave

'eingreifen *v*|*i* (*irr, greifen, sep, -ge-, h*) step in, interfere; **'Eingriff** *m* intervention, interference; MED operation

'einhaken *v*|*t* (*sep, -ge-, h*) hook in; **sich ~** link arms, take s.o.'s arm

'Einhalt *m*: **~ gebieten** (*dat* to); **'einhalten** *v*|*t* (*irr, halten, sep, -ge-, h*) keep

'einhängen (*sep, -ge-, h*) **1.** *v*|*t* hang in; TEL hang up (*receiver*); **sich ~ → einhaken; 2.** *v*|*i* TEL hang up

'einheimisch *adj* native, local; ECON home, domestic; **'Einheimische** *m, f* (-*n*; -*n*) local, native

'Einheit *f* (-; -*en*) unit; POL unity

'einheitlich *adj* uniform; homogeneous

'Einheits... *in cpds* ...*preis etc*: standard

'einhellig ['ainhɛlıç] *adj* unanimous

'einholen *v*|*t* (*sep, -ge-, h*) catch up with (*a. fig*); make up for *lost time*; make (*inquiries*) (*über acc* about); seek (*advice*) (*bei* from); ask for *permission etc*; strike (*sail*); **~ gehen** go shopping

'Einhorn *n* MYTH unicorn

'einhüllen *v*|*t* (*sep, -ge-, h*) wrap (up); *fig* shroud

'einig ['ainıç] *adj*: **sich ~ sein** agree; **sich nicht ~ sein** disagree, differ

'einige ['ainıgə] *indef pron* some, a few, several

'einigen ['ainıgən] *v*|*t* (*ge-, h*) **sich ~ über** (*acc*) agree on

'einigermaßen ['ainıgə'ma:sən] *adv* quite, fairly; not too bad

'einiges *indef pron* some, something; quite a lot

'Einigkeit *f* (-; *no pl*) unity; agreement

'Einigung *f* (-; -*en*) agreement, settlement; POL unification

'einjagen *v*|*t* (*sep, -ge-, h*) **j-m e-n Schrecken ~** give s.o. a fright, frighten *or* scare s.o.

'einjährig [-jɛːrıç] *adj* one-year-old; **~e Pflanze** annual

'einkalku,lieren *v*|*t* (*no -ge-, h*) take into account, allow for

'Einkauf *m* purchase; **Einkäufe machen → einkaufen 2; 'einkaufen** (*sep, -ge-, h*) **1.** *v*|*t* buy, ECON *a.* purchase; **2.** *v*|*i* go shopping

'Einkaufs... *in cpds* shopping ...; **~bummel** *m* shopping spree; **~preis** *m* ECON purchase price; **~wagen** *m* grocery *or* shopping cart, *Br* (supermarket) trolley; **~zentrum** *n* (shopping) mall, *Br* shopping centre

'ein|kehren *v*|*i* (*sep, -ge-, sein*) stop (*in dat* at); **~klammern** *v*|*t* (*sep, -ge-, h*) put in brackets

'Einklang *m* (-[*e*]*s*; *no pl*) MUS unison; *fig* harmony

'ein|kleiden *v*|*t* (*sep, -ge-, h*) clothe (*a. fig*); **~klemmen** *v*|*t* (*sep, -ge-, h*) squeeze, jam; **eingeklemmt sein** be stuck, be jammed; **~kochen** (*sep, -ge-*) **1.** *v*|*t* (*h*) preserve; **2.** *v*|*i* (*sein*) boil down

'Einkommen *n* (-*s*; -) income; **~steuererklärung** *f* income-tax return

'einkreisen *v*|*t* (*sep, -ge-, h*) encircle, surround

'Einkünfte ['ainkʏnftə] *pl* income

'einladen *v*|*t* (*irr, laden, sep, -ge-, h*) invite; load; **~d** *adj* inviting

'Einladung *f* (-; -*en*) invitation

'Einlage *f* (-; -*n*) ECON investment; MED arch support; THEA, MUS interlude

'Einlass *m* (-*es*; *no pl*) admission, admittance; **'einlassen** *v*|*t* (*irr, lassen, sep, -ge-, h*) let in; run (*a bath*); **sich ~ auf** (*acc*) get involved in; let o.s. in for; agree to; **sich mit j-m ~** get involved with s.o.

'Einlauf *m* SPORT finish; MED enema

'einlaufen (*irr, laufen, sep, -ge-*) **1.** *v*|*i* (*sein*) come in (*a.* SPORT); *water*: run in;

MAR enter port; *fabric:* shrink; **2.** v/t (h)
break *new shoes in;* **sich ~** warm up
'einleben v/refl (sep, -ge-, h) settle in
'einlegen v/t (sep, -ge-, h) put in; set
(*hair*); GASTR pickle; MOT change into
'Einlegesohle f insole
'einleiten v/t (sep, -ge-, h) start; introduce; MED induce; TECH dump,
discharge (*sewage*); **~d** adj introductory
'Einleitung f introduction
'ein|lenken v/i (sep, -ge-, h) come round;
~leuchten v/i (sep, -ge-, h) be evident,
be obvious; *das leuchtet mir (nicht)*
ein that makes (doesn't make) sense to
me; **~liefern** v/t (sep, -ge-, h) take (*ins*
Gefängnis to prison; *in die Klinik* to
[the] hospital); **~lösen** v/t (sep, -ge-,
h) redeem; cash (*check*); **~machen**
v/t (sep, -ge-, h) preserve
'einmal adv once; some *or* one day,
sometime; *auf ~* suddenly; at the same
time, at once; *noch ~* once more *or*
again; *noch ~ so ... (wie)* twice as ...
(as); *es war ~* once (upon a time) there
was; *haben Sie schon ~ ...?* have you
ever ...?; *schon ~ dort gewesen sein*
have been there before; *nicht ~* not
even
'Einmal... *in cpds* disposable ...
Einmal'eins n (-; no pl) multiplication
table
einmalig ['ainma:lıç] adj single; *fig*
unique; F fabulous
'Einmann... *in cpds* one-man ...
'Einmarsch m entry; MIL invasion
'einmar,schieren v/i (no -ge-, sein)
march in; **~ in** (acc) MIL invade
'einmischen v/refl (sep, -ge-, h) meddle
(*in* acc in, with), interfere (with)
'Einmündung f junction
einmütig [-my:tıç] adj unanimous
'Einmütigkeit f (-; no pl) unanimity
'Einnahmen ['ainna:mən] pl takings, re-
ceipts; 'einnehmen v/t (irr, nehmen,
sep, -ge-, h) take (a. MIL); earn, make;
'einnehmend adj engaging
'einnicken v/i (sep, -ge-, sein) doze off
'einnisten v/refl (sep, -ge-, h) *sich bei*
j-m ~ park o.s. on s.o.
'Einöde f (-; -n) desert, wilderness
'ein|ordnen v/t (sep, -ge-, h) put in its
proper place; file; *sich ~* MOT get in
lane; **~packen** v/t (sep, -ge-, h) pack

(up); wrap up; **~parken** v/t *and* v/i (sep,
-ge-, h) park (*between two cars*); **~pfer-**
chen v/t (sep, -ge-, h) pen in; coop up;
~pflanzen v/t (sep, -ge-, h) plant; *fig*
implant (a. MED); **~planen** v/t (sep,
-ge-, h) allow for; **~prägen** v/t (sep,
-ge-, h) impress; *sich et. ~* keep s.th. in
mind; memorize s.th.; **~quartieren** F
v/t (no -ge-, h) put s.o. up (*bei j-m* at
s.o.'s place); *sich ~ bei* (dat) move in
with; **~rahmen** v/t (sep, -ge-, h) frame;
~räumen v/t (sep, -ge-, h) put away;
furnish; *fig* grant, concede; **~reden**
(sep, -ge-, h) **1.** v/t: *j-m et. ~* talk s.o.
into (believing) s.th.; **2.** v/i: *auf j-n ~*
keep on at s.o.; **~reiben** v/t (irr, reiben,
sep, -ge-, h) rub; **~reichen** v/t (sep,
h) hand *or* send in; **~reihen** v/t (sep,
-ge-, h) place (among); *sich ~* take
one's place
'einreihig [-raiç] adj single-breasted
'Einreise f entry (a. *in cpds*)
'einreisen v/i (sep, -ge-, sein) enter (*in*
ein Land a country)
'ein|reißen (irr, reißen, sep, -ge-) **1.** v/t
(h) tear; pull down; **2.** v/i (sein) tear;
fig spread; **~renken** v/t (sep, -ge-, h)
MED set; *fig* straighten out
'einrichten v/t (sep, -ge-, h) furnish; establish; arrange; *sich ~* furnish one's
home; *sich ~ auf* (acc) prepare for; 'Einrichtung f (-; -en) furnishings; fittings;
TECH installation(s), facilities; institution, facility
'einrücken (sep, -ge-) **1.** v/i (sein) MIL
join the forces; march in; **2.** v/t (h)
PRINT indent
eins [ains] pron *and* adj one; one thing;
es ist alles ~ it's all the same (thing)
Eins f (-; -en) one; *grade:* excellent, A
einsam ['ainza:m] adj lonely, lonesome;
solitary; 'Einsamkeit f (-; no pl) loneliness; solitude
'einsammeln v/t (sep, -ge-, h) collect
'Einsatz m TECH inset, insert; stake(s)
(a. *fig*); MUS entry; *fig* effort(s), zeal;
use, employment; MIL action, mission;
deployment; *im ~* in action; *unter ~*
des Lebens at the risk of one's life
'einsatz|bereit adj ready for action;
~freudig adj dynamic, zealous
'einschalten v/t (sep, -ge-, h) ELECTR
switch *or* turn on; call s.o. in; *sich ~*
step in; 'Einschaltquote f TV rating

'ein|schärfen v/t (sep, -ge-, h) urge (j-m et. s.o. to do s.th.); ~schätzen v/t (sep, -ge-, h) estimate; judge; rate; **falsch ~** misjudge; ~schenken v/t (sep, -ge-, h) pour (out); ~schicken v/t (sep, -ge-, h) send in; ~schieben v/t (irr, schieben, sep, -ge-, h) slip in; insert; ~schlafen v/i (irr, schlafen, sep, -ge-, h) fall asleep, go to sleep; ~schläfern [-ʃlɛː-fən] v/t (sep, -ge-, h) put to sleep

einschl. ABBR of **einschließlich** incl., including

'Einschlag m strike, impact; fig touch

'einschlagen v/i (irr, schlagen, sep, -ge-, h) **1.** v/t knock in (or out); break (in), smash; wrap up; take (road etc); turn (wheels); → **Laufbahn**; **2.** v/i lightning etc: strike; fig be a success

'einschlägig [-ʃlɛːɡɪç] adj relevant

'ein|schleusen fig v/t (sep, -ge-, h) infiltrate (**in** acc into); ~schließen v/t (irr, schließen, sep, -ge-, h) lock in or up; enclose; MIL surround, encircle; fig include; ~schließlich prp (gen) including, ... included; ~ included; ~schmeicheln v/refl (sep, -ge-, h) **sich ~ bei** ingratiate o.s. with; ~schnappen v/i (sep, -ge-, sein) snap shut; fig go into a huff; → **eingeschnappt**

'einschneidend fig adj drastic; far-reaching; 'Einschnitt m cut; notch; fig break

'einschränken v/t (sep, -ge-, h) restrict, reduce (both: **auf** acc to); cut down on; **sich ~** economize; 'Einschränkung f (-; -en) restriction, reduction, cut; **ohne ~** without reservation

'Einschreibebrief m registered letter

'einschreiben v/t (irr, schreiben, sep, -ge-, h) enter; book; enrol(l) (a. MIL); (**sich**) **~ lassen** enrol(l) (o.s.) (for)

'einschreiten fig v/i (irr, schreiten, sep, -ge-, sein) step in, intervene; **~ (gegen)** take (legal) measures (against)

'einschüchtern v/t (sep, -ge-, h) intimidate; bully; 'Einschüchterung f (-; -en) intimidation

'einschulen v/t (sep, -ge-, h) **eingeschult werden** start school

'Einschuss m bullet hole

'einschweißen v/t (sep, -ge-, h) shrink--wrap

'einsegnen v/t (sep, -ge-, h) REL conse-

crate; confirm; 'Einsegnung f (-; -en) REL consecration; confirmation

'einsehen v/t (irr, sehen, sep, -ge-, h) see, realize; **das sehe ich nicht ein!** I don't see why!; 'Einsehen n: **ein ~ haben** show some understanding

'einseifen v/t (sep, -ge-, h) soap; lather; F fig **j-n ~** take s.o. for a ride

'einseitig [-zaɪtɪç] adj one-sided; MED, POL, JUR unilateral

'ein|senden v/t (irr, senden,] sep, -ge-, h) send in; 'Einsendeschluss m closing date (for entries)

'einsetzen (sep, -ge-, h) **1.** v/t put in, insert; appoint; use, employ; TECH put into service; ECON invest, stake; bet; risk; **sich ~** try hard, make an effort; **sich ~ für** stand up for; **2.** v/i set in, start

'Einsicht f (-; -en) a) insight, b) (no pl) understanding; **zur ~ kommen** listen to reason; **~ nehmen in** (acc) take a look at; 'einsichtig adj understanding; reasonable

'Einsiedler m (-s; -) hermit

'einsilbig [-zɪlbɪç] adj monosyllabic; fig taciturn

'ein|spannen v/t (sep, -ge-, h) harness; TECH clamp, fix; F rope s.o. in; ~sparen v/t (sep, -ge-, h) save, economize on; ~sperren v/t (sep, -ge-, h) lock or shut up; ~spielen v/t (sep, -ge-, h) bring in; **sich ~** warm up; fig get going; → **eingespielt**

'Einspielergebnisse pl film: box-office returns

'einspringen v/i (irr, springen, sep, -ge-, sein) **für j-n ~** take s.o.'s place

'Einspritz... in cpds MOT fuel-injection

'Einspruch m objection (a. JUR), protest; POL veto; appeal

'einspurig [-ʃpuːrɪç] adj RAIL single--track; MOT single-lane

einst [aɪnst] adv once, at one time

'Einstand m start; tennis: deuce

'ein|stecken v/t (sep, -ge-, h) pocket (a. fig); ELECTR plug in; mail, post; fig take; ~stehen v/i (irr, stehen, sep, -ge-, h) **~ für** stand up for; ~steigen v/i (irr, steigen, sep, -ge-, sein) get in; get on (bus etc); **alles ~!** RAIL all aboard!; ~stellen v/t (sep, -ge-, h) engage, employ, hire; give up; stop; SPORT equal; TECH adjust (**auf** acc to); radio:

tune in (to); OPT, PHOT focus (on); *die Arbeit ~* (go on) strike, walk out; *das Feuer ~* MIL cease fire; *sich ~ auf* (*acc*) adjust to; be prepared for

'Einstellung *f* attitude (*zu* towards); employment; cessation; TECH adjustment; OPT, PHOT focus(s)ing; *film*: take

'Einstellungsgespräch *n* interview

Einstieg ['ainʃtiːk] *m* (-[e]*s*; -e) entrance, entry (*a*. POL, ECON)

'Einstiegsdroge *f* gateway drug

einstig ['ainstɪç] *adj* former, one-time

'einstimmen *v/i* (*sep*, *-ge-*, *h*) MUS join in

'einstimmig [-ʃtɪmɪç] *adj* unanimous

'einstöckig [-ʃtœkɪç] *adj* one-storied, *Br* one-storey(ed)

'ein|stu,dieren *v/t* (*no -ge-*, *h*) THEA rehearse; **~stufen** *v/t* (*sep*, *-ge-*, *h*) grade, rate

'Einstufungsprüfung *f* placement test

'einstufig [-ʃtuːfɪç] *adj* single-stage

'Einsturz *m*, 'einstürzen *v/i* (*sep*, *-ge-*, *sein*) collapse

'einst'weilen *adv* for the present

'einstweilig [-vailɪç] *adj* temporary

'ein|tauschen *v/t* (*sep*, *-ge-*, *h*) exchange (*gegen* for); **~teilen** *v/t* (*sep*, *-ge-*, *h*) divide (*in acc* into); organize

'einteilig [-tailɪç] *adj* one-piece

'Einteilung *f* (-; -*en*) division; organization; arrangement

'eintönig [-tøːnɪç] *adj* monotonous

'Eintönigkeit *f* (-; *no pl*) monotony

'Eintopf *m* GASTR stew

'Eintracht *f* (-; *no pl*) harmony, unity

'einträchtig *adj* harmonious, peaceful

Eintrag ['aintraːk] *m* (-[e]*s*; *Einträge* ['aintrɛːgə]) entry (*a*. ECON), registration; 'eintragen *v/t* (*irr, tragen, sep, -ge-, h*) enter (*in acc* in); register (*bei* with); enrol(l) (with); *fig* earn; *sich ~* register, *hotel*: a. check in

einträglich ['aintrɛːklɪç] *adj* profitable

'ein|treffen *v/i* (*irr, treffen, sep, -ge-, sein*) arrive; happen; come true; **~trei-ben** *fig v/t* (*irr, treiben, sep, -ge-, h*) collect; **~treten** (*irr, treten, sep, -ge-*) **1.** *v/i* (*sein*) enter; happen, take place; *~ für* stand up for, support; *~ in* (*acc*) join (*club etc*); **2.** *v/t* (*h*) kick in (*door etc*); *sich et. ~* run s.th. into one's foot

'Eintritt *m* entry; admission; *~ frei!* admission free!; *~ verboten!* keep out!

'Eintritts|geld *n* entrance *or* admission (fee); **~karte** *f* (admission) ticket

'einüben *v/t* (*sep*, *-ge-*, *h*) practise; rehearse

'einverstanden *adj*: *~ sein* agree (*mit* to); *~!* agreed!; 'Einverständnis *n* (-*ses*; *no pl*) agreement

Einwand ['ainvant] *m* (-[e]*s*; *Einwände* ['ainvɛndə]) objection (*gegen* to)

'Einwanderer *m*, 'Einwanderin *f* immigrant; 'einwandern *v/i* (*sep*, *-ge-*, *sein*) immigrate; 'Einwanderung *f* immigration

'einwandfrei *adj* perfect, faultless

einwärts ['ainvɛrts] *adv* inward(s)

'Einweg... *...rasierer, ...spritze etc*: disposable; **~flasche** *f* non-returnable bottle; **~packung** *f* throwaway pack

'einweichen *v/t* (*sep*, *-ge-*, *h*) soak

'einweihen *v/t* (*sep*, *-ge-*, *h*) dedicate, *Br* inaugurate; *j-n ~ in* (*acc*) F let s.o. in on; 'Einweihung *f* (-; *-en*) dedication, *Br* inauguration

'einweisen *v/t* (*irr, weisen, sep, -ge-, h*) *j-n ~ in* (*acc*) send (*esp* JUR commit) s.o. to; instruct s.o. in, brief s.o. on

'einwenden *v/t* (*irr, wenden,*] *sep*, *-ge-*, *h*) object (*gegen* to)

'Einwendung *f* (-; *-en*) objection

'einwerfen *v/t* (*irr, werfen, sep, -ge-, h*) throw in (*a. fig, SPORT a. v/i*); break (*window*); mail, *Br* post; insert (*coin*)

'einwickeln *v/t* (*sep*, *-ge-*, *h*) wrap (up); F take *s.o.* in

'Einwickelpa,pier *n* wrapping-paper

einwilligen ['ainvilɪgən] *v/i* (*sep*, *-ge-*, *h*) consent (*in acc* to), agree (to)

'Einwilligung *f* (-; *-en*) consent (*in acc* to), agreement

'einwirken *v/i* (*sep*, *-ge-*, *h*) *~ auf* (*acc*) act (up)on; *fig* work on *s.o.*

'Einwirkung *f* effect, influence

Einwohner ['ainvoːnɐ] *m* (-*s*; -), 'Einwohnerin *f* (-; *-nen*) inhabitant; 'Einwohnermeldeamt *n* registration office

'Einwurf *m* slot; SPORT throw-in

'Einzahl *f* (-; *no pl*) LING singular

'einzahlen *v/t* (*sep*, *-ge-*, *h*) pay in

'Einzahlung *f* payment, deposit

einzäunen ['aintsɔynən] *v/t* (*sep*, *-ge-*, *h*) fence in

Einzel ['aintsəl] *n* (-*s*; -) *tennis*: singles

'Einzel... *in cpds ...bett, ...zimmer etc*: single ...; **~fall** *m* special case; **~gänger**

[-gɛɳɐ] m (-s; -) F loner; **~haft** f solitary confinement; **~handel** m retail trade; **~händler** m retailer; **~haus** n detached house

'**Einzelheit** f (-; -en) detail

'**einzeln** adj single; odd (shoe etc); **Einzelne** pl several, some; **der Einzelne** the individual; **~ eintreten** enter one at a time; **~ angeben** specify; **im Einzelnen** in detail; **jeder Einzelne** each and every one

'**einziehen** (irr, ziehen, sep, -ge-) **1.** v/t (h) draw in; esp TECH retract; duck; strike (sail etc); MIL draft, Br call up; confiscate; withdraw (license etc); make (inquiries); **2.** v/i (sein) move in; march in; soak in

einzig ['aintsɪç] adj only; single; **kein Einziger ...** not a single ...; **das Einzige** the only thing; **der (die) Einzige** the only one; **~artig** adj unique, singular

'**Einzug** m moving in; entry

Eis [ais] n (-es; no pl) ice; GASTR ice cream; **~ am Stiel** ice lolly; **~bahn** f skating rink; **~bär** m ZO polar bear; **~becher** m sundae; **~bein** n GASTR (pickled) pork knuckles; **~berg** m iceberg; **~brecher** m (-s; -) MAR icebreaker; **~diele** f ice-cream parlo(u)r

Eisen ['aizən] n (-s; -) iron

'**Eisenbahn** f railroad, Br railway; train set; '**Eisenbahner** [-baːnɐ] m (-s; -) railroadman, Br railwayman

'**Eisenbahnwagen** m (railroad) car, Br coach, railway carriage

'**Eisen|erz** n iron ore; **~gießerei** f iron foundry; **~hütte** f TECH ironworks

'**Eisenwaren** pl hardware, ironware; **~handlung** f hardware store, Br ironmonger's

eisern ['aizɐn] adj iron (a. fig), of iron

'**eisgekühlt** adj iced

'**Eishockey** n hockey, Br ice hockey

eisig ['aizɪç] adj icy (a. fig)

'**eis|kalt** adj ice-cold

'**Eiskunst|lauf** m (-[e]s; no pl) figure skating; **~läufer(in)** figure skater

'**Eis|meer** n polar sea; **~re,vue** f ice show; **~schnelllauf** m speed skating; **~scholle** f ice floe; **~verkäufer** m iceman; **~würfel** m ice cube; **~zapfen** m icicle; **~zeit** f (-; no pl) GEOL ice age

eitel ['aitəl] adj vain; '**Eitelkeit** f (-; no pl) vanity

Eiter ['aitɐ] m (-s; no pl) MED pus

'**Eiterbeule** f MED abscess, boil

'**eitern** v/i (ge-, h) MED fester

eitrig ['aitrɪç] adj MED purulent, festering

'**Eiweiß** n (-es; no pl) white of egg; BIOL protein

'**eiweiß|arm** adj low in protein, low-protein; **~reich** adj rich in protein, high-protein

'**Eizelle** f BIOL egg cell, ovum

Ekel ['eːkəl] **1.** m (-s; no pl) disgust (vor dat at), loathing (for); **~ erregend →** **ekelhaft**; **2.** F n (-s; -) beast

'**ekelhaft**, '**ek(e)lig** adj sickening, disgusting, repulsive

'**ekeln** v/refl and v/impers (ge-, h) **ich ekle mich davor** it makes me sick

Ekstase [ɛk'staːzə] f (-; -n) ecstasy

Elan [e'laːn] m (-s; no pl) vigo(u)r

elastisch [e'lastɪʃ] adj elastic, flexible

Elch [ɛlç] m (-[e]s; -e) ZO elk; moose

Elefant [ele'fant] m (-en; -en) ZO elephant; **Ele'fantenhochzeit** F f ECON jumbo merger

elegant [ele'gant] adj elegant

Eleganz [ele'gants] f (-; no pl) elegance

Elektriker [e'lɛktrikɐ] m (-s; -) electrician; **elektrisch** [e'lɛktrɪʃ] adj electrical; electric; **elektrisieren** [elɛktri'ziːrən] v/t (no -ge-, h) electrify

Elektrizität [elɛktritsi'tɛːt] f (-; no pl) electricity; **Elektrizi'tätswerk** n (electric) power station

Elektrogerät [e'lɛktro-] n electric appliance

Elektronik [elɛk'troːnɪk] f electronics; electronic system; **elektronisch** [elɛk'troːnɪʃ] adj electronic

E'lektrora,sierer m (-s; -) electric razor

Elektro|technik [e'lɛktro-] f electrical engineering; **~'techniker** m electrical engineer

Element [ele'mɛnt] n (-[e]s; -e) element

elementar [elemɛn'taːr] adj elementary

elend ['eːlɛnt] adj miserable

'**Elend** n (-s; no pl) misery

'**Elendsviertel** n slums

elf [ɛlf] adj eleven

Elf f (-; -en) eleven; soccer: team

Elfe ['ɛlfə] f (-; -n) elf, fairy

'**Elfenbein** n ivory

Elf'meter m (-s; -) soccer: penalty; **~punkt** m penalty spot; **~schießen** n penalty shoot-out

energisch

'elfte *adj* eleventh

Elite [e'li:tə] *f* (-; *-n*) elite

Ellbogen ['ɛl-] *m* ANAT elbow

Elster ['ɛlstə] *f* (-; *-n*) ZO magpie

elterlich ['ɛltəlɪç] *adj* parental

Eltern ['ɛltən] *pl* parents

'Elternhaus *n* (one's parents') home

'elternlos *adj* orphan(ed)

'Eltern|teil *m* parent; **~vertretung** *f* appr Parent-Teacher Association

Email [e'mai] *n* (-s; -s), Emaille [e'maljə] *f* (-; *-n*) enamel

Emanze [e'mantsə] F *f* (-; *-n*) women's libber; **Emanzipation** [emantsipa'tsjoːn] *f* (-; *-en*) emancipation; women's lib(eration); **emanzipieren** [emantsi'piːrən] *v/refl* (*no -ge-, h*) become emancipated

Embargo [ɛm'bargo] *n* (-s; -s) ECON embargo

Embolie [ɛmbo'liː] *f* (-; *-n*) MED embolism

Embryo ['ɛmbryo] *m* (-s; -en [ɛmbry'oːnən]) BIOL embryo

Emigrant [emi'grant] *m* (-en; -en), Emi'grantin *f* (-; *-nen*) emigrant, *esp* POL refugee; **Emigration** [emigra'tsjoːn] *f* (-; *-en*) emigration; **in der ~** in exile; **emigrieren** [emi'griːrən] *v/i* (*no -ge-, sein*) emigrate

Emission [emi'sjoːn] *f* (-; *-en*) PHYS emission; ECON issue

empfahl [ɛm'pfaːl] *pret of* **empfehlen**

Empfang [ɛm'pfaŋ] *m* (-[e]s; Empfänge [ɛm'pfɛŋə]) reception (*a*. radio, hotel), welcome; receipt (**nach, bei** on)

emp'fangen *v/t* (*irr, fangen, no -ge-, h*) receive; welcome; **Emp'fänger(in)** (-s; -/-; *-nen*) receiver (*m a*. radio); addressee

emp'fänglich *adj* susceptible (**für** to)

Empfängnis [ɛm'pfɛŋnɪs] *f* (-; *no pl*) MED conception; **~verhütung** *f* MED contraception, birth control

Emp'fangs|bescheinigung *f* receipt; **~dame** *f* receptionist

empfehlen [ɛm'pfeːlən] *v/t* (*irr, no -ge-, h*) recommend; **emp'fehlenswert** *adj* advisable; **Emp'fehlung** *f* (-; *-en*) recommendation

empfinden [ɛm'pfɪndən] *v/t* (*irr, finden, no -ge-, h*) feel (**als** ... to be ...); **empfindlich** [ɛm'pfɪntlɪç] *adj* sensitive (**für, gegen** to) (*a*. PHOT, CHEM); tender; delicate; touchy; irritable (*a*. MED); severe (*punishment etc*); **~e Stelle** sore spot

Emp'findlichkeit *f* (-; *-en*) sensitivity; PHOT speed; delicacy; touchiness

empfindsam [ɛm'pfɪntzaːm] *adj* sensitive

Emp'findung *f* (-; *-en*) sensation; perception; feeling, emotion

empfohlen [ɛm'pfoːlən] *pp of* **empfehlen**

empor [ɛm'poːr] *adv* up, upward(s)

empören [ɛm'pøːrən] *v/t* (*no -ge-, h*) outrage; shock; **sich ~ (über** acc) be outraged *or* shocked (at); **~d** *adj* shocking, outrageous

Em'pörkömmling [-kœmlɪŋ] *contp m* (-s; -e) upstart

empört [ɛm'pøːrt] *adj* indignant (**über** acc at), shocked (at); **Em'pörung** *f* (-; *no pl*) indignation

emsig ['ɛmzɪç] *adj* busy; **'Emsigkeit** *f* (-; *no pl*) activity

Ende ['ɛndə] *n* (-s; *no pl*) end; *film*: ending; **am ~** at the end; in the end, finally; **zu ~** over; *time*: up; **zu ~ gehen** come to an end; **zu ~ lesen** finish reading; **er ist ~ zwanzig** he is in his late twenties; **~ Mai** at the end of May; **~ der achtziger Jahre** in the late eighties; *radio*: **~!** over!; **'enden** *v/i* (*ge-, h*) (come to an) end; stop; finish; F **~ als** end up as

'Endergebnis *n* final result

'endgültig *adj* final, definitive

Endlagerung ['ɛnt-] *f* final disposal (*of radioactive waste*)

'endlich *adv* finally, at last

'endlos *adj* endless

'End|runde *f*, **~spiel** *n* SPORT final(s); **~spurt** *m* SPORT final spurt (*a*. fig); **~stati,on** *f* RAIL terminus, terminal; **~summe** *f* (sum) total

'Endung *f* (-; *-en*) LING ending

Energie [enɛr'giː] *f* (-; *-n*) energy; TECH, ELECTR power

ener'giebewusst *adj* energy-conscious

Ener'giekrise *f* energy crisis

ener'gielos *adj* lacking in energy

Ener'gie|quelle *f* source of energy; **~sparen** *n* energy saving, conservation of energy; **~versorgung** *f* power supply

energisch [e'nɛrgɪʃ] *adj* energetic, vigorous

eng [εŋ] *adj* narrow; tight; cramped; *fig* close; **~ beieinander** close(ly) together

Engagement [ãgaʒə'mãː] *n* (-s; -s) THEA *etc* engagement; POL commitment; **engagieren** [ãga'ʒiːrən] *v/t* (*no* -ge-, h) engage; **sich ~ für** be very involved in; **engagiert** [ãga'ʒiːɐt] *adj* involved, committed

Enge ['εŋə] *f* (-; *no pl*) narrowness; cramped conditions; **in die ~ treiben** drive into a corner

Engel ['εŋəl] *m* (-s; -) angel

'**England** England; **Engländer** ['εŋlεndɐ] *m* (-s; -) Englishman; **die ~** *pl* the English; **Engländerin** ['εŋlεndərin] *f* (-; *-nen*) Englishwoman

'**englisch** *adj* English; **auf Englisch** in English

'**Englischunterricht** *m* English lesson(s) *or* class(es); teaching of English

'**Engpass** *m* bottleneck (*a. fig*)

'**engstirnig** [-ʃtɪrnɪç] *adj* narrow-minded

Enkel ['εŋkəl] *m* (-s; -) grandchild; grandson

'**Enkelin** *f* (-; *-nen*) granddaughter

enorm [e'nɔrm] *adj* enormous; F terrific

Ensemble [ã'sãːbl] *n* (-s; -s) THEA company; cast

entarten [εnt'ʔaːrtən] *v/i* (*no* -ge-, sein), **ent'artet** *adj* degenerate; **Ent'artung** *f* (-; *-en*) degeneration

entbehren [εnt'beːrən] *v/t* (*no* -ge-, h) do without; spare; miss; **entbehrlich** [εnt'beːrlɪç] *adj* dispensable; superfluous; **Ent'behrung** *f* (-; *-en*) want, privation

ent'binden (*irr, binden, no* -ge-, h) **1.** *f* MED have the baby; **2.** *v/t*: **j-n ~ von** *fig* relieve s.o. of; **entbunden werden von** MED give birth to

Ent'bindung *f* (-; *-en*) MED delivery

Ent'bindungsstati,on *f* MED maternity ward

entblößen [εnt'bløːsən] *v/t* (*no* -ge-, h) bare, uncover

ent'decken *v/t* (*no* -ge-, h) discover

Ent'decker *m* (-s; -), **Ent'deckerin** *f* (-; *-nen*) discoverer

Ent'deckung *f* (-; *-en*) discovery

Ente ['εntə] *f* (-; *-n*) ZO duck; F *fig* hoax

ent'ehren *v/t* (*no* -ge-, h) dishono(u)r

enteignen [εnt'ʔaɪgnən] *v/t* (*no* -ge-, h)

expropriate; dispossess *s.o.*

Ent'eignung *f* (-; *-en*) expropriation; dispossession

ent'erben *v/t* (*no* -ge-, h) disinherit

entern ['εntɐn] *v/t* (*ge-*, h) MAR board

ent'fachen [εnt'faxən] *v/t* (*no* -ge-, h) kindle, *fig a.* rouse; **~fallen** *v/i* (*irr, fallen, no* -ge-, sein) be cancelled; **~ auf** (*acc*) fall to s.o. ('s share); **es ist mir ~** it has slipped my memory; **~falten** *v/t* (*no* -ge-, h) unfold; *fig* develop; **sich ~** unfold; *fig* develop (**zu** into)

entfernen [εnt'fεrnən] *v/t* (*no* -ge-, h) remove (*a. fig*); **sich ~** leave; **ent'fernt** *adj* distant (*a. fig*); **weit** (**zehn Meilen**) **~** far (10 miles) away; **Ent'fernung** *f* (-; *-en*) distance; removal

Ent'fernungsmesser *m* (-s; -) PHOT range finder

ent'flammbar *adj* (in)flammable

entfremden [εnt'frεmdən] *v/t* (*no* -ge-, h) estrange (*dat* from); **Ent'fremdung** *f* (-; *-en*) estrangement, alienation

ent'führen *v/t* (*no* -ge-, h) kidnap; AVIAT hijack; **Ent'führer** *m* (-s; -) kidnapper; AVIAT hijacker; **Ent'führung** *f* (-; *-en*) kidnapping; AVIAT hijacking

ent'gegen *prp* (*dat*) *and adv* contrary to; toward(s); **~gehen** *v/i* (*irr, gehen, sep, -ge-, sein*) go to meet

ent'gegengesetzt *adj* opposite

ent'gegenkommen *v/i* (*irr, kommen, sep, -ge-, sein*) come to meet; *fig* **j-m ~** meet s.o. halfway; **~d** *fig adj* obliging

ent'gegennehmen *v/t* (*irr, nehmen, sep, -ge-, h*) accept, receive; **~sehen** *v/i* (*irr, sehen, sep, -ge-, h*) await; look forward to *s.th.*; **~setzen** *v/t* (*sep, -ge-, h*) **j-m Widerstand ~** put up resistance to s.o.; **~treten** *v/i* (*irr, treten, sep, -ge-, sein*) walk towards; oppose; face

entgegnen [εnt'geːgnən] *v/i* (*no* -ge-, h) reply, answer; retort

Ent'gegnung *f* (-; *-en*) reply; retort

ent'gehen *v/i* (*irr, gehen, no* -ge-, sein) escape; miss

entgeistert [εnt'gaɪstɐt] *adj* aghast

Entgelt [εnt'gεlt] *n* (-[e]s; -e) remuneration; fee

ent'giften [εnt'gɪftən] *v/t* (*no* -ge-, h) decontaminate; **~gleisen** [εnt'glaɪzən] *v/i* (*no* -ge-, sein) RAIL be derailed; *fig* blunder; **~'gleiten** *fig v/i* (*irr, gleiten, no* -ge-, sein) get out of control; **~grä-**

ten [ɛnt'grɛ:tən] *v/t (no -ge-, h)* bone, fil(l)et

ent'halten *v/t (irr, halten, no -ge-, h)* contain, hold; include; **sich ~** *(gen)* abstain *or* refrain from; **ent'haltsam** *adj* abstinent; moderate; **Ent'haltsamkeit** *f (-; no pl)* abstinence; moderation

Ent'haltung *f (-; -en)* abstention

ent'härten *v/t (no -ge-, h)* soften

enthaupten [ɛnt'hauptən] *v/t (no -ge-, h)* behead, decapitate

ent'hüllen *v/t (no -ge-, h)* uncover; unveil; *fig* reveal, disclose; **Ent'hüllung** *f (-; -en)* unveiling; *fig* revelation, disclosure

Enthusiasmus [ɛntu'zjasmus] *m (-; no pl)* enthusiasm; **Enthusiast(in)** [-'zjast (-ɪn)] *(-en, -en/-; -nen)* enthusiast; *film,* SPORT F fan; **enthusi'astisch** *adj* enthusiastic

ent|'kleiden *v/t and v/refl (no -ge-, h)* undress, strip; **~'kommen** *v/i (irr, kommen, no -ge-, sein)* escape *(dat* from); **~'korken** *v/t (no -ge-, h)* uncork

entkräften [ɛnt'krɛftən] *v/t (no -ge-, h)* weaken *(a. fig)*; **Ent'kräftung** *f (-; -en)* weakening, exhaustion

ent'laden *v/t (irr, laden, no -ge-, h)* unload; *esp* ELECTR discharge; **sich ~** *esp* ELECTR discharge; *fig* explode

Ent'ladung *f (-; -en)* unloading; *esp* ELECTR discharge; *fig* explosion

ent'lang *prp (dat) and adv* along; **hier ~, bitte!** this way, please!; **die Straße** *etc* **~** along the street *etc*

entlarven [ɛnt'larfən] *v/t (no -ge-, h)* unmask, expose

ent'lassen *v/t (irr, lassen, no -ge-, h)* dismiss, F fire, give *s.o.* the sack; MED discharge; JUR release

Ent'lassung *f (-; -en)* dismissal; MED discharge; JUR release

ent'lasten *v/t (no -ge-, h)* relieve *s.o.* of some of his work; clear *s.o.* of a charge; **den Verkehr ~** relieve the traffic congestion; **Ent'lastung** *f (-; -en)* relief; JUR exoneration

Ent'lastungszeuge *m* JUR witness for the defense *(Br* defence)

ent'laufen *v/i (irr, laufen, no -ge-, sein)* run away *(dat* from)

ent'legen *adj* remote, distant

ent|'locken *v/t (no -ge-, h)* draw, elicit *(dat* from); **~'lohnen** *v/t (no -ge-, h)*

pay (off); **~'lüften** *v/t (no -ge-, h)* ventilate; **~machten** [ɛnt'maxtən] *v/t (no -ge-, h)* deprive *s.o.* of his power; **~militarisieren** [ɛntmilitari'zi:rən] *v/t (no -ge-, h)* demilitarize; **~mündigen** [ɛnt'myndɪgən] *v/t (no -ge-, h)* JUR place under disability; **~mutigen** [ɛnt'mu:tɪgən] *v/t (no -ge-, h)* discourage; **~nehmen** *v/t (irr, nehmen, no -ge-, h)* take *(dat* from); **~ aus** (with-) draw from; *fig* gather *or* learn from; **~'puppen** *v/refl (no -ge-, h)* **sich ~ als** turn out to be; **~'rahmen** *v/t (no -ge-, h)* skim; **~'reißen** *v/t (irr, reißen, no -ge-, h)* snatch (away) *(dat* from); **~'rinnen** *v/i (irr, rinnen, no -ge-, sein)* escape *(dat* from); **~'rollen** *v/t (no -ge-, h)* unroll

ent'rüsten *v/t (no -ge-, h)* fill with indignation; **sich ~** become indignant *(über acc* at *s.th.,* with *s.o.)*; **ent'rüstet** *adj* indignant *(über acc* at *s.th.,* with *s.o.)*; **Ent'rüstung** *f (-; -en)* indignation

Entsafter [ɛnt'zaftə] *m (-s; -)* juice extractor

ent'salzen *v/t (no -ge-, h)* desalinize

ent'schädigen *v/t (no -ge-, h)* compensate; **Ent'schädigung** *f (-; -en)* compensation

ent'schärfen *v/t (no -ge-, h)* defuse *(a. fig)*

ent'scheiden *v/t and v/i and v/refl (irr, scheiden, no -ge-, h)* decide *(für* on, in favo[u]r of; *gegen* against); settle; **er kann sich nicht ~** he can't make up his mind; **~d** *adj* decisive; crucial

Ent'scheidung *f (-; -en)* decision

entschieden [ɛnt'ʃi:dən] *adj* decided, determined, resolute; **~ dafür** strongly in favo(u)r of it; **Ent'schiedenheit** *f (-; no pl)* determination

ent'schließen *v/refl (irr, schließen, no -ge-, h)* decide, determine, make up one's mind; **Ent'schließung** *f (-; -en)* POL resolution

entschlossen [ɛnt'ʃlɔsən] *adj* determined, resolute; **Ent'schlossenheit** *f (-; no pl)* determination, resoluteness

Ent'schluss *m* decision, resolution

entschlüsseln [ɛnt'ʃlʏsəln] *v/t (no -ge-, h)* decipher, decode

entschuldigen [ɛnt'ʃuldɪgən] *v/t (no -ge-, h)* excuse; **sich ~** apologize *(bei* to; *für* for); excuse o.s.; **~ Sie!** (I'm) sorry!; excuse me!; **Ent'schuldigung** f (-; -en) excuse; apology; **um ~ bitten** apologize; **~!** (I'm) sorry!; excuse me!

ent'setzen v/t (no -ge-, h) shock; horrify; **Ent'setzen** n (-s; no pl) horror, terror; **ent'setzlich** adj horrible, dreadful, terrible; atrocious; **ent'setzt** adj shocked; horrified

ent'sichern v/t (no -ge-, h) release the safety catch of; **~'sinnen** v/refl (irr, **sinnen**, no -ge-, h) remember, recall

ent'sorgen v/t (no -ge-, h) dispose of

Ent'sorgung f (-; -en) (waste) disposal

ent'spannen v/t and v/refl (no -ge-, h) relax; **sich ~** a. take it easy; fig ease (up); **ent'spannt** adj relaxed

Ent'spannung f (-; -en) relaxation; POL détente

ent'spiegelt adj OPT non-glare

ent'sprechen v/i (irr, **sprechen**, no -ge-, h) correspond to; answer to a description; meet (requirements etc); **~d** adj corresponding (dat to); appropriate

Ent'sprechung f (-; -en) equivalent

ent'springen v/i (irr, **springen**, no -ge-, sein) river: rise

entstehen v/i (irr, **stehen**, no -ge-, sein) come into being; arise; emerge, develop; **~ aus** originate from

Ent'stehung f (-; -en) origin

ent'stellen v/t (no -ge-, h) disfigure, deform; fig distort; **Ent'stellung** f (-; -en) disfigurement, deformation, distortion (a. fig)

entstört [ɛnt'ʃtøːɐt] adj ELECTR interference-free

ent'täuschen v/t (no -ge-, h) disappoint; **Ent'täuschung** f (-; -en) disappointment

entwaffnen [ɛnt'vafnən] v/t (no -ge-, h) disarm

Ent'warnung f all clear (signal)

ent'wässern v/t (no -ge-, h) drain; **Ent'wässerung** f (-; -en) drainage; CHEM dehydration

'entweder cj: **~ ... oder** either ... or

ent'weichen v/i (irr, **weichen**, no -ge-, sein) escape (aus from); **~'weihen** v/t (no -ge-, h) desecrate; **~'wenden** v/t (no -ge-, h) pilfer, steal; **~'werfen** v/t (irr, **werfen**, no -ge-, h) design; draw up

ent'werten v/t (no -ge-, h) lower the value of (a. fig); cancel; **Ent'wertung** f (-; -en) devaluation; cancellation

ent'wickeln v/t and v/refl (no -ge-, h) develop (a. PHOT) (**zu** into); **Ent'wicklung** f (-; -en) development, BIOL a. evolution; adolescence, age of puberty

Ent'wicklungs|helfer m, **~helferin** f POL, ECON development aid volunteer; Peace Corps volunteer; Br VSO worker; **~hilfe** f development aid; **~land** n POL developing country

ent'wirren [ɛnt'vɪrən] v/t (no -ge-, h) disentangle (a. fig); **~'wischen** v/i (no -ge-, sein) get away

ent'würdigend adj degrading

Ent'wurf m outline, (rough) draft, plan; design; sketch

ent'wurzeln v/t (no -ge-, h) uproot; **~'ziehen** v/t (irr, **ziehen**, no -ge-, h) take away (dat from); revoke (license etc); deprive of rights etc; CHEM extract; **sich j-m (e-r Sache) ~** evade s.o. (s.th.)

Ent'ziehungs|anstalt f (Br drug) abuse clinic; **~kur** f detoxi(fi)cation (treatment), a. F drying out

entziffern [ɛnt'tsɪfɐn] v/t (no -ge-, h) decipher, make out

ent'zücken v/t (no -ge-, h) charm, delight; **Ent'zücken** n (-s; no pl) delight; **ent'zückend** adj delightful, charming, F sweet; **ent'zückt** adj delighted (**über** acc, **von** at, with)

Ent'zug m withdrawal; revocation

Ent'zugserscheinung f MED withdrawal symptom

entzündbar [ɛnt'tsʏntbaːɐ] adj (in-)flammable; **ent'zünden** v/refl (no -ge-, h) catch fire; MED become inflamed; **Ent'zündung** f (-; -en) MED inflammation

ent'zwei adv in two, to pieces

Enzyklopädie [ɛntsyklopɛ'diː] f (-; -n) encyclop(a)edia

Epidemie [epide'miː] f (-; -n) MED epidemic (disease)

Epilog [epi'loːk] m (-[e]s; -e [epi'loːgə]) epilog, Br epilogue

episch ['eːpɪʃ] adj epic

Episode [epi'zoːdə] f (-; -n) episode

Epoche [e'pɔxə] f (-; -n) epoch, period, era

Epos ['eːpɔs] n (-; Epen ['eːpən]) epic (poem)

er [eːɐ] pers pron he; it

Er'achten n: **meines ~s** in my opinion

erfreuen

Erbanlage ['ɛrp-] f BIOL genes, genetic code

erbarmen [ɛɐ'barmən] v/refl (no -ge-, h) **sich j-s ~** take pity on s.o.

erbärmlich [ɛɐ'bɛrmlɪç] adj pitiful, pitiable; miserable; mean

er'barmungslos adj pitiless, merciless

er'bauen v/t (no -ge-, h) build, construct; **Er'bauer** m (-s; -) builder, constructor

er'baulich adj edifying; **Er'bauung** fig f (-; -en) edification, uplift

Erbe ['ɛrbə] **1.** m (-n; -n) heir; **2.** n (-s; no pl) inheritance, heritage

erben ['ɛrbən] v/t (ge-, h) inherit

erbeuten [ɛɐ'bɔʏtən] v/t (no -ge-, h) MIL capture; thief: get away with

'Erbfaktor m BIOL gene

Erbin ['ɛrbɪn] f (-; -nen) heir, heiress

er'bitten v/t (irr, **bitten**, no -ge-, h) ask for, request

erbittert [ɛɐ'bɪtɐt] adj fierce, furious

'Erbkrankheit f MED hereditary disease

erblich ['ɛrplɪç] adj hereditary

er'blicken v/t (no -ge-, h) see, catch sight of

erblinden [ɛɐ'blɪndən] v/i (no -ge-, sein) go blind

er'brechen v/t and v/refl (irr, **brechen**, no -ge-, h) MED vomit

Erbschaft ['ɛrpʃaft] f (-; -en) inheritance, heritage

Erbse ['ɛrpsə] f (-; -n) BOT pea; (**grüne**) **~n** green peas

'Erbstück n heirloom

Erd|apfel ['ɛrt-] Austrian m potato; **~ball** m (-[e]s; no pl) globe; **~beben** n (-s; -) earthquake; **~beere** f BOT strawberry; **~boden** m earth, ground

Erde ['ɛrdə] f (-; -n) a) (no pl) earth, b) ground, soil; → **eben**; **'erden** v/t (ge-, h) ELECTR earth, ground

erdenklich [ɛɐ'dɛŋklɪç] adj imaginable

Erd|gas ['ɛrt-] n natural gas; **~geschoss** n, **~geschoß** Austrian n first (Br ground) floor

er'dichten v/t (no -ge-, h) invent, make up; **er'dichtet** adj invented, made-up

erdig ['ɛːrdɪç] adj earthy

'Erd|klumpen m clod, lump of earth; **~kruste** f earth's crust; **~kugel** f globe; **~kunde** f (-; no pl) geography; **~leitung** f ELECTR ground (Br earth) connection; underground pipe(line);

~nuss f BOT peanut; **~öl** n (mineral) oil, petroleum; **~reich** n ground, earth

erdreisten [ɛɐ'draistən] v/refl (no -ge-, h) F have the nerve

er'drosseln v/t (no -ge-, h) throttle

er'drücken v/t (no -ge-, h) crush (to death); **~d** fig adj overwhelming

'Erd|rutsch m (-[e]s; -e) landslide (a. POL); **~teil** m GEOGR continent

er'dulden v/t (no -ge-, h) suffer, endure

'Erdumlaufbahn f earth orbit

'Erdung f (-; -en) ELECTR grounding, Br earthing

'Erdwärme f GEOL geothermal energy

er'eifern v/refl (no -ge-, h) get excited

ereignen [ɛɐ'ʔaignən] v/refl (no -ge-, h) happen, occur; **Ereignis** [ɛɐ'ʔaignɪs] n (-ses; -se) event, occurrence

er'eignisreich adj eventful

Erektion [erɛk'tsjoːn] f (-; -en) erection

Eremit [ere'miːt] m (-en; -en) hermit, anchorite

er'fahren[1] v/t (irr, **fahren**, no -ge-, h) hear; learn; experience

er'fahren[2] adj experienced

Er'fahrung f (-; -en) (work) experience

Er'fahrungsaustausch m exchange of experience; **er'fahrungsgemäß** adv as experience shows

er'fassen v/t (no -ge-, h) grasp; record, register; cover, include; EDP collect

er'finden v/t (irr, **finden**, no -ge-, h) invent; **Er'finder(in)** (-s; -/-; -nen) inventor; **erfinderisch** [ɛɐ'fɪndərɪʃ] adj inventive; **Er'findung** f (-; -en) invention; **Er'findungskraft** f (-; no pl) inventiveness

Erfolg [ɛɐ'fɔlk] m (-[e]s; -e) success; result; **viel ~!** good luck!; **~ versprechend** promising; **er'folgen** v/i (no -ge-, sein) happen, take place; **er'folglos** adj unsuccessful; futile; **Er'folglosigkeit** f (-; no pl) lack of success; **er'folgreich** adj successful; **Er'folgserlebnis** n sense of achievement

erforderlich [ɛɐ'fɔrdəlɪç] adj necessary, required; **er'fordern** v/t (no -ge-, h) require, demand; **Erfordernis** [ɛɐ'fɔrdənɪs] n (-ses; -se) requirement, demand

er'forschen v/t (no -ge-, h) explore; investigate, study; **Er'forscher** m explorer; **Er'forschung** f exploration

er'freuen v/t (no -ge-, h) please

erfreulich [ɛɐˈfrɔylɪç] *adj* pleasing, pleasant; gratifying

er'freut *adj* pleased (**über** *acc* at, about); **sehr ~!** pleased to meet you

er'frieren *v/i* (*irr, frieren, no -ge-, sein*) freeze to death; **Er'frierung** *f* (*-; -en*) MED frostbite

er'frischen *v/t and v/refl* (*no -ge-, h*) refresh (o.s.); **~d** *adj* refreshing

Er'frischung *f* (*-; -en*) refreshment

erfroren [ɛɐˈfroːrən] *adj* frostbitten; BOT killed by frost

er'füllen *fig v/t* (*no -ge-, h*) fulfil(l); keep (*promise etc*); serve (*purpose etc*); meet (*requirements etc*); **~ mit** fill with; **sich ~** be fulfilled, come true; **Er'füllung** *f* (*-; -en*) fulfil(l)ment; **in ~ gehen** come true

ergänzen [ɛɐˈɡɛntsən] *v/t* (*no -ge-, h*) complement (**einander** each other); supplement, add; **~d** *adj* complementary, supplementary

Er'gänzung *f* (*-; -en*) completion; supplement, addition

ergattern [ɛɐˈɡatɐn] F *v/t* (*no -ge-, h*) (manage to) get hold of

er'geben (*irr, geben, no -ge-, h*) **1.** *v/t* amount *or* come to; **2.** *v/refl* surrender; *fig* arise; **sich ~ aus** result from; **sich ~ in** (*acc*) resign o.s. to

Er'gebenheit *f* (*-; no pl*) devotion

Ergebnis [ɛɐˈɡeːpnɪs] *n* (*-ses; -se*) result, SPORT *a.* score; outcome

er'gebnislos *adj* without result

er'gehen *v/i* (*irr, gehen, no -ge-, sein*) order *etc*: be issued (**an** *acc* to); **wie ist es dir ergangen?** how did things go with you?; **et. über sich ~ lassen** (patiently) endure s.th.

ergiebig [ɛɐˈɡiːbɪç] *adj* productive, rich; **Er'giebigkeit** *f* (*-; no pl*) (high) yield; productiveness

er'gießen *v/refl* (*irr, gießen, no -ge-, h*) **sich ~ über** (*acc*) pour down on

er'grauen *v/i* (*no -ge-, sein*) turn gray (*Br* grey)

er'greifen *v/t* (*irr, greifen, no -ge-, h*) seize, grasp, take hold of; take (*measures etc*); take up; *fig* move, touch

ergriffen [ɛɐˈɡrɪfən] *fig adj* moved

Er'griffenheit *f* (*-; no pl*) emotion

er'gründen *v/t* (*no -ge-, h*) find out, fathom

er'haben *adj* raised, elevated; *fig* sublime; **~ sein über** (*acc*) be above

er'halten[1] *v/t* (*irr, halten, no -ge-, h*) get, receive; keep, preserve; protect; support, maintain (*family etc*)

er'halten[2] *adj*: **gut ~** in good condition

erhältlich [ɛɐˈhɛltlɪç] *adj* obtainable, available

Er'haltung *f* (*-; no pl*) preservation; upkeep

er'hängen *v/t* (*no -ge-, h*) hang (**sich** o.s.)

er'heben *v/t* (*irr, heben, no -ge-, h*) raise (*a.* voice), lift; **sich ~** rise up (**gegen** against)

erheblich [ɛɐˈheːplɪç] *adj* considerable

Er'hebung *f* (*-; -en*) survey; revolt

erheitern [ɛɐˈhaitɐn] *v/t* (*no -ge-, h*) cheer up, amuse; **erhellen** *v/t* (*no -ge-, h*) light up; *fig* throw light upon; **erhitzen** [ɛɐˈhɪtsən] *v/t* (*no -ge-, h*) heat; **sich ~** get hot; **er'hoffen** *v/t* (*no -ge-, h*) hope for

erhöhen [ɛɐˈhøːən] *v/t* (*no -ge-, h*) raise; increase; **Er'höhung** *f* (*-; -en*) increase

er'holen *v/refl* (*no -ge-, h*) recover; relax, rest; **erholsam** [ɛɐˈhoːlzaːm] *adj* restful, relaxing; **Er'holung** *f* (*-; no pl*) recovery; relaxation

Er'holungsheim *n* rest home

erinnern [ɛɐˈʔɪnɐn] *v/t* (*no -ge-, h*) **j-n ~ an** (*acc*) remind s.o. of; **sich ~ an** (*acc*) remember, recall; **Erinnerung** [ɛɐˈʔɪnərʊŋ] *f* (*-; -en*) memory (**an** *acc* of); remembrance, souvenir; keepsake; **zur ~** in memory of

er'kalten [ɛɐˈkaltən] *v/i* (*no -ge-, sein*) cool down (*a. fig*)

er'kälten [ɛɐˈkɛltən] *v/refl* (*no -ge-, h*) **sich ~** catch (a) cold; (**stark**) **erkältet sein** have a (bad) cold; **Er'kältung** *f* (*-; -en*) cold

erkennbar [ɛɐˈkɛnbaːɐ] *adj* recognizable; **er'kennen** *v/t* (*irr, kennen, no -ge-, h*) recognize (**an** *dat* by), know (by); see, realize; **er'kenntlich** *adj*: **sich** (*j-m*) **~ zeigen** show (s.o.) one's gratitude; **Er'kenntnis** *f* (*-; -se*) realization; discovery; *pl* findings

Er'kennungs|dienst *m* (police) records department; **~melo,die** *f* signature tune; **~zeichen** *n* badge; AVIAT markings

Erker [ˈɛrkɐ] *m* (*-s; -*) ARCH bay; **~fenster** *n* ARCH bay window

er'klären v/t (no -ge-, h) explain (**j-m** to s.o.); declare; **j-n** (offiziell) **für ... ~** pronounce s.o. ...; **~d** adj explanatory
erklärlich [ɛɐ'klɛːrlɪç] adj explainable; **er'klärt** adj declared; **Er'klärung** f (-; -en) explanation; declaration; definition; **e-e ~ abgeben** make a statement
er'klingen v/i (irr, **klingen**, no -ge-, sein) (re)sound, ring (out)
erkranken [ɛɐ'krankən] v/i (no -ge-, sein) fall ill, get sick; **~ an** (dat) get; **Er'krankung** f (-; -en) illness, sickness
erkunden [ɛɐ'kundən] v/t (no -ge-, h) explore
erkundigen [ɛɐ'kundɪɡən] v/refl (no -ge-, h) inquire (**nach** about s.th.; after s.o.); make inquiries (**bei** j-m) **nach dem Weg ~** ask (s.o.) the way; **Er'kundigung** f (-; -en) inquiry
Er'kundung f (-; -en) exploration; MIL reconnaissance
Erlagschein [ɛɐ'laːk-] Austrian m money-order form
er'lahmen v/i (no -ge-, sein) flag
Erlass [ɛɐ'las] m (-es; -e) decree; JUR remission; **er'lassen** v/t (irr, **lassen**, no -ge-, h) issue; enact (bill etc); **j-m et. ~** release s.o. from s.th.
erlauben [ɛɐ'laubən] v/t (no -ge-, h) allow, permit; **sich et. ~** permit o.s. (or dare) to do s.th.; treat o.s. to s.th.
Erlaubnis [ɛɐ'laupnɪs] f (-; no pl) permission; authority; **um ~ bitten** ask s.o.'s permission; **~schein** m permit
erläutern [ɛɐ'lɔytən] v/t (no -ge-, h) explain, illustrate; **Er'läuterung** f (-; -en) explanation; annotation
Erle ['ɛrlə] f (-; -n) BOT alder
er'leben v/t (no -ge-, h) experience; go through; see; have; **das werden wir nicht mehr ~** we won't live to see that
Erlebnis [ɛɐ'leːpnɪs] n (-ses; -se) experience; adventure
er'lebnisreich adj eventful
erledigen [ɛɐ'leːdɪɡən] v/t (no -ge-, h) take care of, do, handle; settle; F finish s.o. (a. SPORT); do s.o. in; **erledigt** [ɛɐ'leːdɪçt] adj finished, settled; F worn out; F **der ist ~!** he is done for
Er'ledigung f (-; -en) a) (no pl) settlement, b) pl things to do, shopping
er'legen v/t (no -ge-, h) HUNT shoot
erleichtern [ɛɐ'laiçtən] v/t (no -ge-, h) ease, relieve; **er'leichtert** adj relieved;

Er'leichterung [-təruŋ] f (-; no pl) relief (**über** acc at)
er'leiden v/t (irr, **leiden**, no -ge-, h) suffer
er'lesen adj choice, select
er'leuchten v/t (no -ge-, h) illuminate
er'liegen v/i (irr, **liegen**, no -ge-, sein) succumb to
Er'liegen n: **zum ~ kommen** (**bringen**) come (bring) to a standstill
erlogen [ɛɐ'loːɡən] adj false; **~ sein** be a lie
Erlös [ɛɐ'løːs] m (-es; -e) proceeds; profit(s)
erlosch [ɛɐ'lɔʃ] pret of **erlöschen**
erloschen [ɛɐ'lɔʃən] **1.** pp of **erlöschen**; **2.** adj extinct (volcano)
er'löschen v/i (irr, no -ge-, sein) go out; fig die; JUR lapse, expire
er'lösen v/t (no -ge-, h) deliver, free (both: **von** from); **Erlöser** [ɛɐ'løːzɐ] m (-s; no pl) REL Savio(u)r; **Er'lösung** f (-; no pl) REL salvation; relief
ermächtigen [ɛɐ'mɛçtɪɡən] v/t (no -ge-, h) authorize; **Er'mächtigung** f (-; -en) authorization; authority
er'mahnen v/t (no -ge-, h) admonish; reprove, warn (a. SPORT)
Er'mahnung f (-; -en) admonition; warning; esp SPORT (first) caution
Er'mangelung f: **in ~** (gen) for want of
ermäßigt [ɛɐ'mɛːsɪçt] adj reduced, cut; **Er'mäßigung** f (-; -en) reduction, cut
er'messen v/t (irr, **messen**, no -ge-, h) assess; judge; **Er'messen** n (-s; no pl) discretion; **nach eigenem ~** at one's own discretion
er'mitteln **1.** v/t (no -ge-, h) find out; determine; **2.** v/i esp JUR investigate; **Er'mittlung** f (-; -en) finding; JUR investigation
er'möglichen v/t (no -ge-, h) make possible
er'morden v/t (no -ge-, h) murder; esp POL assassinate; **Er'mordung** f (-; -en) murder; esp POL assassination
ermüden [ɛɐ'myːdən] (no -ge-) **1.** v/t (h) tire, fatigue; **2.** v/i (sein) tire, get tired, fatigue (a. TECH); **Er'müdung** f (-; no pl) fatigue, tiredness
er'muntern [ɛɐ'muntən] v/t (no -ge-, h) encourage; stimulate; **Er'munterung** f (-; -en) encouragement; incentive
ermutigen [ɛɐ'muːtɪɡən] v/t (no -ge-, h)

E

encourage; **~d** *adj* encouraging

Er'mutigung *f* (-; -en) encouragement

er'nähren *v/t* (*no -ge-*, *h*) feed; support (*family etc*); **sich ~ von** live on; **Er-'nährer** *m* (-s; -) breadwinner, supporter; **Er'nährung** *f* (-; *no pl*) nutrition, food, diet

er'nennen *v/t* (*irr*, **nennen**, *no -ge-*, *h*) **j-n ~ zu** appoint s.o. (to be)

Er'nennung *f* (-; -en) appointment

erneuern [ɛɐ'nɔyɐn] *v/t* (*no -ge-*, *h*) renew; **Er'neuerung** *f* (-; -en) renewal

er'neut 1. *adj* renewed **2.** *adv* once more

erniedrigen [ɛɐ'niːdrɪɡən] *v/t* (*no -ge-*, *h*) humiliate; **sich ~** degrade o.s.

Er'niedrigung *f* (-; -en) humiliation

ernst [ɛrnst] *adj* serious, earnest; **~ nehmen** take s.o. or s.th. seriously

Ernst *m* (-es; *no pl*) seriousness, earnest; **im ~(?)** seriously(?); **ist das dein ~?** are you serious?

'ernsthaft, 'ernstlich *adj* serious

Ernte [ɛrntə] *f* (-; -n) harvest; crop(s)

'Erntedankfest *n* Thanksgiving (Day), *Br* harvest festival

'ernten *v/t* (*ge-*, *h*) harvest, reap (*a. fig*)

er'nüchtern *v/t* (*no -ge-*, *h*) sober, *fig a.* disillusion; **Er'nüchterung** *f* (-; -en) sobering up; *fig* disillusionment

Eroberer [ɛɐ'ʔoːbərɐ] *m* (-s; -) conqueror; **erobern** [ɛɐ'ʔoːbɐn] *v/t* (*no -ge-*, *h*) conquer; **Er'oberung** *f* (-; -en) conquest (*a. fig*)

er'öffnen *v/t* (*no -ge-*, *h*) open; inaugurate; disclose *s.th.* (*j-m* to s.o.)

Er'öffnung *f* (-; -en) opening; inauguration; disclosure

erörtern [ɛɐ'ʔœrtɐn] *v/t* (*no -ge-*, *h*) discuss; **Er'örterung** *f* (-; -en) discussion

Erotik [e'roːtɪk] *f* (-; *no pl*) eroticism

erotisch [e'roːtɪʃ] *adj* erotic

er'pressen *v/t* (*no -ge-*, *h*) blackmail; extort; **Er'presser(in)** (-s; -/-; -nen) blackmailer; **Er'pressung** *f* (-; -en) blackmail(ing); extortion

er'proben *v/t* (*no -ge-*, *h*) try, test

er'raten *v/t* (*irr*, **raten**, *no -ge-*, *h*) guess

er'rechnen *v/t* (*no -ge-*, *h*) calculate, work *s.th.* out

erregbar [ɛɐ'reːkbaːɐ] *adj* excitable; irritable

er'regen *v/t* (*no -ge-*, *h*) excite, *sexually: a.* arouse; *fig* rouse; cause; **sich ~** get excited; **~d** *adj* exciting, thrilling

Er'reger *m* (-s; -) MED germ, virus

Er'regung *f* (-; -en) excitement

erreichbar [ɛɐ'raiçbaːɐ] *adj* within reach (*a. fig*); available; **leicht ~** within easy reach; **nicht ~** out of reach; not available; **er'reichen** *v/t* (*no -ge-*, *h*) reach; catch (*train etc*); **es ~, dass ...** succeed in doing s.th.; **et. ~** get somewhere; **telefonisch zu ~ sein** have a (*Br* be on the) phone

er'richten *v/t* (*no -ge-*, *h*) put up, erect; *fig* found, *esp* ECON set up

Er'richtung *f* (-; -en) erection; *fig* establishment

er'ringen *v/t* (*irr*, **ringen**, *no -ge-*, *h*) win, gain; achieve

er'röten *v/i* (*no -ge-*, *sein*) blush

Errungenschaft [ɛɐ'rʊŋənʃaft] *f* (-; -en) achievement; **m-e neueste ~** my latest acquisition

Ersatz [ɛɐ'zats] *m* (-es; *no pl*) replacement; substitute; surrogate; compensation; damages; **als ~ für** in exchange for; **~dienst** *m* → **Zivildienst**; **~mann** *m* (-[e]s; *-leute*) substitute (*a.* SPORT); **~mine** *f* refill; **~reifen** *m* MOT spare tire (*Br* tyre); **~spieler** *m* SPORT substitute; **~teil** *n* TECH spare part

er'schaffen *v/t* (*irr*, **schaffen**, *no -ge-*, *h*) create

er'schallen *v/i* ([*irr*, **schallen**,] *no -ge-*, *sein*) (re)sound, ring (out)

er'scheinen *v/i* (*irr*, **scheinen**, *no -ge-*, *sein*) appear, F turn up; be published; **Er'scheinen** *n* (-s; *no pl*) appearance; publication; **Er'scheinung** *f* (-; -en) appearance; apparition; phenomenon

er'schießen *v/t* (*irr*, **schießen**, *no -ge-*, *h*) shoot (dead); **erschlaffen** [ɛɐ'ʃlafən] *v/i* (*no -ge-*, *sein*) go limp; *fig* weaken; **er'schlagen** *v/t* (*irr*, **schlagen**, *no -ge-*, *h*) kill; **er'schließen** *v/t* (*irr*, **schließen**, *no -ge-*, *h*) open up; develop

erschollen [ɛɐ'ʃɔlən] *pp of* **erschallen**

er'schöpfen *v/t* (*no -ge-*, *h*) exhaust; **er'schöpft** *adj* exhausted

Er'schöpfung *f* (-; *no pl*) exhaustion

erschrak [ɛɐ'ʃraːk] *pret of* **erschrecken** 2

er'schrecken 1. *v/t* (*no -ge-*, *h*) frighten; scare; **2.** *v/i* (*irr*, *no -ge-*, *sein*) be frightened (*über acc* at); **~d** *adj* alarming; terrible erschrocken [ɛɐˈʃrɔkən] *pp of* **erschrecken** 2

erschüttern [ɛɐˈʃʏtən] *v/t (no -ge-, h)* shake; *fig a.* shock; *fig* move

Er'schütterung *f (-; -en)* shock *(a. fig)*; TECH vibration

erschweren [ɛɐˈʃveːrən] *v/t (no -ge-, h)* make more difficult; aggravate

er'schwindeln *v/t (no -ge-, h)* obtain *s.th.* by fraud; *(sich) et. von j-m ~* swindle s.o. out of s.th.

er'schwingen *v/t (irr, schwingen, no -ge-, h)* afford; **er'schwinglich** *adj* within one's means, affordable; reasonable *(price)*

er'sehen *v/t (irr, sehen, no -ge-, h)* see, learn, gather *(all: aus* from)

ersetzbar [ɛɐˈzɛtsbaːɐ] *adj* replaceable; reparable; **er'setzen** *v/t (no -ge-, h)* replace *(durch* by); compensate for; *j-m et. ~* reimburse s.o. for s.th.

er'sichtlich *adj* evident, obvious

er'sparen *v/t (no -ge-, h)* save; *j-m et. ~* spare s.o. s.th.

Ersparnisse [ɛɐˈʃpaːɐnɪsə] *pl* savings

erst [eːɐst] *adv* first; at first; *~ jetzt (gestern)* only now (yesterday); *~ nächste Woche* not before *or* until next week; *es ist ~ neun Uhr* it's only nine o'clock; *eben ~* just (now); *~ recht* all the more; *~ recht nicht* even less; *→ einmal*

er'starren *v/i (no -ge-, sein)* stiffen; *fig* freeze; **er'starrt** *adj* stiff; numb

erstatten *v/t (no -ge-, h)* refund, reimburse *(j-m et.* s.o. for s.th.); *Bericht ~* (give a) report *(über acc* on); *Anzeige ~* report to the police

'Erstaufführung *f* THEA first night *or* performance, premiere, *film: a.* first run

er'staunen *v/t (no -ge-, h)* surprise, astonish; **Er'staunen** *n (-s; no pl)* surprise, astonishment; *in ~ (ver)setzen* astonish; **er'staunlich** *adj* surprising, astonishing; **er'staunt** *adj* astonished

'Erstausgabe *f* first edition

'erst'beste *adj* first; any old

'erste *adj* first; *auf den ~n Blick* at first sight; *fürs Erste* for the time being; *als Erste(r)* first; *zum ~n Mal(e)* for the first time; *am Ersten* on the first

er'stechen *v/t (irr, stechen, no -ge-, h)* stab

'erstens *adv* first(ly), in the first place

'Erstere: *der (die, das) ~* the former

er'sticken *v/t (no -ge-, h) and v/i (sein)* choke, suffocate; **Er'stickung** *f (-; no pl)* suffocation

'erst|klassig [-klasıç] *adj* first-class, F *a.* super; *~malig* [-maːlıç] *adj* first; *~mals* [-maːls] *adv* for the first time

er'streben *v/t (no -ge-, h)* strive after

er'strebenswert *adj* desirable

er'strecken *v/refl (no -ge-, h)* extend, stretch *(bis, auf acc* to; *über acc* over); *sich ~ über (acc) a.* cover

'Erstschlag *m* MIL first strike

er'suchen *v/t (no -ge-, h)* request

er'tappen *v/t (no -ge-, h)* catch; *→ Tat*

er'tönen *v/i (no -ge-, sein)* (re)sound

Ertrag [ɛɐˈtraːk] *m (-[e]s; Erträge* [ɛɐˈtrɛːgə]*)* AGR yield, produce, TECH *a.* output; ECON proceeds, returns

er'tragen *v/t (irr, tragen, no -ge-, h)* bear, endure; stand

erträglich [ɛɐˈtrɛːklıç] *adj* bearable, tolerable

er'tränken *v/t (no -ge-, h)* drown

er'trinken *v/i (irr, trinken, no -ge-, sein)* drown

erübrigen [ɛɐˈʔyːbrɪgən] *v/t (no -ge-, h)* spare; *sich ~* be unnecessary

er'wachen *v/i (no -ge-, sein)* wake (up); *esp fig* awake, awaken

Erw. ABBR *of Erwachsene(r)* adult(s)

er'wachsen[1] *v/i (irr, wachsen, no -ge-, sein)* arise *(aus* from)

er'wachsen[2] *adj* grown-up, adult

Er'wachsene *m, f (-n; -n)* adult; *nur für ~!* adults only!; **Er'wachsenenbildung** *f* adult education

erwägen [ɛɐˈvɛːgən] *v/t (irr, wägen, no -ge-, h)* consider, think *s.th.* over; **Er'wägung** *f (-; -en)* consideration; *in ~ ziehen* take into consideration

erwähnen [ɛɐˈvɛːnən] *v/t (no -ge-, h)* mention; **Er'wähnung** *f (-; -en)* mention(ing)

er'wärmen *v/t and v/refl (no -ge-, h)* warm (up); *fig sich ~ für* warm to

Er'wärmung *f (-; -en)* warming up; *~ der Erdatmosphäre* global warming

er'warten *v/t (no -ge-, h)* expect; wait for, await; **Er'wartung** *f (-; -en)* expectation, anticipation

er'wartungsvoll *adj and adv* full of expectation, expectant(ly) er'wecken *fig v/t (no -ge-, h)* awaken; arouse; → **Anschein**

er'weisen *v/t (irr, **weisen**, no -ge-, h)* do (*service etc*); show (*respect etc*); **sich ~ als** prove to be

erweitern [ɛɐ̯'vaitən] *v/t and v/refl (no -ge-, h)* extend, enlarge; *esp* ECON expand; **Er'weiterung** *f (-; -en)* extension, enlargement, expansion

Erwerb [ɛɐ̯'vɛrp] *m (-[e]s; -e)* acquisition; purchase; income; **er'werben** *v/t (irr, **werben**, no -ge-, h)* acquire (*a. fig*); purchase

er'werbs|los *adj* unemployed; **~tätig** *adj* (gainfully) employed, working; **~unfähig** *adj* unable to work

Er'werbung *f (-; -en)* acquisition; purchase

erwidern [ɛɐ̯'vi:dən] *v/t (no -ge-, h)* reply, answer; return (*visit etc*)

Er'widerung *f (-; -en)* reply, answer; return

er'wischen *v/t (no -ge-, h)* catch, get; **ihn hat's erwischt** he's had it

er'wünscht *adj* desired; desirable; welcome

er'würgen *v/t (no -ge-, h)* strangle

Erz [e:ɐ̯ts] *n (-es; -e)* ore

er'zählen *v/t (no -ge-, h)* tell; narrate; **man hat mir erzählt** I was told

Er'zähler *m (-s; -)*, **Er'zählerin** *f (-; -nen)* narrator

Er'zählung *f (-; -en)* (short) story, tale

'Erzbischof *m* REL archbishop

'Erzbistum *n* REL archbishopric

'Erzengel *m* REL archangel

er'zeugen *v/t (no -ge-, h)* ECON produce (*a. fig*); TECH make, manufacture; ELECTR generate; *fig* cause, create; **Er'zeuger** *m (-s; -)* ECON producer; **Er'zeugnis** *n (-ses; -se)* ECON product (*a. fig*); **Er'zeugung** *f (-; -en)* ECON production

er'ziehen *v/t (irr, **ziehen**, no -ge-, h)* bring up, raise; educate; **j-n zu et. ~** teach s.o. to be *or* to do s.th.

Erzieher [ɛɐ̯'tsi:ɐ] *m (-s; -)*, **Erzieherin** [ɛɐ̯'tsi:ərɪn] *f (-; -nen)* educator; teacher; (qualified) kindergarten teacher; **er'zieherisch** *adj* educational, pedagogic(al); **Er'ziehung** *f (-; no pl)* upbringing; education

Er'ziehungs|anstalt *f* reform (*Br* approved) school; **~berechtigte** *m, f*

(*-n; -n*) parent or guardian; **~wesen** *n (-s; no pl)* educational system

er'zielen *v/t (no -ge-, h)* achieve; SPORT score

erzogen [ɛɐ̯'tso:gən] *adj:* **gut ~ sein** be well-bred; **schlecht ~ sein** be ill-bred

er'zwingen *v/t (irr, **zwingen**, no -ge-, h)* (en)force

es [ɛs] *pers pron* it; he; she; **~ gibt** there is, there are; **ich bin ~** it's me; **ich hoffe ~** I hope so; **ich kann ~** I can (do it)

Esche ['ɛʃə] *f (-; -n)* BOT ash (tree)

Esel ['e:zəl] *m (-s; -)* zo donkey, ass (*a.* F)

'Eselsbrücke *f* mnemonic

'Eselsohr *fig n* dog-ear

Eskorte [ɛs'kɔrtə] *f (-; -n)* MIL escort, MAR *a.* convoy

essbar ['ɛsbaːɐ̯] *adj* eatable; edible

essen ['ɛsən] *v/t and v/i (irr, ge-, h)* eat; **zu Mittag ~** (have) lunch; **zu Abend ~** have supper (*or* dinner); **~ gehen** eat *or* dine out; **'Essen** *n (-s; -)* food; meal; dish; dinner

'Essens|marke *f* meal ticket; **~zeit** *f* lunchtime; dinner *or* supper time

Essig ['ɛsɪç] *m (-s; -e)* vinegar

'Essiggurke *f* pickled gherkin, pickle

Ess|löffel *m* tablespoon; **~stäbchen** *pl* chopsticks; **~tisch** *m* dining table; **~zimmer** *n* dining room

Estrich ['ɛstrɪç] *m (-s; -e)* ARCH flooring, subfloor; *Swiss:* loft, attic, garret

etablieren [eta'bli:rən] *v/refl (no -ge-, h)* establish o.s.

Etage [e'ta:ʒə] *f (-; -n)* floor, stor(e)y; **auf der ersten ~** on the second (*Br* first) floor; **E'tagenbett** *n* bunk bed

Etappe [e'tapə] *f (-; -n)* stage, SPORT *a.* leg

Etat [e'ta:] *m (-s; -s)* budget

Ethik ['e:tɪk] *f (-; no pl)* ethics

ethisch ['e:tɪʃ] *adj* ethical

ethnisch ['ɛtnɪʃ] *adj* ethnic

Etikett [eti'kɛt] *n (-[e]s; -e[n])* label (*a. fig*); (price) tag; **Eti'kette** *f (-; -n)* etiquette; **etikettieren** [etikɛ'ti:rən] *v/t (no -ge-, h)* label

etliche ['ɛtlɪçə] *indef pron* several, quite a few

Etui [ɛt'viː] *n (-s; -s)* case

etwa ['ɛtva] *adv* about, around; perhaps, by any chance; **nicht ~, dass** not that; **etwaig** ['ɛtvaɪç] *adj* any

etwas ['ɛtvas] **1.** *indef pron* something;

anything; **2.** *adj* some; any; **3.** *adv* a little, somewhat

EU [eːˈuː] ABBR *of* **Europäische Union** EU, European Union

euch [ɔʏç] *pers pron* you; **~ (selbst)** yourselves; **euer** [ˈɔʏɐ] *poss pron* your; **der (die, das) Eu(e)re** yours

Eule [ˈɔʏlə] *f* (-; -n) zo owl; **~n nach Athen tragen** carry coals to Newcastle

euresgleichen [ˈɔʏrəsˈɡlaɪçən] *pron* people like you, F *contp* the likes of you

Euro... [ˈɔʏro] *in cpds* ...*cheque etc*: Euro...

Europa [ɔʏˈroːpa] Europe; **~...** *in cpds* European; **Europäer** [ɔʏroˈpɛːɐ] *m* (-s; -), **Europäerin** [-ˈpɛːərɪn] *f* (-; -nen), **euro'päisch** *adj* European; **Europäische Gemeinschaft** European Community

Euter [ˈɔʏtɐ] *n* (-s; -) udder

ev. ABBR *of* **evangelisch** Prot., Protestant

evakuieren [evakuˈiːrən] *v/t* (*no -ge-*, h) evacuate

evangelisch [evaŋˈɡeːlɪʃ] *adj* REL Protestant; **~-lutherisch** Lutheran

Evangelium [evaŋˈɡeːljʊm] *n* (-s; -lien) Gospel

eventuell [eventuˈɛl] **1.** *adj* possible; **2.** *adv* possibly, perhaps

evtl. ABBR *of* **eventuell** poss., possibly

ewig [ˈeːvɪç] *adj* eternal; F constant, endless; **auf ~** for ever; **'Ewigkeit** *f* (-; *no pl*) eternity; F **eine ~** (for) ages

exakt [ɛˈksakt] *adj* exact, precise

Ex'aktheit *f* (-; *no pl*) exactness, precision

Examen [ɛˈksaːmən] *n* (-s; *Examina* [ɛˈksaːmina]) exam, examination

Exekutive [ɛksekuˈtiːvə] *f* (-; -n) POL executive (power)

Exemplar [ɛksɛmˈplaːɐ] *n* (-s; -e) specimen; copy

exerzieren [ɛksɛrˈtsiːrən] *v/i* (*no -ge-*, h) MIL drill

Exil [ɛˈksiːl] *n* (-s; -e) exile

Existenz [ɛksɪsˈtɛnts] *f* (-; -en) existence; living, livelihood; **~kampf** *m* struggle for survival; **~minimum** *n* subsistence level

existieren [ɛksɪsˈtiːrən] *v/i* (*no -ge-*, h) exist; live (**von** on)

exklusiv [ɛkskluˈziːf] *adj* exclusive, select

exotisch [ɛˈksoːtɪʃ] *adj* exotic

Expansion [ɛkspanˈzjoːn] *f* (-; -en) expansion

Expedition [ɛkspediˈtsjoːn] *f* (-; -en) expedition

Experiment [ɛksperiˈmɛnt] *n* (-[e]s; -e), **experimentieren** [ɛksperimɛnˈtiːrən] *v/i* (*no -ge-*, h) experiment

Experte [ɛksˈpɛrtə] *m* (-n; -n), **Ex'pertin** *f* (-; -nen) expert (**für** on)

explodieren [ɛksploˈdiːrən] *v/i* (*no -ge-*, sein) explode (*a. fig*), burst; **Explosion** [ɛksploˈzjoːn] *f* (-; -en) explosion (*a. fig*); **explosiv** [-ˈziːf] *adj* explosive

Export [ɛksˈpɔrt] *m* (-[e]s; -e) a) (*no pl*) export(ation), b) exports

exportieren [ɛkspɔrˈtiːrən] *v/t* (*no -ge-*, h) export

Express [ɛksˈprɛs] *m* (-es; *no pl*) RAIL express; **per ~** by special delivery, Br express

extra [ˈɛkstra] *adv* extra; separately; F on purpose; **~ für dich** especially for you

Extra *n* (-s; -s), **~blatt** *n* extra

Extrakt [ɛksˈtrakt] *m* (-[e]s; -e) extract

extravagant [ɛkstravaˈɡant] *adj* flamboyant

extrem [ɛksˈtreːm] *adj*, **Ex'trem** *n* (-s; -e) extreme; **Extremist(in)** [ɛkstreˈmɪst(ɪn)] (-en; -en/-; -nen), **extre'mistisch** *adj* extremist, ultra

Exzellenz [ɛkstseˈlɛnts] *f* (-; -en) Excellency

exzentrisch [ɛksˈtsɛntrɪʃ] *adj* eccentric

Exzess [ɛksˈtsɛs] *m* (-ses; -se) excess

F

Fa. ABBR of **Firma** firm; Messrs.

Fabel ['fa:bəl] f (-; -n) fable (a. fig) **'fabelhaft** adj fantastic, wonderful

Fabrik [fa'bri:k] f (-; -en) factory, works, shop; **Fabrikant** [fabri'kant] m (-en; -en) factory owner; manufacturer

Fa'brikarbeiter m factory worker

Fabrikat [fabri'ka:t] n (-[e]s; -e) make, brand; product

Fabrikation [fabrika'tsjo:n] f (-; -en) manufacturing, production

Fabrikati'onsfehler m flaw

Fa'brikbesitzer m factory owner; **~ware** f manufactured product(s)

Fach [fax] n (-[e]s; Fächer ['feçɐ]) compartment; pigeonhole; shelf; PED, UNIV subject; → **Fachgebiet**; **~arbeiter** m skilled worker; **~arzt** m, **~ärztin** f specialist (für in); **~ausbildung** f professional training; **~ausdruck** m technical term; **~buch** n specialist book

Fächer ['feçɐ] m (-s; -) fan

'Fachfrau f expert; **~gebiet** n line, field; trade, business; **~geschäft** n dealer (specializing in ...); **~hochschule** f appr (techical) college, esp Br polytechnic; **~kenntnisse** pl specialized knowledge

'fachkundig adj competent, expert

'fachlich adj professional, specialized

'Fachliteratur f specialized literature; **~mann** m (-[e]s; -leute) expert

'fachmännisch [-mɛnɪʃ] adj expert

'Fachschule f technical school or college

fachsimpeln ['faxzɪmpəln] v/i (ge-, h) talk shop

'Fachwerk n framework; **~werkhaus** n half-timbered house; **~zeitschrift** f (professional or specialist) journal

Fackel ['fakəl] f (-; -n) torch; **~zug** m torchlight procession

fade ['fa:də] adj GASTR tasteless, flat; stale; fig dull, boring

Faden ['fa:dən] m (-s; Fäden ['fɛ:dən]) thread (a. fig); **'fadenscheinig** adj threadbare; fig flimsy (excuse etc)

fähig ['fɛ:ɪç] adj capable (zu of [doing] s.th.), able (to do s.th.); **'Fähigkeit** f (-; -en) (cap)ability; talent, gift

fahl [fa:l] adj pale, ashen (face)

fahnden ['fa:ndən] v/i (ge-, h) search (nach for); **'Fahndung** f (-; -en) search; **'Fahndungsliste** f wanted list

Fahne ['fa:nə] f (-; -n) flag; mst fig banner; F **e-e ~ haben** reek of alcohol

'Fahneneid m MIL desertion; **~flucht** f (-; no pl) MIL desertion; **~stange** f flagpole, flagstaff

Fahrbahn ['fa:ɐ-] f road(way), pavement; MOT lane

'fahrbar adj mobile

Fähre ['fɛ:rə] f (-; -n) ferry(boat)

fahren ['fa:rən] (irr, ge-) **1.** v/i (sein) go; bus etc: run; leave; MOT drive; ride; **mit dem Auto (Zug, Bus etc) ~** go by car (train, bus etc); **über e-e Brücke etc ~** cross a bridge etc; **mit der Hand über et. ~** run one's hand over s.th.; **was ist denn in dich gefahren?** what's got into you?; **2.** v/t (h) drive (car etc); ride (bicycle etc); carry

Fahrer ['fa:rɐ] m (-s; -) driver; **~flucht** f hit-and-run offense (Br offence)

Fahrerin f (-; -nen) driver

Fahrgast ['fa:ɐ-] m passenger; **~geld** n fare; **~gelegenheit** f means of transport(ation); **~gemeinschaft** f car pool; **~gestell** n MOT chassis; AVIAT → **Fahrwerk**; **~karte** f ticket

'Fahrkartenautomat m ticket machine; **~entwerter** m (-s; -) ticket-cancel(l)ing machine; **~schalter** m ticket window

'fahrlässig adj careless, reckless (a. JUR); **grob ~** grossly negligent

'Fahrlehrer m driving instructor

'Fahrplan m timetable, schedule

'fahrplanmäßig 1. adj scheduled; **2.** adv according to schedule; on time

'Fahrpreis m fare; **~prüfung** f driving test; **~rad** n bicycle, F bike; **~schein** m ticket; **~schule** f driving school; **~schüler** m MOT student driver, Br learner (driver); PED non-local student; **~stuhl** m elevator, Br lift; **~stunde** f driving lesson

Fahrt [fa:ɐt] f (-; -en) ride, MOT a. drive; trip, journey, MAR voyage, cruise; speed (a. MOT); **in voller ~** at full speed

Fährte ['fɛ:ɐtə] f (-; -n) track (a. fig)

'Fahrtenschreiber *m* MOT tachograph

'Fahrwasser *n* MAR fairway

'Fahrwerk *n* AVIAT landing gear

'Fahrzeug *n* (-[e]s *-e*) vehicle

Fairness ['fɛːʀnɪs] *f* (-; *no pl*) fair play

Faktor ['faktoːɐ] *m* (-s; *-en* [fak'toːʀən]) factor

Fakultät [fakʊl'tɛːt] *f* (-; *-en*) UNIV faculty, department

Falke ['falkə] *m* (-*n*; *-n*) ZO hawk, falcon

Fall [fal] *m* (-[e]s; *Fälle* ['fɛlə]) fall; LING, JUR, MED case; *auf jeden ~* in any case; *auf keinen ~* on no account; *für den ~, dass ...* in case ...; *gesetzt den ~, dass* suppose (that); *zu ~ bringen* fig defeat

Falle ['falə] *f* (-; *-n*) trap (*a. fig*)

fallen ['falən] *v/i* (*irr, ge-, sein*) fall (*a. rain etc*), drop; *~ lassen* drop (*a. fig*); MIL be killed (in action); *ein Tor fiel* SPORT a goal was scored

fällen ['fɛlən] *v/t* (*ge-, h*) fell, cut down (*tree*); JUR pass (*sentence*); make (*a decision etc*)

fällig ['fɛlɪç] *adj* due; payable

'Fall|obst *n* windfall; **~rückzieher** *m* soccer: overhead kick

falls [fals] *cj* if, in case; *~ nicht* unless

'Fallschirm *m* parachute; **~jäger** *m* MIL paratrooper; **~springen** *n* MIL parachuting; SPORT skydiving; **~springer** *m* MIL parachutist; SPORT skydiver

'Falltür *f* trapdoor

falsch [falʃ] *adj and adv* wrong; false (*a. fig*); forged; *~ gehen* watch: be wrong; *et. ~ aussprechen* (*schreiben, verstehen etc*) mispronounce (misspell, misunderstand *etc*) s.th.; *~ verbunden!* TEL sorry, wrong number

fälschen ['fɛlʃən] *v/t* (*ge-, h*) forge, fake; counterfeit; **'Fälscher** *m* (-s; -) forger

'Falsch|geld *n* counterfeit or false money; **~münzer** [-mʏntsɐ] *m* (-s; -) counterfeiter; **~spieler** *m* cheat

'Fälschung *f* (-; *-en*) forgery; counterfeit; **'fälschungssicher** *adj* forgery-proof

Falt... ['falt-] *in cpds ...bett, ...boot etc*: folding ...; **Falte** ['faltə] *f* (-; *-n*) fold; wrinkle; pleat; crease; **'falten** *v/t* (*ge-, h*) fold; **'Faltenrock** *m* pleated skirt

Falter ['faltɐ] *m* (-s; -) ZO butterfly

faltig ['faltɪç] *adj* wrinkled

familiär [famiˈljɛːɐ] *adj* personal; informal; *~e Probleme* family problems

Familie [faˈmiːljə] *f* (-; *-n*) family (*a.* ZO, BOT)

Fa'milien|angelegenheit *f* family affair; **~anschluss** *m*: *~ haben* live as one of the family; **~name** *m* family (*or* last) name, surname; **~packung** *f* family size (package); **~planung** *f* family planning; **~stand** *m* marital status; **~vater** *m* family man

Fanatiker [faˈnaːtikɐ] *m* (-s; -), **Fa'natikerin** *f* (-; *-nen*), **fa'natisch** *adj* fanatic; **Fanatismus** [fanaˈtɪsmʊs] *m* (-; *no pl*) fanaticism

fand [fant] *pret of* **finden**

Fang [faŋ] *m* (-[e]s; *Fänge* ['fɛŋə]) catch (*a. fig*); **'fangen** *v/t* (*irr, ge-, h*) catch (*a. fig*); *sich wieder ~* get a grip on o.s. again; *Fangen spielen* play tag (*Br* catch); **'Fangzahn** *m* ZO fang

Fantasie [fantaˈziː] *f* (-; *-n*) imagination; fantasy; **fanta'sielos** *adj* unimaginative; **fanta'sieren** *v/i* (*no -ge-, h*) daydream; MED be delirious; F talk nonsense; **fanta'sievoll** *adj* imaginative; **Fantast** [fanˈtast] *m* (-*en*; *-en*) dreamer; **fan'tastisch** *adj* fantastic, F *a.* great, terrific

Farbband ['farp-] *n* (typewriter) ribbon

Farbe ['farbə] *f* (-; *-n*) colo(u)r; paint; complexion; tan; *card games*: suit

'farbecht *adj* colo(u)r-fast

färben ['fɛrbən] *v/t* (*ge-, h*) dye; *esp fig* colo(u)r; *sich rot ~* turn red; → *abfärben*

'farben|blind *adj* colo(u)r-blind; **~froh**, **~prächtig** *adj* colo(u)rful

'Farb|fernsehen *n* colo(u)r television; **~fernseher** *m* colo(u)r TV set; **~film** *m* colo(u)r film; **~foto** *n* colo(u)r photo

farbig ['farbɪç] *adj* colo(u)red; stained (*glass*); *fig* colo(u)rful; **Farbige** ['farbɪgə] *m, f* (-*n*; *-n*) → *Schwarze*

'Farbkasten *m* paintbox

'farblos *adj* colo(u)rless (*a. fig*)

'Farbstift *m* colo(u)red pencil, crayon

'Farbstoff *m* dye; GASTR colo(u)ring

'Farbton *m* shade, tint

'Färbung *f* (-; *-en*) colo(u)ring; hue

Farnkraut ['farn-] *n* BOT fern

Fasan [faˈzaːn] *m* (-[e]s; *-e[n]*) ZO pheasant

Faschismus [faˈʃɪsmʊs] *m* (-; *no pl*) POL fascism; **Faschist** [faˈʃɪst] *m* (-*en*; *-en*), **fa'schistisch** *adj* POL fascist

F

faseln ['faːzəln] F v/i (ge-, h) drivel

Faser ['faːzɐ] f (-; -n) fiber, Br fibre; grain; **faserig** ['faːzərɪç] adj fibrous; **'fasern** v/i (ge-, h) fray

Fass [fas] n (-es; Fässer ['fɛsɐ]) cask, barrel; **vom ~** on tap

Fassade [fa'saːdə] f (-; -n) ARCH facade, front (a. fig)

'Fassbier n draft (Br draught) beer

fassen ['fasən] (ge-, h) **1.** v/t take hold of, grasp; seize; catch (criminal); hold, take; set (jewels); fig grasp, understand; pluck up (courage); make (a decision); **sich ~** compose o.s.; **sich kurz ~** be brief; **es ist nicht zu ~** that's incredible **2.** v/i: **~ nach** reach for

'Fassung f (-; -en) a) setting; frame (of glasses); ELECTR socket; draft(ing); wording, version, b) (no pl) composure; **die ~ verlieren** lose one's composure; **j-n aus der ~ bringen** put s.o. out

'fassungslos adj stunned; speechless

'Fassungsvermögen n capacity

fast [fast] adv almost, nearly; **~ nie (nichts)** hardly ever (anything)

fasten ['fastən] v/i (ge-, h) fast

'Fastenzeit f REL Lent

'Fastnacht f → **Karneval**

fatal [fa'taːl] adj unfortunate; awkward; disastrous

fauchen ['fauxən] v/i (ge-, h) ZO hiss

faul [faul] adj rotten, bad, GASTR a. spoiled; fig lazy; F fishy; **~e Ausrede** lame excuse; **'faulen** v/i (ge-, h, sein) rot, go bad; decay

faulenzen ['faulɛntsən] v/i (ge-, h) laze, loaf (about); **'Faulenzer(in)** ['-tsɐ (-tsərɪn)] (-s; -/-; -nen) lazybones; contp loafer

'Faulheit f (-; no pl) laziness

faulig ['faulɪç] adj rotten

Fäulnis ['fɔylnɪs] f (-; no pl) rottenness, decay (a. fig)

'Faulpelz F m → **Faulenzer**

'Faultier n ZO sloth

Faust [faust] f (-; Fäuste ['fɔystə]) fist; **auf eigene ~** on one's own initiative; **~handschuh** m mitten; **~regel** f (als **~** as a) rule of thumb; **~schlag** m punch

Favorit [favo'riːt] m (-en; -en), **Favo'ritin** f (-; -nen) favo(u)rite

Fax [faks] n (-; -[e]) fax; fax machine

faxen ['faksən] v/i and v/t (ge-, h) fax, send a fax (to)

'Faxgerät n fax machine

FCKW [ɛftseːkaːˈveː] ABBR of **Fluorchlorkohlenwasserstoff** chlorofluorocarbon, CFC

Feber ['feːbɐ] Austrian m (-s; -), **Februar** ['feːbruaːɐ] m (-s; -e) February

fechten ['fɛçtən] v/i (irr, ge-, h) SPORT fence; fig fight; **'Fechten** n (-s; no pl) SPORT fencing; **Fechter(in)** ['fɛçtɐ (-tərɪn)] (-s; -/-; -nen) SPORT fencer

Feder ['feːdɐ] f (-; -n) feather; plume; nib; TECH spring; **~ball** m SPORT badminton; shuttlecock; **~bett** n comforter, Br duvet; **~gewicht** n SPORT featherweight; **~halter** m penholder

'feder|leicht adj (as) light as a feather

'Federmäppchen [-mɛpçən] n (-s; -) pencil case

'federn (ge-, h) **1.** v/i be springy; **2.** v/t TECH spring; **~d** adj springy, elastic

'Federstrich m stroke of the pen

Federung ['feːdərʊŋ] f (-; -en) springs; MOT suspension; **e-e gute ~ haben** be well sprung

'Federzeichnung f pen-and-ink drawing

Fee [feː] f (-; -n) fairy

fegen ['feːgən] v/t (ge-, h) and fig v/i (sein) sweep

fehl [feːl] adj: **~ am Platze** out of place

'Fehlbetrag m deficit

'fehlen v/i (ge-, h) be missing; be absent; **ihm fehlt (es an)** ... he is lacking ...; **du fehlst uns** we miss you; **was dir fehlt, ist ...** what you need is ...; **was fehlt Ihnen?** what's wrong with you?

Fehler ['feːlɐ] m (-s; -) mistake; fault, TECH a. defect, flaw; EDP error

'fehlerfrei adj faultless, flawless

'fehlerhaft adj faulty; full of mistakes; TECH defective

'Fehlermeldung f EDP error message

'Fehl|ernährung f malnutrition; **~geburt** f MED miscarriage; **~griff** m mistake; wrong choice

'Fehlschlag m failure; **'fehlschlagen** v/i (irr, schlagen, sep, -ge-, sein) fail

'Fehl|start m false start; **~tritt** m slip; fig lapse; **~zündung** f MOT backfire (a. **~ haben**)

Feier ['faɪɐ] f (-; -n) celebration; party

'Feierabend m end of a day's work;

closing time; evening (at home); ~ **ma-chen** finish (work), F knock off; **nach** ~ after work

'**feierlich** adj solemn; festive

'**Feierlichkeit** f (-; -en) a) (no pl) solemnity, b) ceremony

'**feiern** v/t and v/i (ge-, h) celebrate; have a party

'**Feiertag** m holiday; **gesetzlicher** ~ public (or legal, Br a. bank) holiday

feig [faik], **feige** ['faigə] adj cowardly; ~ **sein** be a coward

Feige ['faigə] f (-; -n) BOT fig

'**Feigheit** f (-; no pl) cowardice

'**Feigling** m (-s; -e) coward

Feile ['failə] f (-; -n), '**feilen** v/t and v/i (ge-, h) file

feilschen ['failʃən] v/i (ge-, h) haggle (**um** about, over)

fein [fain] adj fine; choice, excellent; keen (ear); delicate; distinguished, F posh; ~**!** good!, okay!

Feind [faint] m (-[e]s; -e ['faində]) enemy (a. fig); ~**bild** n enemy image

Feindin ['faindin] f (-; -nen) enemy

'**feindlich** adj hostile; MIL enemy

'**Feindschaft** f (-; no pl) hostility

'**feindselig** adj hostile (**gegen** to)

'**Feindseligkeit** f (-; no pl) hostility

feinfühlig ['fainfy:lıç] adj sensitive

'**Feingefühl** n (-[e]s; no pl) sensitiveness

'**Feinheit** f (-; -en) a) (no pl) fineness; keenness; delicacy, b) pl niceties

Fein|kostgeschäft n delicatessen; ~**me,chaniker** m precision mechanic

'**Feinschmecker** m (-s; -) gourmet

feist [faist] adj fat, stout

Feld [fɛlt] n (-[e]s; -er ['fɛldə]) field (a. fig); chess: square; ~**arbeit** f AGR work in the fields; fieldwork; ~**bett** n cot, Br camp bed; ~**flasche** f water bottle, canteen; ~**lerche** f ZO skylark; ~**marschall** m MIL field marshal

'**Feldstecher** [-ʃtɛçɐ] m (-s; -) field glasses

'**Feldwebel** [-ve:bəl] m (-s; -) MIL sergeant

'**Feldzug** m MIL campaign (a. fig)

Felge ['fɛlgə] f (-; -n) rim; SPORT circle

Fell [fɛl] n (-[e]s; -e) ZO coat; skin, fur

Fels [fɛls] m (-en; -en) rock

'**Felsbrocken** m boulder

Felsen ['fɛlzən] m (-s; -) rock

felsig ['fɛlzıç] adj rocky

'**Felsspalte** f crevice

'**Felsvorsprung** m ledge

feminin [femi'ni:n] adj feminine (a. LING); contp effeminate; **Feminismus** [femi'nısmʊs] m (-; no pl) feminism; **Feministin** [femi'nıstın] f (-; -nen), **fe-mi'nistisch** adj feminist

Fenchel ['fɛnçəl] m (-s; no pl) BOT fennel

Fenster ['fɛnstɐ] n (-s; -) window; ~**bank** f (-; -bänke), ~**brett** n windowsill; ~**flügel** m casement; ~**laden** m shutter; ~**rahmen** m window frame; ~**scheibe** f (window)pane

Ferien ['fe:rjən] pl vacation, esp Br holiday(s pl); ~ **haben** be on vacation; ~**haus** n vacation home, cottage; ~**lager** n summer camp; ~**wohnung** f vacation rental, Br holiday apartment

Ferkel ['fɛrkəl] n (-s; -) ZO piglet; F pig

fern [fɛrn] adj and adv far(away), far-off, distant; **von** ~ from a distance; ~ **halten** keep away (**von** from); **es liegt mir** ~ **zu** far be it from me to

'**Fernamt** n telephone exchange

Fern'bedienung f remote control

'**fernbleiben** v/i (irr, **bleiben**, sep, -ge-, sein) stay away (dat from)

Ferne ['fɛrnə] f (-; no pl) distance; **aus der** ~ from a distance

ferner ['fɛrnɐ] adv further(more); in addition, also

'**Fern|fahrer** m long-haul truck driver, F trucker, Br long-distance lorry driver; ~**gespräch** n TEL long-distance call

'**ferngesteuert** adj remote-controlled; MIL guided (missile etc)

'**Fern|glas** n binoculars; ~**heizung** f district heating; ~**ko,pierer** m fax machine; ~**kurs** m correspondence course; ~**laster** F m (-s; -) MOT longhaul truck, Br long-distance lorry; ~**lenkung** f remote control; ~**licht** n MOT full (or high) beam

'**Fernmelde|satel,lit** m communications satellite; ~**technik** f, ~**wesen** n (-s; no pl) telecommunications

'**Fern|rohr** n telescope; ~**schreiben** n, ~**schreiber** m telex

'**fernsehen** v/i (irr, **sehen**, sep, -ge-, h) watch television; '**Fernsehen** n (-s; no pl) television (**im** on); '**Fernseher** F m (-s; -) TV (set); TV viewer

'**Fernseh|schirm** m (TV) screen; **~sen-dung** f TV program(me)

Fernsprechamt n telephone exchange

'**Fernsteuerung** f remote control

'**Fernverkehr** m long-distance traffic

Ferse ['fɛrzə] f (-; -n) ANAT heel (a. fig)

fertig ['fɛrtɪç] adj ready; finished; **~ bringen** manage; iro be capable of; **~ machen** finish (a. F s.o.); get s.th. ready; F give s.o. hell, do s.o. in; **sich ~ machen** get ready; (**mit et.**) **~ sein** have finished (s.th.); **mit et. ~ werden** cope with a problem etc; F **völlig ~** dead beat

'**Fertig|gericht** n ready(-to-serve) meal; **~haus** n prefabricated house, F prefab

'**Fertigkeit** f (-; -en) skill

'**Fertigstellung** f (-; no pl) completion

fesch [fɛʃ] Austrian adj smart, chic

Fessel ['fɛsəl] f (-; -n) shackle (a. fig); ANAT ankle; **fesseln** v/t (ge-, h) bind, tie (up); fig fascinate

fest [fɛst] adj firm (a. fig); solid; fast; fig fixed (idea etc); sound (sleep); steady (girlfriend etc); **~ schlafen** be fast asleep

Fest n (-[e]s; -e) celebration; party; REL festival, feast; → **froh**

'**festbinden** v/t (irr, **binden**, sep, -ge-, h) fasten, tie (**an** dat to)

'**Festessen** n banquet, feast

'**festfahren** v/refl (irr, **fahren**, sep, -ge-, h) get stuck

'**Festhalle** f (festival) hall

'**festhalten** (irr, **halten**, sep, -ge-, h) **1.** v/i: **~ an** (dat) stick to; **2.** v/t hold on to; hold s.o. or s.th. tight; **sich ~ an** (dat) hold on to

festigen ['fɛstɪgən] v/t (ge-, h) strengthen; **sich ~** grow firm or strong

Festigkeit ['fɛstɪçkaɪt] f (-; no pl) firmness; strength

'**Festland** n mainland; the Continent

'**festlegen** v/t (sep, -ge-, h) fix, set; **sich ~ auf** (acc) commit o.s. to s.th.

'**festlich** adj festive

'**festmachen** v/t (sep, -ge-, h) fasten, fix (**an** dat to); MAR moor; ECON fix

'**Festnahme** [-na:mə] f (-; -n), '**festnehmen** v/t (irr, **nehmen**, sep, -ge-, h) arrest

'**Festplatte** f EDP hard disk

'**fest|schrauben** v/t (sep, -ge-, h) screw (on) tight; **~setzen** v/t (sep, -ge-, h) fix; **~sitzen** v/i (irr, **sitzen**, sep, -ge-, h) be

stuck; be (left) stranded

'**Festspiele** pl festival

'**feststehen** v/i (irr, **stehen**, sep, -ge-, h) be certain; date etc: be fixed; **~d** adj established (fact etc); set (phrase etc)

'**feststellen** v/t (sep, -ge-, h) find (out); establish; see, notice; state; TECH lock, arrest; '**Feststellung** f (-; -en) finding(s); realization; statement

'**Festtag** m holiday; REL religious holiday; F red-letter day

'**Festung** f (-; -en) fortress

'**Festwertspeicher** m EDP read-only memory, ROM

'**Festzug** m procession

fett [fɛt] adj fat (a. fig); PRINT bold; **~ gedruckt** boldface, in bold type (or print); **Fett** n (-[e]s; -e) fat; dripping; shortening; TECH grease; '**fettarm** adj low-fat, pred low in fat; '**Fettfleck** m grease spot; **fettig** ['fɛtɪç] adj greasy

'**Fettnäpfchen** n: **ins ~ treten** put one's foot in it

Fetzen ['fɛtsən] m (-s; -) shred; rag; scrap (of paper etc)

feucht [fɔʏçt] adj moist, damp; humid

Feuchtigkeit ['fɔʏçtɪçkaɪt] f (-; no pl) moisture; dampness; humidity

feudal [fɔʏ'da:l] adj POL feudal; F posh, Br swish

Feuer ['fɔʏɐ] n (-s; -) fire (a. fig); **j-m ~ geben** give s.o. a light; **~ fangen** catch fire; fig fall for s.o.; **~a,larm** m fire alarm; **~bestattung** f cremation; **~ei-fer** m ardo(u)r

'**feuerfest** adj fireproof, fire-resistant

'**Feuergefahr** f danger of fire

'**feuergefährlich** adj inflammable

'**Feuer|leiter** f fire escape; **~löscher** [-lœʃɐ] m (-s; -) fire extinguisher; **~melder** [-mɛldɐ] m (-s; -) fire alarm

feuern ['fɔʏɐn] v/i and v/t (ge-, h) fire (a. F s.o.)

'**feuer'rot** adj blazing red; crimson

'**Feuer|schiff** n lightship; **~stein** m flint; **~wache** f fire station; **~waffe** f firearm, gun; **~wehr** f (-; -en) fire brigade (or department); fire truck (Br engine); **~wehrmann** m (-[e]s, -männer, -leute) fireman, fire fighter; **~werk** n fireworks; **~werkskörper** m firework, firecracker; **~zeug** n (cigarette) lighter

feurig ['fɔʏrɪç] adj fiery, ardent

Fiasko ['fjasko] *n* (-s; -s) fiasco, (complete) failure

Fibel ['fi:bəl] *f* (-; -n) primer, first reader

Fiber ['fi:bɐ] *f* fiber, *Br* fibre; **~glas** *n* fiberglass, *Br* fibreglass

Fichte ['fɪçtə] *f* (-; -n) BOT spruce, F *mst* pine *or* fir (tree)

ficken ['fɪkən] V *v/i and v/t* (ge-, h) fuck

Fieber ['fi:bɐ] *n* (-s; *no pl*) MED temperature, fever (*a. fig*); **~ haben** (**messen**) have a (take *s.o.'s*) temperature; **~senkend** MED antipyretic

'fieberhaft *adj* MED feverish (*a. fig*)

'fiebern *v/i* (ge-, h) MED have *or* run a temperature; **~ nach** *fig* crave for

'Fieberthermo,meter *n* fever (*Br* clinical) thermometer

fiel [fi:l] *pret of* **fallen**

fies [fi:s] F *adj* mean, nasty

Figur [fi'gu:ɐ] *f* (-; -en) figure

Filet [fi'le:] *n* (-s; -s) GASTR fil(l)et

Filiale [fi'lja:lə] *f* (-; -n) branch

Film [fɪlm] *m* (-[e]s; -e) film; movie, *esp Br* (motion) picture; *the* movies, *Br the* cinema; **e-n ~ einlegen** PHOT load a camera; **~aufnahme** *f* filming, shooting; take, shot

filmen ['fɪlmən] (ge-, h) **1.** *v/t* film, shoot; **2.** *v/i* make a film

'Film|gesellschaft *f* motion-picture (*Br* film) company; **~kamera** *f* motion-picture (*Br* film) camera; **~kas,sette** *f* film magazine, cartridge; **~pro,jektor** *m* film (*or* movie) projector; **~regis,seur** *m* film director; **~schauspieler(in)** film (*or* screen, movie) actor (actress); **~studio** *n* film studio(s); **~the,ater** *n → Kino*; **~verleih** *m* film distributors; **~vorführer** *m* (-s; -) projectionist

Filter ['fɪltɐ] *m, esp* TECH *n* (-s; -) filter

'Filterkaffee *m* filter coffee

'filtern *v/t* (ge-, h) filter

'Filterziga,rette *f* filter(-tipped) cigarette, filter tip

Filz [fɪlts] *m* (-es; -e) felt; F POL corruption, sleaze; **'filzen** F *v/t* (ge-, h) frisk

'Filz|schreiber [-ʃraibɐ] *m* (-s; -), **~stift** *m* felt(-tipped) pen

Finale [fi'na:lə] *n* (-s; -) finale; SPORT final(s)

Finanz|amt [fi'nants-] *n* tax office; Internal (*Br* Inland) Revenue; **~be-amte** *m* tax officer

Finanzen [fi'nantsən] *pl* finances

finanziell [finan'tsjel] *adj* financial

finanzieren [finan'tsi:rən] *v/t* (*no -ge-, h*) finance

Fi'nanz|mi,nister *m* minister of finance; Secretary of the Treasury; *Br* Chancellor of the Exchequer; **~minis-,terium** *n* ministry of finance; Treasury Department, *Br* Treasury; **~wesen** *n* (-s; *no pl*) finance

Findelkind ['fɪndəl-] *n* JUR foundling

finden *v/t* (*irr, ge-, h*) find; think, believe; **ich finde ihn nett** I think he's nice; **wie ~ Sie ...?** how do you like ...?; **~ Sie (nicht)?** do (don't) you think so?; **das wird sich ~** we'll see

Finder ['fɪndɐ] *m* (-s; -) finder

'Finderlohn *m* finder's reward

findig ['fɪndɪç] *adj* clever

fing [fɪŋ] *pret of* **fangen**

Finger ['fɪŋɐ] *m* (-s; -) ANAT finger; **~ab-druck** *m* fingerprint; **~fertigkeit** *f* (-; *no pl*) manual skill; **~hut** *m* thimble; BOT foxglove; **~nagel** *m* ANAT fingernail; **~spitze** *f* fingertip; **~spitzengefühl** *n* (-[e]s; *no pl*) sure instinct; tact

fingiert [fɪŋ'gi:rt] *adj* faked; fictitious

Fink [fɪŋk] *m* (-en; -en) ZO finch

Finne ['fɪnə] *m* (-n; -n), **Finnin** ['fɪnɪn] *f* (-; -nen) Finn; **'finnisch** *adj* Finnish

Finnland ['fɪn-] Finland

finster ['fɪnstɐ] *adj* dark, gloomy; *fig* grim; shady

'Finsternis *f* (-; -se) darkness, gloom

Finte ['fɪntə] *f* (-; -n) trick; SPORT feint

Firma ['fɪrma] *f* (-; -men) firm, company

firmen ['fɪrmən] *v/t* (ge-, h) REL confirm

'Firmung *f* (-; -en) REL confirmation

First [fɪrst] *m* (-[e]s; -e) ARCH ridge

Fisch [fɪʃ] *m* (-[e]s; -e) ZO fish; *pl* ASTR Pisces; **er ist (ein) ~** he's (a) Pisces

'Fischdampfer *m* trawler

fischen ['fɪʃən] *v/t and v/i* (ge-, h) fish

Fischer ['fɪʃɐ] *m* (-s; -) fisherman; **~... in** *cpds* ...**boot**, ...**dorf** *etc*: fishing ...

Fischerei [fɪʃə'rai] *f* (-; *no pl*) fishing

'Fisch|fang *m* (-[e]s; *no pl*) fishing; **~gräte** *f* fishbone; **~grätenmuster** *n* herring-bone (pattern); **~gründe** *pl* fishing grounds; **~händler** *m* fish dealer, *esp Br* fishmonger; **~kutter** *m* smack; **~laich** *m* spawn; **~stäbchen** *n* GASTR fish stick (*Br* finger); **~zucht**

f fish farming; **~zug** *m* catch, haul (*both a. fig*)

Fisole [fi'zo:lə] *Austrian f* (-; -n) BOT string bean

Fistel ['fɪstəl] *f* (-; -n) MED fistula

'Fistelstimme *f* falsetto

fit [fɪt] *adj* fit; **sich ~ halten** keep fit

'Fitness *f* (-; *no pl*) fitness; **~center** *n* health club, fitness center, gym

fix [fɪks] *adj* ECON fixed; F quick; F smart, bright; F **~ und fertig sein** be dead beat; be a nervous wreck; **~e Idee** PSYCH obsession

fixen ['fɪksən] *F v/i* (ge-, h) shoot, fix; be a junkie; **Fixer** F *m* (-s; -) junkie, mainliner

fixieren [fɪ'ksi:rən] *v/t* (no -ge-, h) fix (*a.* PHOT); stare *at s.o.*

'Fixstern *m* ASTR fixed star

FKK [ɛfka:'ka:] *ABBR of Freikörperkultur* nudism

FK'K-Strand *m* nudist beach

flach [flax] *adj* flat; level, even, plane; *fig* shallow

Fläche ['flɛçə] *f* (-; -n) surface (*a.* MATH); area (*a.* MATH); expanse, space

'flächendeckend *adj* exhaustive

'Flächen|inhalt *m* MATH (surface) area; **~maß** *n* square *or* surface measure

'Flachland *n* (-[e]s; *no pl*) lowland, plain

Flachs [flaks] *m* (-es; *no pl*) BOT flax

flackern ['flakɐn] *v/i* (ge-, h) flicker

Fladenbrot ['fla:dən-] *n* round flat bread (*or* loaf)

Flagge ['flagə] *f* (-; -n) flag

'flaggen *v/i* (ge-, h) fly a flag *or* flags

Flak [flak] *f* (-; -) MIL anti-aircraft gun

Flamme ['flamə] *f* (-; -n) flame (*a. fig*)

Flanell [fla'nɛl] *m* (-s; -e) flannel

Flanke ['flaŋkə] *f* (-; -n) flank, side; *soccer:* cross; SPORT flank vault

flankieren [flaŋ'ki:rən] *v/t* (no -ge-, h) flank

Flasche ['flaʃə] *f* (-; -n) bottle; baby's bottle; F *contp* dead loss

'Flaschen|bier *n* bottled beer; **~hals** *m* neck of a bottle; **~öffner** *m* bottle opener; **~pfand** *n* (bottle) deposit; **~zug** *m* TECH block and tackle, pulley

flatterhaft ['flatɐhaft] *adj* fickle, flighty

flattern ['flatɐn] *v/i* (ge-, sein) flutter; TECH (h) wobble

flau [flau] *adj* queasy; *fig* flat; ECON slack

Flaum [flaum] *m* (-[e]s; *no pl*) down, fluff, fuzz

Flausch [flauʃ] *m* (-es; -e) fleece

flauschig ['flauʃɪç] *adj* fleecy, fluffy

Flausen ['flauzən] F *pl* (funny) ideas

Flaute ['flautə] *f* (-; -n) MAR calm; ECON slack period

Flechte ['flɛçtə] *f* (-; -n) plait, braid; BOT, MED lichen; '**flechten** *v/t* (*irr,* ge-, h) plait, braid (*hair*); weave (*basket*)

Fleck [flɛk] *m* (-[e]s; -e) stain, mark; speck; dot; blot(ch); *fig* place, spot; patch; **blauer ~** bruise; **vom ~ weg** on the spot; **nicht vom ~ kommen** not get anywhere; '**Flecken** *m* → *Fleck*

'Fleckenentferner *m* stain remover

'fleckenlos *adj* spotless (*a. fig*)

fleckig ['flɛkɪç] *adj* spotted; stained

'Fledermaus ['fle:dɐ-] *f* ZO bat

Flegel ['fle:gəl] *m* (-s; -) lout, boor

'flegelhaft *adj* loutish

'Flegeljahre *pl* awkward age

'flegeln F *contp v/refl* (ge-, h) lounge

flehen ['fle:ən] *v/i* (ge-, h) beg; pray (**um** for); **flehentlich** ['fle:əntlɪç] *adj* imploring, entreating

Fleisch [flaiʃ] *n* (-[e]s; *no pl*) flesh (*a. fig*); GASTR meat; **~ fressend** BOT, ZO carnivorous; **~brühe** *f* (meat) broth, consommé

Fleischer ['flaiʃɐ] *m* (-s; -) butcher

Fleischerei [flaiʃə'rai] *f* (-; -en) butcher's (shop)

'Fleischhauer [-hauɐ] *Austrian m* (-s; -) butcher

fleischig ['flaiʃɪç] *adj* fleshy

'fleischlos *adj* meatless

'Fleischwolf *m* meat grinder, Br mincer

Fleiß [flais] *m* (-es; *no pl*) diligence, hard work; **fleißig** ['flaisɪç] *adj* diligent, hard-working; **~ sein** work hard

fletschen ['flɛtʃən] *v/t* (ge-, h) bare

flexibel ['flɛksi:bəl] *adj* flexible

Flexibilität [flɛksibili'tɛ:t] *f* (-; *no pl*) flexibility

flicken ['flɪkən] *v/t* (ge-, h) mend, repair, *a. fig* patch (up); '**Flicken** *m* (-s; -) patch; '**Flickwerk** *n* patchwork (*a. fig*); '**Flickzeug** *n* TECH repair kit

Flieder ['fli:dɐ] *m* (-s; -) BOT lilac

Fliege ['fli:gə] *f* (-; -n) ZO fly; bow tie

'fliegen v/i (irr, ge-, sein) and v/t (h) fly (a. ~ **lassen**); F fall; F be fired, F get the sack; be kicked out of school; F ~ **auf** (acc) really go for; F **in die Luft** ~ blow up

'Fliegen n (-s; no pl) flying; aviation

'Fliegen|fänger m flypaper; ~**fenster** n flyscreen; ~**gewicht** n SPORT flyweight; ~**gitter** n wire mesh (screen); ~**klatsche** f flyswatter; ~**pilz** m BOT fly agaric

Flieger ['fli:gɐ] m (-s; -) MIL airman; F plane; cycling: sprinter; ~**a,larm** m air-raid warning

fliehen ['fli:ən] v/i (irr, ge-, sein) flee, run away (both: **vor** dat from)

'Fliehkraft f PHYS centrifugal force

Fliese ['fli:zə] f (-; -n), 'fliesen v/t (ge-, h) tile; 'Fliesenleger m (-s; -) tiler

Fließband ['fli:s-] n (-[e]s; -bänder) TECH assembly line; conveyor belt

fließen ['fli:sən] v/i (irr, ge-, sein) flow (a. fig); run; ~**d 1.** adj flowing; running; LING fluent; **2.** adv: **er spricht ~ Englisch** he speaks English fluently or fluent English

'Fließheck n MOT fastback

flimmern ['flɪmɐn] v/i (ge-, h) shimmer; film: flicker

flink [flɪŋk] adj quick, nimble

Flinte ['flɪntə] f (-; -n) shotgun; F gun

Flipper ['flɪpɐ] F m (-s; -) pinball machine; 'flippern v/i (ge-, h) play pinball

Flirt [flœrt] m (-s; -s) flirtation

flirten ['flœrtən] v/i (ge-, h) flirt

Flittchen ['flɪtçən] F n (-s; -) floozie

Flitter ['flɪtɐ] m (-s; -) tinsel (a. fig), spangles; ~**wochen** pl honeymoon

flitzen ['flɪtsən] F v/i (ge-, sein) flit, whizz, shoot

flocht [flɔxt] pret of **flechten**

Flocke ['flɔkə] f (-; -n) flake

flockig ['flɔkɪç] adj fluffy, flaky

flog [flo:k] pret of **fliegen**

floh [flo:] pret of **fliehen**

Floh m (-[e]s; Flöhe ['flø:ə]) ZO flea

'Flohmarkt m flea market

Florett [flo'rɛt] n (-[e]s; -e) foil

florieren [flo'ri:rən] v/i (no ge-, h) flourish, prosper

Floskel ['flɔskəl] f (-; -n) empty or cliché(d) phrase

floss [flɔs] pret of **fließen**

Floß [flo:s] n (-es; Flöße ['flø:sə]) raft, float

Flosse ['flɔsə] f (-; -n) ZO fin, a. SPORT flipper

Flöte ['flø:tə] f (-; -n) MUS flute; recorder

flott [flɔt] adj brisk (pace); F smart, chic; MAR afloat

Flotte ['flɔtə] f (-; -n) MAR fleet; navy

'Flottenstützpunkt m MIL naval base

Fluch [flu:x] m (-[e]s; Flüche ['fly:çə]) curse; swear word; **fluchen** ['flu:xən] v/i (ge-, h) swear, curse

Flucht [flʊxt] f (-; -en) flight (**vor** dat from); escape, getaway (**aus** dat from)

'fluchtartig adv hastily

'Fluchtauto n getaway car

flüchten ['flʏçtən] v/i (ge-, sein) flee (**nach, zu** to), run away; escape, get away; **flüchtig** ['flʏçtɪç] adj quick; superficial; careless; fugitive, criminal etc: on the run, at large; ~**er Blick** glance; ~**er Eindruck** glimpse

'Flüchtigkeitsfehler m slip

Flüchtling ['flʏçtlɪŋ] m fugitive; POL refugee

'Flüchtlingslager n refugee camp

Flug [flu:k] m (-[e]s; Flüge ['fly:gə]) flight; **im** ~(**e**) rapidly, quickly; ~**abwehrra,kete** f MIL anti-aircraft missile; ~**bahn** f trajectory; ~**ball** m tennis: volley; ~**begleiter(in** f) flight attendant; ~**blatt** n handbill, leaflet; ~**dienst** m air service

Flügel ['fly:gəl] m (-s; -) ZO wing (a. SPORT); TECH blade; windmill: sail; MUS grand piano; ~**mutter** f TECH wing nut; ~**schraube** f TECH thumb screw; ~**stürmer** m SPORT wing forward; ~**tür** f folding door

'Fluggast m (air) passenger

flügge ['flʏgə] adj full-fledged

'Flug|gesellschaft f airline; ~**hafen** m airport; ~**linie** f air route; → **Fluggesellschaft**; ~**lotse** m air traffic controller; ~**plan** m air schedule; ~**platz** m airfield, airport; ~**schein** m (flight) ticket; ~**schreiber** m (-s; -) flight recorder, black box; ~**sicherung** f air traffic control; ~**verkehr** m air traffic

'Flugzeug n (-[e]s; -e) (air)plane, aircraft, Br a. aeroplane; **mit dem** ~ by air or plane; ~**absturz** m air or plane crash; ~**entführung** f hijacking, skyjacking; ~**halle** f hangar; ~**träger** m

MAR MIL aircraft carrier
Flunder ['flʊndɐ] f (-; -n) ZO flounder
flunkern ['flʊŋkɐn] v/i (ge-, h) fib; brag
Fluor ['fluːoːɐ] n (-s; no pl) CHEM fluorine; fluoride
'**Fluorchlorkohlenwasserstoff** m CHEM chlorofluorocarbon, CFC
Flur [fluːɐ] m (-[e]s; -e) hall; corridor
Fluss [flʊs] m (-es; Flüsse ['flʏsə]) river; stream; **im ~** fig in (a state of) flux
fluss'**abwärts** adv downstream
fluss'**aufwärts** adv upstream
'**Flussbett** n river bed
flüssig ['flʏsɪç] adj liquid; melted; fig fluent; ECON available; '**Flüssigkeit** f (-; -en) a) a liquid, b) (no pl) liquidity; fig fluency; '**Flüssigkris,tallanzeige** f liquid crystal display, LCD
'**Fluss|lauf** m course of a river; ~**pferd** n ZO hippopotamus, F hippo; ~**ufer** n riverbank, riverside
flüstern ['flʏstɐn] v/i and v/t (ge-, h) whisper
Flut [fluːt] f (-; -en) flood (a. fig); high tide; **es ist ~** the tide is in; ~**licht** n floodlights; ~**welle** f tidal wave
focht [fɔxt] pret of **fechten**
Fohlen ['foːlən] n (-s; -) ZO foal; colt; filly
Föhn¹ [føːn] m (-[e]s; -e) hairdrier
Föhn² m (-[e]s; -e) METEOR foehn, föhn
föhnen ['føːnən] v/t (ge-, h) blow-dry
Folge ['fɔlɡə] f (-; -n) result, consequence; effect; succession; order; series; TV etc: sequel, episode; aftermath; MED aftereffect
folgen ['fɔlɡən] v/i (ge-, sein) follow; obey; **hieraus folgt, dass** from this it follows that; **wie folgt** as follows; ~**d** adj following, subsequent
folgendermaßen ['fɔlɡəndɐ'maːsən] adv as follows
'**folgenschwer** adj momentous
'**folgerichtig** adj logical; consistent
folgern ['fɔlɡɐn] v/t (ge-, h) conclude (**aus** dat from); **Folgerung** ['fɔlɡərʊŋ] f (-; -en) conclusion
folglich ['fɔlklɪç] cj consequently, thus, therefore
folgsam ['fɔlkzaːm] adj obedient
Folie ['foːljə] f (-; -n) foil; transparency
Folter ['fɔltɐ] f (-; -n) torture; **auf die ~ spannen** tantalize; '**foltern** v/t (ge-, h) torture, fig a. torment

Fön® m → **Föhn¹**
Fonds [fõː] m (-; -) ECON fund
fönen v/t → **föhnen**
Fontäne [fɔn'tɛːnə] f (-; -n) jet, spout; gush
Förder|band ['fœrdɐ-] n TECH conveyor belt; ~**korb** m mining: cage
fordern ['fɔrdɐn] v/t (ge-, h) demand, esp JUR a. claim; ECON ask, charge
fördern ['fœrdɐn] v/t (ge-, h) promote; support (a. UNIV), sponsor; PED tutor, provide remedial classes for; TECH mine
Forderung ['fɔrdərʊŋ] f (-; -en) demand, claim (a. JUR); ECON charge
Förderung ['fœrdərʊŋ] f (-; -en) promotion, advancement; support, sponsorship; UNIV etc: grant; PED tutoring, remedial classes; TECH mining
Forelle [fo'rɛlə] f (-; -n) ZO trout
Form [fɔrm] f (-; -en) form, shape, SPORT a. condition; TECH mo(u)ld; **gut in ~** in great form; **formal** [fɔr'maːl] adj formal; **Formalität** [fɔrmali'tɛːt] f (-; -en) formality
Format [fɔr'maːt] n (-[e]s; -e) size; format; fig caliber, Br calibre
formatieren [fɔrma'tiːrən] v/t (no -ge-, h) EDP format; **Forma'tierung** f (-; -en) EDP formatting
Formel ['fɔrməl] f (-; -n) formula
formell [fɔr'mɛl] adj formal
formen ['fɔrmən] v/t (ge-, h) shape, form; fig mo(u)ld
'**Formfehler** m irregularity
formieren [fɔr'miːrən] v/t and v/refl (no -ge-, h) form (up)
förmlich ['fœrmlɪç] **1.** adj formal; fig regular; **2.** adv formally; fig literally
'**formlos** adj shapeless; fig informal
'**formschön** adj well-designed
Formular [fɔrmu'laːɐ] n (-s; -e) form, blank
formulieren [fɔrmu'liːrən] v/t (no -ge-, h) word, phrase; formulate; express
Formu'lierung f (-; -en) wording, phrasing; formulation; expression, phrase
forsch [fɔrʃ] adj dashing
forschen ['fɔrʃən] v/i (ge-, h) research, do research; **~ nach** search for
Forscher ['fɔrʃɐ] m (-s; -), '**Forscherin** f (-; -nen) explorer; (research) scientist; **Forschung** ['fɔrʃʊŋ] f (-; -en) research (work)

Forst [fɔrst] *m* (-[e]s; -e[n]) forest

Förster ['fœrstə] *m* (-s; -) forester; forest ranger

'**Forstwirtschaft** *f* (-; *no pl*) forestry

fort [fɔrt] *adv* off, away; gone; missing

Fort [foːr] *n* (-s; -s) MIL fort

'**fortbestehen** *v/i* (*irr*, **stehen**, *sep*, *no -ge-*, *h*)

'**fortbewegen** *v/refl* (*sep*, *no -ge-*, *h*) move; '**Fortbewegung** *f* moving; (lo-co)motion

'**Fortbildung** *f* (-, *no pl*) further education *or* training

'**fort**|**fahren** *v/i* (*irr*, **fahren**, *sep*, *-ge-*) a) (*sein*) leave, go away, MOT *a.* drive off, b) (*h*) continue, go *or* keep on (*et. zu tun* doing s.th.); **~führen** *v/t* (*sep*, *-ge-*, *h*) continue, carry on; **~gehen** *v/i* (*irr*, **gehen**, *sep*, *-ge-*, *sein*) go away, leave

'**fortgeschritten** *adj* advanced

'**fortlaufend** *adj* consecutive, successive

'**fortpflanzen** *v/refl* (*sep*, *-ge-*, *h*) BIOL re-produce; *fig* spread; '**Fortpflanzung** *f* BIOL reproduction

'**fortschreiten** *v/i* (*irr*, **schreiten**, *sep*, *-ge-*, *sein*) advance, proceed, progress; **~d** *adj* progressive

'**Fortschritt** *m* progress

'**fortschrittlich** *adj* progressive

'**fortsetzen** *v/t* (*sep*, *-ge-*, *h*) continue, go on with; '**Fortsetzung** *f* (-; *-en*) con-tinuation; *film etc*: sequel; **~ folgt** to be continued; '**Fortsetzungsro,man** *m* serialized novel

'**fortwährend** *adj* continual, constant

fossil [fɔ'siːl] *adj*, **Fos'sil** *n* (-s; *-ien*) GEOL fossil (*a. fig F*)

Foto ['foːto] *n* (-s; -s) photo(graph); *ein ~ machen* (*von*) take a photo (of)

'**Fotoalbum** *n* photo album

'**Fotoappa,rat** *m* camera

Fotograf [foto'graːf] *m* (-en; -en) pho-tographer; **Fotografie** [fotogra'fiː] *f* (-; -n) a) (*no pl*) photography, b) photo-graph, picture; **fotografieren** [fotogra'fiːrən] *v/t and v/i* (*no -ge-*, *h*) take a photo(graph) *or* picture (of); *sich ~ lassen* have one's picture taken; **Fo-to'grafin** *f* (-; -nen) photographer

Fotoko'**pie** *f* photocopy; **fotoko'pieren** *v/t* (*no -ge-*, *h*) (photo)copy

'**Fotomo,dell** *n* model

'**Fotozelle** *f* photoelectric cell

Fotze ['fɔtsə] V *f* (-; -n) cunt

Foul [faul] *n* (-s; -s) SPORT foul; **foulen** ['faulən] *v/t and v/i* (*ge-*, *h*) SPORT foul

Foyer [foa'jeː] *n* (-s; -s) foyer, lobby, lounge

Fr. ABBR *of* **Frau** Mrs, Ms

Fracht [fraxt] *f* (-; -en) freight, load, MAR, AVIAT *a.* cargo; ECON freight, *Br* carriage; **~brief** *m* RAIL bill of lading (*a.* MAR), *Br* consignment note

Frachter ['fraxtə] *m* (-s; -) MAR freight-er

Frack [frak] *m* (-[e]s; **Fräcke** ['frɛkə]) tails, tailcoat

Frage ['fraːgə] *f* (-; -n) question; *e-e ~ stellen* ask a question; → *infrage*

'**Fragebogen** *m* question(n)aire

'**fragen** *v/t and v/i* (*ge-*, *h*) ask (**nach** for; **wegen** about); *nach dem Weg* (*der Zeit*) ~ ask the way (time); *sich ~* won-der

'**Frage**|**wort** *n* LING interrogative; **~zei-chen** *n* LING question mark

fraglich ['fraːklɪç] *adj* doubtful, uncer-tain; ... in question

fraglos ['fraːkloːs] *adv* undoubtedly, unquestionably

Fragment [fra'gmɛnt] *n* (-[e]s; -e) frag-ment

fragwürdig ['fraːk-] *adj* dubious, F sha-dy

Fraktion [frak'tsjoːn] *f* (-; -en) (parlia-mentary) group *or* party

Frakti'**onsführer** *m* PARL floor leader, *Br* chief whip

Franc [frãː] *m* (-; -s), **Franken** ['fraŋkən] *m* (-; -) franc

frankieren [fraŋ'kiːrən] *v/t* (*no -ge-*, *h*) stamp; frank

Frankreich ['fraŋkraiç] France

Franse ['franzə] *f* (-; -n) fringe

fransig ['franzɪç] *adj* frayed

Franzose [fran'tsoːzə] *m* (-n; -n) Frenchman; *die ~n pl* the French

Französin [fran'tsøːzɪn] *f* (-; -nen) Frenchwoman

französisch [fran'tsøːzɪʃ] *adj* French

fraß [fraːs] *pret of* **fressen**

Fraß F *contp m* (-es; *no pl*) muck

Fratze ['fratsə] *f* (-; -n) grimace

'**fratzenhaft** *adj* distorted

Frau [frau] *f* (-; -en) woman; wife; *~ X* Mrs (*or* Ms) X

Frauchen ['frauçən] *n* mistress (*of dog*)

'**Frauen**|**arzt** *m*, **~ärztin** *f* gyn(a)ecologist; **~bewegung** f: **die ~** POL women's lib(eration)

'**frauenfeindlich** adj sexist

'**Frauen|haus** n women's shelter (Br refuge); **~klinik** f gyn(a)ecological hospital; **~rechtlerin** [-rɛçtlərɪn] f (-; -nen) feminist

Fräulein ['frɔʏlaɪn] n (-s; -) Miss

'**fraulich** adj womanly, feminine

frech [frɛç] adj sassy, Br cheeky

'**Frechheit** f (-; no pl) F Br cheek

frei [fraɪ] adj free (**von** from, of); independent; freelance; vacant; candid, frank; SPORT unmarked; **ein ~er Tag** a day off; **morgen haben wir ~** there is no school tomorrow; **im Freien** outdoors; → **Fuß**

'**Freibad** n open-air swimming-pool

'**freibekommen** v/t (irr, **kommen**, sep, no -ge-, h) **e-n Tag ~** get a day off

'**freiberuflich** adj freelance, self-employed

'**Freiexem,plar** n free copy

'**Freigabe** f (-; no pl) release

'**freigeben** (irr, **geben**, sep, -ge-, h) **1.** v/t release; **e-n Tag ~** etc give a day off; **2.** v/i: **j-m ~** give s.o. time off

'**freigebig** [-ge:bɪç] adj generous

'**Freigepäck** n AVIAT baggage allowance

'**freihaben** F v/i (irr, **haben**, sep, -ge-, h) have a day off (Br a. a holiday)

'**Freihafen** m free port

'**freihalten** v/t (irr, **halten**, sep, -ge-, h) keep, save (seat etc); treat (s.o.)

'**Frei|handel** m free trade; **~handelszone** f free trade area

'**freihändig** [-hɛndɪç] adv with no hands

'**Freiheit** f (-; -en) freedom, liberty; **sich ~en herausnehmen gegen** take liberties with

'**Freiheitsstrafe** f JUR prison sentence

'**Freikarte** f free ticket

'**freikaufen** v/t (sep, -ge-, h) ransom

'**Freikörperkul,tur** f (-; no pl) nudism

'**freilassen** v/t (irr, **lassen**, sep, -ge-, h) release, set free; '**Freilassung** f (-; -en) release

'**Freilauf** m freewheel (a. **im ~ fahren**)

'**freilich** adv indeed, of course

'**Freilicht-** in cpds open-air ...

'**freimachen** v/t (sep, -ge-, h) post: stamp; **sich ~** undress; **sich ~ von** free o.s. from; → **Oberkörper**

'**Freimaurer** m freemason

'**freimütig** [-my:tɪç] adj candid, frank

'**freischaffend** adj freelance

'**freischwimmen** v/refl (irr, **schwimmen**, sep, -ge-, h) pass a 15-minute swimming test

'**freisprechen** v/t (irr, **sprechen**, sep, -ge-, h) esp REL absolve (**von** from); JUR acquit (of); '**Freispruch** m JUR acquittal

'**Freistaat** m POL free state

'**frei|stehen** v/i (irr, **stehen**, sep, -ge-, h) be unoccupied; SPORT be unmarked; **es steht dir frei zu** inf you are free to inf; **~stellen** v/t (sep, -ge-, h) **j-n ~** exempt s.o. (**von** from) (a. MIL); **j-m et. ~** leave s.th. (up) to s.o.

'**Frei|stil** m freestyle; **~stoß** m soccer: free kick; **~stunde** f PED free period; **~tag** m Friday; **~tod** m suicide; **~treppe** f outdoor stairs; **~übungen** pl exercises; **~wild** fig n fair game

'**freiwillig** adj voluntary; **sich ~ melden** volunteer (**zu** for); **Freiwillige** ['fraɪvɪlɪgə] m, f (-n; -n) volunteer

'**Freizeit** f free or leisure time; **~gestaltung** f leisure-time activities; **~kleidung** f leisurewear; **~park** m amusement park; **~zentrum** n leisure center (Br centre)

'**freizügig** adj permissive; film etc: explicit

fremd [frɛmt] adj strange; foreign; unknown; **ich bin auch ~ hier** I'm a stranger here myself; '**fremdartig** adj strange, exotic; **Fremde** ['frɛmdə] m, f (-n; -n) stranger; foreigner

'**Fremden|führer** m, **~führerin** f (-; -nen) (tourist) guide; **~hass** m xenophobia; **~legi,on** f Foreign Legion; **~verkehr** m tourism; **~verkehrsbü,ro** n tourist office; **~zimmer** n guest room; **~ (zu vermieten)** rooms to let

'**fremdgehen** F v/i (irr, **gehen**, sep, -ge-, sein) be unfaithful (to one's wife or husband), play around

'**Fremd|körper** m MED foreign body; fig alien element; **~sprache** f foreign language; **~sprachensekre,tärin** f bilingual secretary

'**fremd|sprachig**, **~sprachlich** adj foreign-language

'**Fremdwort** n (-[e]s; -wörter) foreign word

Frequenz [fre'kvɛnts] f (-; -en) PHYS frequency

Fresse ['frɛsə] V f (-; -n) big (fat) mouth

'fressen v/t (irr, ge-, h) ZO eat, feed on; F gobble (up); fig devour

Freude ['frɔydə] f (-; -n) joy, delight; pleasure; ~ haben an (dat) take pleasure in

'Freuden|geschrei n shouts of joy, cheers; ~haus F n brothel; ~tag m red-letter day; ~tränen pl tears of joy

'freudestrahlend adj radiant (with joy)

freudig ['frɔydɪç] adj joyful, cheerful; happy (event etc)

freudlos ['frɔyt-] adj joyless, cheerless

freuen ['frɔyən] v/t (ge-, h) es freut mich, dass I'm glad or pleased (that); sich ~ über (acc) be pleased or glad about; sich ~ auf (acc) look forward to

Freund [frɔynt] m (-[e]s; -e ['frɔyndə]) friend; boyfriend; Freundin ['frɔyndɪn] f (-; -nen) friend; girlfriend

'freundlich adj friendly, kind, nice; fig cheerful (room etc); 'Freundlichkeit f (-; no pl) friendliness, kindness

'Freundschaft f (-; -en) friendship; ~ schließen make friends

'freundschaftlich adj friendly

'Freundschaftsspiel n SPORT friendly (game)

Frevel ['freːfəl] m (-s; -) outrage (an dat, gegen on)

Frieden ['friːdən] m (-s; no pl) peace; im ~ in peacetime; lass mich in ~! leave me alone!

'Friedens|bewegung f peace movement; ~forschung f peace studies; ~verhandlungen pl peace negotiations or talks; ~vertrag m peace treaty

friedfertig ['friːt-] adj peaceable

'Friedhof m cemetery, graveyard

'friedlich adj peaceful

'friedliebend adj peace-loving

frieren ['friːrən] v/i (irr, ge-, h) freeze; ich friere I am or feel cold; I'm freezing

Fries [friːs] m (-es; -e) ARCH frieze

Frikadelle [frika'dɛlə] f (-; -n) meatball

frisch [frɪʃ] adj fresh; clean (shirt etc); ~ gestrichen! wet (or fresh) paint!

Frische ['frɪʃə] f (-; no pl) freshness

'Frischhalte|beutel m polythene bag; ~folie f plastic wrap, Br. cling film

Friseur [fri'zøːɐ] m (-s; -e) hairdresser;

barber; ~sa,lon m hairdresser's (shop), barber's shop

Friseuse [fri'zøːzə] f (-; -n) hairdresser

frisieren [fri'ziːrən] v/t (no -ge-, h) do s.o.'s hair; F soup up

Frisör etc → Friseur etc

Frist [frɪst] f (-; -en) (fixed) period of time; deadline; term (a. ECON)

fristen ['frɪstən] v/t (ge-, h) sein Dasein ~ scrape a living

'fristlos adj without notice

Frisur [fri'zuːɐ] f (-; -en) hairstyle, hairdo

Fritten ['frɪtən] F pl fries, Br chips; frittieren [fri'tiːrən] v/t (no -ge-, h) deep-fry

frivol [fri'voːl] adj frivolous; suggestive

froh [froː] adj glad (über acc about); cheerful; happy; ~es Fest! happy holiday!; Merry Christmas!

fröhlich ['frøːlɪç] adj cheerful, happy, merry; 'Fröhlichkeit f (-; no pl) cheerfulness, merriment

fromm [frɔm] adj pious, devout; meek; steady (horse); ~er Wunsch pious hope

Frömmigkeit ['frœmɪçkaɪt] f (-; no pl) religiousness, piety

Fronleichnam [froːn-] m (-[e]s; no pl) REL Corpus Christi

Front [frɔnt] f (-; -en) front (a. fig), ARCH a. face, MIL a. line; in ~ liegen SPORT be ahead

frontal [frɔn'taːl] adj MOT head-on

Fron'talzusammenstoß m MOT head-on collision

'Frontantrieb m MOT front-wheel drive

fror [froːɐ] pret of frieren

Frosch [frɔʃ] m (-[e]s; Frösche ['frœʃə]) ZO frog; ~mann m frogman; ~perspek,tive f worm's-eye view; ~schenkel pl GASTR frog's legs

Frost [frɔst] m (-[e]s; Fröste ['frœstə]) frost; ~beule f chilblain

frösteln ['frœstəln] v/i (ge-, h) feel chilly, shiver (a. fig)

'frostig adj frosty, fig a. chilly

'Frostschutzmittel n MOT antifreeze

Frottee [frɔ'teː] n, m (-[s]; -s) terry (-cloth); frottieren [frɔ'tiːrən] v/t (no -ge-, h) rub down

Frucht [frʊxt] f (-; Früchte ['frʏçtə]) BOT fruit (a. fig); 'fruchtbar adj BIOL fertile, esp fig a. fruitful; 'Fruchtbarkeit f (-;

no pl) fertility; *fig* fruitfulness

'**fruchtlos** *adj* fruitless, futile

'**Fruchtsaft** *m* fruit juice

früh [fry:] *adj and adv* early; *zu ~ kom-men* be early; *~ genug* soon enough; *heute* (*morgen*) *~* this (tomorrow) morning; '**Frühaufsteher** *m* (*-s; -*) early riser (F bird); **Frühe** ['fry:ə] *f: in aller ~* (very) early in the morning

früher ['fry:ɐ] **1.** *adj* former; previous; **2.** *adv* in former times, at one time; *~ oder später* sooner or later; *ich habe ~* (*einmal*) ... I used to ...

'**frühestens** *adv* at the earliest

'**Früh|geburt** *f* MED premature birth; premature baby; *~jahr* *n* spring; *~jahrsputz* *m* spring cleaning

früh'morgens *adv* early in the morning

'**frühreif** *adj* precocious

'**Frühstück** *n* breakfast (*zum* for)

'**frühstücken** *v/i* (*ge-, h*) (have) breakfast

Frust [frʊst] F *m* (*-[e]s; no pl*) frustration

Frustration [frʊstra'tsjo:n] *f* (*-; -en*) frustration; **frustrieren** [frʊs'tri:rən] *v/t* (*no -ge-, h*) frustrate

frz. ABBR *of* **französisch** Fr., French

Fuchs [fʊks] *m* (*-es; Füchse* ['fyksə]) ZO fox (*a. fig*); sorrel; *~jagd* *f* foxhunt(ing); *~schwanz* *m* TECH handsaw

'**fuchs'teufels'wild** F *adj* hopping mad

fuchteln ['fʊxtəln] *v/i* (*ge-, h*) *~ mit* wave *s.th.* around

Fuge ['fu:gə] *f* (*-; -n*) TECH joint; MUS fugue

fügen ['fy:gən] *v/refl* (*ge-, h*) submit (*in acc, dat* to *s.th.*)

fühlbar ['fy:l-] *fig adj* noticeable; considerable; **fühlen** ['fy:lən] *v/t and v/i and v/refl* (*ge-, h*) feel, *fig a.* sense; *sich wohl ~* feel well

Fühler ['fy:lɐ] *m* (*-s; -*) ZO feeler (*a. fig*)

fuhr [fu:ɐ] *pret of* **fahren**

führen ['fy:rən] (*ge-, h*) **1.** *v/t* lead; guide; take; run; manage; ECON sell, deal in; keep (*account, books etc*); have (*a talk etc*); bear (*name etc*); MIL command; *j-n ~ durch* show s.o. round; *sich ~* conduct o.s.; **2.** *v/i* lead (*zu* to, *a. fig*), SPORT *a.* be leading, be ahead; *~d adj* leading

Führer ['fy:rɐ] *m* (*-s; -*) leader (*a.* POL); guide; head, chief; guide(book)

'**Führerschein** *m* MOT driver's license, *Br* driving licence

'**Führung** *f* (*-; -en*) a) (*no pl*) leadership, control; ECON management, b) (guided) tour; *gute ~* good conduct; *in ~ gehen* (*sein*) SPORT take (be in) the lead; '**Führungszeugnis** *n* certificate of (good) conduct

Fuhrunternehmen ['fu:ɐ-] *n* trucking company, *Br* haulage contractors

'**Fuhrwerk** *n* horse-drawn vehicle

Fülle ['fʏlə] *f* (*-; no pl*) crush; *fig* wealth, abundance; GASTR body

füllen *v/t and v/refl* (*ge-, h*) fill (*a.* MED), stuff (*a.* GASTR)

Füller ['fʏlɐ] *m* (*-s; -*), '**Füllfederhalter** *m* fountain pen

füllig ['fʏlɪç] *adj* stout, portly

'**Füllung** *f* (*-; -en*) filling (*a.* MED), stuffing (*a.* GASTR)

fummeln ['fʊməln] F *v/i* (*ge-, h*) fiddle, tinker (*both*: *an dat* with); F grope

Fund [fʊnt] *m* (*-[e]s; -e* ['fʊndə]) discovery; find

Fundament [fʊnda'mɛnt] *n* (*-[e]s; -e*) ARCH foundation(s), *fig a.* basis

Fundamentalist [fʊndamenta'lɪst] *m* (*-en; -en*) fundamentalist

'**Fundbü,ro** *n* lost and found (office), *Br* lost-property office

'**Fundgrube** *fig f* treasure trove

Fundi ['fʊndi] F *m* (*-s; -s*) POL radical Green

fundiert [fʊn'di:ɐt] *adj* well-founded (*argument etc*); sound (*knowledge*)

fünf [fʏnf] *adj* five; *grade*: F, N, *Br* fail, poor, E; '**Fünfeck** *n* (*-[e]s; -e*) pentagon; '**fünffach** *adj* fivefold

'**Fünfkampf** *m* SPORT pentathlon

'**Fünflinge** *pl* quintuplets

'**fünfte** *adj* fifth; '**Fünftel** *n* (*-s; -*) fifth

'**fünftens** *adv* fifth(ly), in the fifth place

'**fünfzehn(te)** *adj* fifteen(th)

fünfzig ['fʏnftsɪç] *adj* fifty

'**fünfzigste** *adj* fiftieth

fungieren [fʊŋ'gi:rən] *v/i* (*no -ge-, h*) *~ als* act as, function as

Funk [fʊŋk] *m* (*-s; no pl*) radio; *über* or *durch ~* by radio

'**Funkama,teur** *m* radio ham

Funke ['fʊŋkə] *m* (*-n; -n*) spark; *fig a.* glimmer; **funkeln** ['fʊŋkəln] *v/i* (*ge-, h*) sparkle, glitter; twinkle

'**funken** *v/t* (*ge-, h*) radio, transmit

Funker ['fʊŋkɐ] *m* (-s; -) radio operator

'**Funk|gerät** *n* radio set; **~haus** *n* broadcasting center (*Br* centre); **~sig,nal** *n* radio signal; **~spruch** *m* radio message; **~stati,on** *f* radio station; **~streife** *f* (radio) patrol car; **~tele,fon** *n* cellular phone

Funktion [fʊŋk'tsjoːn] *f* (-; -en) function; **Funktionär** [fʊŋktsjo'nɛːɐ] *m* (-s; -e) functionary, official (*a.* SPORT); **funktionieren** [fʊŋktsjo'niːrən] *v/i* (no -ge-, h) work

'**Funkturm** *m* radio tower

Funkverkehr *m* radio communication

für [fyːɐ] *prp* (acc) for; in favo(u)r of; on behalf of; **~ immer** forever; **Tag ~ Tag** day by day; **Wort ~ Wort** word by word; **jeder ~ sich** everyone by himself; **was ~ ...?** what (kind or sort of) ...?; **das Für und Wider** the pros and cons

Furche ['fʊrçə] *f* (-; -n) furrow; rut

Furcht [fʊrçt] *f* (-; no pl) fear, dread (*both*: **vor** *dat* of); **aus ~(, dass)** for fear (that); **~ erregend** frightening

'**furchtbar** *adj* terrible, awful

fürchten ['fʏrçtən] *v/t and v/i* (ge-, h) fear, be afraid of; dread; **~ um** fear for; **sich ~** be scared; be afraid (**vor** *dat* of); **ich fürchte, ...** I'm afraid ...

fürchterlich ['fʏrçtəlɪç] *→* **furchtbar**

'**furcht|los** *adj* fearless; **~sam** *adj* timid

füreinander *adv* for each other

Furnier [fʊr'niːɐ] *n* (-[e]s; -e), **furnieren** [fʊr'niːrən] *v/t* (no -ge-, h) veneer

'**Fürsorge** *f* (-; no pl) care; **öffentliche ~** (public) welfare (work); **~empfänger** *m* social security beneficiary

'**fürsorglich** [-zɔrklɪç] *adj* considerate

'**Für|sprache** *f* intercession (**für** for; **bei** with); **~sprech** *m* (-[e]s; -e) *Swiss:* lawyer; **~sprecher(in)** advocate (*a. fig*)

Fürst [fʏrst] *m* (-en; -en) prince

'**Fürstentum** *n* (-s; -tümer [-tyːmɐ]) principality

'**Fürstin** *f* (-; -nen) princess

'**fürstlich** *adj* princely (*a. fig*)

Furt [fʊrt] *f* (-; -en) ford

Furunkel [fu'rʊŋkəl] *m* (-s; -) MED boil, furuncle

'**Fürwort** *n* (-[e]s; -wörter) LING pronoun

Furz [fʊrts] *m* (-es; -e), '**furzen** *v/i* (ge-, h) fart

Fusion [fu'zjoːn] *f* (-; -en) ECON merger, amalgamation

fusionieren [fuzjo'niːrən] *v/i* (no -ge-, h) ECON merge, amalgamate

Fuß [fuːs] *m* (-es; *Füße* ['fyːsə] ANAT foot; stand; stem; **zu ~** on foot; **zu ~ gehen** walk; **gut zu ~ sein** be a good walker; **~ fassen** become established; **auf freiem ~** at large

'**Fußball** *m* a) (no pl) soccer, *Br* football, b) soccer ball, *Br* football

'**Fußballer** [-balɐ] *m* (-s; -) footballer

'**Fußball|feld** *n* football field; **~rowdy** *m* (football) hooligan; **~spiel** *n* soccer or football match; **~spieler(in)** football player, footballer; **~toto** *n* football pools

'**Fußboden** *m* floor; flooring; **~heizung** *f* underfloor heating

'**Fußbremse** *f* MOT footbrake

Fussel ['fʊsəl] *f* (-; -n), *m* (-s; -[n]) piece of lint (*Br* fluff); *pl* lint, *Br* fluff; '**fusselig** ['fʊsəlɪç] *adj* linty, *Br* covered in fluff; '**fusseln** *v/i* (ge-, h) shed a lot of lint (*Br* fluff), F mo(u)lt

'**Fußgänger** [-gɛŋɐ] *m* (-s; -), '**Fußgängerin** *f* (-; -nen) pedestrian; '**Fußgängerzone** *f* (pedestrian or shopping) mall, *Br* pedestrian precinct

'**Fußgeher** *Austrian m → Fußgänger*

'**Fuß|gelenk** *n* ANAT ankle; **~matte** *f* doormat; **~note** *f* footnote; **~pflege** *f* pedicure; MED podiatry, *Br.* chiropody; **~pfleger(in)** podiatrist, *Br* chiropodist; **~pilz** *m* MED athlete's foot; **~sohle** *f* ANAT sole (of the foot); **~spur** *f* footprint; track; **~stapfen** *pl*: **in j-s ~ treten** follow in s.o.'s footsteps; **~tritt** *m* kick; **~weg** *m* foothpath; **e-e Stunde ~** an hour's walk

Futter[1] ['fʊtɐ] *n* (-s; no pl) AGR feed, fodder, food

'**Futter**[2] *n* (-s; -) lining

Futteral [fʊtə'raːl] *n* (-s; -e) case; cover

füttern[1] ['fʏtɐn] *v/t* (ge-, h) AGR feed

'**füttern**[2] *v/t* (ge-, h) line

'**Futternapf** *m* (feeding) bowl

Fütterung ['fʏtərʊŋ] *f* (-; -en) feeding (time)

Futur [fu'tuːɐ] *n* (-s; -e) future (*a.* LING)

G

gab [gaːp] *pret of* **geben**

Gabe ['gaːbə] *f* (-; -n) gift, present; MED dose; *fig* talent, gift; *milde* ~ alms

Gabel ['gaːbəl] *f* (-; -n) fork; TEL cradle

'gabeln *v/refl* (ge-, h) fork, branch

'Gabelstapler [-ʃtaːplə] *m* (-s; -) TECH fork-lift (truck)

Gabelung ['gaːbəluŋ] *f* (-; -en) fork(ing)

gackern ['gakən] *v/i* (ge-, h) cluck, cackle (*a. fig*)

gaffen ['gafən] *v/i* (ge-, h) gawk, gawp, F rubberneck; **Gaffer** ['gafə] *m* (-s; -) F rubberneck(er), *Br* nosy parker

Gage ['gaːʒə] *f* (-; -n) fee

gähnen ['gɛːnən] *v/i* (ge-, h) yawn

Gala ['gaːla] *f* (-; -s) gala

galant [ga'lant] *adj* gallant, courteous

Galeere [ga'leːrə] *f* (-; -n) MAR galley

Galerie [galə'riː] *f* (-; -n) gallery

Galgen ['galgən] *m* (-s; -) gallows; **~frist** *f* reprieve; **~hu,mor** *m* gallows humo(u)r; **~vogel** F *m* crook

Galle ['galə] *f* (-; -n) ANAT gall; bile

'Gallen|blase *f* ANAT gall bladder; **~stein** *m* MED gallstone

Gallert ['galɛt] *n* (-[es]; -e), **Gallerte** [ga'lɛrtə] *f* (-; -n) jelly

Galopp [ga'lɔp] *m* (-s; -s, -e) gallop

galoppieren [galɔ'piːrən] *v/i* (*no* -ge-, *sein*) gallop

galt [galt] *pret of* **gelten**

gammeln ['gaməln] F *v/i* (ge-, h) loaf (about), bum around; **Gammler(in)** ['gamlɐ (-lərin)] F (-s; -/-; -nen) loafer, bum

Gämse ['gɛmzə] *f* (-; -n) ZO chamois

gang [gaŋ] *adj*: ~ *und gäbe* nothing unusual, (quite) usual

Gang [gaŋ] *m* (-[e]s; *Gänge* ['gɛŋə]) walk, gait, way *s.o.* walks; ARCH passage, *a.* AVIAT *etc* aisle; corridor; MOT gear; GASTR course; *et. in ~ bringen* get s.th. going, start s.th.; *in ~ kommen* get started; *im ~(e) sein* be (going) on, be in progress; *in vollem ~(e)* in full swing

gängeln ['gɛŋəln] *v/t* (ge-, h) lead *s.o.* by the nose

gängig ['gɛŋɪç] *adj* current; ECON sal(e)able

'Gangschaltung *f* MOT gears

Ganove [ga'noːvə] F *m* (-n; -n) crook

Gans [gans] *f* (-; *Gänse* ['gɛnzə]) ZO goose

Gänse|blümchen ['gɛnzə-] *n* BOT daisy; **~braten** *m* roast goose; **~haut** *f* (-; *no pl*) gooseflesh; *dabei kriege ich e-e ~* F it gives me the creeps; **~marsch** *m* (-[e]s; *no pl*) single *or* Indian file

Gänserich ['gɛnzərɪç] *m* (-s; -e) ZO gander

ganz [gants] **1.** *adj* whole, entire, total; F undamaged; full (*hour etc*); *den ~en Tag* all day; *die ~e Zeit* all the time; *auf der ~en Welt* all over the world; *sein ~es Geld* all his money; **2.** *adv* completely, totally; very; quite, rather, fairly; ~ *allein* all by oneself; ~ *aus Holz* all wood *etc*; ~ *und gar* completely, totally; ~ *und gar nicht* not at all, by no means; ~ *wie du willst* just as you like; *nicht* ~ not quite; → *voll*

Ganze ['gantsə] *n* (-n; *no pl*) whole; *das* ~ the whole thing; *im ~n* in all, altogether; *im großen ~n* on the whole; *aufs ~ gehen* go all out

gänzlich ['gɛntslɪç] *adv* completely, entirely

'Ganztags|beschäftigung *f* full-time job; **~schule** *f* all-day school(ing)

gar [gaːɐ] **1.** *adj* GASTR done; **2.** *adv*: ~ *nicht* not at all; ~ *nichts* nothing at all; ~ *zu* ... (a bit) too ...

Garage [ga'raːʒə] *f* (-; -n) garage

Garantie [garan'tiː] *f* (-; -n) guarantee, *esp* ECON warranty; **garantieren** [garan'tiːrən] *v/t and v/i* (*no* -ge-, h) guarantee (*für et.* s.th.)

Garbe ['garbə] *f* (-; -n) AGR sheaf

Garde ['gardə] *f* (-; -n) guard; MIL (the) Guards

Garderobe [gardə'roːbə] *f* (-; -n) a) (*no pl*) wardrobe, clothes, b) checkroom, *Br* cloakroom; THEA dressing room

Garde'roben|frau *f* checkroom (*Br* cloakroom) attendant; **~marke** *f* coatcheck (*Br* cloakroom) ticket; **~ständer** *m* coat stand *or* rack

Gardine [gar'diːnə] *f* (-; -n) curtain

Gar'dinenstange *f* curtain rod

gären ['gɛ:rən] v/i ([irr,] ge-, h, sein) ferment, work

Garn [garn] n (-[e]s; -e) yarn; thread; cotton

Garnele [gar'ne:lə] f (-; -n) ZO shrimp; prawn

garnieren [gar'ni:rən] v/t (no -ge-, h) garnish (a. fig)

Garnison [garni'zo:n] f (-; -en) MIL garrison, post

Garnitur [garni'tu:ɐ] f (-; -en) set; suite

Garten ['gartən] m (-s; Gärten ['gɛrtən]) garden; **~arbeit** f gardening; **~bau** m (-[e]s; no pl) horticulture; **~erde** f (garden) mo(u)ld; **~fest** n garden party; **~geräte** pl gardening tools; **~haus** n summerhouse; **~lo,kal** n beer garden; outdoor restaurant; **~schere** f pruning shears; **~stadt** f garden city; **~zwerg** m (garden) gnome

Gärtner ['gɛrtnɐ] m (-s; -) gardener

Gärtnerei [gɛrtnə'rai] f (-; -en) truck farm, Br market garden

Gärtnerin f (-; -nen) gardener

Gärung ['gɛ:rʊŋ] f (-; -en) fermentation

Gas [ga:s] n (-es; -e ['ga:zə]) gas; **~ geben** MOT accelerate, F step on the gas

gasförmig [-fœrmɪç] adj gaseous

Gas|hahn m gas valve (or cock, Br tap); **~heizung** f gas heating; **~herd** m gas cooker or stove; **~kammer** f gas chamber; **~la,terne** f gas (street) lamp; **~leitung** f gas main; **~maske** f gas mask; **~ofen** m gas stove; **~pe,dal** n MOT gas pedal, Br accelerator (pedal)

Gasse ['gasə] f (-; -n) lane, alley

Gast [gast] m (-[e]s; Gäste ['gɛstə]) guest; visitor; customer

Gastarbeiter m, **Gastarbeiterin** f foreign worker

Gästebuch ['gɛstə-] n visitors' book

Gästezimmer n guest (or spare) room

gastfreundlich adj hospitable

Gastfreundschaft f hospitality

Gastgeber [-ge:bɐ] m (-s; -) host

Gastgeberin [-ge:bərɪn] f (-; -nen) hostess

Gast|haus n, **~hof** m restaurant, inn

gastieren [gas'ti:rən] v/i (no -ge-, h) give performances; THEA guest, give a guest performance

gastlich adj hospitable

Gast|mannschaft f SPORT visiting team; **~spiel** n THEA guest perform-ance; **~stätte** f restaurant; **~stube** f taproom; restaurant; **~wirt** m landlord; **~wirtschaft** f restaurant, inn

Gaswerk n TECH gasworks

Gaszähler m TECH gas meter

Gatte ['gatə] m (-n; -n) husband

Gatter ['gatə] n (-s; -) fence; gate

Gattin ['gatɪn] f (-; -nen) wife

Gattung ['gatʊŋ] f (-; -en) type, class, sort; BIOL genus; species

GAU [gau] (ABBR of **größter anzunehmender Unfall**) m (-[s]; no pl) worst case scenario, Br maximum credible accident, MCA

Gaul [gaul] m (-[e]s; Gäule ['gɔylə]) nag

Gaumen ['gaumən] m (-s; -) ANAT palate

Gauner ['gaunɐ] m (-s; -), **Gaunerin** f (-; -nen) F crook

Gaze ['ga:zə] f (-; -n) gauze

Gazelle [ga'tsɛlə] f (-; -n) ZO gazelle

geb. ABBR of **geboren** b., born

Gebäck [gə'bɛk] n (-[e]s; -e) pastry; cookies, Br biscuits

ge'backen pp of **backen**

Gebälk [gə'bɛlk] n (-[e]s; -e) timber-work, beams

gebar [gə'ba:ɐ] pret of **gebären**

Gebärde [gə'bɛ:ɐdə] f (-; -n) gesture

ge'bärden v/refl (no -ge-, h) behave, act (**wie** like)

gebären [gə'bɛ:rən] v/t (irr, no -ge-, h) give birth to; **Gebärmutter** [gə'bɛ:ɐ-] f ANAT uterus, womb

Gebäude [gə'bɔydə] n (-s; -) building, structure

Ge'beine pl bones, mortal remains

geben ['ge:bən] v/t (irr, ge-, h) give (**j-m et.** s.o. s.th.); hand, pass; deal (cards); make; **sich ~** pass; get better; **von sich ~** utter, let out; **j-m die Schuld ~** blame s.o.; **es gibt** there is, there are; **was gibt es?** what's up?; what's for lunch etc?; TV etc what's on?; **das gibt's nicht** that can't be true; that's out

Gebet [gə'be:t] n (-[e]s; -e) prayer

ge'beten pp of **bitten**

Gebiet [gə'bi:t] n (-[e]s; -e) region, area; esp POL territory; fig field

ge'bieterisch adj imperious

ge'bietsweise adv regionally; **~ Regen** local showers

Gebilde [gə'bɪldə] n (-s; -) thing, object

gebildet [gə'bɪldət] adj educated

Gebirge [gə'bɪrgə] n (-s; -) mountains

gebirgig [gəˈbɪrgɪç] adj mountainous
Ge'birgs|bewohner m mountain--dweller; **~zug** m mountain range
Ge'biss n (-es; -e) (set of) teeth; (set of) false teeth, denture(s)
ge'bissen pp of **beißen**
Gebläse [gəˈblɛːzə] n (-s; -) TECH blower, (MOT air) fan
ge'blasen pp of **blasen**
geblichen [gəˈblɪçən] pp of **bleichen**
geblieben [gəˈbliːbən] pp of **bleiben**
geblümt [gəˈblyːmt] adj floral
gebogen [gəˈboːgən] 1. pp of **biegen**; 2. adj bent, curved
geboren [gəˈboːrən] 1. pp of **gebären**; 2. adj born; **ein ~er Deutscher** German by birth; **~e Smith** née Smith; **ich bin am ... ~** I was born on the ...
geborgen [gəˈbɔrgən] 1. pp of **bergen**; 2. adj safe, secure; **Ge'borgenheit** f (-; no pl) safety, security
geborsten [gəˈbɔrstən] pp of **bersten**
Gebot [gəˈboːt] n (-[e]s; -e) REL commandment; fig rule; necessity; auction etc: bid
geboten [gəˈboːtən] pp of **bieten**
gebracht [gəˈbraxt] pp of **bringen**
gebrannt [gəˈbrant] pp of **brennen**
ge'braten pp of **braten**
Ge'brauch m (-[e]s; no pl) use; application; **ge'brauchen** v/t (no -ge-, h) use; employ; **gut (schlecht) zu ~ sein** be useful (useless); **ich könnte ... ~** I could do with ...; **gebräuchlich** [gəˈbrɔyçlɪç] adj common, usual; current
Ge'brauchsanweisung f directions or instructions for use
ge'brauchsfertig adj ready for use; instant (coffee etc)
Ge'brauchsgrafiker m commercial artist
ge'braucht adj used, ECON a. second--hand
Ge'brauchtwagen m MOT used or second-hand car; **~händler** m used car dealer
Ge'brechen n (-s; -) defect, handicap
gebrechlich [gəˈbrɛçlɪç] adj frail; infirm; **Ge'brechlichkeit** f (-; no pl) frailty; infirmity
gebrochen [gəˈbrɔxən] pp of **brechen**
Ge'brüder pl brothers
Gebrüll [gəˈbrʏl] n (-[e]s; no pl) roar (-ing)

Gebühr [gəˈbyːɐ] f (-; -en) charge (a. TEL), fee; postage; due; **gebührend** [gəˈbyːrənt] adj due; proper
ge'bühren|frei adj free of charge; TEL toll-free, Br nonchargeable; **~pflichtig** adj chargeable; **~e Straße** toll road; **~e Verwarnung** fine
gebunden [gəˈbʊndən] 1. pp of **binden**; 2. adj bound, fig a. tied
Geburt [gəˈbuːrt] f (-; -en) birth; **Deutscher von ~** German by birth
Ge'burten|kon,trolle f, **~regelung** f birth control
ge'burten|schwach adj low-birthrate; **~stark** adj; **~e Jahrgänge** baby boom
Ge'burtenziffer f birthrate
gebürtig [gəˈbʏrtɪç] adj by birth
Ge'burts|anzeige f birth announcement; **~datum** n date of birth; **~fehler** m congenital defect; **~helfer(in)** obstetrician; **~jahr** n year of birth; **~land** n native country; **~ort** m birthplace; **~tag** m birthday; **~tagsfeier** f birthday party; **~tagskind** n birthday boy (or girl); **~urkunde** f birth certificate
Gebüsch [gəˈbʏʃ] n (-[e]s; -e) bushes, shrubbery
gedacht [gəˈdaxt] pp of **denken**
Gedächtnis [gəˈdɛçtnɪs] n (-ses; -se) memory; **aus dem ~** from memory; **zum ~ an** (acc) in memory (or commemoration) of; **im ~ behalten** keep in mind, remember; **~lücke** f memory lapse; **~schwund** m MED amnesia; blackout; **~stütze** f memory aid
Gedanke [gəˈdaŋkə] m (-n; -n) thought; idea; **was für ein ~!** what an idea!; **in ~n** absorbed in thought; absent--minded; **sich ~n machen über** (acc) think about; be worried or concerned about; **j-s ~n lesen** read s.o.'s mind
Ge'danken|austausch m exchange of ideas; **~gang** m train of thought
ge'dankenlos adj thoughtless
Ge'danken|strich m dash; **~übertragung** f telepathy
Gedeck [gəˈdɛk] n (-[e]s; -e) cover; **ein ~ auflegen** set a place
gedeihen [gəˈdaɪən] v/i (irr, no -ge-, sein) thrive, prosper; grow; flourish
ge'denken v/i (irr, **denken**, no -ge-, h) (gen) think of; commemorate; mention
Gedenk|feier [gəˈdɛŋk-] f commemoration; **~mi,nute** f: **e-e ~** a moment's (Br

minute's) silence; **~stätte** f, **~stein** m memorial; **~tafel** f plaque

Gedicht [gə'dɪçt] n (-[e]s; -e) poem

gediegen [gə'diːgən] adj solid; tasteful

gedieh [gə'diː] pret of **gedeihen**

gediehen [gə'diːən] pp of **gedeihen**

Gedränge [gə'drɛŋə] n (-s; -) crowd, F crush; **ge'drängt** fig adj concise

gedroschen [gə'drɔʃən] pp of **dreschen**

ge'drückt fig adj depressed

gedrungen [gə'drʊŋən] 1. pp of **dringen**; 2. adj squat, stocky; thickset

Geduld [gə'dʊlt] f (-; no pl) patience; **ge'dulden** v/refl (no -ge-, h) wait (patiently); **geduldig** [gə'dʊldɪç] adj patient; **Ge'duldspiel** n puzzle (a. fig)

gedurft [gə'dʊrft] pp of **dürfen**

geehrt [gə'ʔeːrt] adj hono(u)red; **Sehr ~er Herr N.** Dear Mr N.

geeignet [gə'ʔaignət] adj suitable; suited, qualified; right

Gefahr [gə'faːr] f (-; -en) danger; threat; risk; **auf eigene ~** at one's own risk; **außer ~** out of danger, safe

gefährden [gə'fɛːrdən] v/t (no -ge-, h) endanger; risk, jeopardize

ge'fahren pp of **fahren**

gefährlich [gə'fɛːrlɪç] adj dangerous; risky

ge'fahrlos adj without risk, safe

Gefährte [gə'fɛːrtə] m (-n; -n), **Ge'fährtin** f (-; -nen) companion

Gefälle [gə'fɛlə] n (-s; -) fall, slope, descent; gradient (a. PHYS)

ge'fallen 1. pp of **fallen**; 2. v/i (irr, **fallen**, no -ge-, h) please; **es gefällt mir (nicht)** I (don't) like it; **wie gefällt dir ...?** how do you like ...?; **sich et. ~ lassen** put up with s.th.

Ge'fallen[1] m (-s; -) favo(u)r; **j-n um e-n ~ bitten** ask a favo(u)r of s.o.

Ge'fallen[2] n: **~ finden an** (dat) enjoy, like

ge'fällig adj pleasant, agreeable; obliging, kind; **j-m ~ sein** do s.o. a favo(u)r

Ge'fälligkeit f (-; -en) a) (no pl) kindness, b) favo(u)r

ge'fangen 1. pp of **fangen**; 2. adj captive; imprisoned; **~ halten** keep s.o. prisoner; **~ nehmen** take s.o. prisoner; fig captivate; **Ge'fangene** m, f (-n; -n) prisoner; convict; **Ge'fangennahme** f (-; no pl) capture; **Ge'fangenschaft** f

(-; no pl) captivity, imprisonment; **in ~ sein** be a prisoner of war

Gefängnis [gə'fɛŋnɪs] n (-ses; -se) prison, jail, Br a. gaol; **ins ~ kommen** go to jail or prison; **~di,rektor** m, governor, warden; **~strafe** f (sentence or term of) imprisonment; **~wärter** m prison guard

Gefäß [gə'fɛːs] n (-es; -e) vessel (a. ANAT), container

gefasst [gə'fast] adj composed; **~ auf** (acc) prepared for

Gefecht [gə'fɛçt] n (-[e]s; -e) MIL combat, action

gefedert [gə'feːdət] adj: **gut ~ sein** MOT have good suspension

gefeit [gə'fait] adj: **~ gegen** immune to

Gefieder [gə'fiːdə] n (-s; -) ZO plumage, feathers

geflochten [gə'flɔxtən] pp of **flechten**

geflogen [gə'floːgən] pp of **fliegen**

geflohen [gə'floːən] pp of **fliehen**

geflossen [gə'flɔsən] pp of **fließen**

Ge'flügel n (-s; no pl) poultry

ge'flügelt adj: **~es Wort** saying

gefochten [gə'fɔxtən] pp of **fechten**

Ge'folge n (-s; -) entourage, retinue, train; **Gefolgschaft** [gə'fɔlkʃaft] f (-; -en) followers

gefragt [gə'fraːkt] adj in demand, popular

gefräßig [gə'frɛːsɪç] adj greedy, voracious

Gefreite [gə'fraitə] m (-n; -n) MIL first class, Br lance corporal

ge'fressen pp of **fressen**

ge'frieren v/i (irr, **frieren**, no -ge-, sein) freeze

Gefrier|fach [gə'friːɐ-] n freezer, freezing compartment; **~fleisch** n frozen meat

ge'friergetrocknet adj freeze-dried

Ge'frier|punkt m freezing point; **~truhe** f freezer, deep-freeze

gefroren [gə'froːrən] pp of **frieren**

Ge'frorene Austrian n (-n; no pl) ice cream

Gefüge [gə'fyːgə] n (-s; -) structure, texture

gefügig [gə'fyːgɪç] adj pliant

Ge'fügigkeit f (-; no pl) pliancy

Gefühl [gə'fyːl] n (-[e]s; -e) feeling; sense; sensation; emotion; **ge'fühllos** adj insensible, numb; unfeeling, heartless; **ge'fühlsbetont** adj (highly) emo-

G

tional; **ge'fühlvoll** adj (full of) feeling; tender; sentimental

gefunden [gə'fʊndən] pp of **finden**

gegangen [gə'gaŋən] pp of **gehen**

gegeben [gə'ge:bən] pp of **geben**

gegen ['ge:gən] prp (acc) against, JUR, SPORT a. versus; about, around; (in return) for; MED etc for; compared with

'**Gegen...** in cpds ...aktion, ...angriff, ...argument, ...frage etc: counter-...; **~besuch** m return visit

Gegend ['ge:gənt] f (-; -en) region, area; countryside; neighbo(u)rhood

gegenei'nander adv against one another or each other

'**Gegen|fahrbahn** f MOT opposite or oncoming lane; **~gewicht** n counterweight; **ein ~ bilden zu et.** counterbalance s.th.; **~kandi,dat** m rival candidate; **~leistung** f quid pro quo; **als ~** in return; **~licht** n (-[e]s; no pl) PHOT back light; **im** or **bei ~** against the light; **~maßnahme** f countermeasure; **~mittel** n MED antidote (a. fig); **~par,tei** f other side; POL opposition; SPORT opposite side; **~richtung** f opposite direction

'**Gegensatz** m contrast; opposite; **im ~ zu** in contrast to or with; '**gegensätzlich** [-zɛtslɪç] adj contrary, opposite

'**Gegenseite** f opposite side

'**gegenseitig** [-zaɪtɪç] adj mutual

'**Gegenseitigkeit** f: **auf ~ beruhen** be mutual

'**Gegen|spieler** m, **~spielerin** f SPORT opponent (a. fig); **~sprechanlage** f intercom (system)

'**Gegenstand** m object (a. fig); fig subject; '**gegenständlich** [-ʃtɛntlɪç] adj art: representational; '**gegenstandslos** adj invalid; irrelevant; art: abstract, nonrepresentational

'**Gegen|stimme** f PARL vote against, no; **nur drei ~n** only three noes; **~stück** n counterpart

'**Gegenteil** n opposite; **im ~** on the contrary; '**gegenteilig** adj contrary, opposite

gegen'über adv and prp (dat) opposite; fig to, toward(s); compared with

Gegen'über n (-s; -) person opposite; neighbo(u)r across the street

gegen'überstehen v/i (irr, **stehen**, sep, -ge-, h) face, be faced with

Gegen'überstellung f confrontation

'**Gegenverkehr** m oncoming traffic

'**Gegenwart** [-vart] f (-; no pl) present (time); presence; LING present (tense)

'**gegenwärtig** [-vɛrtɪç] **1.** adj present, current; **2.** adv at present

'**Gegen|wehr** [-ve:ɐ] f (-; no pl) resistance; **~wert** m equivalent (value); **~wind** m head wind

'**gegenzeichnen** v/t (sep, -ge-, h) countersign

'**Gegenzug** m countermove; RAIL train coming from the opposite direction

gegessen [gə'gɛsən] pp of **essen**

geglichen [gə'glɪçən] pp of **gleichen**

geglitten [gə'glɪtən] pp of **gleiten**

geglommen [gə'glɔmən] pp of **glimmen**

Gegner ['ge:gnɐ] m (-s; -), '**Gegnerin** f (-; -nen) opponent (a. SPORT), adversary; MIL enemy

'**gegnerisch** adj opposing; MIL (of the) enemy, hostile

'**Gegnerschaft** f (-; -en) opposition

gegolten [gə'gɔltən] pp of **gelten**

gegoren [gə'go:rən] pp of **gären**

gegossen [gə'gɔsən] pp of **gießen**

ge'graben pp of **graben**

gegriffen [gə'grɪfən] pp of **greifen**

gehabt [gə'ha:pt] pp of **haben**

Gehackte [gə'haktə] n → **Hackfleisch**

Gehalt [gə'halt] **1.** m (-[e]s; no pl) content; **2.** n (-[e]s; **Gehälter** [gə'hɛltɐ]) salary

ge'halten pp of **halten**

Ge'halts|empfänger m salaried employee; **~erhöhung** f raise, Br increase or rise in salary

ge'haltvoll adj substantial; nutritious

gehangen [gə'haŋən] pp of **hängen** 1

gehässig [gə'hɛsɪç] adj malicious, spiteful; **Ge'hässigkeit** f (-; no pl) malice, spite(fulness)

ge'hauen pp of **hauen**

Gehäuse [gə'hɔʏzə] n (-s; -) case, box; TECH casing; ZO shell; BOT core

Gehege [gə'he:gə] n (-s; -) enclosure

geheim [gə'haɪm] adj secret; **et. ~ halten** keep s.th. (a) secret

Ge'heim|a,gent m secret agent; **~dienst** m secret service

Geheimnis [gə'haɪmnɪs] n (-ses; -se) secret; mystery

ge'heimnisvoll adj mysterious

Ge'heim|nummer f TEL unlisted (Br

ex-directory) number; **~poli,zei** f secret police; **~schrift** f code, cipher

ge'heißen pp of heißen

gehemmt [gə'hɛmt] adj inhibited, self--conscious

gehen ['ge:ən] v/i (irr, ge-, sein) go; walk; leave; TECH work (a. fig); ECON sell; fig last; **einkaufen (schwimmen) ~** go shopping (swimming); **~ wir!** let's go!; **wie geht es dir (Ihnen)?** how are you?; **es geht mir gut (schlecht)** I'm fine (not feeling well); **~ in** (acc) go into; **~ nach** road etc: lead to; window etc: face; fig go or judge by; **das geht nicht** that's impossible; **das geht schon** that's o.k.; **es geht nichts über** (acc) ... there is nothing like ...; **worum geht es?** what is it about?; **darum geht es (nicht)** that's (not) the point; **sich ~ lassen** let o.s. go

geheuer [gə'hɔyɐ] adj: **nicht (ganz) ~** eerie, creepy, F fishy

Geheul [gə'hɔyl] n (-[e]s; no pl) howling

Ge'hirn n (-[e]s; -e) ANAT brain(s); **~erschütterung** f MED concussion (of the brain); **~schlag** m MED (cerebral) apoplexy; **~wäsche** f brainwashing

gehoben [gə'ho:bən] **1.** pp of heben; **2.** adj elevated; high(er); **~e Stimmung** high spirits

Gehöft [gə'hœft] n (-[e]s; -e) farm(stead)

geholfen [gə'hɔlfən] pp of helfen

Gehölz [gə'hœlts] n (-es; -e) wood, coppice, copse

Gehör [gə'hø:ɐ] n (-[e]s; -e) (sense of) hearing; ear; **nach dem ~** by ear; **sich ~ verschaffen** make o.s. heard

ge'horchen v/i (no -ge-, h) obey; **nicht ~** disobey

ge'hören v/i (no -ge-, h) belong (dat or zu to); **gehört dir das?** is this yours?; **es gehört sich (nicht)** it is proper or right (not done); **das gehört nicht hierher** that's not to the point

ge'hörig **1.** adj due, proper; necessary; decent; **zu et. ~** belonging to s.th.; **2.** adv properly, thoroughly

ge'hörlos adj deaf; **die Gehörlosen** the deaf

gehorsam [gə'ho:rza:m] adj obedient

Ge'horsam m (-s; no pl) obedience

'Gehsteig m, 'Gehweg m sidewalk, Br pavement

Geier ['gaiɐ] m (-s; -) ZO vulture, buzzard

Geige ['gaigə] f (-; -n) MUS violin, F fiddle; **(auf der) ~ spielen** play (on) the violin

'Geigen|bogen m MUS (violin) bow; **~kasten** m MUS violin case

'Geiger ['gaigɐ] m (-s; -), Geigerin ['gaigərin] f (-; -nen) MUS violinist

'Geigerzähler m PHYS Geiger counter

geil [gail] adj V hot, horny; contp lecherous, lewd; BOT rank; F awesome, Br brill, ace

Geisel ['gaizəl] f (-; -n) hostage; **~nehmer** [-ne:mɐ] m (-s; -) kidnap(p)er

Geißel ['gaisəl] fig f (-; -n) scourge

Geist [gaist] m (-[e]s; -er) a) (no pl) spirit; soul; mind; intellect; wit, b) ghost; **der Heilige ~** REL the Holy Ghost or Spirit

Geister|bahn f [gaistɐ] f tunnel of horror, Br ghost train; **~fahrer** F m MOT wrong-way driver

'geisterhaft adj ghostly

'geistesabwesend adj absent-minded

'Geistes|arbeiter m brainworker; **~blitz** m brainstorm, Br brainwave

'Geistesgegenwart f presence of mind; 'geistesgegenwärtig adj alert; quick-witted

'geistesgestört adj mentally disturbed, deranged

'geisteskrank adj mentally ill

'Geisteskrankheit f mental illness

'geistesschwach adj feeble-minded

'Geisteswissenschaften pl the arts, the humanities

'Geisteszustand m mental state

geistig ['gaistɪç] adj mental; intellectual; spiritual; **~ behindert** mentally handicapped; **~e Getränke** spirits

'geistlich adj religious; spiritual; ecclesiastical; clerical; 'Geistliche m (-n; -n) clergyman; priest; minister; **die ~n** the clergy

'geistlos adj trivial, inane, silly

'geistreich, 'geistvoll adj witty, clever

Geiz [gaits] m (-es; no pl) stinginess

'Geizhals m miser, niggard

geizig ['gaitsɪç] adj stingy, miserly

Ge'jammer F n (-s; no pl) wailing, complaining

gekannt [gə'kant] pp of kennen

G

Gekläff [gə'klɛf] F n (-[e]s; no pl) yapping

Geklapper [gə'klapɐ] F n (-s; no pl) clatter(ing)

Geklimper F n (-s; no pl) tinkling

geklungen [gə'kluŋən] pp of **klingen**

gekniffen [gə'knɪfən] pp of **kneifen**

ge'kommen pp of **kommen**

gekonnt [gə'kɔnt] 1. pp of **können**; 2. adj masterly

gekränkt [gə'krɛŋkt] adj hurt, offended

Gekritzel [gə'krɪtsəl] contp n (-s; no pl) scrawl, scribble

gekrochen [gə'krɔxən] pp of **kriechen**

gekünstelt [gə'kʏnstəlt] adj affected; artificial

Gelächter [gə'lɛçtɐ] n (-s; no pl) laughter

ge'laden pp of **laden**

Ge'lage n (-s; -) feast; carouse

Gelände [gə'lɛndə] n (-s; -) area, country, ground; site; fig convenient, opportune; *... in cpds ...lauf, ...ritt, ...wagen etc:* cross-country ...

Geländer [gə'lɛndɐ] n (-s; -) banisters; handrail, rail(ing); parapet

ge'lang pret of **gelingen**

ge'langen v/i (no -ge-, sein) ~ **an** (acc) or **nach** reach, arrive at, get or come to; ~ **in** (acc) get or come into; fig **zu et.** ~ gain or win or achieve s.th.

ge'lassen 1. pp of **lassen**; 2. adj calm, composed, cool

Gelatine [ʒela'tiːnə] f (-; no pl) gelatin(e)

ge'laufen pp of **laufen**

ge'läufig adj common, current; familiar

gelaunt [gə'launt] adj: **schlecht** (**gut**) ~ **sein** be in a bad (good) mood

gelb [gɛlp] adj yellow

'gelblich adj yellowish

'Gelbsucht f (-; no pl) MED jaundice

Geld [gɛlt] n (-[e]s; -er ['gɛldɐ]) money; **zu** ~ **machen** turn into cash

'Geld|angelegenheiten pl money or financial matters or affairs; ~**anlage** f investment; ~**ausgabe** f expense; ~**automat** m automatic teller machine, ATM, autoteller, Br cash dispenser; ~**beutel** m, ~**börse** f purse; ~**buße** f fine, penalty; ~**geber(in)** [-geːbɐ (-bərɪn)] (-s; -/-; -nen) financial backer; investor

'geldgierig adj greedy for money

'Geld|knappheit f, ~**mangel** m lack of money; ECON (financial) stringency; ~**mittel** pl funds, means, resources; ~**schein** m bill, Br (bank)note; ~**schrank** m safe; ~**sendung** f remittance; ~**strafe** f fine; ~**stück** n coin; ~**verlegenheit** f financial embarrassment; ~**verschwendung** f waste of money; ~**waschanlage** f money laundering scheme; ~**wechsel** m exchange of money; ~**wechsler** [-vɛkslɐ] m (-s; -) change machine

Gelee [ʒe'leː] n, m (-s; -s) jelly; gel

ge'legen 1. pp of **liegen**; **2.** adj situated, located; fig convenient, opportune; **Ge'legenheit** f (-; -en) occasion; opportunity, chance; **bei** ~ on occasion

Ge'legenheits|arbeit f casual or odd job; ~**arbeiter** m casual labo(u)rer, odd-job man; ~**kauf** m bargain

gelegentlich [gə'leːgəntlɪç] adv occasionally

gelehrig [gə'leːrɪç] adj docile

Gelehrsamkeit [gə'leːrzaːmkait] f (-; no pl) learning; **gelehrt** [gə'leːrt] adj learned; **Ge'lehrte** m, f (-n; -n) scholar, learned man or woman

Geleise [gə'laizə] n → **Gleis**

Geleit [gə'lait] n (-[e]s; -e) escort

ge'leiten v/t (no -ge-, h) accompany, conduct, escort

Ge'leitzug m MAR, MIL convoy

Gelenk [gə'lɛŋk] n (-[e]s; -e) ANAT, TECH joint; **ge'lenkig** adj flexible (a. TECH); lithe, supple

gelernt [gə'lɛrnt] adj skilled, trained

ge'lesen pp of **lesen**

geliebt [gə'liːpt] adj (be)loved, dear

Ge'liebte 1. m (-n; -n) lover; **2.** f (-n; -n) mistress

geliehen [gə'liːən] pp of **leihen**

gelingen [gə'lɪŋən] v/i (irr, no -ge-, sein) succeed, manage; turn out well; **es gelang mir, et. zu tun** I succeeded in doing (I managed to do) s.th.; **Ge'lingen** n (-s; no pl) success; **gutes** ~! good luck!

gelitten [gə'lɪtən] pp of **leiden**

gelogen [gə'loːgən] pp of **lügen**

gelten ['gɛltən] v/i and v/t (irr, ge-, h) be worth; fig count for; be valid; SPORT count; ECON be effective; ~ **für** apply to; ~ **als** be regarded or looked upon as, be considered or supposed to be;

generell

~ *lassen* accept (*als* as); **~d** *adj* accepted; ~ *machen* assert; *s-n Einfluss* (*bei j-m*) ~ *machen* bring one's influence to bear (on s.o.)

'Geltung *f* (-; *no pl*) prestige; weight; *zur* ~ *kommen* show to advantage

'Geltungsbedürfnis *n* (-*ses*; *no pl*) need for recognition

Gelübde [gə'lʏpdə] *n* (-*s*; -) vow

gelungen [gə'lʊŋən] **1.** *pp of* **gelingen**; **2.** *adj* successful, a success

gemächlich [gə'mɛːçlɪç] *adj* leisurely

ge'mahlen *pp of* **mahlen**

Gemälde [gə'mɛːldə] *n* (-*s*; -) painting, picture; **~gale,rie** *f* art (*or* picture) gallery

gemäß [gə'mɛːs] *prp* (*dat*) according to

gemäßigt [gə'mɛːsɪçt] *adj* moderate; temperate (*climate etc*)

gemein [gə'maɪn] *adj* mean; dirty, filthy (*joke etc*), BOT, ZO common

Gemeinde [gə'maɪndə] *f* (-; -*n*) POL municipality; local government; REL parish; congregation; **~rat** *m* (member of the) city (*Br* local) council; **~rätin** [-rɛːtɪn] *f* (-; -*nen*) member of the city (*Br* local) council; **~steuern** *pl* local taxes, *Br* (local) rates

ge'meingefährlich *adj*; **~er Mensch** public enemy

Ge'meinheit *f* (-; -*en*) a) (*no pl*) meanness, b) mean thing (to do *or* say), F dirty trick

ge'meinnützig [-nʏtsɪç] *adj* non-profit, *Br* non-profitmaking

Ge'meinplatz *m* commonplace

ge'meinsam **1.** *adj* common, joint; mutual; **2.** *adv* together

Ge'meinschaft *f* (-; -*en*) community

Ge'meinschafts|arbeit *f* teamwork; **~kunde** *f* (-; *no pl*) PED social studies; **~produkti,on** *f* coproduction; **~raum** *m* recreation room, lounge

Ge'meinsinn *m* (-[*e*]*s*; *no pl*) public spirit; (sense of) solidarity

ge'meinverständlich *adj* popular

Ge'meinwohl *n* public welfare

ge'messen **1.** *pp of* **messen**; **2.** *adj* measured; formal; grave

Gemetzel [gə'mɛtsəl] *n* (-*s*; -) slaughter, massacre

gemieden [gə'miːdən] *pp of* **meiden**

Gemisch [gə'mɪʃ] *n* (-[*e*]*s*; -*e*) mixture (*a.* CHEM)

gemocht [gə'mɔxt] *pp of* **mögen**

gemolken [gə'mɔlkən] *pp of* **melken**

Gemse → **Gämse**

Gemurmel [gə'mʊrməl] *n* (-*s*; *no pl*) murmur, mutter

Gemüse [gə'myːzə] *n* (-*s*; -) vegetable(s); greens; **~händler** *m* greengrocer('s)

gemusst [gə'mʊst] *pp of* **müssen**

Gemüt [gə'myːt] *n* (-[*e*]*s*; -*er*) mind, soul; heart; nature, mentality

ge'mütlich *adj* comfortable, snug, cozy, *Br* cosy; peaceful, pleasant, relaxed; *mach es dir* ~ make yourself at home; **Ge'mütlichkeit** *f* (-; *no pl*) snugness, coziness, *Br* cosiness; cozy (*Br* cosy) *or* relaxed atmosphere

Ge'mütsbewegung *f* emotion

ge'mütskrank *adj* emotionally disturbed

Ge'mütszustand *m* state of mind

Gen [geːn] *n* (-*s*; -*e*) BIOL gene

genannt [gə'nant] *pp of* **nennen**

genas [gə'naːs] *pret of* **genesen** 1

genau [gə'nau] **1.** *adj* exact, precise, accurate; careful, close; strict; *Genaueres* further details; **2.** *adv*: ~ *um 10 Uhr* at 10 o'clock sharp; ~ *der ...* that very ...; ~ *zuhören* listen closely; *es* ~ *nehmen* (*mit et.*) be particular (about s.th.); **Ge'nauigkeit** *f* (-; *no pl*) accuracy, precision, exactness

ge'nauso *adv* → **ebenso**

genehmigen [gə'neːmɪgən] *v/t* (*no -ge-*, *h*) permit, allow; approve

Ge'nehmigung *f* (-; -*en*) permission; approval; permit; licen|se, *Br* -ce

geneigt [gə'naɪkt] *adj* inclined (*zu* to)

General [genə'raːl] *m* (-*s*; *Generäle* [genə'rɛːlə]) MIL general; **~di,rektor** *m* ECON president, *Br* chairman; **~konsul** *m* consul general; **~konsu,lat** *n* consulate general; **~probe** *f* THEA dress rehearsal; **~sekre,tär** *m* secretary-general; **~stab** *m* MIL general staff; **~streik** *m* general strike; **~versammlung** *f* general meeting; **~vertreter** *m* ECON sole agent

Generation [genəra'tsjoːn] *f* (-; -*en*) generation; **Generati'onenkon,flikt** *m* generation gap

Generator [genə'raːtoːr] *m* (-*s*; -*en* [-ra'toːrən]) ELECTR generator

generell [genə'rɛl] *adj* general, universal

genesen [gə'ne:zən] **1.** *v/i* (*irr*, *no -ge-*, *sein*) recover (*von* from), get well; **2.** *pp of genesen 1* enjoy

Ge'nesung *f* (*-*; *no pl*) recovery

Genetik [ge'ne:tɪk] *f* (*-*; *no pl*) BIOL genetics; **ge'netisch** *adj* BIOL genetic; **~er Fingerabdruck** genetic fingerprint

genial [ge'nja:l] *adj* brilliant, of genius

Genialität [genjali'tɛ:t] *f* (*-*; *no pl*) genius

Genick [gə'nɪk] *n* (*-[e]s*; *-e*) ANAT (back *or* nape of the) neck

Genie [ʒe'ni:] *n* (*-s*; *-s*) genius

genieren [ʒe'ni:rən] *v/refl* (*no -ge-*, *h*) be embarrassed

genießen [gə'ni:sən] *v/t* (*irr*, *no -ge-*, *h*) enjoy

Genießer [gə'ni:sɐ] *m* (*-s*; *-*) gourmet

Genitiv ['ge:niti:f] *m* (*-s*; *-e*) LING genitive *or* possessive (case)

genommen [gə'nɔmən] *pp of nehmen*

genormt [gə'nɔrmt] *adj* standardized

genoss [gə'nɔs] *pret of genießen*

Genosse [gə'nɔsə] *m* (*-n*; *-n*) POL comrade; F pal, buddy, *Br* mate

genossen [gə'nɔsən] *pp of genießen*

Ge'nossenschaft *f* (*-*; *-en*) cooperative

Ge'nossin *f* (*-*; *-nen*) POL comrade

'Gentechnik *f*, **'Gentechnolo,gie** *f* genetic engineering

genug [gə'nu:k] *adj* enough, sufficient

Genüge [gə'ny:gə] *f*: *zur ~* (well) enough, sufficiently

ge'nügen *v/i* (*no -ge-*, *h*) be enough, be sufficient; *das genügt* that will do; **~d** *adj* enough, sufficient; plenty of

genügsam [gə'ny:kza:m] *adj* easily satisfied; frugal; modest; **Ge'nügsamkeit** *f* (*-*; *no pl*) modesty; frugality

Ge'nugtuung *f* (*-*; *no pl*) satisfaction

Genus [gə'nʊs] *n* (*-*; *Genera* ['ge:nera']) LING gender

Genuss [gə'nʊs] *m* (*-es*; *Genüsse* [gə'nysə]) a) pleasure, b) (*no pl*) consumption; *ein ~* a real treat; *food: a.* delicious; **~mittel** *n* excise item, *Br* (semi-)luxury

Geografie, Geographie [geogra'fi:] *f* (*-*; *no pl*) geography; **geografisch, geographisch** [geo'gra:fɪʃ] *adj* geographic(al)

Geologe [geo'lo:gə] *m* (*-n*; *-n*) geologist; **Geologie** [geolo'gi:] *f* (*-*; *no pl*) geology; **Geo'login** *f* (*-*; *-nen*) geologist;

geologisch [geo'lo:gɪʃ] *adj* geologic(al)

Geometrie [geome'tri:] *f* (*-*; *no pl*) geometry; **geometrisch** [geo'me:trɪʃ] *adj* geometric(al)

Gepäck [gə'pɛk] *n* (*-[e]s*; *no pl*) baggage, luggage; **~ablage** *f* baggage (*or* luggage) rack; **~aufbewahrung** *f* baggage room, *Br* left-luggage office; **~kon,trolle** *f* baggage check, *Br* luggage inspection; **~schalter** *m* baggage (*or* luggage) counter; **~schein** *m* baggage check, *Br* luggage ticket; **~träger** *m* porter; *bicycle*: carrier

gepanzert [gə'pantsɛt] *adj* MOT armo(u)red

Gepard ['ge:part] *m* (*-s*; *-e*) ZO cheetah

gepfiffen [gə'pfɪfən] *pp of pfeifen*

gepflegt [gə'pfle:kt] *adj* well-groomed, neat; *fig* cultivated

Gepflogenheit [gə'pflo:gənhait] *f* (*-*; *-en*) habit, custom

Geplapper [gə'plapɐ] F *n* (*-s*; *no pl*) babbling, chatter(ing)

Geplauder [gə'plaudɐ] *n* (*-s*; *no pl*) chat(ting)

Gepolter [gə'pɔltɐ] *n* (*-s*; *no pl*) rumble

gepriesen [gə'pri:zən] *pp of preisen*

Gequassel [gə'kvasəl] F *n* (*-s*; *no pl*), **Gequatsche** [gə'kvatʃə] F *n* (*-s*; *no pl*) blather, blabber

gequollen [gə'kvɔlən] *pp of quellen*

gerade [gə'ra:də] **1.** *adj* straight (*a. fig*); even (*number*); direct; upright, erect (*posture*); **2.** *adv* just; *nicht ~* not exactly; *das ist es ja ~!* that's just it!; *~ deshalb* that's just why; *~ rechtzeitig* just in time; *warum ~ ich?* why me of all people?; *da wir ~ von ... sprechen* speaking of ...; **Ge'rade** *f* (*-n*; *-n*) MATH (straight) line; SPORT straight; *linke* (*rechte*) *~ boxing*: straight left (right)

gerade'aus *adv* straight on *or* ahead; **~he'raus** *adj* straightforward, frank

ge'radestehen *v/i* (*irr*, *stehen*, *sep*, *-ge-*, *h*) stand straight; *~ für* answer for

ge'radewegs *adv* straight, directly

ge'radezu *adv* simply

gerannt [gə'rant] *pp of rennen*

Gerät [gə'rɛ:t] *n* (*-[e]s*; *-e*) device; F gadget; appliance; (*kitchen*) utensil; *radio*, TV set; *coll, a.* SPORT *etc* equipment; SPORT apparatus; TECH tool; instrument

ge'raten 1. pp of raten; 2. v/i (irr, raten, no -ge-, sein) turn out (gut well); ~ an (acc) come across; ~ in (acc) get into; in Brand ~ catch fire

Ge'räteturnen n apparatus gymnastics

Ge'ratewohl n: aufs ~ at random

geräumig [gə'rɔymɪç] adj spacious, roomy

Geräusch [gə'rɔyʃ] n (-[e]s; -e) sound, noise; ge'räuschlos 1. adj noiseless (a. TECH); 2. adv without a sound; ge'räuschvoll adj noisy

gerben ['gɛrbən] v/t (ge-, h) tan

Gerberei [gɛrbə'rai] f (-; -en) tannery

ge'recht adj just, fair; (j-m, e-r Sache) ~ werden do justice to; meet (demands etc); Ge'rechtigkeit f (-; no pl) justice

Ge'rede F n (-s; no pl) talk; gossip

gereizt [gə'raitst] adj irritable

Ge'reiztheit f (-; no pl) irritability

Gericht¹ [gə'rɪçt] n (-[e]s; -e) GASTR dish

Ge'richt² n (-[e]s; -e) JUR court; vor ~ stehen (stellen) stand (bring to) trial; vor ~ gehen go to court

Ge'richtlich adj JUR judicial, legal

Ge'richtsbarkeit f (-; no pl) JUR jurisdiction

Ge'richts|gebäude n JUR law court(s), courthouse; ~hof m JUR law court; ~medi,zin f JUR forensic medicine; ~saal m JUR courtroom; ~verfahren n JUR lawsuit; ~verhandlung f JUR hearing; trial; ~vollzieher [-fɔltsiːɐ] m (-s; -) JUR marshal, Br bailiff

gerieben [gə'riːbən] pp of reiben

gering [gə'rɪŋ] adj little, small; slight, minor; low; ~ schätzen think little of

ge'ringfügig adj slight, minor; petty

ge'ringschätzig [-ʃɛtsɪç] adj contemptuous

ge'ringst adj least; nicht im Geringsten not in the least

ge'rinnen v/i (irr, rinnen, no -ge-, sein) coagulate; curdle; clot

Ge'rippe n (-s; -) skeleton (a. fig); TECH framework

gerissen [gə'rɪsən] 1. pp of reißen; 2. F adj cunning, smart

geritten [gə'rɪtən] pp of reiten

germanisch [gɛr'maːnɪʃ] adj Germanic; Germanist(in) [gɛrma'nɪst(ɪn)] (-en; -en/-; -nen) student of (or graduate in) German

gern [gɛrn] adv willingly, gladly; ~ ha-

ben like, be fond of; et. (sehr) ~ tun like (love) to do s.th.; ich möchte ~ I'd like (to); ~ geschehen! not at all, (you're) welcome

gerochen [gə'rɔxən] pp of riechen

Geröll [gə'rœl] n (-[e]s; -e) scree; boulders

geronnen [gə'rɔnən] pp of rinnen

Gerste ['gɛrstə] f (-; -n) BOT barley

'Gerstenkorn n MED sty(e)

Gerte ['gɛrtə] f (-; -n) switch, rod, twig

Geruch [gə'rʊx] m (-[e]s; Gerüche [gə'ryçə]) smell; odo(u)r; scent

ge'ruchlos adj odo(u)rless

Ge'ruchsinn m (sense of) smell

Gerücht [gə'rʏçt] n (-[e]s; -e) rumo(u)r

ge'rufen pp of rufen

gerührt [gə'ryːrt] adj touched, moved

Ge'rümpel [gə'rʏmpəl] n (-s; no pl) lumber, junk

Gerundium [ge'rʊndiʊm] n (-s; -ien) LING gerund

gerungen [gə'rʊŋən] pp of ringen

Gerüst [gə'rʏst] n (-[e]s; -e) frame (-work); scaffold(ing); stage

ge'salzen pp of salzen

ge'samt [gə'zamt] adj whole, entire, total, all

Ge'samt... in cpds ...ergebnis etc: mst total ...; ~ausgabe f complete edition; ~schule f comprehensive school

gesandt [gə'zant] pp of senden

Gesandte [gə'zantə] m, (-/n; -n) POL envoy; Ge'sandtschaft f (-; -en) legation, mission

Gesang [gə'zaŋ] m (-[e]s; Gesänge [gə'zɛŋə]) singing; song; voice; ~buch n REL hymn book; ~(s)lehrer(in) singing teacher; ~verein m choral society, glee club

Gesäß [gə'zɛːs] n (-es; -e) ANAT buttocks, bottom

ge'schaffen pp of schaffen¹

Geschäft [gə'ʃɛft] n (-[e]s; -e) business, store, Br shop; bargain

ge'schäftig adj busy, active

Ge'schäftigkeit f (-; no pl) activity

ge'schäftlich 1. adj business ...; commercial; 2. adv on business

Ge'schäfts|brief m business letter; ~frau f businesswoman; ~freund m business friend; ~führer m manager; ~führung f management; ~inhaber m proprietor; ~mann m businessman

ge'schäftsmäßig *adj* businesslike
Ge'schäfts|ordnung *f* PARL standing orders; rules (of procedure); ~**partner** *m* (business) partner; ~**räume** *pl* (business) premises; ~**reise** *f* business trip; ~**schluss** *m* closing time; **nach ~ a.** after business hours; ~**stelle** *f* office; ~**straße** *f* shopping street; ~**träger** *m* POL chargé d'affaires
'ge'schäftstüchtig *adj* efficient, smart
Ge'schäfts|verbindung *f* business connection; ~**viertel** *n* commercial district; downtown; ~**zeit** *f* office *or* business hours; ~**zweig** *m* branch *or* line (of business)
geschah [gə'ʃaː] *pret of* geschehen 1
geschehen [gə'ʃeːən] **1.** *v/i* (*irr, no -ge-, sein*) happen, occur, take place; be done; *es geschieht ihm recht* it serves him right; **2.** *pp of* geschehen 1
gescheit [gə'ʃaɪt] *adj* clever, bright, F brainy
Geschenk [gə'ʃɛŋk] *n* (-[e]s; -e) present, gift; ~**packung** *f* gift box
Geschichte [gə'ʃɪçtə] *f* (-; -*n*) a) story, b) (*no pl*) history, c) F business, thing
ge'schichtlich *adj* historical
Ge'schichts|schreiber *m* (-s; -), ~**wissenschaftler** *m* historian
Geschick [gə'ʃɪk] *n* (-[e]s; -e) fate, destiny; → **Ge'schicklichkeit** *f* (-; *no pl*) skill; dexterity; **ge'schickt** *adj* skil(l)ful, skilled; dext(e)rous; *fig* clever
geschieden [gə'ʃiːdən] **1.** *pp of* scheiden; **2.** *adj* divorced, *marriage:* dissolved
geschienen [gə'ʃiːnən] *pp of* scheinen
Geschirr [gə'ʃɪr] *n* (-[e]s; -e) a) dishes, china, b) (*no pl*) kitchen utensils, pots and pans, crockery, c) harness; ~ **spülen** wash *or* do the dishes
Ge'schirrspüler *m* (-s; -) dishwasher
geschissen [gə'ʃɪsən] *pp of* scheißen
ge'schlafen *pp of* schlafen
ge'schlagen *pp of* schlagen
Geschlecht [gə'ʃlɛçt] *n* (-[e]s; -er) a) (*no pl*) sex, b) kind, species, c) family, line(age); generation, d) LING gender
Ge'schlechts|krankheit *f* MED venereal disease; ~**reife** *f* puberty; ~**teile** *pl* genitals; ~**trieb** *m* sexual instinct *or* urge; ~**verkehr** *m* (sexual) intercourse; ~**wort** *n* LING article

geschlichen [gə'ʃlɪçən] *pp of* schleichen
geschliffen [gə'ʃlɪfən] **1.** *pp of* schleifen²; **2.** *adj* cut; *fig* polished
geschlossen [gə'ʃlɔsən] **1.** *pp of* schließen; **2.** *adj* closed
geschlungen [gə'ʃlʊŋən] *pp of* schlingen
Geschmack [gə'ʃmak] *m* (-[e]s; Geschmäcke [gə'ʃmɛkə]) taste (*a. fig*); flavo(u)r; ~ **finden an** (*dat*) develop a taste for; **ge'schmacklos** *adj a. fig* tasteless; **Ge'schmacklosigkeit** *f* (-; *no pl*) tastelessness; *das war e-e ~* that was in bad taste; **Ge'schmack(s-) sache** *f* matter of taste; **ge'schmackvoll** *adj* tasteful, in good taste
geschmeidig [gə'ʃmaɪdɪç] *adj* supple, pliant
geschmissen [gə'ʃmɪsən] *pp of* schmeißen
geschmolzen [gə'ʃmɔltsən] *pp of* schmelzen
geschnitten [gə'ʃnɪtən] *pp of* schneiden
geschoben [gə'ʃoːbən] *pp of* schieben
Geschöpf [gə'ʃœpf] *n* (-[e]s; -e) creature
geschoren [gə'ʃoːrən] *pp of* scheren
Geschoss [gə'ʃɔs] *n* (-es; -e), Geschoß [gə'ʃoːs] *Austrian n* (-es; -e) projectile, missile; stor(e)y, floor
ge'schossen *pp of* schießen
Ge'schrei F *n* (-s; *no pl*) shouting, yelling; screams; crying; *fig* fuss
geschrieben [gə'ʃriːbən] *pp of* schreiben
geschrie(e)n [gə'ʃriː(ə)n] *pp of* schreien
geschritten [gə'ʃrɪtən] *pp of* schreiten
geschunden [gə'ʃʊndən] *pp of* schinden
Geschütz [gə'ʃʏts] *n* (-es; -e) MIL gun, cannon
Geschwader [gə'ʃvaːdə] *n* (-s; -) MIL MAR squadron; AVIAT group, *Br* wing
Geschwätz [gə'ʃvɛts] F *n* (-es; *no pl*) chatter, babble; gossip; *fig* nonsense
ge'schwätzig *adj* talkative; gossipy
geschweige [gə'ʃvaɪgə] *cj:* ~ (**denn**) let alone
geschwiegen [gə'ʃviːgən] *pp of* schweigen
geschwind [gə'ʃvɪnt] *adj* quick, swift
Geschwindigkeit [gə'ʃvɪndɪçkaɪt] *f* (-;

-en) speed; fastness, quickness; PHYS velocity; **mit e-r ~ von ...** at a speed *or* rate of ...

Ge'schwindigkeits|begrenzung *f* speed limit; **~überschreitung** *f* MOT speeding

Geschwister [gə'ʃvɪstɐ] *pl* brother(s) and sister(s); JUR siblings

geschwollen [gə'ʃvɔlən] **1.** *pp of* **schwellen** 1; **2.** *adj* MED swollen; *fig* bombastic, pretentious, pompous

geschwommen [gə'ʃvɔmən] *pp of* **schwimmen**

geschworen [gə'ʃvoːrən] *pp of* **schwören**; **Ge'schworene** *m, f* (*-n; -n*) member of a jury; **die ~n** the jury

Geschwulst [gə'ʃvʊlst] *f* (*-; Geschwülste* [gə'ʃvʏlstə]) MED growth, tumo(u)r

geschwunden [gə'ʃvʊndən] *pp of* **schwinden**

geschwungen [gə'ʃvʊŋən] *pp of* **schwingen**

Geschwür [gə'ʃvyːɐ] *n* (*-s; -e*) MED abscess, ulcer

ge'sehen *pp of* **sehen**

Geselchte [gə'zɛlçtə] *Austrian n* (*-n; no pl*) GASTR smoked meat

Geselle [gə'zɛlə] *m* (*-n; -n*) journeyman

ge'sellen *v/refl* (*no -ge-, h*) **sich zu j-m ~** join s.o.

ge'sellig *adj* sociable; ZO *etc* social; **~es Beisammensein** get-together

Ge'sellin *f* (*-; -nen*) trained woman *hairdresser etc*, journeywoman

Gesellschaft [gə'zɛlʃaft] *f* (*-; -en*) society; company; party; ECON company, corporation; **j-m ~ leisten** keep s.o. company

ge'sellschaftlich *adj* social

Ge'sellschafts... *in cpds* ...*kritik,* ...*ordnung etc*: social ...; **~reise** *f* group tour; **~spiel** *n* parlo(u)r game; **~tanz** *m* ballroom dance

gesessen [gə'zɛsən] *pp of* **sitzen**

Gesetz [gə'zɛts] *n* (*-es; -e*) JUR law; act; **~buch** *n* JUR code (of law); **~entwurf** *m* PARL bill

ge'setzgebend *adj* JUR legislative

Ge'setzgeber *m* (*-s; -*) JUR legislator

Ge'setzgebung *f* (*-; -en*) JUR legislation

ge'setzlich 1. *adj* legal; lawful; **2.** *adv*: **~ geschützt** JUR patented, registered

ge'setzlos *adj* lawless

ge'setzmäßig *adj* legal, lawful

gesetzt [gə'zɛtst] **1.** *adj* staid, dignified; mature (*age*); **2.** *cj*: **~ den Fall(, dass)** ... supposing (that)

ge'setzwidrig *adj* illegal, unlawful

Gesicht [gə'zɪçt] *n* (*-[e]s; -er*) face; **zu ~ bekommen** catch sight of

Ge'sicht|ausdruck *m* look, expression; **~farbe** *f* complexion; **~punkt** *m* point of view, aspect, angle; **~zug** *m* feature

Gesindel [gə'zɪndəl] *n* (*-s; no pl*) trash, *the* riff-raff

gesinnt [gə'zɪnt] *adj* minded; **j-m feindlich ~ sein** be ill-disposed towards s.o.

Ge'sinnung *f* (*-; -en*) mind; attitude; POL conviction(s)

ge'sinnungslos *adj* unprincipled

ge'sinnungstreu *adj* loyal

Ge'sinnungswechsel *m* about-face, *Br* about-turn

gesittet [gə'zɪtət] *adj* civilized, well-mannered

gesoffen [gə'zɔfən] *pp of* **saufen**

gesogen [gə'zoːgən] *pp of* **saugen**

gesotten [gə'zɔtən] *pp of* **sieden**

gespalten [gə'ʃpaltən] *pp of* **spalten**

Gespann [gə'ʃpan] *n* (*-[e]s; -e*) team (*a. fig*)

gespannt [gə'ʃpant] *adj* tense (*a. fig*); **~ sein auf** (*acc*) be anxious to see; **ich bin ~, ob (wie)** I wonder if (how)

Gespenst [gə'ʃpɛnst] *n* (*-[e]s; -er*) ghost, apparition, *esp fig* specter, *Br* spectre

ge'spenstisch *adj* ghostly, F spooky

gespie(e)n [gə'ʃpiː(ə)n] *pp of* **speien**

Gespinst [gə'ʃpɪnst] *n* (*-[e]s; -e*) web, tissue (*both a. fig*)

gesponnen [gə'ʃpɔnən] *pp of* **spinnen**

Gespött [gə'ʃpœt] *n* (*-[e]s; no pl*) mockery, ridicule; **j-n zum ~ machen** make a laughingstock of s.o.

Gespräch [gə'ʃprɛːç] *n* (*-[e]s; -e*) talk (*a. POL*), conversation; TEL call

ge'sprächig *adj* talkative

gesprochen [gə'ʃprɔxən] *pp of* **sprechen**

gesprossen [gə'ʃprɔsən] *pp of* **sprießen**

gesprungen [gə'ʃprʊŋən] *pp of* **springen**

Gespür [gə'ʃpyːɐ] *n* (*-s; no pl*) flair, nose

Gestalt [gə'ʃtalt] *f* (*-; -en*) shape, form; figure; **ge'stalten** *v/t* (*no -ge-, h*) ar-

G

range; design; **Ge'staltung** f (-; -en) arrangement; design; decoration

gestanden [gə'ʃtandən] pp of **stehen**

ge'ständig adj: ~ **sein** confess; have confessed

Geständnis [gə'ʃtɛntnɪs] n (-ses; -se) confession (a. fig)

Gestank [gə'ʃtaŋk] m (-[e]s; no pl) stench, stink

gestatten [gə'ʃtatən] v/t (no -ge-, h) allow, permit

Geste ['gɛstə] f (-; -n) gesture (a. fig)

ge'stehen v/t and v/i (irr, **stehen**, no -ge-, h) confess

Ge'stein n (-[e]s; -e) rock, stone

Gestell [gə'ʃtɛl] n (-[e]s; -e) stand, base, pedestal; shelves; frame

gestern ['gɛstɐn] adv yesterday; ~ **Abend** last night

gestiegen [gə'ʃtiːgən] pp of **steigen**

gestochen [gə'ʃtɔxən] pp of **stechen**

gestohlen [gə'ʃtoːlən] pp of **stehlen**

gestorben [gə'ʃtɔrbən] pp of **sterben**

ge'stoßen pp of **stoßen**

gestreift [gə'ʃtraift] adj striped

gestrichen [gə'ʃtrɪçən] pp of **streichen**

gestrig ['gɛstrɪç] adj yesterday's, of yesterday

gestritten [gə'ʃtrɪtən] pp of **streiten**

Gestrüpp [gə'ʃtryp] n (-[e]s; -e) brushwood, undergrowth; fig jungle, maze

gestunken [gə'ʃtuŋkən] pp of **stinken**

Gestüt [gə'ʃtyːt] n (-[e]s; -e) stud

Gesuch [gə'zuːx] n (-[e]s; -e) application, request

gesund [gə'zʊnt] adj healthy; healthful, fig a. sound; ~**er Menschenverstand** common sense; **(wieder)** ~ **werden** get well (again), recover; **Ge'sundheit** f (-; no pl) health; **auf j-s** ~ **trinken** drink to s.o.'s health; ~**!** bless you!; **ge'sundheitlich 1.** adj: ~**er Zustand** state of health; **aus** ~**en Gründen** for health reasons; **2.** adv: ~ **geht es ihm gut** he is in good health

Ge'sundheitsamt n Public Health Department (Br Office)

ge'sundheitsschädlich adj bad for one's health

Ge'sundheits|zeugnis n health certificate; ~**zustand** m state of health

gesungen [gə'zʊŋən] pp of **singen**

gesunken [gə'zʊŋkən] pp of **sinken**

getan [gə'taːn] pp of **tun**

Getöse [gə'tøːzə] n (-s; no pl) din, (deafening) noise

ge'tragen pp of **tragen**

Getränk [gə'trɛŋk] n (-[e]s; -e) drink, beverage; **Ge'tränkeauto,mat** m drinks machine

Getreide [gə'traidə] n (-s; -) cereals, grain, Br a. corn; ~**ernte** f grain harvest (or crop)

ge'treten pp of **treten**

Getriebe [gə'triːbə] n (-s; -) MOT transmission

ge'trieben [gə'triːbən] pp of **treiben**

getroffen [gə'trɔfən] pp of **treffen**

getrogen [gə'troːgən] pp of **trügen**

getrost [gə'troːst] adv safely

getrunken [gə'trʊŋkən] pp of **trinken**

Getue [gə'tuːə] F n (-s; no pl) fuss

Getümmel [gə'tyməl] n (-s; -) turmoil

Gewächs [gə'vɛks] n (-es; -e) plant; MED growth

ge'wachsen 1. pp of **wachsen**[1]; **2.** fig adj: **j-m** ~ **sein** be a match for s.o.; **e-r Sache** ~ **sein** be equal to s.th., be able to cope with s.th.

Ge'wächshaus n greenhouse, hothouse

gewagt [gə'vaːkt] adj daring; fig risqué

gewählt [gə'vɛːlt] adj refined

Gewähr [gə'vɛːɐ] f: ~ **übernehmen (für)** guarantee; **ge'währen** v/t (no -ge-, h) grant, allow; **ge'währleisten** v/t (no -ge-, h) guarantee

Gewahrsam [gə'vaːɐzaːm] m: **et. (j-n) in** ~ **nehmen** take s.th. in safekeeping (s.o. into custody)

Gewalt [gə'valt] f (-; -en) a) (no pl) force, violence, b) power; **mit** ~ by force; **höhere** ~ act of God; **häusliche** ~ domestic violence; **in s-e** ~ **bringen** seize by force; **die** ~ **verlieren über** (acc) lose control over; ~**herrschaft** f tyranny

ge'waltig adj powerful, mighty; enormous

ge'waltlos adj nonviolent; **Ge'waltlosigkeit** f (-; no pl) nonviolence

ge'waltsam 1. adj violent; **2.** adv by force; ~ **öffnen** force open

ge'walttätig adj violent

Ge'walttätigkeit f (-; -en) a) (no pl) violence, b) act of violence

Ge'waltverbrechen n crime of violence

Gewand [gə'vant] n (-[e]s; Gewänder

[gə'vɛndə]) robe, gown; REL vestment

gewandt [gə'vant] **1.** pp of **wenden** (v/refl); **2.** adj nimble; skil(l)ful; clever

Ge'wandtheit f (-; no pl) nimbleness; skill; ease

gewann [gə'van] pret of **gewinnen**

ge'waschen pp of **waschen**

Gewässer [gə'vɛsə] n (-s; -) body of water; pl waters

Gewebe [gə've:bə] n (-s; -) fabric; BIOL tissue

Gewehr [gə'veːɐ] n (-[e]s; -e) gun; rifle; shotgun; **~kolben** m (rifle) butt; **~lauf** m (rifle or gun) barrel

Geweih [gə'vai] n (-[e]s; -e) ZO antlers, horns

Gewerbe [gə'vɛrbə] n (-s; -) trade, business; **~schein** m trade licen|se, Br -ce; **~schule** f vocational or trade school

gewerblich [gə'vɛrplɪç] adj commercial, industrial; **gewerbsmäßig** [gə'vɛrps-] adj professional

Gewerkschaft [gə'vɛrkʃaft] f (-; -en) labor union, Br (trade) union

Ge'werkschaft(l)er m (-s; -), Ge'werkschaft(l)erin f (-; -nen) labor (Br trade) unionist; ge'werkschaftlich adj, Ge'werkschafts... in cpds labor (Br trade) union ...

ge'wesen pp of **sein**[1]

gewichen [gə'vɪçən] pp of **weichen**

Gewicht [gə'vɪçt] n (-[e]s; -e) weight; importance; **~ legen auf** (acc) stress

gewiesen [gə'viːzən] pp of **weisen**

gewillt [gə'vɪlt] adj willing, ready

Gewimmel [gə'vɪməl] n (-s; no pl) throng

Gewinde [gə'vɪndə] n (-s; -) TECH thread; **ein ~ bohren in** (acc) tap

Gewinn [gə'vɪn] m (-[e]s; -e) ECON profit (a. fig); gain(s); prize; winnings; **~ bringend** profitable

ge'winnen v/t and v/i (irr, no -ge-, h) win; gain; **~d** fig adj winning, engaging

Gewinner [gə'vɪnɐ] m (-s; -), Ge'winnerin f (-; -nen) winner

Ge'winnzahl f winning number

Gewirr [gə'vɪr] n (-[e]s; no pl) tangle; maze

gewiss [gə'vɪs] **1.** adj certain; **2.** adv certainly

Ge'wissen n (-s; -) conscience

ge'wissenhaft adj conscientious

ge'wissenlos adj unscrupulous

Ge'wissens|bisse pl pricks or pangs of conscience; **~frage** f question of conscience; **~gründe** pl: **aus ~n** for reasons of conscience

Ge'wissheit f (-; no pl) certainty; **mit ~** know etc for certain or sure

Gewitter [gə'vɪtɐ] n (-s; -) thunderstorm; **~regen** m thundershower; **~wolke** f thundercloud

gewoben [gə'voːbən] pp of **weben**

gewogen [gə'voːgən] pp of **wiegen**[1] and **wägen**

gewöhnen [gə'vøːnən] v/t and v/refl (no -ge-, h) **sich** (j-n) **~ an** (acc) get (s.o.) used to; **Gewohnheit** f (-; -en) habit (**et. zu tun** of doing s.th.); ge'wohnheitsmäßig adj habitual

gewöhnlich [gə'vøːnlɪç] adj common, ordinary, usual; vulgar, F common

gewohnt [gə'voːnt] adj usual; **et. (zu tun) ~ sein** be used or accustomed to (doing) s.th.

Gewölbe [gə'vœlbə] n (-s; -) vault

gewölbt [gə'vœlpt] adj arched

gewonnen [gə'vɔnən] pp of **gewinnen**

geworben [gə'vɔrbən] pp of **werben**

geworden [gə'vɔrdən] pp of **werden**

geworfen [gə'vɔrfən] pp of **werfen**

gewrungen [gə'vruŋən] pp of **wringen**

Gewühl [gə'vyːl] n (-[e]s; no pl) crowd, crush

gewunden [gə'vundən] **1.** pp of **winden**; **2.** adj winding

Gewürz [gə'vʏrts] n (-es; -e) spice; **~gurke** f pickle(d gherkin)

gewusst [gə'vust] pp of **wissen**

gezackt [gə'tsakt] adj jagged, serrated

Ge'zeiten pl tide(s)

Gezeter [gə'tseːtɐ] contp n (-s; no pl) (shrill) clamo(u)r; nagging

geziert [gə'tsiːrt] adj affected

gezogen [gə'tsoːgən] pp of **ziehen**

Gezwitscher [gə'tsvɪtʃɐ] n (-s; no pl) chirp(ing), twitter(ing)

gezwungen [gə'tsvuŋən] **1.** pp of **zwingen**; **2.** adj forced, unnatural

Gicht [gɪçt] f (-; no pl) MED gout

Giebel ['giːbəl] m (-s; -) gable

Gier [giːɐ] f (-; no pl) greed(iness) (**nach** for); **gierig** ['giːrɪç] adj greedy (**nach**, **auf** acc for, after)

gießen ['giːsən] v/t and v/i (irr, ge-, h) pour; TECH cast; water

Gieße'rei f (-; -en) TECH foundry

'Gießkanne f watering pot (*Br* can)

Gift [gɪft] n (-[e]s; -e) poison, zo *a.* venom (*a. fig*); **giftig** *adj* poisonous; venomous (*a. fig*); poisoned; MED toxic

'Gift|müll m toxic waste; **~mülldepo-,nie** f toxic waste dump; **~schlange** f zo poisonous *or* venomous snake; **~stoff** m poison *or* toxic substance; pollutant; **~zahn** m zo poison fang

Gigant [gi'gant] m (-en; -en) giant

gi'gantisch *adj* gigantic

ging [gɪŋ] *pret of* **gehen**

Gipfel ['gɪpfəl] m (-s; -) top, peak, summit, *fig a.* height; **~konfe,renz** f POL summit (meeting *or* conference)

'gipfeln v/i (ge-, h) culminate (**in** *dat* in)

Gips [gɪps] m (-es; -e) plaster (of Paris); **in ~** MED in (a) plaster (cast); **~abdruck** m, **~abguss** m plaster cast

'gipsen v/t (ge-, h) plaster (*a.* F MED)

'Gipsverband m MED plaster cast

Giraffe [gi'rafə] f (-; -n) zo giraffe

Girlande [gɪr'landə] f (-; -n) garland, festoon

Girokonto ['ʒiːro-] n checking (*or* current) account; postal check (*Br* giro) account

Gischt [gɪʃt] m (-[e]s; -e), f (-; -en) (sea) spray, spindrift

Gitarre [gi'tarə] f (-; -n) MUS guitar

Gitarrist [gita'rɪst] m (-en; -en) guitarist

Gitter ['gɪtə] n (-s; -) lattice; grating; F **hinter ~n** (**sitzen**) (be) behind bars

'Gitterbett n crib, *Br* cot

'Gitterfenster n lattice (window)

Glanz [glants] m (-es; *no pl*) shine, gloss (*a.* TECH), luster, *Br* lustre, brilliance (*a. fig*); *fig* splendo(u)r, glamo(u)r

glänzen ['glɛntsən] v/i (ge-, h) shine, gleam; glitter, glisten; **~d** *adj* shining, shiny, bright; PHOT glossy; *fig* brilliant, excellent

'Glanz|leistung f brilliant achievement; **~zeit** f heyday

Glas [glaːs] n (-es; *Gläser* ['glɛːzə]) glass

Glaser ['glaːzə] m (-s; -) glazier

gläsern ['glɛːzən] *adj* (of) glass

'Glas|faser f, **~fiber** f glass fiber (*Br* fibre); **~hütte** f TECH glassworks

glasieren [gla'ziːrən] v/t (*no* -ge-, h) glaze; GASTR ice, frost

glasig ['glaːzɪç] *adj* glassy

'glasklar *adj* crystal-clear (*a. fig*)

'Glasscheibe f (glass) pane

Glasur [gla'zuːɐ] f (-; -en) glaze; GASTR icing

glatt [glat] *adj* smooth (*a. fig*); slippery; *fig* clear; F **~ gehen** work (out well), go (off) well; **Glätte** ['glɛtə] f (-; *no pl*) smoothness (*a. fig*); slipperiness

'Glatteis n (glare, *Br* black) ice; **es herrscht ~** the roads are icy; F **j-n aufs ~ führen** mislead s.o.

glätten ['glɛtən] v/t (ge-, h) smooth; *Swiss:* → **bügeln**

Glatze ['glatsə] f (-; -n) bald head; **e-e ~ haben** be bald

Glaube ['glaubə] m (-ns; *no pl*) belief, *esp* REL faith (*both:* **an** acc in)

'glauben v/t *and* v/i (ge-, h) believe; think, guess; **~ an** (acc) believe in (*a.* REL)

'Glaubens|bekenntnis n REL creed, profession *or* confession of faith; **~leh-re** f, **~satz** m dogma, doctrine

glaubhaft ['glauphaft] *adj* credible, plausible

gläubig ['glɔʏbɪç] *adj* religious; devout; **die Gläubigen** the faithful

Gläubiger ['glɔʏbɪgə] m (-s; -), 'Gläubigerin f (-; -nen) ECON creditor

'glaubwürdig *adj* credible; reliable

gleich [glaɪç] 1. *adj* same; equal (*right etc*); **auf die ~e Art** (in) the same way; **zur ~en Zeit** at the same time; **das ist mir ~** it's all the same to me; **ganz ~, wann** *etc* no matter when *etc*; **das Gleiche** the same; (*ist*) **~ ...** MATH equals ..., is ...; **~ bleibend** constant, steady; **~ gesinnt** like-minded; **~ lautend** identical; **2.** *adv* equally, alike; at once, right away; in a moment *or* minute; **~ groß** (**alt**) of the same size (age); **~ nach** (**neben**) right after (next to); **~ gegenüber** just opposite *or* across the street; **es ist ~ 5 Uhr** it's almost 5 o'clock; **~ aussehen** (**gekleidet sein**) look (be dressed) alike; **bis ~!** see you soon *or* later!; **gleichaltrig** ['glaɪç'?al-trɪç] *adj* (of) the same age

'gleichberechtigt *adj* equal, having equal rights; '**Gleichberechtigung** f (-; *no pl*) equal rights

'gleichen v/i/i (*irr*, ge-, h) (dat) be *or* look like

'gleichfalls *adv* also, likewise; **danke, ~!** (thanks), the same to you

'gleichförmig [-fœrmɪç] *adj* uniform

'Gleichgewicht *n* (-[*e*]*s*; *no pl*) balance (*a. fig*)

'gleichgültig *adj* indifferent (**gegen** to); careless; *das* (*er*) *ist mir* ~ I don't care (for him); 'Gleichgültigkeit *f* (-; *no pl*) indifference

'Gleichheit *f* (-; *no pl*) equality

'gleichkommen *v/i* (*irr, kommen, sep, -ge-, sein*) *e-r Sache* ~ amount to s.th.; *j-m* ~ equal s.o. (*an dat* in)

'gleichmäßig *adj* regular; constant; even

'gleichnamig [-na:mɪç] *adj* of the same name

'Gleichnis *n* (-*ses*; -*se*) parable

'gleichsam *adv* as it were, so to speak

'gleichseitig [-zaitɪç] *adj* MATH equilateral

'gleich|setzen, ~stellen *v/t* (*sep, -ge-, h*) equate (*dat* to, with); put *s.o.* on an equal footing (with)

'Gleichstrom *m* ELECTR direct current

'Gleichung *f* (-; -*en*) MATH equation

'gleichwertig *adj* equally good; *j-m* ~ *sein* be a match for s.o. (*a.* SPORT)

'gleichzeitig *adj* simultaneous; *beide* ~ both at the same time

Gleis [glais] *n* (-*es*; -*e*) RAIL rail(s), track(s), line; platform, gate

gleiten ['glaitən] *v/i* (*irr, ge-, sein*) glide, slide; ~*d adj*: ~*e Arbeitszeit* flexible working hours, flextime, *Br a.* flexitime

'Gleitflug *m* glide

'Gleitschirm|fliegen *n* paragliding; ~*flieger m* paraglider

Gletscher ['glɛtʃɐ] *m* (-*s*; -) glacier; ~*spalte f* crevasse

glich [glɪç] *pret of gleichen*

Glied [gli:t] *n* (-*es*; *Glieder* ['gli:dɐ]) ANAT limb; penis; TECH link

gliedern ['gli:dɐn] *v/t* (*ge-, h*) structure; divide (*in acc* into)

'Gliederung *f* (-; -*en*) structure, arrangement; outline

'Gliedmaßen *pl* ANAT limbs, extremities

glimmen ['glɪmən] *v/i* ([*irr*] *ge-, h*) glow; smo(u)lder

'Glimmstängel F *m* (-*s*; -) cigarette, *Br sl* fag

glimpflich ['glɪmpflɪç] **1.** *adj* lenient, mild; **2.** *adv*: ~ *davonkommen* get off lightly

glitschig ['glɪtʃɪç] *adj* slippery

glitt [glɪt] *pret of gleiten*

glitzern ['glɪtsɐn] *v/i* (*ge-, h*) glitter, sparkle, glint

global [glo'ba:l] *adj* global

Globus ['glo:bus] *m* (-[*ses*]; -*se*) globe

Glocke ['glɔkə] *f* (-; -*n*) bell

'Glocken|blume *f* bluebell; ~*spiel n* chimes; ~*turm m* bell tower, belfry

glomm [glɔm] *pret of glimmen*

glorreich ['glo:ɐraiç] *adj* glorious

Glotze ['glɔtsə] F *f* (-; -*n*) TV the tube, *Br* goggle box; 'glotzen F *v/i* (*ge-, h*) goggle, gape, stare

Glück [glʏk] *n* (-[*e*]*s*; *no pl*) (good) luck, fortune; happiness; ~ *haben* be lucky; *zum* ~ fortunately; *viel* ~*!* good luck!

Glucke ['glʊkə] *f* (-; -*n*) ZO sitting hen; *fig* hen

gluckern ['glʊkɐn] *v/i* (*ge-, h*) gurgle

'glücklich *adj* happy; ~*er Zufall* lucky chance

'glücklicher'weise *adv* fortunately

'Glücks|bringer *m* (-*s*; -) lucky charm; ~*fall m* lucky chance; ~*pfennig m* lucky penny; ~*pilz m* lucky fellow; ~*spiel n* game of chance; *coll* gambling; ~*spieler m* gambler; ~*tag m* lucky day

'glückstrahlend *adj* radiant

'Glückwunsch *m* congratulations; *herzlichen* ~*!* congratulations!; happy birthday!

Glühbirne ['gly:-] *f* ELECTR light bulb

glühen ['gly:ən] *v/i* (*ge-, h*) glow (*a. fig*)

'glühend ['gly:ənt] *adj* glowing; red-hot (*iron*); *fig* burning; ~ *heiß* blazing hot

'Glühwein *m* mulled wine

Glut [glu:t] *f* (-; -*en*) (glowing) fire; embers; live coals; *fig* ardo(u)r

'Gluthitze *f* blazing heat

GmbH [ge:ʔɛmbe:'ha:] ABBR *of Gesellschaft mit beschränkter Haftung* private limited liability company

Gnade ['gna:də] *f* (-; -*n*) mercy, *esp* REL *a.* grace; favo(u)r

'Gnaden|frist *f* reprieve; ~*gesuch n* JUR petition for mercy

'gnadenlos *adj* merciless

gnädig ['gnɛ:dɪç] *adj* gracious; *esp* REL merciful

Gold [gɔlt] *n* (-[*e*]*s*; *no pl*) gold; ~*barren m* gold bar or ingot; *coll* bullion

golden ['gɔldən] *adj* gold; *fig* golden

'Goldfisch m ZO goldfish
'goldgelb adj golden (yellow)
'Gold|gräber [-grɛːbɐ] m (-s; -) gold digger; ~grube fig goldmine, bonanza
goldig ['gɔldɪç] F adj sweet, lovely, cute
'Gold|mine f goldmine; ~münze f gold coin; ~schmied m goldsmith; ~stück n gold coin
Golf¹ [gɔlf] m (-[e]s; -e) GEOGR gulf
Golf² n (-s; no pl) SPORT golf; ~platz m golf course; ~schläger m golf club; ~spieler m golfer
Gondel ['gɔndəl] f (-; -n) gondola; cabin
Gong ['gɔŋ-] m (-s; -s) gong
gönnen ['gœnən] v/t (ge-; h) j-m et. not (be)grudge s.o. s.th.; j-m et. nicht ~ (be)grudge s.o. s.th.; sich et. ~ allow o.s. s.th., treat o.s. to s.th.
gönnerhaft ['gœnɐhaft] adj patronizing
gor [goːɐ] pret of gären
Gorilla [go'rɪla] m (-s; -s) ZO gorilla
goss [gɔs] pret of gießen
Gosse ['gɔsə] f (-; -n) gutter (a. fig)
Gotik ['goːtɪk] f (-; no pl) ARCH Gothic style or period; 'gotisch adj Gothic
Gott [gɔt] m (-[e]s; Götter ['gœtɐ]) REL God, Lord; MYTH god; ~ sei Dank(!) thank God(!); um ~es Willen! for heaven's sake!; 'gottergeben adj resigned (to the will of God)
'Gottesdienst m REL (divine) service
'gottesfürchtig [-fyrçtɪç] adj god-fearing
'Gotteslästerer [-lɛstərɐ] m (-s; -) blasphemer; 'Gotteslästerung f (-; -en) blasphemy
'Gottheit f (-; -en) deity, divinity
Göttin ['gœtɪn] f (-; -nen) goddess
'göttlich ['gœtlɪç] adj divine
gott'lob int thank God or goodness!
'gottlos adj godless, wicked
'gottverlassen F adj godforsaken
'Gottvertrauen n trust in God
Götze ['gœtsə] m (-n; -n), 'Götzenbild n idol
Gouverneur [guvɛr'nøːɐ] m (-s; -e) governor
Grab [graːp] n (-[e]s; Gräber ['grɛːbɐ]) grave; tomb
graben ['graːbən] v/t and v/i (irr, ge-, h) dig, ZO a. burrow; 'Graben m (-s; Gräben ['grɛːbən]) ditch; MIL trench
'Grab|mal n monument; tomb; ~rede f funeral address; ~schrift f epitaph;

~stätte f burial place; grave, tomb; ~stein m tombstone, gravestone
Grad [graːt] m (-[e]s; -e) degree; MIL etc rank, grade; 15 ~ Kälte 15 degrees below zero; ~einteilung f graduation
graduell [gra'duɛl] adj in degree
Graf [graːf] m (-en; -en) count, Br earl
Graffiti [gra'fiːti] pl graffiti
Grafik ['graːfɪk] f (-; -en) a) (no pl) graphic arts, b) print, c) MATH, TECH graph, diagram, d) (no pl) art(work), illustrations, e) (no pl) EDP graphics
'Grafiker m (-s; -), 'Grafikerin f (-; -nen) graphic artist
Gräfin ['grɛːfɪn] f (-; -nen) countess
grafisch ['graːfɪʃ] adj graphic
Grafologie f → Graphologie
'Grafschaft f (-; -en) county
Gramm [gram] n (-s; -e) gram
Grammatik [gra'matɪk] f (-; -en) grammar; gram'matisch adj grammatical
Granat [gra'naːt] m (-[e]s; -e) MIN garnet
Gra'nate f (-; -n) MIL shell
Gra'nat|splitter m MIL shell splinter; ~werfer m MIL mortar
grandios [gran'djoːs] adj magnificent, grand
Granit [gra'niːt] m (-s; -e) granite
Graphik [graf etc → Grafik etc
Graphologie [grafolo'giː] f (-; no pl) graphology
Gras [graːs] n (-es; Gräser ['grɛːzɐ]) grass; grasen ['graːzən] v/i (ge-, h) graze; 'Grashalm m blade of grass
grassieren [gra'siːrən] v/i (no -ge-, h) rage, be rife
grässlich ['grɛslɪç] adj hideous, atrocious
Gräte ['grɛːtə] f (-; -n) (fish)bone
Gratifikation [gratifika'tsjoːn] f (-; -en) gratuity, bonus
gratis ['graːtɪs] adv free (of charge)
Grätsche ['grɛːtʃə] f (-; -n), 'grätschen v/i (ge-, h) straddle; soccer: stride tackle
Gratulant [gratu'lant] m (-en; -en), Gratu'lantin f (-; -nen) congratulator; Gratulation [-la'tsjoːn] f (-; -en) congratulation; gratulieren [-'liːrən] v/i (no -ge-, h) congratulate (j-m zu et. s.o. on s.th.); j-m zum Geburtstag ~ wish s.o. many happy returns (of the day)
grau [grau] adj gray, Br grey
'Graubrot n rye bread

Gräuel ['grɔʏəl] m (-s; -) horror

'Gräueltat f atrocity

'grauen v/i (ge-, h) **mir graut es vor** (dat) I dread (the thought of)

'Grauen n (-s; -) horror

'grauenhaft, 'grauenvoll adj horrible, horrifying

Graupel ['graupəl] f (-; -n) sleet, soft hail

grausam ['grauzaːm] adj cruel

'Grausamkeit f (-; -en) cruelty

grausig ['grauzɪç] adj → **grauenhaft**

'Grauzone f fig gray (Br grey) area

gravieren [gra'viːrən] v/t (no -ge-, h) engrave; **~d** adj serious

Gravur [gra'vuːr] f (-; -en) engraving

Grazie ['graːtsiə] f (-; no pl) grace

graziös [gra'tsjøːs] adj graceful

greifen ['graifən] (irr, ge-, h) **1.** v/t seize, grasp, grab, take or catch hold of; **2.** v/i fig take effect; **~ nach** reach for; grasp at

Greis [grais] m (-es; -e) (very) old man; **greisenhaft** ['graizənhaft] adj senile (a. MED); **Greisin** ['graizɪn] f (-; -nen) (very) old woman

grell [grɛl] adj glaring; shrill

Grenze ['grɛntsə] f (-; -n) border; boundary; fig limit; **grenzen** v/i (ge-, h) **~ an** (acc) border on

'grenzenlos adj boundless

'Grenz|fall m borderline case; **~land** n borderland, frontier; **~linie** f borderline, POL demarcation line; **~stein** m boundary stone; **~übergang** m frontier crossing (point), checkpoint

Greuel → **Gräuel**

Grieche ['griːçə] m (-n; -n) Greek; 'Griechenland Greece; 'Griechin f (-; -nen), 'griechisch adj Greek

Grieß [griːs] m (-es; -e) semolina

griff [grɪf] pret of **greifen**

Griff m (-[e]s; -e) grip, grasp; handle

'griffbereit adj at hand, handy

Grill [grɪl] m (-s; -s) grill

Grille ['grɪlə] f (-; -n) ZO cricket

'grillen v/t (ge-, h) grill, barbecue

Grimasse [gri'masə] f (-; -n) grimace; **~n schneiden** pull faces

grimmig ['grɪmɪç] adj grim

grinsen ['grɪnzən] v/i (ge-, h) grin (**über** acc at); **höhnisch** or **spöttisch ~ über** (acc) sneer (at); 'Grinsen n (-s; no pl) grin; **höhnisches** or **spöttisches ~** sneer

Grippe ['grɪpə] f (-; -n) MED influenza, F flu

Grips [grɪps] F m (-es; no pl) brains

grob [groːp] **1.** adj coarse (a. fig); fig gross; crude; rude; rough; **2.** adv: **~ geschätzt** at a rough estimate

'Grobheit f (-; no pl) coarseness; roughness; rudeness

grölen ['grøːlən] F v/t and v/i (ge-, h) bawl

Groll [grɔl] m (-[e]s; no pl) grudge, ill will; 'grollen v/i (ge-, h) **j-m** bear s.o. a grudge

Groschen ['grɔʃən] m (-s; -) Austrian groschen; F ten-pfennig piece, ten pfennigs

groß [groːs] adj big; large (a. family); tall; grown-up; F big (brother etc); fig great (a. fun, trouble, pain etc); capital (letter); **~es Geld** bills, Br notes; **~e Ferien** summer vacation, Br summer holiday(s); **Groß und Klein** young and old; **im Großen und Ganzen** on the whole; F **~ in et. sein** be great at (doing) s.th.; **wie ~ ist es?** what size is it?; **wie ~ bist du?** how tall are you?

'großartig adj great, F a. terrific

'Großaufnahme f film: close-up

Größe ['grøːsə] f (-; -n) size; height; esp MATH quantity; fig greatness; celebrity

'Großeltern pl grandparents

'großen'teils adv to a large or great extent, largely

'Größenwahn m megalomania (a. fig)

'Groß|fa,milie f extended family; **~handel** m ECON wholesale (trade); **~händler** m ECON wholesale dealer, wholesaler; **~handlung** f ECON wholesale business; **~indus,trie** f big industry; big business; **~industri,elle** m big industrialist, F tycoon; **~macht** f POL great power; **~markt** m ECON hypermarket; wholesale market; **~maul** F n braggart; **~mutter** f grandmother; **~raum** m conurbation, metropolitan area; **der ~ München** Greater Munich, the Greater Munich area; **~raumflugzeug** n wide-bodied jet

'großschreiben v/t (irr, schreiben, sep, -ge-, h) capitalize; 'Großschreibung f (use of) capitalization

'großsprecherisch [-ʃprɛçərɪʃ] adj boastful

'großspurig [-ʃpuːrɪç] adj arrogant

'Großstadt f big city; **'großstädtisch** adj of or in a big city, urban

'größten'teils adv mostly, mainly

'großtun v/i (irr, tun, sep, -ge-, h) show off; **sich mit et. ~** brag about s.th.

'Großvater m grandfather

'Großverdiener m (-s; -) big earner

'Großwild n big game

'großziehen v/t (irr, ziehen, sep, -ge-, h) raise, rear; bring up

'großzügig adj generous, liberal; ... on a large scale; spacious

'Großzügigkeit f (-; no pl) generosity, liberality; spaciousness

grotesk [gro'tɛsk] adj grotesque

Grotte ['grɔtə] f (-; -n) grotto

grub [gru:p] pret of **graben**

Grübchen ['gry:pçən] n (-s; -) dimple

Grube ['gru:bə] f (-; -n) pit; mine

Grübelei [gry:bə'lai] f (-; -en) pondering, musing

grübeln ['gry:bəln] v/i (ge-, h) ponder, muse (**über** acc on, over)

Gruft [gruft] f (-; Grüfte ['gryftə]) tomb, vault

grün [gry:n] adj green; **Grün** n (-s; -) green; **im ~en** in the country

'Grünanlage f park

Grund [grunt] m (-[e]s; Gründe ['gryndə]) reason; cause; ground, AGR a. soil; bottom; **~ und Boden** property, land; **aus diesem ~(e)** for this reason; **von ~ auf** entirely; **im ~e (genommen)** actually, basically; → **aufgrund**; → **zugrunde**

'Grund... in cpds ...bedeutung, ...bedingung, ...regel, ...prinzip, ...wortschatz etc: mst basic ...; **~begriffe** pl basics, fundamentals; **~besitz** m property, land; **~besitzer** m landowner

gründen ['gryndən] v/t (ge-, h) found (a. family), set up, establish; **sich ~ auf** (dat) be based or founded on

Gründer ['gryndɐ] m (-s; -), **'Gründerin** f (-; -nen) founder

grund'falsch adj absolutely wrong

'Grund|fläche f MATH base; ARCH area; **~gedanke** m basic idea; **~geschwindigkeit** f AVIAT ground speed; **~gesetz** n POL Basic (Constitutional) Law (for the Federal Republic of Germany); **~lage** f foundation, fig a. basis; pl (basic) elements

'grundlegend adj fundamental, basic

gründlich ['gryntlıç] adj thorough

'Grundlinie f tennis etc: base line

'grundlos adj groundless, unfounded

'Grundmauer f foundation

Grün'donnerstag m REL Maundy or Holy Thursday

'Grund|rechnungsart f MATH basic arithmetical operation; **~riss** m ARCH ground plan; **~satz** m principle

grundsätzlich ['gruntzɛtslıç] **1.** adj fundamental; **2.** adv: **ich bin ~ dagegen** I am against it on principle

'Grund|schule f elementary (or grade) school, Br primary (or junior) school; **~stein** m ARCH foundation stone; fig foundations; **~stück** n plot (of land), lot; (building) site; premises; **~stücksmakler** m realtor, Br real estate agent

'Gründung f (-; -en) foundation, establishment, setting up

'grundver'schieden adj totally different

'Grund|wasser n ground water; **~zahl** f cardinal number; **~zug** m main feature, characteristic

Grüne ['gry:nə] m, f (-n; -n) POL Green

'Grünfläche f green space

'grünlich adj greenish

'Grünspan m (-[e]s; no pl) verdigris

grunzen ['gruntsən] v/i and v/t (ge-, h) grunt

Gruppe ['grupə] f (-; -n) group

'Gruppenreise f group tour

gruppieren [gru'pi:rən] v/t (no -ge-, h) group, arrange in groups; **sich ~** form groups

Grusel... ['gru:zəl-] in cpds ...film etc: horror ...; **'gruselig** adj eerie, creepy; spine-chilling; **'gruseln** v/t and v/refl (ge-, h) **es gruselt mich** F it gives me the creeps

Gruß [gru:s] m (-es; Grüße ['gry:sə]) greeting(s); MIL salute; **viele Grüße an** (acc) ... give my regards (or love) to ...; **mit freundlichen Grüßen** yours sincerely; **herzliche Grüße** best wishes; love

grüßen ['gry:sən] v/t (ge-, h) greet, F say hello to; MIL salute; **~ Sie ihn von mir** give my regards (or love) to him

gucken ['gukən] v/i (ge-, h) look

'Guckloch n peephole

Güggeli ['gygəli] n (-s; -) Swiss chicken

gültig ['gyltıç] adj valid; current

'**Gültigkeit** f (-; no pl) validity; **s-e ~ verlieren** expire

Gummi ['gumi] m, n (-s; -[s]) rubber; **~band** n (-[e]s; -bänder) rubber (esp Br a. elastic) band; **~bärchen** pl gummy bears; **~baum** m BOT rubber tree; rubber plant; **~bon,bon** m, n gumdrop

gummieren [gʊˈmiːrən] v/t (no -ge-, h) gum

'**Gummi|knüppel** m truncheon; **~stiefel** m rubber boot, esp Br wellington (boot); **~zug** m elastic

Gunst [gʊnst] f (-; no pl) favo(u)r, goodwill; → **zugunsten**

günstig ['gynstɪç] adj favo(u)rable (**für** to); convenient; **im ~sten Fall** at best; **~e Gelegenheit** chance

Gurgel ['gʊrgəl] f (-; -n) throat; **j-m an die ~ springen** fly at s.o.'s throat; '**gurgeln** v/i (ge-, h) MED gargle

Gurke ['gʊrkə] f (-; -n) BOT cucumber

gurren ['gʊrən] v/i (ge-, h) ZO coo

Gurt [gʊrt] m (-[e]s; -e) belt (a. MOT and AVIAT); strap

Gürtel ['gyrtəl] m (-s; -) belt; **~reifen** m MOT radial (tire, Br tyre)

GUS [gʊs, geːˈʔuːˈʔɛs] ABBR of **Gemeinschaft Unabhängiger Staaten** CIS, Commonwealth of Independent States

Guss [gʊs] m (-es; Güsse ['gʏsə]) downpour; TECH casting; GASTR icing; fig **aus e-m ~** of a piece; '**Gusseisen** n cast iron; '**gusseisern** adj cast-iron

gut [guːt] 1. adj good; fine; **ganz ~** not bad; **also ~!** all right (then)!; **schon ~!** never mind!; (**wieder**) **~ werden** come right (again), be all right; **~e Reise!** have a nice trip!; **sei bitte so ~ und ...** would you be so good as to or good enough to ...; **in et. ~ sein** be good at (doing) s.th.; 2. adv well; **look**, **taste** etc good; **du hast es ~** you are lucky; **es ist ~ möglich** it may well be; **es gefällt mir ~** I (do) like it; **~ gebaut** well-built; **~ gelaunt** in a good mood; **~ gemacht!** well done!; **mach's ~!** take care (of yourself)!; **~ gehen** go (off) well, work out well or all right; **wenn alles ~ geht** if nothing goes wrong; **mir geht es ~** I'm (doing) well; **Gut** n (-[e]s; Güter ['gyːtɐ]) estate; pl goods

'**Gutachten** n (-s; -) (expert) opinion; certificate; **Gutachter** ['guːtʔaxtɐ] m (-s; -) expert

'**gutartig** adj good-natured; MED benign

Gutdünken ['guːtdʏŋkən] n: **nach ~** at one's discretion

Gute ['guːtə] n (-n; no pl) good; **~s tun** do good; **alles ~!** all the best!, good luck!

Güte ['gyːtə] f (-; no pl) goodness, kindness; ECON quality; F **meine ~!** good gracious!

Güter|bahnhof ['gyːtɐ-] m freight depot, Br goods station; **~gemeinschaft** f JUR community of property; **~trennung** f JUR separation of property; **~verkehr** m freight (Br goods) traffic; **~wagen** m freight car, Br goods wag(g)on; **~zug** m freight (Br goods) train

'**gutgläubig** adj credulous

'**Guthaben** n (-s; -) ECON credit (balance)

'**gutheißen** v/t (irr, heißen, sep, -ge-, h) approve (of)

'**gutherzig** adj kind(-hearted)

gütig ['gyːtɪç] adj good, kind(ly)

gütlich ['gyːtlɪç] adv: **sich ~ einigen** come to an amicable settlement

'**gutmachen** v/t (sep, -ge-, h) make up for, repay

'**gutmütig** [-myːtɪç] adj good-natured

'**Gutmütigkeit** f (-; no pl) good nature

'**Gutsbesitzer** m, '**Gutsbesitzerin** f (-; -nen) estate owner

'**Gutschein** m coupon, esp Br voucher

'**gutschreiben** v/t (irr, schreiben, sep, -ge-, h) **j-m et.** credit s.th. to s.o.'s account; '**Gutschrift** f credit

'**Gutshaus** n manor (house)

'**Gutshof** m estate, manor

'**Gutsverwalter** m steward, manager

'**gutwillig** adj willing

Gymnasium [gʏmˈnaːzjʊm] n (-s; -ien) high school, Br appr grammar school

Gymnastik [gʏmˈnastɪk] f (-; no pl) exercises, gymnastics; **gym'nastisch** adj: **~e Übungen** physical exercises

Gynäkologe [gynɛkoˈloːgə] m (-n; -n), **Gynäko'login** f (-; -nen) MED gyn(a)ecologist

H

Haar [haːɐ] *n (-[e]s; -e* [ˈhaːrə]) hair; **sich die ~e kämmen (schneiden lassen)** comb one's hair (have one's hair cut); **sich aufs ~ gleichen** look absolutely identical; **um ein ~** by a hair's breadth
'Haarausfall *m* loss of hair
'Haarbürste *f* hairbrush
haaren [ˈhaːrən] *v/i and v/refl (ge-, h)* ZO lose its hair; *fur:* shed hairs
'Haaresbreite *f:* **um ~** by a hair's breadth
'haarfein *adj* (as) fine as a hair
'Haarfestiger *m (-s; -)* setting lotion
'Haargefäß *n* ANAT capillary (vessel)
'haargenau F *adv* precisely; **(stimmt) ~!** dead right!
haarig [ˈhaːrɪç] *adj* hairy
'haarklein F *adv* to the last detail
'Haar|klemme *f* bobby pin, *Br* hair clip; **~nadel** *f* hairpin; **~nadelkurve** *f* hairpin bend; **~netz** *n* hair-net
'haarscharf F *adv* by a hair's breadth
'Haar|schnitt *m* haircut; **~spalterei** *f (-; no pl)* hair-splitting; **~spange** *f* barrette, *Br* (hair) slide; **~spray** *m, n* hairspray
'haarsträubend *adj* hair-raising
'Haar|teil *n* hairpiece; **~trockner** *m* hair dryer; **~wäsche** *f*, **~waschmittel** *n* shampoo; **~wasser** *n* hair tonic; **~wuchs** *m:* **starken ~ haben** have a lot of hair; **~wuchsmittel** *n* hair restorer
haben [ˈhaːbən] *v/t (irr, ge-, h)* have (got); **Hunger ~** be hungry; **Durst ~** be thirsty; **Ferien (Urlaub) ~** be on vacation (*Br* holiday); **er hat Geburtstag** it's his birthday; **welche Farbe hat ...?** what colo(u)r is ...?; **zu ~ sein** be available; F **sich ~** make a fuss; F **was hast du?** what's the matter with you?; F **da ~ wir's!** there we are!; → **Datum**
'Haben *n (-s; no pl)* ECON credit
Habgier [ˈhaːp-] *f* greed(iness)
'habgierig *adj* greedy
Habicht [ˈhaːbɪçt] *m (-s; -e)* ZO hawk
'Habseligkeiten *pl* belongings
Hacke [ˈhakə] *f (-; -n)* hoe; (pick-)axe; ANAT heel; **'hacken** *v/t (ge-, h)* chop; AGR hoe; ZO peck

'Hackentrick *m* soccer: backheeler
Hacker [ˈhakɐ] *m (-s; -)* EDP hacker
'Hack|fleisch *n* ground (*Br* minced) meat; **~ordnung** *f* ZO pecking order
Hafen [ˈhaːfən] *m (-s; Häfen* [ˈhɛːfən]) harbo(u)r, port; **~arbeiter** *m* docker, longshoreman; **~stadt** *f* (sea)port
Hafer [ˈhaːfɐ] *m (-s; -)* BOT oats; **~brei** *m* oatmeal, *Br* porridge; **~flocken** *pl* (rolled) oats; **~schleim** *m* gruel
Haft [haft] *f (-; no pl)* JUR confinement, imprisonment; **in ~** under arrest
'haftbar *adj* responsible, JUR liable
'Haftbefehl *m* JUR warrant of arrest
'haften *v/i (ge-, h)* stick, adhere (**an** *dat* to); **~ für** JUR answer for, be liable for
Häftling [ˈhɛftlɪŋ] *m (-s; -e)* prisoner, convict
'Haftpflicht *f* JUR liability; **~versicherung** *f* liability insurance; MOT third party insurance
Haftung *f (-; -en)* responsibility, JUR liability; **mit beschränkter ~** limited
Hagel [ˈhaːgəl] *m (-s; no pl)* hail, fig *a.* shower, volley; **'Hagelkorn** *n* hailstone; **'hageln** *v/i (ge-, h)* hail (*a. fig*); **'Hagelschauer** *m* hail shower
hager [ˈhaːgɐ] *adj* lean, gaunt, haggard
Hahn [haːn] *m (-[e]s; Hähne* [ˈhɛːnə]) ZO cock, rooster; TECH (water) tap, faucet
Hähnchen [ˈhɛːnçən] *n (-s; -)* ZO chicken
'Hahnenkamm *m* ZO cockscomb
Hai [hai] *m (-[e]s; -e)*, **~fisch** *m* ZO shark
häkeln [ˈhɛːkəln] *v/t and v/i (ge-, h)* crochet
Haken [ˈhaːkən] *m (-s; -)* hook (*a. boxing*), peg; check, *Br* tick; F snag, catch
'Hakenkreuz *n* swastika
halb [halp] *adj and adv* half; **e-e ~e Stunde** half an hour; **ein ~es Pfund** half a pound; **zum ~en Preis** at half-price; **auf ~em Wege (entgegenkommen)** (meet) halfway; **~ so viel** half as much; F **(mit j-m) halbe-halbe machen** go halves *or* fifty-fifty (with s.o.); **~ gar** GASTR underdone
'Halbbruder *m* half-brother
'Halbdunkel *n* semi-darkness
Halbe [ˈhalbə] *f (-n; -n)* pint (of beer)

'**halbfett** adj GASTR medium-fat; PRINT semi-bold

'**Halbfi,nale** n SPORT semifinal

'**Halbgott** m demigod

'**halbherzig** adj half-hearted

halbieren [hal'biːrən] v/t (no -ge-, h) halve; MATH bisect

'**Halbinsel** f peninsula

'**Halbjahr** n six months; '**halbjährig** [-jɛːrɪç] adj six-month; '**halbjährlich** **1.** adj half-yearly; **2.** adv half-yearly, twice a year

'**Halbkreis** m semicircle

'**Halbkugel** f hemisphere

'**halblaut 1.** adj low, subdued; **2.** adv in an undertone

'**Halbleiter** m ELECTR semiconductor

'**halbmast** adv (at) half-mast

'**Halb|mond** m half-moon, crescent; **~pensi,on** f (-; no pl) esp Br half board; **~schlaf** m doze; **~schuh** m (low) shoe; **~schwester** f half-sister

'**halbtags** adv: **~ arbeiten** work part-time; '**Halbtagsarbeit** f (-; no pl) part-time job; '**Halbtagskraft** f part-time worker, F part-timer

'**halbwegs** [-'veːks] adv reasonably

'**Halbwüchsige** [-vyːksɪgə] m, f (-n; -n) adolescent

'**Halbzeit** f SPORT half (time); **~stand** m SPORT half-time score

Halde ['haldə] f (-; -n) slope; dump

half [half] pret of **helfen**

Hälfte ['hɛlftə] f (-; -n) half; **die ~ von** half of

Halfter ['halftɐ] **1.** m, n (-s; -) halter; **2.** n (-s; -), f (-; -n) holster

Halle ['halə] f (-; -n) hall; lounge; **in der ~** SPORT etc indoors

'**hallen** v/i (ge-, h) resound, reverberate

'**Hallenbad** n indoor swimming pool

'**Hallensport** m indoor sports

Halm [halm] m (-[e]s; -e) BOT blade; ha(u)lm, stalk; straw

Hals [hals] m (-es; Hälse ['hɛlzə]) ANAT neck; throat; **~ über Kopf** helter-skelter; F **sich vom ~ schaffen** get rid of; F **es hängt mir zum ~ (e) (he)raus** I'm fed up with it; fig **bis zum ~** up to one's neck; **~band** n (-[e]s; -bänder) necklace; collar; **~entzündung** f MED sore throat; **~kette** f necklace; **~schmerzen** pl: **~ haben** have a sore throat

'**halsstarrig** [-ʃtarɪç] adj stubborn, obstinate

'**Halstuch** n neckerchief; scarf

Halt m (-[e]s; -e, -s) a) (no pl) hold; support (a. fig); fig stability, b) stop; **~ machen** stop; fig **vor nichts ~ machen** stop at nothing

halt [halt] int stop!, MIL halt!

'**haltbar** adj durable; GASTR not perishable; fig tenable; **~ bis ...** best before ...

'**Haltbarkeitsdatum** n best-by (or best-before) date

halten ['haltən] (irr, ge-, h) **1.** v/t hold; keep (animal, promise etc); make (speech); give (lecture); take (Br a. in) a paper etc; SPORT save; **~ für** regard as; (mis)take for; **viel (wenig) ~ von** think highly (little) of; **sich ~** last; GASTR keep; **sich gut ~** fig do well; **sich ~ an** (acc) keep to; **2.** v/i hold, last; stop, halt; ice: bear; rope etc: hold; **~ zu** stand by, F stick to; **Halter(in)** ['haltɐ(-tərɪn)] (-s; -/-; -nen) owner; TECH holder

'**Haltestelle** f stop, RAIL a. station

'**Halteverbot** n MOT no stopping (area)

'**haltlos** adj unsteady; fig baseless

'**Haltung** f (-; -en) posture; fig attitude (**zu** towards)

hämisch ['hɛːmɪʃ] adj malicious, sneering

Hammel ['haməl] m (-s; -) ZO wether

'**Hammelfleisch** n GASTR mutton

Hammer ['hamɐ] m (-s; Hämmer ['hɛmɐ]) hammer (a. SPORT); **hämmern** ['hɛmɐn] v/t and v/i (ge-, h) hammer

Hämorrhoiden, Hämorriden [hɛmɔro'iːdən] pl MED h(a)emorrhoids, F Br piles

Hampelmann ['hampəl-] m jumping jack

Hamster ['hamstɐ] m (-s; -) ZO hamster

'**hamstern** v/t and v/i (ge-, h) hoard

Hand [hant] f (-; Hände ['hɛndə]) hand; **von ~, mit der ~** by hand; **an ~ von** (or gen) by means of; **zur ~** at hand; **aus erster (zweiter) ~** first-hand (second-hand); **an die ~ nehmen** take by the hand; **sich die ~ geben** shake hands; **aus der ~ legen** lay aside; **~ voll** handful; **Hände hoch (weg)!** hands up (off)!; **~arbeit** f a) (no pl) manual labo(u)r, b) needlework; **es ist ~** it is handmade; **~ball** m SPORT (European) handball; **~betrieb** *m* TECH manual operation; **~breit** *adj* (-; -) hand's breadth; **~bremse** *f* MOT handbrake; **~buch** *n* manual, handbook

Händedruck ['hɛndə-] *m* (-[e]s; -drücke) handshake

Handel ['handəl] *m* (-s; *no pl*) commerce, business; trade; market; transaction, deal, bargain; **~ treiben** ECON trade (**mit** with s.o.); **'handeln** *v/i* (*ge-, h*) act, take action; bargain (**um** for), haggle (over); **mit j-m ~** ECON trade with s.o.; **~ mit** deal in; **~ von** deal with, be about; **es handelt sich um** it concerns, it is about; it is a matter of

'Handels|abkommen *n* trade agreement; **~bank** *f* (-; *-banken*) commercial bank; **~bi,lanz** *f* balance of trade

'handelseinig *adj*: **~ werden** come to terms

'Handels|gesellschaft *f* (trading) company; **~kammer** *f* chamber of commerce; **~schiff** *n* merchant ship; **~schule** *f* commercial school; **~vertreter** *m* (traveling) salesman, *Br* sales representative; **~ware** *f* commodity, merchandise

'Handfeger [-feːgɐ] *m* (-s; -) handbrush; **~fertigkeit** *f* manual skill

'handfest *adj* solid

'Handfläche *f* ANAT palm

'handgearbeitet *adj* handmade

'Hand|gelenk *n* ANAT wrist; **~gepäck** *n* hand baggage (*Br* luggage); **~gra,nate** *f* MIL hand grenade

'handgreiflich [-graiflɪç] *adj*: **~ werden** turn violent, get tough

'handhaben *v/t* (*ge-, h*) handle, manage; TECH operate

'Handkantenschlag *m* chop

'Händler ['hɛndlɐ] *m* (-s; -), **'Händlerin** *f* (-; *-nen*) dealer, trader

'handlich *adj* handy, manageable

'Handlung ['handlʊŋ] *f* (-; *-en*) act, action; *film etc*: story, plot

'Handlungs|reisende *m* sales representative, travel(l)ing salesman; **~weise** *f* conduct, behavio(u)r

'Hand|rücken *m* ANAT back of the hand; **~schellen** *pl* handcuffs; **j-m ~ anlegen** handcuff s.o.; **~schlag** *m* handshake; **~schrift** *f* hand(writing)

'handschriftlich *adj* handwritten

'Hand|schuh *m* glove; **~spiel** *n* soccer:

hand ball; **~stand** *m* handstand; **~tasche** *f* handbag, purse; **~tuch** *n* towel; **~wagen** *m* handcart; **~werk** *n* craft, trade

'Handwerker [-vɛrkɐ] *m* (-s; -) craftsman; workman

'Handwerkszeug *n* (kit of) tools

'Handwurzel *f* ANAT wrist

Handy ['hɛndi] *n* (-s; -s) mobile (phone)

Hanf [hanf] *m* (-es; *no pl*) BOT hemp; cannabis

Hang [haŋ] *m* (-[e]s; *Hänge* ['hɛŋə]) a) slope, b) (*no pl*) *fig* inclination (**zu** for), tendency (towards)

Hänge|brücke ['hɛŋə-] *f* suspension bridge; **~lampe** *f* hanging lamp; **~matte** *f* hammock

hängen ['hɛŋən] **1.** *v/i* (*irr, ge-, h*) hang (**an** *dat* on *the wall etc*; from *the ceiling etc*); **~ bleiben** get caught (**an** *a. fig*); **~ bleiben an** (*dat*) get caught on; **~ an** (*dat*) be fond of; be devoted to; **alles, woran ich hänge** everything that is dear to me; **2.** *v/t* (*ge-, h*) hang (**an** *acc* on)

hänseln ['hɛnzəln] *v/t* (*ge-, h*) tease (**wegen** about)

Hanswurst [hans'vʊrst] *m* (-[e]s; -e) fool, clown

Hantel ['hantəl] *f* (-; *-n*) dumbbell

hantieren [han'tiːrən] *v/i* (*no -ge-, h*) **~ mit** handle; **~ an** (*dat*) fiddle about with

Happen ['hapən] *m* (-s; -) morsel, bite; snack

Hardware ['haːdwɛə] *f* (-; -s) EDP hardware

Harfe ['harfə] *f* (-; *-n*) MUS harp

Harfenist [harfə'nɪst] *m* (-en; -en), **Harfe'nistin** *f* (-; *-nen*) MUS harpist

Harke ['harkə] *f* (-; *-n*), **'harken** *v/t* (*ge-, h*) rake

harmlos ['harmloːs] *adj* harmless

Harmonie [harmo'niː] *f* (-; *-n*) harmony (*a.* MUS); **harmo'nieren** *v/i* (*no -ge-, h*) harmonize (**mit** with); **harmonisch** [har'moːnɪʃ] *adj* harmonious

Harn [harn] *m* (-[e]s; -e) MED urine

'Harnblase *f* ANAT (urinary) bladder

'Harnröhre *f* ANAT urethra

Harpune [har'puːnə] *f* (-; *-n*) harpoon

harpunieren [harpu'niːrən] *v/t* (*no -ge-, h*) harpoon

hart [hart] **1.** *adj* hard, F *a.* tough; SPORT rough; severe; **~ gekocht** hard-boiled; **2.** *adv* hard

Härte ['hɛrtə] f (-; -n) hardness; toughness; roughness; severity; esp JUR hardship; **~fall** m case of hardship

'**härten** v/t (ge-, h) harden

'**Hartfaserplatte** f hardboard

'**Hartgeld** n coin(s)

'**hartgesotten** [-gəzɔtən] adj hard-boiled

'**hartherzig** adj hard-hearted

'**hartnäckig** [-nɛkıç] adj stubborn, obstinate; persistent

Harz [haːrts] n (-es; -e) resin; rosin

'**harzig** adj resinous

Hasch [haʃ] F n (-s; no pl) hash

'**haschen** F v/i (ge-, h) smoke hash

Haschisch ['haʃıʃ] n (-[s]; no pl) hashish

Hase ['haːzə] m (-n; -n) ZO hare

Haselmaus ['haːzəl-] f ZO dormouse

'**Haselnuss** f BOT hazelnut

'**Hasenscharte** f MED harelip

Hass [has] m (-es; no pl) hatred, hate (**auf** acc, **gegen** of, for)

hassen ['hasən] v/t (ge-, h) hate

hässlich ['hɛslıç] adj ugly, fig a. nasty

Hast [hast] f (-; no pl) hurry, haste; rush

hasten ['hastən] v/i (ge-, sein) hurry, hasten, rush

'**hastig** adj hasty, hurried

hätscheln ['hɛːtʃəln] v/t (ge-, h) fondle; contp pamper

hatte ['hatə] pret of **haben**

Haube ['haubə] f (-; -n) bonnet (a. Br MOT); cap; ZO crest; MOT hood

Hauch [haux] m (-[e]s; -e) breath; whiff; fig touch, trace; **hauchen** ['hauxən] v/t (ge-, h) breathe

hauen F v/t ([irr.] ge-, h) hit, thrash; TECH hew; **sich ~** (have a) fight

Haufen ['haufən] m (-s; -) heap, pile (both a. F); F crowd; **häufen** ['hɔyfən] v/t (ge-, h) heap (up), pile (up); **sich ~** fig become more frequent, be on the increase; **häufig** ['hɔyfıç] **1.** adj frequent; **2.** adv frequently, often

Haupt [haupt] n (-[e]s; Häupter ['hɔyptə]) head, fig a. leader; **~bahnhof** m main or central station; **~beschäftigung** f chief occupation; **~bestandteil** m chief ingredient; **~darsteller(in)** leading actor (actress), lead

Häuptelsa,lat ['hɔyptəl-] Austrian m BOT lettuce

'**Haupt|fach** n UNIV major, Br main subject; **~film** m feature (film); **~gericht** n GASTR main course; **~gewinn** m first prize; **~grund** m main reason; **~leitung** f TECH main

Häuptling ['hɔyptlıŋ] m (-s; -e) chief

'**Haupt|mann** m (-[e]s; -leute) MIL captain; **~me,nü** n EDP main menu; **~merkmal** n chief characteristic; **~per,son** F f center (Br centre) of attention; **~quar,tier** n headquarters; **~rolle** f THEA etc lead(ing part)

'**Hauptsache** f main thing or point

'**hauptsächlich** adj main, chief, principal

'**Haupt|satz** m LING main clause; **~sendezeit** f TV prime time, Br peak time (or viewing hours); **~speicher** m EDP main memory; **~stadt** f capital; **~straße** f main street; main road; **~verkehrsstraße** f arterial road; **~verkehrszeit** f rush or peak hour(s); **~versammlung** f general meeting; **~wohnsitz** m main place of residence; **~wort** n (-[e]s; -wörter) LING noun

Haus [haus] n (-es; Häuser ['hɔyzə]) house; building; **zu ~e** at home, in; **nach ~e kommen** (**bringen**) come or get (take) home; **~angestellte** m, f domestic (servant); **~apo,theke** f medicine cabinet; **~arbeit** f housework; **~arzt** m, **~ärztin** f family doctor; **~aufgaben** pl PED homework, assignment; **s-e ~n machen** a. fig do one's homework; **~bar** f cocktail cabinet; **~besetzer** m (-s; -) squatter; **~besetzung** f squatting; **~besitzer** m house owner; **~einweihung** f house-warming (party)

hausen ['hauzən] v/i (ge-, h) live; fig play havoc

'**Hausflur** m (entrance) hall, hallway

'**Hausfrau** f housewife

'**Hausfriedensbruch** m JUR trespass

'**hausgemacht** adj homemade

'**Haushalt** m (-[e]s; -e) household; PARL budget; (j-m) **den ~ führen** keep house (for s.o.); '**Haushälterin** [-hɛltərın] f (-; -nen) housekeeper

'**Haushalts|geld** n housekeeping money; **~plan** m PARL budget; **~waren** pl household articles

'**Haus|herr** m head of the household; host; **~herrin** f lady of the house; hostess '**haushoch** *adj* huge; crushing (*defeat etc*)

hausieren [hau'ziːrən] *v/i* (*no* -ge-, h) peddle, hawk (*mit et.* s.th.) (*a. fig*); **Hau'sierer** *m* (-s; -) pedlar, hawker

häuslich ['hɔʏslɪç] *adj* domestic; home-loving

'**Haus|mädchen** *n* (house)maid; **~mann** *m* house husband; **~mannskost** *f* plain fare; **~meister** *m* caretaker, janitor; **~mittel** *n* household remedy; **~ordnung** *f* house rules; **~rat** *m* (-[e]s; *no pl*) household effects; **~schlüssel** *m* front-door key; **~schuh** *m* slipper

Hausse ['hoːs(ə)] *f* (-; -n) ECON rise, boom

'**Haus|suchung** *f* (-; -en) house search; **~tier** *n* domestic animal; **~tür** *f* front door; **~verwaltung** *f* property management; **~wirt** *m* landlord; **~wirtin** *f* landlady; **~wirtschaft** *f* (-; *no pl*) housekeeping; **~wirtschaftslehre** *f* domestic science, home economics; **~wirtschaftsschule** *f* domestic science (*or* home economics) school

Haut [haut] *f* (-; *Häute* ['hɔʏtə]) skin; complexion; *bis auf die ~ durchnässt* soaked to the skin; **~abschürfung** *f* MED abrasion; **~arzt** *m*, **~ärztin** *f* dermatologist; **~ausschlag** *m* MED rash

'**hauteng** *adj* skin-tight

'**Haut|farbe** *f* colo(u)r of the skin; complexion; **~krankheit** *f* skin disease; **~pflege** *f* skin care; **~schere** *f* cuticle scissors

Hbf. ABBR *of* *Hauptbahnhof* cent. sta., central station

H-Bombe ['haːbɔmbə] *f* MIL H-bomb

Hebamme ['heːpʔamə] *f* (-; -n) midwife

Hebebühne ['heːbə-] *f* MOT car hoist

Hebel ['heːbəl] *m* (-s; -) TECH lever

heben ['heːbən] *v/t* (*irr*, ge-, h) lift, raise (*a. fig*); heave; hoist; *fig a.* improve; *sich ~* rise, go up

Hecht [hɛçt] *m* (-[e]s; -e) ZO pike

'**hechten** *v/i* (ge-, *sein*) dive (*nach* for); SPORT do a long-fly

Heck [hɛk] *n* (-[e]s; -e) MAR stern; AVIAT tail; MOT rear

Hecke ['hɛkə] *f* (-; -n) BOT hedge

'**Heckenrose** *f* BOT dogrose

'**Heckenschütze** *m* MIL sniper

'**Heckscheibe** *f* MOT rear window

Heer [heːɐ] *n* (-[e]s; -e) MIL army, *fig a.* host

Hefe ['heːfə] *f* (-; -n) yeast

Heft [hɛft] *n* (-[e]s; -e) notebook; exercise book; booklet; issue, number

heften ['hɛftən] *v/t* (ge-, h) fix, fasten, attach (*an acc* to); pin (to); tack, baste; stitch

Hefter ['hɛftɐ] *m* (-s; -) stapler; file

heftig ['hɛftɪç] *adj* violent, fierce; heavy

'**Heftklammer** *f* staple

'**Heftpflaster** *n* bandage, Band Aid®, *Br* (adhesive *or* sticking) plaster

Hehl [heːl] *n*: *kein ~ aus et. machen* make no secret of s.th.

Hehler ['heːlɐ] *m* (-s; -) JUR receiver of stolen goods, *sl* fence

Hehlerei [heːlə'raɪ] *f* (-; -en) JUR receiving stolen goods

Heide¹ ['haɪdə] *m* (-n; -n) REL heathen

Heide² *f* (-; -n) heath(land)

'**Heidekraut** *n* (-[e]s; *no pl*) BOT heather, heath

'**Heiden|angst** F *f*: *e-e ~ haben* be scared stiff; **~geld** F *n*: *ein ~ a* fortune; **~lärm** F *m*: *ein ~ a* hell of a noise; **~spaß** F *m*: *e-n ~ haben* have a ball

'**Heidentum** *n* (-s; *no pl*) REL heathenism; **Heidin** ['haɪdɪn] *f* (-; -nen), '**heidnisch** ['haɪdnɪʃ] *adj* REL heathen

heikel ['haɪkəl] *adj* delicate, tricky; tender; F fussy

heil [haɪl] *adj* safe, unhurt; undamaged, whole, intact; **Heil** *n* (-s; *no pl*) REL grace; *sein ~ versuchen* try one's luck

Heiland ['haɪlant] *m* (-[e]s; *no pl*) REL Savio(u)r, Redeemer

'**Heilanstalt** *f* sanatorium, sanitarium; mental asylum

'**Heilbad** *n* health resort, spa

'**heilbar** *adj* curable

heilen ['haɪlən] **1.** *v/t* (ge-, h) cure; **2.** *v/i* (ge-, *sein*) heal (up)

'**Heilgym,nastik** *f* physiotherapy

heilig ['haɪlɪç] *adj* REL holy; sacred (*a. fig*); *~ sprechen* canonize

Heilig'abend *m* Christmas Eve

Heilige ['haɪlɪgə] *m*, *f* (-n; -n) REL saint

heiligen ['haɪlɪgən] *v/t* (ge-, h) REL sanctify (*a. fig*), hallow

'**Heiligtum** *n* (-s; *-tümer* [-tyːmɐ]) REL sanctuary, shrine

'**Heilkraft** *f* healing *or* curative power; '**heilkräftig** *adj* curative

'**Heilkraut** *n* BOT medicinal herb
'**heillos** *fig adj* utter, hopeless
'**Heil|mittel** *n* remedy, cure (*both a. fig*);
~**praktiker(in)** [-praktikɐ (-kərɪn)] (-*s*;
-/-; -*nen*) nonmedical practitioner;
~**quelle** *f* (medicinal) mineral spring
'**heilsam** *fig adj* salutary
'**Heilsar,mee** *f* Salvation Army
'**Heilung** *f* (-; -*en*) cure; healing
heim [haim] *adv* home
Heim *n* (-[*e*]*s*; -*e*) *a* (*no pl*) home, b)
hostel; **Heim...** *in cpds ...computer,
...mannschaft, ...sieg, ...spiel etc*: home
Heimat ['haima:t] *f* (-; *no pl*) home;
home country; home town; **in der
(meiner)** ~ at home; '**heimatlos** *adj*
homeless; '**Heimatstadt** *f* home town;
'**Heimatvertriebene** *m, f* expellee
heimisch ['haimɪʃ] *adj* home, domestic;
BOT, ZO *etc* native; *fig* homelike,
hom(e)y; *sich* ~ *fühlen* feel at home
'**Heimkehr** [-ke:ɐ] *f* (-; *no pl*) return
(home); '**heimkehren** *v/i* (*sep*, -*ge*-,
sein) return home, come back
'**heimlich** *adj* secret; '**Heimlichkeit** *f* (-;
-*en*) *a* (*no pl*) secrecy, b) *pl* secrets
'**Heimreise** *f* journey home
'**heimsuchen** *v/t* (*sep*, -*ge*-, *h*) strike
'**heimtückisch** *adj* insidious (*a*. MED);
treacherous
'**heimwärts** [-vɛrts] *adv* homeward(s)
'**Heimweg** *m* way home
'**Heimweh** *n* (-*s*; *no pl*) homesickness; ~
haben be homesick
'**Heimwerker** [-vɛrkɐ] *m* (-*s*; -) do-it-
-yourselfer
Heirat ['haira:t] *f* (-; -*en*) marriage
heiraten ['haira:tən] *v/t and v/i* (*ge*-, *h*)
marry, get married (to)
'**Heirats|antrag** *m* proposal of (mar-
riage); *j-m e-n* ~ *machen* propose to
s.o.; ~**schwindler** *m* marriage impostor; ~**vermittler(in)** (-*s*; -/-; -*nen*) marriage broker; ~**vermittlung** *f* marriage
bureau
heiser ['haizɐ] *adj* hoarse, husky
'**Heiserkeit** *f* (-; *no pl*) hoarseness, hus-
kiness
heiß [hais] *adj* hot, *fig a.* passionate, ardent; *mir ist* ~ I am or feel hot
heißen ['haisən] *v/i* (*irr*, *ge*-, *h*) be called;
mean; *wie* ~ *Sie?* what's your name?;
wie heißt das? what do you call this?;
was heißt ... auf Englisch? what is ...

in English?; *es heißt im Text* it says in
the text; *das heißt* that is (ABBR *d.h.*
i.e.)
heiter ['haitɐ] *adj* cheerful; humorous
(*film etc*); METEOR fair; *fig aus ~em
Himmel* out of the blue; '**Heiterkeit** *f*
(-; *no pl*) cheerfulness; amusement
heizbar ['haitsba:ɐ] *adj* heated; **heizen**
['haitsən] *v/t and v/i* (*ge*-, *h*) heat; *mit
Kohlen* ~ burn coal; **Heizer** ['haitsɐ]
m (-*s*; -) MAR, RAIL stoker
'**Heiz|kessel** *m* boiler; ~**kissen** *n* elec-
tric cushion; ~**körper** *m* radiator;
~**kraftwerk** *n* thermal power-station;
~**materi,al** *n* fuel; ~**öl** *n* fuel oil
'**Heizung** *f* (-; -*en*) heating
Held [hɛlt] *m* (-*en*; -*en* ['hɛldən]) hero
heldenhaft ['hɛldənhaft] *adj* heroic
'**Heldentat** *f* heroic deed
'**Heldentum** *n* (-*s*; *no pl*) heroism
Heldin ['hɛldɪn] *f* (-; -*nen*) heroine
helfen ['hɛlfən] *v/i* (*irr*, *ge*-, *h*) help, aid;
assist; *j-m bei et.* ~ help s.o. with *or* in
(doing) s.th.; ~ *gegen* MED *etc* be good
for; *er weiß sich zu* ~ he can manage;
es hilft nichts it's no use
Helfer ['hɛlfɐ] *m* (-*s*; -), '**Helferin** *f* (-;
-*nen*) helper, assistant
'**Helfershelfer** *contp m* accomplice
hell [hɛl] *adj* bright (*light, flame etc*);
light (*color etc*); light-colo(u)red (*dress
etc*); clear (*voice etc*); pale (*beer*); *fig*
bright, clever; *es wird schon* ~ it's getting light already; ~**blau** *adj* light blue;
~**blond** *adj* very fair; ~**hörig** *adj* quick
of hearing; ARCH poorly soundproofed;
~ *werden* prick up one's ears
'**Hellseher** *m* (-*s*; -), '**Hellseherin** *f* (-;
-*nen*) clairvoyant
Helm [hɛlm] *m* (-[*e*]*s*; -*e*) helmet
Hemd [hɛmt] *n* (-[*e*]*s*; -*en* ['hɛmdən])
shirt; vest; ~**bluse** *f* shirt; ~**blusen-
kleid** *n* shirtwaist, *Br* shirt-waister
Hemisphäre [hemi'sfɛ:rə] *f* (-; -*n*) hemisphere
hemmen ['hɛmən] *v/t* (*ge*-, *h*) check,
stop; hamper; '**Hemmung** *f* (-; -*en*)
PSYCH inhibition; scruple
'**hemmungslos** *adj* unrestrained; unscrupulous
Hengst [hɛŋst] *m* (-[*e*]*s*; -*e*) ZO stallion
Henkel ['hɛŋkəl] *m* (-*s*; -) handle
Henker ['hɛŋkɐ] *m* (-*s*; -) hangman, ex-
ecutioner

H

Henne ['hɛnə] f (-; -n) ZO hen

her [heːɐ] adv here; *das ist lange ~* that was a long time ago

herab [hɛ'rap] adv down; **~lassen** fig v/refl (irr, **lassen**, sep, -ge-, h) condescend; **~lassend** adj condescending; **~sehen** fig v/i (irr, **sehen**, sep, -ge-, h) ~ *auf* (acc) look down upon; **~setzen** v/t (sep, -ge-, h) reduce; fig disparage

heran [hɛ'ran] adv close, near; ~ *an* (acc) up or near to; **~gehen** v/i (irr, **gehen**, sep, -ge-, sein) ~ *an* (acc) walk up to; fig set about a task etc; **~kommen** v/i (irr, **kommen**, sep, -ge-, sein) come near (a. fig); **~wachsen** v/i (irr, **wachsen**, sep, -ge-, sein) grow (up) (*zu* into)

He'ranwachsende m, f (-n; -n) adolescent

he'ranwinken v/t (sep, -ge-, h) hail (taxi etc)

herauf [hɛ'rauf] adv up (here); upstairs; **~beschwören** v/t (irr, **schwören**, sep, no -ge-, h) call up; bring on, provoke

heraus [hɛ'raus] adv out; fig *aus* (dat) ... ~ out of ...; *zum Fenster ~* out of the window; ~ *mit der Sprache!* speak out!, out with it!; **~bekommen** v/t (irr, **kommen**, sep, no -ge-, h) get out; get back (change); fig find out; **~bringen** v/t (irr, **bringen**, sep, -ge-, h) bring out; PRINT publish; THEA stage; fig find out; **~finden** (irr, **finden**, sep, -ge-, h) **1.** v/t find; fig find out, discover; **2.** v/i find one's way out

He'rausforderer m (-s; -) challenger; **he'rausfordern** v/t (sep, -ge-, h) challenge; provoke, F ask for it; **He'rausforderung** f challenge; provocation

he'rausgeben v/t (irr, **geben**, sep, -ge-, h) give back; give up; PRINT publish; issue; give change (*auf* acc for); **He'rausgeber(in)** [-geːbɐ (-bərɪn)] (-s; -/-; -nen) publisher

he'raus|kommen v/i (irr, **kommen**, sep, -ge-, sein) come out; book: be published; stamps: be issued; ~ *aus* get out of; F *groß* ~ be a great success; **~nehmen** v/t (irr, **nehmen**, sep, -ge-, h) take out; SPORT take s.o. off the team; fig *sich et.* ~ take liberties, go too far; **~putzen** v/t and v/refl (sep, -ge-, h) spruce (o.s.) up; **~reden** v/refl (sep, -ge-, h) make excuses; talk one's way

out; **~stellen** v/t (sep, -ge-, h) put out; fig emphasize; *sich ~ als* turn out or prove to be; **~strecken** v/t (sep, -ge-, h) stick out; **~suchen** v/t (sep, -ge-, h) pick out; *j-m et.* ~ find s.o. s.th.

herb [hɛrp] adj tart; dry (wine etc); fig harsh; bitter

her'bei adv up, over, here; **~eilen** v/i (sep, -ge-, sein) come running up; **~führen** fig v/t (sep, -ge-, sein) cause, bring about

Herberge ['hɛrbɛrgə] f (-; -n) inn; lodging; hostel

Herbst [hɛrpst] m (-[e]s; -e) fall, autumn

Herd [heːɐt] m (-[e]s; -e) ['heːɐdə] cooker, stove; fig center, Br centre; MED focus, seat

Herde ['heːɐdə] f (-; -n) ZO herd (a. fig contp); flock (of sheep, geese etc)

herein [hɛ'raɪn] adv in (here); ~! come in!; **~brechen** v/i (irr, **brechen**, sep, -ge-, sein) night: fall; ~ *über* (acc) befall s.o.; **~fallen** F v/i (irr, **fallen**, sep, -ge-, sein) be taken in (*auf* acc by); **~legen** F v/t (sep, -ge-, h) take s.o. in

her'fallen v/i (irr, **fallen**, sep, -ge-, sein) ~ *über* (acc) attack (a. fig)

'Hergang m: *j-m den ~ schildern* tell s.o. what happened

her'geben v/t (irr, **geben**, sep, -ge-, h) give up, part with; *sich ~ zu* lend o.s. to

Hering ['heːrɪŋ] m (-s; -e) ZO herring

'herkommen v/i (irr, **kommen**, sep, -ge-, sein) come (here); ~ *von* come from, fig a. be caused by

'herkömmlich [-kœmlɪç] adj conventional (a. MIL)

'Herkunft [-kʊnft] f (-; no pl) origin; birth, descent

heroisch [he'roːɪʃ] adj heroic

Herr [hɛr] m (-n; -en) gentleman; master; REL the Lord; ~ *Brown* Mr Brown; ~ *der Lage* master of the situation

'Herren|bekleidung f menswear; **~doppel** n tennis: men's doubles; **~einzel** n tennis: men's singles

'herrenlos adj abandoned; stray (dog)

'Herrentoilette f men's restroom (Br toilet or lavatory)

'herrichten v/t (sep, -ge-, h) get ready, F fix

herrisch ['hɛrɪʃ] adj imperious

herrlich ['hɛrlɪç] adj marvel(l)ous, wonderful, F fantastic; **'Herrlichkeit** *f* (-; *-en*) glory

'Herrschaft *f* (-; *no pl*) rule, power, control (*a. fig*) (**über** *acc* over); **die ~ verlieren über** (*acc*) lose control of

herrschen ['hɛrʃən] *v/i* (*ge-, h*) rule; **es herrschte ...** there was ...; **Herrscher(-in)** ['hɛrʃɐ (-ʃərɪn)] (*-s; -/-; -nen*) ruler; sovereign, monarch; **'herrschsüchtig** *adj* domineering, F bossy

'herrühren *v/i* (*sep, -ge-, h*) ~ **von** come from, be due to

'herstellen *v/t* (*sep, -ge-, h*) make, produce; *fig* establish; **'Herstellung** *f* (-; *no pl*) production; *fig* establishment; **'Herstellungskosten** *pl* production cost(s)

herüber [hɛ'ry:bɐ] *adv* over (here), across

herum [hɛ'rʊm] *adv* (a)round; F **anders ~** the other way round; **~führen** *v/t* (*sep, -ge-, h*) **j-n** (**in der Stadt** *etc*) **~** show s.o. (a)round (the town *etc*); **~kommen** F *v/i* (*irr, kommen, sep, -ge-, sein*) (**weit** *or* **viel**) **~** get around; **um et. ~** *fig* get (a)round s.th.; **~kriegen** F *v/t* (*sep, -ge-, h*) **j-n zu et. ~** get s.o. round to (doing) s.th.; **~lungern** F *v/i* (*sep, -ge-, h*) F loaf *or* hang around; **~reichen** *v/t* (*sep, -ge-, h*) pass *or* hand round; **~sprechen** *v/refl* (*irr, sprechen, sep, -ge-, h*) get around; **~treiben** F *v/refl* (*irr, treiben, sep, -ge-, h*) gad *or* knock about

He'rumtreiber F *m* (*-s; -*), **He'rumtreiberin** F *f* (-; *-nen*) tramp, loafer

herunter [hɛ'rʊntɐ] *adv* down; downstairs; **~gekommen** *adj* run-down; seedy, shabby; **~hauen** F *v/t* (*sep, -ge-, h*) **j-m e-e ~** smack *or* slap s.o. ('s face); **~machen** F *v/t* (*sep, -ge-, h*) run s.o. *or* s.th. down; **~spielen** F *v/t* (*sep, -ge-, h*) play s.th. down

hervor [hɛ'fo:ɐ] *adv* out of *or* from, forth; **~bringen** *v/t* (*irr, bringen, sep, -ge-, h*) bring out, produce (*a. fig*); yield; utter; **~gehen** *v/i* (*irr, gehen, sep, -ge-, sein*) **~ aus** (*dat*) follow from; **als Sieger ~** come off victorious; **~heben** *v/t* (*irr, heben, sep, -ge-, h*) stress, emphasize; **~ragend** *adj* outstanding, excellent, superior; prominent, eminent; **~rufen** *v/t* (*irr, rufen, sep, -ge-, h*) cause, bring about; create; **~ste-**

chend *adj* striking; **~tretend** *adj* prominent; protruding; bulging; **~tun** *v/refl* (*irr, tun, sep, -ge-, h*) distinguish o.s. (**als** as)

Herz [hɛrts] *n* (*-ens; -en*) ANAT heart (*a. fig*); *cards*: heart(s); **j-m das ~ brechen** break s.o.'s heart; **sich ein ~ fassen** take heart; **mit ganzem ~en** whole-heartedly; **schweren ~ens** with a heavy heart; **sich et. zu ~en nehmen** take s.th. to heart; **es nicht übers ~ bringen zu** *inf* not have the heart to *inf*; **et. auf dem ~en haben** have s.th. on one's mind; **ins ~ schließen** take to one's heart; **~anfall** *m* heart attack

'Herzens|lust *f*: **nach ~** to one's heart's content; **~wunsch** *m* heart's desire, dearest wish

'Herzfehler *m* cardiac defect

'herzhaft *adj* hearty; savo(u)ry

'herzig *adj* sweet, lovely, cute

'Herz|infarkt *m* MED cardiac infarct (-ion), F *mst* heart attack, coronary; **~klopfen** *n* (*-s; no pl*) palpitation; **er hatte ~** (**vor** *dat*) his heart was throbbing (with)

'herzkrank *adj* suffering from (a) heart disease

'herzlich 1. *adj* cordial, hearty; warm, friendly; **2.** *adv*: **~ gern** with pleasure

'herzlos *adj* heartless

Herzog ['hɛrtso:k] *m* (*-s; Herzöge* ['hɛrtsø:gə]) duke; **Herzogin** ['hɛrtso:gɪn] *f* (-; *-nen*) duchess

'Herz|schlag *m* heartbeat; MED heart failure; **~schrittmacher** *m* MED (cardiac) pacemaker; **~transplantati,on** *f* MED heart transplant

'herzzerreißend *adj* heart-rending

Hetze ['hɛtsə] *f* (-; *no pl*) hurry, rush; POL *etc* agitation, campaign(ing) (**gegen** against); **'hetzen 1.** *v/t* (*ge-, h*) rush; ZO hunt, chase; **e-n Hund auf j-n ~** set a dog on s.o.; **2.** *v/i* a) (*ge-, sein*) hurry, rush, b) (*ge-, h*) POL *etc* agitate (**gegen** against); **'hetzerisch** *adj* inflammatory; **'Hetzjagd** *f* hunt(ing), chase (*a. fig*); *fig* rush; **'Hetzkam,pagne** *f* POL smear campaign

Heu [hɔʏ] *n* (*-[e]s; no pl*) hay

'Heuboden *m* hayloft

Heuchelei [hɔʏçə'laɪ] *f* (-; *-en*) hypocrisy; cant; **heucheln** ['hɔʏçəln] *v/i and v/t* (*ge-, h*) feign, simulate; **Heuch-**

H

ler(in) ['hɔyçlɐ (-lərɪn)] (-s; -/-; -nen) hypocrite; **heuchlerisch** ['hɔyçlərɪʃ] adj hypocritical

heuer ['hɔyɐ] Austrian adv this year

Heuer ['hɔyɐ] f (-; -n) MAR pay; **'heuern** v/t (ge-, h) hire, MAR a. sign on

heulen ['hɔylən] v/i (ge-, h) howl; F contp bawl; MOT roar; siren: whine

'Heuschnupfen m MED hay fever

'Heuschrecke f (-; -n) ZO grasshopper; locust

heute ['hɔytə] adv today; ~ Abend this evening, tonight; ~ früh, ~ Morgen this morning; ~ in acht Tagen a week from now; ~ vor acht Tagen a week ago today; **heutig** ['hɔytɪç] adj today's; of today, present(-day); **'heutzutage** adv nowadays, these days

Hexe ['hɛksə] f (-; -n) witch (a. fig); alte ~ (old) hag; **'hexen** v/i (ge-, h) practice witchcraft; F work miracles

'Hexen|kessel m inferno; ~schuss m (-es; no pl) MED lumbago

hieb [hi:p] pret of **hauen**

Hieb [hi:p] m (-[e]s; -e ['hi:bə]) blow, stroke; punch; lash, cut; pl beating; thrashing

hielt [hi:lt] pret of **halten**

hier [hi:ɐ] adv here, in this place; present; ~ entlang! this way!

hi'nab adv → **hinunter**

hieran ['hi:'ran] adv from or in this; **hierauf** ['hi:'rauf] adv on it or this; after this, then; **hieraus** ['hi:'raus] adv from or out of this; **hier'bei** adv here, in this case; on this occasion; **hier'durch** adv by this, hereby, this way; **hier'für** adv for this; **hier'her** adv (over) here, this way; **hierin** ['hi:'rɪn] adv in this; **hier'mit** adv with this; **hier'nach** adv after this; according to this; **hierüber** ['hi:'ry:bə] adv about this (subject); **hierunter** ['hi:'rʊntə] adv under this; among these; understand etc by this or that; **hier'von** adv of or from this; **hier'zu** adv to this

hiesig ['hi:zɪç] adj local; ein Hiesiger one of the locals

hieß [hi:s] pret of **heißen**

Hilfe ['hɪlfə] f (-; -n) help; aid (a. ECON), assistance (a. MED), relief (für to); erste ~ first aid; um ~ rufen cry for help; ~! help!; → **mithilfe**; ~me,nü n EDP help menu; ~ruf m call (or cry) for help; ~stellung f support (a. fig)

'hilf|los adj helpless; ~reich adj helpful

'Hilfsakti,on f relief action

'Hilfsarbeiter m, **'Hilfsarbeiterin** f unskilled worker

'hilfsbedürftig adj needy

'hilfsbereit adj helpful, ready to help; **'Hilfsbereitschaft** f (-; no pl) readiness to help, helpfulness

'Hilfs|mittel n aid, TECH a. device; ~organisati,on f relief organization; ~verb n LING auxiliary (verb)

Himbeere ['hɪmbe:rə] f BOT raspberry

Himmel ['hɪml] m (-s; -) sky; REL heaven (a. fig); um ~s willen for Heaven's sake; → **heiter**

'Himmelfahrt REL Ascension (Day)

'Himmels|körper m AST celestial body; ~richtung f direction; cardinal point

himmlisch ['hɪmlɪʃ] adj heavenly, fig a. marvel(l)ous

hin [hɪn] **1.** adv there; bis ~ zu as far as; noch lange ~ still a long way off; auf s-e Bitte (s-n Rat) ~ at his request (advice); ~ und her to and fro, back and forth; ~ und wieder now and then; ~ und zurück there and back; RAIL round trip, round-trip ticket, esp Br return (ticket); **2.** F pred adj ruined; done for; gone

'hinarbeiten v/i (sep, -ge-, h) ~ auf (acc) work towards

hi'nauf adv up (there); upstairs; die Straße etc ~ up the street etc; ~gehen v/i (irr, gehen, sep, -ge-, sein) go up, fig a. rise

hi'naus adv out; aus ... ~ out of ...; in (acc) ... ~ out into ...; ~ (mit dir)! (get) out!, out you go!; ~gehen v/i (irr, gehen, sep, -ge-, sein) go out(side); ~ über (acc) go beyond; ~ auf (acc) window: look out onto; ~laufen v/i (irr, laufen, sep, -ge-, sein) run out(side); ~ auf (acc) come out at; ~schieben v/t (irr, schieben, sep, -ge-, h) put off, postpone; ~stellen v/t (sep, -ge-, h) SPORT send s.o. off (the field); ~werfen v/t (irr, werfen, sep, -ge-, h) throw out (aus etc), fig a. kick out; (give s.o. the) sack, fire; ~wollen v/i (irr, wollen, sep, -ge-, h) ~ auf (acc) aim (or drive or get) at; hoch ~ aim high

'Hinblick m: im ~ auf (acc) in view of, with regard to

'hinbringen *v/t* (*irr*, **bringen**, *sep*, *-ge-*, *h*) take there

hinderlich ['hɪndəlɪç] *adj* hindering, impeding; *j-m ~ sein* be in s.o.'s way

hindern ['hɪndɐn] *v/t* (*ge-*, *h*) hinder, hamper; *~ an* (*dat*) prevent from

Hindernis ['hɪndɐnɪs] *n* (*-ses*; *-se*) obstacle (*a. fig*); *~rennen n* steeplechase

Hindu ['hɪndu] *m* (*-[s]*; *-[s]*) Hindu

Hinduismus [hɪndu'ɪsmʊs] *m* (*-*; *no pl*) hinduism

hin'durch *adv* through; *das ganze Jahr etc ~* throughout the year *etc*

hi'nein *adv* in; *~ mit dir!* in you go!; *~gehen v/i* (*irr*, **gehen**, *sep*, *-ge-*, *sein*) go in; *~ in* (*acc*) go into

'hinfallen *v/i* (*irr*, **fallen**, *sep*, *-ge-*, *sein*) fall (down)

'hinfällig *adj* frail, infirm; invalid

hing [hɪŋ] *pret of* **hängen** 1

'Hingabe *f* (*-*; *no pl*) devotion (*an acc* to); 'hingeben *v/t* (*irr*, **geben**, *sep*, *-ge-*, *h*) give (up); *sich ~* (*dat*) give o.s. to; devote o.s. to

'hinhalten *v/t* (*irr*, **halten**, *sep*, *-ge-*, *h*) hold out; *j-n ~* put s.o. off

hinken ['hɪŋkən] *v/i* a) (*ge-*, *h*) (walk with a) limp, b) (*ge-*, *sein*) limp

'hinkommen *v/i* (*irr*, **kommen**, *sep*, *-ge-*, *sein*) get there; *~kriegen* F *v/t* (*sep*, *-ge-*, *h*) manage

'hinlänglich *adj* sufficient

'hinlegen *v/t* (*sep*, *-ge-*, *h*) lay *or* put down; *sich ~* lie down; *~nehmen v/t* (*irr*, **nehmen**, *sep*, *-ge-*, *h*) put up with

'hinreißen *v/t* (*irr*, **reißen**, *sep*, *-ge-*, *h*) carry away; *~d adj* entrancing; breathtaking

'hinrichten *v/t* (*sep*, *-ge-*, *h*) execute; 'Hinrichtung *f* (*-*; *-en*) execution

'hinsetzen *v/t* (*sep*, *-ge-*, *h*) set *or* put down; *sich ~* sit down

'Hinsicht *f* (*-*; *no pl*) respect; *in gewisser ~* in a way; 'hinsichtlich *prp* (*gen*) with respect *or* regard to

'Hinspiel *n* SPORT first leg

'hinstellen *v/t* (*sep*, *-ge-*, *h*) put (down); *~ als* make *s.o. or s.th.* appear to be

hinten ['hɪntən] *adv* at the back; MOT in the back; *von ~* from behind

hinter ['hɪntɐ] *prp* (*dat*) behind

'Hinter... *in cpds* ...achse, ...eingang, ...rad *etc*: rear ...; *~bein n* hind leg

Hinterbliebenen [-'bliːbənən] *pl the* bereaved; *esp* JUR surviving dependents

hinterei'nander *adv* one after the other; *dreimal ~* three times in a row

'Hintergedanke *m* ulterior motive

hinter'gehen *v/t* (*irr*, **gehen**, *no -ge-*, *h*) deceive

'Hintergrund *m* background (*a. fig*)

'Hinterhalt *m* ambush; 'hinterhältig [-hɛltɪç] *adj* insidious, underhand(ed)

'Hinterhaus *n* rear building

hinter'her *adv* behind, after; afterwards

'Hinterhof *m* backyard

'Hinterkopf *m* back of the head

hinter'lassen *v/t* (*irr*, **lassen**, *no -ge-*, *h*) leave (behind); Hinter'lassenschaft *f* (*-*; *-en*) property (left), estate

hinter'legen *v/t* (*no -ge-*, *h*) deposit (*bei* with)

'Hinterlist *f* deceit(fulness); (underhanded) trick; 'hinterlistig *adj* deceitful; underhand(ed)

'Hintermann *m* person (car *etc*) behind (one); *fig mst pl* person behind the scenes, brain(s), mastermind

'Hintern F *m* (*-s*; *-*) bottom, backside, behind, *Br* bum

'hinterrücks [-ryks] *adv* from behind

'Hinter|seite *f* back; *~teil F n → Hintern*; *~treppe f* back stairs; *~tür f* back door

hinter'ziehen *v/t* (*irr*, **ziehen**, *no -ge-*, *h*) evade (*taxes*)

'Hinterzimmer *n* back room

hi'nüber *adv* over, across; *~ sein* F be ruined; GASTR be spoilt

hi'nunter *adv* down; downstairs; *die Straße ~* down the road

Hinweg ['hɪnveːk] *m* way there

hinweg [hɪn'vɛk] *adv*: *über* (*acc*) ... *~ over* ...; *~kommen v/i* (*irr*, **kommen** *sep*, *-ge-*, *sein*) *~ über* (*acc*) get over; *~sehen v/i* (*irr*, **sehen**, *sep*, *-ge-*, *h*) *~ über* (*acc*) ignore; *~setzen v/refl* (*sep*, *-ge-*, *h*) *sich ~ über* (*acc*) ignore, disregard

Hinweis ['hɪnvaɪs] *m* (*-es*; *-e*) reference (*auf acc* to); hint, tip (as to, regarding); indication (of), clue (as to); 'hinweisen (*irr*, **weisen**, *sep*, *-ge-*, *h*) 1. *v/t*: *j-n ~ auf* (*acc*) draw *or* call s.o.'s attention to; 2. *v/i*: *~ auf* (*acc*) point at *or* to, indicate; *fig* point out, indicate; hint at

'Hinweis|schild *n*, *~tafel f* sign, notice

'hinwerfen *v/t* (*irr*, **werfen**, *sep*, *-ge-*, *h*)

throw down; **~ziehen** *v/refl* (*irr, ziehen, sep, -ge-, h*) extend (**bis zu** to), stretch (to); drag on

hin'zu|fügen *v/t* (*sep, -ge-, h*) add (**zu** to) (*a. fig*); **~kommen** *v/i* (*irr, kommen, sep, -ge-, sein*) be added; **hinzu kommt, dass** add to this ..., and what is more, ...; **~ziehen** *v/t* (*irr, ziehen, sep, -ge-, h*) call in, consult

Hirn [hɪrn] *n* (*-[e]s; -e*) ANAT brain; *fig* brain(s), mind; **~gespinst** *n* fantasy

Hirsch [hɪrʃ] *m* (*-[e]s; -e*) ZO stag; **~weih** *n* ZO antlers; **~kuh** *f* ZO hind

Hirse ['hɪrzə] *f* (*-; -n*) BOT millet

Hirte ['hɪrtə] *m* (*-n; -n*) herdsman; shepherd (*a. fig*)

hissen ['hɪsən] *v/t* (*ge-, h*) hoist

Historiker [hɪs'toːrikɐ] *m* (*-s; -*), **His-'torikerin** *f* (*-; -nen*) historian; **his-'torisch** *adj* historical; historic (*event etc*)

Hitliste ['hɪtlɪstə] *f* top 40 *etc*, charts

Hitze ['hɪtsə] *f* (*-; no pl*) heat

Hitzewelle *f* heat wave

hitzig *adj* hot-tempered, peppery; heated (*debate etc*)

Hitzkopf *m* hothead

Hitzschlag *m* MED heatstroke

HIV-negativ [haːʔiˈfauː] *adj* MED HIV negative; **~positiv** *adj* MED HIV positive; **~Positive** *m, f* (*-n; -n*) MED HIV carrier

H-Milch ['haː-] *f Br* long-life milk

hob [hoːp] *pret of* **heben**

Hobby ['hɔbi] *n* (*-s; -s*) hobby

Hobby... *in cpds* amateur ...

Hobel ['hoːbəl] *m* (*-s; -*) TECH plane

Hobelbank *f* (*-; -bänke*) TECH carpenter's bench

hobeln *v/t* (*ge-, h*) TECH plane

hoch [hoːx] *adj and adv* high; tall; *fig* heavy (*fine etc*); distinguished (*guest*); great, old (*age*); deep (*snow*); **10 ~ 4** MATH 10 to the power of 4; **3000 Meter ~** *fly etc* at an altitude of 3,000 meters; **in hohem Maße** highly, greatly; **~ verschuldet** heavily in debt; F **das ist mir zu ~** that's above me

Hoch *n* (*-s; -s*) METEOR high (*a. fig*)

Hochachtung *f* (*deep*) respect (**vor** *dat* for); **'hochachtungsvoll** *adv* Yours sincerely

Hoch|bau *m* (*-[e]s; no pl*) **Hoch- und Tiefbau** structural and civil engineer-

ing; **~betrieb** F *m* (*-[e]s; no pl*) rush

'hochdeutsch *adj* High *or* standard German

'Hoch|druck *m* high pressure (*a. fig*); **~ebene** *f* plateau, tableland; **~form** *f*: **in ~** in top form *or* shape; **~fre,quenz** *f* ELECTR high frequency; **~gebirge** *n* high mountains; **~genuss** *m* real treat

'hochgezüchtet *adj* ZO, TECH highbred, TECH *a.* sophisticated; MOT tuned up, F souped up

'hochhackig [-hakɪç] *adj* high-heeled

'Hoch|haus *n* high rise, tower block; **~konjunk,tur** *f* ECON boom; **~land** *n* highlands; **~leistungs...** *in cpds* ...*sport etc*: high-performance ...

Hochmut *m* arrogance; **'hochmütig** [-myːtɪç] *adj* arrogant

'Hochofen *m* TECH blast furnace

'hochpro,zentig *adj* high-proof

'Hoch|rechnung *f* projection; POL computer prediction; **~sai,son** *f* peak (*or* height of the) season; **~schulab-schluss** *m* degree; **~schulausbildung** *f* higher education; **~schule** *f* university; college; academy; **~seefischerei** *f* deep-sea fishing; **~sommer** *m* midsummer; **~spannung** *f* ELECTR high tension (*a. fig*) *or* voltage; **~sprung** *m* SPORT high jump

höchst [høːçst] **1.** *adj* highest, *fig a.* supreme; extreme; **2.** *adv* highly, most, extremely; **'Höchst...** *in cpds* mst maximum ..., top ...

'Hochstapler [-ʃtaːplɐ] *m* (*-s; -*), **'Hoch-staplerin** *f* (*-; -nen*) impostor, swindler

'höchstens *adv* at (the) most, at best

'Höchst|form *f* SPORT top form *or* shape; **~geschwindigkeit** *f* top speed (**mit** at); speed limit; **~leistung** *f* SPORT record (performance); TECH maximum output; **~maß** *n* maximum (**an** *dat* of)

'höchstwahr'scheinlich *adv* most likely *or* probably

'Hochtechnolo,gie *f* high technology, hi tech

'hochtrabend *adj* pompous

'Hochverrat *m* high treason

'Hochwasser *n* high tide; flood

'hochwertig [-veːrtɪç] *adj* high-grade, high-quality

Hochzeit ['hɔxtsait] *f* (*-; -en*) wedding

'Hochzeits... *in cpds* ...*geschenk*,

...kleid, ...tag etc: wedding ...; **~reise** f honeymoon

Hocke ['hɔkə] f (-; -n) crouch, squat

'hocken v/i (ge-, h) squat, crouch; F sit

Hocker ['hɔkɐ] m (-s; -) stool

Höcker ['hœkɐ] m (-s; -) ZO hump

Hockey ['hɔki] n (-s; no pl) SPORT field hockey, Br ice hockey

Hoden ['ho:dən] m (-s; -) ANAT testicle

Hof [ho:f] m (-[e]s; Höfe ['hø:fə]) yard; AGR farm; court(yard); court; **~dame** f lady-in-waiting

hoffen ['hɔfən] v/i and v/t (ge-, h) hope (**auf** acc for); trust (in); **das Beste ~** hope for the best; **ich hoffe es** I hope so; **ich hoffe nicht, ich will es nicht ~** I hope not; **'hoffentlich** adv I hope, let's hope, hopefully; **'Hoffnung** f (-; -en) hope (**auf** acc of); **sich ~en machen** have hopes; **die ~ aufgeben** lose hope

'hoffnungslos adj hopeless

'hoffnungsvoll adj hopeful; promising

höflich ['hø:flɪç] adj polite, courteous (**zu** to); **'Höflichkeit** f (-; no pl) politeness, courtesy

Höhe ['hø:ə] f (-; -n) height; AVIAT, MATH, ASTR, GEOGR altitude; peak (a. fig); fig amount; level; extent (of damage etc); MUS pitch; **auf gleicher ~ mit** on a level with; **in die ~** up; F **ich bin nicht ganz auf der ~** I'm not feeling up to the mark

Hoheit f (-; no pl) POL sovereignty; Highness

'Hoheits|gebiet n territory; **~gewässer** pl territorial waters; **~zeichen** n national emblem

'Höhen|luft f mountain air; **~messer** m altimeter; **~ruder** n AVIAT elevator; **~sonne** f MED ultraviolet lamp, sunlamp; **~zug** m mountain chain

'Höhepunkt m climax, culmination, height, peak; highlight

hohl [ho:l] adj hollow (a. fig)

Höhle ['hø:lə] f (-; -n) cave, cavern; ZO hole, burrow; den, lair

'Hohl|maß n measure of capacity; **~raum** m hollow, cavity; **~spiegel** m concave mirror

Hohn [ho:n] m (-[e]s; no pl) derision, scorn; **'Hohngelächter** n jeers, jeering laughter; **höhnisch** ['hø:nɪʃ] adj derisive, scornful; **~es Lächeln** sneer

holen ['ho:lən] v/t (ge-, h) (go and) get,

fetch, go for; draw (breath); call (s.o., the police etc); **~** lassen send for; **sich ~** catch, get (a cold etc); seek (advice)

Holland ['hɔlant] Holland, the Netherlands; **Holländer** ['hɔlɛndɐ] m (-s; -) Dutchman; **'Hol'länderin** [-dərɪn] f (-; -nen) Dutchwoman; **'holländisch** adj Dutch

Hölle ['hœlə] f (-; no pl) hell

'Höllenlärm F m a hell of a noise

Holler ['hɔlɐ] Austrian m (-s; -) BOT elder

höllisch ['hœlɪʃ] adj infernal, F hellish

holperig ['hɔlpərɪç] adj bumpy (a. fig), rough, uneven; fig clumsy (style etc)

holpern ['hɔlpɐn] v/i (ge-, sein) jolt, bump; fig be bumpy

Holunder [ho'lʊndɐ] m (-s; -) BOT elder

Holz [hɔlts] n (-es; Hölzer ['hœltsɐ]) wood; lumber, Br a. timber; **aus ~** (made) of wood, wooden; **~ hacken** chop wood; **~blasinstru,ment** n MUS woodwind (instrument)

hölzern ['hœltsɐn] adj wooden, fig a. clumsy

'Holz|fäller [-fɛlə] m (-s; -) woodcutter, lumberjack; **~hammer** m mallet; fig sledgehammer

holzig ['hɔltsɪç] adj woody; stringy

'Holz|kohle f charcoal; **~schnitt** m woodcut; **~schnitzer** m wood carver; **~schuh** m clog; **~weg** fig m: **auf dem ~ sein** be barking up the wrong tree; **~wolle** f wood shavings, excelsior; **~wurm** m ZO woodworm

homöopathisch [homøo'pa:tɪʃ] adj hom(o)eopathic

homosexuell [homoze'ksʊɛl] adj, **Homosexu'elle** m, f (-n; -n) homosexual

Honig ['ho:nɪç] m (-s; -e) honey

'Honigwabe f honeycomb

Honorar [hono'ra:ɐ] n (-s; -e) fee

honorieren [hono'ri:rən] v/t (no -ge-, h) pay (a fee to); fig appreciate, reward

Hopfen ['hɔpfən] m (-s; -) BOT hop; brewing: hops

hoppla ['hɔpla] int (wh)oops!

hopsen ['hɔpsən] F v/i (ge-, sein) hop, jump

Hörappa,rat ['hø:ɐ-] m hearing aid

hörbar ['hø:ɐbaːɐ] adj audible

horchen ['hɔrçən] v/i (ge-, h) listen (**auf** acc to); eavesdrop; **Horcher** ['hɔrçɐ] m (-s; -) eavesdropper

H

Horde ['hɔrdə] *f* (-; -n) horde (*a.* ZO), *contp a.* mob, gang

hören ['hø:rən] *v/i and v/t* (*ge*-, *h*) hear; listen to; obey, listen; **~ auf** (*acc*) listen to; **von j-m ~** hear from (*or* of, about) s.o.; **er hört schwer** his hearing is bad; **hör(t) mal!** listen!; look (here)!; **nun** *or* **also hör(t) mal!** wait a minute!, now look *or* listen here!; **Hörer** ['hø:rɐ] *m* (-s; -) listener; TEL receiver; **'Hörerin** [-rərɪn] *f* (-; -nen) listener

Hör|fehler ['hø:ɐ-] *m* MED hearing defect; **~gerät** *n* hearing aid

hörig ['hø:rɪç] *adj*: **j-m ~ sein** be s.o.'s slave

Horizont [hori'tsɔnt] *m* (-[e]s; -e) horizon (*a. fig*); **s-n ~ erweitern** broaden one's mind; **das geht über meinen ~** that's beyond me; **horizontal** [horitsɔn'ta:l] *adj* horizontal

Hormon [hɔr'mo:n] *n* (-s; -e) hormone

Horn [hɔrn] *n* (-[e]s; *Hörner* ['hœrnɐ]) horn; **~haut** *f* horny skin, callus(es); ANAT cornea

Hornisse [hɔr'nɪsə] *f* (-; -n) ZO hornet

Horoskop [horo'sko:p] *n* (-s; -e) horoscope

Hör|rohr ['hø:ɐ-] *n* MED stethoscope; **~saal** *m* lecture hall, auditorium; **~spiel** *n* radio play; **~weite** *f*: **in (au-ßer) ~** within (out of) earshot

Höschen ['hø:sçən] *n* (-s; -) panties

Hose ['ho:zə] *f* (-; -n) (**e-e ~** a pair of) pants, *Br* trousers; slacks; shorts

Hosen|anzug *m* pants (*Br* trouser) suit; **~rock** *m* (**ein ~** a pair of) culottes; **~schlitz** *m* fly; **~tasche** *f* trouser pocket; **~träger** *pl* (a pair of) suspenders *or Br* braces

Hospital [hɔspi'ta:l] *n* (-s; *-täler* [-'tɛ:lɐ]) hospital

Hostie ['hɔstjə] *f* (-; -n) REL host

Hotel [ho'tɛl] *n* (-s; -s) hotel; **~di,rektor** *m* hotel manager; **~fach** *n* (-[e]s; *no pl*) hotel business; **~zimmer** *n* hotel room

HP ABBR *of* **Halbpension** half-board

Hr(n). ABBR *of* **Herrn** Mr

Hubraum ['hu:p-] *m* MOT cubic capacity

hübsch [hʏpʃ] *adj* pretty, nice(-looking), cute; *fig* nice, lovely

Hubschrauber ['hu:pʃraubɐ] *m* (-s; -) helicopter; **~landeplatz** *m* heliport

Huf [hu:f] *m* (-[e]s; -e) ZO hoof

'Hufeisen *n* horseshoe

Hüfte ['hʏftə] *f* (-; -n) ANAT hip

'Hüftgelenk *n* ANAT hip joint

'Hüftgürtel *m* girdle

Hügel ['hy:gəl] *m* (-s; -) hill; **'hügelig** *adj* hilly; **'Hügelland** *n* downs

Huhn [hu:n] *n* (-[e]s; *Hühner* ['hy:nɐ]) ZO chicken; hen; **Hühnchen** ['hy:nçən] *n* (-s; -) chicken; F **mit j-m ein ~ zu rup-fen haben** have a bone to pick with s.o.

'Hühner|auge *n* MED corn; **~brühe** *f* chicken broth; **~ei** *n* hen's egg; **~farm** *f* poultry *or* chicken farm; **~hof** *m* poultry *or* chicken yard; **~leiter** *f* chicken ladder; **~stall** *m* henhouse

huldigen ['hʊldɪgən] *v/i* (*ge*-, *h*) pay homage to; *fig* indulge in

Hülle ['hʏlə] *f* (-; -n) cover(ing), wrap (-ping); jacket, *Br* sleeve; sheath; **in ~ und Fülle** in abundance; **'hüllen** *v/t* (*ge*-, *h*) **~ in** (*acc*) wrap (up) in, cover in

Hülse ['hʏlzə] *f* (-; -n) BOT pod; husk; TECH case; **'Hülsenfrüchte** *pl* pulse

human [hu'ma:n] *adj* humane

humanitär [humani'tɛ:ɐ] *adj* humanitarian; **Humanität** [humani'tɛ:t] *f* (-; *no pl*) humanity

Hummel ['hʊməl] *f* (-; -n) ZO bumblebee

Hummer ['hʊmɐ] *m* (-s; -) ZO lobster

Humor [hu'mo:ɐ] *m* (-s; *no pl*) humo(u)r; (*keinen*) **~ haben** have a (no) sense of humo(u)r; **Humorist** [humo'rɪst] *m* (-en; -en) humorist; **humo-'ristisch, hu'morvoll** *adj* humorous

humpeln ['hʊmpəln] *v/i* a) (*ge*-, *h*) hobble, b) (*ge*-, *sein*) limp

Hund [hʊnt] *m* (-[e]s; -e) ZO dog

Hunde|hütte ['hʊndə-] *f* doghouse, *Br* kennel; **~kuchen** *m* dog biscuit; **~leine** *f* lead, leash

'hunde'müde *adj* dog-tired

hundert ['hʊndɐt] *adj* a *or* one hundred; **zu hunderten** by the hundreds

'hundertfach *adj* hundredfold

Hundert'jahrfeier *f* centenary, centennial; **'hundertjährig** [-jɛ:rɪç] *adj* a hundred years old; a hundred years of

'hundertste *adj* hundredth

Hündin ['hʏndɪn] *f* (-; -nen) ZO bitch

hündisch ['hʏndɪʃ] *adj* doglike, slavish

Hüne ['hy:nə] *m* (-n; -n) giant

'Hünengrab *n* dolmen

Hunger ['hʊŋɐ] *m* (-s; *no pl*) hunger; **~ bekommen** get hungry; **~ haben** be hungry; **vor ~ sterben** die of starvation, starve to death

'**Hungerlohn** m starvation wages

'**hungern** v/i (ge-, h) go hungry, starve

'**Hungersnot** f famine

'**Hungerstreik** m hunger strike

'**Hungertod** m (death from) starvation

hungrig ['hʊŋrɪç] adj hungry (**nach, auf** acc for)

Hupe ['huːpə] f (-; -n) MOT horn

'**hupen** v/i (ge-, h) MOT sound one's horn, hoot, honk

hüpfen ['hʏpfən] v/i (ge, sein) hop, skip; ball etc: bounce

Hürde ['hʏrdə] f (-; -n) hurdle, fig a. obstacle; ZO fold, pen

'**Hürdenlauf** m SPORT hurdles

'**Hürdenläufer** m, '**Hürdenläuferin** f SPORT hurdler

Hure ['huːrə] f (-; -n) whore, prostitute

huschen ['hʊʃən] v/i (ge, sein) flit, dart

hüsteln ['hyːstəln] v/i (ge-, h) cough slightly; iro hem; **husten** ['huːstən] v/i (ge-, h), '**Husten** m (-s; no pl) cough

'**Husten|bon,bon** m, n cough drop; **~saft** m PHARM cough syrup

Hut[1] [huːt] m (-[e]s; Hüte ['hyːtə]) hat; **den ~ aufsetzen** (**abnehmen**) put on (take off) one's hat

Hut[2] f: **auf der ~ sein** be on one's guard (**vor** dat against)

hüten ['hyːtən] v/t (ge-, h) guard, protect, watch over; ZO herd, mind; look after; **das Bett ~** be confined to (one's) bed; **sich ~ vor** (dat) beware of; **sich ~, et. zu tun** be careful not to do s.th.

'**Hutkrempe** f (hat) brim

hutschen ['hʊtʃən] Austrian v/t and v/i → **schaukeln**

Hütte ['hʏtə] f (-; -n) hut; contp shack; cottage, cabin; mountain hut; TECH ironworks

Hyäne ['hyːɛːnə] f (-; -n) ZO hy(a)ena

Hyazinthe [hya'tsɪntə] f (-; -n) BOT hyacinth

Hydrant [hy'drant] m (-en; -en) hydrant

hydraulisch [hy'draulɪʃ] adj hydraulic

Hydrokultur ['hyːdro-] f hydroponics

Hygiene [hy'gjeːnə] f (-; no pl) hygiene

hygienisch [hy'gjeːnɪʃ] adj hygienic

Hypnose [hyp'noːzə] f (-; -n) hypnosis; **Hypnotiseur** [hypnoti'zøːʀ] m (-s; -e) hypnotist; **hypnotisieren** [hypnoti-'ziːʀən] v/t (no -ge-, h) hypnotize

Hypotenuse [hypote'nuːzə] f (-; -n) MATH hypotenuse

Hypothek [hypo'teːk] f (-; -en) ECON mortgage; **e-e ~ aufnehmen** take out a mortgage

Hypothese [hypo'teːzə] f (-; -n) hypothesis, supposition; **hypothetisch** [hypo'teːtɪʃ] adj hypothetical

Hysterie [hystə'riː] f (-; -n) hysteria

hysterisch [hys'teːrɪʃ] adj hysterical

i.A. ABBR of **im Auftrag** p.p., per procuration

ICE [iːtseːˈʔeː] ABBR of **Intercityexpresszug** intercity express (train)

ich [ɪç] pers pron I; **~ selbst** (I) myself; **~ bin's** it's me

ideal [ide'aːl] adj, **Ide'al** n (-s; -e) ideal; **Idealismus** [idea'lɪsmʊs] m (-; no pl) idealism; **Idea'list(in)** (-en; -en/-, -nen) idealist

Idee [i'deː] f (-; -n) idea

identifizieren [idɛntifi'tsiːʀən] v/t (no -ge-, h) identify; **sich ~ mit** identify with; **identisch** [i'dɛntɪʃ] adj identical

Identitätskarte [idɛnti'tɛːts-] Austrian f identity card

Ideologe [ideo'loːgə] m (-n; -n) ideologist; **Ideologie** [ideolo'giː] f (-; -n) ideology; **ideo'logisch** adj ideological

idiomatisch [idio'maːtɪʃ] adj LING idiomatic; **~er Ausdruck** idiom

Idiot [i'djoːt] m (-en; -en) idiot

Idi'otenhügel F m skiing: nursery slope

idi'otisch adj idiotic

Idol [i'doːl] n (-s; -e) idol

Idyll [i'dʏl] n (-s; -e), **I'dylle** f (-; -n) idyl(l); **i'dyllisch** adj idyllic

Igel ['iːgəl] m (-s; -) ZO hedgehog

Iglu ['iːglu] m (-s; -s) igloo

ignorieren [ıgno'riːrən] *v/t (no -ge-, h)* ignore, disregard

i.H. *ABBR of* **im Hause** on the premises

ihr [iːɐ] *poss pron* her; *pl* their; **Ihr** your; **ihrerseits** ['iːrɐzaits] *adv* on her (*pl* their) part; **ihresgleichen** ['iːrəs-] *indef pron* her (*pl* their) equals, people like herself (*pl* themselves); **ihretwegen** ['iːrət-] *adv* for her (*pl* their) sake

Ikone [i'koːnə] *f (-; -n)* icon (*a.* EDP)

illegal ['ılegaːl] *adj* JUR illegal

illegitim [ılegi'tiːm] *adj* JUR illegitimate

Illusion [ılu'zjoːn] *f (-; -en)* illusion

illusorisch [ılu'zoːrıʃ] *adj* illusory

Illustration [ılʊstra'tsjoːn] *f (-; -en)* illustration; **illustrieren** [ılʊs'triːrən] *v/t (no -ge-, h)* illustrate; **Illustrierte** [ılʊs'triːrtə] *f (-n; -n)* magazine

im [ım] *prep* in the; **~ Bett** in bed; **~ Kino** *etc* at the cinema *etc*; **~ Erdgeschoss** on the first (*Br* ground) floor; **~ Mai** in May; **~ Jahre 1997** in (the year) 1997; **~ Stehen** (while) standing up; → **Stehen**

imaginär [imagi'nɛːɐ] *adj* imaginary

Imbiss ['ımbıs] *m (-es; -e)* snack

Imbissstube *f* snack bar

imitieren [imi'tiːrən] *v/t (no -ge-, h)* imitate

Imker ['ımkɐ] *m (-s; -)* beekeeper

immatrikulieren [ımatriku'liːrən] *v/t and v/refl (no -ge-, h)* UNIV enrol(l), register

immer ['ımɐ] *adv* always, all the time; **~ mehr** more and more; **~ wieder** again and again; **für ~** for ever, for good

Immergrün *n* BOT evergreen

immer'hin *adv* after all

immer'zu *adv* all the time, constantly

Immigrant [ımi'grant] *m (-en; -en)*, **Immi'grantin** *f (-; -nen)* immigrant

Immissionen [ımı'sjoːnən] *pl* (harmful effects of) noise, pollutants *etc*

Immobilien [ımo'biːljən] *pl* real estate; **~makler** *m* realtor, real estate agent

immun [ı'muːn] *adj* immune (**gegen** to, against, from); **~ machen** → **immunisieren** [ımuni'ziːrən] *v/t (no -ge-, h)* immunize; **Immunität** [ımuni'tɛːt] *f (-; no pl)* immunity; **Im'munschwäche** *f (-; -n)* **Erworbene ~** MED AIDS

Imperativ ['ımperatiːf] *m (-s; -e)* LING imperative (mood)

Imperfekt ['ımperfɛkt] *n (-s; -e)* LING past (tense)

Imperialismus [ımperja'lısmʊs] *m (-; no pl)* imperialism; **Imperialist** [ımperja'lıst] *m (-en; -en)*, **imperia'listisch** *adj* imperialist

impfen ['ımpfən] *v/t (ge-, h)* MED vaccinate

Impf|pass *m* MED vaccination card; **~schein** *m* MED vaccination certificate; **~stoff** *m* MED vaccine, serum

Impfung *f (-; -en)* MED vaccination

imponieren [ımpo'niːrən] *v/i (no -ge-, h)* **j-m ~** impress s.o.

Import [ım'pɔrt] *m (-[e]s; -e)* ECON import(ation); **Importeur** [ımpɔr'tøːɐ] *m (-s; -e)* ECON importer; **importieren** [-'tiːrən] *v/t (no -ge-, h)* ECON import

imposant [ımpo'zant] *adj* impressive, imposing

imprägnieren [ımprɛ'gniːrən] *v/t (no -ge-, h)*, **imprägniert** [ımprɛ'gniːɐt] *adj* waterproof

improvisieren [ımprovi'ziːrən] *v/t and v/i (no -ge-, h)* improvise

Impuls [ım'pʊls] *m (-es; -e)* impulse; stimulus

impulsiv [ımpʊl'ziːf] *adj* impulsive

imstande [ım'ʃtandə] *adj*: **~ sein zu** *inf* be capable of *ger*

in [ın] *prep (dat and acc)* **1.** in, at; within, inside; into, in; **überall ~** all over; **~ der Stadt** in town; **~ der Schule** at school; **~ die Schule** to school; **~s Kino** to the cinema; **~s Bett** to bed; **warst du schon mal ~ ...?** have you ever been to ...?; → **im**; **2.** in, at; during; **~ dieser (der nächsten) Woche** this (next) week; **~ diesem Alter (Augenblick)** at this age (moment); **~ der Nacht** at night; **heute ~ acht Tagen** a week from now; **heute ~ e-m Jahr** this time next year; → **im**; **3.** in, at; **gut sein ~** *(dat)* be good at; **~ Eile** in a hurry; **~ Behandlung (Reparatur)** under treatment (repair); **~s Deutsche** into German; → **im**; **4.** F **~ sein** be in

Inbegriff *m* epitome

inbegriffen *adj* ECON included

in'dem *cj* while, as; by *doing s.th.*

Inder ['ındɐ] *m (-s; -)*, **Inderin** ['ındərın] *f (-; -nen)* Indian

Indian ['ındjaːn] *Austrian m (-s; -e)* ZO turkey (cock)

Indianer [ın'djaːnɐ] *m (-s; -)*, **Indianerin**

[ɪn'dja:nərɪn] f (-; -nen) Native American, (American) Indian

Indien ['ɪndjən] India

Indikativ ['ɪndikati:f] m (-s; -e) LING indicative (mood)

indirekt ['ɪndirɛkt] adj indirect, LING a. reported

indisch ['ɪndɪʃ] adj Indian

indiskret [ɪndɪskre:t] adj indiscreet

Indiskretion [ɪndɪskre'tsjo:n] f (-; -en) indiscretion

indiskutabel [ɪndɪsku'ta:bəl] adj out of the question

individuell [ɪndivi'duɛl] adj, **Individuum** [ɪndi'vi:duʊm] n (-s; -en) individual

Indiz [ɪn'di:ts] n (-es; -ien) indication, sign; pl JUR circumstantial evidence

industrialisieren [ɪndʊstriali'zi:rən] v/t (no -ge-, h) industrialize; **Industriali'sierung** f (-; no pl) industrialization

Industrie [ɪndʊs'tri:] f (-; -n) industry

Indus'triegebiet n industrial area

industriell [ɪndʊstri'ɛl] adj industrial

Industri'elle m (-n; -n) industrialist

inei'nander adv into one another; ~ **verliebt** in love with each other; ~ **greifen** TECH interlock (a. fig)

Infanterie ['ɪnfantəri:] f (-; -n) MIL infantry; **Infanterist** ['ɪnfantərɪst] m (-en; -en) MIL infantryman

Infektion [ɪnfɛk'tsjo:n] f (-; -en) MED infection; **Infekti'onskrankheit** f infectious disease

Infinitiv ['ɪnfiniti:f] m (-s; -e) LING infinitive (mood)

infizieren [ɪnfi'tsi:rən] v/t (no -ge-, h) MED infect

Inflation [ɪnfla'tsjo:n] f (-; -en) inflation

in'folge prp (gen) owing to, due to

infolge'dessen adv consequently

Informatik [ɪnfɔr'ma:tɪk] f (-; no pl) computer science; **Infor'matiker(in)** [ɪnfɔr'ma:tikɐ (-kərɪn)] (-s; -/-; -nen) computer scientist

Information [ɪnfɔrma'tsjo:n] f (-; -en) information; **die neuesten ~en** the latest information

informieren [ɪnfɔr'mi:rən] v/t (no -ge-, h) inform; **falsch ~** misinform

in'frage: ~ **stellen** question; put in jeopardy; ~ **kommen** be possible (person: eligible); **nicht ~ kommen** be out of the question

infrarot ['ɪnfra-] adj PHYS infrared

'Infrastruk,tur f infrastructure

Ing. ABBR of **Ingenieur** eng., engineer

Ingenieur [ɪnʒe'njø:ɐ] m (-s; -e), **Inge-'nieurin** f (-; -nen) engineer

Ingwer ['ɪŋvɐ] m (-s; no pl) ginger

Inhaber ['ɪnha:bɐ] m (-s; -), **'Inhaberin** f (-; -nen) owner, proprietor (proprietress); holder

Inhalt ['ɪnhalt] m (-[e]s; -e) contents; volume, capacity; fig meaning

'Inhalts,angabe f summary; ~**verzeichnis** n table of contents

Initiative [initsja'ti:və] f (-; -n) initiative; **die ~ ergreifen** take the initiative

inklusive [ɪnklu'zi:və] prp ECON including

inkonsequent ['ɪnkɔnzekvɛnt] adj inconsistent

In-'Kraft-Treten n (-s; no pl) coming into force, taking effect

'Inland n (-[e]s; no pl) home (country); ~**flug** m domestic (or internal) flight

inländisch ['ɪnlɛndɪʃ] adj domestic, home, inland

Inlett ['ɪnlɛt] n (-[e]s; -e) ticking

in'mitten prp (gen) in the middle of

innen ['ɪnən] adv inside; **nach ~** inwards

'Innen,archi,tekt m, ~**archi,tektin** f interior designer; ~**architek,tur** f interior design; ~**mi,nister(in)** minister of the interior; Secretary of the Interior, Br Home Secretary; ~**minis,terium** n ministry of the interior; Department of the Interior, Br Home Office; ~**poli,tik** f domestic politics

'innenpo,litisch adj domestic, internal

'Innenseite f: **auf der ~** (on the) inside

'Innenstadt f downtown, (city or town) center or Br centre

inner ['ɪnɐ] adj inside; fig inner; MED, POL internal; **Innere** ['ɪnərə] n (-n; no pl) interior, inside

Innereien [ɪnə'raiən] pl GASTR offal

'innerhalb prp (gen) within

'innerlich adj internal (a. MED)

innert ['ɪnɐt] Swiss prp (gen or dat) with in

innig ['ɪnɪç] adj tender, affectionate

Innung ['ɪnʊŋ] f (-; -en) guild

'inoffiziell adj unofficial

ins [ɪns] → **in**

Insasse ['ɪnzasə] m (-n; -n) inmate; MOT passenger; **'Insassenversicherung** f MOT passenger insurance; **'Insassin** f

(-; -nen) inmate; MOT passenger

insbe'sondere adv (e)specially, particularly

'Inschrift f inscription, legend

Insekt [ɪn'zɛkt] n (-s; -en) ZO insect, bug

In'sektenstich m insect bite

Insel ['ɪnzəl] f (-; -n) island

'Inselbewohner m islander

Inserat [ɪnze'raːt] n (-[e]s; -e) advertisement, F ad; **inserieren** [ɪnze'riːrən] v/t and v/i (no -ge-, h) advertise

insge'heim adv secretly

insge'samt adv altogether, in all

inso'fern 1. adv as far as that goes; **2.** cj: **~ als** in so far as

Inspektion [ɪnspɛk'tsjoːn] f (-; -en) inspection; MOT service

Inspektor [ɪn'spɛktoːɐ] m (-s; -en [ɪnspɛk'toːrən]), **Inspek'torin** f (-; -nen) inspector

inspizieren [ɪnspi'tsiːrən] v/t (no -ge-, h) inspect

Installateur [ɪnstala'tøːɐ] m (-s; -e) plumber; (gas or electrical) fitter

installieren [ɪnsta'liːrən] v/t (no -ge-, h) put in, fit, install(l)

instand [ɪn'ʃtant] adv: **~ halten** keep in good condition or repair; TECH maintain; **~ setzen** repair

In'standhaltung f (-; no pl) maintenance

'instandig adv: **j-n ~ bitten** implore s.o.

In'standsetzung f (-; -en) repair

Instanz [ɪn'stants] f (-; -en) authority; JUR instance

Instinkt [ɪn'stɪŋkt] m (-[e]s; -e) instinct

instinktiv [ɪnstɪŋk'tiːf] adv instinctively

Institut [ɪnsti'tuːt] n (-[e]s; -e) institute

Institution [ɪnstitu'tsjoːn] f (-; -en) institution

Instrument [ɪnstru'mɛnt] n (-[e]s; -e) instrument

inszenieren [ɪnstse'niːrən] v/t (no -ge-, h) (put on) stage; film: direct; fig stage

Insze'nierung f (-; -en) production

intellektuell [ɪntɛlɛk'tuɛl] adj, **Intellektu'elle** m, f (-n; -n) intellectual, F highbrow

intelligent [ɪntɛli'gɛnt] adj intelligent

Intelligenz [ɪntɛli'gɛnts] f (-; -en) intelligence; **~quoti,ent** m I.Q.

Intendant [ɪntɛn'dant] m (-en; -en), **Inten'dantin** f (-; -nen) THEA etc director

intensiv [ɪntɛn'ziːf] adj intensive; intense; **Inten'sivkurs** m crash course

interessant [ɪntəre'sant] adj interesting; **Interesse** [ɪntə'rɛsə] n (-s; -n) interest (**an** dat, **für** in)

Inte'ressengebiet n field of interest

Interessent [ɪntəre'sɛnt] m (-en; -en), **Interes'sentin** f (-; -nen) interested person; ECON prospect, Br prospective buyer

interessieren [ɪntəre'siːrən] v/t (no -ge-, h) interest (**für** in); **sich ~ für** take an interest in; be interested in

intern [ɪn'tɛrn] adj internal

Internat [ɪntɛr'naːt] n (-[e]s; -e) boarding school

internatio'nal [ɪntɛ-] adj international

Internist [ɪntɛr'nɪst] m (-en; -en), **Inter'nistin** f (-; -nen) MED internist

Interpretation [ɪntɛrpreta'tsjoːn] f (-; -en) interpretation; analysis

interpretieren [ɪntɛrpre'tiːrən] v/t (no -ge-, h) interpret, anal|lyze, Br -lyse

Interpunktion [ɪntɛrpuŋk'tsjoːn] f (-; no pl) punctuation

Intervall [ɪntɛr'val] n (-[e]s; -e) interval

intervenieren [ɪntɛrve'niːrən] v/i (no -ge-, h) intervene

Interview ['ɪntɛrvjuː] n (-s; -s), **interviewen** [ɪntɛr'vjuːən] v/t (no -ge-, h) interview

intim [ɪn'tiːm] adj intimate (**mit** with) (a. sexually); **Intimität** [ɪntimi'tɛːt] f (-; no pl) intimacy; **In'timsphäre** f privacy

intolerant ['ɪntolerant] adj intolerant (**gegen** of); **Intoleranz** ['ɪntolerants] f (-; no pl) intolerance

intransitiv ['ɪntranzitiːf] adj LING intransitive

Intrige [ɪn'triːgə] f (-; -n) intrigue, scheme, plot; **intrigieren** [ɪntri'giːrən] v/i (no -ge-, h) (plot and) scheme

Invalide [ɪnva'liːdə] m (-n; -n) invalid; **Inva'lidenrente** f disability pension

Invalidität [ɪnvalidi'tɛːt] f (-; no pl) disablement, disability

Inventar [ɪnvɛn'taːɐ] n (-s; -e) inventory, stock

Inventur [ɪnvɛn'tuːɐ] f (-; -en) ECON stocktaking; **~ machen** take stock

investieren [ɪnvɛs'tiːrən] v/t (no -ge-, h) ECON invest (a. fig); **Investition** [ɪnvɛsti'tsjoːn] f (-; -en) ECON investment

inwiefern [ɪnvi'fɛrn] cj and adv in what respect or way

inwie'weit *cj and adv* to what extent
'Inzucht *f* inbreeding
in'zwischen *adv* meanwhile, in the meantime; by now

irdisch ['ɪrdɪʃ] *adj* earthly, worldly
Ire ['iːrə] *m* (*-n*; *-n*) Irishman; *pl* the Irish
irgend ['ɪrgənt] *adv in cpds*: some...; any...; **wenn ~ möglich** if at all possible; **wenn du ~ kannst** if you possibly can; F **~ so ein ...** some ...; **~'ein(e)** *indef pron* some(one); any(one); **~'ein** *indef pron* some; any; **~etwas** something; anything; **~jemand** someone, somebody; anyone, anybody; **~'wann** *adv* sometime (or other); (at) any time; **~'wie** *adv* somehow (or other); **~'wo** *adv* somewhere; anywhere
Irin ['iːrɪn] *f* (*-*; *-nen*) Irishwoman; **irisch** ['iːrɪʃ] *adj* Irish; **Irland** ['ɪrlant] Ireland
Ironie [iro'niː] *f* (*-*; *no pl*) irony
ironisch [i'roːnɪʃ] *adj* ironic(al)
irre ['ɪrə] *adj* mad, crazy, insane; confused; F super, terrific
'Irre *m*, *f* (*-n*; *-n*) madman (madwoman), lunatic; **wie ein ~r** like mad *or* a madman
'irreführen *v/t* (*sep*, *-ge-*, *h*) mislead, lead astray; **~d** *adj* misleading
'irre|gehen *v/i* (*irr*, **gehen**, *sep*, *-ge-*, *sein*) go astray, *fig a.* be wrong; **~machen** *v/t* (*sep*, *-ge-*, *h*) confuse

irren ['ɪrən] **1.** *v/refl* (*ge-*, *h*) be wrong, be mistaken; **sich ~** be wrong; **sich in et.** **~** get s.th. wrong; **2.** *v/i* (*ge-*, *sein*) wander, stray, err
irritieren [ɪri'tiːrən] *v/t* (*no -ge-*, *h*) irritate; F confuse
'Irrlicht *n* (*-[e]s*; *-er*) will-o'-the-wisp
'Irrsinn *m* (*-[e]s*; *no pl*) madness
'irrsinnig *adj* insane, mad; F terrific
Irrtum ['ɪrtuːm] *m* (*-s*; *Irrtümer* ['ɪrtyːmɐ]) error, mistake; **im ~ sein** be mistaken; **'irrtümlich** *adv* by mistake
Ischias ['ɪʃias] *m*, *n*, *f* (*-*; *no pl*) MED sciatica
Islam [ɪs'laːm] *m* (*-[s]*; *no pl*) Islam
Island ['iːslant] Iceland
Isländer ['iːslɛndɐ] *m* (*-s*; *-*), **'Isländerin** [-dərɪn] *f* (*-*; *-nen*) Icelander
'isländisch *adj* Icelandic
Isolierband [izo'liːɐ-] *n* (*-[e]s*; *-bänder*) insulating tape; **isolieren** [izo'liːrən] *v/t* (*no -ge-*, *h*) isolate; ELECTR, TECH insulate; **Iso'lierstati,on** *f* MED isolation ward; **Iso'lierung** *f* (*-*; *-en*) isolation; ELECTR, TECH insulation
Israel ['ɪsraeːl] Israel
Israeli [ɪsra'eːli] *m* (*-[s]*; *-[s]*), *f* (*-*; *-[s]*), **israelisch** [ɪsra'eːlɪʃ] *adj* Israeli
Italien [i'taːljən] Italy; **Italiener** [ita'ljeːnɐ] *m* (*-s*; *-*), **Itali'enerin** [-nərɪn] *f* (*-*; *-nen*), **itali'enisch** *adj* Italian

J

J

ja [jaː] *adv* yes, F *a.* yeah; PARL yea, aye; **wenn ~** if so; **da ist er ~!** well, there he is!; **ich sagte es Ihnen ~** I told you so; **ich bin ~ (schließlich) ...** after all, I am ...; **tut es 1bcja nicht!** don't you dare do it!; **sei 1bcja vorsichtig!** do be careful!; **vergessen Sie es 1bcja nicht!** be sure not to forget it!; **~, weißt du nicht?** why, don't you know?; **du kommst doch, ~?** you're coming, aren't you?
Jacht [jaxt] *f* (*-*; *-en*) MAR yacht
Jacke ['jakə] *f* (*-*; *-n*) jacket; coat
Jackett [ʒa'kɛt] *n* (*-s*; *-s*) jacket, coat
Jagd [jaːkt] *f* (*-*; *-en*) hunt(ing) (*a. fig*); shoot(ing); *fig* chase; → **Jagdrevier**,

auf (die) ~ gehen go hunting *or* shooting; **~ machen auf** (*acc*) hunt (for); *a.* chase *s.o.*; **~aufseher** *m* gamekeeper; **~flugzeug** *n* MIL fighter (plane); **~hund** *m* ZO hound; **~hütte** *f* (hunting) lodge; **~re,vier** *n* hunting ground; **~schein** *m* hunting *or* shooting licen|se, *Br* -ce
jagen ['jaːgən] *v/t and v/i* (*ge-*, *h*) hunt; shoot; *fig* race, dash; hunt, chase; *j-n* **aus dem Haus** *etc* **~** drive *or* chase s.o. out of the house *etc*
Jäger ['jeːgɐ] *m* (*-s*; *-*) hunter, huntsman
Jaguar ['jaːguaːr] *m* (*-s*; *-e*) ZO jaguar
jäh [jeː] *adj* sudden; steep
Jahr [jaːɐ] *n* (*-[e]s*; *-e* ['jaːrə]) year; **ein**

drei viertel ~ nine months; *einmal im* ~ once a year; *im* ~ *e 1995* in (the year) 1995; *ein 10* ~ *e altes Auto* a ten-year--old car; *mit 18* ~ *en, im Alter von 18* ~ *en* at (the age of) eighteen; *heute vor e-m* ~ a year ago today; *die 80er-Jahre* the eighties

jahr'aus *adv:* ~, **jahrein** year in, year out; year after year

'**Jahrbuch** *n* yearbook, annual

jahrelang ['ja:rəlaŋ] **1.** *adj* longstanding, (many) years of; **2.** *adv* for (many) years

Jahres... ['ja:rəs...] *in cpds* ...*bericht*, ...*bilanz*, ...*einkommen etc:* annual ...; ~**anfang** *m* beginning of the year; ~**ende** *n* end of the year; ~**tag** *m* anniversary; ~**wechsel** *m* turn of the year; ~**zahl** *f* date, year; ~**zeit** *f* season, time of (the) year

'**Jahrgang** *m* age group; PED year, class (*1995* of '95); GASTR vintage

Jahr'hundert *n* (-*s; -e*) century; ~**wende** *f* turn of the century

jährlich ['jɛ:rlɪç] **1.** *adj* annual, yearly; **2.** *adv* every year, yearly, once a year

'**Jahrmarkt** *m* fair

Jahr'tausend *n* (-*s; -e*) millennium

Jahr'zehnt *n* (-[*e*]*s; -e*) decade

'**Jähzorn** *m* violent (fit of) temper

'**jähzornig** *adj* hot-tempered

Jalousie [ʒalu'zi:] *f* (-; -*n*) (venetian) blind

Jammer ['jamɐ] *m* (-*s; no pl*) misery; *es ist ein* ~ it is a pity; **jämmerlich** ['jɛmɐlɪç] *adj* miserable, wretched, pitiful, sorry; ~ *versagen* fail miserably; **'jammern** *v/i* (*ge-, h*) moan, lament (*über acc* over, about); complain (of, about); **jammer'schade** *adj:* *es ist* ~, *dass* it's a crying shame that

Janker ['jaŋkɐ] *Austrian m* (-*s; -*) jacket

Jänner ['jɛnɐ] *Austrian m* (-*s; -*), **Januar** ['janua:r] *m* (-[*s*]; -*e*) January

Japan ['ja:pan] Japan; **Japaner** [ja'pa:nɐ] *m* (-*s; -*), **Ja'panerin** [-nərɪn] *f* (-; -*nen*), **ja'panisch** *adj* Japanese

Jargon [ʒar'gõ:] *m* (-*s; -s*) jargon; slang

'**Jastimme** *f* PARL aye, yea

jäten ['jɛ:tən] *v/t* (*ge-, h*) weed

Jauche ['jauxə] *f* (-; -*n*) liquid manure

jauchzen ['jauxtsən] *v/i* (*ge-, h*) shout for *or* with joy; exult, rejoice

Jause ['jauzə] *Austrian f* (-; -*n*) snack

ja'wohl *adv* (that's) right, (yes,) indeed

je [je:] *adv and cj* ever; each; per; *der beste Film, den ich* ~ *gesehen habe* the best film I have ever seen; ~ *zwei (Pfund)* two (pounds) each; *drei Mark* ~ *Kilo* three marks per kilo; ~ *nach Größe (Geschmack)* according to size (taste); ~ *nachdem(, wie)* it depends (on how); ~ *..., desto ...* the ... the ...

Jeans [dʒi:nz] *pl, a. f* (-; -) (*e-e* ~ a pair of) jeans; ~**jacke** *f* denim jacket

jede ['je:də], **jeder** ['je:dɐ], **jedes** ['je:dəs] *indef pron* every; any; each; either; *jeder weiß (das)* everybody knows; *du kannst jeden fragen* (you can) ask anyone; *jeder von uns (euch)* each of us (you); *jeder, der* whoever; *jeden zweiten Tag* every other day; *jeden Augenblick* any moment now; *jedes Mal* every time; *jedes Mal wenn* whenever

'**jeden'falls** *adv* in any case, anyhow

'**jedermann** *indef pron* everyone, everybody

'**jeder'zeit** *adv* any time, always

je'doch *cj* however

je'her *adv:* *von* ~ always

jemals ['je:ma:ls] *adv* ever

jemand ['je:mant] *indef pron* someone, somebody; anyone, anybody

jene ['je:nə], **jener** ['je:nɐ], **jenes** ['je:nəs] *dem pron* that (one); *pl* those; *dies und jenes* this and that

jenseitig ['je:nzaitɪç] *adj* opposite

jenseits ['je:nzaits] *adv and prp* (*gen*) on the other side (of), beyond (*a. fig*)

'**Jenseits** *n* (-; *no pl*) next world, hereafter

jetzig ['jɛtsɪç] *adj* present; existing

jetzt [jɛtst] *adv* now, at present; *bis* ~ up to now, so far; *erst* ~ only now; ~ *gleich* right now *or* away; *für* ~ for the present; *von* ~ *an* from now on

jeweilig ['je:vailɪç] *adj* respective

jeweils ['je:vails] *adv* each; at a time

Jh. ABBR *of Jahrhundert* cent., century

Jochbein ['jɔx-] *n* ANAT cheekbone

Jockei ['dʒɔke] *m* (-*s; -s*) jockey

Jod [jo:t] *n* (-[*e*]*s; no pl*) CHEM iodine

jodeln ['jo:dəln] *v/i* (*ge-, h*) yodel

Joga → *Yoga*

joggen ['dʒɔgən] *v/i* (*ge-, h*) jog

Jogger ['dʒɔgɐ] *m* (-*s; -*) jogger

Jogging ['dʒɔgɪŋ] *n* (*-s*; *no pl*) jogging; **~anzug** *m* tracksuit; **~hose** *f* tracksuit trousers

Joghurt, Jogurt ['jo:gʊrt] *m, n,* (*-[s]*; *-[s]*) yog(h)urt, yoghourt

Johannisbeere [jo'hanɪs-] *f*: **rote ~** redcurrant; **schwarze ~** blackcurrant

johlen ['jo:lən] *v/i* (*ge-, h*) howl, yell

Jolle ['jɔlə] *f* (*-*; *-n*) MAR dinghy

Jongleur [ʒõ'glø:ɐ] *m* (*-s*; *-e*) juggler

jonglieren [ʒõ'gli:rən] *v/t and v/i* (*no -ge-, h*) juggle

Joule [dʒu:l] *n* (*-[s]*; *-*) PHYS joule

Journalismus [ʒʊrna'lɪsmʊs] *m* (*-*; *no pl*) journalism; **Journalist(in)** [ʒʊrna-'lɪst(ɪn)] (*-en*; *-en/-*; *-nen*) journalist

jr. → **jun.**

Jubel ['ju:bəl] *m* (*-s*; *no pl*) cheering, cheers; rejoicing; **jubeln** *v/i* (*ge-, h*) cheer, shout for joy; rejoice

Jubiläum [jubi'lɛːʊm] *n* (*-s*; *-läen*) anniversary; **50-jähriges ~** fiftieth anniversary, (golden) jubilee

jucken ['jʊkən] *v/t and v/i* (*ge-, h*) itch; **es juckt mich am ...** my ... itches

Jude ['ju:də] *m* (*-n*; *-n*) Jewish person; **er ist ~** he is Jewish; **Jüdin** ['jy:dɪn] *f* (*-*; *-nen*) Jewish woman *or* girl; **sie ist ~** she is Jewish; **jüdisch** ['jy:dɪʃ] *adj* Jewish

Judo ['ju:do] *n* (*-[s]*; *no pl*) SPORT judo

Jugend ['ju:gənt] *f* (*-*; *no pl*) youth; **die ~** young people; **~amt** *n* youth welfare office; **~arbeitslosigkeit** *f* youth unemployment

jugendfrei *adj*: **~er Film** G(-rated) (*Br* U[-rated]) film; **nicht ~** X-rated

Jugendfürsorge *f* youth welfare; **~gericht** *n* JUR juvenile court; **~herberge** *f* youth hostel; **~klub** *m* youth club; **~kriminali,tät** *f* juvenile delinquency

jugendlich *adj* youthful, young

Jugendliche *m, f* (*-n*; *-n*) young person, *m a.* youth, JUR *a.* juvenile

Jugendstil *m* (*-s*; *no pl*) Art Nouveau; **~strafanstalt** *f* detention center (*Br* centre), reformatory; **~verbot** *n* for adults only; → **jugendfrei**; **~zentrum** *n* youth center (*Br* centre)

Juli ['ju:li] *m* (*-[s]*; *-s*) July

Jumbojet ['jʊmbo-] *m* jumbo (jet)

jun. ABBR *of* **junior** Jun., jun., Jnr., Jr., junior

jung [jʊŋ] *adj* young

Junge[1] ['jʊŋə] *m* (*-n*; *-n*) boy; lad; *cards*: jack, knave

Junge[2] *n* (*-n*; *-n*) ZO young; puppy; kitten; cub; **~ bekommen** *or* **werfen** have young

jungenhaft *adj* boyish

Jungenstreich *m* boyish prank

jünger ['jʏŋɐ] *adj* younger

Jünger *m* (*-s*; *-*) REL disciple (*a. fig*)

Jungfer ['jʊŋfɐ] *f* (*-*; *-n*) **alte ~** old maid

Jungfernfahrt *f* MAR maiden voyage; **~flug** *m* AVIAT maiden flight

Jungfrau *f* virgin; ASTR Virgo; **er ist ~** he's (a) Virgo; **~geselle** *m* bachelor, single (man); **~gesellin** *f* bachelor girl, single (woman); *esp* XUR spinster

jüngste ['jʏŋstə] *adj* youngest; *fig* latest; **in ~r Zeit** lately, recently; **das Jüngste Gericht** the Last Judg(e)ment; **der Jüngste Tag** Doomsday

Juni ['ju:ni] *m* (*-[s]*; *-s*) June

junior ['ju:njoːɐ] *adj*, **'Junior** *m* (*-s*; *-en* [ju'njo:rən]), **Juni'orin** *f* (*-*; *-nen*) junior (*a.* SPORT).

Jupe [ʒy:p] *Swiss m* (*-s*; *-s*) skirt

Jura ['ju:ra]: **~ studieren** study (the) law

juridisch [ju'ri:dɪʃ] *Austrian* → **juristisch**; **Jurist(in)** [ju'rɪst(ɪn)] (*-en*; *-en/-*; *-nen*) lawyer; law student; **ju'ristisch** *adj* legal

Jurorenkomitee [ju'ro:rən-] *Austrian n* → **Jury**

Jury [ʒy'ri:] *f* (*-*; *-s*) jury

justieren [jʊs'ti:rən] *v/t* (*no -ge-, h*) TECH adjust, set

Justiz [jʊs'ti:ts] *f* (*-*; *no pl*) (administration of) justice, (the) law; **~beamte** *m* judicial officer; **~irrtum** *m* error of justice; **~mi,nister** *m* minister of justice; Attorney General, *Br* Lord Chancellor; **~minis,terium** *n* ministry of justice; Department of Justice

Jute ['ju:tə] *f* (*-*; *no pl*) jute

Juwel [ju've:l] *m, n* (*-s*; *-en*) jewel, gem (*both a. fig*); *pl* jewel(le)ry

Juwelier [juve'li:ɐ] *m* (*-s*; *-e*) jewel(l)er

K

Kabarett [kaba'rɛt] *n* (*-s*; *-s*) (political) revue

Kabel ['ka:bəl] *n* (*-s*; *-*) cable

'**Kabelfernsehen** *n* cable TV

Kabeljau ['ka:bəljau] *m* (*-s*; *-e*, *-s*) ZO cod(fish)

Kabine [ka'bi:nə] *f* (*-*; *-n*) cabin; cubicle; SPORT dressing room; TECH car; TEL *etc* booth; **Ka'binenbahn** *f* cable railway

Kabinett [kabi'nɛt] *n* (*-s*; *-e*) POL cabinet

Kabis ['ka:bɪs] *Swiss m* (*-*; *no pl*) green cabbage

Kabriolett [kabrio'lɛt] *n* (*-s*; *-s*) MOT convertible

Kachel ['kaxəl] *f* (*-*; *-n*), '**kacheln** *v/t* (*ge-*, *h*) tile; '**Kachelofen** *m* tiled stove

Kadaver [ka'da:vɐ] *m* (*-s*; *-*) carcass

Kadett [ka'dɛt] *m* (*-en*; *-en*) MIL cadet

Käfer ['kɛ:fɐ] *m* (*-s*; *-*) ZO beetle, bug

Kaffee ['kafe] *m* (*-s*; *-s*) coffee; **~ kochen** make coffee; **~ mit Milch** white coffee; **~auto,mat** *m* coffee machine; **~bohne** *f* coffee bean; **~haus** [ka'fe:-] *Austrian n* café, coffee house; **~kanne** *f* coffee pot; **~ma,schine** *f* coffeemaker; **~mühle** *f* coffee grinder

Käfig ['kɛ:fɪç] *m* (*-s*; *-e*) cage (*a. fig*)

kahl [ka:l] *adj* bald; *fig* bare (*rock, wall etc*); barren, bleak (*landscape*)

Kahn [ka:n] *m* (*-[e]s*; *Kähne* ['kɛ:nə]) boat; barge

Kai [kai] *m* (*-s*; *-s*) quay, wharf

Kaiser ['kaizɐ] *m* (*-s*; *-*) emperor

Kaiserin ['kaizərɪn] *f* (*-*; *-nen*) empress

'**Kaiserreich** *n* empire

Kajüte [ka'jy:tə] *f* (*-*; *-n*) MAR cabin

Kakao [ka'kau] *m* (*-s*; *-s*) cocoa; (hot) chocolate; chocolate milk

Kaktee [kak'te:] *f* (*-*; *-n*), **Kaktus** ['kaktʊs] *m* (*-*; *Kakteen*) BOT cactus

Kalb [kalp] *n* (*-[e]s*; *Kälber* ['kɛlbɐ]) ZO calf; **kalben** ['kalbən] *v/i* (*ge-*, *h*) calve

'**Kalbfleisch** *n* veal

'**Kalbs|braten** *m* roast veal; **~schnitzel** *n* veal cutlet; escalope (of veal)

Kaldaunen [kal'daunən] *pl* GASTR tripe

Kalender [ka'lɛndɐ] *m* (*-s*; *-*) calendar; **~jahr** *n* calendar year

Kali ['ka:li] *n* (*-s*; *no pl*) CHEM potash

Kaliber [ka'li:bɐ] *n* (*-s*; *-*) caliber, *Br* calibre (*a. fig*)

Kalk [kalk] *m* (*-[e]s*; *-e*) lime; GEOL limestone, chalk; MED calcium; '**kalken** *v/t* (*ge-*, *h*) whitewash; AGR lime; '**kalkig** *adj* limy; '**Kalkstein** *m* limestone

kalo'rien|arm *adj*, **~redu,ziert** *adj* low--calorie, low in calories; **~reich** *adj* high-calorie, high *or* rich in calories

kalt [kalt] *adj* cold; *mir ist* ~ I'm cold; *es* (*mir*) *wird* ~ it's (I'm) getting cold; ~ *bleiben* *fig* keep (one's) cool; *das lässt mich kalt* that leaves me cold

'**kaltblütig** [-bly:tɪç] **1.** *adj* cold-blooded (*a. fig*); **2.** *adv* in cold blood

Kälte ['kɛltə] *f* (*-*; *no pl*) cold; *fig* coldness; *vor* ~ *zittern* shiver with cold; *fünf Grad* ~ five degrees below zero; **~einbruch** *m* cold snap; **~grad** *m* degree below zero; **~peri,ode** *f* cold spell

'**kaltmachen** *v/t* (*sep*, *-ge-*, *h*) bump off

kam [ka:m] *pret of* **kommen**

Kamee [ka'me:ə] *f* (*-*; *-n*) cameo

Kamel [ka'me:l] *n* (*-s*; *-e*) ZO camel

Ka'melhaar *n* (*-[e]s*; *no pl*) camelhair

Kamera ['kaməra] *f* (*-*; *-s*) camera

Kamerad [kamə'ra:t] *m* (*-en*; *-en* [-'ra:dən]) companion, F mate, pal, buddy; **Kameradin** [-'ra:dɪn] *f* (*-*; *-nen*) companion

Kame'radschaft *f* (*-*; *no pl*) comradeship

'**Kameramann** *m* cameraman

'**Kamera,korder** *m* (*-s*; *-*) camcorder

Kamille [ka'mɪlə] *f* (*-*; *-n*) BOT camomile

Kamin [ka'mi:n] *m* (*-s*; *-e*) fireplace; chimney (*a.* MOUNT); *am* ~ by the fire(side); **~kehrer** [-ke:rɐ] *m* (*-s*; *-*) chimney sweep; **~sims** *m*, *n* mantelpiece

Kamm [kam] *m* (*-[e]s*; *Kämme* ['kɛmə]) comb, ZO *a.* crest (*a. fig*)

kämmen ['kɛmən] *v/t* (*ge-*, *h*) comb; *sich* (*die Haare*) ~ comb one's hair

Kammer ['kamɐ] *f* (*-*; *-n*) (small) room; storeroom, closet; garret; POL, ECON chamber; JUR division

'**Kammermu,sik** *f* chamber music

'**Kammgarn** *n* worsted (yarn)

Kampagne [kam'panjə] f (-; -n) campaign

Kampf [kampf] m (-[e]s; Kämpfe ['kɛmpfə]) fight (a. fig), struggle (a. fig), esp MIL combat, battle (a. fig); SPORT contest, match; boxing: fight, bout; fig conflict; '**kampfbereit** adj ready for battle (MIL combat); **kämpfen** ['kɛmpfən] v/i (ge-, h) fight (**gegen** against; **mit** with; **um** for) (a. fig); struggle (a. fig); fig contend, wrestle

Kampfer ['kampfɐ] m (-s; no pl) CHEM camphor

Kämpfer ['kɛmpfɐ] m (-s; -), '**Kämpferin** f (-; -nen) fighter (a. fig); **kämpferisch** ['kɛmpfərɪʃ] adj fighting, aggressive (a. fig)

'Kampf|flugzeug n MIL combat aircraft; **~kraft** f (-; no pl) fighting strength; **~richter** m SPORT judge; **~sportarten** pl martial arts

Kanada ['kanada] Canada; **Kanadier** [ka'naːdjɐ] m (-s; -), **Ka'nadierin** [-djərɪn] f (-; -nen), **ka'nadisch** adj Canadian

Kanal [ka'naːl] m (-s; Kanäle [ka'nɛːlə]) canal; channel (a. TV, TECH, fig); sewer, drain; **der ~** the (English) Channel

Kanalisation [kanaliza'tsjoːn] f (-; -en) sewerage (system); canalization

kanalisieren [kanali'ziːrən] v/t (no -ge-, h) sewer; canalize; fig channel

Ka'naltunnel m Channel Tunnel, F Chunnel

Kanarienvogel [ka'naːrjən-] m canary

Kandidat [kandi'daːt] m (-en; -en), **Kandi'datin** f (-; -nen) candidate; **Kandidatur** [kandida'tuːɐ] f (-; -en) candidacy, Br a. candidature; **kandidieren** [kandi'diːrən] v/i (no -ge-, h) stand or run for election; **~ für ...** run for the office of ...

Känguru, Känguruh ['kɛŋguru] n (-s; -s) ZO kangaroo

Kaninchen [ka'niːnçən] n (-s; -) ZO rabbit

Kanister [ka'nɪstɐ] m (-s; -) (fuel) can

Kanne ['kanə] f (-; -n) pot; can

Kannibale [kani'baːlə] m (-n; -n) cannibal

kannte ['kantə] pret of **kennen**

Kanon ['kaːnɔn] m (-s; -s) MUS canon, round

Kanone [ka'noːnə] f (-; -n) MIL gun; cannon; F ace, esp SPORT a. crack

Kante ['kantə] f (-; -n) edge; '**kanten** v/t (ge-, h) set on edge; tilt; edge (skis)

'Kanten m (-s; -) crust

kantig ['kantɪç] adj angular, square(d)

Kantine [kan'tiːnə] f (-; -n) canteen

Kanton [kan'toːn] m (-s; -e) POL canton

Kanu ['kaːnu] n (-s; -s) canoe

Kanüle [ka'nyːlə] f (-; -n) MED cannula, (drain) tube

Kanzel ['kantsəl] f (-; -n) REL pulpit; AVIAT cockpit

Kanzlei [kants'lai] f (-; -en) office

Kanzler ['kantslɐ] m (-s; -) chancellor

Kap [kap] n (-s; -s) cape, headland

Kapazität [kapatsi'tɛːt] f (-; -en) capacity; fig authority

Kapelle [ka'pɛlə] f (-; -n) REL chapel; MUS band

Ka'pellmeister m MUS conductor

kapern ['kaːpɐn] v/t (ge-, h) MAR capture, seize

kapieren [ka'piːrən] F v/t (no -ge-, h) get; **kapiert?** got it?

Kapital [kapi'taːl] n (-s; -e, -ien) ECON capital, funds; **~anlage** f investment

Kapitalismus [kapita'lɪsmʊs] m (-; no pl) capitalism; **Kapita'list** m (-en; -en), **kapita'listisch** adj capitalist

Kapi'talverbrechen n capital crime, JUR felony

Kapitän [kapi'tɛːn] m (-s; -e) captain (a. SPORT)

Kapitel [ka'pɪtəl] n (-s; -) chapter (a. fig); F fig story

Kapitulation [kapitula'tsjoːn] f (-; -en) capitulation, surrender (a. fig)

kapitulieren [kapitu'liːrən] v/i (no -ge-, h) capitulate, surrender (a. fig)

Kaplan [ka'plaːn] m (-s; Kapläne [ka'plɛːnə]) REL curate

Kappe ['kapə] f (-; -n) cap, TECH a. top, hood; '**kappen** v/t (ge-, h) cut (rope); lop, top (tree)

Kapsel ['kapsəl] f (-; -n) capsule

kaputt [ka'pʊt] F adj broken (a. fig); TECH out of order; fig dead beat; ruined; **~gehen** F v/i (irr, gehen, sep, -ge-, sein) break; MOT etc break down; fig break up; **~machen** F v/t (sep, -ge-, h) break, wreck (a. fig), ruin (a. fig)

Kapuze [ka'puːtsə] f (-; -n) hood; cowl

Karabiner [kara'biːnɐ] m (-s; -) carbine; **~haken** m karabiner, snaplink

Karaffe [ka'rafə] f (-; -n) decanter

Karambolage [karambo'la:ʒə] f (-; -n) collision, crash

Karat [ka'ra:t] n (-[e]s; -e) carat

Karate [ka'ra:tə] n (-[s]; no pl) SPORT karate

Karawane [kara'va:nə] f (-; -n) caravan

Kardinal [kardi'na:l] m (-s; Kardinäle [kardi'nɛ:lə]) REL cardinal

Karfiol [kar'fjo:l] Austrian m (-s; no pl) BOT cauliflower

Kar'freitag [ka:ɐ̯-] m REL Good Friday

karg [kark], **kärglich** ['kɛrklɪç] adj meag|er, Br -re, scanty; frugal; poor

kariert [ka'ri:ɐt] adj checked, checkered, Br chequered; squared

Karies ['ka:rjɛs] f (-; no pl) MED (dental) caries

Karikatur [karika'tu:ɐ] f (-; -en) mst cartoon, esp fig caricature; **Karikaturist** [karikatu'rɪst] m (-en; -en) cartoonist

karikieren [kari'ki:rən] v/t (no -ge-, h) caricature

Karneval ['karnəval] m (-s; -e, -s) carnival

Karo ['ka:ro] n (-s; -s) square, check; cards: diamonds

Karosserie [karɔsə'ri:] f (-; -n) MOT body

Karotte [ka'rɔtə] f (-; -n) BOT carrot

Karpfen ['karpfən] m (-s; -) ZO carp

Karre ['karə] f (-; -n), **'Karren** m (-s; -) cart; wheelbarrow; F MOT jalopy

Karriere [ka'rje:rə] f (-; -n) career; ~ **machen** work one's way up, get to the top

Karte ['kartə] f (-; -n) card; ticket; GEOGR map; chart; GASTR menu; **gute** (**schlechte**) ~n a good (bad) hand

Kartei [kar'tai] f (-; -en) card index; ~**karte** f index or file card

'Karten|haus n house of cards (a. fig); MAR chartroom; ~**spiel** n card game; deck (Br pack) of cards; ~**tele,fon** n cardphone; ~**vorverkauf** m advance booking; box office

Kartoffel [kar'tɔfəl] f (-; -n) BOT potato; ~**brei** m mashed potatoes; ~**chips** pl (potato) chips, Br crisps; ~**kloß** m, ~**knödel** m potato dumpling; ~**puffer** m potato fritter; ~**schalen** pl potato peelings; ~**schäler** m potato peeler

Karton [kar'tɔŋ] m (-s; -s) cardboard; pasteboard; cardboard box

Karussell [karʊ'sɛl] n (-s; -s) roundabout, car(r)ousel, merry-go-round

Karwoche ['ka:ɐ-] f REL Holy Week

Kaschmir ['kaʃmiːɐ] m (-s; -e) cashmere

Käse ['kɛ:zə] m (-s; -) cheese

Kaserne [ka'zɛrnə] f (-; -n) barracks

Ka'sernenhof m barrack square

käsig ['kɛ:zɪç] adj cheesy; pasty

Kasino [ka'zi:no] n (-s; -s) casino; MIL (officers') mess

Kasperle ['kaspɐlə] n, m (-s; -) Punch; ~**the,ater** n Punch and Judy show

Kassa ['kasa] Austrian f (-; Kassen), **Kasse** ['kasə] f (-; -n) till; cash register; checkout (counter); cash desk; cashier's counter; THEA etc box office; F **gut** (**knapp**) **bei Kasse sein** be flush (be a bit hard up)

'Kassen|beleg m, ~**bon** f sales slip, Br receipt; ~**erfolg** m THEA etc box-office success; ~**pati,ent** m MED health plan (Am medicaid, Br NHS) patient; ~**schlager** f m blockbuster; ~**wart** [-vart] m (-[e]s; -e) treasurer

Kassette [ka'sɛtə] f (-; -n) box, case; MUS, TV, PHOT etc cassette; casket

Kas'setten... in cpds ...rekorder etc: cassette ...

kassieren [ka'si:rən] v/t and v/i (no -ge-, h) collect, take (the money)

Kassierer [ka'si:rɐ] m (-s; -), **Kas'sie-rerin** f (-; -nen) cashier; teller; collector

Kastanie [kas'ta:njə] f (-; -n) BOT chestnut

Kasten ['kastən] m (-s; Kästen ['kɛstən]) box (a. F TV, SPORT etc); case; chest

kastrieren [kas'tri:rən] v/t (no -ge-, h) MED, VET castrate

Kasus ['ka:zʊs] m (-; -) LING case

Katalog [kata'lo:k] m (-[e]s; -e) catalog(ue Br)

Katalysator [kataly'za:to:ɐ] m (-s; -en [-za'to:rən]) CHEM catalyst; MOT catalytic converter

Katapult [kata'pʊlt] m, n (-[e]s; -e), **katapultieren** [katapʊl'ti:rən] v/t (no -ge-, h) catapult

katastrophal [katastro'fa:l] adj disastrous (a. fig), **Katastrophe** [katas'tro:fə] f (-; -n) catastrophe, disaster (a. fig)

Kata'strophen|gebiet n disaster area; ~**schutz** m disaster control

Katechismus [katɛˈçɪsmʊs] *m* (-; -*men*) REL catechism

Kategorie [kategoˈriː] *f* (-; -*n*) category

Kater [ˈkaːtɐ] *m* (-*s*; -) ZO male cat, tomcat; F hangover

kath. ABBR *of* **katholisch** Cath., Catholic

Kathedrale [kateˈdraːlə] *f* (-; -*n*) cathedral

Katholik [katoˈliːk] *m* (-*en*; -*en*), **Katho'likin** *f* (-; -*nen*), **katholisch** [kaˈtoːlɪʃ] *adj* (Roman) Catholic

Kätzchen [ˈkɛtsçən] *n* (-*s*; -) ZO kitten, pussy (*a.* BOT)

Katze [ˈkatsə] *f* (-; -*n*) ZO cat; kitten

Kauderwelsch [ˈkaʊdɐvɛlʃ] *n* (-[*s*]; *no pl*) gibberish

kauen [ˈkaʊən] *v/t and v/i* (*ge-, h*) chew

kauern [ˈkaʊɐn] *v/i and v/refl* (*ge-, h*) crouch, squat

Kauf [kaʊf] *m* (-[*e*]*s*; *Käufe* [ˈkɔʏfə]) purchase (*a.* ECON), F buy; purchasing, buying; **ein guter** ~ a bargain, F a good buy; **zum** ~ **anbieten** offer for sale

'**kaufen** *v/t* (*ge-, h*) buy (*a.* fig), purchase

Käufer [ˈkɔʏfɐ] *m* (-*s*; -), '**Käuferin** *f* (-; -*nen*) buyer; customer

'**Kauffrau** *f* (-; -*en*) businesswoman

'**Kaufhaus** *n* department store; **~kraft** *f* (-; *no pl*) purchasing power

käuflich [ˈkɔʏflɪç] *adj* for sale; *fig* venal

'**Kaufmann** *m* (-[*e*]*s*; -*leute*) businessman; dealer, trader, merchant; storekeeper, *Br mst* shopkeeper; grocer

'**kaufmännisch** [-mɛnɪʃ] *adj* commercial, business; **~er Angestellter** clerk

'**Kaufvertrag** *m* contract of sale

'**Kaugummi** *m* (-*s*; -*s*) chewing gum

kaum [kaʊm] *adv* hardly; ~ **zu glauben** hard to believe

Kaution [kaʊˈtsjoːn] *f* (-; -*en*) security; JUR bail

Kautschuk [ˈkaʊtʃʊk] *m* (-*s*; -*e*) (india) rubber

Kavalier [kavaˈliːɐ] *m* (-*s*; -*e*) gentleman

Kaviar [ˈkaːvjar] *m* (-*s*; -*e*) caviar(e)

keck [kɛk] *adj* cheeky, saucy, pert

Kegel [ˈkeːɡəl] *m* (-*s*; -) skittle, pin; MATH, TECH cone; **~bahn** *f* bowling (*esp Br* skittle) alley

'**kegelförmig** [-fœrmɪç] *adj* conical

'**Kegelkugel** *f* bowling (*esp Br* skittle) ball

'**kegeln** *v/i* (*ge-, h*) bowl, go bowling, *esp Br* play (*at*) skittles *or* ninepins

Kehle [ˈkeːlə] *f* (-; -*n*) ANAT throat

'**Kehlkopf** *m* ANAT larynx

Kehre [ˈkeːrə] *f* (-; -*n*) (sharp) bend

'**kehren** *v/t* (*ge-, h*) sweep; **j-m den Rücken** ~ turn one's back on s.o.

Kehricht [ˈkeːrɪçt] *m* (-*s*; *no pl*) sweepings; **~schaufel** *f* dustpan

kehrtmachen [ˈkeːɐt-] *v/i* (*sep, -ge-, h*) turn back

keifen [ˈkaɪfən] *v/i* (*ge-, h*) nag, bitch

Keil [kaɪl] *m* (-[*e*]*s*; -*e*) wedge; gusset

Keiler [ˈkaɪlɐ] *m* (-*s*; -) ZO wild boar

'**Keilriemen** *m* MOT fan belt

Keim [kaɪm] *m* (-[*e*]*s*; -*e*) BIOL, MED germ; BOT bud, sprout; *fig* seed(s)

'**keimen** *v/i* (*ge-, h*) BOT germinate, sprout; *fig* form, grow; stir

'**keimfrei** *adj* MED sterile

'**keimtötend** *adj* MED germicidal

'**Keimzelle** *f* BIOL germ cell

kein [kaɪn] *indef pron* **1.** *adj:* ~(*e*) no, not any; ~ **anderer** no one else; ~(*e*) ... **mehr** not any more ...; ~ **Geld** (~*e Zeit*) **mehr** no money (time) left; ~ **Kind mehr** no longer a child; **2.** *su:* ~*er*, ~*e*, ~(*e*)*s* none, no one, nobody; ~*er* **von beiden** neither (of the two); ~*er* **von uns** none of us; '**keines'falls** *adv* by no means, under no circumstances; '**keineswegs** [-ˈveːks] *adv* by no means, not in the least; '**keinmal** *adv* not once, not a single time

Keks [keːks] *m, n* (-*es*, -*e*) cookie, *Br* biscuit

Kelch [kɛlç] *m* (-[*e*]*s*; -*e*) cup (*a.* BOT); REL chalice

Kelle [ˈkɛlə] *f* (-; -*n*) GASTR ladle, scoop; TECH trowel; signaling disk

Keller [ˈkɛlɐ] *m* (-*s*; -) cellar; → **~geschoss** *n*, **~geschoß** *Austrian n* basement; **~wohnung** *f* basement (apartment, *esp Br* flat)

Kellner [ˈkɛlnɐ] *m* (-*s*; -) waiter

Kellnerin [ˈkɛlnərɪn] *f* (-; -*nen*) waitress

keltern [ˈkɛltɐn] *v/t* (*ge-, h*) press

kennen [ˈkɛnən] *v/t* (*irr, ge-, h*) know, be acquainted with; ~ **lernen** get to know, become acquainted with; meet *s.o.*; **als ich ihn** ~ **lernte** when I first met him; **Kenner** [ˈkɛnɐ] *m* (-*s*; -), '**Kennerin** *f* (-; -*nen*) expert; **kenntlich** [ˈkɛntlɪç] *adj* recognizable (**an** *dat* by); **Kenntnis**

K

f (-; -se) knowledge; **gute ~se in** (*dat*) a good knowledge of

'Kennwort *n* password

'Kennzeichen *n* mark, sign; (distinguishing) feature, characteristic; MOT license (*Br* registration) number

'kennzeichnen *v/t* (ge-, h) mark; *fig* characterize

kentern ['kɛntɐn] *v/i* (ge-, sein) MAR capsize

Keramik [ke'raːmɪk] *f* (-; -en) ceramics

Kerbe ['kɛrbə] *f* (-; -n) notch

Kerker ['kɛrkɐ] *m* (-s; -) dungeon

Kerl [kɛrl] F *m* (-e) F *m* (-s; -e) fellow, guy; *armer ~* poor devil; *ein anständiger ~* a decent sort

Kern [kɛrn] *m* (-[e]s; -e) BOT pip, seed, stone, kernel; TECH core (*a. fig*) PHYS nucleus; **~...** in cpds ...energie, ...forschung, ...physik, ...reaktor, ...technik etc: nuclear ...; **~fach** *n* PED basic subject; **~fa,milie** *f* nuclear family; **~gehäuse** *n* BOT core

'kernge'sund *adj* F (as) sound as a bell

'kernig ['kɛrnɪç] *adj* full of seeds (*Br* pips); *fig* robust; pithy

'Kernkraft *f* PHYS nuclear power; **~gegner** *m* anti-nuclear activist; **~werk** *n* nuclear power station *or* plant

'kernlos *adj* BOT seedless

'Kernspaltung *f* PHYS nuclear fission

'Kernwaffen *pl* MIL nuclear weapons; 'kernwaffenfrei *adj*: **~e Zone** MIL nuclear-free zone; 'Kernwaffenversuch *m* MIL nuclear test

'Kernzeit *f* ECON core time

Kerze ['kɛrtsə] *f* (-; -n) candle; SPORT shoulder stand

kess [kɛs] F *adj* cheeky, saucy, pert

Kessel ['kɛsəl] *m* (-s; -) kettle; TECH boiler; tank

Kette ['kɛtə] *f* (-; -n) chain (*a. fig*); necklace; **e-e ~** form a line

'Ketten... in cpds ...antrieb, ...laden, ...rauchen, ...raucher, ...reaktion etc: chain ...

'ketten *v/t* (ge-, h) chain (**an** *acc* to)

'Kettenfahrzeug *n* tracked vehicle

Ketzer ['kɛtsɐ] *m* (-s; -) heretic

Ketzerei [kɛtsə'raɪ] *f* (-; -en) heresy

keuchen ['kɔʏçən] *v/i* (ge-, h) pant, gasp

'Keuchhusten *m* MED whooping cough

Keule ['kɔʏlə] *f* (-; -n) club; GASTR leg

keusch [kɔʏʃ] *adj* chaste

'Keuschheit *f* (-; *no pl*) chastity

Kfz [kaː'ʔɛf'tsɛt] ABBR of *Kraftfahrzeug* motor vehicle; **Kf'z-Brief** *m*, **Kf'z--Schein** *m* vehicle registration document; **Kf'z-Steuer** *f* road *or* automobile tax; **Kf'z-Werkstatt** *f* garage

KG [kaː'geː] ABBR of *Kommanditgesellschaft* ECON limited partnership

kichern ['kɪçɐn] *v/i* (ge-, h) giggle

Kiebitz ['kiːbɪts] *m* (-es; -e) ZO peewit, lapwing; F kibitzer

Kiefer[1] ['kiːfɐ] *m* (-s; -) ANAT jaw(bone)

'Kiefer[2] *f* (-; -n) BOT pine(tree)

Kiel [kiːl] *m* (-[e]s; -e) MAR keel; **~flosse** *f* AVIAT tail fin; **~raum** *m* MAR bilge; **~wasser** *n* (-s; -) MAR wake (*a. fig*)

Kieme ['kiːmə] *f* (-n; -n) ZO gill

Kies [kiːs] *m* (-es; -e) gravel (*a.* **mit ~ bestreuen**); F dough

Kiesel ['kiːzəl] *m* (-s; -) pebble

Kilo ['kiːlo] *n* (-s; -) → *Kilogramm*

Kilo|'gramm [kilo-] *n* kilogram(me); **~hertz** [-'hɛrts] *n* (-; -) kilohertz; **~meter** *m* kilometer, *Br* kilometre; **~'watt** *n* ELECTR kilowatt

Kind [kɪnt] *n* (-[e]s; -er [-kɪndɐ]) child; **ein ~ erwarten** be expecting a baby

'Kinder|arzt *m*, **~ärztin** *f* p(a)ediatrician; **~garten** *m* kindergarten, nursery school; **~gärtnerin** [-gɛrtnərɪn] *f* (-; -nen) nursery-school *or* kindergarten teacher; **~geld** *n* child benefit; **~hort** [-hɔrt] *m* (-[e]s; -e), **~krippe** *f* day nursery; **~lähmung** *f* MED polio(-myelitis)

'kinderlieb *adj* fond of children

'kinderlos *adj* childless

'Kinder|mädchen *n* nurse(maid), nanny; **~spiel** *fig n*: **ein ~ sein** be child's play; **~stube** *fig f* manners, upbringing; **~wagen** *m* baby carriage, buggy, *Br* pram; **~zimmer** *n* children's room

'Kindes|alter ['kɪndəs-] *n* childhood; infancy; **~entführung** *f* kidnap(p)ing; **~misshandlung** *f* child abuse

'Kindheit *f* (-; *no pl*) (**von ~ an** from) childhood

'kindisch ['kɪndɪʃ] *adj* childish

'kindlich *adj* childlike

Kinn [kɪn] *n* (-[e]s; -e) ANAT chin; **~backe** *f*, **~backen** *m* (-s; -) ANAT jaw(-bone); **~haken** *m* *boxing*: hook (to the chin), uppercut

Kino ['ki:no] n (-s; -s) a) (no pl) motion pictures, esp Br cinema, F *the* movies, b) movie theater, esp Br cinema

'**Kino|besucher** m, '**Kinogänger** [-gɛŋɐ] m (-s; -) moviegoer, Br cinemagoer

Kippe ['kɪpə] f (-; -n) F butt, esp Br stub; SPORT upstart

'**kippen 1.** v/i (ge-, sein) tip or topple (over); **2.** v/t (ge-, h) tilt, tip over or up

Kirche ['kɪrçə] f (-; -n) church; **in die ~ gehen** go to church

'**Kirchen|buch** n parish register; **~diener** m sexton; **~gemeinde** f parish; **~jahr** n Church or ecclesiastical year; **~lied** n hymn; **~mu,sik** f sacred or church music; **~schiff** n ARCH nave; **~steuer** f church tax; **~stuhl** m pew; **~tag** m church congress

'**Kirchgang** m churchgoing; '**Kirchgänger** [-gɛŋɐ] m (-s; -) churchgoer

'**kirchlich** adj church, ecclesiastical

'**Kirchturm** m steeple; spire; church tower

Kirsche ['kɪrʃə] f (-; -n) BOT cherry

Kissen ['kɪsən] n (-s; -) pillow; cushion; **~bezug** m, **~hülle** f pillowcase, pillowslip

Kiste ['kɪstə] f (-; -n) box, chest; crate

Kitsch [kɪtʃ] m (-[e]s; no pl) kitsch; trash; F slush

'**kitschig** adj kitschy, trashy; slushy

Kitt [kɪt] m (-[e]s; -e) cement; putty

Kittel ['kɪtəl] m (-s; -) smock; overall; MED (white) coat

'**kitten** v/t (ge-, h) cement; putty

Kitzel ['kɪtsəl] m (-s; -) tickle, fig a. thrill, kick; '**kitzeln** v/i and v/t (ge-, h) tickle; **Kitzler** ['kɪtslɐ] m (-s; -) ANAT clitoris; **kitzlig** ['kɪtslɪç] adj ticklish (a. fig)

kläffen ['klɛfən] v/i (ge-, h) yap, yelp

klaffend ['klafənt] adj gaping; yawning

Klage ['kla:gə] f (-; -n) complaint; lament; JUR action, (law)suit

'**klagen** v/i (ge-, h) complain (**über** acc of, about; **bei** to); lament; JUR go to court; **gegen j-n** ~ JUR sue s.o.

Kläger ['klɛ:gɐ] m (-s; -), '**Klägerin** f (-; -nen) JUR plaintiff

kläglich ['klɛ:klɪç] → **jämmerlich**

Klamauk [kla'mauk] m (-s; no pl) racket; THEA etc slapstick

klamm [klam] adj numb; clammy

Klammer ['klamɐ] f (-; -n) TECH cramp,

clamp; clip; clothespin, Br (clothes) peg; MED brace; MATH, PRINT bracket(s); '**klammern** v/t (ge-, h) fasten or clip together; **sich ~ an** (acc) cling to

klang [klaŋ] pret of **klingen**

Klang m (-[e]s; **Klänge** ['klɛŋə]) sound; tone; clink; ringing

'**klangvoll** adj sonorous; fig illustrious

Klappe ['klapə] f (-; -n) flap; hinged lid; MOT tailgate, Br tailboard; TECH, BOT, ANAT valve; F trap; '**klappen** (ge-, h) **1.** v/t: **nach oben ~** lift up, raise; put or fold up; **nach unten ~** lower, put down; **es lässt sich (nach hinten) ~** it folds (backward); **2.** v/i clap, clack; F work, work out (well)

Klapper ['klapɐ] f (-; -n) rattle

'**klappern** v/i (ge-, h) clatter, rattle (**mit et.** s.th.)

'**Klapperschlange** f ZO rattlesnake

Klapp|fahrrad ['klap-] n folding bicycle; **~fenster** n top-hung window; **~messer** n jack knife, clasp knife

klapprig ['klaprɪç] adj MOT rattly, ramshackle; F shaky

'**Klappsitz** m folding or tip-up seat

'**Klappstuhl** m folding chair

'**Klapptisch** m folding table

Klaps [klaps] m (-es; -e) slap, pat; smack

klar [kla:ɐ] adj clear (a. fig); **ist dir ~, dass ...?** do you realize that ...?; **das ist mir (nicht ganz) ~** I (don't quite) understand; **(na) ~!** of course!; **alles ~?** everything okay?

Kläranlage ['klɛ:ɐ-] f sewage works

klären ['klɛ:rən] v/t (ge-, h) TECH purify, treat; fig clear up; settle; SPORT clear (the ball)

'**Klarheit** f (-; no pl) clearness, fig a. clarity

Klarinette [klari'nɛtə] f (-; -n) MUS clarinet

'**Klarsicht...** in cpds transparent

Klasse ['klasə] f (-; -n) class (a. POL), PED a. grade, Br form; classroom; F ~ **sein** be super, be fantastic

'**Klassen|arbeit** f (classroom) test; **~buch** n classbook, Br (class) register; **~kame,rad** m classmate; **~lehrer(in)** homeroom teacher, Br form teacher, a. form master (mistress); **~sprecher** m class representative; **~zimmer** n classroom

klassifizieren [klasifi'tsi:rən] v/t (no

K

-ge-, h) classify; **'Klassifi'zierung** f (-; -en) classification

Klassiker ['klasɪkɐ] m (-s; -) classic

klassisch ['klasɪʃ] adj classic(al)

Klatsch [klatʃ] F m (-es; no pl) gossip

'Klatschbase f gossip

'klatschen v/i and v/t (ge-, h) clap, applaud; F slap, bang; splash; F gossip; **in die Hände ~** clap one's hands

'klatschhaft adj gossipy

'Klatschmaul F n (old) gossip

'klatsch'nass F adj soaking wet

klauben ['klaʊbən] Austrian v/t (ge-, h) pick; gather

Klaue ['klaʊə] f (-; -n) ZO claw; pl fig clutches

klauen ['klaʊən] F v/t (ge-, h) pinch

Klausel ['klaʊzəl] f (-; -n) JUR clause; condition

Klausur [klaʊ'zuːɐ] f (-; -en) test (paper), exam(ination)

Klavier [kla'viːɐ] n (-s; -e) MUS piano; ~ **spielen** play the piano; ~**kon,zert** n MUS piano concerto; piano recital

Klebeband ['kleːbə-] n (-[e]s; -bänder) adhesive tape; **kleben** ['kleːbən] (ge-, h) **1.** v/t glue, paste; stick; **2.** v/i stick, cling (**an** dat to) (a. fig); **klebrig** ['kleːbrɪç] adj sticky

Kleb|stoff ['kleːp-] m adhesive; glue; ~**streifen** m adhesive tape

kleckern ['klɛkɐn] F (ge-, h) **1.** v/i make a mess; **2.** v/t spill

Klecks [klɛks] F m (-es; -e) (ink)blot; blob; **klecksen** ['klɛksən] F v/i (ge-, h) blot, make blots

Klee [kleː] m (-s; no pl) BOT clover

'Kleeblatt n cloverleaf

Kleid [klaɪt] n (-[e]s; -er ['klaɪdɐ]) dress; pl clothes; **kleiden** ['klaɪdən] v/t (ge-, h) dress, clothe; **j-n gut ~** suit s.o.; **sich gut** etc ~ dress well etc

Kleider|bügel ['klaɪdɐ-] m (coat) hanger; ~**bürste** f clothes brush; ~**haken** m coat hook; ~**schrank** m wardrobe; ~**ständer** m coat stand; ~**stoff** m dress material

'kleidsam adj becoming

'Kleidung f (-; no pl) clothes, clothing

'Kleidungsstück n article of clothing

Kleie ['klaɪə] f (-; -n) AGR bran

klein [klaɪn] adj small, esp F little (a. finger, brother); short; **von ~ auf** from an early age; **ein ~ wenig** a little bit; **Groß**

und Klein young and old; **die Kleinen** the little ones; ~ **schneiden** cut up (into small pieces)

'Klein|anzeige f want ad, Br small ad; ~**bildkamera** f 35 mm camera; ~**fa,mi-lie** f nuclear family; ~**geld** n (small) change; ~**holz** n matchwood

Kleinigkeit ['klaɪnɪçkaɪt] f (-; -en) little thing, trifle; little something; **e-e ~ sein** be nothing, be child's play

'Kleinkind n baby, infant

'Kleinkram F m odds and ends

'kleinlaut adj subdued

'kleinlich adj small-minded, petty; mean; pedantic, fussy

'Kleinstadt f small town; **'kleinstäd-tisch** adj small-town, provincial

'Kleintrans,porter m MOT pick-up

'Kleinwagen m MOT small or compact car, F runabout

Kleister ['klaɪstɐ] m (-s; -) paste

Klemme ['klɛmə] f (-; -n) TECH clamp; (hair) clip; F **in der ~ sitzen** be in a fix or tight spot; **'klemmen** v/i and v/t (ge-, h) jam; stick; be stuck, be jammed; **sich ~** jam one's finger or hand

Klempner ['klɛmpnɐ] m (-s; -) plumber

Klepper ['klɛpɐ] m (-s; -) ZO nag

Klerus ['kleːrʊs] m (-; no pl) REL clergy

Klette ['klɛtə] f (-; -n) BOT bur(r); fig leech

klettern ['klɛtɐn] v/i (ge-, sein) climb; **auf e-n Baum ~** climb (up) a tree

'Kletterpflanze f BOT climber

Klient [kli'ɛnt] m (-en; -en), **Kli'entin** f (-; -nen) client

Klima ['kliːma] n (-s; -s) climate, fig a. atmosphere

'Klimaanlage f air-conditioning

klimatisch [kli'maːtɪʃ] adj climatic

klimpern ['klɪmpɐn] v/i (ge-, h) jingle, chink (**mit** et. s.th.); F MUS strum (away) (**auf** dat on)

Klinge ['klɪŋə] f (-; -n) blade

Klingel ['klɪŋəl] f (-; -n) bell

'Klingelknopf m bell (push)

'klingeln v/i (ge-, h) ring (the bell); **es klingelt** the (door)bell is ringing

'klingen v/i (irr, ge-, h) sound; bell, metal etc: ring; glasses etc: clink

Klinik ['kliːnɪk] f (-; -en) hospital; clinic

klinisch ['kliːnɪʃ] adj clinical

Klinke ['klɪŋkə] f (-; -n) (door) handle

Klippe ['klɪpə] f (-; -n) cliff, rock(s); fig obstacle

klirren ['klɪrən] v/i (ge-, h) window: rattle; glasses etc: clink; broken glass: tinkle; swords: clash; keys, coins: jingle

Klischee [kli'ʃeː] n (-s; -s) cliché

klobig ['kloːbɪç] adj bulky, clumsy

klopfen ['klɔpfən] (ge-, h) **1.** v/i heart etc: beat, throb; knock (**an** acc at, on); tap, pat; **es klopft** there's a knock at the door; **2.** v/t beat; knock; drive (nail etc)

Klosett [klo'zɛt] n (-s; -s/-e) lavatory, toilet; **~brille** f toilet seat; **~pa,pier** n toilet paper

Kloß [kloːs] m (-es; Klöße ['kløːsə]) clod, lump (a. fig); GASTR dumpling

Kloster ['kloːstɐ] n (-s; Klöster ['kløːstɐ]) REL monastery; convent

Klotz [klɔts] m (-es; Klötze ['klœtsə]) block; log

Klub [klʊp] m (-s; -s) club

'**Klubsessel** m lounge chair

Kluft [klʊft] f (-; Klüfte ['klʏftə]) gap (a. fig); abyss

klug [kluːk] adj intelligent, clever, F bright, smart; wise; **daraus (aus ihm) werde ich nicht ~** I don't know what to make of it (him)

'**Klugheit** f (-; no pl) intelligence, cleverness, F brains; good sense; knowledge

Klumpen ['klʊmpən] m (-s; -) lump; clod; nugget; '**Klumpfuß** m MED club foot; '**klumpig** adj lumpy; cloddish

knabbern ['knabən] v/t and v/i (ge-, h) nibble, gnaw

Knabe ['knaːbə] m (-n; -n) boy

'**knabenhaft** adj boyish

Knäckebrot ['knɛkə-] n crispbread

knacken ['knakən] v/t and v/i (ge-, h) crack; twig: snap; fire, radio: crackle

Knacks F m (-es; -e) crack; fig defect

Knall [knal] m (-[e]s; -e) bang; crack, report; pop; F **e-n ~ haben** be nuts

'**Knallbon,bon** m, n cracker

'**knallen** v/i and v/t (ge-, h) bang; slam; crack; pop; F crash (**gegen** into); F **j-m e-e ~** slap s.o.('s face)

'**knallig** F adj flashy, loud

'**Knallkörper** m firecracker

knapp [knap] adj scarce; scanty, meager, Br meagre (food, pay etc); bare (a. majority etc); limited (time etc); narrow (escape etc); tight (dress etc);

brief; **~ an Geld** (**Zeit** etc) short of money (time etc); **mit ~er Not** only just, barely; **j-n ~ halten** keep s.o. short

Knappe ['knapə] m (-n; -n) miner

'**Knappheit** f (-; no pl) shortage

Knarre ['knarə] f (-; -n) rattle; F gun

'**knarren** v/i (ge-, h) creak

Knast [knast] F m (-[e]s; Knäste ['knɛstə]) sl clink; **~bruder** F m jailbird

knattern ['knatɐn] v/i (ge-, h) crackle; MOT roar

Knäuel ['knɔʏəl] m, n (-s; -) ball; tangle

Knauf [knauf] m (-[e]s; Knäufe ['knɔʏfə]) knob; pommel

knaus(e)rig ['knauz(ə)rɪç] F adj stingy

knautschen ['knautʃən] v/t and v/i (ge-, h) crumple

'**Knautschzone** f MOT crumple zone

Knebel ['kneːbəl] m (-s; -), '**knebeln** v/t (ge-, h) gag (a. fig)

Knecht [knɛçt] m (-[e]s; -e) farmhand; fig slave; **~schaft** fig f (-; no pl) slavery

kneifen ['knaifən] v/t and v/i (irr, ge-, h) pinch (**j-m in den Arm** s.o.'s arm); F chicken out; '**Kneifzange** f pincers

Kneipe ['knaipə] F f (-; -n) saloon, bar, esp Br pub

kneten ['kneːtən] v/t (ge-, h) knead; mo (u)ld; '**Knetmasse** f Plasticine®, Play-Doh®

Knick [knɪk] m (-[e]s; -e, -s) fold, crease; bend; '**knicken** v/t (ge-, h) fold, crease; bend; break; **nicht ~!** do not bend!

Knicks [knɪks] m (-es; -e) curts(e)y; **e-n ~ machen** → '**knicksen** v/i (ge-, h) curts(e)y (**vor** dat to)

Knie [kniː] n (-s; - ['kniːə, kniː]) ANAT knee; **~beuge** f SPORT knee bend; **~kehle** f ANAT hollow of the knee

knien [kniːn] v/i (ge-, h) kneel, be on one's knees (**vor** dat before)

'**Kniescheibe** f ANAT kneecap

'**Kniestrumpf** m knee-(length) sock

kniff [knɪf] pret of **kneifen**

Kniff m (-[e]s; -e) crease, fold; pinch; trick, knack

kniff(e)lig ['knɪf(ə)lɪç] adj tricky

knipsen ['knɪpsən] v/t and v/i (ge-, h) F PHOT take a picture (of); punch, clip

Knirps [knɪrps] m (-es; -e) little guy

knirschen ['knɪrʃən] v/i (ge-, h) crunch; **mit den Zähnen ~** grind or gnash one's teeth

K

knistern ['knɪstɐn] v/i (ge-, h) crackle; rustle

knittern ['knɪtɐn] v/t and v/i (ge-, h) crumple, crease, wrinkle

Knoblauch ['knoːplaux] m (-[e]s; no pl) BOT garlic

Knöchel ['knœçəl] m (-s; -) ANAT ankle; knuckle

Knochen ['knɔxən] m (-s; -) ANAT bone

'Knochenbruch m MED fracture

knochig ['knɔxɪç] adj bony

Knödel ['knøːdəl] m (-s; -) dumpling

Knolle ['knɔlə] f (-; -n) BOT tuber; bulb

Knopf [knɔpf] m (-es; Knöpfe ['knœpfə]), knöpfen ['knœpfən] v/t (ge-, h) button

'Knopfloch n buttonhole

Knorpel ['knɔrpəl] m (-s; -) GASTR gristle; ANAT cartilage

knorrig ['knɔrɪç] adj gnarled, knotted

Knospe ['knɔspə] f (-; -n), 'knospen v/i (ge-, h) BOT bud

knoten [knoːtən] v/t (ge-, h) knot, make a knot in; 'Knoten m (-s; -) knot (a. fig); 'Knotenpunkt m center, Br centre; RAIL junction

knüllen ['knʏlən] v/t and v/i (ge-, h) crumple

Knüller ['knʏlɐ] F m (-s; -) smash (hit); scoop

knüpfen ['knʏpfən] v/t (ge-, h) tie; weave

Knüppel ['knʏpəl] m (-s; -) stick, cudgel; truncheon; ~schaltung f MOT floor shift

knurren ['knʊrən] v/i (ge-, h) growl, snarl; fig grumble (über acc at); stomach: rumble

knusp(e)rig ['knʊsp(ə)rɪç] adj crisp, crunchy

knutschen ['knuːtʃən] F v/i (ge-, h) pet, neck, smooch

k.o. [kaːˈʔoː] adj knocked out; fig beat

Kobold ['koːbɔlt] m (-[e]s; -e) (hob)goblin, imp (a. fig)

Koch [kɔx] m (-s; Köche ['kœçə]) cook; chef; ~buch n cookbook, Br cookery book

'kochen (ge-, h) 1. v/t cook; boil (eggs etc); make (coffee etc); 2. v/i cook, do the cooking; boil (a. fig); gut ~ be a good cook; F vor Wut ~ boil with rage; ~d heiß boiling hot

Kocher ['kɔxɐ] m (-s; -) ELECTR cooker

Köchin ['kœçɪn] f (-; -nen) cook; chef

'Koch|löffel m (wooden) spoon; ~nische f kitchenette; ~platte f hotplate; ~salz n common salt; ~topf m saucepan, pot

Köder ['køːdɐ] m (-s; -) bait, decoy (both a. fig), lure; 'ködern v/t (ge-, h) bait, decoy (both a. fig)

Kodex ['koːdɛks] m (-es; -, -e) code

kodieren [ko'diːrən] v/t (no -ge-, h) (en-)code; Ko'dierung f (-; -en) (en-)coding

Koffein [kɔfeˈiːn] n (-s; no pl) caffeine

Koffer ['kɔfɐ] m (-s; -) (suit)case; trunk; ~radio n portable (radio); ~raum m MOT trunk, Br boot

Kognak ['kɔnjak] m (-s; -s) (French) brandy, cognac

Kohl [koːl] m (-[e]s; -e) BOT cabbage

Kohle ['koːlə] f (-; -n) coal; ELECTR carbon; F dough

'Kohle,hy,drat n carbohydrate

'Kohlen... in cpds ...dioxid etc: CHEM carbon ...; ~bergwerk n coalmine, colliery; ~ofen m coal-burning stove

'Kohlensäure f CHEM carbonic acid; GASTR F fizz; 'kohlensäurehaltig adj carbonated, F fizzy

'Kohlen|stoff m CHEM carbon; ~wasserstoff m CHEM hydrocarbon

'Kohle|pa,pier n carbon paper; ~zeichnung f charcoal drawing

'Kohlkopf m BOT (head of) cabbage

Kohlrabi [-'raːbi] m (-s; -s) BOT kohlrabi

Koje ['koːjə] f (-; -n) MAR berth, bunk

Kokain [kokaˈiːn] n (-s; no pl) cocaine

kokett [ko'kɛt] adj coquettish

kokettieren [kokɛˈtiːrən] v/i (no -ge-, h) flirt; fig ~ mit toy with

Kokosnuss ['koːkɔs-] f BOT coconut

Koks [koːks] m (-es; no pl) coke; F dough; sl coke, snow

Kolben ['kɔlbən] m (-s; -) butt; TECH piston; ~stange f TECH piston rod

Kolibri ['koːlibri] m (-s; -s) ZO humming bird

Kolleg [kɔ'leːk] n (-s; -s) UNIV course (of lectures)

Kollege [kɔ'leːgə] m (-n; -n), Kol'legin f (-; -nen) colleague

Kollegium [kɔ'leːgjʊm] n (-s; -ien) UNIV faculty, Br teaching staff

Kollekte [kɔ'lɛktə] f (-; -n) REL collection

Kollektion [kɔlɛkˈtsjoːn] f (-; -en) ECON collection; range

kollektiv [kɔlɛkˈtiːf] adj, **Kollekˈtiv** n (-s; -e) collective (a. in cpds)

Koller [ˈkɔlɐ] F m (-s; -) fit; rage

kollidieren [kɔliˈdiːrən] v/i (no -ge-, sein) collide; **Kollision** [kɔliˈzjoːn] f (-; -en) collision, fig a. clash, conflict

Kölnischwasser [ˈkœlnɪʃ-] n (-s; -) (eau de) cologne

Kolonie [koloˈniː] f (-; -n) colony

kolonisieren [koloniˈziːrən] v/t (no -ge-, h) colonize; **Koloniˈsierung** f (-; -en) colonization

Kolonne [koˈlɔnə] f (-; -n) column; MIL convoy; gang, crew

Koloss [koˈlɔs] m (-es; -e) colossus, fig a. giant (of a man)

kolossal [kolɔˈsaːl] adj gigantic

Kombi [ˈkɔmbi] m (-[s]; -s) MOT station wagon, Br estate (car)

Kombination [kɔmbinaˈtsjoːn] f (-; -en) combination; set; coveralls, Br overalls; flying suit; soccer: combined move

kombinieren [kɔmbiˈniːrən] (no -ge-, h) **1.** v/t combine; **2.** v/i reason

Kombüse [kɔmˈbyːzə] f (-; -n) MAR galley

Komet [koˈmeːt] m (-en; -en) ASTR comet

Komfort [kɔmˈfoːɐ] m (-s; no pl) (modern) conveniences; luxury

komfortabel [kɔmfɔrˈtaːbəl] adj comfortable; well-appointed; luxurious

Komik [ˈkoːmɪk] f (-; no pl) humo(u)r; comic effect; **Komiker** [ˈkoːmikɐ] m (-s; -) comedian; **komisch** [ˈkoːmɪʃ] adj comic(al), funny; strange, odd

Komitee [komiˈteː] n (-s; -s) committee

Komma [ˈkɔma] n (-s; -s, -ta) comma; **sechs ~ vier** six point four

Kommandant [kɔmanˈdant] m (-en; -en), **Kommandeur** [kɔmanˈdøːɐ] m (-s; -e) MIL commander, commanding officer; **kommandieren** [kɔmanˈdiːrən] v/i and v/t (no -ge-, h) command, be in command of; **Kommando** [kɔˈmando] n (-s; -s) command; order; MIL command; **Komˈmandobrücke** f MAR (navigating) bridge

kommen [ˈkɔmən] v/i (irr, ge-, sein) come; arrive; get; reach; **zu spät ~** be late; **weit ~** get far; **zur Schule ~** start school; **ins Gefängnis ~** go to jail; ~

lassen send for s.o., call s.o.; order s.th.; ~ **auf** (acc) think of, hit upon; remember; **hinter et.** ~ find s.th. out; **um et.** ~ lose s.th.; miss s.th.; **zu et.** ~ come by s.th.; **wieder zu sich** ~ come round or to; **wohin kommt ...?** where does ... go?; **daher kommt es, dass** that's why; **woher kommt es, dass ...?** why is it that ...?, F how come ...?

Kommentar [kɔmɛnˈtaːɐ] m (-s; -e) commentary; **kein ~!** no comment

Kommentator [kɔmɛnˈtaːtoːr] m (-s; -en [-taˈtoːrən]), **Kommentatorin** [-taˈtoːrɪn] f (-; -nen) commentator

kommentieren [kɔmɛnˈtiːrən] v/t (no -ge-, h) comment (on)

kommerzialisieren [kɔmɛrtsjaliˈziːrən] v/t (no -ge-, h) commercialize

Kommissar [kɔmɪˈsaːɐ] m (-s; -e) commissioner; superintendent

Kommission [kɔmɪˈsjoːn] f (-; -en) mission; committee

Kommode [kɔˈmoːdə] f (-; -n) bureau, Br chest (of drawers)

Kommunal... [kɔmuˈnaːl-] in cpds ...politik etc: local ...; **Kommune** [kɔˈmuːnə] f (-; -n) commune

Kommunikation [kɔmunikaˈtsjoːn] f (-; no pl) communication

Kommunion [kɔmuˈnjoːn] f (-; -en) REL (Holy) Communion

Kommunismus [kɔmuˈnɪsmʊs] m (-; no pl) POL communism; **Kommunist** [kɔmuˈnɪst] m (-en; -en), **Kommunistin** f (-; -nen), **kommuˈnistisch** adj POL communist

Komödie [koˈmøːdjə] f (-; -n) comedy; ~ **spielen** put on an act, play-act

kompakt [kɔmˈpakt] adj compact

Komˈpaktanlage f stereo system, music center (Br centre)

Kompanie [kɔmpaˈniː] f (-; -n) MIL company

Kompass [ˈkɔmpas] m (-es; -e) compass

kompatibel [kɔmpaˈtiːbəl] adj compatible (a. EDP)

komplett [kɔmˈplɛt] adj complete

Komplex [kɔmˈplɛks] m (-es; -e) complex (a. PSYCH)

Kompliment [kɔmpliˈmɛnt] n (-[e]s; -e) compliment; **j-m ein ~ machen** pay s.o. a compliment

Komplize [kɔmˈpliːtsə] m (-n; -n) accomplice

komplizieren [kɔmpli'tsiːrən] v/t (no -ge-, h) complicate; **kompliziert** [kɔmpli'tsiːrt] adj complicated, complex

Kom'plizin f (-; -nen) accomplice

Komplott [kɔm'plɔt] n (-[e]s; -e) plot, conspiracy

komponieren [kɔmpo'niːrən] v/t and v/i (no -ge-, h) MUS compose; write; **Komponist** [kɔmpo'nɪst] m (-en; -en) MUS composer; **Komposition** [kɔmpozi'tsjoːn] f (-; -en) MUS composition

Kompott [kɔm'pɔt] n (-[e]s; -e) GASTR compot(e), stewed fruit

Kompresse [kɔm'prɛsə] f (-; -n) MED compress

komprimieren [kɔmpri'miːrən] v/t (no -ge-, h) compress

Kompromiss [kɔmpro'mɪs] m (-es; -e) compromise; **kompro'misslos** adj uncompromising

kompromittieren [kɔmprɔmɪ'tiːrən] v/t (no -ge-, h) compromise (**sich** o.s.); **~d** adj compromising

Kondensator [kɔndɛn'zaːtɔr] m (-s; -en [-za'toːrən]) ELECTR capacitor; TECH condenser; **kondensieren** [kɔndɛn'ziːrən] v/t (no -ge-, h) condense

Kondensmilch [kɔn'dɛns-] f condensed milk

Kondition [kɔndi'tsjoːn] f (-; -en) a) condition, b) (no pl) SPORT condition, shape, form; **gute ~** (great) stamina

konditional [kɔnditsjo'naːl] adj LING conditional

Konditi'onstraining n fitness training

Konditor [kɔn'diːtɔr] m (-s; -en [-di'toːrən]) confectioner, pastrycook

Konditorei [kɔndito'raɪ] f (-; -en) cake shop; café, tearoom; **~waren** pl confectionery

Kondom [kɔn'doːm] n, m (-s; -e) condom

Kondukteur [kɔndʊk'tøːr] Swiss m (-s; -e) → **Schaffner**

Konfekt [kɔn'fɛkt] n (-[e]s; -e) sweets, chocolates

Konfektion [kɔnfɛk'tsjoːn] f (-; no pl) ready-made clothing; **Konfekti'ons-** in cpds ready-made ..., off-the-peg ...

Konferenz [kɔnfe'rɛnts] f (-; -en) conference

Konfession [kɔnfe'sjoːn] f (-; -en) religion, denomination; **konfessionell** [kɔnfɛsjo'nɛl] adj confessional, denominational; **Konfessi'onsschule** f denominational school

Konfirmand [kɔnfɪr'mant] m (-en; -en), **Konfir'mandin** f (-; -nen) REL confirmand; **Konfirmation** [kɔnfɪrma'tsjoːn] f (-; -en) REL confirmation; **konfirmieren** [kɔnfɪr'miːrən] v/t (no -ge-, h) confirm

konfiszieren [kɔnfɪs'tsiːrən] v/t (no -ge-, h) JUR confiscate

Konfitüre [kɔnfi'tyːrə] f (-; -n) jam

Konflikt [kɔn'flɪkt] m (-[e]s; -e) conflict

konfrontieren [kɔnfrɔn'tiːrən] v/t (no -ge-, h) confront

konfus [kɔn'fuːs] adj confused, mixed-up

Kongress [kɔn'grɛs] m (-es; -e) convention, Br congress

König ['køːnɪç] m (-s; -e) king

Königin ['køːnɪgɪn] f (-; -nen) queen

königlich ['køːnɪklɪç] adj royal

Königreich ['køːnɪk-] n kingdom

Konjugation [kɔnjuga'tsjoːn] f (-; -en) LING conjugation; **konjugieren** [kɔnju'giːrən] v/t (no -ge-, h) LING conjugate

Konjunktiv ['kɔnjʊŋktiːf] m (-s; -e) LING subjunctive (mood)

Konjunktur [kɔnjʊŋk'tuːr] f (-; -en) economic situation

konkret [kɔn'kreːt] adj concrete

Konkurrent [kɔnku'rɛnt] m (-en; -en), **Konkur'rentin** f (-; -nen) competitor, rival; **Konkurrenz** [kɔnku'rɛnts] f (-; no pl) competition; **die ~** one's competitors; **außer ~** not competing; → **konkurrenzlos**

konkur'renzfähig adj competitive

Konkur'renzkampf m competition

konkur'renzlos adj without competition, unrival(l)ed

konkurrieren [kɔnku'riːrən] v/i (no -ge-, h) compete

Konkurs [kɔn'kʊrs] m (-es; -e) ECON, JUR bankruptcy; **in ~ gehen** go bankrupt; **~masse** f JUR bankrupt's estate

können ['kœnən] v/t and v/i (irr, ge-, h), v/aux (irr, no -ge-, h) can, be able to; may, be allowed to; **kann ich gehen** etc? can or may I go?; **du kannst nicht** you cannot or can't; **ich kann nicht mehr** I can't go on; I can't manage or eat any more; **es kann sein** it may be; **ich kann nichts dafür** it's not my fault; *e-e Sprache* ~ know *or* speak a language

'**Können** *n* (-*s*; *no pl*) ability, skill

Könner ['kœnɐ] *m* (-*s*; -), '**Könnerin** *f* (-; -*nen*) master, expert; *esp* SPORT ace, crack

konnte ['kɔntə] *pret of* **können**

konsequent [kɔnze'kvɛnt] *adj* consistent; **Konsequenz** [kɔnze'kvɛnts] *f* (-; -*en*) a) (*no pl*) consistency, b) consequence

konservativ [kɔnzɛrva'tiːf] *adj* conservative

Konserven [kɔn'zɛrvən] *pl* canned (*Br a.* tinned) foods; ~**büchse** *f*, ~**dose** *f* can, *Br a.* tin; ~**fa,brik** *f* cannery

konservieren [kɔnzɛr'viːrən] *v/t* (*no -ge-*, *h*) preserve; **Konser'vierungsmittel** *n* preservative

Konsonant [kɔnzo'nant] *m* (-*en*; -*en*) LING consonant

konstruieren [kɔnstru'iːrən] *v/t* (*no -ge-*, *h*) construct; design

Konstrukteur [kɔnstruk'tøːɐ] *m* (-*s*; -*e*) TECH designer; **Konstruktion** [kɔnstruk'tsjoːn] *f* (-; -*en*) construction

Konsul ['kɔnzul] *m* (-*s*; -*n*) consul

Konsulat [kɔnzu'laːt] *n* (-[*e*]*s*; -*e*) consulate

konsultieren [kɔnzul'tiːrən] *v/t* (*no -ge-*, *h*) consult

Konsum[1] [kɔn'zuːm] *m* (-*s*; *no pl*) consumption

Konsum[2] ['kɔnzuːm] *m* (-*s*; -*s*) co-operative (society *or* store), F co-op

Konsument [kɔnzu'mɛnt] *m* (-*en*; -*en*), **Konsu'mentin** *f* (-; -*nen*) consumer; **Kon'sumgesellschaft** *f* consumer society; **konsumieren** [kɔnzu'miːrən] *v/t* (*no -ge-*, *h*) consume

Kontakt [kɔn'takt] *m* (-[*e*]*s*; -*e*) contact (*a.* ELECTR); ~ **aufnehmen** get in touch; ~ **haben** *or* **in** ~ **stehen mit** be in contact *or* touch with; **den** ~ **verlieren** lose touch; **kon'taktfreudig** *adj* sociable

Kon'taktlinsen *pl* OPT contact lenses

Konter ['kɔntɐ] *m* (-*s*; -), '**kontern** *v/i* (*ge-*, *h*) counter (*a. fig*)

Kontinent [kɔnti'nɛnt] *m* (-[*e*]*s*; -*e*) continent

Konto ['kɔnto] *n* (-*s*; *Konten*) account

'**Kontoauszug** *m* (bank) statement

Kontrast [kɔn'trast] *m* (-[*e*]*s*; -*e*) contrast (*a.* PHOT, TV *etc*)

Kontrolle [kɔn'trɔlə] *f* (-; -*n*) control; supervision; check(up)

Kontrolleur [kɔntrɔ'løːɐ] *m* (-*s*; -*e*), **Kontrol'leurin** *f* (-; -*nen*) inspector, RAIL *a.* conductor

kontrollieren [kɔntrɔ'liːrən] *v/t* (*no -ge-*, *h*) check; check up on *s.o.*; control

Kon'trollpunkt *m* checkpoint

Kontroverse [kɔntro'vɛrzə] *f* (-; -*n*) controversy

konventionell [kɔnvɛntsjo'nɛl] *adj* conventional

Konversation [kɔnvɛrza'tsjoːn] *f* (-; -*en*) conversation; **Konversati'onslexikon** *n* encyclop(a)edia

Konzentration [kɔntsɛntra'tsjoːn] *f* (-; -*en*) concentration

Konzentrati'onslager *n* concentration camp

konzentrieren [kɔntsɛn'triːrən] *v/t and v/refl* (*no -ge-*, *h*) concentrate; **sich auf et.** ~ concentrate on s.th.

Konzept [kɔn'tsɛpt] *n* (-[*e*]*s*; -*e*) (rough) draft; conception; *j-n aus dem* ~ *bringen* put s.o. out

Konzern [kɔn'tsɛrn] *m* (-[*e*]*s*; -*e*) ECON combine, group

Konzert [kɔn'tsɛrt] *n* (-[*e*]*s*; -*e*) MUS concert; concerto; ~**halle** *f*, ~**saal** *m* concert hall, auditorium

Konzession [kɔntsɛ'sjoːn] *f* (-; -*en*) concession; license, *Br* licence

Kopf [kɔpf] *m* (-[*e*]*s*; *Köpfe* ['kœpfə]) head (*a. fig*); top; *fig a.* brains, mind; ~ **hoch!** chin up!; *j-m über den* ~ **wachsen** outgrow s.o.; *fig* be too much for s.o.; **sich den** ~ **zerbrechen** (*über acc*) rack one's brains (over); **sich et. aus dem** ~ **schlagen** put s.th. out of one's mind; ~ **an** ~ neck and neck; ~**ball** *m* SPORT header; headed goal; ~**bedeckung** *f* headgear; **ohne** ~ bareheaded

köpfen ['kœpfən] *v/t* (*ge-*, *h*) behead, decapitate; SPORT head (*ins Tor* home)

'**Kopf|ende** *n* head *or* top; ~**hörer** *pl* headphones; ~**jäger** *m* headhunter; ~**kissen** *n* pillow

'**kopflos** *adj* headless; *fig* panicky

'**Kopf|rechnen** *n* mental arithmetic; ~**sa,lat** *m* BOT lettuce; ~**schmerzen** *pl* headache; ~**sprung** *m* SPORT header; ~**stand** *m* SPORT headstand;

~tuch n scarf, (head)kerchief

kopf'über adv headfirst (a. fig)

'Kopfweh n → **Kopfschmerzen**

'Kopfzerbrechen n: **j-m ~ machen** give s.o. a headache

Kopie [ko'pi:] f (-; -n), **ko'pieren** v/t (no -ge-, h) copy; **Kopiergerät** [ko'pi:ɐ-] n copier; **Ko'pierstift** m indelible pencil

Koppel¹ ['kɔpəl] f (-; -n) paddock

'Koppel² n (-s; -) MIL belt

'koppeln v/t (ge-, h) couple; dock

Koralle [ko'ralə] f (-; -n) ZO coral

Korb [kɔrp] m (-[e]s; Körbe ['kœrbə]) basket; **~möbel** pl wicker furniture

Kord [kɔrt] m (-[e]s; -e) corduroy

Kordel ['kɔrdəl] f (-; -n) cord

'Kordhose f corduroys

Korinthe [ko'rɪntə] f (-; -n) currant

Kork [kɔrk] m (-[e]s; -e) BOT cork

'Korkeiche f BOT cork oak

Korken ['kɔrkən] m (-s; -) cork; **~zieher** [-tsiːɐ] m (-s; -) corkscrew

Korn¹ [kɔrn] n (-[e]s; Körner ['kœrnɐ]) BOT a) grain; seed, b) (no pl) grain, Br a. corn, c) (pl -e) TECH front sight

Korn² F m (-[e]s; -e) (grain) schnapps

körnig ['kœrnɪç] adj grainy

Körper ['kœrpɐ] m (-s; -) body (a. PHYS, CHEM), MATH a. solid, **~bau** m (-[e]s; no pl) build, physique

'körperbehindert adj (physically) disabled or handicapped

'Körpergeruch m body odo(u)r, BO; **~größe** f height; **~kraft** f physical strength

'körperlich adj physical

'Körperpflege f personal hygiene

'Körperschaft f (-; -en) corporation, (corporate) body

'Körperteil m part of the body; **~verletzung** f JUR bodily injury

korrekt [kɔ'rɛkt] adj correct

Korrektur [kɔrɛk'tuːɐ] f (-; -en) correction; PED etc grading, Br marking

Korrespondent [kɔrɛspɔn'dɛnt] m (-en; -en), **Korrespon'dentin** f (-; -nen) correspondent; **Korrespondenz** [-'dɛnts] f (-; -en) correspondence; **korrespondieren** [-'diːrən] v/i (no -ge-, h) correspond (**mit** with)

Korridor ['kɔridoːɐ] m (-s; -e) corridor; hall

korrigieren [kɔri'giːrən] v/t (no -ge-, h) correct; PED etc grade, Br mark

korrupt [kɔ'rʊpt] adj corrupt(ed)

Korruption [kɔrʊp'tsjoːn] f (-; -en) corruption

Korsett [kɔr'zɛt] n (-s; -s) corset (a. fig)

Kosename ['koːzə-] m pet name

Kosmetik [kɔs'meːtɪk] f (-; no pl) beauty culture; cosmetics, toiletries

Kosmetikerin [kɔs'meːtɪkərɪn] f (-; -nen) beautician, cosmetician

Kost [kɔst] f (-; no pl) food, diet; board

'kostbar adj precious, valuable; costly

'Kostbarkeit f (-; -en) precious object, treasure (a. fig)

kosten¹ ['kɔstən] v/t (ge-, h) cost, be; fig take (time etc); **was** or **wie viel kostet ...?** how much it ...?

'kosten² v/t (ge-, h) taste, try

'Kosten pl cost(s); price; expenses; charges; **auf j-s ~** at s.o.'s expense

'kostenlos 1. adj free; **2.** adv free of charge

köstlich ['kœstlɪç] adj delicious; fig priceless; **sich ~ amüsieren** have great fun, F have a ball

'Kostprobe f taste, sample (a. fig)

'kostspielig adj expensive, costly

Kostüm [kɔs'tyːm] n (-s; -e) costume, dress; suit; **~fest** n fancy-dress ball

Kot [koːt] m (-[e]s; no pl) excrement, ZO a. droppings

Kotelett [kɔtə'lɛt] n (-s; -s) chop, cutlet

Koteletten [kɔtə'lɛtən] pl sideburns

'Kotflügel m MOT fender, Br wing

kotzen ['kɔtsən] V v/i (ge-, h) puke

Krabbe ['krabə] f (-; -n) ZO shrimp; prawn

krabbeln ['krabəln] v/i (ge-, sein) crawl

Krach [krax] m (-[e]s; Kräche ['krɛçə]) a) crash, bang, b) (no pl) noise, c) F quarrel, fight

krachen ['kraxən] v/i (ge-, h) crack, bang, crash

Kracher ['kraxɐ] m (-s; -) (fire)cracker

krächzen ['krɛçtsən] v/t and v/i (ge-, h) croak

Kraft [kraft] f (-; Kräfte ['krɛftə]) strength, force (a. POL), power (a. ELECTR, TECH, POL); **in ~ sein** (**setzen, treten**) JUR etc be in (put into, come into) force; **~brühe** f GASTR consommé, clear soup; **~fahrer(in)** driver, motorist; **~fahrzeug** n motor vehicle

kräftig ['krɛftɪç] adj strong (a. fig), powerful; substantial (food); good

'kraftlos adj weak, feeble

'Kraft|probe f test of strength; ~stoff m
MOT fuel; ~verschwendung f waste of
energy; ~werk n power station
Kragen ['kra:gən] m (-s; -) collar
Krähe ['krɛ:ə] f (-; -n) ZO crow
krähen ['krɛ:ən] v/i (ge-, h) crow
Krake ['kra:kə] m (-n; -n) ZO octopus
Kralle ['kralə] f (-; -n) ZO claw (a. fig)
'krallen v/refl (ge-, h) cling (**an** acc on),
clutch (at)
Kram [kra:m] F m (-[e]s; no pl) stuff,
(one's) things
Krampf [krampf] m (-[e]s; Krämpfe
['krɛmpfə]) MED cramp; spasm, convulsion; ~ader f MED varicose vein
'krampfhaft fig adj forced (smile etc);
desperate (attempt etc)
Kran [kra:n] m (-[e]s; Kräne ['krɛ:nə])
TECH crane
Kranich ['kra:nıç] m (-s; -e) ZO crane
krank [kraŋk] adj ill, sick; ~ werden get
sick, Br fall ill; 'Kranke m, f (-n; -n) sick
person, patient; die ~n the sick
kränken ['krɛŋkən] v/t (ge-, h) hurt
(s.o.'s feelings), offend
'Kranken|bett n sickbed; ~geld n sick-
ness benefit; ~gym,nastik f physiotherapy; ~haus n hospital; ~kasse
f health insurance scheme; in e-r ~
sein be a member of a health insurance scheme or plan; ~pflege f nursing; ~pfleger m male nurse; ~schein
m health insurance certificate;
~schwester f nurse; ~versicherung
f health insurance; ~wagen m ambulance; ~zimmer n sickroom
'krankhaft adj morbid (a. fig)
'Krankheit f (-; -en) illness, sickness, disease
'Krankheitserreger m germ
kränklich ['krɛŋklıç] adj sickly, ailing
Kränkung ['krɛŋkuŋ] f (-; -en) insult, offense, Br offence
Kranz [krants] m (-es; Kränze ['krɛntsə])
wreath; fig ring, circle
krass [kras] adj crass, gross; blunt
Krater ['kra:tɐ] m (-s; -) crater
kratzen ['kratsən] v/t and v/refl (ge-, h)
scratch (o.s.); scrape (**von** off)
Kratzer ['kratsɐ] m (-s; -) scratch (a.
MED)
kraulen ['kraulən] 1. v/t (ge-, h) stroke;
run one's fingers through; 2. v/i (ge-,
sein) SPORT do the crawl

kraus [kraus] adj curly (hair); wrinkled
Krause ['krauzə] f (-; -n) ruff; friz(z)
kräuseln ['krɔyzəln] v/t and v/refl (ge-,
h) curl, friz(z); water: ripple
Kraut [kraut] n (-[e]s; Kräuter ['krɔytɐ])
BOT herb; tops, leaves; cabbage
Krawall [kra'val] m (-s; -e) riot; F row,
racket
Krawatte [kra'vatə] f (-; -n) tie
kreativ [krea'ti:f] adj creative
Kreativität [kreativi'tɛ:t] f (-; no pl)
creativity
Kreatur [krea'tu:ɐ] f (-; -en) creature
Krebs [kre:ps] m ZO crayfish; MED can-
cer; AST Cancer; sie ist (ein) ~ she's
(a) Cancer; ~ erregend MED carcino-
genic
Krebs... MED cancerous; ~geschwulst f
MED carcinoma; ~kranke m, f cancer
patient
Kredit [kre'di:t] m (-[e]s; -e) ECON credit;
loan; ~hai m loan shark; ~karte f credit
card, pl coll F plastic money
Kreide ['kraidə] f (-; -n) chalk; crayon
Kreis [krais] m (-es; -e) circle (a. fig); POL
district, county; ~bahn f AST orbit
kreischen ['kraiʃən] v/i (ge-, h) screech;
squeal
Kreisel ['kraizəl] m (-s; -) (spinning) top;
PHYS gyro(scope); 'kreiseln v/i (ge-, h,
sein) spin around
kreisen ['kraizən] v/i (ge-, h, sein) (move
in a) circle, revolve, rotate; circulate
'kreisförmig [-fœrmıç] adj circular
'Kreislauf m MED, ECON circulation;
BIOL cycle (a. fig), TECH, ELECTR a. cir-
cuit; ~störungen pl MED circulatory
trouble
'Kreis|säge f circular saw; ~verkehr m
traffic circle, Br roundabout
Krempe ['krɛmpə] f (-; -n) brim
Kren [kre:n] Austrian m (-[e]s; no pl)
GASTR horseradish
Krepp [krɛp] m (-s; -s) crepe
Kreuz [krɔyts] n (-es; -e) cross (a. fig);
ANAT (small of the) back; cards:
club(s); MUS sharp; über ~ crosswise;
F j-n aufs ~ legen take s.o. in; kreuzen
['krɔytsən] 1. v/t and v/refl (ge-, h) cross;
clash; 2. v/i (ge-, sein) MAR cruise
Kreuzer ['krɔytsɐ] m (-s; -) MAR cruiser
'Kreuzfahrer m HIST crusader
'Kreuzfahrt f MAR cruise
kreuzigen ['krɔytsıgən] v/t (ge-, h) cru-

cify; '**Kreuzigung** f (-; -en) crucifixion
'**Kreuzotter** f ZO adder
'**Kreuzschmerzen** pl backache
'**Kreuzung** f (-; -en) RAIL, MOT crossing, junction; intersection; crossroads; BIOL cross(breed)ing; cross(breed); fig cross
'**Kreuzverhör** n JUR cross-examination; **ins ~ nehmen** cross-examine
'**kreuzweise** adv crosswise, crossways
'**Kreuz|worträtsel** n crossword (puzzle); ~**zug** HIST m crusade
kriechen ['kri:çən] v/i (irr, ge-, sein) creep, crawl; fig **vor j-m ~** toady to s.o.
Kriecher ['kri:çɐ] contp m (-s; -) toady
'**Kriechspur** f MOT slow lane
Krieg [kri:k] m (-[e]s; -e ['kri:ɡə]) war; **~ führen gegen** be at war with
kriegen ['kri:ɡən] F v/t (ge-, h) get; catch
Krieger ['kri:ɡɐ] m (-s; -) warrior
'**Kriegerdenkmal** n war memorial
kriegerisch ['kri:ɡərɪʃ] adj warlike, martial
'**Kriegführung** f (-; no pl) warfare
'**Kriegs|beil** fig n: **das ~ begraben** bury the hatchet; ~**dienstverweigerer** m (-s; -) conscientious objector; ~**erklärung** f declaration of war; ~**gefangene** m prisoner of war, P.O.W.; ~**gefangenschaft** f captivity; ~**recht** n JUR martial law; ~**schauplatz** m theater (Br theatre) of war; ~**schiff** n warship; ~**teilnehmer** m (war) veteran, Br ex-serviceman; ~**treiber** [-traibɐ] m (-s; -) POL warmonger; ~**verbrechen** n war crime; ~**verbrecher** m war criminal
Krimi ['kri:mi] F m (-s; -s) (crime) thriller, detective novel
Kriminal|beamte [krimi'na:l-] m detective, plain-clothesman; ~**polizei** f criminal investigation department; ~**roman** m → **Krimi**
kriminell [krimi'nɛl] adj, **Kriminelle** m, f (-n; -n) criminal
Krippe ['krɪpə] f (-; -n) crib, manger (a. REL); REL crèche, Br crib
Krise ['kri:zə] f (-; -n) crisis
'**Krisenherd** m esp POL trouble spot
Kristall[1] ['krɪs'tal] m (-s; -e) crystal
Kris'tall[2] n (s; no pl), ~**glas** n crystal
kristallisieren [krɪstali'zi:rən] v/i and v/refl (no -ge-, h) crystallize
Kriterium [kri'te:rjʊm] n (-s; -ien) criterion (**für** of)
Kritik [kri'ti:k] f (-; -en) criticism; THEA,

MUS etc review, critique; **gute ~en** a good press; ~ **üben an** (dat) criticize;
Kritiker(in) ['kri:tikɐ (-kərɪn)] (-s; -/-; -nen) critic; **kri'tiklos** adj uncritical; **kritisch** ['kri:tɪʃ] adj critical (a. fig) (**gegenüber** of); **kritisieren** [kriti'zi:rən] v/t (no -ge-, h) criticize
kritzeln ['krɪtsəln] v/t and v/i (ge-, h) scrawl, scribble
kroch [krɔx] pret of **kriechen**
Krokodil [kroko'di:l] n (-s; -e) ZO crocodile
Krone ['kro:nə] f (-; -n) crown; coronet
krönen ['krø:nən] v/t (ge-, h) crown; **j-n zum König ~** crown s.o. king
'**Kronleuchter** m chandelier
'**Kronprinz** m crown prince
'**Kronprin,zessin** f crown princess
'**Krönung** f (-; -en) coronation; fig crowning event, climax, high point
Kropf [krɔpf] m (-[e]s; Kröpfe ['krœpfə]) MED goiter, Br goitre; ZO crop
Kröte ['krø:tə] f (-; -n) ZO toad
Krücke ['krʏkə] f (-; -n) crutch
Krug [kru:k] m (-[e]s; Krüge ['kry:ɡə]) jug, pitcher; mug, stein; tankard
Krümel ['kry:məl] m (-s; -) crumb
krümelig ['kry:məlɪç] adj crumbly
'**krümeln** v/t and v/i (ge-, h) crumble
krumm [krʊm] adj crooked (a. fig), bent
'**krummbeinig** [-bainɪç] adj bow-legged
krümmen ['krʏmən] v/t (ge-, h) bend (a. TECH), crook; **sich ~** bend; writhe (with pain); '**Krümmung** f (-; -en) bend, curve; GEOGR, MATH, MED curvature
Krüppel ['krʏpəl] m (-s; -) cripple
Kruste ['krʊstə] f (-; -n) crust
Kto. ABBR of **Konto** a/c, account
Kübel ['ky:bəl] m (-s; -) bucket, pail; tub
Kubik|meter [ku'bi:k-] n, m cubic meter (Br metre); ~**wurzel** f MATH cube root
Küche ['kʏçə] f (-; -n) kitchen; GASTR cooking, cuisine; **kalte** (**warme**) ~ cold (hot) meals
Kuchen ['ku:xən] m (-s; -) cake; tart, pie
'**Küchen|geräte** pl kitchen utensils (or appliances); ~**geschirr** n kitchen crockery, kitchenware; ~**herd** m cooker; ~**schrank** m (kitchen) cupboard
Kuckuck ['kʊkʊk] m (-s; -s) ZO cuckoo
Kufe ['ku:fə] f (-; -n) runner; AVIAT skid
Kugel ['ku:ɡəl] f (-; -n) ball; bullet; MATH, GEOGR sphere; SPORT shot

'**kugelförmig** [-fœrmɪç] *adj* ballshaped, *esp* ASTR, MATH spheric(al)

'**Kugelgelenk** *n* TECH, ANAT ball (and socket) joint

'**Kugellager** *n* TECH ball bearing

'**kugeln** *v/i* (*ge-, sein*) *and v/t* (*h*) roll

'**Kugelschreiber** [-ʃraibɐ] *m* (*-s; -*) ballpoint (pen)

'**kugelsicher** *adj* bulletproof

'**Kugelstoßen** *n* (*-s; no pl*) SPORT shot put(ting); '**Kugelstoßer** [-ʃtoːsɐ] *m* (*-s; -*), '**Kugelstoßerin** [-ʃtoːsərɪn] *f* (*-; -nen*) SPORT shot-putter

Kuh [kuː] *f* (*-; Kühe* ['kyːə]) ZO cow

kühl [kyːl] *adj* cool (*a. fig*); '**Kühle** *f* (*-; no pl*) cool(ness); '**kühlen** *v/t* (*ge-, h*) cool; chill; refrigerate; refresh

Kühler ['kyːlɐ] *m* (*-s; -*) MOT radiator

'**Kühlerhaube** *f* MOT hood, *Br* bonnet

'**Kühlmittel** *n* coolant

'**Kühlraum** *m* cold-storage room

'**Kühlschrank** *m* fridge, refrigerator

'**Kühltruhe** *f* deep-freeze, freezer

'**Kühlwasser** *n* MOT cooling water

kühn [kyːn] *adj* bold

'**Kühnheit** *f* (*-; no pl*) boldness

'**Kuhstall** *m* cowshed

Küken ['kyːkən] *n* (*-s; -*) ZO chick (*a. fig*)

Kukuruz ['kukuruts] *Austrian m → Mais*

Kuli ['kuːli] F *m* (*-s; -s*) ballpoint

Kulissen [ku'lɪsən] *pl* THEA wings; scenery; *hinter den ~* backstage, *esp fig* behind the scenes

Kult [kʊlt] *m* (*-[e]s; -e*) cult; rite, ritual (act)

kultivieren [kʊlti'viːrən] *v/t* (*no -ge-, h*) cultivate

Kultur [kʊl'tuːɐ] *f* (*-; -en*) culture (*a.* BIOL), civilization; AGR cultivation

Kul'turbeutel *m* toilet bag

kulturell [kʊltu'rɛl] *adj* cultural

Kul'tur|geschichte *f* history of civilization; ~**volk** *n* civilized people; ~**zentrum** *n* cultural center (*Br* centre)

Kultusmi,nister ['kʊltus-] *m* minister of education and cultural affairs

Kummer ['kʊmɐ] *m* (*-s; no pl*) grief, sorrow; trouble, worry; ~ *haben mit* have trouble *or* problems with

kümmerlich ['kʏmɐlɪç] *adj* miserable, poor, scanty; **kümmern** ['kʏmɐn] *v/refl and v/t* (*ge-, h*) *sich ~ um* look after, take care of, mind; care *or* worry about, be interested in

Kumpel ['kʊmpəl] *m* (*-s; -*) miner; F mate, buddy, pal

Kunde ['kʊndə] *m* (*-n; -n*) customer, client; '**Kundendienst** *m* after-sales service; (customer) service; service department; TECH servicing

Kundgebung ['kʊntɡeːbʊŋ] *f* (*-; -en*) meeting, rally, demonstration

kündigen ['kʏndɪɡən] *v/i and v/t* (*ge-, h*) cancel; *j-m ~* give s.o. his/her/one's notice; dismiss s.o., F sack *or* fire s.o.

'**Kündigung** *f* (*-; -en*) cancellation; (period of) notice

Kundin ['kʊndɪn] *f* (*-; -nen*) customer, client

Kundschaft ['kʊntʃaft] *f* (*-; -en*) customers, clients

Kunst [kʊnst] *f* (*-; Künste* ['kʏnstə]) art; skill; ~**...** *in cpds* ...herz, ...leder, ...licht *etc*: artificial ...; ~**akade,mie** *f* academy of arts; ~**ausstellung** *f* art exhibition; ~**dünger** *m* AGR artificial fertilizer; ~**erziehung** *f* PED art (education); ~**faser** *f* man-made *or* synthetic fiber (*Br* fibre); ~**fehler** *m* professional blunder; ~**fliegen** *n* stunt flying, aerobatics; ~**geschichte** *f* history of art; ~**gewerbe** *n*, ~**handwerk** *n* arts and crafts

Künstler ['kʏnstlɐ] *m* (*-s; -*), **Künstlerin** ['kʏnstlərɪn] *f* (*-; -nen*) artist, MUS, THEA *a.* performer

künstlerisch ['kʏnstlərɪʃ] *adj* artistic

künstlich ['kʏnstlɪç] *adj* artificial; false; synthetic; man-made

'**Kunst|schwimmen** *n* water ballet; ~**seide** *f* rayon; ~**springen** *n* springboard diving; ~**stoff** *m* plastic; ~**stück** *n* trick, stunt, *esp fig* feat; ~**turnen** *n* gymnastics; ~**turner** *m* gymnast

'**kunstvoll** *adj* artistic; elaborate

'**Kunstwerk** *n* work of art

Kupfer ['kʊpfɐ] *n* (*-s; no pl*) copper (*aus* of); ~**stich** *m* copperplate (engraving)

Kupon [ku'põː] *m* (*-s; -s*) coupon

Kuppe ['kʊpə] *f* (*-; -n*) (rounded) hilltop; ANAT head

Kuppel ['kʊpəl] *f* (*-; -n*) ARCH dome; cupola

Kuppelei [kʊpə'lai] *f* (*-; -en*) JUR procuring

'**kuppeln** *v/i* (*ge-, h*) MOT put the clutch in *or* out; **Kupplung** ['kʊplʊŋ] *f* (*-; -en*) MOT clutch

Kur [kuːɐ] f (-; -en) course of treatment; cure

Kür [kyːɐ] f (-; -en) SPORT free skating; free exercises

Kurbel ['kʊrbəl] f (-; -n) crank, handle; **'kurbeln** v/t (ge-, h) crank; wind (up etc); **'Kurbelwelle** f TECH crankshaft

Kürbis ['kyrbɪs] m (-ses; -se) BOT pumpkin, gourd, squash

'Kurgast m visitor

kurieren [ku'riːrən] v/t (no -ge-, h) cure (**von** of)

kurios [ku'rjoːs] adj curious, odd, strange

'Kürlauf m SPORT free skating

'Kurort m health resort, spa

Kurpfuscher ['kuːɐpfuʃɐ] m (-s; -) quack (doctor)

Kurs [kʊrs] m (-es; -e) AVIAT, MAR course (a. fig); PED class(es); ECON (exchange) rate; (stock) price; **~buch** n railroad (Br railway) guide

Kürschner ['kyrʃnɐ] m (-s; -) furrier

kursieren [kʊr'ziːrən] v/i (no -ge-, h) circulate (a. fig)

Kurve ['kʊrvə] f (-; -n) curve (a. MATH and fig); bend, turn; **'kurvenreich** adj winding, full of bends; F curvaceous

kurz [kʊrts] adj short; brief; **~e Hose** shorts; (**bis**) **vor ~em** (until) recently; (**erst**) **seit ~em** (only) for a short time; **~ vorher** (**darauf**) shortly before (after[wards]); **~ vor uns** just ahead of us; **~ nacheinander** in quick succession; **~ fortgehen** etc go away for a short time or a moment; **sich ~ fassen** be brief, put it briefly; **~ gesagt** in short; **zu ~ kommen** go short; **~ angebunden** curt

'Kurzarbeit f ECON short time

'kurzarbeiten v/i (sep, ge-, h) ECON work short time

'kurzatmig [-ʔaːtmɪç] adj short of breath

Kürze ['kʏrtsə] f (-; no pl) shortness; brevity; **in ~** soon, shortly, before long

'kürzen v/t (ge-, h) shorten (**um** by); abridge; cut, reduce (a. MATH)

kurzerhand ['kʊrtsɐ'hant] adv without hesitation, on the spot

'kurzfristig 1. adj short-term; **2.** adv at short notice

'Kurzgeschichte f short story

'kurzlebig [-leːbɪç] adj short-lived

kürzlich ['kʏrtslɪç] adv recently, not long ago

'Kurz|nachrichten pl news summary; **~schluss** m ELECTR short circuit, F short; **~schrift** f shorthand

'kurzsichtig adj nearsighted, Br shortsighted

'Kurzstrecke f short distance

'Kürzung f (-; -en) cut, reduction (a. MATH)

'Kurzwaren pl notions, Br haberdashery

'kurzweilig [-vaɪlɪç] adj entertaining

'Kurzwelle f PHYS, radio: short wave

kuschelig ['kʊʃəlɪç] F adj cozy, Br cosy, snug; **kuscheln** ['kʊʃəln] v/refl (ge-, h) snuggle, cuddle (**an** acc up to; **in** acc in)

Kusine f → **Cousine**

Kuss [kʊs] m (-es; Küsse ['kʏsə]) kiss

'kussecht adj kiss-proof

küssen ['kʏsən] v/t (ge-, h) kiss

Küste ['kʏstə] f (-; -n) coast; shore; **an der ~** on the coast; **an die ~** ashore

'Küsten|gewässer pl coastal waters; **~schifffahrt** f coastal shipping; **~schutz** m, **~wache** f coast guard

Küster ['kʏstɐ] m (-s; -) REL verger, sexton

Kutsche ['kʊtʃə] f (-; -n) carriage, coach; **Kutscher** ['kʊtʃɐ] m (-s; -) coachman

Kutte ['kʊtə] f (-; -n) (monk's) habit

Kutteln ['kʊtəln] pl GASTR tripe

Kutter ['kʊtɐ] m (-s; -) MAR cutter

Kuvert [ku'veːɐ] n (-s; -s) envelope

Kybernetik [kybɐr'neːtɪk] f (-; no pl) cybernetics

L

labil [la'biːl] *adj* unstable

Labor [la'boːɐ] *n* (-s; -e) laboratory, F lab; **Laborant(in)** [labo'rant(ɪn)] (-en; -en/-; -nen) laboratory assistant

Labyrinth [laby'rɪnt] *n* (-[e]s; -e) labyrinth, maze (*both a. fig*)

Lache ['laxə] *f* (-; -n) pool, puddle

lächeln ['lɛçəln] *v/i* (ge-, h), **'Lächeln** *n* (-s; *no pl*) smile

lachen ['laxən] *v/i* (ge-, h) laugh (**über** *acc* at); **'Lachen** *n* (-s; *no pl*) laugh (-ter); *j-n zum ~ bringen* make s.o. laugh; **lächerlich** ['lɛçɐlɪç] *adj* ridiculous; **~ machen** ridicule, make fun of; *sich ~ machen* make a fool of o.s.

Lachs [laks] *m* (-es; -e) ZO salmon

Lack [lak] *m* (-[e]s; -e) varnish; lacquer; MOT paint(work)

lackieren [la'kiːrən] *v/t* (*no* -ge-, h) varnish; lacquer; paint (*a.* MOT)

'Lackschuhe *pl* patent-leather shoes

Ladefläche ['laːdə-] *f* loading space

Ladegerät *n* ELECTR battery charger

'Ladehemmung *f* MIL jam

laden ['laːdən] *v/t* (*irr, ge-, h*) load; ELECTR charge; EDP boot (up); *fig et. auf sich ~* burden o.s. with s.th.

Laden *m* (-s; *Läden* ['lɛːdən]) store, *Br* shop; shutter; **~dieb** *m* shoplifter; **~diebstahl** *m* shoplifting; **~inhaber** *m* storekeeper, *Br* shopkeeper; **~kasse** *f* till; **~schluss** *m* closing time; *nach ~* after hours; **~tisch** *m* counter

'Laderampe *f* loading platform *or* ramp

'Laderaum *m* MAR hold

'Ladung *f* (-; -en) load, freight; AVIAT, MAR cargo; ELECTR, MIL charge; *e-e ~ ...* a load of ...

lag [laːk] *pret of* **liegen**

Lage ['laːgə] *f* (-; -n) situation, position (*both a. fig*); location; layer; round (*of beer etc*); *in schöner* (*ruhiger*) *~* beautifully (peacefully) situated; *in der ~ sein zu inf* be able to *inf*, be in a position to *inf*

Lager ['laːgɐ] *n* (-s; -) bed; camp (*a. fig*); ECON stock, store; GEOL deposit; TECH bearing; *et. auf ~ haben* have s.th. in store (*a. fig for s.o.*); **~feuer** *n* campfire; **~haus** *n* warehouse

'lagern (*ge-, h*) **1.** *v/i* camp; ECON be stored; **2.** *v/t* store, keep; MED lay, rest; *kühl ~* keep in a cool place

'Lagerraum *m* storeroom

Lagerung ['laːgərʊŋ] *f* (-; *no pl*) storage

Lagune [la'guːnə] *f* (-; -n) lagoon

lahm [laːm] *adj* lame; **~ legen → lähmen**; **lahmen** ['laːmən] *v/i* (ge-, h) be lame (*auf dat* in)

lähmen ['lɛːmən] *v/t* (ge-, h) paralyze, *Br* paralyse; bring *traffic etc* to a standstill

'Lähmung *f* (-; -en) MED paralysis

Laib [laip] *m* (-[e]s; -e (*laibə*)) loaf

Laich [laiç] *m* (-[e]s; -e), **laichen** ['laiçən] *v/i* (ge-, h) spawn

Laie ['laiə] *m* (-n; -n) layman; amateur

'laienhaft *adj* amateurish

'Laienspiel *n* amateur play

Laken ['laːkən] *n* (-s; -) sheet; bath towel

Lakritze [la'krɪtsə] *f* (-; -n) liquorice

lallen ['lalən] *v/i and v/t* (ge-, h) speak drunkenly; *baby:* babble

Lamm [lam] *n* (-[e]s; *Lämmer* ['lɛmɐ]) ZO lamb; **~fell** *n* lambskin

Lampe ['lampə] *f* (-; -n) lamp, light; bulb

'Lampenfieber *n* stage fright

'Lampenschirm *m* lampshade

Lampion [lam'pjõː] *m* (-s; -s) Chinese lantern

Land [lant] *n* (-[e]s; *Länder* ['lɛndɐ]) land; country; AGR ground, soil; ECON land, property; *an ~ gehen* MAR go ashore; *auf dem ~e* in the country; *aufs ~ fahren* go into the country; *au-ßer ~es gehen* go abroad; **~arbeiter** *m* farmhand; **~bevölkerung** *f* country *or* rural population

Landebahn ['landə-] *f* AVIAT runway

land'einwärts *adv* up-country, inland

landen ['landən] *v/i* (ge-, sein) land; *fig ~ in* (*dat*) end up in

'Landenge *f* neck of land, isthmus

'Landeplatz *m* AVIAT landing field

Länderspiel ['lɛndɐ-] *n* SPORT international match

'Landes|grenze *f* national border; **~in-nere** *n* interior; **~re,gierung** *f* Land (*Austrian* Provincial) government; **~sprache** *f* national language

'landesüblich *adj* customary

'**Landes**|**verrat** *m* treason; **~verräter** *m* traitor (to one's country); **~verteidigung** *f* national defen\se, *Br* -ce

'**Land**|**flucht** *f* rural exodus; **~friedensbruch** *m* JUR breach of the public peace; **~gericht** *n* JUR *appr* regional superior court; **~gewinnung** *f* reclamation of land; **~haus** *n* country house, cottage; **~karte** *f* map; **~kreis** *m* district

landläufig *adj* customary, current, common

ländlich ['lɛntlɪç] *adj* rural; rustic

'**Land**|**rat** *m*, **~rätin** [-rɛːtɪn] *f* (-; -nen) *appr* District Administrator; **~ratte** F *f* MAR landlubber

'**Landschaft** *f* (-; -en) countryside; scenery; *esp* PAINT landscape

'**landschaftlich** *adj* scenic

'**Landsmann** *m* (-[e]s; -*leute*) (fellow) countryman; '**Landsmännin** [-mɛnɪn] *f* (-; -nen) fellow countrywoman

'**Land**|**straße** *f* country (*or* ordinary) road; **~streicher(in)** tramp; **~streitkräfte** *pl* MIL land forces; **~tag** *m* Land parliament

'**Landung** *f* (-; -en) landing, AVIAT *a.* touchdown

'**Landungssteg** *m* MAR gangway

'**Land**|**vermesser** [-fɛrmɛsɐ] *m* (-s; -) land surveyor; **~vermessung** *f* (-; -en) land surveying; **~weg** *m*: *auf dem ~e* by land; **~wirt(in)** farmer

'**Landwirtschaft** *f* (-; *no pl*) agriculture, farming; '**landwirtschaftlich** *adj* agricultural

'**Landzunge** *f* GEOGR promontory, spit

lang [laŋ] *adj and adv* long (time); F tall; *drei Jahre (einige Zeit) ~* for three years (some time); *den ganzen Tag ~* all day long; *seit ~em* for a long time; *vor ~er Zeit* (a) long (time) ago; *über kurz oder ~* sooner or later; *~ ersehnt* long-hoped-for; *~ erwartet* long-awaited; *gleich ~* the same length

'**langatmig** [-ʔaːtmɪç] *adj* long-winded

lange ['laŋə] *adv* (for a) long (time); *es ist schon ~ her(, seit)* it has been a long time (since); *(noch) nicht ~ her* not long ago; *noch ~* hin still a long way off; *es dauert nicht ~* it won't take long; *ich bleibe nicht ~ fort* I won't be long; *wie ~ noch?* how much longer?

Länge ['lɛŋə] *f* (-; -n) length; GEOGR longitude; *der ~ nach* (at) full length; *(sich) in die ~ ziehen* stretch (*a. fig*)

langen ['laŋən] F *v/i* (*ge-*, *h*) reach (*nach* for); be enough; *mir langt es* I've had enough, *fig a.* I'm sick of it

'**Längen**|**grad** *m* GEOGR degree of longitude; **~maß** *n* linear measure

'**Langeweile** *f* (-; *no pl*) boredom; *~ haben* be bored; *aus ~* to pass the time

langfristig *adj* long-term

langjährig [-jɛːrɪç] *adj* longstanding; *~e Erfahrung* many years of experience

'**Langlauf** *m* (-[e]s; *no pl*) SPORT cross-country (skiing)

langlebig [-leːbɪç] *adj* long-lived

länglich ['lɛŋlɪç] *adj* longish, oblong

längs [lɛŋs] **1.** *prp* (*gen*) along(side); **2.** *adv* lengthwise

langsam *adj* slow; **~er werden** *or* **fahren** slow down

'**Lang**|**schläfer** [-flɛːfɐ] *m* (-s; -), **~schläferin** [-fərɪn] *f* (-; -nen) late riser; **~spielplatte** *f* long-playing record, *mst* LP

längst [lɛŋst] *adv* long ago *or* before; *~ vorbei* long past; *ich weiß es ~* I have known it for a long time; **längstens** ['lɛŋstəns] *adv* at (the) most

'**Langstrecken...** *in cpds* long-distance ...; AVIAT, MIL long-range ...

langweilen *v/t* (*ge-*, *h*) bore; *sich ~* be bored; '**langweilig** [-vailɪç] *adj* boring, dull; **~e Person** bore

'**Langwelle** *f* PHYS, *radio:* long wave

'**langwierig** [-viːrɪç] *adj* lengthy, protracted (*a.* MED)

Lanze ['lantsə] *f* (-; -n) lance, spear

Lappalie [la'paːljə] *f* (-; -n) trifle

Lappen ['lapən] *m* (-s; -) (piece of) cloth; rag (*a. fig*)

läppisch ['lɛpɪʃ] *adj* silly; ridiculous

Lärche ['lɛrçə] *f* (-; -n) BOT larch

Lärm [lɛrm] *m* (-s; *no pl*) noise

lärmen ['lɛrmən] *v/i* (*ge-*, *h*) be noisy; **~d** *adj* noisy

Larve ['larfə] *f* (-; -n) mask; ZO larva

las [laːs] *pret of* **lesen**

lasch [laʃ] F *adj* slack, lax

Lasche ['laʃə] *f* (-; -n) flap; tongue

Laser ['leːzɐ] *m* (-s; -) PHYS laser; **~drucker** *m* EDP laser printer; **~strahl** *m* PHYS laser beam; **~technik** *f* laser technology

lassen ['lasən] v/t (irr, ge-, h) and v/aux (irr, no -ge-, h) let, leave; **j-n et. tun ~** let s.o. do s.th.; allow s.o. to do s.th.; make s.o. do s.th.; **j-n (et.) zu Hause ~ leave** s.o. (s.th.) at home; **j-n allein (in Ruhe) ~** leave s.o. alone; **sich die Haare schneiden ~** have or get one's hair cut; **sein Leben ~ (für)** lose (give) one's life (for); **rufen ~** send for, call in; **es lässt sich machen** it can be done; **lass alles so, wie (wo) es ist** leave everything as (where) it is; **er kann das Rauchen etc nicht ~** he can't stop smoking etc; **lass das!** stop it! → **grüßen, kommen**

lässig ['lɛsɪç] adj casual; careless

Last [last] f (-; -en) load, burden, weight (all a. fig); **j-m zur ~ fallen** be a burden to s.o.; **j-m et. zur ~ legen** charge s.o. with s.th.; **lasten** ['lastən] v/i (ge-, h) ~ **auf** (dat) a. fig weigh or rest (up)on

'Lastenaufzug m freight elevator, Br goods lift

Laster¹ ['lastɐ] m (-s; -) → **Lastwagen**

'Laster² n (-s; -) vice

lästern ['lɛstɐn] v/i (ge-, h) ~ **über** (acc) run down

lästig ['lɛstɪç] adj troublesome, annoying; **(j-m) ~ sein** be a nuisance (to s.o.)

'Last|kahn m barge; **~tier** n pack animal; **~wagen** m MOT truck, Br a. lorry; **~wagenfahrer** m MOT truck (Br a. lorry) driver, trucker

Latein [la'taɪn] n (-s; no pl) Latin

La'teina,merika Latin America; **La-'teinameri,kaner(in)**, **la'teinameri,ka-nisch** adj Latin American

la'teinisch adj Latin

Laterne [la'tɛrnə] f (-; -n) lantern; streetlight

La'ternenpfahl m lamppost

Latte ['latə] f (-; -n) lath; pale; SPORT bar

'Lattenzaun m paling, picket fence

Lätzchen ['lɛtsçən] n (-s; -) bib

Laub [laup] n (-[e]s; no pl) foliage, leaves; **'Laubbaum** m deciduous tree

Laube ['laubə] f (-; -n) arbo(u)r

'Laubfrosch m ZO tree frog

'Laubsäge f fretsaw

Lauch [laux] m (-[e]s; -e) BOT leek

Lauer ['lauɐ] f: **auf der ~ liegen** or **sein** lie in wait; **'lauern** v/i (ge-, h) lurk; ~ **auf** (acc) lie in wait for

Lauf [lauf] m (-[e]s; **Läufe** ['lɔɪfə]) run; course; gun: barrel; **im ~(e) der Zeit** in the course of time; **~bahn** f career; **~diszi,plin** f SPORT track event

laufen ['laufən] v/i and v/t (irr, ge-, sein) run (a. TECH, MOT, ECON); walk; fig work, run; **j-n ~ lassen** let s.o. go; let s.o. off; **~d 1.** fig adj present, current (a. ECON); continual; **auf dem Laufenden sein** be up to date; **2.** adv continuously; regularly; always

Läufer ['lɔɪfɐ] m (-s; -) runner (a. carpet); chess: bishop; **'Läuferin** f (-; -nen) runner

'Lauf|gitter n playpen; **~masche** f run, Br ladder; **~schritt** m: **im ~** on the double; **~schuhe** pl walking shoes; SPORT trainers; **~steg** m footbridge; TECH, fashion: catwalk; MAR gangway

Lauge ['laugə] f (-; -n) suds; CHEM lye

Laune ['launə] f (-; -n) mood, temper; **gute (schlechte) ~ haben** be in a good (bad) mood or temper; **launenhaft**, **'launisch** adj moody; bad-tempered

Laus [laus] f (-; **Läuse** ['lɔɪzə]) ZO louse

Lauschangriff ['lauʃ-] m bugging operation; **lauschen** ['lauʃən] v/i (ge-, h) listen (dat to); eavesdrop

lauschig ['lauʃɪç] adj snug, cozy, Br cosy

laut¹ [laut] **1.** adj loud; noisy; **2.** adv loud(ly); **vorlesen** read (out) aloud; **(sprich) ~er, bitte!** speak up, please!

laut² prp (gen or dat) according to

Laut m (-[e]s; -e) sound, noise

lauten ['lautən] v/i (ge-, h) read; be

läuten ['lɔɪtən] v/i and v/t (ge-, h) ring; **es läutet (an der Tür)** the (door)bell is ringing

lauter ['lautɐ] adv sheer (nonsense etc); nothing but; (so) many

lautlos adj silent, soundless; hushed

'Lautschrift f phonetic transcription

'Lautsprecher m TECH (loud)speaker

'Lautstärke f loudness, ELECTR a. (sound) volume; **mit voller ~** at full blast; **~regler** m volume control

lauwarm ['lau-] adj lukewarm (a. fig)

Lava ['la:va] f (-; Laven) GEOL lava

Lavabo [la'va:bo] Swiss n → **Waschbecken**

Lavendel [la'vɛndəl] m (-s; -) BOT lavender

L

Lawine [la'vi:nə] f (-; -n) avalanche

Lazarett [latsa'rɛt] n (-[e]s; -e) (military) hospital

leben ['le:bən] (ge-, h) **1.** v/i live; be alive; **von et. ~** live on s.th.; **2.** v/t live; '**Leben** n (-s; -) life; **am ~ bleiben** stay alive; survive; **am ~ sein** be alive; **ums ~ bringen** kill; **sich das ~ nehmen** take one's (own) life, commit suicide; **ums ~ kommen** lose one's life, be killed; **um sein ~ laufen (kämpfen)** run (fight) for one's life; **das tägliche ~** everyday life; **mein ~ lang** all my life; '**lebend** adj living; **lebendig** [le'bɛndɪç] adj living, alive; fig lively

'**Lebens|abend** m old age, the last years of one's life; **~bedingungen** pl living conditions; **~dauer** f life-span; TECH (service) life; **~erfahrung** f experience of life; **~erwartung** f life expectancy

'**lebensfähig** adj MED viable (a. fig)

'**Lebensgefahr** f mortal danger; **in (unter) ~** in danger (at the risk) of one's life; '**lebensgefährlich** adj dangerous (to life), perilous

'**lebensgroß** adj life-size(d)

'**Lebensgröße** f: **e-e Statue in ~** a life-size(d) statue

'**Lebenshaltungskosten** pl cost of living

'**lebenslänglich 1.** adj lifelong; **~e Freiheitsstrafe** JUR life sentence; **2.** adv for life

'**Lebenslauf** m personal record, curriculum vitae

'**lebenslustig** adj fond of life

'**Lebensmittel** pl food(stuffs); groceries; **~geschäft** n grocery, supermarket

'**lebensmüde** adj tired of life

'**Lebens|notwendigkeit** f vital necessity; **~retter(in)** lifesaver, rescuer; **~standard** m standard of living; **~unterhalt** m livelihood; **s-n ~ verdienen** earn one's living (**als** as; **mit** out of, by); **~versicherung** f life insurance; **~weise** f way of life

'**lebenswichtig** adj vital, essential

'**Lebenszeichen** n sign of life

'**Lebenszeit** f lifetime; **auf ~** for life

Leber ['le:bɐ] f (-; -n) ANAT liver; **~fleck** m mole; **~tran** m cod-liver oil

'**Lebewesen** n living being, creature

lebhaft ['le:phaft] adj lively; heavy (traffic etc)

'**Lebkuchen** m gingerbread

'**leblos** adj lifeless (a. fig)

'**Lebzeiten** pl: **zu s-n ~** in his lifetime

lechzen ['lɛçtsən] v/i (ge-, h) **~ nach** thirst for

leck [lɛk] adj leaking, leaky

Leck n (-[e]s; -s) leak

lecken[1] ['lɛkən] v/t and v/i (ge-, h) a. **~ an** (dat) lick

lecken[2] v/i (ge-, h) leak

lecker ['lɛkɐ] adj delicious, tasty, F yummy; '**Leckerbissen** m delicacy, treat (a. fig)

Leder ['le:dɐ] n (-s; -) leather; '**ledern** adj leather(n); '**Lederwaren** pl leather goods

ledig ['le:dɪç] adj single, unmarried

lediglich ['le:dɪklɪç] adv only, merely

Lee [le:] f (-; no pl) MAR lee; **nach ~** leeward

leer [le:ɐ] **1.** adj empty (a. fig); vacant (house etc); blank (page etc); ELECTR dead, Br flat; **~ stehend** unoccupied, vacant; **2.** adv: **~ laufen** TECH idle; **Leere** ['le:rə] f (-; no pl) emptiness (a. fig); '**leeren** v/t and v/refl (ge-, h) empty; '**Leergut** n empties; '**Leerlauf** m TECH idling; neutral (gear); fig running on the spot; '**Leertaste** f space bar; '**Leerung** f (-; -en) post collection

legal [le'ga:l] adj legal, lawful

legalisieren [legali'zi:rən] v/t (no -ge-, h) legalize; **Legali'sierung** f (-; -en) legalization

Legasthenie [legaste'ni:] f (-; -n) PSYCH dyslexia, F word blindness

Legastheniker [legas'te:nikɐ] m (-s; -), **Legas'thenikerin** f (-; -nen) PSYCH dyslexic

legen ['le:gən] v/t and v/i (ge-, h) lay (a. eggs); place, put; set (hair); **sich ~** lie down; fig calm down; pain: wear off

Legende [le'gɛndə] f (-; -n) legend

leger [le'ʒe:ɐ] adj casual, informal

Legislative [legɪsla'ti:və] f (-; -n) legislative power

legitim [legi'ti:m] adj legitimate

Lehm [le:m] m (-[e]s; -e) loam; clay

lehmig ['le:mɪç] adj loamy, F muddy

Lehne ['le:nə] f (-; -n) back(rest); arm (rest); '**lehnen** v/t and v/i lean (a. **sich ~**) rest (**an acc, gegen** against; **auf acc**

on); **sich aus dem Fenster** ~ lean out of the window; **'Lehnsessel** *m*, **'Lehnstuhl** *m* armchair, easy chair

Lehrbuch ['le:r-] *n* textbook

Lehre ['le:rə] *f* (-; -*n*) science; theory; REL, POL teachings, doctrine; moral; *Br a.* master; ECON apprenticeship; **in der** ~ **sein** be apprenticed (**bei** to); **das wird ihm e-e** ~ **sein** that will teach him a lesson

'lehren *v/t* (*ge-, h*) teach, instruct; show

Lehrer ['le:rɐ] *m* (-s; -) teacher, instructor, *Br a.* master; ~**ausbildung** *f* teacher training

Lehrerin ['le:rərɪn] *f* (-; -*nen*) (lady) teacher, *Br a.* mistress

'Lehrer|kollegium *n* (teaching) staff; ~**zimmer** *n* staff or teachers' room

'Lehr|gang *m* course (of instruction *or* study); training course; ~**herr** *m* master; ~**jahr** *n* year (of apprenticeship)

Lehrling ['le:rlɪŋ] *m* (-s; -e) apprentice, trainee

'Lehr|meister *m* ~**meisterin** *f* master; *fig* teacher; ~**mittel** *pl* teaching aids; ~**plan** *m* curriculum, syllabus; ~**probe** *f* demonstration lesson

'lehrreich *adj* informative, instructive

'Lehr|stelle *f* apprenticeship; vacancy for an apprentice; ~**stuhl** *m* professorship; ~**tochter** *Swiss f* apprentice; ~**vertrag** *m* indenture(s); ~**zeit** *f* apprenticeship

Leib [laip] *m* (-[e]s; *Leiber* ['laibɐ]) body; belly, ANAT abdomen; stomach; **bei lebendigem** ~**e** alive; **mit** ~ **und Seele** (with) heart and soul

Leibeserziehung ['laibəs-] *f* PED physical education, ABBR PE; ~**kräfte** *pl*: **aus** ~**n** with all one's might

'Leibgericht *n* GASTR favo(u)rite dish

leibhaftig [laip'haftɪç] *adj*: **der** ~**e Teufel** the devil incarnate; ~**es Ebenbild** living image; **ich sehe ihn noch** ~ **vor mir** I can see him (before me) now

'leiblich *adj* physical

'Leib|rente *f* life annuity; ~**wache** *f*, ~**wächter** *m* bodyguard; ~**wäsche** *f* underwear

Leiche ['laiçə] *f* (-; -*n*) (dead) body, corpse

leichen'blass *adj* deadly pale

'Leichen|halle *f* mortuary; ~**schauhaus** *n* morgue; ~**verbrennung** *f* cremation; ~**wagen** *m* hearse

leicht [laiçt] *adj* light (*a. fig*); easy, simple; slight, minor; TECH light(weight); ~**möglich** quite possible; ~ **gekränkt** easily offended; **es fällt mir (nicht)** ~ (**zu** *inf*) I find it easy (difficult) (to *inf*); **das ist** ~ **gesagt** it's not as easy as that; **es geht** ~ **kaputt** it breaks easily; **et.** ~ **nehmen** not worry about s.th.; make light of s.th.; **nimm's** ~**!** never mind!, don't worry about it!; ~**verständlich** easy to understand

'Leicht|ath,let *m* SPORT (track-and-field) athlete; ~**ath,letik** *f* SPORT track and field (events), athletics; ~**ath,letin** *f* SPORT (track-and-field) athlete; ~**gewicht** *n* SPORT lightweight

'leichtgläubig *adj* credulous

Leichtigkeit ['laiçtiçkait] *f*: **mit** ~ easily, with ease

'leichtlebig [-le:biç] *adj* happy-go-lucky

'Leichtme,tall *n* light metal

'Leichtsinn *m* (-[e]s; *no pl*) carelessness; recklessness; **'leichtsinnig** *adj* careless; reckless

Leid [lait] *n* (-[e]s; *no pl*) sorrow, grief; pain; **es tut mir** ~ I'm sorry (**um** for; **wegen** about; **dass ich zu spät komme** for being late)

leiden ['laidən] *v/t and v/i* (*irr, ge-, h*) suffer (**an** *dat*, **unter** *dat* from); **j-n gut** ~ **können** like s.o.; **ich kann ... nicht** ~ I don't like ...; I can't stand ...; **'Leiden** *n* (-s; -) suffering(s); MED disease

'Leidenschaft *f* (-; -*en*) passion

'leidenschaftlich *adj* passionate; vehement

'Leidensgenosse *m*, **'Leidensgenossin** *f* fellow sufferer

leider ['laidɐ] *adv* unfortunately; ~ **ja** (**nein**) I'm afraid so (not)

'leidlich *adj* passable, F so-so

'Leidtragende *m, f* (-*n*; -*n*) mourner; **er ist der** ~ **dabei** he is the one who suffers for it

'Leidwesen *n*: **zu m-m** ~ to my regret

Leierkasten *m* ['laiɐ-] *m* barrel organ; ~**mann** *m* organ grinder

leiern ['laiɐn] *v/i and v/t* (*ge-, h*) crank (up); *fig* drone

Leihbücherei ['lai-] *f* public library

leihen ['laiən] *v/t* (*irr, ge-, h*) lend; rent (*Br* hire) out; borrow (**von** from); rent, hire

'**Leih|gebühr** f rental, lending fee;
~**haus** n pawnshop, pawnbroker's
(shop); ~**mutter** F f surrogate mother;
~**wagen** m MOT rented (Br hire) car
'**leihweise** adv on loan
Leim [laim] m (-[e]s; -e), **leimen** ['laimən]
v/t (ge-, h) glue
Leine ['lainə] f (-; -n) line; lead, leash
Leinen ['lainən] n (-s; -) linen; canvas; **in**
~ **gebunden** clothbound
'**Leinenschuh** m canvas shoe
'**Lein|samen** m BOT linseed; ~**tuch** n
(linen) sheet; ~**wand** f linen; PAINT
canvas; screen
leise ['laizə] adj quiet, a. low, soft (voice,
a. music etc); fig slight, faint; ~**r stellen**
turn (the volume) down
Leiste ['laistə] f (-; -n) ledge; ANAT groin
'**leisten** v/t (ge-, h) do, work; achieve, accomplish; render (service etc); take
(oath); **gute Arbeit** ~ do a good job;
sich et. ~ treat o.s. to s.th.; **ich kann**
es mir (nicht) ~ I can('t) afford it
'**Leistung** f (-; -en) performance;
achievement; PED a. (piece of) work,
result, TECH a. output; service, benefit
'**Leistungsdruck** m (-[e]s; no pl) pressure, stress
'**leistungsfähig** adj efficient; (physically) fit; '**Leistungsfähigkeit** f (-; no
pl) efficiency (a. TECH, ECON); fitness
'**Leistungskon,trolle** f (achievement
or proficiency) test; ~**kurs** m PED appr
special subject; ~**sport** m competitive
sport(s)
Leitar,tikel ['lait-] m editorial, esp Br
leader, leading article
leiten ['laitən] v/t (ge-, h) lead, guide (a.
fig), conduct (a. PHYS, MUS); run (a.
PED), be in charge of, manage; TV etc
direct; host; ~**d** adj leading; PHYS con-
ductive; ~**e Stellung** key position; ~**er**
Angestellter executive
Leiter[1] ['laitə] f (-; -n) ladder
'**Leiter**[2] m (-s; -) leader; conductor (a.
PHYS, MUS); ECON etc head, manager;
chairman; → **Schulleiter**
Leiterin ['laitərın] f (-; -nen) leader;
head; chairwoman
'**Leit|faden** m manual, guide; ~**planke** f
MOT guardrail, Br crash barrier;
~**spruch** m motto
'**Leitung** f (-; -en) ECON management;
head office; administration; chairman-
ship; organization; THEA etc direction;
TECH main, pipe(s); ELECTR, TEL line;
die ~ **haben** be in charge; **unter der**
~ **von** MUS conducted by
'**Leitungsrohr** n pipe
'**Leitungswasser** n tap water
Lektion [lɛk'tsjoːn] f (-; -en) lesson
Lektüre [lɛk'tyːrə] f (-; -n) reading (matter); PED reader
Lende ['lɛndə] f (-; -n) ANAT loin; GASTR
sirloin
lenken ['lɛŋkən] v/t (ge-, h) steer, drive;
fig guide s.o.; direct (traffic etc)
Lenker ['lɛŋkə] m (-s; -) handlebar
'**Lenkrad** n MOT steering wheel
'**Lenkung** f (-; -en) MOT steering (system)
Leopard [leo'part] m (-en; -en) ZO
leopard
Lerche ['lɛrçə] f (-; -n) ZO lark
lernen ['lɛrnən] v/t and v/i (ge-, h) learn;
study; **er lernt leicht** he is a quick
learner; **lesen** ~ learn (how) to read
'**Lernmittelfreiheit** f free books etc
lesbar ['leːsbaːɐ] adj readable
Lesbierin ['lɛsbjərın] f (-; -nen), **les-**
bisch ['lɛsbɪʃ] adj lesbian
'**Lesebuch** ['leːzə-] n reader
'**Leselampe** f reading lamp
lesen ['leːzən] v/i and v/t (irr, ge-, h)
read; AGR harvest
'**lesenswert** adj worth reading
Leser ['leːzɐ] m (-s; -) reader
'**Leseratte** F f bookworm
'**Leserbrief** m letter to the editor
'**Leserin** f (-; -nen) reader
'**leserlich** adj legible
'**Lesestoff** m reading matter
'**Lesezeichen** n bookmark
'**Lesung** f (-; -en) reading (a. PARL)
Letzt [lɛtst] f: **in** ~**r Zeit** ~ in the end
letzte ['lɛtstə] adj last; latest; **zum** ~**n**
Mal(e) for the last time; **in** ~**r Zeit** recently; **als Letzter ankommen** etc ar-
rive etc last; **Letzter sein** be last (a.
SPORT); **das ist das Letzte!** that's the
limit!; '**letztens** adv finally; **erst** ~ just
recently; **letztere** ['lɛtstərə] adj latter;
der (die, das) Letztere the latter
Leuchtanzeige ['lɔʏçt-] f luminous or
LED display light; **leuchten** ['lɔʏçtən]
v/i (ge-, h) shine; glow; '**Leuchten** n (-s;
no pl) shining; glow; '**leuchtend** adj
shining (a. fig); bright; **Leuchter**

['lɔʏçtɐ] m (-s; -) candlestick

'Leucht|farbe f luminous paint; **~re-
,klame** f neon sign(s); **~(stoff)röhre** f
ELECTR fluorescent lamp; **~turm** m
lighthouse; **~ziffer** f luminous figure

leugnen ['lɔʏɡnən] v/t and v/i (ge-, h)
deny (**et. getan zu haben** having done
s.th.)

Leute ['lɔʏtə] pl people, F folks

Leutnant ['lɔʏtnant] m (-s; -s) MIL second lieutenant

Lexikon ['leksikɔn] n (-s; -ka, -ken)
encyclop(a)edia; dictionary

Libelle [li'bɛlə] f (-; -n) ZO dragonfly

liberal [libe'raːl] adj liberal

Libero ['liːbero] m (-s; -s) soccer:
sweeper

licht [lɪçt] adj bright; fig lucid

Licht n (-[e]s; -er ['lɪçtɐ]) a) light, b) (no
pl) brightness; **~ machen** switch or
turn on the light(s)

'Licht|bild n photo(graph); slide; **~bil-
dervortrag** m slide lecture; **~blick** m
ray of hope; bright moment

lichtempfindlich adj sensitive to light;
PHOT sensitive; 'Lichtempfindlichkeit
f (light) sensitivity; PHOT speed

lichten ['lɪçtən] v/t (ge-, h) clear; **den
Anker ~** MAR weigh anchor; **sich ~** get
thin(ner); fig be thinning (out)

'Licht|geschwindigkeit f speed of
light; **~griffel** m light pen; **~hupe** f
MOT (headlight) flash(er); **die ~ betätigen** flash one's lights; **~jahr** n light
year; **~ma,schine** f MOT generator;
~orgel f colo(u)r organ; **~pause** f
blueprint; **~schacht** m well; **~schalter**
m (light) switch

'lichtscheu fig adj shady

'Licht|schutzfaktor m sun protection
factor, SPF; **~strahl** m ray or beam of
light (a. fig)

Lichtung f (-; -en) clearing

Lid [liːt] n (-[e]s; Lider ['liːdɐ]) ANAT
(eye)lid; **~schatten** m eye shadow

lieb [liːp] adj dear; nice, kind; good; **~
gewinnen** get fond of; **~ ha-
ben**, love, be fond of; Liebe ['liːbə] f
(-; no pl) love (**zu** of, for); **aus ~ zu** out
of love for; **~ auf den ersten Blick** love
at first sight; 'lieben v/t (ge-, h) love, a.
be in love with s.o.; make love to

'liebenswert adj lovable, charming,
sweet

'liebenswürdig adj kind; 'Liebenswürdigkeit f (-; -en) kindness

lieber ['liːbɐ] adv rather, sooner; **~ haben** prefer, like better; **ich möchte ~
(nicht)** ... I'd rather (not) ...; **du solltest ~ (nicht)** ... you had better (not) ...

'Liebes|brief m love letter; **~erklärung**
f: **j-m e-e ~ machen** declare one's love
to s.o.; **~kummer** m: **~ haben** be love-
sick; **~paar** n lovers

'liebevoll adj loving, affectionate

Liebhaber ['liːphaːbɐ] m (-s; -) lover (a.
fig); **~... in** cpds **...preis, ...stück** etc: collector's ...; Liebhaberei [liːphaːbə'raɪ] f
(-; -en) hobby

Liebkosung [liːp'koːzʊŋ] f (-; -en) caress

'lieblich adj lovely, charming, sweet (a.
wine)

'Liebling m (-s; -e) darling; favo(u)rite

'Lieblings... in cpds mst favo(u)rite

'lieblos adj unloving, cold; unkind
(words etc); fig careless

Lied [liːt] n (-[e]s; -er ['liːdɐ]) song; tune

liederlich ['liːdɐlɪç] adj slovenly, sloppy

Liedermacher ['liːdɐ-] m (-s; -) singer-
-songwriter

lief [liːf] pret of laufen

L

Lieferant [liːfə'rant] m (-en; -en) ECON
supplier; lieferbar ['liːfɐbaːɐ] adj ECON
available; 'Lieferfrist f ECON term of
delivery; liefern ['liːfɐn] v/t (ge-, h)
ECON deliver; **j-m et. ~** supply s.o. with
s.th.; Lieferung ['liːfərʊŋ] f (-; -en)
ECON delivery; supply

'Lieferwagen m MOT (delivery) van

Liege ['liːɡə] f (-; -n) couch

liegen ['liːɡən] v/i (irr, ge-, h) lie, a. be
(situated); (**krank**) **im Bett ~** be (ill) in
bed; **nach Osten (der Straße) ~** face
east (the street); **daran liegt es(, dass)**
that's (the reason) why; **es (er) liegt
mir nicht** F it (he) is not my cup of tea;
mir liegt viel (wenig) daran it means a
lot (doesn't mean much) to me; **~ bleiben** stay in bed; be left behind; **~ lassen** leave (behind); F **j-n links ~ lassen** ignore s.o., give s.o. the cold
shoulder

'Liege|sitz m reclining seat; **~stuhl** m
deckchair; **~stütz** m (-es; -e) SPORT
push-up, Br press-up; **~wagen** m RAIL
couchette

lieh [liː] pret of leihen

ließ [li:s] *pret of* **lassen**

Lift [lɪft] *m* (-[e]s; -e, -s) elevator, *Br* lift; ski lift

Liga ['li:ga] *f* (-; *Ligen*) league, SPORT *a.* division

Likör [li'køːɐ] *m* (-s; -e) liqueur

lila ['li:la] *adj* purple, violet

Lilie ['li:liə] *f* (-; -n) BOT lily

Liliputaner [lilipu'taːnɐ] *m* (-s; -) dwarf, midget

Limonade [limo'naːdə] *f* (-; -n) pop; lemon soda, *Br* lemonade

Limousine [limu'ziːnə] *f* (-; -n) MOT sedan, *Br* saloon car; limousine

Linde ['lɪndə] *f* (-; -n) BOT lime (tree), linden

lindern ['lɪndɐn] *v/t* (ge-, h) relieve, ease, alleviate; **Linderung** ['lɪndərʊŋ] *f* (-; *no pl*) relief, alleviation

Lineal [line'aːl] *n* (-s; -e) ruler

Linie ['li:niə] *f* (-; -n) line; **auf s-e ~ achten** watch one's weight

'Linien|flug *m* AVIAT scheduled flight; **~richter** *m* SPORT linesman

'linientreu *adj* POL: **~ sein** follow the party line

linieren [li'niːrən], **liniieren** [lini'iːrən] *v/t* (*no ge-*, h) rule, line

linke ['lɪŋkə] *adj* left (*a.* POL); **auf der ~n Seite** on the left(-hand side); **'Linke** *m, f* (-n; -n) POL leftist; left-winger

linkisch ['lɪŋkɪʃ] *adj* awkward, clumsy

links [lɪŋks] *adv* on the left (*a.* POL); on the wrong side; **nach ~** (to the) left; **~ von** to the left of

Links... *in cpds* ...*verkehr etc:* left-hand

Links'außen *m* (-; -) SPORT outside left, left wing

'Linkshänder [-hɛndɐ] *m* (-s; -), **'Linkshänderin** *f* (-; -nen) left-hander

'Linksradi,kale *m, f* (-n; -n) POL left-wing extremist

Linse ['lɪnzə] *f* (-; -n) ANAT lentil; OPT lens

Lippe ['lɪpə] *f* (-; -n) ANAT lip

'Lippenstift *m* lipstick

liquidieren [likvi'diːrən] *v/t* (*no ge-*, h) ECON liquidate (*a.* POL)

lispeln ['lɪspəln] *v/i* (ge-, h) (have a) lisp

List [lɪst] *f* (-; -en) a) trick, b) (*no pl*) cunning

Liste ['lɪstə] *f* (-; -n) list; roll

listig ['lɪstɪç] *adj* cunning, tricky, sly

Liter ['liːtɐ] *n, m* (-s; -) liter, *Br* litre

literarisch [lɪtəˈraːrɪʃ] *adj* literary

Literatur [lɪtəraˈtuːɐ] *f* (-; -en) literature; **~... in cpds** ...*kritik etc:* *mst* literary

Litfaßsäule ['lɪtfas-] *f* advertising pillar

litt [lɪt] *pret of* **leiden**

Lizenz [li'tsɛnts] *f* (-; -en) license, *Br* licence

Lkw, LKW ['ɛlkave] *m* (-[s]; -) ABBR *of* **Lastkraftwagen** truck, *Br a.* lorry

Lob [loːp] *n* (-[e]s; *no pl*) praise; **loben** ['loːbən] *v/t* (ge-, h) praise; **'lobenswert** *adj* praiseworthy, laudable

Loch [lɔx] *n* (-[e]s; *Löcher* ['lœçɐ]) hole (*a. fig*); puncture; **lochen** ['lɔxən] *v/t* (ge-, h) punch (*a.* TECH); **Locher** ['lɔxɐ] *m* (-s; -) punch

Locke ['lɔkə] *f* (-; -n) curl; lock

locken[1] ['lɔkən] *v/t and v/refl* (ge-, h) curl

locken[2] *v/t* (ge-, h) lure, entice, *fig a.* attract, tempt

'Locken|kopf *m* curly head; **~wickler** [-vɪklɐ] *m* (-s; -) curler, roller

locker ['lɔkɐ] *adj* loose; slack; *fig* relaxed; **'lockern** *v/t* (ge-, h) loosen, slacken; relax (*a. fig*); **sich ~** loosen, (be)come loose; SPORT limber up; *fig* relax

lockig ['lɔkɪç] *adj* curly, curled

'Lockvogel *m* decoy (*a. fig*)

lodern ['loːdɐn] *v/i* (ge-, h) blaze, flare

Löffel ['lœfəl] *m* (-s; -) spoon; ladle

'löffeln *v/t* (ge-, h) spoon up

log [loːk] *pret of* **lügen**

Logbuch ['lɔk-] *n* MAR log

Loge ['loːʒə] *f* (-; -n) THEA box; lodge

Logik ['loːgɪk] *f* (-; *no pl*) logic

logisch ['loːgɪʃ] *adj* logical

'logischer'weise *adv* obviously

Lohn [loːn] *m* (-[e]s; *Löhne* ['løːnə]) ECON wages, pay(ment); *fig* reward; **~empfänger** *m* wageworker, *Br* wage earner

lohnen ['loːnən] *v/refl* (ge-, h) be worth (while), pay; **es** (*die Mühe*) **lohnt sich** it's worth it (the trouble); **das Buch** (*der Film*) **lohnt sich** the book (film) is worth reading (seeing); **~d** *adj* paying; *fig* rewarding

'Lohn|erhöhung *f* raise, *Br* increase in wages, rise; **~steuer** *f* income tax; **~stopp** *m* wage freeze; **~tüte** *f* pay packet

Loipe ['lɔʏpə] *f* (-; -n) (cross-country) course

Lokal [lo'kaːl] *n* (-s; -e) restaurant; bar, saloon, *esp Br* pub

Lo'kal... *in cpds mst* local

Lok [lɔk] *f* (-; -s) → **Lokomotive**; **~füh-rer** *m* RAIL engineer, *Br* train driver

Lokomotive [lokomo'tiːvə] *f* (-; -n) RAIL engine

Lorbeer ['lɔrbeːɐ] *m* (-s; -en) BOT laurel; GASTR bay leaf

Lore ['loːrə] *f* (-; -n) TECH tipcart

los [loːs] *adj and adv* off; *dog etc*: loose; **~ sein** be rid of; **was ist ~?** what's the matter?, F what's up?; what's going on (here)?; **hier ist nicht viel ~** there's nothing much going on here; F **da ist was ~!** that's where the action is!; F **al-so ~!** okay, let's go!

Los [loːs] *n* (-es; -e ['loːzə]) lot, *fig a.* fate; (lottery) ticket, number

losbinden *v/t* (*irr*, **binden**, *sep*, *-ge-*, *h*) untie

Löschblatt ['lœʃ-] *n* blotting paper

löschen ['lœʃən] *v/t* (*ge-*, *h*) extinguish, put out; quench (*thirst*); blot (*ink*); wipe off *the blackboard*; erase, EDP *a*. delete; slake (*lime*); MAR unload

'Löschpa,pier *n* blotting paper

lose ['loːzə] *adj* loose

Lösegeld ['løːzə-] *n* ransom

losen ['loːzən] *v/i* (*ge-*, *h*) draw lots (**um** for)

lösen ['løːzən] *v/t* (*ge-*, *h*) undo (*knot etc*); loosen, relax; TECH release; take off; solve (*problem etc*); settle (*conflict etc*); buy, get (*ticket etc*); dissolve (*a.* CHEM); **sich ~** come loose *or* undone; *fig* free o.s. (**von** from)

'los|fahren *v/i* (*irr*, **fahren**, *sep*, *-ge-*, *sein*) leave; drive off; **~gehen** *v/i* (*irr*, **gehen**, *sep*, *-ge-*, *sein*) leave; start, begin; *shot etc*: go off; **auf j-n ~** go for s.o.; **ich gehe jetzt los** I'm off now; **~ketten** *v/t* (*sep*, *-ge-*, *h*) unchain; **~kommen** *v/i* (*irr*, **kommen**, *sep*, *-ge-*, *sein*) get away (**von** from); **~lassen** *v/t* (*irr*, **lassen**, *sep*, *-ge-*, *h*) let go; **den Hund ~ auf** (*acc*) set the dog on; **~legen** F *v/i* (*sep*, *-ge-*, *h*) get cracking

löslich ['løːslɪç] *adj* CHEM soluble

'los|machen *v/t* (*sep*, *-ge-*, *h*) → **lösen**; **~reißen** *v/t* (*irr*, **reißen**, *sep*, *-ge-*, *h*) tear off; **sich ~** break away; *esp fig* tear o.s. away (*both*: **von** from); **~sagen** *v/refl* (*sep*, *-ge-*, *h*) **sich ~ von** break

with; **~schlagen** *v/i* (*irr*, **schlagen**, *sep*, *-ge-*, *h*) strike (**auf j-n** out at s.o.); **~schnallen** *v/t* (*sep*, *-ge-*, *h*) unbuckle; **sich ~** MOT, AVIAT unfasten one's seatbelt; **~stürzen** *v/i* (*sep*, *-ge-*, *sein*) **~ auf** (*acc*) rush at

Losung ['loːzʊŋ] *f* (-; -en) MIL password; *fig* slogan

Lösung ['løːzʊŋ] *f* (-; -en) solution (*a. fig*); settlement

'Lösungsmittel *n* solvent

'loswerden *v/t* (*irr*, **werden**, *sep*, *-ge-*, *sein*) get rid of; spend (*money*); lose

'losziehen *v/i* (*irr*, **ziehen**, *sep*, *-ge-*, *sein*) set out, take off, march away

Lot [loːt] *n* (-[e]s; -e) plumbline

löten ['løːtən] *v/t* (*ge-*, *h*) TECH solder

Lotion [lo'tsjoːn] *f* (-; -en) lotion

Lotse ['loːtsə] *m* (-n; -n), **'lotsen** *v/t* (*ge-*, *h*) MAR pilot

Lotterie [lɔtə'riː] *f* (-; -n) lottery; **~gewinn** *m* prize; **~los** *n* lottery ticket

Lotto ['lɔto] *n* (-s; -s) lotto, bingo; *Br* national lottery; *in Germany*: Lotto; (*im*) **~ spielen** do Lotto; **~schein** *m* Lotto coupon; **~ziehung** *f* Lotto draw

Löwe ['løːvə] *m*(-n; -n) ZO lion; AST Leo; **er ist** (*ein*) **~** he's a (a) Leo

'Löwenzahn *m* BOT dandelion

Löwin ['løːvɪn] *f* (-; -nen) ZO lioness

loyal [loa'jaːl] *adj* loyal, faithful

Luchs [lʊks] *m* (-es; -e) ZO lynx

Lücke ['lʏkə] *f* (-; -n) gap (*a. fig*); **Lü-ckenbüßer** *m* stopgap; **'lückenhaft** *adj* full of gaps; *fig* incomplete; **'lücken-los** *adj* without a gap; *fig* complete; **'Lückentest** *m* PSYCH completion *or* fill-in test

lud [luːt] *pret of* **laden**

Luft [lʊft] *f* (-; *no pl*) air; **an der frischen ~** (out) in the fresh air; (**frische**) **~ schöpfen** get a breath of fresh air; **die ~ anhalten** catch (*esp fig a*. hold) one's breath; **tief ~ holen** take a deep breath; **in die ~ sprengen** (F **fliegen**) blow up

'Luft|angriff *m* air raid; **~ballon** *m* balloon; **~bild** *n* aerial photograph *or* view; **~blase** *f* air bubble; **~brücke** *f* airlift

'luftdicht *adj* airtight

'Luftdruck *m* (-[e]s; *no pl*) PHYS, TECH air pressure

lüften ['lʏftən] v/t and v/i (ge-, h) air, ventilate; fig reveal

'**Luft|fahrt** f (-; no pl) aviation, aeronautics; **~feuchtigkeit** f (atmospheric) humidity; **~gewehr** n airgun

'**luftig** adj airy; breezy; light (dress etc)

'**Luft|kissen** n air cushion; **~kissenfahrzeug** n hovercraft; **~krankheit** f air-sickness; **~krieg** m air warfare; **~kurort** m (climatic) health resort

'**luftleer** adj: **~er Raum** vacuum

'**Luft|linie** f: **50 km ~** 50 km as the crow flies; **~post** f air mail; **~pumpe** f air pump; bicycle pump; **~röhre** f ANAT windpipe, trachea; **~schlange** f streamer; **~schloss** n castle in the air; **~sprünge** pl: **~ machen vor Freude** jump for joy

'**Lüftung** f (-; -en) airing; TECH ventilation

'**Luft|veränderung** f change of air; **~verkehr** m air traffic; **~verschmutzung** f air pollution; **~waffe** f MIL air force; **~weg** m: **auf dem ~** by air; **~zug** m draft, Br draught

Lüge ['lyːɡə] f (-; -n) lie; '**lügen** v/i (irr, ge-, h) lie, tell a lie or lies; **das ist gelogen** that's a lie; **Lügner(in)** ['lyːɡnɐ (-nərɪn)] (-s; -/-; -nen) liar; '**lügnerisch** [-nərɪʃ] adj false

Luke ['luːkə] f (-; -n) hatch; skylight

Lümmel ['lʏməl] F m (-s; -) rascal

lumpen ['lʊmpən] F v/t: **sich nicht ~ lassen** be generous

'**Lumpen** m (-s; -) rag; **in ~** in rags; **~pack** F n sl bastards

lumpig ['lʊmpɪç] F adj: **für ~e zwei Mark** for a paltry two marks

Lunge ['lʊŋə] f (-; -n) ANAT lungs; (**auf**) **~ rauchen** inhale

'**Lungen|entzündung** f MED pneumonia; **~flügel** m ANAT lung; **~zug** m: **e-n ~ machen** inhale

Lupe ['luːpə] f (-; -n) magnifying glass; **unter die ~ nehmen** scrutinize (closely)

Lust [lʊst] f (-; Lüste ['lʏstə]) a) (no pl) desire, interest; pleasure, delight, b) lust; **~ haben auf et.** (**et. zu tun**) feel like (doing) s.th.; **hättest du ~ auszugehen?** would you like to go out?, how about going out?; **ich habe keine ~** I don't feel like it, I'm not in the mood for it; **die ~ an et. verlieren** (**j-m die ~ an et. nehmen**) (make s.o.) lose all interest in s.th.

lüstern ['lʏstɐn] adj greedy (**nach** for)

lustig ['lʊstɪç] adj funny; cheerful; **er ist sehr ~** he is full of fun; **es war sehr ~** it was great fun; **sich ~ machen über** (acc) make fun of

'**lustlos** adj listless, indifferent

'**Lustmord** m sex murder

'**Lustspiel** n THEA comedy

lutschen ['lʊtʃən] v/i and v/t (ge-, h) suck

Luv [luːf] f (-; no pl) MAR windward, weather side

luxuriös [lʊksuˈrjøːs] adj luxurious

Luxus ['lʊksʊs] m (-; no pl) luxury; **~ar,tikel** m luxury (article); **~ausführung** f deluxe version; **~ho,tel** n five--star (or luxury) hotel

'**Lymphdrüse** ['lʏmf-] f ANAT lymph gland

lynchen ['lʏnçən] v/t (ge-, h) lynch

Lyrik ['lyːrɪk] f (-; no pl) poetry

Lyriker ['lyːrɪkɐ] m (-s; -), '**Lyrikerin** f (-; -nen) (lyric) poet

lyrisch ['lyːrɪʃ] adj lyrical (a. fig)

M

machbar ['maxbaːɐ] *adj* feasible

machen ['maxən] *v/t (ge-, h)* do; make; GASTR make, prepare; fix (*a. fig*); be, come to, amount to; take, pass (*test etc*); make, go on (*a trip etc*); **Hausaufgaben ~** do one's homework; **da(gegen) kann man nichts ~** it can't be helped; **mach, was du willst!** do as you please!; (**nun**) **mach mal** *or* **schon!** hurry up!, come on *or* along now!; **mach's gut!** take care (of yourself)!, good luck!; (**das**) **macht nichts** it doesn't matter; **mach dir nichts d(a)raus!** never mind!, don't worry!; **das macht mir nichts aus** I don't mind *or* care; **was** *or* **wie viel macht das?** how much is it?; **sich et. (nichts) ~ aus** (not) care about; (not) care for

'Machenschaften *pl* machinations; **unsaubere ~** sleaze (*esp* POL)

Macher ['maxɐ] *m (-s; -)* man of action, doer

Macho ['matʃo] *m (-s; -s)* macho

Macht [maxt] *f (-; Mächte* ['mɛçtə]) power (*über acc* of); **an der ~** in power; **mit aller ~** with all one's might

'Machthaber [-haːbɐ] *m (-s; -)* POL ruler

mächtig ['mɛçtɪç] *adj* powerful, mighty (*a. F*); enormous, huge

'Machtkampf *m* struggle for power

'machtlos *adj* powerless

'Macht|missbrauch *m* abuse of power; **~poli,tik** *f* power politics; **~übernahme** *f* takeover; **~wechsel** *m* transition of power

Mädchen ['mɛːtçən] *n (-s; -)* girl; maid

'mädchenhaft *adj* girlish

'Mädchen|name *m* girl's name; maiden name; **~schule** *f* girls' school

Made ['maːdə] *f (-; -n)* ZO maggot; worm

Mädel ['mɛːdəl] *n (-s; -s)* girl

'madig *adj* maggoty, worm-eaten; F *j-m et. ~ machen* spoil s.th. for s.o.

Magazin [maga'tsiːn] *n (-s; -e)* magazine (*a.* MIL, PHOT, TV); store(room), warehouse

Magd [maːkt] *f (-; Mägde* ['mɛːktə]) (female) farmhand

Magen ['maːgən] *m (-s; Mägen* ['mɛːgən]) ANAT stomach; **~beschwerden** *pl* MED stomach trouble; **~geschwür** *n* MED (stomach) ulcer; **~schmerzen** *pl* stomachache

mager ['maːgɐ] *adj* lean, thin, skinny; GASTR low-fat (*cheese*), lean (*meat*), skim (*milk*); *fig* meager, *Br* meagre

Magie [ma'giː] *f (-; no pl)* magic

magisch ['maːgɪʃ] *adj* magic(al)

Magister [ma'gɪstɐ] *m (-s; -)* UNIV Master of Arts *or* Science; *Austrian →* **Apotheker**

Magistrat [magɪs'traːt] *m (-[e]s; -e)* municipal council

Magnet [ma'gneːt] *m (-[e]s, -en; -e[n])* magnet (*a. fig*); **~... in cpds** ...band, ...feld, ...nadel etc: magnetic ...

mag'netisch *adj* magnetic (*a. fig*)

magnetisieren [magneti'ziːrən] *v/t (no -ge-, h)* magnetize

Mahagoni [maha'goːni] *n (-s; no pl)* mahogany

mähen ['mɛːən] *v/t (ge-, h)* mow; cut; AGR reap; **'Mähdrescher** [-drɛʃɐ] *m (-s; -)* AGR combine (harvester)

mahlen ['maːlən] *v/t (irr, ge-, h)* grind; mill

'Mahlzeit *f (-; -en)* meal; feed(ing)

Mähne ['mɛːnə] *f (-; -n)* ZO mane (*a. F*)

mahnen ['maːnən] *v/t (ge-, h)* remind; ECON send *s.o.* a reminder

'Mahngebühr *f* reminder fee

'Mahnmal *n* memorial

'Mahnung *f (-; -en)* reminder

Mai [mai] *m (-[e]s; -e)* May; *der Erste ~* May Day; **~baum** *m* maypole; **~glöckchen** *n* BOT lily of the valley; **~käfer** *m* ZO cockchafer

Mais [mais] *m (-es; -e)* BOT corn, *Br* maize

Majestät [majɛs'tɛːt] *f: Seine (Ihre, Eure) ~* His (Her, Your) Majesty

majes'tätisch *adj* majestic

Majonäse *f →* **Mayonnaise**

Major [ma'joːɐ] *m (-s; -e)* MIL major

makaber [ma'kaːbɐ] *adj* macabre

Makel ['maːkəl] *m (-s; -)* blemish (*a. fig*)

mäkelig ['mɛːkəlɪç] F *adj* picky, *esp Br* choos(e)y

'makellos *adj* immaculate (*a. fig*)

mäkeln ['mɛːkəln] F v/i (ge-, h) carp, pick, nag (an dat at)

Makler ['maːklɐ] m (-s; -) ECON real estate agent; broker; **~gebühr** f fee, commission

'Maklerin f (-; -nen) ECON → **Makler**

mal [maːl] adv MATH times, multiplied by; by; F → **einmal**; **12 ~ 5 ist (gleich) 60** 12 times or multiplied by 5 is or equals 60; **ein 7 ~ 4 Meter großes Zimmer** a room 7 meters by 4

Mal¹ n (-[e]s; -e) time; **zum ersten (letzten) ~(e)** for the first (last) time; **mit e-m ~(e)** all of a sudden; **ein für alle ~(e)** once and for all

Mal² n mark

malen ['maːlən] v/t (ge-, h) paint

Maler ['maːlɐ] m (-s; -) painter

Malerei [maːlə'raɪ] f (-; -en) painting

Malerin ['maːlərɪn] f (-; -nen) (woman) painter

'malerisch fig adj picturesque

'Malkasten m paintbox

'malnehmen → **multiplizieren**

Malz [malts] n (-es; no pl) malt

'Malzbier n malt beer

Mama ['mama] F f (-; -s) mom(my), Br mum(my)

Mammut ['mamʊt] n (-s; -e, -s) ZO mammoth

man [man] indef pron you, one; they, people; **wie schreibt ~ das?** how do you spell it?; **~ sagt, dass** they or people say (that); **~ hat mir gesagt** I was told

Manager ['mɛnɪdʒɐ] m (-s; -), **'Managerin** f (-; -nen) ECON executive; SPORT manager

manch [manç], **~er** ['mançɐ], **~e** ['mançə], **~es** ['mançəs] indef pron (mst pl) some; quite a few, many

'manchmal adv sometimes, occasionally

Mandant [man'dant] m (-en; -en), **Man'dantin** f (-; -nen) JUR client

Mandarine [manda'riːnə] f (-; -n) BOT tangerine

Mandat [man'daːt] n (-[e]s; -e) POL mandate; seat; **Mandatar** [manda'taːɐ] Austrian m → **Abgeordnete**

Mandel ['mandəl] f (-; -n) BOT almond; ANAT tonsil; **~entzündung** f MED tonsillitis

Manege [ma'neːʒə] f (-; -n) (circus) ring

Mangel¹ ['maŋəl] m (-s; Mängel ['mɛŋəl]) a) (no pl) lack (an dat of), shortage, b) TECH defect, fault; shortcoming; **aus ~ an** (dat) for lack of

'Mangel² f (-; -n) mangle

'mangelhaft adj poor (quality etc); defective (goods etc); PED poor, unsatisfactory, failing

'mangeln v/t (ge-, h) mangle

'mangels prp (gen) for lack or want of

'Mangelware f: **~ sein** be scarce

Manie [ma'niː] f (-; -n) mania (a. fig)

Manieren [ma'niːrən] pl manners

manierlich [ma'niːrlɪç] adv: **sich ~ betragen** behave (decently)

Manifest [mani'fɛst] n (-[e]s; -e) manifesto

manipulieren [manipu'liːrən] v/t (no -ge-, h) manipulate

Mann [man] m (-[e]s; Männer ['mɛnɐ]) man; husband

Männchen ['mɛnçən] n (-s; -) ZO male

'Manndeckung f SPORT man-to-man marking

Mannequin ['manəkɛ̃] n (-s; -s) model

mannigfach ['manɪçfax], **'mannigfaltig** adj many and various

männlich ['mɛnlɪç] adj BIOL male; masculine (a. LING)

'Mannschaft f (-; -en) SPORT team; MAR, AVIAT crew

Manöver [ma'nøːvɐ] n (-s; -), **manövrieren** [manø'vriːrən] v/i (no -ge-, h) maneuver, Br manoeuvre

Mansarde [man'zardə] f (-; -n) room or apartment in the attic

Manschette [man'ʃɛtə] f (-; -n) cuff; TECH gasket

Man'schettenknopf m cuff-link

Mantel ['mantəl] m (-s; Mäntel ['mɛntəl]) coat; tire: casing, bicycle: tire (Br tyre) cover; TECH jacket, shell

Manuskript [manu'skrɪpt] n (-[e]s; -e) manuscript; copy

Mappe ['mapə] f (-; -n) briefcase; school bag, satchel; folder

Märchen ['mɛːrçən] n (-s; -) fairytale (a. fig); **~land** n (-[e]s; no pl) fairyland

Marder ['mardɐ] m (-s; -) ZO marten

Margarine [marga'riːnə] f (-; no pl) margarine

Margerite [margə'riːtə] f (-; -n) BOT marguerite

Marienkäfer [ma'riːən-] *m* ZO lady bug, *Br* ladybird

Marihuana [mari'huaːna] *n* (-s; *no pl*) marijuana, *sl* grass; **~ziga,rette** *f sl* joint

Marille [ma'rɪlə] *Austrian f* (-; -*n*) BOT apricot

Marine [ma'riːnə] *f* (-; -*n*) MIL navy

ma'rineblau *adj* navy blue

Marionette [marjo'nɛtə] *f* (-; -*n*) puppet (*a. fig*); **Mario'nettenthe,ater** *n* puppet show

Mark¹ [mark] *f* (-; -) mark

Mark² *n* (-[e]s; *no pl*) marrow; BOT pulp

Marke ['markə] *f* (-; -*n*) ECON brand; TECH make; trademark; stamp; badge, tag; mark; **markieren** [mar'kiːrən] *v/t* (*no -ge-, h*) mark (*a.* SPORT); F *fig* act; **Mar'kierung** *f* (-; -*en*) mark

Markise [mar'kiːzə] *f* (-; -*n*) awning, sun blind

Markt [markt] *m* (-[e]s; *Märkte* ['mɛrktə]) ECON market; **auf den ~ bringen** put on the market; **~platz** *m* market place; **~wirtschaft** *f* market economy

Marmelade [marmə'laːdə] *f* (-; -*n*) jam

Marmor ['marmoːɐ] *m* (-s; -*e*) marble

Marsch¹ [marʃ] *m* (-[e]s; *Märsche* ['mɛrʃə]) march (*a.* MUS)

Marsch² *f* (-; -*en*) GEOGR marsh, fen

Marschall ['marʃal] *m* (-s; *Marschälle* ['marʃɛlə]) MIL marshal

'Marschbefehl *m* MIL marching orders

marschieren [mar'ʃiːrən] *v/i* (*no -ge-, sein*) march

Marsmensch ['mars-] *m* Martian

Marter ['martɐ] *f* (-; -*n*) torture

'martern *v/t* (*ge-, h*) torture

'Marterpfahl *m* stake

Martinshorn ['martiːns-] *n* (police *etc*) siren

Märtyrer ['mɛrtyrɐ] *m* (-s; -), **'Märtyrerin** *f* (-; -*nen*) martyr (*a. fig*)

Marxismus [mar'ksɪsmʊs] *m* (-; *no pl*) POL Marxism; **Marxist** [mar'ksɪst] *m* (-*en*; -*en*), **mar'xistisch** *adj* POL Marxist

März [mɛrts] *m* (-[es]; -*e*) March

Marzipan [martsi'paːn] *n* (-s; -*e*) marzipan

Masche ['maʃə] *f* (-; -*n*) stitch; mesh; F trick

'Maschendraht *m* wire netting

Maschine [ma'ʃiːnə] *f* (-; -*n*) machine;

MOT engine; AVIAT plane; motorcycle; **~ schreiben** type

Ma'schinen|bau *m* (-[e]s; *no pl*) mechanical engineering; **~gewehr** *n* MIL machinegun

ma'schinenlesbar *adj* EDP machine--readable

Ma'schinen|öl *n* engine oil; **~pis,tole** *f* MIL submachine gun, machine pistol; **~schaden** *m* engine trouble *or* failure; **~schlosser** *m* (engine) fitter

Masern ['maːzɐn] *pl* MED measles

Maserung ['maːzərʊŋ] *f* (-; -*en*) grain

Maske ['maskə] *f* (-; -*n*) mask (*a.* EDP)

'Maskenball *m* fancy-dress ball

'Maskenbildner [-bɪldnɐ] *m* (-s; -), **'Maskenbildnerin** *f* (-; -*nen*) THEA *etc* make-up artist

maskieren [mas'kiːrən] *v/t* (*no -ge-, h*) mask; **sich ~** put on a mask

maskulin [masku'liːn] *adj* masculine (*a.* LING)

maß [maːs] *pret of* **messen**

Maß¹ *n* (-*es*; -*e*) measure (**für** of); dimensions, measurements, size; *fig* extent, degree; **~e und Gewichte** weights and measures; **nach ~ (gemacht)** made to measure; **in gewissem (hohem) ~e** to a certain (high) degree; **in zunehmendem ~e** increasingly; **~ halten** be moderate (**in** *dat* in)

Maß² *f* (-; -[*e*]) liter (*Br* litre) of beer

Massage [ma'saːʒə] *f* (-; -*n*) massage

Massaker [ma'saːkɐ] *n* (-s; -) massacre

Masse ['masə] *f* (-; -*n*) mass; substance; bulk; F **e-e** *Geld etc* loads *or* heaps of; **die (breite) ~**, POL **die ~n** *pl* the masses

'Maßeinheit *f* unit of measure(ment)

'Massen... in *cpds* **...medien, ...mörder** *etc*: mass ...; **~andrang** *m* crush

'massenhaft F *adv* masses *or* loads of

'Massen|karambo,lage *f* MOT pileup; **~produkti,on** *f* ECON mass production

Masseur [ma'søːɐ] *m* (-s; -*e*) masseur

Masseurin [ma'søːrɪn] *f* (-; -*nen*), **Masseuse** [ma'søːzə] *f* (-; -*n*) masseuse

'maßgebend, **'maßgeblich** [-geːplɪç] *adj* authoritative

massieren [ma'siːrən] *v/t* (*no -ge-, h*) massage

massig ['masɪç] *adj* massive, bulky

mäßig ['mɛːsɪç] *adj* moderate; poor

M

mäßigen ['mɛːsɪɡən] v/t and v/refl (ge-, h) moderate; **'Mäßigung** f (-; no pl) moderation; restraint

massiv [ma'siːf] adj solid

Mas'siv n (-s; -e) GEOL massif

'Maßkrug m beer mug, stein

'maßlos adj immoderate; gross (exaggeration)

'Maßnahme [-naːmə] f (-; -n) measure, step

'Maßregel f rule; **'maßregeln** v/t (ge-, h) reprimand; discipline

'Maßstab m scale; fig standard; **im ~ 1:10** on the scale of 1:10

maßstabgetreu adj true to scale

'maßvoll adj moderate

Mast[1] [mast] m (-[e]s; -en) MAR, TECH mast

Mast[2] f (-; -en) AGR fattening

'Mastdarm m ANAT rectum

mästen ['mɛstən] v/t (ge-, h) AGR fatten; F stuff s.o.

masturbieren [mastur'biːrən] v/i (no -ge-, h) masturbate

Match [mɛtʃ] n (-[e]s; -s, -e) game, Br match; **~ball** n tennis: match point

Material [mate'rjaːl] n (-s; -ien) material (a. fig); TECH materials

Materialismus [materja'lɪsmʊs] m (-; no pl) PHILOS materialism; **Materialist** [-'lɪst] m (-en; -en) materialist; **materia'listisch** adj materialistic

Materie [ma'teːrjə] f (-; -n) matter (a. fig); phys subject (matter); **materiell** [mate'rjɛl] adj material

Mathematik [matema'tiːk] f (-; no pl) mathematics; **Mathematiker** [mate'maːtikɐ] m (-s; -) mathematician; **mathe'matisch** adj mathematical

Matinee [mati'neː] f (-; -n) THEA etc morning performance

Matratze [ma'tratsə] f (-; -n) mattress

Matrize [ma'triːtsə] f (-; -n) stencil

Matrose [ma'troːzə] m (-n; -n) MAR sailor, seaman

Matsch [matʃ] F m (-[e]s; no pl) mud, slush; **'matschig** adj muddy, slushy

matt [mat] adj weak; exhausted, worn out; dull, pale (color); PHOT mat(t); frosted (glass); chess: checkmate

Matte ['matə] f (-; -n) mat

Mattigkeit ['matɪçkait] f (-; no pl) exhaustion, weakness

'Mattscheibe f screen; PHOT focus(s)ing screen; F (boob) tube, Br telly, box

Matura [ma'tuːra] Austrian, Swiss f → **Abitur**

Mauer ['mauɐ] f (-; -n) wall; **~blümchen** fig n wallflower; **~werk** n (-[e]s; no pl) masonry, brickwork

'mauern v/i (ge-, h) lay bricks

Maul [maul] n (-[e]s; Mäuler ['mɔʏlɐ]) ZO mouth; sl **halt's ~!** shut up!

maulen ['maulən] F v/i (ge-, h) grumble, sulk, pout

'Maul|korb m muzzle (a. fig); **~tier** n mule; **~wurf** m ZO mole; **~wurfshaufen** m, **~wurfshügel** m molehill

Maurer ['maurɐ] m (-s; -) bricklayer; **~kelle** f trowel; **~meister** m master bricklayer; **~po,lier** m foreman bricklayer

Maus [maus] f (-; Mäuse ['mɔʏzə]) ZO mouse (a. EDP)

'Mausefalle ['mauzə-] f mousetrap

Mauser ['mauzɐ] f (-; no pl) ZO mo(u)lt (-ing); **in der ~ sein** be mo(u)lting

Maut [maut] Austrian f (-; -en) toll; **~straße** f turnpike, toll road

maximal [maksi'maːl] **1.** adj maximum; **2.** adv at (the) most; **Maximum** ['maksimʊm] n (-s; -ma) maximum

Mayonnaise [majɔ'nɛːzə] f (-; -n) GASTR mayonnaise

Mäzen [mɛ'tseːn] m (-s; -e) patron; SPORT sponsor

Mechanik [me'çaːnɪk] f (-; -en) a) (no pl) PHYS mechanics, b) TECH mechanism; **Mechaniker** [me'çaːnikɐ] m (-s; -) mechanic; **mechanisch** [me'çaːnɪʃ] adj TECH mechanical; **mechanisieren** [meçani'ziːrən] v/t (no -ge-, h) mechanize; **Mechani'sierung** f (-; -en) mechanization; **Mechanismus** [meça'nɪsmʊs] m (-; -men) TECH mechanism; works

meckern ['mɛkɐn] v/i (ge-, h) ZO bleat; F grumble, bitch (**über** acc at, about)

Medaille [me'daljə] f (-; -n) medal

Me'daillengewinner m medal(l)ist

Medaillon [medal'jõː] n (-s; -s) locket

Medien ['meːdjən] pl mass media; teaching aids; audio-visual aids

Medikament [medika'mɛnt] n (-[e]s; -e) drug; medicine

meditieren [medi'tiːrən] v/i (no -ge-, h) meditate (**über** acc on)

Medizin [medi'tsiːn] f (-; -en) a) (no pl)

M

(science of) medicine, b) medicine, remedy (**gegen** for)

Mediziner [medi'tsi:nɐ] *m* (-s; -), **Medizinerin** *f* (-; -nen) (medical) doctor; UNIV medical student

medizinisch [medi'tsi:nɪʃ] *adj* medical

Meer [me:ɐ] *n* (-[e]s; -e ['me:rə]) sea (*a. fig*), ocean; **~enge** *f* GEOGR straits

Meeres|boden ['me:rəs-] *m* seabed; **~früchte** *pl* GASTR seafood; **~spiegel** *m* sea level

Meerjungfrau *f* MYTH mermaid

Meerrettich *m* (-s; -e) horseradish

Meerschweinchen [-ʃvainçən] *n* (-s; -) ZO guinea pig

Megabyte [mega'bait] *n* EDP megabyte

Mehl [me:l] *n* (-[e]s; -e) flour; meal

mehlig ['me:lɪç] *adj* mealy

Mehlspeise *Austrian f* sweet (dish)

mehr [me:ɐ] *indef pron and adv* more; **immer ~** more and more; **nicht ~** no longer, not any longer (*or* more); **noch ~** even more; **es ist kein ... ~ da** there isn't any ... left

mehrdeutig [-dɔytɪç] *adj* ambiguous

mehrere ['me:rərə] *adj and indef pron* several

Mehrheit *f* (-; -en) majority

Mehrkosten *pl* extra costs

mehrmals *adv* several times

Mehr|wegflasche *f* returnable (*or* deposit) bottle; **~wertsteuer** *f* ECON value-added tax (ABBR VAT); **~zahl** *f* (-; *no pl*) majority; LING plural (form)

Mehrzweck... *in cpds* ...*fahrzeug etc*: multi-purpose ...

meiden ['maidən] *v/t* (*irr*, ge-, h) avoid

Meile ['mailə] *f* (-; -n) mile

meilenweit *adv* (for) miles

mein [main] *poss pron and adj* my; **das ist ~er** (**~e**, **~[e]s**) that's mine

Meineid *m* JUR perjury

meinen ['mainən] *v/t* (ge-, h) think, believe; mean; say; **~ Sie** (*wirklich*)**?** do you (really) mean so?; **wie ~ Sie das?** what do you mean by that?; **sie ~ es gut** they mean well; **ich habe es nicht so gemeint** I didn't mean it; **wie ~ Sie?** (I beg your) pardon?

meinet|wegen ['mainət-] *adv* for my sake; because of me; F I don't mind *or* care

Meinung *f* (-; -en) opinion (**über** *acc*, **von** about, of); **meiner ~ nach** in my opinion; **der ~ sein, dass** be of the opinion that, feel *or* believe that; **s-e ~ äußern** express one's opinion; **s-e ~ ändern** change one's mind; **ich bin Ihrer** (*anderer*) **~** I (don't) agree with you; **j-m die ~ sagen** give s.o. a piece of one's mind

Meinungs|austausch *m* exchange of views (**über** *acc* on); **~forscher** *m* pollster; **~freiheit** *f* (-; *no pl*) freedom of speech *or* opinion; **~umfrage** *f* opinion poll; **~verschiedenheit** *f* disagreement (**über** *acc* about)

Meise ['maizə] *f* (-; -n) ZO titmouse

Meißel ['maisəl] *m* (-s; -) chisel

meißeln *v/t and v/i* (ge-, h) chisel, carve

meist [maist] **1.** *adj* most; **das ~e** (**davon**) most of it; **die ~en** (**von ihnen**) most of them; **die ~en Leute** most people; **die ~e Zeit** most of the time; **2.** *adv* → **meistens**; **am ~en** (the) most; most (of all); **meistens** ['maistəns] *adv* usually; most of the time

Meister ['maistɐ] *m* (-s; -) master (*a. fig*); SPORT champion, F champ

meisterhaft 1. *adj* masterly; **2.** *adv* in a masterly manner *or* way

Meisterin *f* (-; -nen) master (*a. fig*); SPORT champion

meistern ['maistɐn] *v/t* (ge-, h) master

Meisterschaft *f* (-; -en) a) (*no pl*) mastery, b) SPORT championship, cup; title

Meister|stück *n*, **~werk** *n* masterpiece

Melancholie [melaŋko'li:] *f* (-; -n) melancholy; **melancholisch** [melaŋ'ko:lɪʃ] *adj* melancholy; **~ sein** feel depressed, F have the blues

Melange [me'lãːʒə] *Austrian f* (-; -n) coffee with milk

melden ['mɛldən] (ge-, h) **1.** *v/t* report s.th. *or* s.o. (**bei** to); radio etc: announce, report; **j-m et. ~** notify s.o. of s.th.; **2.** *v/refl*: **sich ~** report (**bei** to, **für**, **zu** for); register (**bei** with); PED etc: put up one's hand; TEL answer the phone; SPORT enter (**für**, **zu** for); volunteer (**für**, **zu** for)

Meldung *f* (-; -en) report, news, announcement; information, notice; notification; registration (**bei** with); SPORT entry (**für**, **zu** for)

melken ['mɛlkən] *v/t* ([*irr*,] ge-, h) milk

Melodie [melo'di:] *f* (-; -n) MUS melody,

tune; **melodisch** [me'lo:dɪʃ] *adj* MUS melodious, melodic

Melone [me'lo:nə] *f* (-; -*n*) BOT melon; F derby, Br bowler (hat)

Memoiren [me'moa:rən] *pl* memoirs

Menge ['mɛŋə] *f* (-; -*n*) amount, quantity; MATH set; F *e-e* ~ *Geld* plenty (*or* lots) of money; → *Menschenmenge*

'**Mengenlehre** *f* (-; *no pl*) MATH set theory; PED new math(ematics)

Mensa ['mɛnza] *f* (-; -*s*, *Mensen*) cafeteria, Br refectory, canteen

Mensch [mɛnʃ] *m* (-*en*; -*en*) human being; man; person, individual; *pl* people; mankind; *kein* ~ nobody; ~! wow!

Menschen|affe *m* ZO ape; ~*fresser* *m* cannibal; ~*freund* *m* philanthropist; ~*handel* *m* slave trade; ~*kenntnis* f: ~ *haben* know human nature; ~*leben* *n* human life

'**menschenleer** *adj* deserted

'**Menschen|menge** *f* crowd; ~*rechte* *pl* human rights; ~*seele* f: *keine* ~ not a (living) soul

'**menschenunwürdig** *adj* degrading; *housing etc*: unfit for human beings

'**Menschen|verstand** m: *gesunder* ~ common sense; ~*würde* *f* human dignity

Menschheit: *die* ~ mankind, the human race

'**menschlich** *adj* human; humane

'**Menschlichkeit** *f* (-; *no pl*) humanity

Menstruation [mɛnstrua'tsjo:n] *f* (-; -*en*) MED menstruation

Mentalität [mɛntali'tɛːt] *f* (-; -*en*) mentality

Menü [me'ny:] *n* (-*s*; -*s*) set meal (*or* lunch); EDP menu

Meridian [meri'dja:n] *m* (-*s*; -*e*) GEOGR, ASTR meridian

merkbar ['mɛrkba:ɐ] *adj* marked, distinct; noticeable; '**Merkblatt** *n* leaflet; **merken** ['mɛrkən] *v/t* (*ge-*, *h*) notice; feel; find (out), discover; *sich et.* ~ remember s.th., keep *or* bear s.th. in mind; '**merklich** *adj* → **merkbar**; '**Merkmal** *n* sign; feature, trait

'**merkwürdig** *adj* strange, odd, curious

'**merkwürdiger'weise** *adv* strangely enough

messbar ['mɛsba:ɐ] *adj* measurable

'**Messbecher** *m* measuring cup

Messe ['mɛsə] *f* (-; -*n*) ECON fair; REL mass; MIL, MAR mess

messen ['mɛsən] *v/t* (*irr*, *ge-*, *h*) measure; take (*temperature etc*); *sich nicht mit j-m* ~ *können* be no match for s.o.; *gemessen an* (*dat*) compared with

Messer ['mɛsɐ] *n* (-*s*; -) knife; *bis aufs* ~ to the knife; *auf des* ~*s Schneide stehen* be on a razor edge, be touch and go (*ob* whether)

Messerstecherei [-ʃtɛçə'rai] *f* (-; -*en*) knife fight

'**Messerstich** *m* stab (with a knife)

Messing ['mɛsɪŋ] *n* (-*s*; *no pl*) brass

'**Messinstru,ment** *n* measuring instrument

'**Messung** *f* (-; -*en*) measuring; reading

Metall [me'tal] *n* (-*s*; -*e*) metal

metallen [me'talən], **me'tallisch** *adj* metallic

Me'tallwaren *pl* hardware

Metamorphose [metamɔr'fo:zə] *f* (-; -*n*) metamorphosis

Metastase [meta'sta:zə] *f* (-; -*n*) MED metastasis

Meteor [mete'o:ɐ] *m* (-*s*; -*e*) ASTR meteor

Meteorit [meteo'ri:t] *m* (-*en*; -*e*[*n*]) ASTR meteorite

Meteorologe [meteoro'lo:gə] *m* (-*n*; -*n*) meteorologist; **Meteorologie** [meteorolo'gi:] *f* (-; *no pl*) meteorology; **Meteoro'login** *f* (-; -*nen*) meteorologist

Meter ['me:tɐ] *n*, *m* (-*s*; -) meter, Br metre; ~*maß* *n* tape measure

Methode [me'to:də] *f* (-; -*n*) method, TECH *a.* technique; **methodisch** [me'to:dɪʃ] *adj* methodical

metrisch ['me:trɪʃ] *adj* metric; ~*es Maßsystem* metric system

Metropole [metro'po:lə] *f* (-; -*n*) metropolis

Metzger ['mɛtsgɐ] *m* (-*s*; -) butcher

Metzgerei [mɛtsgə'rai] *f* (-; -*en*) butcher's (shop)

Meute ['mɔytə] *f* (-; -*n*) pack (of hounds); *fig* mob, pack

Meuterei [mɔytə'rai] *f* (-; -*en*) mutiny; **Meuterer** ['mɔytərɐ] *m* (-*s*; -) mutineer; **meutern** ['mɔytɐn] *v/i* (*ge-*, *h*) mutiny (*gegen* against)

MEZ ABBR *of* **Mitteleuropäische Zeit** CET, Central European Time

miau [mi'au] *int* ZO meow, Br miaow

miauen [mi'auən] v/i (no -ge-, h) zo meow, Br miaow

mich [mɪç] pers pron me; ~ (selbst) myself

mied [miːt] pret of meiden

Mieder ['miːdɐ] n (-s; -) corset(s); bodice; ~höschen n pantie girdle; ~waren pl foundation garments

Miene ['miːnə] f (-; -n) expression, look, air; gute ~ zum bösen Spiel machen grin and bear it

mies [miːs] F adj rotten, lousy

Miete ['miːtə] f (-; -n) rent; hire charge; zur ~ wohnen be a tenant; lodge (bei with); 'mieten v/t (ge-, h) rent; (take on) lease; AVIAT, MAR charter; ein Auto etc ~ rent (Br hire) a car; Mieter(in) ['miːtɐ (-tərɪn)] (-s; -/-; -nen) tenant, lodger

'Mietshaus n apartment building or house, Br block of flats, tenement

'Mietvertrag m lease (contract)

'Mietwohnung f apartment, Br (rented) flat

Migräne [mi'grɛːnə] f (-; -n) MED migraine

Mikro ['miːkro] F n (-s; -s) mike

Mikro... ['miːkro-] in cpds ...chip, ...computer, ...elektronik, ...film, ...prozessor etc: micro...

Mikrofon [mikro'foːn] n (-s; -e) microphone

Mikroskop [mikro'skoːp] n (-s; -e) microscope; mikro'skopisch adj microscopic(al)

Mikrowelle ['miːkro-] F f, 'Mikrowellenherd m microwave oven

Milbe ['mɪlbə] f (-; -n) zo mite

Milch [mɪlç] f (-; no pl) milk; ~geschäft n dairy, creamery; ~glas n frosted glass

milchig ['mɪlçɪç] adj milky

'Milch|kaffee m white coffee; ~kännchen n (milk) jug; ~kanne f milk can; ~mann F m milkman; ~mixgetränk n milk shake; ~produkte pl dairy products; ~pulver n powdered milk; ~reis m rice pudding; ~straße f ASTR Milky Way, Galaxy; ~tüte f milk carton; ~wirtschaft f dairy farming; ~zahn m milk tooth

mild [mɪlt] adj mild, soft; gentle

milde ['mɪldə] adv mildly; ~ ausgedrückt to put it mildly

'Milde f (-; no pl) mildness, gentleness; leniency, mercy

mildern ['mɪldɐn] v/t (ge-, h) lessen, soften; ~d adj: ~e Umstände JUR mitigating circumstances

'mildtätig adj charitable

Milieu [mi'ljøː] n (-s; -s) environment; social background

Militär [mili'tɛːɐ] n (-s; no pl) the military, armed forces; army; ~dienst m (-[e]s; no pl) military service; ~diktatur f military dictatorship; ~gericht n court martial

militärisch [mili'tɛːrɪʃ] adj military

Militarismus [milita'rɪsmʊs] m (-; no pl) militarism; Militarist [milita'rɪst] m (-en; -en) militarist; milita'ristisch adj militaristic

'Mili'tärre'gierung f military government

Milliarde [mɪl'jardə] f (-; -n) billion, Br old use a. a thousand million(s)

Millimeter ['mɪlimeːtɐ] m, n (-s; -) millimet|er, Br -re; ~pa,pier n graph paper

Million [mɪl'ioːn] f (-; -en) million

Millionär [mɪljoˈnɛːɐ] m (-s; -e), Millio-'närin f (-; -nen) millionaire

Milz [mɪlts] f (-; no pl) ANAT spleen

Mimik ['miːmɪk] f (-; no pl) facial expression

minder ['mɪndɐ] 1. adj → geringer, weniger; 2. adv less; nicht ~ no less

'Minderheit f (-; -en) minority

'minderjährig [-jɛːrɪç] adj: ~ sein be under age, be a minor; 'Minderjährige [-jɛːrɪgə] m, f (-n; -n) minor

'Minderjährigkeit f (-; no pl) minority

'minderwertig adj inferior, of inferior quality; 'Minderwertigkeit f (-; no pl) inferiority; ECON inferior quality

'Minderwertigkeitskom,plex m PSYCH inferiority complex

mindest ['mɪndəst] adj least; das Mindeste the (very) least; nicht im 2en not in the least, not at all

'Mindest... in cpds ...alter, ...einkommen, ...lohn etc: minimum ...

mindestens ['mɪndəstəns] adv at least

'Mindest|haltbarkeitsdatum n pull date, Br best-before (or best-by, sell-by) date; ~maß n minimum; auf ein ~ herabsetzen reduce to a minimum

Mine ['miːnə] f (-; -n) mine (a. MAR, MIL); lead; cartridge; refill

M

Mineral [minə'raːl] n (-s; -e, -ien) mineral; **Mineralogie** [minералo'giː] f (-; no pl) mineralogy

Mine'ralöl n mineral oil

Mine'ralwasser n mineral water

Miniatur [minja'tuːɐ] f (-; -en) miniature

Minigolf ['mini-] n miniature (Br crazy) golf

minimal [mini'maːl] adj, adv minimal; minimum; at least; **Minimum** ['miːnimʊm] n (-s; -ma) minimum

Minirock ['mini-] m miniskirt

Minister [mi'nistɐ] m (-s; -), **Mi'nisterin** f (-; -nen) minister, secretary, Br a. secretary of state

Ministerium [minis'teːriʊm] n (-s; -ien) ministry, department, Br a. office

Mi'nisterpräsi,dent m, **Mi'nisterpräsi,dentin** f prime minister

minus ['miːnʊs] adv MATH minus; **bei 10 Grad ~** at 10 degrees below zero

Minute [mi'nuːtə] f (-; -n) minute

Mi'nutenzeiger m minute hand

Mio ABBR of **Million(en)** m, million

mir [miːɐ] pers pron (to) me

Mischbatte,rie ['miʃ-] f mixing faucet, Br mixer tap

'Mischbrot n wheat and rye bread

mischen ['miʃən] v/t (ge-, h) mix; blend (tea etc); shuffle (cards); **sich ~** mingle or mix (**unter** with)

'Mischling m (-s; -e) esp contp half--caste; BOT, ZO hybrid; mongrel

'Mischmasch F m (-[e]s; -e) hotch-potch, jumble

'Misch|ma,schine f TECH mixer; **~pult** n radio, TV: mixer, mixing console

'Mischung f (-; -en) mixture; blend; assortment

'Mischwald m mixed forest

miserabel [mizə'raːbəl] F adj lousy, rotten

miss'achten [mis-] v/t (no -ge-, h) disregard, ignore; despise

Miss'achtung f disregard; contempt; neglect (all: gen of)

'Missbildung f (-; -en) deformity, malformation

miss'billigen v/t (no -ge-, h) disapprove of

'Missbrauch m abuse (a. JUR); misuse; **miss'brauchen** v/t (no -ge-, h) abuse; misuse

miss'deuten v/t (no -ge-, h) misinterpret

'Misserfolg m failure; F flop

'Missernte f bad harvest, crop failure

miss'fallen v/i (irr, **fallen**, no -ge-, h) **j-m ~** displease s.o.; '**Missfallen** n (-s; no pl) displeasure, dislike

'missgebildet adj deformed, malformed; '**Missgeburt** f deformed child or animal; freak

'Missgeschick n (-[e]s; -e) mishap

miss'glücken v/i (no -ge-, sein) fail

miss'gönnen v/t (no -ge-, h) **j-m et. ~** envy s.o. s.th.

'Missgriff m mistake

miss'handeln v/t (no -ge-, h) ill-treat, maltreat (a. fig); batter

Miss'handlung f ill-treatment, maltreatment, esp JUR assault and battery

Mission [mi'sjoːn] f (-; -en) mission (a. POL and fig); **Missionar(in)** [misjo'naːɐ (-'naːrin)] (-s; -e/-; -nen) missionary

'Missklang m dissonance, discord (both a. fig)

'Misskre,dit m discredit

misslang [mis'laŋ] pret of **misslingen**; **misslingen** [mis'liŋən] v/i (irr, no -ge-, sein) fail; **misslungen** [mis'lʊŋən] pp of **misslingen**; **das ist mir ~** I've bungled it

'missmutig adj bad-tempered, grumpy, glum

miss'raten 1. v/i (irr, **raten**, no -ge-, sein) fail; turn out badly; 2. adj wayward

miss'trauen v/i (no -ge-, h) distrust; '**Misstrauen** n (-s; no pl) distrust, suspicion (both: **gegenüber** of)

'Misstrauens|antrag m PARL motion of no confidence; **~votum** n PARL vote of no confidence

misstrauisch ['mistrauiʃ] adj distrustful, suspicious

'Missverhältnis n disproportion

'Missverständnis n (-ses; -se) misunderstanding; '**missverstehen** v/t (irr, **stehen**, no -ge-, h) misunderstand

'Misswahl f beauty contest or competition

Mist [mist] m (-[e]s; no p) AGR dung, manure; F trash, rubbish

'Mistbeet n AGR hotbed

Mistel ['mistəl] f (-; -n) BOT mistletoe

'Mistgabel *f* AGR dung fork

'Misthaufen *m* AGR manure heap

mit [mɪt] *prp* (*dat*) *and adv* with; ~ **Gewalt** by force; ~ **Absicht** on purpose; ~ **dem Auto** (*der Bahn etc*) by car (train *etc*); ~ **20 Jahren** at the age of) 20; ~ **100 Stundenkilometern** at 100 kilometers per hour; ~ **einem Mal**(**e**) all of a sudden; (all) at the same time; ~ **lauter Stimme** in a loud voice; ~ **anderen Worten** in other words; **ein Mann** ~ **dem Namen ...** a man by the name of ...; *j-n* ~ **Namen kennen** know s.o. by name; ~ **der Grund dafür, dass** one of the reasons why; ~ **der Beste** one of the best

'Mitarbeit *f* cooperation; assistance; PED activity, class participation

'Mitarbeiter *m*, 'Mitarbeiterin *f* colleague; employee; assistant; **freie**(**r**) **Mitarbeiter**(**in**) freelance

'mit|bekommen F *v/t* (*irr*, **kommen**, *sep*, *no* -*ge*-, *h*) get; catch; **~benutzen** *v/t* (*sep*, *no* -*ge*-, *h*) share

'Mit|bestimmungsrecht *n* (right of) codetermination; worker participation; **~bewerber**(**in**) (rival) competitor; fellow applicant; **~bewohner**(**in**) roommate, *Br* flatmate

'mitbringen *v/t* (*irr*, **bringen**, *sep*, -*ge*-, *h*) bring *s.th. or s.o.* with one; *j-m et.* ~ bring s.o. s.th.; **Mitbringsel** ['mɪt-brɪŋzəl] F *n* (-*s*; -) little present; souvenir

'Mitbürger *m*, 'Mitbürgerin *f* fellow citizen

mitei'nander *adv* with each other, with one another; together, jointly

'miterleben *v/t* (*sep*, *no* -*ge*-, *h*) live to see

'Mitesser *m* MED blackhead

'mitfahren *v/i* (*irr*, **fahren**, *sep*, -*ge*-, *sein*) **mit** *j-m* ~ drive *or* go with s.o.; *j-n* ~ **lassen** give s.o. a lift

'Mitfahr|gelegenheit *f* lift; **~zen,trale** *f* car pool(ing) service

'mitfühlend *adj* sympathetic

'mitgeben *v/t* (*irr*, **geben**, *sep*, -*ge*-, *h*) *j-m et.* ~ give s.o. s.th. (to take along)

'Mitgefühl *n* (-[*e*]*s*; *no pl*) sympathy

'mitgehen *v/i* (*irr*, **gehen**, *sep*, -*ge*-, *sein*) **mit** *j-m* ~ go *or* come along with s.o.; F **et.** ~ **lassen** walk off with s.th.

'Mitgift *f* (-; -*en*) dowry

'Mitglied *n* member (**bei** of)

'Mitgliedsbeitrag *m* subscription

'Mitgliedschaft *f* (-; -*en*) membership

'mithaben *v/t* (*irr*, **haben**, *sep*, -*ge*-, *h*) **ich habe kein Geld mit** I haven't got any money with me *or* on me

'Mithilfe *f* (-; *no pl*) assistance, help, cooperation (**bei** in; **von** of)

mit'hilfe *prp*: ~ **von** (*or gen*) with the help of, *fig a.* by means of

'mithören *v/t* (*sep*, -*ge*-, *h*) listen in to; overhear

'Mitinhaber *m*, 'Mitinhaberin *f* joint owner

'mitkommen *v/i* (*irr*, **kommen**, *sep*, -*ge*-, *sein*) come along (**mit** with); *fig* keep pace (**mit** with), follow; PED get on, keep up (with the class)

'Mitlaut *m* LING consonant

'Mitleid *n* (-[*e*]*s*; *no pl*) pity (**mit** for); **aus** ~ out of pity; ~ **haben mit** feel sorry for

'mitleidig ['mɪtlaidɪç] *adj* compassionate, sympathetic

'mitleidslos *adj* pitiless

'mitmachen (*sep*, -*ge*-, *h*) **1.** *v/i* join in; **2.** *v/t* take part in; follow (*a fashion etc*); F go through

'Mitmenschen: **die** ~ one's fellow human beings; people

'mitnehmen *v/t* (*irr*, **nehmen**, *sep*, -*ge*-, *h*) take *s.th. or s.o.* with one; *j-n* (**im Auto**) ~ give s.o. a lift

'mitreden *v/t* (*sep*, -*ge*-, *h*) **et. mitzureden haben** (**bei**) have a say (in)

'mitreißen *v/t* (*irr*, **reißen**, *sep*, -*ge*-, *h*) drag along; *fig* carry away (*mst passive*); **~d** *fig adj* electrifying (*speech etc*)

'mitschneiden *v/t* (*irr*, **schneiden**, *sep*, -*ge*-, *h*) radio, TV record, tape(-record)

'mitschreiben (*irr*, **schreiben**, *sep*, -*ge*-, *h*) **1.** *v/t* take down; take, do (*a test*); **2.** *v/i* take notes

'Mitschuld *f* (-; *no pl*) partial responsibility; 'mitschuldig *adj*: ~ **sein** be partly to blame (**an** *dat* for)

'Mitschüler *m*, 'Mitschülerin *f* classmate; schoolmate, fellow student

'mitspielen *v/i* (*sep*, -*ge*-, *h*) SPORT, MUS play; join in *a game etc*; **in e-m Film** *etc* ~ be *or* appear in a film *etc*

'Mitspieler *m*, 'Mitspielerin *f* partner, SPORT *a.* team-mate

Mittag ['mɪtaːk] *m* (-*s*; -*e*) noon, midday;

M

heute ~ at noon today; *zu* ~ *essen* (have) lunch; **essen** ~ lunch; *was gibt es zum* ~? what's for lunch?

'**mittags** *adv* at noon; *12 Uhr* ~ 12 o'clock noon

'**Mittags|pause** *f* lunch break; **~ruhe** *f* midday rest; **~schlaf** *m* after-dinner nap; **~zeit** *f* lunchtime

Mitte ['mɪtə] *f* (-; *no pl*) middle; center, *Br* centre (*a*. POL); ~ *Juli* in the middle of July; ~ *dreißig* in one's mid thirties

'**mitteilen** *v/t* (*sep, -ge-, h*) *j-m et.* ~ inform s.o. of s.th.; '**mitteilsam** *adj* communicative; '**Mitteilung** *f* (-; *-en*) report, information, message

Mittel ['mɪtəl] *n* (-*s*; -) means, way; measure; PHARM remedy (*gegen* for); *a. fig*) average; MATH mean; PHYS medium; *pl* means, money

'**Mittelalter** *n* (-*s*; *no pl*) Middle Ages

'**mittelalterlich** *adj* medi(a)eval

'**Mittel|ding** *n* cross (*zwischen* between); **~feld** *n* SPORT midfield; **~feldspieler(in)** midfield player, midfielder; **~finger** *m* ANAT middle finger

'**mittelfristig** *adj* medium-term

'**Mittelgewicht** *n* (-[*e*]*s*; *no pl*) SPORT middleweight (class)

'**mittelgroß** *adj* of medium height; medium-sized

'**Mittel|klasse** *f* middle class (*a*. MOT); **~linie** *f* SPORT halfway line

'**mittellos** *adj* without means

'**mittelmäßig** *adj* average

'**Mittelpunkt** *m* center, *Br* centre (*a. fig*)

'**mittels** *prp* (*gen*) by (means of), through

'**Mittelschule** *f* → *Realschule*

'**Mittel|strecke** *f* SPORT middle distance; **~streckenra,kete** *f* MIL medium-range missile; **~streifen** *m* MOT median strip, *Br* central reservation; **~stufe** *f* PED junior highschool, *Br* middle school; **~stürmer(in)** SPORT center (*Br* centre) forward; **~weg** *m* middle course; **~welle** *f* radio: medium wave (ABBR AM); **~wort** *n* (-[*e*]*s*; *-wörter*) LING participle

mitten ['mɪtən] *adv*: ~ *in* (*auf, unter dat*) in the midst or middle of

mitten'drin F *adv* right in the middle

mitten'durch F *adv* right through (the middle); right in two

Mitternacht ['mɪtɐnaxt] *f* midnight

mittlere ['mɪtlərə] *adj* middle, central; average, medium

mittlerweile ['mɪtlɐ'vailə] *adv* meanwhile, (in the) meantime

Mittwoch ['mɪtvɔx] *m* (-[*s*]; *-e*) Wednesday

mit'unter *adv* now and then

'**Mitverantwortung** *f* share of the responsibility

'**mitwirken** *v/i* (*sep, -ge-, h*) take part (*bei* in); '**Mitwirkende** *m, f* (*-n; -n*) THEA, MUS performer; *pl* THEA the cast; '**Mitwirkung** *f* (-; *no pl*) participation

mixen ['mɪksən] *v/t* (*ge-, h*) mix

'**Mixbecher** *m* shaker; **Mixer** ['mɪksɐ] *m* (-*s*; -) mixer; '**Mixgetränk** *n* mixed drink, cocktail, shake

Möbel ['møːbəl] *pl* furniture; **~spediti,on** *f* removal firm; **~stück** *n* piece of furniture; **~wagen** *m* moving (*Br* furniture) van

mobil [mo'biːl] *adj* mobile; ~ *machen* MIL mobilize

Mobiliar [mobi'ljaːɐ] *n* (-*s*; *no pl*) furniture

Mo'biltele,fon *n* mobile phone

möblieren [mø'bliːrən] *v/t* (*no -ge-, h*) furnish

mochte ['mɔxtə] *pret of* **mögen**

Mode ['moːdə] *f* (-; *-n*) fashion; *in* ~ in fashion; ~ *sein* be in fashion, F be in; *die neueste* ~ the latest fashion; *mit der* ~ *gehen* follow the fashion; *in* (*aus der*) ~ *kommen* come into (go out of) fashion

Modell [mo'dɛl] *n* (-*s*; *-e*) model; *j-m* ~ *stehen or sitzen* pose or sit for s.o.; **~bau** *m* model construction; **~baukasten** *m* model construction kit; **~eisenbahn** *f* model railway

modellieren [modɛ'liːrən] *v/t* (*no -ge-, h*) mould

Modem ['moːdɛm] *m, n* (-*s*; *-s*) EDP modem

'**Modenschau** *f* fashion show

Moderator [mode'raːtoːɐ] *m* (-*s*; *-en* [modera'to:rən]), **Modera'torin** *f* (-; *-nen*) TV *etc* presenter, host, anchorman (anchorwoman)

moderieren [mode'riːrən] *v/t* (*no -ge-, h*) TV *etc* present, host

moderig ['moːdərɪç] *adj* musty, mo(u)ldy

modern[1] ['mo:dɐn] *v/i* (*ge-, h, sein*) mo(u)ld, rot, decay

modern[2] [mo'dɛrn] *adj* modern; fashionable

modernisieren [modɛrni'zi:rən] *v/t* (*no -ge-, h*) modernize, bring up to date

'**Mode|schmuck** *m* costume jewel(le)ry; **~schöpfer(in)** fashion designer; **~waren** *pl* fashionwear; **~wort** *n* (*-[e]s; -wörter*) vogue word, F in word; **~zeichner(in)** fashion designer; **~zeitschrift** *f* fashion magazine

modisch ['mo:dɪʃ] *adj* fashionable, stylish

Modul[1] [mo'du:l] *n* (*-s; -e*) EDP module

Modul[2] ['mo:dʊl] *m* (*-s;-n*) MATH, TECH module

Mofa ['mo:fa] *n* (*-s; -s*) (small) moped, motorized bicycle

mogeln ['mo:gəln] F *v/i* (*ge-, h*) cheat; crib

mögen ['mø:gən] *v/t* (*irr, ge-, h*) and *v/aux* (*irr, no -ge-, h*) like; **er mag sie (nicht)** he likes (doesn't like) her; **lieber ~** like better, prefer; **nicht ~** dislike; **was möchten Sie?** what would you like?; **ich möchte, dass du es weißt** I'd like you to know (it); **ich möchte lieber bleiben** I'd rather stay; **es mag sein (, dass)** it may be (that)

möglich ['mø:klɪç] **1.** *adj* possible; **alle ~en** all sorts of; **sein Möglichstes tun** do what one can; do one's utmost; **nicht ~!** you don't say (so)!; **so bald (schnell, oft) wie ~** as soon (quickly, often) as possible; **2.** *adv:* **~st bald** *etc* as soon *etc* as possible; '**möglicher-'weise** *adv* possibly; '**Möglichkeit** *f* (*-; -en*) possibility; opportunity; chance; **nach ~** if possible

Mohammedaner [mohame'da:nɐ] *m* (*-s; -*), **mohamme'danisch** *adj* Muslim

Mohn [mo:n] *m* (*-[e]s; -e*) BOT poppy

Möhre ['mø:rə] *f* (*-; -n*), **Mohrrübe** ['mo:rɐ] *f* BOT carrot

Molch [mɔlç] *m* (*-[e]s; -e*) ZO salamander

Mole ['mo:lə] *f* (*-; -n*) MAR mole, jetty

Molekül [mole'ky:l] *n* (*-s; -e*) CHEM molecule

molk [mɔlk] *pret of* **melken**

Molkerei [mɔlkə'rai] *f* (*-; -en*) dairy

Moll [mɔl] *n* (*-; no pl*) MUS minor (key); **a-Moll** A minor

mollig ['mɔlɪç] F *adj* snug, cozy, Br cosy; plump, chubby

Moment [mo'mɛnt] *m* (*-[e]s; -e*) moment; (*e-n*) **~ bitte!** just a moment please!; **im ~** at the moment

Monarch [mo'narç] *m* (*-en; -en*) monarch; **Monarchie** [monar'çi:] *f* (*-; -n*) monarchy; **Monarchin** [mo'narçɪn] *f* (*-; -nen*) monarch; **Monarchist** [monar'çɪst] *m* (*-en; -en*) monarchist

Monat ['mo:nat] *m* (*-[e]s; -e*) month; **zweimal im** or **pro ~** twice a month

'**monatelang** *adv* for months

'**monatlich** *adj and adv* monthly

'**Monats|binde** *f* sanitary napkin (*Br* towel); **~karte** *f* commuter ticket, *Br* (monthly) season ticket

Mönch [mœnç] *m* (*-[e]s; -e*) monk; friar

Mond [mo:nt] *m* (*-[e]s; -e* ['mo:ndə]) moon; **~finsternis** *f* lunar eclipse

'**mondhell** *adj* moonlit

'**Mond|landefähre** *f* lunar module; **~landung** *f* moon landing; **~oberfläche** *f* moon surface, lunar soil; **~schein** *m* (*-[e]s; no pl*) moonlight; **~sichel** *f* crescent; **~umkreisung** *f*, **~umlaufbahn** *f* lunar orbit

Monitor ['mo:nito:ɐ] *m* (*-s; -en* [moni'to:rən]) TV *etc* monitor

Monolog [mono'lo:k] *m* (*-[e]s; -e*) monolog(ue *Br*)

Monopol [mono'po:l] *n* (*-s; -e*) ECON monopoly

monoton [mono'to:n] *adj* monotonous

Monotonie [monoto'ni:] *f* (*-; -n*) monotony

Monoxid ['mo:nɔksi:t] *n* CHEM monoxide

Monster ['mɔnstɐ] *n* (*-s; -*) monster

Montag ['mo:nta:k] *m* (*-[e]s; -e*) Monday

Montage [mɔn'ta:ʒə] *f* (*-; -n*) TECH assembly; installation; **auf ~ sein** be away on a field job; **~band** *n* (*-[e]s; -bänder*) TECH assembly line; **~halle** *f* TECH assembly house

Monteur [mɔn'tø:ɐ] *m* (*-s; -e*) TECH fitter; *esp* MOT, AVIAT mechanic

montieren [mɔn'ti:rən] *v/t* (*no -ge-, h*) TECH assemble; fit, attach; instal(l)

Moor [mo:ɐ] *n* (*-[e]s; -e*) bog, moor (-land); **moorig** ['mo:rɪç] *adj* boggy

Moos [mo:s] *n* (*-es; -e*) BOT moss

moosig ['mo:zɪç] *adj* mossy

M

Moped ['mo:pɛt] *n (-s; -s)* moped

Mops [mɔps] *m (-es; Möpse* ['mœpsə]*)* ZO pug(dog)

Moral [mo'ra:l] *f (-; no pl)* morals, moral standards; MIL *etc* morale; **mo'ralisch** *adj* moral; **moralisieren** [morali'zi:rən] *v/i (no -ge-, h)* moralize

Morast [mo'rast] *m (-[e]s; -e* [mo'rɛstə]*)* morass; mire, mud

Mord [mɔrt] *m (-[e]s; -e* ['mɔrdə]*)* murder (*an dat* of); MIL *etc* morale; **e-n ~ begehen** commit murder; **~anschlag** *m esp* POL assassination attempt

Mörder ['mœrdɐ] *m (-s; -),* **'Mörderin** *f (-; -nen)* murderer; (hired) killer; *esp* POL assassin

'Mord|kommissi,on *f* homicide division, *Br* murder squad; **~pro,zess** *m* JUR murder trial

'Mords|angst F *f:* **e-e ~ haben** be scared stiff; **~glück** F *n* stupendous luck; **~kerl** F *m* devil of a fellow; **~wut** F *f:* **e-e ~ haben** be in a hell of a rage

'Mord|verdacht *m* suspicion of murder; **~versuch** *m* attempted murder

morgen ['mɔrgən] *adv* tomorrow; **~ Abend (früh)** tomorrow night (morning); **~ Mittag** at noon tomorrow; **~ in e-r Woche** a week from tomorrow; **~ um diese Zeit** this time tomorrow; **... von ~** tomorrow's ..., ... of tomorrow

'Morgen *m (-s; -)* morning; AGR acre; **heute ~** this morning; **am (frühen) ~** (early) in the morning; **am nächsten ~** the next morning; **~essen** *Swiss* **~** breakfast; **~grauen** *n* dawn; **im** *or* **bei ~** at dawn; **~land** *n (-[e]s; no pl)* Orient; **~mantel** *m,* **~rock** *m* dressing gown

'morgens *adv* in the morning; **von ~ bis abends** from morning till night

morgig ['mɔrgɪç] *adj* tomorrow's ...

Morphium ['mɔrfjʊm] *n (-s; no pl)* PHARM morphine

morsch [mɔrʃ] *adj* rotten; **~ werden** rot

Morsealpha,bet [m'mɔrzə-] *n* Morse code

Mörser ['mœrzɐ] *m (-s; -)* mortar *(a.* MIL*)*

'Morsezeichen *n* Morse signal

Mörtel ['mœrtəl] *m (-s; -)* mortar

Mosaik [moza'i:k] *n (-s; -en)* mosaic

Mosa'ikstein *m* piece

Moschee [mɔ'ʃe:] *f (-; -n)* mosque

Moskito [mɔs'ki:to] *m (-s; -s)* ZO mosquito

Moslem ['mɔslɛm] *m (-s; -s),* **moslemisch** [mɔs'le:mɪʃ] *adj,* **Moslime** [-'li:mə] *f (-; -n)* Muslim

Most [mɔst] *m (-[e]s; -e)* grape juice; cider

Motiv [mo'ti:f] *n (-s; -e)* motive; PAINT, MUS motif; **Motivation** [motiva'tsjo:n] *f (-; -en)* motivation; **motivieren** [moti'vi:rən] *v/t (no -ge-, h)* motivate

Motor ['mo:to:ɐ, mo'to:ɐ] *m (-s; -en* [mo'to:rən]*)* motor, engine; **~boot** *n* motor boat; **~haube** *f* hood, *Br* bonnet

motorisieren [motori'zi:rən] *v/t (no -ge-, h)* motorize

'Motor|leistung *f* (engine) performance; **~rad** *n* motorcycle, F motorbike; **~ fahren** ride a motorcycle; **~radfahrer(in)** motorcyclist, biker; **~roller** *m* (motor) scooter; **~säge** *f* power saw; **~schaden** *m* engine trouble (*or* failure)

Motte ['mɔtə] *f (-; -n)* ZO moth

'Mottenkugel *f* mothball

'mottenzerfressen *adj* moth-eaten

Motto ['mɔto] *n (-s; -s)* motto

Möwe ['mø:və] *f (-; -n)* ZO (sea)gull

Mücke ['mʏkə] *f (-; -n)* ZO gnat, midge, mosquito; **aus e-r ~ e-n Elefanten machen** make a mountain out of a molehill; **'Mückenstich** *m* gnat bite

müde ['my:də] *adj* tired; weary; sleepy; **~ sein (werden)** be (get) tired (fig *e-r Sache* of s.th.)

'Müdigkeit *f (-; no pl)* tiredness

Muff [mʊf] *m (-[e]s; -e)* muff

Muffe ['mʊfə] *f (-; -n)* TECH sleeve, socket

Muffel ['mʊfəl] F *m (-s; -)* sourpuss

muff(e)lig ['mʊf(ə)lɪç], **muffig** ['mʊfɪç] F *adj* musty; *contp* sulky, sullen

Mühe ['my:ə] *f (-; -n)* trouble; effort; difficulty (*mit* with *s.th.*); **(nicht) der ~ wert** (not) worth the trouble; *j-m* **~ machen** give s.o. trouble; **sich ~ geben** try hard; **sich die ~ sparen** save o.s. the trouble; **mit ~ und Not** (just) barely

'mühelos *adv* without difficulty

mühen ['my:ən] *v/refl (ge-, h)* struggle, work hard

'mühevoll *adj* laborious

Mühle ['my:lə] *f (-; -n)* mill; morris

Mühsal ['myːzaːl] *f* (-; -e) toil

mühsam ['myːzaːm], **'mühselig 1.** *adj* laborious; **2.** *adv* with difficulty

Mulatte [mu'latə] *m* (-n; -n), **Mu'lattin** *f* (-; -nen) mulatto

Mulde ['muldə] *f* (-; -n) hollow

Mull [mul] *m* (-[e]s; -e) muslin; *esp* MED gauze

Müll [myl] *m* (-s; *no pl*) garbage, trash, *Br* refuse, rubbish; **~abfuhr** *f* garbage (*Br* refuse) collection; **~beseitigung** *f* waste disposal; **~beutel** *m* garbage bag, *Br* dustbin liner

'Mullbinde *f* MED gauze bandage

'Müll|con,tainer *m* garbage (*Br* rubbish) skip; **~depo,nie** *f* dump; **~eimer** *m* garbage can, *Br* dustbin; **~fahrer** *m* garbage man, *Br* dustman; **~halde** *f* dump; **~haufen** *m* garbage (*Br* rubbish) heap; **~kippe** *f* dump; **~schlucker** *m* garbage (*Br* refuse) chute; **~tonne** *f* garbage can, *Br* dustbin; **~verbrennungsanlage** *f* (waste) incineration plant; **~wagen** *m* garbage truck, *Br* dustcart

Multiplikation [multiplika'tsjoːn] *f* (-; -en) MATH multiplication; **multiplizieren** [multipli'tsiːrən] *v/t* (*no -ge-, h*) MATH multiply (**mit** by)

Mumie ['muːmjə] *f* (-; -n) mummy

Mumps [mumps] *m, f* (-; *no pl*) MED mumps

Mund [munt] *m* (-[e]s; *Münder* ['myndə]) mouth; F **den ~ voll nehmen** talk big; **halt den ~!** shut up!; **~art** *f* dialect

münden ['myndən] *v/i* (*ge-, h, sein*) **~ in** (*acc*) *river etc*: flow into; *road etc*: lead into

'Mundgeruch *m* bad breath

'Mundhar,monika *f* MUS mouth organ, harmonica

mündig ['myndɪç] *adj* emancipated; **~ (werden)** JUR (come) of age

mündlich ['myntlɪç] *adj* oral; verbal

'Mundstück *n* mouthpiece; tip

'Mündung *f* (-; -en) *river*: mouth; *gun*: muzzle

'Mund|wasser *n* mouthwash; **~werk** *n*: **ein gutes ~ haben** have the gift of the gab; **ein loses ~** a loose tongue; **~winkel** *m* corner of the mouth

'Mund-zu-'Mund-Beatmung *f* (-; -en) MED mouth-to-mouth resuscitation, F kiss of life

Munition [muni'tsjoːn] *f* (-; -en) ammunition

munkeln ['muŋkəln] F *v/t* (*ge-, h*) **man munkelt, dass** rumo(u)r has it that

Münster ['mynstɐ] *n* (-s; -) cathedral, minster

munter ['muntɐ] *adj* awake; lively; merry

Münze ['myntsə] *f* (-; -n) coin; medal

'Münz|einwurf *m* (coin) slot; **~fernsprecher** *m* pay phone; **~tank (auto,mat)** *m* coin-operated (gas, *Br* petrol) pump; **~wechsler** *m* (-s; -) change machine

mürbe ['myrbə] *adj* tender; brittle; GASTR crisp; **'Mürbeteig** *m* short pastry; shortcake

Murmel ['murməl] *f* (-; -n) marble

murmeln *v/t and v/i* (*ge-, h*) murmur

'Murmeltier *n* ZO marmot

murren ['murən] *v/i* (*ge-, h*) complain (**über** *acc* about)

mürrisch ['myrɪʃ] *adj* sullen; grumpy

Mus [muːs] *n* (-es; -e) mush; stewed fruit

Muschel ['muʃəl] *f* (-; -n) ZO mussel; shell

Museum [mu'zeːum] *n* (-s; *Museen*) museum

Musik [mu'ziːk] *f* (-; *no pl*) music

musikalisch [muzi'kaːlɪʃ] *adj* musical

Mu'sik|anlage *f* hi-fi *or* stereo set; **~auto,mat** *m*, **~box** *f* juke box

Musiker ['muːzikɐ] *m* (-s; -), **'Musikerin** *f* (-; -nen) musician

Mu'sik|instru,ment *n* musical instrument; **~ka,pelle** *f* band; **~kas,sette** *f* music cassette; **~lehrer(in)** music teacher; **~stunde** *f* music lesson

musisch ['muːzɪʃ] *adv*: **~ interessiert (begabt)** fond of (gifted for) fine arts and music

musizieren [muzi'tsiːrən] *v/i* (*no -ge-, h*) make music

Muskat [mus'kaːt] *m* (-[e]s; -e), **~nuss** *f* BOT nutmeg

Muskel ['muskəl] *m* (-s; -n) ANAT muscle; **~kater** F *m* aching muscles; **~zerrung** *f* MED pulled muscle

muskulös [musku'løːs] *adj* muscular, brawny

Müsli ['myːsli] *n* (-s; -) GASTR granola, *Br* muesli

Muss *n* (-; *no pl*) necessity; **es ist ein ~** it is a must

M

Muße ['muːsə] *f* (-; *no pl*) leisure; spare time

müssen ['mʏsən] *v/i* (*irr, ge-, h*) and *v/aux* (*irr, no -ge-, h*) must, have (got) to; *du musst den Film sehen!* you must see the film!; *ich muss jetzt (m-e) Hausaufgaben machen* I have (got) to do my homework now; *sie muss krank sein* she must be ill; *du musst es nicht tun* you need not do it; *das müsstest du (doch)* wissen you ought to know (that); *sie müsste zu Hause sein* she should (ought to) be (at) home; *das müsste schön sein!* that would be nice!; *du hättest ihm helfen ~* you ought to have helped him

müßig ['myːsɪç] *adj* idle; useless

musste ['mʊstə] *pret of* **müssen**

Muster ['mʊstɐ] *n* (-*s*; -) pattern; sample; model

'**muster|gültig, ~haft** *adj* exemplary; *sich ~ benehmen* behave perfectly

'**Musterhaus** *n* showhouse

'**mustern** *v/t* (*ge-, h*) eye *s.o.*; size *s.o.* up; MIL *gemustert werden* F have one's medical; **Musterung** ['mʊstərʊŋ] *f* (-; *-en*) MIL medical (examination for military service)

Mut [muːt] *m* (-[*e*]*s*; *no pl*) courage; *j-m ~ machen* encourage *s.o.*; *den ~ verlieren* lose courage; → *zumute*

mutig ['muːtɪç] *adj* courageous, brave

'**mutlos** *adj* discouraged

'**mutmaßen** *v/t* (*ge-, h*) speculate

'**mutmaßlich** *adj* probable; presumed

'**Mutprobe** *f* test of courage

Mutter ['mʊtɐ] *f* (-; *Mütter* ['mʏtɐ]) mother; TECH nut; **~boden** *m*, **~erde** *f* AGR topsoil

mütterlich ['mʏtɐlɪç] *adj* motherly

'**mütterlicherseits** *adv*: **Onkel** *etc* **~** maternal uncle *etc*

'**Mutterliebe** *f* motherly love

'**mutterlos** *adj* motherless

'**Mutter|mal** *n* birthmark, mole; **~milch** *f* mother's milk; **~schaftsurlaub** *m* maternity leave; **~schutz** *m* JUR legal protection of expectant and nursing mothers; **~söhnchen** *contp n* sissy; **~sprache** *f* mother tongue; **~sprachler** [-ʃpraːxlɐ] *m* (-*s*; -) native speaker; **~tag** *m* Mother's Day

Mutti ['mʊti] F *f* (-; *-s*) mom(my), *esp Br* mum(my)

'**mutwillig** *adj* wanton

Mütze ['mʏtsə] *f* (-; *-n*) cap

MwSt *ABBR of* **Mehrwertsteuer** VAT, value-added tax

mysteriös [mʏste'rjøːs] *adj* mysterious

mystisch ['mʏstɪʃ] *adj* mystic(al)

mythisch ['myːtɪʃ] *adj* mythical

Mythologie [mytolo'giː] *f* (-; *-n*) mythology

Mythos ['myːtɔs] *m* (-; *Mythen*) myth

N *ABBR of* **Nord(en)** N, north

na [na] *int* well?; *~ und?* so what?; *~ gut!* all right then; *~ ja* (oh) well; *~(, ~)!* come on!, come now!; *~ so (et)was!* what do you say!; *~, dann nicht!* oh, forget it!; *~ also!* there you are!; *~, warte!* just you wait!

Nabe ['naːbə] *f* (-; *-n*) TECH hub

Nabel ['naːbəl] *m* (-*s*; -) ANAT navel

'**Nabelschnur** *f* ANAT umbilical chord

nach [naːx] *prp* (*dat*) *and adv* to, to-ward(s), for; after; *time*: after, past; according to, by; *~ Hause* home; *abfahren ~* leave for; *~ rechts (Süden)* to the right (south); *~ oben* up(stairs); *~*

unten down(stairs); *~ vorn (hinten)* to the front (back); *der Reihe ~* one after the other; *s-e Uhr ~ dem Radio stellen* set one's watch by the radio; *~ m-r Uhr* by my watch; *suchen (fragen) ~* look (ask) for; *~ Gewicht (Zeit)* by weight (the hour); *riechen (schmecken) ~* smell (taste) of; *und ~ und* gradually; *~ wie vor* as before, still

'**nachahmen** [-aːmən] *v/t* (*sep, -ge-, h*) imitate, copy; take off

'**Nachahmung** *f* (-; *-en*) imitation

Nachbar ['naxbaːɐ] *m* (-*n*; -*n*), '**Nachbarin** *f* (-; *-nen*) neighbo(u)r; '**Nachbar-**

schaft f (-; no pl) neighbo(u)rhood, vicinity

'**Nachbau** m (-[e]s; -ten) TECH reproduction; '**nachbauen** v/t (sep, -ge-, h) copy, reproduce

'**Nachbildung** f (-; -en) copy, imitation; replica; dummy

'**nachblicken** v/i (sep, -ge-, h) look after

nach'**dem** cj after, when; **je ~ wie** depending on how

'**nachdenken** v/i (irr, **denken**, sep, -ge-, h) think; **~ über** (acc) think about, think s.th. over

'**nachdenklich** adj thoughtful; **es macht e-n ~** it makes you think

'**Nachdruck**¹ m (-[e]s; no pl) emphasis, stress

'**Nachdruck**² (-[e]s; -e) reprint

'**nachdrucken** v/t (sep, -ge-, h) reprint

'**nachdrücklich** [-drʏklɪç] adj emphatic; forceful; **~ raten** (**empfehlen**) advise (recommend) strongly

'**nacheifern** v/i (sep, -ge-, h) **j-m ~** emulate s.o.

nach**ei**'**nander** adv one after the other, in (or by) turns

'**nacherzählen** v/t (sep, no -ge-, h) retell; '**Nacherzählung** f (-; -en) PED reproduction

'**Nachfolge** f (-; no pl) succession; **j-s ~ antreten** succeed s.o.; '**nachfolgen** v/i (sep, -ge-, sein) (dat) succeed s.o.; '**Nachfolger(in)** [-fɔlɡɐ (-ɡərɪn)] (-s; -/-; -nen) successor

'**nachforschen** v/i (sep, -ge-, h) investigate; '**Nachforschung** f (-; -en) investigation, inquiry

'**Nachfrage** f (-; -n) inquiry; ECON demand; '**nachfragen** v/i (sep, -ge-, h) inquire, ask

'**nach|fühlen** v/t (sep, -ge-, h) **j-m et. ~** understand how s.o. feels; **~füllen** v/t (sep, -ge-, h) refill; **~geben** v/i (irr, **geben**, sep, -ge-, h) give in (way); fig give in

'**Nachgebühr** f (-; -en) post surcharge

'**nachgehen** v/i (irr, **gehen**, sep, -ge-, sein) follow (a. fig); watch; be slow; **e-r Sache ~** investigate s.th.; **s-r Arbeit ~** go about one's work

'**Nachgeschmack** m (-[e]s; no pl) aftertaste (a. fig)

'**nachgiebig** [-giːbɪç] adj yielding, soft (both a. fig); '**Nachgiebigkeit** f (-; no pl) yieldingness, softness (both a. fig)

'**nachhaltig** [-haltɪç] adj lasting, enduring

nach'**hause** Austrian adv home

nach'**her** adv afterwards; **bis ~!** see you later!, so long!

'**Nachhilfe** f help, assistance; PED → **~stunden** pl, **~unterricht** m PED private lesson(s), coaching

'**nachholen** v/t (sep, -ge-, h) make up for, catch up on

'**Nachkomme** m (-n; -n) descendant, pl esp JUR issue; '**nachkommen** v/i (irr, **kommen**, sep, -ge-, sein) follow, come later; (dat) comply with

'**Nachkriegs...** in cpds postwar ...

Nachlass ['naːxlas] m (-es; -lässe [-lɛsə]) ECON reduction, discount; JUR estate

'**nachlassen** v/i (irr, **lassen**, sep, -ge-, h) decrease, diminish, go down; effect etc: wear off; student etc: slacken one's effort; interest etc: flag; health etc: fail, deteriorate

'**nachlässig** adj careless, negligent

'**nach|laufen** v/i (irr, **laufen**, sep, -ge-, sein) run after; **~lesen** v/t (irr, **lesen**, sep, -ge-, h) look up; **~machen** v/t (sep, -ge-, h) imitate, copy; counterfeit, forge

'**Nachmittag** m afternoon; **heute ~** this afternoon

'**nachmittags** adv in the afternoon

Nachnahme ['naːxnaːmə] f (-; -n) ECON cash on delivery; **per ~ schicken** send C.O.D.

'**Nach|name** m surname, last (or family) name; **~porto** n surcharge

'**nachprüfen** v/t (sep, -ge-, h) check (up), make sure (of)

'**nachrechnen** v/t (sep, -ge-, h) check

'**Nachrede** f: **üble ~** malicious gossip; JUR defamation (of character), slander

Nachricht ['naːxrɪçt] f (-; -en) news; message; report; information, notice; pl news (report), newscast; **e-e gute** (**schlechte**) ~ good (bad) news; **Sie hören ~en** here is the news

'**Nachrichten|dienst** m news service; MIL intelligence service; **~satel,lit** m communications satellite; **~sprecher** (**-in**) newscaster, esp Br newsreader; **~technik** f telecommunications

'**Nachruf** m obituary

'**nach|rüsten** v/i (sep, -ge-, h) POL, MIL close the armament gap; **~sagen** v/t (sep, -ge-, h) **j-m Schlechtes ~** speak badly of s.o.; **man sagt ihm nach, dass er ...** he is said to inf

'Nachsai,son *f* off-peak season; **in der ~** out of season

'nachschlagen (*irr*, **schlagen**, *sep*, *-ge-*, *h*) **1.** *v/t* look up; **2.** *v/i*: **~ in** (*dat*) consult; **'Nachschlagewerk** *n* reference book

'Nach|schlüssel *m* duplicate (*or* skeleton) key; **~schrift** *f* postscript; dictation; **~schub** *m esp* MIL supplies

'nach|sehen (*irr*, **sehen**, *sep*, *-ge-*, *h*) **1.** *v/i* follow with one's eyes; (have a) look; **~ ob** (go and) see whether; **2.** *v/t* look *or* go over *or* through; correct, mark; check (*a.* TECH); **~senden** *v/t* ([*irr*, **senden**,] *sep*, *-ge-*, *h*) send on, forward; **bitte ~!** *post* please forward!

'Nachsilbe *f* LING suffix

'nachsitzen *v/i* (*irr*, **sitzen**, *sep*, *-ge-*, *h*) stay in (after school), be kept in; **~ lassen** keep in, detain

'Nachspann *m* (*-[e]s*; *-e*) film: credits *pl*

'Nachspiel *n* sequel, consequences

'nachspielen *v/i* (*sep*, *-ge-*, *h*) SPORT **5 Minuten ~ lassen** allow 5 minutes for injury time; **'Nachspielzeit** *f esp* soccer: injury time

'nach|spio,nieren *v/i* (*no* *-ge-*, *h*) spy (up)on; **~sprechen** *v/t* (*irr*, **sprechen**, *sep*, *-ge-*, *h*) *j-m et.* **~** say *or* repeat s.th. after s.o.

nächst'beste ['nɛːçst] *adj* first, F any old; next-best, second-best

nächste ['nɛːçstə] *adj* next; nearest (*a. relative*); **in den ~n Tagen (Jahren)** in the next few days (years); **in ~r Zeit** in the near future; **was kommt als Nächstes?** what comes next?; **der Nächste, bitte!** next please!

'nachstehen *v/i* (*irr*, **stehen**, *sep*, *-ge-*, *h*) *j-m in nichts* **~** be in no way inferior to s.o.

'nachstellen (*sep*, *-ge-*, *h*) **1.** *v/t* put back (*watch*); TECH (re)adjust; **2.** *v/i*: *j-m* **~** be after s.o.; **'Nachstellung** *f* (*-*; *-en*) persecution

'Nächstenliebe *f* charity

Nacht [naxt] *f* (*-*; *Nächte* ['nɛçtə]) night; **Tag u.** **~** night and day; **die ganze ~** all night (long); **heute Nacht** tonight; last night

'Nachtdienst *m* night duty; **~ haben** PHARM be open all night

'Nachteil *m* disadvantage, drawback; **im ~ sein** be at a disadvantage (**gegenüber** compared with); **'nachteilig** [-tailɪç] *adj* disadvantageous

'Nacht|essen *Swiss n →* **Abendbrot**, **~falter** *m* ZO moth; **~hemd** *n* nightgown, nightdress; F nightie; nightshirt

Nachtigall ['naxtɪɡal] *f* (*-*; *-en*) ZO nightingale

'Nachtisch *m* (*-[e]s*; *no pl*) dessert; sweet

nächtlich ['nɛçtlɪç] *adj* nightly; at *or* by night

'Nachtlo,kal *n* nightclub

Nachtrag ['naːxtraːk] *m* (*-[e]s*; *-träge* [-trɛːɡə]) supplement; **'nachtragen** *fig* *v/t* (*irr*, **tragen**, *sep*, *-ge-*, *h*) *j-m et.* **~** bear s.o. a grudge; **'nachtragend** *adj* unforgiving; **'nachträglich** [-trɛːklɪç] *adj* additional; later; belated

nachts *adv* at night, in the night(time)

'Nachtschicht *f* night shift; **~ haben** be on night shift

'nachtschlafend *adj*: **zu ~er Zeit** in the middle of the night

'Nachtisch *m* bedside table

'Nachttopf *m* chamber pot

'Nachtwächter *m* night watchman

'nachwachsen *v/i* (*irr*, **wachsen**, *sep*, *-ge-*, *sein*) grow again

'Nachwahl *f* PARL special election, *Br* by-election

Nachweis ['naːxvais] *m* (*-es*; *-e*) proof, evidence; **'nachweisbar** *adj* demonstrable; *esp* CHEM *etc* detectable

'nachweisen *v/t* (*irr*, **weisen**, *sep*, *-ge-*, *h*) prove; *esp* CHEM *etc* detect

'nachweislich *adv* as can be proved

'Nach|welt *f* (*-*; *no pl*) posterity; **~wirkung** *f* aftereffect(s), *pl a.* aftermath; **~wort** *n* (*-[e]s*; *-worte*) epilog(ue)

'Nachwuchs *m* (*-es*; *no pl*) young talent, F new blood; **~... in cpds** ...autor, ...schauspieler *etc*: talented *or* promising young ..., up-and-coming ...

'nach|zahlen *v/t* (*sep*, *-ge-*, *h*) pay extra; **~zählen** *v/t* (*sep*, *-ge-*, *h*) count over (again), check

'Nachzahlung *f* additional *or* extra payment

Nachzügler ['naːxtsyːklɐ] *m* (*-s*; *-*) straggler, latecomer

Nacken ['nakən] *m* (*-s*; *-*) ANAT (back *or* nape of the) neck; **~stütze** *f* headrest

nackt [nakt] *adj* naked; *esp* PAINT, PHOT nude; bare (*a. fig*); *fig* plain; **völlig ~** stark naked; **sich ~ ausziehen** strip; **~ baden** swim in the nude; *j-n ~ malen* paint s.o. in the nude

Nadel ['na:dəl] *f* (-; -*n*) needle; pin; brooch; **~baum** *m* BOT conifer(ous tree); **~öhr** *n* eye of a needle; **~stich** *m* pinprick (*a. fig*)

Nagel ['na:gəl] *m* (-*s*; *Nägel* ['nɛ:gəl]) nail; *an den Nägeln kauen* bite one's nails; **~lack** *m* nail varnish *or* polish

'**nageln** *v/t* (*ge-*, *h*) nail (*an acc*, *auf acc* to)

'**nagel|neu** F *adj* brand-new

'**Nagelpflege** *f* manicure

nagen ['na:gən] (*ge-*, *h*) **1.** *v/i* gnaw (*an dat* at); *an e-m Knochen ~* pick a bone; **2.** *v/t* gnaw; '**Nagetier** *n* ZO rodent

'**Nahaufnahme** *f* PHOT *etc* close-up

nahe [na:ə] *adj* near, close (*bei* to); nearby; *j-m ~ gehen* affect s.o. deeply; **~ kommen** (*dat*) come close to; **~ legen** suggest; **~ liegen** seem likely; **~ liegend** likely, obvious; **Nähe** ['nɛ:ə] *f* (-; *no pl*) nearness; neighbo(u)r-hood, vicinity; *in der ~ des Bahnhofs* near the station; *ganz in der ~* quite near, close by; *in deiner ~* near you

nahen ['na:ən] *v/i* (*ge-*, *sein*) approach

nähen ['nɛ:ən] *v/t and v/i* (*ge-*, *h*) sew; make

Nähere ['nɛ:ərə] *n* (-*n*; *no pl*) details, particulars

nähern ['nɛ:ən] *v/refl* (*ge-*, *h*) approach, get near(er) *or* close(r) (*dat* to)

'**nahezu** *adv* nearly, almost

'**Nähgarn** *n* (sewing) cotton

'**Nahkampf** *m* MIL close combat

nahm [na:m] *pret of* **nehmen**

'**Nähma,schine** *f* sewing machine

'**Nähnadel** *f* (sewing) needle

nähren ['nɛ:rən] *v/t* (*ge-*, *h*) feed; *fig* nurture

nahrhaft ['na:ɐhaft] *adj* nutritious, nourishing

Nährstoff ['nɛ:ɐ-] *m* nutrient

Nahrung ['na:rʊŋ] *f* (-; *no pl*) food, nourishment; AGR feed; diet

'**Nahrungsmittel** *pl* food(stuffs)

Nährwert *m* nutritional value

Naht [na:t] *f* (-; *Nähte* ['nɛ:tə]) seam; MED suture

'**Nahverkehr** *m* local traffic; '**Nahver-**

kehrszug *m* local *or* commuter train

'**Nähzeug** *n* sewing kit

naiv [na'i:f] *adj* naive; **Naivität** [naivi'tɛ:t] *f* (-; *no pl*) naivety

Name ['na:mə] *m* (-*ns*; -*n*) name; *im ~n von* on behalf of; *nur dem ~n nach* in name only; '**namenlos** *adj* nameless; *fig a.* unspeakable; '**namens** *adv* by (the) name of, named, called

'**Namens|tag** *m* name day; **~vetter** *m* namesake; **~zug** *m* signature

namentlich ['na:məntlɪç] *adj and adv* by name

nämlich ['nɛ:mlɪç] *adv* that is (to say), namely; you see *or* know

nannte ['nantə] *pret of* **nennen**

Napf [napf] *m* (-[*e*]*s*; *Näpfe* ['nɛpfə]) bowl, basin

Narbe ['narbə] *f* (-; -*n*) scar

narbig ['narbɪç] *adj* scarred

Narkose [nar'ko:zə] *f* (-; -*n*) MED an(a)esthesia; *in ~* under an an(a)es-thetic

Narr [nar] *m* (-*en*; -*en*) fool; *j-n zum ~en halten* fool s.o.; '**narrensicher** *adj* foolproof; **närrisch** ['nɛrɪʃ] *adj* foolish; **~ vor** (*dat*) mad with

Narzisse [nar'tsɪsə] *f* (-; -*n*) BOT daffodil

nasal [na'za:l] *adj* nasal

naschen ['naʃən] *v/i and v/t* (*ge-*, *h*) nibble (*an dat* at); *gern ~* have a sweet tooth; **Nascherei** [naʃə'raiən] *pl* dainties, goodies, sweets; '**naschhaft** *adj* sweet-toothed

Nase ['na:zə] *f* (-; -*n*) ANAT nose (*a. fig*); *sich die ~ putzen* blow one's nose; *in der ~ bohren* pick one's nose; F *die ~ voll haben* (*von*) be fed up (with)

'**Nasen|bluten** *n* MED nosebleed; **~loch** *n* nostril; **~spitze** *f* tip of the nose

Nashorn *n* ZO rhinoceros, F rhino

nass [nas] *adj* wet; *triefend ~* soaking (wet); **Nässe** ['nɛsə] *f* (-; *no pl*) wet (-ness); '**nässen** (*ge-*, *h*) **1.** *v/t* wet; **2.** *v/i* MED weep

'**nasskalt** *adj* damp and cold, raw

Nation [na'tsjo:n] *f* (-; -*en*) nation

national [natsjo'na:l] *adj* national

Natio'nalhymne *f* national anthem

Nationalismus [natsjona'lɪsmʊs] *m* (-; *no pl*) nationalism; **Nationalität** [natsjonali'tɛ:t] *f* (-; -*en*) nationality

Natio'nal|mannschaft *f* SPORT national team; **~park** *m* national park

N

Natio'nalsozia,lismus *m* HIST National Socialism, *contp* Nazism; **Natio'nalsozia,list** *m*, **natio'nalsozia,listisch** *adj* HIST National Socialist, *contp* Nazi

Natter ['natɐ] *f* (-; -n) ZO adder, viper (*a. fig*)

Natur [na'tuːɐ] *f* (-; -en) nature; **von ~ (aus)** by nature

Naturalismus [natura'lɪsmʊs] *m* (-; *no pl*) naturalism

Na'tur|ereignis *n*, **~erscheinung** *f* natural phenomenon; **~forscher** *m* naturalist; **~geschichte** *f* natural history; **~gesetz** *n* law of nature

na'turgetreu *adj* true to life; lifelike

Na'turkata,strophe *f* (natural) catastrophe *or* disaster, act of God

natürlich [na'tyːɐlɪç] **1.** *adj* natural; **2.** *adv* naturally, of course

Na'tur|schätze *pl* natural resources; **~schutz** *m* nature conservation; **unter ~** protected; **~schützer** [-ʃʏtsɐ] *m* (-s; -) conservationist; **~schutzgebiet** *n* nature reserve; national park; **~volk** *n* primitive race; **~wissenschaft** *f* (natural) science

n. Chr. ABBR *of* **nach Christus** AD, anno domini

Nebel ['neːbəl] *m* (-s; -) fog; mist; haze; smoke; **~horn** *n* foghorn; **~leuchte** *f* MOT fog light

neben ['neːbən] *prp* (*dat and acc*) beside, next to; besides; apart from; compared with; **~ anderem** among other things; **setz dich ~ mich** sit by me or by my side

neben'an *adv* next door

neben'bei *adv* in addition, at the same time; **~ (gesagt)** by the way

'Nebenberuf *m* second job, sideline; 'nebenberuflich *adv* as a sideline

'Nebenbuhler [-buːlɐ] *m* (-s; -), 'Nebenbuhlerin *f* (-; -nen) rival

nebenei'nander *adv* side by side; next (door) to each other; **~ bestehen** coexist

'Neben|einkünfte *pl*, **~einnahmen** *pl* extra money; **~fach** *n* PED *etc* minor (subject), *Br* subsidiary subject; **~fluss** *m* tributary; **~gebäude** *n* next-door *or* adjoining building; annex(e); **~haus** *n* house next door; **~kosten** *pl* extras; **~mann** *m*: **dein ~** the person next to

you; **~pro,dukt** *n* by-product; **~rolle** *f* THEA supporting role, minor part (*a. fig*); cameo (role); **~sache** *f* minor matter; **das ist ~** that's of little *or* no importance

'nebensächlich *adj* unimportant

'Neben|satz *m* LING subordinate clause; **~stelle** *f* TEL extension; **~straße** *f* side street; minor road; **~strecke** *f* RAIL branch line; **~tisch** *m* next table; **~verdienst** *m* extra earnings; **~wirkung** *f* side effect; **~zimmer** *n* adjoining room

neblig ['neːblɪç] *adj* foggy; misty; hazy

necken ['nɛkən] *v/t* (*ge-, h*) tease

Neckerei [nɛkə'raɪ] *f* (-; -en) teasing

'neckisch *adj* playful, teasing

Neffe ['nɛfə] *m* (-n; -n) nephew

negativ ['neːɡatiːf] *adj* negative

'Negativ *n* (-s; -e) PHOT negative

Neger ['neːɡɐ] *m* (-s; -), **Negerin** ['neːɡərɪn] *f* (-; -nen) → *Schwarze*

nehmen ['neːmən] *v/t* (*irr, ge-, h*) take (*a. sich ~*); **j-m et. ~** take s.th. (away) from s.o. (*a. fig*); **sich e-n Tag frei ~** take a day off; **j-n an die Hand ~** take s.o. by the hand

Neid [naɪt] *m* (-es; *no pl*) envy; **reiner ~** sheer envy; **neidisch** ['naɪdɪʃ] *adj* envious (*auf acc*)

Neige ['naɪɡə] *f*: **zur ~ gehen** draw to its close; run out

'neigen (*ge-, h*) **1.** *v/t and refl* bend, incline; **2.** *v/i*: **zu et. ~** tend to (do) s.th.

'Neigung *f* (-; -en) inclination (*a. fig*), slope, incline; *fig* tendency

nein [naɪn] *adv* no

Nektar ['nɛktaːɐ] *m* (-s; -e) BOT nectar

Nelke ['nɛlkə] *f* (-; -n) BOT carnation; GASTR clove

nennen ['nɛnən] *v/t* (*irr, ge-, h*) name, call; mention; **sich ~** call o.s., be called; **man nennt ihn ...** he is called ...; **das nenne ich ...!** that's what I call ...!

'nennenswert *adj* worth mentioning

Nenner ['nɛnɐ] *m* (-s; -) MATH denominator

'Nennwert *m* ECON nominal *or* face value; **zum ~** at par

Neo..., neo... [neo-] *in cpds* ...fascist *etc*: neo-...

Neon ['neːɔn] *n* (-s; *no pl*) CHEM neon

'Neonröhre *f* neon tube

Nepp [nɛp] F *m* (-s; *no pl*) rip-off

207
nichtsdestoweniger

neppen ['nɛpən] F v/t (ge-, h) fleece, rip s.o. off

Nerv [nɛrf] m (-s; -en) ANAT nerve; **j-m auf die ~en fallen** or **gehen** get on s.o.'s nerves; **die ~en behalten (verlieren)** keep (lose) one's head

nerven ['nɛrfən] F v/t and v/i (ge-, h) be a pain in the neck (**j-n** to s.o.)

'Nervenarzt m, 'Nervenärztin f neurologist

'nervenaufreibend adj nerve-racking

'Nerven|belastung f nervous strain; **~kitzel** m thrill, F kick(s)

'nervenkrank adj mentally ill

'Nerven|säge F f pain in the neck; **~sys,tem** n nervous system; **~zusammenbruch** m nervous breakdown

nervös [nɛr'vøːs] adj nervous

Nervosität [nɛrvozi'tɛːt] f (-; no pl) nervousness

Nerz [nɛrts] m (-es; -e) ZO mink

Nessel ['nɛsəl] f (-; -n) BOT nettle

Nest [nɛst] n (-[e]s; -er ['nɛstɐ]) ZO nest; F contp one-horse town

nett [nɛt] adj nice; kind; **so ~ sein und et.** (or **et. zu**) **tun** be so kind as to do s.th.

netto ['nɛto] adv ECON net

Netz [nɛts] n (-es; -e) net; RAIL, TEL, EDP network; ELECTR mains; **am ~ sein** EDP be in the network; **~haut** f ANAT retina; **~karte** f RAIL area season ticket

neu [nɔy] adj new; fresh; fig modern; **neuere Sprachen** modern languages; **neueste Nachrichten (Mode)** latest news (fashion); **von neuem** anew, afresh; **seit neu(st)em** since (very) recently; **viel Neues** a lot of new things; **was gibt es Neues?** what's the news?, what's new?; **~artig** adj novel

'Neubau m (-[e]s; -ten) new building; **~gebiet** n new housing estate

neuerdings ['nɔyɐdɪŋs] adv lately, recently

Neuerer ['nɔyɐrɐ] m (-s; -) innovator; 'Neuerung f (-; -en) innovation

'Neugestaltung f reorganization, reformation

Neugier f, Neugierde ['nɔygiːɐdə] f (-; no pl) curiosity; 'neugierig adj curious (**auf** acc about); F contp nos(e)y; **ich bin ~, ob** I wonder if; 'Neugierige [-giːrɪgə] contp pl rubbernecks

Neuheit f (-; -en) novelty

Neuigkeit ['nɔyɪçkait] f (-; -en) (piece of) news

'Neujahr n New Year('s Day); **Prost ~!** Happy New Year!

'neulich adv the other day

Neuling ['nɔylɪŋ] m (-s; -e) newcomer, F greenhorn

'neumodisch contp adj newfangled

'Neumond m new moon

neun [nɔyn] adj nine; **neunte** adj ninth; 'Neuntel n (-s; -) ninth (part); 'neuntens adv ninthly; 'neunzehn adj nineteen; 'neunzehnte adj nineteenth; 'neunzig adj ninety; 'neunzigste adj ninetieth

Neurose [nɔy'roːzə] f (-; -n) MED neurosis; neurotisch [nɔy'roːtɪʃ] adj MED neurotic

'neusprachlich adj modern-language

neutral [nɔy'traːl] adj neutral

Neutralität [nɔytrali'tɛːt] f (-; no pl) neutrality

Neutronen... [nɔy'troːnən-] PHYS in cpds ...bombe etc: neutron ...

Neutrum ['nɔytrum] n (-s; -tra) LING neuter

'Neuverfilmung f remake

'neuwertig adj as good as new

'Neuzeit f (-; no pl) modern times

nicht [nɪçt] adv not; **überhaupt ~** not at all; **~ (ein)mal, gar ~ erst** not even; **~ mehr** not any more or longer; **sie ist nett (wohnt hier), ~ (wahr)?** she's nice (lives here), isn't (doesn't) she?; **~ so... wie** not as ... as; **noch ~** not yet; **~ besser (als)** no (or not any) better (than); **ich (auch) ~** I don't or I'm not (either); **(bitte) ~!** (please) don't!

'Nicht... in cpds ...mitglied, ...schwimmer etc: mst non-...; **~beachtung** f disregard; non-observance

Nichte ['nɪçtə] f (-; -n) niece

nichtig ['nɪçtɪç] adj trivial; JUR void, invalid

'Nichtraucher m, 'Nichtraucherin f non-smoker

nichts indef pron nothing, not anything; **~ (anderes) als** nothing but; **gar ~** nothing at all; F **das ist ~** that's no good; **~sagend** meaningless; **Nichts** n (-s; no pl) nothing(ness); **aus dem ~ appear** etc from nowhere; **build** etc from nothing

nichtsdesto'weniger adv nevertheless

'**nichtsnutzig** [-nʊtsıç] *adj* good-
-for-nothing, worthless

'**Nichtstuer** *m* (-s; -) do-nothing,
F bum

nicken ['nıkən] *v/i* (ge-, h) nod (one's
head)

nie [ni:] *adv* never, at no time; *fast ~*
hardly ever; *~ und nimmer* never ever

nieder ['ni:dər] **1.** *adj* low; **2.** *adv* down

'**Niedergang** *m* (-[e]s; *no pl*) decline

'**niedergeschlagen** *adj* depressed,
(feeling) down

'**Niederlage** *f* defeat, F beating

'**niederlassen** *v/refl* (*irr, lassen, sep,
-ge-, h*) settle (down); ECON set up (*als*
as); '**Niederlassung** *f* (-; -en) ECON establishment; branch

'**niederlegen** *v/t* (*sep, -ge-, h*) lay down
(*a. office etc*); *die Arbeit ~* (go on)
strike, down tools, F walk out; *sich ~*
lie down; go to bed; **~metzeln** *v/t* (*sep,
-ge-, h*) massacre

'**Niederschlag** *m* METEOR rain(fall);
PHYS fallout; CHEM precipitate; *boxing:*
knock-down; '**niederschlagen** *v/t* (*irr,
schlagen, sep, -ge-, h*) knock down;
cast down (*eyes*); *fig* put down (*revolt
etc*); JUR quash; *sich ~* CHEM precipitate

'**niederschmettern** *fig v/t* (*sep, -ge-, h*)
shatter, crush

'**niederträchtig** *adj* base, mean

Niederung ['ni:dərʊŋ] *f* (-; -en) low-
land(s)

niedlich ['ni:tlıç] *adj* pretty, sweet, cute

niedrig ['ni:drıç] *adj* low (*a. fig*); *fig* light
(*sentence etc*); *~ fliegen* fly low

niemals ['ni:ma:ls] → *nie*

niemand ['ni:mant] *indef pron* nobody,
no one, not anybody; *~ von ihnen*
none of them; '**Niemandsland** *n*
(-[e]s; *no pl*) no-man's-land

Niere ['ni:rə] *f* (-; -n) ANAT kidney

nieseln ['ni:zəln] *v/i* (ge-, h) drizzle

'**Nieselregen** *m* drizzle

niesen ['ni:zən] *v/i* (ge-, h) sneeze

Niete[1] ['ni:tə] *f* (-; -n) TECH rivet

Niete[2] *f* (-; -n) blank; F failure

Nikolaustag ['nıkolaus-] *m* St. Nicho-
las' Day

Nikotin [niko'ti:n] *n* (-s; *no pl*) CHEM
nicotine

Nilpferd ['ni:l-] *n* ZO hippopotamus, F
hippo

Nippel ['nıpəl] *m* (-s; -) TECH nipple

nippen ['nıpən] *v/i* (ge-, h) sip (*an dat* at)

nirgends ['nırgənts] *adv* nowhere

Nische ['ni:ʃə] *f* (-; -n) niche, recess

nisten ['nıstən] *v/i* (ge-, h) ZO nest

'**Nistplatz** *m* ZO nesting place

Niveau [ni'vo:] *n* (-s; -s) level, *fig a.* standard

Nixe ['nıksə] *f* (-; -n) water nymph, mermaid

noch [nɔx] *adv* still; *~ nicht* not yet; *~
nie* never before; *er hat nur ~ 5
Mark (Minuten)* he has only 5 marks
(minutes) left; (*sonst*) *~ et.?* anything
else?; *ich möchte ~ et.* (*Tee*) I'd like
some more (tea); *~ ein(e, -n)...*, *bitte*
another ..., please; *~ einmal* once more
or again; *~ zwei Stunden* another two
hours, two hours to go; *~ besser
(schlimmer)* even better (worse); *~
gestern* only yesterday; *und wenn
es ~ so ... ist* however (*or* no matter
how) ... it may be

'**nochmalig** [-ma:lıç] *adj* new, renewed

'**nochmals** *adv* once more *or* again

Nockerl ['nɔkəl] *Austrian n* (-s; -n)
GASTR small dumpling

Nomade [no'ma:də] *m* (-n; -n), **No'ma-
din** *f* (-; -nen) nomad

Nominativ ['no:minati:f] *m* (-s; -e) LING
nominative (case)

nominieren [nomi'ni:rən] *v/t* (*no ge-, h*)
nominate

Nonne ['nɔnə] *f* (-; -n) REL nun

'**Nonnenkloster** *n* REL convent

Norden ['nɔrdən] *m* (-s; *no pl*) north;
nach ~ north(wards); **nordisch** ['nɔr-
dıʃ] *adj* northern; SPORT *~e Kombination* Nordic Combined

nördlich ['nœrtlıç] **1.** *adj* north(ern);
northerly; **2.** *adv:* *~ von* north of

'**Nordlicht** ['nɔrt-] *n* (-[e]s; -er) ASTR
northern lights

Nord'osten *m* northeast; **nord'östlich**
adj northeast(ern); northeasterly

'**Nordpol** *m* North Pole

Nord'westen *m* northwest

nord'westlich *adj* northwest(ern);
northwesterly

'**Nordwind** *m* north wind

nörgeln ['nœrgəln] *v/i* (ge-, h) nag (*an
dat* at)

Nörgler ['nœrglə] *m* (-s; -), '**Nörglerin** *f*
(-; -nen) nagger

Norm [nɔrm] f (-; -en) standard, norm

normal [nɔr'maːl] adj normal; F **nicht ganz ~** not quite right in the head

Nor'mal... esp TECH in cpds ...maß, ...zeit etc: standard ...; **~ben‚zin** n regular (gas, Br petrol)

normalerweise [nɔr'maːlə'vaizə] adv normally, usually

normalisieren [nɔrmali'ziːrən] v/refl (no -ge-, h) return to normal

normen ['nɔrmən] v/t (ge-, h) standard-ize

Norwegen ['nɔrveːgən] Norway

Norweger ['nɔrveːgɐ] m (-s; -), 'Norwe-gerin [-gərin] f (-; -nen), 'norwegisch adj Norwegian

Not [noːt] f (-; Nöte ['nøːtə]) need; want; poverty; hardship; misery; difficulty; emergency; distress; **~ leidend** needy; **in ~ sein** be in trouble; **zur ~** if need be, if necessary

Notar [no'taːɐ] m (-s; -e), No'tarin f (-; -nen) JUR notary (public)

'Not|aufnahme f MED emergency room, Br casualty; **~ausgang** m emergency exit; **~behelf** m (-[e]s; -e) make-shift, expedient; **~bremse** f emergency brake; **~dienst** m emergency duty

'notdürftig adj scanty; temporary

Note ['noːtə] f (-; -n) note (a. MUS and POL); ECON bill, esp Br (bank)note; PED grade, Br mark; pl MUS (sheet) music; **~n lesen** read music

Notebook ['noʊtbʊk] n (-s; -s) EDP note-book

'Notendurchschnitt m PED etc average

'Notenständer m music stand

'Notfall m emergency

'notfalls adv if necessary

'notgedrungen adv: **et. ~ tun** be forced to do s.th.

notieren [no'tiːrən] v/t (no -ge-, h) make a note of, note (down); ECON quote

nötig ['nøːtɪç] adj necessary; **~ haben** need; **~ brauchen** need badly; **das Nö-tigste** the (bare) necessities or essentials; **nötigen** ['nøːtɪgən] v/t (ge-, h) force, compel; press, urge; 'Nötigung f (-; -en) coercion; JUR intimidation

Notiz [no'tiːts] f (-; -en) note; **keine ~ nehmen von** take no notice of, ignore; **sich ~en machen** take notes; **~block** m memo pad, Br notepad; **~buch** n notebook

'Notlage f awkward (or difficult) situa-tion; difficulties; emergency

'notlanden v/i (-ge-, sein) AVIAT make an emergency landing; 'Notlandung f AVIAT emergency landing

'Notlösung f expedient

'Notlüge f white lie

notorisch [no'toːrɪʃ] adj notorious

'Not|ruf m TEL emergency call; **~rufsäu-le** f TEL emergency phone; **~sig‚nal** n emergency or distress signal; **~stand** m state of (national) emergency; **~standsgebiet** n disaster area; ECON depressed area; **~standsgesetze** pl POL emergency laws; **~verband** m MED emergency dressing

'Notwehr f (-; no pl) JUR self-defense, Br self-defence

'notwendig adj necessary

'Notwendigkeit f (-; -en) necessity

'Notzucht f (-; no pl) JUR rape

Novelle [no'vɛlə] f (-; -n) novella; PARL amendment

November [no'vɛmbɐ] m (-[s]; -) No-vember

Nr. ABBR of **Nummer** No., no., num-ber

Nu [nuː] m: **im ~** in no time

Nuance [nyã'sə] f shade

nüchtern ['nʏçtɐn] adj sober (a. fig); matter-of-fact; **auf ~en Magen** on an empty stomach; **~ werden (machen)** sober up

'Nüchternheit f (-; no pl) sobriety

Nudel ['nuːdəl] f (-; -n) noodle

nuklear [nukle'aːɐ] adj nuclear

null [nʊl] adj zero, Br nought; TEL 0; SPORT nil, nothing; tennis: love; **~ Grad** zero degrees; **~ Fehler** no mistakes; **gleich Null sein** be nil

'Null|di‚ät f low-calorie (or F starvation) diet; **~punkt** m zero (point or fig level); **~ta‚rif** m free fare(s); **zum ~** free (of charge)

Numerus clausus ['nuːmerʊs 'klauzʊs] m (-; no pl) UNIV restricted admission (s)

Nummer ['nʊmɐ] f (-; -n) number; issue; size; nummerieren [nʊmə'riːrən] v/t (no -ge-, h) number

'Nummernschild n MOT license plate, Br numberplate

nun [nuːn] adv now; well

nur [nuːɐ] adv only, just; merely; nothing but; *er tut ~ so* he's just pretending; *~ so (zum Spaß)* just for fun; *warte ~!* just you wait!; *mach ~!, ~ zu!* go ahead!; → *Erwachsene*

Nuss [nʊs] *f* (-; *Nüsse* ['nʏsə]) BOT nut; **~baum** *m* walnut (tree); **~knacker** *m* nutcracker; **~schale** *f* nutshell

Nüstern ['nʏstɐn] *pl* ZO nostrils

Nutte ['nʊtə] F *f* (-; -n) hooker, *sl* tart

Nutzanwendung ['nʊts-] *f* practical application; **'nutzbar** *adj* usable; **~ machen** utilize; exploit; harness; **'nutzbringend** *adj* profitable, useful

nütze ['nʏtsə] *adj* useful; *zu nichts ~ sein* be (of) no use; be good for nothing

Nutzen ['nʊtsən] *m* (-s; -) use; profit, gain; advantage; **~ ziehen aus** (*dat*) benefit *or* profit from *or* by; **zum ~ von** (*or gen*) for the benefit of

'nutzen, 'nützen (*ge-, h*) **1.** *v/i: j-m ~* be of use to s.o.; *es nützt nichts* (*es zu tun*) it's no use (doing it); **2.** *v/t* use, make use of; take advantage of

nützlich ['nʏtslɪç] *adj* useful, helpful; advantageous; *sich ~ machen* make o.s. useful

'nutzlos *adj* useless, (of) no use

'Nutzung *f* (-; -en) use, utilization

Nylon® ['naɪlɔn] *n* (-s; *no pl*) nylon; **~strümpfe** *pl* nylon stockings

Nymphe ['nʏmfə] *f* (-; -n) nymph

O

O ABBR *of Osten* E, east

o *int* oh!; *o weh!* oh dear!

o. Ä. ABBR *of oder Ähnliche(s)* or the like

Oase [o'a:zə] *f* (-; -n) oasis (*a. fig*)

ob [ɔp] *cj* whether, if; *als ~* as if, as though; *und ~!* and how!, you bet!

Obacht ['o:baxt] *f: ~ geben auf* (*acc*) pay attention to; (*gib*) *~!* watch out!

Obdach ['ɔpdax] *n* (-[e]s; *no pl*) shelter

'obdachlos *adj* homeless, without shelter; **'Obdachlose** *m, f* (-*n*; -*n*) homeless person; **'Obdachlosen,syl** *n* shelter for the homeless

Obduktion [ɔpdʊk'tsjo:n] *f* (-; -en) MED autopsy

obduzieren [ɔpdu'tsi:rən] *v/t* (*no -ge-, h*) MED perform an autopsy on

oben ['o:bən] *adv* above; up; on (the) top; at the top (*a. fig*); on the surface; upstairs; *da ~* up there; *von ~ bis unten* from top to bottom (*or* toe); *links ~* (at the) top left; *siehe ~* see above; F *~ ohne* topless; *von ~ herab* *fig* patronizing(ly), condescending(ly); *~ erwähnt or genannt* above-mentioned; *~'an adv* at the top; *~'auf adv* on the top; on the surface; F feeling great; *~'drein adv* besides, into the bargain, at that; *~'hin adv* superficially

Ober ['o:bɐ] *m* (-s; -) waiter

'Ober|arm *m* ANAT upper arm; **~arzt** *m*, **~ärztin** *f* assistant medical director; **~befehl** *m* MIL supreme command; **~begriff** *n* generic term; **~bürgermeister** *m* mayor, *Br* Lord Mayor

obere ['o:bərə] *adj* upper, top, *fig a.* superior

'Oberfläche *f* surface (*a. fig*) (*an dat* on); **'oberflächlich** *adj* superficial

'oberhalb *prp* (*gen*) above

'Ober|hand *f: die ~ gewinnen* (*über acc*) get the upper hand (of); **~haupt** *n* head, chief; **~haus** *n* (-es; *no pl*) *Br* PARL House of Lords; **~hemd** *n* shirt; **~herrschaft** *f* (-; *no pl*) supremacy

Oberin ['o:bərɪn] *f* (-; -nen) REL Mother Superior

'oberirdisch *adj* above ground; ELECTR overhead

'Ober|kellner *m* head waiter; **~kiefer** *m* ANAT upper jaw; **~körper** *m* upper part of the body; *den ~ freimachen* strip to the waist; **~leder** *n* uppers; **~leitung** *f* chief management; ELECTR overhead contact line; **~lippe** *f* ANAT upper lip

Obers ['o:bɐs] *Austrian n* (-; *no pl*) GASTR cream

'Oberschenkel *m* ANAT thigh

'Oberschule *f appr* highschool, *Br* grammar school

Oberst ['o:bɛst] m (-en; -en) MIL colonel

oberste ['o:bəstə] adj up(per)most, top (most); highest; fig chief, first

'Oberstufe f appr senior highschool, Br appr senior classes; ~teil n top

ob'gleich cj (al)though

Obhut ['ɔphu:t] f (-; no pl) care, charge; in s-e ~ nehmen take care or charge of

obig ['o:bɪç] adj above(-mentioned)

Objekt [ɔp'jɛkt] n (-[e]s; -e) object (a. LING); ECON property

objektiv [ɔpjɛk'ti:f] adj objective; impartial, unbias(s)ed

Objek'tiv n (-s; -e) PHOT (object) lens

Objektivität [ɔpjɛktivi'tɛ:t] f (-; no pl) objectivity; impartiality

Oblate [o'bla:tə] f (-; -n) wafer; REL host

obligatorisch [obliga'to:rɪʃ] adj compulsory

Oboe [o'bo:ə] f (-; -n) MUS oboe

Oboist [obo'ɪst] m (-en; -en) MUS oboist

Observatorium [ɔpzɛrva'to:rjʊm] n (-s; -ien) ASTR observatory

Obst [o:pst] n (-[e]s; no pl) fruit; ~garten m orchard; ~kon,serven pl canned fruit; ~laden m fruit store, esp Br fruiterer's (shop); ~torte f fruit pie (Br flan)

obszön [ɔps'tsø:n] adj obscene, filthy

ob'wohl cj (al)though

Occasion [ɔka'zjo:n] Swiss f (-; -en) bargain, good buy

Ochse ['ɔksə] m (-n; -n) ZO ox, bullock; F blockhead

od. ABBR of oder or

öde ['ø:də] adj deserted, desolate; waste; fig dull, dreary, tedious

oder ['o:də] cj or; ~ aber or else, otherwise; ~ vielmehr or rather; ~ so or so; er kommt doch, ~? he's coming, isn't he?; du kennst ihn ja nicht, ~ doch? you don't know him, or do you?

Ofen ['o:fən] m (-s; Öfen ['ø:fən]) stove; oven; TECH furnace; ~heizung f stove heating; ~rohr n stovepipe

offen ['ɔfən] 1. adj open (a. fig); vacant (post); fig frank; 2. adv: ~ gesagt frankly (speaking); ~ s-e Meinung sagen speak one's mind (freely); ~ stehen be open (fig j-m to s.o.); ECON be outstanding

offenbar adj obvious, evident; apparent; offenbaren [-'ba:rən] v/t (ge-, h)

reveal, disclose, show; Offen'barung f (-; -en) revelation

'Offenheit f (-; no pl) openness, frankness

'offenherzig adj open-hearted, frank, candid; fig revealing (dress)

'offensichtlich adj → offenbar

offensiv [ɔfɛn'zi:f] adj, Offensive [ɔfɛn'zi:və] f (-; -n) offensive

öffentlich ['œfəntlɪç] adj public; ~e Verkehrsmittel pl public transport; ~e Schulen pl public (Br state) schools; ~ auftreten appear in public

'Öffentlichkeit f (-; no pl) the public; in aller ~ in public, openly; an die ~ bringen make public

offiziell [ɔfi'tsjɛl] adj official

Offizier [ɔfi'tsi:ə] m (-s; -e) MIL (commissioned) officer

öffnen ['œfnən] v/t and v/refl (ge-, h) open; Öffner ['œfnɐ] m (-s; -) opener; 'Öffnung f (-; -en) opening

'Öffnungszeiten pl business or office hours

oft [ɔft] adv often, frequently

oh [o:] int o(h)!

ohne ['o:nə] prp (acc) and cj without; ~ mich! count me out!; ~ ein Wort (zu sagen) without (saying) a word

ohne|'gleichen adj unequal(l)ed, unparalleled; ~'hin adv anyhow, anyway

Ohnmacht ['o:nmaxt] f (-; -en) MED unconsciousness; fig helplessness; in ~ fallen faint, pass out; 'ohnmächtig adj MED unconscious; fig helpless; ~ werden faint, pass out

Ohr [o:ə] n (-[e]s; -en ['o:rən]) ANAT ear; F j-n übers ~ hauen cheat s.o.; bis über die ~en verliebt (verschuldet) head over heels in love (over your head in debt)

Öhr [ø:ə] n (-[e]s; -e ['ø:rə]) eye

Ohrenarzt ['o:rən-] m ear specialist

'ohrenbetäubend adj deafening

'Ohren|schmerzen pl earache; ~schützer pl earmuffs; ~zeuge m earwitness

'Ohrfeige f slap in the face (a. fig); 'ohrfeigen [-faigən] v/t (ge-, h) j-n ~ slap s.o.'s face

'Ohr|läppchen [-lɛpçən] n (-s; -) ANAT earlobe; ~ring m earring

oje [o'je:] int oh dear!, dear me!

Ökologe [øko'lo:gə] m (-n; -n) ecologist;

Ökologie [øko:loˈgi:] *f* (-; *no pl*) ecology; **ökologisch** [økoˈlo:gɪʃ] *adj* ecological

Ökonomie [økonoˈmi:] *f* (-; *no pl*) economy; ECON economics; **ökonomisch** [økoˈno:mɪʃ] *adj* economical; ECON economic

Ökosy,stem [ˈø:ko-] *n* ecosystem

Oktave [ɔkˈta:və] *f* (-; *-n*) MUS octave

Oktober [ɔkˈto:bɐ] *m* (-[*s*]; -) October

ökumenisch [økuˈme:nɪʃ] *adj* REL ecumenical

Öl [ø:l] *n* (-[*e*]*s*; *Öle*) oil; petroleum; **nach ~ bohren** drill for oil; **auf ~ sto-ßen** strike oil; **'Ölbaum** *m* BOT olive (tree)

Oldtimer [ˈɔʊldtaɪmɐ] *m* (-*s*; -) MOT veteran car

ölen [ˈø:lən] *v/t* (*ge-*, *h*) oil, TECH *a.* lubricate

'Öl∥farbe *f* oil (paint); **~feld** *n* oilfield; **~förderland** *n* oil-producing country; **~förderung** *f* oil production; **~gemälde** *n* oil painting; **~heizung** *f* oil heating

ölig [ˈø:lɪç] *adj* oily, greasy (*both a. fig*)

oliv [oˈli:f] *adj* olive

Olive [oˈli:və] *f* (-; *-n*) BOT olive

'Öl∥leitung *f* (oil) pipeline; **~messtab** *m* MOT dipstick; **~pest** *f* oil pollution; **~quelle** *f* oil well; **~sar,dine** *f* canned (*Br a.* tinned) sardine; **~tanker** *m* MAR oil tanker; **~teppich** *m* oil slick; **~stand** *m* oil level

'Ölung *f* (-; *no pl*) oiling, TECH *a.* lubrication; **Letzte ~** REL extreme unction

'Öl∥wanne *f* MOT oil pan, *Br* sump; **~wechsel** *m* MOT oil change; **~zeug** *n* oilskins

Olympia... [oˈlʏmpja-] *in cpds* ...*mannschaft*, ...*medaille etc*: Olympic ...

Olympiade [olʏmˈpja:də] *f* (-; *-n*) SPORT Olympic Games, Olympics

Oma [ˈo:ma] F *f* (-; *-s*) grandma

Omi [ˈo:mi] F *f* (-; *-s*) granny

Omnibus [ˈɔmnibʊs] *m* → **Bus**

onanieren [onaˈni:rən] *v/i* (*no ge-*, *h*) masturbate

Onkel [ˈɔŋkəl] *m* (-*s*; -) uncle

Online... [ˈɔnlaɪn-] EDP online ...

Opa [ˈo:pa] F *m* (-*s*; *-s*) grandpa

Oper [ˈo:pɐ] *f* (-; *-n*) MUS opera; opera (house)

Operation [opəraˈtsjo:n] *f* (-; *-en*) MED operation; **e-e ~ vornehmen** perform an operation; **Operati'onssaal** *m* MED operating room (*Br* theatre)

Operette [opəˈrɛtə] *f* (-; *-n*) MUS operetta

operieren [opəˈri:rən] (*no -ge-*, *h*) **1.** *v/t* MED *j-n ~* operate on s.o. (*wegen* for); **operiert werden** be operated on, have an operation; **sich ~ lassen** undergo an operation; **2.** *v/i* MED, MIL operate; proceed

Opernsänger(in) opera singer

Opfer [ˈɔpfɐ] *n* (-*s*; -) sacrifice; offering; victim; **ein ~ bringen** make a sacrifice; (*dat*) **zum ~ fallen** fall victim to

'opfern *v/t and v/i* (*ge-*, *h*) sacrifice

Opium [ˈo:pjʊm] *n* (-*s*; *no pl*) opium

Opposition [ɔpoziˈtsjo:n] *f* (-; *-en*) opposition (*a.* PARL)

Optik [ˈɔptik] *f* (-; *no pl*) optics; PHOT optical system

Optiker [ˈɔptikɐ] *m* (-*s*; -), **'Optikerin** *f* (-; *-nen*) optician

optimal [ɔptiˈma:l] *adj* optimum, best

Optimismus [ɔptiˈmɪsmʊs] *m* (-; *no pl*) optimism; **Optimist(in)** [ɔptiˈmɪst(ɪn)] (-*en*; -*en*/-; *-nen*) optimist; **opti'mistisch** *adj* optimistic

Option [ɔpˈtsjo:n] *f* (-; *-en*) option

optisch [ˈɔptiʃ] *adj* optical

Orange [oˈrã:ʒə] *f* (-; *-n*) BOT orange

Orchester [ɔrˈkɛstɐ] *n* (-*s*; -) MUS orchestra

Orchidee [ɔrçiˈde:] *f* (-; *-n*) bot orchid

Orden [ˈɔrdən] *m* (-*s*; -) medal, decoration; *esp* REL order

'Ordensschwester *f* REL sister, nun

ordentlich [ˈɔrdəntlɪç] **1.** *adj* tidy, neat, orderly; proper; thorough; decent (*a.* F); respectable; full (*member etc*); JUR ordinary; reasonable (*performance etc*); F good, sound; **2.** *adv*: **s-e Sache ~ machen** do a good job; **sich ~ benehmen** (*anziehen*) behave (dress) properly *or* decently

ordinär [ɔrdiˈnɛ:ɐ] *adj* vulgar; common

ordnen [ˈɔrdnən] *v/t* (*ge-*, *h*) put in order; arrange, sort (out); file; settle

Ordner [ˈɔrdnɐ] *m* (-*s*; -) file; folder; attendant, guard

'Ordnung *f* (-; *no pl*) order; orderliness, tidiness; arrangement; system, set-up; class; **in ~** all right; TECH *etc* in (good) order; **in ~ bringen** put right (*a. fig*);

tidy up; repair, fix (a. fig); (in) ~ **halten** keep (in) order; **et. ist nicht in ~ (mit)** there is s.th. wrong (with)

'**ordnungsgemäß 1.** adj correct, regular; **2.** adv duly, properly

'**Ordnungs|strafe** f JUR fine, penalty; **~zahl** f MATH ordinal number

Organ [ɔr'ga:n] n (-s; -e) organ; **~empfänger** m MED organ recipient; **~handel** m sale of (transplant) organs

Organisation [ɔrganiza'tsjo:n] f (-; -en) organization; **Organisator** [ɔrgani'za:to:r] m (-s; -en [-za'to:rən]) organizer; **Organisa'torin** f (-; -nen) organizer; **organisatorisch** [-za'to:rɪʃ] adj organizational

organisch [ɔr'ga:nɪʃ] adj organic

organisieren [ɔrgani'zi:rən] v/t organize; F get (hold of); **sich ~** organize; ECON unionize; **organisiert** [ɔr'gani'zi:rt] adj organized; ECON unionized

Organismus [ɔrga'nɪsmʊs] m (-; -men) BIOL organism

Organist [ɔrga'nɪst] m (-en; -en), **Orga'nistin** f (-; -nen) MUS organist

Or'ganspender m MED (organ) donor

Orgasmus [ɔr'gasmʊs] m (-; -men) orgasm

Orgel ['ɔrgəl] f (-; -n) MUS organ

'**Orgelpfeife** f MUS organ pipe

Orgie ['ɔrgjə] f (-; -n) orgy

Orientale [ɔrjɛn'ta:lə] m (-n; -n), **Orien'talin** f (-; -nen), **orien'talisch** adj oriental

orientieren [ɔrjɛn'ti:rən] v/t (no -ge-, h) inform (**über** acc about), brief (on); **sich ~** orient(ate) o.s. (a. fig) (**nach** by); inform o.s.; **Orien'tierung** f (-; no pl) orientation, fig a. information; **die ~ verlieren** lose one's bearings

Orien'tierungssinn m (-[e]s; no pl) sense of direction

original [origi'na:l] adj original; real, genuine; TV live; **Origi'nal** n (-s; -e) original; fig real (or quite a) character

Origi'nal... in cpds ...aufnahme, ...ausgabe etc: original ...; **~übertragung** f live broadcast or program(me)

originell [origi'nɛl] adj original; ingenious; witty

Orkan [ɔr'ka:n] m (-[e]s; -e) hurricane

or'kanartig adj violent; fig thunderous

Ort [ɔrt] m (-[e]s; -e) place; village, (small) town; spot, point; scene; **vor ~** mining: at the (pit) face; fig in the field, on the spot

orten ['ɔrtən] v/t (ge-, h) locate, spot

orthodox [ɔrto'dɔks] adj orthodox

Orthographie [ɔrtogra'fi:] f (-; -n) orthography

Orthopäde [ɔrto'pɛ:də] m (-n; -n), **Ortho'pädin** f (-; -nen) MED orthop(a)edic specialist

örtlich ['œrtlɪç] adj local

'**Ortsbestimmung** f AVIAT, MAR location; LING adverb of place

'**Ortschaft** f → **Ort**

'**Ortsgespräch** n TEL local call

'**Ortskenntnis** f: **~ besitzen** know a place

'**Ortsnetz** n TEL local exchange

'**Ortszeit** f local time

Öse ['ø:zə] f (-; -n) eye; eyelet

Ostblock ['ɔst-] m (-[e]s; no pl) HIST POL East(ern) Bloc

Osten ['ɔstən] m (-s; no pl) east; POL the East; **nach ~** east(wards)

Oster|ei ['o:stɐ-] n Easter egg; **~hase** m Easter bunny or rabbit

Ostern ['o:stɐn] n (-; -) Easter (**zu, an** at); **frohe ~!** Happy Easter!

Österreicher ['ø:stəraiçɐ] m (-s; -), '**Österreicherin** [-raiçərin] f (-; -nen), '**österreichisch** adj Austrian

östlich ['œstlɪç] **1.** adj east(ern); easterly; **2.** adv: **~ von** (to the) east of

ostwärts ['ɔstvɛrts] adv east(wards)

'**Ostwind** m east wind

Otter ['ɔtɐ] ZO **1.** m (-s; -) otter; **2.** f (-; -n) adder, viper

outen ['autən] v/t (ge-, h) out

Ouvertüre [uver'ty:rə] f (-; -n) MUS overture

oval [o'va:l] adj, **O'val** n (-s; -e) oval

Oxid [ɔ'ksi:t] n (-[e]s; -e [ɔ'ksi:də]) CHEM oxide; **oxidieren** [ɔksi'di:rən] v/t (no -ge-, h) and v/i (h, sein) CHEM oxidize; **Oxyd** n → **Oxid**

Ozean ['o:tsea:n] m (-s; -e) ocean, sea

Ozon [o'tso:n] n (-s; no pl) CHEM ozone

o'zonfreundlich adj ozone-friendly

O'zon|loch n ozone hole; **~schicht** f ozone layer; **~schild** m ozone shield; **~werte** pl ozone levels

P

paar [paːɐ] *indef pron*: **ein ~** a few, some, F a couple of; **ein ~ Mal** a few times

Paar *n* (-[e]s; -e) pair; couple; **ein ~ (neue) Schuhe** a (new) pair of shoes

paaren ['paːrən] *v/t and v/refl* (ge-, h) ZO mate; *fig* combine

'Paarlauf *m* SPORT pair skating

'Paarung *f* (-; -en) ZO mating, copulation; SPORT matching

'paarweise *adv* in pairs, in twos

Pacht [paxt] *f* (-; -en) lease; rent

'pachten *v/t* (ge-, h) (take on) lease

Pächter ['peçtɐ] *m* (-s; -), 'Pächterin *f* (-; -nen) leaseholder; AGR tenant

'Pacht|vertrag *m* lease; ~zins *m* rent

Pack¹ [pak] *m → Packen

Pack² *contp n* (-[e]s; *no pl*) rabble

Päckchen ['pɛkçən] *n* (-s; -) pack, Br packet; small parcel; **packen** ['pakən] *v/t and v/i* (ge-, h) pack; make up (*parcel etc*); grab, seize (**an** *dat* by); *fig* grip; **'Packen** *m* (-s; -) pack, pile (*a. fig*); **Packer** ['pakɐ] *m* (-s; -) packer; removal man; **'Packpa,pier** *n* packing *or* brown paper; **'Packung** *f* (-; -en) package, box; pack, Br packet

Pädagoge [pɛda'goːgə] *m* (-n; -n), **Pädagogin** *f* (-; -nen) teacher; education(al)ist

päda'gogisch *adj* pedagogic, educational; **~e Hochschule** college of education

Paddel ['padəl] *n* (-s; -) paddle

'Paddelboot *n* canoe

'paddeln *v/i* (ge-, h, sein) paddle, canoe

Page ['paːʒə] *m* (-n; -n) page(boy)

Paket [pa'keːt] *n* (-[e]s; -e) package; parcel; **~karte** *f* parcel post slip, Br parcel mailing form; **~post** *f* parcel post; **~schalter** *m* parcel counter; **~zustellung** *f* parcel delivery

Pakt [pakt] *m* (-[e]s; -e) POL pact

Palast [pa'last] *m* (-[e]s; Paläste [pa'lɛstə]) palace

Palme ['palmə] *f* (-; -n) BOT palm (tree)

Palm'sonntag *m* REL Palm Sunday

Pampelmuse ['pampəlmuːzə] *f* (-; -n) BOT grapefruit

paniert [pa'niːɐt] *adj* GASTR breaded

Panik ['paːnɪk] *f* (-; -en) panic; **in ~ geraten (versetzen)** panic; **in ~ -stricken**, F panicky; **panisch** ['paːnɪʃ] *adj*: **~e Angst** mortal terror

Panne ['panə] *f* (-; -n) breakdown, MOT *a.* engine trouble; *fig* mishap

'Pannenhilfe *f* MOT breakdown service

Panter, Panther ['pantɐ] *m* (-s; -) ZO panther

Pantoffel [pan'tɔfəl] *m* (-s; -n) slipper; **~held** F *m* henpecked husband

Pantomime [panto'miːmə] THEA **1.** *f* (-; -n) mime, dumb show; **2.** *m* (-n; -n) mime (artist); **panto'mimisch** *adv*: **~ darstellen** mime

Panzer ['pantsɐ] *m* (-s; -) armo(u)r (*a. fig*); MIL tank; ZO shell; **~glas** *n* bulletproof glass

'panzern *v/t* (ge-, h) armo(u)r; → **gepanzert**

'Panzerschrank *m* safe

Panzerung ['pantsərʊŋ] *f* (-; -en) armo(u)r plating

Papa [pa'paː] F *m* (-s; -s) dad(dy), pa

Papagei [papa'gai] *m* (-en; -en) ZO parrot

Papeterie [papetə'riː] *Swiss f* (-; -n) stationer('s shop)

Papier [pa'piːɐ] *n* (-s; -e) paper; *pl* papers, documents; identification (paper)

Pa'pier... *in cpds* ...geld, ...handtuch, ...serviette, ...tüte *etc*: *mst* paper ...; **~geschäft** *n* stationer's (store, Br shop); **~korb** *m* wastepaper basket; **~krieg** F *m* red tape; **~schnitzel** *pl* scraps of paper; **~waren** *pl* stationery

Pappe ['papə] *f* (-; -n) cardboard, pasteboard

Pappel ['papəl] *f* (-; -n) BOT poplar

'Papp|kar,ton *m* cardboard box, carton; **~teller** *m* paper plate

Paprika ['paprika] *m* (-s; -[s]) a) BOT sweet pepper, b) (*no pl*) GASTR paprika

Papst [paːpst] *m* (-[e]s; Päpste ['pɛːpstə]) pope; **'päpstlich** *adj* papal

Parade [pa'raːdə] *f* (-; -n) parade; *soccer etc*: save; *boxing, fencing*: parry

Paradeiser [para'daizɐ] *Austrian m* (-s; -) BOT tomato

Paradies [para'diːs] *n* (*-es; -e*) paradise

paradiesisch [para'diːzɪʃ] *fig adj* heavenly, delightful

paradox [para'dɔks] *adj* paradoxical

Paragraph [para'graːf] *m* (*-en; -en*) JUR article, section; paragraph

parallel [para'leːl] *adj*, **Paral'lele** *f* (*-; -n*) parallel

Parasit [para'ziːt] *m* (*-en; -en*) parasite

Parfüm [par'fyːm] *n* (*-s; -s*) perfume, *Br a.* scent; **Parfümerie** [parfymə'riː] *f* (*-; -n*) perfumery; **parfümieren** [parfy-'miːrən] *v/t* (*no -ge-, h*) perfume, scent; *sich ~* put on perfume

parieren [pa'riːrən] *v/t* and *v/i* (*no -ge-, h*) SPORT parry, *fig a.* counter (**mit** with); pull up (*horse*); obey

Park [park] *m* (*-s; -s*) park

parken ['parkən] *v/t* and *v/i* (*ge-, h*) MOT park; **Parken verboten!** no parking!

Parkett [par'kɛt] *n* (*-[e]s; -e, -s*) parquet (floor); THEA orchestra, *Br* stalls; dance floor

'**Park|gebühr** *f* parking fee; **~(hoch-)haus** *n* parking garage, *Br* multi-storey car park

parkieren [par'kiːrən] *Swiss v/t and v/i* → **parken**

'**Park|kralle** *f* wheel clamp; **~lücke** *f* parking space; **~platz** *m* parking lot, *Br* car park; → **Parklücke**; **e-n ~ suchen** (**finden**) look for (find) somewhere to park the car; **~scheibe** *f* parking disk (*Br* disc); **~sünder** *m* parking offender; **~uhr** *f* MOT parking meter; **~wächter** *m* park keeper; MOT parking lot (*Br* car park) attendant

Parlament [parla'mɛnt] *n* (*-[e]s; -e*) parliament; **parlamentarisch** [parlamɛn'taːrɪʃ] *adj* parliamentary

Parodie [paro'diː] *f* (*-; -n*), **paro'dieren** *v/t* (*no -ge-, h*) parody

Parole [pa'roːlə] *f* (*-; -n*) MIL password; *fig* watchword, POL *a.* slogan

Partei [par'tai] *f* (*-; -en*) party (*a.* POL); *j-s ~ ergreifen* take sides with s.o., side with s.o.; **par'teiisch** *adj* partial (*für* to); prejudiced (*gegen* against)

par'teilos *adj* POL independent

Par'tei|mitglied *n* POL party member; **~pro,gramm** *n* POL platform; **~tag** *m* POL convention; **~zugehörigkeit** *f* POL party membership

Parterre [par'tɛrə] *n* (*-s; -s*) first (*Br* ground) floor

Partie [par'tiː] *f* (*-; -n*) game, SPORT *a.* match; part, passage (*a.* MUS); **e-e gute** *etc* **~ sein** be a good *etc* match

Partisan [parti'zaːn] *m* (*-s, -en; -en*), **Parti'sanin** *f* (*-; -nen*) MIL partisan, guerilla

Partitur [parti'tuːr] *f* (*-; -en*) MUS score

Partizip [parti'tsiːp] *n* (*-s; -ien*) LING participle

Partner ['partnɐ] *m* (*-s; -*), '**Partnerin** *f* (*-; -nen*) partner

'**Partnerschaft** *f* (*-; -en*) partnership

'**Partnerstadt** *f* twin town

paschen ['paʃən] *Austrian v/t and v/i* (*ge-, h*) smuggle; **Pascher** ['paʃɐ] *Austrian m* (*-s; -*) smuggler

Pass [pas] *m* (*-es; Pässe* ['pɛsə]) passport; SPORT, GEOGR pass; **langer ~** SPORT long ball

Passage [pa'saːʒə] *f* (*-; -n*) passage

Passagier [pasa'ʒiːr] *m* (*-s; -e*) passenger; **~flugzeug** *n* passenger plane; airliner

Passa'gierin *f* (*-; -nen*) passenger

Passah ['pasa] *n* (*-s; no pl*), '**Passahfest** *n* REL Passover

Passant [pa'sant] *m* (*-en; -en*), **Pas'santin** *f* (*-; -nen*) passerby

'**Passbild** *n* passport photo(graph)

passen ['pasən] **1.** *v/i* (*ge-, h*) fit (*j-m* s.o.; *auf* or *für* or *zu et.* s.th.); suit (*j-m* s.o.), be convenient; *cards*, SPORT pass; **~ zu** go with, match; **sie ~ gut zueinander** they are well suited to each other; *passt es Ihnen morgen?* would tomorrow suit you or be all right (with you)?; *das (es) passt mir gar nicht* I don't like that (him) at all; *das passt (nicht) zu ihm* that's just like him (not like him, not his style); **~d** *adj* fitting; matching; suitable, right

passierbar [pa'siːrbaːr] *adj* passable

passieren [pa'siːrən] (*no -ge-*) **1.** *v/i* (*sein*) happen; **2.** *v/t* (*h*) pass (through)

Pas'sierschein *m* pass, permit

Passion [pa'sjoːn] *f* (*-; -en*) passion; REL Passion

passiv ['pasiːf] *adj* passive

'**Passiv** *n* (*-s; no pl*) LING passive (voice)

Paste ['pastə] *f* (*-; -n*) paste

Pastell [pas'tɛl] *n* (*-[e]s; -e*) PAINT pastel

Pastete [pas'teːtə] *f* (*-; -n*) GASTR pie

Pate ['pa:tə] m (-n; -n) godfather; **'Patenkind** n godchild

'Patenschaft f (-; -en) sponsorship

Patent [pa'tɛnt] n (-[e]s; -e) patent; MIL commission; **~amt** n patent office; **~anwalt** m JUR patent agent

patentieren [patɛn'tiːrən] v/t (no -ge-, h) patent; **(sich) et. ~ lassen** take out a patent for s.th.

Pa'tentinhaber m patentee

pathetisch [pa'te:tɪʃ] adj pompous

Patient [pa'tsjɛnt] m (-en; -en), Pa'tientin f (-; -nen) MED patient

Patin ['pa:tɪn] f (-; -nen) godmother

Patriot [patri'oːt] m (-en; -en) patriot

patri'otisch adj patriotic

Patrone [pa'troːnə] f (-; -n) cartridge

Patrouille [pa'trʊljə] f (-; -n) MIL patrol; **patrouillieren** [patrʊl'jiːrən] v/i (no -ge-, h) MIL patrol

Patsche ['patʃə] F f: **in der ~ sitzen** be in a fix or jam

'patschen F v/i (ge-, h) (s)plash

'patsch'nass adj soaking wet

patzen ['patsən] F v/i (ge-, h), **Patzer** ['patsɐ] F m (-s; -) blunder

Pauke ['paʊkə] f (-; -n) MUS bass drum; kettledrum

'pauken F v/i and v/t (ge-, h) cram

Pauschale [paʊ'ʃaːlə] f (-; -n) lump sum

Pau'schalgebühr f flat rate; **~reise** f package tour; **~urteil** n sweeping judg(e)ment

Pause¹ ['paʊzə] f (-; -n) recess, Br break, esp THEA, SPORT intermission, Br interval; pause; rest (a. MUS)

'Pause² f (-; -n) TECH tracing

'pausen v/t (ge-, h) TECH trace

'pausenlos adj uninterrupted, nonstop

'Pausenzeichen n radio: interval signal; PED bell

pausieren [paʊ'ziːrən] v/i (no -ge-, h) pause, rest

Pavian ['paːvjaːn] m (-s; -e) ZO baboon

Pavillon ['pavɪljɔŋ] m (-s; -s) pavilion

Pazifist [patsi'fɪst] m (-en; -en), Pazi'fistin f (-; -nen), pazi'fistisch adj pacifist

PC [peː'tseː] m (-[s]; -[s]) ABBR of **personal computer** PC

Pech [pɛç] n (-s; no pl) pitch; F bad luck; **~strähne** F f run of bad luck; **~vogel** F m unlucky fellow

pedantisch [pe'dantɪʃ] adj pedantic, fussy

Pegel ['peːgəl] m (-s; -) level (a. fig)

peilen ['paɪlən] v/t (ge-, h) sound

peinigen ['paɪnɪgən] v/t (ge-, h) torment

Peiniger ['paɪnɪgɐ] m (-s; -) tormentor

peinlich ['paɪnlɪç] adj embarrassing; **~ genau** meticulous (**bei**, **in** dat in); **es war mir ~** I was or felt embarrassed

Peitsche ['paɪtʃə] f (-; -n), **'peitschen** v/t (ge-, h) whip

'Peitschenhieb m lash

Pelle ['pɛlə] f (-; -n) skin; peel; **'pellen** v/t (ge-, h) peel; **'Pellkar,toffeln** pl potatoes (boiled) in their jackets

Pelz [pɛlts] m (-es; -e) fur; skin

pelzgefüttert adj fur-lined

'Pelzgeschäft n fur(rier's) store (Br shop)

pelzig ['pɛltsɪç] adj furry; MED furred

'Pelzmantel m fur coat

'Pelztiere pl furred animals, furs

Pendel ['pɛndəl] n (-s; -) pendulum

'pendeln v/i (ge-, h) swing; RAIL etc shuttle; commute

'Pendeltür f swing door

'Pendelverkehr m RAIL etc shuttle service; commuter traffic; **Pendler(in)** ['pɛndlɐ (-lərɪn)] (-s; -/-; -nen) RAIL etc commuter

Penis ['peːnɪs] m (-s; -se) ANAT penis

Penner ['pɛnɐ] F m (-s; -) tramp, bum

Pension [pã'sjoːn] f (-; -en) (old age) pension; boarding-house, private hotel; **in ~ sein** be retired; **Pensionär** [pãsjo'nɛːɐ (-'nɛːrɪn)] (-s; -e/-; -nen) (old age) pensioner; boarder; **Pensionat** [pãsjo'naːt] n (-[e]s; -e) boarding school

pensionieren [pãsjo'niːrən] v/t (no -ge-, h) pension (off); **sich ~ lassen** retire; **Pensio'nierung** f (-; -en) retirement

Pensionist [pãsjo'nɪst] Austrian, Swiss m (-en; -en) (old age) pensioner

Pensi'onsgast m boarder

Pensum ['pɛnzʊm] n (-s; Pensen, Pensa) (work) quota, stint

per [pɛr] prp (acc) per; by

perfekt [pɛr'fɛkt] adj perfect; **~ machen** settle

'Perfekt n (-s; -e) LING present perfect

Pergament [pɛrga'mɛnt] n (-[e]s; -e) parchment

Periode [pe'rjo:də] *f* (-; -n) period, MED *a.* menstruation

periodisch [pe'rjo:dɪʃ] *adj* periodic(al)

Peripherie [perife'ri:] *f* (-; -n) periphery, outskirts; ~**geräte** *pl* EDP peripheral equipment

Perle ['pɛrlə] *f* (-; -n) pearl; bead

'perlen *v/i* (*ge-*, *h*) sparkle, bubble

'Perlenkette *f* pearl necklace

'Perlmuschel *f* ZO pearl oyster

Perlmutt ['pɛrlmʊt] *n* (-s; *no pl*) mother-of-pearl

Perron [pe'rõ:] *m* (-s; -s) Swiss platform

Perser ['pɛrzɐ] *m* (-s; -) Persian; **Perserin** ['pɛrzərɪn] *f* (-; -nen) Persian carpet; **Perserin** ['pɛrzərɪn] *f* (-; -nen) Persian (woman); **Persien** ['pɛrzjən] Persia; **persisch** ['pɛrzɪʃ] *adj* Persian

Person [pɛr'zo:n] *f* (-; -en) person, THEA *etc a.* character; *ein Tisch für drei* ~*en* a table for three

Personal [pɛrzo'na:l] *n* (-s; *no pl*) staff, personnel; *zu wenig* ~ *haben* be understaffed; ~**abbau** *m* staff reduction; ~**abteilung** *f* personnel department; ~**ausweis** *m* identity card; ~**chef** *m* staff manager

Personalien [pɛrzo'na:ljən] *pl* particulars, personal data

Perso'nalpro,nomen *n* LING personal pronoun

Per'sonen|(kraft)wagen (ABBR **PKW**) *m* (Br *a.* motor)car, auto(mobile); ~**zug** *m* passenger train; local *or* commuter train

personifizieren [pɛrzonifi'tsi:rən] *v/t* (*no -ge-*, *h*) personify

persönlich [pɛr'zø:nlɪç] *adj* personal

Per'sönlichkeit *f* (-; -en) personality

Perücke [pe'rʏkə] *f* (-; -n) wig

pervers [pɛr'vɛrs] *adj* perverted; ~**er Mensch** pervert

Pessimismus [pɛsi'mɪsmʊs] *m* (-; *no pl*) pessimism; **Pessimist(in)** [pɛsi'mɪst(ɪn)] (-en; -en/-; -nen) pessimist; **pessi'mistisch** *adj* pessimistic

Pest [pɛst] *f* (-; *no pl*) MED plague

Pestizid [pɛsti'tsi:t] *n* (-s; -e) pesticide

Petersilie [pe:tɐ'zi:ljə] *f* (-; -n) BOT parsley

Petroleum [pe'tro:leʊm] *n* (-s; *no pl*) kerosene, Br paraffin; ~**lampe** *f* kerosene (Br paraffin) lamp

petzen ['pɛtsən] F *v/i* (*ge-*, *h*) tell tales, Br *a.* sneak

Pfad [pfa:t] *m* (-[e]s; -e ['pfa:də]) path, track; ~**finder** *m* boy scout; ~**finderin** [-fɪndərɪn] *f* (-; -nen) girl scout, Br girl guide

Pfahl [pfa:l] *m* (-[e]s; Pfähle ['pfɛ:lə]) stake; post; pole

Pfand [pfant] *n* (-[e]s; Pfänder ['pfɛndɐ]) security; pawn, pledge; deposit; forfeit

'Pfandbrief *m* ECON mortgage bond

pfänden ['pfɛndən] *v/t* (*ge-*, *h*) seize

'Pfandhaus *n* → **Leihhaus**

'Pfandleiher [-laiɐ] *m* (-s; -) pawnbroker

'Pfandschein *m* pawn ticket

'Pfändung *f* (-; -en) JUR seizure

Pfanne ['pfanə] *f* (-; -n) pan, skillet

'Pfannkuchen *m* pancake

Pfarrbezirk ['pfar-] *m* parish

Pfarrer ['pfarɐ] *m* (-s; -) vicar; pastor; (parish) priest

'Pfarr|gemeinde *f* parish; ~**haus** *n* parsonage; rectory, vicarage; ~**kirche** *f* parish church

Pfau [pfau] *m* (-[e]s; -en) ZO peacock

Pfeffer ['pfɛfɐ] *m* (-s; -) pepper; ~**kuchen** *m* gingerbread; ~**minze** [-mɪntsə] *f* (-; *no pl*) BOT peppermint

'pfeffern *v/t* (*ge-*, *h*) pepper

'Pfefferstreuer *m* (-s; -) pepper caster

pfeffrig ['pfɛfrɪç] *adj* peppery

Pfeife ['pfaifə] *f* (-; -n) whistle; pipe (*a.* MUS); '**pfeifen** *v/i and v/t* (*irr*, *ge-*, *h*) whistle (*j-m* to s.o.); F ~ *auf* (*acc*) not give a damn about

Pfeil [pfail] *m* (-[e]s; -e) arrow

Pfeiler ['pfailɐ] *m* (-s; -) pillar; pier

Pfennig ['pfɛnɪç] *m* (-s; -e) pfennig; *fig* penny

Pferch [pfɛrç] *m* (-[e]s; -e) fold, pen

'pferchen *v/t* (*ge-*, *h*) cram (*in acc* into)

Pferd [pfe:ɐt] *n* (-[e]s; -e) ZO horse (*a.* SPORT); *zu* ~*e* on horseback

Pferde|geschirr ['pfe:ɐdə-] *n* harness; ~**koppel** *f* paddock; ~**rennen** *n* horserace; ~**stall** *m* stable; ~**stärke** *f* TECH horsepower; ~**wagen** *m* (horse-drawn) carriage

pfiff [pfɪf] *pret of* **pfeifen**

Pfiff *m* (-[e]s; -e) whistle

pfiffig ['pfɪfɪç] *adj* smart

Pfingsten ['pfɪŋstən] *n* (-; -) REL Pentecost, Br Whitsun (*zu*, *an* at)

Pfingst'montag *m* REL Whit Monday

'Pfingstrose *f* BOT peony

Pfingst'sonntag *m* REL Pentecost, *Br* Whit Sunday

Pfirsich ['pfɪrzɪç] *m* (-*s*; -*e*) BOT peach

Pflanze ['pflantsə] *f* (-; -*n*) plant; **~n fressend** ZO herbivorous

'pflanzen *v/t* (ge-, h) plant

'Pflanzenfett *n* vegetable fat

'pflanzlich *adj* vegetable

'Pflanzung *f* (-; -*en*) plantation

Pflaster ['pflastɐ] *n* (-*s*; -) pavement; MED Band-Aid®, *Br* plaster

'pflastern *v/t* (ge-, h) pave

'Pflasterstein *m* paving stone

Pflaume ['pflaumə] *f* (-; -*n*) BOT plum

Pflege ['pfle:gə] *f* (-; *no pl*) care; MED nursing; *fig* cultivation; TECH maintenance; **j-n in ~ nehmen** take s.o. into one's care; **~... in** *cpds* ...eltern, ...kind, ...sohn *etc*: foster ...; ...heim, ...kosten, ...personal *etc*: nursing ...

'pflegebedürftig *adj* needing care

'Pflegefall *m* constant-care patient

'pflegeleicht *adj* wash-and-wear, easy-care

'pflegen *v/t* (ge-, h) care for, look after, *esp* MED *a.* nurse; TECH maintain; *fig* cultivate; keep up (*custom etc*); **sie pflegte zu sagen** she used to or would say; **Pfleger** ['pfle:gɐ] *m* (-*s*; -) male nurse; **Pflegerin** ['pfle:gərɪn] *f* (-; -*nen*) nurse; **'Pflegestelle** *f* nursing place

Pflicht [pflɪçt] *f* (-; -*en*) duty (**gegen** to); SPORT compulsory events

'pflichtbewusst *adj* conscientious

'Pflicht|bewusstsein *n* sense of duty; **~erfüllung** *f* performance of one's duty; **~fach** *n* PED compulsory subject

'pflicht|gemäß, **~getreu** *adj* dutiful; **~vergessen** *adv*: **~ handeln** neglect one's duty

'Pflichtversicherung *f* compulsory insurance

Pflock [pflɔk] *m* (-[*e*]*s*; *Pflöcke* ['pflœkə]) peg, pin; plug

pflücken ['pflʏkən] *v/t* (ge-, h) pick, gather

Pflug [pflu:k] *m* (-[*e*]*s*; *Pflüge* ['pfly:gə]), **pflügen** ['pfly:gən] *v/t and v/i* (ge-, h) plow, *Br* plough

Pforte ['pfɔrtə] *f* (-; -*n*) gate, door, entrance; **Pförtner** ['pfœrtnɐ] *m* (-*s*; -) doorman, doorkeeper, porter

Pfosten ['pfɔstən] *m* (-*s*; -) post

Pfote ['pfo:tə] *f* (-; -*n*) ZO paw (*a.* F)

pfropfen ['pfrɔpfən] *v/t* (ge-, h) stopper; cork; plug; AGR graft; F cram, stuff

'Pfropfen *m* (-*s*; -) stopper; cork; plug; MED clot

pfui [pfui] *int* ugh!; *audience*: boo!

Pfund [pfʊnt] *n* (-[*e*]*s*; -*e* ['pfʊndə]) pound (*453,59 g*); pound (sterling); **10 ~** ten pounds

'pfundweise *adv* by the pound

pfuschen ['pfʊʃən] *v/i* (ge-, h), **Pfuscherei** [pfʊʃə'rai] F *f* (-; -*en*) bungle, botch

Pfütze ['pfʏtsə] *f* (-; -*n*) puddle, pool

Phänomen [fɛno'me:n] *n* (-*s*; -*e*) phenomenon; **phänomenal** [fɛnome'na:l] *adj* phenomenal

Phantasie *etc* → **Fantasie** *etc*

pharmazeutisch [farma'tsɔʏtɪʃ] *adj* pharmaceutic(al)

Phase ['fa:zə] *f* (-; -*n*) phase (*a.* ELECTR), stage

Philosoph [filo'zo:f] *m* (-*en*; -*en*) philosopher; **Philosophie** [filozo'fi:] *f* (-; -*n*) philosophy; **philosophieren** [filozo'fi:rən] *v/i* (*no* -ge-, h) philosophize (**über** *acc* on); **Philo'sophin** *f* (-; -*nen*) (woman) philosopher; **philosophisch** [filo'zo:fɪʃ] *adj* philosophical

phlegmatisch [flɛ'gma:tɪʃ] *adj* phlegmatic

Phonetik [fo'ne:tɪk] *f* (-; *no pl*) phonetics; **pho'netisch** *adj* phonetic

Phosphor ['fɔsfo:ɐ] *m* (-*s*; -*e*) CHEM phosphorus

Photo... → **Foto...**

Phrase ['fra:zə] *contp f* (-; -*n*) cliché (phrase)

Physik [fy'zi:k] *f* (-; *no pl*) physics

physikalisch [fyzi'ka:lɪʃ] *adj* physical

Physiker ['fy:zikɐ] *m* (-*s*; -), **'Physikerin** *f* (-; -*nen*) physicist

physisch ['fy:zɪʃ] *adj* physical

Pianist [pja'nɪst] *m* (-*en*; -*en*), **Pia'nistin** *f* (-; -*nen*) MUS pianist

Piano ['pja:no] *n* (-*s*; -*s*) MUS piano

Picke ['pɪkə] *f* (-; -*n*) TECH pick(axe)

Pickel[1] ['pɪkəl] *m* (-*s*; -) TECH pick(axe)

Pickel[2] *m* (-*s*; -) MED pimple; **pickelig** ['pɪkəlɪç] *adj* MED pimpled, pimply

picken ['pɪkən] *v/i and v/t* (ge-, h) ZO peck, pick

Picknick ['pɪknɪk] *n* (-*s*; -*e*, -*s*) picnic

'picknicken *v/i* (ge-, h) (have a) picnic

piekfein ['piːk-] F *adj* posh

piep(s)en ['piːp(s)ən] *v/i* (*ge-*, *h*) chirp, cheep; ELECTR bleep

Pietät [pje'tɛːt] *f* (-; *no pl*) reverence; piety; **pie'tätlos** *adj* irreverent; **pie'tätvoll** *adj* reverent

Pik [piːk] *n* (-[s]; -[s]) *cards*: spade(s)

pikant [pi'kant] *adj* piquant, spicy (*both a. fig*)

Pilger ['pɪlɡɐ] *m* (-s; -) pilgrim; **'Pilgerfahrt** *f* pilgrimage; **'Pilgerin** *f* (-; *-nen*) pilgrim; **'pilgern** *v/i* (*ge-*, *sein*) (go on a) pilgrimage

Pille ['pɪlə] *f* (-; *-n*) pill; F *die ~ nehmen* be on the pill

Pilot [pi'loːt] *m* (*-en*; *-en*), **Pi'lotin** *f* (-; *-nen*) pilot

Pilz [pɪlts] *m* (*-es*; *-e*) BOT mushroom (*a. fig*); toadstool; MED fungus; **~e suchen (gehen)** go mushrooming

Pinguin ['pɪŋɡuiːn] *m* (-s; *-e*) ZO penguin

pinkeln ['pɪŋkəln] F *v/i* (*ge-*, *h*) (have a) pee, piddle

Pinsel ['pɪnzəl] *m* (-s; -) (paint)brush

'Pinselstrich *m* brushstroke

Pinzette [pɪn'tsɛtə] *f* (-; *-n*) tweezers

Pionier [pjo'niːɐ] *m* (-s; *-e*) pioneer, MIL *a.* engineer

Pirat [pi'raːt] *m* (*-en*; *-en*) pirate

Pisse ['pɪsə] V *f* (-; *no pl*), **'pissen** V *v/i* (*ge-*, *h*) piss

Piste ['pɪstə] *f* (-; *-n*) course; AVIAT runway

Pistole [pɪs'toːlə] *f* (-; *-n*) pistol, gun

Pkw, PKW ['peːkaːveː] *m* (-[s]; -[s]) ABBR *of* **Personenkraftwagen** (*Br a.* motor)car, automobile

Plache ['plaxə] *Austrian f* (-; *-n*) awning, tarpaulin

placieren *etc* → **platzieren** *etc*

plädieren [plɛ'diːrən] *v/i* (*no -ge-*, *h*) JUR plead (*für* for); **Plädoyer** [plɛdoa'jeː] *n* (-s; -s) JUR final speech, pleading

Plage ['plaːɡə] *f* (-; *-n*) trouble, misery; plague; nuisance, F pest; **'plagen** *v/t* (*ge-*, *h*) trouble; bother; pester; *sich ~* toil, drudge

Plakat [pla'kaːt] *n* (-[e]s; *-e*) poster, placard, bill

Plakette [pla'kɛtə] *f* (-; *-n*) plaque, badge

Plan [plaːn] *m* (-[e]s; *Pläne* ['plɛːnə]) plan; intention

Plane ['plaːnə] *f* (-; *-n*) awning, tarpaulin

'planen *v/t* (*ge-*, *h*) plan, make plans for

Planet [pla'neːt] *m* (*-en*; *-en*) ASTR planet

planieren [pla'niːrən] *v/t* (*no -ge-*, *h*) TECH level, plane, grade

Planke ['plaŋkə] *f* (-; *-n*) plank, (thick) board

plänkeln ['plɛŋkəln] *v/i* (*ge-*, *h*) skirmish

'planlos *adj* without plan; aimless

'planmäßig 1. *adj* scheduled (*arrival etc*); **2.** *adv* according to plan

Plan(t)schbecken ['planʃ-] *n* paddling pool

plan(t)schen ['planʃən] *v/i* (*ge-*, *h*) splash

Plantage [plan'taːʒə] *f* (-; *-n*) plantation

Plappermaul ['plapɐ-] F *n* chatterbox

plappern ['plapɐn] F *v/i* (*ge-*, *h*) chatter, prattle, babble, jabber

plärren ['plɛrən] F *v/i* and *v/t* (*ge-*, *h*) blubber; bawl; *radio*: blare

Plastik¹ ['plastɪk] *f* (-; *-en*) sculpture

'Plastik² *n* (-s; *no pl*) plastic; **~... in cpds** *...besteck etc*: plastic ...

plastisch ['plastɪʃ] *adj* plastic; three-dimensional; *fig* graphic

Platin ['plaːtiːn] *n* (-s; *no pl*) platinum

plätschern ['plɛtʃɐn] *v/i* (*ge-*, *h*) ripple (*a. fig*), splash

platt [plat] *adj* flat, level, even; *fig* trite; F flabbergasted

Platte ['platə] *f* (-; *-n*) sheet, plate; slab; board; panel; MUS record, disk, *Br* disc; EDP disk; GASTR dish; F bald pate; *kalte ~* GASTR plate of cold cuts (*Br* meats)

plätten ['plɛtən] *v/t* (*ge-*, *h*) iron, press

'Platten|spieler *m* record player; **~teller** *m* turntable

'Plattform *f* platform

Plattfuß *m* MED flat foot

'Plattheit *fig f* (-; *-en*) triviality; platitude

Plättli ['plɛtli] *Swiss n* (-s; -s) tile

Platz [plats] *m* (*-es*; *Plätze* ['plɛtsə]) place, spot; site; room, space; square; circus; seat; **es ist (nicht) genug ~** there's (there isn't) enough room; **~ machen für** make room for; make way for; **~ nehmen** take a seat, sit down; **ist dieser ~ noch frei?** is this seat taken?; **j-n vom ~ stellen** SPORT send s.o. off; **auf eigenem ~** SPORT at home; **auf die Plätze, fertig, los!** SPORT on your marks, get set, go!

'Platz|anweiser *m* (-s; -) usher; **~anweiserin** *f* (-; *-nen*) usherette

Plätzchen ['plɛtsçən] *n* (-s; -) (little)

place, spot; GASTR cookie, Br biscuit

platzen ['platsən] *v/i* (*ge-*, *sein*) burst (*a. fig*); crack, split; explode (*a. fig* **vor** *dat* with), blow up; F come to grief *or* nothing, fall through, blow up, *sl* go phut; break up

platzieren [pla'tsi:rən] *v/t* (*no -ge-*, *h*) place; **sich** ~ SPORT be placed

Plat'zierung *f* (*-; -en*) place, placing

'**Platzkarte** *f* reservation (ticket)

Plätzli ['plɛtsli] *Swiss n* (*-s; -*) cutlet

'**Platz|pa,trone** *f* blank (cartridge); **~re-gen** *m* cloudburst, downpour; **~re-ser,vierung** *f* seat reservation; **~ver-weis** *m*: **e-n ~ erhalten** SPORT be sent off; **~wart** *m* (*-s; -e*) SPORT ground-keeper, *Br* groundsman; **~wunde** *f* MED cut, laceration

Plauderei [plaudə'rai] *f* (*-; -en*) chat

plaudern ['plaudɐn] *v/i* (*ge-*, *h*) (have a) chat

plauschen ['plauʃən] *Austrian v/i* (have a) chat

pleite ['plaitə] F *adj* broke; ~ **gehen** go broke

'**Pleite** F *f* (*-; -n*) bankruptcy; *fig* flop

Plombe ['plɔmbə] *f* (*-; -n*) TECH seal; MED filling; **plombieren** [plɔm'bi:rən] *v/t* (*no -ge-*, *h*) TECH seal; MED fill

plötzlich ['plœtslɪç] **1.** *adj* sudden; **2.** *adv* suddenly, all of a sudden

plump [plʊmp] *adj* clumsy; **plumps** *int* thud, plop; **plumpsen** ['plʊmpsən] *v/i* (*ge-*, *sein*) thud, plop, flop

Plunder ['plʊndɐ] F *m* (*-s; no pl*) trash, junk

Plünderer ['plʏndərɐ] *m* (*-s; -*) looter, plunderer; **plündern** ['plʏndɐn] *v/i and v/t* (*ge-*, *h*) plunder, loot

Plural ['plu:ra:l] *m* (*-s; -e*) LING plural

plus [plʊs] *adv* plus

Plusquamperfekt ['plʊskvamperfɛkt] *n* (*-s; -e*) LING past perfect

Pneu [pnɔy] *Swiss m* (*-s; -s*) tire, *Br* tyre

Po [po:] F *m* (*-s; -s*) bottom, behind

Pöbel ['pø:bəl] *m* (*-s; no pl*) mob, rabble

pochen ['pɔxən] *v/i* (*ge-*, *h*) knock, rap (*both*: **an** *acc* at)

Pocke ['pɔkə] *f* (*-; -n*) MED pock

'**Pocken** *pl* MED smallpox; **~impfung** *f* MED smallpox vaccination

Podest [po'dɛst] *n*, *m* (*-[e]s; -e*) platform; *fig* pedestal

Podium ['po:djʊm] *n* (*-s; -ien*) podium,

platform; '**Podiumsdiskussi,on** *f* panel discussion

Poesie [poe'zi:] *f* (*-; -n*) poetry

Poet [po'e:t] *m* (*-en; -en*), **Po'etin** *f* (*-; -nen*) poet

poetisch [po'e:tɪʃ] *adj* poetic(al)

Pointe ['poɛ̃:tə] *f* (*-; -n*) point, punch line

Pokal [po'ka:l] *m* (*-s; -e*) goblet; SPORT cup; **~endspiel** *n* SPORT cup final; **~sie-ger** *m* SPORT cup winner; **~spiel** *n* SPORT cup tie

pökeln ['pø:kəln] *v/t* (*ge-*, *h*) salt

Pol [po:l] *m* (*-s; -e*) GEOGR pole

polar [po'la:r] *adj* polar

Pole ['po:lə] *m* (*-n; -n*) Pole

'**Polen** Poland

Polemik [po'le:mɪk] *f* (*-; -en*) polemic(s); **po'lemisch** *adj* polemic(al)

polemisieren [polemi'zi:rən] *v/i* (*no -ge-*, *h*) polemize

Police [po'li:sə] *f* (*-; -n*) policy

Polier [po'li:ɐ] *m* (*-s; -e*) TECH foreman

polieren [po'li:rən] *v/t* (*no -ge-*, *h*) polish

Polin ['po:lɪn] *f* (*-; -nen*) Pole, Polish woman

Politik [poli'ti:k] *f* (*-; no pl*) politics; policy (*a. fig*); **Politiker(in)** [po'li:tikɐ (-kərɪn)] (*-s; -/-; -nen*) politician; **politisch** [po'li:tɪʃ] *adj* political; **politisie-ren** [politi'zi:rən] *v/i* (*no -ge-*, *h*) talk politics

Polizei [poli'tsai] *f* (*-; no pl*) police; **~au-to** *n* police car; **~beamt|e** *m*, **-in** *f* police officer

poli'zeilich *adj* (of *or* by the) police

Poli'zei|prä,sidium *n* police headquarters; **~re,vier** *n* police station; precinct, *Br* district; **~schutz** *m*: **unter** ~ under police guard; **~streife** *f* police patrol; **~stunde** *f* closing time; **~wache** *f* police station

Polizist [poli'tsɪst] *m* (*-en; -en*) policeman; **Poli'zistin** *f* (*-; -nen*) policewoman

polnisch ['pɔlnɪʃ] *adj* Polish

Polster ['pɔlstɐ] *n* (*-s; -*) upholstery; cushion; pad(ding); *fig* bolster; **~gar-ni,tur** *f* three-piece suite; **~möbel** *pl* upholstered furniture

'**polstern** *v/t* (*ge-*, *h*) upholster; pad

'**Polster|sessel** *m* easy chair, armchair; **~stuhl** *m* upholstered chair

Polsterung ['pɔlstərʊŋ] *f* (*-; -en*) upholstery; padding poltern ['pɔltɐn] v/i (ge-, h) rumble; fig bluster

Pommes frites [pɔm'frɪt] pl French fries, French fried potatoes, Br chips

Pomp [pɔmp] m (-[e]s; no pl) pomp

pompös [pɔm'pøːs] adj showy

Pony¹ ['pɔni] n (-s; -s) ZO pony

Pony² m (-s; -s) fringe, bangs

Popgruppe ['pɔp-] f MUS pop group

'Popmu,sik f pop music

populär [popu'lɛːɐ] adj popular

Popularität [populari'tɛːt] f (-; no pl) popularity

Pore ['poːrə] f (-; -n) pore

Porno ['pɔrno] F m (-s; -s), ~film m porn (film), blue movie; ~heft n porn magazine

porös [po'røːs] adj porous

Portemonnaie [pɔrtmɔ'neː] n (-s; -s) purse

Portier [pɔr'tjeː] m (-s; -s) doorman, porter

Portion [pɔr'tsjoːn] f (-; -en) portion, share; helping, serving

Portmonee → Portemonnaie

Porto ['pɔrto] n (-s; -s, -ti) postage

Porträt [pɔr'trɛː] n (-s; -s) portrait

porträtieren [pɔrtrɛ'tiːrən] v/t (no -ge-, h) portray

Portugal ['pɔrtugal] Portugal

Portugiese [pɔrtu'giːzə] m (-n; -n), Portu'giesin f (-; -nen), portu'giesisch adj Portuguese

Porzellan [pɔrtse'laːn] n (-s; -e) china, porcelain

Posaune [po'zaunə] f (-; -n) MUS trombone; fig trumpet

Pose ['poːzə] f (-; -n) pose, attitude

Position [pozi'tsjoːn] f (-; -en) position (a. fig)

positiv ['poːzitiːf] adj positive

possessiv [pɔsɛ'siːf] adj LING possessive; Posses'sivpro,nomen n LING possessive pronoun

Post [pɔst] f (-; no pl) mail, esp Br post; letters; mit der ~ by post or mail; ~amt n post office; ~anweisung f money order; ~beamt|e m, -in f post office clerk; ~bote m mailman, Br postman

Posten ['pɔstən] m (-s; -) post; job, position; MIL sentry; ECON item; lot, parcel

'Postfach n (PO) box

postieren [pɔs'tiːrən] v/t (no -ge-, h) post, station, place; sich ~ station o.s.

'Postkarte f postcard

'Postkutsche f stagecoach

'postlagernd adj (in care of) general delivery, Br poste restante

'Post|leitzahl f zip code, Br post(al) code; ~mi,nister m Postmaster General; ~scheck m postal check (Br cheque); ~sparbuch n post-office savings book; ~stempel m postmark

'postwendend adv by return mail, Br by return (of post)

'Post|wertzeichen n (postage) stamp; ~zustellung f postal or mail delivery

Potenz [po'tɛnts] f (-; -en) a) (no pl) MED potency, b) MATH power

Pracht [praxt] f (-; no pl) splendo(u)r, magnificence

prächtig ['prɛçtıç] adj splendid, magnificent, fig a. great, super

prägen ['prɛːgən] v/t (ge-, h) stamp, coin (a. fig)

prahlen ['praːlən] v/i (ge-, h) brag, boast (both: mit it); talk big, show off; Prahler ['praːlɐ] m (-s; -) boaster, braggart; Prahlerei [praːlə'rai] f (-; -en) boasting, bragging; 'prahlerisch adj boastful, showy

Praktikant [prakti'kant] m (-en; -en), Prakti'kantin f (-; -nen) trainee; Praktiken ['praktikən] pl practices; 'Praktikum n (-s; -ka) practical training; 'praktisch 1. adj practical; useful, handy; ~er Arzt general practitioner; 2. adv practically; virtually; praktizieren [prakti'tsiːrən] v/t (no -ge-, h) practice (Br practise) medicine or law

Prälat [prɛ'laːt] m (-en; -en) REL prelate

Praline [pra'liːnə] f (-; -n) chocolate

prall [pral] adj tight; well-rounded; bulging; blazing (sun)

prallen ['pralən] v/i (ge-, sein) ~ gegen (or auf acc) crash or bump into

Prämie ['prɛːmjə] f (-; -n) premium; prize; bonus; prämieren [prɛ'miːrən], prämiieren [prɛmi'iːrən] v/t (no -ge-, h) award a prize to

Pranke ['praŋkə] f (-; -n) ZO paw (a. F)

Präparat [prɛpa'raːt] n (-[e]s; -e) preparation

präparieren [prɛpa'riːrən] v/t (no -ge-, h) prepare; MED, BOT, ZO dissect

P

Präposition [prɛpozi'tsjoːn] f (-; -en) LING preposition

Prärie [prɛ'riː] f (-; -n) prairie

Präsens ['prɛːzɛns] n (-; -sentia [prɛ'zɛntsja]) LING present (tense)

präsentieren [prɛzɛn'tiːrən] v/t (no -ge-, h) present; offer

Präservativ [prɛzɛrva'tiːf] n (-s; -e) condom

Präsident [prɛzi'dɛnt] m (-en; -en), **Präsi'dentin** f (-; -nen) president; chairman (chairwoman); **präsidieren** [prɛzi'diːrən] v/i preside (**in** dat over)

Präsidium [prɛ'ziːdjʊm] n (-s; -ien) presidency

prasseln ['prasəln] v/i (ge-, h) rain etc: patter; fire: crackle

Präteritum [prɛ'teːritʊm] n (-s; -ta) LING past (tense)

Praxis ['praksɪs] f (-; Praxen) a) (no pl) practice (a. MED, JUR), b) MED doctor's office, Br surgery

Präzedenzfall [prɛtse'dɛnts-] m precedent

präzis [prɛ'tsiːs], **präzise** [prɛ'tsiːzə] adj precise; **Präzision** [prɛtsi'zjoːn] f (-; no pl) precision

predigen ['preːdɪgən] v/i and v/t (ge-, h) preach

Prediger ['preːdɪgə] m (-s; -), **'Predigerin** f (-; -nen) preacher

Predigt ['preːdɪçt] f (-; -en) sermon

Preis [prais] m (-es; -e) price (a. fig); prize; film etc: award; reward; **um jeden ~** at all costs

'Preisausschreiben n competition

Preiselbeere ['praizəl-] f BOT cranberry

preisen ['praizən] v/t (irr, ge-, h) praise

'Preiserhöhung f rise or increase in price(s)

'preisgeben v/t (irr, geben, sep, -ge-, h) abandon; reveal, give away

'preisgekrönt adj prize-winning; film etc: award-winning

'Preis|gericht n jury; **~lage** f price range; **~liste** f price list; **~nachlass** m discount; **~rätsel** n competition; **~richter(in)** judge; **~schild** n price tag; **~stopp** m price freeze; **~träger(in)** prizewinner

'preiswert adj cheap

prellen ['prɛlən] v/t (ge-, h) fig cheat (**um** out of); **sich et. ~** MED bruise s.th.;

'Prellung f (-; -en) MED contusion, bruise

Premiere [prə'mjeːrə] f (-; -n) THEA etc first night, première

Premier|mi,nister [prə'mjeː-] m, **Pre'miermi,nisterin** f prime minister

Presse ['prɛsə] f (-; -n) a) (no pl) press, b) squeezer; **~...** in cpds: no pl) ...agentur, ...konferenz, ...fotograf etc: press ...; **~freiheit** f freedom of the press; **~meldung** f news item

'pressen v/t (ge-, h) press; squeeze

'Presse|tri,büne f press box; **~vertreter** m reporter

'Pressluft f compressed air; **~...** in cpds ...bohrer, ...hammer etc: pneumatic ...

Prestige [prɛs'tiːʒə] n (-s; no pl) prestige; **~verlust** m loss of prestige or face

Preuße ['prɔysə] m (-n; -n), **'Preußin** f (-; -nen), **'preußisch** adj Prussian

prickeln ['prɪkəln] v/i (ge-, h) prickle; tingle

pries [priːs] pret of **preisen**

Priester ['priːstə] m (-s; -) priest; **Priesterin** ['priːstərɪn] f (-; -nen) priestess; **'priesterlich** adj priestly

prima ['priːma] F adj great, super

primär [pri'mɛːɐ] adj primary

Primar|arzt [pri'maːɐ-] Austrian m → **Oberarzt**; **~schule** Swiss f → **Grundschule**

Primel ['priːməl] f (-; -n) BOT primrose

primitiv [primi'tiːf] adj primitive

Prinz [prɪnts] m (-en; -en) prince

Prinzessin [prɪn'tsɛsɪn] f (-; -nen) princess

'Prinzgemahl m prince consort

Prinzip [prɪn'tsiːp] n (-s; -ien) principle (**aus** on; **in** in); **prinzipiell** [prɪntsi'pjɛl] adv as a matter of principle

Prise ['priːzə] f (-; -n) **e-e ~ Salz** etc a pinch of salt etc

Prisma ['prɪsma] n (-s; -men) prism

Pritsche ['prɪtʃə] f (-; -n) plank bed; MOT platform

privat [pri'vaːt] adj private; personal

Pri'vat... in cpds ...leben, ...schule, ...detektiv etc: private ...; **~angelegenheit** f personal or private matter or affair; **das ist m-e ~** that's my own business

Privileg [privi'leːk] n (-[e]s; -gien [privi'leːgjən]) privilege

pro [proː] prp (acc) per; **2 Mark ~ Stück** two marks each

Pro *n*: **das ~ und Kontra** the pros and cons

Probe ['pro:bə] *f* (-; -*n*) trial, test; sample; THEA rehearsal; MATH proof; **auf ~** on probation; **auf die ~ stellen** put to the test; **~alarm** *m* test alarm; test drill; **~aufnahmen** *pl* film: screen test; **~fahrt** *f* test drive; **~flug** *m* test flight

'proben *v/i* and *v/t* (ge-, h) THEA *etc* rehearse

'probeweise *adv* on trial; on probation

'Probezeit *f* (time of) probation

probieren [pro'bi:rən] *v/t* (*no* ge-, h) try; taste

Problem [pro'ble:m] *n* (-*s*; -*e*) problem

problematisch [proble'ma:tɪʃ] *adj* problematic(al)

Produkt [pro'dʊkt] *n* (-[*e*]*s*; -*e*) product (*a.* MATH); result

Produktion [prodʊk'tsjo:n] *f* (-; -*en*) production; output

produktiv [prodʊk'ti:f] *adj* productive

Produktivität [prodʊktivi'tɛ:t] *f* (-; *no pl*) productivity

Produzent [produ'tsɛnt] *m* (-*en*; -*en*), **Produ'zentin** *f* (-; -*nen*) producer; **produzieren** [produ'tsi:rən] *v/t* (*no* ge-, h) produce

professionell [profɛsjo'nɛl] *adj* professional

Professor [pro'fɛso:ɐ] *m* (-*s*; -*en* [profɛ'so:rən]), **Profes'sorin** *f* (-; -*nen*) professor

Professur [profɛ'su:ɐ] *f* (-; -*en*) professorship, chair (**für** of)

Profi ['pro:fi] *m* (-*s*; -*s*) pro; **~...** *in cpds* ...*boxer*, ...*fußballer etc*: professional

Profil [pro'fi:l] *n* (-*s*; -*e*) profile; MOT tread; **profilieren** [profi'li:rən] *v/refl* (*no* ge-, h) distinguish o.s.

Profit [pro'fi:t] *m* (-[*e*]*s*; -*e*) profit

profitieren [profi'ti:rən] *v/i* (*no* ge-, h) profit (**von** *or* **bei et.** from *or* by s.th.)

Prognose [pro'gno:zə] *f* (-; -*n*) prediction; METEOR forecast; MED prognosis

Programm [pro'gram] *n* (-*s*; -*e*) program (me *Br*), TV *a.* channel; EDP program; **~fehler** *m* EDP program error, bug

programmieren [progra'mi:rən] *v/t* (*no* ge-, h) program (*a.* EDP)

Programmierer [progra'mi:rɐ] *m* (-*s*; -), **Program'miererin** *f* (-; -*nen*) EDP programmer

Projekt [pro'jɛkt] *n* (-[*e*]*s*; -*e*) project

Projektion [projɛk'tsjo:n] *f* (-; -*en*) projection; **Projektor** [pro'jɛkto:ɐ] *m* (-*s*; -*en* [projɛk'to:rən]) projector

proklamieren [prokla'mi:rən] *v/t* (*no* -ge-, h) proclaim

Prokurist [proku'rɪst] *m* (-*en*; -*en*), **Proku'ristin** *f* (-; -*nen*) authorized signatory

Proletarier [prole'ta:rjɐ] *m* (-*s*; -), **proletarisch** [-'ta:rɪʃ] *adj* proletarian

Prolog [pro'lo:k] *m* (-*s*; -*e*) prologue

Promillegrenze [pro'mɪlə-] *f* (blood) alcohol limit

prominent [promi'nɛnt] *adj* prominent

Prominenz [promi'nɛnts] *f* (-; *no pl*) notables; high society

Promotion [promo'tsjo:n] *f* (-; -*en*) UNIV doctorate; **promovieren** [promo'vi:rən] *v/i* (*no* -ge-, h) do one's doctorate

prompt [prɔmpt] *adj* prompt; quick

Pronomen [pro'no:mən] *n* (-*s*; -*mina*) LING pronoun

Propeller [pro'pɛlɐ] *m* (-*s*; -) propeller

Prophet [pro'fe:t] *m* (-*en*; -*en*) prophet; **pro'phetisch** *adj* prophetic

prophezeien [profe'tsaiən] *v/t* (*no* -ge-, h) prophesy, predict; **Prophe'zeiung** *f* (-; -*en*) prophecy, prediction

Proportion [propɔr'tsjo:n] *f* (-; -*en*) proportion

Proporz [pro'pɔrts] *m* (-*es*; -*e*) POL proportional representation

Prosa ['pro:za] *f* (-; *no pl*) prose

Prospekt [pro'spɛkt] *m* (-[*e*]*s*; -*e*) prospectus; brochure, pamphlet

prost [pro:st] *int* cheers!

Prostituierte [prostitu'i:ɐtə] *f* (-*n*; -*n*) prostitute

Protest [pro'tɛst] *m* (-[*e*]*s*; -*e*) protest; **aus ~ in** (*or* as a) protest

Protestant [protɛs'tant] *m* (-*en*; -*en*), **Protes'tantin** *f* (-; -*nen*), **protes'tantisch** *adj* REL Protestant

protestieren [protɛs'ti:rən] *v/i* (*no* -ge-, h) protest

Prothese [pro'te:zə] *f* (-; -*n*) MED artificial limb; denture

Protokoll [proto'kɔl] *n* (-*s*; -*e*) record, minutes; protocol; (**das**) **~ führen** take *or* keep the minutes; **zu ~ nehmen** JUR record; **~führer** *m* keeper of the minutes

protokollieren [protoko'li:rən] *v/t* and

v/i (no -ge-, h) take the minutes (of); JUR record

protzen ['prɔtsən] F *v/i (ge-, h)* show off (**mit et.** s.th.)

protzig ['prɔtsɪç] *adj* showy, flashy

Proviant [pro'vjant] *m (-s; no pl)* provisions, food

Provinz [pro'vɪnts] *f (-; -en)* province; *fig* country; **provinziell** [provɪn'tsjɛl] *adj* provincial (*a. contp*)

Provision [provi'zjoːn] *f (-; -en)* ECON commission

provisorisch [provi'zoːrɪʃ] *adj* provisional, temporary

provozieren [provo'tsiːrən] *v/t (no -ge-, h)* provoke

Prozent [pro'tsɛnt] *n (-[e]s; -e)* per cent; F *pl* discount; **~satz** *m* percentage

prozentual [protsɛn'tuaːl] *adj* proportional; **~er Anteil** percentage

Prozess [pro'tsɛs] *m (-es; -e)* process (*a. TECH, CHEM etc*); JUR action; lawsuit; case; trial; *j-m den ~ machen* take s.o. to court; *e-n ~ gewinnen (verlieren)* win (lose) a case; **prozessieren** [protsɛ'siːrən] *v/i (no -ge-, h)* JUR go to court; *gegen j-n ~* bring an action against s.o., take s.o. to court

Prozession [protsɛ'sjoːn] *f (-; -en)* procession

Prozessor [pro'tsɛsoːɐ] *m (-s; -en* [protsɛ'soːrən]*)* EDP processor

prüde ['pryːdə] *adj* prudish; **~ sein** be a prude

prüfen ['pryːfən] *v/t (ge-, h)* PED *etc* examine, test (*a. TECH*); check; inspect (*a. TECH*); *fig* consider; **~d** *adj* searching

Prüfer ['pryːfɐ] *m (-s; -),* **'Prüferin** *f (-; -nen)* PED *etc* examiner; *esp* TECH tester

Prüfling ['pryːflɪŋ] *m (-s; -e)* candidate

'Prüfstein *m* touchstone (*für* of)

'Prüfung *f (-; -en)* examination, F exam; test; check(ing), inspection; *e-e ~ machen (bestehen, nicht bestehen)* take (pass, fail) an exam(ination)

'Prüfungsarbeit *f* examination *or* test paper

Prügel ['pryːɡəl] F *pl (e-e Tracht) ~ bekommen* get a (good) beating *or* hiding *or* thrashing; **Prüge'lei** F *f (-; -en)* fight; **'prügeln** F *v/t (ge-, h)* beat, flog; *sich ~* (have a) fight; **'Prügelstrafe** *f* corporal punishment

Prunk [prʊŋk] *m (-[e]s; no pl)* splen-

do(u)r, pomp; **'prunkvoll** *adj* splendid, magnificent

PS [peː'ʔɛs] ABBR *of* **Pferdestärke** horsepower, HP

Psalm [psalm] *m (-s; -en)* REL psalm

Pseudonym [psɔydo'nyːm] *n (-s; -e)* pseudonym

pst [pst] *int* sh!, ssh!; psst!

Psyche ['psyːçə] *f (-; -n)* mind, psyche

Psychiater [psy'çjaːtɐ] *m (-s; -),* **Psy'chiaterin** *f (-; -nen)* psychiatrist; **psychiatrisch** [psy'çjaːtrɪʃ] *adj* psychiatric

psychisch ['psyːçɪʃ] *adj* mental, MED *a.* psychic

Psychoana'lyse [psyço-] *f* psychoanalysis

Psychologe [psyço'loːɡə] *m (-n; -n)* psychologist (*a. fig*); **Psychologie** [psyçolo'giː] *f (-; no pl)* psychology; **Psycho'login** *f (-; -nen)* psychologist; **psycho'logisch** *adj* psychological

Psychose [psy'çoːzə] *f (-; -n)* MED psychosis

psychosomatisch [psyçozo'maːtɪʃ] *adj* MED psychosomatic

Pubertät [puber'tɛːt] *f (-; no pl)* puberty

Publikum ['puːblikʊm] *n (-s; no pl)* audience, TV *a.* viewers; *radio:* a. listeners; SPORT crowd, spectators; ECON customers; public

publizieren [publi'tsiːrən] *v/t (no -ge-, h)* publish

Pudding ['pʊdɪŋ] *m (-s; -e, -s)* pudding, *esp Br* blancmange

Pudel ['puːdəl] *m (-s; -)* ZO poodle

Puder ['puːdɐ] *m (-s; -)* powder

Puderdose *f* powder compact

'pudern *v/t (ge-, h)* powder; *sich ~* powder one's face

'Puderzucker *m* confectioner's (*Br* icing) sugar

Puff¹ [pʊf] F *m (-s; -s)* brothel

Puff² *m (-[e]s; Püffe* ['pyfə]*)* hump; poke

Puffer ['pʊfɐ] *m (-s; -)* RAIL buffer (*a. fig*)

'Puffmais *m* popcorn

Pulli ['pʊli] F *m (-s; -s)* (light) sweater

Pullover [pʊ'loːvɐ] *m (-s; -)* sweater, pullover

Puls [pʊls] *m (-es; -e)* MED pulse; pulse rate; **~ader** *f* ANAT artery

pulsieren [pʊl'ziːrən] *v/i (no -ge-, h)* MED pulsate (*a. fig*)

Pult [pʊlt] *n (-[e]s; -e)* desk

Pulver ['pʊlvɐ] n (-s; -) powder; F cash, sl dough; **pulv(e)rig** ['pʊlv(ə)rıç] adj powdery; **pulverisieren** [pʊlveri'zi:rən] v/t (no -ge-, h) pulverize

'**Pulverkaffee** m instant coffee

'**Pulverschnee** m powder snow

pumm(e)lig ['pʊm(ə)lıç] F adj chubby, plump, tubby

Pumpe ['pʊmpə] f (-; -n) TECH pump

'**pumpen** v/i and v/t TECH pump; F lend; borrow

Punker ['paŋkɐ] F m (-s; -), '**Punkerin** f (-; -nen) punk

Punkt [pʊŋkt] m (-[e]s; -e) point (a. fig); dot; full stop, period; fig spot, place; **um ~ zehn** (Uhr) at ten (o'clock) sharp; **nach ~en gewinnen** etc SPORT win etc on points

punktieren [pʊŋk'ti:rən] v/t (no -ge-, h) dot; MED puncture

pünktlich ['pʏŋktlıç] adj punctual; ~ **sein** be on time; '**Pünktlichkeit** f (-; no pl) punctuality

'**Punkt|sieger** m SPORT winner on points; **~spiel** n SPORT league game

Pupille [pu'pılə] f (-; -n) ANAT pupil

Puppe ['pʊpə] f (-; -n) doll, F a. chick; THEA puppet (a. fig); MOT dummy; ZO chrysalis, pupa

'**Puppen|spiel** n puppet show; **~stube** f

doll's house; **~wagen** m doll carriage, Br doll's pram

pur [pu:ɐ] adj pure (a. fig); whisky etc: straight, Br neat

Purpur ['pʊrpʊr] m (-s; no pl) crimson

'**purpurrot** adj crimson

Purzelbaum ['pʊrtsəl-] m somersault; **e-n ~ schlagen** turn a somersault

purzeln ['pʊrtsəln] v/i (ge-, sein) tumble

Pute ['pu:tə] f (-; -n) ZO turkey (hen)

Puter ['pu:tɐ] m (-s; -) ZO turkey (cock)

Putsch [pʊtʃ] m (-[e]s; -e) putsch, coup (d'état); '**putschen** v/i (ge-, h) revolt, make a putsch

Putz [pʊts] m (-es; no pl) ARCH plaster (ing); **unter ~** ELECTR concealed

putzen ['pʊtsən] (ge-, h) **1.** v/t clean; polish; wipe; **sich die Nase ~** blow one's nose; **sich die Zähne ~** brush one's teeth; **2.** v/i do the cleaning; ~ (**gehen**) work as a cleaner

'**Putzfrau** f cleaner, cleaning woman or lady

putzig ['pʊtsıç] adj funny, cute

'**Putzlappen** m cleaning rag

'**Putzmittel** n clean(s)er; polish

Puzzle ['pazəl] n (-s; -s) jigsaw (puzzle)

Pyjama [py'dʒa:ma] m (-s; -s) pajamas, Br pyjamas

Pyramide [pyra'mi:də] f (-; -n) pyramid

Q

Quacksalber ['kvakzalbɐ] m (-s; -) quack (doctor)

Quadrat [kva'dra:t] n (-[e]s; -e) square; **ins ~ erheben** MATH square; **~... in** cpds ...meile, ...meter, ...wurzel, ...zahl etc: square ...; **qua'dratisch** adj square; MATH quadratic

quaken ['kva:kən] v/i (ge-, h) duck: quack; frog: croak

quäken ['kvɛ:kən] v/i (ge-, h) squeak

Qual [kva:l] f (-; -en) pain, torment, agony; anguish

quälen ['kvɛ:lən] v/t (ge-, h) torment (a. fig); torture; fig pester, plague

Qualifikation [kvalifika'tsjo:n] f (-; -en) qualification; **Qualifikati'ons...** in cpds ...spiel etc: qualifying ...

qualifizieren [kvalifi'tsi:rən] v/t and v/refl (no -ge-, h) qualify

Qualität [kvali'tɛ:t] f (-; -en) quality

qualitativ [kvalita'ti:f] adj and adv in quality

Quali'täts... in cpds ...arbeit, ...waren etc: high-quality ...

Qualm [kvalm] m (-[e]s; no pl) (thick) smoke; **qualmen** ['kvalmən] v/i (ge-, h) smoke; F be a heavy smoker

'**qualvoll** adj very painful; agonizing

Quantität [kvanti'tɛ:t] f (-; -en) quantity;

quantitativ [kvantita'ti:f] adj and adv in quantity

Quantum ['kvantʊm] n (-s; Quanten) amount, fig a. share

Quarantäne [karan'tɛ:nə] f (-; -n) (**un-**

ter ~ stellen put in) quarantine

Quark [kvark] m (-s; no pl) curd, cottage cheese

Quartal [kvar'ta:l] n (-s; -e) quarter (of a year)

Quartett [kvar'tɛt] n (-[e]s; -e) MUS quartet(te)

Quartier [kvar'ti:ɐ] n (-s; -e) accommodation; *Swiss:* quarter

Quarz [kva:ɐts] m (-es; -e) MIN quartz

Quatsch [kvatʃ] F m (-[e]s; no pl) nonsense, rubbish, *sl* rot, crap, bullshit; **~ machen** fool around; joke, F kid

quatschen ['kvatʃən] F v/i (ge-, h) talk rubbish; chat

Quecksilber ['kvɛksɪlbɐ] n (-s; no pl) mercury, quicksilver

Quelle ['kvɛlə] f (-n) spring, source (a. *fig*), well, *fig a.* origin; **'quellen** v/i (*irr*, ge-, *sein*) pour (**aus** from)

'Quellenangabe f reference

quengeln ['kvɛŋəln] F v/i (ge-, h) whine

quer [kve:ɐ] adv across; crosswise; **kreuz und ~** all over the place; **kreuz und ~ durch Deutschland fahren** travel all over Germany; **Quere** ['kve:rə] f: F **j-m in die ~ kommen** get in s.o.'s way

'Querfeld'einlauf m SPORT cross-country race

'Querlatte f SPORT crossbar

'Querschläger m MIL ricochet

'Querschnitt m cross-section (a. *fig*)

'querschnitt(s)gelähmt adj MED paraplegic

'Querstraße f intersecting road; **zweite ~ rechts** second turning on the right

Querulant [kveru'lant] m (-en; -en), **Queru'lantin** f (-; -nen) querulous person

quetschen ['kvɛtʃən] v/t and v/refl (ge-, h) squeeze; MED bruise (o.s.)

'Quetschung f (-; -en) MED bruise

quiek(s)en ['kvi:k(s)ən] v/i (ge-, h) squeak, squeal

quietschen ['kvi:tʃən] v/i (ge-, h) squeal; screech; squeak, creak

quitt [kvɪt] adj: **mit j-m ~ sein** be quits or even with s.o. (a. *fig*)

quittieren [kvɪ'ti:rən] v/t (no -ge-, h) ECON give a receipt for

'Quittung f (-; -en) receipt; *fig* answer

quoll [kvɔl] pret of **quellen**

Quote ['kvo:tə] f (-; -n) quota; share; rate

'Quotenregelung f quota system

Quotient [kvo'tsjɛnt] m (-en; -en) MATH quotient

R

Rabatt [ra'bat] m (-[e]s; -e) ECON discount, rebate

Rabe ['ra:bə] m (-n; -n) ZO raven

rabiat [ra'bja:t] adj rough, tough

Rache ['raxə] f (-; no pl) revenge; **aus ~ für** in revenge for

Rachen ['raxən] m (-s; -) ANAT throat

rächen ['rɛçən] v/t (ge-, h) avenge s.th.; revenge s.o.; **sich an j-m für et.~** revenge o.s. or take revenge on s.o. for s.th.; **Rächer** ['rɛçɐ] m (-s; -) avenger

rachsüchtig ['rax-] adj revengeful, vindictive

Rad [ra:t] n (-[e]s; Räder ['rɛ:dɐ]) wheel; bicycle, F bike; **~ fahren** cycle, ride a bicycle, F bike; **ein ~ schlagen** peacock: spread its tail; SPORT turn a (cart)wheel

Radar [ra'da:ɐ] m, n (-s; -e) radar; **~falle** f MOT speed trap; **~kon,trolle** f MOT radar speed check; **~schirm** m radar screen; **~stati,on** f radar station

radeln ['ra:dəln] F v/i (ge-, *sein*) bike

Rädelsführer ['rɛ:dəls-] m ringleader

Räderwerk ['rɛ:dɐ-] n TECH gearing

'Radfahrer m (-s;-), 'Radfahrerin f (-; -nen) cyclist

radieren [ra'di:rən] v/t (no -ge-, h) erase, rub out; *art:* etch

Radiergummi [ra'di:ɐ-] m eraser, Br a. rubber

Ra'dierung f (-; -en) *art:* etching

Radieschen [ra'di:sçən] n (-s; -) BOT (red) radish

radikal [radi'ka:l] adj, **Radi'kale** m, f (-n; -n) radical; **Radikalismus** [radika'lısmʊs] *m* (-; *no pl*) radicalism

Radio ['ra:djo] *n* (-s; -s) radio; **im ~** on the radio; **~ hören** listen to the radio

radioak'tiv [radjo-] *adj* PHYS radioactive; **~er Niederschlag** fall-out

Radioaktivi'tät *f* (-; *no pl*) radioactivity

'Radiowecker *m* clock radio

Radius ['ra:djʊs] *m* (-s; *Radien*) radius

'Rad|kappe *f* hubcap; **~rennbahn** *f* cycling track; **~rennen** *n* cycle race; **~sport** *m* cycling; **~sportler** *m* cyclist; **~weg** *m* cycle track *or* path, bikeway

raffen ['rafən] *v/t* (*ge-, h*) gather up; **an sich ~** grab

Raffinerie [rafinə'ri:] *f* (-; *-n*) CHEM refinery

Raffinesse [rafi'nɛsə] *f* (-; *-n*) a) (*no pl*) shrewdness, b) refinement

raffiniert [rafi'ni:ɐt] *adj* refined (*a. fig*); *fig* shrewd, clever

ragen ['ra:gən] *v/i* (*ge-, h*) tower (up), rise (high)

Rahe ['ra:ə] *f* (-; *-n*) MAR yard

Rahm [ra:m] *m* (-[e]s; *no pl*) cream

rahmen ['ra:mən] *v/t* (*ge-, h*) frame; PHOT mount; **'Rahmen** *m* (-s; -) frame; *fig* framework; setting; scope; **aus dem ~ fallen** be out of the ordinary

Rakete [ra'ke:tə] *f* (-; *-n*) rocket, MIL *a.* missile; **ferngelenkte ~** guided missile; **e-e ~ abfeuern (starten)** launch a rocket *or* missile

Ra'keten|antrieb *m* rocket propulsion; **mit ~** rocket-propelled; **~basis** *f* MIL rocket *or* missile base *or* site

rammen ['ramən] *v/t* (*ge-, h*) ram; MOT *etc* hit, collide with

Rampe ['rampə] *f* (-; *-n*) (loading) ramp

'Rampenlicht *n* (-[e]s; *no pl*) THEA footlights; *fig* limelight

Ramsch [ramʃ] F *m* (-es; *no pl*) junk

Rand [rant] *m* (-[e]s; *Ränder* ['rɛndɐ]) edge, border; brink (*a. fig*); rim; brim; margin; **am ~(e) des Ruins** *etc* on the brink of ruin *etc*

randalieren [randa'li:rən] *v/i* (*no -ge-, h*) kick up a racket; **Randalierer** [randa'li:rɐ] *m* (-s; -) rowdy, hooligan

'Rand|bemerkung *f* marginal note; *fig* comment; **~gruppe** *f* fringe group

'randlos *adj* rimless

'Randstreifen *m* MOT shoulder

rang [raŋ] *pret of* **ringen**

Rang *m* (-[e]s; *Ränge* ['rɛŋə]) position,

rank (*a.* MIL); THEA balcony, *Br* circle; *pl* SPORT terraces

rangieren [raŋ'ʒi:rən] (*no -ge-, h*) **1.** *v/t* RAIL switch, *Br* shunt; **2.** *fig v/i* rank (**vor j-m** before s.o.)

'Rangordnung *f* hierarchy

Ranke ['raŋkə] *f* (-; *-n*) BOT tendril

'ranken *v/refl* (*ge-, h*) BOT creep, climb

rann [ran] *pret of* **rinnen**

rannte ['rantə] *pret of* **rennen**

Ranzen ['rantsən] *m* (-s; -) knapsack; satchel

ranzig ['rantsɪç] *adj* rancid, rank

Rappe ['rapə] *m* (-n; *-n*) ZO black horse

rar [ra:ɐ] *adj* rare, scarce

Rarität [rari'tɛ:t] *f* (-; *-en*) a) (curiosity, b) (*no pl*) rarity

rasch [raʃ] *adj* quick, swift; prompt

rascheln ['raʃəln] *v/i* (*ge-, h*) rustle

rasen ['ra:zən] *v/i* a) (*ge-, sein*) F MOT race, tear, speed, b) (*ge-, h*) rage; **~ vor Begeisterung** roar with enthusiasm

'Rasen *m* (-s; -) lawn, grass

'rasend *adj* breakneck; raging; agonizing; splitting; thunderous

'Rasen|mäher *m* lawn mower; **~platz** *m* lawn; *tennis*: grass court

Raserei [ra:zə'raɪ] *f* (-; *-en*) a) (*no pl*) frenzied rage; frenzy, madness, b) F MOT reckless driving

Rasier|appa,rat [ra'zi:ɐ-] *m* (safety) razor; *esp* **elektrischer ~** shaver; **~creme** *f* shaving cream

rasieren [ra'zi:rən] *v/t and v/refl* (*no -ge-, h*) shave

Ra'sier|klinge *f* razor blade; **~messer** *n* (straight) razor; **~pinsel** *m* shaving brush; **~seife** *f* shaving soap; **~wasser** *n* aftershave (lotion)

Rasse ['rasə] *f* (-; *-n*) race; ZO breed

'Rassehund *m* ZO pedigree dog

Rassel ['rasəl] *f* (-; *-n*), **'rasseln** *v/i* (*ge-, h*) rattle

'Rassen... *in cpds* **...diskriminierung,** **...konflikt, ...probleme** *etc*: *mst* racial **...; ~trennung** *f* POL (racial) segregation; HIST apartheid; **~unruhen** *pl* race riots

rassig ['rasɪç] *adj* classy

rassisch ['rasɪʃ] *adj* racial

Rassismus [ra'sɪsmʊs] *m* (-; *no pl*) POL racism; **Ras'sist(in)** (-en; -en/-; *-nen*), **ras'sistisch** *adj* POL racist

R

Rast [rast] f (-; -en) rest, stop; break; **rasten** ['rastən] v/i (ge-, h) rest, stop, take a break; **'rastlos** adj restless

'Rastplatz m resting place; MOT rest area, Br lay-by

'Raststätte f MOT service area

Rasur [ra'zuːɐ] f (-; -en) shave

Rat [raːt] m (-[e]s; Räte ['rɛːtə]) a) (no pl) (piece of) advice, b) council; **j-n um ~ fragen** ask s.o.'s advice; **j-s ~ befolgen** take s.o.'s advice

Rate ['raːtə] f (-; -n) rate; ECON instal(l)-ment; **auf ~n** by instal(l)ments

raten ['raːtən] v/t and v/i (irr, ge-, h) advise; guess; solve; **j-m zu et. ~** advise s.o. to do s.th.; **rate mal!** (have a) guess!

'Ratenzahlung f → Abzahlung

'Rateteam n TV etc panel

'Ratgeber [-geːbɐ] m (-s; -), **'Ratgeberin** f (-; -nen) adviser, counsel(l)or; m guide (über acc to)

'Rathaus n city (Br town) hall

ratifizieren [ratifi'tsiːrən] v/t (no -ge-, h) ratify

Ration [ra'tsioːn] f (-; -en) ration

rational [ratsio'naːl] adj rational

rationell [ratsio'nɛl] adj efficient; economical

rationieren [ratsio'niːrən] v/t (no -ge-, h) ration

'ratlos adj at a loss

'ratsam adj advisable, wise

'Ratschlag m piece of advice; **ein paar gute Ratschläge** some good advice

Rätsel ['rɛːtsəl] n (-s; -) puzzle; riddle (both a. fig); mystery

'rätselhaft adj puzzling; mysterious

Ratte ['ratə] f (-; -n) ZO rat (a. contp)

rattern ['ratɐn] v/i (ge-, h, sein) rattle, clatter

rau [rau] adj rough, rugged (both a. fig); harsh; chapped; sore

Raub [raup] m (-[e]s; no pl) robbery; loot, booty; prey; **~bau** m (-[e]s; no pl) overexploitation (an dat of); **~ mit s-r Gesundheit treiben** ruin one's health

rauben ['raubən] v/t (ge-, h) rob, steal; kidnap; **j-m et. ~** rob s.o. of s.th. (a. fig)

Räuber ['rɔʏbɐ] m (-s; -) robber

'Raub|fisch m predatory fish; **~mord** m murder with robbery; **~mörder** m murderer and robber; **~tier** n beast of prey;

~überfall m holdup, (armed) robbery; mugging; **~vogel** m bird of prey; **~zug** m raid

Rauch [raux] m (-[e]s; no pl) smoke; CHEM etc fume; **rauchen** ['rauxən] v/i and v/t (ge-, h) smoke; CHEM etc fume; **Rauchen verboten!** no smoking; **Pfeife ~** smoke a pipe; **Raucher(in)** ['rauxɐ (-xərɪn)] (-s; -/-; -nen) smoker (m a. RAIL)

Räucher... ['rɔʏçɐ-] in cpds **~aal**, ...speck etc: smoked ...

'räuchern v/t (ge-, h) smoke

'Räucherstäbchen n joss stick

'Rauchfahne f trail of smoke

'rauchig adj smoky

'Rauch|waren pl tobacco products; furs; **~zeichen** n smoke signal

Räude ['rɔʏdə] f (-; -n) VET mange

'räudig adj VET mangy

raufen ['raufən] v/t (ge-, h) **1.** v/t: **sich die Haare ~** tear one's hair; **2.** v/i fight, scuffle; **Rauferei** [raufə'rai] f (-; -en) fight, scuffle

Raum [raum] m (-[e]s; Räume ['rɔʏmə]) room; space; area; (outer) space; **~anzug** m spacesuit; **~deckung** f SPORT zone marking

räumen ['rɔʏmən] v/t (ge-, h) leave, move out of; check out of; clear (von of); evacuate (a. MIL); **s-e Sachen in ...** (acc) ~ put one's things (away) in ...

'Raum|fahrer F m spaceman; **~fahrt** f (-; no pl) space travel or flight; astronautics; **~fahrt...** in cpds ...technik, ...zentrum etc: space ...; **~fähre** f space shuttle; **~flug** m space flight; **~inhalt** m volume; **~kapsel** f space capsule; **~labor** n space lab

räumlich ['rɔʏmlɪç] adj three-dimensional

'Raum|schiff n spacecraft; spaceship; **~sonde** f space probe; **~station** f space station

'Räumung f (-; -en) clearance; evacuation (a. MIL); JUR eviction

'Räumungsverkauf m ECON clearance sale

raunen ['raunən] v/i (ge-, h) whisper, murmur

Raupe ['raupə] f (-; -n) ZO caterpillar, TECH a. track; **'Raupenschlepper** m MOT caterpillar tractor

'Raureif m hoarfrost

raus [raus] F *int* get out (of here)!

Rausch [rauʃ] *m* (-*es*; *Räusche* ['rɔʏʃə]) drunkenness, intoxication; F high; *fig* ecstasy; **e-n ~ haben** be drunk; **s-n ~ ausschlafen** sleep it off

rauschen ['rauʃən] *v/i* a) (*ge-, h*) water etc: rush; *brook*: murmur; *storm*: roar, b) (*ge-, sein*) sweep; **~d** *adj* thunderous (*applause*); **~es Fest** lavish celebration

'**Rauschgift** *n* drug(s), narcotic(s); **~de-zer,nat** *n* narcotics or drugs squad; **~handel** *m* drug traffic(king); **~händ-ler** *m* drug trafficker, F pusher

räuspern ['rɔʏspən] *v/refl* (*ge-, h*) clear one's throat

Razzia ['ratsja] *f* (-; -*ien*) raid, roundup

Reagenzglas [rea'gɛnts-] *n* CHEM test tube

reagieren [rea'giːrən] *v/i* (*no -ge-, h*) CHEM, MED react (*auf acc* to), *fig a.* respond (to); **Reaktion** [reak'tsjoːn] *f* (-; -*en*) CHEM, MED, PHYS, POL reaction (*auf acc* to), *fig a.* response (to)

Reaktor [re'aktoːɐ] *m* (-*s*; -*en* [re-ak'toːrən]) PHYS (nuclear or atomic) reactor

real [re'aːl] *adj* real; concrete

realisieren [reali'ziːrən] *v/t* (*no -ge-, h*) realize

Realismus [rea'lɪsmʊs] *m* (-; *no pl*) realism; **rea'listisch** *adj* realistic

Realität [reali'tɛːt] *f* (-; *no pl*) reality

Re'alschule *f appr* (junior) highschool, *Br* secondary (modern) school

Rebe ['reːbə] *f* (-; -*n*) BOT vine

Rebell [re'bɛl] *m* (-*en*; -*en*) rebel

rebellieren [rebɛ'liːrən] *v/i* (*no -ge-, h*) rebel, revolt, rise (*all*: **gegen** against)

Re'bellin *f* (-; -*nen*) rebel

re'bellisch *adj* rebellious

Rebhuhn ['reːp-] *n* ZO partridge

'**Rebstock** *m* BOT vine

Rechen ['reçən] *m* (-*s*; -), '**rechen** *v/t* (*ge-, h*) rake

'**Rechen|aufgabe** *f* MATH (arithmetical) problem; **~fehler** *m* MATH arithmetical error, miscalculation; **~ma,schine** *f* calculator; computer

'**Rechenschaft** *f*: **~ ablegen über** (*acc*) account for; **zur ~ ziehen** call to account (**wegen** for)

'**Rechen|schieber** *m* MATH slide rule; **~werk** *n* EDP arithmetic unit; **~zent-**

rum *n* computer center (*Br* centre)

rechnen ['rɛçnən] *v/i* and *v/t* (*ge-, h*) calculate, reckon, work out, do sums; count; **~ mit** *fig* expect; count on; *mit mir kannst du nicht ~!* count me out!

'**Rechnen** *n* (-*s*; *no pl*) arithmetic

Rechner ['rɛçnɐ] *m* (-*s*; -) calculator; computer

'**rechnerabhängig** *adj* EDP online

rechnerisch ['rɛçnərɪʃ] *adj* arithmetical

'**rechnerunabhängig** *adj* EDP offline

'**Rechnung** *f* (-; -*en*) MATH calculation; problem, sum; ECON invoice, bill, check; *die ~, bitte!* can I have the check, please?; *das geht auf m-e* ~ that's on me

recht [rɛçt] **1.** *adj* right; correct; POL right-wing; *auf der ~en Seite* on the right(-hand side); *mir ist es ~* I don't mind; **2.** *adv* right(ly), correctly; rather, quite; *ich weiß nicht ~* I don't really know; *es geschieht ihm ~* it serves him right; *erst ~* all the more; *erst ~ nicht* even less; *du kommst gerade ~* (*zu*) you're just in time (for)

Recht *n* (-[*e*]*s*; -*e*) a) right, claim (*both*: *auf acc* to), b) (*no pl*) JUR law; justice; *gleiches ~* equal rights; **~ haben** be right; *j-m ~ geben* agree with s.o.; *im ~ sein* be in the right; *er hat es mit* (*vollem*) **~ getan** he was (perfectly) right to do so; *ein ~ auf et. ha-ben* be entitled to s.th.

'**Rechteck** *n* (-[*e*]*s*; -*e*) rectangle

'**rechteckig** *adj* rectangular

'**rechtfertigen** *v/t* (*ge-, h*) justify

'**Rechtfertigung** *f* (-; -*en*) justification

'**rechtlich** *adj* JUR legal

'**rechtlos** *adj* without rights; outcast

'**rechtmäßig** *adj* JUR lawful; legitimate; legal; '**Rechtmäßigkeit** *f* (-; *no pl*) JUR lawfulness, legitimacy

rechts [rɛçts] *adv* on the right(-hand side); *nach ~* to the right

Rechts... *in cpds* POL right-wing ...; **~an-spruch** *m* legal claim (*auf acc* to); **~anwalt** *m*, **~anwältin** [-anvɛltɪn] *f* (-; -*nen*) lawyer

Rechts'außen *m* (-; -) *soccer*: outside right

'**rechtschaffen** *adj* honest

'**Recht|schreibfehler** *m* spelling mistake; **~schreibung** *f* (-; *no pl*) spelling, orthography

R

'rechtsextre,mistisch *adj* POL extreme right

'Rechtsfall *m* JUR (law) case

'Rechtshänder [-hɛndɐ] *m* (-s; -), **Rechtshänderin** *f* (-; -nen) right-handed person; **sie ist Rechtshänderin** she is right-handed

'Rechtsprechung *f* (-; *no pl*) jurisdiction

'rechtsradi,kal *adj* POL extreme right-wing

'Rechtsschutz *m* legal protection; legal costs insurance

'rechtswidrig *adj* JUR illegal, unlawful

'rechtwink(e)lig *adj* rectangular

'rechtzeitig **1.** *adj* punctual; **2.** *adv* in time (**zu** for)

Reck [rɛk] *n* (-[e]s; -e) horizontal bar

recken ['rɛkən] *v/t* (ge-, h) stretch; **sich~** stretch o.s.

recyceln [ri'saikəln] *v/t* (*no* ge-, h) recycle; **Recyclingpa,pier** [ri'saiklɪŋ-] *n* recycled paper

Redakteur [redak'tøːɐ] *m* (-s; -e), **Redak'teurin** *f* (-; -nen) editor

Redaktion [redak'tsjoːn] *f* (-; -en) a) (*no pl*) editing, b) editorial staff, editors, c) editorial office *or* department

redaktionell [redaktsjo'nɛl] *adj* editorial

Rede ['reːdə] *f* (-; -n) speech, address; talk (**von** of); **e-e ~ halten** make a speech; **direkte (indirekte) ~** LING direct (reported *or* indirect) speech; **j-n zur ~ stellen** take s.o. to task; **nicht der ~ wert** not worth mentioning

'redegewandt *adj* eloquent

reden ['reːdən] *v/i and v/t* (ge-, h) talk, speak (*both:* **mit** to; **über** *acc* about, of); **ich möchte mit dir ~** I'd like to talk to you; **die Leute ~** people talk; **j-n zum Reden bringen** make s.o. talk

'Redensart *f* saying, phrase

redlich ['reːtlɪç] *adj* upright, honest; **sich ~(e) Mühe geben** do one's best

Redner ['reːdnɐ] *m* (-s; -), **'Rednerin** *f* (-; -nen) speaker

'Rednerpult *n* speaker's desk

redselig ['reːtzeːlɪç] *adj* talkative

reduzieren [redu'tsiːrən] *v/t* (*no* ge-, h) reduce (**auf** *acc* to)

Reeder ['reːdɐ] *m* (-s; -) shipowner

Reederei [reːdə'rai] *f* (-; -en) shipping company

reell [re'ɛl] *adj* reasonable, fair (*price*); real (*chance*); solid (*firm*)

Referat [refe'raːt] *n* (-[e]s; -e) paper; report; lecture; **ein ~ halten** read a paper

Referendar [referɛn'daːɐ] *m* (-s; -e), **Referen'darin** *f* (-; -nen) *appr* trainee teacher

Referent [refe'rɛnt] *m* (-en; -en), **Refe'rentin** *f* (-; -nen) speaker; **Referenz** [refe'rɛnts] *f* (-; -en) reference; **referieren** [refe'riːrən] *v/i* (*no* ge-, h) (give a) report *or* lecture (**über** *acc* on)

reflektieren [reflɛk'tiːrən] *v/t and v/i* (*no* ge-, h) reflect (*fig* **über** *acc* [up]on)

Reflex [re'flɛks] *m* (-es; -e) reflex

reflexiv [reflɛ'ksiːf] *adj* LING reflexive

Reform [re'fɔrm] *f* (-; -en) reform

Reformator [refɔr'maːtoːɐ] *m* (-s; -en [-ma'toːrən]), **Reformer(in)** [re'fɔrmɐ (-mərɪn)] (-s; -/-; -nen) reformer

Re'formhaus *n* health food store (*Br* shop)

reformieren [refɔr'miːrən] *v/t* (*no* ge-, h) reform

Refrain [rə'frɛː] *m* (-s; -s) refrain, chorus

Regal [re'gaːl] *n* (-s; -e) shelf (unit), shelves

rege ['reːgə] *adj* lively; busy; active

Regel ['reːgəl] *f* (-; -n) rule; MED period, menstruation; **in der ~** as a rule

'regelmäßig *adj* regular

regeln ['reːgəln] *v/t* (ge-, h) regulate, TECH a. adjust; ECON settle

'regelrecht *adj* regular (*a.* F)

'Regeltechnik *f* control engineering

'Regelung *f* (-; -en) regulation; adjustment; ECON settlement; TECH control

'regelwidrig *adj* against the rule(s); SPORT unfair; **~es Spiel** foul play

regen ['reːgən] *v/t and v/refl* (ge-, h) move, stir

'Regen *m* (-s; -) rain; **starker ~** heavy rain(fall); **~bogen** *m* rainbow; **~bogenhaut** *f* ANAT iris; **~guss** *m* (heavy) shower, downpour; **~mantel** *m* raincoat; **~schauer** *m* shower; **~schirm** *m* umbrella; **~tag** *m* rainy day; **~tropfen** *m* raindrop; **~wald** *m* rain forest; **~wasser** *n* rainwater; **~wetter** *n* rainy weather; **~wurm** *m* ZO earthworm; **~zeit** *f* rainy season, the rains

Regie [re'ʒiː] *f* (-; *no pl*) THEA, *film etc*: direction; **unter der ~ von** directed by

Re'gieanweisung *f* stage direction

regieren [re'gi:rən] (*no* -*ge*-, *h*) **1.** *v/i*
reign; **2.** *v/t* govern (*a.* LING), rule

Re'gierung *f* (-; -*en*) government, administration; reign

Re'gierungs|bezirk *m* administrative district; **~chef** *m* head of government; **~wechsel** *m* change of government

Regime [re'ʒi:m] *n* (-*s*; -) POL regime

Re'gimekritiker *m* POL dissident

Regiment [regi'mɛnt] *n* (-[*e*]*s*; -*er*) a) (*no pl*) rule (*a. fig*), b) MIL regiment

Regisseur [reʒɪ'søːɐ] *m* (-*s*; -*e*), **Regis-'seurin** *f* (-; -*nen*) THEA, *film etc*: director, THEA Br a. producer

Register [re'gɪstɐ] *n* (-*s*; -) register (*a.* MUS), record; index; **registrieren** [regɪs'tri:rən] *v/t* (*no* -*ge*-, *h*) register, record; *fig* note; **Registrierkasse** [regɪs'tri:ɐ-] *f* cash register

Reglement [reglə'mãː] *n* (-*s*; -*s*) regulation, order, rule

Regler ['re:glɐ] *m* (-*s*; -) TECH control

regnen ['re:gnən] *v/i* (*ge*-, *h*) rain (*a. fig*); **es regnet in Strömen** it's pouring with rain; **'regnerisch** *adj* rainy

regulär [regu'lɛːɐ] *adj* regular; normal

regulierbar [regu'li:ɐbaːɐ] *adj* adjustable; controllable

regulieren [regu'li:rən] *v/t* (*no* -*ge*-, *h*) regulate, adjust; control

'Regung *f* (-; -*en*) movement, motion; emotion; impulse

'regungslos *adj* motionless

Reh [re:] *n* (-[*e*]*s*; -*e*) ZO deer, roe; doe; GASTR venison

rehabilitieren [rehabili'ti:rən] *v/t* (*no* -*ge*-, *h*) rehabilitate

'Reh|bock *m* ZO (roe)buck; **~keule** *f* GASTR leg of venison; **~kitz** *n* ZO fawn

Reibe ['raibə] *f* (-; -*n*), **Reibeisen** ['raip-] *n* (-*s*; -) grater, rasp

reiben ['raibən] *v/i and v/t* (*irr*, *ge*-, *h*) rub; grate, grind; **sich die Augen (Hände) ~** rub one's eyes (hands)

'Reibung *f* (-; -*en*) TECH *etc* friction

'reibungslos *adj* TECH *etc* frictionless; *fig* smooth

reich [raiç] *adj* rich (**an** *dat* in), wealthy; abundant

Reich *n* (-[*e*]*s*; -*e*) empire, kingdom (*a.* REL, BOT, ZO); *fig* world

reichen ['raiçən] (*ge*-, *h*) **1.** *v/t* reach; hand, pass; give, hold out (*one's hand*); **2.** *v/i* last, do; **~ bis** reach *or* come up

to; **das reicht** that will do; F **mir reicht's!** I've had enough

'reichhaltig *adj* rich

'reichlich **1.** *adj* rich, plentiful; plenty of; **2.** *adv* rather; generously

'Reichtum *m* (-*s*; *no pl*) wealth (**an** *dat* of) (*a. fig*)

'Reichweite *f* reach; AVIAT, MIL *etc* range; **in (außer) (j-s) ~** within (out of) (s.o.'s) reach

reif [raif] *adj* ripe, *esp fig* mature

Reif *m* (-[*e*]*s*; *no pl*) white frost, hoar-frost

Reife ['raifə] *f* (-; *no pl*) ripeness, *esp fig* maturity; **'reifen** *v/i* (*ge*-, *sein*) ripen, mature (*both a. fig*)

Reifen ['raifən] *m* (-*s*; -) hoop; MOT *etc* tire, Br tyre; **~panne** *f* MOT flat tire (Br tyre), puncture, F flat

'Reifeprüfung *f* → **Abitur**

'reiflich *adj* careful

Reihe ['raiə] *f* (-; -*n*) line, row; number; series; **der ~ nach** in turn; **ich bin an der ~** it's my turn

'Reihenfolge *f* order

'Reihenhaus *n* row (Br terraced) house

'reihenweise *adv* in rows; F *fig* by the dozen

Reiher ['raiɐ] *m* (-*s*; -) ZO heron

Reim [raim] *m* (-[*e*]*s*; -*e*) rhyme

reimen ['raimən] *v/t and v/refl* (*ge*-, *h*) rhyme (**auf** *acc* with)

rein [rain] *adj* pure (*a. fig*); clean; *fig* clear (*conscience*); plain (*truth*); mere, sheer, nothing but

'Reinfall F *m* flop; let-down

'Reingewinn *m* ECON net profit

'reinhauen F *v/i* (*sep*, -*ge*-, *h*) tuck in

'Reinheit *f* (-; *no pl*) purity (*a. fig*); cleanness

reinigen ['rainigən] *v/t* (*ge*-, *h*) clean; cleanse (*a.* MED); dry-clean; *fig* purify

'Reinigung *f* (-; -*en*) clean(s)ing; *fig* purification; (dry) cleaners; **chemi-sche ~** dry cleaning; dry cleaner's

'Reinigungsmittel *n* cleaning agent, cleaner, detergent

'reinlich *adj* clean; cleanly

'reinrassig *adj* ZO purebred, pedigree; thoroughbred

'Reinschrift *f* fair copy

Reis [rais] *m* (-*es*; -*e*) BOT rice

Reise ['raizə] *f* (-; -*n*) trip; journey; tour; MAR voyage; **auf ~n sein** be travel(l)ing; **e-e ~ machen** take a trip; **gute ~!** have a nice trip!; **~andenken** n souvenir; **~bü¸ro** n travel agency or bureau; **~führer** m guide(book); **~gesellschaft** f tourist party; tour operator; **~kosten** pl travel(l)ing expenses; **~krankheit** f travel sickness; **~leiter(in)** tour guide or manager, Br courier

'reisen v/i (ge-, sein) travel; **durch Frankreich ~** tour France; **ins Ausland ~** go abroad; '**Reisende** m, f (-n; -n) travel(l)er; tourist; passenger

'Reise|pass n passport; **~scheck** m travel(l)er's check (Br cheque); **~tasche** f travel(l)ing bag, holdall

Reisig ['raɪzɪç] n (-s; no pl) brushwood

Reißbrett ['raɪs-] n drawing board

reißen ['raɪsən] (irr, ge-) **1.** v/t (h) tear (**in Stücke** to pieces), rip; pull, drag; ZO kill; F crack (jokes); SPORT knock down; **an sich ~** seize, snatch, grab; **2.** v/i (sein) break, burst; **sich um et. ~** scramble for (or to get) s.th.; **~d** adj torrential

Reißer ['raɪsɐ] F m (-s; -) thriller; hit

reißerisch ['raɪsərɪʃ] adj sensational, loud

'Reiß|verschluss m zipper; **den ~ an et. öffnen (schließen)** unzip (zip up) s.th.; **~zwecke** f thumbtack, Br drawing pin

reiten ['raɪtən] (irr, ge-) **1.** v/i (sein) ride, go on horseback; **2.** v/t (h) ride

'Reiten n (-s; no pl) horseback riding

Reiter ['raɪtɐ] m (-s; -) rider, horseman

Reiterin ['raɪtərɪn] f (-; -nen) rider, horsewoman

'Reitpferd n saddle or riding horse

Reiz [raɪts] m (-es; -e) charm, attraction, appeal; thrill; MED, PSYCH stimulus; (**für j-n**) **den ~ verlieren** lose one's appeal (for s.o.); 'reizbar adj irritable, excitable; reizen ['raɪtsən] (ge-, h) **1.** v/t irritate (a. MED), annoy; ZO bait; provoke; appeal to, attract; tempt; challenge; **2.** v/i cards: bid; '**reizend** adj charming, delightful; lovely, sweet, cute; '**reizlos** adj unattractive

'Reizung f (-; -en) irritation (a. MED)

'reizvoll adj attractive; challenging

'Reizwort n (-[e]s; -wörter) emotive word

rekeln ['reːkəln] F v/refl (ge-, h) loll

Reklamation [reklama'tsjoːn] f (-; -en) complaint

Reklame [re'klaːmə] f (-; -n) advertising, publicity; advertisement, F ad; **~ machen für** advertise, promote

reklamieren [rekla'miːrən] v/i (no -ge-, h) complain (**wegen** about), protest (against)

Rekord [re'kɔrt] m (-[e]s; -e) record; **e-n ~ aufstellen** set or establish a record

Rekrut [re'kruːt] m (-en; -en) MIL recruit

rekrutieren [rekru'tiːrən] v/t (no -ge-, h) recruit

Rektor ['rɛktoːɐ] m (-s; -en [rɛk'toːrən]) principal, Br headmaster; UNIV president, Br rector; **Rektorin** [rɛk'toːrɪn] f (-; -nen) principal, Br headmistress; UNIV president, Br rector

relativ [rela'tiːf] adj relative

Relief [re'ljɛf] n (-s; -s) relief

Religion [reli'gjoːn] f (-; -en) religion

religiös [reli'gjøːs] adj religious

Reling ['reːlɪŋ] f (-; -s) MAR rail

Reliquie [re'liːkvjə] f (-; -n) relic

Rempelei [rɛmpə'laɪ] F f (-; -en), **rempeln** ['rɛmpəln] F v/t (ge-, h) jostle

Rennbahn ['rɛn-] f racecourse, racetrack; cycling track

'Rennboot n racing boat; speedboat

rennen ['rɛnən] v/i and v/t (irr, ge-, sein) run; '**Rennen** n (-s; -) race (a. fig); heat

'Renn|fahrer m, **~fahrerin** f racing driver; racing cyclist; **~läufer** m ski racer; **~pferd** n racehorse; racer; **~rad** n racing bicycle, racer; **~sport** m racing; **~stall** m racing stable; **~wagen** m race (Br racing) car, racer

renommiert [reno'miːɐt] adj renowned

renovieren [reno'viːrən] v/t (no -ge-, h) renovate, F do up; redecorate

rentabel [rɛn'taːbəl] adj ECON profitable, paying

Rente ['rɛntə] f (-; -n) (old age) pension; **in ~ gehen** retire

'Renten|alter n retirement age; **~versicherung** f pension scheme

Rentier ['rɛntiːɐ] n (-s; -e) ZO reindeer

rentieren [rɛn'tiːrən] v/refl (no -ge-, h) ECON pay; fig be worth it

Rentner ['rɛntnɐ] m (-s; -), '**Rentnerin** [-nərɪn] f (-; -nen) (old age) pensioner

Reparatur [repara'tuːɐ] f (-; -en) repair; **~werkstatt** f repair shop; MOT garage reparieren [repa'ri:rən] v/t (no -ge-, h) repair, mend, F fix

Reportage [repɔr'ta:ʒə] f (-; -n) report

Reporter [re'pɔrtɐ] m (-s; -), **Re'porterin** f (-; -nen) reporter

Repräsentant [reprɛzɛn'tant] m (-en; -en) representative; **Repräsentantenhaus** n PARL House of Representatives; **Repräsen'tantin** f (-; -nen) representative; **repräsentieren** [reprɛzɛn'ti:rən] v/t (no -ge-, h) represent

Repressalie [reprɛ'sa:ljə] f (-; -n) reprisal

Reproduktion [reprodʊk'tsjo:n] f (-; -en) reproduction, print

reproduzieren [reprodʊ'tsi:rən] v/t (no -ge-, h) reproduce

Reptil [rɛp'ti:l] n (-s; -ien) ZO reptile

Republik [repu'bli:k] f (-; -en) republic

Republikaner [republi'ka:nɐ] m (-s; -), **Republi'kanerin** f (-; -nen), **republi'kanisch** adj POL republican

Reservat [rezɛr'va:t] n (-[e]s; -e) (p)reserve; reservation

Reserve [re'zɛrvə] f (-; -n) reserve (a. MIL); **~... in** cpds ...kanister, ...rad etc: spare ...

reservieren [rezɛr'vi:rən] v/t (no -ge-, h) reserve (a. **~ lassen**); **j-m e-n Platz ~** keep or save a seat for s.o.; **reserviert** [rezɛr'vi:rt] adj reserved (a. fig); aloof; **Reser'viertheit** f (-; no pl) aloofness

Residenz [rezi'dɛnts] f (-; -en) residence

Resignation [rezigna'tsjo:n] f (-; no pl) resignation; **resignieren** [rezɪ'gni:rən] v/i (no -ge-, h) give up; **resigniert** [rezɪ'gni:rt] adj resigned

Resozialisierung f (-; -en) rehabilitation

Respekt [re'spɛkt] m (-[e]s; no pl) respect (**vor** dat for); **respektieren** [respɛk'ti:rən] v/t (no -ge-, h) respect

re'spektlos adj irreverent, disrespectful; **re'spektvoll** adj respectful

Ressort [rɛ'sɔːr] n (-s; -s) department, province

Rest [rɛst] m (-[e]s; -e) rest; pl remains, remnants; GASTR leftovers; F **das gab ihm den ~** that finished him (off)

Restaurant [rɛsto'rãː] n (-s; -s) restaurant

restaurieren [rɛsto'ri:rən] v/t (no -ge-, h) restore

'Restbetrag m remainder

'restlich adj remaining

'restlos adv completely

Resultat [rezʊl'ta:t] n (-[e]s; -e) result (a. SPORT), outcome

Retorte [re'tɔrtə] f (-; -n) CHEM retort

Re'tortenbaby F n test-tube baby

retten ['rɛtən] v/t (ge-, h) save, rescue (both: **aus** dat, **vor** dat from)

Retter ['rɛtɐ] m (-s; -), **'Retterin** f (-; -nen) rescuer

Rettich ['rɛtɪç] m (-s; -e) BOT radish

Rettung f (-; -en) rescue (**aus** dat, **vor** dat from); **das war s-e ~** that saved him

'Rettungs|boot n lifeboat; **~mannschaft** f rescue party; **~ring** m life belt, life buoy; **~schwimmer** m lifeguard

Reue ['rɔʏə] f (-; no pl) remorse, repentance (both: **über** acc for)

reumütig ['rɔʏmy:tɪç] adj repentant

Revanche [re'vãːʃ(ə)] f (-; -n) revenge

revanchieren [revã'ʃi:rən] v/refl (no -ge-, h) have one's revenge (**bei, an** dat on); make it up (**bei j-m** to s.o.)

Revers [re've:r] n, m (-; -) lapel

revidieren [revi'di:rən] v/t (no -ge-, h) revise; ECON audit

Revier [re'vi:r] n (-s; -e) district; ZO territory (a. fig); → **Polizeirevier**

Revision [revi'zjo:n] f (-; -en) revision; ECON audit; JUR appeal

Revolte [re'vɔltə] f (-; -n), **revoltieren** [revɔl'ti:rən] v/i (no -ge-, h) revolt

Revolution [revolu'tsjo:n] f (-; -en) revolution; **revolutionär** [revolutsjo'nɛːɐ] adj, **Revolutio'när(in)** (-s; -e/-; -nen) revolutionary

Revolver [re'vɔlvɐ] m (-s; -) revolver, F gun

Revue [re'vy:] f (-; -n) THEA (musical) show

R

Rezept [re'tsɛpt] n (-[e]s; -e) MED prescription; GASTR recipe (a. fig)

Rezession [retsɛ'sjo:n] f (-; -en) ECON recession

Rhabarber [ra'barbɐ] m (-s; no pl) BOT rhubarb

rhetorisch [re'to:rɪʃ] adj rhetorical

Rheuma ['rɔʏma] n (-s; no pl) MED rheumatism

rhythmisch ['rʏtmɪʃ] adj rhythmic(al)

Rhythmus ['rʏtmʊs] m (-; -men) rhythm

Ribisel ['ri:bi:zəl] Austrian f (-; -[n]) → **Johannisbeere**

richten ['rɪçtən] v/t (ge-, h) fix; get s.th. ready, prepare; do (room, one's hair); (**sich**) ~ **an** (acc) address (o.s.) to; put a question to; ~ **auf** (acc) direct or turn to; point or aim camera, gun etc at; ~ **gegen** direct against; **sich** ~ **nach** go by, act according to; follow (fashion etc); depend on; **ich richte mich ganz nach dir** I leave it to you

Richter ['rɪçtɐ] m (-s; -), '**Richterin** f (-; -nen) judge

'**richterlich** adj judicial

'**Richtgeschwindigkeit** f MOT recommended speed

richtig ['rɪçtɪç] **1.** adj right; correct, proper; true; real; **2.** adv: ~ **nett** (**böse**) really nice (angry); **et.** ~ **machen** do s.th. right; **m-e Uhr geht** ~ my watch is right; fig ~ **stellen** put or set right

'**Richtigkeit** f (-; no pl) correctness

'**Richt|linien** pl guidelines; ~**preis** m ECON recommended price

'**Richtung** f (-; -en) direction; POL leaning; PAINT etc style; '**richtungslos** adj aimless, disorient(at)ed

'**richtungweisend** adj pioneering

rieb [riːp] pret of **reiben**

riechen ['riːçən] v/i and v/t (irr, ge-, h) smell (**nach** of; **an** dat at)

rief [riːf] pret of **rufen**

Riegel ['riːɡəl] m (-s; -) bolt, bar

Riemen ['riːmən] m (-s; -) strap; TECH belt; MAR oar

Riese ['riːzə] m (-n; -n) giant (a. fig)

rieseln ['riːzəln] v/i (ge-, sein) trickle; rain: drizzle; snow: fall gently

Riesen... in cpds mst giant ..., gigantic ..., enormous ...; ~**erfolg** m huge success, film etc: a. smash hit

'**riesengroß**, '**riesenhaft** → **riesig**

'**Riesenrad** n Ferris wheel

riesig ['riːzɪç] adj enormous, gigantic, giant

'**Riesin** f (-; -nen) giantess (a. fig)

riet [riːt] pret of **raten**

Riff [rɪf] n (-[e]s; -e) GEOGR reef

Rille ['rɪlə] f (-; -n) groove

Rind [rɪnt] n (-[e]s; -er ['rɪndɐ]) ZO cow, pl cattle; GASTR beef

Rinde ['rɪndə] f (-; -n) BOT bark; GASTR rind; crust

Rinder|braten ['rɪndɐ-] m roast beef; ~**herde** f herd of cattle

'**Rind|fleisch** n GASTR beef; ~**(s)leder** n cowhide; ~**vieh** n ZO cattle

Ring [rɪŋ] m (-[e]s; -e) ring (a. fig); MOT ring road; subway etc: circle (line)

'**Ringbuch** n loose-leaf or ring binder

ringeln ['rɪŋəln] v/refl (ge-, h) curl, coil (a. ZO)

'**Ringelnatter** f ZO grass snake

'**Ringelspiel** Austrian n → **Karussell**

ringen ['rɪŋən] (irr, ge-, h) **1.** v/i SPORT wrestle (**mit** with), fig a. struggle (against, with; **um** for); **nach Atem** ~ gasp (for breath); **2.** v/t wring

Ringen n (-s; no pl) SPORT wrestling

Ringer ['rɪŋɐ] m (-s; -) SPORT wrestler

'**ringförmig** [-fœrmɪç] adj circular

'**Ringkampf** m SPORT wrestling match

'**Ringrichter** m SPORT referee

rings adv: ~ **um** around

'**ringshe'rum**, '**rings'um**, '**ringsum'her** adv all around; everywhere

Rinne ['rɪnə] f (-; -n) groove, channel; gutter; '**rinnen** v/i (irr, ge-, sein) run; flow, stream; **Rinnsal** ['rɪnzaːl] n (-s; -e) trickle

'**Rinnstein** m gutter

Rippe ['rɪpə] f (-; -n) ANAT rib

'**Rippenfell** n ANAT pleura; ~**entzündung** f MED pleurisy

'**Rippenstoß** m nudge in the ribs

Risiko ['riːziko] n (-s; -s, -ken) risk; **ein** (**kein**) ~ **eingehen** take a risk (no risks); **auf eigenes** ~ at one's own risk

riskant [rɪs'kant] adj risky

riskieren [rɪs'kiːrən] v/t (no -ge-, h) risk

riss [rɪs] pret of **reißen**

Riss m (-es; -e) tear, rip, split (a. fig); crack; MED chap, laceration; **rissig** ['rɪsɪç] adj chapped; cracky, cracked

Rist [rɪst] m (-es; -e) ANAT instep

ritt [rɪt] pret of **reiten**

Ritt m (-[e]s; -e) ride (on horseback)

Ritter ['rɪtɐ] m (-s; -) knight; **j-n zum** ~ **schlagen** knight s.o.

'**ritterlich** fig adj chivalrous

Ritz [rɪts] m (-es; -e), **Ritze** ['rɪtsə] f (-; -n) crack, chink; spot

Rivale [ri'vaːlə] m (-n; -n), **Ri'valin** f (-; -nen) rival; **rivalisieren** [rivali'ziːrən] v/i (no -ge-, h) compete; **Rivalität** [rivali'tɛːt] f (-; -en) rivalry

rk., **r.-k.** ABBR of **römisch-katholisch** RC, Roman Catholic

Robbe ['rɔbə] f (-; -n) ZO seal

Robe ['roːbə] f (-; -n) robe, gown

Roboter ['rɔbɔtɐ] m (-s; -) robot

robust [ro'bʊst] adj robust, strong, tough

roch [rɔx] pret of **riechen**

röcheln ['rœçəln] (ge-, h) 1. v/i moan; 2. v/t gasp

Rock [rɔk] m (-[e]s; Röcke ['rœkə]) skirt

Rodelbahn ['roːdəl-] f toboggan run

rodeln ['roːdəln] v/i (ge-, sein) sled(ge), coast; SPORT toboggan

'Rodelschlitten m sled(ge); toboggan

roden ['roːdən] v/t (ge-, h) clear; stub

Rogen ['roːgən] m (-s; -) (hard) roe

Roggen ['rɔgən] m (-s; -) BOT rye

roh [roː] adj raw; rough; fig brutal; **mit ~er Gewalt** with brute force

'Rohbau m (-[e]s; -ten) carcass

'Rohkost f raw vegetables and fruit

'Rohling m (-s; -e) TECH blank; fig brute

'Rohmateri,al n raw material

'Rohöl n crude (oil)

Rohr [roːɐ] n (-[e]s; -e ['roːrə]) TECH pipe, tube; duct; BOT reed; cane

Röhre ['røːrə] f (-; -n) pipe, tube (a. TV), TV etc valve

'Rohr|leitung f duct, pipe(s); plumbing; pipeline; **~stock** m cane; **~zucker** m cane sugar

'Rohstoff m raw material

Rollbahn ['rɔl-] f AVIAT runway

Rolle ['rɔlə] f (-; -n) roll (a. SPORT), TECH a. roller; coil; caster, castor; THEA part, role (both a. fig); **e-e ~ Garn** a spool of thread, Br a reel of cotton; **das spielt keine ~** that doesn't matter, that makes no difference; **Geld spielt k-e ~** money is no object

'rollen v/i (ge-, sein) and v/t (ge-, h) roll

Roller ['rɔlɐ] m (-s; -) (motor) scooter

'Roll|film m PHOT roll film; **~kragen** m turtleneck, esp Br polo neck; **~laden** m rolling shutter

Rollo ['rɔlo] n (-s; -s) shades, Br (roller) blind

'Rollschuh m roller skate; **~ laufen** roller-skate; **~bahn** f roller-skating rink; **~läufer** m roller skater

'Rollstuhl m wheelchair

'Rolltreppe f escalator

Roman [ro'maːn] m (-s; -e) novel

Romanik [ro'maːnɪk] f (-; no pl) ARCH Romanesque (style or period)

romanisch [ro'maːnɪʃ] adj LING Romance; ARCH Romanesque

Romanist [roma'nɪst] m (-en; -en), **Roma'nistin** f (-; -nen) student of Romance languages

Ro'manschriftsteller m, **Ro'manschriftstellerin** f novelist

Romantik [ro'mantɪk] f (-; no pl) romance; HIST Romanticism

romantisch [ro'mantɪʃ] adj romantic

Römer ['røːmɐ] m (-s; -), '**Römerin** f (-; -nen), **römisch** ['røːmɪʃ] adj Roman

Rommee ['rɔme] n (-s; -s) rummy

röntgen ['rœntgən] v/t (ge-, h) MED X-ray

'Röntgen|appa,rat m MED X-ray apparatus; **~aufnahme** f, **~bild** n MED X-ray; **~strahlen** pl PHYS X-rays; **~untersuchung** f MED X-ray

rosa ['roːza] adj pink; fig rose-colo(u)red; **Rose** ['roːzə] f (-; -n) BOT rose

'Rosenkohl m BOT Brussels sprouts

'Rosenkranz m REL rosary

rosig ['roːzɪç] adj rosy (a. fig)

Rosine [ro'ziːnə] f (-; -n) raisin

'Rosshaar n (-[e]s; no pl) horsehair

Rost [rɔst] m (-[e]s; -e) a) (no pl) CHEM rust, b) TECH grate; GASTR grid(iron), grill; **rosten** ['rɔstən] v/i (ge-, sein) rust

rösten ['rœstən] v/t (ge-, h) roast (a. F); toast; fry

'Rostfleck m rust stain; '**rostfrei** adj rustproof, stainless; '**rostig** adj rusty

rot [roːt] adj red (a. POL); **~ glühend** red-hot; **~ werden** blush; **in den ~en Zahlen** ECON in the red

Rot n (-s; -) red; **die Ampel steht auf ~** the lights are red; **bei ~** at red

rotblond adj sandy(-haired)

Röte ['røːtə] f (-; no pl) redness, red (colo[u]r); fig blush

Röteln ['røːtəln] pl MED German measles

röten ['røːtən] v/refl (ge-, h) redden; flush

'rothaarig adj red-haired

'Rothaarige m, f (-n; -n) redhead

rotieren [ro'tiːrən] v/i (no -ge-, h) rotate

'Rotkehlchen n (-s; -) ZO robin

'Rotkohl m BOT red cabbage

rötlich ['røːtlɪç] adj reddish

'Rot|stift m red crayon or pencil; **~wein** m red wine; **~wild** n ZO (red) deer

Rotznase ['rɔts-] F f snotty nose

Route ['ruːtə] f (-; -n) route

R

Routine [ru'ti:nə] f (-; *no pl*) routine; experience; **~sache** f routine (matter)
routiniert [ruti'ni:ɐt] *adj* experienced
Rübe ['ry:bə] f (-; -*n*) BOT turnip; (sugar) beet
Rubin [ru'bi:n] m (-*s*; -*e*) MIN ruby
Rübli ['ry:pli] *Swiss* n (-*s*; -) BOT carrot
Rubrik [ru'bri:k] f (-; -*en*) heading; column
Ruck [rʊk] m (-[*e*]*s*; -*e*) jerk, jolt, start; *fig* POL swing
Rückantwortschein ['rʏk-] m reply coupon
'ruckartig *adj* jerky, abrupt
'rückbezüglich *adj* LING reflexive
'Rückblende f flashback (*auf acc* to)
'Rückblick m review (*auf acc* of); **im ~** in retrospect
rücken ['rʏkən] **1.** v/t (ge-, h) move, shift, push; **2.** v/i (ge-, *sein*) move; move over; **näher ~** approach
'Rücken m (-*s*; -) ANAT back (*a. fig*); **~deckung** *fig* f backing, support; **~lehne** f back(rest); **~mark** n ANAT spinal cord; **~schmerzen** pl backache; **~schwimmen** n backstroke; **~wind** m following wind, tailwind; **~wirbel** m ANAT dorsal vertebra
'Rück|erstattung f (-; -*en*) refund; **~fahrkarte** f round-trip ticket, *Br a.* return (ticket); **~fahrt** f return trip; **auf der ~** on the way back; **~fall** m relapse
'rückfällig *adj*: **~ werden** relapse
'Rückflug m return flight
'Rückgabe f (-; *no pl*) return
'Rückgang m drop, fall; ECON recession
'rückgängig *adj*: **~ machen** cancel
'Rück|gewinnung f (-; *no pl*) recovery; **~grat** n ANAT spine, backbone (*both a. fig*); **~halt** m (-[*e*]*s*; *no pl*) support; **~hand** f, **~handschlag** m tennis: backhand; **~kauf** m ECON repurchase
Rückkehr ['rʏkke:ɐ] f (-; *no pl*) return; **nach s-r ~ aus ...** on his return from ...
'Rück|kopplung f ELECTR feedback (*a. fig*); **~lage** f (-; -*n*) reserve(s); savings; **~lauf** m TECH rewind
'rückläufig *adj* falling, downward
'Rücklicht n (-[*e*]*s*; -*er*) MOT rear light, taillight
rücklings ['rʏklɪŋs] *adv* backward(s); from behind
'Rückporto n return postage

'Rückreise f → **Rückfahrt**
Rucksack ['rʊkzak] m rucksack, backpack; **~tou,rismus** m backpacking; **~tou,rist** m backpacker
'Rück|schlag m SPORT return; *fig* setback; **~schluss** m conclusion; **~schritt** m *fig* step back(ward); **~seite** f back; reverse; flip side; **~sendung** f return
'Rücksicht f (-; -*en*) consideration, regard; **aus** (**ohne**) **~ auf** (*acc*) out of (without any) consideration *or* regard for; **~ nehmen auf** (*acc*) show consideration for; **'rücksichtslos** *adj* inconsiderate (**gegen** of); thoughtless (of); ruthless; reckless; **'rücksichtsvoll** *adj* considerate (**gegen** of), thoughtful
'Rück|sitz m MOT back seat; **~spiegel** m MOT rear-view mirror; **~spiel** n SPORT return match; **~stand** m CHEM residue; **mit der Arbeit** (**e-m Tor**) **im ~ sein** be behind with one's work (down by one goal)
'rückständig *adj* backward; underdeveloped; **~e Miete** arrears of rent
'Rück|stau m MOT tailback; **~stelltaste** f backspace key; **~tritt** m resignation; withdrawal; TECH → **~trittbremse** f coaster (*Br* back-pedal) brake
rückwärts ['rʏkvɛrts] *adv* backward(s); **~ aus** (*dat*) **... fahren** back out of ...; **~ in** (*acc*) **... fahren** back into ...
'Rückwärtsgang m MOT reverse (gear)
'Rückweg m way back
'ruckweise *adv* jerkily, in jerks
'rückwirkend *adj* retroactive
'Rück|wirkung f reaction (**auf acc** upon); **~zahlung** f repayment; **~zieher** m (-*s*; -) soccer: overhead kick; F **e-n ~ machen** back (*or* chicken) out (**von** of); **~zug** m retreat
Rüde ['ry:də] m (-*n*; -*n*) ZO male (dog *ect*)
Rudel ['ru:dəl] n (-*s*; -) ZO pack; herd
Ruder ['ru:dɐ] n (-*s*; -) AVIAT, MAR rudder; SPORT oar; **am ~** at the helm (*a. fig*); **~boot** n rowing boat, rowboat
Ruderer ['ru:dərɐ] m (-*s*; -) rower, oarsman; **'Ruderin** f (-; -*nen*) rower, oarswoman; **'rudern** v/i and v/t (ge-, h) row
'Ruder|re,gatta f (rowing) regatta, boat race; **~sport** m rowing
Ruf [ru:f] m (-[*e*]*s*; -*e*) call (*a. fig*); cry; shout; *fig* reputation; **'rufen** v/i and v/t (*irr*, ge-, h) call (*a. doctor etc*); cry;

shout; **~ nach** call for (a. fig); **~ lassen** send for; **um Hilfe ~** call or cry for help

'Rufnummer f telephone number

'Rufweite f: **in (außer) ~** within (out of) call(ing distance)

Rüge ['ry:gə] f (-; -n) reproof, reproach (both: **wegen** for); **'rügen** v/t (ge-, h) reprove, reproach

Ruhe ['ru:ə] f (-; no pl) quiet, calm; silence; rest; peace; calm(ness); **zur ~ kommen** come to rest; **j-n in ~ lassen** leave s.o. in peace; **lass mich in ~!** leave me alone!; **et. in ~ tun** take one's time (doing s.th.); **die ~ behalten** F keep (one's) cool, play it cool; **sich zur ~ setzen** retire; **~, bitte!** (be) quiet, please!; **'ruhelos** adj restless

'ruhen v/i (ge-, h) rest (**auf** dat on)

'Ruhe|pause f break; **~stand** m (-[e]s; no pl) retirement; **~störer** m (-s; -) esp JUR disturber of the peace; **~tag** m a day's rest; **Montag ~** closed on Mondays

ruhig ['ru:ɪç] adj quiet; silent; calm; cool; TECH smooth; **~ bleiben** F keep (one's) cool, play it cool

Ruhm [ru:m] m (-[e]s; no pl) fame, esp POL, MIL etc glory; **rühmen** ['ry:mən] v/t (ge-, h) praise (**wegen** for); **sich e-r Sache ~** boast of s.th.; **rühmlich** ['ry:mlɪç] adj laudable, praiseworthy

'ruhmlos adj inglorious

'ruhmreich adj glorious

Ruhr [ru:ɐ] f (-; no pl) MED dysentery

Rühreier ['ry:ɐʔaiɐ] pl scrambled eggs

rühren ['ry:rən] v/t (ge-, h) stir; move (a. fig); fig touch, affect; **das hätte mich gar nicht** that leaves me cold; **rührt euch!** MIL (stand) at ease!; **~d** fig adj touching, moving; very kind

rührig ['ry:rɪç] adj active, busy

rührselig ['ry:ʁ-] adj sentimental

'Rührung f (-; no pl) emotion

Ruin [ru'i:n] m (-s; no pl) ruin

Ruine [ru'i:nə] f (-; -n) ruin

ruinieren [rui'ni:rən] v/t (no -ge-, h) ruin

rülpsen ['rʏlpsən] v/i (ge-, h), **Rülpser** ['rʏlpsɐ] m (-s; -) belch

Rumäne [ru'mɛ:nə] m (-n; -n) Romanian; **Rumänien** Romania; **Ru'mänin** f (-; -nen), **ru'mänisch** adj Romanian

Rummel ['rʊməl] F m (-s; no pl) (hustle and) bustle; F ballyhoo; **~platz** F m amusement park, fairground

rumoren [ru'mo:rən] v/i (no -ge-, h) rumble

Rumpelkammer ['rʊmpəl-] F f lumber room

rumpeln ['rʊmpəln] F v/i (ge-, h, sein) rumble

Rumpf [rʊmpf] m (-es; Rümpfe ['rʏmpfə]) ANAT trunk; MAR hull; AVIAT fuselage

rümpfen ['rʏmpfən] v/t (ge-, h) **die Nase ~** turn up one's nose (**über** acc at), sneer (at)

rund [rʊnt] **1.** adj round (a. fig); **2.** adv about; **~ um** a(round); **'Rundblick** m panorama; **Runde** ['rʊndə] f (-; -n) round (a. fig and SPORT); racing: lap; **s-e ~ machen in** (dat) patrol; **die ~ machen** go the round(s)

'Rundfahrt f tour (**durch** round)

'Rundfunk m (-s; no pl) radio; broadcasting corporation; **im ~** on the radio; **im ~ übertragen** or **senden** broadcast; **~hörer(in)** listener, pl a. (radio) audience; **~sender** m broadcasting or radio station

'Rundgang m tour (**durch** of)

'rundhe'raus adv frankly, plainly

'rundhe'rum adv all around

'rundlich adj plump, chubby

'Rund|reise f tour (**durch** of); **~schau** f review; **~schreiben** n circular (letter); **~spruch** Swiss m → **Rundfunk**

'Rundung f (-; -en) curve

'rundweg ['-vɛk] adv flatly, plainly

runter ['rʊntɐ] F adv → **herunter**

Runzel ['rʊntsəl] f (-; -n) wrinkle

runz(e)lig ['rʊnts(ə)lɪç] adj wrinkled

'runzeln v/t (ge-, h) **die Stirn ~** frown (**über** acc at)

Rüpel ['ry:pəl] m (-s; -) lout

rupfen ['rʊpfən] v/t (ge-, h) pluck

Rüsche ['ry:ʃə] f (-; -n) frill, ruffle

Ruß [ru:s] m (-es; no pl) soot

Russe ['rʊsə] m (-n; -n) Russian

Rüssel ['rʏsəl] m (-s; -) ZO trunk; snout

rußen ['ru:sən] v/i (ge-, h) smoke

rußig ['ru:sɪç] adj sooty

Russin ['rʊsɪn] f (-; -nen), **russisch** ['rʊsɪʃ] adj Russian

'Russland Russia

rüsten ['rʏstən] (ge-, h) **1.** v/i MIL arm; **2.** v/refl get ready, prepare (**zu, für** for); arm o.s. (**gegen** for)

rüstig ['rʏstɪç] adj vigorous, sprightly

R

rustikal [rʊstiˈkaːl] adj rustic
'Rüstung f (-; -en) MIL armament;
armo(u)r
'Rüstungs|indus,trie f armament in-
dustry; **~wettlauf** m arms race
'Rüstzeug n equipment
Rute ['ruːtə] f (-; -n) rod (a. fig), switch

Rutschbahn ['rʊtʃ-] f, **Rutsche** ['rʊtʃə] f
(-; -n) slide, chute; 'rutschen v/i (ge-,
sein) slide, slip; glide; MOT etc skid; **rutschig** ['rʊtʃɪç] adj slippery
'rutschsicher adj MOT etc non-skid
rütteln ['rʏtəln] (ge-, h) **1.** v/t shake; **2.** v/i
jolt; *an der Tür ~* rattle at the door

S

S ABBR of **Süd(en)** S, south
S. ABBR of **Seite** p., page
s. ABBR of **siehe** see
Saal [zaːl] m (-[e]s; Säle ['zɛːlə]) hall
Saat [zaːt] f (-; -en) a) (no pl) sowing, b)
seed(s) (a. fig); crop(s)
Sabbat ['zabat] m (-s; -e) sabbath (day)
sabbern ['zabɐn] F v/i (ge-, h) slobber,
slaver
Säbel ['zɛːbəl] m (-s; -) saber, Br sabre
(a. SPORT), sword; 'säbeln F v/t (ge-, h)
cut, hack
Sabotage [zaboˈtaːʒə] f (-; -n) sabotage;
Saboteur [zaboˈtøːɐ] m (-s; -e) saboteur; **sabotieren** [zaboˈtiːrən] v/t (no
-ge-) sabotage
Sach|bearbeiter ['zax-] m, **~bearbeite-
rin** f official in charge; **~beschädi-
gung** f damage to property; **~buch** n
specialized book, pl coll nonfiction
'sachdienlich adj: **~e Hinweise** relevant information
Sache ['zaxə] f (-; -n) thing; matter; business; issue, problem, question; cause;
JUR matter, case; pl things, clothes;
zur ~ kommen (bei der ~ bleiben)
come (keep) to the point; *nicht zur
~ gehören* be irrelevant
'sachgerecht adj proper
'Sachkenntnis f expert knowledge
'sachkundig adj expert
'sachlich adj matter-of-fact, businesslike; unbias(s)ed, objective; practical,
technical; *~ richtig* factually correct
sächlich ['zɛçlɪç] adj LING neuter
'Sachre,gister n (subject) index
'Sachschaden m damage to property
sacht [zaxt] adj soft, gentle; slow
'Sach|verhalt m (-[e]s; -e) facts (of the
case); **~verstand** m know-how; **~ver-**

ständige m, f (-n; -n) expert; JUR expert witness; **~wert** m (-[e]s; no pl) real
value; **~zwänge** pl inherent necessities
Sack [zak] m (-[e]s; Säcke ['zɛkə]) sack,
bag; V balls; **sacken** ['zakən] F v/i (ge-,
sein) sink; **'Sackgasse** f blind alley (a.
fig), dead end (a. fig), fig impasse
Sadismus [zaˈdɪsmʊs] m (-; no pl) sa-
dism; **Sadist** [zaˈdɪst] m (-en; -en) sadist; **sa'distisch** adj sadistic
säen ['zɛːən] v/t and v/i (ge-, h) sow (a.
fig)
Safari [zaˈfaːri] f (-; -s) safari; **~park** m
wildlife reserve, safari park
Saft [zaft] m (-[e]s; Säfte ['zɛftə]) juice;
BOT sap (both a. fig); **saftig** ['zaftɪç]
adj juicy (a. fig); lush; F fancy (prices
etc)
Sage ['zaːgə] f (-; -n) legend, myth
Säge ['zɛːgə] f (-; -n) saw
'Sägemehl n sawdust
sagen ['zaːgən] v/i and v/t (ge-, h) say;
j-m et. ~ tell s.o. s.th.; *die Wahrheit
~* tell the truth; *er lässt dir ~* he asked
me to tell you; *~ wir ...* (let's) say ...;
man sagt, er sei reich he is said to be
rich; *er lässt sich nichts ~* he will not
listen to reason; *das hat nichts zu ~* it
doesn't matter; *et. (nichts) zu ~ haben
(bei)* have a say (no say) (in); *~ wollen
mit* mean by; *das sagt mir nichts* it
doesn't mean anything to me; *unter
uns gesagt* between you and me
sägen ['zɛːgən] v/t and v/i (ge-, h) saw
'sagenhaft adj legendary; F fabulous,
incredible, fantastic
'Sägespäne pl sawdust
'Sägewerk n sawmill
sah [zaː] pret of **sehen**
Sahne ['zaːnə] f (-; no pl) cream

239

Satire

Saison [zɛˈzõː] f (-; -s) season; *in der ~* in season

sai'sonbedingt adj seasonal

Saite [ˈzaitə] f (-; -n) MUS string, chord (a. fig); **'Saiteninstru,ment** n MUS string(ed) instrument

Sakko [ˈzako] m, n (-s; -s) (sports) jacket, sport(s) coat

Sakristei [zakrɪsˈtai] f (-; -en) REL vestry, sacristy

Salat [zaˈlaːt] m (-[e]s; -e) BOT lettuce; GASTR salad; **~sauce** f salad dressing

Salbe [ˈzalbə] f (-; -n) ointment

'Salbung f (-; -en) unction

'salbungsvoll adj unctuous

Saldo [ˈzaldo] m (-s; -s, -di) ECON balance

Salon [zaˈlõː] m (-s; -s) salon; MAR saloon; drawing room

salopp [zaˈlɔp] adj casual; contp sloppy

Salpeter [zalˈpeːtɐ] m (-s; no pl) CHEM saltpeter (Br -petre), niter, Br nitre

Salto [ˈzalto] m (-s; -s, -ti) somersault

Salut [zaˈluːt] m (-[e]s; -e) MIL salute; ~ *schießen* fire a salute

salutieren [zaluˈtiːrən] v/i (no -ge-, h) MIL (give a) salute

Salve [ˈzalvə] f (-; -n) MIL volley (a. fig) salute

Salz [zalts] n (-es; -e) salt

'Salzbergwerk n salt mine

salzen [ˈzaltsən] v/t ([irr.] ge-, h) salt

salzfrei [ˈzaltsfrai] adj salt-free, no-salt diet

salzig [ˈzaltsɪç] adj salty

'Salz|kar,toffeln pl boiled potatoes; **~säure** f (-; no pl) CHEM hydrochloric acid; **~stange** f pretzel (Br salt) stick; **~streuer** m (-s; -) salt shaker, Br salt cellar; **~wasser** n salt water

Same [ˈzaːmə] m (-n; -n), **'Samen** m (-s -) BOT seed (a. fig); BIOL sperm, semen

'Samen|bank f (-; -en) MED, VET sperm bank; **~erguss** m ejaculation; **~korn** n BOT seedcorn

Sammel... [ˈzaməl-] in cpds ...begriff, ...bestellung, ...konto etc: collective ...; **~büchse** f collecting box

'sammeln v/t (ge-, h) collect; gather, pick; accumulate; *sich ~* assemble; fig compose o.s.

Sammler [ˈzamlɐ] m (-s; -), **'Sammlerin** f (-; -nen) collector

'Sammlung f (-; -en) collection

Samstag [ˈzamstaːk] m (-[e]s; -e) Saturday

samt [zamt] prp (dat) together or along with

Samt m (-[e]s; -e) velvet

sämtlich [ˈzɛmtlɪç] adj: **~e** pl all the; the complete works etc

Sanatorium [zanaˈtoːrjʊm] n (-s; -ien) sanatorium, sanitarium

Sand [zant] m (-[e]s; -e) sand

Sandale [zanˈdaːlə] f (-; -n) sandal

Sandalette [zandaˈlɛtə] f (-; -n) high--heeled sandal

'Sand|bahn f SPORT dirt track; **~bank** f (-; -bänke) sandbank; **~boden** m sandy soil; **~burg** f sandcastle

sandig [ˈzandɪç] adj sandy

'Sand|mann m, **~männchen** n sandman; **~pa,pier** n sandpaper; **~sack** m sand bag; **~stein** m sandstone; **~strand** m sandy beach

sandte [ˈzantə] pret of **senden**

'Sanduhr f hourglass

sanft [zanft] adj gentle, soft; mild; easy (death)

'sanftmütig [-myːtɪç] adj gentle, mild

sang [zaŋ] pret of **singen**

Sänger [ˈzɛŋɐ] m (-s; -), **Sängerin** [ˈzɛŋərɪn] f (-; -nen) singer

sanieren [zaˈniːrən] v/t (no -ge-, h) redevelop (a. ECON), rehabilitate (a. ARCH)

Sa'nierung f (-; -en) redevelopment, rehabilitation; **Sa'nierungsgebiet** n redevelopment area

sanität [zaniˈtɛːɐ] adj sanitary

Sanitäter [zaniˈtɛːtɐ] m (-s; -) paramedic; MIL medic, Br medical orderly

sank [zaŋk] pret of **sinken**

Sankt [zaŋkt] Saint, ABBR St

Sardelle [zarˈdɛlə] f (-; -n) ZO anchovy

Sardine [zarˈdiːnə] f (-; -n) ZO sardine

Sarg [zark] m (-[e]s; Särge [ˈzɛrɡə]) casket, esp Br coffin

Sarkasmus [zarˈkasmʊs] m (-; no pl) sarcasm; **sar'kastisch** adj sarcastic

saß [zaːs] pret of **sitzen**

Satan [ˈzaːtan] m (-s; -e) Satan; fig devil

Satellit [zatɛˈliːt] m (-en; -en) satellite (a. fig); **über ~** by or via satellite

Satel'liten... in cpds ...bild, ...staat, ...stadt, ...-TV: satellite ...

Satin [zaˈtɛ̃ː] m (-s; -s) satin; sateen

Satire [zaˈtiːrə] f (-; -n) satire (**auf** acc

upon); **Satiriker** [za'ti:rikə] *m* (-s; -) satirist; **sa'tirisch** *adj* satiric(al)

satt [zat] *adj* F full (up); **ich bin ~** I've had enough, F I'm full (up); **sich ~ es-sen** eat one's fill (**an** *dat* of); F **~ haben** be tired *or* F sick of, be fed up with

Sattel ['zatəl] *m* (-s; *Sättel* ['zɛtəl]) saddle; **'satteln** *v/t* (*ge-*, *h*) saddle; **'Sat-telschlepper** *m* MOT semi-trailer truck, *Br* articulated lorry

sättigen ['zɛtɪgən] (*ge-*, *h*) **1.** *v/t* satisfy; feed; CHEM, PHYS saturate; **2.** *v/i* be substantial, be filling; **'Sättigung** *f* (-; *-en*) satiety; CHEM, ECON saturation (*a. fig*)

Sattler ['zatlɐ] *m* (-s; -) saddler

Sattlerei [zatlə'rai] *f* (-; *-en*) saddlery

Satz [zats] *m* (-es; *Sätze* ['zɛtsə]) leap; LING sentence; *tennis etc*: set; MUS movement; MUS rate; **~aussage** *f* LING predicate; **~bau** *m* (-[e]s; *no pl*) LING syntax; construction; **~gegenstand** *m* LING subject

Satzung ['zatsʊŋ] *f* (-; *-en*) statute

'Satzzeichen *n* LING punctuation mark

Sau [zau] *f* (-; *Säue* ['zɔyə]) ZO sow; HUNT wild sow; F swine, pig

sauber ['zaubɐ] *adj* clean (*a. fig*); pure; neat (*a. fig*), tidy; decent; *iro* fine, nice; **~ halten** keep clean (**sich** o.s.); **~ ma-chen** clean (up); **'Sauberkeit** *f* (-; *no pl*) clean(li)ness; tidiness, neatness; purity; decency; **säubern** ['zɔybɐn] *v/t* (*ge-*, *h*) clean (up); cleanse (*a.* MED); **~ von** clear (POL *a.* purge) of

'Säuberung(sakti,on) *f* POL purge

sauer ['zauɐ] *adj* sour (*a. fig*), acid (*a.* CHEM); GASTR pickled; F mad (**auf** *acc* at), cross (with); **~ werden** turn sour; F get mad; **saurer Regen** acid rain

säuerlich ['zɔyɐlɪç] *adj* sharp; F wry

'Sauerstoff *m* (-[e]s; *no pl*) CHEM oxygen; **~gerät** *n* MED oxygen apparatus; **~zelt** *n* MED oxygen tent

'Sauerteig *m* leaven

saufen ['zaufən] *v/t and v/i* (*irr*, *ge-*, *h*) ZO drink; F booze; **Säufer(in)** ['zɔyfɐ (-fərɪn)] F (-s; -/-; *-nen*) drunkard, F boozer

saugen ['zaugən] *v/i and v/t* ([*irr*] *ge-*, *h*) suck (**an et.** [at] s.th.)

säugen ['zɔygən] *v/t* (*ge-*, *h*) suckle (*a.* ZO), nurse, breastfeed

'Säugetier *n* mammal

saugfähig ['zauk-] *adj* absorbent

Säugling ['zɔyklɪŋ] *m* (-s; *-e*) baby, infant

'Säuglings|heim *n* (baby) nursery; **~pflege** *f* infant care; **~schwester** *f* baby nurse; **~stati,on** *f* neonatal care unit; **~sterblichkeit** *f* infant mortality

Säule ['zɔylə] *f* (-; *-n*) column; pillar (*a. fig*); **'Säulengang** *m* colonnade

Saum [zaum] *m* (-[e]s; *Säume* ['zɔymə]) hem(line); seam; **säumen** ['zɔymən] *v/t* (*ge-*, *h*) hem; border, edge; line

Sauna ['zauna] *f* (-; -s, *Saunen*) sauna

Säure ['zɔyrə] *f* (-; *-n*) CHEM acid

'säurehaltig [-haltɪç] *adj* acid

sausen ['zauzən] *v/i a*) (*ge-*, *sein*) F rush, dash, b) (*ge-*, *h*) ears: buzz; *wind*: howl

'Saustall *m* pigsty (*a.* F contp)

Saxophon [zakso'fo:n] *n* (-s; *-e*) MUS saxophone, F sax

S-Bahn ['ɛsba:n] *f* rapid transit, *Br* suburban train

Schabe ['ʃa:bə] *f* (-; *-n*) ZO cockroach

'schaben *v/t* (*ge-*, *h*) scrape (**von** from)

schäbig ['ʃɛ:bɪç] *adj* shabby, *fig a.* mean

Schablone [ʃa'blo:nə] *f* (-; *-n*) stencil; *fig* stereotype

Schach [ʃax] *n* (-s; *no pl*) chess; **~!** check!; **~ und matt!** checkmate!; **j-n in ~ halten** keep s.o. in check; **~brett** *n* chessboard; **~feld** *n* square; **~fi,gur** *f* chessman, piece

schach'matt *adj*: **j-n ~ setzen** checkmate s.o.

'Schachspiel *n* (game of) chess; chess-board and men

Schacht [ʃaxt] *m* (-[e]s; *Schächte* ['ʃɛçtə]) shaft, *mining*: *a.* pit

Schachtel ['ʃaxtəl] *f* (-; *-n*) box; carton; **e-e ~ Zigaretten** a pack (*esp Br* packet) of cigarettes

'Schachzug *m* move (*a. fig*)

schade ['ʃa:də] *pred adj*: **es ist ~** it's a pity; **wie ~!** what a pity *or* shame!; **zu ~ sein für** be too good for

Schädel ['ʃɛ:dəl] *m* (-s; -) ANAT skull; **~bruch** *m* MED fracture of the skull

schaden ['ʃa:dən] *v/i* (*ge-*, *h*) damage, do damage to, harm, hurt; **der Gesund-heit ~** be bad for one's health; **das schadet nichts** it doesn't matter; **es könnte ihm nicht ~** it wouldn't hurt him

'**Schaden** *m* (*-s; Schäden* ['ʃɛːdən]) damage (*an dat* to); *esp* TECH trouble, defect (*a.* MED); *fig* disadvantage, ECON loss; ***j-m ~ zufügen*** do s.o. harm; **~ersatz** *m* damages; **~ leisten** pay damages; **~freude** *f:* **~ empfinden über** (*acc*) gloat over

'**schadenfroh** *adv* gloatingly

schadhaft ['ʃaːthaft] *adj* damaged; defective, faulty; leaking (*pipes*)

schädigen ['ʃɛːdɪɡən] *v/t* (*ge-, h*) damage, harm

schädlich ['ʃɛːtlɪç] *adj* harmful, injurious; bad (for your health)

Schädling ['ʃɛːtlɪŋ] *m* (*-s; -e*) BIOL pest

'**Schädlings|bekämpfung** *f* pest control; **~bekämpfungsmittel** *n* pesticide

'**Schadstoff** ['ʃaːt-] *m* harmful substance; pollutant

'**schadstoffarm** *adj* MOT low-emission

Schaf [ʃaːf] *n* (*-[e]s; -e*) ZO sheep

'**Schafbock** *m* ZO ram

Schäfer ['ʃɛːfɐ] *m* (*-s; -*) shepherd; **~hund** *m* sheepdog; ***Deutscher ~*** German shepherd, *esp Br* Alsatian

'**Schaffell** *n* sheepskin; ZO fleece

schaffen[1] ['ʃafən] *v/t* (*irr, ge-, h*) create

'**schaffen**[2] (*ge-, h*) **1.** *v/t* cause, bring about; manage, get s.th. done; take; ***es ~*** make it, *a.* succeed; **2.** *v/i* work; ***j-m zu ~ machen*** cause s.o. trouble; ***sich zu ~ machen an*** (*dat*) tamper with

Schaffner ['ʃafnɐ] *m* (*-s;-*), '**Schaffnerin** *f* (*-; -nen*) conductor; *Br* RAIL guard

Schafott [ʃaˈfɔt] *n* (*-[e]s; -e*) scaffold

Schaft [ʃaft] *m* (*-[e]s; Schäfte* ['ʃɛftə]) shaft; stock; shank; leg

'**Schafwolle** *f* sheep's wool

'**Schafzucht** *f* sheep breeding

schäkern ['ʃɛːkən] *v/i* (*ge-, h*) joke; flirt

schal [ʃaːl] *adj* stale, flat, *fig a.* empty

Schal *m* (*-s; -s*) scarf

Schale ['ʃaːlə] *f* (*-; -n*) bowl, dish; GASTR shell; peel, skin; **schälen** ['ʃɛːlən] *v/t* (*ge-, h*) peel, pare; ***sich ~ skin:*** peel (off)

Schall [ʃal] *m* (*-[e]s; -e*) sound; **~dämpfer** *m* silencer (*a. Br* MOT), MOT muffler

'**schalldicht** *adj* soundproof

schallen ['ʃalən] *v/i* (*[irr,] ge-, h*) sound; ring (out); **~des Gelächter** roars of laughter

'**Schall|geschwindigkeit** *f* speed of

sound; **~mauer** *f* sound barrier; **~platte** *f* record, disk, *Br* disc; **~welle** *f* PHYS sound wave

schalten ['ʃaltən] *v/i* and *v/t* (*ge-, h*) switch, turn; MOT shift (*esp Br* change) gear; F get it; react; **Schalter** ['ʃaltɐ] *m* (*-s; -*) counter; RAIL ticket window; AVIAT desk; ELECTR switch

'**Schalt|hebel** *m* MOT gear lever; TECH, AVIAT control lever; ELECTR switch lever; **~jahr** *n* leap year; **~tafel** *f* ELECTR switchboard, control panel; **~uhr** *f* time switch

'**Schaltung** *f* (*-; -en*) MOT gearshift; ELECTR circuit

Scham [ʃaːm] *f* (*-; no pl*) shame; ***vor ~*** with shame; **schämen** ['ʃɛːmən] *v/refl* (*ge-, h*) be *or* feel ashamed (*gen, wegen* of); ***du solltest dich (was) ~!*** you ought to be ashamed of yourself!

'**Scham|gefühl** *n* (*-[e]s; no pl*) sense of shame; **~haare** *f* pubic hair

'**schamhaft** *adj* bashful

'**schamlos** *adj* shameless; indecent

Schande ['ʃandə] *f* (*-; no pl*) shame, disgrace; **schänden** ['ʃɛndən] *v/t* (*ge-, h*) disgrace; desecrate; rape

'**Schandfleck** ['ʃant-] *m* eyesore

'**schändlich** ['ʃɛntlɪç] *adj* disgraceful

'**Schandtat** *f* atrocity

Schanze ['ʃantsə] *f* (*-; -n*) SPORT ski jump

Schar [ʃaːɐ] *f* (*-; -en* ['ʃaːrən]) troop, band; F horde; crowd; ZO flock

'**scharen** *v/refl* (*ge-, h*) ***sich ~ um*** gather round

scharf [ʃarf] *adj* sharp (*a. fig*), PHOT *a.* in focus; clear; savage, fierce (*dog*); live (*ammunition*), armed (*bomb etc*); GASTR hot; F hot, sexy; F **~ sein auf** (*acc*) be keen on; **~ (ein)stellen** PHOT focus; F **~e Sachen** hard liquor

Schärfe ['ʃɛrfə] *f* (*-; -n*) sharpness (*a.* PHOT), *fig* severity, fierceness

'**schärfen** *v/t* (*ge-, h*) sharpen

'**Scharf|richter** *m* executioner; **~schütze** *m* sharpshooter; sniper

'**scharfsichtig** *adj* sharp-sighted; *fig* clear-sighted

'**Scharfsinn** *m* (*-[e]s; no pl*) acumen

'**scharfsinnig** *adj* sharp-witted, shrewd

Scharlach ['ʃarlax] *m* (*-s; no pl*) scarlet; MED scarlet fever

'**scharlachrot** *adj* scarlet

S

Scharlatan [ʃarˈlaːtan] *m* (-s; -e) charlatan, fraud

Scharnier [ʃarˈniːɐ] *n* (-s; -e) TECH hinge

Schärpe [ˈʃɛrpə] *f* (-; -n) sash

scharren [ˈʃarən] *v/i* (ge-, h) scrape, scratch

schartig [ˈʃartɪç] *adj* jagged, notchy

Schaschlik [ˈʃaʃlɪk] *m, n* (-s; -s) GASTR shish kebab

Schatten [ˈʃatən] *m* (-s; -) shadow (*a. fig*); shade; **im ~** in the shade

'**schattenhaft** *adj* shadowy

Schattierung [ʃaˈtiːrʊŋ] *f* (-; -en) shade; *fig* colo(u)r

schattig [ˈʃatɪç] *adj* shady

Schatz [ʃats] *m* (-es; *Schätze* [ˈʃɛtsə]) treasure; *fig* darling; **~amt** *n* POL Treasury Department, *Br* Treasury

schätzen [ˈʃɛtsən] *v/t* (ge-, h) estimate, value (**auf** *acc* at); appreciate; think highly of; F reckon, guess

'**Schatz|kammer** *f* treasury (*a. fig*); **~kanzler** *m* Chancellor of the Exchequer; **~meister(in)** treasurer

'**Schätzung** *f* (-; -en) estimate; valuation

Schau [ʃau] *f* (-; -en) show, exhibition; **zur ~ stellen** show, display

Schauder [ˈʃaudɐ] *m* (-s; -) shudder

'**schauderhaft** *adj* horrible, dreadful

'**schaudern** *v/i* (ge-, h) shudder, shiver (*both:* **vor** *dat* with)

schauen [ˈʃauən] *v/i* (ge-, h) look (**auf** *acc* at)

Schauer [ˈʃauɐ] *m* (-s; -) METEOR shower; shudder, shiver; **~geschichte** *f* horror story (*a. fig*)

'**schauerlich** *adj* dreadful, horrible

Schaufel [ˈʃaufəl] *f* (-; -n) shovel; dustpan; '**schaufeln** *v/t* (ge-, h) shovel; dig

'**Schaufenster** *n* shop window; **~auslage** *f* window display; **~bummel** *m*: **e-n ~ machen** go window-shopping; **~dekoration** *f* window dressing

Schaukel [ˈʃaukəl] *f* (-; -n) swing

'**schaukeln** (ge-, h) **1.** *v/i* swing; *boat etc*: rock; **2.** *v/t* rock

'**Schaukel|pferd** *n* rocking horse; **~stuhl** *m* rocking chair, rocker

'**Schaulustige** [-lʊstɪɡə] *pl* (curious) onlookers, F rubbernecks

Schaum [ʃaum] *m* (-[e]s; *Schäume* [ˈʃɔymə]) foam; froth; lather; spray; **schäumen** [ˈʃɔymən] *v/i* (ge-, h) foam (*a. fig*); froth; lather; spray

'**Schaumgummi** *m* foam rubber

schaumig [ˈʃaumɪç] *adj* foamy, frothy

'**Schaumlöscher** *m* foam extinguisher

'**Schauplatz** *m* scene

'**Schaupro,zess** *m* JUR show trial

schaurig [ˈʃaurɪç] *adj* creepy; horrible

'**Schauspiel** *n* THEA play; *fig* spectacle

'**Schauspieler(in)** actor (actress)

'**Schauspielschule** *f* drama school

'**Schausteller** [-ʃtɛlə] *m* (-s; -) showman

Scheck [ʃɛk] *m* (-s; -s) ECON check, *Br* cheque; **~heft** *n* checkbook, *Br* chequebook

scheckig [ˈʃɛkɪç] *adj* spotty

'**Scheckkarte** *f* check cashing (*Br* cheque) card

scheffeln [ˈʃɛfəln] F *v/t* (ge-, h) rake in

Scheibe [ˈʃaibə] *f* (-; -n) disk, *Br* disc; slice; pane; target

'**Scheiben|bremse** *f* MOT disk (*Br* disc) brake; **~wischer** *n* MOT windshield (*Br* windscreen) wiper

Scheide [ˈʃaidə] *f* (-; -n) sheath; scabbard; ANAT vagina; '**scheiden** [*irr, ge-*) **1.** *v/t* (h) separate, part (*both:* **von** from); divorce; **sich ~ lassen** get a divorce, **von j-m:** divorce s.o.; **2.** *v/i* (*sein*) part; **~ aus** (*dat*) retire from

'**Scheideweg** *m* crossroads

'**Scheidung** *f* (-; -en) divorce

'**Scheidungsklage** *f* JUR divorce suit

Schein[1] [ʃain] *m* (-[e]s; -e) certificate; blank, *Br* form; bill, *Br* note

Schein[2] *m* (-[e]s; *no pl*) light; *fig* appearance; **et. (nur) zum ~ tun** (only) pretend to do s.th.

'**scheinbar** *adj* seeming, apparent

scheinen [ˈʃainən] *v/i* (*irr*, ge-, h) shine; *fig* seem, appear, look

'**scheinheilig** *adj* hypocritical

'**Scheinwerfer** *m* searchlight; MOT headlight; THEA spotlight

Scheiß... [ˈʃais-] V *in cpds* damn ..., fucking ..., *esp Br* bloody ...

Scheiße [ˈʃaisə] V *f* (-; *no pl*), '**scheißen** V *v/i* (*irr*, ge-, h) shit, crap

Scheit [ʃait] *n* (-[e]s; -e) piece of wood

Scheitel [ˈʃaitəl] *m* (-s; -) parting

'**scheiteln** *v/t* (ge-, h) part

Scheiterhaufen [ˈʃaitə-] *m* pyre; HIST stake

scheitern [ˈʃaitən] *v/i* (ge-, *sein*) fail, go wrong

Schelle ['ʃɛlə] f (-; -n) (little) bell; TECH clamp, clip

Schellfisch ['ʃɛl-] m ZO haddock

Schelm [ʃɛlm] m (-[e]s; -e) rascal

schelmisch ['ʃɛlmɪʃ] adj impish

Schema ['ʃeːma] n (-s; -s, -ta) pattern, system; **schematisch** [ʃeˈmaːtɪʃ] adj schematic; mechanical

Schemel ['ʃeːməl] m (-s; -) stool

schemenhaft ['ʃeːmən-] adj shadowy

Schenkel ['ʃɛŋkəl] m (-s; -) ANAT thigh; shank; MATH leg

schenken ['ʃɛŋkən] v/t (ge-, h) give (as a present) (**zu** to)

'**Schenkung** f (-; -en) JUR donation

Scherbe ['ʃɛrbə] f (-; -n), '**Scherben** m (-s; -) (broken) piece, fragment

Schere ['ʃeːrə] f (-; -n) scissors; ZO claw

scheren[1] ['ʃeːrən] v/t (irr, ge-, h) ZO shear; BOT clip; cut

'**scheren**[2] v/refl (ge-, h) **sich ~ um** bother about

Scherereien [ʃeːrəˈraiən] pl trouble, bother

Schermaus ['ʃeːr-] Austrian f ZO mole

Scherz [ʃɛrts] m (-es; -e) joke; **im** (**zum**) **~** for fun; **scherzen** ['ʃɛrtsən] v/i (ge-, h) joke (**über** acc at); '**scherzhaft** adj joking; **~ gemeint** meant as a joke

scheu [ʃɔy] adj shy (a. ZO); bashful; **~ machen** frighten; **Scheu** f (-; no pl) shyness; awe; **scheuen** ['ʃɔyən] (ge-, h) **1.** v/i shy (**vor** dat at), take fright (at); **2.** v/t shun, avoid; fear; **sich ~, et. zu tun** be afraid of doing s.th.

scheuern ['ʃɔyərn] v/t and v/i (ge-, h) scrub, scour; chafe

'**Scheuertuch** n floor cloth

'**Scheuklappen** pl blinders, Br blinkers (both a. fig)

Scheune ['ʃɔynə] f (-; -n) barn

Scheusal ['ʃɔyzaːl] n (-s; -e) monster (a. fig)

scheußlich ['ʃɔyslɪç] adj horrible (a. F), atrocious

Schicht [ʃɪçt] f (-; -en) layer; coat; film; ECON shift; class; **schichten** ['ʃɪçtən] v/t (ge-, h) arrange in layers, pile up

'**schichtweise** adv in layers

schick [ʃɪk] adj smart, chic, stylish

schicken ['ʃɪkən] v/t (ge-, h) send (**nach**, **zu** to); **das schickt sich nicht** that isn't done

Schickeria [ʃɪkəˈriːa] F f (-; no pl) smart

set, beautiful people, trendies

Schickimicki [ʃɪkiˈmɪki] F contp m (-s; -s) trendy

Schicksal ['ʃɪkzaːl] n (-s; -e) fate, destiny; lot

Schiebe|dach ['ʃiːbə-] n MOT sliding roof, sunroof; **~fenster** n sliding window; sash window

schieben ['ʃiːbən] v/t (irr, ge-, h) push

Schieber ['ʃiːbɐ] m (-s; -) TECH slide; bolt; F profiteer

'**Schiebetür** f sliding door

'**Schiebung** F f (-; -en) swindle, fix (a. SPORT)

schied [ʃiːt] pret of **scheiden**

Schiedsrichter ['ʃiːts-] m, '**Schiedsrichterin** f soccer: referee; tennis: umpire; judge, esp pl a. jury

schief [ʃiːf] adj crooked, not straight; sloping, oblique (a. MATH); leaning; fig false; F **~ gehen** go wrong

Schiefer ['ʃiːfɐ] m (-s; -) GEOL slate

'**Schiefertafel** f slate

schielen ['ʃiːlən] v/i (ge-, h) squint, be cross-eyed

schien [ʃiːn] pret of **scheinen**

Schienbein ['ʃiːn-] n ANAT shin(bone)

Schiene ['ʃiːnə] f (-; -n) TECH etc rail; MED splint

'**schienen** v/t (ge-, h) MED splint

Schießbude ['ʃiːs-] f shooting gallery

schießen ['ʃiːsən] v/i and v/t (irr, ge-, h) shoot, fire (both: **auf** acc at); SPORT score; **Schießerei** [ʃiːsəˈrai] f (-; -en) shooting; gunfight

'**Schießpulver** n gunpowder; **~scharte** f MIL loophole, embrasure; **~scheibe** f target; **~stand** m shooting range

Schiff [ʃɪf] n (-[e]s; -e) MAR ship, boat; ARCH nave; **mit dem ~** by boat

Schiffahrt f → **Schiffahrt**

'**schiffbar** adj navigable

'**Schiffbau** m (-[e]s; no pl) shipbuilding

'**Schiffbruch** m shipwreck (a. fig); **~ erleiden** be shipwrecked

Schiffer ['ʃɪfɐ] m (-s; -) sailor; skipper

Schiffahrt f (-; no pl) shipping, navigation

'**Schiffs|junge** m ship's boy; **~ladung** f shipload; cargo; **~schraube** f (ship's) propeller; **~werft** f shipyard

Schikane [ʃiˈkaːnə] f (-; -n) a. pl harassment; **aus reiner ~** out of sheer spite; F **mit allen ~n** with all the trimmings

S

schikanieren [ʃika'ni:rən] *v/t* (*no -ge-, h*) harass; bully

Schild[1] [ʃilt] *n* (*-[e]s; -er* [ʃildə]) sign, plate

Schild[2] *m* (*-[e]s; -e*) shield

'Schilddrüse *f* ANAT thyroid (gland)

schildern ['ʃildɐn] *v/t* (*ge-, h*) describe; depict, portray

Schilderung ['ʃildərʊŋ] *f* (*-; -en*) description, portrayal; account

'Schildkröte *f* ZO tortoise; turtle

Schilf [ʃilf] *n* (*-[e]s; no pl*) BOT reed(s)

schillern ['ʃilɐn] *v/i* (*ge-, h*) be iridescent; **~d** *adj* iridescent; *fig* dubious

Schimmel ['ʃiml] *m* ZO white horse; BOT mo(u)ld; **schimm(e)lig** ['ʃim(ə)lɪç] *adj* mo(u)ldy, musty; **~schimmeln** *v/i* (*ge-, h, sein*) go mo(u)ldy

Schimmer ['ʃimɐ] *m* (*-s; -*) glimmer (*a. fig*), gleam, *fig a.* touch

'schimmern *v/i* (*ge-, h*) shimmer, glimmer, gleam

Schimpanse [ʃim'panzə] *m* (*-n; -n*) ZO chimpanzee

schimpfen ['ʃimpfən] *v/i and v/t* (*ge-, h*) scold (*mit j-m* s.o.); F tell *s.o.* off, bawl *s.o.* out; **~ über** (*acc*) complain about

'Schimpfwort *n* swearword

Schindel ['ʃindl] *f* (*-; -n*) shingle

schinden ['ʃindən] *v/t* (*irr, ge-, h*) maltreat; slave-drive; **sich ~** drudge, slave away; **Schinder** ['ʃindɐ] *m* (*-s; -*) slave driver; **Schinderei** [ʃində'rai] *f* (*-; -en*) slavery, drudgery

Schinken ['ʃiŋkən] *m* (*-s; -*) ham

Schippe ['ʃipə] *f* (*-; -n*), **'schippen** *v/t* (*ge-, h*) shovel

Schirm [ʃirm] *m* (*-[e]s; -e*) umbrella; sunshade; TV, EDP *etc*: screen; shade; peak, visor; **~herr(in)** patron, sponsor; **~herrschaft** *f* patronage, sponsorship; **unter der ~ von** under the auspices of; **~mütze** *f* peaked cap; **~ständer** *m* umbrella stand

schiss [ʃis] *pret of* **scheißen**

Schlacht [ʃlaxt] *f* (*-; -en*) battle (**bei** of)

'schlachten *v/t* (*ge-, h*) slaughter, kill, butcher

Schlachter ['ʃlaxtɐ] *m* (*-s; -*) butcher

'Schlacht|feld *n* MIL battlefield, battleground; **~haus** *n*, **~hof** *m* slaughterhouse; **~plan** *m* MIL plan of action (*a. fig*); **~schiff** *n* MIL battleship

Schlacke ['ʃlakə] *f* (*-; -n*) cinders; GEOL, METALL slag

Schlaf [ʃla:f] *m* (*-[e]s; no pl*) sleep; **e-n leichten (festen) ~ haben** be a light (sound) sleeper; F *fig* **im ~** blindfold

'Schlafanzug *m* pajamas, *Br* pyjamas

Schläfe ['ʃlɛːfə] *f* (*-; -n*) ANAT temple

schlafen ['ʃlaːfən] *v/i* (*irr, ge-, h*) sleep (*a. fig*); **~ gehen, sich ~ legen** go to bed; **fest ~** be fast asleep; **j-n ~ legen** put s.o. to bed *or* to sleep

schlaff [ʃlaf] *adj* slack (*a. fig*); flabby; limp

'Schlaf|gelegenheit *f* sleeping accommodation; **~krankheit** *f* MED sleeping sickness; **~lied** *n* lullaby

'schlaflos *adj* sleepless

'Schlaflosigkeit *f* (*-; no pl*) sleeplessness, MED insomnia

'Schlafmittel *n* MED sleeping pill(s)

'Schlafmütze *fig f* sleepyhead; slowpoke, *Br* slowcoach

schläfrig ['ʃlɛːfrɪç] *adj* sleepy, drowsy

'Schlaf|saal *m* dormitory; **~sack** *m* sleeping bag; **~ta,blette** *f* sleeping pill

'schlaftrunken *adj* (very) drowsy

'Schlaf|wagen *m* RAIL sleeping car, sleeper; **~wandler(in)** [-vandlɐ (-lərɪn)] (*-s; -/-; -nen*) sleepwalker, somnambulist; **~zimmer** *n* bedroom

Schlag [ʃla:k] *m* (*-[e]s; Schläge* ['ʃlɛːgə]) blow (*a. fig*); slap; punch; pat, tap; *a. tennis*: stroke; ELECTR shock (*a. fig*); MED beat; *pl* beating; **→ Schlaganfall**; **~ader** *f* ANAT artery; **~anfall** *m* MED (apoplectic) stroke

'schlagartig 1. *adj* sudden, abrupt; **2.** *adv* all of a sudden, abruptly

'Schlagbaum *m* barrier

'Schlagbohrer *m* TECH percussion drill

schlagen ['ʃlaːgən] (*irr, ge-, h*) **1.** *v/t* hit, beat (*a.* GASTR *and fig*), strike, knock, fell, cut (down); *a.* fight (**um** over); **sich geschlagen geben** admit defeat; **2.** *v/i* hit, beat (*a. heart etc*), strike (*a. clock*), knock; **an** *or* **gegen et.** ~ hit s.th., bump *or* crash into s.th.

Schlager ['ʃlaːgɐ] *m* (*-s; -*) MUS hit (*a. fig*), (pop) song

Schläger ['ʃlɛːgɐ] *m* (*-s; -*) *tennis etc*: racket; *table tennis, cricket, baseball*: bat; *golf*: club; *hockey*: stick; *contp* thug; **Schlägerei** [ʃlɛːgə'rai] *f* (*-; -en*) fight, brawl

'**schlagfertig** *adj* quick-witted; **~e Antwort** (witty) repartee

'**Schlag|instru,ment** *n* MUS percussion instrument; **~kraft** *f* (*-; no pl*) striking power (*a.* MIL); **~loch** *n* pot-hole; **~obers** *Austrian n*, **~sahne** *f* whipped cream; **~seite** *f* MAR list; **~ haben** be listing; **~stock** *m* baton, truncheon; **~wort** *n* catchword, slogan; **~zeile** *f* headline

'**Schlagzeug** *n* MUS drums

'**Schlagzeuger** [-tsɔʏɡɐ] *m* (*-s; -*) MUS drummer

schlaksig ['ʃlaːksɪç] *adj* lanky, gangling

Schlamm [ʃlam] *m* (*-[e]s; -e*) mud

schlammig ['ʃlamɪç] *adj* muddy

Schlampe ['ʃlampə] F *f* (*-; -n*) slut

schlampig ['ʃlampɪç] F *adj* sloppy

schlang [ʃlaŋ] *pret of* **schlingen**

Schlange ['ʃlaŋə] *f* (*-; -n*) ZO snake, serpent (*a. fig*); *fig* line, *esp Br* queue; **~ stehen** line up, stand in line, *esp Br* queue (up) (**nach** for); **schlängeln** ['ʃlɛŋəln] *v/refl* (*ge-, h*) wind *or* weave (one's way), *person:* worm one's way

'**Schlangenlinie** *f* serpentine line; **in ~n fahren** weave

schlank [ʃlaŋk] *adj* slim, slender; **j-n ~ machen** make s.o. look slim; **~e Unternehmensstruktur** ECON lean management; '**Schlankheitskur** *f:* **e-e ~ machen** be slimming

schlapp [ʃlap] F *adj* worn out; weak; **Schlappe** ['ʃlapə] F *f* (*-; -n*) setback, beating; '**schlappmachen** F *v/i* (*sep, -ge-, h*) flake out; '**Schlappschwanz** F *m* weakling, wimp

schlau [ʃlaʊ] *adj* clever, smart, bright; sly, cunning, crafty

Schlauch [ʃlaʊx] *m* (*-[e]s; Schläuche* ['ʃlɔʏçə]) tube; hose; **~boot** *n* (inflatable *or* rubber) dinghy

Schlaufe ['ʃlaʊfə] *f* (*-; -n*) loop

schlecht [ʃlɛçt] *adj* bad; poor; **mir ist (wird) ~** I feel (I'm getting) sick to my stomach; **~ aussehen** look ill; **sich ~ fühlen** feel bad; **~ werden** GASTR go bad; **es geht ihm sehr ~** he is in a bad way; **~ gelaunt** in a bad temper *or* mood, bad-tempered; F **j-n ~ machen** run s.o. down, backbite s.o.

schleichen ['ʃlaɪçən] *v/i* (*irr, ge-, sein*) creep (*a. fig*), sneak; '**Schleichweg** *m* secret path; '**Schleichwerbung** *f* plugging; **für et. ~ machen** plug s.th.

Schleier ['ʃlaɪɐ] *m* (*-s; -*) veil (*a. fig*); haze; '**schleierhaft** *adj:* F **es ist mir ~** it's a mystery to me

Schleife ['ʃlaɪfə] *f* (*-; -n*) bow; ribbon; AVIAT, EDP, ELECTR, GEOGR loop

schleifen[1] ['ʃlaɪfən] *v/t and v/i* (*ge-, h*) drag (along); rub

'**schleifen**[2] (*irr, ge-, h*) grind (*a.* TECH), sharpen; sand(paper); cut; F drill *s.o.* hard

Schleifer ['ʃlaɪfɐ] *m* (*-s; -*), '**Schleifma,schine** *f* TECH grinder

'**Schleifpa,pier** *n* sandpaper

'**Schleifstein** *m* grindstone; whetstone

Schleim [ʃlaɪm] *m* (*-[e]s; -e*) slime; MED mucus; '**Schleimhaut** *f* ANAT mucous membrane; **schleimig** ['ʃlaɪmɪç] *adj* slimy (*a. fig*); MED mucous

schlemmen ['ʃlɛmən] *v/i* (*ge-, h*) feast

schlendern ['ʃlɛndɐn] *v/i* (*ge-, sein*) stroll, saunter, amble

schlenkern ['ʃlɛŋkɐn] *v/i and v/t* (*ge-, h*) dangle, swing (**mit den Armen** one's arms)

schleppen ['ʃlɛpən] *v/t* (*ge-, h*) drag (*a. fig*), MOT, MAR tow; **sich ~** drag (on); **~d** *adj* dragging; *fig* drawling

Schlepper ['ʃlɛpɐ] *m* (*-s; -*) MAR tug; MOT tractor

'**Schlepp|lift** *m* T-bar (lift), drag lift, ski tow; **~tau** *n* tow-rope; **im (ins) ~** in tow (*a. fig*)

Schleuder ['ʃlɔʏdɐ] *f* (*-; -n*) catapult, slingshot; TECH spin drier

'**schleudern** (*ge-, h*) **1.** *v/t* fling, hurl (*both a. fig*); spin-dry; **2.** *v/i* MOT skid; '**Schleudersitz** *m* AVIAT ejection (*esp Br* ejector) seat

schleunigst ['ʃlɔʏnɪçst] *adv* immediately

Schleuse ['ʃlɔʏzə] *f* (*-; -n*) sluice; lock

schlich [ʃlɪç] *pret of* **schleichen**

schlicht [ʃlɪçt] *adj* plain, simple

schlichten ['ʃlɪçtən] *v/t* (*ge-, h*) settle

'**Schlichtung** *f* (*-; -en*) settlement

schlief [ʃliːf] *pret of* **schlafen**

schließen ['ʃliːsən] *v/t and v/i* (*irr, ge-, h*) shut, close (down); *fig* close, finish; **~ aus** (*dat*) conclude from; **nach ... zu ~** judging by ...

Schließfach ['ʃliːs-] *n* safe-deposit box; RAIL *etc:* (left luggage) locker

schließlich ['ʃliːslɪç] *adv* finally; eventually, in the end; after all

schliff [ʃlɪf] *pret of* **schleifen**²

Schliff *m* [-[e]s; -e] cut; polish (*a. fig*)

schlimm [ʃlɪm] *adj* bad; awful; *das ist nicht* or *halb so ~* it's not as bad as that; *das Schlimme daran* the bad thing about it

'**schlimmsten'falls** *adv* at the worst

Schlinge ['ʃlɪŋə] *f* (-; -n) loop; noose; HUNT snare (*a. fig*); MED sling

Schlingel ['ʃlɪŋəl] *m* (-s; -) rascal

schlingen ['ʃlɪŋən] *v/t* (*irr, ge-, h*) wind; twist; tie; wrap (*um* [a]round); gobble; *sich um et. ~* wind (a)round s.th.

schlingern ['ʃlɪŋɐn] *v/i* (*ge-, h*) MAR roll

'**Schlingpflanze** *f* BOT creeper, climber

Schlips [ʃlɪps] *m* (-es; -e) necktie, *esp Br* tie

schlitteln ['ʃlɪtəln] *Swiss v/i* (*ge-, sein*) go sledging, go tobogganing

Schlitten ['ʃlɪtən] *m* (-s; -) sled, *Br* sledge; sleigh; SPORT toboggan; *~ fahren* go sledging, go tobogganing

Schlittschuh ['ʃlɪt-] *m* ice-skate (*a. ~ laufen*); *~läufer(in)* ice-skater

Schlitz [ʃlɪts] *m* (-es; -e) slit; slot

schlitzen ['ʃlɪtsən] *v/t ge-, h*) slit, slash

schloss [ʃlɔs] *pret of* **schließen**

Schloss (-es; *Schlösser* ['ʃlœsɐ]) TECH lock; ARCH castle, palace; *ins ~ fallen door*: slam shut; *hinter ~ und Riegel* locked up, under lock and key

Schlosser ['ʃlɔsɐ] *m* (-s; -) metalwork-er; locksmith; **Schlosserei** [ʃlɔsə'raɪ] *f* (-; -en) metalwork shop

schlottern ['ʃlɔtɐn] *v/i* (*ge-, h*) shake, tremble (*both: vor dat* with); *fig* slumber

Schlucht [ʃlʊxt] *f* (-; -en) canyon, gorge, ravine

schluchzen ['ʃlʊxtsən] *v/i* (*ge-, h*), **Schluchzer** ['ʃlʊxtsɐ] *m* (-s; -) sob

Schluck [ʃlʊk] *m* (-[e]s; -e) draught, swallow; sip; gulp; '**Schluckauf** *m* (-s; *no pl*) hiccups; (*e-n*) *~ haben* have (the) hiccups; **schlucken** ['ʃlʊkən] *v/t and v/i* (*ge-, h*) swallow (*a. fig*)

'**Schluckimpfung** *f* MED oral vaccina-tion

schlug [ʃluːk] *pret of* **schlagen**

Schlummer ['ʃlʊmɐ] *m* (-s; *no pl*) slum-ber; '**schlummern** *v/i* (*ge-, h*) lie asleep; *fig* slumber

schlüpfen ['ʃlʏpfən] *v/i* (*ge-, sein*) slip, slide; ZO hatch (out); **Schlüpfer**

['ʃlʏpfɐ] *m* (-s; -) briefs, panties

schlüpfrig ['ʃlʏpfrɪç] *adj* slippery; *contp* risqué, off-colo(u)r

Schlupfwinkel ['ʃlʊpf-] *m* hiding place

schlurfen ['ʃlʊrfən] *v/i* (*ge-, sein*) shuffle (along)

schlürfen ['ʃlʏrfən] *v/t and v/i* (*ge-, h*) slurp

Schluss [ʃlʊs] *m* (-es; *no pl*) end; con-clusion; ending; *~ machen* finish; break up; *~ machen mit* stop s.th., put an end to s.th.; *zum ~* finally; (*ganz*) *bis zum ~* to the (very) end; *~ für heute!* that's all for today!

Schlüssel ['ʃlʏsəl] *m* (-s; -) key (*für, zu* to); *~bein n* ANAT collarbone; *~blume f* BOT cowslip; primrose; *~bund m, n* bunch of keys; *~kind F n* latchkey child; *~loch n* keyhole; *~wort n* key-word, EDP *a.* password

'**Schlussfolgerung** *f* conclusion

schlüssig ['ʃlʏsɪç] *adj* conclusive; *sich ~ werden* make up one's mind (*über acc* about)

'**Schluss|licht** *n* MOT *etc*: tail-light; *~pfiff* *m* SPORT final whistle; *~phase f* final stage(s); *~verkauf* *m* ECON (end--of-season) sale

schmächtig ['ʃmɛçtɪç] *adj* slight, thin, frail

schmackhaft ['ʃmakhaft] *adj* tasty

schmal [ʃmaːl] *adj* narrow; thin, slender (*a. fig*); **schmälern** ['ʃmɛːlɐn] *v/t* (*ge-, h*) detract from

'**Schmalfilm** *m* cinefilm

'**Schmalspur** *f* RAIL narrow ga(u)ge

'**Schmalspur...** *fig in cpds* small-time ...

Schmalz [ʃmalts] *n* (-es; -e) grease; lard

schmalzig ['ʃmaltsɪç] F *adj* schmaltzy, mushy, *Br* soapy

schmarotzen [ʃma'rɔtsən] F *v/i* (*no -ge-, h*) sponge (*bei* on)

Schmarotzer [ʃma'rɔtsɐ] *m* (-s; -) BOT, ZO parasite, *fig a.* sponger

schmatzen ['ʃmatsən] *v/i* smack (one's lips), eat noisily

schmecken ['ʃmɛkən] *v/i and v/t* (*ge-, h*) taste (*nach* of); *gut* (*schlecht*) *~* taste good (bad); (*wie*) *schmeckt dir ...?* (how) do you like ...? (*a. fig*); *es schmeckt süß* (*nach nichts*) it has a sweet (no) taste

Schmeichelei [ʃmaɪçə'laɪ] *f* (-; -en) flattery; **'schmeichelhaft** *adj* flattering; **'schmeicheln** *v/i* (*ge-*, *h*) flatter (*j-m* s.o.); **Schmeichler(in)** ['ʃmaiçlɐ (-lərɪn)] (*-s*; -/-; -*nen*) flatterer; **schmeichlerisch** ['ʃmaiçlərɪʃ] *adj* flattering

schmeißen ['ʃmaisən] F *v/t* and *v/i* (*irr*, *ge-*, *h*) throw, chuck; slam; *mit Geld um sich ~* throw one's money about

'Schmeißfliege *f* ZO blowfly, bluebottle

schmelzen ['ʃmɛltsən] *v/i* (*irr*, *ge-*, *sein*) and *v/t* (*h*) melt; thaw; TECH smelt **'Schmelz|ofen** *m* (s)melting furnace; **~tiegel** *m* melting pot (*a. fig*)

Schmerz [ʃmɛrts] *m* (*-es*; *-en*) pain (*a. fig*), ache; *fig* grief, sorrow

schmerzen ['ʃmɛrtsən] *v/i* and *v/t* (*ge-*, *h*) hurt (*a. fig*), ache; *esp fig* pain

'schmerzfrei *adj* without pain

'schmerzhaft *adj* painful

'schmerzlich *adj* painful, sad

'schmerzlos *adj* painless

'Schmerzmittel *n* PHARM painkiller

'schmerzstillend *adj* painkilling

Schmetterling ['ʃmɛtɐlɪŋ] *m* (*-s*; *-e*) ZO butterfly

schmettern ['ʃmɛtɐn] (*ge-*, *h*) **1.** *v/t* smash (*a.* tennis); F MUS belt out; **2.** *v/i* a) (*sein*) crash, slam, b) MUS blare

Schmied [ʃmiːt] *m* (*-[e]s*; *-e*) (black-)smith; **Schmiede** ['ʃmiːdə] *f* (*-*; *-n*) forge, smithy; **'Schmiedeeisen** *n* wrought iron; **'schmieden** *v/t* (*ge-*, *h*) forge; *fig* make (*plans etc*)

schmiegen ['ʃmiːgən] *v/refl* (*ge-*, *h*) *sich ~ an* (*acc*) snuggle up to; *dress etc*: cling to

Schmiere ['ʃmiːrə] *f* (*-*; *-n*) grease

'schmieren *v/t* (*ge-*, *h*) TECH grease, oil, lubricate; spread (*butter etc*); *contp* scribble, scrawl; **Schmiererei** [ʃmiːrə'rai] *f* (*-*; *-en*) scrawl; graffiti

schmierig ['ʃmiːrɪç] *adj* greasy; dirty; filthy; *contp* slimy

Schmiermittel ['ʃmiːɐ-] *n* TECH lubricant

Schminke ['ʃmɪŋkə] *f* (*-*; *-n*) make-up (*a.* THEA); **'schminken** *v/t* (*ge-*, *h*) make s.o. up; *sich ~* make o.s. or one's face up

Schmirgelpa,pier ['ʃmɪrgəl-] *n* emery paper

schmiss [ʃmɪs] *pret of* **schmeißen**

schmollen ['ʃmɔlən] *v/i* (*ge-*, *h*) sulk, be sulky, pout

schmolz [ʃmɔlts] *pret of* **schmelzen**

schmoren ['ʃmoːrən] *v/t* and *v/i* (*ge-*, *h*) GASTR braise, stew (*a. fig*)

Schmuck [ʃmʊk] *m* (*-[e]s*; *no pl*) jewel(le)ry, jewels; decoration(s), ornament(s); **schmücken** ['ʃmʏkən] *v/t* (*ge-*, *h*) decorate; **'schmucklos** *adj* unadorned; plain; **'Schmuckstück** *n* piece of jewel(le)ry; *fig* gem

Schmuggel ['ʃmʊgəl] *m* (*-*; *no pl*), **Schmuggelei** [ʃmʊgə'lai] *f* (*-*; *-en*) smuggling; **'schmuggeln** *v/t* and *v/i* (*ge-*, *h*) smuggle; **'Schmuggelware** *f* smuggled goods; **Schmuggler** ['ʃmʊglɐ] *m* (*-s*; *-*) smuggler

schmunzeln ['ʃmʊntsəln] *v/i* (*ge-*, *h*) smile to o.s.

schmusen ['ʃmuːzən] F *v/i* (*ge-*, *h*) (kiss and) cuddle, smooch

Schmutz [ʃmʊts] *m* (*-es*; *no pl*) dirt, filth, *fig a.* smut; **~fleck** *m* smudge

schmutzig ['ʃmʊtsɪç] *adj* dirty, filthy (*both a. fig*); *~ werden*, *sich ~ machen* get dirty

Schnabel ['ʃnaːbəl] *m* (*-s*; *Schnäbel* ['ʃnɛːbəl]) ZO bill, beak

Schnalle ['ʃnalə] *f* (*-*; *-n*) buckle

'schnallen *v/t* (*ge-*, *h*) buckle; *et. ~ an* (*acc*) strap s.th. to

schnalzen ['ʃnaltsən] *v/i* (*ge-*, *h*) snap one's fingers; click one's tongue

schnappen ['ʃnapən] (*ge-*, *h*) **1.** *v/i* snap, snatch (*both*: *nach* at); F *nach Luft ~* gasp for breath; **2.** F *v/t* catch

'Schnappschuss *m* PHOT snapshot

Schnaps [ʃnaps] *m* (*-es*; *Schnäpse* ['ʃnɛpsə]) spirits, schnapps, F booze

schnarchen ['ʃnarçən] *v/i* (*ge-*, *h*) snore

schnarren ['ʃnarən] *v/i* (*ge-*, *h*) rattle; *voice*: rasp

schnattern ['ʃnatɐn] *v/i* (*ge-*, *h*) ZO cackle; chatter (*a.* F)

schnauben ['ʃnaubən] *v/i* and *v/t* (*ge-*, *h*) snort; *sich die Nase ~* blow one's nose

schnaufen ['ʃnaufən] *v/i* (*ge-*, *h*) breathe hard, pant, puff

Schnauze ['ʃnautsə] *f* (*-*; *-n*) ZO snout, mouth, muzzle; F AVIAT, MOT nose; TECH spout; V trap, kisser; V *die ~ halten* keep one's trap shut

Schnecke ['ʃnɛkə] *f* (*-*; *-n*) ZO snail; slug

'Schnecken|haus *n* ZO snail shell;

S

~tempo n: **im ~** at a snail's pace

Schnee [ʃneː] m (-s; no pl) snow (a. sl.); **~räumen** remove snow; **~ball** m snowball; **~ballschlacht** f snowball fight

'**schneebedeckt** adj snow-capped

'**Schnee|fall** m snowfall; **~flocke** f snowflake; **~gestöber** [-ɡəʃtøːbɐ] n (-s; -) snow flurry; **~glöckchen** n BOT snowdrop; **~grenze** f snow line; **~mann** m snowman; **~matsch** m slush; **~mo,bil** n snowmobile; **~pflug** m snowplow, Br snowplough; **~regen** m sleet; **~sturm** m snowstorm, blizzard; **~verwehung** f snowdrift

'**schneeweiß** adj snow-white

Schneewittchen [ʃneːˈvɪtçən] n (-s; no pl) Snow White

Schneid [ʃnaɪt] F m (-[e]s; no pl) grit, guts; **~brenner** m TECH cutting torch

Schneide [ˈʃnaɪdə] f (-; -n) edge

'**schneiden** v/t and v/i (irr, ge-, h) cut (a. fig, film etc: a. edit); GASTR carve

Schneider [ˈʃnaɪdɐ] m (-s; -) tailor; **Schneiderei** [ʃnaɪdəˈraɪ] f (-; -en) a) (no pl) tailoring, dressmaking, b) tailor's or dressmaker's shop; **Schneiderin** f (-; -nen) dressmaker; seamstress; '**schneidern** v/i and v/t (ge-, h) do dressmaking; make, sew

'**Schneidezahn** m incisor

schneidig [ˈʃnaɪdɪç] adj dashing; smart

schneien [ˈʃnaɪən] v/i (ge-, h) snow

schnell [ʃnɛl] adj fast, quick; prompt; rapid; **es geht ~** it won't take long; **(mach[t]) ~!** hurry up!

'**Schnell...** in cpds ...dienst, ...paket, ...zug etc: mst express ...

schnellen [ˈʃnɛlən] v/t (ge-, h) and v/i (ge-, sein) shoot, spring

'**Schnellhefter** m folder

Schnelligkeit [ˈʃnɛlɪçkaɪt] f (-; no pl) speed; quickness, rapidity

'**Schnell|imbiss** m snack bar; **~straße** f expressway, thruway, Br motorway

schnetzeln [ˈʃnɛtsəln] esp Swiss v/t (ge-, h) GASTR chop up

Schnippchen [ˈʃnɪpçən] n: F **j-m ein ~ schlagen** outwit s.o.

schnippisch [ˈʃnɪpɪʃ] adj sassy, pert

schnipsen [ˈʃnɪpsən] v/i (ge-, h) snap one's fingers

schnitt [ʃnɪt] pret of **schneiden**

Schnitt m (-[e]s; -e) cut (a. fig); average

'**Schnittblumen** pl cut flowers

Schnitte [ˈʃnɪtə] f (-; -n) slice; open sandwich

schnittig [ˈʃnɪtɪç] adj stylish; MOT sleek

Schnitt|lauch m BOT chives; **~muster** n pattern; **~punkt** m (point of) intersection; **~stelle** f film etc: cut; EDP interface; **~wunde** f MED cut

Schnitzel[1] [ˈʃnɪtsəl] n (-s; -) GASTR cutlet; **Wiener ~** schnitzel

Schnitzel[2] n, m (-s; -) chip; scrap

schnitzen [ˈʃnɪtsən] v/t (ge-, h) carve, cut (in wood); **Schnitzer** [ˈʃnɪtsɐ] m (-s; -) (wood) carver; **Schnitzerei** [ʃnɪtsəˈraɪ] f (-; -en) (wood) carving

Schnorchel [ˈʃnɔrçəl] m (-s; -), '**schnorcheln** v/i (ge-, h) snorkel

Schnörkel [ˈʃnœrkəl] m (-s; -) flourish; ARCH scroll

schnorren [ˈʃnɔrən] F v/t (ge-, h) mooch, Br cadge

schnüffeln [ˈʃnʏfəln] v/i (ge-, h) sniff (**an** dat at); F snoop (about or around)

Schnuller [ˈʃnʊlɐ] m (-s; -) pacifier, Br dummy

Schnulze [ˈʃnʊltsə] F f (-; -n) tearjerker; schmal(t)zy song

Schnulzensänger F m, '**Schnulzensängerin** f crooner

schnulzig [ˈʃnʊltsɪç] F adj schmal(t)zy

Schnupfen [ˈʃnʊpfən] m (-s; -) MED cold; **e-n ~ haben (bekommen)** have a (catch [a]) cold

'**Schnupftabak** m snuff

schnuppern [ˈʃnʊpɐn] v/i (ge-, h) sniff (**an et.** [at] s.th.)

Schnur [ʃnuːɐ] f (-; Schnüre [ˈʃnyːrə]) string, cord; ELECTR flex

Schnürchen [ˈʃnyːɐçən] n: **wie am ~** like clockwork

schnüren [ˈʃnyːrən] v/t (ge-, h) lace (up); tie up

'**schnurgerade** adv dead straight

'**schnurlos** adj: **~es Telefon** cordless phone

Schnürlsamt [ˈʃnyːɐl-] Austrian m corduroy

Schnurrbart [ˈʃnʊr-] m m(o)ustache

schnurren [ˈʃnʊrən] v/i (ge-, h) purr

Schnür|schuh [ˈʃnyːɐ-] m laced shoe; **~senkel** [-zɛŋkəl] m (-s; -) shoestring, Br shoelace

schnurstracks [ˈʃnuːɐˈʃtraks] adv direct(ly), straight; straight away

schob [ʃoːp] pret of **schieben**

Schober ['ʃoːbɐ] *m* (-s; -) haystack, hayrick; barn

Schock [ʃɔk] *m* (-[e]s; -s) MED shock; **unter ~ stehen** be in (a state of) shock

schocken ['ʃɔkən] F *v/t* (ge-, h) shock

schockieren [ʃɔ'kiːrən] *v/t* (no -ge-, h) shock

Schokolade [ʃoko'laːdə] *f* (-; -*n*) chocolate; **e-e Tafel ~** a bar of chocolate

scholl [ʃɔl] *pret of* **schallen**

Scholle ['ʃɔlə] *f* (-; -*n*) clod; (ice)floe; ZO flounder, *Br* plaice

schon [ʃoːn] *adv* already; ever; even; **~ damals** even then; **~ 1968** as early as 1968; **~ der Gedanke** the very idea; **ist sie ~ da (zurück)?** has she come (is she back) yet?; **habt ihr ~ gegessen?** have you eaten yet?; **bist du ~ einmal dort gewesen?** have you ever been there?; **ich wohne hier ~ seit zwei Jahren** I've been living here for two years now; **ich kenne ihn ~, aber** I do know him, but; **er macht das ~** he'll do it all right; **~ gut!** never mind!, all right!

schön [ʃøːn] **1.** *adj* beautiful, lovely; METEOR *a.* fine, fair; nice (*a.* F *iro*) **(na,)** ~ all right; **2.** *adv:* **~ warm (kühl)** nice and warm (cool); **ganz ~ teuer (schnell)** pretty expensive (fast); **j-n ganz ~ erschrecken (überraschen)** give s.o. quite a start (surprise)

schonen ['ʃoːnən] *v/t* (ge-, h) take care of, go easy on (*a.* TECH); spare; **sich ~** take it easy; save o.s. *or* one's strength; **~d 1.** *adj* gentle; mild; **2.** *adv:* **~ umgehen mit** take (good) care of; handle with care; go easy on

'**Schönheit** *f* (-; -*en*) beauty

'**Schönheitspflege** *f* beauty care

'**Schonung** *f* (-; -*en*) a) (*no pl*) (good) care; rest; preservation, b) tree nursery

'**schonungslos** *adj* relentless, brutal

schöpfen ['ʃœpfən] *v/t* (ge-, h) scoop, ladle; draw (*water*); → **Luft, Verdacht**

Schöpfer ['ʃœpfɐ] *m* (-s; -), '**Schöpferin** *f* (-; -*nen*) creator

schöpferisch ['ʃœpfərɪʃ] *adj* creative

'**Schöpfung** *f* (-; -*en*) creation

schor [ʃoːɐ] *pret of* **scheren**

Schorf [ʃɔrf] *m* (-[e]s; -e) MED scab

Schornstein ['ʃɔrnʃtaɪn] *m* chimney; MAR, RAIL funnel; **~feger** *m* chimney-sweep

schoss [ʃɔs] *pret of* **schießen**

Schoß [ʃoːs] *m* (-es; *Schöße* ['ʃøːsə]) lap; womb

Schote ['ʃoːtə] *f* (-; -*n*) BOT pod, husk

Schotte ['ʃɔtə] *m* (-*n*; -*n*) Scot(sman); *pl* the Scots, the Scottish (people)

Schotter ['ʃɔtɐ] *m* (-s; -) gravel, road metal

Schottin ['ʃɔtn] *f* (-; -*nen*) Scotswoman

'**schottisch** *adj* Scots, Scottish; Scotch

'**Schottland** Scotland

schräg [ʃrɛːk] **1.** *adj* slanting, sloping, oblique; diagonal; **2.** *adv:* **~ gegenüber** diagonally opposite

Schramme ['ʃramə] *f* (-; -*n*), '**schrammen** *v/t and v/i* (ge-, h) scratch (*a.* MED)

Schrank [ʃraŋk] *m* (-[e]s; *Schränke* ['ʃrɛŋkə]) cupboard; closet; wardrobe

Schranke ['ʃraŋkə] *f* (-; -*n*) barrier (*a. fig*), RAIL *a.* gate; JUR bar; *pl* limits, bounds

'**schrankenlos** *fig adj* boundless

'**Schrankenwärter** *m* RAIL gatekeeper

'**Schrankwand** *f* wall units

Schraube ['ʃraubə] *f* (-; -*n*), '**schrauben** *v/t* (ge-, h) TECH screw

'**Schrauben|schlüssel** *m* TECH spanner, wrench; **~zieher** *m* TECH screwdriver

Schraubstock ['ʃraup-] *m* vise, *Br* vice

Schreck [ʃrɛk] *m* (-[e]s; -e) fright, shock; **j-m e-n ~ einjagen** give s.o. a fright, scare s.o.

Schrecken ['ʃrɛkən] *m* (-s; -) terror, fright; horror(s); '**Schreckensnachricht** *f* dreadful news

'**schreckhaft** *adj* jumpy; skittish

'**schrecklich** *adj* awful, terrible; horrible, dreadful, atrocious

Schrei [ʃrai] *m* (-[e]s; -e) cry, shout, yell, scream (*all:* **um, nach** for)

schreiben ['ʃraibən] *v/t and v/i* (irr, ge-, h) write (*j-m* to s.o.; **über** *acc* about); type; spell; **falsch ~** misspell; **wie schreibt man ...?** how do you spell ...?

'**Schreiben** *n* (-s; -) letter

'**Schreib|fehler** *m* spelling mistake; **~heft** *n* exercise book; **~kraft** *f* typist; **~ma,schine** *f* typewriter; **~materi,al** *n* writing materials, stationery; **~schutz** *m* EDP write *or* file protection; **~tisch** *m* desk

'**Schreibung** *f* (-; -*en*) spelling

'**Schreibwaren** *pl* stationery; **~ge-**

S

schäft n stationer's, stationery shop

'**Schreibzen,trale** f typing pool

schreien ['ʃraiən] v/i and v/t (irr, ge-, h) cry, shout, yell, scream (all: **um, nach** [out] for); ~ **vor Schmerz** (**Angst**) cry out with pain (in terror); **es war zum Schreien** it was a scream; ~**d** fig adj loud (colors); flagrant (abuse etc), glaring (injustices etc)

Schreiner ['ʃrainɐ] m (-s; -) → **Tischler**

schreiten ['ʃraitən] v/i (irr, ge-, sein) stride

schrie [ʃriː] pret of **schreien**

schrieb [ʃriːp] pret of **schreiben**

Schrift [ʃrɪft] f (-; -en) (hand)writing, hand; PRINT type; character, letter; pl works, writings; **die Heilige** ~ REL the Scriptures; ~**art** f script; PRINT typeface; ~**deutsch** n standard German

'**schriftlich** adj written; ~ **übersetzen** translate in writing

'**Schriftsteller** [-ʃtɛlɐ] m (-s; -), '**Schriftstellerin** f (-; -nen) author, writer

'**Schrift|verkehr** m, ~**wechsel** m correspondence; ~**zeichen** n character, letter

schrill [ʃrɪl] adj shrill (a. fig), piercing

schritt [ʃrɪt] pret of **schreiten**

Schritt m (-[e]s; -e) step (a. fig); pace; fig ~**e unternehmen** take steps; ~ **fahren!** MOT dead slow; ~**macher** m SPORT pacemaker (a. MED), pacesetter

'**schrittweise** adv step by step, gradually

schroff [ʃrɔf] adj steep; jagged; fig gruff

Schrot [ʃroːt] m, n (-[e]s; -e) a) (no pl) coarse meal, b) HUNT (small) shot; pellet; ~**flinte** f shotgun

Schrott [ʃrɔt] m (-[e]s; -e) scrap (metal)

'**Schrotthaufen** m scrap heap

'**Schrottplatz** m scrapyard

schrubben ['ʃrʊbən] v/t (ge-, h) scrub, scour

schrumpfen ['ʃrʊmpfən] v/i (ge-, sein) shrink

Schub [ʃuːp] m (-[e]s; Schübe ['ʃyːbə]) → **Schubkraft**; ~**fach** n drawer; ~**karren** m wheelbarrow; ~**kasten** m drawer; ~**kraft** f PHYS, TECH thrust; ~**lade** f drawer

Schubs [ʃʊps] F m (-es; -e), **schubsen** ['ʃʊpsən] F v/t (ge-, h) push

schüchtern ['ʃʏçtɐn] adj shy, bashful

'**Schüchternheit** f (-; no pl) shyness, bashfulness

schuf [ʃuːf] pret of **schaffen**[1]

Schuft [ʃʊft] m (-[e]s; -e) contp bastard

schuften ['ʃʊftən] F v/i (ge-, h) slave away, drudge

Schuh [ʃuː] m (-[e]s; -e) shoe; **j-m et. in die ~e schieben** put the blame for s.th. on s.o.; ~**anzieher** m shoehorn; ~**creme** f shoe polish; ~**geschäft** n shoe store (Br shop); ~**löffel** m shoehorn; ~**macher** m shoemaker; ~**putzer** [-pʊtsə] m (-s; -) shoeshine boy

'**Schul|abbrecher** m (-s; -) dropout; ~**abgänger** [-apgɛŋɐ] m (-s; -) school leaver; ~**amt** n school board, Br education authority; ~**arbeit** f schoolwork; pl homework; ~**besuch** m (school) attendance; ~**bildung** f education; ~**buch** n textbook

Schuld [ʃʊlt] f (-; -en ['ʃʊldən]) a) (no pl) JUR guilt, esp REL sin, b) mst pl debt; **j-m die ~** (**an et.**) **geben** blame s.o. (for s.th.); **es ist** (**nicht**) **deine** ~ it is(n't) your fault; ~**en haben** (**machen**) be in (run into) debt; → **zuschulden**; '**schuldbewusst** adj: ~**e Miene** guilty look; **schulden** ['ʃʊldən] v/t (ge-, h) **j-m et.** ~ owe s.o. s.th.; **schuldig** ['ʃʊldɪç] adj esp JUR guilty (**an** dat of); responsible or to blame (for); **j-m et.** ~ **sein** owe s.o. s.th.; **Schuldige** ['ʃʊldɪgə] m, f (-n; -n) culprit; JUR guilty person, offender

'**schuldlos** adj innocent

Schuldner ['ʃʊldnɐ] m (-s; -); '**Schuldnerin** f (-; -nen) debtor

'**Schuldschein** m ECON promissory note, IOU (= I owe you)

Schule ['ʃuːlə] f (-; -n) school (a. fig); **höhere** ~ appr (senior) high school, Br secondary school; **auf** or **in der** ~ at school; **in die** or **zur** ~ **gehen** (**kommen**) go to (start) school

'**schulen** v/t (ge-, h) train, school

Schüler ['ʃyːlɐ] m (-s; -) student, schoolboy, esp Br a. pupil; ~**austausch** m student exchange (program[me])

Schülerin ['ʃyːlərɪn] f (-; -nen) student, schoolgirl, esp Br a. pupil

'**Schülervertretung** f appr student government (Br council)

'**Schul|ferien** pl vacation, Br holidays; ~**fernsehen** n educational TV; ~**funk** *m* schools programmes; **~gebäude** *n* school (building); **~geld** *n* school fee(s), tuition; **~heft** *n* exercise book; **~hof** *m* school yard, playground; **~ka,me,rad** *m* schoolfellow; **~leiter** *m* principal, *Br* headmaster, head teacher; **~leiterin** *f* principal, *Br* headmistress; **~mappe** *f* schoolbag; satchel; **~ordnung** *f* school regulations

'**schulpflichtig** *adj:* **~es Kind** school--age child

'**Schul|schiff** *n* training ship; **~schluss** *m* end of school (*or* term); **nach ~** after school; **~schwänzer** [-ʃvɛntsɐ] *m* (-s; -) truant; **~stunde** *f* lesson, class, period; **~tasche** *f* schoolbag

Schulter ['ʃʊltɐ] *f* (-; -n) ANAT shoulder

'**Schulterblatt** *n* ANAT shoulder-blade

'**schulterfrei** *adj* strapless

'**schultern** *v/t* (ge-, h) shoulder

'**Schultertasche** *f* shoulder bag

'**Schulwesen** *n* (-s; *no pl*) education(al system)

schummeln ['ʃʊməln] F *v/i* (ge-, h) cheat

Schund [ʃʊnt] *m* (-[e]s; *no pl*) trash, rubbish, junk

schund [ʃʊnt] *pret* **of schinden**

Schuppe ['ʃʊpə] *f* (-; -n) ZO scale; *pl* MED dandruff

'**Schuppen** *m* (-s; -) shed, *esp* F *contp* shack

schuppig ['ʃʊpɪç] *adj* ZO scaly

schüren ['ʃyːrən] *v/t* (ge-, h) stir up (*a. fig*)

schürfen ['ʃʏrfən] *v/i* (ge-, h) prospect (**nach** for)

'**Schürfwunde** *f* MED graze, abrasion

Schurke ['ʃʊrkə] *m* (-n; -n) *esp* THEA *etc* villain

Schurwolle ['ʃuːɐ-] *f* virgin wool

Schürze ['ʃʏrtsə] *f* (-; -n) apron

Schuss [ʃʊs] *m* (-es; *Schüsse* ['ʃʏsə]) shot; GASTR dash; SPORT shot, *soccer:* *a.* strike; *skiing:* schuss (*a.* **~ fahren**); *sl* shot, fix; F **gut in ~ sein** be in good shape

Schüssel ['ʃʏsəl] *f* (-; -n) bowl, dish; basin

'**Schuss|waffe** *f* firearm; **~wunde** *f* MED gunshot *or* bullet wound

Schuster ['ʃuːstɐ] *m* (-s; -) shoemaker

Schutt [ʃʊt] *m* (-[e]s; *no pl*) rubble, debris

'**Schüttelfrost** *m* MED shivering fit, *the* shivers

schütteln ['ʃʏtəln] *v/t* (ge-, h) shake

schütten ['ʃʏtən] *v/t* (ge-, h) pour; throw

Schutz [ʃʊts] *m* (-es; *no pl*) protection (**gegen**, **vor** *dat* against), defense, *Br* defence (against, from); shelter (from); safeguard (against); cover; **~blech** *n* fender, *Br* mudguard; **~brille** *f* goggles

Schütze ['ʃʏtsə] *m* (-n; -n) MIL rifleman; hunter; SPORT scorer; ASTR Sagittarius; **er ist (ein) ~** he's a(n) Sagittarius; **ein guter ~** a good shot

schützen ['ʃʏtsən] *v/t* (ge-, h) protect (**gegen**, **vor** *dat* against, from), defend (against, from), guard (against, from); shelter (from); safeguard

'**Schutzengel** *m* guardian angel

'**Schützengraben** *m* MIL trench

'**Schutzgeld** *n* protection money; **~erpressung** *f* protection racket

'**Schutz|haft** *f* JUR protective custody; **~heilige** *m*, *f* patron (saint); **~impfung** *f* MED protective inoculation; vaccination; **~kleidung** *f* protective clothing

Schützling ['ʃʏtslɪŋ] *m* (-s; -e) protégé(e)

'**schutzlos** *adj* unprotected; defenseless, *Br* defenceless

'**Schutz|maßnahme** *f* safety measure; **~pa,tron** *m* REL patron (saint); **~umschlag** *m* dust cover; **~zoll** *m* ECON protective duty (*or* tariff)

schwach [ʃvax] *adj* weak (*a. fig*); poor; faint; delicate, frail; **schwächer werden** grow weak; decline; fail; fade

Schwäche ['ʃvɛçə] *f* weakness (*a. fig*); MED infirmity; *fig* drawback, short-coming; **e-e ~ haben für** be partial to; '**schwächen** *v/t* (ge-, h) weaken (*a. fig*); lessen; '**schwächlich** *adj* weakly, feeble; delicate, frail; '**Schwächling** *m* (-s; -e) weakling (*a. fig*), softy, sissy

'**schwachsinnig** *adj* feeble-minded; F stupid, idiotic

'**Schwachstrom** *m* ELECTR low-voltage current

Schwager ['ʃvaːgɐ] *m* (-s; *Schwäger* ['ʃvɛːgɐ]) brother-in-law; **Schwägerin** ['ʃvɛːgərɪn] *f* (-; -nen) sister-in-law

Schwalbe ['ʃvalbə] *f* (-; -n) ZO swallow; *soccer:* dive

Schwall [ʃval] *m* (-[e]s; -e) gush, *esp fig a.* torrent schwamm [ʃvam] pret of **schwimmen**

Schwamm m (-[e]s; Schwämme ['ʃvɛmə]) sponge; BOT fungus; F dry rot

Schwammerl ['ʃvaməl] Austrian m (-s; -[n]) → **Pilz**

schwammig ['ʃvamɪç] adj spongy; puffy; fig woolly

Schwan [ʃvaːn] m (-[e]s; Schwäne ['ʃvɛːnə]) ZO swan

schwand [ʃvant] pret of **schwinden**

schwang [ʃvaŋ] pret of **schwingen**

schwanger ['ʃvaŋɐ] adj pregnant

'Schwangerschaft f (-; -en) pregnancy; **'Schwangerschaftsabbruch** m abortion

schwanken ['ʃvaŋkən] v/i (ge-, h) sway, roll (a. MAR); stagger; fig ~ **zwischen ... und ...** waver between ... and ...; prices: range from ... to ...; **'Schwankung** f (-; -en) change, variation (a. ECON)

Schwanz [ʃvants] m (-es; Schwänze ['ʃvɛntsə]) ZO tail (a. AVIAT, ASTR); V cock

schwänzen ['ʃvɛntsən] v/i and v/t (ge-, h) (**die Schule**) ~ play truant (F hooky)

Schwarm [ʃvarm] m (-[e]s; Schwärme ['ʃvɛrmə]) swarm; crowd, F bunch; ZO shoal, school; F dream; idol

schwärmen ['ʃvɛrmən] v/i a) (ge-, sein) ZO swarm, b) (ge-, h) ~ **für** be mad about; dream of; have a crush on s.o.; ~ **von** rave about

Schwarte ['ʃvartə] f (-; -n) rind; F contp (old) tome

schwarz [ʃvarts] adj black (a. fig); **~es Brett** bulletin board, Br notice board; ~ **auf weiß** in black and white

'Schwarzarbeit f (-; no pl) illicit work

'Schwarzbrot n rye bread

Schwarze ['ʃvartsə] m, f (-n; -n) black (man or woman); pl the Blacks

schwärzen ['ʃvɛrtsən] v/t (ge-, h) blacken

'Schwarz|fahrer m fare dodger; **~händler** m black marketeer; **~markt** m black market; **~seher** m pessimist; (TV) license (Br licence) dodger

Schwarz'weiß... in cpds ...film, ...fernseher etc: black-and-white ...

schwatzen ['ʃvatsən], schwätzen ['ʃvɛtsən] v/i (ge-, h) chat(ter); PED talk

Schwätzer ['ʃvɛtsɐ] contp m (-s; -), 'Schwätzerin f (-; -nen) loudmouth

schwatzhaft ['ʃvatshaft] adj chatty

Schwebe|bahn ['ʃveːbə-] f cableway, ropeway; **~balken** m SPORT beam

schweben ['ʃveːbən] v/i (ge-, h) be suspended; ZO, AVIAT hover (a. fig); glide; esp JUR be pending; **in Gefahr** ~ be in danger

Schwede ['ʃveːdə] m (-n; -n) Swede

Schweden ['ʃveːdən] Sweden

Schwedin ['ʃveːdɪn] f (-; -nen) Swede

'schwedisch adj Swedish

Schwefel ['ʃveːfəl] m (-s; no pl) CHEM sulfur, Br sulphur; **~säure** f CHEM sulfuric (Br sulphuric) acid

Schweif [ʃvaif] m (-[e]s; -e) ZO tail (a. ASTR); schweifen ['ʃvaifən] v/i (ge-, sein) wander (a. fig), roam

schweigen ['ʃvaigən] v/i (irr, ge-, h) be silent; 'Schweigen n (-s; no pl) silence; 'schweigend adj silent

schweigsam ['ʃvaikzaːm] adj quiet, taciturn, reticent

Schwein [ʃvain] n (-[e]s; -e) ZO pig, hog; F contp (filthy) pig; swine, bastard; F ~ **haben** be lucky; 'Schweinebraten m roast pork; 'Schweinefleisch n pork; Schweinerei [ʃvainə'rai] f F f (-; -en) mess; fig dirty trick; dirty or crying shame; filth(y story or joke)

'Schweinestall m pigsty (a. fig)

'schweinisch F adj filthy, obscene

'Schweinsleder n pigskin

Schweiß [ʃvais] m (-es; no pl) sweat, perspiration

schweißen v/t (ge-, h) TECH weld

Schweißer m (-s; -) TECH welder

'schweißgebadet adj soaked in sweat

'Schweißgeruch m body odo(u)r, BO

Schweiz [ʃvaits] Switzerland

Schweizer ['ʃvaitsɐ] m (-s; -), adj Swiss

Schweizerin ['ʃvaitsərɪn] f (-; -nen) Swiss woman or girl

schweizerisch ['ʃvaitsərɪʃ] adj Swiss

schwelen ['ʃveːlən] v/i (ge-, h) smo(u)lder (a. fig)

schwelgen ['ʃvɛlgən] v/i (ge-, h) ~ **in** (dat) revel in

Schwelle ['ʃvɛlə] f (-; -n) threshold (a. fig); RAIL tie, Br sleeper

'schwellen 1. v/i (irr, ge-, sein) swell; 2. v/t (ge-, h) swell

'Schwellung f (-; -en) MED swelling

Schwemme ['ʃvɛmə] f (-; -n) ECON glut, oversupply; 'schwemmen v/t (ge-, h) **an Land** ~ wash ashore

Schwengel ['ʃvɛŋəl] *m* (*-s*; *-*) clapper; handle

schwenken ['ʃvɛŋkən] *v/t* (*ge-*, *h*) *and v/i* (*ge-*, *sein*) swing, wave

schwer [ʃveːɐ] **1.** *adj* heavy; *fig* difficult, hard; GASTR strong, rich; MED *etc* serious, severe; heavy, violent (*storm etc*); **~e Zeiten** hard times; **100 Pfund ~ sein** weigh a hundred pounds; **2.** *adv:* **~ arbeiten** work hard; **→ hören; ~ beschädigt** seriously disabled; *j-m* **~ fallen** be difficult for s.o.; **es fällt ihm ~ zu ...** he finds it difficult to ...; **~ verdaulich** indigestible, heavy (*both a. fig*); **~ verständlich** difficult *or* hard to understand; **~ verwundet** seriously wounded

Schwere ['ʃveːrə] *f* (*-*; *no pl*) weight (*a. fig*); *fig* seriousness

'schwerfällig *adj* awkward, clumsy

'Schwergewicht *n* (*-[e]s*; *no pl*) heavyweight; *fig* (main) emphasis

'schwerhörig *adj* hard of hearing

'Schwer|industrie *f* heavy industry; **~kraft** *f* (*-*; *no pl*) PHYS gravity; **~metall** *n* heavy metal

'schwermütig [-myːtɪç] *adj* melancholy; **~ sein** have the blues

'Schwerpunkt *m* center (*Br* centre) of gravity; *fig* (main) emphasis

Schwert [ʃveːɐt] *n* (*-[e]s*; *-er*) sword

'Schwerverbrecher *m* dangerous criminal, JUR felon

'schwerwiegend *fig adj* weighty, serious

Schwester ['ʃvɛstɐ] *f* (*-*; *-n*) sister, REL *a.* nun; MED nurse

schwieg [ʃviːk] *pret of* **schweigen**

Schwieger... ['ʃviːgɐ-] *in cpds* ...*eltern*, ...*mutter*, ...*sohn etc*: ...*in-law*

Schwiele ['ʃviːlə] *f* (*-*; *-n*) MED callus

schwielig ['ʃviːlɪç] *adj* horny

schwierig ['ʃviːrɪç] *adj* difficult, hard

'Schwierigkeit *f* (*-*; *-en*) difficulty, trouble; *in* **~en geraten** get *or* run into trouble; **~en haben**, *et.* **zu tun** have difficulty in doing s.th.

Schwimmbad ['ʃvɪm-] *n* (indoor) swimming pool; **schwimmen** ['ʃvɪmən] *v/i* (*irr*, *ge-*, *sein*) swim; float; **~ gehen** go swimming

'Schwimm|flosse *f* swimfin, *Br* flipper; **~gürtel** *m* swimming belt; **~haut** *f* ZO

web; ~lehrer *m* swimming instructor; **~weste** *f* life jacket

Schwindel ['ʃvɪndəl] *m* (*-s*; *no pl*) MED giddiness, dizziness; F swindle, fraud; **~ erregend** dizzy

'schwindeln F *v/i* (*ge-*, *h*) fib, tell fibs

schwinden ['ʃvɪndən] *v/i* (*irr*, *ge-*, *sein*) dwindle, decline

Schwindler ['ʃvɪndlɐ] F *m* (*-s*; *-*), **'Schwindlerin** *f* (*-*; *-nen*) swindler, crook; liar

schwindlig ['ʃvɪndlɪç] *adj* MED dizzy, giddy; *mir ist* **~** I feel dizzy

Schwinge ['ʃvɪŋə] *f* (*-*; *-n*) ZO wing

schwingen *v/i and v/t* (*irr*, *ge-*, *h*) swing; wave; PHYS oscillate; vibrate

'Schwingung *f* (*-*; *-en*) PHYS oscillation; vibration

Schwips [ʃvɪps] F *m:* **e-n ~ haben** be tipsy

schwirren ['ʃvɪrən] *v/i* a) (*ge-*, *sein*) whirr, whizz, *esp* ZO buzz (*a. fig*), b) (*ge-*, *h*) *mir schwirrt der Kopf* my head is buzzing

schwitzen ['ʃvɪtsən] *v/i* (*ge-*, *h*) sweat, perspire

schwoll [ʃvɔl] *pret of* **schwellen** 1

schwor [ʃvoːɐ] *pret of* **schwören**

schwören ['ʃvøːrən] *v/i and v/t* (*irr*, *ge-*, *h*) swear; JUR take an *or* the oath; *fig* **~ auf** (*acc*) swear by

schwul [ʃvuːl] F *adj* gay; *contp* queer

schwül [ʃvyːl] *adj* sultry (*a. fig*), close

schwülstig ['ʃvʏlstɪç] *adj* bombastic, pompous

Schwung [ʃvʊŋ] *m* (*-[e]s; Schwünge* ['ʃvʏŋə]) swing; *fig* verve, pep; drive; *in* **~ kommen** get going; *et. in* **~ bringen** get s.th. going; **'schwungvoll** *adj* full of energy *or* verve; MUS swinging

Schwur [ʃvuːɐ] *m* (*-[e]s; Schwüre* ['ʃvyːrə]) oath; **~gericht** *n* JUR jury court

sechs [zɛks] *adj* six; *grade:* F, *Br a.* poor; **'Sechseck** *n* (*-[e]s; -e*) hexagon; **'sechseckig** *adj* hexagonal; **'sechsfach** *adj* sixfold; **'sechsmal** *adv* six times; **Sechs'tagerennen** *n* SPORT six-day race; **'sechstägig** [-tɛːgɪç] *adj* lasting *or* of six days; **'sechste** *adj* sixth; **Sechstel** ['zɛkstəl] *n* (*-s*; *-*) sixth (part); **'sechstens** *adv* sixthly, in the sixth place; **sechzehn(te)** ['zɛçtseːn(tə)] *adj* sixteen(th); **sechzig**

['zɛçtsɪç] *adj* sixty; '**sechzigste** *adj* six-
tieth

See¹ [ze:] *m* (-s; -n) lake

See² *f* (-; *no pl*) sea, ocean; **auf ~** at sea;
auf hoher ~ on the high seas; **an der ~**
at the seaside; **zur ~ gehen (fahren)** go
to sea (be a sailor); **in ~ stechen** put to
sea; **~bad** *n* seaside resort; **~fahrt** *f*
navigation; **~gang** *m* (-[e]s; *no pl*): **ho-**
her ~ heavy sea; **~hafen** *m* seaport;
~hund *m* ZO seal; **~karte** *f* nautical
chart

'seekrank *adj* seasick

'Seekrankheit *f* seasickness

Seele ['ze:lə] *f* (-; -n) soul (*a. fig*)

'seelenlos *adj* soulless

'Seelenruhe *f* peace of mind; **in aller ~**
as cool as you please

seelisch ['ze:lɪʃ] *adj* mental

'Seelsorge *f* (-; *no pl*) pastoral care

'Seelsorger [-zɔrgɐ] *m* (-s; -), '**Seelsor-**
gerin *f* (-; -nen) pastor

'See|macht *f* sea power; **~mann** *m*
(-[e]s; -leute) seaman, sailor; **~meile** *f*
nautical mile; **~not** *f* (-; *no pl*)
distress (at sea); **~notkreuzer** *m* MAR
rescue cruiser; **~räuber** *m* pirate; **~rei-**
se *f* voyage, cruise; **~rose** *f* BOT water
lily; **~sack** *m* kit bag; **~schlacht** *f* MIL
naval battle; **~streitkräfte** *pl* MIL naval
forces, navy

'seetüchtig *adj* seaworthy

'See|warte *f* naval observatory; **~weg** *m*
sea route; **auf dem ~** by sea; **~zeichen**
n seamark; **~zunge** *f* ZO sole

Segel ['ze:gəl] *n* (-s; -) sail; **~boot** *n* sail-
boat, *Br* sailing boat; **~fliegen** *n* gliding; **~flugzeug** *n* glider

'segeln *v/i* (ge-, sein) sail, SPORT *a.* yacht

'Segel|schiff *n* sailing ship; sailing ves-
sel; **~sport** *m* sailing, yachting; **~tuch** *n*
canvas, sailcloth

Segen ['ze:gən] *m* (-s; -) blessing (*a. fig*)

Segler ['ze:glɐ] *m* (-s; -) yachtsman

Seglerin ['ze:glərɪn] *f* (-; -nen) yachts-
woman

segnen ['ze:gnən] *v/t* (ge-, h) bless

'Segnung *f* (-; -nen) blessing

Sehbeteiligung ['ze:-] *f* (TV) ratings

sehen ['ze:ən] *v/i* and *v/t* (*irr*, ge-, h) see;
watch; notice; **~ nach** look after; look
for; **sich ~ lassen** show up; **das sieht**
man (kaum) it (hardly) shows; **siehst**
du (you) see; I told you; **siehe oben**

(**unten**, **Seite ...**) see above (below,
page ...); '**sehenswert** *adj* worth seeing; '**Sehenswürdigkeit** *f* (-; -en) place
etc worth seeing, sight, *pl* sights

'Sehkraft *f* (-; *no pl*) eyesight, vision

Sehne ['ze:nə] *f* (-; -n) ANAT sinew;
string

sehnen ['ze:nən] *v/refl* (ge-, h) long
(**nach** for), yearn (for); **sich danach**
~ zu *inf* be longing to *inf*

'Sehnerv *m* ANAT optic nerve

sehnig ['ze:nɪç] *adj* sinewy, GASTR *a.*
stringy

sehnlichst ['ze:nlɪçst] *adj* dearest

'Sehnsucht *f*, '**sehnsüchtig** *adj* longing, yearning

sehr [ze:ɐ] *adv* before *adj* and *adv*: very;
with *verbs*: very much, greatly

'Sehtest *m* sight test

seicht [zaɪçt] *adj* shallow (*a. fig*)

Seide ['zaɪdə] *f* (-; -n), '**seiden** *adj* silk

'Seidenpa.pier *n* tissue paper

'Seidenraupe *f* ZO silkworm

seidig ['zaɪdɪç] *adj* silky

Seife ['zaɪfə] *f* (-; -n) soap

'Seifen|blase *f* soap bubble; **~lauge** *f*
(soap)suds; **~oper** *f* TV soap opera;
~schale *f* soap dish; **~schaum** *m*
lather

seifig ['zaɪfɪç] *adj* soapy

Seil [zaɪl] *n* (-[e]s; -e) rope

'Seilbahn *f* cable railway

'seilspringen *v/i* (*only inf*) skip

sein¹ [zaɪn] *v/i* (*irr*, ge-, sein) be; exist; **et.**
~ lassen stop *or* quit (doing) s.th.

sein² *poss pron* his, her, its; **~er**, **~e**,
~(e)s his, hers

Sein *n* (-s; *no pl*) being; existence

seiner|seits ['zaɪnɐzaɪts] *adv* for his
part; **~'zeit** *adv* then, in those days

seines'gleichen ['zaɪnəs-] *pron* his
equals

seinet'wegen ['zaɪnət-] → **meinetwe-**
gen

seit [zaɪt] *prp* and *cj* since; **~ 1982** since
1982; **~ drei Jahren** for three years
(now); **~ langem (kurzem)** for a long
(short) time; **~'dem 1.** *adv* since then,
since that time, ever since; **2.** *cj* since

Seite ['zaɪtə] *f* (-; -n) side (*a. fig*); page;
auf der linken ~ on the left(-hand
side); *fig* **auf die e-n (anderen) ~** on
the one (other) hand

'Seiten|ansicht *f* side view, profile;

~**blick** m sidelong glance; ~**hieb** m sideswipe; ~**linie** f esp soccer: touchline

seitens ['zaɪtəns] prp (gen) on the part of, by

'**Seitensprung** F m: **e-n ~ machen** cheat (on one's wife or husband)

'**Seitenstechen** n (-s; no pl) MED a stitch (in the side)

'**seitlich** adj side ..., at the side(s)

'**seitwärts** [-vɛrts] adv sideways, to the side

Sekretär [zekre'tɛːɐ] m (-s; -e) secretary; bureau; **Sekretariat** [-ta'rjaːt] n (-[e]s; -e) secretary's office; **Sekretärin** [-'tɛːrɪn] f (-; -nen) secretary

Sekt [zɛkt] m (-[e]s; -e) sparkling wine, champagne

Sekte ['zɛktə] f (-; -n) sect

Sektion [zɛk'tsjoːn] f (-; -en) section; MED autopsy

Sektor ['zɛktoːɐ] m (-s; -en [zɛk'toːrən]) sector; fig field

Sekunde [ze'kʊndə] f (-; -n) second; **auf die ~** to the second

Se'**kundenzeiger** m second(s) hand

selbe ['zɛlbə] adj same

selber ['zɛlbɐ] pron → **selbst** 1

selbst [zɛlbst] 1. pron: **ich (du etc) ~ I** (you etc) myself (yourself etc); **mach es ~** do it yourself; **et. ~ tun** do s.th. by oneself; **von ~** by itself; **~ gemacht** homemade; 2. adv even

'**Selbstachtung** f self-respect

'**selbständig** etc → **selbstständig** etc

'**Selbst|bedienung**(**sladen** m) f self-service (store, Br shop); ~**befriedigung** f masturbation; ~**beherrschung** f self-control; ~**bestimmung** f self-determination

'**selbstbewusst** adj self-confident, self-assured; '**Selbstbewusstsein** n self-confidence

'**Selbst|bildnis** n self-portrait; ~**erhaltungstrieb** m survival instinct; ~**erkenntnis** f (-; no pl) self-knowledge

'**selbstgerecht** adj self-righteous

'**Selbst|hilfe** f self-help; ~**hilfegruppe** f self-help group; ~**kostenpreis** m: **zum ~** ECON at cost (price)

'**selbstkritisch** adj self-critical

'**Selbstlaut** m LING vowel

'**selbstlos** adj unselfish

'**Selbst|mord** m, ~**mörder(in)** suicide

'**selbstmörderisch** adj suicidal

'**selbstsicher** adj self-confident, self-assured

'**selbstständig** adj independent, self-reliant; self-employed; '**Selbstständigkeit** f (-; no pl) independence

'**Selbststudium** n (-s; no pl) self-study

'**selbst|süchtig** adj selfish, ego(t)istic(al); ~**tätig** adj automatic

'**Selbsttäuschung** f self-deception

'**selbstverständlich** 1. adj natural; **das ist ~** that's a matter of course; 2. adv of course, naturally; **~! a.** by all means!; '**Selbstverständlichkeit** f (-; -en) matter of course

'**Selbst|verteidigung** f self-defense, Br self-defence; ~**vertrauen** n self-confidence, self-reliance; ~**verwaltung** f self-government, autonomy; ~**wähldienst** m TEL automatic long-distance dial(l)ing service

'**selbstzufrieden** adj self-satisfied

selchen ['zɛlçən] Austrian → **räuchern**

selig ['zeːlɪç] adj REL blessed; late; fig overjoyed

Sellerie ['zɛləri] m (-s; -[s]), f (-; -) BOT celeriac; celery

selten ['zɛltən] 1. adj rare; **~ sein** be rare, be scarce; 2. adv rarely, seldom

'**Seltenheit** f (-; no pl) rarity

seltsam ['zɛltzaːm] adj strange, odd

Semester [ze'mɛstɐ] n (-s; -) UNIV semester, esp Br term

Semikolon [zemi'koːlɔn] n (-s; -s) LING semicolon

Seminar [zemi'naːɐ] n (-s; -e) UNIV department; seminar; REL seminary; teacher training college

sen. ABBR of **senior** sen., Sen., Sr, Snr, senior

Senat [ze'naːt] m (-[e]s; -e) senate

Senator [ze'naːtoːɐ] m (-s; -en [zena'toːrən]), **Sena'torin** f (-; -nen) senator

Sendemast m ELECTR mast

senden ['zɛndən] v/t ([irr], ge-, h) send (**mit der Post** by mail, Br by post); ELECTR broadcast, transmit, a. televise

Sender ['zɛndɐ] m (-s; -) radio or television station; ELECTR transmitter

'**Sende|reihe** f TV or radio series; ~**schluss** m close-down, F sign-off; ~**zeichen** n call letters (Br sign); ~**zeit** f air time

'**Sendung** f (-; -en) broadcast, program (-me), a. telecast; ECON consignment,

S

shipment; **auf ~ sein** be on the air

Senf [zɛnf] *m* (-[e]s; -e) mustard (*a.* BOT)

senil [ze'ni:l] *adj* senile; **Senilität** [zenili'tɛːt] *f* (-; *no pl*) senility

Senior ['ze:njoːɐ] **1.** *m* (-s; -en [ze-'njoːrən]) senior (*a.* SPORT); senior citizen; **2.** *adj* senior

Seni'orenheim *n* old people's home

Seni'orin *f* (-; -nen) senior citizen

Senke ['zɛŋkə] *f* (-; -n) GEOGR depression, hollow; **'senken** *v/t* (ge-; *h*) lower (*a.* one's voice); *a.* bow (one's head); ECON *a.* reduce, cut; **sich ~** drop, go *or* come down

'senkrecht *adj* vertical

Sensation [zɛnza'tsjoːn] *f* (-; -en) sensation; **sensationell** [zɛnzatsjo'nɛl] *adj*, **Sensati'ons...** in cpds ...blatt *etc*: sensational (...)

Sense ['zɛnzə] *f* (-; -n) AGR scythe

sensibel [zɛn'ziːbəl] *adj* sensitive

sensibilisieren [zɛnzibili'ziːrən] *v/t* (*no -ge-, h*) sensitize (**für** to)

sentimental [zɛntimɛn'taːl] *adj* sentimental; **Sentimentalität** [zɛntimɛntali'tɛːt] *f* (-; -en) sentimentality

September [zɛp'tɛmbɐ] *m* (-[s]; -) September

Serenade [zere'naːdə] *f* (-; -n) MUS serenade

Serie ['zeːrjə] *f* (-; -n) series, TV *etc a.* serial; set; **in ~** produce *etc* in series

'serienmäßig *adj* series(-produced); standard

'Serien|nummer *f* serial number; **~wagen** *m* MOT standard-type car

seriös [ze'rjøːs] *adj* respectable; honest; serious

Serum ['zeːrʊm] *n* (-s; -ren, -ra) serum

Service[1] [zɛr'viːs] *n* (-[s]; -) set; service

Service[2] ['zøːɐvɪs] *m, n* (-; -s) service

servieren [zɛr'viːrən] *v/t* (*no -ge-, h*) serve; **Serviererin** [zɛr'viːrərɪn] *f* (-; -nen) waitress; **Serviertochter** [zɛr-'viːɐ-] *Swiss f* waitress

Serviette [zɛr'vjɛtə] *f* (-; -n) napkin, *esp Br* serviette

Servo|bremse ['zɛrvo-] *f* MOT servo *or* power brake; **~lenkung** *f* MOT servo(-assisted) *or* power steering

Sessel ['zɛsəl] *m* (-s; -) armchair, easy chair; **~lift** *m* chair lift

sesshaft ['zɛshaft] *adj*: **~ werden** settle (down)

Set [zɛt] *n, m* (-s; -s) place mat

setzen ['zɛtsən] *v/t and v/i* (ge-; *h*) put, set (*a.* PRINT, AGR, MAR), AGR *a.* plant; place; seat *s.o.*; **~ über** (*acc*) jump over; cross (*river*); **~ auf** (*acc*) bet on, back; **sich ~** sit down; CHEM *etc* settle; **sich ~ auf** (*acc*) get on, mount; **sich ~ in** (*acc*) get into; **sich zu j-m ~** sit beside *or* with s.o.; **~ Sie sich bitte!** take *or* have a seat!

Setzer ['zɛtsɐ] *m* (-s; -) PRINT compositor, typesetter; **Setzerei** [zɛtsə'rai] *f* (-; -en) PRINT composing room

Seuche ['zɔʏçə] *f* (-; -n) epidemic (disease)

seufzen ['zɔʏftsən] *v/i* (ge-; *h*), **Seufzer** ['zɔʏftsɐ] *m* (-s; -) sigh

Sexismus [zɛ'ksɪsmʊs] *m* (-; *no pl*) sexism; **Sexist** [zɛ'ksɪst] *m* (-en; -en), **se-'xistisch** *adj* sexist

Sexual... [zɛ'ksuaːl-] in cpds ...erziehung, ...leben, ...trieb *etc*: sex(ual) ...; **~verbrechen** *n* sex crime

sexuell [zɛ'ksuɛl] *adj* sexual; **~e Belästigung** (sexual) harassment

sexy ['zɛksi] *adj* sexy

sezieren [ze'tsiːrən] *v/t* (*no -ge-, h*) MED dissect (*a. fig*); perform an autopsy on

Showgeschäft ['ʃoʊ-] *n* (-[e]s; *no pl*) show business

sich [zɪç] *refl pron* oneself; himself, herself, itself; *pl* themselves; yourself, *pl* yourselves; **~ ansehen** look at oneself; look at each other

Sichel ['zɪçəl] *f* (-; -n) AGR sickle; ASTR crescent

sicher ['zɪçɐ] **1.** *adj* safe (**vor** *dat* from), secure (from); *esp* TECH proof (**gegen** against); *fig* certain, sure; reliable; **(sich) ~ sein** be sure (**e-r Sache** of s.th.; **dass** that); **2.** *adv* safely; **~!** of course, sure(ly); certainly; probably; **du hast** (**bist**) **~ ...** you must have (be) ...

'Sicherheit *f* (-; -en) a) (*no pl*) security (*a.* MIL, POL, ECON); safety (*a.* TECH); *fig* certainty; skill; **(sich) in ~ bringen** get to safety, b) ECON cover

'Sicherheits... *esp* TECH in cpds ...glas, ...nadel, ...schloss *etc*: safety ...; **~gurt** *m* seat belt, safety belt; **~maßnahme** *f* safety (POL security) measure

'sicherlich *adv → sicher 2*

'sichern *v/t* (ge-; *h*) protect, safeguard;

secure (a. MIL, TECH); EDP save; **sich ~** secure o.s. (**gegen**, **vor** dat against, from); **'sicherstellen** v/t (sep, -ge-, h) secure; guarantee; **Sicherung** ['zɪçərʊŋ] f (-; -en) securing; safeguard (-ing); TECH safety device; ELECTR fuse; **'Sicherungs|kasten** m ELECTR fuse box; **~ko,pie** f EDP backup; **e-e ~ machen (von)** back up

Sicht [zɪçt] f (-; no pl) visibility; view; **in ~ kommen** come into sight or view; **auf lange ~** in the long run; **'sichtbar** adj visible; **sichten** ['zɪçtən] v/t (ge-, h) sight; fig sight (through or out)

'Sichtkarte f season ticket

'sichtlich adv visibly

'Sichtweite f visibility; **in (außer) ~** within (out of) sight

sickern ['zɪkən] v/i (ge-, sein) trickle, ooze, seep

sie [ziː] pers pron she; it; pl they; **Sie** you

Sieb [ziːp] n (-[e]s; -e) sieve; strainer

sieben[1] ['ziːbən] v/t (ge-, h) sieve, sift

'sieben[2] adj seven

Sieben'**meter** m SPORT penalty shot or throw

siebte ['ziːptə] adj, **'Siebtel** n (-s; -) seventh; **siebzehn(te)** ['ziːp-] adj seventeen(th); **siebzig** ['ziːptsɪç] adj seventy; **'siebzigste** adj seventieth

siedeln ['ziːdəln] v/i (ge-, h) settle

sieden ['ziːdən] v/t and v/i ([irr], ge-, h) boil, simmer

'Siedepunkt m boiling point (a. fig)

Siedler ['ziːdlɐ] m (-s; -) settler

Siedlung ['ziːdlʊŋ] f (-; -en) settlement; housing development

Sieg [ziːk] m (-[e]s; -e) victory, SPORT a. win

Siegel ['ziːɡəl] n (-s; -) seal, signet

'Siegellack m sealing wax

'siegeln v/t (ge-, h) seal

siegen ['ziːɡən] v/i (ge-, h) win

Sieger ['ziːɡɐ] m (-s; -), **Siegerin** ['ziːɡərɪn] f (-; -nen) winner

'siegreich adj winning; victorious

Signal [zɪ'ɡnaːl] n (-s; -e), **signalisieren** [zɪɡnali'ziːrən] v/t (no -ge-, h) signal

signieren [zɪ'ɡniːrən] v/t (no -ge-, h) sign

Silbe ['zɪlbə] f (-; -n) syllable

'Silbentrennung f LING syllabification

Silber ['zɪlbɐ] n (-s; no pl) silver; silverware; **'silbergrau** adj silver-gray (Br -grey); **'Silberhochzeit** f silver

wedding; **'silbern** adj silver

Silhouette [zi'luɛtə] f (-; -n) silhouette; skyline

Silikon [zili'koːn] n (-s; -e) CHEM silicone

Silizium [zi'liːtsjʊm] n (-s; no pl) CHEM silicon

Silvester [zɪl'vɛstɐ] n (-s; -) New Year's Eve

Sims [zɪms] m, n (-es; -e) ledge; windowsill

simulieren [zimu'liːrən] v/t and v/i TECH etc simulate; sham

simultan [zimʊl'taːn] adj simultaneous

Sinfonie [zɪnfo'niː] f (-; -n) MUS symphony

singen ['zɪŋən] v/t and v/i (irr, ge-, h) sing (**richtig** [**falsch**] in [out of] tune)

Singular ['zɪŋɡulaːɐ] m (-s; -e) LING singular

'Singvogel ['zɪŋ-] m ZO songbird

sinken ['zɪŋkən] v/i (irr, ge-, sein) sink (a. fig), go down (a. ECON), ASTR a. set; prices etc: fall, drop

Sinn [zɪn] m (-[e]s; -e) sense (**für** of); mind; meaning; point, idea; **im ~ ha-ben** have in mind; **es hat keinen ~** (**zu warten** etc) it's no use or good (waiting etc); **'Sinnbild** n symbol

'sinnentstellend adj distorting

Sinnes|organ ['zɪnəs-] n sense organ; **~täuschung** f hallucination; **~wandel** m change of mind

'sinnlich adj sensuous; sensory; sensual; **'Sinnlichkeit** f (-; no pl) sensuality

'sinnlos adj senseless; useless

'sinnverwandt adj synonymous

'sinnvoll adj meaningful; useful; wise, sensible

Sintflut ['zɪnt-] f the Flood

Sippe ['zɪpə] f (-; -n) (extended) family, clan

Sirene [zi'reːnə] f (-; -n) siren

Sirup ['ziːrʊp] m (-s; -e) sirup, Br syrup; treacle, molasses

Sitte ['zɪtə] f (-; -n) custom, tradition; pl morals; manners

'Sittenlosigkeit f (-; no pl) immorality

'Sittenpoli,zei f vice squad

'sittenwidrig adj immoral

'Sittlichkeitsverbrechen n sex crime

Situation [zitua'tsjoːn] f (-; -en) situation; position

Sitz [zɪts] m (-es; -e) seat; fit; **~blo,ckade** f sit-down demonstration

sitzen ['zıtsən] v/i (irr, ge-, h) sit (**an** dat at; **auf** dat on); be; fit; F do time; ~ **bleiben** keep one's seat; PED have to repeat a year; F ~ **bleiben auf** (dat) be left with; F **j-n** ~ **lassen** leave s.o. in the lurch, let s.o. down

'**Sitzplatz** m seat

'**Sitzstreik** m sit-down strike

'**Sitzung** f (-; -en) session (a. PARL), meeting, conference

Skala ['ska:la] f (-; -en) scale, fig a. range

Skalp [skalp] m (-s; -e), **skalpieren** [skal'pi:rən] v/t (no -ge-, h) scalp

Skandal [skan'da:l] m (-s; -e) scandal; **ein** ~ **sein** be scandalous; **skandalös** [skanda'lø:s] adj scandalous, shocking

Skelett [ske'lɛt] n (-[e]s; -e) skeleton

Skepsis ['skɛpsıs] f (-; no pl) skepticism, Br scepticism; **Skeptiker** ['skɛptikɐ] m (-s; -) skeptic, Br sceptic; **skeptisch** ['skɛptıʃ] adj skeptical, Br sceptical

Ski [ʃiː] m (-s; -er ['ʃiːɐ]) ski; ~ **laufen** or **fahren** ski; **~fahrer(in)** skier; **~fliegen** n ski flying; **~lift** m ski lift; **~piste** f ski run; **~schuh** m ski boot; **~sport** m skiing; **~springen** n ski jumping

Skizze ['skıtsə] f (-; -n), **skizzieren** [skı'tsi:rən] v/t (no -ge-, h) sketch

Sklave ['skla:və] m (-n; -n) slave (a. fig); **Sklaverei** [skla:və'rai] f (-; no pl) slavery; **Sklavin** f (-; -nen) slave (a. fig); '**sklavisch** adj slavish (a. fig)

Skonto ['skɔnto] m, n (-s; -s) ECON (cash) discount

Skorpion [skɔr'pjo:n] m (-s; -e) ZO scorpion; ASTR Scorpio; **er ist** (**ein**) ~ he's (a) Scorpio

Skrupel ['skru:pəl] m (-s; -) scruple, qualm; '**skrupellos** adj unscrupulous

Skulptur [skʊlp'tu:ɐ] f (-; -en) sculpture

Slalom ['sla:ləm] m (-s; -s) slalom

Slawe ['sla:və] m (-n; -n), '**Slawin** f (-; -nen) Slav; '**slawisch** adj Slav(ic)

Slip [slıp] m (-s; -s) briefs, panties

'**Slipeinlage** f panty liner

Slipper ['slıpɐ] m (-s; -) loafer, esp Br slip-on (shoe)

Slowake [slo'va:kə] m (-n; -n) Slovak

Slowakei [slova'kai] f Slovakia

Slo'wakin f (-; -nen), **slo'wakisch** adj Slovak

Smaragd [sma'rakt] m (-[e]s; -e) MIN, **sma'ragdgrün** adj emerald

Smoking ['smo:kıŋ] m (-s; -s) tuxedo, Br dinner jacket

Snob [snɔp] m (-s; -s) snob; **Snobismus** [sno'bısmʊs] m (-; no pl) snobbery; **sno'bistisch** adj snobbish

so [zo:] **1.** adv so; like this or that, this or that way; thus; such; (**nicht**) ~ **groß wie** (not) as big as; ~ **ein(e)** such a; ~ **sehr** so (F that) much; **und** ~ **weiter** and so on; **oder** ~ **et.** or s.th. like that; **oder** ~ or so; ~, **fangen wir an!** well or all right, let's begin!; F ~ **weit sein** be ready; **es ist** ~ **weit** it's time; ~ **genannt** so-called; **doppelt** ~ **viel** twice as much; ~ **viel wie möglich** as much as possible; **2.** cj so, therefore; ~ **dass** so that; **3.** int: ~! all right!, o.k.!; that's it!; **ach** ~! I see

s.o. ABBR of **siehe oben** see above

so'**bald** [zo-] cj as soon as

Socke ['zɔkə] f (-; -n) sock

Sockel ['zɔkəl] m (-s; -) base; pedestal

Sodbrennen ['zo:t-] n (-s; no pl) MED heartburn

soeben [zo'e:bən] adv just (now)

Sofa ['zo:fa] n (-s; -s) sofa, settee, davenport

sofern [zo'fɛrn] cj if, provided that; ~ **nicht** unless

soff [zɔf] pret of **saufen**

sofort [zo'fɔrt] adv at once, immediately, right away

So'fortbildkamera f PHOT instant camera

Software ['zɔftwɛːɐ] f EDP software; **~pa,ket** n software package

sog [zo:k] pret of **saugen**

Sog m (-[e]s; -e) suction, MAR a. wake

sogar [zo'ga:ɐ] adv even

Sohle ['zo:lə] f (-; -n) sole; mining: floor

Sohn [zo:n] m (-[e]s; Söhne ['zø:nə]) son

Sojabohne ['zo:ja-] f BOT soybean

so'**lange** [zo-] cj as long as

Solar... [zo'la:ɐ-] in cpds ...energie etc: solar ...

solch [zɔlç] dem pron such, like this or that

Sold [zɔlt] m (-[e]s; -e) MIL pay

Soldat [zɔl'da:t] m (-en; -en), **Sol'datin** f (-; -nen) soldier

Söldner ['zœldnɐ] m (-s; -) MIL mercenary

Sole ['zo:lə] f (-; -n) brine, salt water

solidarisch [zoli'da:rıʃ] adj: **sich** ~ **er-**

klären mit declare one's solidarity with

solide [zo'liːdə] *adj* solid, *fig a.* sound; reasonable (*prices*); steady (*person*)

Solist [zo'lɪst] *m* (-en; -en), **So'listin** *f* (-; *-nen*) soloist

Soll [zɔl] *n* (-[s]; -[s]) ECON debit; target, quota; **~ und Haben** debit and credit

sollen ['zɔlən] *v/i* (*ge-*, *h*) and *v/aux* (*irr*, *no -ge-*, *h*) be to; be supposed to; (*was*) **soll ich ...?** (what) shall I ...?; **du solltest (nicht) ...** you should(n't) ...; you ought(n't) to; **was soll das?** what's the idea?

Solo ['zoːlo] *n* (-s, -s, Soli) *esp* MUS solo; SPORT solo attempt *etc*

so'mit [zo-] *cj* thus, so, consequently

Sommer ['zɔmɐ] *m* (-s; -) summer (time); **im ~** in (the) summer; **~ferien** *pl* summer vacation (*Br* holidays); **~frische** *f* summer resort

'sommerlich *adj* summery

'Sommersprosse *f* freckle

'sommersprossig *adj* freckled

'Sommerzeit *f* summertime; daylight saving (*Br* summer) time

Sonate [zo'naːtə] *f* (-; *-n*) MUS sonata

Sonde ['zɔndə] *f* (-; *-n*) probe (*a.* MED)

Sonder... ['zɔndɐ-] *in cpds* **...angebot**, **...ausgabe**, **...flug**, **...preis**, **...wunsch**, **...zug** *etc*: special ...

'sonderbar *adj* strange, F funny

'Sonderling *m* (-s; -e) eccentric

'Sondermüll *m* hazardous (*or* special toxic) waste; **~depo,nie** *f* special waste dump

sondern ['zɔndɐn] *cj* but; **nicht nur ...**, **~ auch ...** not only ... but also ...

'Sonderschule *f* special school (for the handicapped *etc*)

Sonnabend ['zɔn-] *m* Saturday

Sonne ['zɔnə] *f* (-; *-n*) sun

sonnen ['zɔnən] *v/refl* (*ge-*, *h*) sunbathe; **'Sonnenaufgang** *m* (*bei* ~ at) sunrise

'Sonnen|bad *n*: **ein ~ nehmen** sunbathe; **~bank** *f* (-; *-bänke*) sunbed; **~blume** *f* BOT sunflower; **~brand** *m* sunburn; **~bräune** *f* suntan; **~brille** *f* sunglasses; **~creme** *f* suntan lotion, *Br* sun cream; **~ener,gie** *f* solar energy; **~finsternis** *f* solar eclipse

'sonnen'klar F *adj* (as) clear as daylight

'Sonnen|kol,lektor *m* solar panel; **~licht** *n* (-[e]s, *no pl*) sunlight; **~öl** *n* suntan oil; **~schein** *m* sunshine;

~schirm *m* sunshade; **~schutz** *m* suntan lotion; **~seite** *f* sunny side (*a. fig*); **~stich** *m* sunstroke; **~strahl** *m* sunbeam; **~sys,tem** *n* solar system; **~uhr** *f* sundial; **~untergang** *m* sunset

sonnig ['zɔnɪç] *adj* sunny (*a. fig*)

Sonntag ['zɔn-] *m* Sunday; (*am*) ~ on Sunday; **'sonntags** *adv* on Sundays

'Sonntagsfahrer *contp m* MOT Sunday driver

sonst [zɔnst] *adv* else; otherwise, or (else); normally, usually; **~ noch et.** (*jemand*)**?** anything (anyone) else?; **~ noch Fragen?** any other questions?; **~ nichts** nothing else; **alles wie ~** everything as usual; **nichts ist wie ~** nothing is as it used to be; **'sonstig** *adj* other

Sopran [zo'praːn] *m* (-s; -e) MUS, **Sopranistin** [zopra'nɪstɪn] *f* (-; *-nen*) MUS soprano

Sorge ['zɔrgə] *f* (-; *-n*) worry; sorrow; trouble; care; **sich ~n machen** (*um*) worry *or* be worried (about); **keine ~!** I don't worry!; **sorgen** ['zɔrgən] (*ge-*, *h*) **1.** *v/i*: **~ für** care for, take care of; **dafür ~, dass** see (to it) that; **2.** *v/refl*: **sich ~ um** worry *or* be worried about

'Sorgenkind *n* problem child

Sorgfalt ['zɔrkfalt] *f* (-; *no pl*) care

sorgfältig ['zɔrkfɛltɪç] *adj* careful

sorglos ['zɔrk-] *adj* carefree; careless

Sorte ['zɔrtə] *f* (-; *-n*) sort, kind, type; **sortieren** [zɔr'tiːrən] *v/t* (*no -ge-*, *h*) sort; arrange; **Sortiment** [zɔrti'mɛnt] *n* (-[e]s; -e) ECON assortment

Soße ['zoːsə] *f* (-; *-n*) sauce; gravy

sott [zɔt] *pret of* **sieden**

Souffleur [zu'fløːɐ] *m* (-s; -e), **Souffleuse** [zu'fløːzə] *f* (-; *-n*) THEA prompter; **soufflieren** [zu'fliːrən] *v/i* (*no -ge-*, *h*) THEA prompt (*j-m* s.o.)

souverän [zuvə'rɛːn] *adj* POL sovereign

Souveränität [zuvərɛni'tɛːt] *f* (-; *no pl*) POL sovereignty

so'viel [zo-] *cj* as far as; **→ so**; **so'weit** *cj* as far as; **→ so**; **so'wie** *cj* as well as, and ... as well; as soon as; **sowie'so** *adv* anyway, anyhow, in any case

Sowjet [zɔ'vjɛt] *m* (-s; -s), **sow'jetisch** *adj* HIST Soviet

so'wohl [zo-] *cj*: **~ Lehrer als (auch) Schüler** both teachers and students

sozial [zo'tsjaːl] *adj* social

Sozi'al... *in cpds* ...arbeiter, ...demokrat, ...versicherung *etc*: social ...; **~hilfe** *f* welfare, *Br* social security; **~ beziehen** be on welfare (*Br* social security)

Sozialismus [zotsja'lɪsmʊs] *m* (-; *no pl*) socialism; **Sozialist(in)** (-en/-; -en/ -nen), **sozia'listisch** *adj* socialist

Sozi'alkunde *f* PED social studies

Sozi'alstaat *m* welfare state

Soziologe [zotsjo'lo:gə] *m* (-n; -n) sociologist; **Soziologie** [zotsjolo'gi:] *f* (-; *no pl*) sociology; **Sozio'login** *f* (-; -nen) sociologist; **soziologisch** [zotsjo'lo:gɪʃ] *adj* sociological

sozu'sagen *adv* so to speak

Spagat [ʃpa'ga:t] *m*: **~ machen** do the splits

Spalier [ʃpa'li:ɐ] *n* (-s; -e) BOT espalier; MIL *etc* lane

Spalt [ʃpalt] *m* (-[e]s; -e) crack, gap; **Spalte** ['ʃpaltə] *f* (-; -n) → **Spalt**; PRINT column; **'spalten** *v/t* ([irr,] *ge*-, h) split (*a. fig*); POL divide; **sich** ~ split (*a. fig*); **'Spaltung** *f* (-; -en) split(ting); PHYS fission; *fig* split; POL division

Span [ʃpa:n] *m* (-[e]s; Späne ['ʃpɛ:nə]) chip; *pl* TECH shavings

Spange ['ʃpaŋə] *f* (-; -n) clasp

Spaniel ['ʃpa:njəl] *m* (-s; -s) ZO spaniel

Spanien ['ʃpa:njən] Spain

Spanier ['ʃpa:njɐ] *m* (-s; -), **Spanierin** ['ʃpa:njərɪn] *f* (-; -nen) Spaniard

spanisch ['ʃpa:nɪʃ] *adj* Spanish

spann [ʃpan] *pret of* **spinnen**

Spann [ʃpan] *m* (-[e]s; -e) ANAT instep

Spanne ['ʃpanə] *f* (-; -n) span

'spannen *v/t* (*ge*-, h) **1.** *v/t* stretch, tighten; put up (*line*); cock (*gun*); draw, bend (*bow*); **2.** *v/i* be (too) tight; **~d** *adj* exciting, thrilling, gripping

'Spannung *f* (-; -en) tension (*a.* TECH, POL, PSYCH); ELECTR voltage; *fig* suspense, excitement

'Spannweite *f* span, *fig a.* range

Spar|buch ['ʃpa:ɐ-] *n* savings book; **~büchse** *f esp Br* money box

sparen ['ʃpa:rən] *v/i* and *v/t* (*ge*-, h) save; economize; **~ für** or **auf** (*acc*) save up for; **Sparer(in)** ['ʃpa:rɐ (-rərɪn)] (-s; -/-; -nen) saver

'Sparschwein(chen) *n* piggy bank

Spargel ['ʃpargəl] *m* (-s; -) BOT asparagus

'Sparkasse *f* savings bank

'Sparkonto *n* savings account

spärlich ['ʃpɛːɐlɪç] *adj* sparse, scant; scanty; poor (*attendance*)

sparsam ['ʃpa:ɐza:m] *adj* economical (**mit** of); **~ leben** lead a frugal life; **~ umgehen mit** use sparingly; go easy on

'Sparsamkeit *f* (-; *no pl*) economy

Spaß [ʃpa:s] *m* (-es; Späße ['ʃpɛ:sə]) fun; joke; **aus** (**nur zum**) ~ (just) for fun; **es macht viel** (**keinen**) ~ it's great (no) fun; **j-m den** ~ **verderben** spoil s.o.'s fun; **er macht nur** ~ he is only joking (F kidding); **keinen** ~ **verstehen** have no sense of humo(u)r

spaßen ['ʃpa:sən] *v/i* (*ge*-, h) joke

spaßig ['ʃpa:sɪç] *adj* funny

'Spaßvogel *m* joker

spät [ʃpɛ:t] *adj and adv* late; **am ~en Nachmittag** late in the afternoon; **wie ~ ist es?** what time is it?; **von früh bis ~** from morning till night; (**fünf Minuten**) **zu ~ kommen** be (five minutes) late; **bis ~er!** see you (later)!; → **früher**

Spaten ['ʃpa:tən] *m* (-s; -) spade

'spätestens *adv* at the latest

Spatz [ʃpats] *m* (-en; -en) ZO sparrow

spazieren [ʃpa'tsi:rən]: **~ fahren** go (take *s.o.*) for a drive; take *s.o.* out; **~ gehen** go for a walk

Spazierfahrt [ʃpa'tsi:ɐ-] *f* drive, ride

Spa'ziergang *m* walk; **e-n ~ machen** go for a walk; **Spa'ziergänger(in)** [-gɛŋɐ (-ŋərɪn)] (-s; -/-; -nen) walker

Specht [ʃpɛçt] *m* (-[e]s; -e) ZO woodpecker

Speck [ʃpɛk] *m* (-[e]s; -e) bacon

speckig ['ʃpɛkɪç] *fig adj* greasy

Spediteur [ʃpedi'tø:ɐ] *m* (-s; -e) shipping agent; remover

Spedition [ʃpedi'tsjo:n] *f* (-; -en) shipping agency; moving (*Br* removal) firm

Speer [ʃpe:ɐ] *m* (-[e]s; -e) spear; SPORT javelin

Speiche ['ʃpaiçə] *f* (-; -n) spoke

Speichel ['ʃpaiçəl] *m* (-s; *no pl*) saliva, spit

Speicher ['ʃpaiçɐ] *m* (-s; -) storehouse; tank, reservoir; ARCH attic; EDP memory, store; **~dichte** *f* EDP bit density; **~kapazi,tät** *f* EDP memory capacity

'speichern *v/t* (*ge*-, h) store (up)

Speicherung ['ʃpaiçərʊŋ] *f* (-; -en) storage

speien ['ʃpaiən] *v/t* (*irr*, *ge*-, h) spit;

spout; *volcano etc*: belch

Speise ['ʃpaizə] *f* (-; -*n*) food; dish; **~eis** *n* ice cream; **~kammer** *f* larder, pantry; **~karte** *f* menu

'**speisen** (*ge-, h*) **1.** *v/i* dine; **2.** *v/t* feed (*a.* ELECTR *etc*)

'**Speise|röhre** *f* ANAT gullet; **~saal** *m* dining hall; **~wagen** *m* RAIL diner, *esp Br* dining car

Spekulant [ʃpeku'lant] *m* (-*en*; -*en*) ECON speculator

Spekulation [ʃpekula'tsjoːn] *f* (-; -*en*) speculation, ECON *a.* venture

spekulieren [ʃpeku'liːrən] *v/i* (*no -ge-, h*) ECON speculate (**auf** *acc* on; **mit** in)

Spende ['ʃpɛndə] *f* (-; -*n*) gift; contribution; donation; **'spenden** *v/t* (*ge-, h*) give (*a. fig*); donate (*a.* MED); **Spender** ['ʃpɛndɐ] *m* (-*s*; -) giver; donor (*a.* MED), **Spenderin** *f* (-; -*nen*) donor (*a.* MED)

spendieren [ʃpɛn'diːrən] *v/t* (*no -ge-, h*) **j-m et. ~** treat s.o. to s.th.

Spengler ['ʃpɛŋlɐ] *Austrian m* → **Klempner**

Sperling ['ʃpɛrlɪŋ] *m* (-*s*; -*e*) ZO sparrow

Sperre ['ʃpɛrə] *f* (-; -*n*) barrier, RAIL *a.* gate; *fig* stop; TECH lock(ing device); barricade; SPORT suspension; PSYCH mental block; ECON embargo

'**sperren** *v/t* (*ge-, h*) close; ECON embargo; cut off; stop (*check*); SPORT suspend; obstruct; **~ in** (*acc*) lock (up) in

'**Sperr|holz** *n* plywood; **~müllabfuhr** *f* removal of bulky refuse

'**Sperrung** *f* (-; -*en*) closing

Spesen ['ʃpeːzən] *pl* expenses

Spezi ['ʃpeːtsi] F *m* (-*s*; -[*s*]) buddy, pal

Spezial|ausbildung [ʃpe'tsjaːl-] *f* special training; **~gebiet** *n* special field, special(i)ty; **~geschäft** *n* specialized shop *or* store

spezialisieren [ʃpetsjali'ziːrən] *v/refl* (*no -ge-, h*) specialize (**auf** *acc* in); **Spezialist(in)** [ʃpetsja'lɪst(ɪn)] (-*en*; -*en*/-; -*nen*) specialist; **Spezialität** [ʃpetsjali'tɛːt] *f* (-; -*en*) special(i)ty; **speziell** [ʃpe'tsjɛl] *adj* specific, particular

spezifisch [ʃpe'tsiːfɪʃ] *adj* specific; **~es Gewicht** specific gravity

Sphäre ['sfɛːrə] *f* (-; -*n*) sphere (*a. fig*)

spicken ['ʃpɪkən] (*ge-, h*) **1.** *v/t* GASTR lard (*a. fig*); **2.** F *v/i* PED crib

spie [ʃpiː] *pret of* **speien**

Spiegel ['ʃpiːgəl] *m* (-*s*; -) mirror (*a. fig*)

'**Spiegelbild** *n* reflection (*a. fig*)

'**Spiegelei** *n* GASTR fried egg

'**spiegel'glatt** *adj* glassy; icy

'**spiegeln** *v/i* and *v/t* (*ge-, h*) reflect (*a. fig*); shine; **sich ~** be reflected (*a. fig*)

'**Spiegelung** *f* (-; -*en*) reflection

Spiel [ʃpiːl] *n* (-[*e*]*s*; -*e*) game (*a. fig*); match; play (*a.* THEA *etc*); gambling; *fig* gamble; **auf dem ~ stehen** be at stake; **aufs ~ setzen** risk; **spielen** ['ʃpiːlən] *v/i* and *v/t* (*ge-, h*) play (*a. fig*) (**um** for); THEA act; perform; gamble; do (*the pools etc*); **Klavier *etc* ~** play the piano *etc*; '**spielend** *fig adv* easily; **Spieler** ['ʃpiːlɐ] *m* (-*s*; -), **Spielerin** ['ʃpiːlərɪn] *f* (-; -*nen*) player; gambler

'**Spiel|feld** *n* (playing) field, pitch; **~film** *m* feature film; **~halle** *f* amusement arcade, game room; **~kame,rad(in)** playmate; **~karte** *f* playing card; **~ka,sino** *n* casino; **~marke** *f* counter, chip; **~plan** *m* THEA *etc* program(me); **~platz** *m* playground; **~raum** *fig m* play, scope; **~regel** *f* rule (of the game); **~sachen** *pl* toys; **~stand** *m* score; **~uhr** *f* music (*Br* musical) box; **~verderber(in)** (-*s*; -/-; -*nen*) spoilsport; **~waren** *pl* toys; **~zeit** *f* THEA, SPORT season; playing (*film*: running) time

'**Spielzeug** *n* toy(s); **~... in cpds ...pistole** *etc*: toy ...

Spieß [ʃpiːs] *m* (-*es*; -*e*) MIL spear; GASTR spit; skewer

spießen ['ʃpiːsən] *v/t* (*ge-, h*) skewer

Spießer ['ʃpiːsɐ] F *contp m* (-*s*; -), '**spie-Big** F *contp adj* philistine

Spinat [ʃpi'naːt] *m* (-[*e*]*s*; -*e*) BOT spinach

Spind [ʃpɪnt] *n, m* (-[*e*]*s*; -*e*) locker

Spindel ['ʃpɪndəl] *f* (-; -*n*) spindle

Spinne ['ʃpɪnə] *f* (-; -*n*) ZO spider

'**spinnen** (*irr, ge-, h*) **1.** *v/t* spin (*a. fig*); **2.** F *contp v/i* be nuts; talk nonsense

Spinner ['ʃpɪnɐ] *m* (-*s*; -), '**Spinnerin** *f* (-; -*nen*) spinner; F *contp* nut, crackpot

'**Spinnrad** *n* spinning wheel

'**Spinnwebe** *f* (-; -*n*) cobweb

Spion [ʃpjoːn] *m* (-*s*; -*e*) spy

Spionage [ʃpjo'naːʒə] *f* (-; *no pl*) espionage; **spionieren** [ʃpjo'niːrən] *v/i* (*no -ge-, h*) spy; F snoop

Spi'onin *f* (-; -*nen*) spy

S

Spirale [ʃpiˈraːlə] f (-; -n), **spiˈralförmig** [-fœrmɪç] adj spiral

Spirituosen [ʃpiriˈtuoːzən] pl spirits

Spiritus [ˈʃpiːritus] m spirit

Spital [ʃpiˈtaːl] Austrian, Swiss n (-s; Spitäler [ʃpiˈtɛːlɐ]) hospital

spitz [ʃpɪts] adj pointed (a. fig); MATH acute; **~e Zunge** sharp tongue

Spitzbogen m ARCH pointed arch

Spitze [ˈʃpɪtsə] f (-; -n) point; tip; ARCH spire; BOT, GEOGR top; head (a. fig); lace; F MOT top speed; **~ sein** F be super, be (the) tops; **an der ~** at the top (a. fig)

Spitzel [ˈʃpɪtsəl] m (-s; -) informer, F stoolpigeon

spitzen [ˈʃpɪtsən] v/t (ge-, h) point, sharpen; purse; ZO prick up (its ears)

'Spitzen... in cpds top ...; hi-tech ...; **~technolo,gie** f high technology, hi tech

'spitzfindig adj quibbling

'Spitzfindigkeit f (-; -en) subtlety

Spitzhacke f pickax(e), pick

Spitzname m nickname

Splitter [ˈʃplɪtɐ] m (-s; -), **splittern** v/i (ge-, h, sein) splinter

splitter'nackt F adj stark naked

sponsern [ˈʃpɔnzɐn] v/t (ge-, h) sponsor

Sponsor [ˈʃpɔnzɐ] m (-s; -en [ʃpɔnˈzoːrən]) sponsor

spontan [ʃpɔnˈtaːn] adj spontaneous

Sporen [ˈʃpoːrən] pl spurs (a. ZO); BIOL spores

Sport [ʃpɔrt] m (-[e]s; no pl) sport(s); PED physical education; **~ treiben** do sports

'Sport... in cpds ...ereignis, ...geschäft, ...hemd, ...verein, ...zentrum etc: mst sports ...; **~kleidung** f sportswear

'Sportler [ˈʃpɔrtlɐ] m (-s; -), **Sportlerin** [ˈʃpɔrtlərɪn] f (-; -nen) athlete

'sportlich adj athletic; casual, sporty

'Sport|nachrichten pl sports news; **~platz** m sports grounds; **~tauchen** n scuba diving; **~wagen** m stroller, Br pushchair; MOT sports car

Spott [ʃpɔt] m (-[e]s; no pl) mockery; derision

'spott'billig F adj dirt cheap

spotten [ˈʃpɔtən] v/i (ge-, h) mock (über acc at); scoff (at); make fun (of)

Spötter [ˈʃpœtɐ] m (-s; -) mocker, scoffer; **'spöttisch** adj mocking, derisive

'Spottpreis m: **für e-n ~** dirt cheap

sprach [ʃpraːx] pret of **sprechen**

Sprache [ˈʃpraːxə] f (-; -n) language (a. fig); speech; **zur ~ kommen (bringen)** come up (bring s.th. up)

'Sprach|fehler m speech defect; **~ge-brauch** m usage; **~la,bor** n language laboratory; **~lehre** f grammar; **~leh-rer(in)** language teacher

'sprachlich 1. adj language ...; **2.** adv: **~ richtig** grammatically correct

'sprachlos adj speechless

'Sprach|rohr fig n mouthpiece; **~unter-richt** m language teaching; **~wissen-schaft** f linguistics

sprang [ʃpraŋ] pret of **springen**

Spraydose [ˈʃpreː-] f spray can, aerosol (can)

Sprechanlage [ˈʃpreç-] f intercom

sprechen [ˈʃpreçən] v/t and v/i (irr, ge-, h) speak (**j-n, mit j-m** to s.o.); talk (to) (both: **über** acc, **von** about, of); **nicht zu ~ sein** be busy; **Sprecher(in)** [ˈʃpreçɐ (-çərɪn)] (-s; -/-; -nen) speaker; announcer; spokesman (spokes-woman); **'Sprechstunde** f office hours; MED office (Br consulting) hours, Br surgery; **'Sprechzimmer** n office, Br a. consulting room

spreizen [ˈʃpraitsən] v/t (ge-, h) spread

sprengen [ˈʃprɛŋən] v/t (ge-, h) blow up; blast; sprinkle; water; fig break up

'Sprengkopf m MIL warhead

'Sprengstoff m MIL explosive

'Sprengung f (-; -en) blasting; blowing up

sprenkeln [ˈʃprɛŋkəln] v/t (ge-, h) speck(le), dot

Spreu [ʃprɔy] f (-; no pl) chaff (a. fig)

Sprichwort [ˈʃpriç-] n proverb, saying

'sprichwörtlich adj proverbial (a. fig)

sprießen [ˈʃpriːsən] v/i (irr, ge-, sein) BOT sprout

'Springbrunnen m fountain

springen [ˈʃprɪŋən] v/i (irr, ge-, sein) jump, leap; **ball** etc: bounce; SPORT dive; **glass** etc: crack; break; burst; **in die Höhe (zur Seite) ~** jump up (aside)

Springer [ˈʃprɪŋɐ] m (-s; -) jumper; div-er; **chess**: knight

'Springflut f spring tide

'Springreiten n show jumping

Spritze [ˈʃprɪtsə] f (-; -n) MED injection, F shot; syringe; **'spritzen 1.** v/i and v/t (*ge-*, *h*) splash; spray (*a.* TECH, AGR); MED inject; give *s.o.* an injection (*of*); **2.** *v/i* (*ge-*, *sein*) spatter; gush (*aus* from); **Spritzer** ['ʃprɪtsɐ] *m* (*-s*; *-*) splash; dash

'Spritzpis,tole *f* TECH spray gun

'Spritztour F *f* MOT spin

spröde ['ʃprøːdə] *adj* brittle (*a.* fig); rough

spross [ʃprɔs] *pret of* **sprießen**

Sprosse ['ʃprɔsə] *f* (*-*; *-n*) rung

Spruch [ʃprʊx] *m* (*-[e]s*; *Sprüche* ['ʃprʏçəl]) saying; decision; ~**band** *n* banner

Sprudel ['ʃpruːdəl] *m* (*-s*; *-*) mineral water; '**sprudeln** *v/i* (*ge-*, *sein*) bubble

Sprühdose ['ʃpryː-] *f* spray can, aerosol (can); **sprühen** ['ʃpryːən] *v/t and v/i* (*ge-*, *h*) spray; throw out (*sparks*)

'Sprühregen *m* drizzle

Sprung [ʃprʊŋ] *m* (*-[e]s*; *Sprünge* ['ʃprʏŋəl]) jump, leap; SPORT dive; crack, fissure; ~**brett** *n* SPORT diving board; springboard; fig stepping stone; ~**schanze** *f* ski jump

Spucke ['ʃpʊkə] F *f* (*-*; *no pl*) spit

'spucken *v/i and v/t* (*ge-*, *h*) spit; F throw up

Spuk [ʃpuːk] *m* (*-[e]s*; *-e*) apparition, ghost; **spuken** ['ʃpuːkən] *v/i* (*ge-*, *h*) ~ *in* (*dat*) haunt; *hier spukt es* this place is haunted

Spule ['ʃpuːlə] *f* (*-*; *-n*) spool, reel; bobbin; ELECTR coil; '**spulen** *v/t* (*ge-*, *h*) spool, wind, reel

spülen ['ʃpyːlən] *v/t and v/i* (*ge-*, *h*) wash up, do the dishes; rinse; flush the toilet

'Spülma,schine *f* dishwasher

Spur [ʃpuːɐ] *f* (*-*; *-en*) track(s); trail; print; lane; trace (*a.* fig); *j-m auf der* ~ *sein* be on *s.o.*'s trail; **spüren** ['ʃpyːrən] *v/t* (*ge-*, *h*) feel, sense; notice

'spurlos *adv* without leaving a trace

'Spurweite *f* RAIL ga(u)ge; MOT track

St. ABBR *of* **Sankt** St, Saint

Staat [ʃtaːt] *m* (*-[e]s*; *-en*) state; POL government; '**Staatenbund** *m* confederacy, confederation; '**staatenlos** *adj* stateless; '**staatlich** 1. *adj* state ...; public, national; 2. *adv:* ~ *geprüft* qualified, registered

'Staats|angehörige *m*, *f* national, citizen, subject; ~**angehörigkeit** *f* (*-*; *no pl*) nationality; ~**anwalt** *m* JUR district

attorney, Br (public) prosecutor; ~**besuch** *m* official *or* state visit; ~**bürger(in)** citizen; ~**chef** *m* head of state; ~**dienst** *m* civil (*or* public) service

'staatseigen *adj* state-owned

'Staatsfeind *m* public enemy

'staatsfeindlich *adj* subversive

'Staats|haushalt *m* budget; ~**kasse** *f* treasury; ~**mann** *m* statesman; ~**oberhaupt** *n* head of (the) state; ~**sekre,tär(-in)** undersecretary of state; ~**streich** *m* coup d'état; ~**vertrag** *m* treaty; ~**wissenschaft** *f* political science

Stab [ʃtaːp] *m* (*-[e]s*; *Stäbe* ['ʃtɛːbə]) staff (*a.* fig); bar; SPORT, MUS baton; SPORT pole

Stäbchen ['ʃtɛːpçən] *pl* chopstick

'Stabhochsprung *m* SPORT pole vault

stabil [ʃtaˈbiːl] *adj* stable (*a.* ECON, POL); solid, strong; sound; **stabilisieren** [ʃtabiliˈziːrən] *v/t* (*no -ge-*, *h*) stabilize; **Stabilität** [-ˈtɛːt] *f* (*-*; *no pl*) stability

stach [ʃtax] *pret of* **stechen**

Stachel ['ʃtaxəl] *m* (*-s*; *-n*) BOT spine, prick; ZO sting; ~**beere** *f* BOT gooseberry; ~**draht** *m* barbed wire

stachelig ['ʃtaxəlɪç] *adj* prickly

'Stachelschwein *n* ZO porcupine

Stadel ['ʃtaːdəl] *Austrian m* (*-s*; *-[n]*) barn

Stadion ['ʃtaːdjɔn] *n* (*-s*; *-ien*) stadium

Stadium ['ʃtaːdjʊm] *n* (*-s*; *-ien*) stage, phase

Stadt [ʃtat] *f* (*-*; *Städte* ['ʃtɛːtə]) town; city; *die* ~ *Berlin* the city of Berlin; *in die* ~ *fahren* go downtown, *esp Br* go (in)to town; ~**bahn** *f* urban railway

Städter ['ʃtɛːtɐ] *m* (*-s*; *-*), '**Städterin** *f* (*-*; *-nen*) city dweller, F townie, *often contp* city slicker

'Stadt|gebiet *n* urban area; ~**gespräch** fig *n* talk of the town

städtisch ['ʃtɛːtɪʃ] *adj* urban; POL municipal

'Stadt|plan *m* city map; ~**rand** *m* outskirts; ~**rat** *m* town council; city council, *Br* town council(l)or; ~**rundfahrt** *f* sightseeing tour; ~**streicher(in)** city vagrant; ~**teil** *m*, ~**viertel** *n* quarter

Staffel ['ʃtafəl] *f* (*-*; *-n*) SPORT relay race *or* team; MIL, AVIAT squadron

Staffelei [ʃtafəˈlaɪ] *f* (*-*; *-en*) PAINT easel

'staffeln *v/t* (*ge-*, *h*) grade, scale

stahl [ʃtaːl] *pret of* **stehlen**

S

Stahl m (-[e]s; Stähle ['ʃtɛːlə]) steel
'**Stahlwerk** n steelworks
stak [ʃtaːk] pret of **stecken** 2
Stall [ʃtal] m (-[e]s; Ställe ['ʃtɛlə]) stable
'**Stallknecht** m stableman
Stamm [ʃtam] m (-[e]s; Stämme ['ʃtɛmə]) BOT stem (a. LING), trunk; tribe, stock; fig regulars; **~...** in cpds ...gast, ...kunde, ...spieler etc: regular ...; **~baum** m family tree; ZO pedigree
stammeln ['ʃtaməln] v/t (ge-, h) stammer
stammen ['ʃta.ən] v/i (ge-, h) **~ aus (von)** come from; be from; **~ von** work of art etc: be by
'**Stammformen** pl LING principal parts, mst tenses
stämmig ['ʃtɛmɪç] adj sturdy; stout
'**Stammkneipe** F f Br local
stampfen ['ʃtampfən] (ge-, h) **1.** v/t mash; **2.** v/i stamp (**mit dem Fuß** one's foot)
stand [ʃtant] pret of **stehen**
Stand m (-[e]s; Stände ['ʃtɛndə]) a) (no pl) stand(ing), standing or upright position; footing, foothold; ASTR position; TECH etc: height, level (a. fig); SPORT score; racing: standings; fig state; social standing, status, b) stand, stall, c) class; profession; **auf den neuesten ~ bringen** bring up to date; **e-n schweren ~ haben** have a hard time (of it); → **außerstande**; → **imstande**; → **instand**; → **zustande**
Standard ['ʃtandart] m (-s; -s) standard
'**Standbild** n statue
Ständchen ['ʃtɛntçən] n (-s; -) MUS serenade
Ständer ['ʃtɛndɐ] m (-s; -) stand; rack
Standesamt ['ʃtandəs-] n marriage license bureau, Br registry office; **standesamtlich** adj: **~e Trauung** civil marriage; '**Standesbeamt|e** m, **-in** f civil magistrate, Br registrar
'**Standfoto** n still
'**standhaft** adj steadfast, firm; **~ bleiben** resist temptation
'**standhalten** v/i (irr, halten, sep, -ge-, h) withstand, resist
ständig ['ʃtɛndɪç] adj constant; permanent (address)
'**Stand|licht** n (-[e]s; no pl) MOT parking light; **~ort** m position; location; MIL post, garrison; **~pauke** F f: **j-m e-e ~ halten** give s.o. a talking-to; **~platz**

m stand; **~punkt** m (point of) view, standpoint; **~recht** n (-[e]s; no pl) MIL martial law; **~spur** f MOT (Br hard) shoulder; **~uhr** f grandfather clock
Stange ['ʃtaŋə] f (-; -n) pole; staff; rod, bar; carton (of cigarettes)
Stängel ['ʃtɛŋəl] m (-s; -) BOT stalk, stem
stank [ʃtaŋk] pret of **stinken**
Stanniol [ʃta'njoːl] n (-s; -e) tin foil
Stanze ['ʃtantsə] f (-; -n), '**stanzen** v/t (ge-, h) TECH punch
Stapel ['ʃtaːpəl] m (-s; -) pile, stack; heap; **vom ~ lassen** MAR launch (a. fig); **vom ~ laufen** MAR be launched
'**Stapellauf** m MAR launch
'**stapeln** v/t (ge-, h) pile (up), stack
stapfen ['ʃtapfən] v/i (ge-, sein) trudge
Star [ʃtaːɐ] m (-[e]s; -e) ZO starling; MED cataract
Star² [ʃtaːɐ] m (-s; -s) THEA etc: star
starb [ʃtarp] pret of **sterben**
stark [ʃtark] **1.** adj strong (a. GASTR); powerful; fig heavy; F super, great; **2.** adv: **~ beeindruckt** greatly impressed; **~ beschädigt** badly damaged; **Stärke** ['ʃtɛrkə] f (-; -n) a) (no pl) strength, power; intensity, b) degree, c) CHEM starch; '**stärken** v/t (ge-, h) strengthen (a. fig); starch; **sich ~** take some refreshment; '**Starkstrom** m ELECTR high-voltage (or heavy) current; **Stärkung** f (-; -en) strengthening; refreshment; '**Stärkungsmittel** n MED tonic
starr [ʃtar] adj stiff; rigid (a. TECH); frozen (face); **~er Blick** (fixed) stare; **~ vor Kälte (Entsetzen)** frozen (scared) stiff; '**starren** v/i (ge-, h) stare (**auf** acc at); '**starrköpfig** [-kœpfɪç] adj stubborn, obstinate; '**Starrsinn** m (-[e]s; no pl) stubbornness, obstinacy
Start [ʃtart] m (-[e]s; -s) start (a. fig); AVIAT take-off; rocket: lift-off
'**Startbahn** f AVIAT runway
'**startbereit** adj ready to start; AVIAT ready for take-off
starten ['ʃtartən] v/i (ge-, sein) and v/t (ge-, h) start (a. F); AVIAT take-off; lift off; launch (a. fig)
Station [ʃta'tsjoːn] f (-; -en) station; MED ward; **stationär** [ʃtatsjo'nɛːɐ] adj: **~er Patient** MED in-patient; **stationieren** [ʃtatsjo'niːrən] v/t (no -ge-, h) MIL sta-

tion; deploy; **Stationsvorsteher** *m* RAIL stationmaster

Statist [ʃtaˈtɪst] *m* (*-en*; *-en*) THEA extra

Statistik [ʃtaˈtɪstɪk] *f* (*-*; *-en*) statistics; **Sta'tistiker** [-tikɐ] *m* (*-s*; *-*) statistician; **sta'tistisch** *adj* statistical

Stativ [ʃtaˈtiːf] *n* (*-s*; *-e*) PHOT tripod

statt [ʃtat] *prp* instead of; **~ et. zu tun** instead of doing s.th.; **~'dessen** instead

Stätte [ˈʃtɛtə] *f* (*-*; *-n*) place; scene

'stattfinden *v/i* (*irr, finden, sep, -ge-, h*) take place; happen

'stattlich *adj* imposing; handsome

Statue [ˈʃtaːtuə] *f* (*-*; *-n*) statue

Statur [ʃtaˈtuːɐ] *f* (*-*; *-en*) build

Status [ˈʃtaːtʊs] *m* (*-*; *-*) state; status; **~sym‚bol** *n* status symbol; **~zeile** *f* EDP status line

Stau [ʃtau] *m* (*-[e]s*; *-s, -e*) MOT traffic jam *or* congestion

Staub [ʃtaup] *m* (*-[e]s*; TECH *-e, Stäube* [ˈʃtɔybə]) dust (*a. ~ wischen*)

'Staubecken *n* reservoir

stauben [ˈʃtaubən] *v/i* (*ge-, h*) give off *or* make dust; **staubig** [ˈʃtaubɪç] *adj* dusty; **'staubsaugen** *v/i* and *v/t* (*ge-, h*) vacuum, F *Br* hoover; **'Staubsauger** *m* vacuum cleaner, F *Br* hoover; **'Staubtuch** *n* duster

'Staudamm *m* dam

Staude [ˈʃtaudə] *f* (*-*; *-n*) BOT herbacious plant

stauen [ˈʃtauən] *v/t* (*ge-, h*) dam up; **sich ~** MOT *etc* be stacked up

staunen [ˈʃtaunən] *v/i* (*ge-, h*) be astonished *or* surprised (*über acc* at)

Staunen *n* (*-s*; *no pl*) astonishment, amazement

Staupe [ˈʃtaupə] *f* (*-*; *-n*) VET distemper

'Stausee *m* reservoir

stechen [ˈʃtɛçən] *v/i* and *v/t* (*irr, ge-, h*) prick; ZO sting, bite; stab; pierce; **mit et. ~ in** (*acc*) stick s.th. in(to); **sich ~** prick o.s.; **~d** *fig adj* piercing (*look*); stabbing (*pain*)

'Stechuhr *f* time clock

Steckbrief [ˈʃtɛk-] *m* JUR "wanted" poster

'steckbrieflich *adv*: **er wird ~ gesucht** JUR a warrant is out against him

'Steckdose *f* ELECTR (wall) socket

stecken [ˈʃtɛkən] (*ge-, h*) **1.** *v/t* stick; put; *esp* TECH insert (*in acc* into); pin (*an acc*

to, on); AGR set, plant; **2.** *v/i* (*[irr]*) be; stick, be stuck; **~ bleiben** get stuck (*a. fig*)

'Steckenpferd *n* hobby horse; *fig* hobby

Stecker [ˈʃtɛkɐ] *m* (*-s*; *-*) ELECTR plug

'Steck|kon‚takt *m* ELECTR plug (connection); **~nadel** *f* pin; **~platz** *m* EDP slot

Steg [ʃteːk] *m* (*-[e]s*; *-e*) footbridge

Stegreif [ˈʃteːkraif] *m*: **aus dem ~** extempore, ad-lib; **aus dem ~ sprechen** *or* **spielen** *etc* extemporize, ad-lib

stehen [ˈʃteːən] *v/i* (*irr, ge-, h*) stand; be; stand up; **es steht ihr** it suits (*or* looks well on) her; **wie steht es** (*or* **das Spiel**)**?** what's the score?; **hier steht, dass** it says here that; **wo steht das?** where does it say so *or* that?; **sich gut (schlecht) ~** be well (badly) off; F **sich gut mit j-m ~** get along well with s.o.; **wie steht es mit ...?** what about ...?; F **darauf stehe ich** it turns me on; **~ bleiben** stop; *esp* TECH come to a standstill (*a. fig*); **~ lassen** leave (untouched); leave behind; **alles ~ und liegen lassen** drop everything; **sich e-n Bart ~ lassen** grow a beard

'Steh|kragen *m* stand-up collar; **~lampe** *f* floor (*Br* standard) lamp; **~leiter** *f* step ladder

stehlen [ˈʃteːlən] *v/t* and *v/i* (*irr, ge-, h*) steal (*a. fig sich ~*)

'Stehplatz *m* standing ticket; *pl* standing room

steif [ʃtaif] *adj* stiff (*vor dat* with)

Steigbügel [ˈʃtaik-] *m* stirrup

steigen [ˈʃtaigən] *v/i* (*irr, ge-, sein*) go, step; climb (*a.* AVIAT); *fig* rise, go up; **~ in** (*auf*) (*acc*) get on (*bus, bike etc*); **~ aus** (*von*) get off (*bus, horse etc*); **aus dem Bett ~** get out of bed

steigern [ˈʃtaigɐn] *v/t* (*ge-, h*) raise, increase; heighten; improve; LING compare; **sich ~** improve, get better

Steigerung [ˈʃtaigərʊŋ] *f* (*-*; *-en*) rise, increase; heightening; improvement; LING comparison

'Steigung *f* (*-*; *-en*) gradient; slope

steil [ʃtail] *adj* steep (*a. fig*)

Stein [ʃtain] *m* (*-[e]s*; *-e*) stone (*a.* BOT, MED), rock; **~bock** *m* ZO rock goat; ASTR Capricorn; **er ist (ein) ~** he's (a) Capricorn; **~bruch** *m* quarry

steinern ['ʃtainɐn] *adj* (of) stone; *fig* stony

'Steingut *n* (-[e]s; -e) earthenware

steinig ['ʃtainɪç] *adj* stony

steinigen ['ʃtainɪɡən] *v/t* (ge-, h) stone

'Steinkohle *f* (hard) coal

'Steinmetz [-mɛts] *m* (-en; -en) stone-mason

'Steinzeit *f* (-; *no pl*) Stone Age

Stellage [ʃtɛˈlaːʒə] *Austrian f* (-; -n) stand, rack, shelf

Stelle ['ʃtɛlə] *f* (-; -n) place; spot; point; job; authority; MATH figure; *freie ~* vacancy, opening; *auf der (zur)* ~ on the spot; *an erster ~ stehen (kommen)* be (come) first; *an j-s ~* in s.o.'s place; *ich an deiner ~* if I were you

'stellen *v/t* (ge-, h) put; set (*trap, clock, task etc*); turn (*up, down etc*); ask (*question*); provide; corner, hunt down (*criminal etc*); *sich ~* give o.s. up, turn o.s. in; *sich gegen (hinter) j-n ~ fig* oppose (back) s.o.; *sich schlafend etc* ~ pretend to be asleep *etc*; *stell dich dorthin!* (go and) stand over there!

'Stellen|angebot *n* vacancy; *ich habe ein ~* I was offered a job; **~anzeige** *f* job ad(vertisement), employment ad; **~gesuch** *n* application for a job

'stellenweise *adv* partly, in places

Stellung *f* (-; -en) position; post, job; *~ nehmen zu* comment on, give one's opinion of; **~nahme** [-naːmə] *f* (-; -n) comment, opinion (*both: zu* on)

'stellungslos *adj* unemployed, jobless

'stellvertretend *adj* acting, deputy, vice-...; **'Stellvertreter(in)** (-s; -/-; -nen) representative; deputy

Stelze ['ʃtɛltsə] *f* (-; -n) stilt

'stelzen *v/i* (ge-, sein) stalk

stemmen ['ʃtɛmən] *v/t* (ge-, h) lift (*weight*); *sich ~ gegen* press o.s. against; *fig* resist *or* oppose s.th.

Stempel ['ʃtɛmpəl] *m* (-s; -) stamp; postmark; hallmark; BOT pistil

'Stempelkissen *n* ink pad

'stempeln (ge-, h) **1.** *v/t* stamp; cancel; hallmark; **2.** F *v/i:* ~ *gehen* be on the dole

Stengel → **Stängel**

Stenografie [ʃtenograˈfiː] *f* (-; -n) shorthand; **stenograˈfieren** *v/t* (*no* ge-, h) take down in shorthand

Stenogramm [ʃtenoˈɡram] *n* (-[e]s; -e) shorthand notes; **Stenotypistin** [-tyˈpɪstɪn] *f* (-; -nen) shorthand typist

Steppdecke ['ʃtɛp-] *f* quilt; **steppen** ['ʃtɛpən] (ge-, h) **1.** *v/t* quilt; stitch; **2.** *v/i* tap dance; **Stepptanz** *m* tap dancing

Sterbebett ['ʃtɛrbə-] *n* deathbed

'Sterbeklinik *f* MED hospice

sterben ['ʃtɛrbən] *v/i* (*irr*, ge-, sein) die (*an dat* of) (*a. fig*); *im Sterben liegen* be dying

sterblich ['ʃtɛrplɪç] *adj* mortal

'Sterblichkeit *f* (-; *no pl*) mortality

Stereo ['ʃteːreo] *n* (-s; -s) stereo

steril [ʃteˈriːl] *adj* sterile; **Sterilisation** [ʃteriliˈza'tsjoːn] *f* (-; -en) sterilization; **sterilisieren** [ʃteriliˈziːrən] *v/t* (*no* ge-, h) sterilize

Stern [ʃtɛrn] *m* (-[e]s; -e) star (*a. fig*)

'Sternbild *n* ASTR constellation; sign of the zodiac

'Sternchen *n* (-s; -) PRINT asterisk

'Sternenbanner *n* Star-Spangled Banner, Stars and Stripes

'Sternenhimmel *m* starry sky

'sternklar *adj* starry

'Stern|kunde *f* (-; *no pl*) astronomy; **~schnuppe** *f* (-; -n) shooting *or* falling star; **~warte** *f* (-; -n) observatory

stetig ['ʃteːtɪç] *adj* continual, constant; steady; **stets** [ʃteːts] *adv* always

Steuer[1] ['ʃtɔʏɐ] *n* (-s; -) MOT (steering) wheel; MAR helm, rudder

Steuer[2] *f* (-; -n) tax (*auf acc* on)

'Steuer|beamte *m* revenue officer; **~berater** *m* tax adviser

'Steuerbord *n* MAR starboard

'Steuer|erklärung *f* tax return; **~ermäßigung** *f* tax allowance

steuerfrei *adj* tax-free

'Steuerhinterziehung *f* tax evasion

'Steuer|knüppel *m* AVIAT control column *or* stick; **~mann** *m* MAR helmsman; *rowing:* cox, coxswain

'steuern *v/t and v/i* (ge-, h) steer, AVIAT, MAR *a.* navigate, pilot, MOT *a.* drive; TECH control (*a. fig*); *fig* direct

'steuerpflichtig *adj* taxable

'Steuerrad *n* MOT steering wheel

'Steuerruder *n* MAR helm, rudder

'Steuersenkung *f* tax reduction

Steuerung ['ʃtɔʏərʊŋ] *f* (-; -en) steering (system); ELECTR, TECH control (*a. fig*)

'**Steuerzahler** *m*, '**Steuerzahlerin** *f* taxpayer

Stich [ʃtɪç] *m* (-[e]s; -e) prick; ZO sting, bite; stab; stitch; *cards:* trick; engraving; *im ~ lassen* desert *or* abandon *s.o., s.th.*, leave *s.o.* in the lurch, let *s.o.* down

Stichelei [ʃtɪçə'laɪ] F *f* (-; -en) dig, gibe

sticheln ['ʃɪçəln] F *v/i* (ge-, h) make digs, gibe (*gegen* at)

'**Stichflamme** *f* jet of flame

'**stichhaltig** *adj* valid, sound; watertight; *nicht ~ sein* F not hold water

'**Stich**|**probe** *f* spot check; **~tag** *m* cutoff date; deadline; **~wahl** *f* POL run-off; **~wort** *n* a) (-[e]s; -e) THEA cue, b) (-[e]s; -wörter) headword; **~e** *pl* notes; *das Wichtigste in ~en* an outline of the main points; **~wortverzeichnis** *n* index; **~wunde** *f* MED stab

sticken ['ʃtɪkən] *v/t and v/i* (ge-, h) embroider; **Stickerei** [ʃtɪkə'raɪ] *f* (-; -en) embroidery

stickig ['ʃtɪkɪç] *adj* stuffy

'**Stickstoff** *m* (-[e]s; *no pl*) CHEM nitrogen

Stief... [ʃtiːf-] *in cpds ...mutter etc:* step...

Stiefel ['ʃtiːfəl] *m* (-s; -) boot

'**Stiefmütterchen** [-mʏtçən] *n* (-s; -) BOT pansy

stieg [ʃtiːk] *pret of* **steigen**

Stiege ['ʃtiːgə] *Austrian f* (-; -n) → **Treppe**

Stiel [ʃtiːl] *m* (-[e]s; -e) handle; stick; stem; BOT stalk

Stier [ʃtiːɐ] *m* (-[e]s; -e) ZO bull; ASTR Taurus; *er ist (ein) ~* he's a(n) Taurus

'**Stierkampf** *m* bullfight

stieß [ʃtiːs] *pret of* **stoßen**

Stift [ʃtɪft] *m* (-[e]s; -e) pen; pencil; crayon; TECH pin; peg

stiften ['ʃtɪftən] *v/t* (ge-, h) donate; *fig* cause; '**Stiftung** *f* (-; -en) donation

Stil [ʃtiːl] *m* (-[e]s; -e) style (*a. fig*); *in großem ~* in (grand) style; *fig* on a large scale; **stilistisch** [ʃti'lɪstɪʃ] *adj* stylistic

still [ʃtɪl] *adj* quiet, silent; still; *sei(d) ~!* be quiet!; *halt ~!* keep still!; *sich ~ verhalten* keep quiet (*or* still)

Stille ['ʃtɪlə] *f* (-; *no pl*) silence, quiet (-ness); *in aller ~* quietly; secretly

Stilleben *n* → **Stillleben**

stillen ['ʃtɪlən] *v/t* (ge-, h) nurse, breast-feed; *fig* relieve (*pain*); satisfy (*curiosity etc*); quench (*one's thirst*)

'**Stillleben** *n* PAINT still life

'**stillhalten** *v/i* (*irr*, **halten**, sep, -ge-, h) keep still

'**stilllegen** *v/t* (sep, -ge-, h) close down

'**stillos** *adj* lacking style, tasteless

'**stillschweigend** *adj* tacit

'**Stillstand** *m* (-[e]s; *no pl*) standstill, stop, *fig a.* stagnation (*a.* ECON); deadlock; '**stillstehen** *v/i* (*irr*, **stehen**, sep, -ge-, h) (have) stop(ped), (have) come to a standstill

'**Stilmöbel** *pl* period furniture

'**stilvoll** *adj* stylish; *~ sein* have style

'**Stimmband** *n* ANAT vocal cord

'**stimmberechtigt** *adj* entitled to vote

Stimme ['ʃtɪmə] *f* (-; -n) voice; POL vote; *sich der ~ enthalten* abstain

stimmen ['ʃtɪmən] (ge-, h) **1.** *v/i* be right, be true, be correct; POL vote (*für* for; *gegen* against); *es stimmt et. nicht* (*damit or mit ihm*) there's s.th. wrong (with it *or* him); **2.** *v/t* MUS tune; *j-n traurig ~* make s.o. sad *etc*

'**Stimmenthaltung** *f* abstention

'**Stimmrecht** *n* right to vote

Stimmung *f* (-; -en) mood; atmosphere; feeling

'**stimmungsvoll** *adj* atmospheric

'**Stimmzettel** *m* ballot (paper)

stinken ['ʃtɪŋkən] *v/i* (*irr*, ge-, h) stink (*a. fig*) (*nach* of)

Stipendium [ʃti'pɛndjʊm] *n* (-s; -ien) UNIV scholarship, grant

stippen ['ʃtɪpən] *v/t* (ge-, h) dip

'**Stippvi,site** F *f* flying visit

Stirn [ʃtɪrn] *f* (-; -en) ANAT forehead; *die ~ runzeln* frown

stöbern ['ʃtøːbɐn] F *v/i* (ge-, h) rummage (about)

stochern ['ʃtɔxɐn] *v/i* (ge-, h) *im Feuer ~* poke the fire; *im Essen ~* pick at one's food; *in den Zähnen ~* pick one's teeth

Stock [ʃtɔk] *m* (-[e]s; Stöcke ['ʃtœkə]) stick; cane; ARCH stor(e)y, floor; *im ersten ~* on the second (*Br* first) floor

'**stock**|**dunkel** F *adj* pitch-dark

stocken ['ʃtɔkən] *v/i* (ge-, h) stop (short); falter; *traffic:* be jammed; **~d 1.** *adj* halting; **2.** *adv:* ~ *lesen* stumble through a text; ~ *sprechen* speak haltingly

'**Stockfleck** *m* mo(u)ld stain

'Stockung f (-; -en) holdup, delay

'Stockwerk n stor(e)y, floor

Stoff [ʃtɔf] m (-[e]s; -e) material, stuff (a. F); fabric, textile; cloth; CHEM, PHYS etc substance; fig subject (matter)

'stofflich adj material

'Stofftier n soft toy animal

'Stoffwechsel m BIOL metabolism

stöhnen ['ʃtøːnən] v/i (ge-, h) groan, moan (a. fig)

Stollen ['ʃtɔlən] m (-s; -) tunnel, gallery

stolpern ['ʃtɔlpərn] v/i (ge-, sein) stumble (**über** acc over), trip (over) (both a. fig)

stolz [ʃtɔlts] adj proud (**auf** acc of)

Stolz m (-es; no pl) pride (**auf** acc in)

stolzieren [ʃtɔl'tsiːrən] v/i (no -ge-, sein) strut, stalk

stopfen ['ʃtɔpfən] v/t (ge-, h) darn, mend; stuff, fill (a. pipe)

Stoppel ['ʃtɔpəl] f (-; -n) stubble

'Stoppelbart m stubbly beard

'stoppelig adj stubbly, bristly

'Stoppelzieher Austrian m corkscrew

stoppen ['ʃtɔpən] v/t and v/i (ge-, h) stop (a. fig); esp SPORT time

'Stopp|licht n (-[e]s; -er) MOT stop light; ~schild n stop sign; ~uhr f stopwatch

Stöpsel ['ʃtœpsəl] m (-s; -) stopper; plug

Storch [ʃtɔrç] m (-[e]s; Störche ['ʃtœrçə]) ZO stork

stören ['ʃtøːrən] v/t and v/i (ge-, h) disturb; trouble; bother, annoy; be in the way; **lassen Sie sich nicht ~!** don't let me disturb you!; **darf ich Sie kurz ~?** may I trouble you for a minute?; **es (er) stört mich nicht** it (he) doesn't bother me, I don't mind (him); **stört es Sie(, wenn ich rauche)?** do you mind (my smoking or if I smoke)?

'Störenfried [-friːt] m (-[e]s; -e) troublemaker; intruder

Störfall ['ʃtøːr-] m TECH accident

störrisch ['ʃtœrɪʃ] adj stubborn, obstinate

'Störung f (-; -en) disturbance; trouble (a. TECH); TECH breakdown; TV, radio: interference

Stoß [ʃtoːs] m (-es; Stöße ['ʃtøːsə]) push, shove; thrust; kick; butt; blow, knock; shock; MOT jolt; bump, esp TECH, PHYS impact; pile, stack; **'Stoßdämpfer** m MOT shock absorber; **stoßen** ['ʃtoːsən] v/t (irr, ge-, h) and v/i (sein) push, shove; thrust; kick; butt; knock, strike; pound;

~ gegen or **an** (acc) bump or run into or against; **sich den Kopf ~ (an** dat) knock one's head (against); **~ auf** (acc) strike (oil etc); fig come across; meet with; **'stoßgesichert** adj shockproof, shock-resistant; **'Stoßstange** f MOT bumper; **'Stoßzahn** m ZO tusk; **'Stoßzeit** f rush hour, peak hours

stottern ['ʃtɔtərn] v/i and v/t (ge-, h) stutter

Str. ABBR of **Straße** St, Street; Rd, Road

'Strafanstalt f prison, penitentiary; **'strafbar** adj punishable, penal; **sich ~ machen** commit an offense (Br offence); **Strafe** ['ʃtraːfə] f (-; -n) punishment; JUR, ECON, SPORT penalty (a. fig); fine; **20 Mark ~ zahlen müssen** be fined 20 marks; **zur ~** as a punishment; **'strafen** v/t (ge-, h) punish

straff [ʃtraf] adj tight; fig strict

'straffrei adj: **~ ausgehen** go unpunished

'Straf|gefangene m, f prisoner, convict; **~gesetz** n criminal law

sträflich ['ʃtrɛːflɪç] **1.** adj inexcusable; **2.** adv: **~ vernachlässigen** neglect badly

'Straf|mi,nute f SPORT penalty minute; **~pro,zess** m JUR criminal action, trial; **~raum** m SPORT penalty area (F box); **~stoß** m SPORT penalty kick; **~tat** f JUR criminal offense (Br offence); crime; **~zettel** m ticket

Strahl [ʃtraːl] m (-[e]s; -en) ray (a. fig); beam; flash; jet; **strahlen** ['ʃtraːlən] v/i (ge-, h) radiate; shine (brightly); fig beam (**vor** with); **'Strahlen...** in cpds PHYS ...schutz etc: radiation ...

'Strahlung f (-; -en) PHYS radiation

Strähne ['ʃtrɛːnə] f (-; -n) strand; streak

stramm [ʃtram] adj tight; **~stehen** MIL stand to attention

strampeln ['ʃtrampəln] v/i (ge-, h) kick

Strand [ʃtrant] m (-[e]s; Strände ['ʃtrɛndə]) beach; **am ~** on the beach

stranden ['ʃtrandən] v/i (ge-, sein) MAR strand; fig fail

'Strand|gut n flotsam and jetsam (a. fig), **~korb** m roofed wicker beach chair

Strang [ʃtraŋ] m (-[e]s; Stränge ['ʃtrɛŋə]) rope; esp ANAT cord

Strapaze [ʃtra'paːtsə] f (-; -n) strain, exertion, hardship; **strapazieren** [ʃtrapa'tsiːrən] v/t (no -ge-, h) wear s.o. or s.th. out, be hard on; **strapazierfähig** *adj* longwearing, *Br* hardwearing

strapaziös [ʃtrapa'tsjøːs] *adj* strenuous

Straße ['ʃtraːsə] *f* (-; -n) road; street; GEOGR strait; **auf der ~** on the road; on (*Br a.* in) the street

'**Straßen|arbeiten** *pl* roadworks; **~bahn** *f* streetcar, *Br* tram; **~ca,fé** *n* sidewalk (*Br* pavement) café; **~karte** *f* road map; **~kehrer** [-keːrə] *m* (-*s*; -) street sweeper; **~kreuzung** *f* crossroads; intersection; **~lage** *f* MOT roadholding; **~rand** *m* roadside; **am ~** at or by the roadside; **~sperre** *f* road block

strategisch [ʃtra'teːgɪʃ] *adj* strategic

sträuben ['ʃtrɔybən] *v/t and v/refl* (*ge-*, *h*) ruffle (up); bristle (up); **sich ~ gegen** struggle against

Strauch [ʃtraux] *m* (-[*e*]*s*; Sträucher ['ʃtrɔyçɐ]) BOT shrub, bush

straucheln ['ʃtrauxəln] *v/i* (*ge-*, *sein*) stumble

Strauß[1] ['ʃtraus] *m* (-*es*; -*e*) ZO ostrich

Strauß[2] *m* (-*es*; Sträuße ['ʃtrɔysə]) bunch, bouquet

Strebe ['ʃtreːbə] *f* (-; -*n*) prop, stay (*a.* AVIAT, MAR); '**streben** *v/i* (*ge-*, *h*) strive (**nach** for, after); **Streber** ['ʃtreːbə] *m* (-*s*; -) pusher; PED *etc* grind, *Br* swot; **strebsam** ['ʃtreːp-] *adj* ambitious

Strecke ['ʃtrɛkə] *f* (-; -*n*) distance (*a.* SPORT, MATH); route; RAIL line; SPORT course; stretch; **zur ~ bringen** kill; *esp fig* hunt down; '**strecken** *v/t* (*ge-*, *h*) stretch (out), extend

Streich [ʃtraiç] *m* (-[*e*]*s*; -*e*) trick, prank, practical joke; **j-m e-n ~ spielen** play a trick *or* joke on s.o.

streicheln ['ʃtraiçəln] *v/t* (*ge-*, *h*) stroke, caress

streichen ['ʃtraiçən] *v/t and v/i* (*irr*, *ge-*, *h*) paint; spread; cross out; cancel; MAR strike; MUS bow; **mit der Hand ~ über** (*acc*) run one's hand over; **~ durch** roam (*acc*); **Streicher(in)** ['ʃtraiçɐ (-çərɪn)] (-*s*; -/-; -*nen*) MUS string player, *pl the* strings

'**Streich|holz** *n* match; **~instru,ment** *n* MUS string instrument; **~or,chester** *n* MUS string orchestra

'**Streichung** *f* (-; -*en*) cancellation; cut

Streife ['ʃtraifə] *f* (-; -*n*) patrol; **auf ~ gehen** go on patrol; **auf ~ sein in** (*dat*) patrol

'**streifen** *v/t and v/i* (*ge-*, *h*) touch, brush (against); MOT scrape against; graze; slip (**von** off); *fig* touch on; **~ durch** roam (*acc*), wander through

'**Streifen** *m* (-*s*; -) stripe; strip

'**Streifenwagen** *m* squad (*Br* patrol) car

'**Streifschuss** *m* MED graze

'**Streifzug** *m* tour (**durch** of)

Streik [ʃtraik] *m* (-[*e*]*s*; -*s*) strike, walkout; **wilder ~** wildcat strike

'**Streikbrecher** *m* strikebreaker, *Br* blackleg, *contp* scab

streiken ['ʃtraikən] *v/i* (*ge-*, *h*) (go *or* be on) strike; *F fig* refuse (to work *etc*)

'**Streikende** *m*, *f* (-*n*; -*n*) striker

'**Streikposten** *m* picket

Streit [ʃtrait] *m* (-[*e*]*s*; -*e*) quarrel; argument; fight; POL *etc* dispute; **~ anfangen** pick a fight *or* quarrel; **~ suchen** be looking for trouble; **streiten** ['ʃtraitən] *v/i and v/refl* (*irr*, *ge-*, *h*) quarrel, argue, fight (*all*: **wegen**, **über** *acc* about, over); **sich ~ um** fight for

'**Streitfrage** *f* (point at) issue

streitig ['ʃtraitɪç] *adj*: **j-m et. ~ machen** dispute s.o.'s right to s.th.

'**Streitkräfte** *pl* MIL (armed) forces

'**streitsüchtig** *adj* quarrelsome

streng [ʃtrɛŋ] *adj* strict; severe; harsh; rigid; **~ genommen** strictly speaking

Strenge ['ʃtrɛŋə] *f* (-; *no pl*) strictness; severity; harshness; rigidity

'**strenggläubig** *adj* REL orthodox

Stress [ʃtrɛs] *m* (-*es*; *no pl*) stress; **im ~** under stress

Streu [ʃtrɔy] *f* (-; -*en*) AGR litter

'**streuen** *v/t and v/i* (*ge-*, *h*) scatter (*a.* PHYS); spread; sprinkle; grit

streunen ['ʃtrɔynən] *v/i* (*ge-*, *sein*), **~d** *adj* stray

strich [ʃtrɪç] *pret of* **streichen**

Strich *m* (-[*e*]*s*; -*e*) line; stroke; F redlight district; F **auf den ~ gehen** walk the streets; **~kode** *m* bar code; **~junge** F *m* male prostitute

'**strichweise** *adv* in parts; **~ Regen** scattered showers

Strick [ʃtrɪk] *m* (-[*e*]*s*; -*e*) cord; rope

stricken ['ʃtrɪkən] *v/t and v/i* (*ge-*, *h*) knit

'**Strick|jacke** *f* cardigan; **~leiter** *f* rope ladder; **~nadel** *f* knitting needle; **~waren** *pl* knitwear; **~zeug** *n* knitting (things)

S

Striemen ['ʃtriːmən] m (-s; -) welt, weal

stritt [ʃtrɪt] pret of **streiten**

strittig ['ʃtrɪtɪç] adj controversial; **~er Punkt** point at issue

Stroh [ʃtroː] n (-[e]s; no pl) straw; thatch; **~dach** n thatch(ed) roof; **~halm** m straw; **~hut** m straw hat; **~witwe** F f grass widow; **~witwer** F m grass widower

Strom [ʃtroːm] m (-[e]s; Ströme ['ʃtrøːmə]) (large) river; current (a. ELECTR); **ein ~ von** a stream of (a. fig); **es gießt in Strömen** it's pouring (with rain)

strom'ab(wärts) adv downstream

strom'auf(wärts) adv upstream

'Stromausfall m ELECTR power failure, blackout

strömen ['ʃtrøːmən] v/i (ge-, sein) stream (a. fig), flow, run; pour (a. fig)

'Stromkreis m ELECTR circuit

'stromlinienförmig adj streamlined

'Stromschnelle f (-; -n) GEOGR rapid

'Stromstärke f ELECTR amperage

'Strömung f (-; -en) current, fig a. trend

Strophe ['ʃtroːfə] f (-; -n) stanza, verse

strotzen ['ʃtrɔtsən] v/i (ge-, h) **~ von** be full of, abound with; **~ vor** (dat) be bursting with

Strudel ['ʃtruːdəl] m (-s; -) whirlpool (a. fig), eddy

Struktur [ʃtrʊk'tuːɐ] f (-; -en) structure, pattern

Strumpf [ʃtrʊmpf] m (-[e]s; Strümpfe ['ʃtrʏmpfə]) stocking

'Strumpfhose f pantyhose, Br tights

struppig ['ʃtrʊpɪç] adj shaggy

Stück [ʃtʏk] n (-[e]s; -e) piece; part; lump; AGR head (a. pl); THEA play; **2 Mark das ~** 2 marks each; **im** or **am ~** in one piece; **in ~e schlagen** (rei-ßen) smash (tear) to pieces; **'stückwei-se** adv bit by bit (a. fig); ECON by the piece

Student [ʃtu'dɛnt] m (-en; -en), **Stu-'dentin** f (-; -nen) student; **Studie** ['ʃtuːdjə] f (-; -n) study (**über** acc of); **'Studienplatz** m university or college place; **studieren** [ʃtu'diːrən] v/t and v/i (no -ge-, h) study, be a student (of) (**an** dat at); **Studium** ['ʃtuːdjum] n (-s; -ien) studies; **das ~ der Medizin** etc the study of medicine etc

Stufe ['ʃtuːfə] f (-; -n) step; level; stage

'Stufenbarren m SPORT uneven parallel bars

Stuhl [ʃtuːl] m (-[e]s; Stühle ['ʃtyːlə]) chair; MED stool; **~gang** m (-[e]s; no pl) MED (bowel) movement; **~lehne** f back of a chair

stülpen ['ʃtʏlpən] v/t (ge-, h) put (**auf** acc, **über** acc over, on)

stumm [ʃtʊm] adj dumb, mute; fig silent

Stummel ['ʃtʊməl] m (-s; -) stub, stump, butt

'Stummfilm m silent film

Stümper ['ʃtʏmpɐ] F m (-s; -) bungler

stumpf [ʃtʊmpf] adj blunt, dull (a. fig)

Stumpf m (-[e]s; Stümpfe ['ʃtʏmpfə]) stump, stub

'stumpfsinnig adj dull; monotonous

Stunde ['ʃtʊndə] f (-; -n) hour; PED class, lesson; period

'Stundenkilo,meter m kilometer (Br kilometre) per hour

'stundenlang 1. adj: **nach ~em Warten** after hours of waiting; **2.** adv for hours (and hours)

'Stunden|lohn m hourly wage; **~plan** m schedule, Br timetable

'stundenweise adv by the hour

'Stundenzeiger m hour hand

stündlich ['ʃtʏntlɪç] **1.** adj hourly; **2.** adv hourly, every hour

Stupsnase ['ʃtʊps-] F f snub nose

stur [ʃtuːɐ] F adj pigheaded

Sturm [ʃtʊrm] m (-[e]s; Stürme ['ʃtʏrmə]) storm (a. fig); **stürmen** ['ʃtʏrmən] v/t or v/i (ge-, h) and v/i (ge-, sein) storm; SPORT attack; rush; **Stürmer(in)** ['ʃtʏrmɐ (-mərɪn)] (-s; -/-; -nen) SPORT forward; esp soccer: striker; **stürmisch** ['ʃtʏrmɪʃ] adj stormy; fig wild, vehement

Sturz [ʃtʊrts] m (-es; Stürze ['ʃtʏrtsə]) fall (a. fig), POL etc: overthrow

stürzen ['ʃtʏrtsən] **1.** v/i (ge-, sein) fall; crash; rush; dash; **schwer ~** have a bad fall; **2.** v/t (ge-, h) throw; POL etc: overthrow; **j-n ins Unglück ~** ruin s.o.; **sich ~ stürzen aus** throw o.s. out of; **sich ~ auf** (acc) throw o.s. at

'Sturzflug m AVIAT nosedive

'Sturzhelm m crash helmet

Stute ['ʃtuːtə] f (-; -n) ZO mare

Stütze ['ʃtʏtsə] f (-; -n) support, prop; fig a. aid

stutzen ['ʃtʊtsən] (ge-, h) **1.** v/t trim, clip;

2. v/i stop short; (begin to) wonder

stützen ['ʃtʏtsən] v/t (ge-, h) support (a. fig); **sich ~ auf** (acc) lean on; fig be based on

'**Stütz|pfeiler** m ARCH supporting column; **~punkt** m MIL base (a. fig)

Styropor® [ʃtyro'poːɐ] n (-s; no pl) Styrofoam®, Br polystyrene

s.u. ABBR of **siehe unten** see below

Subjekt [zʊp'jɛkt] n (-[e]s; -e) LING subject; contp character

subjektiv [zʊpjɛk'tiːf] adj subjective

Substantiv ['zʊpstanti:f] n (-s; -e) LING noun

Substanz [zʊp'stants] f (-; -en) substance (a. fig)

subtrahieren [zʊptra'hiːrən] v/t (no -ge-, h) MATH subtract; **Subtraktion** [zʊptrak'tsjoːn] f (-; -en) MATH subtraction

subventionieren [zʊpvɛntsjo'niːrən] v/t (no -ge-, h) subsidize

Suche ['zuːxə] f (-; no pl) search (**nach** for); **auf der ~ nach** in search of; '**suchen** v/t and v/i (ge-, h) look for; search for; **gesucht: ...** wanted: ...; **was hat er hier zu ~?** what's he doing here?; **er hat hier nichts zu ~** he has no business to be here; **Sucher** ['zuːxɐ] m (-s; -) PHOT viewfinder

Sucht [zʊxt] f (-; Süchte ['zʏçtə]) addiction (**nach** to); mania (for); **süchtig** ['zʏçtɪç] adj: **~ sein** be addicted to drugs etc, be a drug etc addict; **Süchtige** ['zʏçtɪgə] m, f (-n; -n) addict

Süden ['zyːdən] m (-s; no pl) south; **nach ~** south(wards)

Südfrüchte ['zyːt-] pl tropical or southern fruits

'**südlich 1.** adj south(ern); southerly; **2.** adv: **~ von** (to the) south of

Süd|osten m southeast; **süd'östlich** adj southeast(ern); southeasterly

'**Südpol** m South Pole

'**südwärts** [-vɛrts] adv southward(s)

Süd|westen m southwest; **süd'westlich** adj southwest(ern); southwesterly

'**Südwind** m south wind

Sülze ['zʏltsə] f (-; -n) GASTR jellied meat

Summe ['zʊmə] f (-; -n) sum (a. fig); amount; (sum) total

summen ['zʊmən] v/i and v/t (ge-, h) buzz, hum

summieren [zʊ'miːrən] v/refl (no -ge-, h) add up (**auf** acc to)

Sumpf [zʊmpf] m (-es; Sümpfe ['zʏmpfə]) swamp, bog

'**sumpfig** adj swampy, marshy

Sünde ['zʏndə] f (-; -n) sin (a. fig)

'**Sündenbock** F m scapegoat

Sünder ['zʏndɐ] m (-s; -), '**Sünderin** f (-; -nen) sinner

sündig ['zʏndɪç] adj sinful; **sündigen** ['zʏndɪgən] v/i (ge-, h) (commit a) sin

Super... ['zuːpɐ-] in cpds ...macht etc: mst super...

'**Super** n (-s; no pl), **~ben,zin** n super or premium (gasoline), Br four-star (petrol)

Superlativ ['zuːpɐlatiːf] m (-s; -e) LING superlative (a. fig)

'**Supermarkt** m supermarket

Suppe ['zʊpə] f (-; -n) soup

'**Suppen...** in cpds ...löffel, ...teller, ...küche etc: soup ...

Surfbrett ['zœːɐf-] n sail board; surfboard; '**surfen** v/i (ge-, h) go surfing

surren ['zʊrən] v/i (ge-, h) whirr; buzz

süß [zyːs] adj sweet, sugary (both a. fig)

Süße ['zyːsə] f (-; no pl) sweetness

'**süßen** v/t (ge-, h) sweeten

Süßigkeiten ['zyːsɪçkaitən] pl sweets, candy

'**süßlich** adj sweetish; contp mawkish, sugary

'**süß'sauer** adj GASTR sweet-and-sour

'**Süßstoff** m sweetener

'**Süßwasser** n fresh water

Symbol [zʏm'boːl] n (-s; -e) symbol; **Symbolik** [zʏm'boːlɪk] f (-; no pl) symbolism; **sym'bolisch** adj symbolic(al)

Symmetrie [zʏme'triː] f (-; -n) symmetry; **symmetrisch** [zʏ'meːtrɪʃ] adj symmetric(al)

Sympathie [zʏmpa'tiː] f (-; -n) liking (**für** for); sympathy; **Sympathisant(in)** [zʏmpati'zant(ɪn)] (-en; -en/-; -nen) sympathizer; **sympathisch** [zʏm'paːtɪʃ] adj nice, likable; **er ist mir ~** I like him

Symphonie [zʏmfo'niː] f (-; -n) etc → **Sinfonie**

Symptom [zʏmp'toːm] n (-s; -e) symptom

Synagoge [zyna'goːgə] f (-; -n) synagogue

synchron [zʏn'kroːn] adj TECH synchro-

nous; **synchronisieren** [zʏnkroni-'ziːrən] *v/t* (*no -ge-, h*) synchronize; *film etc:* dub
synonym [zyno'nyːm] *adj* synonymous
Syno|nym *n* (*-s; -e*) synonym
Synthese [zʏn'teːzə] *f* (*-; -n*) synthesis
synthetisch [zʏn'teːtɪʃ] *adj* synthetic

System [zʏs'teːm] *n* (*-s; -e*) system
systematisch [zʏste'maːtɪʃ] *adj* systematic, methodical
Sys'temfehler *m* EDP system error
Szene ['stseːnə] *f* (*-; -n*) scene (*a. fig*)
Szenerie [stsenə'riː] *f* (*-; -n*) scenery; setting

T

Tabak ['taːbak] *m* (*-s; -e*) tobacco; **~geschäft** *n* tobacconist's; **~waren** *pl* tobacco products
Tabelle [ta'bɛlə] *f* (*-; -n*) table (*a.* MATH, SPORT)
Ta'bellen|kalkulati,on *f* EDP spreadsheet; **~platz** *m* SPORT position
Tablett [ta'blɛt] *n* (*-[e]s; -s*) tray
Tablette [ta'blɛtə] *f* (*-; -n*) tablet
tabu [ta'buː] *adj,* **Ta'bu** *n* (*-s; -s*) taboo
Tabulator [tabu'laːtoːɐ] *m* (*-s; -en* [-la'toːrən]) tabulator
Tachometer [taxo'meːtɐ] *m, n* (*-s; -*) MOT speedometer
Tadel ['taːdəl] *m* (*-s; -*) blame; censure, reproof, rebuke; **'tadellos** *adj* faultless; blameless; excellent; perfect
'tadeln *v/t* (*ge-, h*) criticize, blame; censure, reprove, rebuke (*all:* **wegen** for)
Tafel ['taːfəl] *f* PED *etc:* blackboard; (bulletin, *esp Br* notice) board; sign; tablet, plaque; GASTR bar (*of chocolate*)
täfeln ['tɛːfəln] *v/t* (*ge-, h*) panel
'Täfelung *f* (*-; -en*) panel(l)ing
Taft [taft] *m* (*-[e]s; -e*) taffeta
Tag [taːk] *m* (*-[e]s; -e* ['taːgə]) day; daylight; **welchen ~ haben wir heute?** what day is it today?; **heute** (**morgen**) **in 14 ~en** two weeks from today (tomorrow); **e-s ~es** one day; **den ganzen ~** all day; **am ~e** during the day; **~ und Nacht** night and day; **am helllichten ~** in broad daylight; **ein freier ~** a day off; **guten ~!** hello!, hi!; how do you do?; (*j-m*) **guten ~ sagen** say hello (to s.o.); F **sie hat ihre ~e** she has her period; **unter ~e** underground; → **zutage**
Tage|bau ['taːgə-] *m* (*-[e]s; -e*) opencast

mining; **~buch** *n* diary; **~ führen** keep a diary
'tagelang *adv* for days
'tagen *v/i* (*ge-, h*) meet, hold a meeting; JUR be in session
'Tages|anbruch *m:* **bei ~** at daybreak, at dawn; **~gespräch** *n* talk of the day; **~karte** *f* day ticket; GASTR menu for the day; **~licht** *n* (*-[e]s; no pl*) daylight; **~mutter** *f* childminder; **~ordnung** *f* agenda; **~stätte** *f* day care center (*Br* centre); **~tour** *f* day trip; **~zeit** *f* time of day; **zu jeder ~** at any hour; **~zeitung** *f* daily (paper)
'tageweise *adv* by the day
täglich ['tɛːklɪç] *adj and adv* daily
'Tagschicht *f* ECON day shift
'tagsüber *adv* during the day
'Tagung *f* (*-; -en*) conference
Taille ['taljə] *f* (*-; -n*) waist; waistline
tailliert [ta'jiːɐt] *adj* waisted, tapered
Takelage [takə'laːʒə] *f* (*-; -n*) MAR rigging
Takt [takt] *m* (*-[e]s; -e*) a) (*no pl*) MUS time, measure, beat, b) MUS bar, c) MOT stroke, d) (*no pl*) tact; **den ~ halten** MUS keep time
Taktik ['taktɪk] *f* (*-; -en*) MIL tactics (*a. fig*); **'taktisch** *adj* tactical
'taktlos *adj* tactless
'Taktstock *m* MUS baton
'Taktstrich *m* MUS bar
'taktvoll *adj* tactful
Tal [taːl] *n* (*-[e]s; Täler* ['tɛːlɐ]) valley
Talar [ta'laːɐ] *m* (*-s; -e*) robe, gown
Talent [ta'lɛnt] *n* (*-[e]s; -e*) talent (*a. person*), gift; **talentiert** [talɛn'tiːɐt] *adj* talented, gifted
Talg [talk] *m* (*-[e]s; -e*) tallow; GASTR suet

Talisman ['ta:lɪsman] *m* (-s; -e) talisman, charm

Talk|master ['tɔ:k-] *m* (-s; -s) TV talk (*Br* chat) show host; **~show** [-ʃoʊ] *f* (-; -s) TV talk (*Br* chat) show

'**Talsperre** *f* dam, barrage

Tampon ['tampɔn] *m* (-s; -s) tampon

Tandler ['tandlə] *Austrian m* (-s; -) second-hand dealer

Tang [taŋ] *m* (-[e]s; -e) BOT seaweed

Tank [taŋk] *m* (-s; -s) tank; **tanken** ['taŋkən] *v/t* (ge-, h) get some gasoline (*Br* petrol), fill up; **Tanker** ['taŋkə] *m* (-s; -) MAR tanker; '**Tankstelle** *f* filling (*or* gas, *Br* petrol) station; '**Tankwart** *m* (-[e]s; -e) gas station (*Br* petrol pump) attendant

Tanne ['tanə] *f* (-; -n) BOT fir (tree)

'**Tannenbaum** *m* Christmas tree

'**Tannenzapfen** *m* BOT fir cone

Tante ['tantə] *f* (-; -n) aunt; **~ Lindy** Aunt Lindy; **~-Emma-Laden** F *m* mom--and-pop store, *Br* corner shop

Tantiemen [tã'tjeːmən] *pl* royalties

Tanz [tants] *m* (-es; *Tänze* ['tɛntsə]), **tanzen** ['tantsən] *v/i* (ge-, h, sein) *and* *v/t* (ge-, h) dance; **Tänzer** ['tɛntsə] *m* (-s; -), **Tänzerin** ['tɛntsərɪn] *f* (-; -nen) dancer

'**Tanz|fläche** *f* dance floor; **~kurs** *m* dancing lessons; **~mu,sik** *f* dance music; **~schule** *f* dancing school

Tapete [ta'peːtə] *f* (-; -n), **tapezieren** [tape'tsiːrən] *v/t* (no ge-, h) wallpaper

tapfer ['tapfə] *adj* brave; courageous

'**Tapferkeit** *f* (-; *no pl*) bravery; courage

Tarif [ta'riːf] *m* (-[e]s; -e) rate(s), tariff; (wage) scale; **~lohn** *m* standard wage(s); **~verhandlungen** *pl* wage negotiations, collective bargaining

tarnen ['tarnən] *v/t* (ge-, h) camouflage; *fig* disguise

'**Tarnung** *f* (-; -en) camouflage

Tasche ['taʃə] *f* (-; -n) bag; pocket

'**Taschen|buch** *n* paperback; **~dieb** *m* pickpocket; **~geld** *n* allowance, *Br* pocket money; **~lampe** *f* flashlight, *Br* torch; **~messer** *n* penknife, pocket-knife; **~rechner** *m* pocket calculator; **~schirm** *m* telescopic umbrella; **~tuch** *n* handkerchief, F hankie; **~uhr** *f* pocket watch

Tasse ['tasə] *f* (-; -n) cup; **e-e ~ Tee** *etc* a cup of tea *etc*

Tastatur [tasta'tuːɐ] *f* (-; -en) keyboard, keys; **Taste** ['tastə] *f* (-; -n) key

tasten ['tastən] (ge-, h) **1.** *v/i* grope (**nach** for), feel (for); fumble (for); **2.** *v/t* touch, feel; **sich ~** feel *or* grope (*a.* *fig*) one's way

'**Tastentele,fon** *n* push-button phone

'**Tastsinn** *m* (-[e]s; *no pl*) sense of touch

tat [taːt] *pret of* **tun**

Tat *f* (-; -en) act, deed; action; JUR offense, *Br* offence; **j-n auf frischer ~ er-tappen** catch in the act

'**tatenlos** *adj* inactive, passive

Täter ['tɛːtə] *m* (-s; -), '**Täterin** *f* (-; -nen) culprit; JUR offender

tätig ['tɛːtɪç] *adj* active; busy; **~ sein bei** be employed with; **~ werden** act, take action; '**Tätigkeit** *f* (-; -en) activity; work; occupation, job; **in ~** in action

'**Tatkraft** *f* (-; *no pl*) energy

'**tatkräftig** *adj* energetic, active

tätlich ['tɛːtlɪç] *adj* violent; **~ werden gegen** assault; '**Tätlichkeiten** *pl* (acts of) violence; JUR assault and battery

'**Tatort** *m* JUR scene of the crime

tätowieren [tɛto'viːrən] *v/t* (no -ge-, h), **Täto'wierung** *f* (-; -en) tattoo

'**Tatsache** *f* fact

'**tatsächlich 1.** *adj* actual, real; **2.** *adv* actually, in fact; really

tätscheln ['tɛːtʃəln] *v/t* (ge-, h) pat, pet

Tatze ['tatsə] *f* (-; -n) ZO paw (*a.* *fig*)

Tau¹ [taʊ] *n* (-[e]s; -e) rope

Tau² *m* (-[e]s; *no pl*) dew

taub [taʊp] *adj* deaf (*fig* **gegen** to); numb, benumbed

Taube ['taʊbə] *f* (-; -n) ZO pigeon; *esp* *fig* dove; '**Taubenschlag** *m* pigeon-house

'**Taubheit** *f* (-; *no pl*) deafness; numbness

'**taubstumm** *adj* deaf-and-dumb

'**Taubstumme** *m*, *f* (-n; -n) deaf mute

tauchen ['taʊxən] **1.** *v/i* dive (**nach** for); SPORT skin-dive; *submarine*: *a.* submerge; stay underwater; **2.** *v/t* (h) dip (**in** *acc* into); duck; **Taucher** ['taʊxə] *m* (-s; -) (SPORT skin) diver; '**Tauchsport** *m* skin diving

tauen ['taʊən] *v/i* (ge-, sein) *and* *v/t* (ge-, h) thaw, melt

Taufe ['taʊfə] *f* (-; -n) baptism, christening; '**taufen** *v/t* (ge-, h) baptize, christen; '**Taufpate** *m* godfather; '**Taufpatin**

f godmother; **'Taufschein** *m* certificate of baptism

taugen ['taugən] *v/i* (*ge-, h*) be good *or* fit *or* of use *or* suited (*all:* **zu**, **für** for); **nichts** ~ be no good; F **taugt es was?** is it any good?; **tauglich** ['tauklıç] *adj esp* MIL fit (for service)

Taumel ['tauməl] *m* (*-s; no pl*) dizziness; rapture, ecstasy; **'taumelig** *adj* dizzy; **'taumeln** *v/i* (*ge-, sein*) stagger, reel

Tausch [tauʃ] *m* (*-[e]s; -e*) exchange, F swap; **tauschen** ['tauʃən] *v/t* (*ge-, h*) exchange, F swap (*both:* **gegen** for); switch; change; **ich möchte nicht mit ihm** ~ I wouldn't like to be in his shoes

täuschen ['tɔyʃən] *v/t* (*ge-, h*) deceive, fool; delude; cheat; *a.* SPORT feint; **sich** ~ deceive o.s.; be mistaken; **sich** ~ **lassen von** be taken in by; **~de Ähnlichkeit** striking similarity; **'Täuschung** *f* (*-; -en*) deception; delusion; JUR deceit; *a.* PED cheating

tausend ['tauzənt] *adj* a thousand

'tausendst *adj* thousandth

'Tausendstel *n* (*-s; -*) thousandth (part)

'Tautropfen *m* dewdrop

'Tauwetter *n* thaw

'Tauziehen *n* (*-s; no pl*) SPORT tug-of-war (*a. fig*)

Taxi ['taksi] *n* (*-s; -s*) taxi(cab), cab

taxieren [ta'ksi:rən] *v/t* (*no -ge-, h*) rate, estimate (**auf** *acc* at)

'Taxistand *m* cabstand, *esp Br* taxi rank

Technik ['tɛçnık] *f* (*-; -en*) a) (*no pl*) technology, engineering, b) technique (*a.* SPORT *etc*), MUS execution

Techniker ['tɛçnıkɐ] *m* (*-s; -*), **'Technikerin** *f* (*-; -nen*) engineer; technician (*a.* SPORT *etc*)

technisch ['tɛçnıʃ] *adj* technical; technological; **~e Hochschule** school *etc* of technology

Technologie [tɛçnolo'gi:] *f* (*-; -n*) technology; **technologisch** [tɛçno'lo:gıʃ] *adj* technological

Tee [te:] *m* (*-s; -s*) tea; (*e-n*) ~ **trinken** have some tea; (*e-n*) ~ **machen** *or* **kochen** make some tea; **~beutel** *m* teabag; **~kanne** *f* teapot; **~löffel** *m* teaspoon

Teer [te:ɐ] *m* (*-[e]s; -e*), **teeren** ['te:rən] *v/t* (*ge-, h*) tar

'Teesieb *n* tea strainer

'Teetasse *f* teacup

Teich [taıç] *m* (*-[e]s; -e*) pool, pond

Teig [taık] *m* (*-[e]s; -e*) dough, paste

teigig ['taıgıç] *adj* doughy, pasty

'Teigwaren *pl* pasta

Teil [taıl] *m*, *n* (*-[e]s; -e*) part; portion, share; component; **zum** ~ partly, in part; **~... in cpds ...erfolg** *etc*: partial ...

'teilbar *adj* divisible

'Teilchen *n* (*-s; -*) particle

teilen ['taılən] *v/t* (*ge-, h*) divide; share

'teilhaben *v/i* (*irr,* **haben**, *sep, -ge-, h*) ~ **an** (*dat*) (have a) share in; **'Teilhaber(in)** [-ha:bɐ (-bərın)] (*-s; -/-; -nen*) ECON partner

'Teilnahme [-na:mə] *f* (*-; no pl*) participation (**an** *dat* in); *fig* interest (in); sympathy (for)

'teilnahmslos *adj* indifferent; *esp* MED apathetic; **'Teilnahmslosigkeit** *f* (*-; no pl*) indifference; apathy

'teilnehmen *v/i* (*irr,* **nehmen**, *sep, -ge-, h*) ~ **an** (*dat*) take part *or* participate in; share (in); **'Teilnehmer(in)** [-ne:mɐ (-mərın)] (*-s; -/-; -nen*) participant; UNIV student; SPORT competitor

teils *adv* partly

'Teilstrecke *f* stage, leg

'Teilung *f* (*-; -en*) division

'teilweise *adv* partly, in part

'Teilzahlung *f* → **Abzahlung, Rate**

Teint [tɛ̃:] *m* (*-s; -s*) complexion

Tel. ABBR *of* **Telefon** tel., telephone

Telefon [tele'fo:n] *n* (*-s; -e*) telephone, phone; **am** ~ on the (tele)phone; ~ **haben** have a (*Br* be on the) (tele)phone; **ans** ~ **gehen** answer the (tele)phone; **~anruf** *m* (tele)phone call; **~anschluss** *m* telephone connection; **~apparat** *m* telephone

Telefonat [telefo'na:t] *n* (*-[e]s; -e*) → **Telefongespräch**

Tele|fon|buch *n* telephone directory, phone book; **~gebühr** *f* telephone charge; **~gespräch** *n* (tele)phone call

telefonieren [telefo'ni:rən] *v/i* (*no -ge-, h*) (tele)phone; be on the phone; **mit j-m** ~ talk to s.o. on the phone

telefonisch [tele'fo:nıʃ] **1.** *adj* telephonic, telephone ...; **2.** *adv* by (tele)phone, over the (tele)phone

Telefonist [telefo'nıst] *m* (*-en; -en*), **Telefonistin** *f* (*-; -nen*) (telephone) operator

Tele'fon|karte f phonecard; ~leitung f telephone line; ~netz n telephone network; ~nummer f (tele)phone number; ~zelle f (tele)phone booth, esp Br (tele)phone box, Br call box; ~zen,tra- le f switchboard

telegrafieren [telegra'fi:rən] v/t and v/i (no -ge-, h) telegraph, wire; cable

telegrafisch [tele'gra:fɪʃ] adj and adv by telegraph, by wire, by cable

Telegramm [tele'gram] n (-s; -e) telegram, wire, cable(gram)

Teleobjektiv ['te:lə-] n telephoto lens

Telephon n → Telefon

Teletext ['te:lə-] m teletext

Teller ['tɛlə] m (-s; -) plate; ~wäscher [-vɛʃə] m (-s; -) dishwasher

Tempel ['tɛmpəl] m (-s; -) temple

Temperament [tɛmpəra'mɛnt] n (-[e]s; -e) temper(ament); life, F pep

tempera'ment|los adj lifeless, dull; ~voll adj full of life or F pep

Temperatur [tɛmpəra'tu:ɐ] f (-; -en) temperature; j-s ~ messen take s.o.'s temperature

Tempo ['tɛmpo] n (-s; -s, -pi) speed; MUS time; mit ~ ... at a speed of ... an hour

Tendenz [tɛn'dɛnts] f (-; -en) tendency, trend; leaning; tendenziös [tɛndɛn'tsjø:s] adj tendentious; tendieren [tɛn'di:rən] v/i (no -ge-, h) tend (zu towards; dazu, et. zu tun to do s.th.)

Tennis ['tɛnɪs] n (-; no pl) tennis; ~platz m tennis court; ~schläger m tennis racket; ~spieler(in) tennis player

Tenor [te'no:ɐ] m (-s; Tenöre [te'nø:rə]) MUS tenor

Teppich ['tɛpɪç] m (-s; -e) carpet

'Teppichboden m fitted carpet, wall- -to-wall carpeting

Termin [tɛr'mi:n] m (-s; -e) date; deadline; engagement; e-n ~ vereinbaren (einhalten, absagen) make (keep, cancel) an appointment

Terminal ['tø:rɛminəl] a) m, n (-s; -s) AVIAT terminal, b) n (-s; -s) EDP terminal

Terrasse [tɛ'rasə] f (-; -n) terrace

ter'rassenförmig [-fœrmɪç] adj terraced, in terraces

Terrine [tɛ'ri:nə] f (-; -n) tureen

Territorium [tɛri'to:rjʊm] n (-s; -ien) territory

Terror ['tɛro:ɐ] m (-s; no pl) terror

terrorisieren [tɛrori'zi:rən] v/t (no -ge-, h) terrorize

Terrorismus [tɛro'rɪsmʊs] m (-; no pl) terrorism; Terrorist(in) [-'rɪst(ɪn)] (-en; -en/-; -nen), terro'ristisch adj terrorist

Testament [tɛsta'mɛnt] n (-[e]s; -e) (last) will; JUR last will and testament

testamentarisch [tɛstamɛn'ta:rɪʃ] adv by will

Testa'mentsvollstrecker m executor

Testbild ['tɛst-] n TV test card

testen ['tɛstən] v/t (no -ge-, h) test

'Testpi,lot m test pilot

Tetanus ['te:tanʊs] m (-; no pl) MED tetanus

teuer ['tɔYɐ] adj expensive; wie ~ ist es? how much is it?

Teufel ['tɔYfəl] m (-s; -) devil (a. fig); wer (wo, was) zum ~ ...? who (where, what) the hell ...? 'Teufelskerl F m devil of a fellow; 'Teufelskreis m vicious circle; 'teuflisch ['tɔYflɪʃ] adj devilish, diabolic(al)

Text [tɛkst] m (-[e]s; -e) text; MUS words, lyrics

Texter ['tɛkstɐ] m (-s; -), 'Texterin f (-; -nen) MUS songwriter

Textil... [tɛks'ti:l-] in cpds textile ...

Textilien [tɛks'ti:ljən] pl textiles

'Textverarbeitung f EDP word processing; 'Textverarbeitungsgerät n EDP word processor

Theater [te'a:tɐ] n (-s; -) theater, Br theatre; F ~ machen (um) make a fuss (about); ~besucher m theatergoer, Br theatregoer; ~karte f theater (Br theatre) ticket; ~kasse f box office; ~stück n play

Thema ['te:ma] n (-s; Themen) subject, topic; MUS theme; das ~ wechseln change the subject

Theologe [teo'lo:gə] m (-n; -n) theologian; Theologie [teolo'gi:] f (-; -n) theology; Theo'login f (-; -nen) theologian; theo'logisch adj theological

Theoretiker [teo're:tikɐ] m (-s; -) theorist; theo'retisch adj theoretical

Theorie [teo'ri:] f (-; -n) theory

Therapeut [tera'pɔYt] m (-en; -en), Thera'peutin f (-; -nen) therapist; Therapie [-'pi:] f (-; -n) therapy

Thermometer [tɛrmo'me:tɐ] n (-s; -) thermometer

Thermosflasche® ['tɛrmɔs-] f thermos®

These ['te:zə] *f* (-; -*n*) thesis

Thon [to:n] *Swiss m* (-*s*; -*e*) tuna (fish)

Thrombose [trɔm'bo:zə] *f* (-; -*n*) MED thrombosis

Thron [tro:n] *m* (-[*e*]*s*; -*e*) throne

'Thronfolger [-fɔlɡɐ] *m* (-*s*; -), 'Thronfolgerin [-fɔlɡərɪn] *f* (-; -*nen*) successor to the throne

Thunfisch ['tu:n-] *m* tuna (fish)

Tick [tɪk] F *m* (-[*e*]*s*; -*s*) quirk

ticken ['tɪkən] *v/i* (*ge*-, *h*) tick

Tiebreak, Tie-Break ['taɪbreɪk] *m*, *n tennis*: tiebreak(er)

tief [ti:f] *adj* deep (*a. fig*); low

Tief *n* (-*s*; -*s*) METEOR depression (*a.* PSYCH, ECON), low (*a. fig*)

Tiefe ['ti:fə] *f* (-; -*n*) depth (*a. fig*)

'Tiefebene *f* lowland(s); ~flieger *m* low-flying air plane; ~gang *m* MAR draft; *fig* draught; *fig* depth; ~ga‚rage *f* parking *or* underground garage, *Br* underground car park

'tiefgekühlt *adj* deep-frozen

'Tiefkühlfach *n* freezing compartment; ~schrank *m*, ~truhe *f* freezer, deep-freeze; ~kost *f* frozen foods

Tier [ti:ɐ] *n* (-[*e*]*s*; -*e*) animal; F *hohes* ~ bigwig, big shot; ~arzt *m*, ~ärztin *f* veterinarian, *Br* veterinary surgeon, *Br* vet; ~freund *m* animal lover; ~garten *m* → *Zoo*; ~heim *n* animal shelter

tierisch ['ti:rɪʃ] *adj* animal; *fig* bestial, brutish

'Tierkreis *m* ASTR zodiac; ~zeichen *n* sign of the zodiac

'Tiermedi‚zin *f* veterinary medicine

Tierquäle‚rei *f* cruelty to animals

'Tierreich *n* animal kingdom; ~schutz *m* protection of animals; ~schutzverein *m* society for the prevention of cruelty to animals; ~versuch *m* MED experiment with animals

Tiger ['ti:ɡɐ] *m* (-*s*; -) ZO tiger

Tigerin ['ti:ɡərɪn] *f* (-; -*nen*) ZO tigress

tilgen ['tɪlɡən] *v/t* (*ge*-, *h*) ECON pay off

Tinte ['tɪntə] *f* (-; -*n*) ink

'Tintenfisch *m* ZO squid

Tipp [tɪp] *m* (-*s*; -*s*) hint, tip; tip-off; *j-m e-n ~ geben* tip s.o. off

tippen ['tɪpən] *v/i* and *v/t* (*ge*-, *h*) tap; type; F guess; do *lotto etc*

Tisch [tɪʃ] *m* (-[*e*]*s*; -*e*) table; *am ~ sitzen* sit at the table; *bei ~* at table; *den ~ decken* (*abräumen*) lay (clear)

the table; ~decke *f* tablecloth; ~gebet *n* REL grace: *das ~ sprechen* say grace

Tischler ['tɪʃlɐ] *m* (-*s*; -) joiner; cabinet-maker

'Tischplatte *f* tabletop; ~rechner *m* desktop computer; ~tennis *n* table tennis; ~tuch *n* tablecloth

Titel ['ti:təl] *m* (-*s*; -) title; ~bild *n* cover picture; ~blatt *n*, ~seite *f* title page; cover, front page

Toast [to:st] *m* (-[*e*]*s*; -*s*), toasten ['to:stən] *v/t* (*ge*-, *h*) toast

toben ['to:bən] *v/i* (*ge*-, *h*) rage (*a. fig*); romp; tobsüchtig ['to:p-] *adj* raving mad; 'Tobsuchtsanfall *m* tantrum

Tochter ['tɔxtɐ] *f* (-; *Töchter* ['tœçtɐ]) daughter; ~gesellschaft *f* ECON subsidiary (company)

Tod [to:t] *m* (-[*e*]*s*; *no pl*) death (*a. fig*) (*durch* from); *tod...* in *cpds* ...*ernst*, ...*müde*, ...*sicher*: dead ...

Todesängste ['to:dəs-] *pl*: ~ ausstehen be scared to death; ~anzeige *f* obituary (notice); ~fall *m* (case of) death; ~kampf *m* agony; ~opfer *n* casualty; ~strafe *f* JUR capital punishment; death penalty; ~ursache *f* cause of death; ~urteil *n* JUR death sentence

'Todfeind *m* deadly enemy

'tod'krank *adj* mortally ill

tödlich ['tø:tlɪç] *adj* fatal; deadly; *esp fig* mortal

'Todsünde *f* mortal *or* deadly sin

Toilette [toa'lɛtə] *f* (-; -*n*) bathroom, *Br* toilet, lavatory; *pl* rest rooms, *Br* ladies' *or* men's rooms

Toi‚letten... in *cpds* ...*papier*, ...*seife etc*: toilet ...; ~tisch *m* dressing table

tolerant [tole'rant] *adj* tolerant (*gegen* of, towards); Toleranz [tole'rants] *f* (-; -*en*) tolerance (*a.* TECH); tolerieren [tole'ri:rən] *v/t* (*no -ge-*, *h*) tolerate

toll [tɔl] *adj* wild; F great, fantastic

'tollkühn *adj* daredevil

'Tollwut *f* VET rabies; 'tollwütig [-vy:tɪç] *adj* VET rabid

Tomate [to'ma:tə] *f* (-; -*n*) BOT tomato

Ton¹ [to:n] *m* (-[*e*]*s*; -*e*) clay

Ton² *m* (-[*e*]*s*; *Töne* ['tø:nə]) tone (*a.* MUS, PAINT), PAINT *a.* shade; sound (*a.* TV, *film*); note; stress; *kein ~* not a word; ~abnehmer *m* ELECTR pickup; ~art *f* MUS key; ~band *n* (-[*e*]*s*;

-bänder) (recording) tape; **~bandgerät** *n* tape recorder

tönen ['tø:nən] (*ge-*, *h*) **1.** *v/i* sound, ring; **2.** *v/t* tinge, tint, shade

'**Ton|fall** *m* tone (of voice); accent; **~film** *m* sound film; **~kopf** *m* ELECTR (magnetic) head; **~lage** *f* MUS pitch; **~leiter** *f* MUS scale

Tonne ['tɔnə] *f* (*-; -n*) barrel; (metric) ton

'**Tontechniker** *m* sound engineer

'**Tönung** *f* (*-; -en*) tint, tinge, shade

Topf [tɔpf] *m* (*-[e]s; Töpfe* ['tœpfə]) pot; saucepan

Topfen ['tɔpfən] *Austrian m* (*-s; no pl*) GASTR curd(s)

Töpfer ['tœpfɐ] *m* (*-s; -*) potter

Töpferei [tœpfə'raɪ] *f* (*-; -en*) pottery

'**Töpferin** *f* (*-; -nen*) potter

'**Töpferscheibe** *f* potter's wheel

'**Töpferware** *f* pottery, earthenware

Tor [to:ɐ] *n* (*-[e]s; -e*) gate; *soccer etc*: goal; *ein ~ schießen* score (a goal); *im ~ stehen* keep goal

Torf [tɔrf] *m* (*-[e]s; -e*) peat

'**Torfmull** *m* peat dust

'**Torhüter** [-hy:tɐ] *m → Torwart*

torkeln ['tɔrkəln] *v/i* (*ge-*, *h*, *sein*) reel, stagger

'**Torlatte** *f* SPORT crossbar

'**Torlinie** *f* SPORT goal line

torpedieren [tɔrpe'di:rən] *v/t* (*no -ge-*, *h*) MIL torpedo (*a. fig*)

'**Tor|pfosten** *m* SPORT goalpost; **~raum** *m* SPORT goalmouth; **~schuss** *m* SPORT shot at goal; **~schütze** *m* SPORT scorer

Torte ['tɔrtə] *f* (*-; -n*) pie, *esp Br* flan; cream cake, gateau

'**Torwart** [-vart] *m* (*-[e]s; -e*) SPORT goalkeeper; *F* goalie

tosen ['to:zən] *v/i* (*ge-*, *h*) roar; thunder; **~d** *adj* thunderous (*applause*)

tot [to:t] *adj* dead (*a. fig*); late; *~ geboren* MED stillborn; *~ umfallen* drop dead

total [to'ta:l] *adj* total, complete

totalitär [totali'tɛ:ɐ] *adj* POL totalitarian

'**Tote** *m*, *f* (*-n; -n*) dead man *or* woman; (dead) body, corpse; *mst pl* casualty; *F the dead*; **töten** ['tø:tən] *v/t* (*ge-*, *h*) kill

'**Totenbett** *n* deathbed

'**toten|blass** *adj* deadly pale

'**Toten|gräber** [-grɛ:bɐ] *m* (*-s; -*) gravedigger; **~kopf** *m* skull; skull and crossbones; **~maske** *f* death mask; **~messe**

f REL mass for the dead, requiem (*a. MUS*); **~schädel** *m* skull; **~schein** *m* death certificate

'**toten**'**still** *adj* deathly still

'**totlachen** *F v/refl* (*sep*, *-ge-*, *h*) kill o.s. laughing

Toto ['to:to] *m*, *F n* (*-s; -s*) football pools

'**Totschlag** *m* (*-[e]s; no pl*) JUR manslaughter; '**totschlagen** *v/t* (*irr*, *schlagen*, *sep*, *-ge-*, *h*) kill; *j-n ~* beat s.o. to death; *die Zeit ~* kill time

'**totschweigen** *v/t* (*irr*, *schweigen*, *sep*, *-ge-*, *h*) hush up

Toupet [tu'pe:] *n* (*-s; -s*) toupee

toupieren [tu'pi:rən] *v/t* (*no -ge-*, *h*) *Br* backcomb

Tour [tu:ɐ] *f* (*-; -en*) tour (*durch* of), trip; excursion; TECH turn, revolution; *auf ~en kommen* MOT pick up speed; *F krumme ~en* underhand methods

Touren... ['tu:rən-] *in cpds* ...*rad etc*: touring ...

Tourismus [tu'rɪsmʊs] *m* (*-; no pl*) tourism; **~geschäft** *n* tourist industry

Tourist [tu'rɪst] *m* (*-en; -en*), **Tou'ristin** *f* (*-; -nen*) tourist; **tou'ristisch** *adj* touristic

Tournee [tʊr'ne:] *f* (*-; -s, -n*) tour; *auf ~ gehen* go on tour

Trab [tra:p] *m* (*-[e]s; no pl*) trot

Trabant [tra'bant] *m* (*-en; -en*) ASTR satellite; **Tra'bantenstadt** *f* satellite town

traben ['tra:bən] *v/i* (*ge-*, *sein*) trot

Traber ['tra:bɐ] *m* (*-s; -*) ZO trotter

'**Trabrennen** *n* trotting race

Tracht [traxt] *f* (*-; -en*) costume; uniform; dress; *F e-e ~ Prügel* a thrashing

trächtig ['trɛçtɪç] *adj* ZO with young, pregnant

Tradition [tradi'tsjo:n] *f* (*-; -en*) tradition; **traditionell** [traditsjo'nɛl] *adj* traditional

traf [tra:f] *pret of* **treffen**

Trafik [tra'fɪk] *Austrian f* (*-; -en*) → **Tabakgeschäft**; **Trafikant** [trafi'kant] *Austrian m* (*-en; -en*) tobacconist

Tragbahre ['tra:k-] *f* stretcher

'**tragbar** *adj* portable; wearable; *fig* bearable; *person*: acceptable

Trage ['tra:gə] *f* (*-; -n*) stretcher

träge ['trɛ:gə] *adj* lazy, indolent; PHYS inert (*a. fig*)

tragen ['tra:gən] (*irr*, *ge-*, *h*) **1.** *v/t* carry;

wear; *fig* bear; **sich gut ~** wear well; **2.** *v/i* BOT bear fruit; *fig* hold; **~d** *adj* ARCH supporting; **~d** *adj* ARCH supporting

Träger ['trɛːgɐ] *m* (-s; -) carrier; porter; (shoulder) strap; TECH support; ARCH girder; *fig* bearer

'**trägerlos** *adj* strapless

'**Tragetasche** *f* carrier bag; carrycot

'**tragfähig** *adj* load-bearing; *fig* sound

'**Tragfläche** *f* AVIAT wing

Trägheit ['trɛːkhait] *f* (-; *no pl*) laziness, indolence; PHYS inertia (*a. fig*)

Tragik ['traːgɪk] *f* (-; *no pl*) tragedy

tragisch ['traːgɪʃ] *adj* tragic

Tragödie [tra'gøːdjə] *f* (-; -n) tragedy

'**Tragriemen** *m* strap; sling

'**Tragweite** *f* range; *fig* significance

Trainer ['trɛːnɐ] *m* (-s; -), '**Trainerin** *f* (-; -nen) SPORT trainer, coach; **trainieren** [trɛ'niːrən] *v/i* and *v/t* (*no -ge-*, *h*) SPORT train, coach

'**Training** *n* (-s; -s) training

'**Trainingsanzug** *m* track suit

Traktor ['traktoːɐ] *m* (-s; -en [trak'toːrən]) MOT tractor

trällern ['trɛlɐn] *v/t* and *v/i* (*ge-*, *h*) warble, trill

Tram [tram] *Austrian f* (-; -s), *Swiss n* (-s; -s) streetcar, *Br* tram

trampeln ['trampəln] *v/i* (*ge-*, *h*) trample, stamp

'**Trampelpfad** *m* beaten track

trampen ['trɛmpən] *v/i* (*ge-*, *sein*) hitchhike; **Tramper(in)** ['trɛmpɐ (-pərɪn)] (-s; -/-; -nen) hitchhiker

Träne ['trɛːnə] *f* (-; -n) tear; **in ~n ausbrechen** burst into tears; '**tränen** *v/i* (*ge-*, *h*) water; '**Tränengas** *n* tear gas

trank [traŋk] *pret of* **trinken**

Tränke ['trɛŋkə] *f* (-; -n) watering place

'**tränken** *v/t* (*ge-*, *h*) ZO water; soak, drench

Transfer [trans'feːɐ] *m* (-s; -s) transfer (*a. SPORT*)

Transformator [transfɔr'maːtoːɐ] *m* (-s; -en [-ma'toːrən]) ELECTR transformer

Transfusion [transfu'zjoːn] *f* (-; -en) MED transfusion

Transistor [tran'zɪstoːɐ] *m* (-s; -en [-zɪs'toːrən]) ELECTR transistor

Transit [tran'ziːt] *m* (-s; -e) transit

transitiv ['tranziːtiːf] *adj* LING transitive

transparent [transpa'rɛnt] *adj* transparent

Transparent *n* (-[e]s; -e) banner

Transplantation [transplanta'tsjoːn] *f* (-; -en), **transplantieren** [-'tiːrən] *v/t* (*no -ge-*, *h*) MED transplant

Transport [trans'pɔrt] *m* (-[e]s; -e) transport; shipment; **transportabel** [transpɔr'taːbəl], **trans'portfähig** *adj* transportable; **transportieren** [transpɔr'tiːrən] *v/t* (*no -ge-*, *h*) transport, ship, carry, MOT *a.* haul

Trans'portmittel *n* (means of) transport(ation); **~unternehmen** *n* hauler, *Br* haulier

Trapez [tra'peːts] *n* (-es; -e) MATH trapezoid, *Br* trapezium; SPORT trapeze

trappeln ['trapəln] *v/i* (*ge-*, *sein*) clatter; patter

trat [traːt] *pret of* **treten**

Traube ['traubə] *f* (-; -n) BOT bunch of grapes; grape; *pl* grapes; *fig* cluster

'**Traubensaft** *m* grape juice

'**Traubenzucker** *m* glucose

trauen ['trauən] (*ge-*, *h*) **1.** *v/t* marry; **2.** *v/i* trust (*j-m s.o.*); **sich ~**, *et. zu tun* dare (to) do s.th.; **ich traute meinen Augen nicht** I couldn't believe my eyes

Trauer ['trauɐ] *f* (-; *no pl*) grief, sorrow; mourning; **in ~** in mourning; **~fall** *m* death; **~feier** *f* funeral service; **~marsch** *m* MUS funeral march

'**trauern** *v/i* (*ge-*, *h*) mourn (**um** for)

'**Trauerrede** *f* funeral oration

'**Trauerzug** *m* funeral procession

träufeln ['trɔyfəln] *v/t* (*ge-*, *h*) drip, trickle

Traum [traum] *m* (-[e]s; **Träume** ['trɔymə]) dream (*a. fig*); **~...**, **~... in cpds** ...**beruf**, ...**mann** *etc*: dream ..., ... of one's dreams; **träumen** ['trɔymən] *v/i* and *v/t* (*ge-*, *h*) dream (*a. fig*) (**von** about, of); **schlecht ~** have bad dreams; **Träumer** ['trɔymɐ] *m* (-s; -) dreamer (*a. fig*); **Träumerei** [trɔymə-'rai] *fig f* (day)dream(s), reverie (*a. MUS*)

träumerisch ['trɔymərɪʃ] *adj* dreamy

traurig ['trauɾɪç] *adj* sad (**über** *acc*, **wegen** about)

'**Traurigkeit** *f* (-; *no pl*) sadness

Trauring ['trau-] *m* wedding ring

'**Trauschein** *m* marriage certificate

'**Trauung** *f* (-; -en) marriage, wedding

279

trommeln

'Trauzeuge *m*, 'Trauzeugin *f* witness to a marriage

Trecker ['trɛkɐ] *m* (-s; -) MOT tractor

Treff [trɛf] F *m* (-s; -s) meeting place

treffen ['trɛfən] *v/t and v/i (irr, ge-, h)* hit (*a. fig*); hurt; meet *s.o.*; take (*measures etc*); *nicht ~* miss; *sich ~ (mit j-m)* meet (*s.o.*); *gut~* PHOT *etc*: capture well; 'Treffen *n* (-s; -) meeting; 'treffend 1. *adj* apt (*remark etc*); 2. *adv:* ~ *gesagt* well put; 'Treffer ['trɛfɐ] *m* (-s; -) hit (*a. fig*), SPORT goal; win; 'Treffpunkt *m* meeting place

Treibeis ['traip-] *n* drift ice

treiben ['traibən] (*irr, ge-*) 1. *v/t* (*h*) drive (*a.* TECH *and fig*); SPORT *etc*: do; push, press *s.o.;* BOT put forth; F do, be up to; 2. *v/i* (*sein*) drift (*a. fig*), float; BOT shoot (up); *sich ~ lassen* drift along (*a. fig*); *~de Kraft* driving force; 'Treiben *n* (-s; *no pl*) doings, goingson; *geschäftiges ~* bustle

'Treib|haus *n* hothouse; *~hauseffekt m* greenhouse effect; *~holz n* driftwood; *~riemen m* TECH driving belt; *~sand m* quicksand; *~stoff m* fuel

trennen ['trɛnən] *v/t* (*ge-, h*) separate; sever; part; divide (*a.* LING, POL); segregate; TEL disconnect; *sich ~* separate (*von* from), part (*a. fig*); *sich ~ von* part with *s.th.;* leave *s.o.;* 'Trennung *f* (-; *-en*) separation; division; segregation

'Trennwand *f* partition

Treppe ['trɛpə] *f* (-; *-n*) staircase, stairs

'Treppen|absatz *m* landing; *~geländer n* banisters; *~haus n* staircase; hall

Tresor [tre'zoːɐ] *m* (-s; -e) safe; strongroom, vault

treten ['treːtən] *v/i and v/t* (*irr, ge-, h*) kick; step (*aus* out of; *in* acc into; *auf* acc on[to]); pedal (away)

treu [trɔy] *adj* faithful (*a. fig*); loyal; devoted; **Treue** ['trɔyə] *f* (-; *no pl*) fidelity, faithfulness, loyalty

'Treuhänder [-hɛndɐ] *m* (-s; -) JUR trustee

'treulos *adj* faithless, disloyal, unfaithful (*all:* gegen to)

Tribüne [tri'byːnə] *f* (-; *-n*) platform; stand

Trichter ['trɪçtɐ] *m* (-s; -) funnel; crater

Trick [trɪk] *m* (-s; -s) trick; *~aufnahme f*

trick shot; *~betrüger(in)* confidence trickster

trieb [triːp] *pret of treiben*

Trieb *m* (-[e]s; -e) ['triːbə] BOT (young) shoot, sprout; *fig* impulse, drive; sex drive; *~feder f* mainspring (*a. fig*)

triefen ['triːfən] *v/i* (*ge-, h*) drip, be dripping (*von* with)

triftig ['trɪftɪç] *adj* weighty; good

Trikot [tri'koː] *n* (-s; -s) SPORT shirt, jersey; leotard

Triller ['trɪlɐ] *m* (-s; -) MUS trill; 'trillern *v/i and v/t* (*ge-, h*) trill; ZO warble

trimmen ['trɪmən] *v/refl* (*ge-, h*) keep fit

'Trimmpfad *m* fitness trail

trinkbar ['trɪŋkbaːɐ] *adj* drinkable

trinken ['trɪŋkən] *v/t and v/i* (*irr, ge-, h*) drink (*auf* acc to); have; *et. zu ~* a drink; **Trinker(in)** ['trɪŋkɐ (-kərɪn)] (-s; -/-; *-nen*) drinker, alcoholic

'Trink|geld *n* tip; *j-m (e-e Mark) ~ geben* tip *s.o.* (one mark); *~spruch m* toast; *~wasser n* drinking water

Trio ['triːo] *n* (-s; -s) MUS trio (*a. fig*)

trippeln ['trɪpəln] *v/i* (*ge-, sein*) mince

Tripper ['trɪpɐ] *m* (-s; -) MED gonorrh(o)ea

Tritt [trɪt] *m* (-[e]s; -e) kick; step

'Trittbrett *n* (-s; *MOT* running board

'Trittleiter *f* stepladder

Triumph [tri'ʊmf] *m* (-[e]s; -e) triumph

triumphal [triʊm'faːl] *adj* triumphant

triumphieren [triʊm'fiːrən] *v/i* (*no -ge-, h*) triumph (*über* acc over)

trocken ['trɔkən] *adj* dry (*a. fig*)

'Trocken... *in cpds* dried ...; drying ...

'Trockenhaube *f* hairdryer

'Trockenheit *f* (-; *no pl*) dryness, AGR drought

'trockenlegen *v/t* (*sep, -ge-, h*) drain; change (*a baby*)

trocknen ['trɔknən] *v/t* (*ge-, h*) and *v/i* (*sein*) dry

Trockner ['trɔknɐ] *m* (-s; -) dryer

Troddel ['trɔdəl] *f* (-; *-n*) tassel

Trödel ['trøːdəl] *m* (-s; *no pl*) junk

trödeln ['trøːdəln] *v/i* (*ge-, h*) dawdle

Trödler ['trøːdlɐ] *m* (-s; -) junk dealer; dawdler

trog [troːk] *pret of trügen*

Trog *m* (-[e]s; Tröge ['trøːgə]) trough

Trommel ['trɔməl] *f* (-; *-n*) MUS drum (*a.* TECH); *~fell n* ANAT eardrum

'trommeln *v/i and v/t* (*ge-, h*) drum

Trommler ['trɔmlɐ] m (-s; -) drummer

Trompete [trɔm'pe:tə] f (-; -n) MUS trumpet; **trom'peten** v/i and v/t (no -ge-, h) trumpet (a. ZO); **Trompeter** [trɔm'pe:tɐ] m (-s; -) trumpeter

Tropen ['tro:pən]: **die ~** pl the tropics; **'Tropen... in cpds** tropical ...

Tropf [trɔpf] m (-[e]s; Tröpfe ['trœpfə]) MED drip

Tröpfchen ['trœpfçən] n (-s; -) droplet

tröpfeln ['trœpfəln] v/i and v/t (ge-, h) drip; **es tröpfelt** it's spitting

tropfen ['trɔpfən] v/i and v/t (ge-, h) drip, drop; **'Tropfen** m (-s; -) drop (a. fig); **ein ~ auf den heißen Stein** a drop in the bucket; **'tropfenweise** adv in drops, drop by drop

Trophäe [tro'fɛ:ə] f (-; -n) trophy (a. fig)

tropisch ['tro:pɪʃ] adj tropical

Trosse ['trɔsə] f (-; -n) cable

Trost [tro:st] m (-[e]s; no pl) comfort, consolation; **ein schwacher ~** cold comfort

trösten ['trø:stən] v/t (ge-, h) comfort, console; **sich ~** console o.s. (**mit** with)

tröstlich ['trø:stlɪç] adj comforting

'trostlos adj miserable; desolate

Trott [trɔt] m (-[e]s; -e) trot; F **der alte ~** the old routine

Trottel ['trɔtəl] F m (-s; -) dope

trottelig ['trɔtəlɪç] F adj dopey

trotten ['trɔtən] v/i (ge-, sein) trot

Trottinett ['trɔtinɛt] Swiss n (-s; -e) scooter

Trottoir [trɔ'toaɐ] Swiss n (-s; -e, -s) sidewalk, Br pavement

trotz [trɔts] prp (gen) in spite of, despite

Trotz m (-es; no pl) defiance; **j-m zum ~** to spite s.o.

'trotzdem adv in spite of it, nevertheless, F anyhow, anyway

trotzen ['trɔtsən] v/i (ge-, h) defy (dat s.o. or s.th.); sulk

trotzig ['trɔtsɪç] adj defiant; sulky

trüb [try:p], **trübe** ['try:bə] adj cloudy; muddy; dim; dull, fig a. gloomy

Trubel ['tru:bəl] m (-s; no pl) (hustle and) bustle

trüben ['try:bən] v/t (ge-, h) cloud; fig spoil, mar

Trübsal ['try:pza:l] f: **~ blasen** mope

'trübselig adj sad, gloomy; dreary

'Trübsinn m (-[e]s; no pl) melancholy,

gloom, low spirits; **'trübsinnig** adj melancholy, gloomy

trug [tru:k] pret of **tragen**

trügen ['try:gən] (irr, ge-, h) **1.** v/t deceive; **2.** v/i be deceptive

trügerisch ['try:gərɪʃ] adj deceptive

'Trugschluss m fallacy

Truhe ['tru:ə] f (-; -n) chest

Trümmer ['trymɐ] pl ruins; debris; pieces, bits

Trumpf [trʊmpf] m (-[e]s; Trümpfe ['trympfə]) trump (card) (a. fig); **~ sein** be trumps; fig **s-n ~ ausspielen** play one's trump card

Trunkenheit f (-; no pl) drunkenness esp JUR; **~ am Steuer** drunk (Br drink) driving

Trunksucht f (-; no pl) alcoholism

Trupp [trʊp] m (-s; -s) band, party; group; **Truppe** ['trʊpə] f (-; -n) MIL troop, pl troops, forces; THEA company, troupe

'Truppen|gattung f MIL branch (of service); **~übungsplatz** m training area

Truthahn ['tru:t-] m ZO turkey

Tscheche ['tʃɛçə] m (-n; -n) Czech; **Tschechien** ['tʃɛçjən] Czech Republic; **'Tschechin** f (-; -nen) Czech; **'tschechisch** adj Czech; **Tschechische Republik** Czech Republic

Tube ['tu:bə] f (-; -n) tube

Tuberkulose [tuberku'lo:zə] f (-; -n) MED tuberculosis

Tuch [tu:x] n (-[e]s) a) (pl -e) cloth, b) (pl Tücher ['ty:çɐ]) scarf

'Tuchfühlung f: **auf ~** in close contact

tüchtig ['tyçtɪç] adj (cap)able, competent; skil(l)ful; efficient; F fig good

'Tüchtigkeit f (-; no pl) (cap)ability, qualities; skill; efficiency

tückisch ['tykɪʃ] adj malicious; MED insidious; treacherous

tüfteln ['tyftəln] F v/i (ge-, h) puzzle (**an** dat over)

Tugend ['tu:gənt] f (-; -en) virtue (a. fig)

Tulpe ['tʊlpə] f (-; -n) BOT tulip

Tumor ['tu:mo:ɐ] m (-s; -en [tu'mo:rən]) MED tumo(u)r

Tümpel ['tympəl] m (-s; -) pool

Tumult [tu'mʊlt] m (-[e]s; -e) tumult, uproar

tun [tu:n] v/t and v/i (irr, ge-, h) do; take (a step etc); F put; **zu ~ haben** have work to do; be busy; **ich weiß (nicht)**,

was ich ~ soll *or* **muss** I (don't) know what to do; **so ~, als ob** pretend to *inf*

Tünche ['tʏnçə] *f* (-; -*n*), **'tünchen** *v/t* (ge-, *h*) whitewash

Tunfisch *m* → **Thunfisch**

Tunke ['tʊŋkə] *f* (-; -*n*) sauce

Tunnel ['tʊnəl] *m* (-*s*; -) tunnel

Tüpfelchen ['tʏpfəlçən] *n*: **das ~ auf dem i** the icing on the cake

tupfen ['tʊpfən] *v/t* (ge-, *h*) dab

'Tupfen *m* (-*s*; -) dot, spot

Tupfer ['tʊpfɐ] *m* (-*s*; -) MED swab

Tür [tyːɐ] *f* (-; -*en* ['tyːrən]) door (*a. fig*); **die ~(en) knallen** slam the door(s); F **j-n vor die ~ setzen** throw s.o. out; **Tag der offenen ~** open house (*Br* day)

Turban ['tʊrbaːn] *m* (-*s*; -*e*) turban

Turbine [tʊr'biːnə] *f* (-; -*n*) TECH turbine

Turbolader ['tʊrbolaːdɐ] *m* (-*s*; -) MOT turbo(charger)

Türke ['tʏrkə] *m* (-*n*; -*n*) Turk; **Türkei** [tʏr'kai] *f* Turkey; **Türkin** ['tʏrkɪn] *f* (-; -*nen*) Turk(ish woman); **'türkisch** *adj* Turkish

'Tür|klingel *f* doorbell; **~klinke** *f* door handle; **~knauf** *m* doorknob

Turm [tʊrm] *m* (-[*e*]*s*; **Türme** ['tʏrmə]) tower; steeple; *chess:* castle, rook

türmen ['tʏrmən] *v/t* (ge-, *h*) pile up (*a. sich ~*)

'Turmspitze *f* spire

'Turmspringen *n* SPORT platform diving

turnen ['tʊrnən] *v/i* (ge-, *h*) SPORT do gymnastics; **'Turnen** *n* (-*s*; *no pl*) SPORT

gymnastics; PED physical education (ABBR PE); **Turner** ['tʊrnɐ] *m* (-*s*; -), **Turnerin** ['tʊrnərɪn] *f* (-; -*nen*) SPORT gymnast

'Turnhalle *f* gymnasium, F gym

'Turnhemd *n* gym shirt

'Turnhose *f* gym shorts

Turnier [tʊr'niːɐ] *n* (-*s*; -*e*) tournament

Tur'niertanz *m* ballroom dancing

'Turn|lehrer(in) gym(nastics) *or* PE teacher; **~schuh** *m* sneaker, *Br* trainer; **~verein** *m* gymnastics club

'Tür|pfosten *m* doorpost; **~rahmen** *m* doorframe; **~schild** *n* doorplate; **~sprechanlage** *f* entryphone

Tusche ['tʊʃə] *f* (-; -*n*) Indian ink; watercolo(u)r

'Tuschkasten *m* paintbox

Tüte ['tyːtə] *f* (-; -*n*) (paper *or* plastic) bag; etc ~ a bag of

TÜV [tʏf] ABBR *of* **Technischer Über-wachungs-Verein** *Br appr* MOT (test), compulsory car inspection; **(nicht) durch den ~ kommen** pass (fail) its *or* one's MOT

Typ [tyːp] *m* (-*s*; -*en*) type; model; F fellow, guy; **Type** ['tyːpə] *f* (-; -*n*) TECH type; F character

Typhus ['tyːfʊs] *m* (-; *no pl*) MED typhoid (fever)

typisch ['tyːpɪʃ] *adj* typical (**für** of)

Tyrann [ty'ran] *m* (-*en*; -*en*) tyrant

Tyrannei [tyra'nai] *f* (-; -*en*) tyranny

tyrannisch [ty'ranɪʃ] *adj* tyrannical

tyrannisieren [tyrani'ziːrən] *v/t* (*no* -ge-, *h*) tyrannize, bully

U

u.a. ABBR *of* **unter anderem** among other things; **und andere** and others

U-Bahn ['uːbaːn] *f* underground, subway, *in London:* tube

übel ['yːbəl] *adj* bad; **mir ist ~** I feel sick; **et. ~ nehmen** be offended by s.th.; **~ riechend** foul-smelling, foul

'Übel *n* (-*s*; -) evil

'Übelkeit *f* (-; -*en*) nausea

'Übeltäter *m*, **'Übeltäterin** *f esp iro* culprit

üben ['yːbən] *v/t and v/i* (ge-, *h*) practice, *Br* practise; **Klavier** *etc* ~ practice the piano *etc*

über ['yːbɐ] *prp* (*dat or acc*) over; above (*a. fig*); more than; across; *fig* about, of, *lecture etc a.* on; **sprechen** (*nachden-ken etc*) ~ (*acc*) talk (think *etc*) about; ~ **Nacht bleiben** stay overnight; ~ **München nach Rom** to Rome via Munich

über'all *adv* everywhere; ~ **in ...** (*dat*) *a.* throughout ..., all over ...

über'anstrengen v/t and v/refl (no -ge-, h) overstrain (o.s.)

über'arbeiten v/t (no -ge-, h) revise; **sich ~** overwork o.s.

überaus adv most, extremely

'überbelichten v/t (no -ge-, h) PHOT overexpose

über'bieten v/t (irr, bieten, no -ge-, h) at auction: outbid (**um** by); fig beat, outdo s.o.

'Überblick m view; fig overview (**über** acc of); general idea, outline

über'blicken v/t (no -ge-, h) overlook; fig be able to calculate

über'bringen v/t (irr, bringen, no -ge-, h) deliver; **Über'bringer(in)** (-s; -/-; -nen) ECON bearer

über'brücken v/t (no -ge-, h) bridge (a. fig); **~dacht** [-'daxt] adj roofed, covered; **~'dauern** v/t (no -ge-, h) outlast, survive; **~'denken** v/t (irr, denken, no -ge-, h) think s.th. over

überdimensio,nal adj oversized

'Überdosis f MED overdose

überdrüssig [-dry.sıç] adj: **~ sein** be weary or sick (gen of)

'über|durchschnittlich adj above-average; **~eifrig** adj overzealous

über'eilen v/t (no -ge-, h) rush; **nichts ~!** don't rush things!; **über'eilt** adj rash, hasty

überei'nander adv on top of each other; talk etc about one another; **die Beine ~ schlagen** cross one's legs

über'einkommen v/i (irr, kommen, sep, -ge-, sein) agree; **Über'einkommen** (-s; -), **Über'einkunft** f (-; -künfte) agreement

über'einstimmen v/i (sep, -ge-, h) tally, correspond (with); **mit j-m ~** agree with s.o. (**in** dat on); **Über'einstimmung** f (-; -en) agreement; correspondence; **in ~ mit** in accordance with

über'fahren v/t (irr, fahren, no -ge-, h) run s.o. over, knock s.o. down

'Überfahrt f MAR crossing

'Überfall m assault (**auf** acc on); hold-up (on, of); mugging (of); MIL raid (on); invasion (of); **über'fallen** v/t (irr, fallen, no -ge-, h) attack, assault; hold up; mug; MIL raid; invade

'überfällig adj overdue

über'fliegen v/t (irr, fliegen, no -ge-, h) fly over or across; fig glance over, skim (through)

'überfließen v/i (irr, fließen, sep, -ge-, sein) overflow

'Überfluss m (-es; no pl) abundance (**an** dat of); affluence; **im ~ haben** abound in; **'überflüssig** adj superfluous

über|'fluten v/t (no -ge-, h) flood (a. fig); **~'fordern** v/t (no -ge-, h) overtax

überfragt [-'fra:kt] adj: F **da bin ich ~** you've got me there

über'führen v/t (no -ge-, h) transport; JUR convict s.o.

Über'führung f (-; -en) transfer; JUR conviction; MOT overpass, Br flyover; footbridge

über'füllt adj overcrowded, packed

über'füttern v/t (no -ge-, h) overfeed

'Übergang m crossing; fig transition

über'geben v/t (irr, geben, no -ge-, h) hand over; MIL surrender; **sich ~** vomit

über'gehen¹ v/t (irr, gehen, no -ge-, h) pass over, ignore

'übergehen² v/i (irr, gehen, sep, -ge-, sein) pass (**zu** on to); **~ in** (acc) change or turn (in)to

'übergeschnappt F adj cracked

'Übergewicht n (~ **haben** be) overweight; fig predominance

'übergewichtig adj overweight

über'glücklich adj overjoyed

'übergreifen v/i (irr, greifen, sep, -ge-, h) **~ auf** (acc) spread to

'Übergriff m infringement (**auf** acc of); (act of) violence

'Übergröße f outsize; **in ~n** outsized, oversize(d)

über'hand: **~ nehmen** become rampant

über'häufen v/t (no -ge-, h) swamp; shower

über'haupt adv ... at all; anyway; **~ nicht (nichts)** not (nothing) at all

überheblich [-'he:plıç] adj arrogant

Über'heblichkeit f (-; no pl) arrogance

über|'hitzen v/t (no -ge-, h) overheat (a. fig); **~höht** [-'hø:t] adj excessive; **~'holen** v/t (no -ge-, h) pass, overtake (a. SPORT); TECH overhaul, service; **~'holt** adj outdated, antiquated; **~'hören** v/t (no -ge-, h) miss, not catch or get; ignore

'überirdisch adj supernatural

'**über'kleben** *v/t* (*no -ge-, h*) paste up, cover

'**überkochen** *v/i* (*sep, -ge-, sein*) boil over

über'kommen *v/t* (*irr,* **kommen***, no -ge-, h*) ... **überkam ihn** he was seized with *or* overcome by ...; ~'**laden** *v/t* (*irr,* **laden***, no -ge-, h*) overload (*a.* ELECTR); *fig* clutter; ~'**lassen** *v/t* (*irr,* **lassen***, no -ge-, h*) **j-m et.** ~ let s.o. have s.th., leave s.th. to s.o. (*a. fig*); **j-n sich selbst** ~ leave s.o. to himself; **j-n s-m Schicksal** ~ leave s.o. to his fate; ~'**lasten** *v/t* (*no -ge-, h*) overload (*a.* ELECTR); *fig* overburden

'**überlaufen**[1] *v/i* (*irr,* **laufen***, sep, -ge-, sein*) run *or* flow over; MIL desert

über'laufen[2] *v/t* (*irr,* **laufen***, no -ge-, h*) **es überlief mich heiß und kalt** I went hot and cold

über'laufen[3] *adj* overcrowded

'**Überläufer** *m* MIL deserter; POL defector

über'leben *v/t and v/i* (*no -ge-, h*) survive (*a. fig*); live through *s.th.*

Über'lebende *m, f* (*-n; -n*) survivor

'**überlebensgroß** *adj* larger than life

über'legen[1] *v/t and v/i* (*no -ge-, h*) think about *s.th.*, think *s.th.* over; consider; **lassen Sie mich** ~ let me think; **ich habe es mir (anders) überlegt** I've made up (changed) my mind

über'legen[2] *adj* superior (*j-m* to s.o.)

Über'legenheit *f* (*-; no pl*) superiority

über'legt *adj* deliberate; prudent

Über'legung *f* (*-; -en*) consideration, reflection

'**überleiten** *v/i* (*sep, -ge-, h*) ~ **zu** lead up *or* over to

über'liefern *v/t* (*no -ge-, h*) hand down, pass on; **Über'lieferung** *f* (*-; -en*) tradition

über'listen *v/t* (*no -ge-, h*) outwit

'**Übermacht** *f* (*-; no pl*) superiority; *esp* MIL superior forces; **in der** ~ **sein** be superior in numbers; '**übermächtig** *adj* superior; *fig* overpowering

'**Übermaß** *n* (*-es; no pl*) excess (**an** *dat* of); '**übermäßig** *adj* excessive

'**übermenschlich** *adj* superhuman

über'mitteln *v/t* (*no -ge-, h*) convey

'**übermorgen** *adv* the day after tomorrow

über'müdet *adj* overtired

'**übermütig** [-my:tɪç] *adj* high-spirited

'**übernächst** *adj the* next but one; ~**e Woche** the week after next

übernachten [-'naxtən] *v/i* (*no -ge-, h*) stay overnight (**bei j-m** at s.o.'s [house], with s.o.), spend the night (at, with)

Über'nachtung *f* (*-; -en*) night; ~ **und Frühstück** bed and breakfast

Übernahme ['y:bɐnaːmə] *f* (*-; -n*) taking (over); adoption

'**übernatürlich** *adj* supernatural

über'nehmen *v/t* (*irr,* **nehmen***, no -ge-, h*) take over; adopt; take (*responsibility etc*); undertake *to do*

über'prüfen *v/t* (*no -ge-, h*) check, examine; verify; *esp* POL screen

Über'prüfung *f* check, examination; verification; screening

über'queren *v/t* (*no -ge-, h*) cross; ~'**ragen** *v/t* (*no -ge-, h*) tower above (*a. fig*); ~'**ragend** *adj* outstanding

überraschen [y:bɐ'raʃən] *v/t* (*no -ge-, h*) surprise; **j-n bei et.** ~ *a.* catch s.o. doing s.th.; **Über'raschung** *f* (*-; -en*) surprise

über'reden *v/t* (*no -ge-, h*) persuade (**et. zu tun** to do s.th.); **j-n zu et.** ~ talk s.o. into (doing) s.th.; **Über'redung** *f* (*-; no pl*) persuasion

überregio,nal *adj* national

über'reichen *v/t* (*no -ge-, h*) present, hand *s.th.* over (*dat* to); ~'**reizen** *v/t* (*no -ge-, h*) overexcite; ~'**reizt** *adj* overwrought, F on edge

Über'rest *m* remains; *pl* relics; GASTR leftovers

über'rumpeln *v/t* (*no -ge-, h*) (take *s.o.* by) surprise; ~'**runden** *v/t* (*no -ge-, h*) SPORT lap

übersät [-'zɛːt] *adj:* ~ **mit** strewn with *garbage*; studded with *stars*

übersättigt [-'zɛtɪçt] *adj* sated, surfeited

'**Überschall...** *in cpds* supersonic ...

über'schatten *v/t* (*no -ge-, h*) overshadow (*a. fig*); ~'**schätzen** *v/t* (*no -ge-, h*) overrate, overestimate

'**Überschlag** *m* AVIAT loop; SPORT somersault; ECON rough estimate

'**überschlagen**[1] (*irr,* **schlagen***, sep, -ge-*) **1.** *v/t* (*h*) cross (*one's legs*); **2.** *v/i* (*sein*) *fig* ~ **in** (*acc*) turn into

über'schlagen[2] (*no -ge-, h*) **1.** *v/t* skip; ECON make a rough estimate of; **2.** *v/refl* turn (right) over; go head over heels; *voice:* break

U

'überschnappen F v/i (no -ge-, sein) crack up

über'schneiden v/refl (irr, schneiden, no -ge-, h) overlap (a. fig); intersect; ~'schreiben v/t (irr, schreiben, no -ge-, h) make s.th. over (dat to); ~'schreiten v/t (irr, schreiten, no -ge-, h) cross; fig go beyond; pass; break (the speed limit etc)

'Überschrift f heading, title; headline; caption

'Überschuss m, 'überschüssig [-ʃy-sɪç] adj surplus

über'schütten v/t (no -ge-, h) ~ mit cover with; shower with; heap s.th. on

'überschwänglich [-ʃvɛŋlɪç] adj effusive

über'schwemmen v/t (no -ge-, h), Über'schwemmung f (-; -en) flood

'überschwenglich → überschwänglich

'Übersee: in (nach) ~ oversea

über'sehen v/t (irr, sehen, no -ge-, h) overlook; ignore

über'setzen[1] v/t (no -ge-, h) translate (in acc into)

'übersetzen[2] (sep, -ge-) 1. v/i (h, sein) cross (über e-n Fluss a river); 2. v/t (h) take over

Übersetzer [-'zɛtsɐ] m (-s; -), Über'setzerin f (-; -nen) translator

Über'setzung f (-; -en) translation (aus dat from; in acc into)

'Übersicht f (-; -en) overview (über acc of); outline, summary

'übersichtlich adj clear(ly arranged)

'übersiedeln v/i (sep, -ge-, sein) move (nach to); 'Übersied(e)lung f move

über'spannen v/t (no -ge-, h) span

über'spannt fig adj eccentric; extravagant

über'spielen v/t (no -ge-, h) record; tape; fig cover up

über'spitzt adj exaggerated

über'springen v/t (irr, springen, no -ge-, h) jump (over), esp SPORT a. clear; fig skip

über'stehen[1] v/t (irr, stehen, no -ge-, h) get over; survive (a. fig), live through

'überstehen[2] v/i (irr, stehen, sep, -ge-, h) jut out

über'steigen fig v/t (irr, steigen, no -ge-, h) exceed; ~'stimmen v/t (no -ge-, h) outvote

'über|streifen v/t (sep, -ge-, h) slip s.th. on; ~'strömen v/i (sep, -ge-, sein) overflow (vor dat with)

'Überstunden pl overtime; ~ machen work overtime

über'stürzen v/t (no -ge-, h) et. ~ rush things; sich ~ events: follow in rapid succession; ~'stürzt adj (over)hasty; rash; ~'teuert adj overpriced; ~'tönen v/t (no -ge-, h) drown (out)

über'tragbar adj transferable; MED contagious

über'tragen[1] adj figurative

über'tragen[2] v/t (irr, tragen, no -ge-, h) broadcast, a. televise; translate; MED, TECH transmit; MED transfuse (blood); JUR, ECON transfer

Über'tragung f (-; -en) radio, TV broadcast; transmission; translation; MED transfusion; JUR, ECON transfer

über'treffen v/t (irr, treffen, no -ge-, h) outstrip, outdo, surpass, beat

über'treiben v/i and v/t (irr, treiben, no -ge-, h) exaggerate; overdo

Über'treibung f (-; -en) exaggeration

über'treten[1] v/i (irr, treten, sep, -ge-, sein) ~ zu go over to, REL convert to

über'treten[2] (irr, treten, no -ge-, h) 1. v/t break, violate; 2. v/i SPORT foul (a jump or throw); Über'tretung f (-; -en) violation, JUR a. offen|se, Br -ce

'Übertritt m change (zu to); REL, POL conversion (to)

übervölkert [-'fœlkɐt] adj overpopulated

über'wachen v/t (no -ge-, h) supervise, oversee; control; observe

Über'wachung f (-; -en) supervision, control; observance; surveillance

überwältigen [-'vɛltɪgən] v/t (no -ge-, h) overwhelm, overpower, fig a. overcome; ~d adj overwhelming, overpowering

über'weisen v/t (irr, weisen, no -ge-, h) ECON transfer (an j-n to s.o.'s account); remit; MED refer (an acc to)

Über'weisung f (-; -en) ECON transfer; remittance; MED referral

'überwerfen[1] v/t (irr, werfen, sep, -ge-, h) slip s.th. on

über'werfen[2] v/refl (irr, werfen, no -ge-, h) sich ~ (mit j-m) fall out with each other (with s.o.)

über'wiegen v/i (irr, wiegen, no -ge-, h)

über'winden v/t (irr, **winden**, no -ge-, h) overcome (a. fig); defeat; **sich ~ zu** inf bring o.s. to inf; **~wintern** ['-vɪntən] v/i (no -ge-, h) spend the winter (**in** dat in); **~'wuchern** v/t (no -ge-, h) overgrow

'**Überzahl** f (-; no pl) majority; **in der ~ sein** outnumber s.o.

über'zeugen v/t (no -ge-, h) convince (**von** of), persuade; **sich ~, dass** make sure that; **~ selbst ~** (go and) see for o.s.; **überzeugt** [-'tsɔykt] adj convinced; **~ sein** a. be or feel (quite) sure; **Über'zeugung** f (-; -en) conviction

'überziehen[1] v/t (irr, **ziehen**, sep, -ge-, h) put s.th. on

über'ziehen[2] v/t (irr, **ziehen**, sep, -ge-, h) put s.th. on

über'ziehen[2] v/t (irr, ziehen, sep, no, -ge-, h) TECH etc cover; ECON overdraw

Über'ziehungskre,dit m ECON overdraft (facility)

'**Überzug** m cover; coat(ing)

üblich ['y:plɪç] adj usual, normal; **es ist ~** it's the custom; **wie ~** as usual

'**U-Boot** n submarine

übrig ['y:brɪç] adj remaining; **die Übrigen** pl the others, the rest; **~ sein** (**haben**) be (have) left; **~ bleiben** be left, remain; **es bleibt mir nichts anderes ~ (als zu** inf) there is nothing else I can do (but inf); **~ lassen** leave

übrigens ['y:brɪgəns] adv by the way

Übung ['y:bʊŋ] f (-; -en) exercise; practice; **in** (**aus der**) **~** in (out of) practice

Ufer ['u:fɐ] n (-s; -) shore; bank; **ans ~** ashore

Uhr [u:ɐ] f (-; -en) ['u:rən]) clock; watch; **um vier ~** at four o'clock

'**Uhr|armband** n watchstrap; **~macher** m (-s; -) watchmaker; **~werk** n clockwork; **~zeiger** m hand; **~zeigersinn** m: **im ~** clockwise; **entgegen dem ~** counterclockwise; Br anticlockwise

Uhu ['u:hu] m (-s; -s) ZO eagle owl

UKW [u:ka:'ve:] ABBR of **Ultrakurzwelle** VHF, very high frequency

Ulk [ʊlk] m (-s; -e) joke; hoax

ulkig ['ʊlkɪç] adj funny

Ulme ['ʊlmə] f (-; -n) BOT elm

Ultimatum [ʊltiˈmaːtʊm] n (-s; -ten) ultimatum; **j-m ein ~ stellen** deliver an ultimatum to s.o.

um [ʊm] prp (acc) and cj (a)round; at;

about, around; **~ Geld** for money; **~ e-e Stunde** (**10 cm**) by an hour (10 cm); **~ ... willen** for the sake of ...; **~ zu** inf (in order) to inf; **~ sein** F be over; **die Zeit ist ~** time's up; **→ umso**

umarmen [ʊmˈʔarmən] v/t (no -ge-, h) (a. **sich ~**) embrace, hug

Um'armung f (-; -en) embrace, hug

'**Umbau** m (-[e]s; -e, -ten) rebuilding, reconstruction; '**umbauen** v/t (sep, -ge-, h) rebuild, reconstruct

'**um|binden** v/t (irr, **binden**, sep, -ge-, h) put s.th. on; **~blättern** v/i (sep, -ge-, h) turn (over) the page; **~bringen** v/t (irr, **bringen**, sep, -ge-, h) kill; **sich ~** kill o.s.; **~buchen** v/t (sep, -ge-, h) change; ECON transfer (**auf** acc to); **~denken** v/i (irr, **denken**, sep, -ge-, h) change one's way of thinking; **~dispo,nieren** v/i (sep, no -ge-, h) change one's plans; **~drehen** v/t (sep, -ge-, h) turn (round); **sich ~** turn round

Um'drehung f (-; -en) turn; PHYS, TECH rotation, revolution

umei'nander adv care etc about or for each other

'**umfahren**[1] v/t (irr, **fahren**, sep, -ge-, h) run down

um'fahren[2] v/t (irr, **fahren**, no -ge-, h) drive (MAR sail) round

'**umfallen** v/i (irr, **fallen**, sep, -ge-, h) fall down or over; collapse; **tot ~** drop dead

'**Umfang** m circumference; size; extent; **in großem ~** on a large scale

'**umfangreich** adj extensive; voluminous

um'fassen fig v/t (no -ge-, h) cover; include; **~d** adj comprehensive; complete

'**umformen** v/t (sep, -ge-, h) turn, change; ELECTR, LING, MATH a. transform, convert (**all: in** acc [in]to)

'**Umformer** m (-s; -) ELECTR converter

'**Umfrage** f opinion poll

'**Umgang** m (-[e]s; no pl) company; **~ haben mit** associate with; **beim ~ mit** when dealing with

'**umgänglich** [-gɛŋlɪç] adj sociable

'**Umgangs|formen** pl manners; **~sprache** f colloquial speech; **die englische ~** colloquial English

um'geben v/t (irr, **geben**, no -ge-, h) surround (**mit** with); **Um'gebung** f (-;

-en) surroundings; environment

'**umgehen**[1] v/i (irr, **gehen**, sep, -ge-, sein) ~ **mit** deal with, handle; ~ **können mit** have a way with, be good with

um'**gehen**[2] v/t (irr, **gehen**, no -ge-, h) avoid; bypass

'**umgehend** adv immediately

Um'**gehungsstraße** f bypass; beltway, Br ring road

umgekehrt ['ʊmgəke:ɐt] **1.** adj reverse; opposite; (**genau**) ~ (just) the other way round; **2.** adv the other way round; **und** ~ and vice versa

'**umgraben** v/t (irr, **graben**, sep, -ge-, h) dig (up), break up

'**Umhang** m cape; '**umhängen** v/t (sep, -ge-, h) put around or over s.o.'s shoulders etc; rehang

'**umhauen** v/t (irr, **hauen**, sep, -ge-, h) fell, cut down; F knock s.o. out

um'**her** adv (a)round, about

um'**herstreifen** v/i (sep, -ge-, sein) roam or wander around

'**umkehren** (sep, -ge-) **1.** v/i (sein) turn back; **2.** v/t (h) reverse

'**Umkehrung** f (-; -en) reversal (a. fig)

'**umkippen** (sep, -ge-) **1.** v/t (h) tip over, upset; **2.** v/i (sein) fall down or over, overturn

um'**klammern** v/t (no -ge-, h), **Um-'klammerung** f (-; -en) clasp, clutch, clench

'**Umkleide**|**ka**,**bine** f changing cubicle; ~**raum** m esp SPORT changing or locker room; THEA dressing room

'**umkommen** v/i (irr, **kommen**, sep, -ge-, sein) be killed (**bei** in), die (**in**); F ~ **vor** (dat) be dying with

'**Umkreis** m: **im** ~ **von** within a radius of; **um'kreisen** v/t (no -ge-, h) circle; ASTR revolve around; satellite etc: orbit

'**umkrempeln** v/t (sep, -ge-, h) roll up

'**Umlauf** m circulation; PHYS, TECH rotation; ECON circular; **im** (**in**) ~ **sein** (**bringen**) be in (put into) circulation, circulate; ~**bahn** f ASTR orbit

'**um**|**laufen** v/i (irr, **laufen**, sep, -ge-, sein) circulate; ~**legen** v/t (sep, -ge-, h) put on; move; share (expenses etc); TECH pull; F do s.o. in, bump s.o. off

'**umleiten** v/t (sep, -ge-, h) divert; '**Umleitung** f (-; -en) detour, Br diversion

'**umliegend** adj surrounding

'**umpacken** v/t (sep, -ge-, h) repack

'**umpflanzen** v/t (sep, -ge-, h) repot

umranden [ʊm'randən] v/t (no -ge-, h), **Um'randung** f (-; -en) edge, border

'**umräumen** v/t (sep, -ge-, h) rearrange

'**umrechnen** v/t (sep, -ge-, h) convert (**in** acc into); '**Umrechnung** f (-; -en) conversion; '**Umrechnungskurs** m exchange rate

'**umreißen** v/t (irr, **reißen**, sep, -ge-, h) knock s.o. down

um'**ringen** v/t (no -ge-, h) surround

'**Umriss** m outline (a. fig), contour

'**um**|**rühren** v/t (sep, -ge-, h) stir; ~**rüsten** v/t (sep, -ge-, h) TECH convert (**auf** acc to); ~**satteln** F v/i (sep, -ge-, h) ~ **von** ... **auf** (acc) ... switch from ... to ...

'**Umsatz** m ECON sales

'**umschalten** v/t and v/i (sep, -ge-, h) switch (over) (**auf** acc to) (a. fig)

'**Umschlag** m envelope; cover, wrapper; jacket; cuff, Br turn-up; MED compress; ECON handling; '**umschlagen** (irr, **schlagen**, sep, -ge-) **1.** v/t (h) cut down, fell; turn up; turn down; ECON handle; **2.** v/i (sein) turn over; fig change (suddenly)

'**Umschlagplatz** m trading center (Br centre)

'**umschnallen** v/t (sep, -ge-, h) buckle on

'**umschreiben**[1] v/t (irr, **schreiben**, sep, -ge-, h) rewrite

um'**schreiben**[2] v/t (irr, **schreiben**, no -ge-, h) paraphrase

Um'**schreibung** f (-; -en) paraphrase

'**Umschrift** f transcription

'**umschulen** v/t (sep, -ge-, h) retrain; transfer to another school

umschwärmt [ʊm'ʃvɛrmt] adj idolized

'**Umschwung** m (drastic) change, esp POL a. swing

um'**segeln** v/t (no -ge-, h) sail round; circumnavigate

'**um**|**sehen** v/refl (irr, **sehen**, sep, -ge-, h) look around (**in e-m Laden** a shop; **nach** for); look back (**nach** at); sich ~ **nach** be looking for; ~**setzen** v/t (sep, -ge-, h) move (a. PED); ECON sell; ~ **in** (acc) convert (in)to; **in die Tat** ~ put into action; **sich** ~ change places

'**umsiedeln** v/i (sep, -ge-, sein) and v/t (h) resettle; → **umziehen**

'**Umsied(e)lung** f (-; -en) resettlement

'**Umsiedler** m (-s; -) resettler

'**umso 1.** *je später etc*, ~ *schlechter etc* the later *etc* the worse *etc*; **2.** ~ *besser* so much the better

um'**sonst** *adv* free (of charge), for nothing; F for free; *fig* in vain

um'**spannen** *v/t (no -ge-, h)* span (*a. fig*)

'**umspringen** *v/i (irr,* **springen***, sep, -ge-, sein)* shift, change (suddenly) (*a. fig*); ~ *mit* treat (badly)

'**Umstand** *m* circumstance; fact; detail; *unter diesen* (*keinen*) *Umständen* under the (no) circumstances; *unter Umständen* possibly; *keine Umstände machen* not cause *s.o.* any trouble; not go to any trouble; no put o.s. out; *in anderen Umständen sein* be expecting

um'**ständlich** ['ʊmʃtɛntlıç] *adj* awkward; complicated; long-winded; *das ist* (*mir*) *viel zu ~* that's far too much trouble (for me)

'**Umstands|kleid** *n* maternity dress; ~**wort** *n (-[e]s; -wörter)* LING adverb

'**Umstehende:** *die* ~*n pl* the bystanders

'**umsteigen** *v/i (irr,* **steigen***, sep, -ge-, sein)* change (*nach* for), RAIL *a.* change trains (for)

'**umstellen** *v/t (sep, -ge-, h)* change (*auf acc* to), make a change *or* changes in, *esp* TECH *a.* switch (over) (to), convert (to); adjust (to); rearrange (*a. furniture*), reorganize; reset (*watch*); *sich ~ auf* (*acc*) change *or* switch (over) to; adjust (o.s.) to, get used to

'**Umstellung** *f (-; -en)* change; switch, conversion; adjustment; rearrangement, reorganization

'**umstimmen** *v/t (sep, -ge-, h)* *j-n ~* change s.o.'s mind

'**umstoßen** *v/t (irr,* **stoßen***, sep, -ge-, h)* knock over, upset (*a. fig*)

um**stritten** [ʊm'ʃtrıtən] *adj* controversial

'**Umsturz** *m* overthrow; '**umstürzen** *v/i (sep, -ge-, sein)* overturn, fall over

'**Umtausch** *m*, '**umtauschen** *v/t (sep, -ge-, h)* exchange (*gegen* for)

'**umwälzend** *adj* revolutionary

'**Umwälzung** *f (-; -en)* radical change

'**umwandeln** *v/t (sep, -ge-, h)* turn (*in acc* into), transform (into), *esp* CHEM, ELECTR, PHYS *a.* convert ([in]to)

'**Umwandlung** *f (-; -en)* transformation, conversion

'**Umweg** *m* roundabout route *or* way (*a. fig*), *esp* MOT *a.* detour; *ein ~ von 10 Minuten* ten minutes out of the way; *fig auf ~en* in a roundabout way

'**Umwelt** *f (-; no pl)* environment

'**Umwelt...** *in cpds mst* environmental ...; ~**forschung** *f* ecology

umwelt|freundlich *adj* environment-friendly, non-polluting; ~**schädlich** *adj* harmful, noxious, polluting

'**Umwelt|schutz** *m* conservation, environmental protection, pollution control; ~**schützer** *m* environmentalist, conservationist; ~**schutzpa,pier** *m* recycled paper; ~**sünder** *m* (environmental) polluter; ~**verschmutzer** *m (-s; -)* polluter; ~**verschmutzung** *f* (environmental) pollution; ~**zerstörung** *f* ecocide

'**umziehen** (*irr,* **ziehen***, sep -ge-*) **1.** *v/i* (*sein*) move (*nach* to); **2.** *v/refl* (*h*) change (one's clothes)

umzingeln [ʊm'tsıŋəln] *v/t (no -ge-, h)* surround, encircle

'**Umzug** *m* move (*nach* to), removal (to); parade

unabhängig ['ʊn-] *adj* independent (*von* of); ~ *davon, ob* (*was*) regardless of whether (what); '**Unabhängigkeit** *f (-; no pl)* independence (*von* from)

unab'sichtlich *adj* unintentional; *et.* ~ *tun* do s.th. by mistake

unab'wendbar *adj* inevitable

'**unachtsam** *adj* careless, negligent

'**Unachtsamkeit** *f (-; no pl)* carelessness, negligence

unan'fechtbar *adj* incontestable

'**un|angebracht** *adj* inappropriate; ~ *sein* be out of place; ~**angemessen** *adj* unreasonable; inadequate; ~**angenehm** *adj* unpleasant; embarrassing

unan'nehmbar *adj* unacceptable

Unannehmlichkeiten ['ʊn'anne:mlıçkaıtən] *pl* trouble, difficulties

unan'sehnlich *adj* unsightly

'**unanständig** *adj* indecent, obscene

unan'tastbar *adj* inviolable

'**unappetitlich** *adj* unappetizing

'**Unart** ['ʊn'a:rt] *f (-; -en)* bad habit

'**unartig** *adj* naughty, bad

'**unaufdringlich** *adj* unobtrusive

'**unauffällig** *adj* inconspicuous, unobtrusive

U

unauf'findbar *adj* not to be found, un-traceable

'unaufgefordert *adv* without being asked, of one's own accord

unaufhörlich [ʊn'aufˈhøːɐlɪç] *adj* continuous

'unaufmerksam *adj* inattentive

'Unaufmerksamkeit *f* (-; *no pl*) inattention, inattentiveness

'unaufrichtig *adj* insincere

unaus|löschlich [ʊn'aus'lœʃlɪç] *adj* indelible; ~stehlich [-'ʃteːlɪç] *adj* unbearable

'unbarmherzig *adj* merciless

'un|beabsichtigt *adj* unintentional; ~beachtet *adj* unnoticed; ~beaufsichtigt *adj* unattended; ~bebaut *adj* undeveloped; ~bedacht [-bədaxt] *adj* thoughtless; ~bedenklich 1. *adj* safe; 2. *adv* without hesitation; ~bedeutend *adj* insignificant; minor; ~bedingt 1. *adj* unconditional, absolute; 2. *adv* by all means, absolutely; *need etc* badly; ~befahrbar *adj* impassable; ~befangen *adj* unprejudiced, unbias(s)ed; unembarrassed; ~befriedigend *adj* unsatisfactory; ~befriedigt *adj* dissatisfied; ~begabt *adj* untalented; ~begreiflich *adj* inconceivable, incomprehensible; ~begrenzt *adj* unlimited, boundless; ~begründet *adj* unfounded

'Unbehagen *n* (-s; *no pl*) uneasiness, discomfort; 'unbehaglich *adj* uneasy, uncomfortable

unbehelligt [ʊnbə'hɛlɪçt] *adj* unmolested

'un|beherrscht *adj* uncontrolled, lacking self-control; ~beholfen [-bəhɔlfən] *adj* clumsy, awkward; ~beirrt *adj* unwavering; ~bekannt *adj* unknown

'Unbekannte *f* (-; *-n*) MATH unknown quantity

'un|bekümmert *adj* light-hearted, cheerful; ~belehrbar *adj*: *er ist* ~ he'll never learn; ~beliebt *adj* unpopular; *er ist überall* ~ nobody likes him; ~bemannt *adj* unmanned; ~bemerkt *adj* unnoticed; ~benutzt *adj* unused; ~bequem *adj* uncomfortable; inconvenient; ~berechenbar *adj* unpredictable; ~berechtigt *adj* unauthorized; unjustified; ~beschädigt *adj* undamaged; ~bescheiden *adj* immodest

un|be'schränkt *adj* unlimited; absolute

(*power*); ~beschreiblich [-bə'ʃraiplɪç] *adj* indescribable; ~be'sehen *adv* unseen; ~besiegbar [-bə'ziːkbaːɐ] *adj* invincible

'un|besonnen *adj* thoughtless, imprudent; rash; ~be'spielbar *adj* SPORT unplayable; ~beständig *adj* unstable; METEOR changeable, unsettled; ~bestätigt *adj* unconfirmed

unbe'stechlich *adj* incorruptible

'unbestimmt *adj* indefinite (*a.* LING); uncertain; vague

un|be'streitbar *adj* indisputable; ~bestritten [-bə'ʃtrɪtən] *adj* undisputed

'un|beteiligt *adj* not involved; indifferent; ~betont *adj* unstressed

unbeugsam [ʊn'bɔykzaːm] *adj* inflexible

'un|bewacht *adj* unwatched, unguarded (*a. fig*); ~bewaffnet *adj* unarmed; ~beweglich *adj* immovable; motionless

unbe'wohnbar *adj* uninhabitable

'unbewohnt *adj* uninhabited; unoccupied, vacant

'unbewusst *adj* unconscious

unbe'zahlbar *fig adj* invaluable, priceless; 'unbezahlt *adj* unpaid

'unblutig 1. *adj* bloodless; 2. *adv* without bloodshed

'unbrauchbar *adj* useless

und [ʊnt] *cj* and; F *na* ~? so what?

'undankbar *adj* ungrateful (*gegen* to); thankless; 'Undankbarkeit *f* (-; *no pl*) ingratitude, ungratefulness

undefi'nierbar *adj* undefinable

un'denkbar *adj* unthinkable

'undeutlich *adj* indistinct; inarticulate; *fig* vague

'undicht *adj* leaky

'unduldsam *adj* intolerant; 'Unduldsamkeit *f* (-; *no pl*) intolerance

undurch'dringlich *adj* impenetrable; ~'führbar *adj* impracticable

'undurch|lässig *adj* impervious, impermeable; ~sichtig *adj* opaque; *fig* mysterious

'uneben *adj* uneven; 'Unebenheit *f* a) (-; *no pl*) unevenness, b) (-; *-en*) bump

'unecht *adj* false; artificial; imitation ...; F *contp* fake, phon(e)y

'unehelich *adj* illegitimate

'unehrenhaft *adj* dishono(u)rable

'unehrlich *adj* dishonest

'**uneigennützig** *adj* unselfish

'**uneinig** *adj*: (*sich*) **~ sein** disagree (*über acc* on); '**Uneinigkeit** *f* (-; *no pl*) disagreement; dissension

un**ein**'**nehmbar** *adj* impregnable

'**un|empfänglich** *adj* insusceptible (*für* to); **~empfindlich** *adj* insensitive (*gegen* to)

un'**endlich** *adj* infinite; endless; never-ending; **Un'endlichkeit** *f* (-; *no pl*) infinity (*a. fig*)

unent|**behrlich** [ʊn'ɛnt'beːɐlɪç] *adj* indispensable; **~geltlich** [-'gɛltlɪç] *adj and adv* free (of charge)

'**unentschieden** *adj* undecided; **~ enden** SPORT end in a draw *or* tie; **es steht~** the score is even; '**Unentschieden** *n* (-*s*; -) SPORT draw, tie

'**unentschlossen** *adj* irresolute

unent'**schuldbar** *adj* inexcusable

unentwegt [ʊn'ɛnt've:kt] *adv* untiringly; continuously

'**un|erfahren** *adj* inexperienced; **~erfreulich** *adj* unpleasant; **~erfüllt** *adj* unfulfilled; **~ergiebig** *adj* unproductive; **~erheblich** *adj* irrelevant (*für* to); insignificant

unerhört ['ʊn'ɛːɐ'høːɐt] *adj* outrageous

'**un|erkannt** *adj* unrecognized; **~erklärlich** *adj* inexplicable; **~erlässlich** *adj* essential, indispensable; **~erlaubt** *adj* unallowed; unauthorized; **~erledigt** *adj* unsettled (*a.* ECON)

uner'**messlich** *adj* immeasurable

unermüdlich [ʊn'ʔɛɐ'myːtlɪç] *adj* indefatigable; untiring

uner'**reichbar** *adj* inaccessible; *esp fig* unattainable; **uner'reicht** *adj* unequal(l)ed

unersättlich [ʊn'ʔɛɐ'zɛtlɪç] *adj* insatiable

'**unerschlossen** *adj* undeveloped

uner|**schöpflich** [ʊn'ʔɛɐ'ʃœpflɪç] *adj* inexhaustible; **~schütterlich** [-'ʃʏtɐlɪç] *adj* imperturbable; **~schwinglich** [-'ʃvɪŋlɪç] *adj* exorbitant; **für j-n ~ sein** be beyond s.o.'s means; **~setzlich** [-'zɛtslɪç] *adj* irreplaceable; **~träglich** [-'trɛːklɪç] *adj* unbearable

'**unerwartet** *adj* unexpected

'**unerwünscht** *adj* unwanted

'**unfähig** *adj* incompetent; incapable (*zu tun* of doing), unable (to *inf*)

'**Unfähigkeit** *f* (-; *no pl*) incompetence; incapacity, inability

'**Unfall** *m* accident; crash

'**Unfallstelle** *f* scene of the accident

un'**fehlbar** *adj* infallible (*a.* REL); unfailing

unförmig ['ʊnfœrmɪç] *adj* shapeless; misshapen; monstrous

'**unfrankiert** *adj* unstamped

'**unfrei** *adj* not free; *post* unpaid

'**unfreiwillig** *adj* involuntary; unconscious (*humor*)

'**unfreundlich** *adj* unfriendly (*zu* to), unkind (to); *fig* cheerless

'**Unfrieden** *m* (-*s*; *no pl*) discord; **~ stiften** make mischief

'**unfruchtbar** *adj* infertile; '**Unfruchtbarkeit** *f* (-; *no pl*) infertility

Unfug ['ʊnfuːk] *m* (-[*e*]*s*; *no pl*) nonsense; **~ treiben** be up to mischief, fool around

Ungar ['ʊŋar] *m* (-*n*; -*n*), '**Ungarin** *f* (-; -*nen*), '**ungarisch** *adj* Hungarian; '**Ungarn** Hungary

'**ungastlich** *adj* inhospitable

'**un|geachtet** *prp* (*gen*) regardless of; despite; **~geahnt** *adj* unthought-of; **~gebeten** *adj* uninvited, unasked; **~gebildet** *adj* uneducated; **~geboren** *adj* unborn; **~gebräuchlich** *adj* uncommon, unusual; **~gebührlich** [-gəbyːɐlɪç] *adj* unseemly; **~gebunden** *fig adj* free, independent; **frei und ~** footloose and fancy-free; **~gedeckt** *adj* ECON uncovered; SPORT unmarked

'**Ungeduld** *f* (-; *no pl*) impatience

'**ungeduldig** *adj* impatient

'**ungeeignet** *adj* unfit; unqualified; inappropriate

ungefähr ['ʊŋəfɛːɐ] **1.** *adj* approximate; rough; **2.** *adv* approximately, roughly, about, around, ... or so; **so ~** something like that

'**ungefährlich** *adj* harmless; safe

'**ungeheuer** *adj* enormous (*a. fig*), huge, vast

'**Ungeheuer** *n* (-*s*; -) monster (*a. fig*)

unge'**heuerlich** *adj* monstrous

'**ungehindert** *adj and adv* unhindered

'**ungehobelt** *fig adj* uncouth, rough

'**ungehörig** *adj* improper, unseemly

'**ungehorsam** *adj* disobedient

Ungehorsam *m* (-*s*; *no pl*) disobedience

U

'un|gekocht adj uncooked; ~gekünstelt adj unaffected; ~gekürzt adj unabridged; ~gelegen adj inconvenient; j-m ~ kommen be inconvenient for s.o.

ungelenk ['ʊngəlɛŋk] adj awkward, clumsy

'ungelernt adj unskilled

'ungemütlich adj uncomfortable; F ~ werden get nasty

'ungenau adj inaccurate; fig vague; 'Ungenauigkeit f (-; -en) inaccuracy

ungeniert ['ʊnʒeniːɐt] adj uninhibited

'un|genießbar adj uneatable; undrinkable; F unbearable; ~genügend adj insufficient; PED poor, unsatisfactory; grade: a. F; ~gepflegt adj neglected; untidy, unkempt; ~gerade adj uneven; odd; ~gerecht adj unfair, unjust

'Ungerechtigkeit f (-; no pl) injustice, unfairness

'ungern adv unwillingly; et. ~ tun hate or not like to do s.th.

'un|geschehen adj: ~ machen undo; ~geschickt adj awkward, clumsy; ~geschliffen adj uncut (diamond etc); unpolished (a. fig); ~geschminkt adj without make-up; fig unvarnished, plain (truth); ~gesetzlich adj illegal, unlawful; ~gestört adj undisturbed; ~gestraft adj: ~ davonkommen get off unpunished (F scot-free); ~gesund adj unhealthy (a. fig); ~geteilt adj undivided (a. fig)

Ungetüm ['ʊngəty:m] n (-s; -e) monster, fig a. monstrosity

'ungewiss adj uncertain; j-n im Ungewissen lassen keep s.o. in the dark (über acc about); 'Ungewissheit f (-; no pl) uncertainty

'ungewöhnlich adj unusual

'ungewohnt adj strange, unfamiliar;

Ungeziefer ['ʊngətsi:fɐ] n (-s; no pl) vermin

'ungezogen adj naughty, bad; spoilt

'ungezwungen adj relaxed, informal; easygoing

'ungläubig adj incredulous, unbelieving (a. REL)

unglaublich [ʊn'glauplɪç] adj incredible, unbelievable

'unglaubwürdig adj implausible; unreliable (witness etc)

'ungleich adj unequal, different; unlike; ~mäßig adj uneven; irregular

'Unglück n (-[e]s; -e) a) (no pl) bad luck, misfortune; misery, b) accident; disaster; 'unglücklich adj unhappy, miserable; unfortunate; 'unglücklicher'weise adv unfortunately

'ungültig adj invalid; für ~ erklären JUR invalidate

'Ungunst f: zu ~en → zuungunsten; 'ungünstig adj unfavo(u)rable; disadvantageous

'ungut adj: ~es Gefühl misgivings (bei et. about s.th.); nichts für ~! no offense (Br offence) meant!

'unhaltbar adj untenable; intolerable; SPORT unstoppable

'unhandlich adj unwieldy

'unhar,monisch adj MUS discordant

'Unheil n (-s; no pl) mischief; evil; disaster; 'unheilbar adj MED incurable

'unheilvoll adj disastrous; sinister

'unheimlich adj creepy, spooky, eerie; F tremendous; F ~ gut terrific, fantastic

'unhöflich adj impolite; rude

'Unhöflichkeit f (-; no pl) impoliteness, rudeness

'un'hörbar adj inaudible

'unhygienisch adj insanitary

Uniform [uni'fɔrm] f (-; -en) uniform

'uninteressant adj uninteresting

uninteressiert ['ʊn'ɪntəresiːɐt] adj uninterested (an dat in)

Union [u'njoːn] f (-; -en) union

Universität [univerzi'tɛːt] f (-; -en) university

Universum [uni'vɛrzʊm] n (-s; no pl) universe

Unke ['ʊŋkə] f (-; -n) ZO toad

'unkenntlich adj unrecognizable

'Unkenntnis f (-; no pl) ignorance

'unklar adj unclear; uncertain; confused, muddled; im Unklaren sein (lassen) be (leave s.o.) in the dark

'unklug adj imprudent, unwise

'Unkosten pl expenses, costs

'Unkraut n (-[e]s; no pl) weed(s); ~ jäten weed (the garden)

unkündbar ['ʊnkʏntbaːɐ] adj permanent (post)

'unlängst adv lately, recently

'unleserlich adj illegible

'unlogisch adj illogical

un'lösbar adj insoluble

'unmännlich adj unmanly, effeminate

'unmäßig adj excessive

'Unmenge f vast quantity or number(s) (von of), F loads (of), tons (of)

'Unmensch m monster, brute

'unmenschlich adj inhuman, cruel

'Unmenschlichkeit f (-; -en) a) (no pl) inhumanity, b) cruelty

un'merklich adj imperceptible

'unmissverständlich adj unmistakable

'unmittelbar 1. adj immediate, direct; 2. adv: ~ nach (hinter) right after (behind)

'unmöbliert adj unfurnished

'unmodern adj out of fashion or style

'unmöglich 1. adj impossible; 2. adv: ich kann es ~ tun I can't possibly do it

'unmoralisch adj immoral

'unmündig adj JUR under age

'unmusikalisch adj unmusical

'unnachahmlich adj inimitable

'unnachgiebig adj unyielding

'unnachsichtig adj strict, severe

unnahbar [ʊn'naːbaːɐ] adj standoffish, cold

'unnatürlich adj unnatural (a. fig); affected

'unnötig adj unnecessary, needless

unnütz ['ʊnnʏts] adj useless

'unordentlich adj untidy; ~ sein room etc: be (in) a mess; 'Unordnung f (-; no pl) disorder, mess

'unparteiisch adj impartial, unbias(s)ed; 'Unparteiische m, f (-n; -n) SPORT referee

'unpassend adj unsuitable; improper; inappropriate

'unpassierbar adj impassable

unpässlich ['ʊnpɛslɪç] adj indisposed

'unpersönlich adj impersonal (a. LING)

'unpolitisch adj unpolitical

'unpraktisch adj impractical

'unpünktlich adj unpunctual

'unrecht adj wrong; j-m ~ tun do s.o. wrong; 'Unrecht n (-[e]s; no pl) injustice, wrong; zu ~ wrong(ful)ly; ~ haben be wrong

'unrechtmäßig adj unlawful

'unregelmäßig adj irregular (a. LING)

'Unregelmäßigkeit f (-; -en) irregularity

'unreif adj unripe; fig immature

'Unreife fig f immaturity

'unrein adj unclean; impure (a. REL)

'Unreinheit f (-; -en) impurity

'unrichtig adj incorrect, wrong

'Unruhe f (-; -n) a) (no pl) restlessness, unrest (a. POL); anxiety, alarm, b) pl disturbances, riots

'unruhig adj restless; uneasy; worried, alarmed; MAR rough

uns [ʊns] pers pron (to) us; each other; ~ (selbst) (to) ourselves; ein Freund von ~ a friend of ours

'un|sachgemäß adj improper; ~sachlich adj unobjective; ~sanft adj rude, rough; ~sauber adj unclean, esp fig a. impure; SPORT unfair; fig underhand; ~schädlich adj harmless; ~scharf adj PHOT blurred, out of focus

un'schätzbar adj inestimable, invaluable

'un|scheinbar adj inconspicuous; plain; ~schicklich adj indecent; ~schlüssig adj irresolute; undecided; ~schön adj unsightly; fig unpleasant

'Unschuld f (-; no pl) innocence; fig virginity

'unschuldig adj innocent (an dat of)

'unselbstständig adj dependent on others; 'Unselbstständigkeit f lack of independence, dependence on others

unser ['ʊnzɐ] poss pron our; ~er, ~e, ~es ours

'unsicher adj unsafe, insecure; self-conscious; uncertain; 'Unsicherheit f (-; -en) a) (no pl) insecurity, unsafeness; self-consciousness, b) uncertainty

'unsichtbar adj invisible

'Unsinn m (-[e]s; no pl) nonsense

'unsinnig adj nonsensical, stupid; absurd

'Unsitte f bad habit; abuse

'unsittlich adj immoral, indecent

'unsozial adj unsocial

'unsportlich adj unathletic; fig unfair

'unsterblich 1. adj immortal (a. fig); 2. adv: ~ verliebt madly in love (in acc with); 'Unsterblichkeit f immortality

'Unstimmigkeit f (-; -en) discrepancy; pl disagreements

'unsympathisch adj disagreeable; er (es) ist mir ~ I don't like him (it)

'untätig adj inactive; idle; 'Untätigkeit f (-; no pl) inactivity

'untauglich adj unfit (a. MIL); incompetent

un'teilbar adj indivisible

unten ['ʊntən] adv (down) below, down

U

(a. **nach ~**); downstairs; **~ auf** (dat) at the bottom of *the page etc*; **siehe ~** see below; **von oben bis ~** from top to bottom

unter ['ʊntɐ] prp under; below (a. fig); among; fig less than; **~ anderem** among other things; **~ uns (gesagt)** between you and me; **~ Wasser** underwater

'Unterarm m ANAT forearm

'unter|belichtet adj PHOT underexposed; **~besetzt** adj understaffed

'Unterbewusstsein n subconscious; **im ~** subconsciously

unter'bieten v/t (irr, bieten, no -ge-, h) underbid; undercut; beat (record); **~binden** fig v/t (irr, binden, no -ge-, h) put a stop to; prevent

unter'brechen v/t (irr, brechen, no -ge-, h) interrupt; **Unter'brechung** f (-; -en) interruption

'unterbringen v/i (irr, bringen, sep, -ge-, h) accommodate, find s.o. a place for, put (in acc into); 'Unterbringung f (-; -en) accommodation

unter'dessen adv in the meantime, meanwhile

unter'drücken v/t (no -ge-, h) oppress; suppress; **Unter'drücker** m (-s; -) oppressor; **Unter'drückung** f (-; -en) oppression; suppression

untere ['ʊntərə] adj lower (a. fig)

'unterentwickelt adj underdeveloped

'unterernährt adj undernourished, underfed; 'Unterernährung f (-; no pl) undernourishment, malnutrition

Unter'führung f (-; -en) underpass, Br a. subway

'Untergang m ASTR setting; MAR sinking; fig downfall; decline; fall; 'untergehen v/i (irr, gehen, sep, -ge-, sein) go down (a. fig), ASTR a. set, MAR a. sink

'untergeordnet adj subordinate, inferior; secondary

'Untergewicht n (-[e]s; no pl), 'untergewichtig adj underweight

unter'graben fig v/t (irr, graben, no -ge-, h) undermine

'Untergrund m subsoil; POL underground; **in den ~ gehen** go underground; **~bahn** f → U-Bahn

'unterhalb prp (gen) below, under

'Unterhalt m (-[e]s; no pl) support,

maintenance (a. JUR); **unter'halten** v/t (irr, halten, no -ge-, h) entertain; support; **sich ~ (mit)** talk (to, with); **sich (gut) ~** enjoy o.s., have a good time; **unter'haltsam** adj entertaining; **Unter'haltung** f (-; -en) talk, conversation; entertainment; **Unter'haltungsindus,trie** f show business

'Unter|händler m negotiator; **~haus** n (-es; no pl) Br PARL House of Commons; **~hemd** n undershirt, Br vest; **~holz** n (-es; no pl) undergrowth; **~hose** f shorts, esp Br underpants, panties, Br pants; **e-e lange ~, lange ~n** (a pair of) long johns

'unterirdisch adj underground

'Unterkiefer m ANAT lower jaw

'Unterkleid n slip

'unterkommen v/i (irr, kommen, sep, -ge-, sein) find accommodation; find work or a job (**bei** with)

Unterkunft ['ʊntɐkʊnft] f (-; -künfte [-kʏnftə]) accommodation, lodging(s); MIL quarters; **~ und Verpflegung** board and lodging

'Unterlage f TECH base; pl documents; data

unter'lassen v/t (irr, lassen, no -ge-, h) omit, fail to do s.th.; stop or quit doing s.th.; **Unter'lassung** f (-; -en) omission (a. JUR)

'unterlegen[1] v/t (sep, -ge-, h) underlay

unter'legen[2] adj inferior (dat to)

Unter'legenheit f (-; no pl) inferiority

'Unterleib m ANAT abdomen, belly

unter'liegen v/i (irr, liegen, no -ge-, sein) be defeated (**j-m** by s.o.), lose (to s.o.); fig be subject to

'Unterlippe f ANAT lower lip

'Untermieter m, 'Untermieterin f roomer, Br lodger

unter'nehmen v/t (irr, nehmen, no -ge-, h) make, take, go on a trip etc; **et. ~** do s.th. (**gegen** about s.th.); take action (**gegen** s.o.); **Unter'nehmen** n (-s; -) firm, business; venture; undertaking, enterprise; MIL operation; **Unter'nehmensberater(in)** management consultant; **Unter'nehmer** m (-s; -) businessman, entrepreneur; employer; **Unter'nehmerin** f (-; -nen) businesswoman; **unter'nehmungslustig** adj active, dynamic; adventurous

'**Unteroffizier** *m* MIL non-commissioned officer

'**unterordnen** *v/t and v/refl* (*sep, -ge-, h*) subordinate (o.s.) (*dat* to)

Unter'redung *f* (*-; -en*) talk(s)

Unterricht ['ʊntərɪçt] *m* (*-[e]s; no pl*) instruction, teaching; PED school, classes, lessons; **unter'richten** *v/i and v/t* (*no -ge-, h*) teach; give lessons; inform (*über acc* of); '**Unterrichtsstunde** *f* lesson, PED *a.* class, period

'**Unterrock** *m* slip

unter'sagen *v/t* (*no -ge-, h*) prohibit

unter'schätzen *v/t* (*no -ge-, h*) underestimate; underrate

unter'scheiden *v/t and v/i* (*irr, scheiden, no -ge-, h*) distinguish (*zwischen* between; *von* from); tell apart; *sich ~* differ (*von* from; *in dat* in; *durch* by); **Unter'scheidung** *f* (*-; -en*) distinction; **Unterschied** ['ʊntərʃiːt] *m* (*-[e]s; -e*) difference; *im ~ zu* unlike, as opposed to; '**unterschiedlich** *adj* different; varying

unter'schlagen *v/t* (*irr, schlagen, no -ge-, h*) embezzle; **Unter'schlagung** *f* (*-; -en*) embezzlement

Unterschlupf ['ʊntərʃlʊpf] *m* (*-[e]s; no pl*) hiding place

unter'schreiben *v/t and v/i* (*irr, schreiben, no -ge-, h*) sign

'**Unterschrift** *f* signature; caption

'**Unterseeboot** *n → U-Boot*

Untersetzer ['ʊntərzɛtsər] *m* (*-s; -*) coaster; saucer

unter'setzt *adj* thickset, stocky

'**Unterstand** *m* shelter, MIL *a.* dugout

unter'stehen (*irr, stehen, no -ge-, h*) **1.** *v/i* (*dat*) be under the control of); **2.** *v/refl* dare; *~ Sie sich* (*et. zu tun*)! don't you dare ([to] do s.th.)!

'**unterstellen**¹ *v/t* (*sep, -ge-, h*) put *s.th.* in; store; *sich ~* take shelter

unter'stellen² *v/t* (*no -ge-, h*) assume; *j-m ~, dass er ...* insinuate that s.o. ...; **Unter'stellung** *f* (*-; -en*) insinuation

unter'streichen *v/t* (*irr, streichen, no -ge-, h*) underline (*a. fig*)

unter'stützen *v/t* (*no -ge-, h*) support; back (up); **Unter'stützung** *f* (*-; -en*) support; aid; welfare (payments)

unter'suchen *v/t* (*no -ge-, h*) examine (*a.* MED), investigate (*a.* JUR); search; CHEM analyze; **Unter'suchung** *f* (*-;*

-en) examination (*a.* MED), investigation (*a.* JUR), *a.* (medical) checkup; CHEM analysis

Unter'suchungs|gefangene *m, f* JUR prisoner on remand; **~gefängnis** *n* JUR remand prison; **~haft** *f*: *in ~ sein* JUR be on remand; **~richter** *m* JUR examining magistrate

Untertan ['ʊntətaːn] *m* (*-s; -en*) subject

'**Untertasse** *f* saucer

'**untertauchen** (*sep, -ge-*) **1.** *v/i* (*sein*) dive, submerge; *fig* disappear; *esp* POL go underground; **2.** *v/t* (*h*) duck

'**Unterteil** *n, m* lower part, bottom

unter'teilen *v/t* (*no -ge-, h*) subdivide; **Unter'teilung** *f* (*-; -en*) subdivision

'**Untertitel** *m* subtitle; *film: a.* caption

'**Unterton** *m* undertone

Unter'treibung *f* (*-; -en*) understatement

'**untervermieten** *v/t* (*no -ge-, h*) sublet

unter'wandern *v/t* (*no -ge-, h*) infiltrate

'**Unterwäsche** *f* underwear

'**Unterwasser...** *in cpds* underwater ...

unterwegs [ʊntə've:ks] *adv* on the *or* one's way (*nach* to)

unter'weisen *v/t* (*irr, weisen, no -ge-, h*) instruct; **Unter'weisung** *f* (*-; -en*) instruction

'**Unterwelt** *f* (*-; no pl*) underworld

unter'werfen *v/t* (*irr, werfen, no -ge-, h*) subject (*dat* to); subjugate; *sich ~* submit (to); **Unter'werfung** *f* (*-; -en*) subjection; submission (*unter acc* to)

unterwürfig [ʊntə'vʏrfɪç] *adj* servile

unter'zeichnen *v/t* (*no -ge-, h*) sign; **Unter'zeichnete** *m, f* (*-n; -n*) the undersigned; **Unter'zeichnung** *f* (*-; -en*) signing

'**unterziehen**¹ *v/t* (*irr, ziehen, sep, -ge-, h*) put *s.th.* on underneath

unter'ziehen² *v/t* (*irr, ziehen, no -ge-, h*) *sich e-r Behandlung, Prüfung etc ~* undergo (*treatment etc*), take (*an examination etc*)

'**Untiefe** *f* shallow, shoal

un'tragbar *adj* unbearable, intolerable; **~'trennbar** *adj* inseparable

untreu *adj* unfaithful (*dat* to)

un'tröstlich *adj* inconsolable; **~trüglich** [ʊn'try:klɪç] *adj* unmistakable

'**Untugend** *f* vice, bad habit

'**unüber|legt** *adj* thoughtless; **~sichtlich** *adj* blind (*bend etc*)

U

unüber|trefflich [ʊnʔyːbɐˈtrɛflɪç] *adj* unsurpassable, matchless; **~troffen** [-ˈtrɔfən] *adj* unequal(l)ed; **~windlich** [-ˈvɪntlɪç] *adj* insuperable, invincible

unum|gänglich [ʊnʔʊmˈgɛŋlɪç] *adj* inevitable; **~schränkt** [-ˈʃrɛŋkt] *adj* unlimited; POL absolute; **~stritten** [-ˈʃtrɪtən] *adj* undisputed; **~wunden** [-ˈvʊndən] *adv* straight out, frankly

ununterbrochen [ˈʊnʔʊntɐbrɔxən] *adj* uninterrupted; continuous

un|ver'änderlich *adj* unchanging; **~ver'antwortlich** *adj* irresponsible; **~ver'besserlich** *adj* incorrigible; **~ver'bindlich** *adj* noncommittal, ECON not binding; **~ver'daulich** *adj* indigestible (*a. fig*)

'unverdient *adj* undeserved

'unverdünnt *adj* undiluted; straight

unver'einbar *adj* incompatible

'unverfälscht *adj* unadulterated

'unverfänglich *adj* harmless

'unverfroren *adj* brazen, impertinent

'unvergänglich *adj* immortal, eternal

unver'gesslich *adj* unforgettable

'unver'gleichlich *adj* incomparable

'unverhältnismäßig *adv* disproportionately; **~ hoch** excessive

'unverheiratet *adj* unmarried, single

unverhofft [ˈʊnfɐhɔft] *adj* unhoped-for; unexpected

unverhohlen [ˈʊnfɐhoːlən] *adj* undisguised, open

'unverkäuflich *adj* not for sale; unsal(e)able

unver'kennbar *adj* unmistakable

'unverletzt *adj* unhurt

unvermeidlich [ʊnfɐˈmaitlɪç] *adj* inevitable

'unvermindert *adj* undiminished

'unvermittelt *adj* abrupt, sudden

'Unvermögen *n* (-s; *no pl*) inability, incapacity

'unvermutet *adj* unexpected

'unvernünftig *adj* unreasonable; foolish

'unverschämt *adj* rude, impertinent; outrageous (*price etc*); '**Unverschämtheit** *f* (-; *-en*) impertinence; **die ~ haben zu** *inf* have the nerve to *inf*

'unverschuldet *adj* through no fault of one's own

unversehens [ˈʊnfɐzeːəns] *adv* unexpectedly, all of a sudden

'un|versehrt *adj* unhurt; undamaged; **~söhnlich** *adj* irreconcilable (*a. fig*), implacable; **~versorgt** *adj* unprovided for; **~verständlich** *adj* unintelligible; **es ist mir ~** I can't see how *or* why, F it beats me; **~versucht** *adj*: **nichts ~ lassen** leave nothing undone

unver'wundbar *adj* invulnerable

unver|wüstlich [ʊnfɐˈvyːstlɪç] *adj* indestructible; **~zeihlich** [-ˈtsailɪç] *adj* inexcusable; **~züglich** [-ˈtsyːklɪç] **1.** *adj* immediate, prompt; **2.** *adv* immediately, without delay

'unvollendet *adj* unfinished

'unvollkommen *adj* imperfect

'unvollständig *adj* incomplete

'unvorbereitet *adj* unprepared

'unvoreingenommen *adj* unprejudiced, unbias(s)ed

'unvorhergesehen *adj* unforeseen

'unvorhersehbar *adj* unforeseeable

'unvorsichtig *adj* careless; '**Unvorsichtigkeit** *f* (-; *no pl*) carelessness

unvor'stellbar *adj* unthinkable

'unvorteilhaft *adj* unbecoming

'unwahr *adj* untrue; '**Unwahrheit** *f* untruth; '**unwahrscheinlich** *adj* improbable, unlikely; F fantastic

unwegsam [ˈʊnveːkzaːm] *adj* difficult, rough (*terrain*)

unweigerlich [ʊnˈvaigɐlɪç] *adv* inevitably

'unweit *prp* (*gen*) not far from

'Unwetter *n* (-s; *-*) disastrous (thunder)storm

'unwichtig *adj* unimportant

unwider|legbar [ʊnviːdɐˈleːkbaːɐ] *adj* irrefutable; **~ruflich** [-ˈruːflɪç] *adj* irrevocable; **~stehlich** [-ˈʃteːlɪç] *adj* irresistible

'Unwille(n) *m* indignation (**über** *acc* at); '**unwillig** *adj* indignant (**über** *acc* at); unwilling, reluctant

'unwillkürlich *adj* involuntary

'unwirklich *adj* unreal

'unwirksam *adj* ineffective

unwirsch [ˈʊnvɪrʃ] *adj* surly, gruff

'unwirtlich [ˈʊnvɪrtlɪç] *adj* inhospitable

'unwirtschaftlich *adj* uneconomic(al)

'unwissend *adj* ignorant

'Unwissenheit *f* (-; *no pl*) ignorance

'unwohl *adj* unwell; uneasy

'unwürdig *adj* unworthy (*gen* of)

unzählig [ʊnˈtsɛːlɪç] *adj* innumerable, countless

unzer'brechlich *adj* unbreakable

unzer'reißbar *adj* untearable

unzer'störbar *adj* indestructible

unzer'trennlich *adj* inseparable

'Unzucht *f* (-; *no pl*) sexual offense (*Br* offence); **'unzüchtig** *adj* indecent; obscene

'unzufrieden *adj* discontent(ed) (*mit* with), dissatisfied (with); **'Unzufriedenheit** *f* discontent, dissatisfaction

'unzugänglich *adj* inaccessible

'unzulänglich *adj* inadequate

'unzulässig *adj* inadmissible

unzu'mutbar *adj* unacceptable; unreasonable

'unzurechnungsfähig *adj* JUR irresponsible; **'Unzurechnungsfähigkeit** *f* (-; *no pl*) JUR irresponsibility

'unzureichend *adj* insufficient

'unzusammenhängend *adj* incoherent

'unzuverlässig *adj* unreliable, untrustworthy; uncertain

üppig [ˈʏpɪç] *adj* luxuriant, lush (*both a. fig*); voluptuous, luscious; opulent; rich

uralt [ˈuːɐˈʔalt] *adj* ancient (*a. iro*)

Uran [uˈraːn] *n* (-s; *no pl*) uranium

Urauf'führung *f* première, first performance (*film:* showing)

urbar [ˈuːɐbaːɐ] *adj* arable; ~ **machen** cultivate; reclaim

'Urbevölkerung *f*, **'Ureinwohner** *pl* aboriginal inhabitants; *in Australia:* Aborigines

'Urenkel *m* great-grandson

'Urenkelin *f* great-granddaughter

'Urgroß... *in cpds* ...**eltern,** ...**mutter,** ...**vater:** great-grand...

Urheberrechte [ˈuːɐheːbɐ-] *pl* copyright (*an dat* on, for)

Urin [uˈriːn] *m* (-s; -e) urine; **urinieren** [uriˈniːrən] *v/i* (*no -ge-*, *h*) urinate

Urkunde [ˈuːɐkʊndə] *f* (-; -n) document; diploma; **'Urkundenfälschung** *f* forgery of documents

Urlaub [ˈuːɐlaup] *m* (-[e]s; -e) vacation, *Br* holiday(s); MIL leave; **in** *or* **im** ~ **sein** (*auf* ~ **gehen**) be (go) on vacation (*Br* holiday); **e-n Tag** (*ein paar Tage*) ~ **nehmen** take a day (a few days) off; **Urlauber(in)** [ˈuːɐlaubɐ (-bərɪn)] (-s; -/-; -nen) vacationist, vacationer, *Br* holidaymaker

Urne [ˈʊrnə] *f* (-; -n) urn; ballot box

'Ursache *f* (-; -n) cause; reason; **keine ~!** not at all, you're welcome

'Ursprung *m* origin

ursprünglich [ˈuːɐʃprʏŋlɪç] *adj* original; natural, unspoilt

Urteil [ˈʊrtail] *n* (-[e]s; -e) judg(e)ment; JUR sentence; **sich ein ~ bilden** form a judg(e)ment (*über acc* about)

urteilen *v/i* (*ge-*, *h*) judge (*über j-n, et. s.o., s.th.;* **nach** by)

'Urwald *m* primeval forest; jungle

urwüchsig [ˈuːɐvyːksɪç] *adj* coarse, earthy

'Urzeit *f* prehistoric times

usw. ABBR *of* **und so weiter** etc., and so on

Utensilien [utɛnˈziːljən] *pl* utensils

Utopie [utoˈpiː] *f* (-; -n) illusion

utopisch [uˈtoːpɪʃ] *adj* utopian; fantastic

V

Vagabund [vagaˈbʊnt] *m* (-en; -en) vagabond, tramp, F bum

vage [ˈvaːgə] *adj* vague

Vakuum [ˈvaːkuʊm] *n* (-s; -kua, -kuen) vacuum

Vampir [ˈvampiːɐ] *m* (-s; -e) ZO vampire (*a. fig*)

Vanille [vaˈnɪljə] *f* (-; *no pl*) vanilla

variabel [vaˈrjaːbəl] *adj* variable

Variante [vaˈrjantə] *f* (-; -n) variant

Variation [varjaˈtsioːn] *f* (-; -en) variation

Varietee, *a.* **Varieté** [varjeˈteː] *n* (-s; -s) vaudeville, *Br* variety theatre, music hall

variieren [variˈiːrən] *v/i and v/t* (*no -ge-*, *h*) vary

Vase [ˈvaːzə] *f* (-; -n) vase

Vater ['faːtɐ] m (-s; *Väter* ['fɛːtɐ]) father

'**Vaterland** n native country

'**Vaterlandsliebe** f patriotism

väterlich ['fɛːtɐlɪç] adj fatherly, paternal

'**Vaterschaft** f (-; -en) JUR paternity

'**Vater'unser** n (-s; -) REL Lord's Prayer

v. Chr. ABBR of *vor Christus* BC, before Christ

V-Ausschnitt ['faʊ-] m V-neck

Vegetarier [vegeˈtaːrjɐ] m (-s; -), **Vegetarierin** f (-; -nen), **vegetarisch** [vegeˈtaːrɪʃ] adj vegetarian

Vegetation [vegetaˈtsjoːn] f (-; -en) vegetation; **vegetieren** [vegeˈtiːrən] v/i (no -ge-, h) vegetate

Veilchen n (-s; -) BOT violet

Velo ['veːlo] Swiss n (-s; -s) bicycle, F bike

Ventil [vɛnˈtiːl] n (-s; -e) TECH valve; fig vent, outlet

Ventilation [vɛntilaˈtsjoːn] f (-; -en) ventilation; **Ventilator** [vɛntiˈlaːtoːr] m (-s; -en [-laˈtoːrən]) fan

verabreden [fɛɐˈʔap-] v/t (no -ge-, h) agree (up)on, arrange; appoint, fix; *sich ~* make a date (or an appointment) (*mit* with); **Ver'abredung** f (-; -en) appointment; date

ver'ab|reichen v/t (no -ge-, h) give; MED administer; **~scheuen** v/t (no -ge-, h) loathe, detest

verabschieden [fɛɐˈʔapʃiːdən] v/t (no -ge-, h) say goodbye to (a. *sich ~ von*); dismiss; JUR pass; **Ver'abschiedung** f (-; -en) dismissal; JUR passing

ver'achten v/t (no -ge-, h) despise; **verächtlich** [fɛɐˈʔɛçtlɪç] adj contemptuous; **Ver'achtung** f (-; no pl) contempt

verallgemeinern [fɛɐˈʔalgəˈmaɪnɐn] v/t (no -ge-, h) generalize

ver'altet adj antiquated, out of date

Veranda [veˈranda] f (-; -den) porch, Br veranda(h)

veränderlich [fɛɐˈʔɛndɐlɪç] adj changeable (a. METEOR), variable (a. MATH, LING); **ver'ändern** v/t and v/refl (no -ge-, h), **Ver'änderung** f change

verängstigt [fɛɐˈʔɛŋstɪçt] adj frightened, scared

ver'anlagen v/t (no -ge-, h) ECON assess; **veranlagt** [fɛɐˈʔanlaːkt] adj inclined (*zu, für* to); **künstlerisch** (**musikalisch**) **~ sein** have a gift or bent for

art (music); **Ver'anlagung** f (-; -en) (pre)disposition (a. MED); talent, gift; ECON assessment

ver'anlassen v/t (no -ge-, h) make arrangements (or arrange) for s.th.; *j-n zu et. ~* make s.o. do s.th.

Ver'anlassung f (-; -en) cause (*zu* for)

ver'|anschaulichen v/t (no -ge-, h) illustrate; **~'anschlagen** v/t (no -ge-, h) estimate (*auf* acc at)

ver'anstalten v/t (no -ge-, h) arrange, organize; hold, give (*concert, party etc*); **Ver'anstaltung** f (-; -en) event, SPORT a. meet, Br meeting

ver'antworten v/t (no -ge-, h) take the responsibility for; **ver'antwortlich** adj responsible; *j-n ~ machen für* hold s.o. responsible for; **Ver'antwortung** f (-; no pl) responsibility; *auf eigene ~* at one's own risk; *j-n zur ~ ziehen* call s.o. to account; **Ver'antwortungsgefühl** n (-[e]s; no pl) sense of responsibility; **ver'antwortungslos** adj irresponsible

ver'|arbeiten v/t (no -ge-, h) process; fig digest; *et. ~ zu* manufacture (or make) s.th. into; **~'ärgern** v/t (no -ge-, h) make s.o. angry, annoy

ver'armt adj impoverished

ver'arschen v/t (no -ge-, h) *j-n ~* take the piss out of s.o.

Verb [vɛrp] n (-s; -en ['vɛrbən]) LING verb

Verband [fɛɐˈbant] m (-es; *Verbände* [fɛɐˈbɛndə]) MED dressing, bandage; ECON association; MIL formation, unit; **~(s)kasten** m MED first-aid kit or box; **~(s)zeug** n MED dressing material

ver'bannen v/t (no -ge-, h) banish (a. fig), exile; **Ver'bannung** f (-; -en) banishment, exile

verbarrika'dieren v/t (no -ge-, h) barricade; block

ver'bergen v/t (irr, **bergen**, no -ge-, h) hide (a. *sich ~*), conceal

ver'bessern v/t (no -ge-, h) improve; correct; **Ver'besserung** f (-; -en) improvement; correction

ver'beugen v/refl (no -ge-, h), **Ver'beugung** f (-; -en) bow (*vor* to)

ver'biegen v/t (irr, **biegen**, no -ge-, h) twist; **~'bieten** v/t (irr, **bieten**, no -ge-, h) forbid; prohibit; → *verboten*

ver'billigen v/t (no -ge-, h) reduce in

price; **verbilligt** [-'bɪlɪçt] *adj* reduced, at reduced prices

verbinden *v/t* (*irr*, **binden**, *no* -ge-, *h*) MED dress, bandage; bandage *s.o.* up; *a.* TECH connect, join, link (up); TEL put *s.o.* through (**mit** to); combine (*a.* CHEM **sich ~**); *fig* unite; associate; *j-m die Augen ~* blindfold s.o.; *damit sind beträchtliche Kosten verbunden* that involves considerable cost(s *pl*); *falsch verbunden!* wrong number!

verbindlich [fɛɐ'bɪntlɪç] *adj* obligatory, compulsory (*a.* PED); obliging

Ver'bindlichkeit *f* (-; -en) a) (*no pl*) obligingness, b) *pl* ECON liabilities

Ver'bindung *f* (-; -en) connection; combination; CHEM compound; UNIV fraternity, *Br* society; *sich in ~ setzen mit* get in touch with; *in ~ stehen* (**bleiben**) be (keep) in touch

verbissen [fɛɐ'bɪsən] *adj* dogged

ver'bittert *adj* bitter, embittered

verblasen [fɛɐ'blaːzən] *v/i* (*no* -ge-, *sein*) fade (*a. fig*)

Verbleib [fɛɐ'blaɪp] *m* (-[e]s; *no pl*) whereabouts; **ver'bleiben** *v/i* (*irr*, **bleiben**, *no* -ge-, *sein*) remain

verbleit [fɛɐ'blaɪt] *adj* leaded

ver'blendet *fig adj* blind

Ver'blendung *fig f* (-; -en) blindness

verblichen [fɛɐ'blɪçən] *adj* faded

verblüffen [fɛɐ'blʏfən] *v/t* (*no* -ge-, *h*) amaze, F flabbergast

Ver'blüffung *f* (-; -en) amazement

ver'blühen *v/i* (*no* -ge-, *sein*) fade, wither (*both a. fig*)

ver'bluten *v/i* (*no* -ge-, *sein*) MED bleed to death

verborgen [fɛɐ'bɔrgən] *adj* hidden, concealed; *im Verborgenen* in secret

Verbot [fɛɐ'boːt] *n* (-[e]s; -e) prohibition, ban (on *s.th.*); **ver'boten** *adj*: *Rauchen ~* no smoking

Ver'brauch *m* (-[e]s; *no pl*) consumption (**an** *dat* of); **ver'brauchen** *v/t* (*no* -ge-, *h*) consume, use up

Verbraucher [fɛɐ'braʊxɐ] *m* (-s; -), **Ver'braucherin** *f* (-; -nen) consumer; **~schutz** *m* consumer protection

Ver'brechen *n* (-s; -) crime; *ein ~ begehen* commit a crime; **Ver'brecher(in)** (-s; -/-; -nen), **ver'brecherisch** *adj* criminal

ver'breiten *v/t and v/refl* (*no* -ge-, *h*) spread (*in dat*, **über** *acc* over, through); circulate

verbreitern [fɛɐ'braɪtɐn] *v/t and v/refl* (*no* -ge-, *h*) widen, broaden

Ver'breitung *f* (-; *no pl*) spread(ing); circulation

ver'brennen *v/i* (*irr*, **brennen**, *no* -ge-, *sein*) *and v/t* (*h*) burn (up); cremate

Ver'brennung *f* (-; -en) burning; cremation; TECH combustion; MED burn

ver'bringen *v/t* (*irr*, **bringen**, *no* -ge-, *h*) spend, pass

verbrüdern [fɛɐ'bryːdɐn] *v/refl* (*no* -ge-, *h*) fraternize; **Verbrüderung** [fɛɐ'bryːdəruŋ] *f* (-; -en) fraternization

ver'brühen *v/t* (*no* -ge-, *h*) scald

ver'buchen *v/t* (*no* -ge-, *h*) book

verbünden [fɛɐ'bʏndən] *v/refl* (*no* -ge-, *h*) ally o.s. (**mit** to, with)

Ver'bündete *m, f* (-n; -n) ally (*a. fig*)

ver'bürgen *v/refl* (*no* -ge-, *h*) **sich ~ für** vouch for, guarantee

ver'büßen *v/t* (*no* -ge-, *h*) **e-e Strafe ~** serve a sentence, serve time

verchromt [fɛɐ'kroːmt] *adj* chromium--plated

Verdacht [fɛɐ'daxt] *m* (-[e]s; -e) suspicion; **~ schöpfen** become suspicious

verdächtig [fɛɐ'dɛçtɪç] *adj* suspicious, suspect; **Verdächtige** [fɛɐ'dɛçtɪgə] *m, f* (-n; -n) suspect; **ver'dächtigen** *v/t* (*no* -ge-, *h*) suspect (*j-n e-r Tat* s.o. of [doing] s.th.); **Ver'dächtigung** *f* (-; -en) suspicion

verdammen [fɛɐ'damən] *v/t* (*no* -ge-, *h*) condemn (**zu** to), damn (*a.* REL); **Ver'dammnis** *f* (-; *no pl*) REL damnation; **ver'dammt 1.** *adj* damned, F *a.* damn, darn(ed), *Br sl a.* bloody; F *~* (*noch mal*)! damn (it)!; **2.** *adv ~ gut etc* damn (*Br sl a.* bloody) good *etc*; **Ver'dammung** *f* (-; -en) condemnation; REL damnation

ver'dampfen *v/t* (*no* -ge-, *h*) *and v/i* (*sein*) evaporate

ver'danken *v/t* (*no* -ge-, *h*) *j-m* (*e-m Umstand*) *et.* **~** owe s.th. to s.o. (s.th.)

verdarb [fɛɐ'darp] *pret of* **verderben**

verdauen [fɛɐ'daʊən] *v/t* (*no* -ge-, *h*) digest (*a. fig*)

ver'daulich *adj* digestible; *leicht* (*schwer*) *~* easy (hard) to digest

Ver'dauung *f* (-; *no pl*) digestion

V

Ver'deck n (-[e]s; -e) top; ver'decken v/t (no -ge-, h) cover (up) (a. fig)

ver'denken v/t (irr, denken, no -ge-) ich kann es ihm nicht ~, (dass er ...) I can't blame him (for doing)

verderben [fɛɐ'dɛrbən] (irr, no -ge-) 1. v/i (sein) spoil (a. fig); GASTR go bad; 2. v/t (h) spoil (a. fig), ruin; sich den Magen ~ upset one's stomach

Ver'derben n (-s; no pl) ruin

verderblich [fɛɐ'dɛrplɪç] adj perishable; leicht ~e Lebensmittel perishables

ver'dichten v/t (no -ge-, h) compress, condense

ver'dienen v/t (no -ge-, h) earn, make; fig deserve

Ver'dienst¹ m (-[e]s; -e) earnings; salary; wages; gain, profit

Ver'dienst² n (-[e]s; -e) merit; es ist sein ~, dass it is thanks to him that

ver'dient adj (well-)deserved

ver'doppeln v/t and v/refl (no -ge-, h) double

verdorben [fɛɐ'dɔrbən] 1. pp of verderben; 2. adj GASTR spoilt, bad (both a. fig); MED stomach

ver'dorren [fɛɐ'dɔrən] v/i (no -ge-, sein) wither, dry up; ~'drängen v/t (no -ge-, h) supplant, supersede; replace; PHYS displace; PSYCH repress, suppress; ~'drehen v/t (no -ge-, h) twist, fig a. distort; die Augen ~ roll one's eyes; j-m den Kopf ~ turn s.o.'s head; ~'dreht F fig adj mixed up; ~'dreifachen v/t and v/refl (no -ge-, h) treble, triple

verdrießen [fɛɐ'driːsən] v/t (irr, no -ge-, h) annoy; verdrießlich [fɛɐ'driːslɪç] adj glum, morose, sullen; verdross [fɛɐ'drɔs] pret of verdrießen; verdrossen [fɛɐ'drɔsən] 1. pp of verdrießen; 2. adj grumpy, sullen; Verdruss [fɛɐ'drʊs] m (-es; -e) annoyance

ver'dummen (no -ge-) 1. v/t (h) make stupid, stultify; 2. v/i (sein) become stultified

ver'dunkeln v/t and v/refl (no -ge-, h) darken; black out; fig obscure

Ver'dunk(e)lung f (-; -en) darkening; blackout; JUR collusion

ver'dünnen v/t (no -ge-, h) dilute

ver'dunsten v/i (no -ge-, sein) evaporate

ver'dursten v/i (no -ge-, sein) die of thirst

verdutzt [fɛɐ'dʊtst] adj puzzled

ver'edeln v/t (no -ge-, h) BOT graft; TECH process, refine; Ver'ed(e)lung f (-; -en) BOT grafting; TECH processing, refinement

ver'ehren v/t (no -ge-, h) admire; adore, worship (both a. fig), esp REL a. revere, venerate; Ver'ehrer(in) (-s; -/-; -nen) admirer, esp film etc: a. fan; Ver'ehrung f (-; no pl) admiration; adoration; worship; esp REL reverence, veneration

vereidigen [fɛɐ'aidɪɡən] v/t (no -ge-, h) swear s.o. in; JUR put s.o. under an oath

Verein [fɛɐ'ain] m (-[e]s; -e) club (a. SPORT); society, association

vereinbar [fɛɐ'ainbaːɐ] adj compatible (mit with); vereinbaren [fɛɐ'ainbaːrən] v/t (no -ge-, h) agree (up)on, arrange; Ver'einbarung f (-; -en) agreement, arrangement

ver'einen → vereinigen

ver'einfachen v/t (no -ge-, h) simplify

Ver'einfachung f (-; -en) simplification

ver'einheitlichen v/t (no -ge-, h) standardize

ver'einigen v/t and v/refl (no -ge-, h) unite (zu into); combine, join

Ver'einigung f (-; -en) union; combination; alliance

ver'einsamen v/i (no -ge-, sein) become lonely or isolated

vereinzelt [fɛɐ'aintsəlt] adj occasional, odd; ~ Regen scattered showers

ver'eiteln v/t (no -ge-, h) prevent; frustrate; ~'enden v/i (no -ge-, sein) esp ZO die, perish; ~'engen v/t and v/refl (no -ge-, h) narrow

ver'erben v/t (no -ge-, h) j-m et. ~ leave (BIOL transmit) s.th. to s.o.; sich ~ (auf acc) be passed on or down (to) (a. BIOL and fig); Ver'erbung f (-; no pl) BIOL heredity; Ver'erbungslehre f BIOL genetics

verewigen [fɛɐ'eːvɪɡən] v/t (no -ge-, h) immortalize

ver'fahren (irr, fahren, no -ge-) 1. v/i (sein) proceed; ~ mit deal with; 2. v/refl (h) MOT get lost

Ver'fahren n (-s; -) procedure, method, esp TECH a. technique, way; JUR (legal) proceedings (gegen against)

Ver'fall m (-[e]s; no pl) decay (a. fig); dilapidation; fig decline; ECON etc expiry;

ver'fallen (*irr, fallen, no -ge-, sein*) **1.** *v/i* decay (*a. fig*), dilapidate; *esp fig* decline; ECON expire; MED waste away; become addicted to; (**wieder**) ~ **in** (*acc*) fall (back) into; ~ **auf** (*acc*) hit (up)on; **2.** *adj* decayed; dilapidated; **j-m** ~ **sein** be s.o.'s slave; **Ver'fallsda-tum** *n* expiry date; GASTR pull date, *Br* best-before (*or* best-by) date; PHARM sell-by date

ver'fälschen *v/t* (*no -ge-, h*) falsify; distort; GASTR adulterate

verfänglich [fɛɐˈfɛŋlɪç] *adj* delicate, tricky; embarrassing, compromising

ver'färben *v/refl* (*no -ge-, h*) discolo(u)r

ver'fassen *v/t* (*no -ge-, h*) write

Verfasser [fɛɐˈfasə] *m* (*-s, -*), **Ver'fassering** *f* (*-; -nen*) author

Ver'fassung *f* (*-; -en*) state (of health *or* of mind), condition; POL constitution

ver'fassungs\|mäßig *adj* POL constitutional; **~widrig** *adj* unconstitutional

ver'faulen *v/i* (*no -ge-, sein*) rot, decay

ver'fechten *v/t* (*irr, fechten, no -ge-, h*), **Ver'fechter(in)** (*-s; -/-; -nen*) advocate

ver'fehlen *v/t* (*no -ge-, h*) miss (**sich** each other); **Ver'fehlung** *f* (*-; -en*) offense, *Br* offence

verfeinden [fɛɐˈfaɪndən] *v/refl* (*no -ge-, h*) become enemies; **ver'feindet** *adj* hostile; ~ **sein** be enemies

verfeinern [fɛɐˈfaɪnən] *v/t and v/refl* (*no -ge-, h*) refine

ver'filmen *v/t* (*no -ge-, h*) film; **Ver'filmung** *f* (*-; -en*) filming; film version

ver'flechten *v/t* (*irr, flechten, no -ge-, h*) intertwine (**a. sich** ~)

ver'fluchen *v/t* (*no -ge-, h*) curse

ver'flucht → **verdammt**

ver'folgen *v/t* (*no -ge-, h*) pursue (*a. fig*); chase, hunt (*both a. fig*); POL, REL persecute; follow (*track etc*); *fear etc:* haunt s.o.; **j-n gerichtlich** ~ prosecute s.o.; **Verfolger** [fɛɐˈfɔlgə] *m* (*-s; -*) pursuer; persecutor; **Ver'folgung** *f* (*-; -en*) pursuit (*a. cycling*); chase, hunt; persecution; **gerichtliche** ~ prosecution

ver'frachten *v/t* (*no -ge-, h*) freight, ship; *F* bundle *s.o., s.th.* (**in** *acc* into)

verfremden [fɛɐˈfrɛmdən] *v/t* (*no -ge-, h*) *esp art:* alienate

ver'früht *adj* premature

verfügbar [fɛɐˈfyːkbaːɐ] *adj* available; **ver'fügen** (*no -ge-, h*) **1.** *v/t* decree, or-

der; **2.** *v/i:* ~ **über** (*acc*) have at one's disposal; **Ver'fügung** *f* (*-; -en*) a) decree, order, b) (*no pl*) disposal; **j-m zur** ~ **stehen** (**stellen**) be (place) at s.o. 's disposal

ver'führen *v/t* (*no -ge-, h*) seduce (**et. zu tun** into doing s.th.); **Ver'führer** *m* (*-s; -*) seducer; **Ver'führerin** *f* (*-; -nen*) seductress; **ver'führerisch** *adj* seductive; tempting; **Ver'führung** *f* (*-; -en*) seduction

vergangen [fɛɐˈgaŋən] *adj* gone, past; **im ~en Jahr** last year; **Ver'gangenheit** *f* (*-; no pl*) past; LING past tense

vergänglich [fɛɐˈgɛŋlɪç] *adj* transitory, transient

vergasen [fɛɐˈgaːzən] *v/t* (*no -ge-, h*) gas; CHEM gasify; **Vergaser** [fɛɐˈgaːzə] *m* (*-s; -*) MOT carburet(t)or

vergaß [fɛɐˈgaːs] *pret of* **vergessen**

ver'geben *v/t* (*irr, geben, no -ge-, h*) give away (*a. fig*); award (*prize etc*); forgive; **ver'gebens** *adv* in vain; **vergeblich** [fɛɐˈgeːplɪç] **1.** *adj* futile; **2.** *adv* in vain; **Ver'gebung** *f* (*-; -en*) forgiveness, pardon

ver'gehen (*irr, gehen, no -ge-, sein*) **1.** *v/i* time *etc:* go by, pass; *pain, effect etc:* wear off; ~ **vor** (*dat*) be dying with; **wie die Zeit vergeht!** how time flies!; **2.** *v/refl* **sich** ~ **an** (*dat*) violate; rape

Vergehen *n* (*-s; -*) JUR offen\|se, *Br* -ce

ver'gelten *v/t* (*irr, gelten, no -ge-, h*) repay; reward; **Ver'geltung** *f* (*-; -en*) retaliation (*a.* MIL)

vergessen [fɛɐˈgɛsən] **1.** *v/t* (*irr, no -ge-, h*) forget; leave; **2.** *pp of* **vergessen** 1; **Ver'gessenheit** *f:* **in** ~ **geraten** fall into oblivion; **vergesslich** [fɛɐˈgɛslɪç] *adj* forgetful

vergeuden [fɛɐˈgɔɪdən] *v/t* (*no -ge-, h*), **Ver'geudung** *f* (*-; -en*) waste

vergewaltigen [fɛɐgəˈvaltɪgən] *v/t* (*no -ge-, h*) rape, violate (*a. fig*); **Verge'waltigung** *f* (*-; -en*) rape, violation (*a. fig*)

vergewissern [fɛɐgəˈvɪsən] *v/refl* (*no -ge-, h*) make sure (**e-r Sache** of s.th.; **ob** whether; **dass** that)

ver'gießen *v/t* (*irr, gießen, no -ge-, h*) shed (*blood, tears*); spill

ver'giften *v/t* (*no -ge-, h*) poison (*a. fig*); contaminate; **Ver'giftung** *f* (*-; -en*) poisoning (*a. fig*); contamination

V

ver'gittert *adj* barred (*window etc*)

Ver'gleich *m* (-[e]s, -e) comparison; JUR compromise; **ver'gleichbar** *adj* comparable (**mit** to, with); **ver'gleichen** *v/t* (*irr*, **gleichen**, *no* -ge-, *h*) compare (**mit** with *or* to); **... ist nicht zu ~ mit** ... cannot be compared to; ... cannot compare with; **verglichen mit** compared to *or* with; **ver'gleichsweise** *adv* comparatively, relatively

ver'glühen *v/i* (*no* -ge-, *sein*) burn out (*or* up)

vergnügen [fɛɐˈgnyːgən] *v/refl* (*no* -ge-, *h*) enjoy o.s. (**mit et.** doing s.th.)

Ver'gnügen *n* (-s; -) pleasure, enjoyment, fun; **mit ~** with pleasure; **viel ~!** have fun!, have a good time!

vergnügt [fɛɐˈgnyːkt] *adj* cheerful

Ver'gnügung *f* (-; -en) pleasure, amusement, entertainment

Ver'gnügungspark *m* amusement park

ver'gnügungssüchtig *adj* pleasure-seeking

Ver'gnügungsviertel *n* nightlife district

ver'golden *v/t* (*no* -ge-, *h*) gild; **~göttern** [fɛɐˈgœtən] *v/t* (*no* -ge-, *h*) idolize, adore; **~'graben** *v/t* (*irr*, **graben**, *no* -ge-, *h*) bury (*a. fig*)

ver'greifen *v/refl* (*irr*, **greifen**, *no* -ge-, *h*) **sich ~ an** (*dat*) lay hands on

vergriffen [fɛɐˈgrɪfən] *adj* out of print

vergrößern [fɛɐˈgrøːsən] *v/t* (*no* -ge-, *h*) enlarge (*a.* PHOT); increase; OPT magnify; **sich ~** increase, grow, expand; **Ver'größerung** *f* (-; -en) increase; PHOT enlargement; OPT magnification; **Ver'größerungsglas** *n* OPT magnifying glass

Vergünstigung [fɛɐˈgʏnstɪgʊŋ] *f* (-; -en) privilege

vergüten [fɛɐˈgyːtən] *v/t* (*no* -ge-, *h*) reimburse, pay (for); **Ver'gütung** *f* (-; -en) reimbursement

ver'haften *v/t* (*no* -ge-, *h*), **Ver'haftung** *f* (-; -en) arrest

ver'halten¹ *v/refl* (*irr*, **halten**, *no* -ge-, *h*) behave, conduct o.s., act; **sich ruhig ~** keep quiet

ver'halten² *adj* restrained; subdued

Ver'halten *n* (-s; *no pl*) behavio(u)r, conduct; **Ver'haltensforschung** *f* behavio(u)ral science; **ver'haltensge-** **stört** *adj* disturbed, maladjusted

Verhältnis [fɛɐˈhɛltnɪs] *n* (-ses; -se) relationship, relations; attitude; proportion, relation, *esp* MATH ratio; F affair; *pl* circumstances, conditions; **über j-s ~se** beyond s.o.'s means; **ver'hältnis-mäßig** *adv* comparatively, relatively

Ver'hältniswort *n* (-[e]s; -wörter) LING preposition

ver'handeln *no* (-ge-, *h*) **1.** *v/i* negotiate; **2.** *v/t* JUR hear; **Ver'handlung** *f* (-; -en) negotiation, talk; JUR hearing; trial; **Ver'handlungsbasis** *f* ECON asking price

ver'hängen *v/t* (*no* -ge-, *h*) cover (**mit** with); impose (**über** *acc* on)

Verhängnis [fɛɐˈhɛŋnɪs] *n* (-ses; -se) fate; disaster; **ver'hängnisvoll** *adj* fatal, disastrous

verharmlosen [fɛɐˈharmloːzən] *v/t* (*no* -ge-, *h*) play s.th. down

verhärmt [fɛɐˈhɛrmt] *adj* careworn

ver'hasst *adj* hated; hateful

ver'hätscheln *v/t* (*no* -ge-, *h*) coddle, pamper, spoil

ver'hauen F *v/t* (*no* -ge-, *h*) spank

verheerend [fɛɐˈheːrənt] *adj* disastrous

ver'heilen *v/i* (*no* -ge-, *sein*) heal (up)

verheimlichen [fɛɐˈhaimlɪçən] *v/t* (*no* -ge-, *h*) hide, conceal

ver'heiraten *v/t* (*no* -ge-, *h*) marry (s.o. off) (**mit** to); **sich ~** get married

ver'heiratet *adj* married (**mit** to)

ver'heißungsvoll *adj* promising

ver'helfen *v/i* (*irr*, **helfen**, *no* -ge-, *h*) **j-m zu et. ~** help s.o. to get s.th.

ver'herrlichen *v/t* (*no* -ge-, *h*) glorify, *contp a.* idolize; **Ver'herrlichung** *f* (-; -en) glorification

ver'hexen *v/t* (*no* -ge-, *h*) bewitch

ver'hindern *v/t* (*no* -ge-, *h*) prevent (**dass j. et. tut** s.o. from doing s.th.); **ver'hindert** *adj* unable to come; F **ein ~er ...** a would-be ...; **Ver'hinderung** *f* (-; -en) prevention

ver'höhnen *v/t* (*no* -ge-, *h*) deride, mock (at), jeer (at)

Verhör [fɛɐˈhøːɐ] *n* (-[e]s; -e) JUR interrogation; **ver'hören** (*no* -ge-, *h*) **1.** *v/t* interrogate, question; **2.** *v/refl* get it wrong

ver'hüllen *v/t* (*no* -ge-, *h*) cover, veil

ver'hungern *v/i* (*no* -ge-, *sein*) die of hunger, starve (to death)

Ver'**hungern** n (-s; no pl) starvation

ver'**hüten** v/t (no -ge-, h) prevent

Ver'**hütung** f (-; -en) prevention

Ver'**hütungsmittel** n MED contraceptive

ver'**irren** v/refl (no -ge-, h) get lost, lose one's way, go astray (a. fig)

Ver'**irrung** f (-; -en) aberration

ver'**jagen** v/t (no -ge-, h) chase or drive away

ver**jähren** [fɛɐˈjɛːrən] v/i (no -ge-, sein) JUR come under the statute of limitations; ver'**jährt** adj JUR statute-barred

ver**jüngen** [fɛɐˈjʏŋən] v/t (no -ge-, h) make s.o. (look) younger, rejuvenate; **sich ~** ARCH, TECH taper (off)

ver'**kabeln** v/t (no -ge-, h) ELECTR cable

Ver'**kauf** m sale; ver'**kaufen** v/t (no -ge-, h) sell; **zu ~** for sale; **sich gut ~** sell well; Ver'**käufer** m (-s; -) (sales)clerk, salesman, Br shop assistant; ECON seller; Ver'**käuferin** f (-; -nen) (sales)clerk, saleslady, Br shop assistant; ver'**käuflich** adj for sale; **schwer ~** hard to sell

Ver**kehr** [fɛɐˈkeːɐ] m (-s; no pl) traffic; transportation, Br transport; fig contact, dealings; intercourse; circulation; **starker (schwacher) ~** heavy (light) traffic; ver'**kehren** (no -ge-, h) **1.** v/i bus etc: run; **~ in** (dat) frequent; **~ mit** associate or mix with; have intercourse with; **2.** v/t turn (**in** acc into); **ins Gegenteil ~** reverse

Ver'**kehrs|ader** f arterial road; **~ampel** f traffic light(s); **~behinderung** f hold-up, delay; JUR obstruction of traffic; **~de,likt** n traffic offense (Br offence); **~flugzeug** n airliner; **~funk** m traffic bulletin; **~insel** f traffic island; **~meldung** f traffic announcement, flash; **~mi,nister** m minister of transportation; **~minis,terium** n ministry of transportation; **~mittel** n means of transportation; **öffentliche ~** public transportation; **~opfer** n road casualty; **~poli,zei** f traffic police; **~rowdy** m F road hog

ver'**kehrssicher** adj MOT roadworthy

Ver'**kehrs|sicherheit** f MOT road safety; roadworthiness; **~stau** m traffic jam; **~sünder(in)** f traffic offender; **~teilnehmer(in)** road user; **~unfall** m traffic accident; (car) crash; **~unter-**

richt m traffic instruction; **~zeichen** n traffic sign

ver'**kehrt** adj and adv wrong; upside down; inside out

ver'**kennen** v/t (irr, kennen, no -ge-, h) mistake, misjudge; **~klagen** v/t (no -ge-, h) JUR sue (**auf** acc, **wegen** for); **~klappen** v/t (no -ge-, h) dump (into the sea); **~kleben** v/t (no -ge-, h) glue (together)

ver'**kleiden** v/t (no -ge-, h) disguise (**als** as), dress s.o. up (as); TECH cover, (en)case; panel; **sich ~** disguise o.s., dress (o.s.) up; Ver'**kleidung** f (-; -en) disguise; TECH cover, encasement; panel(l)ing; MOT fairing

ver**kleinern** [fɛɐˈklainɐn] v/t (no -ge-, h) make smaller, reduce, diminish; Ver'**kleinerung** [fɛɐˈklainɐrʊŋ] f (-; -en) reduction

ver'**klingen** v/i (irr, klingen, no -ge-, sein) die away

ver'**knallt** F adj: **~ sein in** (acc) be madly in love with, have a crush on

ver'**knoten** v/t (no -ge-, h) knot; **~knüpfen** v/t (no -ge-, h) knot together; fig connect, combine; **~kohlen** v/i (no -ge-, sein) char; **~kommen 1.** v/i (irr, kommen, no -ge-, sein) become run-down or dilapidated; go to seed; GASTR go bad; **2.** adj run-down, dilapidated; neglected; depraved, rotten (to the core); **~korken** v/t (no -ge-, h) cork (up); **~körpern** v/t (no -ge-, h) personify; embody; esp THEA impersonate; **~kriechen** v/refl (irr, kriechen, no -ge-, h) hide; **~krümmt** adj crooked, curved (a. MED); **~krüppelt** adj crippled; **~kümmern** v/i (no -ge-, sein) BIOL become stunted; **~kümmert** adj BIOL stunted

ver**künden** [fɛɐˈkʏndən] v/t (no -ge-, h) announce; proclaim; JUR pronounce; REL preach; Ver'**kündung** f (-; -en) announcement; proclamation; JUR pronouncement; REL preaching

ver'**kürzen** v/t (no -ge-, h) shorten; reduce; **~laden** v/t (irr, laden, no -ge-, h) load (**auf** acc onto; **in** acc into)

Ver**lag** [fɛɐˈlaːk] m (-[e]s; -e [-ˈlaːɡə]) publishing house or company, publisher(s)

ver'**lagern** v/t and v/refl (no -ge-, h) shift (**auf** acc to)

ver'langen v/t (no -ge-, h) ask for; demand; claim; charge; take, call for; **Ver'langen** n (-s; -) desire (**nach** for); longing (for), yearning (for); **auf ~** by request; ECON on demand

verlängern [fɛɐ'lɛŋən] v/t (no -ge-, h) lengthen, make longer; prolong, extend (a. ECON); **Verlängerung** [fɛɐ'lɛŋərʊŋ] f (-; -en) lengthening; prolongation, extension; SPORT overtime, Br extra time

ver'langsamen v/t and v/refl (no -ge-, h) slacken, slow down (both a. fig)

ver'lassen (irr, **lassen**, no -ge-, h) **1.** v/t leave; abandon, desert; **2.** v/refl: **sich ~ auf** (acc) rely or depend on

ver'lässlich [fɛɐ'lɛslɪç] adj reliable, dependable

Ver'lauf m course; **ver'laufen** (irr, **laufen**, no -ge-) **1.** v/i (sein) run; go; end (up); **2.** v/refl get lost, lose one's way

ver'leben v/t (no -ge-, h) spend; have

ver'legen[1] v/t (no -ge-, h) move; mislay; TECH lay; put off, postpone; publish

ver'legen[2] adj embarrassed

Ver'legenheit f (-; -en) a) (no pl) embarrassment, b) embarrassing situation

Verleger [fɛɐ'le:gɐ] m (-s; -), **Ver'legerin** f (-; -nen) publisher

Verleih [fɛɐ'lai] m (-[e]s; -e) a) (no pl) hire, rental, b) film: distributor(s)

ver'leihen v/t (irr, **leihen**, no -ge-, h) lend, loan; MOT etc rent (Br hire) out; award (prize etc); grant (privilege etc); **Ver'leihung** f (-; -en) award(ing), presentation; grant(ing)

ver'leiten v/t (no -ge-, h) **j-n zu et. ~** make s.o. do s.th., lead s.o. to do s.th.

ver'lernen v/t (no -ge-, h) forget

ver'lesen v/t (irr, **lesen**, no -ge-, h) **1.** v/t read (or call) out; **2.** v/refl make a slip (in reading); misread s.th.

verletzen [fɛɐ'lɛtsṇ] v/t (no -ge-, h) hurt, injure, fig a. offend; **sich ~** hurt o.s., get hurt; **~d** adj offensive

Ver'letzte m, f (-n; -n) injured person; pl the injured; **Ver'letzung** f (-; -en) injury, esp pl a. hurt; JUR violation

ver'leugnen v/t (no -ge-, h) deny; renounce

verleumden [fɛɐ'lɔymdṇ] v/t (no -ge-, h) defame; JUR slander, libel; **ver'leumderisch** adj JUR slanderous,

libel(l)ous; **Ver'leumdung** f (-; -en) JUR slander; libel

ver'lieben v/refl (no -ge-, h) fall in love (**in** acc with); **verliebt** [fɛɐ'li:pt] adj in love (**in** acc with); amorous (look etc); **Ver'liebte** m, f (-n; -n) lover

verlieren [fɛɐ'li:rən] v/t and v/i (irr, no -ge-, h) lose; **Ver'lierer(in)** (-s; -/-; -nen) loser

ver'loben v/refl (no -ge-, h) get engaged (**mit** to); **Verlobte** [fɛɐ'lo:ptə] **1.** m (-n; -n) fiancé; **2.** f (-n; -n) fiancée; **Ver'lobung** f (-; -en) engagement

ver'locken v/t (no -ge-, h) tempt; **~d** adj tempting

Ver'lockung f (-; -en) temptation

verlogen [fɛɐ'lo:gən] adj untruthful, lying

verlor [fɛɐ'lo:ɐ] pret of **verlieren**

verloren [fɛɐ'lo:rən] **1.** pp of **verlieren**; **2.** adj lost; wasted; **~ gehen** be or get lost

ver'losen v/t (no -ge-, h) raffle (off); **Ver'losung** f (-; -en) raffle

Verlust [fɛɐ'lʊst] m (-[e]s; -e) loss (a. fig); pl esp MIL casualties

ver'machen v/t (no -ge-, h) leave, will

Vermächtnis [fɛɐ'mɛçtnɪs] n (-ses; -se) legacy (a. fig)

ver'markten v/t (no -ge-, h) market, merchandize; **Ver'marktung** f (-; -en) marketing, merchandizing

ver'mehren v/t and v/refl increase (**um** by), multiply (by) (a. BIOL); BIOL reproduce, esp ZO a. breed; **Ver'mehrung** f (-; -en) increase; BIOL reproduction

vermeidbar [fɛɐ'maitba:ɐ] adj avoidable; **ver'meiden** v/t (irr, **meiden**, no -ge-, h) avoid

vermeintlich [fɛɐ'maintlɪç] adj supposed, alleged

ver'mengen v/t (no -ge-, h) mix, mingle, blend

Vermerk [fɛɐ'mɛrk] m (-[e]s; -e) note

ver'merken v/t (no -ge-, h) make a note of

ver'messen[1] v/t (irr, **messen**, no -ge-, h) measure; survey

ver'messen[2] adj presumptuous

Ver'messung f (-; -en) measuring; survey(ing)

ver'mieten v/t (no -ge-, h) let, rent, lease (out); rent (Br hire) out (cars etc); **zu ~** for rent, Br to let, for hire

Ver'mieter *n* (*-s*; -) landlord

Ver'mieterin *f* (-; *-nen*) landlady

Ver'mietung *f* (-; *-en*) letting, renting

ver'mischen *v/t and v/refl* (*no -ge-*, *h*) mix, mingle, blend (*mit* with); **ver-'mischt** *adj* mixed; miscellaneous

vermissen [fɛɐˈmɪsən] *v/t* (*no -ge-*, *h*) miss; **ver'misst** *adj* missing; **die Ver-missten** *pl* the missing

ver'mitteln (*no -ge-*, *h*) **1.** *v/t* arrange; give, convey (*impression etc*); **j-m et. ~ get** *or* find s.o. s.th.; **2.** *v/i* mediate (**zwischen** between); **Ver'mittler** *m* (*-s*; -) mediator, go-between; ECON agent, broker; **Ver'mittlung** *f* (-; *-en*) mediation; arrangement; agency, office; (telephone) exchange; operator

ver'modern *v/i* (*no -ge-*, *sein*) rot, mo(u)lder

Ver'mögen *n* (*-s*; -) fortune, property, possessions; ECON assets

ver'mögend *adj* well-to-do, well-off

vermummen [fɛɐˈmʊmən] *v/refl* (*no -ge-*, *h*) mask o.s., disguise o.s.

vermuten [fɛɐˈmuːtən] *v/t* (*no -ge-*, *h*) suppose, expect, think, guess; **ver'mut-lich** *adv* probably; **Ver'mutung** *f* (-; *-en*) supposition; speculation

vernachlässigen [fɛɐˈnaːxlɛsɪɡən] *v/t* (*no -ge-*, *h*), **Ver'nachlässigung** *f* (-; *-en*) neglect

ver'narben *v/i* (*no -ge-*, *sein*) scar over; *fig* heal

ver'narrt *adj*: **~ in** (*acc*) mad *or* crazy about

ver'nehmen *v/t* (*irr*, **nehmen**, *no -ge-*, *h*) JUR question, interrogate

ver'nehmlich *adj* clear, distinct

Ver'nehmung *f* (-; *-en*) JUR interroga-tion, examination

ver'neigen *v/refl* (*no -ge-*, *h*), **Ver'nei-gung** *f* (-; *-en*) bow (*vor dat* to) (*a. fig*)

ver'neinen (*no -ge-*, *h*) **1.** *v/t* deny; **2.** *v/i* say no, answer in the negative; **~d** *adj* negative

Ver'neinung *f* (-; *-en*) denial, negative (*a.* LING)

ver'nichten *v/t* (*no -ge-*, *h*) destroy; **~d** *adj* devastating (*a. fig*); crushing

Ver'nichtung *f* (-; *-en*) destruction; ex-termination

Vernunft [fɛɐˈnʊnft] *f* (-; *no pl*) reason; **~ annehmen** listen to reason; **j-n zur ~ bringen** bring s.o. to reason

vernünftig [fɛɐˈnʏnftɪç] *adj* sensible, reasonable (*a.* ECON); F decent

ver'öden *v/i* (*no -ge-*, *sein*) become de-serted

ver'öffentlichen *v/t* (*no -ge-*, *h*) publish; **Ver'öffentlichung** *f* (-; *-en*) publication

ver'ordnen *v/t* (*no -ge-*, *h*) order, MED *a.* prescribe (**gegen** for); **Ver'ordnung** *f* (-; *-en*) order; MED prescription

ver'pachten *v/t* (*no -ge-*, *h*) lease

Ver'pächter *m* lessor

ver'packen *v/t* (*no -ge-*, *h*) pack (up); TECH package; wrap up

Ver'packung *f* (-; *-en*) pack(ag)ing; wrapping; **Ver'packungsmüll** *m* superfluous packaging

ver'passen *v/t* (*no -ge-*, *h*) miss; **~'pat-zen** F *v/t* (*no -ge-*, *h*) mess up, spoil; **~pesten** [fɛɐˈpɛstən] *v/t* (*no -ge-*, *h*) pollute, foul, contaminate; stink up (*Br* out); **~'petzen** F *v/t* (*no -ge-*, *h*) *j-n* ~ tell on s.o. (*bei* to); **~'pfänden** *v/t* (*no -ge-*, *h*) pawn; *fig* pledge

ver'pflanzen *v/t* (*no -ge-*, *h*), **Ver'pflan-zung** *f* (-; *-en*) transplant (*a.* MED)

ver'pflegen *v/t* (*no -ge-*, *h*) feed

Ver'pflegung *f* (-; *-en*) food

ver'pflichten *v/t* (*no -ge-*, *h*) oblige; en-gage; **sich ~, et. zu tun** undertake (ECON agree) to do s.th.; **ver'pflichtet** *adj*: **~ sein (sich ~ fühlen) et. zu tun** be (feel) obliged to do s.th.; **Ver'pflich-tung** *f* (-; *-en*) obligation; duty; ECON, JUR liability; engagement; commit-ment

ver'pfuschen F *v/t* (*no -ge-*, *h*) bungle, botch

ver'plappern *v/refl* (*no -ge-*, *h*) blab

verpönt [fɛɐˈpøːnt] *adj* taboo

ver'prügeln F *v/t* (*no -ge-*, *h*) beat *s.o.* up

Ver'putz *m* (*-es*; *no pl*), **ver'putzen** *v/t* (*no -ge-*, *h*) ARCH plaster

verquollen [fɛɐˈkvɔlən] *adj* face *etc*: puffy, swollen; *wood*: warped

Verrat [fɛɐˈraːt] *m* (*-[e]s*; *no pl*) betrayal (*an dat* of); treachery (to); JUR treason (to); **ver'raten** *v/t* (*irr*, **raten**, *no -ge-*, *h*) betray, give away (*both a. fig*); **sich ~** betray o.s., give o.s. away

Verräter [fɛɐˈrɛːtɐ] *m* (*-s*; -), **Ver'räterin** *f* (-; *-nen*) traitor

verräterisch [fɛɐˈrɛːtərɪʃ] *adj* treache-rous; *fig* telltale

ver'rechnen (*no -ge-*, *h*) **1.** *v/t* offset

(**mit** against); **2.** *v/refl* miscalculate, make a mistake (*a. fig*); **sich um e-e Mark ~** be one mark out

Ver'rechnungsscheck *m* ECON voucher cheque, *Br* crossed cheque

ver'regnet *adj* rainy

ver'reisen *v/i* (*no -ge-, sein*) go away (**geschäftlich** on business); **ver'reist** *adj* away (**geschäftlich** on business)

verrenken [fɛɐˈrɛŋkən] *v/t* (*no -ge-, h*) MED dislocate, luxate; **sich et. ~** MED dislocate s.th.; **sich den Hals ~** crane one's neck; **Ver'renkung** *f* (-; -en) MED dislocation, luxation

ver'richten *v/t* (*no -ge-, h*) do, perform, carry out

ver'riegeln *v/t* (*no -ge-, h*) bolt, bar

verringern [fɛɐˈrɪŋɐn] *v/t* (*no -ge-, h*) decrease, lessen (*both a. sich ~*), reduce, cut down; **Ver'ringerung** *f* (-; -en) reduction, decrease

ver'rosten *v/t* (*no -ge-, sein*) rust, get rusty (*a. fig*)

verrotten [fɛɐˈrɔtən] *v/i* (*no -ge-, sein*) rot; **ver'rottet** *adj* rotten

ver'rücken *v/t* (*no -ge-, h*) move, shift

ver'rückt *adj* mad, crazy (*both a. fig* **nach** about); **wie ~** like mad; **~ werden** go mad, go crazy; **j-n ~ machen** drive s.o. mad; **Ver'rückte** *m, f* (-*n; -n*) madman (madwoman), lunatic, maniac (*all a. F*); **Ver'rücktheit** *f* (-; -en) a) (*no pl*) madness, craziness, b) crazy thing

Ver'ruf *m:* **in ~ bringen** bring discredit (up)on; **in ~ kommen** get into discredit

ver'rufen *adj* disreputable, notorious

ver'rutschen *v/i* (*no -ge-, sein*) slip, get out of place

Vers [fɛrs] *m* (-*es; -e* [ˈfɛrzə]) verse; line

ver'sagen *v/t* (*no -ge-, h*) **1.** *v/i* fail (*a.* MED.), MOT *etc a.* break down; *gun etc:* misfire; **2.** *v/t* deny, refuse; **Ver'sagen** *n* (-*s; no pl*) failure; **Ver'sager** *m* (-*s; -*) failure

ver'salzen *v/t* (*no -ge-, h*) oversalt

ver'sammeln *v/t* (*no -ge-, h*) gather, assemble; **sich ~** *a.* meet; **Ver'sammlung** *f* (-; -en) assembly, meeting

Versand [fɛɐˈzant] *m* (-[e]s; *no pl*) dispatch, shipment; **~... in** *cpds* **...haus, ...katalog** *etc:* mail-order ...

ver'säumen *v/t* (*no -ge-, h*) miss; **~ et. zu tun** fail to do s.th.; **Versäumnis** [fɛɐˈzɔymnɪs] *n* (-*ses; -se*) omission

ver'schaffen *v/t* (*no -ge-, h*) get, find; **sich ~** obtain; **~'schämt** *adj* bashful; **~'schanzen** *v/refl* (*no -ge-, h*) entrench o.s. (*a. fig* **hinter** behind); **~'schärfen** *v/t* (*no -ge-, h*) aggravate; tighten up; increase; **sich ~** get worse; **~'schenken** *v/t* (*no -ge-, h*) give away (*a. fig*); **~'scherzen** *v/t* (*no -ge-, h*) forfeit; **~'scheuchen** *v/t* (*no -ge-, h*) chase away (*a. fig*); **~'schicken** *v/t* (*no -ge-, h*) send off, *esp* ECON *a.* dispatch

ver'schieben *v/t* (*irr, schieben, no -ge-, h*) move, shift (*a. sich ~*); postpone, put off; **Ver'schiebung** *f* (-; -en) shift(ing); postponement

verschieden [fɛɐˈʃiːdən] *adj* different (**von** from); **~e** *... pl* various ..., several...; **~artig** *adj* different; various

Ver'schiedenheit *f* (-; -en) difference

ver'schiedentlich *adv* repeatedly

ver'schiffen *v/t* (*no -ge-, h*) ship

Ver'schiffung *f* (-; -en) shipment

ver'schimmeln *v/t* (*no -ge-, sein*) get mo(u)ldy; **~'schlafen** (*irr, schlafen, no -ge-, h*) **1.** *v/i* oversleep; **2.** *v/t* sleep through; **3.** *adj* sleepy (*a. fig*)

Ver'schlag *m* shed

ver'schlagen[1] *v/t* (*irr, schlagen, no -ge-, h*) **j-m den Atem ~** take s.o.'s breath away; **j-m die Sprache ~** leave s.o. speechless; **es hat ihn nach X ~** he ended up in X

ver'schlagen[2] *adj* sly, cunning

verschlechtern [fɛɐˈʃlɛçtɐn] *v/t and v/refl* (*no -ge-, h*) make (*refl* get) worse, worsen, deteriorate

Ver'schlechterung *f* (-; -en) deterioration; change for the worse

ver'schleiern *v/t* (*no -ge-, h*) veil (*a. fig*)

Verschleiß [fɛɐˈʃlais] *m* (-*es; no pl*) wear (and tear); **ver'schleißen** *v/t* (*irr, no -ge-, h*) wear out

ver'schleppen *v/t* (*no -ge-, h*) carry off; POL displace; draw out, delay; MED neglect; **~'schleudern** *v/t* (*no -ge-, h*) waste; ECON sell dirt cheap; **~'schließen** *v/t* (*irr, schließen, no -ge-, h*) close (*a. fig* one's eyes); lock (up)

ver'schlingen *v/t* (*irr, schlingen, no -ge-, h*) devour (*a. fig*); gulp (down)

verschliss [fɛɐˈʃlɪs] *pret of* **verschleißen**; **verschlissen** [fɛɐˈʃlɪsən] *pp of* **verschleißen**

verschlossen [fɛɐˈʃlɔsən] *adj* closed;

fig aloof, reserved; **Ver'schlossenheit** *f* (-; *no pl*) aloofness

ver'schlucken (*no -ge-, h*) **1.** *v/t* swallow (*fig* up); **2.** *v/refl* choke; *ich habe mich verschluckt* it went down the wrong way

Ver'schluss *m* fastener; clasp; catch; lock; cover, lid; cap, top; PHOT shutter; *unter ~* under lock and key

ver'schlüsseln *v/t* (*no -ge-, h*) (en)code, (en)cipher

verschmähen [fɛɐ'ʃmɛːən] *v/t* (*no -ge-, h*) disdain, scorn

ver'schmelzen *v/i* (*irr*, **schmelzen**, *no -ge-, sein*) *and v/t* (*h*) merge, fuse (*both a.* ECON, POL *etc*); melt; **Ver'schmelzung** *f* (-; *-en*) fusion (*a. fig*)

ver'schmerzen *v/t* (*no -ge-, h*) get over *s.th.*; ~'**schmieren** *v/t* (*no -ge-, h*) smear, smudge

verschmitzt [fɛɐ'ʃmɪtst] *adj* mischievous

ver'schmutzen (*no -ge-*) **1.** *v/t* (*h*) soil, dirty; pollute; **2.** *v/i* (*sein*) get dirty; get polluted; ~'**schnaufen** F *v/i and v/refl* (*no -ge-, h*) stop for breath

ver'schneit *adj* snow-covered, snowy

Ver'schnitt *m* blend; waste

verschnupft [fɛɐ'ʃnʊpft] *adj*: ~ *sein* MED have a cold; F be in a huff

ver'schnüren *v/t* (*no -ge-, h*) tie up

verschollen [fɛɐ'ʃɔlən] *adj* missing; JUR presumed dead

ver'schonen *v/t* (*no -ge-, h*) spare; *j-n mit et.* ~ spare *s.o. s.th.*

verschönern [fɛɐ'ʃøːnɐn] *v/t* (*no -ge-, h*) embellish; **Verschönerung** [fɛɐ'ʃøːnə-rʊŋ] *f* (-; *-en*) embellishment

verschossen [fɛɐ'ʃɔsən] *adj* faded; F ~ *sein in* (*acc*) have a crush on

verschränken [fɛɐ'ʃrɛŋkən] *v/t* (*no -ge-, h*) fold; cross (*one's legs*)

ver'schreiben (*irr*, **schreiben**, *no -ge-, h*) **1.** *v/t* MED prescribe (**gegen** for); **2.** *v/refl* make a slip of the pen

ver'schreibungspflichtig *adj* PHARM available on prescription only

verschroben [fɛɐ'ʃroːbən] *adj* eccentric, odd

ver'schrotten *v/t* (*no -ge-, h*) scrap

ver'schüchtert *adj* intimidated

ver'schulden *v/t* (*no -ge-, h*) be responsible for, cause; be the cause of; *sich ~* get into debt; **ver'schuldet** *adj* in debt

ver'schütten *v/t* (*no -ge-, h*) spill; bury *s.o.* (*alive*)

verschwägert [fɛɐ'ʃvɛːgɐt] *adj* related by marriage

ver'schweigen *v/t* (*irr*, **schweigen**, *no -ge-, h*) keep *s.th.* a secret, hide

verschwenden [fɛɐ'ʃvɛndən] *v/t* (*no -ge-, h*) waste; **Verschwender** [fɛɐ-'ʃvɛndɐ] *m* (*-s; -*) spendthrift; **verschwenderisch** [fɛɐ'ʃvɛndərɪʃ] *adj* wasteful, extravagant; lavish; **Ver-'schwendung** *f* (-; *-en*) waste

verschwiegen [fɛɐ'ʃviːgən] *adj* discreet; hidden, secret; **Ver'schwiegenheit** *f* (-; *no pl*) secrecy, discretion

ver'schwimmen *v/i* (*irr*, **schwimmen**, *no -ge-, sein*) become blurred

ver'schwinden *v/i* (*irr*, **schwinden**, *no -ge-, sein*) disappear, vanish; F **verschwinde!** beat it!; **Ver'schwinden** *n* (*-s; no pl*) disappearance

verschwommen [fɛɐ'ʃvɔmən] *adj* blurred (*a.* PHOT), *fig a.* vague, hazy

ver'schwören *v/refl* (*irr*, **schwören**, *no -ge-, h*) conspire, plot; **Verschwörer** [fɛɐ'ʃvøːrɐ] *m* (*-s; -*) conspirator; **Ver-'schwörung** *f* (-; *-en*) conspiracy, plot

verschwunden [fɛɐ'ʃvʊndən] *adj* missing

ver'sehen (*irr*, **sehen**, *no -ge-, h*) **1.** *v/t* hold (*an office etc*); ~ *mit* provide with; **2.** *v/refl* make a mistake; **Ver'sehen** *n* (*-s; -*) mistake, error; *aus ~* → **versehentlich** [fɛɐ'zeːəntlɪç] *adv* by mistake, unintentionally

Versehrte [fɛɐ'zeːɐtə] *m, f* (*-n; -n*) disabled person

ver'sengen *v/t* (*no -ge-, h*) singe, scorch; ~'**senken** *v/t* (*no -ge-, h*) sink; *sich ~ in* (*acc*) become absorbed in

ver'sessen *adj*: ~ *auf* (*acc*) keen on, mad *or* crazy about

ver'setzen *v/t* (*no -ge-, h*) move, shift; transfer; PED promote, *Br* move up; give (*s.o. a kick etc*); pawn; AGR transplant; F *j-n* ~ stand *s.o.* up; *j-n in die Lage* ~ *zu inf* put *s.o.* in a position to *inf*; enable *s.o.* to *inf*; *sich in j-s Lage* ~ put o.s. in *s.o.'s* place; **Ver'setzung** *f* (-; *-en*) transfer; PED promotion

ver'seuchen *v/t* (*no -ge-, h*) contaminate; **Ver'seuchung** *f* (-; *-en*) contamination

ver'sichern *v/t* (*no -ge-, h*) ECON insure

(**bei** with); assure (**j-m et.** s.o. of s.th.), assert; **sich ~** insure (**dass** that); make sure (**dass** that); **Ver'sicherte** m, f (-n; -n) the insured; **Ver'sicherung** f (-; -en) insurance; assurance, assertion

Ver'sicherungs|gesellschaft f insurance company; **~po,lice** f, **~schein** m insurance policy

ver|'sickern v/i (no -ge-, sein) trickle away; **~'siegeln** v/t (no -ge-, h) seal; **~'siegen** v/i (no -ge-, sein) dry up, run dry; **~'silbern** v/t (no -ge-, h) silver-plate; F turn s.th. into cash; **~'sinken** v/i (irr, sinken, no -ge-, sein) sink; → versunken

Version [ver'zjo:n] f (-; -en) version

'Versmaß n meter, Br metre

versöhnen [fɛɐˈzøːnən] v/t (no -ge-, h) reconcile; **sich (wieder) ~** make it up (**mit** with); **ver'söhnlich** adj conciliatory; **Ver'söhnung** f (-; -en) reconciliation; esp POL appeasement

ver'sorgen v/t (no -ge-, h) provide (**mit** with), supply (with); support; take care of, look after; **Ver'sorgung** f (-; no pl) supply (**mit** with); support; care

ver'späten v/refl (no -ge-, h) be late; **ver'spätet** adj belated, late, RAIL etc a. delayed; **Ver'spätung** f (-; -en) being or coming late, RAIL etc delay; **20 Minuten ~ haben** be 20 minutes late

ver'speisen v/t (no -ge-, h) eat (up)

ver'sperren v/t (no -ge-, h) bar, block (up), obstruct (a. view); lock

ver'spielen v/t (no -ge-, h) lose; **ver'spielt** adj playful

ver'spotten v/t (no -ge-, h) make fun of, ridicule

ver'sprechen (irr, sprechen, no -ge-, h) **1.** v/t promise (a. fig); **sich zu viel ~ (von)** expect too much (of); **2.** v/refl make a mistake or slip; **Ver'sprechen** n (-s; -) promise; **ein ~ geben** (**halten, brechen**) make (keep, break) a promise; **Ver'sprecher** F m (-s; -) slip (of the tongue)

ver'staatlichen v/t (no -ge-, h) ECON nationalize; **Ver'staatlichung** f (-; -en) ECON nationalization

Verstädterung [fɛɐˈʃtɛːtərʊŋ] f (-; -en) urbanization

Verstand [fɛɐˈʃtant] m (-[e]s; no pl) mind, intellect; reason, (common) sense; intelligence, brains; **nicht bei**

~ out of one's mind, not in one's right mind; **den ~ verlieren** go out of one's mind; **verstandesmäßig** [fɛɐˈʃtandəsmɛːsɪç] adj rational

ver'ständig adj reasonable, sensible

verständigen [fɛɐˈʃtɛndɪɡən] v/t (no -ge-, h) inform (**von** of), notify (of); call (doctor, police etc); **sich ~** communicate; come to an agreement (**über** acc on); **Ver'ständigung** f (-; no pl) communication (a. TEL); agreement

verständlich [fɛɐˈʃtɛntlɪç] adj audible; intelligible; comprehensible; understandable; **schwer (leicht) ~** difficult (easy) to understand; **j-m et. ~ machen** make s.th. clear to s.o.; **sich ~ machen** make o.s. understood

Verständnis [fɛɐˈʃtɛntnɪs] n (-ses; no pl) comprehension, understanding; sympathy; (**viel) ~ haben** be (very) understanding; **~ haben für** understand; appreciate

ver'ständnislos adj uncomprehending; blank (look etc)

ver'ständnisvoll adj understanding, sympathetic; knowing (look etc)

ver'stärken v/t (no -ge-, h) reinforce (a. TECH, MIL); strengthen (a. TECH); radio, PHYS amplify; intensify; **Ver'stärker** m (-s; -) amplifier; **Ver'stärkung** f (-; -en) strengthening; reinforcement(s MIL); amplification; intensification

ver'stauben v/i (no -ge-, sein) get dusty

verstauchen [fɛɐˈʃtauxən] v/t (no -ge-, h), **Ver'stauchung** f (-; -en) MED sprain

ver'stauen v/t (no -ge-, h) stow away

Versteck [fɛɐˈʃtɛk] n (-[e]s; -e) hiding place, hideout, hideaway

ver'stecken v/t and v/refl (no -ge-, h) hide (a. fig); **Verstecken spielen** play (at) hide-and-seek

ver'stehen v/t (irr, stehen, no -ge-, h) understand, F get; catch; see; realize; know; **es ~ zu** inf know how to inf; **zu ~ geben** give s.o. to understand, suggest; **ich verstehe!** I see!; **et. ~** misunderstand; **was ~ Sie unter ...?** what do you mean or understand by ...?; **sich (gut) ~** get along (well) (**mit** with); **es versteht sich von selbst** it goes without saying

ver'steifen (no -ge-, h) **1.** v/t stiffen (a. **sich ~**); TECH strut, brace; **2.** v/refl: **sich auf et. ~** insist on (doing) s.th.

ver'steigern v/t (no -ge-, h) auction off
Ver'steigerung f (-; -en) auction (sale)
ver'steinern v/i (no -ge-, sein) petrify (a. fig)
ver'stellbar adj adjustable
ver'stellen v/t (no -ge-, h) block; move; set s.th. wrong or the wrong way; TECH adjust, regulate; disguise (one's voice etc); **sich ~** pretend
Ver'stellung f (-; no pl) disguise, make-believe, (false) show
ver'steuern v/t (no -ge-, h) pay duty or tax on
verstiegen [fɛɐˈʃtiːgən] adj high-flown
ver'stimmen v/t (no -ge-, h) MUS put out of tune; fig annoy; **ver'stimmt** adj annoyed; MUS out of tune; MED upset; **Ver'stimmung** f (-; -en) annoyance
ver|stockt [fɛɐˈʃtɔkt] adj stubborn, obstinate; **~stohlen** [fɛɐˈʃtoːlən] adj furtive, stealthy
ver'stopfen v/t (no -ge-, h) plug (up); block, jam; MED constipate; **ver'stopft** adj MED constipated; **Ver'stopfung** f (-; -en) block(age); MED constipation
verstorben [fɛɐˈʃtɔrbən] adj late, deceased; **Ver'storbene** m, f (-n; -n) the deceased; **die ~n** the deceased
verstört [fɛɐˈʃtøːɐt] adj upset; distracted; wild (look etc)
Ver'stoß m offense, Br offence (**gegen** against), violation (of)
ver'stoßen (irr, stoßen, no -ge-, h) **1.** v/t expel (**aus** from); disown; **2.** v/i: **~ gegen** offend against, violate
ver'strahlt adj (radioactively) contaminated
ver'streichen (irr, streichen, no -ge-) **1.** v/i (sein) time: pass, go by; date: expire; **2.** v/t (h) spread
ver'streuen v/t (no -ge-, h) scatter
verstümmeln [fɛɐˈʃtʏməln] v/t (no -ge-, h) mutilate (a. fig); **Ver'stümmelung** f (-; -en) mutilation (a. fig)
ver'stummen v/i (no -ge-, sein) grow silent; stop; die down
Versuch [fɛɐˈzuːx] m (-[e]s; -e) attempt, try; trial, test; PHYS experiment; **mit et. (j-m) e-n ~ machen** give s.th. (s.o.) a try; **ver'suchen** v/t (no -ge-, h) try, attempt; taste; REL tempt; **es ~** have a try (at it)
Ver'suchs... in cpds ...bohrung etc: test ..., trial ...; **~ka,ninchen** n guinea pig;

~stadium n experimental stage; **~tier** n laboratory or test animal
ver'suchsweise adv by way of trial
Ver'suchung f (-; -en) temptation; **j-n in ~ führen** tempt s.o.
versunken [fɛɐˈzʊŋkən] fig adj: **~ in** (acc) absorbed or lost in
ver'süßen v/t (no -ge-, h) sweeten
ver'tagen v/t and v/refl (no -ge-, h) adjourn; **Ver'tagung** f (-; -en) adjournment
ver'tauschen v/t (no -ge-, h) exchange (**mit** for)
verteidigen [fɛɐˈtaidɪgən] v/t (no -ge-, h) defend (**sich** o.s.); **Verteidiger(in)** [fɛɐˈtaidɪgɐ (-gərɪn)] (-s; -/-; -nen) defender, SPORT a. back; fig advocate; **Ver'teidigung** f (-; -en) defense, Br defence
Ver'teidigungs... in cpds ...politik etc: mst defense ..., Br defence ...; **~mi,nister** m Secretary of Defense, Br Minister of Defence; **~minis,terium** n Department of Defense, Br Ministry of Defence
ver'teilen v/t (no -ge-, h) distribute; hand out; **Ver'teiler** m (-s; -) distributor; **Ver'teilung** f (-; -en) distribution
ver'tiefen v/t and v/refl (no -ge-, h) deepen (a. fig); **sich ~ in** (acc) become absorbed in; **Ver'tiefung** f (-; -en) hollow, depression, dent; fig deepening
vertikal [vɛrtiˈkaːl] adj, **Verti'kale** f (-; -n) vertical
ver'tilgen v/t (no -ge-, h) exterminate; F consume; **Ver'tilgung** f (-; no pl) extermination
vertonen [fɛɐˈtoːnən] v/t (no -ge-, h) set to music
Vertrag [fɛɐˈtraːk] m (-[e]s; Verträge [fɛɐˈtrɛːgə]) contract; POL treaty
ver'tragen v/t (irr, tragen, no -ge-, h) endure, bear, stand; **ich kann ... nicht ~** ... doesn't agree with me; **I can't stand ...; er kann viel ~** he can take a lot; he can hold his drink; F **ich (es) könnte ... ~** I (it) could do with ...; **sich (gut) ~** get along (well) (**mit** with); **sich wieder ~** make it up
ver'traglich adv by contract
verträglich [fɛɐˈtrɛːklɪç] adj easy to get on with; GASTR (easily) digestible
ver'trauen v/t (no -ge-, h) trust (**auf** acc in); **Ver'trauen** n (-s; no pl) confidence,

trust, faith; **im ~** (**gesagt**) between you and me; **wenig ~ erweckend aussehen** inspire little confidence

Ver'trauens|frage f: **die ~ stellen** PARL ask for a vote of confidence; **~sache** f: **das ist ~** that is a matter of confidence; **~stellung** f position of trust

ver'trauensvoll adj trustful, trusting

Ver'trauensvotum n PARL vote of confidence

ver'trauenswürdig adj trustworthy

ver'traulich adj confidential; familiar

ver'traut adj familiar; close

Ver'traute m, f (-n; -n) confidant(e f)

Ver'trautheit f (-; no pl) familiarity

ver'treiben v/t (irr, treiben, no -ge-, h) drive or chase away (a. fig); pass (the time); ECON sell; ~ **aus** drive out of; **Ver'treibung** f (-; -en) expulsion (**aus** from)

ver'treten v/t (irr, treten, no -ge-, h) substitute for, replace, stand in for; POL, ECON represent; PARL a. sit for; JUR act for s.o.; **j-s Sache ~** JUR plead s.o.'s cause; **die Ansicht ~, dass** argue that; **sich den Fuß ~** sprain one's ankle; **f sich die Beine ~** stretch one's legs

Ver'treter m (-s; -), **Ver'treterin** f (-; -nen) substitute, deputy; POL, ECON representative, ECON agent; MED locum

Ver'tretung f (-; -en) substitution, replacement; substitute, stand-in, a. supply teacher; ECON, POL representation

Vertrieb [fɛɐ'triːp] m (-[e]s; no pl) ECON sale, distribution

Vertriebene [fɛɐ'triːbənə] m, f (-n; -n) POL refugee

ver'trocknen v/i (no -ge-, sein) dry up; ~**'trödeln** F v/t (no -ge-, h) dawdle away, waste; ~**'trösten** v/t (no -ge-, h) put s.o. off; ~**'tuschen** F v/t (no -ge-, h) cover up; ~**'übeln** v/t (no -ge-, h) take amiss; **ich kann es ihr nicht ~** I can't blame her for it; ~**'üben** v/t (no -ge-, h) commit

verunglücken [fɛɐ'ʔʊnɡlʏkən] v/i (no -ge-, sein) have an accident; fig go wrong; **tödlich ~** die in an accident

ver'ursachen v/t (no -ge-, h) cause

ver'urteilen v/t (no -ge-, h) condemn (**zu** to) (a. fig), sentence (to), convict (**wegen** of); **Ver'urteilung** f (-; -en) condemnation (a. fig)

ver'vielfachen v/t (no -ge-, h) multiply

vervielfältigen [fɛɐ'fiːlfɛltɪɡən] v/t (no -ge-, h) copy, duplicate; **Ver'vielfältigung** f (-; -en) duplication; copy

ver'vollkommnen v/t (no -ge-, h) perfect; improve

vervollständigen [fɛɐ'fɔlʃtɛndɪɡən] v/t (no -ge-, h) complete

ver|'wachsen adj MED deformed, crippled; fig ~ **mit** deeply rooted in, bound up with; ~**'wackelt** F adj PHOT blurred

ver'wahren v/t (no -ge-, h) keep (in a safe place); **sich ~ gegen** protest against

verwahrlost [fɛɐ'vaːɐloːst] adj uncared-for, neglected

ver'walten v/t (no -ge-, h) manage, esp POL a. administer; **Ver'walter** m (-s; -) manager; administrator; **Ver'waltung** f (-; -en) administration, management; **Ver'waltungs...** in cpds ...gericht, ...kosten etc: administrative ...

ver'wandeln v/t (no -ge-, h) change, turn (both a. **sich ~**), esp PHYS, CHEM a. transform, convert (all: **in** acc into); **Ver'wandlung** f (-; -en) change, transformation; conversion

verwandt [fɛɐ'vant] adj related (**mit** to); **Ver'wandte** m, f (-n; -n) relative; (**alle**) **m-e ~n** (all) my relatives or relations; **der nächste ~** the next of kin; **Ver'wandtschaft** f (-; -en) a) relationship, b) (no pl) relations

ver'warnen v/t (no -ge-, h) Br caution; SPORT book; **Ver'warnung** f (-; -en) Br caution; SPORT booking

ver'waschen adj washed-out

ver'wässern v/t (no -ge-, h) water down (a. fig)

ver'wechseln v/t (no -ge-, h) confuse (**mit** with), mix up (with), mistake (for); **Ver'wechs(e)lung** f (-; -en) mistake, F mix-up

ver'wegen adj daring, bold

Ver'wegenheit f (-; no pl) boldness, daring

ver'weichlicht adj soft

ver'weigern v/t (no -ge-, h) refuse; disobey; **Ver'weigerung** f (-; -en) denial, refusal

ver'weilen v/i (no -ge-, h) stay; fig rest

Verweis [fɛɐ'vais] m (-es; -e) reprimand, reproof; reference (**auf** acc to)

V

ver'weisen v/t (irr, **weisen**, no -ge-, h) refer (**auf** acc, **an** acc to); expel (gen from)

ver'welken v/i (no -ge-, sein) wither, fig a. fade

ver'wenden v/t (no -ge-, h) use; spend (time etc) (**auf** acc on); **Ver'wendung** f (-; -en) use; **keine ~ haben für** have no use for

ver'werfen v/t (irr, **werfen**, no -ge-, h) drop, give up; reject

ver'werten v/t (no -ge-, h) use, make use of

verwesen [fɛɐ'veːzən] v/i (no -ge-, sein), **Ver'wesung** f (-; no pl) decay

ver'wickeln fig v/t (no -ge-, h) involve; **sich ~ in** (acc) get caught in; **ver'wickelt** fig adj complicated; **~ sein** (**werden**) **in** (acc) be (get) involved in; **Ver'wicklung** fig f (-; -en) involvement; complication

ver'wildern v/i (no -ge-, sein) grow (or run) wild; **ver'wildert** adj wild (a. fig), overgrown

ver'winden v/t (irr, **winden**, no -ge-, h) get over s.th.

ver'wirklichen v/t (no -ge-, h) realize; **sich ~** come true; **sich selbst ~** fulfil(l) o.s.; **Ver'wirklichung** f (-; -en) realization

ver'wirren v/t (no -ge-, h) tangle (up); fig confuse; **ver'wirrt** fig adj confused; **Ver'wirrung** fig f (-; -en) confusion

ver'wischen v/t (no -ge-, h) blur (a. fig); cover (track etc)

verwittern [fɛɐ'vɪtən] v/i (no -ge-, sein) GEOL weather

ver'witwet adj widowed

verwöhnen [fɛɐ'vøːnən] v/t (no -ge-, h) spoil; **ver'wöhnt** adj spoilt

verworren [fɛɐ'vɔrən] adj confused, muddled; complicated

verwundbar [fɛɐ'vʊntbaːɐ] adj vulnerable (a. fig); **ver'wunden** v/t (no -ge-, h) wound

ver'wunderlich adj surprising

Verwunderung [fɛɐ'vʊndəruŋ] f (-; no pl) (**zu m-r** etc **~** to my etc) surprise

Ver'wundete m, f (-n; -n) wounded (person), casualty

Ver'wundung f (-; -en) wound, injury

ver'wünschen v/t (no -ge-, h), **Ver'wünschung** f (-; -en) curse

ver'wüsten v/t (no -ge-, h) lay waste,

devastate, ravage; **Ver'wüstung** f (-; -en) devastation, ravage

ver'zählen v/refl (no -ge-, h) count wrong; **~zärteln** [fɛɐ'tsɛrtəln] v/t (no -ge-, h) coddle, pamper; **~'zaubern** v/t (no -ge-, h) enchant, fig a. charm; **~ in** (acc) turn into; **~'zehren** v/t (no -ge-, h) consume (a. fig)

ver'zeichnen v/t (no -ge-, h) record, keep a record of, list; fig achieve; suffer; **Ver'zeichnis** n (-ses; -se) list, catalog(ue); record, register; index

verzeihen [fɛɐ'tsaiən] v/t and v/i (irr, no -ge-, h) forgive s.o.; pardon, excuse s.th.; **ver'zeihlich** adj pardonable; **Ver'zeihung** f (-; no pl) pardon; (j-n) **um ~ bitten** apologize (to s.o.); **~!** (I'm) sorry!; excuse me!

ver'zerren v/t (no -ge-, h) distort (a. fig); **sich ~** become distorted

Ver'zerrung f (-; -en) distortion

Verzicht [fɛɐ'tsɪçt] m (-[e]s; -e) renunciation (**auf** acc of); mst giving up, doing without etc

ver'zichten v/i (no -ge-, h) **~ auf** (acc) do without; give up; renounce (a. JUR)

verzieh [fɛɐ'tsiː] pret of **verzeihen**

ver'ziehen (irr, **ziehen**, no -ge-) 1. v/i (sein) move (**nach** to); 2. v/t (h) spoil; **das Gesicht ~** make a face; **sich ~** wood: warp; storm etc: pass (over); F disappear; 3. pp of **verzeihen**

ver'zieren v/t (no -ge-, h) decorate

Ver'zierung f (-; -en) decoration, ornament

ver'zinsen v/t (no -ge-, h) pay interest on; **sich ~** yield interest

Ver'zinsung f (-; -en) interest

ver'zögern v/t (no -ge-, h) delay; **sich ~** be delayed; **Ver'zögerung** f (-; -en) delay

ver'zollen v/t (no -ge-, h) pay duty on; **et.** (**nichts**) **zu ~ haben** have s.th. (nothing) to declare

verzückt [fɛɐ'tsʏkt] adj ecstatic; **Ver'zückung** f (-; -en) ecstasy; **in ~ geraten** go into ecstasies or raptures (**wegen**, **über** acc over)

Verzug [fɛɐ'tsuːk] m (-[e]s; no pl) delay; ECON default

ver'zweifeln v/i (no -ge-, h) despair (**an** dat of); **ver'zweifelt** adj desperate, despairing

Ver'zweiflung f (-; no pl) despair; **j-n**

V

zur ~ bringen drive s.o. to despair
verzweigen [fɛˈtsvaigən] v/refl (no -ge-, h) branch
verzwickt [fɛˈtsvɪkt] F adj tricky
Veteran [veteˈraːn] m (-en; -en) MIL veteran (a. fig)
Veterinär [veteriˈnɛːɐ] m (-s; -e), **Veteri'närin** f (-; -nen) veterinarian, Br veterinary surgeon, F vet
Veto ['veːto] n (-s; -s) veto; **(s)ein ~ einlegen gegen** veto
Vetter [fɛtɐ] m (-s; -n) cousin
'Vetternwirtschaft f (-; no pl) nepotism
vgl. ABBR of **vergleiche** cf., confer
VHS ABBR of **Volkshochschule** adult education program(me); adult evening classes
Vibration [vibraˈtsjoːn] f (-; -en) vibration; **vibrieren** [viˈbriːrən] v/i (no -ge-, h) vibrate
Video ['viːdeo] n (-s; -s) video (a. in cpds ...aufnahme, ...clip, ...kamera, ...kassette, ...recorder etc); **auf ~ aufnehmen** video(tape); tape; **~band** n videotape; **~text** m teletext
Videothek [video'teːk] f (-; -en) video (tape) library; video store (Br shop)
Vieh [fiː] n (-[e]s; no pl) cattle; **20 Stück ~** 20 head of cattle; **~bestand** m livestock; **~händler** m cattle dealer
'viehisch contp adj bestial, brutal
'Vieh|markt m cattle market; **~zucht** f cattle breeding, stockbreeding; **~züchter** m cattle breeder, stockbreeder
viel [fiːl] adj and adv a lot (of), plenty (of), F lots of; **~e** many; **nicht ~** not much; **nicht ~e** not many; **sehr ~** a great deal (of); **sehr ~e** very many, a lot (of); **das ~e Geld** all that money; **ziemlich ~** quite a lot (of); **ziemlich ~e** quite a few; **~ besser** much better; **~ teurer** much more expensive; **e-r zu ~** one too many; **~ zu~** far too much; **~ zu wenig** not nearly enough; **~ lieber** much rather; **wie ~** how much (pl many); **~ beschäftigt** very busy; **~ sagend** meaningful; **~ versprechend** promising; **'vieldeutig** [-dɔytɪç] adj ambiguous; **vielerlei** ['fiːlɐ'lai] adj all kinds or sorts of; **'vielfach 1.** adj multiple; **2.** adv in many cases, (very) often; **'Vielfalt** f (-; no pl) (great) variety (gen of); **'vielfarbig** adj multicolo(u)red
vielleicht [fiˈlaiçt] adv perhaps, maybe;

~ ist er ... he may or might be ...
'vielmals adv: (ich) danke (Ihnen) ~ thank you very much; **entschuldigen Sie ~** I'm very sorry, I do apologize
viel'mehr cj rather
'vielseitig [-zaitiç] adj versatile
'Vielseitigkeit f (-; no pl) versatility
vier [fiːɐ] adj four; **zu viert sein** be four; **auf allen ~en** on all fours; **unter ~ Augen** in private, privately
'Vierbeiner [-bainɐ] m (-s; -) ZO quadruped, four-legged animal
'vierbeinig adj four-legged
Viereck n quadrangle, quadrilateral
'viereckig adj quadrangular, square
Vierer ['fiːrɐ] m (-s; -) rowing: four
'vierfach adj fourfold; **~e Ausfertigung** four copies
'vierfüßig [-fyːsɪç] adj four-footed
'Vierfüßler [-fyːslɐ] m (-s; -) ZO quadruped
'vierhändig [-hɛndɪç] adj MUS four-handed
'vierjährig [-jɛːrɪç] adj four-year-old, of four
Vierlinge ['fiːrlɪŋə] pl quadruplets, quads
'viermal adv four times
'Vierradantrieb m MOT four-wheel drive
'vierseitig [-zaitɪç] adj MATH quadrilateral
'vierspurig [-ʃpuːrɪç] adj MOT four-lane
'vierstöckig [-ʃtœkɪç] adj four-storied, Br four-storey ...
'Viertaktmotor m four-stroke engine
vierte ['fiːrtə] adj fourth
Viertel ['fɪrtəl] n (-s; -) fourth (part); quarter; **(ein) ~ vor (nach)** (a) quarter to (past); **~fi,nale** n SPORT quarter finals
Viertel'jahr n three months
'vierteljährlich 1. adj quarterly; **2.** adv every three months, quarterly
vierteln ['fɪrtəln] v/t (ge-, h) quarter
'Viertel|note f MUS quarter note, Br crotchet; **~pfund** n quarter of a pound
Viertel'stunde f quarter of an hour
viertens ['fiːrtəns] adv fourthly
vierzehn ['fɪrtseːn] adj fourteen; **~ Tage** two weeks, esp Br a. a fortnight
'vierzehnte adj fourteenth
vierzig ['fɪrtsɪç] adj forty
'vierzigste adj fortieth

Villa ['vɪla] f (-; Villen) villa

violett [vio'lɛt] adj violet, purple

Violine [vio'liːnə] f (-; -n) MUS violin

Virtuelle Realität [vɪr'tuɛlə] f EDP virtual reality, Cyberspace

virtuos [vɪr'tuoːs] adj virtuoso ..., masterly; **Virtuose** [vɪr'tuoːzə] m (-n; -n) virtuoso; **Virtuosität** [vɪrtuoziˈtɛːt] f (-; no pl) virtuosity

Virus ['viːrʊs] n, m (-; Viren) MED virus

Visier [vi'ziːɐ] n (-s; -e) sights; visor

Vision [vi'zjoːn] f (-; -en) vision

Visite [vi'ziːtə] f (-; -n) MED round

Vi'sitenkarte f (visiting) card

Visum ['viːzʊm] n (-s; Visa) visa

vital [vi'taːl] adj vigorous; **Vitalität** [vitaliˈtɛːt] f (-; no pl) vigo(u)r

Vitamin [vita'miːn] n (-s; -e) vitamin

Vitrine [vi'triːnə] f (-; -n) (glass) cabinet; showcase

Vize... ['fiːtsə-] in cpds ...präsident etc: vice(-)...

Vogel ['foːgəl] m (-s; Vögel ['føːgəl]) ZO bird; F **den ~ abschießen** take the cake

'Vogelbauer n birdcage

'vogelfrei adj outlawed

'Vogel|futter n birdseed; **~kunde** f ornithology; **~käfig** m birdcage

vögeln ['føːgəln] V v/t and v/i (ge-, h) screw

'Vogel|nest n bird's nest; **~perspektive** f bird's-eye view; **~scheuche** f scarecrow (a. fig); **~schutzgebiet** n bird sanctuary; **~warte** f ornithological station; **~zug** m bird migration

Vokabel [vo'kaːbəl] f (-; -n) word; pl → **Vokabular** [vokabu'laːɐ] n (-s; -e) vocabulary

Vokal [vo'kaːl] m (-s; -e) LING vowel

Volant [vo'lãː] m Austrian m → **Lenkrad**

Volk [fɔlk] n (-[e]s; Völker ['fœlkɐ]) people, nation; the people; ZO swarm; **ein Mann aus dem ~e** a man of the people

Völker|kunde f ethnology; **~mord** m genocide; **~recht** n (-[e]s; no pl) international law; **~wanderung** f migration of peoples; F mass exodus

Volks|abstimmung f POL referendum; **~fest** n funfair; **~hochschule** f adult evening classes; **~lied** n folk song; **~mund** m: **im ~** in the vernacular; **~mu,sik** f folk music; **~repu,blik** f

people's republic; **~schule** HIST f → **Grundschule**; **~sport** m popular sport; **~sprache** f vernacular; **~stamm** m tribe, race; **~tanz** m folk dance; **~tracht** f national costume

'volkstümlich [-tyːmlɪç] adj popular, folk ...; traditional

'Volks|versammlung f public meeting; **~wirt** m economist; **~wirtschaft** f (national) economy; → **~wirtschaftslehre** f economics; **~zählung** f census

voll [fɔl] 1. adj full (a. fig); full up (a. F); F plastered; thick, rich (hair); **~er** full of, filled with, a. covered with dirt etc; 2. adv fully; completely, totally, wholly; pay etc in full, the full price; hit etc full, straight, right; **~ entwickelt** fully developed; **~ füllen** (gießen) fill (up); **~ machen** fill (up); F soil, dirty; **um das Unglück ~ zu machen** to crown it all; **(nicht) für ~ nehmen** (not) take seriously; **~ packen** load (mit with) (a. fig); **~ stopfen** stuff, fig a. cram, pack (all: mit with); **bitte ~ tanken!** MOT fill her up, please!

'vollauf adv perfectly, quite

'vollauto,matisch adj fully automatic

Vollbart m (full) beard

'Vollbeschäftigung f full employment

'Vollblut... in cpds full-blooded (a. fig)

'Vollblüter [-blyːtɐ] m (-s; -) ZO thoroughbred

voll'bringen v/t (irr, bringen, no -ge-, h) accomplish, achieve; perform

'Volldampf m full steam; F **mit ~** (at) full blast

voll'enden v/t (no -ge-, h) finish, complete; **voll'endet** adj completed; fig perfect; **vollends** ['fɔlɛnts] adv completely; **Voll'endung** f (-; no pl) finishing, completion; fig perfection

voll'führen v/t (no -ge-, h) perform

'Vollgas n (-es; no pl) MOT full throttle; **~ geben** F step on it

völlig ['fœlɪç] 1. adj complete, absolute, total; 2. adv completely; **~ unmöglich** absolutely impossible

'volljährig [-jɛːrɪç] adj JUR **~ sein (werden)** be (come) of age; **noch nicht ~** under age; **'Volljährigkeit** f (-; no pl) JUR majority

voll'kommen adj perfect; → **völlig**

Voll'kommenheit f (-; no pl) perfection

'Voll|kornbrot n wholemeal bread;

V

~macht f (-; -en) full power(s), authority; JUR power of attorney; **~ haben** be authorized; **~milch** f full-cream milk; **~mond** m full moon; **~pensi,on** f full board

'**vollschlank** adj plump

'**vollständig** adj complete; → **völlig**

voll'**strecken** v/t (no -ge-, h) JUR execute; **Voll'streckung** f (-; -en) JUR execution

'**Volltreffer** m direct hit; bull's eye (a. fig); **~versammlung** f plenary session

'**vollwertig** adj full

'**Vollwertkost** f wholefoods

vollzählig ['fɔltsɛːlɪç] adj complete

voll'**ziehen** v/t (irr, ziehen, no -ge-, h) execute; perform; **sich ~** take place; **Voll'ziehung** f (-; no pl), **Voll'zug** m (-[e]s; no pl) execution

Volontär [volɔn'tɛːʀ] m (-s; -e), **Volon-'tärin** f (-; -nen) unpaid trainee

Volt [vɔlt] n (-; -) ELECTR volt

Volumen [vo'luːmən] n (-s; -, -mina) volume; size

von [fɔn] prp from; instead of gen: of; passive: by; about s.o. or s.th.: of; **südlich ~** south of; **weit ~** far from; **~ Hamburg** from Hamburg; **~ nun an** from now on; **ein Freund ~ mir** a friend of mine; **die Freunde ~ Alice** Alice's friends; **ein Brief (Geschenk) ~ Tom** a letter (gift) from Tom; **ein Buch (Bild) ~ Orwell (Picasso)** a book (painting) by Orwell (Picasso); **der König (Bürgermeister etc) ~ ...** the King (Mayor etc) of ...; **ein Kind ~ 10 Jahren** a child of ten; **müde ~ der Arbeit** tired from work; **es war nett (gemein) ~ dir** it was nice (mean) of you; **reden (hören) ~** talk (hear) about or of; **~ Beruf (Geburt)** by profession (birth); **~ selbst** by itself; **~ mir aus!** I don't mind or care

von'**statten** adv: **~ gehen** go, come off

vor [foːʀ] prp (dat and acc) in front of; outside; before; ... ago; with; for; **~ der Klasse** in front of the class; **~ der Schule** in front of or outside the school; before school; **~ kurzem (e-r Stunde)** a short time (an hour) ago; **5 Minuten ~ 12** five (minutes) to twelve; **~ j-m liegen** be or lie ahead of s.o. (a. fig and SPORT); **~ sich hin** smile etc to o.s.; **sicher ~** safe from; **~ Kälte** with cold; **~ Angst** for fear; **~ allem**

above all; **~ sich gehen** go on, happen

'**Vorabend** m eve (a. fig)

'**Vorahnung** f presentiment, foreboding

voran [fo'ʀan] adv at the head (dat of), in front (of), before; **Kopf ~** head first; **~gehen** v/i (irr, gehen, sep, -ge-, sein) go in front or first; esp fig lead the way; **~kommen** v/i (irr, kommen, sep, -ge-, sein) get on or along (a. fig), make headway

'**Voranzeige** f preannouncement; film: trailer

'**vorarbeiten** v/i (sep, -ge-, h) work in advance; fig pave the way

'**Vorarbeiter** m foreman

voraus [fo'ʀaus] adv ahead (dat of); **im Voraus** in advance, beforehand

vo'**rausgehen** v/i (irr, gehen, sep, -ge-, sein) precede; → **vorangehen**

vo'**rausgesetzt** cj: **~, dass** provided that

vo'**raussage** f (-; -n) prediction; METEOR forecast; **vo'raussagen** v/t (sep, -ge-, h) predict; forecast

vo'**raus|schicken** v/t (sep, -ge-, h) send on ahead; **~sehen** v/t (irr, sehen, sep, -ge-, h) foresee, see s.th. coming

vo'**raussetzen** v/t (sep, -ge-, h) assume; take s.th. for granted

vo'**raussetzung** f (-; -en) condition, prerequisite; assumption; **die ~en erfüllen** meet the requirements

Vo'raussicht f (-; no pl) foresight; **aller ~ nach** in all probability

vo'**raussichtlich** adv probably; **er kommt ~ morgen** he is expected to arrive tomorrow

'**Vorauszahlung** f advance payment

'**Vorbedeutung** f omen

'**Vorbedingung** f prerequisite

Vorbehalt ['foːʀbəhalt] m (-[e]s; -e) reservation; '**vorbehalten 1.** v/t (irr, halten, sep, no -ge-, h) **sich (das Recht) ~ zu** inf reserve the right to inf; **2.** adj reserved; '**vorbehaltlos 1.** adj unconditional; **2.** adv without reservation

vor'bei adv time: over, past; finished; gone; space: past, by; **jetzt ist alles ~** it's all over now; **~! I** missed!; **~fahren** v/i (irr, fahren, sep, -ge-, sein) go (or drive) past (**an** dat s.o. or s.th.), pass (s.o. or s.th.); **~gehen** v/i (irr, gehen, sep, -ge-, sein) walk past (**an** dat s.o. or s.th.), pass (a. fig go by, pass; shot etc: miss; **~ kommen** v/i (irr,

kommen, sep, -ge-, sein) pass (**an** dat s.th.); get past (**an** obstacle etc); F drop in (**bei j-m** on s.o.); fig avoid; **~lassen** v/t (irr, **lassen**, sep, -ge-, h) let s.o. pass

'**Vorbemerkung** f preliminary remark

'**vorbereiten** v/t and v/refl (sep, no -ge-, h) prepare (**auf** acc for); '**Vorbereitung** f (-; -en) preparation (**auf** acc for)

'**vorbestellen** v/t (sep, no -ge-, h) book (or order) in advance; reserve (room, seat etc); '**Vorbestellung** f (-; -en) advance booking; reservation

'**vorbestraft** adj: ~ **sein** have a police record

'**vorbeugen** (sep, -ge-, h) **1.** v/i prevent (**e-r Sache** s.th.); **2.** v/refl bend forward; **~d** adj preventive, MED a. prophylactic

'**Vorbeugung** f (-; -en) prevention

'**Vorbild** n model, pattern; (**j-m**) **ein ~ sein** set an example (to s.o.); **sich j-n zum ~ nehmen** follow s.o.'s example

'**vorbildlich** adj exemplary

'**Vorbildung** f education(al background)

'**vor|bringen** v/t (irr, **bringen**, sep, -ge-, h) bring forward; say, state; **~da‚tieren** v/t (no -ge-, h) antedate; postdate

Vorder... ['fɔrdɐ-] in cpds ...**achse**, ...**rad**, ...**sitz**, ...**tür**, ...**zahn** etc: front ...

vordere ['fɔrdərə] adj front

'**Vorder|grund** m foreground (a. fig); **~mann** m: **mein ~** the man or boy in front of me; **~seite** f front (side); head

'**vor|dräng(e‚l)n** v/refl (sep, -ge-, h) cut into line, Br jump the queue; **~dringen** v/i (irr, **dringen**, sep, -ge-, sein) advance; ~ (**bis**) zu work one's way through to (a. fig); **~dringlich 1.** adj (most) urgent; **2.** adv: **et. ~ behandeln** give s.th. priority

'**Vordruck** m (-[e]s; -e) form, blank

'**voreilig** adj hasty, rash, precipitate; **~e Schlüsse ziehen** jump to conclusions

'**voreingenommen** adj prejudiced, bias(s)ed; '**Voreingenommenheit** f (-; no pl) prejudice, bias

'**vorenthalten** v/t (irr, **halten**, sep, no -ge-, h) keep back, withhold (both: **j-m et.** s.th. from s.o.)

'**Vorentscheidung** f preliminary decision

'**vorerst** adv for the present, for the time being

Vorfahr ['foːɐfaːɐ] m (-en; -en) ancestor

'**vorfahren** v/i (irr, **fahren**, sep, -ge-, sein) drive up (or on); '**Vorfahrt** f (-; no pl) right of way, priority

'**Vorfall** m incident, occurrence, event

'**vor|fallen** v/i (irr, **fallen**, sep, -ge-, sein) happen, occur; **~finden** v/t (irr, **finden**, sep, -ge-, h) find

'**Vorfreude** f anticipation

'**vorführen** v/t (sep, -ge-, h) show, present; perform (trick etc); demonstrate; JUR bring (**j-m** before s.o.); '**Vorführer** m demonstrator; '**Vorführung** f presentation, show(ing); performance; demonstration; JUR production

'**Vorführwagen** m MOT demonstrator, Br demonstration car

'**Vorgabe** f handicap

'**Vorgang** m event, occurrence, happening; file, record(s); BIOL, TECH process; **e-n ~ schildern** give an account of what happened; **Vorgänger(in)** ['foːɐɡɛŋɐ (-ɡərɪn)] (-s; -/-; -nen) predecessor

'**Vorgarten** m front yard (Br garden)

'**vorgeben** v/t (irr, **geben**, sep, -ge-, h) SPORT give; fig use s.th. as a pretext

'**Vorgebirge** n foothills

'**vorgefasst** adj preconceived

'**vorgefertigt** adj prefabricated

'**Vorgefühl** n presentiment

'**vorgehen** v/i (irr, **gehen**, sep, -ge-, sein) go on; come first; act; JUR sue (**gegen j-n** s.o.); proceed; watch: be fast; '**Vorgehen** n (-s; no pl) procedure

'**vorgeschichtlich** adj prehistoric

'**Vorgeschmack** m foretaste (**auf** acc of); **~gesetzte** m, f (-n; -n) superior, F boss

'**vorgestern** adv the day before yesterday

'**vorgreifen** v/i (irr, **greifen**, sep, -ge-, h) anticipate s.o. or s.th.

'**vorhaben** v/t (irr, **haben**, sep, -ge-, h) plan, intend; **haben Sie heute Abend et. vor?** have you anything on tonight?; **was hat er jetzt wieder vor?** what is he up to now?; '**Vorhaben** n (-s; -) plan(s), intention; TECH, ECON a. project

'**Vorhalle** f (entrance) hall, lobby

'**vorhalten** (irr, **halten**, sep, -ge-, h) **1.** v/t: **j-m et. ~** hold s.th. in front of s.o.; fig blame s.o. for (doing) s.th.; **2.** v/i last;

V

'**Vorhaltungen** *pl* reproaches; **j-m ~ machen (für et.)** reproach s.o. (with s.th., for being ...)

'**Vorhand** *f* (-; *no pl*) *tennis:* forehand

vorhanden [foːɐ̯'handən] *adj* available; in existence; **~ sein** exist; **es ist nichts mehr ~** there's nothing left; **Vor'handensein** *n* (-s; *no pl*) existence

'**Vorhang** *m* curtain

'**Vorhängeschloss** *n* padlock

vor'her *adv* before, earlier; in advance, beforehand

vor'herbestimmen *v/t* (*sep, no -ge-, h*) predetermine

vorherig [foːɐ̯'heːrɪç] *adj* previous

'**Vorherrschaft** *f* (-; *no pl*) predominance; '**vorherrschen** *v/i* (*sep, -ge-, h*) predominate, prevail; '**vorherrschend** *adj* predominant, prevailing

vor'hersehbar *adj* foreseeable

vor'hersehen *v/t* (*irr, sehen, sep, -ge-, h*) foresee

vor'hin *adv* a (little) while ago

'**Vorhut** *f* (-; *-en*) MIL vanguard

vorig ['foːrɪç] *adj* last; former, previous

vorjährig ['foːrjɛːrɪç] *adj* of last year, last year' ...

'**Vorkämpfer** *m*, '**Vorkämpferin** *f* champion, pioneer

Vorkehrungen ['foːɐ̯keːrʊŋən] *pl:* **~ treffen** take precautions

'**Vorkenntnisse** *pl* previous knowledge *or* experience (**in** *dat* of)

'**vorkommen** *v/i* (*irr, kommen, sep, -ge-, sein*) be found; happen; **es kommt mir ... vor** it seems ... to me

'**Vorkommen** *n* (-s; -) MIN deposit(s)

Vorkommnis ['foːɐ̯kɔmnɪs] *n* (-ses; -se) occurrence, incident, event

'**Vorkriegs...** *in cpds* prewar ...

'**vorladen** *v/t* (*irr, laden, sep, -ge-, h*) JUR summon; '**Vorladung** *f* (-; *-en*) JUR summons

'**Vorlage** *f* model; pattern; copy; presentation; PARL bill; *soccer etc:* pass

'**vorlassen** *v/t* (*irr, lassen, sep, -ge-, h*) let *s.o.* go first; let *s.o.* pass; **vorgelassen werden** be admitted (**bei** to)

'**Vorlauf** *m* recorder: fast-forward; SPORT (preliminary) heat; '**Vorläufer** *m* forerunner, precursor; '**vorläufig 1.** *adj* provisional, temporary; **2.** *adv* for the present, for the time being

'**vorlaut** *adj* pert, cheeky

'**Vorleben** *n* (-s; *no pl*) former life, past

'**vorlegen** *v/t* (*sep, -ge-, h*) present; produce; show

'**Vorleger** *m* (-s; -) rug; mat

'**vorlesen** *v/t* (*irr, lesen, sep, -ge-, h*) read out (aloud); **j-m et. ~** read s.th. to s.o.; '**Vorlesung** *f* (-; *-en*) lecture (**über** *acc on*; **vor** *dat* to); **e-e ~ halten** (give a) lecture

'**vorletzte** *adj* last but one; **~ Nacht (Woche)** the night (week) before last

vor'lieb: **~ nehmen mit** make do with

'**Vorliebe** *f* (-; *-n*) preference, special liking

'**vorliegen** *v/i* (*irr, liegen, sep, -ge-, h*) **es liegen (keine) ... vor** there are (no) ...; **was liegt gegen ihn vor?** what is he charged with?; **~d** *adj* present, in question

'**vorlügen** *v/t* (*irr, lügen, sep, -ge-, h*) **j-m et. ~** tell s.o. lies; **~machen** *v/t* (*sep, -ge-, h*) **j-m et. ~** show s.th. to s.o., show s.o. how to do s.th.; *fig* fool s.o.

'**Vormachtstellung** *f* supremacy

'**Vormarsch** *m* MIL advance (*a. fig*)

'**vormerken** *v/t* (*sep, -ge-, h*) **j-n ~** put s.o.'s name down

'**Vormittag** *m* morning; **heute ~** this morning

'**vormittags** *adv* in the morning; **sonntags ~** on Sunday mornings

'**Vormund** *m* (-[e]s; -e) JUR guardian; **~schaft** *f* (-; *-en*) JUR guardianship

vorn [fɔrn] *adv* in front; **nach ~** forward; **von ~** from the front; from the beginning; **j-n von ~(e) sehen** see s.o.'s face; **noch einmal von ~(e) (anfangen)** (start) all over again

'**Vorname** *m* first *or* Christian name, forename

vornehm ['foːɐ̯neːm] *adj* distinguished; noble; fashionable, exclusive, F smart, posh; **die ~e Gesellschaft** (high) society; **~ tun** put on airs

'**vornehmen** *v/t* (*irr, nehmen, sep, -ge-, h*) carry out, do; make (*changes etc*); **sich et. ~** decide *or* resolve to do s.th.; make plans for s.th.; **sich fest vorgenommen haben zu** *inf* have the firm intention to *inf*, be determined to *inf*

'**vornherein** *adv:* **von ~** from the start *or* beginning

'**Vorort** *m* suburb; **~(s)zug** *m* suburban *or* local *or* commuter train

'**Vorposten** *m* outpost (*a.* MIL)

'**vorprogram,mieren** *v/t* (*sep, no -ge-, sein*) (pre)program(me); *fig* **das war vorprogrammiert** that was bound to happen

'**Vorrang** *m* (*-[e]s; no pl*) precedence (**vor** *dat* over), priority (over)

'**Vorrat** *m* (*-[e]s; -räte*) store, stock, supply (*all:* **an** *dat* of); GASTR provisions; ECON resources, reserves; **e-n ~ anlegen an** (*dat*) stockpile; **vorrätig** ['foːrɛːtɪç] *adj* available; ECON in stock

'**Vorrecht** *n* privilege

'**Vorredner** *m* previous speaker

'**Vorrichtung** *f* TECH device

'**vorrücken** (*sep, -ge-*) **1.** *v/t* (*h*) move forward; **2.** *v/i* (*sein*) advance

'**Vorrunde** *f* SPORT preliminary round

'**vorsagen** *v/i* (*sep, -ge-, h*) *j-m* **~** prompt s.o.

'**Vorsai,son** *f* off-peak season

'**Vorsatz** *m* resolution; intention; JUR intent; **vorsätzlich** ['foːrzɛtslɪç] *adj* intentional; *esp* JUR wil(l)ful

'**Vorschau** *f* preview (**auf** *acc* of), *film*, TV *a.* trailer

'**Vorschein** *m*: **zum ~ bringen** produce; *fig* bring out; **zum ~ kommen** appear; *fig* come to light

'**vor|schieben** *v/t* (*irr, schieben, sep, -ge-, h*) push forward; slip (*bolt*); use as a pretext; **~schießen** F *v/t* (*irr, schießen, sep, -ge-, h*) advance (*money*)

'**Vorschlag** *m* suggestion, proposal (*a.* PARL *etc*); **den ~ machen →** '**vorschlagen** *v/t* (*irr, schlagen, sep, -ge-, h*) suggest, propose

'**Vorschlussrunde** *f* SPORT semifinal

'**vorschnell** *adj* hasty, rash

'**vorschreiben** *fig v/t* (*irr, schreiben, sep, -ge-, h*) prescribe; tell; **ich lasse mir nichts ~** I won't be dictated to;

'**Vorschrift** *f* rule, regulation; instruction, direction; **Dienst nach ~ machen** work to rule

'**vorschrifts|mäßig** *adj* correct, proper; **~widrig** *adj and adv* contrary to regulations

'**Vorschub** *m*: **~ leisten** (*dat*) encourage; JUR aid and abet

'**Vorschul...** *in cpds* pre-school ...

'**Vorschule** *f* preschool

'**Vorschuss** *m* advance

'**vorschützen** *v/t* (*sep, -ge-, h*) use *s.th.* as a pretext

'**vorsehen** (*irr, sehen, sep, -ge-, h*) **1.** *v/t* plan; provide; **~ für** intend (*or* designate) for; **2.** *v/refl* be careful, take care, watch out (**vor** *dat* for)

'**Vorsehung** *f* (*-; no pl*) providence

'**vorsetzen** *v/t* (*sep, -ge-, h*) *j-m* **et. ~** put *s.th.* before *s.o.*; offer *s.o. s.th.*

'**Vorsicht** *f* (*-; no pl*) caution, care; **~!** look *or* watch out!, (be) careful!; **~, Stufe!** mind the step!; '**vorsichtig** *adj* careful, cautious; '**vorsichtshalber** [-halbɐ] *adv* to be on the safe side; '**Vorsichtsmaßnahme** *f* precaution, precautionary measure; **~n treffen** take precautions

'**Vorsilbe** *f* LING prefix

'**vorsingen** *v/t and v/i* (*irr, singen, sep, -ge-, h*) *j-m* **et. ~** sing *s.th.* to *s.o.*; (have an) audition

'**Vorsitz** *m* chair(manship), presidency; **den ~ haben** (**übernehmen**) be in (take) the chair, preside (**bei** over, at)

'**Vorsitzende** *m, f* (*-n; -n*) chairman (chairwoman), president

'**Vorsorge** *f* (*-; no pl*) precaution; **~ treffen** take precautions; **~untersuchung** *f* MED preventive checkup

'**vorsorglich 1.** *adj* precautionary; **2.** *adv* as a precaution

'**Vorspann** *m* (*-[e]s; -e*) *film etc*: credits

'**Vorspeise** *f* hors d'œuvre, *Br* starter

'**Vorspiel** *n* MUS prelude (*a. fig*); foreplay; '**vorspielen** *v/t* (*sep, -ge-, h*) *j-m* **et. ~** play *s.th.* to *s.o.*

'**vorsprechen** *v/t, v/i* (*irr, sprechen, sep, -ge-, h*) **1.** *v/t* pronounce (*j-m* for *s.o.*); **2.** *v/i* call (**bei** at); THEA (have an) audition

'**vorspringen** *fig v/i* (*irr, springen, sep, -ge-, sein*) project, protrude (*both a.* ARCH); '**Vorsprung** *m* ARCH projection; SPORT lead; **e-n ~ haben** be leading (**von** by); *esp fig* **e-n ~ von zwei Jahren haben** be two years ahead

'**Vorstadt** *f* suburb

'**Vorstand** *m* ECON board (of directors); managing committee (*of a club etc*)

'**vorstehen** *v/i* (*irr, stehen, sep, -ge-, h*) project, protrude

'**vorstellen** *v/t* (*sep, -ge-, h*) introduce (**sich** o.s.; *j-n j-m* s.o. to s.o.); put *watch* forward (*um* by); *fig* mean; **sich ~** (*j-n als* ...) ~ imagine s.th. (s.o. as ...); **so stelle ich mir ... vor** that's my idea of ...; **sich ~ bei** have an interview with *a firm etc*; '**Vorstellung** *f* (-; *-en*) introduction; interview; THEA performance, *film etc*: *a.* show; idea; expectation

'Vorstellungs|kraft *f* (-; *no pl*), **~vermögen** *n* (-*s*; *no pl*) imagination

Vorstopper ['fo:rʃtɔpɐ] *m* (-*s*; -) SPORT center (*Br* centre) back

'Vorstoß *m* MIL advance; *fig* attempt

'Vorstrafe *f* previous conviction

'vorstrecken *v/t* (*sep*, *-ge-*, *h*) advance (*money*)

'Vorstufe *f* preliminary stage

'vortäuschen *v/t* (*sep*, *-ge-*, *h*) feign, fake

'Vorteil *m* advantage (*a.* SPORT); benefit, profit; **die ~e und Nachteile** the pros and cons; '**vorteilhaft** *adj* advantageous, profitable; '**Vorteilsregel** *f* SPORT advantage rule

Vortrag ['fo:rtra:k] *m* (-[*e*]*s*; *Vorträge* ['fo:rtrɛːgə]) talk, *esp* UNIV lecture; MUS *etc* recital; *e-n* ~ *halten* give a talk or lecture (*vor dat* to; *über acc* on)

'vortragen *v/t* (*irr*, *tragen*, *sep*, *-ge-*, *h*) express, state; MUS *etc* perform, play; recite (*poem etc*)

'vortreten *v/i* (*irr*, *treten*, *sep*, *-ge-*, *sein*) step forward; *fig* protrude, stick out

'Vortritt *m* (-[*e*]*s*; *no pl*) precedence; *j-m den* ~ *lassen* let s.o. go first

vorüber [fo'ry:bɐ] *adv*: ~ *sein* be over; **~gehen** *v/i* (*irr*, *gehen*, *sep*, *-ge-*, *sein*) pass, go by; **~gehend** *adj* temporary

'Vorübung *f* preparatory exercise

'Voruntersuchung *f* JUR, MED preliminary examination

'Vorurteil *n* prejudice; '**vorurteilslos** *adj* unprejudiced, unbias(s)ed

'Vorverkauf *m* THEA advance booking

'vorverlegen *v/t* (*sep*, *no -ge-*, *h*) advance

'Vorwahl *f* TEL area (*Br* STD or dialling) code; POL primary, *Br* preliminary election

'Vorwand *m* pretext, excuse

vorwärts ['fo:rvɛrts] *adv* forward, on (-ward), ahead; **~!** come on!, let's go!; **~kommen** make headway (*a. fig*)

vorweg [fo:ɐ'vɛk] *adv* beforehand

vor'wegnehmen *v/t* (*irr*, *nehmen*, *sep*, *-ge-*, *h*) anticipate

'vor|weisen *v/t* (*irr*, *weisen*, *sep*, *-ge-*, *h*) produce, show; **et. ~ können** boast s.th.; **~werfen** *fig v/t* (*irr*, *werfen*, *sep*, *-ge-*, *h*) **j-m et. ~** reproach s.o. with s.th.

'vorwiegend *adv* predominantly, chiefly, mainly, mostly

'vorwitzig *adj* cheeky, pert

'Vorwort *n* (-[*e*]*s*; -*e*) foreword; preface

'Vorwurf *m* reproach; *j-m Vorwürfe machen* (*wegen*) reproach s.o. (for); '**vorwurfsvoll** *adj* reproachful

'Vorzeichen *n* omen, sign (*a.* MATH)

'vorzeigen *v/t* (*sep*, *-ge-*, *h*) show; produce

'vorzeitig *adj* premature, early

'vorziehen *v/t* (*irr*, *ziehen*, *sep*, *-ge-*, *h*) draw; *fig* prefer

'Vorzimmer *n* anteroom; outer office; *Austrian* → **Hausflur**

'Vorzug *m* advantage; merit

vorzüglich [fo:ɐ'tsy:klıç] *adj* excellent, exquisite

'vorzugsweise *adv* preferably

Votum ['vo:tom] *n* (-*s*; *-ta*, *-ten*) vote

VP ABBR *of Vollpension* full board; (full) board and lodging

vulgär [vʊl'gɛːɐ] *adj* vulgar

Vulkan [vʊl'ka:n] *m* (-*s*; -*e*) volcano; **~ausbruch** *m* volcanic eruption

vul'kanisch *adj* volcanic

V

W

W ABBR of **West(en)** W, west; **Watt** W, watt(s)

Waage ['va:gə] f (-; -n) scale(s Br); balance; ASTR Libra; **sich die ~ halten** balance each other; **er ist (e-e) ~** he's (a) Libra; **'waagerecht** adj horizontal

Waagschale ['va:k-] f scale

Wabe ['va:bə] f (-; -n) honeycomb

wach [vax] adj awake; **~ werden** wake (up), esp fig awake

Wache ['vaxə] f (-; -n) guard (a. MIL); sentry; MAR, MED etc watch; police station; **~ haben** be on guard (MAR watch); **~ halten** keep watch; **'wachen** v/i (ge-, h) (keep) watch (**über** acc over)

'Wachhund m watchdog

'Wachmann m (-[e]s; -männer, -leute) watchman; Austrian → **Polizist**

Wacholder [va'xɔldɐ] m (-s; -) BOT juniper

'wach|rufen v/t (irr, **rufen**, sep, -ge-, h) call up, evoke; **~rütteln** v/t (sep, -ge-, h) rouse (a. fig)

Wachs [vaks] n (-es; -e) wax

wachsam ['vaxza:m] adj watchful, on one's guard, vigilant; **'Wachsamkeit** f (-; no pl) watchfulness, vigilance

wachsen¹ ['vaksən] v/i (irr, ge-, sein) grow (a. **sich ~ lassen**), fig a. increase

'wachsen² v/t (ge-, h) wax

'Wachs|fi,gurenkabi,nett n waxworks; **~tuch** n oilcloth

'Wachstum n (-s; no pl) growth, fig a. increase

Wachtel ['vaxtəl] f (-; -n) ZO quail

Wächter ['vɛçtɐ] m (-s; -) guard

'Wachtmeister m (-s; no pl) patrolman, Br (police) constable

'Wach(t)turm m watchtower

wackelig ['vakəlıç] adj shaky (a. fig); loose (tooth); **'wackeln** v/i (ge-, h) shake; table etc: wobble; tooth: be loose; PHOT move; **~ mit** waggle

Wade ['va:də] f (-; -n) ANAT calf

Waffe ['vafə] f (-; -n) weapon (a. fig), pl a. arms

Waffel ['vafəl] f (-; -n) waffle; wafer

'Waffen|gewalt f: **mit ~** by force of arms; **~schein** m gun license (Br licence); **~stillstand** m armistice (a. fig); truce

wagen ['va:gən] v/t (ge-, h) dare; risk; **sich ~** venture

'Wagen m (-s; -) MOT car; RAIL car, Br carriage

wägen ['vɛ:gən] lit v/t (irr, ge-, h) weigh (one's words etc)

'Wagen|heber m TECH jack; **~ladung** f cartload

Waggon [va'gõ:] m (-s, -s) (railroad) car, Br (railway) carriage; freight car, Br goods waggon

Wagnis ['va:knıs] n (-ses; -se) venture, risk

Wa'gon m → **Waggon**

Wahl [va:l] f (-; -en) choice; alternative; selection; POL election; voting, poll; vote; **die ~ haben (s-e treffen)** have the (make one's) choice; **keine (andere) ~ haben** have no choice or alternative; **'wahlberechtigt** adj POL entitled to vote; **'Wahlbeteiligung** f POL poll, (voter) turnout; **hohe (niedrige) ~** heavy (light) poll; **'Wahlbezirk** m → **Wahlkreis**

wählen ['vɛ:lən] v/t and v/i (ge-, h) choose, pick, select; POL vote (for); elect; TEL dial; **'Wähler** m (-s; -) voter

'Wahlergebnis n election result

wählerisch ['vɛ:lərıʃ] adj F picky (**in** dat about), esp Br choos(e)y

'Wählerschaft f (-; -en) electorate, voters

'Wahl|fach n PED etc elective, optional subject; **~ka,bine** f voting (esp Br polling) booth; **~kampf** m election campaign; **~kreis** m electoral district, Br constituency; **~lo,kal** n polling place (Br station)

'wahllos adj indiscriminate

'Wahl|pro,gramm n election platform; **~recht** n (-[e]s; no pl) (right to) vote, suffrage, franchise; **~rede** f election speech

'Wählscheibe f TEL dial

'Wahl|sieg m election victory; **~sieger** m election winner; **~spruch** m motto;

~urne f ballot box; **~versammlung** f election rally

'**Wahnsinn** m (-[e]s; no pl) madness (a. F), insanity

'**wahnsinnig 1.** adj mad (a. F), insane, F a. crazy; F awful, terrible; **2.** F adv terribly, awfully; madly (in love)

'**Wahnsinnige** m, f (-n; -n) madman (madwoman), lunatic, maniac (all a. F)

'**Wahnvorstellung** f delusion, hallucination

wahr [vaːɐ] adj true; real; genuine

wahren ['vaːrən] v/t (ge-, h) protect; **den Schein ~** keep up appearances

während ['vɛːrənt] **1.** prp (gen) during; **2.** cj while; whereas

'**wahrhaft, wahr'haftig** adv really, truly

'**Wahrheit** f (-; -en) truth

'**wahrheits|gemäß, ~getreu** adj true, truthful; **~liebend** adj truthful

wahrnehmbar ['vaːɐneːmbaːɐ] adj noticeable, perceptible; '**wahrnehmen** v/t (irr, **nehmen**, sep, -ge-, h) perceive, notice; seize, take (chance etc); look after (s.o.'s interests etc); '**Wahrnehmung** f (-; -en) perception

'**wahrsagen** v/i (sep, -ge-, h) **j-m ~** tell s.o. his fortune; **sich ~ lassen** have one's fortune told; '**Wahrsager** [-zaːgɐ] m (-s; -), '**Wahrsagerin** [-zaːgərɪn] f (-; -nen) fortune-teller

wahr'scheinlich 1. adj probable, likely; **2.** adv probably, (very or most) likely; **~ gewinnt er (nicht)** he is (not) likely to win; **Wahr'scheinlichkeit** f (-; -en) probability, likelihood

Währung ['vɛːrʊŋ] f (-; -en) currency

'**Währungs...** in cpds ...politik, ...reform etc: monetary ...

'**Wahrzeichen** n landmark

Waise ['vaɪzə] f (-; -n) orphan; **~ werden** be orphaned

'**Waisenhaus** n orphanage

Wal [vaːl] m (-[e]s; -e) zo whale

Wald [valt] m (-[e]s; Wälder ['vɛldɐ]) wood(s), forest; **~brand** m forest fire

'**waldreich** adj wooded

'**Waldsterben** n dying of forests

'**Walfang** m whaling

'**Walfänger** m whaler

Walkman® m (-s; -men) personal stereo, Walkman®

Wall [val] m (-[e]s; Wälle ['vɛlə]) mound; MIL rampart

Wallach ['valax] m (-[e]s; -e) zo gelding

wallen ['valən] v/i (ge-, sein) flow

'**Wallfahrer** m, '**Wallfahrerin** f pilgrim

'**Wallfahrt** f pilgrimage

'**Walnuss** f BOT walnut

'**Walross** n zo walrus

Walze ['valtsə] f (-; -n) roller; cylinder; TECH, MUS barrel

'**walzen** v/t (ge-, h) roll (a. TECH)

wälzen ['vɛltsən] v/t (ge-, h) roll (a. **sich ~**); fig turn s.th. over in one's mind

Walzer ['valtsə] m (-s; -) MUS waltz (a. **~ tanzen**)

wand [vant] pret of **winden**

Wand f (-; Wände ['vɛndə]) wall, fig a. barrier

Wandale [van'daːlə] m (-n; -n) vandal; **Wandalismus** [vanda'lɪsmʊs] m (-; no pl) vandalism

Wandel ['vandəl] m (-s; no pl), '**wandeln** v/t and v/refl (ge-, h) change

Wanderer ['vandərə] m (-s; -), '**Wanderin** f (-; -nen) hiker

wandern ['vandən] v/i (ge-, sein) hike; ramble (about); eyes etc: roam, wander

'**Wander|po,kal** m challenge cup; **~preis** m challenge trophy; **~schuhe** pl walking shoes; **~tag** m (school) outing or excursion

'**Wanderung** f (-; -en) walking tour, hike; zo etc migration

'**Wand|gemälde** n mural; **~ka,lender** m wall calendar; **~karte** f wallchart

Wandlung ['vandlʊŋ] f (-; -en) change

'**Wand|schrank** m closet, Br built-in cupboard; **~tafel** f blackboard

wandte ['vantə] pret of **wenden**

'**Wandteppich** m tapestry

Wange ['vaŋə] f (-; -n) ANAT cheek

Wankelmotor ['vaŋkəl-] m rotary piston or Wankel engine

wankelmütig ['vaŋkəlmyːtɪç] adj fickle

wanken ['vaŋkən] v/i (ge-, sein) stagger, reel; fig rock

wann [van] interr adv when, (at) what time; **seit ~?** (for) how long?, since when?

Wanne ['vanə] f (-; -n) tub (a. F); bath (tub)

Wanze ['vantsə] f (-; -n) zo bug (a. F)

Wapitihirsch [va'piːti-] m zo elk

Wappen ['vapən] n (-s; -) (coat of) arms

'**Wappenkunde** f heraldry

wappnen ['vapnən] fig v/refl (ge-, h) arm o.s.

war [vaːɛ] pret of **sein**[1]

warb [varp] pret of **werben**

Ware ['vaːrə] f (-; -n) coll mst goods; article; product

'**Waren|haus** n department store; **~lager** n stock; **~probe** f sample; **~zeichen** n trademark

warf [varf] pret of **werfen**

warm [varm] adj warm (a. fig); GASTR hot; **schön ~** nice and warm; **~ halten** keep warm; **~ machen** warm (up)

Wärme ['vɛrmə] f (-; no pl) warmth; PHYS heat; **~iso,lierung** f heat insulation

'**wärmen** v/t (ge-, h) warm

'**Wärmflasche** f hot-water bottle

'**warmherzig** adj warm-hearted

Warm|wasser|bereiter m (-s; -) water heater; **~versorgung** f hot-water supply

'**Warn|blinkanlage** f MOT warning flasher; **~dreieck** n MOT warning triangle

warnen ['varnən] v/t (ge-, h) warn (**vor** dat of, against); **j-n davor ~, et. zu tun** warn s.o. not to do s.th.

'**Warn|schild** n danger sign; **~sig,nal** n warning signal; **~streik** m token strike

'**Warnung** f (-; -en) warning

warten[1] ['vartən] v/i (ge-, h) wait (**auf** acc for); **j-n ~ lassen** keep s.o. waiting

'**warten**[2] v/t (ge-, h) TECH service, maintain

Wärter ['vɛrtɐ] m (-s; -), '**Wärterin** f (-; -nen) attendant; ZO keeper

'**Warte|liste** f waiting list; **~saal** m, **~zimmer** n waiting room

'**Wartung** f (-; -en) TECH maintenance

warum [va'rʊm] interr adv why

Warze ['vartsə] f (-; -n) MED wart

was [vas] **1.** interr pron what; **~ gibt's?** what is it?, F what's up?; what's for lunch etc?; **~ soll's?** so what?; **~ machen Sie?** what are you doing?; what do you do?; **~ kostet ...?** how much is ...?; **~ für ...?** what kind or sort of ...?; **~ für e-e Farbe (Größe)?** what colo(u)r (size)?; **~ für ein Unsinn** what nonsense!; **~ für e-e gute Idee!** what a good idea!; **2.** rel pron what; **~ (auch) immer** whatever; **alles, ~ ich habe**

(**brauche**) all I have (need); **ich weiß nicht, ~ ich tun (sagen) soll** I don't know what to do (say); **..., ~ mich ärgerte...**, which made me angry; **3.** F indef pron → **etwas**

waschbar ['vaʃbaːɛ] adj washable

'**Waschbecken** n washbowl, Br washbasin

Wäsche ['vɛʃə] f (-; -n) a) washing, b) (no pl) laundry; linen; underwear; **in der ~** in the wash; **schmutzige ~ waschen** wash one's dirty linen in public

'**waschecht** adj washable; fast (color); fig trueborn, genuine

'**Wäsche|klammer** f clothespin, Br clothes peg; **~leine** f clothesline

waschen ['vaʃən] v/t and v/refl (irr, ge-, h) wash; **sich die Haare (Hände) ~** wash one's hair (hands)

Wäscherei [vɛʃə'rai] f (-; -en) laundry

'**Waschlappen** m washcloth, Br flannel, facecloth; **~ma,schine** f washing machine, F washer

'**waschma,schinenfest** adj machine-washable

Wasch|mittel n, **~pulver** n washing powder; **~raum** m lavatory, washroom; **~sa,lon** m laundromat, Br launderette; **~straße** f MOT car wash

Wasser ['vasɛ] n (-s; -) water; **~ball** m beach ball; SPORT water polo; **~bett** n water bed; **~dampf** m steam

'**wasserdicht** adj waterproof; esp MAR watertight (a. fig)

'**Wasser|fall** m waterfall; falls; **~farbe** f water colo(u)r; **~flugzeug** n seaplane; **~graben** m SPORT water jump; **~hahn** m tap, faucet

wässerig ['vɛsərɪç] adj watery; **j-m den Mund ~ machen** make s.o.'s mouth water

'**Wasser|kessel** m kettle; **~klo,sett** n water closet, W.C.; **~kraft** f (-; no pl) water power; **~kraftwerk** n hydroelectric power station or plant; **~lauf** m watercourse; **~leitung** f waterpipe(s); **~mangel** m (-s; no pl) water shortage; **~mann** m (-[e]s; no pl) ASTR Aquarius; **er ist (ein) ~** he's (an) Aquarius

'**wassern** v/i (ge-, h) AVIAT touch down on water; spacecraft: splash down

wässern ['vɛsɐn] v/t (ge-, h) water; AGR irrigate; GASTR soak; PHOT rinse

'**Wasserpflanze** f BOT aquatic plant

'**Wasserrohr** *n* TECH water pipe
'**Wasserscheide** *f* GEOGR watershed
'**wasserscheu** *adj* afraid of water
'**Wasser|ski 1.** *m* water ski; **2.** *n* (-*s*; *no pl*) water skiing; ~ **fahren** water-ski; ~**spiegel** *m* water level; ~**sport** *m* water *or* aquatic sports, aquatics; ~**spülung** *f* TECH flushing cistern; *Toilette mit* ~ (flush) toilet, W.C.; ~**stand** *m* water level; ~**stoff** *m* (-[*e*]*s*; *no pl*) CHEM hydrogen; ~**stoffbombe** *f* MIL hydrogen bomb, H-bomb; ~**strahl** *m* jet of water; ~**straße** *f* waterway; ~**tier** *n* aquatic animal; ~**verschmutzung** *f* water pollution; ~**versorgung** *f* water supply; ~**waage** *f* (*Br* spirit) level; ~**weg** *m* waterway; *auf dem* ~ by water; ~**welle** *f* water wave; ~**werk(e** *pl*) *n* waterworks; ~**zeichen** *n* watermark

waten ['vaːtən] *v/i* (*ge-*, *sein*) wade
watscheln ['vaːtʃəln] *v/i* (*ge-*, *sein*) waddle
Watt[1] [vat] *n* (-*s*; -) ELECTR watt
Watt[2] *n* (-[*e*]*s*; -*en*) GEOGR mud flats
Watte ['vatə] *f* (-; -*n*) cotton wool
wattiert [va'tiːrt] *adj* padded; quilted
weben ['veːbən] *v/t and v/i* ([*irr*,] *ge-*, *h*) weave; **Weber** ['veːbɐ] *m* (-*s*; -) weaver; **Weberei** [veːbə'raɪ] *f* (-; -*en*) weaving mill; '**Weberin** *f* (-; -*nen*) weaver; **Webstuhl** ['veːp-] *m* loom
Wechsel ['vɛksəl] *m* (-*s*; -) change; exchange; ECON bill of exchange; allowance; '**Wechselgeld** *n* (small) change
wechselhaft *adj* changeable
'**Wechseljahre** *pl* MED menopause
'**Wechselkurs** *m* ECON exchange rate
'**wechseln** *v/t and v/i* (*ge-*, *h*) change; exchange; vary; ~**d** *adj* varying
'**wechselseitig** [-zaɪtɪç] *adj* mutual, reciprocal
'**Wechsel|strom** *m* ELECTR alternating current; ~**stube** *f* ECON exchange office; ~**wirkung** *f* interaction
wecken ['vɛkən] *v/t* (*ge-*, *h*) wake (up), F call; *fig* awaken (*memories etc*); rouse (*s.o.'s curiosity etc*)
Wecker ['vɛkɐ] *m* (-*s*; -) alarm (clock)
wedeln ['veːdəln] *v/i* (*ge-*, *h*) wave (*mit et.* s.th.); *skiing*: wedel; *mit dem Schwanz* ~ wag its tail
weder ['veːdɐ] *cj*: ~ ... *noch* ... neither ... nor ...

Weg [veːk] *m* (- [*e*]*s*; -*e* ['veːgə]) way (*a. fig*); road (*a. fig*); path; route; walk; *auf friedlichem* (*legalem*) ~ by peaceful (legal) means; *j-m aus dem* ~ *gehen* get (*fig* keep) out of s.o.'s way; *j-n aus dem* ~ *räumen* put s.o. out of the way; *vom* ~ *abkommen* lose one's way; → **halb**
weg [vɛk] *adv* away; gone; off; F in raptures (*von* over, about); *Finger* ~! (keep your) hands off!; *nichts wie* ~! let's get out of here!; F ~ *sein* be out; ~**bleiben** F *v/i* (*irr, bleiben, sep, -ge-, sein*) stay away; be left out; ~**bringen** F *v/t* (*irr, bringen, sep, -ge-, h*) take away; ~ *von* get s.o. away from
wegen ['veːgən] *prp* (*gen*) because of; for the sake of; due *or* owing to; JUR for
wegfahren ['vɛk-] (*irr, fahren, sep, -ge-*) **1.** *v/i* (*sein*) leave; **2.** *v/t* (*h*) take away, remove
wegfallen *v/i* (*irr, fallen, sep, -ge-, sein*) be dropped; stop; be stopped
Weggang ['vɛk-] *m* (-[*e*]*s*; *no pl*) leaving; '**weggehen** *v/i* (*irr, gehen, sep, -ge-, sein*) go away (*a. fig*), leave; stain *etc*: come off; ECON sell
weg|jagen ['vɛk-] *v/t* (*sep, -ge-, h*) drive *or* chase away; ~**kommen** F *v/i* (*irr, kommen, sep, -ge-, sein*) get away; get lost; *gut* ~ come off well; *mach, dass du wegkommst!* get out of here!, *sl* get lost!; ~**lassen** *v/t* (*irr, lassen, sep, -ge-, h*) let s.o. go; leave s.th. out; ~**laufen** *v/i* (*irr, laufen, sep, -ge-, sein*) run away ([*vor*] *j-m* from s.o.) (*a. fig*); ~**legen** *v/t* (*sep, -ge-, h*) put away; ~**nehmen** *v/t* (*irr, nehmen, sep, -ge-, h*) take away (*von* from); take up (*room, time*); steal (*a. s.o.'s girlfriend etc*); *j-m et.* ~ take s.th. (away) from s.o.; ~**räumen** *v/t* (*sep, -ge-, h*) clear away, remove; ~**schaffen** *v/t* (*sep, -ge-, h*) remove; ~**schicken** *v/t* (*sep, -ge-, h*) send away *or* off; ~**sehen** *v/i* (*irr, sehen, sep, -ge-, h*) look away; ~**setzen** *v/t* (*sep, -ge-, h*) move
Wegweiser ['veːkvaɪzɐ] *m* (-*s*; -) signpost; *fig* guide
Wegwerf... ['vɛkvɛrf-] *in cpds* ...*geschirr*, ...*besteck*, ...*rasierer etc*: throwaway ..., disposable ...; ...*flasche etc*: non-returnable ...; '**wegwerfen** *v/t* (*irr, werfen, sep, -ge-, h*) throw away

W

weg|wischen ['vɛk-] v/t (sep, -ge-, h) wipe off; **~ziehen** (irr, ziehen, sep, -ge-) **1.** v/i (sein) move away; **2.** v/t (h) pull away

weh [veː] adv: ~ **tun** → **wehtun**

wehen ['veːən] v/i (ge-, h) blow; wave

'Wehen pl MED labo(u)r

wehmütig ['veːmyːtɪç] adj melancholy; wistful

Wehr[1] [veːr] n (-[e]s; -e ['veːrə]) weir

Wehr[2] f: **sich zur ~ setzen** → **wehren**

'Wehrdienst m (-[e]s; no pl) military service; **~verweigerer** m (-s; -) conscientious objector

wehren ['veːrən] v/refl (ge-, h) defend o.s. (**gegen** against), fight (a. fig **gegen et.** s.th.); **'wehrlos** adj defenseless, Br defenceless; fig helpless

'Wehrpflicht f (-; no pl) compulsory military service; **'wehrpflichtig** adj liable to military service; **'Wehrpflichtige** m (-n; -n) draftee, Br conscript

'wehtun hurt (**j-m** s.o.; fig s.o.'s feelings); be aching; **sich (am Finger) ~** hurt o.s. (hurt one's finger)

Weib [vaip] n (-[e]s; -er ['vaibɐ]) contp woman; bitch; **'Weibchen** n (-s; -) ZO female; **weibisch** ['vaibɪʃ] adj effeminate, F sissy; **'weiblich** adj female; feminine (a. LING)

weich [vaiç] adj soft (a. fig), tender; GASTR done; soft-boiled (egg); **~ werden** soften; fig give in; F **j-n ~ machen** soften s.o. up

Weiche ['vaiçə] f (-; -n) RAIL switch, points

weichen ['vaiçən] v/i (irr, ge-, sein) give way (**dat** to), yield (to); go (away)

'weichlich adj soft, effeminate, F sissy

'Weichling m (-s; -e) weakling, F softy, sissy

'Weichspüler m (-s; -) fabric softener

'Weichtier n ZO mollusc, Br mollusk

Weide[1] ['vaidə] f (-; -n) BOT willow

Weide[2] f (-; -n) AGR pasture; **auf die (der) ~** to (at) pasture; **'Weideland** n pasture(land), range; **'weiden** v/t and v/i (ge-, h) graze, pasture; fig **sich ~ an** (dat) feast on; contp gloat over

weigern ['vaigɐn] v/refl (ge-, h) refuse

Weigerung ['vaigərʊŋ] f (-; -en) refusal

Weihe ['vaiə] f (-; -n) REL consecration; ordination; **'weihen** v/t (ge-, h) consecrate; **zum Priester ~** ordain s.o. priest

Weiher ['vaiɐ] m (-s; -) pond

Weihnachten ['vainaxtən] n (-; -) Christmas, F Xmas

'Weihnachts|abend m Christmas Eve; **~baum** m Christmas tree; **~einkäufe** pl Christmas shopping; **~geschenk** n Christmas present; **~lied** n (Christmas) carol; **~mann** m Father Christmas, Santa Claus; **~markt** m Christmas fair; **~tag** m Christmas Day; **zweiter ~** day after Christmas, esp Br Boxing Day; **~zeit** f Christmas season

'Weih|rauch m REL incense; **~wasser** n (-s; no pl) REL holy water

weil [vail] cj because; since, as

'Weilchen n: **ein ~** a little while

Weile ['vailə] f: **e-e ~** a while

Wein [vain] m (-[e]s; -e) wine; BOT vine; **~(an)bau** m (-[e]s; no pl) wine growing; **~beere** f grape; **~berg** m vineyard; **~brand** m brandy

weinen ['vainən] v/i (ge-, h) cry (**vor dat** with; **nach** for; **wegen** about, over); weep (**um** for, over; **über** acc at; **vor dat** for, with); **weinerlich** ['vainɐlɪç] adj tearful; whining

'Wein|fass n wine cask or barrel; **~flasche** f wine bottle; **~händler** m wine merchant; **~hauer** m Austrian m → **Winzer**, **~karte** f wine list; **~keller** m wine cellar or vault, vaults; **~kellerei** f winery; **~kenner** m wine connoisseur; **~lese** f vintage; **~presse** f wine press; **~probe** f wine tasting; **~rebe** f BOT vine

'weinrot adj claret

'Weinstock m BOT vine

'Weintraube f → **Traube**

weise ['vaizə] adj wise

Weise f (-; -n) way; MUS tune; **auf diese (die gleiche) ~** this (the same) way; **auf m-e (s-e) ~** my (his) way

weisen ['vaizən] v/t and v/i (irr, ge-, h) show; **j-n von der Schule ~** expel s.o. from school; **~ auf** (acc) point to or at; **von sich ~** reject; repudiate

Weisheit ['vaishait] f (-; -en) wisdom; **mit s-r ~ am Ende sein** be at one's wit's end

'Weisheitszahn m wisdom tooth

weismachen ['vais-] F v/t: **j-m ~, dass** make s.o. believe that; **du kannst mir nichts ~** you can't fool me

weiß [vais] adj white; **~ werden** or **machen** whiten; **'Weißbrot** n white bread;

W

'Weiße *m, f (-n; -n)* white, white man (woman), *pl the* whites

'weißen *v/t (ge-, h)* whitewash

'Weißkohl *m,* **'Weißkraut** *n* BOT (green, *Br* white) cabbage

'weißlich *adj* whitish

'Weißwein *m* white wine

Weisung ['vaizʊŋ] *f (-; -en)* instruction, directive

weit [vait] **1.** *adj* wide, *clothes: a.* big; long *(way, trip etc)*; **2.** *adv* far, a long way *(von* from); **~ weg** far away *(von* from); **von ~em** from a distance; **~ und breit** far and wide; **bei ~em** by far; **bei ~em nicht so ...** not nearly as ...; **~ über** *(acc)* well over; **~ besser** far or much better; **zu ~ gehen** go too far; **es ~ bringen** go far; **wir haben es ~ gebracht** we have come a long way; **~ blickend** *fig* farsighted; **~ reichend** far-reaching; **~ verbreitet** widespread

'weit'ab *adv* far away *(von* from)

'weit'aus *adv* (by) far, much

Weite ['vaitə] *f (-; -n)* width; vastness, expanse; *esp* SPORT distance

'weiten *v/t and v/refl (ge-, h)* widen

weiter ['vaitɐ] *adv* on, further; *(mach)* **~!** go on!; *(geh)* **~!** move on!; **und so ~** and so on *or* forth, et cetera; **nichts ~** nothing else; **~arbeiten** *v/i (sep, -ge-, h)* go on working; **~bilden** *v/refl (sep, -ge-, h)* improve one's knowledge; continue one's education *or* training

'Weiterbildung *f (-; no pl)* further education *or* training

weitere ['vaitərə] *adj* further, additional; **alles Weitere** the rest; **bis auf ~s** until further notice; **ohne ~s** easily; **Weiteres** more, (further) details

'weiter|geben *v/t (irr, geben, sep, -ge-, h)* pass *(dat, an acc* to) *(a. fig)*; **~gehen** *v/i (irr, gehen, sep, -ge-, sein)* move on; *fig* continue, go on

'weiter|hin *adv* further(more); **et. ~ tun** go on doing s.th., continue to do s.th.

'weiter|kommen *v/i (irr, kommen, sep, -ge-, sein)* get on *(fig* in life); **~leben** *v/i (sep, -ge-, h)* live on, *fig a.* survive; **~machen** *v/t and v/i (sep, -ge-, h)* go or carry on, continue

'Weiterverkauf *m* resale

'weit|gehend 1. *adj* considerable; **2.** *adv* largely; **~läufig** *adj* spacious; distant

(relative); **~sichtig** *adj* MED farsighted *(a. fig), Br* longsighted

'Weitsprung *m* broad *(Br* long) jump

'Weitwinkelobjek,tiv *n* PHOT wide--angle lens

Weizen ['vaitsən] *m (-s; -)* BOT wheat

welche ['vɛlçə], **welcher** ['vɛlçɐ], **welches** ['vɛlçəs] **1.** *interr pron* what, which; **welcher?** which one?; **welcher von beiden?** which of the two?; **2.** *rel pron* who, that; which, that; **3.** F **welche** *indef pron* some, any

welk [vɛlk] *adj* faded, withered; flabby

welken ['vɛlkən] *v/i (ge-, sein)* fade, wither

'Wellblech ['vɛl-] *n* corrugated iron

Welle ['vɛlə] *f (-; -n)* wave *(a.* PHYS *and fig)*; TECH shaft; **'wellen** *v/t and v/refl (ge-, h)* wave

'Wellenlänge *f* ELECTR wavelength

'Wellensittich [-zɪtɪç] *m (-s; -e)* ZO budgerigar, F budgie

wellig ['vɛlɪç] *adj* wavy

Welt [vɛlt] *f (-; -en)* world; **die ganze ~** the whole world; **auf der ganzen ~** all over *or* throughout the world; **das beste** *etc* **... der ~** the best *etc* ... in the world, the world's best *etc* ...; **zur ~ kommen** be born; **zur ~ bringen** give birth to

'Weltall *n* universe

'weltberühmt *adj* world-famous

Weltergewicht ['vɛltɐ-] *n (-[e]s; no pl)*, **'Weltergewichtler** *m (-s; -)* SPORT welterweight

'weltfremd *adj* naive, unrealistic

'Weltfriede(n) *m* world peace

'Weltgeschichte *f* world history

'weltklug *adj* worldlywise

'Weltkrieg *m* world war; **der Zweite ~** World War II

'Weltkugel *f* globe

'weltlich *adj* worldly

'Welt|litera,tur *f* world literature; **~macht** *f* POL world power; **~markt** *m* ECON world market; **~meer** *n* ocean; **~meister(in)** world champion; **~meisterschaft** *f* world championship; *esp soccer:* World Cup; **~raum** *m (-[e]s; no pl)* (outer) space; **~reich** *n* empire; **~reise** *f* world trip; **~re,kord** *m* world record; **~ruf** *m (von ~* of) worldwide reputation; **~stadt** *f* metropolis; **~untergang** *m* end of the world

'**weltweit** *adj* worldwide

'**Weltwirtschaft** *f* world economy

'**Weltwirtschaftskrise** *f* worldwide economic crisis

'**Weltwunder** *n* wonder of the world

Wende ['vɛndə] *f* (-; -*n*) turn (*a. swimming*); change; **~kreis** *m* ASTR, GEOGR tropic; MOT turning circle

Wendeltreppe ['vɛndəl-] *f* spiral staircase

'**wenden** *v/t and v/i* (*ge-*, *h*) *and v/refl* ([*irr,*] *ge-*, *h*) turn (**nach** to; **gegen** against); MOT turn (round); GASTR turn over; **sich an j-n um Hilfe ~** turn to s.o. for help; **bitte ~** please turn over, pto

'**Wendepunkt** *m* turning point

wendig ['vɛndɪç] *adj* MOT, MAR maneuverable, *Br* manoeuvrable; *fig* nimble

'**Wendung** *f* (-; -*en*) turn, *fig a.* change; expression, phrase

wenig ['ve:nɪç] *indef pron and adv* little; **~(e)** *pl* few; **nur ~e** only few; only a few; (**in**) **~er als** (in) less than; **am ~sten** least of all; **er spricht ~** he doesn't talk much; (**nur**) **ein (klein) ~** (just) a little (bit)

'**wenigstens** *adv* at least

wenn [vɛn] *cj* when; if; **~ ... nicht** if ... not, unless; **~ auch** (al)though, even though; **wie** *or* **als ~** as though, as if; **ich nur ... wäre!** if only I were ...!; **~ auch noch so ...** no matter how ...; **und ~ nun ...?** what if ...?

wer [ve:ɐ] **1.** *interr pron* who, which; **~ von euch?** which of you?; **2.** *rel pron* who; **~ auch (immer)** who(so)ever; **3.** F *indef pron* somebody, anybody

Werbe|abteilung ['vɛrbə-] *f* publicity department; **~agen,tur** *f* advertising agency; **~feldzug** *m* advertising campaign; **~fernsehen** *n* commercial television; **~film** *m* promotion(al) film; **~funk** *m* radio commercials

werben ['vɛrbən] (*irr,* *ge-*, *h*) **1.** *v/i* advertise (**für et.** for s.th.), promote (s.th.), give *s.th.* or *s.o.* publicity; *esp* POL make propaganda (**für** for), canvass (for); **~ um** court (*a. fig*); **2.** *v/t* recruit; canvass, solicit

'**Werbesendung** *f*, '**Werbespot** [-ʃpɔt] *m* (-*s*; -*s*) (TV) commercial

'**Werbung** *f* (-; *no pl*) advertising, (sales) promotion; *a.* POL *etc* publicity, propa-

ganda; recruitment; **~ machen für et.** advertise s.th.

Werdegang ['ve:ɐdə-] *m* career

werden ['ve:ɐdən] *v/i* (*irr,* *ge-*, *sein*) *and v/aux* become, get; turn, go; grow; turn out; **wir ~** we will (*or* shall), we are going to; **geliebt ~** be loved (**von** by); **was willst du ~?** what do you want to be?; **mir wird schlecht** I'm going to be sick; F **es wird schon wieder (~)** it'll be all right

werfen ['vɛrfən] *v/i and v/t* (*irr,* *ge-*, *h*) throw (*a.* ZO ([*mit*] *et. nach* s.th. at); drop (*bombs*); cast (*shadow*)

Werft [vɛrft] *f* (-; -*en*) MAR shipyard, dockyard

Werk [vɛrk] *n* (-[*e*]*s*; -*e*) work, deed; TECH mechanism; ECON works, factory; **ans ~ gehen** set *or* go to work; **~bank** *f* (-; -*bänke*) TECH workbench; **~meister** *m* TECH foreman

'**Werkstatt** *f* (-; -*stätten*) workshop; MOT garage

'**Werktag** *m* workday

'**werktags** *adv* on workdays

'**werktätig** *adj* working

'**Werkzeug** *n* tool (*a. fig*); *coll* tools; instrument; **~macher** *m* toolmaker

wert [ve:ɐt] *adj* worth; **die Mühe (e-n Versuch) ~** worth the trouble (a try); *fig* **nichts ~** no good; **Wert** *m* (-[*e*]*s*; -*e*) value, *esp fig a.* worth; use; *pl* data, figures; **... im ~(e) von 20 Dollar** 20 dollars' worth of ...; **großen ~ legen auf** (*acc*) set great store by

werten ['ve:ɐtən] *v/t* (*ge-*, *h*) value; *a.* SPORT rate, judge

'**Wertgegenstand** *m* article of value

'**wertlos** *adj* worthless

'**Wertpa,piere** *pl* securities

'**Wertsachen** *pl* valuables

'**Wertung** *f* (-; -*en*) valuation; *a.* SPORT rating, judging; score, points

'**wertvoll** *adj* valuable

Wesen ['ve:zən] *n* (-*s*; -) being, creature; *fig* essence; nature, character; **viel ~s machen um** make a fuss about

'**wesentlich** *adj* essential; considerable; **im Wesentlichen** on the whole

weshalb [vɛsˈhalp] *interr adv* → **warum**

Wespe ['vɛspə] *f* (-; -*n*) ZO wasp

Weste ['vɛstə] *f* (-; -*n*) vest, *Br* waistcoat

Westen ['vɛstən] *m* (-*s*; *no pl*) west; POL West

W

Western ['vɛstən] m (-s; -) western

'**westlich 1.** adj western; westerly; POL West(ern); **2.** adv: ~ **von** (to the) west of

'**Westwind** m west(erly) wind

Wettbewerb ['vɛtbəvɛrp] m (-[e]s; -e) competition (a. ECON), contest

'**Wettbü,ro** n betting office

Wette ['vɛtə] f (-; -n) bet; **e-e ~ abschlie-ßen** make a bet; **um die ~ laufen** etc race (**mit j-m** s.o.)

'**wetteifern** v/i (ge-, h) compete (**mit** with; **um** for)

'**wetten** v/i and v/t (ge-, h) bet; **mit j-m um 10 Dollar ~** bet s.o. ten dollars; **~ auf** (acc) bet on, back

Wetter ['vɛtə] n (-s; -) weather

'**Wetterbericht** m weather report

'**Wetterfahne** f weather vane

'**wetterfest** adj weatherproof

'**Wetter|karte** f weather chart; **~lage** f weather situation; **~leuchten** n sheet lightning; **~vorhersage** f weather forecast; **~warte** f weather station

'**Wett|kampf** m competition, contest; **~kämpfer(in)** contestant, competitor; **~lauf** m race (a. fig **mit** against); **~läufer(in)** runner

'**wettmachen** v/t (sep, -ge-, h) make up for

'**Wettrennen** n race

'**Wettrüsten** n (-s; no pl) arms race

'**Wettstreit** m contest, competition

wetzen ['vɛtsən] v/t (ge-, h) whet, sharpen

wich [vɪç] pret of **weichen**

wichtig ['vɪçtɪç] adj important

'**Wichtigkeit** f (-; no pl) importance

'**wickeln** ['vɪkəln] v/t (ge-, h) change (baby); **~ in** (acc) wrap in; **~ um** wrap (a)round

Widder ['vɪdə] m (-s; -) ZO ram; ASTR Aries; **er ist (ein) ~** he's (an) Aries

wider ['vi:də] prp (acc) against; **~ Willen** against one's will; **~ Erwarten** contrary to expectations

'**Widerhaken** m barb

'**widerhallen** v/i (sep, -ge-, h) resound (**von** with)

wider'legen v/t (no -ge-, h) refute, disprove

'**widerlich** adj sickening, disgusting

'**widerrechtlich** adj illegal, unlawful

'**Widerruf** m JUR revocation; withdrawal; **wider'rufen** v/t (irr, rufen, no -ge-, h) revoke; withdraw

Widersacher ['vi:dɛzaxə] m (-s; -) adversary, rival

'**Widerschein** m reflection

wider'setzen v/refl (no -ge-, h) (dat) oppose, resist

'**widersinnig** adj absurd

'**widerspenstig** ['vi:dəʃpɛnstɪç] adj unruly, stubborn

'**widerspiegeln** v/t (sep, -ge-, h) reflect (a. fig); **sich ~ in** (dat) be reflected in

wider'sprechen v/i (irr, sprechen, no -ge-, h) (dat) contradict

'**Widerspruch** m contradiction

widersprüchlich ['vi:dəʃprʏçlɪç] adj contradictory

'**widerspruchslos** adv without contradiction

'**Widerstand** m resistance (a. ELECTR), opposition; **~ leisten** offer resistance (dat to); '**widerstandsfähig** adj resistant (a. TECH); **wider'stehen** v/i (irr, stehen, no -ge-, h) (dat) resist

wider'streben v/i (no -ge-, h) **es widerstrebt mir, dies zu tun** I hate doing or to do that; **~d** adv reluctantly

widerwärtig ['vi:dəvɛrtɪç] adj disgusting

'**Widerwille** m aversion (**gegen** to), dislike (of, for); disgust (at)

'**widerwillig** adj reluctant, unwilling

widmen ['vɪtmən] v/t (ge-, h) dedicate; '**Widmung** f (-; -en) dedication

wie [vi:] **1.** interr adv how; **~ geht es Gordon?** how is Gordon?; **~ ist er?** what's he like?; **~ ist das Wetter?** what's the weather like?; **~ heißen Sie?** what's your name?; **~ nennt man ...?** what do you call ...?; **~ wäre (ist, steht) es mit ...?** what or how about ...?; **~ viele ...?** how many ...?; **2.** cj like; as; **~ neu (verrückt)** like new (mad); **doppelt so ...** twice as ... as; **~ (zum Beispiel)** such as, like; **~ üblich** as usual; **~ er sagte** as he said; **ich zeige (sage) dir, ~ (...)** I'll show (tell) you how (...)

wieder ['vi:də] adv again; in cpds often re...; **immer ~** again and again; **~ aufbauen** reconstruct; **~ aufnehmen** resume; **~ beleben** MED resuscitate, revive (a. fig); **~ erkennen** recognize (an dat by); **~ finden** find (what one has lost); fig regain; **~ gutmachen** make up for; **~ herstellen** restore; **~**

sehen see *or* meet again; **~ verwendbar** reusable; **~ verwerten** TECH recycle

Wieder|'aufbau m (-[e]s; no pl) reconstruction, rebuilding; **~'aufbereitung** f TECH recycling, reprocessing (a. NUCL); **~'aufbereitungsanlage** f TECH reprocessing plant; **~'aufleben** n (-s; no pl) revival; **~'aufnahme** f (-; no pl) resumption

'wiederbekommen v/t (irr, **kommen**, sep, no -ge-, h) get back

'Wieder|belebung f (-; -en) MED resuscitation; **~belebungsversuch** m MED attempt at resuscitation

'wiederbringen v/t (irr, **bringen**, sep, -ge-, h) bring back; return

Wieder'einführung f reintroduction

Wiederentdeckung f rediscovery

'Wiedergabe f TECH reproduction, playback; **'wiedergeben** v/t (irr, **geben**, sep, -ge-, h) give back, return; fig describe; TECH play back, reproduce

Wieder'gutmachung f (-; -en) reparation

'wiederholen¹ v/t (sep, -ge-, h) (go and) get *s.o.* or *s.th.* back

wieder'holen² v/t (no -ge-, h) repeat; PED revise, review; THEA replay; **sich ~** repeat o.s. (a. fig); **wieder'holt** adv repeatedly, several times

Wieder'holung f (-; -en) repetition; PED review; TV etc rerun; SPORT replay

Wiederkehr ['viːdeːkeːɐ] f (-; no pl) return; recurrence; **'wiederkehren** v/i (sep, -ge-, sein) return; recur

'wiederkommen v/i (irr, **kommen**, sep, -ge-, sein) come back, return

Wiedersehen n (-s; -) seeing *s.o.* again; reunion; **auf ~!** goodbye!

wiederum ['viːdərʊm] adv again; on the other hand

'Wieder|vereinigung f reunion, esp POL a. reunification; **~verkauf** m resale; **~verwendung** f reuse; **~verwertung** f (-; -en) TECH recycling; **~wahl** f POL re-election

Wiege ['viːɡə] f (-; -n) cradle

wiegen¹ ['viːɡən] v/t and v/i (irr, ge-, h) weigh

wiegen² v/t (ge-, h) rock (**in den Schlaf** to sleep)

'Wiegenlied n lullaby

wiehern ['viːɐn] v/i (ge-, h) ZO neigh

wies [viːs] pret of **weisen**

Wiese ['viːzə] f (-; -n) meadow

Wiesel ['viːzəl] n (-s; -) ZO weasel

wieso [vi'zoː] interr adv → **warum**

wieviel [vi'fiːlt] adj: **zum ~en Male?** how many times?

wild [vɪlt] adj wild (a. fig) (F **auf** acc about); violent; **~er Streik** wildcat strike

Wild n (-[e]s; no pl) HUNT game; GASTR mst venison; **~bach** m torrent

Wilde ['vɪldə] m, f (-n; -n) savage; F **wie ein ~r** like mad

Wilderer ['vɪldərɐ] m (-s; -) poacher

'wildern v/i (ge-, h) poach

'Wildhüter m gamekeeper

'Wildkatze f ZO wild cat

'Wildleder n suede

'Wildnis f (-; -se) wilderness

'Wild|park m, **~reser,vat** n game park or reserve; **~schwein** n ZO wild boar

Wille ['vɪlə] m (-ns; no pl) will; intention; **s-n ~n durchsetzen** have or get one's own way; **j-m s-n ~n lassen** let s.o. have his (own) way

willenlos adj weak(-willed)

'Willenskraft f (-; no pl) willpower; **durch ~ erzwingen** will

willensstark adj strong-willed

willig ['vɪlɪç] adj willing

will'kommen adj welcome (a. **~ heißen**) (**in** dat to)

willkürlich ['vɪlkyːrlɪç] adj arbitrary; random

wimmeln ['vɪməln] v/i (ge-, h) **~ von** be teeming with

wimmern ['vɪmɐn] v/i (ge-, h) whimper

Wimpel ['vɪmpəl] m (-s; -) pennant

Wimper ['vɪmpɐ] f (-; -n) eyelash; **ohne mit der ~ zu zucken** without turning a hair; **'Wimperntusche** f mascara

Wind [vɪnt] m (-[e]s; -e ['vɪndə]) wind

Winde ['vɪndə] f (-; -n) winch, windlass, hoist

Windel ['vɪndəl] f (-; -n) diaper, Br nappy

winden ['vɪndən] v/t (irr, ge-, h) wind, TECH a. hoist; **sich ~** wind (one's way); writhe (with pain etc)

'Windhund m ZO greyhound

windig ['vɪndɪç] adj windy

'Wind|mühle f windmill; **~pocken** pl MED chickenpox; **~richtung** f direction

W

of the wind; **~schutzscheibe** f MOT windshield, Br windscreen; **~stärke** f wind force

'**windstill** adj, '**Windstille** f calm

'**Windstoß** m gust

'**Windsurfen** n windsurfing

'**Windung** f (-; -en) bend, turn (a. TECH)

Wink [vɪŋk] m (-[e]s; -e) sign; fig hint

Winkel ['vɪŋkəl] m (-s; -) corner; MATH angle; '**winkelig** adj angular; crooked

winken ['vɪŋkən] v/i (ge-, h) wave (one's hand etc), wave; beckon

winseln ['vɪnzəln] v/i (ge-, h) whimper, whine

Winter ['vɪntɐ] m (-s; -) winter

'**winterlich** adj wintry

'**Winter|reifen** m MOT snow tire (Br tyre); **~schlaf** m ZO hibernation; **~spiele** pl: **Olympische ~** SPORT Winter Olympics; **~sport** m winter sports

Winzer ['vɪntsɐ] m (-s; -) winegrower

winzig ['vɪntsɪç] adj tiny, diminutive

Wipfel ['vɪpfəl] m (-s; -) (tree)top

Wippe ['vɪpə] f (-; -n), '**wippen** v/i (ge-, h) seesaw

wir [viːɐ] pers pron we; **~ drei** the three of us; F **~ sind's!** it's us!

Wirbel ['vɪrbəl] m (-s; -) whirl (a. fig); ANAT vertebra

'**wirbeln** v/i (ge-, sein) whirl

'**Wirbel|säule** f ANAT spinal column, spine; **~sturm** m cyclone, tornado; **~tier** n vertebrate; **~wind** m whirlwind

wirken ['vɪrkən] (ge-, h) **1.** v/i work; be effective (**gegen** against); look; **anregend** etc **~** have a stimulating etc effect (**auf** acc [up]on); **~ als** act as; **2.** v/t weave; fig work (miracles etc)

wirklich ['vɪrklɪç] adj real, actual; true, genuine; '**Wirklichkeit** f (-; -en) reality; **in ~** in reality, actually

wirksam ['vɪrkzaːm] adj effective

'**Wirkung** f (-; -en) effect

'**wirkungslos** adj ineffective

'**wirkungsvoll** adj effective

wirr [vɪr] adj confused, mixed-up; hair: tousled; **Wirren** ['vɪrən] pl disorder, confusion; **Wirrwarr** ['vɪrvar] m (-s; no pl) confusion, mess, welter

Wirt [vɪrt] m (-[e]s; -e) landlord; '**Wirtin** f (-; -nen) landlady; '**Wirtschaft** f (-; -en) ECON, POL economy; business; → **Gastwirtschaft**; '**wirtschaften** v/i (ge-, h) keep house; manage one's money or

affairs or business; economize; **gut (schlecht) ~** be a good (bad) manager; '**Wirtschafterin** f (-; -nen) housekeeper; '**wirtschaftlich** adj economic; economical; '**Wirtschafts...** ECON in cpds ...gemeinschaft, ...gipfel, ...krise, ...system, ...wunder etc: economic ...

'**Wirtshaus** n → **Gastwirtschaft**

wischen ['vɪʃən] v/t (ge-, h) wipe; **Staub ~** dust

wispern ['vɪspɐn] v/t and v/i (ge-, h) whisper

wissbegierig ['vɪs-] adj curious

wissen ['vɪsən] v/t and v/i (irr, ge-, h) know; **ich möchte ~** I'd like to know, I wonder; **soviel ich weiß** as far as I know; **weißt du** you know; **weißt du noch?** (do you) remember?; **woher weißt du das?** how do you know?; **man kann nie ~** you never know; **ich will davon (von ihm) nichts ~** I don't want anything to do with it (him)

'**Wissen** n (-s; no pl) knowledge; know-how; **m-s ~s** as far as I know

'**Wissenschaft** f (-; -en) science

'**Wissenschaftler** m (-s; -), '**Wissenschaftlerin** f (-; -nen) scientist

'**wissenschaftlich** adj scientific

'**wissenswert** adj worth knowing; **Wissenswertes** useful facts; **alles Wissenswerte (über** acc) all you need to know (about)

wittern ['vɪtɐn] v/t (ge-, h) scent, smell (both a. fig)

Witwe ['vɪtvə] f (-; -n) widow

Witwer ['vɪtvɐ] m (-s; -) widower

Witz [vɪts] m (-es; -e) joke; **~e reißen** crack jokes

witzig ['vɪtsɪç] adj funny; witty

wo [voː] adv where; **~ ... doch** when, although

wob [voːp] pret of **weben**

wobei [voˈbaɪ] adv: **~ bist du?** what are you at?; **~ mir einfällt** which reminds me

Woche ['vɔxə] f (-; -n) week

'**Wochen...** in cpds ...lohn, ...markt, ...zeitung etc: weekly ...; **~ende** n weekend; **am ~** on (Br at) the weekend

'**wochenlang 1.** adj: **~es Warten** (many) weeks of waiting; **2.** adv for weeks

'**Wochenschau** f film: newsreel

'**Wochentag** m weekday

wöchentlich ['vœçəntlɪç] **1.** *adj* weekly; **2.** *adv* weekly, every week; *einmal ~* once a week

wodurch [vo'dʊrç] *adv* how; through which

wofür [vo'fy:ɐ] *adv* for which; *~?* what (...) for?

wog [vo:k] *pret of* **wiegen**[1] *and* **wägen**

Woge ['vo:gə] *f* (-; -n) wave, *esp* fig *a.* surge; breaker; **'wogen** *v/i* (*ge*-, *h*) surge, heave (*both a.* fig)

woher [vo'he:ɐ] *adv* where ... from; *~ weißt du (das)?* how do you know?

wohin [vo'hɪn] *adv* where (... to)

wohl [vo:l] *adv and cj* well; probably, I suppose; *sich ~ fühlen* be well; feel good; feel at home (*bei* with); *ich fühle mich nicht ~* I don't feel well; *j-m ~ tun* do s.o. good; *~ oder übel* willy-nilly, whether you *etc* like it or not; *~ kaum* hardly

Wohl *n* (-[e]s; *no pl*) well-being; *auf j-s ~ trinken* drink to s.o.('s health); *zum ~!* to your health!; F cheers!

'wohlbehalten *adv* safely

'Wohlfahrtsstaat *m* welfare state

'wohl|gemerkt *adv* mind you; *~genährt* *adj* well-fed; *~gesinnt* *adj: j-m ~ sein* be well-disposed towards s.o.; *~habend* *adj* well-off, well-to-do

wohlig ['vo:lɪç] *adj* snug, cozy, *Br* cosy

'Wohl|stand *m* (-[e]s; *no pl*) prosperity, affluence; *~standsgesellschaft* *f* affluent society

'Wohltat *f* (-; *no pl*) pleasure; relief; blessing; **'Wohltäter(in)** benefactor (benefactress); **'wohltätig** *adj* charitable; *für ~e Zwecke* for charity

'Wohltätigkeits... *in cpds* ...ball, ...konzert *etc*: charity ...

'wohlverdient *adj* well-deserved

'wohlwollend *adj* benevolent

wohnen ['vo:nən] *v/i* (*ge*-, *h*) live (*in dat* in; *bei j-m* with s.o.); stay (*in dat* at; *bei* with)

'Wohngebiet *n* residential area

'Wohngemeinschaft *f*: (*mit j-m*) *in e-r ~ leben* share an apartment (*Br* a flat) *or* a house (with s.o.)

wohnlich ['vo:nlɪç] *adj* comfortable, snug, cozy, *Br* cosy

'Wohnmo,bil *n* (-s; -e) camper, motor home (*Br* caravan)

'Wohn|siedlung *f* housing develop-

ment (*Br* estate); *~sitz* *m* residence; *ohne festen ~* of no fixed abode

'Wohnung *f* (-; *-en*) apartment, *Br* flat; *m-e etc ~* my *etc* place

'Wohnungs|amt *n* housing office; *~bau* *m* (-[e]s; *no pl*) house building; *~not* *f* housing shortage

'Wohnwagen *m* trailer, *Br* caravan; mobile home

'Wohnzimmer *n* sitting *or* living room

wölben ['vœlbən] *v/refl* (*ge*-, *h*), **'Wölbung** *f* (-; *-en*) vault, arch

Wolf [vɔlf] *m* (-[e]s; *Wölfe* ['vœlfə]) ZO wolf

Wolke ['vɔlkə] *f* (-; -n) cloud

'Wolkenbruch *m* cloudburst

'Wolkenkratzer *m* (-s; -) skyscraper

'wolkenlos *adj* cloudless

wolkig ['vɔlkɪç] *adj* cloudy, clouded

Woll... [vɔl-] *in cpds* ...schal, ...socken *etc*: wool(l)en ...; *~decke* *f* blanket

Wolle ['vɔlə] *f* (-; -n) wool

wollen ['vɔlən] *v/t and v/i* (*ge*-, *h*) *and v/aux* (*no -ge-*, *h*) want (to); *lieber ~* prefer; *~ wir (gehen* etc*)?* shall we (go *etc*)?; *~ Sie bitte ...* will *or* would you please ...; *wie (was, wann) du willst* as (whatever, whenever) you like; *sie will, dass ich komme* she wants me to come; *ich wollte, ich wäre (hätte) ...* I wish I were (had) ...

womit [vo'mɪt] *adv* with which; *~?* what ... with?

Wonne ['vɔnə] *f* (-; -n) joy, delight

woran [vo'ran] *adv: ~ denkst du?* what are you thinking of?; *~ liegt es, dass ...?* how is it that ...?; *~ sieht man, welche (ob) ...?* how can you tell which (if) ...?

worauf [vo'rauf] *adv* after which; on which; *~?* what ... on?; *~ wartest du?* what are you waiting for?

woraus [vo'raus] *adv* from which; *~ ist es?* what's it made of?

worin [vo'rɪn] *adv* in which; *~?* where?

Wort [vɔrt] *n* (-[e]s; -e, *Wörter* ['vœrtɐ]) word; *mit anderen ~en* in other words; *sein ~ geben (halten, brechen)* give (keep, break) one's word; *j-n beim ~ nehmen* take s.o. at his word; *ein gutes ~ einlegen für* put in a good word for; *j-m ins ~ fallen* cut s.o. short

'Wortart *f* LING part of speech

Wörter|buch ['vœrtɐ-] *n* dictionary;

~verzeichnis n vocabulary, list of words

'**Wortführer** m spokesman; '**Wortführerin** f spokeswoman

'**wortkarg** adj taciturn

wörtlich ['vœrtlɪç] adj literal; **~e Rede** LING direct speech

'**Wort|schatz** m vocabulary; **~spiel** n pun; **~stellung** f LING word order

worüber [vo'ry:bə] adv about which; **~ lachen Sie?** what are you laughing at or about?

worum [vo'rʊm] adv about which; **~ handelt es sich?** what is it about?

worunter [vo'rʊntɐ] adv among which; **~?** what ... under?

wovon [vo'fɔn] adv about which; **~ redest du?** what are you talking about?

wovor [vo'fo:ɐ] adv of which; **~ hast du Angst?** what are you afraid of?

wozu [vo'tsu:] adv: **~ er mir rät** what he advised me to do; **~?** what (...) for?; why?

Wrack [vrak] n (-[e]s; -s) MAR wreck (a. fig)

wrang [vraŋ] pret of **wringen**

wringen ['vrɪŋən] v/t (irr, ge-, h) wring

Wucher ['vu:xɐ] m (-s; no pl) usury

Wucherer ['vu:xərɐ] m (-s; -) usurer

'**wuchern** v/i (ge-, h) grow (fig be) rampant; **Wucherung** ['vu:xərʊŋ] f (-; -en) MED growth

Wuchs [vu:ks] m (-es; no pl) growth; build

wuchs [vu:ks] pret of **wachsen**¹

Wucht [vʊxt] f (-; no pl) force; impact

'**wuchtig** adj massive; powerful

wühlen ['vy:lən] v/i (ge-, h) dig; ZO root; rummage (**in** dat, through)

Wulst [vʊlst] m (-es; Wülste ['vYlstə]), f (-; Wülste) bulge; roll (of fat)

'**wulstig** ['vʊlstɪç] adj bulging; thick

wund [vʊnt] adj MED sore; **~e Stelle** MED sore; **~er Punkt** fig sore point

Wunde ['vʊndə] f (-; -n) MED wound

Wunder ['vʊndɐ] n (-s; -) miracle, fig a. wonder; **~ wirken** work wonders; (**es ist**) **kein ~, dass du müde bist** no wonder you are tired; '**wunderbar** adj wonderful, marvel(l)ous

'**Wunderkind** n infant prodigy

'**wunderlich** adj funny, odd; senile

'**wundern** v/refl (ge-, h) be surprised or astonished (**über** acc at)

'**wundervoll** adj wonderful

'**Wundstarrkrampf** m (-es; no pl) MED tetanus

Wunsch [vʊnʃ] m (-[e]s; Wünsche ['vYnʃə]) wish; request; **auf j-s ~** at s.o.'s request; **auf eigenen ~** at one's own request; (**je**) **nach ~** as desired

wünschen ['vYnʃən] v/t (ge-, h) wish; **sich et.** (**zu Weihnachten** etc) **~** want s.th. (for Christmas etc); **das habe ich mir** (**schon immer**) **gewünscht** that's what I (always) wanted; **alles, was man sich nur ~ kann** everything one could wish for; **ich wünschte, ich wäre** (**hätte**) ... I wish I were (had) ...

'**wünschenswert** adj desirable

wurde ['vʊrdə] pret of **werden**

Würde ['vYrdə] f (-; -n) dignity

'**würdelos** adj undignified

'**Würdenträger** m dignitary

'**würdevoll** adj dignified

würdig ['vYrdɪç] adj worthy (gen of); dignified; **würdigen** ['vYrdɪgən] v/t (ge-, h) appreciate; **j-n keines Blickes ~** ignore s.o. completely; '**Würdigung** f (-; -en) appreciation

Wurf [vʊrf] m (-[e]s; Würfe ['vYrfə]) throw; ZO litter

Würfel ['vYrfəl] m (-s; -) cube (a. MATH); dice; '**würfeln** v/i (ge-, h) throw dice (**um** for); play dice; GASTR dice; **e-e Sechs ~** throw a six

'**Würfelzucker** m lump sugar

'**Wurfgeschoss** n missile

würgen ['vYrgən] v/i and v/t (ge-, h) choke; throttle s.o.

Wurm [vʊrm] m (-[e]s; Würmer ['vYrmɐ]) ZO worm; **wurmen** ['vʊrmən] F v/t (ge-, h) gall s.o.; '**wurmstichig** ['vʊrmʃtɪçɪç] adj worm-eaten

Wurst [vʊrst] f (-; Würste ['vYrstə]) sausage

Würstchen ['vYrstçən] n (-s; -) small sausage, frankfurter, wiener; hot dog

Würze ['vYrtsə] f (-; -n) spice (a. fig)

Wurzel ['vʊrtsəl] f (-; -n) root (a. MATH); **~n schlagen** take root (a. fig)

'**wurzeln** v/i (ge-, h) **~ in** (dat) be rooted in (a. fig)

'**würzen** v/t (ge-, h) spice, season, flavo(u)r; **würzig** ['vYrtsɪç] adj spicy, well-seasoned

wusch [vu:ʃ] pret of **waschen**

wusste ['vʊstə] pret of **wissen**

W

Wust [vu:st] F *m* (-[e]s; *no pl*) tangled mass

wüst [vy:st] *adj* waste; confused; wild, dissolute

Wüste ['vy:stə] *f* (-; -*n*) desert

Wut [vu:t] *f* (-; *no pl*) rage, fury; **e-e ~ haben** be furious (**auf** *acc* with)

'**Wutanfall** *m* fit of rage

wüten ['vy:tən] *v/i* (*ge-, h*) rage (*a. fig*); **~d** *adj* furious (**auf** *acc* with; **über** *acc* at), F mad (at)

'**wutschnaubend** *adj* fuming

X, Y

X-Beine ['ıksbainə] *pl* knock-knees; **sie hat ~** she's knock-kneed

x-beinig ['ıksbainıç] *adj* knock-kneed

x-be'liebig *adj*: **jede(r, -s) x-Beliebige ...** any ... you like, F any old ...

'**x-mal** F *adv* umpteen times

x-te ['ıkstə] *adj*: **zum ~n Male** for the umpteenth time

Xylophon [ksylo'fo:n] *n* (-*s*; -*e*) MUS xylophone

Yacht [jaxt] *f* (-; -*en*) MAR yacht

Yoga ['jo:ga] *m, n* (-[*s*]; *no pl*) yoga

Z

Zacke ['tsakə] *f* (-; -*n*), **'Zacken** *m* (-*s*; -) (sharp) point; tooth; **zackig** ['tsakıç] *adj* serrated; jagged; *fig* smart

zaghaft ['tsa:khaft] *adj* timid

zäh [tse:] *adj* tough (*a. fig*), **~flüssig** *adj* thick, viscous; *fig* slow-moving (*traffic*)

Zähigkeit ['tse:ıçkait] *f* (-; *no pl*) toughness, *fig a.* stamina

Zahl [tsa:l] *f* (-; -*en*) number; figure

'**zahlbar** *adj* payable (**an** *acc* to; **bei** at)

zählbar ['tse:lba:r] *adj* countable

zahlen ['tsa:lən] *v/i and v/t* (*ge-, h*) pay; **~, bitte!** the check (*Br* bill), please!

zählen ['tse:lən] *v/t and v/i* (*ge-, h*) count (**bis** up to; *fig* **auf** *acc* on); **~ zu** rank with *the best etc*

'**zahlenmäßig** **1.** *adj* numerical; **2.** *adv*: **j-m ~ überlegen sein** outnumber s.o.

Zähler ['tse:lɐ] *m* (-*s*; -) counter (*a.* TECH); MATH numerator; ELECTR *etc* meter

'**Zahlkarte** *f* *post* deposit (*Br* paying-in) slip

'**zahllos** *adj* countless

'**Zahlmeister** *m* MIL paymaster; MAR purser

'**zahlreich** **1.** *adj* numerous; **2.** *adv* in great number

'**Zahltag** *m* payday

'**Zahlung** *f* (-; -*en*) payment

'**Zählung** *f* (-; -*en*) count; POL census

'**Zahlungs|aufforderung** *f* request for payment; **~bedingungen** *pl* terms of payment; **~befehl** *m* order to pay

'**zahlungsfähig** *adj* solvent

'**Zahlungs|frist** *f* term of payment; **~mittel** *n* currency; **gesetzliches ~** legal tender; **~schwierigkeiten** *pl* financial difficulties; **~ter,min** *m* date of payment

'**zahlungsunfähig** *adj* insolvent

'**Zählwerk** *n* TECH counter

'**Zahlwort** *n* LING numeral

zahm [tsa:m] *adj* tame (*a. fig*)

zähmen ['tse:mən] *v/t* (*ge-, h*) tame (*a. fig*); **'Zähmung** *f* (-; *no pl*) taming

Zahn [tsa:n] *m* (-[e]s; *Zähne* ['tse:nə]) tooth, TECH *a.* cog; **~arzt** *m*, **~ärztin** *f* dentist, dental surgeon; **~bürste** *f* toothbrush; **~creme** *f* toothpaste

zahnen ['tsa:nən] *v/i* (*ge-, h*) cut one's teeth, teethe

'**Zahnfleisch** *n* gums

'**zahnlos** *adj* toothless

'**Zahn|lücke** *f* gap between the teeth; **~medi,zin** *f* dentistry; **~pasta, ~paste** *f* toothpaste; **~radbahn** *f* rack railroad; **~schmerzen** *pl* toothache; **~spange** *f* MED brace; **~stein** *m* tartar; **~stocher** *m* (-s; -) toothpick

Zange ['tsaŋə] *f* (-; -n) TECH pliers; pincers; tongs; MED forceps; ZO pincer

zanken ['tsaŋkən] *v/r*/*refl* (ge-, h) quarrel (*wegen* about; *um* over), fight, argue (about; over)

zänkisch ['tsɛŋkɪʃ] *adj* quarrelsome

Zäpfchen ['tsɛpfçən] *n* (-s; -) ANAT uvula; PHARM suppository

zapfen ['tsapfən] *v/t* (ge-, h) tap

Zapfen *m* (-s; -) faucet, *Br* tap; TECH peg, pin; bung; tenon; pivot; BOT cone

Zapfenstreich *m* MIL tattoo, taps

Zapf|hahn *m* faucet, *Br* tap; MOT nozzle; **~säule** *f* MOT gasoline (*Br* petrol) pump

zappelig ['tsapəlıç] *adj* fidgety

zappeln ['tsapəln] *v/i* (ge-, h) fidget, wriggle

zappen ['zɛpən] F *v/i* (ge-, h) TV zap

zart [tsaːɐt] *adj* tender; gentle; **~ fühlend** sensitive

Zartgefühl *n* (-[e]s; *no pl*) delicacy (of feeling), sensitivity, tact

zärtlich ['tsɛːɐtlıç] *adj* tender, affectionate (*zu* with); **Zärtlichkeit** *f* (-; -en) a) (*no pl*) tenderness, affection, b) caress

Zauber ['tsaubɐ] *m* (-s; -) magic, spell, charm (*all a. fig*), *fig* enchantment; **Zauberei** [tsaubə'rai] *f* (-; -en) magic, witchcraft; **Zauberer** ['tsaubərɐ] *m* (-s; -) magician, sorcerer, wizard (*a. fig*); **zauberhaft** *fig adj* enchanting, charming; **Zauberin** ['tsaubərın] *f* (-; -nen) sorceress

Zauber|kraft *f* magic power; **~künstler** *m* magician, conjurer; **~kunststück** *n* conjuring trick

zaubern (ge-, h) 1. *v/i* practise magic; do conjuring tricks; 2. *v/t* conjure (up)

Zauberspruch *m* spell

zaudern ['tsaudɐn] *v/i* (ge-, h) hesitate

Zaum [tsaum] *m* (-[e]s; *Zäume* ['tsɔymə]) bridle; *im ~ halten* control (*sich* o.s.), keep in check

zäumen ['tsɔymən] *v/t* (ge-, h) bridle

Zaumzeug *n* (-[e]s; -e) bridle

Zaun [tsaun] *m* (-[e]s; *Zäune* ['tsɔynə]) fence; **~gast** *m* onlooker; **~pfahl** *m* pale

---

z.B. ABBR *of* **zum Beispiel** e.g., for example, for instance

Zebra ['tseːbra] *n* (-s; -s) ZO zebra

Zebrastreifen *m* MOT zebra crossing

Zeche ['tsɛçə] *f* (-; -n) check, *Br* bill; (coal) mine, pit; *die ~ bezahlen müssen* F have to foot the bill

Zeh [tseː] *m* (-s; -en), **Zehe** ['tseːə] *f* (-; -n) ANAT toe; *große* (*kleine*) *~* big (little) toe; **Zehennagel** *m* ANAT toenail

Zehenspitze *f* tip of the toe; *auf ~n gehen* (walk on) tiptoe

zehn [tseːn] *adj* ten; **zehnfach** *adj* tenfold; **zehnjährig** [-jɛːrıç] *adj* ten-year-old (*boy etc*); ten-year *anniversary etc*; *absence etc* of ten years

Zehnkampf *m* SPORT decathlon

zehnmal *adv* ten times; **zehnte** *adj* tenth; **Zehntel** *n* (-s; -) tenth; **zehntens** *adv* tenthly

Zeichen ['tsaiçən] *n* (-s; -) sign; mark; signal; *zum ~ gen* as a token of; **~block** *m* sketch pad; **~brett** *n* drawing board; **~dreieck** *n* MATH set square; **~folge** *f* EDP string; **~lehrer(in)** art teacher; **~setzung** *f* (-; *no pl*) LING punctuation; **~sprache** *f* sign language; **~trickfilm** *m* (animated) cartoon

zeichnen ['tsaiçnən] *v/i and v/t* (ge-, h) draw; mark (*a. fig*); sign; *fig* leave its mark on *s.o.*; **Zeichnen** *n* (-s; *no pl*) drawing; PED art; **Zeichner** ['tsaiçnɐ] *m* (-s; -) *mst* graphic artist; draftsman, *Br* draughtsman; **Zeichnung** *f* (-; -en) drawing; diagram; ZO marking

Zeigefinger ['tsaigə-] *m* ANAT forefinger, index finger; **zeigen** ['tsaigən] (ge-, h) 1. *v/t* show (*a. sich ~*); 2. *v/i*: *~ nach* point to; (*mit dem Finger*) *~ auf* (*acc*) point (one's finger) at; **Zeiger** ['tsaigɐ] *m* (-s; -) hand; TECH pointer, needle; **Zeigestock** *m* pointer

Zeile ['tsailə] *f* (-; -n) line (*a. TV*); *j-m ein paar ~n schreiben* drop s.o. a line

Zeit [tsait] *f* (-; -en) time; age, era; LING tense; *vor einiger ~* some time ago, a while ago; *in letzter ~* lately, recently; *in der* (*or zur*) *~ gen* in the days of; *... aller ~en* ... of all time; *die ~ ist um* time's up; *e-e ~ lang* for some time, for a while; *sich ~ lassen* take one's time; *es wird ~, dass ...* it's time to *inf*; *das*

---

waren noch ~*en* those were the days; → *zurzeit*

'Zeit|abschnitt *m* period (of time); ~**alter** *n* age; ~**bombe** *f* time bomb (*a. fig*); ~**druck** *m*: *unter ~ stehen* be pressed for time; ~**fahren** *n* (*-s; no pl*) cycling: time trials

'zeitgemäß *adj* modern, up-to-date

'Zeitgenosse *m*, 'Zeitgenossin *f*, 'zeitgenössisch [-gənœsɪʃ] *adj* contemporary

'Zeit|geschichte *f* (*-; no pl*) contemporary history; ~**gewinn** *m* (*-[e]s; no pl*) gain of time; ~**karte** *f* season ticket

zeit'lebens *adv* all one's life

'zeitlich 1. *adj* time ...; 2. *adv*: *et. ~ planen* or *abstimmen* time s.th.

'zeitlos *adj* timeless; classic

'Zeit|lupe *f*: *in ~* in slow motion; ~**not** *f*: *in ~ sein* be pressed for time; ~**punkt** *m* moment; ~**raffer** *m*: *im ~* in quick motion

'zeitraubend *adj* time-consuming

'Zeitraum *m* period (of time)

'Zeitschrift *f* magazine

Zeitung ['tsaɪtʊŋ] *f* (*-; -en*) (news)paper

'Zeitungs|abonne,ment *n* subscription to a paper; ~**ar,tikel** *m* newspaper article; ~**ausschnitt** *m* (newspaper) clipping (*Br* cutting); ~**junge** *m* paper boy; ~**kiosk** *m* newspaper kiosk; ~**no,tiz** *f* press item; ~**pa,pier** *n* newspaper; ~**stand** *m* newsstand; ~**verkäufer(in)** *f* newsdealer, *Br* news vendor

'Zeitverlust *m* (*-[e]s; no pl*) loss of time

'Zeitverschiebung *f* AVIAT time lag

'Zeitverschwendung *f* waste of time

'Zeitvertreib [-fɛɐtraip] *m* (*-[e]s; -e*) pastime; *zum ~* to pass the time

'zeitweilig ['tsaɪtvaɪlɪç] *adj* temporary

'zeitweise *adv* at times, occasionally

'Zeitwort *n* (*-[e]s; -wörter*) LING verb

'Zeitzeichen *n* radio: time signal

'Zeitzünder *m* MIL time fuse

Zelle ['tselə] *f* (*-; -n*) cell

Zellstoff ['tsɛl-] *m*, Zellulose [tselu-'loːzə] *f* (*-; -n*) TECH cellulose

Zelt [tsɛlt] *n* (*-[e]s; -e*) tent; zelten ['tsɛltən] *v/i* (*ge-, h*) camp; 'Zeltlager *n* camp; 'Zeltplatz *m* campsite

Zement [tseˈmɛnt] *m* (*-[e]s; -e*), zementieren [tsemɛnˈtiːrən] *v/t* (*no -ge-, h*) cement

Zenit [tseˈniːt] *m* (*-[e]s; no pl*) zenith

zensieren [tsɛnˈziːrən] *v/t* (*no -ge-, h*) censor; PED mark, grade; Zensor ['tsɛnzoːɐ] *m* (*-s; -en* [tsɛnˈzoːrən]) censor; Zensur [tsɛnˈzuːɐ] *f* (*-; -en* [tsɛnˈzuːrən]) a) (*no pl*) censorship, b) PED mark, grade

Zentimeter [tsɛntiˈmeːtɐ] *n*, *m* (*-s; -*) centimeter, *Br* centimetre

Zentner ['tsɛntnɐ] *m* (*-s; -*) 50 kilograms, metric hundredweight

zentral [tsɛnˈtraːl] *adj* central

Zentrale [tsɛnˈtraːlə] *f* (*-; -n*) head office; headquarters; TEL switchboard; TECH control room

Zen'tral|heizung *f* central heating; ~**verriegelung** *f* MOT central locking

Zentrum ['tsɛntrʊm] *n* (*-s; Zentren*) center, *Br* centre

Zepter ['tsɛptɐ] *n* (*-s; -*) scepter, *Br* sceptre

zer'brechen *v/i* (*irr, brechen, no -ge-, sein*) *and v/t* (*h*) break; → *Kopf*

zer'brechlich *adj* fragile

zer'bröckeln *v/t* (*no -ge-, h*) *and v/i* (*sein*) crumble

zer'drücken *v/t* (*no -ge-, h*) crush

Zeremonie [tseremoˈniː] *f* (*-; -n*) ceremony

zeremoniell [tseremoˈnjɛl] *adj*, Zeremoni'ell *n* (*-s; -e*) ceremonial

Zer'fall *m* (*-[e]s; no pl*) disintegration, decay; zer'fallen *v/i* (*irr, fallen, no -ge-, sein*) disintegrate, decay; *~ in* (*acc*) break up into

zer'fetzen *v/t* (*no -ge-, h*) tear to pieces; *~* 'fressen *v/t* (*irr, fressen, no -ge-, h*) eat (holes in); CHEM corrode; *~* 'gehen *v/i* (*irr, gehen, no -ge-, sein*) melt, dissolve; *~* 'hacken *v/t* (*no -ge-, h*) chop (*a.* ELECTR)

zerknirscht [tsɛɐˈknɪrʃt] *adj* remorseful

zer'|knittern *v/t* (*no -ge-, h*) (c)rumple, crease; *~* 'knüllen *v/t* (*no -ge-, h*) crumple up; *~* 'kratzen *v/t* (*no -ge-, h*) scratch; *~* 'krümeln *v/t* (*no -ge-, h*) crumble; *~* 'lassen *v/t* (*irr, lassen, no -ge-, h*) melt; *~* 'legen *v/t* (*no -ge-, h*) take apart *or* to pieces; TECH dismantle; GASTR carve; CHEM, LING, *fig* analyze, *Br* analyse

zer'lumpt *adj* ragged, tattered

zer'mahlen *v/t* (*no -ge-, h*) grind

zer'mürben *v/t* (*no -ge-, h*) wear down

Z

zer'**quetschen** v/t (no -ge-, h) crush

Zerrbild ['tsɛr-] n caricature

zer'**reiben** v/t (irr, **reiben**, no -ge-, h) rub to powder, pulverize

zer'**reißen** (irr, **reißen**, no -ge-) **1.** v/t (h) tear up or to pieces; **sich die Hose ~** tear one's trousers; **2.** v/i (sein) tear; break

zerren ['tsɛrən] (ge-, h) **1.** v/t tug, drag, pull (a. MED); **2.** v/i: ~ **an** (dat) tug (or strain) at

'**Zerrung** f (-; -en) MED pulled muscle

zer'**rütten** [tsɛr'rytən] v/t (no -ge-, h) ruin; **zer'rüttet** adj: ~**e Ehe (Verhältnisse)** broken marriage (home)

zer'**sägen** v/t (no -ge-, h) saw up; ~**schellen** [-'ʃɛlən] v/i (no -ge-, sein) be smashed, AVIAT a. crash; ~'**schlagen 1.** v/t (irr, **schlagen**, no -ge-, h) smash (to pieces); fig smash; **sich ~** come to nothing; **2.** adj: **sich ~ fühlen** be (all) worn out, F be dead beat; ~'**schmettern** v/t (no -ge-, h) smash (to pieces), shatter (a. fig); ~'**schneiden** v/t (irr, **schneiden**, no -ge-, h) cut (up); ~'**setzen** v/t (no -ge-, h) CHEM decompose (a. **sich ~**); fig corrupt, undermine; ~'**splittern** v/t (no -ge-, h) and v/i (sein) split (up), splinter; shatter; ~'**springen** v/i (irr, **springen**, no -ge-, sein) crack; shatter; ~'**stampfen** v/t (no -ge-, h) pound; GASTR mash

zer'**stäuben** v/t (no -ge-, h) spray; **Zerstäuber** [tsɛr'ʃtɔybɐ] m (-s; -) atomizer, sprayer

zer'**stören** v/t (no -ge-, h) destroy, ruin (both a. fig); **Zer'störer** m (-s; -) destroyer (a. MAR); **zer'störerisch** adj destructive; **Zer'störung** f (-; -en) destruction

zer'**streuen** v/t and v/refl (no -ge-, h) scatter, disperse; break up (crowd etc); fig take s.o.'s (refl one's) mind off things; **zer'streut** fig adj absent-minded; **Zer'streutheit** f (-; no pl) absent-mindedness; **Zer'streuung** fig f (-; -en) diversion, distraction

zer'**stückeln** v/t (no -ge-, h) cut up or (in)to pieces; dismember (body)

Zertifikat [tsɛrtifi'ka:t] n (-[e]s; -e) certificate

zer'**treten** v/t (irr, **treten**, no -ge-, h) crush (a. fig)

zer'**trümmern** v/t (no -ge-, h) smash

zerzaust [tsɛr'tsaust] adj tousled, dishevel(l)ed

Zettel ['tsɛtəl] m (-s; -) slip (of paper); note; label, sticker

Zeug [tsɔyk] n (-[e]s; -e) stuff (a. F); things; **er hat das ~ dazu** he's got what it takes; **dummes ~** nonsense

Zeuge ['tsɔygə] m (-n; -n) witness

'**zeugen**[1] v/i (ge-, h) JUR give evidence (**für** for); fig ~ **von** testify to

'**zeugen**[2] v/t (ge-, h) BIOL procreate; father

'**Zeugen**|**aussage** f JUR testimony, evidence; ~**bank** f (-; -bänke) JUR witness stand (Br box)

Zeugin f (-; -nen) JUR (female) witness

Zeugnis ['tsɔyknɪs] n (-ses; -se) report card, Br (school) report; certificate, diploma; reference; pl credentials

'**Zeugung** f (-; -en) BIOL procreation

z. H(d). ABBR of **zu Händen** attn, attention

Zickzack ['tsɪktsak] m (-[e]s; -e) (a. **im ~ fahren**) zigzag

Ziege ['tsi:gə] f (-; -n) ZO (nanny) goat; F contp (**blöde**) ~ (silly old) cow

Ziegel ['tsi:gəl] m (-s; -) brick; tile

'**Ziegeldach** n tiled roof

Ziegelei [tsi:gə'lai] f (-; -en) brickyard

'**Ziegelstein** m brick

'**Ziegen**|**bock** m ZO billy goat; ~**leder** n kid (leather); ~**peter** [-pe:tɐ] m (-s; -) MED mumps

ziehen ['tsi:ən] (irr, -ge-) **1.** v/t (h) pull, draw; take off one's hat (**vor** dat to) (a. fig); AGR grow; pull or take out (**aus** of); **j-n ~ an** (dat) pull s.o. by; **auf sich ~** attract (attention etc); **sich ~** run; stretch; → **Länge, Erwägung; 2.** v/i a) (h) pull (**an** dat at), b) (sein) move; ZO etc migrate; go; travel; wander, roam; **es zieht** there's a draft (Br draught)

Ziehharmonika ['tsi:harmo:nika] f (-; -s) MUS accordion

'**Ziehung** f (-; -en) draw

Ziel [tsi:l] n (-[e]s; -e) aim, target, mark (all a. fig), fig a. goal, objective; destination; SPORT finish; **sich ein ~ setzen** set o.s. a goal; **sein ~ erreichen** reach one's goal; **sich zum ~ gesetzt haben, et. zu tun** aim to do or at doing s.th.

'**Zielband** n (-[e]s; -bänder) SPORT tape

zielen ['tsi:lən] v/i (ge-, h) (take) aim (auf acc at)

'**Ziellinie** f SPORT finishing line

'**ziellos** adj aimless

'**Zielscheibe** f target, fig a. object

zielstrebig ['tsi:lʃtre:bɪç] adj purposeful, determined

ziemlich ['tsi:mlɪç] **1.** adj quite a; **2.** adv rather, fairly, quite, F pretty; **~ viele** quite a few

Zierde ['tsi:ɐdə] f (-; -n) (zur as a) decoration; **zieren** ['tsi:rən] v/t (ge-, h) decorate; **sich ~** be coy; make a fuss

zierlich ['tsi:ɐlɪç] adj dainty; petite

'**Zierpflanze** ['tsi:ɐ-] f ornamental plant

Ziffer ['tsɪfɐ] f (-; -n) figure

'**Zifferblatt** n dial, face

Zigarette [tsiga'rɛtə] f (-; -n) cigarette

Ziga'retten|auto,mat m cigarette machine; **~stummel** m cigarette end, stub, butt

Zigarre [tsi'garə] f (-; -n) cigar

Zigeuner [tsi'gɔynɐ] m (-s; -), **Zi'geunerin** [-nərɪn] f (-; -nen) gypsy, Br gipsy

Zimmer ['tsɪmɐ] n (-s; -) room; apartment; **~einrichtung** f furniture; **~mädchen** n (chamber)maid; **~mann** m carpenter

'**zimmern** v/t (ge-, h) build, make

'**Zimmer|pflanze** f indoor plant; **~service** m room service; **~suche** f: **auf ~ sein** be looking (or hunting) for a room; **~vermittlung** f accommodation office

zimperlich ['tsɪmpɐlɪç] adj prudish; soft, F sissy

Zimt [tsɪmt] m (-[e]s; -e) cinnamon

Zink [tsɪŋk] n (-[e]s; no pl) CHEM zinc

Zinke ['tsɪŋkə] f (-; -n) tooth; prong

Zinn [tsɪn] n (-[e]s; no pl) CHEM tin; pewter

Zins [tsɪns] m (-es; -en) ECON interest (a. pl); **3% ~en bringen** bear interest at 3%; '**zinslos** adj ECON interest-free; '**Zinssatz** m ECON interest rate

Zipfel ['tsɪpfəl] m (-s; -) corner; point; tail; GASTR end; **~mütze** f pointed cap

zirka ['tsɪrka] adv about, approximately

Zirkel ['tsɪrkəl] m (-s; -) circle (a. fig); MATH compasses, dividers

zirkulieren [tsɪrku'li:rən] v/i (no -ge-, h) circulate

Zirkus ['tsɪrkʊs] m (-; -se) circus

zirpen ['tsɪrpən] v/i (ge-, h) chirp

zischen ['tsɪʃən] v/i and v/t (ge-, h) hiss; fat etc: sizzle; fig whiz(z)

ziselieren [tsizə'li:rən] v/t (no -ge-, h) TECH chase

Zitat [tsi'ta:t] n (-[e]s; -e) quotation, F quote; **zitieren** [tsi'ti:rən] v/t (no -ge-, h) quote, cite (a. JUR), JUR summon

Zitrone [tsi'tro:nə] f (-; -n) BOT lemon

Zi'tronen|limo,nade f lemon soda or pop, Br (fizzy) lemonade; **~saft** m lemon juice; **~schale** f lemon peel

zitterig ['tsɪtərɪç] adj shaky; **zittern** ['tsɪtɐn] v/i (ge-, h) tremble, shake (both: vor dat with)

zivil [tsi'vi:l] adj civil, civilian

Zi'vil n (-s; no pl) civilian clothes; **Polizist in** plainclothes policeman

Zi'vildienst m MIL alternative service (in lieu of military service)

Zivilisation [tsiviliza'tsjo:n] f (-; -en) civilization; **zivilisieren** [tsivili'zi:rən] v/t (no -ge-, h) civilize

Zivilist [tsivi'lɪst] m (-en; -en) civilian

Zi'vilrecht n (-[e]s; no pl) JUR civil law

Zi'vilschutz m civil defen|se, Br -ce

Znüni ['tsny:ni] Swiss m, n (-s; -) mid-morning snack, tea (or coffee) break

zog [tso:k] pret of **ziehen**

zögern ['tsø:gɐn] v/i (ge-, h) hesitate; '**Zögern** n (-s; no pl) hesitation

Zoll¹ [tsɔl] m (-[e]s; -) inch

Zoll² m (-[e]s; Zölle ['tsœlə]) a) (no pl) customs, b) duty

'**Zollabfertigung** f customs clearance

'**Zollbeamte** m customs officer

'**Zollerklärung** f customs declaration

'**zollfrei** adj duty-free

'**Zollkon,trolle** f customs examination

'**zollpflichtig** adj liable to duty

'**Zollstock** m (folding) rule

Zone ['tso:nə] f (-; -n) zone

Zoo [tso:] m (-s; -s) zoo

'**Zoohandlung** f pet shop

Zoologe [tsoo'lo:gə] m (-n; -n) zoologist; **Zoologie** [tsoolo'gi:] f (-; no pl) zoology; **Zoo'login** f (-; -nen) zoologist; **zoo'logisch** adj zoological

Zopf [tsɔpf] m (-[e]s; Zöpfe ['tsœpfə]) plait; pigtail

Zorn [tsɔrn] m (-[e]s; no pl) anger

zornig ['tsɔrnɪç] adj angry

Zote ['tso:tə] f (-; -n) filthy joke, obscenity

zottelig ['tsɔtəlɪç] adj shaggy

Z

z.T. ABBR *of* **zum Teil** partly

zu [tsu:] **1.** *prp (dat)* to, toward(s); at; *purpose:* for; **~ Fuß (Pferd)** on foot (horseback); **~ Hause (Ostern** *etc)* at home (Easter *etc*); **~ Weihnachten** give *etc* for Christmas; **Tür (Schlüssel)** **~ ...** door (key) to ...; **~ m-r Überraschung** to my surprise; **wir sind ~ dritt** there are three of us; **~ zweien** two by two; **~ e-r Mark** at *or* for one mark; SPORT **1 ~ 1** one all; **2 ~ 1 gewinnen** win two one, win by two goals *etc* to one; → **zum, zur. 2.** *adv* too; F closed, shut; **~ viel** too much, too many; **~ wenig** too little, too few; **3.** *cj* to; **es ist ~ erwarten** it is to be expected

Zubehör ['tsu:bəhø:ɐ] *n (-[e]s; -e)* accessories

'**zubereiten** *v/t (sep, no -ge-, h)* prepare; '**Zubereitung** *f (-; -en)* preparation

'**zu|binden** *v/t (irr, binden, sep, -ge-, h)* tie (up); **~bleiben** *v/i (irr, bleiben, sep, -ge-, sein)* stay shut; **~blinzeln** *v/i (sep, -ge-, h) (dat)* wink at

'**Zubringer** *m (-s; -)*, **~straße** *f* MOT feeder (road), access road

Zucht [tsʊxt] *f (-; -en)* breed; ZO breeding; BOT cultivation; **züchten** ['tsʏçtən] *v/t (ge-, h)* ZO breed; BOT grow, cultivate; **Züchter(in)** ['tsʏçtɐ (-tərɪn)] *m (-s; -/-; -nen)* ZO breeder; BOT grower

'**Zuchtperle** *f* culture(d) pearl

zucken ['tsʊkən] *v/i (ge-, h)* jerk; twitch (**mit et.** s.th.); wince; *lightning:* flash

zücken ['tsʏkən] *v/t (ge-, h)* draw (*weapon*); F pull out (*one's wallet etc*)

Zucker ['tsʊkɐ] *m (-s; -)* sugar; **~dose** *f* sugar bowl; **~guss** *m* icing, frosting

'**zuckerkrank** *adj*, '**Zuckerkranke** *m, f (-n; -n)* MED diabetic

'**Zuckerkrankheit** *f* MED diabetes

'**Zuckermais** *m* sweet corn

'**zuckern** *v/t (ge-, h)* sugar

'**Zuckerrohr** *n* BOT sugarcane

'**Zuckerrübe** *f* BOT sugar beet

'**Zuckerwatte** *f* candy floss

'**Zuckerzange** *f* sugar tongs

'**Zuckung** *f (-; -en)* twitch(ing); tic; convulsion, spasm

'**zudecken** *v/t (sep, -ge-, h)* cover (up)

zudem [tsu'de:m] *adv* besides, moreover

'**zudrehen** *v/t (sep, -ge-, h)* turn off; **j-m**

den Rücken ~ turn one's back on s.o.

'**zudringlich** *adj:* **~ werden** F get fresh (**j-m gegenüber** with s.o.)

'**zudrücken** *v/t (sep, -ge-, h)* close, push s.th. shut; → **Auge**

zuerst [tsu'?e:ɐst] *adv* first; at first; first (of all), to begin with

'**Zufahrt** *f* approach; drive(way)

'**Zufahrtsstraße** *f* access road

'**Zufall** *m* chance; **durch ~** by chance, by accident; '**zufallen** *v/i (irr, fallen, sep, -ge-, sein)* door *etc:* slam (shut); *fig* fall to s.o.; **mir fallen die Augen zu** I can't keep my eyes open; '**zufällig 1.** *adj* accidental, chance ...; **2.** *adv* by accident, by chance; **~ tun** happen to do

'**Zuflucht** *f:* **~ suchen (finden)** look for (find) refuge *or* shelter (**vor** *dat* from; **bei** with); **(s-e) ~ nehmen zu** resort to

zufrieden [tsu'fri:dən] *adj* content(ed), satisfied; **sich ~ geben mit** content o.s. with; **j-n ~ lassen** leave s.o. alone; **~ stellen** satisfy; **~ stellend** satisfactory; **Zu'friedenheit** *f (-; no pl)* contentment, satisfaction

'**zufrieren** *v/i (irr, frieren, sep, -ge-, sein)* freeze up *or* over

'**zufügen** *v/t (sep, -ge-, h)* do, cause; **j-m Schaden ~ a.** harm s.o.

Zufuhr ['tsu:fu:ɐ] *f (-; -en)* supply

Zug [tsu:k] *m (-[e]s; Züge* ['tsy:gə]*)* RAIL train; procession; line; parade; *fig* feature; trait; tendency; *chess etc:* move (*a. fig*); *swimming:* stroke; pull (*a.* TECH), PHYS *a.* tension; *smoking:* puff; draft, *Br* draught; PED stream; **im ~e** *gen* in the course of; **in e-m ~** at one go; **~ um ~** step by step; **in groben Zügen** in broad outlines

'**Zugabe** *f* addition; THEA encore

'**Zugang** *m* access (*a. fig*); '**zugänglich** [-gɛnlɪç] *adj* accessible (**für** to) (*a. fig*)

'**Zugbrücke** *f* drawbridge

'**zugeben** *v/t (irr, geben, sep, -ge-, h)* add; *fig* admit

'**zugehen** *v/i (irr, gehen, sep, -ge-, sein)* F *door etc:* close, shut; **~ auf** *(acc)* walk up to, approach (*a. fig*); **es geht auf 8 Uhr zu** it's getting on for 8; **es ging lustig zu** we had a lot of fun

'**Zugehörigkeit** *f (-; no pl)* membership

Zügel ['tsy:gəl] *m (-s; -)* rein (*a. fig*)

'**zügeln 1.** *v/t (ge-, h)* curb, control, bridle; **2.** *Swiss v/i (ge-, sein)* move

'Zugeständnis *n* concession

'zugestehen *v/t* (*irr, **stehen**, sep, no -ge-, h*) concede, grant

'zugetan *adj* attached (*dat* to)

'Zugführer *m* RAIL conductor, *Br* guard

zugig ['tsu:gɪç] *adj* drafty, *Br* draughty

'Zugkraft *f* a) TECH traction, b) (*no pl*) attraction, draw, appeal

'zugkräftig *adj*: **~ sein** be a draw

zu'gleich [tsu-] *adv* at the same time

'Zugluft *f* (-; *no pl*) draft, *Br* draught

'Zugma,schine *f* MOT tractor

'zugreifen *v/i* (*irr, **greifen**, sep, -ge-, h*) grab (at) it; *fig* grab the opportunity; **greifen Sie zu!** help yourself!; **mit ~** lend a hand

'Zugriffscode *m* EDP access code

'Zugriffszeit *f* EDP access time

zugrunde [tsu'grʊndə] *adv*: **~ gehen** (**an** *dat*) perish (of); **e-r Sache et. ~ legen** base s.th. on s.th.; **~ richten** ruin

zugunsten [tsu'gʊnstən] *prp* (*gen*) in favo(u)r of

zu'gute [tsu-] *adv*: **j-m et. ~ halten** give s.o. credit for s.th.; make allowances for s.o.'s ...; **j-m ~ kommen** be for the benefit of s.o.

'Zugvogel *m* ZO bird of passage

'zuhalten *v/t* (*irr, **halten**, sep, -ge-, h*) keep shut; **sich die Ohren (Augen) ~** cover one's ears (eyes) with one's hands; **sich die Nase ~** hold one's nose

Zuhälter ['tsu:hɛltɐ] *m* (*-s; -*) pimp

Zuhause [tsu'hauzə] *n* (*-s; no pl*) home

zu'hause *Austrian adv* at home

'zuhören *v/i* (sep, -ge-, h*) listen (*dat* to)

'Zuhörer *m*, **'Zuhörerin** *f* listener, *pl a. the* audience

'zujubeln *v/i* (sep, -ge-, h*) cheer

'zukleben *v/t* (sep, -ge-, h*) seal

'zuknöpfen *v/t* (sep, -ge-, h*) button (up)

'zukommen *v/i* (*irr, **kommen**, sep, -ge-, sein*) **~ auf** (*acc*) come up to; *fig* be ahead of; **die Dinge auf sich ~ lassen** wait and see

Zukunft ['tsu:kʊnft] *f* (-; *no pl*) future (*a.* LING)

'zukünftig 1. *adj* future; **2.** *adv* in future

'zulächeln *v/i* (sep, -ge-, h*) smile at

'Zulage *f* bonus

'zulangen F *v/i* (sep, -ge-, h*) tuck in

'zulassen *v/t* (*irr, **lassen**, sep, -ge-, h*) F keep s.th. closed; *fig* allow; MOT *etc* license, register; **j-n zu et. ~** admit s.o. to

s.th.; **'zulässig** *adj* admissible (*a.* JUR); **~ sein** be allowed; **'Zulassung** *f* (-; *-en*) admission; MOT *etc* license, *Br* licence

'zulegen *v/t* (sep, -ge-, h*) add; F **sich ... ~** get o.s. s.th.; adopt (*name*)

zu'letzt [tsu-] *adv* in the end; *come etc* last; finally; **wann hast du ihn ~ gesehen?** when did you last see him?

zu'liebe [tsu-] *adv*: **j-m ~** for s.o.'s sake

zum [tsʊm] *prp* **zu dem → zu**; **~ ersten Mal** for the first time; *et.* **~ Kaffee** *etc* with one's coffee; **~ Schwimmen** *etc* **gehen** go swimming *etc*

'zumachen *v/t* (sep, -ge-, h*) **1.** *v/t* close, shut; button (up); **2.** *v/i* close (down)

'zumauern *v/t* (sep, -ge-, h*) brick *or* wall up

zumutbar ['tsu:mu:tba:ɐ] *adj* reasonable; **zu'mute** [tsu-] *adv*: **mir ist ... ~** I feel ...; **'zumuten** *v/t* (sep, -ge-, h*) **j-m et. ~** expect s.th. of s.o.; **sich zu viel ~** overtax o.s.; **'Zumutung** *f*: **das ist e-e ~** that's asking *or* expecting a bit much

zu'nächst [tsu-] *adv* → **zuerst**

'zunageln *v/t* (sep, -ge-, h*) nail up

'zunähen *v/t* (sep, -ge-, h*) sew up

Zunahme ['tsu:na:mə] *f* (-; *-n*) increase

'Zuname *m* surname

zünden ['tsʏndən] *v/i* (ge-, h*) kindle; ELECTR, MOT ignite, fire; **~d** *fig adj* stirring

Zünder ['tsʏndɐ] *m* (*-s; -*) MIL fuse; *pl Austrian* matches

Zünd|holz ['tsʏnt-] *n* match; **~kerze** *f* MOT spark plug; **~schlüssel** *m* MOT ignition key; **~schnur** *f* fuse

'Zündung *f* (-; *-en*) MOT ignition

'zunehmen *v/i* (*irr, **nehmen**, sep, -ge-, h*) increase (*an dat* in); put on weight; *moon:* wax; *days:* grow longer

'Zuneigung *f* (-; *-en*) affection

Zunft [tsʊnft] HIST *f* (-; *Zünfte* ['tsʏnftə]) guild

Zunge [tsʊŋə] *f* (-; *-n*) ANAT tongue; **es liegt mir auf der ~** it's on the tip of my tongue

züngeln ['tsʏŋəln] *v/i* (ge-, h*) *flames:* lick, flicker

'Zungenspitze *f* tip of the tongue

'zunicken *v/i* (sep, -ge-, h*) (*dat*) nod at

zunutze [tsu'nʊtsə] *adv*: **sich et. ~ machen** make (good) use of s.th.; take advantage of s.th.

Z

zupfen [tsʊpfən] v/t and v/i (ge-, h) pull (**an** dat at), pick, pluck (at) (a. MUS)

zur [tsuːɐ] prp **zu der** → **zu**; ~ **Schule** (**Kirche**) **gehen** go to school (church); ~ **Hälfte** half (of it or them); ~ **Belohnung** etc as a reward etc

'**zurechnungsfähig** adj JUR responsible; '**Zurechnungsfähigkeit** f (-; no pl) JUR responsibility

zu'recht|finden v/refl (irr, **finden**, sep, -ge-, h) find one's way; fig cope, manage; ~**kommen** v/i (irr, **kommen**, sep, -ge-, sein) get along (**mit** with); cope (with); ~**legen** v/t (sep, -ge-, h) arrange; fig **sich et.** ~ think s.th. out; ~**machen** F v/t (sep, -ge-, h) get ready, prepare, fix; **sich** ~ do s.o. up; ~**rücken** v/t (sep, -ge-, h) put s.th. straight (a. fig)

zu'rechtweisen v/t (irr, **weisen**, sep, -ge-, h) reprimand, **Zu'rechtweisung** f reprimand

'**zu|reden** v/i (sep, -ge-, h) **j-m** ~ encourage s.o.; ~**reiten** v/t (irr, **reiten**, sep, -ge-, h) break in; ~**richten** F fig v/t (sep, -ge-, h) **übel** ~ batter, a. beat s.o. up badly, a. make a mess of s.th., ruin

zurück [tsuˈrʏk] adv back; behind (a. fig), ~**behalten** v/t (irr, **halten**, sep, no -ge-, h) keep back, retain; ~**bekommen** v/t (irr, **kommen**, sep, no -ge-, h) get back; ~**bleiben** v/i (irr, **bleiben**, sep, -ge-, sein) stay behind, be left behind; fall behind (a. PED etc); ~**blicken** v/i (sep, -ge-, h) look back (**auf** acc at, fig on); ~**bringen** v/t (irr, **bringen**, sep, -ge-, h) bring or take back, return; ~**da,tieren** v/t (sep, no -ge-, h) backdate (**auf** acc to); ~**fallen** fig v/i (irr, **fallen**, sep, -ge-, sein) fall behind, SPORT a. drop back; ~**finden** v/i (irr, **finden**, sep, -ge-, h) find one's way back (**nach**, **zu** to); fig return (to); ~**fordern** v/t (sep, -ge-, h) reclaim; ~**führen** v/t (sep, -ge-, h) lead back; ~ **auf** (acc) attribute to; ~**geben** v/t (irr, **geben**, sep, -ge-, h) give back, return; ~**geblieben** fig adj backward; retarded; ~**gehen** v/i (irr, **gehen**, sep, -ge-, sein) go back, return; fig decrease; go down, drop; ~**gezogen** fig adj secluded; ~**greifen** v/i (irr, **greifen**, sep, -ge-, h) ~ **auf** (acc) fall back (up)on

zu'rückhalten v/t (irr, **halten**, sep, -ge-, h) **1.** v/t hold back; **2.** v/refl control o.s.; be careful; ~**d** adj reserved

Zu'rückhaltung f (-; no pl) reserve

zu'rück|kehren v/i (sep, -ge-, sein) return; ~**kommen** v/i (irr, **kommen**, sep, -ge-, sein) come back, return (both fig **auf** acc to); ~**lassen** v/t (irr, **lassen**, sep, -ge-, h) leave (behind); ~**legen** v/t (sep, -ge-, h) put back; put aside, save (money); cover, do (miles); ~**nehmen** v/t (irr, **nehmen**, sep, -ge-, h) take back (a. fig); ~**rufen** v/t (irr, **rufen**, sep, -ge-, h) **1.** v/t call back (a. TEL); ECON recall; **ins Gedächtnis** ~ recall; **2.** v/i TEL call back; ~**schlagen** v/t (irr, **schlagen**, sep, -ge-, h) **1.** v/t beat off; tennis: return; fold back; **2.** v/i hit back; MIL retaliate (a. fig); ~**schrecken** v/i (sep, -ge-, sein) ~ **vor** (dat) shrink from; **vor nichts** ~ stop at nothing; ~**setzen** v/t (sep, -ge-, h) MOT back (up); fig neglect s.o.; ~**stehen** v/i (irr, **stehen**, sep, -ge-, h) stand aside; ~**stellen** v/t (sep, -ge-, h) put back (a. watch); put aside; MIL defer; ~**strahlen** v/t (sep, -ge-, h) reflect; ~**treten** v/i (irr, **treten**, sep, -ge-, sein) step or stand back; resign (**von e-m Amt** [**Posten**] one's office [post]); ECON, JUR withdraw (**von** from); ~**weichen** v/i (irr, **weichen**, sep, -ge-, sein) fall back (a. MIL.); ~**weisen** v/t (irr, **weisen**, sep, -ge-, h) turn down; JUR dismiss; ~**zahlen** v/t (sep, -ge-, h) pay back (a. fig); ~**ziehen** v/t (irr, **ziehen**, sep, -ge-, h) draw back; fig withdraw; **sich** ~ retire, withdraw, MIL a. retreat

'**Zuruf** m shout; '**zurufen** v/t (irr, **rufen**, sep, -ge-, h) **j-m et.** ~ shout s.th. to s.o.

zur'zeit adv at the moment, at present

'**Zusage** f promise; assent

'**zusagen** v/i and v/t (sep, -ge-, h) accept (an invitation); (dat) suit, appeal to; **s-e Hilfe** ~ promise to help

zusammen [tsuˈzamən] adv together; **alles** ~ (all) in all; **das macht** ~ ... that makes ... altogether

Zu'sammenarbeit f (-; no pl) cooperation; **in** ~ **mit** in collaboration with; **zu'sammenarbeiten** v/i (sep, -ge-, h) cooperate, collaborate

zu'sammenbeißen v/t (irr, **beißen**, sep, -ge-, h) **die Zähne** ~ clench one's teeth

zu'sammenbrechen v/i (irr, **brechen**, sep, -ge-, sein) break down, collapse (both a. fig); **Zu'sammenbruch** m breakdown, collapse

zu'sammen|fallen v/i (irr, **fallen**, sep, -ge-, sein) coincide; **~falten** v/t (sep, -ge-, h) fold up

zu'sammenfassen v/t (sep, -ge-, h) summarize, sum up; **Zu'sammenfassung** f (-; -en) summary

zu'sammen|fügen v/t (sep, -ge-, h) join (together); **~gesetzt** adj compound; **~halten** v/i and v/t (irr, **halten**, sep, -ge-, h) hold together (a. fig); F stick together

Zu'sammenhang m (-[e]s; -hänge) connection; context; **im ~ stehen** (**mit**) be connected (with)

zu'sammenhängen v/i (irr, **hängen**, sep, -ge-, h) be connected; **~d** adj coherent

zu'sammenhang(s)los adj incoherent, disconnected

zu'sammen|klappen v/i (sep, -ge-, sein) and v/t (h) TECH fold up; F break down; **~kommen** v/i (irr, **kommen**, sep, -ge-, sein) meet

Zu'sammenkunft [-kunft] f (-; -künfte [-kynftə]) meeting

zu'sammen|legen (sep, -ge-, h) 1. v/t combine; fold up; 2. v/i club together; **~nehmen** v/t (irr, **nehmen**, sep, -ge-, h) muster (up); **sich ~** pull o.s. together; **~packen** v/t (sep, -ge-, h) pack up; **~passen** v/i (sep, -ge-, h) harmonize; match; **~rechnen** v/t (sep, -ge-, h) add up; **~reißen** F v/refl (irr, **reißen**, sep, -ge-, h) pull o.s. together; **~rollen** v/t (sep, -ge-, h) roll up; **sich ~** coil up; **~rotten** [-rɔtən] v/refl (sep, -ge-, h) band together; **~rücken** (sep, -ge-) 1. v/t (h) move closer together; 2. v/i (sein) move up; **~schlagen** v/t (irr, **schlagen**, sep, -ge-, h) clap (hands); click (one's heels); beat s.o. up; smash (up)

zu'sammenschließen v/refl (irr, **schließen**, sep, -ge-, h) join, unite; **Zu'sammenschluss** m union

zu'sammen|schreiben v/t (irr, **schreiben**, sep, -ge-, h) write in one word; **~schrumpfen** v/i (sep, -ge-, sein) shrink

zu'sammensetzen v/t (sep, -ge-, h) put together; TECH assemble; **sich ~ aus** (dat) consist of, be composed of; **Zu'sammensetzung** f (-; -en) composi-

tion; CHEM, LING compound; TECH assembly

zu'sammenstellen v/t (sep, -ge-, h) put together; arrange

Zu'sammenstoß m collision (a. fig), crash; impact; fig clash; **zu'sammenstoßen** v/i (irr, **stoßen**, sep, -ge-, sein) collide (a. fig; **mit** with); run or bump into; fig have a clash with

zu'sammentreffen v/i (irr, **treffen**, sep, -ge-, sein) meet, encounter; coincide (**mit** with); **Zu'sammentreffen** n (-s; -) meeting; coincidence; encounter

zu'sammen|treten v/i (irr, **treten**, sep, -ge-, sein) meet; **~tun** v/refl (irr, **tun**, sep, -ge-, h) join (forces), F team up; **~wirken** v/i (sep, -ge-, h) combine; **~zählen** v/t (sep, -ge-, h) add up; **~ziehen** (irr, **ziehen**, sep, -ge-) 1. v/t and v/refl (h) contract; 2. v/i (sein) move in (**mit** with); **~zucken** v/i (sep, -ge-, sein) wince, flinch

'Zusatz m addition; chemical etc additive; **~... in** cpds mst additional ..., supplementary ...; auxiliary ...; **zusätzlich** ['tsu:zɛtslɪç] adj additional, extra

'zuschauen v/i (sep, -ge-, h) look on (**bei et.** at s.th.); **j-m ~** watch s.o. (**bei et.** doing s.th.)

Zuschauer ['tsu:ʃauɐ] m (-s; -), **'Zuschauerin** f (-; -nen) spectator; TV viewer, pl a. the audience

'Zuschauerraum m auditorium

'Zuschlag m extra charge; RAIL etc excess fare; bonus; auction: knocking down; **'zuschlagen** v/t (irr, **schlagen**, sep, -ge-, h) and v/t (h) door etc: slam or bang shut; boxing etc: hit, strike (a blow); fig act; **j-m et. ~** auction: knock s.th. down to s.o.

'zu|schließen v/t (irr, **schließen**, sep, -ge-, h) lock (up); **~schnallen** v/t (sep, -ge-, h) buckle (up); **~schnappen** v/i (sep, -ge-) a) (h) dog: snap, b) (sein) door etc: snap shut; **~schneiden** v/t (irr, **schneiden**, sep, -ge-, h) cut out; cut (to size); **~schnüren** v/t (sep, -ge-, h) tie (or lace) up; **~schrauben** v/t (sep, -ge-, h) screw shut; **~schreiben** v/t (irr, **schreiben**, sep, -ge-, h) ascribe or attribute (dat to)

'Zuschrift f letter

zuschulden [tsu:'ʃuldən] adv: **sich et.**

(*nichts*) ~ **kommen lassen** do s.th. (nothing) wrong

'**Zuschuss** *m* allowance; subsidy

'**zuschütten** *v/t* (*sep, -ge-, h*) fill up

'**zusehen** → **zuschauen**

zusehends ['tsu:se:ənts] *adv* noticeably; rapidly

'**zusetzen** (*sep, -ge-, h*) **1.** *v/t* add; lose (*money*); **2.** *v/i* lose money; *j-m* ~ press s.o. (hard)

'**zuspielen** *v/t* (*sep, -ge-, h*) SPORT pass

'**zuspitzen** *v/t* (*sep, -ge-, h*) point; **sich** ~ become critical

'**Zuspruch** *m* (-[*e*]*s; no pl*) encouragement; words of comfort

'**Zustand** *m* condition, state, F shape

zustande [tsu'ftandə] *adv:* ~ **bringen** bring about, manage (to do); ~ **kommen** come about; **es kam nicht** ~ it didn't come off

'**zuständig** *adj* responsible (**für** for), in charge (of)

'**zustehen** *v/i* (*irr, stehen, sep, -ge-, h*) *j-m steht et.* (**zu tun**) **zu** s.o. is entitled to (do) s.th.

'**zustellen** *v/t* (*sep, -ge-, h*) post: deliver; '**Zustellung** *f* post: delivery

'**zustimmen** *v/i* (*sep, -ge-, h*) agree (*dat* to s.th.; with s.o.); '**Zustimmung** *f* approval, consent; (*j-s*) ~ **finden** meet with (s.o.'s) approval

'**zustoßen** *v/i* (*irr, stoßen, sep, -ge-, sein*) *j-m* ~ happen to s.o.

zutage [tsu'ta:gə] *adv:* ~ **bringen** (**kommen**) bring (come) to light

'**Zutaten** *pl* ingredients

'**zuteilen** *v/t* (*sep, -ge-, h*) assign, allot; '**Zuteilung** *f* (-; -en) allotment; ration

'**zutragen** *v/refl* (*irr, tragen, sep, -ge-, h*) happen

'**zutrauen** *v/t* (*sep, -ge-, h*) *j-m et.* ~ credit s.o. with s.th.; **sich zu viel** ~ overrate o.s.

zutraulich ['tsu:traulıç] *adj* trusting; ZO friendly

'**zutreffen** *v/i* (*irr, treffen, sep, -ge-, h*) be true; ~ **auf** (*acc*) apply to, go for; ~**d** *adj* true, correct

'**zutrinken** *v/i* (*irr, trinken, sep, -ge-, h*) *j-m* ~ drink to s.o.

'**Zutritt** *m* (-[*e*]*s; no pl*) admission; access; ~ **verboten!** no admittance!

zu'ungunsten *adv* to s.o.'s disadvantage

zuverlässig ['tsu:fɛɐlɛsıç] *adj* reliable, dependable; safe; '**Zuverlässigkeit** *f* (-; *no pl*) reliability, dependability

Zuversicht ['tsu:fɛɐzıçt] *f* (-; *no pl*) confidence; '**zuversichtlich** *adj* confident, optimistic

zuviel → **zu**

zu'vor [tsu-] *adv* before, previously; first

zu'vorkommen *v/i* (*irr, kommen, sep, -ge-, sein*) anticipate; prevent; *j-m* ~ *a.* F beat s.o. to it; ~**d** *adj* obliging; polite

Zuwachs ['tsu:vaks] *m* (-*es; no pl*) increase, growth; '**zuwachsen** *v/i* (*irr, wachsen, sep, -ge-, sein*) become overgrown; MED close

zu'weilen [tsu-] *adv* occasionally, now and then

'**zuweisen** *v/t* (*irr, weisen, sep, -ge-, h*) assign

'**zuwenden** *v/t and v/refl* ([*irr, wenden,*] *sep, -ge-, h*) turn to (*a. fig*)

'**Zuwendung** *f* (-; -en) a) payment, b) (*no pl*) attention; (loving) care, love, affection

zuwenig → **zu**

'**zuwerfen** *v/t* (*irr, werfen, sep, -ge-, h*) slam (shut); *j-m et.* ~ throw s.o. s.th.; *j-m e-n Blick* ~ cast a glance at s.o.

zu'wider [tsu-] *adj:* ... *ist mir* ~ I hate or detest ...; ~**handeln** *v/i* (*sep, -ge-, h*) (*dat*) act contrary to; violate

'**zuwinken** *v/i* (*sep, -ge-, h*) wave to; signal to; ~**zahlen** *v/t* (*sep, -ge-, h*) pay extra; ~**ziehen** (*irr, ziehen, sep, -ge-*) **1.** *v/t* (h) draw (*curtains etc*); pull tight; *fig* consult; **sich** ~ MED catch; **2.** *v/i* (*sein*) move in

zuzüglich ['tsu:tsy:klıç] *prp* (*gen*) plus

Zvieri ['tsfi:ri] Swiss *m, n* (-*s; -s*) afternoon snack, tea or coffee break

zwang [tsvaŋ] *pret of* **zwingen**

Zwang *m* (-[*e*]*s; Zwänge* ['tsvɛŋə]) compulsion, constraint; restraint; coercion; force; ~ **sein** be compulsory; **zwängen** ['tsvɛŋən] *v/t* (*ge-, h*) press, squeeze, force; '**zwanglos** *adj* informal; casual; '**Zwanglosigkeit** *f* (-; *no pl*) informality

'**Zwangs|arbeit** *f* JUR hard labo(u)r; ~**herrschaft** *f* (-; *no pl*) despotism, tyranny; ~**lage** *f* predicament

'**zwangsläufig** *adv* inevitably

'**Zwangs|maßnahme** f sanction; **~voll-streckung** f JUR compulsory execution; **~vorstellung** f PSYCH obsession
'**zwangsweise** adv by force
'**zwanzig** ['tsvantsɪç] adj twenty
'**zwanzigste** adj twentieth
zwar [tsva:ɐ] adv: **ich kenne ihn ~, aber ...** I do know him, but ..., I know him all right, but ...; **und ~** that is (to say), namely
Zweck [tsvɛk] m (-[e]s; -e) purpose, aim; **s-n ~ erfüllen** serve its purpose; **es hat keinen ~ (zu warten** etc) it's no use (waiting etc); '**zwecklos** adj useless
'**zweckmäßig** adj practical; wise; TECH, ARCH functional; '**Zweckmäßigkeit** f (-; no pl) practicality, functionality
zwecks prp (gen) for the purpose of
zwei [tsvai] adj two
'**zweibeinig** [-bainɪç] adj two-legged
'**Zweibettzimmer** n twin-bedded room
'**zweideutig** [-dɔytɪç] adj ambiguous; off-colo(u)r
Zweier ['tsvaiɐ] m (-s; -) rowing: pair
zweierlei ['tsvaiɐ'lai] adj two kinds of
'**zweifach** adj double, twofold
Zweifa'milienhaus n duplex, Br two-family house
Zweifel ['tsvaifəl] m (-s; -) doubt
'**zweifelhaft** adj doubtful, dubious
'**zweifellos** adv undoubtedly, no or without doubt
'**zweifeln** v/i (ge-, h) **~ an** (dat) doubt s.th., have one's doubts about
Zweig [tsvaik] m (-[e]s; -e) BOT branch (a. fig); twig; **~geschäft** n, **~niederlassung** f, **~stelle** f branch
'**zweijährig** [-jɛːrɪç] adj two-year-old, of two (years)
'**Zweikampf** m duel
'**zweimal** adv twice
'**zweimalig** adj (twice) repeated
'**zwei|motorig** [-mo:to:rɪç] adj twin-engined; **~reihig** [-raiɪç] adj double-breasted (suit); **~schneidig** adj double-edged, two-edged (both a. fig); **~seitig** [-zaitɪç] adj two-sided; reversible; POL bilateral; EDP double-sided
'**Zweisitzer** [-zɪtsɐ] m (-s; -) esp MOT two-seater
'**zwei|sprachig** [-ʃpra:xɪç] adj bilingual; **~stimmig** [-ʃtɪmɪç] adj MUS ... for two voices; **~stöckig** [-ʃtœkɪç] adj two-storied, Br two-storey ...

zweit [tsvait] adj second; **ein ~er ...** another ...; **jede(r, -s) ~e ...** every other ...; **aus ~er Hand** second-hand; **wir sind zu ~** there are two of us
'**zweitbeste** adj second-best
'**zweiteilig** adj two-piece (suit etc)
zweitens ['tsvaitəns] adv secondly
'**zweitklassig** [-klasɪç] adj, '**zweitrangig** [-raŋɪç] adj second-class or -rate
Zwerchfell ['tsvɛrç-] n ANAT diaphragm
Zwerg [tsvɛrk] m (-[e]s; -e [tsvɛrgə]) dwarf; gnome; fig midget; **~... in cpds** BOT dwarf ...; ZO pygmy ...
Zwetsch(g)e ['tsvɛtʃ(g)ə] f (-; -n) BOT plum
zwicken ['tsvikən] v/t and v/i (ge-, h) pinch, nip
Zwieback ['tsvi:bak] m (-[e]s; -e, -bäcke [-bɛkə]) rusk, zwieback
Zwiebel ['tsvi:bəl] f (-; -n) GASTR onion; BOT bulb
'**Zwiegespräch** ['tsvi:-] n dialog(ue)
'**Zwielicht** n (-[e]s; no pl) twilight
'**Zwiespalt** m (-[e]s; -e) conflict
'**zwiespältig** [-ʃpɛltɪç] adj conflicting
'**Zwietracht** f (-; no pl) discord
Zwilling ['tsvilɪŋ] m (-s; -e) twin; pl ASTR Gemini; **er ist (ein) ~** he's a(n) Gemini
'**Zwillings|bruder** m twin brother; **~schwester** f twin sister
Zwinge ['tsviŋə] f (-; -n) TECH clamp
zwingen ['tsviŋən] v/t (irr, ge-, h) force, compel; **~d** adj compelling; cogent
Zwinger ['tsviŋɐ] m (-s; -) kennels
zwinkern ['tsviŋkɐn] v/i (ge-, h) wink, blink
Zwirn [tsvɪrn] m (-[e]s; -e) thread, yarn, twist
zwischen ['tsviʃən] prp (dat and acc) between; among
'**zwischen'durch** F adv in between
'**Zwischen|ergebnis** n intermediate result; **~fall** m incident; **~händler** m ECON middleman; **~landung** f AVIAT stopover; **ohne ~** nonstop
'**Zwischen|raum** m space, interval; **~ruf** m (loud) interruption; pl heckling; **~rufer** m (-s; -) heckler; **~spiel** n interlude; **~stati,on** f stop(over); **~machen (in** dat) stop over (in); **~wand** f partition (wall); **~zeit** f: **in der ~** in the meantime, meanwhile
Zwist [tsvist] m (-[e]s; -e) discord

Z

zwitschern ['tsvɪtʃɐn] v/i (ge-, h) twitter, chirp

Zwitter ['tsvɪtɐ] m (-s; -) BIOL hermaphrodite

zwölf [tsvœlf] adj twelve; **um ~ (Uhr)** at twelve (o'clock); at noon; at midnight

'**zwölfte** adj twelfth

Zyankali [tsyaːnˈkaːli] n (-s; no pl) CHEM potassium cyanide

Zyklus ['tsyːklʊs] m (-; -klen) cycle; series, course

Zylinder [tsiˈlɪndɐ] m (-s; -) top hat; MATH, TECH cylinder; **zylindrisch** [tsiˈlɪndrɪʃ] adj cylindrical

Zyniker ['tsyːnikɐ] m (-s; -) cynic

zynisch ['tsyːnɪʃ] adj cynical

Zynismus [tsyˈnɪsmʊs] m (-; -men) cynicism

Zypresse [tsyˈprɛsə] f (-; -n) BOT cypress

Zyste ['tsʏstə] f (-; -n) MED cyst

z.Z(t). ABBR of **zur Zeit** at the moment, at present

PART II

ENGLISH-GERMAN
DICTIONARY

A

A, a A, a *n*; *from A to Z* von A bis Z
A grade Eins
a *before vowel:* **an** *indef art* ein(e); per, pro, je; *not a(n)* kein(e); *all of a size* alle gleich groß; *100 dollars a year* 100 Dollar im Jahr; *twice a week* zweimal die *or* in der Woche
a·back: *taken ~* überrascht, verblüfft; bestürzt
a·ban·don aufgeben, preisgeben; verlassen; überlassen; *be found ~ed* MOT *etc* verlassen aufgefunden werden
a·base erniedrigen, demütigen
a·base·ment Erniedrigung *f*, Demütigung *f*
a·bashed verlegen
ab·at·toir *Br* Schlachthof *m*
ab·bess REL Äbtissin *f*
ab·bey REL Kloster *n*; Abtei *f*
ab·bot REL Abt *m*
ab·bre·vi·ate (ab)kürzen
ab·bre·vi·a·tion Abkürzung *f*, Kurzform *f*
ABC Abc *n*, Alphabet *n*
ab·di·cate *Amt, Recht etc* aufgeben, verzichten auf (*acc*); *~ (from) the throne* abdanken
ab·di·ca·tion Verzicht *m*; Abdankung *f*
ab·do·men ANAT Unterleib *m*
ab·dom·i·nal ANAT Unterleibs...
ab·duct JUR *j-n* entführen
ab·er·ra·tion Verirrung *f*
a·bet → *aid* 1
ab·hor verabscheuen
ab·hor·rence Abscheu *m* (*of* vor *dat*)
ab·hor·rent zuwider (*to dat*); abstoßend
a·bide *v/i: ~ by the law etc* sich an das Gesetz *etc* halten; *v/t: he can't ~ him* er kann ihn nicht ausstehen
a·bil·i·ty Fähigkeit *f*
ab·ject verächtlich, erbärmlich; *in ~ poverty* in äußerster Armut
ab·jure abschwören; entsagen (*dat*)
a·blaze in Flammen; *fig* glänzend, funkelnd (*with* vor *dat*)
a·ble fähig; geschickt; *be ~ to inf* in der Lage sein zu *inf*, können
a·ble-bod·ied kräftig
ab·nor·mal abnorm, ungewöhnlich; anomal

a·board an Bord; *all ~!* MAR alle Mann *or* Reisenden an Bord!; RAIL alles einsteigen!; *~ a bus* in e-m Bus; *go ~ a train* in e-n Zug einsteigen
a·bode *a. place of ~* Aufenthaltsort *m*, Wohnsitz *m*; *of or with no fixed ~* ohne festen Wohnsitz
a·bol·ish abschaffen, aufheben
ab·o·li·tion Abschaffung *f*, Aufhebung *f*
A-bomb → *atom(ic) bomb*
a·bom·i·na·ble abscheulich, scheußlich; *a·bom·i·nate* verabscheuen; *a·bom·i·na·tion* Abscheu *m*
ab·o·rig·i·nal 1. eingeboren, Ur...; **2.** Ureinwohner *m*
ab·o·rig·i·ne Ureinwohner *m*
a·bort *v/t* abbrechen (*a.* MED *Schwangerschaft*); MED *Kind* abtreiben; *v/i* fehlschlagen, scheitern; MED e-e Fehlgeburt haben; *a·bor·tion* MED Fehlgeburt *f*; Schwangerschaftsabbruch *m*, Abtreibung *f*; *have an ~* abtreiben (lassen)
a·bor·tive misslungen, erfolglos
a·bound reichlich vorhanden sein; Überfluss haben, reich sein (*in* an *dat*); voll sein (*with* von)
a·bout 1. *prp* um (... herum); bei (*dat*); (irgendwo) herum in (*dat*); um, gegen, etwa; im Begriff, dabei; über (*acc*); *I had no money ~ me* ich hatte kein Geld bei mir; **2.** *adv* herum, umher; in der Nähe; etwa, ungefähr
a·bove 1. *prp* über (*dat or acc*), oberhalb (*gen*); *fig* über, erhaben über (*acc*); *~ all* vor allem; **2.** *adv* oben; darüber; **3.** *adj* obig, oben erwähnt
a·breast nebeneinander; *keep ~ of, be ~ of fig* Schritt halten mit
a·bridge (ab-, ver)kürzen
a·bridge(e)·ment Kürzung *f*; Kurzfassung *f*
a·broad im *or* ins Ausland; überall(hin); *the news soon spread ~* die Nachricht verbreitete sich rasch
a·brupt abrupt; jäh; schroff
ab·scess MED Abszess *m*
ab·sence Abwesenheit *f*; Mangel *m*
ab·sent 1. abwesend; fehlend; nicht vor-

handen; **be ~** fehlen (*from school* in der Schule; *from work* am Arbeitsplatz); **2. ~ o.s. from** fernbleiben (*dat*) or von; **ab·sent-mind·ed** zerstreut, geistesabwesend

ab·so·lute absolut; unumschränkt; vollkommen; unbedingt; CHEM rein, unvermischt

ab·so·lu·tion REL Absolution *f*

ab·solve freisprechen, lossprechen

ab·sorb absorbieren, aufsaugen, einsaugen; *fig* ganz in Anspruch nehmen

ab·sorb·ing *fig* fesselnd, packend

ab·stain sich enthalten (*from gen*)

ab·ste·mi·ous enthaltsam; mäßig

ab·sten·tion Enthaltung *f*; POL Stimmenthaltung *f*

ab·sti·nence Abstinenz *f*, Enthaltsamkeit *f*

ab·sti·nent abstinent, enthaltsam

ab·stract 1. abstrakt; **2.** *das* Abstrakte; Auszug *m*; **3.** abstrahieren; entwenden

ab·stract·ed *fig* zerstreut

ab·strac·tion Abstraktion *f*; abstrakter Begriff

ab·surd absurd; lächerlich

a·bun·dance Überfluss *m*; Fülle *f*; Überschwang *m*

a·bun·dant reich, reichlich

a·buse 1. Missbrauch *m*; Beschimpfung (en *pl*) *f*; **~ of drugs** Drogenmissbrauch *m*; **~ of power** Machtmissbrauch *m*; **2.** missbrauchen; beschimpfen; **a·bu·sive** beleidigend, Schimpf...

a·but (an)grenzen (**on** an *acc*)

a·byss Abgrund *m* (*a. fig*)

ac·a·dem·ic 1. Hochschullehrer *m*; **2.** akademisch; **a·cad·e·mi·cian** Akademiemitglied *n*; **a·cad·e·my** Akademie *f*; **~ of music** Musikhochschule *f*

ac·cede: ~ zustimmen (*dat*); Amt antreten; *Thron* besteigen

ac·cel·e·rate *v/t* beschleunigen; *v/i* schneller werden, MOT *a.* beschleunigen, Gas geben

ac·cel·e·ra·tion Beschleunigung *f*

ac·cel·e·ra·tor MOT Gaspedal *n*

ac·cent 1. Akzent *m* (*a.* LING); **2.** → **ac·cen·tu·ate** akzentuieren, betonen

ac·cept annehmen; akzeptieren; hinnehmen; **ac·cept·a·ble** annehmbar; *person:* tragbar; **ac·cept·ance** Annahme *f*; Aufnahme *f*

ac·cess Zugang *m* (**to** zu); *fig* Zutritt *m*

(**to** bei, zu); EDP Zugriff *m* (**to** auf *acc*); **easy of ~** zugänglich (*person*)

ac·ces·sa·ry → accessory

ac·cess code EDP Zugriffskode *m*

ac·ces·si·ble (leicht) zugänglich

ac·ces·sion (Neu)Anschaffung *f* (**to** für); Zustimmung *f* (**to** zu); Antritt *m* (*e-s Amtes*); **~ to power** Machtübernahme *f*; **~ to the throne** Thronbesteigung *f*

ac·ces·so·ry JUR Komplize *m*, Komplizin *f*, Mitschuldige *m*, *f*; *mst pl* Zubehör *n*, *fashion: a.* Accessoires *pl*, TECH *a.* Zubehörteile *pl*

ac·cess| road Zufahrts- or Zubringerstraße *f*; **~ time** EDP Zugriffszeit *f*

ac·ci·dent Unfall *m*, Unglück *n*, Unglücksfall *m*; NUCL Störfall *m*; **by ~** zufällig

ac·ci·den·tal zufällig; versehentlich

ac·claim feiern (**as** als)

ac·cla·ma·tion lauter Beifall; Lob *n*

ac·cli·ma·tize (sich) akklimatisieren or eingewöhnen

ac·com·mo·date unterbringen; Platz haben für, fassen; anpassen (**to** *dat* or an *acc*)

ac·com·mo·da·tion Unterkunft *f*, Unterbringung *f*; **~ of·fice** Zimmervermittlung *f*

ac·com·pa·ni·ment MUS Begleitung *f*

ac·com·pa·ny begleiten (*a.* MUS)

ac·com·plice JUR Komplize *m*, Komplizin *f*, Helfershelfer(in)

ac·com·plish erreichen; leisten

ac·com·plished fähig, tüchtig

ac·com·plish·ment Fähigkeit *f*, Talent *n*

ac·cord 1. Übereinstimmung *f*; **of one's own ~** von selbst; **with one ~** einstimmig; **2.** übereinstimmen (**with** mit)

ac·cor·dance: in ~ with entsprechend (*dat*)

ac·cord·ing: ~ to laut; nach

ac·cord·ing·ly folglich, also; (dem)entsprechend

ac·cost *j-n* ansprechen

ac·count 1. ECON Rechnung *f*, Berechnung *f*; Konto *n*; Rechenschaft *f*; Bericht *m*; **by all ~s** nach allem, was man so hört; **of no ~** ohne Bedeutung; **on no ~** auf keinen Fall; **on ~ of** wegen; **take into ~**, **take ~ of** in Betracht or Erwägung ziehen, berücksichtigen;

turn s.th. to (*good*) ~ et. (gut) ausnutzen; **keep ~s** die Bücher führen; **call to** ~ zur Rechenschaft ziehen; **give (an)** ~ **of** Rechenschaft ablegen über (*acc*); **give an** ~ **of** Bericht erstatten über (*acc*); **2.** *v/i*: ~ **for** Rechenschaft über et. ablegen; (sich) erklären
ac·count·a·ble verantwortlich; erklärlich
ac·coun·tant ECON Buchhalter(in)
ac·count·ing ECON Buchführung *f*
acct ABBR *of* **account** Konto *n*
ac·cu·mu·late (sich) (an)häufen *or* ansammeln
ac·cu·mu·la·tion Ansammlung *f*
ac·cu·mu·la·tor ELECTR Akkumulator *m*
ac·cu·ra·cy Genauigkeit *f*
ac·cu·rate genau
ac·cu·sa·tion Anklage *f*; Anschuldigung *f*, Beschuldigung *f*
ac·cu·sa·tive *a.* ~ **case** LING Akkusativ *m*
ac·cuse JUR anklagen; beschuldigen (*of* gen); **the ~d** der *or* die Angeklagte, die Angeklagten *pl*
ac·cus·er JUR Ankläger(in)
ac·cus·ing anklagend, vorwurfsvoll
ac·cus·tom gewöhnen (**to** an *acc*)
ac·cus·tomed gewohnt, üblich; gewöhnt (**to** an *acc*, zu *inf*)
ace Ass *n* (*a*. *fig*); **have an** ~ **in the hole** (*Br* **up one's sleeve**) *fig* (noch) e-n Trumpf in der Hand haben; **within an** ~ um ein Haar
ache 1. schmerzen, wehtun; **2.** *anhaltender* Schmerz
a·chieve zustande bringen; Ziel erreichen; **a·chieve·ment** Zustandebringen *n*, Leistung *f*, Ausführung *f*
ac·id 1. sauer; *fig* beißend, bissig; **2.** CHEM Säure *f*; **a·cid·i·ty** Säure *f*
ac·id rain saurer Regen
ac·knowl·edge anerkennen; zugeben; *Empfang* bestätigen
ac·knowl·edg(e)·ment Anerkennung *f*; (*Empfangs*)Bestätigung *f*; Eingeständnis *n*
a·corn BOT Eichel *f*
a·cous·tics Akustik *f*
ac·quaint bekannt machen; ~ **s.o. with s.th.** j-m et. mitteilen; **be ~ed with** kennen; **ac·quaint·ance** Bekanntschaft *f*; Bekannte *m*, *f*

ac·quire erwerben; sich aneignen
ac·qui·si·tion Erwerb *m*; Anschaffung *f*, Errungenschaft *f*
ac·quit JUR freisprechen (*of* von); ~ **o.s. well** s-e Sache gut machen
ac·quit·tal JUR Freispruch *m*
a·cre Acre *m* (*4047 qm*)
ac·rid scharf, beißend
ac·ro·bat Akrobat(in)
ac·ro·bat·ic akrobatisch
a·cross 1. *adv* hinüber, herüber; (quer) durch; drüben, auf der anderen Seite; über Kreuz; **2.** *prp* (quer) über (*acc*); (quer) durch; auf der anderen Seite von (*or gen*), jenseits (*gen*); über (*dat*); **come** ~, **run** ~ *fig* stoßen auf (*acc*)
act 1. *v/i* handeln; sich verhalten *or* benehmen; (ein)wirken; funktionieren; (Theater) spielen; *v/t* THEA spielen (*a. fig*), *Stück* aufführen; ~ **as** fungieren als; **2.** Handlung *f*, Tat *f*; JUR Gesetz *n*; THEA Akt *m*; **act·ing** THEA Spiel(en) *n*
ac·tion Handlung *f* (*a*. THEA), Tat *f*; *film etc*: Action *f*; Funktionieren *n*; (Ein-)Wirkung *f*; JUR Klage *f*, Prozess *m*; MIL Gefecht *n*, Einsatz *m*; **take** ~ handeln
ac·tive aktiv; tätig, rührig; lebhaft (*a*. ECON), rege; wirksam
ac·tiv·ist *esp* POL Aktivist(in)
ac·tiv·i·ty Tätigkeit *f*; Aktivität *f*; Betriebsamkeit *f*; *esp* ECON Lebhaftigkeit *f*; ~ **va·ca·tion** Aktivurlaub *m*
ac·tor Schauspieler *m*
ac·tress Schauspielerin *f*
ac·tu·al wirklich, tatsächlich, eigentlich
ac·u·men Scharfsinn *m*
ac·u·punc·ture MED Akupunktur *f*
a·cute akut (*shortage, pain etc*); brennend (*problem etc*); scharf (*hearing etc*); scharfsinnig; MATH spitz (*angle*)
ad F → **advertisement**
ad·a·mant unerbittlich
a·dapt anpassen (**to** *dat or* an *acc*); *Text* bearbeiten (**from** nach); TECH umstellen (**to** auf *acc*); umbauen (**to** für)
a·dapt·a·ble anpassungsfähig
ad·ap·ta·tion Anpassung *f*; Bearbeitung *f*
a·dapt·er, **a·dapt·or** ELECTR Adapter *m*
add *v/t* hinzufügen; ~ **up** zusammenzählen, addieren; *v/i*: ~ **to** vermehren, beitragen zu, hinzukommen zu; ~ **up**

MATH ergeben; F sich summieren; *fig* e-n Sinn ergeben; **~ up to** *fig* hinauslaufen auf (*acc*)
ad·der zo Natter *f*
ad·dict Süchtige *m, f; alcohol (drug)* ~ Alkoholsüchtige (Drogen- *or* Rauschgiftsüchtige); (*Fußball- etc*) Fanatiker (in), (*Film- etc*)Narr *m*
ad·dic·ted süchtig, abhängig (**to** von); **be ~ to alcohol (drugs)** alkoholsüchtig (drogenabhängig *or* -süchtig) sein
ad·dic·tion Sucht *f*, Süchtigkeit *f*
ad·di·tion Hinzufügen *n*; Zusatz *m*; Zuwachs *m*; ARCH Anbau *m*; MATH Addition *f*; **in ~** außerdem; **in ~ to** außer (*dat*)
ad·di·tion·al zusätzlich
ad·dress **1.** *Worte* richten (**to** an *acc*), *j-n* anreden *or* ansprechen; **2.** Adresse *f*, Anschrift *f*; Rede *f*, Ansprache *f*
ad·dress·ee Empfänger(in)
ad·ept erfahren, geschickt (**at, in** in *dat*)
ad·e·qua·cy Angemessenheit *f*
ad·e·quate Angemessen
ad·here (**to**) kleben, haften (an *dat*); *fig* festhalten (an *dat*); **ad·her·ence** Anhaften *n*; *fig* Festhalten *n*; **ad·her·ent** Anhänger(in)
ad·he·sive **1.** klebend; **2.** Klebstoff *m*; ~ **plas·ter** MED Heftpflaster *n*; ~ **tape** Klebeband *n*, Klebstreifen *m*; MED Heftpflaster *n*
ad·ja·cent angrenzend, anstoßend (**to** an *acc*); benachbart
ad·jec·tive LING Adjektiv *n*, Eigenschaftswort *n*
ad·join (an)grenzen an (*acc*)
ad·journ *v/t* verschieben, (*v/i* sich) vertagen; **ad·journ·ment** Vertagung *f*, Verschiebung *f*
ad·just anpassen; TECH einstellen, regulieren; **ad·just·a·ble** TECH verstellbar, regulierbar; **ad·just·ment** Anpassung *f*; TECH Einstellung *f*
ad·lib aus dem Stegreif (sprechen *or* spielen)
ad·min·is·ter verwalten; PHARM geben, verabreichen; ~ **justice** Recht sprechen
ad·min·is·tra·tion Verwaltung *f*; POL Regierung *f*; Amtsperiode *f*
ad·min·is·tra·tive Verwaltungs...
ad·min·is·tra·tor Verwaltungsbeamte *m*

ad·mi·ra·ble bewundernswert; großartig
ad·mi·ral MAR Admiral *m*
ad·mi·ra·tion Bewunderung *f*
ad·mire bewundern; verehren
ad·mir·er Verehrer *m*
ad·mis·si·ble zulässig
ad·mis·sion Eintritt *m*, Zutritt *m*; Aufnahme *f*; Eintrittsgeld *n*; Eingeständnis *n*; ~ **free** Eintritt frei
ad·mit *v/t* zugeben; (her)einlassen (**to**, **into** in *acc*), eintreten lassen; zulassen (**to** zu); **ad·mit·tance** Einlass *m*, Eintritt *m*, Zutritt *m*; **no ~** Zutritt verboten
ad·mon·ish ermahnen; warnen (**of**, **against** vor *dat*)
a·do Getue *n*, Lärm *m*; **without more or further** ~ ohne weitere Umstände
ad·o·les·cence Jugend *f*, Adoleszenz *f*
ad·o·les·cent **1.** jugendlich, heranwachsend; **2.** Jugendliche *m, f*
a·dopt adoptieren; übernehmen; **~ed child** Adoptivkind *n*
a·dop·tion Adoption *f*
a·dop·tive parents Adoptiveltern *pl*
a·dor·a·ble F bezaubernd, entzückend
ad·o·ra·tion Anbetung *f*, Verehrung *f*
a·dore anbeten, verehren
a·dorn schmücken, zieren
a·dorn·ment Schmuck *m*, Verzierung *f*
a·droit geschickt
a·dult **1.** erwachsen; **2.** Erwachsene *m, f*; **~s only** nur für Erwachsene!; ~ **ed·uca·tion** Erwachsenenbildung *f*
a·dul·ter·ate verfälschen, *Wein* panschen
a·dul·ter·er Ehebrecher *m*
a·dul·ter·ess Ehebrecherin *f*
a·dul·ter·ous ehebrecherisch
a·dul·ter·y Ehebruch *m*
ad·vance **1.** *v/i* vordringen, vorrücken (*a. time*); Fortschritte machen; *v/t* vorrücken; *Argument etc* vorverlegen; *Argument etc* vorbringen; *Geld* vorstrecken, F vorschießen; (be)fördern; *Preis* erhöhen; *Wachstum etc* beschleunigen; **2.** Vorrücken *n*, Vorstoß *m* (*a. fig*); Fortschritt *m*; ECON Vorschuss *m*; Erhöhung *f*; **in ~** im Voraus
ad·vanced fortgeschritten; ~ **for one's years** weit *or* reif für sein Alter
ad·vance·ment Fortschritt *m*, Verbesserung *f*

ad·van·tage Vorteil *m* (*a.* SPORT); **~ rule** SPORT Vorteilsregel *f*; **take ~ of** ausnutzen

ad·van·ta·geous vorteilhaft

ad·ven·ture Abenteuer *n*, Wagnis *n*

ad·ven·tur·er Abenteurer *m*

ad·ven·tur·ess Abenteu(r)erin *f*

ad·ven·tur·ous abenteuerlich; verwegen, kühn

ad·verb LING Adverb *n*, Umstandswort *n*

ad·ver·sa·ry Gegner(in)

ad·ver·tise ankündigen, bekannt machen; inserieren; Reklame machen (für)

ad·ver·tise·ment Anzeige *f*, Inserat *n*

ad·ver·tis·ing 1. Reklame *f*, Werbung *f*; **2.** Reklame..., Werbe...; **~ a·gen·cy** Werbeagentur *f*; **~ cam·paign** Werbefeldzug *m*

ad·vice Rat(schlag) *m*; ECON Benachrichtigung *f*; **take medical ~** e-n Arzt zu Rate ziehen; **take my ~** hör auf mich

ad·vice| cen·ter, *Br* **~ cen·tre** Beratungsstelle *f*

ad·vis·a·ble ratsam

ad·vise *v/t* j-*n* beraten; j-*m* raten; *esp* ECON benachrichtigen, avisieren; *v/i* sich beraten

ad·vis·er *esp Br*, **ad·vis·or** Berater *m*

ad·vi·so·ry beratend

ad·vo·cate 1. befürworten, verfechten; **2.** Befürworter(in), Verfechter(in)

aer·i·al 1. luftig; Luft...; **2.** Antenne *f*

aer·i·al pho·to·graph, **~ view** Luftaufnahme *f*, Luftbild *n*

aero... Aero..., Luft...

aer·o·bics SPORT Aerobic *n*

aer·o·drome *esp Br* Flugplatz *m*

aer·o·dy·nam·ic aerodynamisch

aer·o·dy·nam·ics Aerodynamik *f*

aer·o·nau·tics Luftfahrt *f*

aer·o·plane *Br* Flugzeug *n*

aer·o·sol Spraydose *f*, Sprühdose *f*

aes·thet·ic *etc* → **esthetic** *etc*

a·far: from ~ von weit her

af·fair Angelegenheit *f*, Sache *f*; F Ding *n*, Sache *f*; Affäre *f*

af·fect beeinflussen; MED angreifen, befallen; bewegen, rühren; e-e Vorliebe haben für; vortäuschen

af·fec·tion Liebe *f*, Zuneigung *f*

af·fec·tion·ate liebevoll, herzlich

af·fil·i·ate *als Mitglied* aufnehmen; angliedern

af·fin·i·ty Affinität *f*; (geistige) Verwandtschaft *f*; Neigung *f* (**for, to** zu)

af·firm versichern; beteuern; bestätigen; **af·fir·ma·tion** Versicherung *f*, Beteuerung *f*; Bestätigung *f*

af·fir·ma·tive 1. bejahend; **2. answer in the ~** bejahen

af·fix (**to**) anheften, ankleben (an *acc*), befestigen (an *dat*); beifügen, hinzufügen (*dat*)

af·flict heimsuchen, plagen; **~ed with** geplagt von, leidend an (*dat*)

af·flic·tion Gebrechen *n*; Elend *n*, Not *f*

af·flu·ence Überfluss *m*; Wohlstand *m*

af·flu·ent reich, reichlich; **~ so·ci·e·ty** Wohlstandsgesellschaft *f*

af·ford sich leisten; gewähren, bieten; **I can ~ it** ich kann es mir leisten

af·front 1. beleidigen; **2.** Beleidigung *f*

a·float MAR flott, schwimmend; **set ~** MAR flottmachen; *fig Gerücht etc* in Umlauf setzen

a·fraid: be ~ of sich fürchten *or* Angst haben vor (*dat*); **I'm ~ she won't come** ich fürchte, sie wird nicht kommen; **I'm ~ I must go now** leider muss ich jetzt gehen

a·fresh von neuem

Af·ri·ca Afrika *n*; **Af·ri·can 1.** afrikanisch; **2.** Afrikaner(in)

af·ter 1. *adv* hinterher, nachher, danach; **2.** *prp* nach; hinter (*dat*) (... her); **~ all** schließlich (doch); **3.** *cj* nachdem; **4.** *adj* später; Nach...; **~ ef·fect** MED Nachwirkung *f* (*a. fig*)

af·ter·glow Abendrot *n*

af·ter·math Nachwirkungen *pl*, Folgen *pl*

af·ter·noon Nachmittag *m*; **this ~** heute Nachmittag; **good ~!** guten Tag!

af·ter·taste Nachgeschmack *m*

af·ter·thought nachträglicher Einfall

af·ter·ward, *Br* **af·ter·wards** nachher, später

a·gain wieder; wiederum; ferner; **~ and ~, time and ~** immer wieder; **as much ~** noch einmal so viel

a·gainst gegen; an (*dat or acc*); **as ~** verglichen mit; **he was ~ it** er war dagegen

age 1. (Lebens)Alter *n*; Zeit(alter *n*) *f*; Menschenalter *n*; (**old**) ~ (hohes) Alter; **at the ~ of** im Alter von; *s.o.* **your**

~ in deinem or Ihrem Alter; (*come*) *of* ~ mündig or volljährig (werden); *be over* ~ die Altersgrenze überschritten haben; *under* ~ minderjährig; unmündig; *wait for* ~*s* F e-e Ewigkeit warten; **2.** alt werden or machen

a·ged¹ alt, betagt

aged²: ~ *twenty* 20 Jahre alt

age·less zeitlos; ewig jung

a·gen·cy Agentur *f*; Geschäftsstelle *f*, Büro *n*

a·gen·da Tagesordnung *f*

a·gent Agent *m* (a. POL), Vertreter *m*; (*Grundstücks- etc*)Makler *m*; CHEM Wirkstoff *m*, Mittel *n*

ag·glom·er·ate (sich) zusammenballen; (sich) (an)häufen

ag·gra·vate erschweren, verschlimmern; F ärgern

ag·gre·gate **1.** sich belaufen auf (*acc*); **2.** gesamt; **3.** Gesamtmenge *f*, Summe *f*; TECH Aggregat *n*

ag·gres·sion Angriff *m*

ag·gres·sive aggressiv, Angriffs...; *fig* energisch

ag·gres·sor Angreifer *m*

ag·grieved verletzt, gekränkt

a·ghast entgeistert, entsetzt

a·gile flink, behend

a·gil·i·ty Flinkheit *f*, Behendigkeit *f*

ag·i·tate *v/t fig* aufregen, aufwühlen; *Flüssigkeit* schütteln; *v/i* POL agitieren, hetzen (*against* gegen)

ag·i·ta·tion Aufregung *f*; POL Agitation *f*

ag·i·ta·tor POL Agitator *m*

a·glow: *be* ~ strahlen (*with* vor)

a·go: *a year* ~ vor e-m Jahr

ag·o·ny Qual *f*; Todeskampf *m*

a·gree *v/i* übereinstimmen; sich vertragen; einig werden, sich einigen (*on* über *acc*); übereinkommen; ~ *to* zustimmen (*dat*), einverstanden sein mit

a·gree·a·ble (*to*) angenehm (für); übereinstimmend (mit)

a·gree·ment Übereinstimmung *f*; Vereinbarung *f*, Abkommen *n*

ag·ri·cul·tur·al landwirtschaftlich

ag·ri·cul·ture Landwirtschaft *f*

a·ground MAR gestrandet; *run* ~ stranden, auf Grund laufen

a·head vorwärts, voraus; vorn; *go* ~*!* nur zu!, mach nur!; *straight* ~ geradeaus

aid **1.** unterstützen, *j-m* helfen (*in* bei); fördern; *he was accused of* ~*ing and abetting* JUR er wurde wegen Beihilfe angeklagt; **2.** Hilfe *f*, Unterstützung *f*

AIDS, Aids MED Aids *n*; *person with* ~ Aids-Kranke *m, f*

ail kränklich sein; **ail·ment** Leiden *n*

aim **1.** *v/i* zielen (*at* auf *acc*, nach); ~ *at fig* beabsichtigen; *be* ~*ing to do s.th.* vorhaben, et. zu tun; *v/t*: ~ *at* Waffe etc richten auf *or* gegen (*acc*); **2.** Ziel *n* (a. *fig*); Absicht *f*; *take* ~ *at* zielen auf (*acc*) *or* nach; **aim·less** ziellos

air¹ **1.** Luft *f*; Luftzug *m*; Miene *f*, Aussehen *n*; *by* ~ auf dem Luftwege; *in the open* ~ im Freien; *on the* ~ im Rundfunk *or* Fernsehen; *be on the* ~ senden; in Betrieb sein; *go off the* ~ die Sendung beenden (*person*); sein Programm beenden (*station*); *give o.s.* ~*s, put on* ~*s* vornehm tun; **2.** (aus)lüften; *fig* an die Öffentlichkeit bringen; erörtern

air² MUS Arie *f*, Weise *f*, Melodie *f*

air·bag MOT Airbag *m*

air·base MIL Luftstützpunkt *m*

air·bed Luftmatratze *f*

air·borne AVIAT in der Luft; MIL Luftlande...

air·brake TECH Druckluftbremse *f*

air·bus AVIAT Airbus *m*, Großraumflugzeug *n*

air-con·di·tioned mit Klimaanlage

air-con·di·tion·ing Klimaanlage *f*

air·craft car·ri·er MAR, MIL Flugzeugträger *m*

air·field Flugplatz *m*

air force MIL Luftwaffe *f*

air host·ess AVIAT Stewardess *f*

air jack·et Schwimmweste *f*

air·lift AVIAT Luftbrücke *f*

air·line AVIAT Fluggesellschaft *f*

air·lin·er AVIAT Verkehrsflugzeug *n*

air·mail Luftpost *f*; *by* ~ mit Luftpost

air·man MIL Flieger *m*

air·plane Flugzeug *n*

air·pock·et AVIAT Luftloch *n*

air pol·lu·tion Luftverschmutzung *f*

air·port Flughafen *m*

air raid MIL Luftangriff *m*

air-raid| pre·cau·tions MIL Luftschutz *m*; ~ shel·ter MIL Luftschutzraum *m*

air route AVIAT Flugroute *f*

air·sick luftkrank
air·space Luftraum *m*
air·strip (behelfsmäßige) Start- und Landebahn
air ter·mi·nal Flughafenabfertigungsgebäude *n*
air·tight luftdicht
air time Sendezeit *f*
air traf·fic AVIAT Flugverkehr *m*
air-traf·fic| con·trol AVIAT Flugsicherung *f*; **~ con·trol·ler** AVIAT Fluglotse *m*
air·way AVIAT Fluggesellschaft *f*
air·wor·thy AVIAT flugtüchtig
air·y luftig
aisle ARCH Seitenschiff *n*; Gang *m*
a·jar halb offen, angelehnt
a·kin verwandt (**to** mit)
a·lac·ri·ty Bereitwilligkeit *f*
a·larm 1. Alarm(zeichen *n*) *m*; Wecker *m*; Angst *f*; **2.** alarmieren; beunruhigen; **~ clock** Wecker *m*
al·bum Album *n* (*a. record*)
al·bu·mi·nous BIOL eiweißhaltig
al·co·hol Alkohol *m*; **al·co·hol·ic 1.** alkoholisch; **2.** Alkoholiker(in)
al·co·hol·ism Alkoholismus *m*, Trunksucht *f*
a·lert 1. wachsam; munter; **2.** Alarm *m*; Alarmbereitschaft *f*; **on the ~** auf der Hut; in Alarmbereitschaft; **3.** warnen (**to** vor *dat*), alarmieren
al·ga BOT Alge *f*
al·ge·bra MATH Algebra *f*
al·i·bi JUR Alibi *n*
a·li·en 1. ausländisch; fremd; **2.** Ausländer(in); Außerirdische *m*, *f*
a·li·en·ate veräußern; entfremden; *esp art*: verfremden; **a·li·en·a·tion** Entfremdung *f*; *esp art*: Verfremdung *f*
a·light 1. in Flammen; **2.** aussteigen; absteigen, absitzen; ZO sich niederlassen; AVIAT landen
a·lign (sich) ausrichten (**with** nach)
a·like 1. *adj* gleich; **2.** *adv* gleich, ebenso
al·i·men·ta·ry nahrhaft; **~ ca·nal** ANAT Verdauungskanal *m*
al·i·mo·ny JUR Unterhalt *m*
a·live lebendig; (noch) am Leben; lebhaft; **~ and kicking** gesund und munter; **be ~ with** wimmeln von
all 1. *adj* all; ganz; jede(r, -s); **2.** *pron* alles; alle *pl*; **3.** *adv* ganz, völlig; **~ at once** auf einmal; **the ~ better** desto besser; **~ but** beinahe, fast; **~ in** F fertig,

ganz erledigt; **~ right** in Ordnung; **for ~ that** dessen ungeachtet, trotzdem; **for ~ I know** soviel ich weiß; **at ~** überhaupt; **not at ~** überhaupt nicht; **the score was two ~** das Spiel stand zwei zu zwei
all-A·mer·i·can typisch amerikanisch; die ganzen USA vertretend
al·lay beruhigen; lindern
al·le·ga·tion *unerwiesene* Behauptung *f*
al·lege behaupten
al·leged angeblich, vermeintlich
al·le·giance Treue *f*
al·ler·gic MED allergisch (**to** gegen)
al·ler·gy MED Allergie *f*
al·le·vi·ate mildern, lindern
al·ley (*enge or* schmale) Gasse; Garten-, Parkweg *m*; *bowling*: Bahn *f*
al·li·ance Bündnis *n*
al·li·ga·tor ZO Alligator *m*
al·lo·cate zuteilen, anweisen
al·lo·ca·tion Zuteilung *f*
al·lot zuteilen, an-, zuweisen
al·lot·ment Zuteilung *f*; Parzelle *f*
al·low erlauben, bewilligen, gewähren; zugeben; ab-, anrechnen, vergüten; **~ for** einplanen, berücksichtigen (*acc*)
al·low·a·ble erlaubt, zulässig
al·low·ance Erlaubnis *f*; Bewilligung *f*; Taschengeld *n*, Zuschuss *m*; Vergütung *f*; *fig* Nachsicht *f*; **make ~(s) for s.th.** et. berücksichtigen
al·loy TECH **1.** Legierung *f*; **2.** legieren
all-round vielseitig
all-round·er Alleskönner *m*; Allroundsportler *m*, -spieler *m*
al·lude anspielen (**to** auf *acc*)
al·lure locken, an-, verlocken
al·lure·ment Verlockung *f*
al·lu·sion Anspielung *f*
all-wheel drive MOT Allradantrieb *m*
al·ly 1. (sich) vereinigen, verbünden (**to**, **with** mit); **2.** Verbündete *m*, *f*, Bundesgenosse *m*, Bundesgenossin *f*; **the Allies** MIL die Alliierten *pl*
al·might·y allmächtig; **the Almighty** REL der Allmächtige
al·mond BOT Mandel *f*
al·most fast, beinah(e)
alms Almosen *n*
a·loft (hoch) (dr)oben
a·lone allein; **let ~**, **leave ~** in Ruhe lassen, bleiben lassen; **let ~ ...** geschweige denn ...

a·long 1. *adv* weiter, vorwärts; da; dahin; **all ~** die ganze Zeit; **~ with** (zusammen) mit; **come ~** mitkommen, mitgehen; **get ~** vorwärts kommen, weiterkommen; auskommen, sich vertragen (**with s.o.** mit j-m); **take ~** mitnehmen; **2.** *prp* entlang (*dat*), längs (*gen*)

a·long·side Seite an Seite; neben

a·loof abseits; reserviert, zurückhaltend, verschlossen; **a·loof·ness** Reserviertheit *f*; Verschlossenheit *f*

a·loud laut

al·pha·bet Alphabet *n*

al·pine (Hoch)Gebirgs..., alpin

al·read·y bereits, schon

al·right → *all right*

Al·sa·tian *esp Br* ZO Deutscher Schäferhund

al·so auch, ferner

al·tar REL Altar *m*

al·ter ändern, sich (ver)ändern; ab-, umändern; **al·ter·a·tion** Änderung *f* (*to an dat*), Veränderung *f*

al·ter·nate 1. abwechseln (lassen); **2.** abwechselnd; **al·ter·nat·ing cur·rent** ELECTR Wechselstrom *m*

al·ter·na·tion Abwechslung *f*; Wechsel *m*

al·ter·na·tive 1. alternativ, wahlweise; **2.** Alternative *f*, Wahl *f*, Möglichkeit *f*

al·though obwohl, obgleich

al·ti·tude Höhe *f*; **at an ~ of** in e-r Höhe von

al·to·geth·er im Ganzen, insgesamt; ganz (und gar), völlig

al·u·min·i·um *Br*, **a·lu·mi·num** Aluminium *n*

al·ways immer, stets

am, AM *ABBR of before noon* (*Latin ante meridiem*) morgens, vorm., vormittags

a·mal·gam·ate (sich) zusammenschließen, ECON *a.* fusionieren

a·mass anhäufen, aufhäufen

am·a·teur Amateur(in); Dilettant(in); Hobby...

a·maze in Erstaunen setzen, verblüffen; **a·maze·ment** Staunen *n*, Verblüffung *f*; **a·maz·ing** erstaunlich

am·bas·sa·dor POL Botschafter *m* (**to** in *e-m Land*); **am·bas·sa·dress** POL Botschafterin *f* (**to** in *e-m Land*)

am·ber Bernstein *m*

am·bi·gu·i·ty Zwei-, Mehrdeutigkeit *f*

am·big·u·ous zwei-, mehr-, vieldeutig

am·bi·tion Ehrgeiz *m*

am·bi·tious ehrgeizig, strebsam

am·ble 1. Passgang *m*; **2.** im Passgang gehen *or* reiten; schlendern

am·bu·lance Krankenwagen *m*

am·bush 1. Hinterhalt *m*; **be** *or* **lie in ~ for s.o.** j-m auflauern; **2.** auflauern (*dat*); überfallen

a·men *int* REL amen

a·mend verbessern, berichtigen; PARL abändern, ergänzen; **a·mend·ment** Bess(e)rung *f*; Verbesserung *f*; PARL Abänderungsantrag *m*, Ergänzungsantrag *m*; Zusatzartikel *m* zur Verfassung; **a·mends** (Schaden)Ersatz *m*; **make ~** Schadenersatz leisten, es wieder gutmachen; **make ~ to s.o. for s.th.** j-n für et. entschädigen

a·men·i·ty *often pl* Annehmlichkeiten *pl*

A·mer·i·ca Amerika *n*; **A·mer·i·can 1.** amerikanisch; **2.** Amerikaner(in)

A·mer·i·can·is·m LING Amerikanismus *m*

A·mer·i·can·ize (sich) amerikanisieren

A·mer·i·can plan Vollpension *f*

a·mi·a·ble liebenswürdig, freundlich

am·i·ca·ble freundschaftlich, *a.* JUR gütlich

a·mid(st) inmitten (*gen*), (mitten) in *or* unter

a·miss verkehrt, falsch, übel; **take s.th. ~** et. übel nehmen, et. verübeln

am·mo·ni·a CHEM Ammoniak *n*

am·mu·ni·tion Munition *f*

am·nes·ty JUR **1.** Amnestie *f*; **2.** begnadigen

a·mok: run ~ Amok laufen

a·mong(st) (mitten) unter, zwischen

am·o·rous verliebt

a·mount 1. (**to**) sich belaufen (auf *acc*); hinauslaufen (auf *acc*); **2.** Betrag *m*, (Gesamt)Summe *f*; Menge *f*

am·per·age ELECTR Stromstärke *f*

am·ple weit, groß, geräumig; reich, reichlich, beträchtlich

am·pli·fi·ca·tion Erweiterung *f*; PHYS Verstärkung *f*

am·pli·fi·er ELECTR Verstärker *m*

am·pli·fy erweitern; ELECTR verstärken

am·pli·tude Umfang *m*, Weite *f*, Fülle *f*; ELECTR, PHYS Amplitude *f* am·pu·tate MED amputieren

a·muck → **amok**

a·muse (**o.s.** sich) amüsieren, unterhalten, belustigen

a·muse·ment Unterhaltung f, Vergnügen n, Zeitvertreib m; ~ **park** Vergnügungspark m, Freizeitpark m

a·mus·ing amüsant, unterhaltend

an → **a**

an·a·bol·ic ster·oid PHARM Anabolikum n

a·nae·mi·a Br → **anemia**

an·aes·thet·ic Br → **anesthetic**

a·nal ANAT anal, Anal...

a·nal·o·gous analog, entsprechend

a·nal·o·gy Analogie f, Entsprechung f

a·na·lyse esp Br, **an·a·lyze** analysieren; zerlegen

a·nal·y·sis Analyse f

an·arch·y Anarchie f, Gesetzlosigkeit f; Chaos n

a·nat·o·mize MED zerlegen; zergliedern; **a·nat·o·my** MED Anatomie f; Zergliederung f, Analyse f

an·ces·tor Vorfahr m, Ahn m

an·ces·tress Vorfahrin f, Ahnfrau f

an·chor MAR 1. Anker m; **at** ~ vor Anker; 2. verankern

an·chor·man TV Moderator m

an·chor·wom·an TV Moderatorin f

an·cho·vy ZO Anschovis f, Sardelle f

an·cient 1. alt, antik; uralt; 2. **the ~s** HIST die Alten, die antiken Klassiker

and und

an·ec·dote Anekdote f

a·ne·mi·a MED Blutarmut f, Anämie f

an·es·thet·ic MED 1. betäubend, Narkose...; 2. Betäubungsmittel n

an·gel Engel m

an·ger 1. Zorn m, Ärger m (**at** über acc); 2. erzürnen, (ver)ärgern

an·gle[1] Winkel m (a. MATH)

an·gle[2] angeln (**for** nach)

an·gler Angler(in)

An·gli·can REL 1. anglikanisch; 2. Anglikaner(in)

An·glo-Sax·on 1. angelsächsisch; 2. Angelsachse m

an·gry zornig, verärgert, böse (**at, with** über acc, mit dat)

an·guish Qual f, Schmerz m

an·gu·lar winkelig; knochig

an·i·mal 1. Tier n; 2. tierisch; ~ **lov·er**

Tierfreund m; ARCH Tierheim n

an·i·mate beleben; aufmuntern, anregen

an·i·mat·ed lebendig; lebhaft, angeregt; ~ **car·toon** Zeichentrickfilm m

an·i·ma·tion Lebhaftigkeit f; Animation f, Herstellung f von (Zeichen-) Trickfilmen; EDP bewegtes Bild

an·i·mos·i·ty Animosität f, Feindseligkeit f

an·kle ANAT (Fuß)Knöchel m

an·nals Jahrbücher pl

an·nex 1. anhängen; annektieren; 2. Anhang m; ARCH Anbau m

an·ni·ver·sa·ry Jahrestag m; Jahresfeier f

an·no·tate mit Anmerkungen versehen; kommentieren

an·nounce ankündigen; bekannt geben; radio, TV ansagen; durchsagen; **an·nounce·ment** Ankündigung f; Bekanntgabe f; radio, TV Ansage f; Durchsage f; **an·nounc·er** radio, TV Ansager(in), Sprecher(in)

an·noy ärgern; belästigen

an·noy·ance Störung f, Belästigung f; Ärgernis n

an·noy·ing ärgerlich, lästig

an·nu·al 1. jährlich, Jahres...; 2. einjährige Pflanze; Jahrbuch n

an·nu·i·ty (Jahres)Rente f

an·nul für ungültig erklären, annullieren; **an·nul·ment** Annullierung f, Aufhebung f

an·o·dyne MED 1. schmerzstillend; 2. schmerzstillendes Mittel

a·noint REL salben

a·nom·a·lous anomal

a·non·y·mous anonym

an·o·rak Anorak m

an·oth·er ein anderer; ein Zweiter; noch eine(r, -s)

an·swer 1. v/t et. beantworten; j-m antworten; entsprechen (dat); Zweck erfüllen; TECH dem Steuer gehorchen; JUR e-r Vorladung Folge leisten; e-r Beschreibung entsprechen; ~ **the bell** or **door** (die Tür) aufmachen; ~ **the telephone** ans Telefon gehen; v/i antworten (**to** auf acc); entsprechen (**to** dat); ~ **s.o. back** freche Antworten geben; widersprechen; ~ **for** einstehen für; 2. Antwort f (**to** auf acc)

an·swer·a·ble verantwortlich

an·swer·ing ma·chine TEL Anrufbeantworter m

ant ZO Ameise f

an·tag·o·nism Feindschaft f

an·tag·o·nist Gegner(in)

an·tag·o·nize bekämpfen; sich j-n zum Feind machen

Ant·arc·tic antarktisch

an·te·ced·ent vorhergehend, früher (**to** als)

an·te·lope ZO Antilope f

an·ten·na¹ ZO Fühler m

an·ten·na² ELECTR Antenne f

an·te·ri·or vorhergehend, früher (**to** als); vorder

an·them MUS Hymne f

an·ti... Gegen..., gegen ... eingestellt, Anti..., anti...

an·ti·air·craft MIL Fliegerabwehr..., Flugabwehr...

an·ti·bi·ot·ic MED Antibiotikum n

an·ti·bod·y BIOL Antikörper m, Abwehrstoff m

an·tic·i·pate voraussehen, ahnen; erwarten; zuvorkommen; vorwegnehmen; **an·tic·i·pa·tion** (Vor)Ahnung f, Erwartung f; Vorwegnahme f; Vorfreude f; **in ~** im Voraus

an·ti·clock·wise Br entgegen dem Uhrzeigersinn

an·tics Mätzchen pl

an·ti·dote Gegengift n, Gegenmittel n

an·ti·for·eign·er vi·o·lence Gewalt f gegen Ausländer

an·ti·freeze Frostschutzmittel n

an·ti·lock brak·ing sys·tem MOT Antiblockiersystem n (ABBR **ABS**)

an·ti·mis·sile MIL Raketenabwehr...

an·ti·nu·cle·ar ac·tiv·ist Kernkraftgegner(in)

an·tip·a·thy Abneigung f

an·ti·quat·ed veraltet

an·tique 1. antik, alt; **2.** Antiquität f

an·tique| deal·er Antiquitätenhändler (in); **~ shop** esp Br, **~ store** Antiquitätenladen m

an·tiq·ui·ty Altertum n, Vorzeit f

an·ti·sep·tic MED **1.** antiseptisch; **2.** antiseptisches Mittel

ant·lers ZO Geweih n

a·nus ANAT After m

an·vil Amboss m

anx·i·e·ty Angst f, Sorge f

anx·ious besorgt, beunruhigt (**about**

wegen); begierig, gespannt (**for** auf acc); bestrebt (**to do** zu tun)

an·y 1. adj and pron (irgend)eine(r, -s), (irgend)welche(r, -s); (irgend)etwas; jede(r, -s) (beliebige); einige pl, welche pl; **not ~** keiner; **2.** adv irgend(wie), ein wenig, (noch) etwas

an·y·bod·y (irgend)jemand; jeder

an·y·how irgendwie; trotzdem, jedenfalls; wie dem auch sei

an·y·one → anybody

an·y·thing (irgend)etwas; alles; **~ but** alles andere als; **~ else?** sonst noch etwas?; **not ~** nichts

an·y·way → anyhow

an·y·where irgendwo(hin); überall

a·part einzeln, für sich; beiseite; **~ from** abgesehen von

a·part·heid POL Apartheid f, Politik f der Rassentrennung

a·part·ment Wohnung f; **~ build·ing, ~ house** Mietshaus n

ap·a·thet·ic apathisch, teilnahmslos, gleichgültig; **ap·a·thy** Apathie f, Teilnahmslosigkeit f

ape ZO (Menschen)Affe m

ap·er·ture Öffnung f

a·pi·a·ry Bienenhaus n

a·piece für jedes Stück, pro Stück, je

a·pol·o·gize sich entschuldigen (**for** für; **to** bei); **a·pol·o·gy** Entschuldigung f; Rechtfertigung f; **make an ~ (for s.th.)** sich (für et.) entschuldigen

ap·o·plex·y MED Schlaganfall m, F Schlag m

a·pos·tle REL Apostel m

a·pos·tro·phe LING Apostroph m

ap·pal(l) erschrecken, entsetzen

ap·pal·ling erschreckend, entsetzlich

ap·pa·ra·tus Apparat m, Vorrichtung f, Gerät n

ap·par·ent offenbar; anscheinend; scheinbar

ap·pa·ri·tion Erscheinung f, Gespenst n

ap·peal 1. JUR Berufung or Revision einlegen, Einspruch erheben, Beschwerde einlegen; appellieren, sich wenden (**to** an acc); **~ to** gefallen (dat), zusagen (dat), wirken auf (acc); j-n dringend bitten (**for** um); **2.** JUR Revision f, Berufung f; Beschwerde f; Einspruch m; Appell m (**to** an acc), Aufruf m; Wirkung f, Reiz m; Bitte f (**to** an *acc*; (*for* um); ~ *for mercy* JUR Gnadengesuch *n*

ap·peal·ing flehend; ansprechend

ap·pear (er)scheinen; sich zeigen; *öffentlich* auftreten; sich ergeben *or* herausstellen; **ap·pear·ance** Erscheinen *n*; Auftreten *n*; Äußere *n*, Erscheinung *f*, Aussehen *n*; Anschein *m*, äußerer Schein; *keep up* ~*s* den Schein wahren; *to or by all* ~*s* allem Anschein nach

ap·pease besänftigen, beschwichtigen; *Durst etc* stillen; *Neugier* befriedigen

ap·pend an-, hinzu-, beifügen

ap·pend·age Anhang *m*; Anhängsel *n*

ap·pen·di·ci·tis MED Blinddarmentzündung *f*

ap·pen·dix Anhang *m*; *a.* **vermiform** ~ ANAT Wurmfortsatz *m*, Blinddarm *m*

ap·pe·tite (*for*) Appetit *m* (auf *acc*); *fig* Verlangen *n* (nach)

ap·pe·tiz·er Appetithappen *m*, appetitanregendes Gericht *or* Getränk

ap·pe·tiz·ing appetitanregend

ap·plaud applaudieren, Beifall spenden; loben

ap·plause Applaus *m*, Beifall *m*

ap·ple BOT Apfel *m*

ap·ple cart: *upset s.o.'s* ~ F j-s Pläne über den Haufen werfen

ap·ple pie (*warmer*) gedeckter Apfelkuchen; **ap·ple-pie or·der**: F *in* ~ in schönster Ordnung

ap·ple sauce Apfelmus *n*; *sl* Schmus *m*, Quatsch *m*

ap·pli·ance Vorrichtung *f*; Gerät *n*; Mittel *n*

ap·plic·a·ble anwendbar (*to* auf *acc*)

ap·pli·cant Antragsteller(in), Bewerber (in) (*for* um)

ap·pli·ca·tion Anwendung *f* (*to* auf *acc*); Bedeutung *f* (*to* für); Gesuch *n* (*for* um); Bewerbung *f* (*for* um)

ap·ply *v/t* (*to*) (auf)legen, auftragen (auf *acc*); anwenden (auf *acc*); verwenden (für); ~ *o.s. to* sich widmen (*dat*); *v/i* (*to*) passen, zutreffen, sich anwenden lassen (auf *acc*); gelten (für); sich wenden (an *acc*); ~ *for* sich bewerben um, *et.* beantragen

ap·point bestimmen, festsetzen; verabreden; ernennen (*s.o. governor* j-n zum ...); berufen (*to* auf *e-n Posten*)

ap·point·ment Bestimmung *f*; Verabre-

dung *f*; Termin *m*; Ernennung *f*, Berufung *f*; Stelle *f*; ~ **book** Terminkalender *m*

ap·por·tion verteilen, zuteilen

ap·prais·al (Ab)Schätzung *f*

ap·praise (ab)schätzen, taxieren

ap·pre·cia·ble nennenswert, spürbar

ap·pre·ci·ate *v/t* schätzen, würdigen; dankbar sein für; *v/i* im Wert steigen

ap·pre·ci·a·tion Würdigung *f*; Dankbarkeit *f*; (*richtige*) Beurteilung *f*; ECON Wertsteigerung *f*

ap·pre·hend ergreifen, fassen; begreifen; befürchten; **ap·pre·hen·sion** Ergreifung *f*, Festnahme *f*; Besorgnis *f*; **ap·pre·hen·sive** ängstlich, besorgt (*for* um; *that* dass)

ap·pren·tice **1.** Auszubildende *m*, *f*, Lehrling *m*, *Swiss* Lehrtochter *f*; **2.** in die Lehre geben; **ap·pren·tice·ship** Lehrzeit *f*, Lehre *f*, Ausbildung *f*

ap·proach 1. *v/i* näher kommen, sich nähern; *v/t* sich nähern (*dat*); herangehen *or* herantreten an (*acc*); **2.** (Heran)Nahen *n*; Einfahrt *f*, Zufahrt *f*, Auffahrt *f*; Annäherung *f*; Methode *f*

ap·pro·ba·tion Billigung *f*, Beifall *m*

ap·pro·pri·ate 1. sich aneignen; verwenden; PARL bewilligen; **2.** (*for*, *to*) angemessen (*dat*), passend (für, zu)

ap·prov·al Billigung *f*; Anerkennung *f*, Beifall *m*; **ap·prove** billigen, anerkennen; **ap·proved** bewährt

ap·prox·i·mate annähernd, ungefähr

a·pri·cot BOT Aprikose *f*

A·pril (ABBR **Apr**) April *m*

a·pron Schürze *f*; ~ **strings**: *be tied to one's mother's* ~ an Mutters Schürzenzipfel hängen

apt geeignet, passend; treffend; begabt; ~ *to* geneigt zu

ap·ti·tude (*for*) Begabung *f* (für), Befähigung *f* (für), Talent *n* (zu)

ap·ti·tude test Eignungsprüfung *f*

aq·ua·plan·ing *Br* MOT Aquaplaning *n*

a·quar·i·um Aquarium *n*

A·quar·i·us ASTR Wassermann *m*; *he* (*she*) *is* (*an*) ~ er (sie) ist (ein) Wassermann

a·quat·ic Wasser...

a·quat·ic plant Wasserpflanze *f*

a·quat·ics, **a·quat·ic sports** Wassersport *m*

aq·ue·duct Aquädukt *m*

Ar·ab Araber(in); **A·ra·bi·a** Arabien n
Ar·a·bic **1.** arabisch; **2.** LING Arabisch n
ar·a·ble AGR anbaufähig; Acker...
ar·bi·tra·ry willkürlich, eigenmächtig
ar·bi·trate entscheiden, schlichten
ar·bi·tra·tion Schlichtung f
ar·bi·tra·tor Schiedsrichter m; Schlichter m
ar·bo(u)r Laube f
arc Bogen m; ELECTR Lichtbogen m
ar·cade Lauben-, Bogengang m; Durchgang m, Passage f
arch¹ **1.** Bogen m; Gewölbe n; **2.** (sich) wölben; krümmen
arch² erste(r, -s), oberste(r, -s), Haupt..., Erz...
arch³ schelmisch
ar·cha·ic veraltet
arch·an·gel Erzengel m
arch·bish·op REL Erzbischof m
ar·cher Bogenschütze m
ar·cher·y Bogenschießen n
ar·chi·tect Architekt(in)
ar·chi·tec·ture Architektur f
ar·chives Archiv n
arch·way (Bogen)Gang m
arc·tic arktisch, nördlich, Polar...
ar·dent feurig, glühend; fig leidenschaftlich, heftig; eifrig
ar·do(u)r Leidenschaft f, Glut f, Feuer n; Eifer m
are du bist, wir or sie or Sie sind, ihr seid
ar·e·a (Boden)Fläche f; Gegend f, Gebiet n; Bereich m
ar·e·a code TEL Vorwahl(nummer) f
Ar·gen·ti·na Argentinien n
Ar·gen·tine **1.** argentinisch; **2.** Argentinier(in)
a·re·na Arena f
ar·gue argumentieren; streiten; diskutieren; **ar·gu·ment** Argument n; Wortwechsel m, Auseinandersetzung f
ar·id dürr, trocken (a. fig)
Ar·ies ASTR Widder m; **he (she) is (an) ~** er (sie) ist (ein) Widder
a·rise entstehen; auftauchen, auftreten
ar·is·toc·ra·cy Aristokratie f, Adel m
ar·is·to·crat Aristokrat(in), Adlige m, f
ar·is·to·crat·ic aristokratisch, adlig
a·rith·me·tic¹ Rechnen n
ar·ith·met·ic² arithmetisch, Rechen...
ar·ith·met·ic u·nit EDP Rechenwerk n
ark Arche f; **Noah's ~** die Arche Noah
arm¹ ANAT Arm m; Armlehne f; **keep**

s.o. at ~'s length sich j-n vom Leibe halten
arm² MIL (sich) bewaffnen; (auf)rüsten
ar·ma·ment MIL Bewaffnung f; Aufrüstung f
arm·chair Lehnstuhl m, Sessel m
ar·mi·stice MIL Waffenstillstand m
ar·mo(u)r **1.** MIL Rüstung f, Panzer m (a. fig, ZO); **2.** panzern
ar·mo(u)red car gepanzertes Fahrzeug
arm·pit ANAT Achselhöhle f
arms Waffen pl; Waffengattung f; **~ con·trol** Rüstungskontrolle f; **~ race** Wettrüsten n, Rüstungswettlauf m
ar·my MIL Armee f, Heer m
a·ro·ma Aroma n, Duft m
ar·o·mat·ic aromatisch, würzig
a·round **1.** adv (rings)herum, (rund-) herum, ringsumher, überall; umher, herum; in der Nähe; da; **2.** prp um, um... herum, rund um; in (dat) ... herum; ungefähr, etwa
a·rouse (auf)wecken; fig aufrütteln, erregen
ar·range (an)ordnen; festlegen, festsetzen; arrangieren (a. MUS); vereinbaren; MUS, THEA bearbeiten
ar·range·ment Anordnung f; Vereinbarung f; Vorkehrung f; MUS Arrangement n, Bearbeitung f (a. THEA)
ar·rears Rückstand m, Rückstände pl
ar·rest JUR **1.** Verhaftung f, Festnahme f; **2.** verhaften, festnehmen
ar·riv·al Ankunft f; Erscheinen n; Ankömmling m; **~s** AVIAT, RAIL etc ,Ankunft' (timetable); **ar·rive** (an)kommen, eintreffen, erscheinen; **~ at** fig erreichen (acc), kommen zu
ar·ro·gance Arroganz f, Überheblichkeit f
ar·ro·gant arrogant, überheblich
ar·row Pfeil m
ar·row·head Pfeilspitze f
ar·se·nic CHEM Arsen n
ar·son JUR Brandstiftung f
art **1.** Kunst f; **2.** Kunst...; **~ exhibition** Kunstausstellung f; → **arts**
ar·te·ri·al ANAT Schlagader...
ar·te·ri·al road Hauptverkehrsstraße f, Verkehrsader f
ar·te·ri·o·scle·ro·sis MED Arteriosklerose f, Arterienverkalkung f
ar·te·ry ANAT Arterie f, Schlagader f; (Haupt)Verkehrsader f

art·ful schlau, verschmitzt

art gal·le·ry Gemäldegalerie *f*

ar·thri·tis MED Arthritis *f*, Gelenkentzündung *f*

ar·ti·choke BOT Artischocke *f*

ar·ti·cle Artikel *m* (*a.* LING)

ar·tic·u·late 1. deutlich (aus)sprechen; **2.** deutlich ausgesprochen; gegliedert

ar·tic·u·lat·ed Gelenk...; **~ lorry** *Br* MOT Sattelschlepper *m*

ar·tic·u·la·tion (deutliche) Aussprache; TECH Gelenk *n*

ar·ti·fi·cial künstlich, Kunst...; **~ person** juristische Person

ar·til·le·ry MIL Artillerie *f*

ar·ti·san Handwerker *m*

art·ist Künstler(in)

ar·tis·tic künstlerisch, Kunst...

art·less schlicht; naiv

arts Geisteswissenschaften *pl*; **Arts Department**, *Br* **Faculty of Arts** philosophische Fakultät

as 1. *adv* so, ebenso; wie; als; **2.** *cj* (gerade) wie, so wie; ebenso wie; als, während; obwohl, obgleich; da, weil; **~ ... ~** (eben)so ... wie; **~ for, ~ to** was ... (an-) betrifft; **~ from** von e-m *Zeitpunkt* an, ab; **~ it were** sozusagen; **~ Hamlet** THEA als Hamlet

as·bes·tos Asbest *m*

as·cend (auf)steigen; ansteigen; besteigen; **as·cen·dan·cy, as·cen·den·cy** Überlegenheit *f*; Einfluss *m*

as·cen·sion Aufsteigen *n* (*esp* ASTR); Aufstieg *m*; **As·cen·sion (Day)** REL Himmelfahrt(stag *m*) *f*

as·cent Aufstieg *m*; Besteigung *f*; Steigung *f*

as·cet·ic asketisch

a·sep·tic MED **1.** aseptisch, keimfrei; **2.** aseptisches Mittel

ash[1] BOT Esche *f*; Eschenholz *n*

ash[2] *a.* **ashes** Asche *f*

a·shamed beschämt; **be ~ of** sich schämen für (*or* gen)

ash·en Aschen...; aschfahl, aschgrau

a·shore am *or* ans Ufer *or* Land

ash·tray Asch(en)becher *m*

Ash Wednes·day Aschermittwoch *m*

A·sia Asien *n*; **A·sian, A·si·at·ic 1.** asiatisch; **2.** Asiat(in)

a·side beiseite (*a.* THEA), seitwärts; **~ from** abgesehen von

ask *v/t* fragen (**s.th.** nach et.); verlangen

(**of, from s.o.** von j-m); bitten (**s.o.** [**for**] **s.th.** j-n um et.; **that** darum, dass); erbitten; **~ (s.o.) a question** (j-m) e-e Frage stellen; *v/i* **~ for** bitten um; fragen nach; **he ~ed for it** *or* **for trouble** er wollte es ja so haben; **to be had for the ~ing** umsonst zu haben sein

a·skance: look ~ at s.o. j-n schief *or* misstrauisch ansehen

a·skew schief

a·sleep schlafend; **be (fast, sound) ~** (fest) schlafen; **fall ~** einschlafen

as·par·a·gus BOT Spargel *m*

as·pect Lage *f*; Aspekt *m*, Seite *f*, Gesichtspunkt *m*

as·phalt 1. Asphalt *m*; **2.** asphaltieren

as·pic GASTR Aspik *m*, Gelee *n*

as·pi·rant Bewerber(in)

as·pi·ra·tion Ambition *f*, Bestrebung *f*

as·pire streben (**to, after** nach)

ass ZO Esel *m*

as·sail angreifen; **be ~ed with doubts** von Zweifeln befallen werden

as·sail·ant Angreifer(in)

as·sas·sin (*esp* politischer) Mörder, Attentäter *m*; **as·sas·sin·ate** *esp* POL ermorden; **be ~d** e-m Attentat *or* Mordanschlag zum Opfer fallen; **as·sas·sin·a·tion** (*of*) (*esp* politischer) Mord (an *dat*), Ermordung *f* (*gen*), Attentat *n* (auf *acc*)

as·sault 1. Angriff *m*, Überfall *m*; **2.** angreifen, überfallen

as·sem·blage Ansammlung *f*; TECH Montage *f*; **as·sem·ble** (sich) versammeln; TECH montieren

as·sem·bly Versammlung *f*, Gesellschaft *f*; TECH Montage *f*; **~ line** TECH Fließband *n*

as·sent 1. Zustimmung *f*; **2.** (**to**) zustimmen (*dat*); billigen (*acc*)

as·sert behaupten; geltend machen; **~ o.s.** sich behaupten, sich durchsetzen

as·ser·tion Behauptung *f*; Erklärung *f*; Geltendmachung *f*

as·sess Kosten etc festsetzen; *Einkommen etc* (zur Steuer) veranlagen (**at** mit); *fig* abschätzen, beurteilen

as·sess·ment Festsetzung *f*, (Steuer-) Veranlagung *f*; *fig* Einschätzung *f*

as·set ECON Aktivposten *m*; *fig* Plus *n*, Gewinn *m*; *pl* ECON Aktiva *pl*; JUR Vermögen(smasse *f*) *n*; Konkursmasse *f*

as·sid·u·ous emsig, fleißig

as·sign an-, zuweisen; bestimmen; zuschreiben; **as·sign·ment** An-, Zuweisung *f*; Aufgabe *f*; Auftrag *m*; JUR Abtretung *f*; Übertragung *f*

as·sim·i·late (sich) angleichen *or* anpassen (**to**, **with** *dat*)

as·sim·i·la·tion Assimilation *f*, Angleichung *f*, Anpassung *f* (*all:* **to** an *acc*)

as·sist *j-m* beistehen, helfen; *j-n* unterstützen; **as·sist·ance** Beistand *m*, Hilfe *f*; **as·sist·ant 1.** stellvertretend, Hilfs...; **2.** Assistent(in), Mitarbeiter(in); (*shop*) ~ *Br* Verkäufer(in)

as·so·ci·ate 1. vereinigen, verbinden, zusammenschließen; assoziieren; ~ **with** verkehren mit; **2.** Teilhaber(in)

as·so·ci·a·tion Vereinigung *f*, Verbindung *f*; Verein *m*

as·sort sortieren, aussuchen, zusammenstellen; **as·sort·ment** ECON (**of**) Sortiment *n* (von), Auswahl *f* (an *dat*)

as·sume annehmen, voraussetzen; übernehmen

as·sump·tion Annahme *f*, Voraussetzung *f*; Übernahme *f*; **the Assumption** REL Mariä Himmelfahrt *f*

as·sur·ance Zusicherung *f*, Versicherung *f*; *esp Br* (Lebens)Versicherung *f*; Sicherheit *f*, Gewissheit *f*; Selbstsicherheit *f*; **as·sure** *j-m* versichern; *esp Br j-s Leben* versichern; **as·sured 1.** sicher; **2.** *esp Br* Versicherte *m*, *f*; **as·sur·ed·ly** ganz gewiss

as·te·risk PRINT Sternchen *n*

asth·ma MED Asthma *n*

as·ton·ish in Erstaunen setzen; **be ~ed** erstaunt sein (**at** über *acc*)

as·ton·ish·ing erstaunlich

as·ton·ish·ment (Er)Staunen *n*, Verwunderung *f*

as·tound verblüffen

a·stray: **go ~** vom Weg abkommen; *fig* auf Abwege geraten; irregehen; **lead ~** *fig* irreführen; verleiten

a·stride rittlings (**of** auf *dat*)

as·trin·gent MED **1.** adstringierend; **2.** Adstringens *n*

as·trol·o·gy Astrologie *f*

as·tro·naut Astronaut *m*, (Welt)Raumfahrer *m*

as·tron·o·my Astronomie *f*

as·tute scharfsinnig; schlau

a·sun·der auseinander, entzwei

a·sy·lum Asyl *n*; **right of ~** Asylrecht *n*

a·sy·lum seek·er Asylant(in), Asylbewerber(in)

at *prp place*: in, an, bei, auf; *direction*: auf, nach, gegen, zu; *occupation*: bei, beschäftigt mit, in; *manner, state*: in, bei, zu, unter; *price etc*: für, um; *time, age*: um, bei; ~ **the baker's** beim Bäcker; ~ **the door** an der Tür; ~ **school** in der Schule; ~ **10 dollars** für 10 Dollar; ~ **18** mit 18 (Jahren); ~ **the age of** im Alter von; ~ **8 o'clock** um 8 Uhr

a·the·ism Atheismus *m*

ath·lete SPORT (Leicht)Athlet(in)

ath·let·ic SPORT athletisch

ath·let·ics SPORT (Leicht)Athletik *f*

At·lan·tic 1. *a.* ~ **Ocean** der Atlantik; **2.** atlantisch

at·mo·sphere Atmosphäre *f* (*a. fig*)

at·mo·spher·ic atmosphärisch

at·oll Atoll *n*

at·om Atom *n*; ~ **bomb** Atombombe *f*

a·tom·ic atomar, Atom...; ~ **age** Atomzeitalter *n*; ~ **bomb** Atombombe *f*; ~ **en·er·gy** Atomenergie *f*; ~ **pile** Atomreaktor *m*; ~ **pow·er** Atomkraft *f*; **~-pow·ered** atomgetrieben; ~ **waste** Atommüll *m*; ~ **weight** CHEM Atomgewicht *n*

at·om·ize atomisieren; *Flüssigkeit* zerstäuben; **at·om·iz·er** Zerstäuber *m*

a·tone: ~ **for** büßen für, *et.* sühnen

a·tone·ment Buße *f*, Sühne *f*

a·tro·cious scheußlich, grässlich; grausam

a·troc·i·ty Scheußlichkeit *f*; Greueltat *f*

at·tach *v/t* (**to**) anheften, ankleben (an *acc*), befestigen, anbringen (an *dat*); *Wert, Wichtigkeit etc* beimessen (*dat*); **be ~ed to** *fig* hängen an; **at·tach·ment** Befestigung *f*; Bindung *f* (**to** an *acc*); Anhänglichkeit *f* (**to** an *acc*)

at·tack 1. angreifen; **2.** Angriff *m*; MED Anfall *m*

at·tempt 1. versuchen; **2.** Versuch *m*; **an ~ on s.o.'s life** ein Mordanschlag *or* Attentat auf *j-n*

at·tend *v/t* (*ärztlich*) behandeln; *Kranke* pflegen; teilnehmen an (*dat*), *Schule, Vorlesung etc* besuchen; *fig* begleiten; *v/i* anwesend sein; erscheinen; ~ **to** *j-n* (*im Laden*) bedienen; **are you being ~ed to?** werden Sie schon bedient?; ~ **to s.th.** etwas erledigen; **at-**

tend·ance Dienst *m*, Bereitschaft *f*; Pflege *f*; Anwesenheit *f*, Erscheinen *n*; Besucher *pl*, Teilnehmer *pl*; Besuch (erzahl *f*) *m*, Beteiligung *f*; **at·tend·ant** Begleiter(in); Aufseher(in); (*Tank*-) Wart *m*

at·ten·tion Aufmerksamkeit *f* (*a. fig*); *pay ∼* aufpassen

at·ten·tive aufmerksam

at·tic Dachboden *m*; Dachkammer *f*

at·ti·tude (Ein)Stellung *f*; Haltung *f*

at·tor·ney Bevollmächtigte *m*, *f*; JUR (Rechts)Anwalt *m*, (Rechts)Anwältin *f*; *power of ∼* Vollmacht *f*

At·tor·ney Gen·er·al JUR Justizminister; *Br* erster Kronanwalt

at·tract anziehen; *Aufmerksamkeit* erregen; *fig* reizen; **at·trac·tion** Anziehung *f*, Anziehungskraft *f*, Reiz *m*; Attraktion *f*, THEA *etc* Zugnummer *f*, Zugstück *n*; **at·trac·tive** anziehend; attraktiv; reizvoll

at·trib·ute[1] zuschreiben (*to dat*); zurückführen (*to* auf *acc*)

at·trib·ute[2] Attribut *n* (*a.* LING), Eigenschaft *f*, Merkmal *n*

at·tune: *∼ to fig* einstellen auf (*acc*)

au·ber·gine BOT Aubergine *f*

au·burn kastanienbraun

auc·tion 1. Auktion *f*, Versteigerung *f*; **2.** *mst ∼ off* versteigern

auc·tion·eer Auktionator *m*

au·da·cious unverfroren, dreist

au·dac·i·ty Unverfrorenheit *f*, Dreistigkeit *f*

au·di·ble hörbar

au·di·ence Publikum *n*, Zuhörer *pl*, Zuschauer *pl*, Besucher *pl*, Leser(kreis *m*) *pl*; Audienz *f*

au·di·o·vis·u·al aids audiovisuelle Unterrichtsmittel *pl*

au·dit ECON **1.** Buchprüfung *f*; **2.** prüfen

au·di·tion MUS Vorsingen *n*; THEA Vorsprechen *n*; *have an ∼* vorsingen, THEA vorsprechen

au·di·tor ECON Buchprüfer *m*; UNIV Gasthörer(in)

au·di·to·ri·um Zuhörer-, Zuschauerraum *m*; Vortrags-, Konzertsaal *m*

Aug ABBR *of* **August** Aug., August *m*

au·ger TECH großer Bohrer

Au·gust (ABBR *Aug*) August *m*

aunt Tante *f*

au pair (girl) Au-pair-Mädchen *n*

aus·pic·es: *under the ∼ of* unter der Schirmherrschaft (*gen*)

aus·tere streng; enthaltsam; dürftig; einfach, schmucklos

Aus·tra·li·a Australien; **Aus·tra·li·an 1.** australisch; **2.** Australier(in)

Aus·tri·a Österreich *n*

Aus·tri·an 1. österreichisch; **2.** Österreicher(in)

au·then·tic authentisch; zuverlässig; echt

au·thor Urheber(in), Autor(in), Verfasser(in), Schriftsteller(in)

au·thor·ess Autorin *f*, Verfasserin *f*, Schriftstellerin *f*

au·thor·i·ta·tive gebieterisch, herrisch; maßgebend

au·thor·i·ty Autorität *f*; Nachdruck *m*, Gewicht *n*; Vollmacht *f*; Einfluss *m* (*over* auf *acc*); Ansehen *n*; Quelle *f*; Autorität *f*, Kapazität *f*; *mst pl* Behörde *f*

au·thor·ize *j-n* autorisieren, ermächtigen, bevollmächtigen

au·thor·ship Urheberschaft *f*

au·to Auto *n*

au·to... auto..., selbst..., Auto..., Selbst...

au·to·bi·og·ra·phy Autobiografie *f*

au·to·graph Autogramm *n*

au·to·mat® Automatenrestaurant *n*

au·to·mate automatisieren

au·to·mat·ic 1. automatisch; **2.** Selbstladepistole *f*, -gewehr *n*; Auto *n* mit Automatik; *∼ tel·ler ma·chine* (ABBR *ATM*) Geld-, Bankautomat *m*

au·to·ma·tion TECH Automation *f*

au·tom·a·ton Roboter *m*

au·to·mo·bile Auto *n*, Automobil *n*

au·ton·o·my POL Autonomie *f*

au·top·sy MED Autopsie *f*

au·to·tel·ler Geld-, Bankautomat *m*

au·tumn Herbst *m*

au·tum·nal herbstlich, Herbst...

aux·il·i·a·ry helfend, Hilfs...

a·vail: *to no ∼* vergeblich

a·vail·a·ble verfügbar, vorhanden; erreichbar; ECON lieferbar, vorrätig, erhältlich

av·a·lanche Lawine *f*

av·a·rice Habsucht *f*

av·a·ri·cious habgierig

a·venge rächen; **a·veng·er** Rächer(in)

av·e·nue Allee *f*; Boulevard *m*, Prachtstraße *f*

B

av·e·rage **1.** Durchschnitt *m*; **2.** durchschnittlich, Durchschnitts...
a·verse abgeneigt (**to** *dat*)
a·ver·sion Widerwille *m*, Abneigung *f*
a·vert abwenden (*a. fig*)
a·vi·a·ry Vogelhaus *n*, Voliere *f*
a·vi·a·tion Luftfahrt *f*
a·vi·a·tor Flieger *m*
av·id gierig (**for** nach); begeistert
av·o·ca·do BOT Avocado *f*
a·void (ver)meiden; ausweichen
a·void·ance Vermeidung *f*
a·vow·al Bekenntnis *n*, (Ein)Geständnis *n*
a·wait erwarten, warten auf (*acc*)
a·wake **1.** wach, munter; **2.** *a.* **a·waken** *v/t* (auf)wecken; *v/i* aufwachen, erwachen;
a·wak·en·ing Erwachen *n*
a·ward **1.** Belohnung *f*; Preis *m*, Auszeichnung *f*; **2.** zuerkennen, *Preis etc* verleihen

a·ware: **be ~ of s.th.** von etwas wissen, sich e-r Sache bewusst sein; **become ~ of s.th.** etwas merken
a·way weg, fort; (weit) entfernt; immer weiter, d(a)rauflos; SPORT Auswärts...; **~ match** SPORT Auswärtsspiel *n*
awe **1.** (Ehr)Furcht *f*, Scheu *f*; **2.** *j-m* (Ehr)Furcht *or* großen Respekt einflößen
aw·ful furchtbar, schrecklich
awk·ward ungeschickt, linkisch; unangenehm; unhandlich, sperrig; ungünstig, ungelegen
awl Ahle *f*, Pfriem *m*
aw·ning Plane *f*; Markise *f*
a·wry schief
ax(e) Axt *f*, Beil *n*
ax·is MATH *etc* Achse *f*
ax·le TECH (Rad)Achse *f*, Welle *f*
ay(e) PARL Jastimme *f*
A-Z *Br appr* Stadtplan *m*
az·ure azurblau, himmelblau

B

B, b B, b *n*
b ABBR *of* **born** geb., geboren
bab·ble **1.** stammeln; plappern, schwatzen; plätschern; **2.** Geplapper *n*, Geschwätz *n*
babe kleines Kind, Baby *n*; F Puppe *f*
ba·boon ZO Pavian *m*
ba·by **1.** Baby *n*, Säugling *m*, kleines Kind; F Puppe *f*; **2.** Baby..., Kinder...; klein; **~ bug·gy, ~ car·riage** Kinderwagen *m*
ba·by·hood Säuglingsalter *n*
ba·by·ish *contp* kindisch
ba·by·mind·er *Br* Tagesmutter *f*
ba·by·sit babysitten
ba·by·sit·ter Babysitter(in)
bach·e·lor Junggeselle *m*
back **1.** Rücken *m*; Rückseite *f*; (Rück)Lehne *f*; hinterer *or* rückwärtiger Teil; SPORT Verteidiger *m*; **2.** *adj* Hinter..., Rück..., hintere(r, -s), rückwärtig; ECON rückständig; alt, zurückliegend; **3.** *adv* zurück, rückwärts; **4.** *v/t* mit e-m Rücken versehen; wetten *or* setzen auf (*acc*); *a.* **~ up** unterstüt-

zen; zurückbewegen; MOT zurückstoßen mit; **~ up** EDP e-e Sicherungskopie machen von; *v/i often* **~ up** sich rückwärts bewegen, zurückgehen *or* -fahren, MOT *a.* zurückstoßen; **~ in(to a parking space)** MOT rückwärts einparken; **~ up** EDP e-e Sicherungskopie machen
back·ache Rückenschmerzen *pl*
back·bite verleumden, schlecht machen
back·bone ANAT Rückgrat *n* (*a. fig*)
back·break·ing erschöpfend, mörderisch
back·chat *Br* freche Antwort(en *pl*)
back·comb *Br* toupieren
back door Hintertür *f*; *fig* Hintertürchen *n*
back·er Unterstützer *m*, Geldgeber *m*
back·fire MOT Früh- *or* Fehlzündung haben; *fig* fehlschlagen
back·ground Hintergrund *m*
back·hand SPORT Rückhand *f*, Rückhandschlag *m*
back·heel·er *soccer*: Hackentrick *m*

back·ing Unterstützung *f*
back num·ber alte Nummer
back·pack *großer* Rucksack
back·pack·er Rucksacktourist(in)
back·pack·ing Rucksacktourismus *m*
back·ped·al brake *Br* Rücktritt *m*, Rücktrittbremse *f*
back seat MOT Rücksitz *m*
back·side Gesäß *n*, F Hintern *m*, Po *m*
back·space (key) EDP Rücktaste *f*
back stairs Hintertreppe *f*
back street Seitenstraße *f*
back·stroke Rückenschwimmen *n*
back talk freche Antwort(en *pl*)
back·track *fig* e-n Rückzieher machen
back·up Unterstützung *f*; TECH Ersatzgerät *n*; EDP Backup *n*, Sicherungskopie *f*; MOT Rückstau *m*
back·ward 1. *adj* Rück..., Rückwärts...; zurückgeblieben; rückständig; *a ~ glance* ein Blick zurück; **2.** *adv a.* **backwards** rückwärts, zurück
back·yard Garten *m* hinter dem Haus; *Br* Hinterhof *m*
ba·con Speck *m*
bac·te·ri·a BIOL Bakterien *pl*
bad schlecht, böse, schlimm; *go ~* schlecht werden, verderben; *he is in a ~ way* es geht ihm schlecht; *he is ~ly off* es geht ihm finanziell schlecht; *~ly wounded* schwer verwundet; *want ~ly* dringend brauchen
badge Abzeichen *n*; Dienstmarke *f*
bad·ger 1. ZO Dachs *m*; **2.** *j-n* plagen, *j-m* zusetzen
bad·min·ton Federball(spiel *n*) *m*, SPORT Badminton *n*
bad-tempered schlecht gelaunt
bag 1. Beutel *m*, Sack *m*; Tüte *f*; Tasche *f*; *~ and baggage* (mit) Sack und Pack; **2.** in e-n Beutel *etc* tun; in Beutel verpacken *or* abfüllen; HUNT zur Strecke bringen; schlottern; *a. ~ out* sich bauschen
bag·gage (Reise)Gepäck *n*; *~ car* RAIL Gepäckwagen *m*; *~ check* Gepäckschein *m*; *~ claim* AVIAT Gepäckausgabe *f*; *~ room* RAIL Gepäckaufbewahrung *f*
bag·gy bauschig; ausgebeult
bag·pipes MUS Dudelsack *m*
bail 1. Bürge *m*; JUR Kaution *f*; *be out on ~* gegen Kaution auf freiem Fuß sein; *go or stand ~ for s.o.* für j-n Kau-

tion stellen; **2.** *~ out* JUR *j-n* gegen Kaution freibekommen; AVIAT (mit dem Fallschirm) abspringen
bai·liff (Guts)Verwalter *m*; *Br* JUR Gerichtsvollzieher *m*
bait 1. Köder *m* (*a. fig*); **2.** mit e-m Köder versehen; *fig* ködern
bake backen, im (Back)Ofen braten; TECH brennen; dörren
bak·er Bäcker *m*
bak·er·y Bäckerei *f*
bak·ing pow·der Backpulver *n*
bal·ance 1. Waage *f*; Gleichgewicht *n* (*a. fig*); ECON Bilanz *f*; Saldo *m*, Kontostand *m*, Guthaben *n*; Restbetrag *m*; *keep one's ~* das Gleichgewicht halten; *lose one's ~* das Gleichgewicht verlieren; *fig* die Fassung verlieren; *~ of payments* ECON Zahlungsbilanz *f*; *~ of power* POL Kräftegleichgewicht *n*; *~ of trade* ECON Handelsbilanz *f*; **2.** *v/t* abwägen; im Gleichgewicht halten, balancieren; ECON ausgleichen; *v/i* balancieren; ECON sich ausgleichen; *~ each other* sich die Waage halten
bal·ance sheet ECON Bilanz *f*
bal·co·ny Balkon *m* (*a. THEA*)
bald kahl
bale¹ ECON Ballen *m*
bale²: *~ out* *Br* AVIAT (mit dem Fallschirm) abspringen
bale·ful hasserfüllt
balk 1. Balken *m*; **2.** stutzen; scheuen
ball¹ 1. Ball *m*; Kugel *f*; ANAT (Hand-, Fuß)Ballen *m*; Knäuel *m*, *n*; Kloß *m*; *start the ~ rolling* den Stein ins Rollen bringen; *play ~* F mitmachen; *long ~* SPORT langer Pass; **2.** ballen; sich zusammenballen
ball² Ball *m*, Tanzveranstaltung *f*
bal·lad Ballade *f*
bal·last 1. Ballast *m*; **2.** mit Ballast beladen
ball bear·ing TECH Kugellager *n*
bal·let Ballett *n*
bal·lis·tics MIL Ballistik *f*
bal·loon 1. Ballon *m*; Sprech-, Denkblase *f*; **2.** sich (auf)blähen
bal·lot 1. Stimmzettel *m*; (geheime) Wahl; **2.** (*for*) stimmen (für), (in geheimer Wahl) wählen (*acc*); *~ box* Wahlurne *f*; *~ pa·per* Stimmzettel *m*
ball·point (pen) Kugelschreiber *m*, F Kuli *m*

ball·room Ballsaal *m*, Tanzsaal *m*

balls V Eier *pl*

balm Balsam *m* (*a. fig*)

balm·y lind, mild

ba·lo·ney F Quatsch *m*

bal·us·trade Balustrade *f*, Brüstung *f*, Geländer *n*

bam·boo BOT Bambus(rohr *n*) *m*

bam·boo·zle F betrügen, *j-n* übers Ohr hauen

ban 1. (amtliches) Verbot, Sperre *f*; REL Bann *m*; **2.** verbieten

ba·nal banal, abgedroschen

ba·na·na Banane *f*

band 1. Band *n*; Streifen *m*; Schar *f*, Gruppe *f*, *contp* Bande *f*; (Musik)Kapelle *f*, (Tanz-, Unterhaltungs)Orchester *n*, (*Jazz-, Rock*)Band *f*; **2.** ~ *together* sich zusammentun *or* -rotten

ban·dage MED **1.** Bandage *f*; Binde *f*; Verband *m*; (Heft)Pflaster *n*; **2.** bandagieren; verbinden (zu)kleben

'Band-Aid® MED (Heft)Pflaster *n*

b **bernachtung** *f* mit Frühstück

ban·dit Bandit *m*

band·lead·er MUS Bandleader *m*

band·mas·ter MUS Kapellmeister *m*

ban·dy krumm

ban·dy-legged säbelbeinig, o-beinig

bang 1. heftiger Schlag; Knall *m*; *mst pl* Pony *m*; **2.** dröhnend (zu)schlagen

ban·gle Armreif *m*, Fußreif *m*

ban·ish verbannen

ban·ish·ment Verbannung *f*

ban·is·ter *a. pl* Treppengeländer *n*

ban·jo MUS Banjo *n*

bank[1] ECON **1.** Bank *f* (*a.* MED); **2.** *v/t* bei e-r Bank einzahlen; *v/i* ein Bankkonto haben (**with** bei)

bank[2] (Erd)Wall *m*; Böschung *f*; (*Fluss- etc*)Ufer *n*; (*Sand-, Wolken*)Bank *f*

bank ac·count Bankkonto *n*

bank bill Banknote *f*, Geldschein *m*

bank·book Sparbuch *n*

bank code ECON Bankleitzahl *f*

bank·er Bankier *m*, Banker *m*; **~'s card** Scheckkarte *f*

bank hol·i·day *Br* gesetzlicher Feiertag *m*

bank·ing ECON **1.** Bankgeschäft *n*, Bankwesen *n*; **2.** Bank...

bank note *Br* → *bank bill*

bank rate ECON Diskontsatz *m*

bank·rupt JUR **1.** Konkursschuldner *m*;

2. bankrott; *go* ~ in Konkurs gehen, Bankrott machen; **3.** *j-n, Unternehmen* Bankrott machen; **bank·rupt·cy** JUR Bankrott *m*, Konkurs *m*

bank sort·ing code → *bank code*

ban·ner Transparent *n*

banns Aufgebot *n*

ban·quet Bankett *n*

ban·ter necken

bap·tism REL Taufe *f*

bap·tize REL taufen

bar 1. Stange *f*, Stab *m*; SPORT (Tor-, Quer-, Sprung)Latte *f*; Riegel *m*; Schranke *f*, Sperre *f*; *fig* Hindernis *m*; (*Gold- etc*)Barren *m*; MUS Taktstrich *m*; *ein* Takt *m*; dicker Strich; JUR (Gerichts)Schranke *f*; JUR Anwaltschaft *f*; Bar *f*, Lokal *n*, Imbissstube *f*; *pl* Gitter *n*; *a* ~ *of chocolate* ein Riegel *or* e-e Tafel Schokolade; *a* ~ *of soap* ein Stück Seife; **2.** zuriegeln, verriegeln; versperren; einsperren; (ver)hindern; ausschließen

barb Widerhaken *m*

bar·bar·i·an 1. barbarisch; **2.** Barbar(in)

bar·be·cue 1. Bratrost *m*, Grill *m*; Barbecue *n*; **2.** auf dem Rost *or* am Spieß braten, grillen

barbed wire Stacheldraht *m*

bar·ber (Herren)Friseur *m*, (-)Frisör *m*

bar code Strichcode *m*

bare 1. nackt, bloß; kahl; leer; **2.** entblößen

bare-faced unverschämt, schamlos

bare·foot, bare·foot·ed barfuß

bare·head·ed barhäuptig

bare·ly kaum

bar·gain 1. Geschäft *n*, Handel *m*; vorteilhaftes Geschäft, Gelegenheitskauf *m*; *a* (*dead*) ~ spottbillig; *it's a* ~! abgemacht!; *into the* ~ obendrein; **2.** (ver)handeln; ~ *sale* Verkauf *m* zu herabgesetzten Preisen; Ausverkauf *m*

barge 1. Lastkahn *m*; **2.** ~ *in* F hereinplatzen (**on** bei)

bark[1] BOT Borke *f*, Rinde *f*

bark[2] **1.** bellen; ~ *up the wrong tree* F auf dem Holzweg sein; an der falschen Adresse sein; **2.** Bellen *n*

bar·ley BOT Gerste *f*; Graupe *f*

barn Scheune *f*, (Vieh)Stall *m*

ba·rom·e·ter Barometer *n*

bar·on Baron *m*; Freiherr *m*

bar·on·ess Baronin *f*; Freifrau *f*

bar·racks MIL Kaserne *f*; *contp* Mietskaserne *f*

bar·rage Staudamm *m*; MIL Sperrfeuer *n*; *fig* (Wort- *etc*)Schwall *m*

bar·rel Fass *n*, Tonne *f*; (*Gewehr*)Lauf *m*; TECH Trommel *f*, Walze *f*

bar·rel or·gan MUS Drehorgel *f*

bar·ren unfruchtbar; trocken

bar·rette Haarspange *f*

bar·ri·cade 1. Barrikade *f*; **2.** verbarrikadieren; sperren

bar·ri·er Schranke *f* (*a. fig*), Barriere *f*, Sperre *f*; Hindernis *n*

bar·ris·ter *Br* JUR Barrister *m*

bar·row Karre *f*

bar·ter 1. Tausch(handel) *m*; **2.** tauschen (*for* gegen)

base¹ gemein

base² 1. Basis *f*; Grundlage *f*; Fundament *n*; Fuß *m*; MIL Standort *m*; MIL Stützpunkt *m*; **2.** gründen, stützen (*on* auf *acc*)

base³ CHEM Base *f*

base·ball SPORT Baseball(spiel *n*) *m*

base·board Scheuerleiste *f*

base·less grundlos

base·line *tennis etc*: Grundlinie *f*

base·ment ARCH Fundament *n*; Kellergeschoss *n*

bash·ful scheu, schüchtern

ba·sic¹ Grund..., grundlegend; **2.** *pl* Grundlagen *f*

ba·sic² CHEM basisch

ba·sic·al·ly im Grunde

ba·sin Becken *n*, Schale *f*, Schüssel *f*; Tal-, Wasser-, Hafenbecken *n*

ba·sis Basis *f*; Grundlage *f*

bask sich sonnen (*a. fig*)

bas·ket Korb *m*

bas·ket·ball SPORT Basketball(spiel *n*) *m*

bass¹ MUS Bass *m*

bass² ZO (Fluss-, See)Barsch *m*

bas·tard Bastard *m*

baste¹ GASTR mit Fett begießen

baste² (an)heften

bat¹ ZO Fledermaus *f*; *as blind as a ~* stockblind

bat² *baseball, cricket* **1.** Schlagholz *n*, Schläger *m*; F *right off the ~* sofort; **2.** am Schlagen sein

batch Stapel *m*, Stoß *m*; *~ pro·cessing* EDP Stapelverarbeitung *f*

bate: *with ~d breath* mit angehaltenem Atem

bath 1. (Wannen)Bad *n*; *pl* Bad *n*, Badeanstalt *f*; Badeort *m*; *have a ~ Br*, *take a ~* baden, ein Bad nehmen; **2.** *Br v/t* *j-n* baden; *v/i* baden, ein Bad nehmen

bathe *v/t* baden (*a*. MED); *v/i* baden, ein Bad nehmen; schwimmen

bath·ing 1. Baden *n*; **2.** Bade...

bath·ing suit → swimsuit

bath·robe Bademantel *m*; Morgenrock *m*, Schlafrock *m*

bath·room Badezimmer *n*; Toilette *f*

bath·tub Badewanne *f*

bat·on Stab *m*; MUS Taktstock *m*; Schlagstock *m*, Gummiknüppel *m*

bat·tal·i·on MIL Bataillon *n*

bat·ter¹ heftig schlagen; misshandeln; verbeulen; *~ down*, *~ in* einschlagen

bat·ter² GASTR Rührteig *m*

bat·ter³ *baseball, cricket*: Schläger *m*, Schlagmann *m*

bat·ter·y ELECTR Batterie *f*; JUR Tätlichkeit *f*, Körperverletzung *f*; *assault and ~* JUR tätliche Beleidigung

bat·ter·y charg·er ELECTR Ladegerät *n*

bat·ter·y-op·e·rat·ed ELECTR batteriebetrieben

bat·tle 1. MIL Schlacht *f* (*of* bei); *fig* Kampf *m* (*for* um); **2.** kämpfen

bat·tle·field, **bat·tle·ground** MIL Schlachtfeld *n*

bat·tle·ments ARCH Zinnen *pl*

bat·tle·ship MIL Schlachtschiff *n*

baulk → balk

Ba·va·ri·a Bayern *n*

Ba·var·i·an 1. bay(e)risch; **2.** Bayer(in)

bawd·y obszön

bawl brüllen, schreien; *~ s.o. out* mit *j-m* schimpfen

bay¹ GEOGR Bai *f*, Bucht *f*; ARCH Erker *m*

bay² *a. ~ tree* BOT Lorbeer(baum) *m*

bay³ 1. ZO bellen, Laut geben; **2.** *hold or keep at ~ j-n* in Schach halten; *et.* von sich fern halten

bay⁴ 1. rotbraun; **2.** ZO Braune *m*

bay·o·net MIL Bajonett *n*

bay·ou GEOGR sumpfiger Flussarm

bay win·dow ARCH Erkerfenster *n*

ba·zaar Basar *m*

BC ABBR *of before Christ* v. Chr., vor Christus

B

be sein; *to form the passive*: werden; stattfinden; *he wants to ~ a doctor etc* er möchte Arzt *etc* werden; *how much are the shoes?* was kosten die Schuhe?; *that's five dollars* das macht *or* kostet fünf Dollar; *she is reading* sie liest gerade; *there is, there are* es gibt

beach Strand *m*; ~ **ball** Wasserball *m*; ~ **bug·gy** MOT Strandbuggy *m*

beach·wear Strandkleidung *f*

bea·con Leucht-, Signalfeuer *n*

bead (*Glas-, Schweiß- etc*)Perle *f*, *pl* REL Rosenkranz *m*

bead·y klein, rund und glänzend

beak ZO Schnabel *m*; TECH Tülle *f*

beam 1. Balken *m*; (Licht)Strahl *m*; AVIAT *etc* Peil-, Leit-, Richtstrahl *m*; 2. ausstrahlen; strahlen (*a. fig with* vor *dat*)

bean BOT Bohne *f*; *be full of ~s* F aufgekrazt sein; → *spill* 1

bear¹ ZO Bär *m*

bear² tragen; zur Welt bringen, gebären; ertragen, aushalten; *I can't ~ him* (*it*) ich kann ihn (es) nicht ausstehen *or* leiden; ~ *out* bestätigen

bear·a·ble erträglich

beard Bart *m*; BOT Grannen *pl*

beard·ed bärtig

bear·er Träger(in); ECON Überbringer(in), Inhaber(in)

bear·ing Ertragen *n*; Betragen *n*; (Körper)Haltung *f*, *fig* Beziehung *f*; Lage *f*, Richtung *f*, Orientierung *f*; *take one's ~s* sich orientieren; *lose one's ~s* die Orientierung verlieren

beast (*a. wildes*) Tier; Bestie *f*

beast·ly scheußlich

beast of prey ZO Raubtier *n*

beat 1. schlagen; (ver)prügeln; besiegen; übertreffen; F ~ *s.o. to it* j-m zuvorkommen; ~ *it!* F hau ab!; *that ~s all!* das ist doch der Gipfel *or* die Höhe!; *that ~s me* F das ist mir zu hoch; ~ *about the bush* wie die Katze um den heißen Brei herumschleichen; ~ *down* ECON drücken, herunterhandeln; ~ *s.o. up* j-n zusammenschlagen; 2. Schlag *m*; MUS Takt(schlag) *m*; *jazz:* Beat *m*; Pulsschlag *m*; Runde *f*, Revier *n*; 3. (*dead*) ~ F wie erschlagen, fix und fertig

beat·en track Trampelpfad *m*; *off* *the* ~ ungewohnt, ungewöhnlich

beat·ing (Tracht *f*) Prügel *pl*

beau·ti·cian Kosmetikerin *f*

beau·ti·ful schön

beau·ty Schönheit *f*; *Sleeping Beauty* Dornröschen *n*; ~ **care** Schönheitspflege *f*; ~ **par·lo(u)r**, ~ **sal·on** Schönheitssalon *m*

bea·ver ZO Biber *m*; Biberpelz *m*

be·cause weil; ~ *of* wegen (*gen*)

beck·on (zu)winken (*dat*)

be·come *v/i* werden (*of* aus); *v/t* sich schicken für; *j-m* stehen, *j-n* kleiden

be·com·ing passend; schicklich; kleidsam

bed 1. Bett *n*; ZO Lager *n*; AGR Beet *n*; Unterlage *f*; ~ *and breakfast* Zimmer *n* mit Frühstück; 2. ~ *down* sein Nachtlager aufschlagen

bed·clothes Bettwäsche *f*

bed·ding Bettzeug *n*; AGR Streu *f*

bed·lam Tollhaus *n*

bed·rid·den bettlägerig

bed·room Schlafzimmer *n*

bed·side: *at the* ~ am (*a. Kranken*)Bett

bed·side lamp Nachttischlampe *f*

bed·sit F, **bed·sit·ter, bed·sit·ting room** *Br* möbliertes Zimmer; Einzimmerappartement *n*

bed·spread Tagesdecke *f*

bed·stead Bettgestell *n*

bed·time Schlafenszeit *f*

bee ZO Biene *f*; *have a ~ in one's bonnet* F e-n Fimmel *or* Tick haben

beech BOT Buche *f*

beech·nut BOT Buchecker *f*

beef GASTR Rindfleisch *n*

beef·bur·ger GASTR *Br* Hamburger *m*

beef tea GASTR (Rind)Fleischbrühe *f*

beef·y F bullig

bee·hive Bienenkorb *m*, Bienenstock *m*

bee·keep·er Imker *m*

bee·line: *make a ~ for* F schnurstracks losgehen auf (*acc*)

beep·er TECH Piepser *m*

beer Bier *n*

beet BOT Runkelrübe *f*, Rote Bete, Rote Rübe

bee·tle ZO Käfer *m*

beet·root BOT *Br* Rote Bete, Rote Rübe

be·fore 1. *adv space*: vorn, voran; *time*: vorher, früher, schon (früher); 2. *cj* bevor, ehe, bis; 3. *prp* vor; **be·fore·hand** zuvor, im Voraus, vorweg

be·friend sich *j-s* annehmen

beg *v/t et.* erbitten (*of s.o.* von j-m); betteln um; *j-n* bitten; *v/i* betteln; (dringend) bitten

be·get (er)zeugen

beg·gar 1. Bettler(in); F Kerl *m*; **2.** *it ~s all description* es spottet jeder Beschreibung

be·gin beginnen, anfangen

be·gin·ner Anfänger(in)

be·gin·ning Beginn *m*, Anfang *m*

be·grudge missgönnen

be·guile täuschen; betrügen (*of, out of* um); sich *die Zeit* vertreiben

be·half: in (*Br* on) *~ of* im Namen von (*or* gen)

be·have sich (gut) benehmen

be·hav·io(u)r Benehmen *n*, Betragen *n*, Verhalten *n*

be·hav·io(u)r·al sci·ence PSYCH Verhaltensforschung *f*

be·head enthaupten

be·hind 1. *adv* hinten, dahinter; zurück; **2.** *prp* hinter (*dat or acc*); **3.** F Hinterteil *n*, Hintern *m*

beige beige

be·ing Sein *n*, Dasein *n*, Existenz *f*; (Lebe)Wesen *n*, Geschöpf *n*; *j-s* Wesen *n*, Natur *f*

be·lat·ed verspätet

belch 1. aufstoßen, rülpsen; *a. ~ out* speien, ausstoßen; **2.** Rülpser *m*

bel·fry Glockenturm *m*, -stuhl *m*

Bel·gium Belgien *n*

Bel·gian 1. belgisch; **2.** Belgier(in)

be·lief Glaube *m* (*in* an *acc*)

be·liev·a·ble glaubhaft

be·lieve glauben (*in* an *acc*); *I couldn't ~ my ears* (*eyes*) ich traute m-n Ohren (Augen) nicht

be·liev·er REL Gläubige *m, f*

be·lit·tle *fig* herabsetzen

bell Glocke *f*; Klingel *f*

bell·boy *Br*, **bell·hop** (Hotel)Page *m*

bel·lig·er·ent kriegerisch; streitlustig, aggressiv; Krieg führend

bel·low 1. brüllen; **2.** Gebrüll *n*

bel·lows Blasebalg *m*

bel·ly 1. Bauch *m*; Magen *m*; **2.** *~ out* (an)schwellen lassen; bauschen

bel·ly·ache F Bauchweh *n*

be·long gehören; *~ to* gehören *dat or* zu

be·long·ings Habseligkeiten *pl*, Habe *f*

be·loved 1. (innig) geliebt; **2.** Geliebte *m, f*

be·low 1. *adv* unten; **2.** *prp* unter (*dat or acc*)

belt 1. Gürtel *m*; Gurt *m*; GEOGR Zone *f*, Gebiet *n*; TECH (Treib)Riemen *m*; **2.** *~ out* MUS schmettern; *a. ~ up* den Gürtel (*gen*) zumachen; *~ up* MOT sich anschnallen; **belt·ed** mit e-m Gürtel

belt·way Umgehungsstraße *f*; Ringstraße *f*

be·moan betrauern, beklagen

bench Sitzbank *f*, Bank *f* (*a.* SPORT); TECH Werkbank *f*; JUR Richterbank *f*; Richter *m or pl*

bend 1. Biegung *f*, Kurve *f*; *drive s.o. round the ~* F j-n noch wahnsinnig machen; **2.** (sich) biegen *or* krümmen; neigen; beugen; *fig* richten (*to, on* auf *acc*)

be·neath → **below**

ben·e·dic·tion REL Segen *m*

ben·e·fac·tor Wohltäter *m*

be·nef·i·cent wohltätig

ben·e·fi·cial wohltuend, zuträglich, nützlich

ben·e·fit 1. Nutzen *m*, Vorteil *m*; Wohltätigkeitsveranstaltung *f*; (Sozial-, Versicherungs- *etc*)Leistung *f*; (Arbeitslosen- *etc*)Unterstützung *f*; (Kranken*etc*)Geld *n*; **2.** nützen; *~ by, ~ from* Vorteil haben von *or* durch, Nutzen ziehen aus

be·nev·o·lence Wohlwollen *n*

be·nev·o·lent wohltätig; wohlwollend

be·nign MED gutartig

bent 1. *~ on doing* entschlossen zu tun; **2.** Hang *m*, Neigung *f*; Veranlagung *f*

ben·zene CHEM Benzol *n*

ben·zine CHEM Leichtbenzin *n*

be·queath JUR vermachen

be·quest JUR Vermächtnis *n*

be·reave berauben

be·ret Baskenmütze *f*

ber·ry BOT Beere *f*

berth 1. MAR Liege-, Ankerplatz *m*; Koje *f*; RAIL (Schlafwagen)Bett *n*; **2.** MAR festmachen, anlegen

be·seech (inständig) bitten (um); anflehen

be·set heimsuchen; *~ with difficulties* mit vielen Schwierigkeiten verbunden

be·side *prp* neben (*dat or acc*); *~ o.s.* außer sich (*with* vor); *~ the point, ~ the question* nicht zur Sache gehörig

be·sides 1. adv außerdem; **2.** prp abgesehen von, außer (dat)
be·siege belagern
be·smear beschmieren
be·spat·ter bespritzen
best 1. adj beste(r, -s) höchste(r, -s), größte(r, -s), meiste; **~ before** GASTR haltbar bis; **2.** adv am besten; **3.** der, die, das Beste; **all the ~!** alles Gute!, viel Glück!; **to the ~ of ...** nach bestem ...; **make the ~ of** das Beste machen aus (dat); **at ~** bestenfalls; **be at one's ~** in Hoch- or Höchstform sein
best-be·fore date, best-by date Mindesthaltbarkeitsdatum n
bes·ti·al fig tierisch, bestialisch
be·stow geben, verleihen (**on** dat)
best-sell·er Bestseller m
bet 1. Wette f; **make a ~** e-e Wette abschließen; **2.** wetten; **~ s.o. ten dollars** mit j-m um zehn Dollar wetten; **you ~** F und ob!
be·tray verraten (a. fig); verleiten
be·tray·al Verrat m
be·tray·er Verräter(in)
bet·ter 1. adj besser; **he is ~** es geht ihm besser; **~ and ~** immer besser; **2.** das Bessere; **get the ~ of** die Oberhand gewinnen über (acc); et. überwinden; **3.** adv besser; mehr; **do ~ than** es besser machen als; **know ~** es besser wissen; **so much the ~** desto besser; **you had ~ go** Br, F **you ~ go** es wäre besser, wenn du gingest; **~ off** (finanziell) besser gestellt; **he is ~ off than I am** es geht ihm besser als mir; **4.** v/t verbessern; v/i sich bessern
be·tween 1. adv dazwischen; **in ~** zwischendurch; F **few and far ~** (ganz) vereinzelt; **2.** prp zwischen (dat or acc); unter (dat); **~ you and me** unter uns or im Vertrauen (gesagt)
bev·el TECH abkanten, abschrägen
bev·er·age Getränk n
bev·y ZO Schwarm m, Schar f
be·ware (**of**) sich in Acht nehmen (vor dat), sich hüten (vor dat); **~ of the dog!** Vorsicht, bissiger Hund!
be·wil·der verwirren
be·wil·der·ment Verwirrung f
be·witch bezaubern, verhexen
be·yond 1. adv darüber hinaus; **2.** prp jenseits (gen); über ... (acc) hinaus
bi... zwei, zweifach, zweimal

bi·as Neigung f; Vorurteil n
bi·as(s)ed voreingenommen; JUR befangen
bi·ath·lete SPORT Biathlet m
bi·ath·lon SPORT Biathlon m
bib (Sabber)Lätzchen n
Bi·ble Bibel f
bib·li·cal biblisch, Bibel...
bib·li·og·ra·phy Bibliografie f
bi·car·bon·ate a. **~ of soda** CHEM doppeltkohlensaures Natron
bi·cen·te·na·ry Br, **bi·cen·ten·ni·al** Zweihundertjahrfeier f
bi·ceps ANAT Bizeps m
bick·er sich zanken or streiten
bi·cy·cle Fahrrad n
bid 1. auction: bieten; **2.** ECON Gebot n, Angebot n
bi·en·ni·al zweijährlich; BOT zweijährig; **bi·en·ni·al·ly** alle zwei Jahre
bier (Toten)Bahre f
big groß; dick, stark; **talk ~** F den Mund voll nehmen
big·a·my Bigamie f
big busi·ness Großunternehmertum n
big·head F Angeber m
big shot, big·wig F hohes Tier
bike F **1.** (Fahr)Rad n; **2.** Rad fahren
bik·er Motorradfahrer(in); Radfahrer(in), Radler(in)
bi·lat·er·al bilateral
bile Galle f (a. fig)
bi·lin·gual zweisprachig
bill¹ ZO Schnabel m
bill² ECON Rechnung f; POL (Gesetzes-) Vorlage f; JUR (An)Klageschrift f; Plakat n; Banknote f, (Geld)Schein m
bill·board Reklametafel f
bill·fold Brieftasche f
bil·li·ards Billard(spiel) n
bil·li·on Milliarde f
bill of de·liv·er·y ECON Lieferschein m; **~ of ex·change** ECON Wechsel m; **~ of sale** JUR Verkaufsurkunde f
bil·low 1. Woge f; (Rauch- etc) Schwaden m; **2.** a. **~ out** sich bauschen or blähen
bil·ly goat ZO Ziegenbock m
bin (großer) Behälter
bi·na·ry MATH, PHYS etc binär, Binär...
bi·na·ry code EDP Binärcode m
bi·na·ry num·ber MATH Binärzahl f
bind v/t (an-, ein-, um-, auf-, fest-, ver-) binden; a. vertraglich binden, ver-

pflichten; einfassen; *v/i* binden

bind·er (*esp Buch*)Binder(in); Einband *m*; Aktendeckel *m*

bind·ing **1.** bindend, verbindlich; **2.** Einband *m*; Einfassung *f*, Borte *f*

bin·go Bingo *n*

bi·noc·u·lars Feldstecher *m*, Fern-, Opernglas *n*

bi·o·chem·is·try Biochemie *f*

bi·o·de·gra·da·ble biologisch abbaubar, umweltfreundlich

bi·og·ra·pher Biograf *m*

bi·og·ra·phy Biografie *f*

bi·o·log·i·cal biologisch

bi·ol·o·gist Biologe *m*, Biologin *f*

bi·ol·o·gy Biologie *f*

bi·o·rhythms Biorhythmus *m*

bi·o·tope Biotop *n*

bi·ped zo Zweifüßer *m*

birch BOT Birke *f*

bird zo Vogel *m*

bird·cage Vogelkäfig *m*

bird of pas·sage zo Zugvogel *m*

bird of prey zo Raubvogel *m*

bird sanc·tu·a·ry Vogelschutzgebiet *n*

bird·seed Vogelfutter *n*

bird's-eye view Vogelperspektive *f*

bi·ro® Kugelschreiber *m*

birth Geburt *f*; Herkunft *f*; **give** ~ **to** gebären, zur Welt bringen

birth cer·tif·i·cate Geburtsurkunde *f*

birth con·trol Geburtenregelung *f*; ~ **pill** MED Antibabypille *f*

birth·day Geburtstag *m*; **happy** ~**!** alles Gute *or* herzlichen Glückwunsch zum Geburtstag!

birth·mark Muttermal *n*

birth·place Geburtsort *m*

birth·rate Geburtenziffer *f*

bis·cuit *Br* Keks *m*, *n*, Plätzchen *n*

bi·sex·u·al bisexuell

bish·op REL Bischof *m*; *chess*: Läufer *m*

bish·op·ric REL Bistum *n*

bi·son zo Bison *m*; Wisent *m*

bit Bisschen *n*, Stück(chen) *n*; Gebiss *n* (*am Zaum*); (Schlüssel)Bart *m*; EDP Bit *n*; **a (little)** ~ ein (kleines) bisschen

bitch zo Hündin *f*, F *contp* Miststück *n*, Schlampe *f*

bit den·si·ty EDP Speicherdichte *f*

bite **1.** Beißen *n*; Biss *m*; Bissen *m*, Happen *m*; TECH Fassen *n*, Greifen *n*; **2.** (an)beißen; zo stechen; GASTR brennen; *fig* schneiden (*cold etc*); beißen

(*smoke etc*); TECH fassen, greifen

bit·ter bitter; *fig* verbittert

bit·ters GASTR Magenbitter *m*

biz F → **business**

black **1.** schwarz; dunkel; finster; **have s.th. in** ~ **and white** et. schwarz auf weiß haben *or* besitzen; **be** ~ **and blue** blaue Flecken haben; **beat s.o.** ~ **and blue** j-n grün und blau schlagen; **2.** schwärzen; ~ **out** verdunkeln; **3.** Schwarz *n*; Schwärze *f*; Schwarze *m*, *f*

black·ber·ry BOT Brombeere *f*

black·bird zo Amsel *f*

black·board (Schul-, Wand)Tafel *f*

black box AVIAT Flugschreiber *m*

black cur·rant BOT schwarze Johannisbeere

black·en *v/t* schwärzen; *fig* anschwärzen; *v/i* schwarz werden

black eye blaues Auge, Veilchen *n*

black·head MED Mitesser *m*

black ice Glatteis *n*

black·ing schwarze Schuhwichse *f*

black·leg *Br* Streikbrecher *m*

black·mail **1.** Erpressung *f*; **2.** *j-n* erpressen; **black·mail·er** Erpresser(in)

black mar·ket Schwarzmarkt *m*

black·ness Schwärze *f*

black·out Verdunkelung *f*; Black-out *m*; ELECTR Stromausfall *m*; Ohnmacht *f*

black pud·ding GASTR Blutwurst *f*

black sheep *fig* schwarzes Schaf

black·smith Schmied *m*

blad·der ANAT Blase *f*

blade TECH Blatt *n*, Schaufel *f*; Klinge *f*; Schneide *f*; BOT Halm *m*

blame **1.** Tadel *m*; Schuld *f*; **2.** tadeln; **be to** ~ **for** schuld sein an (*dat*)

blame·less untadelig

blanch *v/t* bleichen; GASTR blanchieren; *v/i* erbleichen, bleich werden

blank **1.** leer; unausgefüllt, unbeschrieben; ECON Blanko...; verdutzt; **2.** Leere *f*; leerer Raum, Lücke *f*; unbeschriebenes Blatt, Formular *n*; *lottery*: Niete *f*; ~ **car·tridge** Platzpatrone *f*; ~ **check** (*Br* **cheque**) ECON Blankoscheck *m*

blan·ket **1.** (Woll)Decke *f*; **2.** zudecken

blare brüllen, plärren (*radio etc*), schmettern (*trumpet*)

blas·pheme lästern

blas·phe·my Gotteslästerung *f*

blast **1.** Windstoß *m*; MUS Ton *m*; TECH

B

Explosion *f*; Druckwelle *f*; Sprengung *f*; **2.** sprengen; *fig* zunichte machen; ~ **off** (**into space**) in den Weltraum schießen; ~ **off** abheben, starten (*rocket*); ~**!** verdammt!; ~ **you!** der Teufel soll dich holen!; ~**ed** verdammt, verflucht

blast fur·nace TECH Hochofen *m*

blast-off Start *m* (*of a rocket*)

bla·tant offenkundig, eklatant

blaze 1. Flamme (*n pl*) *f*, Feuer *n*; heller Schein; *fig* Ausbruch *m*; **2.** brennen, lodern; leuchten

blaz·er Blazer *m*

bla·zon Wappen *n*

bleach bleichen

bleak öde, kahl; rau; *fig* trüb, freudlos, finster

blear·y trübe, verschwommen

bleat ZO **1.** Blöken *n*; **2.** blöken

bleed *v/i* bluten; *v/t* MED zur Ader lassen; F schröpfen

bleed·ing MED Blutung *f*; Aderlass *m*

bleep 1. Piepton *m*; **2.** *j-n* anpiepsen

bleep·er Br F Piepser *m*

blem·ish 1. (*a.* Schönheits)Fehler *m*; Makel *m*; **2.** entstellen

blend 1. (sich) (ver)mischen; GASTR verschneiden; **2.** Mischung *f*; GASTR Verschnitt *m*

blend·er Mixer *m*, Mixgerät *n*

bless segnen; preisen; **be ~ed with** gesegnet sein mit; (**God**) ~ **you!** alles Gute!; Gesundheit!; ~ **me!**, ~ **my heart!**, ~ **my soul!** F du meine Güte!

bless·ed selig, gesegnet; F verflixt

bless·ing Segen *m*

blight BOT Mehltau *m*

blind 1. blind (*fig* **to** gegen[über]); unübersichtlich; **2.** Rouleau *n*, Rollo *n*; **the** ~ die Blinden *pl*; **3.** blenden; *fig* blind machen (**to** für, gegen)

blind al·ley Sackgasse *f*

blind·ers Scheuklappen *pl*

blind·fold 1. blindlings; **2.** *j-m* die Augen verbinden; **3.** Augenbinde *f*

blind·ly *fig* blindlings

blind·ness Blindheit *f*; Verblendung *f*

blind·worm ZO Blindschleiche *f*

blink 1. Blinzeln *n*; **2.** blinzeln, zwinkern; blinken

blink·ers Br Scheuklappen *pl*

bliss Seligkeit *f*, Wonne *f*

blis·ter MED, TECH **1.** Blase *f*; **2.** Blasen

hervorrufen auf (*dat*); Blasen ziehen *or* TECH werfen

blitz MIL **1.** heftiger Luftangriff; **2.** schwer bombardieren

bliz·zard Blizzard *m*, Schneesturm *m*

bloat·ed (an)geschwollen, (auf)gedunsen; *fig* aufgeblasen

bloat·er GASTR Bückling *m*

blob Klecks *m*

block 1. Block *m*, Klotz *m*; Baustein *m*, (Bau)Klötzchen *n*; (*Schreib-, Notiz-*)Block *m*; (Häuser)Block *m*; TECH Verstopfung *f*; *fig* geistige *etc* Sperre; **2.** (**of flats**) Br Wohn-, Mietshaus *n*; **2.** *a.* ~ **up** (ab-, ver)sperren, blockieren, verstopfen

block·ade 1. Blockade *f*; **2.** blockieren

block·bust·er F Kassenmagnet *m*, Kassenschlager *m*

block·head F Dummkopf *m*

block let·ters Blockschrift *f*

blond 1. Blonde *m*; **2.** blond; hell (*skin*)

blonde 1. blond; **2.** Blondine *f*

blood Blut *n*; **in cold** ~ kaltblütig; ~ **bank** MED Blutbank *f*; ~ **clot** MED Blutgerinnsel *n*; ~ **cor·pus·cle** MED Blutkörperchen *n*

blood·cur·dling grauenhaft

blood do·nor MED Blutspender(in)

blood group MED Blutgruppe *f*

blood·hound ZO Bluthund *m*

blood pres·sure MED Blutdruck *m*

blood·shed Blutvergießen *n*

blood·shot blutunterlaufen

blood·thirst·y blutdürstig

blood ves·sel ANAT Blutgefäß *n*

blood test MED Blutprobe *f*

blood·y blutig; Br F verdammt, verflucht

bloom 1. Blume *f*, Blüte *f*; *fig* Blüte(zeit) *f*; **2.** blühen; *fig* (er)strahlen

blos·som 1. Blüte *f*; **2.** blühen; *fig* ~ **into** erblühen zu

blot 1. Klecks *m*; *fig* Makel *m*; **2.** beklecksen

blotch Klecks *m*; Hautfleck *m*

blotch·y fleckig

blot·ter (Tinten)Löscher *m*

blot·ting pa·per Löschpapier *n*

blouse Bluse *f*

blow¹ Schlag *m* (*a. fig*), Stoß *m*

blow² *v/i* blasen, wehen; keuchen; schnaufen; explodieren; platzen (*tire*); ELECTR durchbrennen; ~ **up** in die Luft fliegen; explodieren; v/t: **~ one's nose** sich die Nase putzen; **~ one's top** F an die Decke gehen (*vor Wut*); **~ out** ausblasen; **~ up** sprengen; PHOT vergrößern

blow-dry föhnen

blow-fly ZO Schmeißfliege f

blow-pipe Blasrohr n

blow-up PHOT Vergrößerung f

blud-geon Knüppel m

blue 1. blau; F melancholisch, traurig, schwermütig; **2.** Blau n; **out of the ~** fig aus heiterem Himmel

blue-ber-ry BOT Blau-, Heidelbeere f

blue-bot-tle ZO Schmeißfliege f

blue-col-lar work-er Arbeiter(in)

blues MUS Blues m; F Melancholie f; **have the ~** F den Moralischen haben

bluff[1] Steilufer n

bluff[2] **1.** Bluff m; **2.** bluffen

blu-ish bläulich

blun-der 1. Fehler m, F Schnitzer m; **2.** e-n (groben) Fehler machen; verpfuschen, F verpatzen

blunt stumpf; fig offen

blunt-ly freiheraus

blur [blɜː] **1.** v/t verwischen; verschmieren; PHOT, TV verwackeln, verzerren; fig trüben; **2.** v/i verschwimmen (a. fig)

blurt: ~ out herausplatzen mit

blush 1. Erröten n, Schamröte f; **2.** erröten, rot werden

blus-ter brausen (*wind*); fig poltern, toben

BMX ABBR of *bicycle motocross* Querfeldeinrennen n; **~ bike** BMX-Rad n

BO ABBR → *body odo(u)r*

boar ZO Eber m; Keiler m

board 1. Brett n; (Anschlag)Brett n; Konferenztisch m; Ausschuss m, Kommission f; Behörde f; Verpflegung f; Pappe f, Karton m; SPORT (Surf)Board n; **on ~ a train** in e-m Zug; **2.** v/t dielen, verschalen; beköstigen; an Bord gehen; MAR entern; RAIL *etc* einsteigen in; v/i in Kost sein, wohnen

board-er Kostgänger(in); Pensionsgast m; Internatsschüler(in)

board game Brettspiel n

board-ing| card AVIAT Bordkarte f; **~ house** Pension f, Fremdenheim n; **~ school** Internat n

board of di-rec-tors ECON Aufsichtsrat m

Board of Trade Handelskammer f; Br Handelsministerium n

board-walk Strandpromenade f

boast 1. Prahlerei f; **2.** (*of, about*) sich rühmen (*gen*), prahlen (mit)

boat Boot n; Schiff n

bob 1. Knicks m; kurzer Haarschnitt; Br HIST F Schilling m; **2.** v/t Haar kurz schneiden; v/i sich auf und ab bewegen; knicksen

bob-bin Spule f (a. ELECTR)

bob-sleigh SPORT Bob m

bod-ice Mieder n; Oberteil n

bod-i-ly körperlich

bod-y Körper m, Leib m; Leiche f; JUR Körperschaft f; Hauptteil m; MOT Karosserie f; MIL Truppenkörper m

bod-y-guard Leibwache f; Leibwächter m

bod-y| o-do(u)r (ABBR *BO*) Körpergeruch m; **~ stock-ing** Body m

bod-y-work MOT Karosserie f

Boer 1. Bure m; **2.** Buren...

bog Sumpf m, Morast m

bo-gus falsch; Schwindel...

boil[1] MED Geschwür n, Furunkel m, n

boil[2] **1.** kochen, sieden; **2.** Kochen n, Sieden n

boil-er (Dampf)Kessel m; Boiler m

boil-er suit Overall m

boil-ing point Siedepunkt m (a. fig)

bois-ter-ous ungestüm; heftig; laut; lärmend

bold kühn, verwegen; keck, dreist, unverschämt; steil; PRINT fett; **as ~ as brass** F frech wie Oskar; **words in ~ print** fett gedruckt; **bold-ness** Kühnheit f, Verwegenheit f; Dreistigkeit f

bol-ster 1. Keilkissen n; **2. ~ up** fig (unter)stützen; j-m Mut machen

bolt 1. Bolzen m; Riegel m; Blitz(strahl) m; plötzlicher Satz, Fluchtversuch m; **2.** *adv:* **~ upright** kerzengerade; **3.** v/t verriegeln; F hinunterschlingen; v/i davonlaufen, ausreißen; ZO scheuen, durchgehen

bomb 1. Bombe f; **the ~** die Atombombe; **2.** bombardieren; **bom-bard** bombardieren; **bomb-er** AVIAT Bomber m; Bombenleger m

bomb-proof bombensicher

bomb-shell Bombe f (a. fig)

bo-nan-za fig Goldgrube f

bond Bund m, Verbindung f; ECON

Schuldverschreibung *f*, Obligation *f*; **in ~ ECON** unter Zollverschluss

bond·age Hörigkeit *f*

bonds *fig* Bande *pl*

bone 1. ANAT Knochen *m*, *pl a.* Gebeine *pl*; **ZO** Gräte *f*; **~ of contention** Zankapfel *m*; ***have a ~ to pick with s.o.*** mit j-m ein Hühnchen zu rupfen haben; ***make no ~s about*** nicht lange fackeln mit; **2.** die Knochen auslösen (aus); entgräten

bon·fire Feuer *n* im Freien; Freudenfeuer *n*

bon·net Haube *f*; *Br* Motorhaube *f*

bo·nus ECON Bonus *m*, Prämie *f*; Gratifikation *f*

bon·y knöchern; knochig

boo *int* buh!; **THEA ~ off the stage**, *soccer*: **~ off the park** auspfeifen

boobs *sl* Titten *pl*

boo·by F Trottel *m*

book 1. Buch *n*; Heft *n*; Liste *f*; Block *m*; **2.** buchen; eintragen; **SPORT** verwarnen; *Fahrkarte etc* lösen; *Platz etc* (vor)bestellen, reservieren lassen; *Gepäck* aufgeben; **~ in** *esp Br* sich (*im Hotel*) eintragen; **~ in at** absteigen in (*dat*); **~ed up** ausgebucht, ausverkauft, belegt

book·case Bücherschrank *m*

book·ing Buchen *n*, (Vor)Bestellung *f*; **SPORT** Verwarnung *f*; **~ clerk** Schalterbeamte *m*, -beamtin *f*; **~ of·fice** Fahrkartenausgabe *f*, -schalter *m*; **THEA** Kasse *f*

book·keep·er ECON Buchhalter(in)

book·keep·ing ECON Buchhaltung *f*, Buchführung *f*

book·let Büchlein *n*, Broschüre *f*

book·mak·er Buchmacher *m*

book·mark(·er) Lesezeichen *n*

book·sell·er Buchhändler(in)

book·shelf Bücherregal *n*

book·shop *esp Br*, **book·store** Buchhandlung *f*

book·worm *fig* Bücherwurm *m*

boom¹ ECON 1. Boom *m*, Aufschwung *m*, Hochkonjunktur *f*, Hausse *f*; **2.** e-n Boom erleben

boom² MAR Baum *m*, Spiere *f*; **TECH** (Kran)Ausleger *m*; *film*, *TV* (Mikrofon)Galgen *m*

boom³ dröhnen, donnern

boor·ish ungehobelt

boost 1. hochschieben; **ECON** in die Höhe treiben; ankurbeln; **ELECTR** verstärken; **TECH** erhöhen; *fig* stärken, Auftrieb geben (*dat*); **2.** Erhöhung *f*; Auftrieb *m*; **ELECTR** Verstärkung *f*

boost·er ECON Auftrieb *m*, Ankurbelung *f*; **ELECTR** Verstärker *m*

boot¹ Stiefel *m*; *Br* **MOT** Kofferraum *m*

boot²: ~ (up) EDP laden

boot³: to ~ obendrein

boot·ee (*Damen*)Halbstiefel *m*

booth (*Markt- etc*)Bude *f*; (*Messe-*)Stand *m*; (*Wahl- etc*)Kabine *f*; (*Telefon*)Zelle *f*

boot·lace Schnürsenkel *m*

boot·y Beute *f*

booze F 1. saufen; **2.** Zeug *n*; Sauferei *f*

bor·der 1. Rand *m*, Saum *m*, Einfassung *f*; Rabatte *f*; Grenze *f*; **2.** einfassen; (um)säumen; grenzen (**on** an *acc*)

bore¹ 1. Bohrloch *n*; **TECH** Kaliber *n*; **2.** bohren

bore² 1. Langweiler *m*; langweilige *or* lästige Sache; **2.** *j-n* langweilen; **be ~d** sich langweilen

bore·dom Lang(e)weile *f*

bor·ing langweilig

bo·rough Stadtteil *m*; Stadtgemeinde *f*; Stadtbezirk *m*

bor·row (sich) *et.* borgen *or* (aus)leihen

bos·om Busen *m*; *fig* Schoß *m*

boss F 1. Boss *m*, Chef *m*; **2.** *a.* **~ about**, **~ around** herumkommandieren

boss·y F herrisch

bo·tan·i·cal botanisch

bot·a·ny Botanik *f*

botch 1. Pfusch *m*; **2.** verpfuschen

both beide(s); **~ ... and ...** sowohl ... als (auch) ...

both·er 1. Belästigung *f*, Störung *f*, Plage *f*, Mühe *f*; **2.** belästigen, stören, plagen; ***don't ~!*** bemühen Sie sich nicht!

bot·tle 1. Flasche *f*; **2.** in Flaschen abfüllen; **~ bank** *Br* Altglascontainer *m*

bot·tle·neck *fig* Engpass *m*

bot·tle o·pen·er Flaschenöffner *m*

bot·tom unterster Teil, Boden *m*, Fuß *m*, Unterseite *f*; Grund *m*; **F** Hintern *m*, Popo *m*; ***be at the ~ of s.th.*** hinter e-r Sache stecken; ***get to the ~ of s.th.*** e-r Sache auf den Grund gehen

bough Ast *m*, Zweig *m*

boul·der Geröllblock *m*, Findling *m*

bounce 1. aufprallen *or* aufspringen (lassen); springen, hüpfen, stürmen;

bravery

ECON F platzen (*check*); **2.** Sprung *m*, Satz *m*; F Schwung *m*

bounc·ing kräftig, stramm

bound[1] unterwegs (*for* nach)

bound[2] *mst pl* Grenze *f*, *fig a.* Schranke *f*

bound[3]**1.** Sprung *m*, Satz *m*; **2.** springen, hüpfen; auf-, abprallen

bound·a·ry Grenze *f*

bound·less grenzenlos

boun·te·ous, boun·ti·ful freigebig, reichlich

boun·ty Freigebigkeit *f*; Prämie *f*

bou·quet Bukett *n* (*a.* GASTR.), Strauß *m*; GASTR. Blume *f*

bout SPORT (*Box-, Ring*)Kampf *m*; MED Anfall *m*

bou·tique Boutique *f*

bow[1] **1.** Verbeugung *f*; **2.** *v/i* sich verbeugen *or* verneigen (*to* vor *dat*); *fig* sich beugen *or* unterwerfen (*to* dat); *v/t* biegen; beugen, neigen

bow[2] MAR Bug *m*

bow[3] Bogen *m*; Schleife *f*

bow·els ANAT Darm *m*; Eingeweide *pl*

bowl[1] Schale *f*, Schüssel *f*, Napf *m*; (*Zucker*)Dose *f*; Becken *n*; (*Pfeifen-*) Kopf *m*

bowl[2]**1.** (*Bowling-, Kegel- etc*)Kugel *f*; **2.** kegeln; rollen (*bowling ball*); *cricket:* werfen

bow-leg·ged o-beinig

bowl·er[1] Bowlingspieler(in); Kegler(in)

bowl·er[2], *a.* **~ hat** *esp Br* Bowler *m*, F Melone *f*

bowl·ing Bowling *n*; Kegeln *n*; **go ~** kegeln; **~ al·ley** Kegelbahn *f*; **~ ball** Kegelkugel *f*

box[1] Kasten *m*, Kiste *f*; Büchse *f*, Dose *f*, Kästchen *n*; Schachtel *f*; Behälter *m*; TECH Gehäuse *n*; Postfach *n*; *Br* (*Telefon*)Zelle *f*; JUR Zeugenstand *m*; THEA Loge *f*; MOT, ZO Box *f*

box[2] **1.** SPORT boxen; F **~ s.o.'s ears** j-n ohrfeigen; **2.** F **a ~ on the ear** e-e Ohrfeige

box[3] [bɒ'aks] BOT Buchsbaum *m*

box·er Boxer *m*

box·ing Boxen *n*, Boxsport *m*

Box·ing Day *Br* der zweite Weihnachtsfeiertag

box num·ber Chiffre(nummer) *f*

box of·fice Theaterkasse *f*

boy Junge *m*, Knabe *m*, Bursche *m*

boy·cott 1. boykottieren; **2.** Boykott *m*

boy·friend Freund *m*

boy·hood Knabenjahre *pl*, Jugend (-zeit) *f*

boy·ish jungenhaft

boy scout Pfadfinder *m*

bra BH *m* (*Büstenhalter*)

brace 1. TECH Strebe *f*, Stützbalken *m*; (*Zahn*)Klammer *f*, (-)Spange *f*; **2.** TECH verstreben, versteifen, stützen

brace·let Armband *n*

brac·es *Br* Hosenträger *pl*

brack·et TECH Träger *m*, Halter *m*; Stütze *f*; PRINT Klammer *f*; (*esp Alters-, Steuer*)Klasse *f*; *lower income ~* niedrige Einkommensgruppe

brack·ish brackig, salzig

brag prahlen (*about* mit)

brag·gart Prahler *m*, F Angeber *m*

braid 1. Zopf *m*; Borte *f*, Tresse *f*; **2.** flechten; mit Borte besetzen

brain ANAT Gehirn *n*, *often pl fig a.* Verstand *m*, Intelligenz *f*, Kopf *m*

brain·storm Geistesblitz *m*

brain·wash *j-n* e-r Gehirnwäsche unterziehen

brain·wash·ing Gehirnwäsche *f*

brain·wave *Br* Geistesblitz *m*

brain·y F gescheit

braise GASTR schmoren

brake TECH **1.** Bremse *f*; **2.** bremsen

brake·light MOT Bremslicht *n*

bram·ble BOT Brombeerstrauch *m*

bran AGR Kleie *f*

branch 1. Ast *m*, Zweig *m*; *fig* Fach *n*; Linie *f* (*des Stammbaumes*); ECON Zweigstelle *f*, Filiale *f*; **2.** sich verzweigen; abzweigen

brand 1. ECON (*Schutz-, Handels*)Marke *f*, Warenzeichen *n*; Markenname *m*; Sorte *f*, Klasse *f*; Brandmal *n*; **2.** einbrennen; brandmarken

bran·dish schwingen

brand name ECON Markenname *m*

brand-new nagelneu

bran·dy Kognak *m*, Weinbrand *m*

brass Messing *n*; F Unverschämtheit *f*

brass band MUS Blaskapelle *f*

bras·sière Büstenhalter *m*

brat *contp* Balg *m*, *n*, Gör *n*

brave 1. tapfer, mutig, unerschrocken; **2.** trotzen; mutig begegnen (*dat*)

brav·er·y Tapferkeit *f*

brawl

B

brawl **1.** Krawall *m*; Rauferei *f*; **2.** Krawall machen; raufen

brawn·y muskulös

bray **1.** ZO Eselsschrei *m*; **2.** ZO schreien; *fig* wiehern

bra·zen unverschämt, unverfroren, frech

Bra·zil Brasilien *n*; **Bra·zil·ian 1.** brasilianisch; **2.** Brasilianer(in)

breach **1.** Bruch *m*; *fig* Verletzung *f*; MIL Bresche *f*; **2.** e-e Bresche schlagen in (*acc*)

bread Brot *n*; **brown ~** Schwarzbrot *n*; **know which side one's ~ is buttered** F s-n Vorteil (er)kennen

breadth Breite *f*

break **1.** Bruch *m*; Lücke *f*; Pause *f* (*Br a.* PED), Unterbrechung *f*; (plötzlicher) Wechsel, Umschwung *m*; (*Tages*)Anbruch *m*; **bad ~** F Pech *n*; **lucky ~** F Dusel *m*, Schwein *n*; **give s.o. a ~** F j-m e-e Chance geben; **take a ~** e-e Pause machen; **without a ~** ununterbrochen; **2.** *v/t* (ab-, auf-, durch-, zer)brechen; zerschlagen, kaputtmachen; ZO *a.* **~ in** zähmen, abrichten, zureiten; *Gesetz, Vertrag etc* brechen; *Kode etc* knacken; *schlechte Nachricht* (schonend) beibringen; *v/i* brechen (*a. fig*); (zer-) brechen; (zer)reißen, kaputtgehen; anbrechen (*Tag*); METEOR umschlagen; *fig* ausbrechen (**into** in *Tränen etc*); **~ away** ab-, losbrechen; sich losmachen *or* losreißen; **~ down** ein-, niederreißen, *Haus* abbrechen; zusammenbrechen (*a. fig*); versagen; MOT e-e Panne haben; *fig* scheitern; **~ in** einbrechen, eindringen; **~ into** einbrechen in (*ein Haus etc*); **~ off** abbrechen, *fig a.* Schluss machen mit; **~ out** ausbrechen; **~ through** durchbrechen; *fig* den Durchbruch schaffen; **~ up** abbrechen, beenden, schließen; (sich) auflösen; *fig* zerbrechen, auseinander gehen

break·a·ble zerbrechlich

break·age Bruch *m*

break·a·way **1.** Trennung *f*; **2.** Splitter...

break·down Zusammenbruch *m* (*a. fig*); TECH Maschinenschaden *m*; MOT Panne *f*; **~ nervous ~** MED Nervenzusammenbruch *m*; **~ lor·ry** *Br* MOT Abschleppwagen *m*; **~ ser·vice** *Br* MOT Pannendienst *m*, Pannenhilfe *f*; **~ truck** *Br* MOT Abschleppwagen *m*

break·fast **1.** Frühstück *n*; **have ~ → 2.** frühstücken

break·through *fig* Durchbruch *m*

break·up Aufhebung *f*; Auflösung *f*

breast ANAT Brust *f*; Busen *m*; *fig* Herz *n*; **make a clean ~ of s.th.** et. offen (ein)gestehen

breast·stroke Brustschwimmen *n*

breath Atem(zug) *m*; Hauch *m*; **be out of ~** außer Atem sein; **waste one's ~** in den Wind reden

breath·a·lyse *Br*, **breath·a·lyze** F (ins Röhrchen) blasen *or* pusten lassen

breath·a·lys·er® *Br*, **breath·alyz·er®** Alkoholtestgerät *n*, F Röhrchen *n*

breathe atmen

breath·less atemlos

breath·tak·ing atemberaubend

breech·es Kniebund-, Reithosen *pl*

breed **1.** ZO Rasse *f*, Zucht *f*; **2.** *v/t* BOT, ZO züchten; *v/i* BIOL sich fortpflanzen

breed·er Züchter(in); Zuchttier *n*; PHYS Brüter *m*

breed·ing BIOL Fortpflanzung *f*; (Tier)Zucht *f*; *fig* Erziehung *f*; (gutes) Benehmen

breeze Brise *f*

breth·ren *esp* REL Brüder *pl*

brew brauen; *Tee* zubereiten, aufbrühen

brew·er (Bier)Brauer *m*

brew·er·y Brauerei *f*

bri·ar → brier

bribe **1.** Bestechungsgeld *n*, -geschenk *n*; Bestechung *f*; **2.** bestechen

brib·er·y Bestechung *f*

brick **1.** Ziegel(stein) *m*, Backstein *m*; *Br* Baustein *m*, (Bau)Klötzchen *n*

brick·lay·er Maurer *m*

brick·yard Ziegelei *f*

brid·al Braut...; **bride** Braut *f*

bride·groom Bräutigam *m*

brides·maid Brautjungfer *f*

bridge **1.** Brücke *f*; **2.** e-e Brücke schlagen über (*acc*); *fig* überbrücken

bri·dle **1.** Zaum *m*; Zügel *m*; **2.** (auf)zäumen; zügeln; **~ path** Reitweg *m*

brief **1.** kurz, bündig; **2.** instruieren, genaue Anweisungen geben (*dat*)

brief·case Aktenmappe *f*

briefs Slip *m*

bri·er BOT Dornstrauch *m*; Wilde Rose *f*

bri·gade MIL Brigade *f*

bright hell, glänzend; klar; heiter; lebhaft; gescheit

bright·en v/t a. ~ **up** heller machen, aufhellen, erhellen; aufheitern; v/i a. ~ **up** sich aufhellen

bright·ness Helligkeit f; Glanz m; Heiterkeit f; Gescheitheit f

brill Br F super, toll

bril·liance, bril·lian·cy Glanz m; fig Brillanz f

bril·liant 1. glänzend; hervorragend, brillant; **2.** Brillant m

brim 1. Rand m; Krempe f; **2.** bis zum Rande füllen or voll sein

brim·ful(l) randvoll

brine Sole f; Lake f

bring bringen, mitbringen, herbringen; j-n dazu bringen (**to do** zu tun); ~ **about** zustande bringen; bewirken; ~ **forth** hervorbringen; ~ **off** et. fertig bringen, schaffen; ~ **on** verursachen; ~ **out** herausbringen; ~ **round** Ohnmächtigen wieder zu sich bringen; Kranken wieder auf die Beine bringen; ~ **up** auf-, großziehen; erziehen; zur Sprache bringen

brink Rand m (a. fig)

brisk flott; lebhaft; frisch

bris·tle 1. Borste f; (Bart)Stoppel f; **2.** a. ~ **up** sich sträuben; zornig werden; strotzen, wimmeln (**with** von)

bris·tly stoppelig, Stoppel...

Brit F Brite m, Britin f

Brit·ain Britannien n

Brit·ish britisch; **the** ~ die Briten pl

Brit·on Brite m, Britin f

brit·tle spröde, zerbrechlich

broach Thema anschneiden

broad breit; weit; hell; deutlich (hint etc); derb (humor etc); stark (accent); allgemein; weitherzig; liberal

broad·cast 1. im Rundfunk or Fernsehen bringen, ausstrahlen, übertragen; senden; **2.** radio, TV Sendung f

broad·cast·er Rundfunk-, Fernsehsprecher(in)

broad·en verbreitern, erweitern

broad jump SPORT Weitsprung m

broad·mind·ed liberal

bro·cade Brokat m

bro·chure Broschüre f; Prospekt m

brogue fester Straßenschuh

broil grillen

broke F pleite, abgebrannt

bro·ken zerbrochen, kaputt; gebrochen (a. fig); zerrüttet

brok·en-heart·ed verzweifelt, untröstlich

bro·ker ECON Makler m

bron·chi·tis MED Bronchitis f

bronze 1. Bronze f; **2.** bronzefarben; Bronze...

brooch Brosche f

brood ZO **1.** Brut f; **2.** Brut...; **3.** brüten (a. fig)

brook Bach m

broom Besen m

broth GASTR Fleischbrühe f

broth·el Bordell n

broth·er Bruder m; ~**(s) and sister(s)** Geschwister pl

broth·er·hood REL Bruderschaft f

broth·er-in-law Schwager m

broth·er·ly brüderlich

brow ANAT (Augen)Braue f; Stirn f; GEOGR Rand m

brow·beat einschüchtern

brown 1. braun; **2.** Braun n; **3.** bräunen; braun werden

browse grasen, weiden; fig schmökern

bruise 1. MED Quetschung f, blauer Fleck; **2.** quetschen; anstoßen; MED e-e Quetschung or e-n blauen Fleck bekommen

brunch Brunch m

brush 1. Bürste f; Pinsel m; ZO (Fuchs-)Rute f; Scharmützel n; Unterholz n; **2.** bürsten; fegen; streifen; **~ against s.o.** j-n streifen; ~ **away**, ~ **off** wegbürsten, abwischen; ~ **aside**, ~ **away** et. abtun; ~ **up (on)** fig aufpolieren, auffrischen

brush·wood Gestrüpp n, Unterholz n

brusque brüsk, barsch

Brus·sels sprouts BOT Rosenkohl m

bru·tal brutal, roh

bru·tal·i·ty Brutalität f

brute 1. brutal; **with ~ force** mit roher Gewalt; **2.** Vieh n; F Untier n, Scheusal n; Rohling m; **brut·ish** fig tierisch

bub·ble 1. Blase f; **2.** sprudeln

buck[1] **1.** ZO Bock m; **2.** bocken

buck[2] F Dollar m

buck·et Eimer m, Kübel m

buck·le 1. Schnalle f, Spange f; **2.** a. ~ **up** zu-, festschnallen; ~ **on** anschnallen

buck·skin Wildleder n

bud 1. BOT Knospe f; fig Keim m; **2.** knospen, keimen

bud·dy F Kamerad m; Kumpel m, Spezi m

B

budge *v/i* sich (von der Stelle) rühren; *v/t* (vom Fleck) bewegen

bud·ger·i·gar ZO Wellensittich *m*

bud·get Budget *n*, Etat *m*; PARL Haushaltsplan *m*

bud·gie F → *budgerigar*

buf·fa·lo ZO Büffel *m*

buff·er TECH Puffer *m*

buf·fet¹ schlagen; ~ *about* durchrütteln, durchschütteln

buf·fet² Büfett *n*, Anrichte *f*

buf·fet³ (*Frühstücks-* etc)Büfett *n*; Theke *f*

bug 1. ZO Wanze *f* (a. F *fig*); Insekt *n*; EDP Programmfehler *m*; 2. F Wanzen anbringen in (*dat*); F ärgern

bug·ging| de·vice Abhörgerät *n*; ~ op·er·a·tion Lauschangriff *m*

bug·gy Kinderwagen *m*; MOT Buggy *m*

bu·gle MUS Wald-, Signalhorn *n*

build 1. (er)bauen, errichten; 2. Körperbau *m*, Figur *f*, Statur *f*; **build·er** Erbauer *m*; Bauunternehmer *m*

build·ing 1. (Er)Bauen *n*; Bau *m*, Gebäude *n*; 2. Bau...; ~ site Baustelle *f*

built-in eingebaut, Einbau...

built-up: ~ area bebautes Gelände or Gebiet; geschlossene Ortschaft

bulb BOT Zwiebel *f*, Knolle *f*; ELECTR (Glüh)Birne *f*

bulge 1. (Aus)Bauchung *f*, Ausbuchtung *f*; 2. sich (aus)bauchen; hervorquellen

bulk Umfang *m*, Größe *f*, Masse *f*; Großteil *m*; **in ~** ECON lose, unverpackt; en gros; **bulk·y** sperrig

bull ZO Bulle *m*, Stier *m*

bull·dog ZO Bulldogge *f*

bull·doze planieren; F einschüchtern

bull·doz·er TECH Bulldozer *m*, Planierraupe *f*

bul·let Kugel *f*

bul·le·tin Bulletin *n*, Tagesbericht *m*

bul·le·tin board schwarzes Brett

bul·let-proof kugelsicher

bull·fight Stierkampf *m*

bul·lion Gold-, Silberbarren *m*

bull·lock ZO Ochse *m*

bull's-eye: **hit the ~** ins Schwarze treffen (a. *fig*)

bul·ly 1. tyrannische Person, Tyrann *m*; 2. einschüchtern, tyrannisieren

bul·wark Bollwerk *n* (a. *fig*)

bum F 1. Gammler *m*; Tippelbruder *m*;

Vagabund *m*; Nichtstuer *m*; 2. *v/t* schnorren; ~ *around* herumgammeln

bum·ble·bee ZO Hummel *f*

bump 1. heftiger Schlag or Stoß; Beule *f*; Unebenheit *f*; 2. stoßen; rammen, auf *ein* Auto auffahren; zusammenstoßen; holpern; ~ *into* j-n zufällig treffen; F ~ *s.o. off* j-n umlegen

bump·er MOT Stoßstange *f*

bump·y holp(e)rig

bun süßes Brötchen; (Haar)Knoten *m*

bunch Bund *n*, Bündel *n*; F Verein *m*, Haufen *m*; ~ *of flowers* Blumenstrauß *m*; ~ *of grapes* Weintraube *f*; ~ *of keys* Schlüsselbund *m*, *n*

bun·dle 1. Bündel *n* (a. *fig*), Bund *n*; *v/t* a. ~ *up* bündeln

bun·ga·low Bungalow *m*

bun·gee elastisches Seil

bun·gee jump·ing Bungeespringen *n*

bun·gle 1. Pfusch *m*; 2. (ver)pfuschen

bunk Koje *f*; → ~ *bed* Etagenbett *n*

bun·ny Häschen *n*

buoy 1. MAR Boje *f*; 2. ~ *up fig* Auftrieb geben (*dat*)

bur·den 1. Last *f*; Bürde *f*; 2. belasten

bu·reau *Br* Schreibtisch *m*; (Spiegel-)Kommode *f*; Büro *n*

bu·reauc·ra·cy Bürokratie *f*

burg·er GASTR Hamburger *m*

bur·glar Einbrecher *m*

bur·glar·ize einbrechen in (*acc*)

bur·glar·y Einbruch *m*

bur·gle *Br* → *burglarize*

bur·i·al Begräbnis *n*

bur·ly stämmig, kräftig

burn 1. MED Verbrennung *f*, Brandwunde *f*; verbrannte Stelle; 2. (ver-, an-) brennen; ~ *down* ab-, niederbrennen; ~ *out* ausbrennen; ~ *up* auflodern; verbrennen; verglühen (*rocket* etc)

burn·ing brennend (a. *fig*)

burp F rülpsen, aufstoßen; ein Bäuerchen machen (lassen)

bur·row 1. ZO Bau *m*; 2. graben; sich eingraben or vergraben

burst 1. Bersten *n*; Riss *m*; *fig* Ausbruch *m*; 2. *v/i* bersten, (zer)platzen; zerspringen; explodieren; ~ *from* sich losreißen von; ~ *in on* or *upon s.o.* bei j-m hereinplatzen; ~ *into tears* in Tränen ausbrechen; ~ *out fig* herausplatzen; *v/t* (auf)sprengen

bur·y begraben, vergraben; beerdigen

bus Omnibus *m*, Bus *m*

bus driv·er Busfahrer *m*

bush Busch *m*; Gebüsch *n*

bush·el Bushel *m*, Scheffel *m* (*Am* 35,24 l, *Br* 36,37 l)

bush·y buschig

busi·ness Geschäft *n*; Arbeit *f*, Beschäftigung *f*; Beruf *m*, Tätigkeit *f*; Angelegenheit *f*; Sache *f*, Aufgabe *f*; *~ of the day* Tagesordnung *f*; *on ~* geschäftlich, beruflich; *you have no ~ doing (or to do) that* Sie haben kein Recht, das zu tun; *that's none of your ~* das geht Sie nichts an; → *mind* 2

busi·ness hours Geschäftszeit *f*

busi·ness·like geschäftsmäßig, sachlich

busi·ness·man Geschäftsmann *m*

busi·ness trip Geschäftsreise *f*

busi·ness·wom·an Geschäftsfrau *f*

bus stop Bushaltestelle *f*

bust¹ Büste *f*

bust²: *go ~* F Pleite gehen

bus·tle 1. geschäftiges Treiben; 2. *~ about* geschäftig hin und her eilen

bus·y 1. beschäftigt; geschäftig; fleißig (*at* bei, an *dat*); belebt (*street*); arbeitsreich (*dat*); TEL besetzt; 2. (*mst ~ o.s.*) beschäftigen (*with* mit)

bus·y·bod·y aufdringlicher Mensch, Gschaftlhuber *m*

bus·y sig·nal TEL Besetztzeichen *n*

but 1. *cj* aber, jedoch; sondern; außer, als; ohne dass; dennoch; *~ then* and(e)rerseits; *he could not ~ laugh* er musste einfach lachen; 2. *prp* außer (*dat*); *all ~ him* alle außer ihm; *the last ~ one* der Vorletzte; *the next ~ one* der Übernächste; *nothing ~* nichts als; *~ for* wenn nicht ... gewesen wäre, ohne; 3. *cj* (*the* [*die or das*] *nicht*); *there is no one ~ knows* es gibt niemand, der es nicht weiß; 4. *adv* nur; erst, gerade; *all ~* fast, beinahe

butch·er 1. Fleischer *m*, Metzger *m*; 2. (*fig* ab)schlachten

but·ler Butler *m*

butt¹ 1. (*Gewehr*)Kolben *m*; (*Zigarren etc*)Stummel *m*, (*Zigaretten*)Kippe *f*; (*Kopf*)Stoß *m*; 2. (mit dem Kopf) stoßen; *~ in* F sich einmischen (*on* in *acc*)

butt² Wein-, Bierfaß *n*; Regentonne *f*

but·ter·cup BOT Butterblume *f*

but·ter·fly ZO Schmetterling *m*, Falter *m*

but·tocks ANAT Gesäß *n*, F *or* ZO Hinterteil *n*

but·ton 1. Knopf *m*; Button *m*, (Ansteck)Plakette *f*, Abzeichen *n*; 2. *mst ~ up* zuknöpfen

but·ton·hole Knopfloch *n*

but·tress Strebepfeiler *m*

bux·om drall, stramm

buy 1. F Kauf *m*; 2. (an-, ein)kaufen (*of, from* von; *at* bei); *Fahrkarte* lösen; *~ out* *j-n* abfinden, auszahlen; *Firma* aufkaufen; *~ up* aufkaufen

buy·er Käufer(in); ECON Einkäufer(in)

buzz 1. Summen *n*, Surren *n*; Stimmengewirr *n*; 2. *v/i* summen, surren; *~ off!* F schwirr ab!, hau ab!

buz·zard ZO Bussard *m*

buzz·er ELECTR Summer *m*

by 1. *prp* (nahe *or* dicht) bei *or* an, neben (*side ~ side* Seite an Seite); vorbei *or* vorüber an; *time*: bis um, bis spätestens (*be back ~ 9.30* sei um 9 Uhr 30 zurück); während, bei (*~ day* bei Tage); per, mit (*~ bus* mit dem Bus; *~ rail* per Bahn); nach, ...weise (*~ the dozen* dutzendweise); nach, gemäß (*~ my watch* nach *or* auf m-r Uhr); von (*~ nature* von Natur aus); von, durch (*a play ~ ...* ein Stück von ...; *~ o.s.* allein); um (*~ an inch* um e-n Zoll); MATH mal (*2 ~ 4*); *geteilt* durch (*6 ~ 3*); 2. *adv* vorbei, vorüber (*go ~* vorbeigehen, -fahren); *time*: vergehen); beiseite (*put ~* beiseite legen, zurücklegen); *~ and large* im Großen und Ganzen

by... Neben...; Seiten...;

bye, bye-bye *int* F Wiedersehen!, tschüs(s)!

by-e·lec·tion PARL Nachwahl *f*

by·gone 1. vergangen; 2. *let ~s be ~s* lass(t) das Vergangene ruhen

by·pass 1. Umgehungsstraße *f*; MED Bypass *m*; 2. umgehen; vermeiden

by-prod·uct Nebenprodukt *n*

by·road Nebenstraße *f*

by·stand·er Zuschauer(in), *pl die* Umstehenden

byte EDP Byte *n*

by·way Nebenstraße *f*

by·word Inbegriff *m*; *be a ~ for* stehen für

C

C, c C, c n

C ABBR *of* **Celsius** C, Celsius; **centigrade** hundertgradig

c ABBR *of* **cent(s)** Cent *m or pl*; **century** Jh., Jahrhundert *n*; **circa** ca., zirca, ungefähr; **cubic** Kubik...

cab Droschke *f*, Taxi *n*; RAIL Führerstand *m*; MOT Fahrerhaus *n*, *a.* TECH Führerhaus *n*

cab·a·ret Varieteedarbietung(en *pl*) *f*

cab·bage BOT Kohl *m*

cab·in Hütte *f*; MAR Kabine *f*, Kajüte *f*; AVIAT Kanzel *f*

cab·i·net Schrank *m*, Vitrine *f*; POL Kabinett *n*

cab·i·net-mak·er Kunsttischler *m*

cab·i·net meet·ing POL Kabinettssitzung *f*

ca·ble 1. Kabel *n*; (Draht)Seil *n*; 2. telegrafieren; *j-m Geld* telegrafisch anweisen; TV verkabeln

ca·ble car Kabine *f*, Wagen *m*

ca·ble·gram (Übersee)Telegramm *n*

ca·ble| rail·way Drahtseil-, Kabinenbahn *f*; ~ **tel·e·vi·sion**, ~ **TV** Kabelfernsehen *n*

cab rank, cab·stand Taxi-, Droschkenstand *m*

cack·la ZO 1. Gegacker *n*, Geschnatter *n*; 2. gackern, schnattern

cac·tus BOT Kaktus *m*

ca·dence MUS Kadenz *f*; (Sprech-)Rhythmus *m*

ca·det MIL Kadett *m*

cadge Br F schnorren

caf·é, caf·e Café *n*

caf·e·te·ri·a Cafeteria *f*, Selbstbedienungsrestaurant *n*, *a.* Kantine *f*, UNIV Mensa *f*

cage 1. Käfig *m*; *mining:* Förderkorb *m*; 2. einsperren

cake 1. Kuchen *m*, Torte *f*; Tafel *f* *Schokolade*, Stück *n* Seife; F **take the ~** den Vogel abschießen; 2. **~d with mud** schmutzverkrustet

ca·lam·i·ty großes Unglück, Katastrophe *f*

cal·cu·late *v/t* kalkulieren; be-, aus-, errechnen; F vermuten; *v/i:* ~ **on** rechnen mit *or* auf (*acc*), zählen auf (*acc*)

cal·cu·la·tion Berechnung *f* (*a. fig*); ECON Kalkulation *f*; *fig* Überlegung *f*

cal·cu·la·tor TECH (Taschen)Rechner *m*

cal·en·dar Kalender *m*

calf¹ ANAT Wade *f*

calf² ZO Kalb *n*

calf·skin Kalb(s)fell *n*

cal·i·ber, *esp Br* cal·i·bre Kaliber *n*

call 1. Ruf *m*; TEL Anruf *m*, Gespräch *n*; Ruf *m*, Berufung *f* (**to** in *ein Amt;* auf *e-n Lehrstuhl*); Aufruf *m*, Aufforderung *f*; Signal *n*; (kurzer) Besuch; **on ~** auf Abruf; **be on ~** MED Bereitschaftsdienst haben; **make a ~** telefonieren; 2. *v/t* (herbei)rufen; (ein)berufen; TEL anrufen; *j-n* berufen, ernennen (**to** zu); nennen; *Aufmerksamkeit* lenken (**to** auf *acc*); **be ~ed** heißen; ~ **s.o. names** j-n beschimpfen, j-n beleidigen; *v/i* rufen; TEL anrufen; e-n (kurzen) Besuch machen (**on s.o., at s.o.'s [house]** bei j-m); ~ **at a port** MAR e-n Hafen anlaufen; ~ **for** rufen nach; *et.* anfordern; *et.* abholen; **to be ~ed for** postlagernd; ~ **on** sich an *j-n* wenden (**for** wegen); appellieren an (*acc*) (**to do** zu tun); ~ **on s.o.** j-n besuchen

call box Br Telefonzelle *f*

call·er Besucher(in); TEL Anrufer(in)

call girl Callgirl *n*

call-in → **phone-in**

call·ing Berufung *f*; Beruf *m*

cal·lous schwielig; *fig* gefühllos

cal·lus Schwiele *f*

calm 1. still, ruhig; 2. (Wind)Stille *f*, Ruhe *f*; 3. *often* ~ **down** besänftigen, (sich) beruhigen

cal·o·rie Kalorie *f*; **high** *or* **rich in ~s** kalorienreich; **low in ~s** kalorienarm, kalorienreduziert

cal·o·rie-con·scious kalorienbewusst

calve ZO kalben

cam·cor·der Camcorder *m*, Kamerarekorder *m*

cam·el ZO Kamel *n*

cam·e·o Kamee *f*; THEA, *film:* kleine Nebenrolle, kurze Szene

cam·e·ra Kamera *f*, Fotoapparat *m*

cam·o·mile BOT Kamille *f*

cam·ou·flage 1. Tarnung *f*; 2. tarnen

camp 1. (*Zelt- etc*)Lager *n*; 2. lagern; ~ **out** zelten, campen

cam·paign 1. MIL Feldzug *m* (*a. fig*); *fig* Kampagne *f*, Aktion *f*; POL Wahlkampf *m*; 2. *fig* kämpfen (**for** für; **against** gegen)

camp bed *Br*, **camp cot** Feldbett *n*

camp·er (van) Campingbus *m*, Wohnmobil *n*

camp·ground, camp·site Lagerplatz *m*; Zeltplatz *m*, Campingplatz *m*

cam·pus Campus *m*, Universitätsgelände *n*

can[1] *v/aux* ich kann, du kannst *etc*; dürfen, können

can[2] 1. Kanne *f*; (Blech-, Konserven-)Dose *f*, (-)Büchse *f*; 2. einmachen, eindosen

Can·a·da Kanada *n*; **Ca·na·di·an 1.** kanadisch; 2. Kanadier(in)

ca·nal Kanal *m* (*a.* ANAT)

ca·nar·y ZO Kanarienvogel *m*

can·cel (durch-, aus)streichen; entwerten; rückgängig machen; absagen; **be ~**(*l*)**ed** ausfallen

Can·cer ASTR Krebs *m*; **he** (**she**) **is** (**a**) **~** er (sie) ist (ein) Krebs

can·cer MED Krebs *m*

can·cer·ous MED Krebs..., krebsbefallen

can·cer pa·tient MED Krebskranke *m, f*

can·did aufrichtig, offen

can·di·date Kandidat(in) (**for** für), Bewerber(in) (**for** um)

can·died kandiert

can·dle Kerze *f*; Licht *n*; **burn the ~ at both ends** mit s-r Gesundheit Raubbau treiben

can·dle·stick Kerzenleuchter *m*, Kerzenständer *m*

can·do(u)r Aufrichtigkeit *f*, Offenheit *f*

can·dy 1. Kandis(zucker) *m*; Süßigkeiten *pl*; 2. kandieren; ~ **floss** Zuckerwatte *f*; ~ **store** Süßwarengeschäft *n*

cane BOT Rohr *n*; (Rohr)Stock *m*

ca·nine Hunde...

canned Dosen..., Büchsen...; ~ **fruit** Obstkonserven *pl*

can·ne·ry Konservenfabrik *f*

can·ni·bal Kannibale *m*

can·non MIL Kanone *f*

can·ny schlau

ca·noe 1. Kanu *n*, Paddelboot *n*; 2. Kanu fahren, paddeln

can·on Kanon *m*; Regel *f*

can o·pen·er Dosen-, Büchsenöffner *m*

can·o·py Baldachin *m*

cant Jargon *m*; Phrase(n *pl*) *f*

can·tan·ker·ous F zänkisch, mürrisch

can·teen *esp Br* Kantine *f*; MIL Feldflasche *f*; Besteck(kasten *m*) *n*

can·ter 1. Kanter *m*; 2. kantern

can·vas Segeltuch *n*; Zelt-, Packleinwand *f*; Segel *pl*; PAINT Leinwand *f*; Gemälde *n*

can·vass 1. POL Wahlfeldzug *m*; ECON Werbefeldzug *m*; 2. *v/t* eingehend untersuchen *or* erörtern *or* prüfen; POL werben um (*Stimmen*); *v/i* POL e-n Wahlfeldzug veranstalten

can·yon GEOGR Cañon *m*, Schlucht *f*

cap 1. Kappe *f*, Mütze *f*; Haube *f*; Zündkapsel *f*; 2. (mit e-r Kappe *etc*) bedecken; *fig* krönen; übertreffen

ca·pa·bil·i·ty Fähigkeit *f*

ca·pa·ble fähig (**of** zu)

ca·pac·i·ty (Raum)Inhalt *m*; Fassungsvermögen *n*; Kapazität *f*; Aufnahmefähigkeit *f*; (TECH Leistungs)Fähigkeit *f* (**for** *ger* zu *inf*); **in my ~ as** in meiner Eigenschaft als

cape[1] GEOGR Kap *n*, Vorgebirge *n*

cape[2] Cape *n*, Umhang *m*

ca·per 1. Kapriole *f*, Luftsprung *m*; **cut ~s →** 2. Freuden- *or* Luftsprünge machen

ca·pil·la·ry ANAT Haar-, Kapillargefäß *n*

cap·i·tal 1. ECON Kapital *n*; Hauptstadt *f*; Großbuchstabe *m*; 2. Kapital...; Tod(es)...; Haupt...; großartig, prima; ~ **crime** JUR Kapitalverbrechen *n*

cap·i·tal·ism ECON Kapitalismus *m*

cap·i·tal·ist ECON Kapitalist *m*

cap·i·tal·ize großschreiben; ECON kapitalisieren

cap·i·tal| let·ter Großbuchstabe *m*; ~ **pun·ish·ment** JUR Todesstrafe *f*

ca·pit·u·late kapitulieren (**to** vor *dat*)

ca·pri·cious launisch

Cap·ri·corn ASTR Steinbock *m*; **he** (**she**) **is** (**a**) **~** er (sie) ist (ein) Steinbock

cap·size MAR *v/i* kentern; *v/t* zum Kentern bringen

cap·sule Kapsel *f*

cap·tain (An)Führer *m*; MAR, ECON Kapitän m; AVIAT Flugkapitän m; MIL Hauptmann m; SPORT (Mannschafts-)Kapitän m, Spielführer m

cap·tion Überschrift f, Titel m; Bildunterschrift f; film: Untertitel m

cap·ti·vate fig gefangen nehmen, fesseln; **cap·tive 1.** gefangen; gefesselt; **hold ~** gefangen halten; **2.** Gefangene m, f; **cap·tiv·i·ty** Gefangenschaft f

cap·ture **1.** Eroberung f; Gefangennahme f; **2.** fangen, gefangen nehmen; erobern; erbeuten; MAR kapern

car Auto n, Wagen m; (Eisenbahn-, Straßenbahn-)Wagen m; Gondel f (of a balloon etc); Kabine f; **by ~** mit dem Auto, im Auto

car·a·mel Karamell m; Karamelle f

car·a·van Karawane f; Br Wohnwagen m; **~ site** Campingplatz m für Wohnwagen

car·a·way BOT Kümmel m

car·bine MIL Karabiner m

car·bo·hy·drate CHEM Kohle(n)hydrat n

car bomb Autobombe f

car·bon CHEM Kohlenstoff m; → **carbon copy, carbon paper**

car·bon cop·y Durchschlag m

car·bon pa·per Kohlepapier n

car·bu·ret·(t)or MOT Vergaser m

car·case Br, **car·cass** Kadaver m, Aas n; GASTR Rumpf m

car·cin·o·gen·ic MED karzinogen, Krebs erregend

car·ci·no·ma MED Krebsgeschwulst f

card Karte f; **play ~s** Karten spielen; **have a ~ up one's sleeve** fig (noch) e-n Trumpf in der Hand haben

card·board Pappe f; **~ box** Pappschachtel f, Pappkarton m

car·di·ac MED Herz...; **~ pace·mak·er** MED Herzschrittmacher m

car·di·gan Strickjacke f

car·di·nal **1.** Grund..., Haupt..., Kardinal...; scharlachrot; **2.** REL Kardinal m

car·di·nal num·ber MATH Kardinalzahl f, Grundzahl f

card in·dex Kartei f

card phone Kartentelefon n

card·sharp·er Falschspieler m

car dump Autofriedhof m

care **1.** Sorge f; Sorgfalt f; Vorsicht f; Obhut f, Pflege f; **needing ~** MED pflegebedürftig; **medical ~** ärztliche Behand-

lung; **take ~ of** aufpassen auf (acc); versorgen; **with ~!** Vorsicht!; **2.** Lust haben (**to** inf zu inf); **~ about** sich kümmern um; **~ for** sorgen für, sich kümmern um; sich etwas machen aus; **I don't ~!** F meinetwegen!; **I couldn't ~ less** F es ist mir völlig egal

ca·reer Karriere f, Laufbahn f; **2.** Berufs...; Karriere...; **3.** rasen

ca·reers| ad·vice Berufsberatung f; **~ ad·vi·sor** Berufsberater m; **~ guidance** Berufsberatung f; **~ of·fice** Berufsberatungsstelle f; **~ of·fi·cer** Berufsberater m

care·free sorgenfrei, sorglos

care·ful vorsichtig; sorgsam bedacht (**of** auf acc); sorgfältig; **be ~!** pass auf!

care·less nachlässig, unachtsam; leichtsinnig, unvorsichtig; sorglos

care·less·ness Nachlässigkeit f, Unachtsamkeit f; Leichtsinn m; Sorglosigkeit f

ca·ress **1.** Liebkosung f; Zärtlichkeit f; **2.** liebkosen, streicheln

care·tak·er Hausmeister m; (Haus etc)Verwalter m

care·worn abgehärmt, verhärmt

car fer·ry Autofähre f

car·go Ladung f

car hire Br Autovermietung f

car·i·ca·ture **1.** Karikatur f, Zerrbild n; **2.** karikieren

car·i·ca·tur·ist Karikaturist m

car·ies, a. **dental ~** MED Karies f

car me·chan·ic Automechaniker m

car·mine Karmin(rot) n

car·na·tion BOT Nelke f

car·nap·per F Autoentführer m

car·ni·val Karneval m

car·niv·o·rous ZO Fleisch fressend

car·ol Weihnachtslied n

carp[1] ZO Karpfen m

carp[2] nörgeln

car park esp Br Parkplatz m; Parkhaus n

car·pen·ter Zimmermann m

car·pet **1.** Teppich m; **fitted ~** Teppichboden m; **sweep s.th. under the ~** fig et. unter den Teppich kehren; **2.** mit Teppich(boden) auslegen

car phone Autotelefon n

car pool Fahrgemeinschaft f

car pool(·ing) ser·vice Mitfahrzentrale f

car·port MOT überdachter Abstellplatz

car rent·al Autovermietung *f*

car re·pair shop Autoreparaturwerkstatt *f*

car·riage Beförderung *f*, Transport *m*; Transportkosten *pl*; Kutsche *f*; *Br* RAIL (Personen)Wagen *m*; (Körper-)Haltung *f*

car·riage·way Fahrbahn *f*

car·ri·er Spediteur *m*; Gepäckträger *m* (*on a bicycle*); MIL Flugzeugträger *m*

car·ri·er bag *Br* Trag(e)tasche *f*, -tüte *f*

car·ri·on 1. Aas *n*; **2.** Aas...

car·rot BOT Karotte *f*, Mohrrübe *f*

car·ry *v/t* bringen, führen, tragen (*a. v/i*), fahren, befördern; (bei sich) haben *or* tragen; *Ansicht* durchsetzen; *Gewinn, Preis* davontragen; *Ernte, Zinsen* tragen; (weiter)führen, *Mauer* ziehen; *Antrag* durchbringen; *be carried* PARL *etc* angenommen werden; **~ the day** den Sieg davontragen; **~ s.th. too far** et. übertreiben, et. zu weit treiben; *get carried away fig* die Kontrolle über sich verlieren; sich hinreißen lassen; **~ forward**, **~ over** ECON übertragen; **~ on** fortsetzen, weiterführen; ECON betreiben; **~ out**, **~ through** aus-, durchführen

car·ry·cot *Br* (Baby)Trag(e)tasche *f*

cart 1. Karren *m*; Wagen *m*; Einkaufswagen *m*; *put the ~ before the horse fig* das Pferd beim Schwanz aufzäumen; **2.** karren

car·ti·lage ANAT Knorpel *m*

cart·load Wagenladung *f*

car·ton Karton *m*; *a ~ of cigarettes* e-e Stange Zigaretten

car·toon Cartoon *m*, *n*; Karikatur *f*; Zeichentrickfilm *m*

car·toon·ist Karikaturist *m*

car·tridge Patrone *f* (*a.* MIL); (Film-) Patrone *f*, (Film)Kassette *f*; Tonabnehmer *m*

cart·wheel: turn ~s Rad schlagen

carve GASTR vorschneiden, zerlegen; TECH schnitzen; meißeln

carv·er (Holz)Schnitzer *m*; Bildhauer *m*; GASTR Tranchierer *m*, Tranchiermesser *n*; **carv·ing** Schnitzerei *f*

car wash Autowäsche *f*; (Auto)Waschanlage *f*, Waschstraße *f*

cas·cade Wasserfall *m*

case[1] **1.** Behälter *m*; Kiste *f*, Kasten *m*; Etui *n*; Gehäuse *n*; Schachtel *f*; (*Glas-*) Schrank *m*; (*Kissen*)Bezug *m*; TECH Verkleidung *f*; **2.** in ein Gehäuse *or* Etui stecken; TECH verkleiden

case[2] Fall *m* (*a.* JUR), LING *a.* Kasus *m*; MED (*Krankheits*)Fall *m*, Patient(in); Sache *f*, Angelegenheit *f*

case·ment Fensterflügel *m*; → ~ **window** Flügelfenster *n*

cash 1. Bargeld *n*; Barzahlung *f*; ~ **down** gegen bar; ~ **on delivery** Lieferung *f* gegen bar; (per) Nachnahme *f*; **2.** einlösen

cash·book ECON Kassenbuch *n*

cash desk Kasse *f*

cash dis·pens·er *esp Br* Geld-, Bankautomat *m*

cash·ier Kassierer(in)

cash·less bargeldlos

cash ma·chine Geld-, Bankautomat *m*

cash·point *Br* → *cash machine*

cash reg·is·ter Registrierkasse *f*

cas·ing (Schutz)Hülle *f*; Verschalung *f*, Verkleidung *f*, Gehäuse *n*

cask Fass *n*

cas·ket Kästchen *n*; Sarg *m*

cas·sette (*Film-, Band-, Musik*)Kassette *f*; ~ **deck** Kassettendeck *n*; ~ **player** Kassettenrekorder *m*; **~ra·di·o** Radiorekorder *m*; **~ re·cord·er** Kassettenrekorder *m*

cas·sock REL Soutane *f*

cast 1. Wurf *m*; TECH Guss(form *f*) *m*; Abguss *m*, Abdruck *m*; Schattierung *f*, Anflug *m*; Form *f*, Art *f*; Auswerfen *n* (*of a fishing line etc*); THEA Besetzung *f*; **2.** (ab-, aus-, hin-, um-, weg)werfen; ZO abwerfen (*skin*); verlieren (*teeth*); verwerfen; gestalten; TECH gießen; *a.* ~ **up** ausrechnen, zusammenzählen; THEA *Stück* besetzen; *Rollen* verteilen (*to* an *acc*); ~ **lots** losen (*for* um); ~ **away** wegwerfen; *be* ~ **down** niedergeschlagen sein; ~ **off** *Kleidung* ausrangieren; MAR losmachen; *Freund etc* fallen lassen; *knitting:* abketten; *v/i:* **about for**, ~ **around for** suchen (nach), *fig a.* sich umsehen nach

cas·ta·net Kastagnette *f*

cast·a·way Schiffbrüchige *m*, *f*

caste Kaste *f* (*a. fig*)

cast·er Laufrolle *f*; *Br* (*Salz-, Zucker- etc*)Streuer *m* cast i·ron Gusseisen *n*

cast-i·ron gusseisern

cas·tle Burg *f*, Schloss *n*; *chess:* Turm *m*

cast·or → **caster**

cast·or oil PHARM Rizinusöl *n*

cas·trate kastrieren

cas·u·al zufällig; gelegentlich; flüchtig; lässig

cas·u·al·ty Unfall *m*; Verunglückte *m*, *f*, Opfer *n*; MIL Verwundete *m*; Gefallene *m*; **casualties** Opfer *pl*, MIL *mst* Verluste *pl*; **~ (de·part·ment)** MED Notaufnahme *f*; **~ ward** MED Unfallstation *f*

cas·u·al wear Freizeitkleidung *f*

cat ZO Katze *f*

cat·a·log, *esp Br* **cat·a·logue 1.** Katalog *m*; Verzeichnis *n*, Liste *f*; **2.** katalogisieren

cat·a·lyt·ic con·vert·er MOT Katalysator *m*

cat·a·pult *Br* Schleuder *f*; Katapult *n*, *m*

cat·a·ract Wasserfall *m*; Stromschnelle *f*; MED grauer Star

ca·tarrh MED Katarr(h) *m*

ca·tas·tro·phe Katastrophe *f*

catch **1.** Fangen *n*; Fang *m*, Beute *f*; Halt *m*; Griff *m*; TECH Haken *m* (*a. fig*); (Tür)Klinke *f*; Verschluss *m*; **2.** *v/t* (auf-, ein)fangen; packen, fassen, ergreifen; überraschen, ertappen; *Blick etc* auffangen; F *Zug etc* (noch) kriegen, erwischen; *et.* erfassen, verstehen; *Atmosphäre etc* einfangen; sich *e-e Krankheit* holen; **~ (a) cold** sich erkälten; **~ the eye** ins Auge fallen; **~ s.o.'s eye** j-s Aufmerksamkeit auf sich lenken; **~ s.o. up** j-n einholen; **be caught up in** verwickelt sein (*acc*); *v/i* sich verfangen, hängen bleiben; fassen, greifen; TECH ineinander greifen; klemmen; einschnappen; **~ up with** einholen

catch·er Fänger *m*

catch·ing packend; MED ansteckend (*a. fig*)

catch·word Schlagwort *n*; Stichwort *n*

catch·y MUS eingängig

cat·e·chis·m REL Katechismus *m*

cat·e·go·ry Kategorie *f*

ca·ter: **~ for** Speisen und Getränke liefern für; *fig* sorgen für

cat·er·pil·lar ZO Raupe *f*

Cat·er·pil·lar® MOT Raupenfahrzeug *n*;

~ trac·tor® MOT Raupenschlepper *m*

cat·gut MUS Darmsaite *f*

ca·the·dral Dom *m*, Kathedrale *f*

Cath·o·lic REL **1.** katholisch; **2.** Katholik (in)

cat·kin BOT Kätzchen *n*

cat·tle Vieh *n*; **~ breed·er** Viehzüchter *m*; **~ breed·ing** Viehzucht *f*; **~ dealer** Viehhändler *m*; **~ mar·ket** Viehmarkt *m*

ca(u)l·dron großer Kessel

cau·li·flow·er BOT Blumenkohl *m*

cause **1.** Ursache *f*; Grund *m*; Sache *f*; **2.** verursachen; veranlassen

cause·less grundlos

cau·tion **1.** Vorsicht *f*; Warnung *f*; Verwarnung *f*; **2.** warnen; verwarnen; JUR belehren

cau·tious behutsam, vorsichtig

cav·al·ry HIST MIL Kavallerie *f*

cave **1.** Höhle *f*; **2.** *v/i:* **~ in** einstürzen

cav·ern (große) Höhle

cav·i·ty Höhle *f*; MED Loch *n*

caw ZO **1.** krächzen; **2.** Krächzen *n*

CD ABBR *of* **compact disk** CD(-Platte) *f*

CD play·er CD-Spieler *m*

CD-ROM ABBR *of* **compact disk read-only memory** CD-ROM

CD vid·e·o CD-Video *n*

cease aufhören; beenden

cease-fire MIL Feuereinstellung *f*; Waffenruhe *f*

cease·less unaufhörlich

ceil·ing (Zimmer)Decke *f*; ECON Höchstgrenze *f*, oberste Preisgrenze

cel·e·brate feiern; **cel·e·brat·ed** gefeiert, berühmt (*for* für, wegen)

cel·e·bra·tion Feier *f*

ce·leb·ri·ty Berühmtheit *f*

cel·e·ry BOT Sellerie *m*, *f*

ce·les·ti·al himmlisch

cel·i·ba·cy Ehelosigkeit *f*

cell BIOL Zelle *f*, ELECTR *a.* Element *n*

cel·lar Keller *m*

cel·list MUS Cellist(in)

cel·lo MUS (Violon)Cello *n*

cel·lo·phane® Cellophan® *n*

cel·lu·lar BIOL Zell(en)...

cel·lu·lar phone Funktelefon *n*

Cel·tic keltisch

ce·ment **1.** Zement *m*; Kitt *m*; **2.** zementieren; (ver)kitten

cem·e·tery Friedhof *m*

cen·sor **1.** Zensor *m*; **2.** zensieren

cen·sor·ship Zensur f
cen·sure 1. Tadel m, Verweis m; **2.** tadeln
cen·sus Volkszählung f
cent Hundert n; Cent m (1/100 Dollar); **per ~** Prozent n
cen·te·na·ry Hundertjahrfeier f, hundertjähriges Jubiläum
cen·ten·ni·al 1. hundertjährig; **2.** → **centenary**
cen·ter 1. Zentrum n, Mittelpunkt m; soccer: Flanke f; **2.** (sich) konzentrieren; zentrieren; **~ back** soccer: Vorstopper m; **~ for·ward** SPORT Mittelstürmer(in); **~ of grav·i·ty** PHYS Schwerpunkt m
cen·ti·grade: 10 degrees ~ 10 Grad Celsius
cen·ti·me·ter, Br **cen·ti·me·tre** Zentimeter m, n
cen·ti·pede ZO Tausendfüß(l)er m
cen·tral zentral; Haupt..., Zentral...; Mittel...; **~ heat·ing** Zentralheizung f
cen·tral·ize zentralisieren
cen·tral| lock·ing MOT Zentralverriegelung f; **~ res·er·va·tion** Br MOT Mittelstreifen m
cen·tre Br → **center**
cen·tu·ry Jahrhundert n
ce·ram·ics Keramik f, keramische Erzeugnisse pl
ce·re·al 1. Getreide...; **2.** BOT Getreide n; Getreidepflanze f; GASTR Getreideflocken pl, Frühstückskost f
cer·e·bral ANAT Gehirn...
cer·e·mo·ni·al 1. zeremoniell; **2.** Zeremoniell n
cer·e·mo·ni·ous zeremoniell; förmlich
cer·e·mo·ny Zeremonie f, Feier f, Feierlichkeit f; Förmlichkeit(en pl) f
cer·tain sicher, gewiss; zuverlässig; bestimmt; gewisse(r, -s); **cer·tain·ly** sicher, gewiss; int sicherlich, bestimmt, natürlich; **cer·tain·ty** Sicherheit f, Bestimmtheit f, Gewissheit f
cer·tif·i·cate Zeugnis n; Bescheinigung f; **~ of (good) conduct** Führungszeugnis n; **General Certificate of Education advanced level (A level)** Br PED appr Abitur(zeugnis) n; **General Certificate of Education ordinary level (O level)** Br PED appr mittlere Reife; **medical ~** ärztliches Attest
cer·ti·fy et. bescheinigen; beglaubigen

cer·ti·tude Sicherheit f, Bestimmtheit f, Gewissheit f
CET ABBR of **Central European Time** MEZ, mitteleuropäische Zeit
cf (Latin **confer**) ABBR of **compare** vgl., vergleiche
CFC ABBR of **chlorofluorocarbon** FCKW, Fluorchlorkohlenwasserstoff m
chafe v/t warm reiben; aufreiben, wund reiben; v/i (sich durch)reiben, scheuern
chaff AGR Spreu f; Häcksel n
chaf·finch ZO Buchfink m
chag·rin 1. Ärger m; **2.** ärgern
chain 1. Kette f; fig Fessel f; **2.** (an)ketten; fesseln
chain re·ac·tion Kettenreaktion f
chain-smoke F Kette rauchen
chain-smok·er Kettenraucher(in)
chain-smok·ing Kettenrauchen n
chain store Kettenladen m
chair Stuhl m; UNIV Lehrstuhl m; ECON etc Vorsitz m; **be in the ~** den Vorsitz führen; **~ lift** Sessellift m
chair·man Vorsitzende m, Präsident m; Diskussionsleiter m; ECON Br Generaldirektor m
chair·man·ship Vorsitz m
chair·wom·an Vorsitzende f, Präsidentin f; Diskussionsleiterin f
chal·ice REL Kelch m
chalk 1. Kreide f; **2.** mit Kreide schreiben or zeichnen
chal·lenge 1. Herausforderung f; **2.** herausfordern
chal·len·ger Herausforderer m
cham·ber TECH, PARL etc Kammer f
cham·ber·maid Zimmermädchen n
cham·ber of com·merce ECON Handelskammer f
cham·ois ZO Gämse f
cham·ois (leath·er) Fensterleder n
champ F SPORT → **champion**
cham·pagne Champagner m
cham·pi·on 1. Verfechter(in), Fürsprecher(in); SPORT Meister(in); **2.** verfechten, eintreten für; **cham·pi·on·ship** SPORT Meisterschaft f
chance 1. Zufall m; Chance f, (günstige) Gelegenheit; Aussicht f (of auf acc); Möglichkeit f; Risiko n; **by ~** zufällig; **take a ~** es darauf ankommen lassen; **take no ~s** nichts riskieren (wollen); **2.** zufällig; **3.** F riskieren

chan·cel·lor Kanzler m

chan·de·lier Kronleuchter m

change 1. Veränderung f, Wechsel m; Abwechslung f; Wechselgeld n; Kleingeld n; **for a ~** zur Abwechslung; **~ for the better (worse)** Bess(e)rung f (Verschlechterung f); 2. v/t (ver)ändern, umändern; (aus)wechseln; (aus-, ver-) tauschen (**for** gegen); umbuchen; MOT, TECH schalten; **~ over** umschalten; umstellen; **~ trains** umsteigen; v/i sich (ver)ändern, wechseln; sich umziehen

change·a·ble veränderlich

change ma·chine Münzwechsler m

change·o·ver Umstellung f (**to** auf acc)

chang·ing room esp SPORT Umkleidekabine f, Umkleideraum m

chan·nel 1. Kanal m (a. fig); (Fernseh- etc)Kanal m, (Fernseh- etc)Programm n; fig Weg m; 2. fig lenken

Chan·nel Tun·nel Kanaltunnel m, Eurotunnel m

chant 1. (Kirchen)Gesang m; Singsang m; 2. in Sprechchören rufen

cha·os Chaos n

chap¹ 1. Riss m; 2. rissig machen or werden; aufspringen

chap² Br F Bursche m, Kerl m

chap·el ARCH Kapelle f; REL Gottesdienst m

chap·lain REL Kaplan m

chap·ter Kapitel n

char verkohlen

char·ac·ter Charakter m; Ruf m, Leumund m; Schriftzeichen n, Buchstabe m; novel etc: Figur f, Gestalt f; THEA Rolle f; **char·ac·ter·is·tic** 1. charakteristisch (**of** für); 2. Kennzeichen n, **char·ac·ter·ize** charakterisieren

char·coal Holzkohle f

charge 1. v/t ELECTR (auf)laden; Gewehr etc laden; j-n beauftragen (**with** mit); j-n beschuldigen or anklagen (**with** e-r Sache) (a. JUR); ECON berechnen, verlangen, fordern (**for** für); MIL angreifen; stürmen; **~ s.o. with s.th.** ECON j-m in Rechnung stellen; v/i: **~ at s.o.** auf j-n losgehen; 2. Ladung f (a. ELECTR etc); (Spreng)Ladung f; Beschuldigung f, a. JUR Anklage (-punkt m) f; ECON Preis m; Forderung f; Gebühr f; a. pl Unkosten pl, Spesen pl; Verantwortung f; Schützling m, Mündel n, m; **free of ~** kostenlos; **be**

in ~ of verantwortlich sein für; **take ~ of** die Leitung etc übernehmen, die Sache in die Hand nehmen

char·i·ot HIST Streit-, Triumphwagen m

cha·ris·ma Charisma n, Ausstrahlung f, Ausstrahlungskraft f

char·i·ta·ble wohltätig

char·i·ty Nächstenliebe f; Wohltätigkeit f; Güte f, Nachsicht f; milde Gabe

char·la·tan Scharlatan m; Quacksalber m, Kurpfuscher m

charm 1. Zauber m; Charme m, Reiz m; Talisman m, Amulett n; 2. bezaubern, entzücken

charm·ing charmant, bezaubernd

chart (See-, Himmels-, Wetter)Karte f; Diagramm n, Schaubild n; pl MUS Charts pl, Hitliste(n pl) f

char·ter 1. Urkunde f; Charta f; Chartern n; 2. chartern, mieten

char·ter flight Charterflug m

char·wom·an Putzfrau f, Raumpflegerin f

chase 1. Jagd f; Verfolgung f; 2. v/t jagen, hetzen; Jagd machen auf (acc); TECH ziselieren; v/i rasen, rennen

chasm Kluft f, Abgrund m

chaste keusch; schlicht

chas·tise züchtigen

chas·ti·ty Keuschheit f

chat 1. Geplauder n, Schwätzchen n, Plauderei f; 2. plaudern

chat show Br TV Talkshow f

chat show host Br TV Talkmaster m

chat·ter 1. plappern; schnattern; klappern; 2. Geplapper n; Klappern n

chat·ter·box F Plappermaul n

chat·ty gesprächig

chauf·feur Chauffeur m

chau·vi F Chauvi m

chau·vin·ist Chauvinist m; F **male ~ pig** Chauvi m; contp Chauvischwein n

cheap billig; fig schäbig, gemein

cheap·en (sich) verbilligen; fig herabsetzen

cheat 1. Betrug m, Schwindel m; Betrüger(in); 2. betrügen; F schummeln

check 1. Schach(stellung f) n; Hemmnis n, Hindernis n (**on** für); Einhalt m; Kontrolle f (**on** gen); Kontrollabschnitt m, -schein m; Gepäckschein m; Garderobenmarke f; ECON Scheck m (**for** über); Häkchen n (**on** a list etc); ECON

Kassenzettel *m*, Rechnung *f*; karierter Stoff; **2.** *v/i* (plötzlich) innehalten; **~** in sich (*in e-m Hotel*) anmelden; einstempeln; AVIAT einchecken; **~ out** (*aus e-m Hotel*) abreisen; ausstempeln; **~ up** (**on**) F (*e-e Sache*) nachprüfen, (*e-e Sache, j-n*) überprüfen; *v/t* hemmen, hindern, aufhalten; zurückhalten; checken, kontrollieren, überprüfen; *auf e-r Liste* abhaken; *Mantel etc in der Garderobe* abgeben; *Gepäck* aufgeben

check card ECON Scheckkarte *f*
checked kariert
check·ers Damespiel *n*
check-in Anmeldung *f*; Einstempeln *n*; AVIAT Einchecken *n*
check-in| coun·ter, **~ desk** AVIAT Abfertigungsschalter *m*
check·ing ac·count ECON Girokonto *n*
check·list Check-, Kontrollliste *f*
check·mate 1. (Schach)Matt *n*; **2.** (schach)matt setzen
check·out Abreise *f*; Ausstempeln *n*
check-out coun·ter Kasse *f*
check·point Kontrollpunkt *m*
check·room Garderobe *f*; Gepäckaufbewahrung *f*
check-up Überprüfung *f*; MED Check-up *m*, Vorsorgeuntersuchung *f*
cheek ANAT Backe *f*, Wange *f*; Br Unverschämtheit *f*; **cheek·y** Br frech
cheer 1. Stimmung *f*, Fröhlichkeit *f*; Hoch *n*, Hochruf *m*, Beifall *m*; Beifallsruf *m*; *pl* SPORT Anfeuerungsrufe *pl*; **three ~s!** dreimal hoch!; **~s!** prost!; **2.** *v/t* mit Beifall begrüßen; *a.* **~ on** anspornen; *a.* **~ up** aufheitern; *v/i* hoch rufen, jubeln; *a.* **~ up** Mut fassen; **~ up!** Kopf hoch!; **cheer·ful** vergnügt
cheer·i·o *int* Br F tschüs(s)!
cheer·lead·er SPORT Einpeitscher *m*, Cheerleader *m*
cheer·less freudlos; unfreundlich
cheer·y vergnügt
cheese Käse *m*
chee·tah ZO Gepard *m*
chef Küchenchef *m*; Koch *m*
chem·i·cal 1. chemisch; **2.** Chemikalie *f*
chem·ist Chemiker(in); Apotheker(in); Drogist(in)
chem·is·try Chemie *f*
chem·ist's shop Apotheke *f*; Drogerie *f*

chem·o·ther·a·py MED Chemotherapie *f*
cheque Br ECON Scheck *m*; **crossed ~** Verrechnungsscheck *m*; **~ ac·count** Br Girokonto *n*; **~ card** Br Scheckkarte *f*
cher·ry BOT Kirsche *f*
chess Schach(spiel) *n*; **a game of ~** e-e Partie Schach
chess·board Schachbrett *n*
chess·man, **chess·piece** Schachfigur *f*
chest Kiste *f*; Truhe *f*; ANAT Brust *f*, Brustkasten *m*; **get s.th. off one's ~** F sich et. von der Seele reden
chest·nut 1. BOT Kastanie *f*; **2.** kastanienbraun
chest of drawers Kommode *f*
chew (zer)kauen
chew·ing gum Kaugummi *m*
chic schick, *Austrian* fesch
chick ZO Küken *n*, junger Vogel; F Biene *f*, Puppe *f* (*girl*)
chick·en ZO Huhn *n*; Küken *n*; GASTR (*Brat*)Hähnchen *n*, (*Brat*)Hühnchen *n*
chick·en-heart·ed furchtsam, feige
chick·en pox MED Windpocken *pl*
chic·o·ry BOT Chicorée *m*, *f*
chief 1. oberste(r, -s), Ober..., Haupt..., Chef...; wichtigste(r, -s); **2.** Chef *m*; Häuptling *m*
chief·ly hauptsächlich
chil·blain MED Frostbeule *f*
child Kind *n*; **from a ~** von Kindheit an; **with ~** schwanger; **~ a·buse** JUR Kindesmisshandlung *f*; **~ ben·e·fit** Br Kindergeld *n*
child·birth Geburt *f*, Niederkunft *f*
child·hood Kindheit *f*; **from ~** von Kindheit an
child·ish kindlich; kindisch
child·like kindlich
child·mind·er Tagesmutter *f*
chill 1. kalt, frostig, kühl (*a. fig*); **2.** Frösteln *n*; Kälte *f*, Kühle *f* (*a. fig*); MED Erkältung *f*; **3.** abkühlen; *j-n* frösteln lassen; kühlen
chill·y kalt, frostig, kühl (*a. fig*)
chime 1. Glockenspiel *n*; Geläut *n*; **2.** läuten; schlagen (*clock*)
chim·ney Schornstein *m*
chim·ney sweep Schornsteinfeger *m*
chimp F, **chim·pan·zee** ZO Schimpanse *m*

chin ANAT Kinn *n*; ~ *up!* Kopf hoch!, halt die Ohren steif!

chi·na Porzellan *n*

Chi·na China *n*

Chi·nese 1. chinesisch; 2. Chinese *m*, Chinesin *f*; LING Chinesisch *n*; *the* ~ die Chinesen *pl*

chink Ritz *m*, Spalt *m*

chip 1. Splitter *m*, Span *m*, Schnitzel *n*, *m*; dünne Scheibe; Spielmarke *f*; EDP Chip *m*; 2. *v/t* schnitzeln; anschlagen, abschlagen; *v/i* abbröckeln

chips (Kartoffel)Chips *pl*; *Br* Pommes frites *pl*, F Fritten *pl*

chi·ro·po·dist Fußpfleger(in), Pediküre *f*

chirp ZO zirpen, zwitschern, piepsen

chis·el 1. Meißel *m*; 2. meißeln

chit-chat Plauderei *f*

chiv·al·rous ritterlich

chive(s) BOT Schnittlauch *m*

chlo·ri·nate *Wasser etc* chloren

chlo·rine CHEM Chlor *n*

chlo·ro·fluo·ro·car·bon (ABBR *CFC*) CHEM Fluorchlorkohlenwasserstoff *m* (ABBR *FCKW*)

chlor·o·form MED 1. Chloroform *n*; 2. chloroformieren

choc·o·late Schokolade *f*; Praline *f*; *pl* Pralinen *pl*, Konfekt *n*

choice 1. Wahl *f*; Auswahl *f*; 2. auserlesen, ausgesucht, vorzüglich

choir ARCH, MUS Chor *m*

choke 1. *v/t* (er)würgen, (*a. v/i*) ersticken; ~ *back Ärger etc* unterdrücken, *Tränen* zurückhalten; ~ *down* hinunterwürgen; *a.* ~ *up* verstopfen; 2. MOT Choke *m*, Luftklappe *f*

cho·les·te·rol MED Cholesterin *n*

choose (aus)wählen, aussuchen

choos·(e)y *F* wählerisch

chop 1. Hieb *m*, (Handkanten)Schlag *m*; GASTR Kotelett *n*; 2. *v/t* (zer)hacken, hauen; ~ *down* fällen; *v/i* hacken

chop·per Hackmesser *n*, Hackbeil *n*; F Hubschrauber *m*

chop·py unruhig (*sea*)

chop·stick Essstäbchen *n*

cho·ral MUS Chor...

cho·rale MUS Choral *m*

chord MUS Saite *f*; Akkord *m*

chore schwierige *or* unangenehme Aufgabe; *pl* Hausarbeit *f*

cho·rus MUS Chor *m*; Kehrreim *m*,

Refrain *m*; Tanzgruppe *f*

Christ REL Christus *m*

chris·ten REL taufen

chris·ten·ing REL 1. Taufe *f*; 2. Tauf...

Chris·tian REL 1. christlich; 2. Christ(in)

Chris·ti·an·i·ty REL Christentum *n*

Chris·tian name Vorname *m*

Christ·mas Weihnachten *n and pl*; *at* ~ zu Weihnachten; ~ *Day* erster Weihnachtsfeiertag; ~ *Eve* Heiliger Abend

chrome Chrom *n*

chro·mi·um CHEM Chrom *n*

chron·ic chronisch; ständig, (an)dauernd

chron·i·cle Chronik *f*

chron·o·log·i·cal chronologisch

chro·nol·o·gy Zeitrechnung *f*; Zeitfolge *f*

chub·by *F* rundlich, pumm(e)lig; pausbäckig

chuck *F* werfen, schmeißen; ~ *out j-n* rausschmeißen; *et.* wegschmeißen; ~ *up Job etc* hinschmeißen

chuck·le 1. ~ (*to o.s.*) (stillvergnügt) in sich hineinlachen; 2. leises Lachen

chum *F* Kamerad *m*, Kumpel *m*

chum·my *F* dick befreundet

chump Holzklotz *m*; F Trottel *m*

chunk Klotz *m*, Klumpen *m*

Chun·nel F → *Channel Tunnel*

church 1. Kirche *f*; 2. Kirch..., Kirchen...

church ser·vice REL Gottesdienst *m*

church·yard Kirchhof *m*

churl·ish grob, flegelhaft

churn 1. Butterfass *n*; 2. buttern; *Wellen* aufwühlen, peitschen

chute Stromschnelle *f*; Rutsche *f*, Rutschbahn *f*; F Fallschirm *m*

ci·der *a.* *hard* ~ Apfelwein *m*; (*sweet*) ~ Apfelmost *m*, Apfelsaft *m*

ci·gar Zigarre *f*

cig·a·rette Zigarette *f*

cinch F todsichere Sache

cin·der Schlacke *f*; *pl* Asche *f*

Cin·der·el·la Aschenbrödel *n*, Aschenputtel *n*

cin·der track SPORT Aschenbahn *f*

cin·e·cam·e·ra (Schmal)Filmkamera *f*

cin·e·film Schmalfilm *m*

cin·e·ma *Br* Kino *n*; Film *m*

cin·na·mon Zimt *m*

ci·pher Geheimschrift *f*, Chiffre *f*; Null *f* (*a. fig*)

383   **classified**

cir·cle 1. Kreis *m*; THEA Rang *m*; *fig* Kreislauf *m*; **2.** (um)kreisen

cir·cuit Kreislauf *m*; ELECTR Stromkreis *m*; Rundreise *f*; SPORT Zirkus *m*; *short* ~ ELECTR Kurzschluss *m*

cir·cu·i·tous gewunden; weitschweifig; ~ *route* Umweg *m*

cir·cu·lar 1. kreisförmig; Kreis...; **2.** Rundschreiben *n*; Umlauf *m*; (Post-) Wurfsendung *f*

cir·cu·late zirkulieren, im Umlauf sein; *v/t* in Umlauf setzen

cir·cu·lat·ing li·bra·ry Leihbücherei *f*

cir·cu·la·tion (*a.* Blut)Kreislauf *m*, Zirkulation *f*; ECON Umlauf *m*; *newspaper etc:* Auflage *f*

cir·cum·fer·ence (Kreis)Umfang *m*

cir·cum·nav·i·gate umschiffen, umsegeln

cir·cum·scribe MATH umschreiben; *fig* begrenzen

cir·cum·spect umsichtig, vorsichtig

cir·cum·stance Umstand *m*; *pl* (Sach-) Lage *f*, Umstände *pl*; Verhältnisse *pl*; *in or under no ~s* unter keinen Umständen, auf keinen Fall; *in or under the ~s* unter diesen Umständen

cir·cum·stan·tial ausführlich; umständlich; ~ *ev·i·dence* JUR Indizien *pl*, Indizienbeweis *m*

cir·cus Zirkus *m*

CIS ABBR of *Commonwealth of Independent States die* GUS, *die* Gemeinschaft unabhängiger Staaten

cis·tern Wasserbehälter *m*; Spülkasten *m*

ci·ta·tion Zitat *n*; JUR Vorladung *f*

cite zitieren; JUR vorladen

cit·i·zen Bürger(in); Städter(in); Staatsangehörige *m*, *f*

cit·i·zen·ship Staatsangehörigkeit *f*

cit·y 1. (Groß)Stadt *f*; *the City* die (Londoner) City; **2.** städtisch, Stadt...; ~ *cen·tre Br* Innenstadt *f*, City *f*; ~ *coun·cil·(l)or* Stadtrat *m*, Stadträtin *f*; ~ *hall* Rathaus *n*; Stadtverwaltung *f*; ~ *slick·er often contp* Städter(in), Stadtmensch *m*; ~ *va·grant* Stadtstreicher(in), Nichtsesshafte *m*, *f*

civ·ic städtisch, Stadt...

civ·ics PED Staatsbürgerkunde *f*

civ·il staatlich, Staats...; (staats)bürgerlich, Bürger...; zivil, Zivil...; JUR zivilrechtlich; höflich

ci·vil·i·an Zivilist *m*

ci·vil·i·ty Höflichkeit *f*

civ·i·li·za·tion Zivilisation *f*, Kultur *f*

civ·i·lize zivilisieren

civ·il rights (Staats)Bürgerrechte *pl*; ~ *ac·tiv·ist* Bürgerrechtler(in); ~ *move·ment* Bürgerrechtsbewegung *f*

civ·il ser·vant Staatsbeamte *m*, -beamtin *f*; ~ *ser·vice* Staatsdienst *m*; ~ *war* Bürgerkrieg *m*

clad gekleidet

claim 1. Anspruch *m*; Anrecht *n* (*to* auf *acc*); Forderung *f*; Behauptung *f*; Claim *m*; **2.** beanspruchen; fordern; behaupten

clair·voy·ant 1. hellseherisch; **2.** Hellseher(in)

clam·ber (mühsam) klettern

clam·my feuchtkalt, klamm

clam·o(u)r 1. Geschrei *n*, Lärm *m*; **2.** lautstark verlangen (*for* nach)

clamp TECH Zwinge *f*

clan Clan *m*, Sippe *f*

clan·des·tine heimlich

clang klingen, klirren; erklingen lassen

clank 1. Gerassel *n*, Geklirr *n*; **2.** rasseln *or* klirren (mit)

clap 1. Klatschen *n*; Schlag *m*, Klaps *m*; **2.** schlagen *or* klatschen (mit)

clar·et roter Bordeaux(wein); Rotwein *m*

clar·i·fy *v/t* (auf)klären, klarstellen; *v/i* sich (auf)klären, klar werden

clar·i·net MUS Klarinette *f*

clar·i·ty Klarheit *f*

clash 1. Zusammenstoß *m*; Konflikt *m*; **2.** zusammenstoßen; *fig* nicht zusammenpassen *or* harmonieren

clasp 1. Haken *m*, Schnalle *f*; Schloss *n*, (Schnapp)Verschluss *m*; Umklammerung *f*; **2.** einhaken, zuhaken; ergreifen, umklammern

clasp knife Taschenmesser *n*

class 1. Klasse *f*; (Bevölkerungs-) Schicht *f*; (Schul)Klasse *f*; (Unterrichts)Stunde *f*; Kurs *m*; Jahrgang *m*; **2.** (in Klassen) einteilen, einordnen, einstufen

clas·sic 1. Klassiker *m*; **2.** klassisch

clas·si·cal klassisch

clas·sic car Klassiker *m*

clas·si·fi·ca·tion Klassifizierung *f*, Einteilung *f*

clas·si·fied klassifiziert; MIL, POL geheim; **~ ad** Kleinanzeige f

clas·si·fy klassifizieren, einstufen

class·mate Mitschüler(in)

class·room Klassenzimmer n

clat·ter 1. Geklapper n; **2.** klappern (mit)

clause JUR Klausel f, Bestimmung f; LING Satz(teil n) m

claw 1. ZO Klaue f, Kralle f; (Krebs-) Schere f; **2.** (zer)kratzen; umkrallen, packen

clay Ton m, Lehm m

clean 1. adj rein; sauber, glatt, eben; sl clean; **2.** adv völlig, ganz und gar; **3.** reinigen, säubern, putzen; **~ out** reinigen; **~ up** gründlich reinigen; aufräumen

clean·er Rein(e)machefrau f, (Fenster- etc)Putzer m; Reinigungsmittel n, Reiniger m; **take to the ~s** et. zur Reinigung bringen; F j-n ausnehmen

clean·ing: do the ~ sauber machen, putzen; **~ la·dy, ~ wom·an** Putzfrau f

clean·li·ness Reinlichkeit f

clean·ly 1. adv sauber; **2.** adj reinlich

cleanse reinigen, säubern

cleans·er Putzmittel n, Reinigungsmittel n, Reiniger m

clear 1. adj klar; hell; rein; deutlich; frei (of von); ECON Netto..., Rein...; **2.** v/t reinigen, säubern; Wald lichten, roden; wegräumen (a. **~ away**); Tisch abräumen; räumen, leeren; Hindernis nehmen; SPORT klären; ECON verzollen; JUR freisprechen; EDP löschen; v/i klar or hell werden; METEOR aufklaren sich verziehen (fog); **~ out** aufräumen; ausräumen, entfernen; F abhauen; **~ up** aufräumen; Verbrechen etc aufklären; METEOR aufklaren

clear·ance Räumung f; TECH lichter Abstand; Freigabe f; **~ sale** ECON Räumungsverkauf m, Ausverkauf m

clear·ing Lichtung f

cleave spalten

cleav·er Hackmesser n

clef MUS Schlüssel m

cleft Spalt m, Spalte f

clem·en·cy Milde f, Nachsicht f

clem·ent mild (a. METEOR)

clench Lippen etc (fest) zusammenpressen; Zähne zusammenbeißen; Faust ballen

cler·gy REL Klerus m, die Geistlichen pl

cler·gy·man REL Geistliche m

clerk Verkäufer(in); (Büro- etc)Angestellte m, f, (Bank-, Post)Beamte m, (-)Beamtin f

clev·er klug, gescheit; geschickt

click 1. Klicken n; **2.** v/i klicken; zu-, einschnappen; mit der Zunge schnalzen; v/t klicken or einschnappen lassen; mit der Zunge schnalzen; **~ on** EDP anklicken

cli·ent JUR Klient(in), Mandant(in); Kunde m, Kundin f, Auftraggeber(in)

cliff Klippe f, Felsen m

cli·mate Klima n

cli·max Höhepunkt m; Orgasmus m

climb klettern; (er-, be)steigen; **~ (up) a tree** auf e-n Baum klettern

climb·er Kletterer m, Bergsteiger(in); BOT Kletterpflanze f

clinch 1. TECH sicher befestigen; (ver)nieten; boxing: umklammern (v/i clinchen); fig entscheiden; **that ~ed it** damit war die Sache entschieden; **2.** boxing: Clinch m

cling (to) festhalten (an dat), sich klammern (an acc); sich (an)schmiegen (an acc)

cling·film® esp Br Frischhaltefolie f

clin·ic Klinik f

clin·i·cal klinisch

clink 1. Klirren n, Klingen n; sl Knast m; **2.** klingen or klirren (lassen); klimpern mit

clip¹ 1. ausschneiden; Schafe etc scheren; **2.** Schnitt m; Schur f; (Film- etc) Ausschnitt m; (Video)Clip m

clip² 1. (Heft-, Büro- etc)Klammer f; (Ohr)Klipp m; **2.** a. **~ on** anklammern

clip·per: (a pair of) ~s (e-e) (Nagel-etc)Schere f, Haarschneidemaschine f

clip·pings Abfälle pl, Schnitzel pl; (Zeitungs- etc)Ausschnitte pl

clit·o·ris ANAT Klitoris f

cloak 1. Umhang m; **2.** fig verhüllen

cloak·room Br Garderobe f; Toilette f

clock 1. (Wand-, Stand-, Turm)Uhr f; **9 o'clock** 9 Uhr; **2.** SPORT Zeit stoppen; **~ in, ~ on** einstempeln; **~ out, ~ off** ausstempeln; **~ ra·di·o** Radiowecker m

clock·wise im Uhrzeigersinn

clock·work Uhrwerk n; **like ~** wie am Schnürchen

clod (Erd)Klumpen m

clog 1. (Holz)Klotz m; Holzschuh m; **2.** a. **~ up** verstopfen

clois·ter ARCH Kreuzgang *m*; REL Kloster *n*

close 1. *adj* geschlossen; knapp (*result etc*); genau, gründlich (*inspection etc*); eng (anliegend); stickig, schwül; eng (*friend*), nah (*relative*); **keep a ~ watch on** scharf im Auge behalten (*acc*); **2.** *adv* eng, nahe, dicht; **~ by** ganz in der Nähe, nahe *or* dicht bei; **3.** Ende *n*, (Ab)Schluss *m*; **come** *or* **draw to a ~** sich dem Ende nähern; Einfriedung *f*; **4.** *v/t* (ab-, ver-, zu)schließen, zumachen; ECON schließen; *Straße* (ab)sperren; *v/i* sich schließen; schließen, zumachen; enden, zu Ende gehen; **~ down** *Geschäft etc* schließen, *Betrieb* stilllegen; *radio*, TV das Programm beenden, Sendeschluss haben; **~ in** bedrohlich nahe kommen; hereinbrechen (*night*); **~ up** (ab-, ver-, zu)schließen; aufschließen, aufrücken

closed geschlossen, F *pred* zu

clos·et (Wand)Schrank *m*

close-up PHOT, *film*: Großaufnahme *f*

clos·ing date Einsendeschluss *m*

clos·ing time Laden-, Geschäftsschluss *m*; Polizeistunde *f* (*of a pub*)

clot 1. Klumpen *m*, Klümpchen *n*; **~ of blood** MED Blutgerinnsel *n*; **2.** gerinnen; Klumpen bilden

cloth Stoff *m*, Tuch *n*; Lappen *m*

cloth·bound in Leinen gebunden

clothe (an-, be)kleiden; einkleiden

clothes Kleider *pl*, Kleidung *f*; Wäsche *f*

clothes bas·ket Wäschekorb *m*

clothes·horse Wäscheständer *m*

clothes·line Wäscheleine *f*

clothes peg *Br*, **clothes·pin** Wäscheklammer *f*

cloth·ing (Be)Kleidung *f*

cloud 1. Wolke *f*; *fig* Schatten *m*; **2.** (sich) bewölken; (sich) trüben

cloud·burst Wolkenbruch *m*

cloud·less wolkenlos

cloud·y bewölkt; trüb; *fig* unklar

clout F Schlag *m*; POL Einfluss *m*

clove[1] GASTR (Gewürz)Nelke *f*; **~ of garlic** Knoblauchzehe *f*

clo·ven hoof ZO Huf *m* der Paarzeher

clo·ver BOT Klee *m*

clown Clown *m*; Hanswurst *m*

club 1. Keule *f*; Knüppel *m*; SPORT Schlagholz *n*; (*Golf*)Schläger *m*; Klub *m*; *pl card game*: Kreuz *n*; **2.** einknüppeln auf (*acc*), niederknüppeln

club·foot MED Klumpfuß *m*

cluck ZO **1.** gackern; glucken; **2.** Gackern *n*; Glucken *n*

clue Anhaltspunkt *m*, Fingerzeig *m*, Spur *f*

clump 1. Klumpen *m*; (*Baum- etc* -) Gruppe *f*; **2.** trampeln

clum·sy unbeholfen, ungeschickt, plump

clus·ter 1. BOT Traube *f*, Büschel *n*; Haufen *m*; **2.** sich drängen

clutch 1. Griff *m*; TECH Kupplung *f*; *fig* Klaue *f*; **2.** (er)greifen; umklammern

clut·ter *fig* überladen

c/o ABBR *of* **care of** c/o, (wohnhaft) bei

Co ABBR *of* **company** ECON Gesellschaft *f*

coach 1. Reisebus *m*; *Br* RAIL (Personen)Wagen *m*; Kutsche *f*; SPORT Trainer(in); PED Nachhilfelehrer(in); **2.** SPORT trainieren; PED *j-m* Nachhilfeunterricht geben

coach·man Kutscher *m*

co·ag·u·late gerinnen (lassen)

coal (Stein)Kohle *f*; **carry ~s to Newcastle** F *Br* Eulen nach Athen tragen

co·a·li·tion POL Koalition *f*; Bündnis *n*, Zusammenschluss *m*

coal·mine, **coal·pit** Kohlengrube *f*

coarse grob; rau; derb; ungeschliffen; gemein

coast 1. Küste *f*; **2.** MAR die Küste entlangfahren; (im Leerlauf (*car*) *or* im Freilauf (*bicycle*) fahren; rodeln

coast·er brake Rücktritt(bremse *f*) *m*

coast·guard (Angehörige *m* der) Küstenwache *f*

coast·line Küstenlinie *f*, -strich *m*

coat 1. Mantel *m*; ZO Pelz *m*, Fell *n*; (*Farb- etc*)Überzug *m*, Anstrich *m*, Schicht *f*; **2.** (an)streichen, überziehen, beschichten

coat hang·er Kleiderbügel *m*

coat·ing (*Farb- etc*)Überzug *m*, Anstrich *m*; Schicht *f*; Mantelstoff *m*

coat of arms Wappen(schild *m*, *n*) *n*

coax überreden, beschwatzen

cob Maiskolben *m*

cob·bled: ~ street Straße *f* mit Kopfsteinpflaster

cob·bler (Flick)Schuster *m*

cob·web Spinn(en)gewebe *n*

co·caine Kokain *n*

cock 1. ZO Hahn *m*; V Schwanz *m*; **2.** aufrichten; ~ **one's ears** die Ohren spitzen

cock·a·too ZO Kakadu *m*

cock·chaf·er ZO Maikäfer *m*

cock·eyed F schielend; (krumm und) schief

Cock·ney Cockney *m*, waschechter Londoner

cock·pit AVIAT Cockpit *n*

cock·roach ZO Schabe *f*

cock·sure F übertrieben selbstsicher

cock·tail Cocktail *m*

cock·y großspurig, anmaßend

co·co BOT Kokospalme *f*

co·coa Kakao *m*

co·co·nut BOT Kokosnuss *f*

co·coon (*Seiden*)Kokon *m*

cod ZO Kabeljau *m*, Dorsch *m*

COD ABBR *of **collect** (Br **cash**) on delivery* per Nachnahme

cod·dle verhätscheln, verzärteln

code 1. Kode *m*; **2.** verschlüsseln, chiffrieren; kodieren

cod·fish → cod

cod·ing Kodierung *f*

cod-liv·er oil Lebertran *m*

co·ed·u·ca·tion PED Gemeinschaftserziehung *f*

co·ex·ist gleichzeitig *or* nebeneinander bestehen *or* leben

co·ex·ist·ence Koexistenz *f*

cof·fee Kaffee *m*; *black (white)* ~ Kaffee ohne (mit) Milch; ~ **bar** Br Café *n*; Imbissstube *f*; ~ **bean** Kaffeebohne *f*; ~ **grind·er** Kaffeemühle *f*; ~ **machine** Kaffeeautomat *m*

cof·fee·mak·er Kaffeemaschine *f*

cof·fee| pot Kaffeekanne *f*; ~ **shop** Café *n*; Imbissstube *f*; ~ **ta·ble** Couchtisch *m*

cof·fin Sarg *m*

cog TECH (Rad)Zahn *m*; → **cog·wheel** TECH Zahnrad *n*

co·her·ence, co·her·en·cy Zusammenhang *m*

co·her·ent zusammenhängend

co·he·sion Zusammenhalt *m*

co·he·sive (*fest*) zusammenhaltend

coif·fure Frisur *f*

coil 1. *a.* ~ *up* aufrollen, (auf)wickeln; sich zusammenrollen; **2.** Spirale *f* (*a.* TECH, MED); Rolle *f*, Spule *f*

coin 1. Münze *f*; **2.** prägen

co·in·cide zusammentreffen; übereinstimmen; **co·in·ci·dence** (*zufälliges*) Zusammentreffen; Zufall *m*

coin-op·e·rat·ed: ~ (*gas*, Br *petrol*) *pump* Münztank(automat) *m*

coke Koks *m* (*a.* F *cocaine*)

Coke® F Coke *n*, Cola *n*, *f*, Coca *n*, *f*

cold 1. kalt; **2.** Kälte *f*; MED Erkältung *f*; *catch (a)* ~ sich erkälten; *have a* ~ erkältet sein

cold-blood·ed kaltblütig

cold cuts GASTR Aufschnitt *m*

cold-heart·ed kaltherzig

cold·ness Kälte *f*

cold sweat Angstschweiß *m*; *he broke out in a* ~ ihm brach der Angstschweiß aus

cold war POL kalter Krieg

cold wave METEOR Kältewelle *f*

cole·slaw Krautsalat *m*

col·ic MED Kolik *f*

col·lab·o·rate zusammenarbeiten

col·lab·o·ra·tion Zusammenarbeit *f*; *in* ~ *with* gemeinsam mit

col·lapse 1. zusammenbrechen (*a.* fig), einstürzen; umfallen; fig scheitern; **2.** Einsturz *m*; fig Zusammenbruch *m*

col·lap·si·ble Klapp..., zusammenklappbar

col·lar 1. Kragen *m*; (*Hunde- etc*)Halsband *n*; **2.** beim Kragen packen; *j-n* festnehmen, F schnappen

col·lar·bone ANAT Schlüsselbein *n*

col·league Kollege *m*, Kollegin *f*, Mitarbeiter(in)

col·lect *v/t* (ein)sammeln; *Daten* erfassen; *Geld* kassieren; *j-n or et.* abholen; *Gedanken etc* sammeln; *v/i* sich (ver-)sammeln; **col·lect·ed** fig gefasst

col·lect·ing box Sammelbüchse *f*

col·lec·tion Sammlung *f*; ECON Eintreibung *f*; REL Kollekte *f*; Abholung *f*

col·lec·tive gesammelt; Sammel...; ~ *bargaining* ECON Tarifverhandlungen

col·lec·tive·ly insgesamt; zusammen

col·lec·tor Sammler(in); Steuereinnehmer *m*; ELECTR Stromabnehmer *m*

col·lege College *n*; Hochschule *f*; höhere Lehranstalt

col·lide zusammenstoßen, kollidieren (*a.* fig)

col·lie·ry Kohlengrube *f*

col·li·sion Zusammenstoß *m*, Kollision *f* (*a. fig*)

col·lo·qui·al umgangssprachlich

co·lon LING Doppelpunkt *m*

colo·nel MIL Oberst *m*

co·lo·ni·al·is·m POL Kolonialismus *m*

col·o·nize kolonisieren, besiedeln

col·o·ny Kolonie *f*

col·o(u)r 1. Farbe *f*; *a. pl* MIL Fahne *f*; MAR Flagge *f*; *what ~ is ...?* welche Farbe hat ...?; **2.** *v/t* färben; anmalen, bemalen, anstreichen; *fig* beschönigen; *v/i* sich (ver)färben; erröten

col·o(u)r bar Rassenschranke *f*

col·o(u)r-blind farbenblind

col·o(u)red bunt; farbig

col·o(u)r·fast farbecht

col·o(u)r film PHOT Farbfilm *m*

col·o(u)r·ful farbenprächtig; *fig* farbig, bunt

col·o(u)r·ing Färbung *f*; Farbstoff *m*; Gesichtsfarbe *f*

col·o(u)r·less farblos

col·o(u)r line Rassenschranke *f*

col·o(u)r| set Farbfernseher *m*; *~* **tel·e·vi·sion** Farbfernsehen *n*

colt ZO (Hengst)Fohlen *n*

col·umn Säule *f*; PRINT Spalte *f*; MIL Kolonne *f*

col·umn·ist Kolumnist(in)

comb 1. Kamm *m*; **2.** kämmen; striegeln

com·bat 1. Kampf *m*; *single ~* Zweikampf *m*; **2.** kämpfen gegen, bekämpfen; **com·ba·tant** MIL Kämpfer *m*

com·bi·na·tion Verbindung *f*, Kombination *f*; **com·bine 1.** (sich) verbinden; **2.** ECON Konzern *m*; AGR *a. ~* *harvester* Mähdrescher *m*

com·bus·ti·ble 1. brennbar; **2.** Brennstoff *m*, Brennmaterial *n*

com·bus·tion Verbrennung *f*

come kommen; *to ~* künftig, kommend; *~ and go* kommen und gehen; *~ to see* besuchen; *~ about* geschehen, passieren; *~ across* auf j-n *or* et. stoßen; *~ along* mitkommen, mitgehen; *~ apart* auseinander fallen; *~ away* sich lösen, ab-, losgehen (*button etc*); *~ back* zurückkommen; *~ by s.th.* zu et. kommen; *~ down* herunterkommen (*a. fig*); einstürzen; sinken (*prices*); überliefert werden; *~ down with* F erkranken an (*dat*); *~ for* abholen kommen, kommen wegen; *~ forward* sich mel-

den; *~ from* kommen aus; kommen von; *~ home* nach Hause (*Austrian, Swiss a.* nachhause) kommen; *~ in* hereinkommen; eintreffen (*news*); einlaufen (*train*); *~ in!* herein!; *~ loose* sich ablösen, abgehen; *~ off* ab-, losgehen (*button etc*); *~ on!* los!, vorwärts!, komm!; *~ out* herauskommen; *~ over* vorbeikommen (*visitor*); *~ round* vorbeikommen (*visitor*); wieder zu sich kommen; *~ through* durchkommen; *Krankheit etc* überstehen, überleben; *~ to* sich belaufen auf (*acc*); wieder zu sich kommen; *~ up to* entsprechen (*dat*), heranreichen an (*acc*)

come·back Come-back *n*

co·me·di·an Komiker *m*

com·e·dy Komödie *f*, Lustspiel *n*

come·ly attraktiv, gut aussehend

com·fort 1. Komfort *m*, Bequemlichkeit *f*; Trost *m*; *cold ~* schwacher Trost; **2.** trösten

com·for·ta·ble komfortabel, behaglich, bequem; tröstlich

com·fort·er Tröster *m*; *esp Br* Schnuller *m*; Steppdecke *f*

com·fort·less unbequem; trostlos

com·fort sta·tion Bedürfnisanstalt *f*

com·ic komisch; Komödien..., Lustspiel...; **com·i·cal** komisch, spaßig

com·ics Comics *pl*, Comic-Hefte *pl*

com·ma LING Komma *n*

com·mand 1. Befehl *m*; Beherrschung *f*; MIL Kommando *n*; **2.** befehlen; MIL kommandieren; verfügen über (*acc*); beherrschen

com·mand·er MIL Kommandeur *m*, Befehlshaber *m*; *~* **in chief** MIL Oberbefehlshaber *m*

com·mand·ment REL Gebot *n*

com·mand mod·ule Kommandokapsel *f*

com·man·do MIL Kommando *n*

com·mem·o·rate gedenken (*gen*)

com·mem·o·ra·tion: *in ~ of* zum Gedenken *or* Gedächtnis an (*acc*)

com·mem·o·ra·tive Gedenk..., Erinnerungs...

com·ment 1. (*on*) Kommentar *m* (zu); Bemerkung *f* (zu); Anmerkung *f* (zu); *no ~!* kein Kommentar!; **2.** *v/i ~ on* e-n Kommentar abgeben zu, sich äußern über (*acc*); *v/t* bemerken (*that* dass) com·men·ta·ry Kommentar *m* (**on** zu)

com·men·ta·tor Kommentator *m*, *ra·dio*, TV *a.* Reporter *m*

com·merce ECON Handel *m*

com·mer·cial **1.** ECON Handels..., Geschäfts...; kommerziell, finanziell; **2.** *radio*, TV Werbespot *m*, Werbesendung *f*; ~ **art** Gebrauchsgrafik *f*; ~ **art·ist** Gebrauchsgrafiker(in)

com·mer·cial·ize kommerzialisieren

com·mer·cial tel·e·vi·sion Werbefernsehen *n*; kommerzielles Fernsehen

com·mis·e·rate: ~ **with** Mitleid empfinden mit

com·mis·e·ra·tion Mitleid *n* (**for** mit)

com·mis·sion **1.** Auftrag *m*; Kommission *f*, Ausschuss *m*; ECON Kommission *f*, Provision *f*; Begehung *f* (*of a crime*); **2.** beauftragen; *et.* in Auftrag geben

com·mis·sion·er Beauftragte *m*, *f*; Kommissar(in)

com·mit anvertrauen, übergeben (**to** *dat*); JUR *j-n* einweisen (**to** in *acc*); *Verbrechen* begehen; *j-n* verpflichten (**to** zu), *j-n* festlegen (**to** auf *acc*)

com·mit·ment Verpflichtung *f*; Engagement *n*

com·mit·tal JUR Einweisung *f*

com·mit·tee Komitee *n*, Ausschuss *m*

com·mod·i·ty ECON Ware *f*, Artikel *m*

com·mon **1.** gemeinsam, gemeinschaftlich; allgemein; alltäglich; gewöhnlich, einfach; **2.** Gemeindeland *n*; **in** ~ gemeinsam (**with** mit)

com·mon·er Bürgerliche *m*, *f*

com·mon law (ungeschriebenes englisches) Gewohnheitsrecht

Com·mon Mar·ket ECON, POL HIST Gemeinsamer Markt

com·mon·place **1.** Gemeinplatz *m*; **2.** alltäglich; abgedroschen

Com·mons: **the** ~, **the House of** ~ *Br* PARL das Unterhaus

com·mon sense gesunder Menschenverstand

Com·mon·wealth: **the** ~ (**of Nations**) das Commonwealth

com·mo·tion Aufregung *f*; Aufruhr *m*, Tumult *m*

com·mu·nal Gemeinde...; Gemeinschafts...; **com·mune** Kommune *f*

com·mu·ni·cate *v/t* mitteilen; *v/i* sich besprechen; sich in Verbindung setzen

(**with s.o.** mit j-m); (durch e-e Tür) verbunden sein

com·mu·ni·ca·tion Mitteilung *f*; Verständigung *f*, Kommunikation *f*; Verbindung *f*; *pl* Kommunikationsmittel *pl*; Verkehrswege *pl*

com·mu·ni·ca·tions sat·el·lite Nachrichtensatellit *m*

com·mu·ni·ca·tive mitteilsam, gesprächig

Com·mu·nion *a.* **Holy** ~ REL (heilige) Kommunion, Abendmahl *n*

com·mu·nis·m POL Kommunismus *m*

com·mu·nist POL **1.** Kommunist(in); **2.** kommunistisch

com·mu·ni·ty Gemeinschaft *f*; Gemeinde *f*

com·mute JUR Strafe *mildernd* umwandeln; RAIL *etc* pendeln

com·mut·er Pendler(in); ~ **train** Pendlerzug *m*, Nahverkehrszug *m*

com·pact **1.** Puderdose *f*; MOT Kleinwagen *m*; **2.** *adj* kompakt; eng, klein; knapp (*style*); ~ **car** MOT Kleinwagen *m*; ~ **disk** (ABBR **CD**) Compact Disc *f*, CD *f*; ~ **disk play·er** CD-Player *m*, CD-Spieler *m*

com·pan·ion Begleiter(in); Gefährte *m*, Gefährtin *f*; Gesellschafter(in); Handbuch *n*, Leitfaden *m*

com·pan·ion·ship Gesellschaft *f*

com·pa·ny Gesellschaft *f*, ECON *a.* Firma *f*; MIL Kompanie *f*; THEA Truppe *f*; **keep s.o.** ~ j-m Gesellschaft leisten

com·pa·ra·ble vergleichbar

com·par·a·tive **1.** vergleichend; verhältnismäßig; **2.** *a.* ~ **degree** LING Komparativ *m*; **com·par·a·tive·ly** vergleichsweise; verhältnismäßig

com·pare **1.** *v/t* vergleichen; ~*d with* im Vergleich zu; *v/i* sich vergleichen lassen; **2.** *beyond* ~, *without* ~ unvergleichlich

com·par·i·son Vergleich *m*

com·part·ment Fach *n*; RAIL Abteil *n*

com·pass Kompass *m*; *pair of* ~*es* Zirkel *m*

com·pas·sion Mitleid *n*

com·pas·sion·ate mitleidig

com·pat·i·ble vereinbar; *be* ~ (*with*) passen (zu), zusammenpassen; EDP *etc* kompatibel sein (mit)

com·pat·ri·ot Landsmann *m*, Landsmännin *f*

com·pel (er)zwingen
com·pel·ling bezwingend
com·pen·sate *j-n* entschädigen; *et.* ersetzen; ausgleichen
com·pen·sa·tion Ersatz *m*; Ausgleich *m*; Schadenersatz *m*, Entschädigung *f*; Bezahlung *f*, Gehalt *n*
com·pere *Br* Conférencier *m*
com·pete sich (mit)bewerben (*for* um); konkurrieren; SPORT (am Wettkampf) teilnehmen
com·pe·tence Können *n*, Fähigkeit *f*
com·pe·tent fähig, tüchtig; fachkundig, sachkundig
com·pe·ti·tion Wettbewerb *m*; Konkurrenz *f*
com·pet·i·tive konkurrierend
com·pet·i·tor Mitbewerber(in); Konkurrent(in); SPORT (Wettbewerbs-)Teilnehmer(in)
com·pile kompilieren, zusammentragen, zusammenstellen
com·pla·cence, **com·pla·cen·cy** Selbstzufriedenheit *f*, Selbstgefälligkeit *f*; **com·pla·cent** selbstzufrieden, selbstgefällig
com·plain sich beklagen *or* beschweren (*about* über *acc*; *to* bei); klagen (*of* über *acc*)
com·plaint Klage *f*, Beschwerde *f*; MED Leiden *n*, *pl* MED *a*. Beschwerden *pl*
com·ple·ment 1. Ergänzung *f*; **2.** ergänzen
com·ple·men·ta·ry (sich) ergänzend
com·plete 1. vollständig; vollzählig; **2.** vervollständigen; beenden, abschließen
com·ple·tion Vervollständigung *f*; Abschluss *m*; **~ test** PSYCH Lückentext *m*
com·plex 1. zusammengesetzt; komplex, vielschichtig; **2.** Komplex *m* (*a*. PSYCH)
com·plex·ion Gesichtsfarbe *f*, Teint *m*
com·plex·i·ty Komplexität *f*, Vielschichtigkeit *f*
com·pli·ance Einwilligung *f*; Befolgung *f*; **in ~ with** gemäß (*dat*)
com·pli·ant willfährig
com·pli·cate komplizieren
com·pli·cat·ed kompliziert
com·pli·ca·tion Komplikation *f* (*a*. MED)
com·plic·i·ty JUR Mitschuld *f*, Mittäterschaft *f* (*in* an *dat*)

com·pli·ment 1. Kompliment *n*; Empfehlung *f*; Gruß *m*; **2.** *v/t j-m* ein Kompliment *or* Komplimente machen (**on** über *acc*)
com·ply (**with**) einwilligen (in *acc*); (*e-e Abmachung etc*) befolgen
com·po·nent Bestandteil *m*; TECH, ELECTR Bauelement *n*
com·pose zusammensetzen, -stellen; MUS komponieren; verfassen; **be ~d of** bestehen *or* sich zusammensetzen aus; **~ o.s.** sich beruhigen
com·posed ruhig, gelassen
com·pos·er MUS Komponist(in)
com·po·si·tion Zusammensetzung *f*; MUS Komposition *f*; PED Aufsatz *m*
com·po·sure Fassung *f*, (Gemüts)Ruhe *f*
com·pound[1] Lager *n*; Gefängnishof *m*; (Tier)Gehege *n*
com·pound[2] **1.** Zusammensetzung *f*; Verbindung *f*; LING zusammengesetztes Wort; **2.** zusammengesetzt; **~ interest** ECON Zinseszinsen *pl*; **3.** *v/t* zusammensetzen; steigern, *esp* verschlimmern
com·pre·hend begreifen, verstehen
com·pre·hen·si·ble verständlich
com·pre·hen·sion Verständnis *n*; Begriffsvermögen *n*, Verstand *m*; **past ~** unfassbar, unfasslich
com·pre·hen·sive 1. umfassend; **2.** *a*. **~ school** *Br* Gesamtschule *f*
com·press zusammendrücken, -pressen; **~ed air** Druckluft *f*
com·pres·sion PHYS Verdichtung *f*; TECH Druck *m*
com·prise einschließen, umfassen; bestehen aus
com·pro·mise 1. Kompromiss *m*; **2.** *v/t* bloßstellen, kompromittieren; *v/i* e-n Kompromiss schließen
com·pro·mis·ing kompromittierend; verfänglich
com·pul·sion Zwang *m*
com·pul·sive zwingend, Zwangs...; PSYCH zwanghaft
com·pul·so·ry obligatorisch; Pflicht..., Zwangs...
com·punc·tion Gewissensbisse *pl*; Reue *f*; Bedenken *pl*
com·pute berechnen; schätzen
com·put·er Computer *m*, Rechner *m*
com·put·er·aid·ed computergestützt;

~-con·trolled computergesteuert

com·put·er| game Computerspiel n; **~ graph·ics** Computergrafik f

com·put·er·ize (sich) auf Computer umstellen; computerisieren; mit Hilfe e-s Computers errechnen or zusammenstellen

com·put·er| pre·dic·tion Hochrechnung f; **~ sci·ence** Informatik f; **~ sci·en·tist** Informatiker m; **~ vi·rus** EDP Computervirus m

com·rade Kamerad m; (Partei)Genosse m

con¹ → **contra**

con² F reinlegen, betrügen

con·ceal verbergen; verheimlichen

con·cede zugestehen, einräumen

con·ceit Einbildung f, Dünkel m

con·ceit·ed eingebildet (**of** auf acc)

con·cei·va·ble denkbar, begreiflich

con·ceive v/i schwanger werden; v/t Kind empfangen; sich et. vorstellen or denken

con·cen·trate (sich) konzentrieren

con·cept Begriff m; Gedanke m

con·cep·tion Vorstellung f, Begriff m; BIOL Empfängnis f

con·cern 1. Angelegenheit f; Sorge f; ECON Geschäft n, Unternehmen n; **2.** betreffen, angehen; beunruhigen

con·cerned besorgt; beteiligt (**in** an dat)

con·cern·ing prp betreffend, hinsichtlich (gen); was ... (acc) (an)betrifft

con·cert MUS Konzert n

con·cert hall Konzerthalle f, -saal m

con·ces·sion Zugeständnis n; Konzession f

con·cil·i·a·to·ry versöhnlich, vermittelnd

con·cise kurz, knapp

con·cise·ness Kürze f

con·clude schließen, beenden; Vertrag etc abschließen; et. folgern, schließen (**from** aus); **to be ~d** Schluss folgt

con·clu·sion (Ab)Schluss m, Ende n; Abschluss m (**of** a contract etc); (Schluss)Folgerung f; → **jump**

con·clu·sive schlüssig

con·coct (zusammen)brauen; fig aushecken, ausbrüten

con·coc·tion Gebräu n; fig Erfindung f

con·crete¹ konkret

con·crete² 1. Beton m; **2.** Beton...; **3.** betonieren

con·cur übereinstimmen

con·cur·rence Zusammentreffen n; Übereinstimmung f

con·cus·sion MED Gehirnerschütterung f

con·demn verurteilen (a. JUR); verdammen; für unbrauchbar or unbewohnbar etc erklären; **~ to death** JUR zum Tode verurteilen; **con·dem·na·tion** Verurteilung f (a. JUR); Verdammung f

con·den·sa·tion Kondensation f; Zusammenfassung f

con·dense kondensieren; zusammenfassen

con·densed milk Kondensmilch f

con·dens·er TECH Kondensator m

con·de·scend sich herablassen

con·de·scend·ing herablassend, gönnerhaft

con·di·ment Gewürz n, Würze f

con·di·tion 1. Zustand m; (körperlicher or Gesundheits)Zustand m; SPORT Kondition f, Form f; Bedingung f; pl Verhältnisse pl, Umstände pl; **on ~ that** unter der Bedingung, dass; **out of ~** in schlechter Verfassung, in schlechtem Zustand; **2.** bedingen; in Form bringen

con·di·tion·al 1. (**on**) bedingt (durch), abhängig (von); **2.** a. ~ **clause** LING Bedingungs-, Konditionalsatz m; a. ~ **mood** LING Konditional m

con·do → **condominium**

con·dole kondolieren (**with** dat)

con·do·lence Beileid n

con·dom Kondom n, m

con·do·min·i·um Eigentumswohnanlage f; Eigentumswohnung f

con·done verzeihen, vergeben

con·du·cive dienlich, förderlich (**to** dat)

con·duct 1. Führung f; Verhalten n, Betragen n; **2.** führen; PHYS leiten; MUS dirigieren; **~ed tour** Führung f (**of** durch); **con·duc·tor** Führer m, Leiter m; (Bus-, Straßenbahn)Schaffner m; RAIL Zugbegleiter m; MUS Dirigent m; PHYS Leiter m; ELECTR Blitzableiter m

cone Kegel m; GASTR Eistüte f; BOT Zapfen m

con·fec·tion Konfekt n

con·fec·tion·er Konditor m

con·fec·tion·e·ry Süßigkeiten pl, Süß-, Konditoreiwaren pl; Konfekt n; Konditorei f; Süßwarengeschäft n

con·fed·e·ra·cy (Staaten)Bund m; **the Confederacy** HIST die Konföderation

con·fed·er·ate 1. verbündet; **2.** Verbündete m, Bundesgenosse m; **3.** (sich) verbünden

con·fed·er·a·tion Bund m, Bündnis n; (Staaten)Bund m

con·fer v/t Titel etc verleihen (**on** dat); v/i sich beraten

con·fe·rence Konferenz f

con·fess gestehen; beichten

con·fes·sion Geständnis n; REL Beichte f

con·fes·sion·al REL Beichtstuhl m

con·fes·sor REL Beichtvater m

con·fi·dant(e) Vertraute m (f)

con·fide: ~ s.th. to s.o. j-m et. anvertrauen; ~ in s.o. sich j-m anvertrauen

con·fi·dence Vertrauen n; Selbstvertrauen n; ~ man → conman; ~ trickster Trickbetrüger m

con·fi·dent überzeugt, zuversichtlich

con·fi·den·tial vertraulich

con·fine begrenzen, beschränken; einsperren; **be ~d of** entbunden werden von; **con·fine·ment** Haft f; Beschränkung f; MED Entbindung f

con·firm bestätigen; bekräftigen; REL konfirmieren, firmen

con·fir·ma·tion Bestätigung f; REL Konfirmation f, Firmung f

con·fis·cate beschlagnahmen

con·fis·ca·tion Beschlagnahme f

con·flict 1. Konflikt m, Zwiespalt m; **2.** im Widerspruch stehen (**with** zu)

con·flict·ing widersprüchlich, zwiespältig

con·form (sich) anpassen (**to** dat, an acc)

con·found verwirren, durcheinander bringen

con·front gegenübertreten, -stehen (dat); sich stellen (dat); konfrontieren

con·fron·ta·tion Konfrontation f

con·fuse verwechseln; verwirren; **con·fused** verwirrt; verlegen; verworren; **con·fu·sion** Verwirrung f; Verlegenheit f; Verwechslung f

con·geal erstarren (lassen); gerinnen (lassen)

con·gest·ed überfüllt; verstopft

con·ges·tion MED Blutandrang m; a. **traffic** ~ Verkehrsstockung f, Verkehrsstörung f, Verkehrsstau m

con·grat·u·late beglückwünschen, j-m gratulieren

con·grat·u·la·tion Glückwunsch m; ~s! ich gratuliere!, herzlichen Glückwunsch!

con·gre·gate (sich) versammeln

con·gre·ga·tion REL Gemeinde f

con·gress Kongress m; **Congress** PARL der Kongress

Con·gress·man PARL Kongressabgeordnete m; **Con·gress·wom·an** PARL Kongressabgeordnete f

con·ic, con·i·cal esp TECH konisch, kegelförmig

co·ni·fer BOT Nadelbaum m

con·jec·ture 1. Vermutung f; **2.** vermuten

con·ju·gal ehelich

con·ju·gate LING konjugieren, beugen

con·ju·ga·tion LING Konjugation f, Beugung f

con·junc·tion Verbindung f; LING Konjunktion f, Bindewort n

con·junc·ti·vi·tis MED Bindehautentzündung f

con·jure zaubern; Teufel etc beschwören; ~ up heraufbeschwören (a. fig)

con·jur·er esp Br → conjuror

con·jur·ing trick Zaubertrickstück n

con·jur·or Zauberer m, Zauberin f, Zauberkünstler(in)

con·man Betrüger m; Hochstapler m

con·nect verbinden; ELECTR anschließen, zuschalten; RAIL, AVIAT etc Anschluss haben (**with** acc)

con·nect·ed verbunden; (logisch) zusammenhängend (speech etc); **be well** ~ gute Beziehungen haben

con·nec·tion, Br **con·nex·ion** Verbindung f, Anschluss m (a. ELECTR, RAIL, AVIAT, TEL); Zusammenhang m; mst pl Beziehungen pl, Verbindungen pl; Verwandte pl

con·quer erobern; (be)siegen

con·quer·or Eroberer m

con·quest Eroberung f (a. fig); erobertes Gebiet

con·science Gewissen n

con·sci·en·tious gewissenhaft; Gewissens...; **con·sci·en·tious·ness** Gewissenhaftigkeit f

con·sci·en·tious ob·jec·tor MIL Wehrdienstverweigerer m

con·scious MED bei Bewusstsein; bewusst; **be ~ of** sich bewusst sein (*gen*)

con·scious·ness Bewusstsein *n* (*a.* MED)

con·script MIL **1.** einberufen; **2.** Wehrpflichtige *m*; **con·scrip·tion** MIL Einberufung *f*; Wehrpflicht *f*

con·se·crate REL weihen; widmen

con·se·cra·tion REL Weihe *f*

con·sec·u·tive aufeinander folgend; fortlaufend

con·sent **1.** Zustimmung *f*; **2.** einwilligen, zustimmen

con·se·quence Folge *f*, Konsequenz *f*; Bedeutung *f*

con·se·quent·ly folglich, daher

con·ser·va·tion Erhaltung *f*; Naturschutz *m*; Umweltschutz *m*; **~ area** (Natur)Schutzgebiet *n*

con·ser·va·tion·ist Naturschützer(in); Umweltschützer(in)

con·ser·va·tive **1.** erhaltend; konservativ; vorsichtig; **2. Conservative** POL Konservative *m*, *f*

con·ser·va·to·ry Treibhaus *n*, Gewächshaus *n*; Wintergarten *m*

con·serve erhalten

con·sid·er *v/t* nachdenken über (*acc*); betrachten als, halten für; sich überlegen, erwägen; in Betracht ziehen, berücksichtigen; *v/i* nachdenken, überlegen

con·sid·e·ra·ble ansehnlich, beträchtlich; **con·sid·e·ra·bly** bedeutend, ziemlich, (sehr) viel

con·sid·er·ate rücksichtsvoll

con·sid·e·ra·tion Erwägung *f*, Überlegung *f*; Berücksichtigung *f*; Rücksicht (nahme) *f*; **take into ~** in Erwägung *or* in Betracht ziehen

con·sid·er·ing in Anbetracht (der Tatsache, dass)

con·sign ECON *Waren* zusenden

con·sign·ment ECON (Waren)Sendung *f*; Zusendung *f*

con·sist: **~ in** bestehen in (*dat*); **~ of** bestehen aus

con·sis·tence, con·sis·ten·cy Konsistenz *f*, Beschaffenheit *f*; Übereinstimmung *f*; Konsequenz *f*

con·sis·tent übereinstimmend, vereinbar (**with** mit); konsequent; SPORT *etc*: beständig

con·so·la·tion Trost *m*

con·sole trösten

con·sol·i·date festigen; *fig* zusammenschließen, -legen

con·so·nant LING Konsonant *m*, Mitlaut *m*

con·spic·u·ous deutlich sichtbar; auffallend

con·spir·a·cy Verschwörung *f*

con·spir·a·tor Verschwörer *m*

con·spire sich verschwören

con·sta·ble *Br* Polizist *m*

con·stant konstant, gleich bleibend; (be)ständig; (an)dauernd

con·stant-care pa·tient MED Pflegefall *m*

con·ster·na·tion Bestürzung *f*

con·sti·pat·ed MED verstopft

con·sti·pa·tion MED Verstopfung *f*

con·stit·u·en·cy POL *Br* Wählerschaft *f*; Wahlkreis *m*

con·stit·u·ent (wesentlicher) Bestandteil; POL Wähler(in)

con·sti·tute ernennen, einsetzen; bilden, ausmachen

con·sti·tu·tion POL Verfassung *f*; Konstitution *f*, körperliche Verfassung

con·sti·tu·tion·al konstitutionell; POL verfassungsmäßig

con·strained gezwungen, unnatürlich

con·strict zusammenziehen

con·stric·tion Zusammenziehung *f*

con·struct bauen, errichten, konstruieren

con·struc·tion Konstruktion *f*; Bau *m*, Bauwerk *n*; **under ~** im Bau (befindlich); **~ site** Baustelle *f*

con·struc·tive konstruktiv

con·struc·tor Erbauer *m*, Konstrukteur *m*

con·sul Konsul *m*

con·su·late Konsulat *n*; **~ gen·e·ral** Generalkonsulat *n*

con·sul gen·e·ral Generalkonsul *m*

con·sult *v/t* konsultieren, um Rat fragen; in *e-m Buch* nachschlagen; *v/i* (sich) beraten

con·sul·tant (fachmännischer) Berater; *Br* Facharzt *m*

con·sul·ta·tion Konsultation *f*, Beratung *f*, Rücksprache *f*

con·sult·ing beratend; **~ hours** *Br* MED Sprechstunde *f*; **~ room** *Br* MED Sprechzimmer *n*

con·sume *v/t Essen etc* zu sich nehmen, verzehren (*a. fig*); verbrauchen, konsumieren; zerstören, vernichten

con·sum·er ECON Verbraucher(in); ~ **so·ci·e·ty** Konsumgesellschaft f

con·sum·mate 1. vollendet; **2.** vollenden; *Ehe* vollziehen

con·sump·tion Verbrauch m

cont ABBR *of **continued*** Forts., Fortsetzung f; fortgesetzt

con·tact 1. Berührung f; Kontakt m; Ansprechpartner(in), Kontaktperson f (a. MED); **make ~s** Verbindungen anknüpfen od herstellen; **2.** sich in Verbindung setzen mit, Kontakt aufnehmen mit; ~ **lens** Kontaktlinse f, -schale f, Haftschale f

con·ta·gious MED ansteckend (a. fig)

con·tain enthalten; *fig* zügeln, zurückhalten; **con·tain·er** Behälter m; ECON Container m; **con·tain·er·ize** ECON auf Containerbetrieb umstellen; in Containern transportieren

con·tam·i·nate verunreinigen; infizieren, vergiften; (a. radioaktiv) verseuchen; **radioactively ~d** verstrahlt; **~d soil** Altlasten pl; **con·tam·i·na·tion** Verunreinigung f; Vergiftung f; (a. radioaktive) Verseuchung f

contd ABBR *of **continued*** (→ **cont**)

con·tem·plate (nachdenklich) betrachten; nachdenken über (acc); erwägen, beabsichtigen

con·tem·pla·tion (nachdenkliche) Betrachtung; Nachdenken n

con·tem·pla·tive nachdenklich

con·tem·po·ra·ry 1. zeitgenössisch; **2.** Zeitgenosse m, Zeitgenossin f

con·tempt Verachtung f

con·temp·ti·ble verachtenswert

con·temp·tu·ous geringschätzig, verächtlich

con·tend kämpfen, ringen (**for** um; **with** mit); **con·tend·er** esp SPORT Wettkämpfer(in)

con·tent[1] Gehalt m, Aussage f, pl Inhalt m; **(table of) ~s** Inhaltsverzeichnis n

con·tent[2] **1.** zufrieden; **2.** befriedigen; ~ **o.s.** sich begnügen

con·tent·ed zufrieden

con·tent·ment Zufriedenheit f

con·test 1. (Wett)Kampf m; Wettbewerb m; **2.** sich bewerben um; bestreiten, a. JUR anfechten

con·tes·tant Wettkämpfer(in), (Wettkampf)Teilnehmer(in)

con·text Zusammenhang m

con·ti·nent Kontinent m, Erdteil m; **the Continent** Br das (europäische) Festland; **con·ti·nen·tal** kontinental, Kontinental...

con·tin·gen·cy Möglichkeit f, Eventualität f; ~ **plan** Notplan m

con·tin·gent 1. **be ~ on** abhängen von; **2.** Kontingent n (a. MIL)

con·tin·u·al fortwährend, unaufhörlich

con·tin·u·a·tion Fortsetzung f; Fortbestand m, Fortdauer f

con·tin·ue v/t fortsetzen, fortfahren mit; beibehalten; **to be ~d** Fortsetzung folgt; v/i fortdauern; andauern, anhalten; fortfahren, weitermachen

con·ti·nu·i·ty Kontinuität f

con·tin·u·ous ununterbrochen; ~ **form** LING Verlaufsform f

con·tort verdrehen; verzerren

con·tor·tion Verdrehung f; Verzerrung f

con·tour Umriss m

con·tra wider, gegen

con·tra·band ECON Schmuggelware f

con·tra·cep·tion MED Empfängnisverhütung f

con·tra·cep·tive MED **1.** empfängnisverhütend; **2.** Verhütungsmittel n

con·tract 1. Vertrag m; **2.** (sich) zusammenziehen; sich e-e Krankheit zuziehen; e-n Vertrag abschließen; sich vertraglich verpflichten

con·trac·tion Zusammenziehung f

con·trac·tor a. **building ~** Bauunternehmer m

con·tra·dict widersprechen (dat)

con·tra·dic·tion Widerspruch m

con·tra·dic·to·ry (sich) widersprechend

con·tra·ry 1. entgegengesetzt (**to** dat); gegensätzlich; ~ **to expectations** wider Erwarten; **2.** Gegenteil n; **on the ~** im Gegenteil

con·trast 1. Gegensatz m; Kontrast m; **2.** v/t gegenüberstellen, vergleichen; v/i sich abheben (**with** von, gegen); im Gegensatz stehen (**with** zu)

con·trib·ute beitragen, beisteuern; spenden (**to** für)

con·tri·bu·tion Beitrag m; Spende f

con·trib·u·tor Beitragende m, f; Mitarbeiter(in)

con·trib·u·to·ry beitragend

con·trite zerknirscht

con·trive zustande bringen; es fertig bringen

con·trol 1. Kontrolle f, Herrschaft f, Macht f, Gewalt f, Beherrschung f; Aufsicht f; TECH Steuerung f; mst pl TECH Steuervorrichtung f; **get** (**have, keep**) **under ~** unter Kontrolle bringen (haben, halten); **get out of ~** außer Kontrolle geraten; **lose ~ of** die Herrschaft or Gewalt or Kontrolle verlieren über; 2. beherrschen, die Kontrolle haben über (acc); e-r Sache Herr werden, (erfolgreich) bekämpfen; kontrollieren, überwachen; ECON (staatlich) lenken, Preise binden; ELECTR, TECH steuern, regeln, regulieren; **~ desk** ELECTR Schalt-, Steuerpult n; **~ pan·el** ELECTR Schalttafel f; **~ tow·er** AVIAT Kontrollturm m, Tower m

con·tro·ver·sial umstritten

con·tro·ver·sy Kontroverse f, Streit m

con·tuse MED sich et. prellen or quetschen; **con·tu·sion** MED Prellung f, Quetschung f

con·va·lesce gesund werden, genesen

con·va·les·cence Rekonvaleszenz f, Genesung f

con·va·les·cent 1. genesend; 2. Rekonvaleszent(in), Genesende m, f

con·vene (sich) versammeln; zusammenkommen; Versammlung einberufen

con·ve·ni·ence Annehmlichkeit f, Bequemlichkeit f; Br Toilette f; **all** (**modern**) **~s** aller Komfort; **at your earliest ~** möglichst bald; **con·ve·ni·ent** bequem; günstig, passend

con·vent REL (Nonnen)Kloster n

con·ven·tion Zusammenkunft f, Tagung f, Versammlung f; Abkommen n; Konvention f, Sitte f; **con·ven·tion·al** herkömmlich, konventionell

con·verge konvergieren; zusammenlaufen, -strömen

con·ver·sa·tion Gespräch n, Unterhaltung f

con·ver·sa·tion·al Unterhaltungs...; **~ English** Umgangsenglisch n

con·verse sich unterhalten

con·ver·sion Umwandlung f, Verwandlung f; Umbau m; Umstellung f (**to** auf acc); REL Bekehrung f, Übertritt m; MATH Umrechnung f; **~ ta·ble** Umrechnungstabelle f

con·vert (sich) umwandeln or verwandeln; umbauen (**into** zu); umstellen (**to** auf acc); REL etc (sich) bekehren; MATH umrechnen

con·vert·er ELECTR Umformer m

con·vert·i·ble 1. umwandelbar, verwandelbar; ECON konvertierbar; 2. MOT Kabrio(lett) n

con·vey befördern, transportieren, bringen; überbringen, übermitteln; Ideen etc mitteilen, vermitteln

con·vey·ance Beförderung f, Transport m; Übermittlung f; Verkehrsmittel n

con·vey·or belt TECH Förderband n

con·vict 1. Verurteilte m, f; Strafgefangene m, f; 2. JUR (**of**) überführen (gen); verurteilen (wegen)

con·vic·tion Überzeugung f; JUR Verurteilung f

con·vince überzeugen

con·voy 1. MAR Geleitzug m, Konvoi m; MOT (Wagen)Kolonne f; (Geleit-)Schutz m; 2. Geleitschutz geben (dat), eskortieren

con·vul·sion MED Zuckung f, Krampf m; **con·vul·sive** MED krampfhaft, krampfartig, konvulsiv

coo ZO gurren (a. fig)

cook 1. Koch m; Köchin f; 2. kochen; F Bericht etc frisieren; **~ up** F sich ausdenken, erfinden

cook·book Kochbuch n

cook·er Br Ofen m, Herd m

cook·e·ry Kochen n; Kochkunst f

cook·e·ry book Br Kochbuch n

cook·ie (süßer) Keks, Plätzchen n

cook·ing GASTR Küche f

cook·y → **cookie**

cool 1. kühl; fig kalt(blütig), gelassen; abweisend; gleichgültig; F klasse, prima, cool; 2. Kühle f, F (Selbst)Beherrschung f; 3. (sich) abkühlen; **~ down, ~ off** sich beruhigen

coon F ZO Waschbär m

coop 1. Hühnerstall m; 2. **~ up, ~ in** einsperren, einpferchen

co-op F Co-op m

co·op·e·rate zusammenarbeiten; mitwirken, helfen

co·op·e·ra·tion Zusammenarbeit f; Mitwirkung f, Hilfe f

co·op·e·ra·tive 1. zusammenarbeitend; kooperativ, hilfsbereit; ECON Gemeinschafts-..., Genossenschafts...; **2.** *a.* **~ society** Genossenschaft *f*; Co-op *m*, Konsumverein *m*; *a.* **~ store** Co-op *m*, Konsumladen *m*

co·or·di·nate 1. koordinieren, aufeinander abstimmen; **2.** koordiniert, gleichgeordnet; **co·or·di·na·tion** Koordinierung *f*, Koordination *f*; harmonisches Zusammenspiel

cop F Bulle *m*

cope: ~ with gewachsen sein (*dat*), fertig werden mit

cop·i·er Kopiergerät *n*, Kopierer *m*

co·pi·ous reich(lich); weitschweifig

cop·per 1. MIN Kupfer *n*; Kupfermünze *f*; **2.** kupfern, Kupfer...

cop·pice, copse Gehölz *n*

cop·y 1. Kopie *f*; Abschrift *f*; Nachbildung *f*; Durchschlag *m*; Exemplar *n*; (*Zeitungs*)Nummer *f*; PRINT Satzvorlage *f*; **fair ~** Reinschrift *f*; **2.** kopieren; abschreiben, e-e Kopie anfertigen von; EDP *Daten* übertragen; nachbilden; nachahmen

cop·y·book Schreibheft *n*

cop·y·ing Kopier...

cop·y·right Urheberrecht *n*, Copyright *n*

cor·al ZO Koralle *f*

cord 1. Schnur *f* (*a.* ELECTR), Strick *m*; Kordsamt *m*; **2.** ver-, zuschnüren

cor·di·al[1] Fruchtsaftkonzentrat *n*; MED Stärkungsmittel *n*

cor·di·al[2] herzlich

cor·di·al·i·ty Herzlichkeit *f*

cord·less schnurlos

cordless phone schnurloses Telefon

cor·don 1. Kordon *m*, Postenkette *f*; **2. ~ off** abriegeln, absperren

cor·du·roy Kord *m*; (**a pair of**) **~s** (e-e) Kordhose

core 1. Kerngehäuse *n*; Kern *m*, *fig a. das* Innerste *n*; **2.** entkernen

core time ECON Kernzeit *f*

cork 1. Kork(en) *m*; **2.** *a.* **~ up** zu-, verkorken; **cork-screw** Korkenzieher *m*

corn[1] **1.** Korn *n*, Getreide *n*; *a.* **Indian ~** Mais *m*; **2.** pökeln

corn[2] MED Hühnerauge *n*

cor·ner 1. Ecke *f*; Winkel *m*; *esp* MOT Kurve *f*; *soccer*: Eckball *m*, Ecke *f*; *fig* schwierige Lage, Klemme *f*; **2.**

Eck...; **3.** in die Ecke (*fig* Enge) treiben; **~ kick** *soccer*: Eckball *m*, Eckstoß *m*; **~ shop** *Br* Tante-Emma-Laden *m*

cor·net MUS Kornett *n*; *Br* GASTR Eistüte *f*

corn·flakes Cornflakes *pl*

cor·nice ARCH Gesims *n*, Sims *m*

cor·o·na·ry 1. ANAT Koronar...; **2.** F MED Herzinfarkt *m*

cor·o·na·tion Krönung *f*

cor·o·net Adelskrone *f*

cor·po·ral MIL Unteroffizier *m*

cor·po·ral pun·ish·ment körperliche Züchtigung

cor·po·rate gemeinsam; Firmen...

cor·po·ra·tion JUR Körperschaft *f*; Stadtverwaltung *f*; ECON (Aktien)Gesellschaft *f*

corpse Leichnam *m*, Leiche *f*

cor·pu·lent beleibt

cor·ral 1. Korral *m*, Hürde *f*, Pferch *m*; **2.** *Vieh* in e-n Pferch treiben

cor·rect 1. korrekt, richtig, *a.* genau (*time*); **2.** korrigieren, verbessern, berichtigen

cor·rec·tion Korrektur *f*, Verbess(e)rung *f*; Bestrafung *f*

cor·rect·ness Richtigkeit *f*

cor·re·spond (**with, to**) entsprechen (*dat*), übereinstimmen (mit); korrespondieren (**with** mit)

cor·re·spon·dence Übereinstimmung *f*; Korrespondenz *f*, Briefwechsel *m*; **~ course** Fernkurs *m*

cor·re·spon·dent 1. entsprechend; **2.** Briefpartner(in); Korrespondent(in)

cor·re·spon·ding entsprechend

cor·ri·dor Korridor *m*, Gang *m*

cor·rob·o·rate bekräftigen, bestätigen

cor·rode zerfressen; CHEM korrodieren, rosten; **cor·ro·sion** CHEM Korrosion *f*; Rost *m*; **cor·ro·sive** CHEM ätzend; *fig* nagend, zersetzend

cor·rupt 1. korrupt, bestechlich, käuflich; *moralisch* verdorben; **2.** bestechen; *moralisch* verderben

cor·rupt·i·ble korrupt, bestechlich, käuflich

cor·rup·tion Verdorbenheit *f*; Unredlichkeit *f*; Korruption *f*; Bestechlichkeit *f*; Bestechung *f*

cor·set Korsett *n*

cos·met·ic 1. kosmetisch, Schönheits...;

2. kosmetisches Mittel, Schönheitsmittel n

cos·me·ti·cian Kosmetiker(in)

cos·mo·naut Kosmonaut m, (Welt-)Raumfahrer n

cos·mo·pol·i·tan 1. kosmopolitisch; **2.** Weltbürger(in)

cost 1. Preis m; Kosten pl; Schaden m; **2.** kosten

cost·ly kostspielig; teuer erkauft

cost of liv·ing Lebenshaltungskosten pl

cos·tume Kostüm n, Kleidung f, Tracht f; ~ **jew·el·(le)ry** Modeschmuck m

co·sy Br → **cozy**

cot Feldbett n; Br Kinderbett n

cot·tage Cottage n, (kleines) Landhaus; Ferienhaus n, Ferienhäuschen n

cot·ton 1. Baumwolle f; Baumwollstoff m; (Baumwoll)Garn n, (Baumwoll-)Zwirn m; (Verband)Watte f; **2.** baumwollen, Baumwoll...

cot·ton·wood BOT e-e amer. Pappel n

cot·ton wool Br (Verband)Watte f

couch Couch f, Sofa n; Liege f

cou·chette RAIL Liegewagenplatz m; a. ~ **coach** Liegewagen m

cou·gar ZO Puma m

cough 1. Husten m; **2.** husten

coun·cil Rat m, Ratsversammlung f; ~ **house** Br gemeindeeigenes Wohnhaus

coun·cil·(l)or Ratsmitglied n, Stadtrat m, Stadträtin f

coun·sel 1. Beratung f; Rat(schlag) m; Br JUR (Rechts)Anwalt m; ~ **for the defense** (Br **defence**) Verteidiger m; ~ **for the prosecution** Anklagevertreter m; **2.** j-m raten; zu et. raten; **~ing center** (Br **~ling centre**) Beratungsstelle f

coun·sel·(l)or (Berufs- etc)Berater(in); JUR (Rechts)Anwalt m

count¹ Graf m

count² 1. Zählung f; JUR Anklagepunkt m; **2.** v/t (ab-, auf-, aus-, nach-, zusammen)zählen; aus-, berechnen; fig halten für, betrachten als; v/i zählen; gelten; **~ ten** bis zehn zählen; **~ down** Geld hinzählen; den Count-down durchführen für, letzte (Start)Vorbereitungen treffen für; **~ on** zählen auf (acc), sich verlassen auf (acc), sicher rechnen mit

count·down Count-down m, n, letzte

(Start)Vorbereitungen pl

coun·te·nance Gesichtsausdruck m; Fassung f, Haltung f

count·er¹ TECH Zähler m; Br Spielmarke f

**coun·ter² **Ladentisch m; Theke f; (Bank-, Post)Schalter m

coun·ter³ 1. (ent)gegen, Gegen...; **2.** entgegentreten (dat), entgegnen (dat), bekämpfen; abwehren

coun·ter·act entgegenwirken (dat); neutralisieren

coun·ter·bal·ance 1. Gegengewicht n; **2.** ein Gegengewicht bilden zu, ausgleichen

coun·ter·clock·wise entgegen dem Uhrzeigersinn

coun·ter·es·pi·o·nage Spionageabwehr f

coun·ter·feit 1. falsch, gefälscht; **2.** Fälschung f; **3.** Geld, Unterschrift etc fälschen; ~ **mon·ey** Falschgeld n

coun·ter·foil Kontrollabschnitt m

coun·ter·mand Befehl etc widerrufen; Ware abbestellen

coun·ter·pane Tagesdecke f

coun·ter·part Gegenstück n; genaue Entsprechung f

coun·ter·sign gegenzeichnen

coun·tess Gräfin f

count·less zahllos

coun·try 1. Land n, Staat m; Gegend f, Landschaft f; **in the ~** auf dem Lande; **2.** Land..., ländlich

coun·try·man Landbewohner m; Bauer m; a. **fellow ~** Landsmann m

coun·try road Landstraße f

coun·try·side (ländliche) Gegend; Landschaft f

coun·try·wom·an Landbewohnerin f; Bäuerin f; a. **fellow ~** Landsmännin f

coun·ty (Land)Kreis m; Br Grafschaft f; ~ **seat** Kreis(haupt)stadt f; ~ **town** Br Grafschaftshauptstadt f

coup Coup m; Putsch m

cou·ple 1. Paar n; **a ~ of** F ein paar; **2.** (zusammen)koppeln; TECH kuppeln; ZO (sich) paaren

cou·pon Gutschein m; Kupon m, Bestellzettel m

cour·age Mut m

cou·ra·geous mutig, beherzt

cou·ri·er Kurier m, Eilbote m; Reiseleiter m

course AVIAT, MAR Kurs m (*a. fig*); SPORT (*Renn*)Bahn f, (*Renn*)Strecke f, (*Golf*)Platz m; Verlauf m; GASTR Gang m; Reihe f, Zyklus m; Kurs m, Lehrgang m; *of ~* natürlich, selbstverständlich; *the ~ of events* der Gang der Ereignisse, der Lauf der Dinge

court **1.** Hof m; kleiner Platz; SPORT Platz m, (Spiel)Feld n; JUR Gericht n, Gerichtshof m; *go to ~* JUR prozessieren; *take s.o. to ~* JUR gegen j-n prozessieren; j-m den Prozess machen; **2.** *j-m* den Hof machen; werben um

cour·te·ous höflich; **cour·te·sy** Höflichkeit f; *by ~ of* mit freundlicher Genehmigung von (*or gen*)

court·house Gerichtsgebäude n

court·ier Höfling m

court·ly höfisch; höflich

court mar·tial MIL Kriegsgericht n

court-mar·tial MIL vor ein Kriegsgericht stellen

court·room Gerichtssaal m

court·ship Werben n

court·yard Hof m

cous·in Cousin m, Vetter m; Cousine f, Kusine f

cove kleine Bucht

cov·er **1.** Decke f; Deckel m; (Buch-)Deckel m, Einband m; Umschlag m; Titelseite f; Hülle f; Überzug m, Bezug m; Schutzhaube f, Schutzplatte f; Abdeckhaube f; Briefumschlag m; GASTR Gedeck n; Deckung f; Schutz m; fig Tarnung f; *take ~* in Deckung gehen; *under plain ~* in neutralem Umschlag; *under separate ~* mit getrennter Post; **2.** (be-, zu)decken; einschlagen, einwickeln; verbergen; decken, schützen; ECON (ab)decken; versichern; *Thema* erschöpfend behandeln; *radio, TV* berichten über (*acc*); sich über *e-e Fläche etc* erstrecken; *Strecke* zurücklegen; SPORT *Gegenspieler* decken; *j-n* beschatten; *~ up* ab-, zudecken; *fig* verheimlichen, vertuschen; *~ up for s.o.* j-n decken

cov·er·age Berichterstattung f (*of* über *acc*)

cov·er girl Covergirl n, Titelblattmädchen n

cov·er·ing Decke f; Überzug m; Hülle f; (*Fußboden*)Belag m

cov·er sto·ry Titelgeschichte f

cow[1] ZO Kuh f

cow[2] einschüchtern

cow·ard **1.** feig(e); **2.** Feigling m

cow·ard·ice Feigheit f

cow·ard·ly feig(e)

cow·boy Cowboy m

cow·er kauern; sich ducken

cow·herd Kuhhirt m

cow·hide Rind(s)leder n

cow·house Kuhstall m

cowl Mönchskutte f; Kapuze f; TECH Schornsteinkappe f

cow·shed Kuhstall m

cow·slip BOT Schlüsselblume f; Sumpfdotterblume f

cox, cox·swain Bootsführer m; *rowing:* Steuermann m

coy schüchtern, scheu

coy·ote ZO Kojote m, Präriewolf m

co·zy **1.** behaglich, gemütlich; **2.** → *egg cosy, tea cosy*

CPU ABBR *of central processing unit* EDP Zentraleinheit f

crab ZO Krabbe f, Taschenkrebs m

crack **1.** Knall m; Sprung m, Riss m; Spalt(e f) m, Ritze f; (heftiger) Schlag; **2.** erstklassig; **3.** *v/i* krachen, knallen, knacken; (zer)springen; überschnappen (*voice*); *a. ~ up* zusammenbrechen; F *~ up* überschnappen; *get ~ing* F loslegen; *v/t* knallen mit (*Peitsche*), knacken mit (*Fingern*); zerbrechen; *Nuss, F Kode, Safe etc* knacken; *~ a joke* e-n Witz reißen; **crack·er** GASTR Cracker m, Kräcker m; Schwärmer m, Knallfrosch m, Knallbonbon m, n

crack·le knattern, knistern, prasseln

cra·dle **1.** Wiege f; **2.** wiegen; betten

craft[1] Boot(e *pl*) n, Schiff(e *pl*) n; Flugzeug(e *pl*) n; (Welt)Raumfahrzeug (e *pl*) n

craft[2] Handwerk n, Gewerbe n; Schlauheit f, List f

crafts·man (Kunst)Handwerker m

craft·y gerissen, listig, schlau

crag Klippe f, Felsenspitze f

cram *v/t* (voll)stopfen; nudeln, mästen; mit *j-m* pauken; *v/i* pauken, büffeln (*for* für)

cramp **1.** MED Krampf m; TECH Klammer f; *fig* Fessel f; **2.** einengen, hemmen

cran·ber·ry BOT Preiselbeere f

crane[1] TECH Kran *m*

crane[2] **1.** ZO Kranich *m*; **2.** den Hals recken; **~ one's neck** sich den Hals verrenken (**for** nach)

crank 1. TECH Kurbel *f*; TECH Schwengel *m*; F Spinner *m*, komischer Kauz; **2.** (an)kurbeln

crank·shaft TECH Kurbelwelle *f*

crank·y wack(e)lig; verschroben; schlecht gelaunt

cran·ny Riss *m*, Ritze *f*

crape Krepp *m*, Flor *m*

crash 1. Krach *m*, Krachen *n*; MOT Unfall *m*, Zusammenstoß *m*; AVIAT Absturz *m*; ECON Zusammenbruch *m*, (Börsen)Krach *m*; **2.** *v/t* zertrümmern; e-n Unfall haben mit; AVIAT abstürzen mit; *v/i* krachend einstürzen, zusammenkrachen; *esp* ECON zusammenbrechen; krachen (**against**, **into** gegen); MOT zusammenstoßen, verunglücken; AVIAT abstürzen; **3.** Schnell..., Sofort...; **~ bar·ri·er** MOT Leitplanke *f*; **~ course** Schnell-, Intensivkurs *m*; **~ di·et** radikale Schlankheitskur; **~ hel·met** Sturzhelm *m*

crash-land AVIAT e-e Bruchlandung machen (mit); **crash land·ing** AVIAT Bruchlandung *f*

crate (Latten)Kiste *f*

cra·ter Krater *m*; Trichter *m*

crave sich sehnen (**for**, **after** nach)

crav·ing heftiges Verlangen

craw·fish → crayfish

crawl 1. Kriechen *n*; **2.** kriechen; krabbeln; kribbeln; wimmeln (**with** von); *swimming*: kraulen; **it makes my skin ~** F mir läuft e-e Gänsehaut über den Rücken

cray·fish ZO Flusskrebs *m*

cray·on Zeichen-, Buntstift *m*

craze Verrücktheit *f*, F Fimmel *m*; **be the ~** Mode sein

cra·zy verrückt (**about** nach)

creak knarren, quietschen

cream GASTR Rahm *m*, Sahne *f*; Creme *f*; *fig* Auslese *f*, Elite *f*; **2.** creme(farben); **cream·y** sahnig; weich

crease 1. (Bügel)Falte *f*; **2.** (zer)knittern

cre·ate (er)schaffen; hervorrufen; verursachen

cre·a·tion Schöpfung *f*

cre·a·tive schöpferisch

cre·a·tor Schöpfer *m*

crea·ture Geschöpf *n*; Kreatur *f*

crèche (Kinder)Krippe *f*; (Weihnachts)Krippe *f*

cre·den·tials Beglaubigungsschreiben *n*; Referenzen *pl*; Zeugnis *n*; Ausweis *m*, Ausweispapiere *pl*

cred·i·ble glaubwürdig

cred·it 1. Glaube(n) *m*; Ruf *m*, Ansehen *n*; Verdienst *n*; ECON Kredit *m*; Guthaben *n*; **~ (side)** Kredit(seite *f*) *n*, Haben *n*; **on ~** auf Kredit; **2.** *j-m* glauben; *j-m* trauen; ECON gutschreiben; **~ s.o. with s.th.** j-m et. zutrauen; j-m et. zuschreiben

cred·i·ta·ble achtbar, ehrenvoll (**to** für)

cred·it card ECON Kreditkarte *f*

cred·i·tor ECON Gläubiger *m*

cred·its *film*: Vorspann *m*, Nachspann *m*

cred·it·wor·thy ECON kreditwürdig

cred·u·lous leichtgläubig

creed REL Glaubensbekenntnis *n*

creek Bach *m*; *Br* kleine Bucht

creep kriechen; schleichen (*a. fig*); **~ in** (sich) hinein- *or* hereinschleichen; sich einschleichen (*mistake etc*); **it makes my flesh ~** mir läuft e-e Gänsehaut über den Rücken

creep·er BOT Kriech-, Kletterpflanze *f*

creep·y unheimlich

cre·mate verbrennen, einäschern

cres·cent Halbmond *m*

cress BOT Kresse *f*

crest ZO Haube *f*, Büschel *n*; (*Hahnen-*) Kamm *m*; Bergrücken *m*, Kamm *m*; (*Wellen*)Kamm *m*; Federbusch *m*; **fa·mily ~** Familienwappen *n*

crest·fal·len niedergeschlagen

cre·vasse GEOL (Gletscher)Spalte *f*

crev·ice GEOL Riss *m*, Spalte *f*

crew AVIAT, MAR Besatzung *f*, Crew *f*, MAR Mannschaft *f*

crib 1. (Futter)Krippe *f*; Kinderbettchen *n*; *esp Br* (Weihnachts)Krippe *f*; F PED Spickzettel *m*; **2.** F abschreiben, spicken

crick: **a ~ in one's back (neck)** ein steifer Rücken (Hals)

crick·et[1] ZO Grille *f*

crick·et[2] SPORT Kricket *n*

crime JUR Verbrechen *n*; *coll* Verbrechen *pl*; **~ nov·el** Kriminalroman *m*

crim·i·nal 1. kriminell; Kriminal...,

Straf...; **2.** Verbrecher(in), Kriminelle *m, f*

crimp kräuseln

crim·son karmesinrot; puterrot

cringe sich ducken

crin·kle 1. Falte *f*, Fältchen *n*; **2.** (sich) kräuseln; knittern

crip·ple 1. Krüppel *m*; **2.** zum Krüppel machen; *fig* lähmen

cri·sis Krise *f*

crisp knusp(e)rig, mürbe; frisch, knackig (*vegetable*); scharf, frisch (*air*); kraus (*hair*)

crisp·bread Knäckebrot *n*

crisps *a.* **potato ~** *Br* (Kartoffel)Chips *pl*

criss-cross 1. Netz *n* sich schneidender Linien; **2.** kreuz und quer ziehen durch; kreuz und quer (ver)laufen

cri·te·ri·on Kriterium *n*

crit·ic Kritiker(in)

crit·i·cal kritisch; bedenklich

crit·i·cis·m Kritik *f* (**of** an *dat*)

crit·i·cize kritisieren; kritisch beurteilen; tadeln

cri·tique Kritik *f*, Besprechung *f*, Rezension *f*

croak ZO krächzen; quaken (*both a. fig*)

cro·chet 1. Häkelei *f*; Häkelarbeit *f*; **2.** häkeln

crock·e·ry Geschirr *n*

croc·o·dile ZO Krokodil *n*

cro·ny F alter Freund

crook 1. Krümmung *f*; Hirtenstab *m*; F Gauner *m*; **2.** (sich) krümmen *or* biegen; **crook·ed** gekrümmt krumm; F unehrlich, betrügerisch

croon schmachtend singen; summen

croon·er Schnulzensänger(in)

crop 1. AGR (Feld)Frucht *f*, Ernte *f*; ZO Kropf *m*; kurzer Haarschnitt; kurz geschnittenes Haar; **2.** ZO abfressen, abweiden; *Haar* kurz schneiden; **~ up** *fig* plötzlich auftauchen

cross 1. Kreuz *n* (*a. fig*); BIOL Kreuzung *f*; *soccer* Flanke *f*; **2.** böse, ärgerlich; **3.** (sich) kreuzen; *Straße* überqueren; *Plan etc* durchkreuzen; BIOL kreuzen; **~ off, ~ out** ausstreichen, durchstreichen; **~ o.s.** sich bekreuzigen; **~ one's arms** die Arme verschränken; **~ one's legs** die Beine übereinander schlagen; **keep one's fingers ~ed** den Daumen drücken

cross·bar SPORT Tor-, Querlatte *f*

cross·breed Mischling *m*, Kreuzung *f*

cross-coun·try Querfeldein..., Gelände...; **~ skiing** Skilanglauf *m*

cross-ex·am·i·na·tion JUR Kreuzverhör *n*; **cross-ex·am·ine** JUR ins Kreuzverhör nehmen

cross-eyed: be ~ schielen

cross·ing (*Straßen- etc*)Kreuzung *f*; Straßenübergang *m*; *Br* Fußgängerüberweg *m*; MAR Überfahrt *f*

cross·road Querstraße *f*

cross·roads (Straßen)Kreuzung *f*, *fig* Scheideweg *m*

cross-sec·tion Querschnitt *m*

cross·walk Fußgängerüberweg *m*

cross·wise kreuzweise

cross·word (puz·zle) Kreuzworträtsel *n*

crotch ANAT Schritt *m*

crotch·et MUS *Br* Viertelnote *f*

crouch 1. sich ducken; **2.** Hockstellung *f*

crow 1. ZO Krähe *f*; Krähen *n*; **2.** krähen

crow·bar TECH Brecheisen *n*

crowd 1. (Menschen)Menge *f*; Masse *f*; Haufen *m*; **2.** sich drängen; *Straßen etc* bevölkern; voll stopfen

crowd·ed überfüllt, voll

crown 1. Krone *f*; **2.** krönen; *Zahn* überkronen; **to ~ it all** zu allem Überfluss

cru·cial entscheidend, kritisch

cru·ci·fix REL Kruzifix *n*

cru·ci·fix·ion REL Kreuzigung *f*

cru·ci·fy REL kreuzigen

crude roh, unbearbeitet; *fig* roh, grob

crude (oil) Rohöl *n*

cru·el grausam; roh, gefühllos

cru·el·ty Grausamkeit *f*; **~ to animals** Tierquälerei *f*; **society for the prevention of ~ to animals** Tierschutzverein *m*; **~ to children** Kindesmisshandlung *f*

cru·et Essig-, Ölfläschchen *n*

cruise 1. Kreuzfahrt *f*, Seereise *f*; **2.** kreuzen, e-e Kreuzfahrt *or* Seereise machen; AVIAT, MOT mit Reisegeschwindigkeit fliegen *or* fahren; **~ mis·sile** MIL Marschflugkörper *m*

cruis·er Kreuzfahrtschiff *n*; MIL MAR Kreuzer *m*; (Funk)Streifenwagen *m*

crumb Krume *f*, Krümel *m*

crum·ble zerkrümeln, zerbröckeln

crum·ple *v/t* zerknittern; *v/i* knittern;

zusammengedrückt werden; **~ zone** MOT Knautschzone f

crunch geräuschvoll (zer)kauen; knirschen

cru·sade HIST Kreuzzug m (a. fig)

crush 1. Gedränge n; **have a ~ on s.o.** für j-n schwärmen, F in j-n verknallt sein; **2.** v/t zerquetschen, zermalmen, zerdrücken; TECH zerkleinern, zermahlen; auspressen; fig nieder-, zerschmettern, vernichten; v/i sich drängen; **~ bar·ri·er** Barriere f, Absperrung f

crust (Brot)Kruste f, (Brot)Rinde f

crus·ta·cean ZO Krebs-, Krusten-, Schalentier n

crust·y krustig

crutch Krücke f

cry 1. Schrei m, Ruf m; Geschrei n; Weinen n; **2.** schreien, rufen (**for** nach); weinen; heulen, jammern

crypt Gruft f, Krypta f

crys·tal Kristall m; Uhrglas n

crys·tal·line kristallen

crys·tal·lize kristallisieren

cub ZO Junge n

cube Würfel m (a. MATH); PHOT Blitzwürfel m; MATH Kubikzahl f

cube root MATH Kubikwurzel f

cu·bic, cu·bi·cal würfelförmig; kubisch; Kubik...

cu·bi·cle Kabine f

cuck·oo ZO Kuckuck m

cu·cum·ber BOT Gurke f; (**as**) **cool as a ~** F eiskalt, kühl und gelassen

cud AGR wiedergekäutes Futter; **chew the ~** wiederkäuen; fig überlegen

cud·dle v/t an sich drücken; schmusen mit; v/i: **~ up** sich kuscheln or schmiegen (**to** an acc)

cud·gel 1. Knüppel m; **2.** prügeln

cue[1] THEA etc Stichwort n (a. fig); fig Wink m

cue[2] billiards: Queue n

cuff[1] Manschette f; (Hosen-, Br Ärmel-)Aufschlag m

cuff[2] **1.** Klaps m; **2.** j-m e-n Klaps geben

cuff link Manschettenknopf m

cui·sine GASTR Küche f

cul·mi·nate gipfeln (**in** in dat)

cu·lottes (**a pair of**) ein) Hosenrock m

cul·prit Schuldige m, f, Täter(in)

cul·ti·vate AGR anbauen, bebauen; kultivieren; Freundschaft etc pflegen

cul·ti·vat·ed AGR bebaut; fig gebildet, kultiviert

cul·ti·va·tion AGR Kultivierung f, Anbau m; fig Pflege f

cul·tu·ral kulturell; Kultur...

cul·ture Kultur f (a. BIOL); ZO Zucht f

cul·tured kultiviert; gezüchtet, Zucht...

cum·ber·some lästig, hinderlich; klobig

cu·mu·la·tive sich (an)häufend, anwachsend; Zusatz...

cun·ning 1. schlau, listig; **2.** List f, Schlauheit f

cup 1. Tasse f; Becher m; Schale f; Kelch m; SPORT Cup m, Pokal m; **2.** **die Hand** hohl machen; **she ~ped her chin in her hand** sie stützte das Kinn in die Hand

cup·board (Geschirr-, Speise-, Br a. Wäsche-, Kleider)Schrank m

cup·board bed Schrankbett n

cup fi·nal SPORT Pokalendspiel n

cu·po·la ARCH Kuppel f

cup tie SPORT Pokalspiel n

cup win·ner SPORT Pokalsieger m

cur Köter m; Schurke m

cu·ra·ble MED heilbar

cu·rate REL Hilfsgeistliche m

cu·ra·tive heilkräftig; **~ power** Heilkraft f

curb 1. Kandare f (a. fig); Bordstein m; **2.** an die Kandare legen (a. fig); fig zügeln

curd a. pl Dickmilch f, Quark m

cur·dle v/t Milch gerinnen lassen; v/i gerinnen, dick werden; **the sight made my blood ~** bei dem Anblick erstarrte mir das Blut in den Adern

cure 1. MED Kur f; (Heil)Mittel n; Heilung f; **2.** MED heilen; GASTR pökeln; räuchern; trocknen

cur·few MIL Ausgangsverbot n, -sperre f

cu·ri·o Rarität f

cu·ri·os·i·ty Neugier f; Rarität f

cu·ri·ous neugierig; wissbegierig; seltsam, merkwürdig

curl 1. Locke f; **2.** (sich) kräuseln or locken; **curl·er** Lockenwickler m; **curl·y** gekräuselt; gelockt, lockig

cur·rant BOT Johannisbeere f; GASTR Korinthe f

cur·ren·cy ECON Währung f; **foreign ~** Devisen pl

cur·rent 1. laufend; gegenwärtig, aktuell; üblich, gebräuchlich; **~ events** Tagesereignisse pl; **2.** Strömung f, Strom m (both a. fig); ELECTR Strom m; **~ account** Br ECON Girokonto n

cur·ric·u·lum Lehr-, Stundenplan m; **~ vi·tae** Lebenslauf m

cur·ry¹ GASTR Curry m, n

cur·ry² Pferd striegeln

curse **1.** Fluch m, Verwünschung f; **2.** (ver)fluchen, verwünschen

curs·ed verflucht

cur·sor EDP Cursor m

cur·so·ry flüchtig, oberflächlich

curt knapp; barsch, schroff

cur·tail Ausgaben etc kürzen; Rechte beschneiden

cur·tain **1.** Vorhang m, Gardine f; **draw the ~s** die Vorhänge auf- or zuziehen; **2. ~ off** mit Vorhängen abteilen

curt·s(e)y **1.** Knicks m; **2.** knicksen (**to** vor dat)

cur·va·ture Krümmung f

curve **1.** Kurve f; Krümmung f, Biegung f; **2.** (sich) krümmen or biegen

cush·ion **1.** Kissen n, Polster n; **2.** polstern; Stoß etc dämpfen

cuss **1.** Fluch m; **2.** (ver)fluchen

cus·tard Eiercreme f, Vanillesoße f

cus·to·dy JUR Haft f; Sorgerecht n

cus·tom Brauch m, Gewohnheit f; ECON Kundschaft f

cus·tom·a·ry üblich

cus·tom-built nach Kundenangaben gefertigt

cus·tom·er Kunde m, Kundin f, Auftraggeber(in)

cus·tom house Zollamt n

cus·tom-made maßgefertigt, Maß...

cus·toms Zoll m; **~ clear·ance** Zollabfertigung f; **~ of·fi·cer, ~ of·fi·cial** Zollbeamte m

cut **1.** Schnitt m; MED Schnittwunde f; GASTR Schnitte f, Stück n; (Zu)Schnitt m (clothes); TECH Schnitt m, Schliff m; Haarschnitt m; fig Kürzung f, Senkung f; cards: Abheben n; **2.** schneiden; ab-, an-, auf-, aus-, be-, durch-, zer-, zuschneiden; Edelstein etc schleifen; Gras mähen, Bäume fällen, Holz hacken; MOT Kurve schneiden; Löhne etc kürzen; Preise herabsetzen, senken; Karten abheben; **~ one's teeth** Zähne bekommen, zahnen; **~ s.o. (dead)** fig F

j-n schneiden; **~ s.o. or s.th. short** j-n or et. unterbrechen, j-m ins Wort fallen; **~ across** quer durch ... gehen; **~ back** Pflanze beschneiden, stutzen; einschränken; **~ down** Bäume fällen; verringern, einschränken, reduzieren; **~ in** F sich einmischen, unterbrechen; **~ in on s.o.** MOT j-n schneiden; **~ off** abschneiden; unterbrechen, trennen; Strom etc sperren; **~ out** (her)ausschneiden; Kleid etc zuschneiden; **be ~ out for** wie geschaffen sein für; **~ up** zerschneiden

cut·back Kürzung f

cute F schlau; niedlich, süß

cu·ti·cle Nagelhaut f

cut·le·ry (Ess)Besteck n

cut·let GASTR Kotelett n; (Kalbs-, Schweine)Schnitzel n; Hacksteak n

cut-off date Stichtag m

cut-price, cut-rate ECON herabgesetzt, ermäßigt; Billig...

cut·ter Zuschneider m; (Glas-, Diamant)Schleifer m; Schneidemaschine f, -werkzeug n; film: Cutter(in); MAR Kutter m

cut·throat **1.** Mörder m; Killer m; **2.** mörderisch

cut·ting **1.** schneidend; scharf; TECH Schneid(e)..., Fräs...; **2.** Schneiden n; BOT Steckling m; esp Br Ausschnitt m

cut·tings Schnipsel pl; Späne pl

cut·ting torch TECH Schneidbrenner m

Cy·ber·space → **virtual reality**

cy·cle¹ Zyklus m; Kreis(lauf) m

cy·cle² **1.** Fahrrad n; **2.** Rad fahren

cy·cle| path, **~ track** (Fahr)Radweg m

cy·cling Radfahren n

cy·clist Radfahrer(in); Motorradfahrer(in)

cy·clone Wirbelsturm m

cyl·in·der Zylinder m, TECH a. Walze f, Trommel f

cyn·ic Zyniker(in); **cyn·i·cal** zynisch; **cyn·i·cism** Zynismus m

cy·press BOT Zypresse f

cyst MED Zyste f

czar → **tsar**

Czech **1.** tschechisch; **~ Republic** Tschechien n, Tschechische Republik; **2.** Tscheche m, Tschechin f; LING Tschechisch n

D

D, d D, d *n*

d ABBR *of* died gest., gestorben

dab 1. Klecks *m*, Spritzer *m*; 2. betupfen, abtupfen

dab·ble bespritzen; ~ at, ~ in sich oberflächlich *or contp* in dilettantischer Weise beschäftigen mit

dachs·hund ZO Dackel *m*

dad F, dad·dy F Papa *m*, Vati *m*

dad·dy long·legs ZO Schnake *f*, Weberknecht *m*

daf·fo·dil BOT gelbe Narzisse *f*

dag·ger Dolch *m*; be at ~s drawn *fig* auf Kriegsfuß stehen (with mit)

dai·ly 1. täglich; the ~ grind *or* rut das tägliche Einerlei; 2. Tageszeitung *f*; Putzfrau *f*

dain·ty 1. zierlich, reizend; wählerisch; 2. Leckerbissen *m*

dair·y Molkerei *f*; Milchwirtschaft *f*; Milchgeschäft *n*

dai·sy BOT Gänseblümchen *n*

dal·ly ~ about herumtrödeln

dam 1. (Stau)Damm *m*; 2. *a.* ~ up stauen, eindämmen

dam·age 1. Schaden *m*, (Be)Schädigung *f*; *pl* JUR Schadenersatz *m*; 2. (be)schädigen

dam·ask Damast *m*

damn 1. verdammen; verurteilen; ~ (it)! F verflucht!, verdammt!; 2. *adj and adv* F → damned; 3. I don't care a ~ F das ist mir völlig gleich(gültig) *or* egal

dam·na·tion Verdammung *f*; REL Verdammnis *f*

damned F verdammt

damn·ing vernichtend, belastend

damp 1. feucht, klamm; 2. Feuchtigkeit *f*; 3. *a.* damp·en an-, befeuchten; dämpfen; damp·ness Feuchtigkeit *f*

dance 1. Tanz *m*; Tanzveranstaltung *f*; 2. tanzen

danc·er Tänzer(in)

danc·ing 1. Tanzen *n*; 2. Tanz...

dan·de·li·on BOT Löwenzahn *m*

dan·druff (Kopf)Schuppen *pl*

Dane Däne *m*, Dänin *f*

dan·ger Gefahr *f*; be out of ~ außer Lebensgefahr sein; ~ ar·e·a Gefahrenzone *f*, Gefahrenbereich *m*

dan·ger·ous gefährlich

dan·ger zone → danger area

dan·gle baumeln (lassen)

Da·nish 1. dänisch; 2. LING Dänisch *n*

dank feucht, nass(kalt)

dare *v/i* es wagen, sich (ge)trauen; I ~ say ich glaube wohl; allerdings; how ~ you! was fällt dir ein!; untersteh dich!; *v/t et.* wagen

dare·dev·il Draufgänger *m*

dar·ing 1. kühn, verwegen, waghalsig; 2. Mut *m*, Kühnheit *f*, Verwegenheit *f*

dark 1. dunkel; finster; *fig* düster, trüb(e); geheim(nisvoll); 2. Dunkel *n*, Dunkelheit *f*; Verwegenheit *f* vor (bei, nach) Einbruch der Dunkelheit; keep s.o. in the ~ about s.th. j-n über et. im Ungewissen lassen

Dark Ag·es das frühe Mittelalter

dark·en (sich) verdunkeln *or* verfinstern

dark·ness Dunkelheit *f*, Finsternis *f*

dark·room PHOT Dunkelkammer *f*

dar·ling 1. Liebling *m*; 2. lieb; F goldig

darn stopfen, ausbessern

dart 1. Wurfpfeil *m*; Sprung *m*, Satz *m*; ~s Darts *n*; 2. *v/t* werfen, schleudern; *v/i* schießen, stürzen

dart·board Dartsscheibe *f*

dash 1. Schlag *m*; Klatschen *n*; GASTR Prise *f* (*of* salt), Schuss *m* (*of* rum etc), Spritzer *m* (*of* lemon etc); Gedankenstrich *m*; SPORT Sprint *m*; *fig* Anflug *m*; a ~ of blue ein Stich ins Blaue; make a ~ for losstürzen auf (acc); 2. *v/t* schleudern, schmettern; *Hoffnung etc* zerstören, zunichte machen; *v/i* stürmen; ~ off davonstürzen

dash·ing schneidig, forsch

da·ta Daten *pl* (*a.* EDP), Angaben *pl*; ~ bank, ~·base EDP Datenbank *f*; ~ cap·ture Datenerfassung *f*; ~ car·ri·er Datenträger *m*; ~ in·put Dateneingabe *f*; ~ me·di·um Datenträger *m*; ~ mem·o·ry Datenspeicher *m*; ~ out·put Datenausgabe *f*; ~ pro·cess·ing Datenverarbeitung *f*; ~ pro·tec·tion JUR Datenschutz *m*; ~ stor·age Datenspeicher *m*; ~ trans·fer Datenübertragung *f*

date[1] BOT Dattel f

date[2] Datum n; Zeit f, Zeitpunkt m; Termin m; Verabredung f; F (Verabredungs)Partner(in); *out of* ~ veraltet, unmodern; *up to* ~ zeitgemäß, modern, auf dem Laufenden; **2.** datieren; F sich verabreden mit, (aus)gehen mit

dat·ed veraltet, überholt

da·tive a. ~ *case* LING Dativ m, dritter Fall

daub (be)schmieren

daugh·ter Tochter f

daugh·ter-in-law Schwiegertochter f

daunt entmutigen

dav·en·port Sofa n

daw zo Dohle f

daw·dle F (herum)trödeln

dawn 1. (Morgen)Dämmerung f; *at* ~ bei Tagesanbruch; **2.** dämmern; ~ *on* fig j-m dämmern

day Tag m; *often pl* (Lebens)Zeit f; *any* ~ jederzeit; *these* ~s heutzutage; *the other* ~ neulich; *the* ~ *after tomorrow* übermorgen; *the* ~ *before yesterday* vorgestern; *open all* ~ durchgehend geöffnet; *let's call it a* ~! machen wir Schluss für heute!, Feierabend!

day·break Tagesanbruch m

day care cen·ter (*Br* **cen·tre**) → **day nursery**

day·dream 1. Tag-, Wachtraum m; **2.** (mit offenen Augen) träumen

day·dream·er Träumer(in)

day·light Tageslicht n; *in broad* ~ am helllichten Tag

day nur·se·ry (Kinder)Tagesstätte f

day off freier Tag

day re·turn Br Tagesrückfahrkarte f

day·time: *in the* ~ am Tag, bei Tage

daze 1. blenden; betäuben; **2.** *in a* ~ benommen, betäubt

dead 1. tot; unempfindlich (*to* für); matt; blind (*window etc*); erloschen; ECON flau; tot (*capital etc*); völlig, total; ~ *stop* völliger Stillstand; *drop* ~ tot umfallen; **2.** *adv* völlig, total; plötzlich, abrupt; genau, direkt; ~ *slow* MOT Schritt fahren!; ~ *tired* todmüde; **3.** *the* ~ die Toten *pl*; *in the* ~ *of winter* im tiefsten Winter; *in the* ~ *of night* mitten in der Nacht

dead·en abstumpfen; (ab)schwächen; dämpfen

dead end Sackgasse f (*a. fig*)

dead heat SPORT totes Rennen

dead·line letzter (Ablieferungs)Termin; Stichtag m

dead·lock fig toter Punkt

dead·locked fig festgefahren

dead loss Totalverlust m; F *he's a* ~ er ist e-e Niete

dead·ly tödlich

deaf 1. taub; **2.** *the* ~ die Tauben *pl*

deaf-and-dumb taubstumm

deaf·en taub machen; betäuben

deaf-mute Taubstumme m, f

deal 1. F Geschäft n, Handel m; Menge f; *it's a* ~! abgemacht!; *a good* ~ ziemlich viel; *a great* ~ sehr viel; **2.** *v/t* (aus-, ver-, zu)teilen; *j-m Karten geben; j-m e-n Schlag* versetzen; *v/i* handeln (*in* mit e-r Ware); sl dealen; *cards:* geben; ~ *with* sich befassen mit, behandeln; ECON Handel treiben mit, Geschäfte machen mit; **deal·er** ECON Händler *cards:* Geber(in); sl Dealer m; **deal·ing** mst pl Umgang m, Beziehungen pl

dean REL, UNIV Dekan m

dear 1. teuer; lieb; *Dear Sir* Sehr geehrter Herr ...; **2.** Liebste m, f, Schatz m; *my* ~ m-e Liebe, mein Lieber; **3.** *int* (*oh*) ~!, ~ *me!* F du liebe Zeit!, ach herrje!; *dear·est* sehnlichst; *dear·ly* innig, von ganzem Herzen; ECON teuer

death Tod m; Todesfall m

death·bed Sterbebett n

death cer·tif·i·cate Totenschein m

death·ly tödlich; ~ *still* totenstill

death war·rant JUR Hinrichtungsbefehl m; fig Todesurteil n

de·bar: ~ *s.o. from* j-n ausschließen aus

de·base erniedrigen; mindern

de·ba·ta·ble umstritten

de·bate 1. Debatte f, Diskussion f; **2.** debattieren, diskutieren

deb·it ECON **1.** Soll n; (Konto)Belastung f; ~ *and credit* Soll und Haben n; **2.** *j-n,* *ein Konto* belasten

deb·ris Trümmer pl, Schutt m

debt Schuld f; *be in* ~ Schulden haben, verschuldet sein; *be out of* ~ schuldenfrei sein; *get into* ~ sich verschulden, Schulden machen

debt·or Schuldner(in)

de·bug TECH, EDP Fehler beseitigen

de·but Debüt n

Dec ABBR *of December* Dez., Dezember m

D

dec·ade Jahrzehnt *n*

dec·a·dent dekadent

de·caf·fein·at·ed koffeinfrei

de·camp F verschwinden

de·cant abgießen; umfüllen

de·cant·er Karaffe *f*

de·cath·lete SPORT Zehnkämpfer *m*

de·cath·lon SPORT Zehnkampf *m*

de·cay 1. zerfallen; verfaulen; kariös *or* schlecht werden (*tooth*); 2. Zerfall *m*; Verfaulen *n*

de·cease *esp* JUR Tod *m*, Ableben *n*

de·ceased *esp* JUR 1. *the* ~ der *or* die Verstorbene; die Verstorbenen *pl*; 2. verstorben

de·ceit Betrug *m*; Täuschung *f*

de·ceit·ful betrügerisch

de·ceive betrügen; täuschen

de·ceiv·er Betrüger(in)

De·cem·ber (ABBR *Dec*) Dezember *m*

de·cen·cy Anstand *m*

de·cent anständig; F annehmbar, (ganz) anständig; F nett

de·cep·tion Täuschung *f*

de·cep·tive trügerisch; *be* ~ täuschen, trügen

de·cide (sich) entscheiden; bestimmen; beschließen, sich entschließen

de·cid·ed entschieden; bestimmt; entschlossen

dec·i·mal MATH 1. *a.* ~ *fraction* Dezimalbruch *m*; 2. Dezimal...

de·ci·pher entziffern

de·ci·sion Entscheidung *f*; Entschluss *m*; Entschlossenheit *f*; *make a* ~ e-e Entscheidung treffen; *reach or come to a* ~ zu e-m Entschluss kommen

de·ci·sive entscheidend; ausschlaggebend; entschieden

deck 1. MAR Deck *n*; Spiel *n*, Pack *m* (Spiel)Karten; 2. ~ *out* schmücken

deck·chair Liegestuhl *m*

dec·la·ra·tion Erklärung *f*; Zollerklärung *f*; de·clare erklären; deklarieren; verzollen

de·clen·sion LING Deklination *f*

de·cline 1. abnehmen, zurückgehen; fallen; verfallen; (höflich) ablehnen; LING deklinieren; 2. Abnahme *f*, Rückgang *m*, Verfall *m*

de·cliv·i·ty (Ab)Hang *m*

de·clutch MOT auskuppeln

de·code entschlüsseln

de·com·pose zerlegen; (sich) zersetzen; verwesen

de·con·tam·i·nate entgasen, entgiften, entseuchen, entstrahlen

de·con·tam·i·na·tion Entseuchung *f*

dec·o·rate verzieren, schmücken; tapezieren; (an)streichen; dekorieren

dec·o·ra·tion Verzierung *f*, Schmuck *m*, Dekoration *f*; Orden *m*

dec·o·ra·tive dekorativ; Zier...

dec·o·ra·tor Dekorateur *m*; Maler *m* und Tapezierer *m*

dec·o·rous anständig

de·co·rum Anstand *m*

de·coy 1. Lockvogel *m* (*a, fig*); Köder *m* (*a. fig*); 2. ködern; locken (*into* in *acc*); verleiten (*into* zu)

de·crease 1. Abnahme *f*; 2. abnehmen; (sich) vermindern

de·cree 1. Dekret *n*, Erlass *m*, Verfügung *f*; *esp* JUR Entscheid *m*, Urteil *n*; 2. verfügen

ded·i·cate widmen

ded·i·cat·ed engagiert

ded·i·ca·tion Widmung *f*; Hingabe *f*

de·duce ableiten; folgern

de·duct Betrag abziehen (*from* von); de·duct·i·ble: *tax-*~ steuerlich absetzbar; de·duc·tion Abzug *m*; (Schluss-)Folgerung *f*, Schluss *m*

deed Tat *f*; Heldentat *f*; JUR (Übertragungs)Urkunde *f*

deep 1. tief (*a. fig*); 2. Tiefe *f*

deep·en (sich) vertiefen, *fig a.* (sich) verstärken

deep freeze 1. tiefkühlen, einfrieren; 2. Tiefkühl-, Gefriertruhe *f*

deep-fro·zen tiefgefroren

deep fry frittieren

deep·ness Tiefe *f*

deer ZO Hirsch *m*; Reh *n*

de·face entstellen; unleserlich machen; ausstreichen

def·a·ma·tion Verleumdung *f*

de·fault 1. JUR Nichterscheinen *n* vor Gericht; SPORT Nichtantreten *n*; ECON Verzug *m*; 2. s-n Verpflichtungen nicht nachkommen, ECON *a.* im Verzug sein; JUR nicht vor Gericht erscheinen; SPORT nicht antreten

de·feat 1. Niederlage *f*; 2. besiegen, schlagen; vereiteln, zunichte machen

de·fect Defekt *m*, Fehler *m*; Mangel *m*

de·fec·tive mangelhaft; schadhaft, defekt

de·fence Br → **defense**

de·fence·less Br → **defenseless**

de·fend (**from**, **against**) verteidigen (gegen), schützen (vor *dat*, gegen)

de·fen·dant Angeklagte *m*, *f*; Beklagte *m*, *f*

de·fend·er Verteidiger(in); SPORT Abwehrspieler(in)

de·fense Verteidigung *f* (*a.* MIL, JUR, SPORT), Schutz *m*; SPORT Abwehr *f*; **witness for the ~** Entlastungszeuge *m*

de·fense·less schutzlos, wehrlos

de·fen·sive 1. Defensive *f*, Verteidigung *f*, Abwehr *f*; 2. defensiv; Verteidigungs..., Abwehr...

de·fer aufschieben, verschieben

de·fi·ance Herausforderung *f*; Trotz *m*

de·fi·ant herausfordernd; trotzig

de·fi·cien·cy Unzulänglichkeit *f*; Mangel *m*

de·fi·cient mangelhaft, unzureichend

def·i·cit ECON Defizit *n*, Fehlbetrag *m*

de·file beschmutzen

de·fine definieren; erklären, bestimmen

def·i·nite bestimmt; endgültig, definitiv

def·i·ni·tion Definition *f*, Bestimmung *f*, Erklärung *f*

de·fin·i·tive endgültig, definitiv

de·flect *v/t* ablenken; *Ball* abfälschen; *v/i* abweichen

de·form entstellen, verunstalten

de·formed deformiert; verunstaltet; verwachsen

de·for·mi·ty Missbildung *f*

de·fraud betrügen (**of** um)

de·frost *v/t Windschutzscheibe etc* entfrosten; *Kühlschrank etc* abtauen, *Tiefkühlkost etc* auftauen; *v/i* ab-, auftauen

deft geschickt, gewandt

de·fy herausfordern; trotzen (*dat*)

de·gen·e·rate 1. entarten; 2. entartet

deg·ra·da·tion Erniedrigung *f*

de·grade erniedrigen, demütigen

de·gree Grad *m*; Stufe *f*; (akademischer) Grad; **by ~s** allmählich; **take one's ~** e-n akademischen Grad erwerben, promovieren

de·hy·drate austrocknen; TECH das Wasser entziehen (*dat*)

de·i·fy vergöttern; vergöttlichen

deign sich herablassen

de·i·ty Gottheit *f*

de·jec·ted niedergeschlagen, mutlos, deprimiert

de·jec·tion Niedergeschlagenheit *f*

de·lay 1. Aufschub *m*; Verzögerung *f*; RAIL *etc* Verspätung *f*; 2. ver-, aufschieben; verzögern; aufhalten; **be ~ed** sich verzögern; RAIL *etc* Verspätung haben

del·e·gate 1. abordnen, delegieren; *Vollmachten etc* übertragen; 2. Delegierte *m*, *f*, bevollmächtigter Vertreter

del·e·ga·tion Übertragung *f*; Abordnung *f*, Delegation *f*

de·lete (aus)streichen; EDP löschen

de·lib·e·rate absichtlich, vorsätzlich; bedächtig, besonnen

de·lib·e·ra·tion Überlegung *f*; Beratung *f*; Bedächtigkeit *f*

del·i·ca·cy Delikatesse *f*, Leckerbissen *m*; Zartheit *f*; Feingefühl *n*, Takt *m*

del·i·cate delikat (*a. fig*), schmackhaft; zart; fein; zierlich; zerbrechlich; heikel; empfindlich

del·i·ca·tes·sen Delikatessen *pl*, Feinkost *f*; Feinkostgeschäft *n*

de·li·cious köstlich

de·light 1. Vergnügen *n*, Entzücken *n*; 2. entzücken, erfreuen; **~ in** (große) Freude haben an (*dat*)

de·light·ful entzückend

de·lin·quen·cy Kriminalität *f*

de·lin·quent 1. straffällig; 2. Straffällige *m*, *f*; → **juvenile** 1

de·lir·i·ous MED im Delirium, fantasierend; **de·lir·i·um** MED Delirium *n*

de·liv·er ausliefern, (ab)liefern; *Briefe* zustellen; *Rede etc* halten; befreien, erlösen; **be ~ed of** MED entbunden werden von

de·liv·er·ance Befreiung *f*

de·liv·er·er Befreier(in)

de·liv·er·y (Ab-, Aus)Lieferung *f*; post Zustellung *f*; Halten *n* (*e-r Rede*); Vortrag(sweise *f*) *m*; MED Entbindung *f*

de·liv·er·y van Br MOT Lieferwagen *m*

dell kleines Tal

de·lude täuschen

del·uge Überschwemmung *f*; *fig* Flut *f*

de·lu·sion Täuschung *f*; Wahn(vorstellung *f*) *m*

de·mand 1. Forderung *f* (**for** nach); Anforderung *f* (**on** an *acc*); Nachfrage *f* (**for** nach), Bedarf *m* (**for** an *dat*); **on**

~ auf Verlangen; **2.** verlangen, fordern; (*fordernd*) fragen nach; erfordern

de·mand·ing anspruchsvoll

de·ment·ed wahnsinnig

demi... Halb..., halb...

de·mil·i·ta·rize entmilitarisieren

dem·o F Demo *f*

de·mo·bi·lize demobilisieren

de·moc·ra·cy Demokratie *f*

dem·o·crat Demokrat(in)

dem·o·crat·ic demokratisch

de·mol·ish demolieren; ab-, ein-, niederreißen; zerstören

dem·o·li·tion Demolierung *f*; Niederreißen *n*, Abbruch *m*

de·mon Dämon *m*; Teufel *m*

dem·on·strate demonstrieren; beweisen; zeigen; vorführen

dem·on·stra·tion Demonstration *f*, *a.* Kundgebung *f*, *a.* Vorführung *f*; ~ **car** *Br* Vorführwagen *m*

de·mon·stra·tive: *be* ~ s-e Gefühle (offen) zeigen

dem·on·stra·tor Demonstrant(in); Vorführer(in); MOT Vorführwagen *m*

de·mor·al·ize demoralisieren

de·mote degradieren

de·mure ernst, zurückhaltend

den ZO Höhle *f* (*a. fig*); F Bude *f*

de·ni·al Ablehnung *f*; Leugnen *n*; Verweigerung *f*; **official** ~ Dementi *f*

den·ims Jeans *pl*

Den·mark Dänemark *n*

de·nom·i·na·tion REL Konfession *f*; ECON Nennwert *m*

de·note bezeichnen; bedeuten

de·nounce (öffentlich) anprangern

dense dicht; *fig* beschränkt, begriffsstutzig; **den·si·ty** Dichte *f*

dent **1.** Beule *f*, Delle *f*; **2.** ver-, einbeulen

den·tal Zahn...; ~ **plaque** Zahnbelag *m*; ~ **plate** (Zahn)Prothese *f*; ~ **surgeon** Zahnarzt *m*, Zahnärztin *f*

den·tist Zahnarzt *m*, Zahnärztin *f*

den·tures (Zahn)Prothese *f*, (künstliches) Gebiss

de·nun·ci·a·tion Denunziation *f*

de·nun·ci·a·tor Denunziant(in)

de·ny abstreiten, bestreiten, dementieren, (ab)leugnen; *j-m et.* verweigern, abschlagen

de·o·do·rant De(s)odorant *n*, Deo *n*

de·part abreisen; abfahren, abfliegen; abweichen (*from* von)

de·part·ment Abteilung *f*, UNIV *a.* Fachbereich *m*; POL Ministerium *n*

De·part·ment| of De·fense Verteidigungsministerium *n*; ~ **of the En·viron·ment** *Br* Umweltministerium *n*; ~ **of the In·te·ri·or** Innenministerium *n*; ~ **of State** *a.* **State Department** Außenministerium *n*

de·part·ment store Kaufhaus *n*, Warenhaus *n*

de·par·ture Abreise *f*; RAIL *etc* Abfahrt *f*; AVIAT Abflug *m*; *fig* Abweichung *f*; ~**s**, Abfahrt'; ~ **gate** AVIAT Flugsteig *m*; ~ **lounge** AVIAT Abflughalle *f*

de·pend: ~ **on** sich verlassen auf (*acc*); abhängen von; angewiesen sein auf (*acc*); *that* ~**s** das kommt darauf an

de·pend·a·ble zuverlässig

de·pend·a·bil·i·ty Zuverlässigkeit *f*

de·pen·dant Angehörige *m*, *f*

de·pen·dence Abhängigkeit *f*; Vertrauen *n*

de·pen·dent **1.** (**on**) abhängig (von); angewiesen (auf *acc*); **2.** → **dependant**

de·plor·a·ble bedauerlich, beklagenswert; **de·plore** beklagen, bedauern

de·pop·u·late entvölkern

de·port ausweisen, *Ausländer a.* abschieben; deportieren

de·pose *j-n* absetzen; JUR unter Eid erklären

de·pos·it **1.** absetzen, abstellen; CHEM, GEOL (sich) ablagern *or* absetzen; deponieren, hinterlegen; ECON *Betrag* anzahlen; **2.** CHEM Ablagerung *f*, GEOL *a.* (*Erz- etc*)Lager *n*; Deponierung *f*, Hinterlegung *f*; ECON Anzahlung *f*; *make a* ~ e-e Anzahlung leisten (**on** für)

dep·ot Depot *n*; Bahnhof *m*

de·prave *moralisch* verderben

de·pre·ci·ate an Wert verlieren

de·press (nieder)drücken; deprimieren, bedrücken

de·pressed deprimiert, niedergeschlagen; ECON flau (*market*); Not leidend (*industry*); ~ **ar·e·a** ECON Notstandsgebiet *n*

de·press·ing deprimierend, bedrückend

de·pres·sion Depression *f*, Niedergeschlagenheit *f*; ECON Depression *f*, Flaute *f*; Senke *f*, Vertiefung *f*; METEOR Tief(druckgebiet) *n*

de·prive: ~ *s.o. of s.th.* j-m et. entziehen *or* nehmen; **de·prived** benachteiligt

dept, Dept ABBR *of* **department** Abt., Abteilung *f*

depth 1. Tiefe *f*; 2. Tiefen...

dep·u·ta·tion Abordnung *f*

dep·u·tize: ~ *for s.o.* j-n vertreten

dep·u·ty (Stell)Vertreter(in); PARL Abgeordnete *m, f; a.* ~ *sheriff* Hilfssheriff *m*

de·rail: *be* ~ed entgleisen

de·ranged geistesgestört

der·by F Melone *f*

der·e·lict heruntergekommen, baufällig

de·ride verhöhnen, verspotten

de·ri·sion Hohn *m*, Spott *m*

de·ri·sive höhnisch, spöttisch

de·rive herleiten (**from** von); (sich) ableiten (**from** von); abstammen (**from** von); ~ *pleasure from* Freude finden *or* haben an (*dat*)

der·ma·tol·o·gist Dermatologe *m*, Hautarzt *m*

de·rog·a·to·ry abfällig, geringschätzig

der·rick TECH Derrickkran *m*; MAR Ladebaum *m*; TECH Bohrturm *m*

de·scend herab-, hinabsteigen, herunter-, hinuntersteigen, -gehen, -kommen; AVIAT niedergehen; abstammen, herkommen (**from** von); ~ *on* herfallen über (*acc*); überfallen (*acc*) (*visitor acc*)

de·scen·dant Nachkomme *m*

de·scent Herab-, Hinuntersteigen *n*, -gehen *n*; AVIAT Niedergehen *n*; Gefälle *n*; Abstammung *f*, Herkunft *f*

de·scribe beschreiben

de·scrip·tion Beschreibung *f*, Schilderung *f*; Art *f*, Sorte *f*; **de·scrip·tive** beschreibend; anschaulich

des·e·crate entweihen

de·seg·re·gate die Rassentrennung aufheben (*in dat*); **de·seg·re·ga·tion** Aufhebung *f* der Rassentrennung

des·ert[1] 1. Wüste *f*; 2. Wüsten...

de·sert[2] *v/t* verlassen, im Stich lassen; *v/i* MIL desertieren

de·sert·er MIL Deserteur *m*

de·ser·tion (JUR *a.* böswilliges) Verlassen; MIL Fahnenflucht *f*

de·serve verdienen

de·serv·ed·ly verdientermaßen

de·serv·ing verdienstvoll

de·sign 1. Design *n*, Entwurf *m*, (TECH Konstruktions)Zeichnung *f*; Design *n*, Muster *n*; (*a.* böse)Absicht; 2. entwerfen, TECH konstruieren; gestalten; ausdenken; bestimmen, vorsehen (**for** für)

des·ig·nate *et. or* j-n bestimmen

de·sign·er Designer(in); TECH Konstrukteur *m*; (*Mode*)Schöpfer(in)

de·sir·a·ble erwünscht, wünschenswert; begehrenswert

de·sire 1. Wunsch *m*, Verlangen *n*, Begierde *f* (**for** nach); 2. wünschen; begehren

de·sist Abstand nehmen (**from** von)

desk Schreibtisch *m*; Pult *n*; Empfang *m*, Rezeption *f*; Schalter *m*

desk·top| com·put·er Desktop-Computer *m*, Tischcomputer *m*, Tischrechner *m*; ~ **pub·lish·ing** (ABBR **DTP**) EDP Desktop-Publishing *n*

des·o·late einsam, verlassen; trostlos

de·spair 1. Verzweiflung *f*; *drive s.o. to* ~ j-n zur Verzweiflung bringen; 2. verzweifeln (*of an dat*)

de·spair·ing verzweifelt

de·spatch → **dispatch**

des·per·ate verzweifelt; F hoffnungslos, schrecklich

des·per·a·tion Verzweiflung *f*

des·pic·a·ble verachtenswert, verabscheuungswürdig

de·spise verachten

de·spite trotz (*gen*)

des·pon·dent mutlos, verzagt

des·pot Despot *m*, Tyrann *m*

des·sert Nachtisch *m*, Dessert *n*

des·ti·na·tion Bestimmung *f*; Bestimmungsort *m*

des·tined bestimmt; MAR *etc* unterwegs (**for** nach)

des·ti·ny Schicksal *n*

des·ti·tute mittellos

de·stroy zerstören, vernichten; *Tier* töten, einschläfern; **de·stroy·er** Zerstörer(in); MAR MIL Zerstörer *m*

de·struc·tion Zerstörung *f*, Vernichtung *f*; **de·struc·tive** zerstörend, vernichtend; zerstörerisch

de·tach (ab-, los)trennen, (los)lösen

de·tached einzeln, frei *or* allein stehend; unvoreingenommen; distanziert; ~ *house* Einzelhaus *n*

de·tach·ment (Los)Lösung *f*, (Ab-) Trennung *f*; MIL (Sonder)Kommando *n*

de·tail 1. Detail *n*, Einzelheit *f*; MIL

(Sonder)Kommando *n*; **in ~** ausführlich; **2.** genau schildern; MIL abkommandieren

de·tailed detailliert, ausführlich

de·tain aufhalten; JUR in (Untersuchungs)Haft behalten

de·tect entdecken, (heraus)finden

de·tec·tion Entdeckung *f*

de·tec·tive Kriminalbeamte *m*, Detektiv *m*; **~nov·el, ~sto·ry** Kriminalroman *m*

de·ten·tion JUR Haft *f*; PED Nachsitzen *n*

de·ter abschrecken (*from* von)

de·ter·gent Reinigungs-, Wasch-, Geschirrspülmittel *n*

de·te·ri·o·rate (sich) verschlechtern, nachlassen; verderben

de·ter·mi·na·tion Entschlossenheit *f*, Bestimmtheit *f*; Entschluss *m*; Feststellung *f*, Ermittlung *f*; **de·ter·mine** et. beschließen, bestimmen; feststellen, ermitteln; (sich) entscheiden; sich entschließen; **de·ter·mined** entschlossen

de·ter·rence Abschreckung *f*

de·ter·rent 1. abschreckend; **2.** Abschreckungsmittel *n*

de·test verabscheuen

de·throne entthronen

de·to·nate *v/t* zünden; *v/i* detonieren, explodieren

de·tour Umweg *m*; Umleitung *f*

de·tract: ~ from ablenken von; schmälern (*acc*)

de·tri·ment Nachteil *m*, Schaden *m*

deuce *cards etc*: Zwei *f*; *tennis*: Einstand *m*

de·val·u·a·tion Abwertung *f*

de·val·ue abwerten

dev·a·state verwüsten

dev·a·stat·ing verheerend, vernichtend; F umwerfend, toll

de·vel·op (sich) entwickeln; *Naturschätze, Bauland* erschließen, *Altstadt etc* sanieren; **de·vel·op·er** PHOT Entwickler *m*; (Stadt)Planer *m*

de·vel·op·ing Entwicklungs...; **~coun·try, ~na·tion** Entwicklungsland *n*

de·vel·op·ment Entwicklung *f*; Erschließung *f*, Sanierung *f*

de·vi·ate abweichen (*from* von)

de·vi·a·tion Abweichung *f*

de·vice Vorrichtung *f*, Gerät *n*; Plan *m*,

Trick *m*; **leave s.o. to his own ~s** j-n sich selbst überlassen

dev·il Teufel *m* (*a. fig*)

dev·il·ish teuflisch

de·vi·ous abwegig; gewunden; unaufrichtig; **~ route** Umweg *m*

de·vise (sich) ausdenken

de·void: ~ of ohne (*acc*)

de·vote widmen (*to dat*); **de·vot·ed** ergeben; hingebungsvoll; eifrig, begeistert; **dev·o·tee** begeisterter Anhänger; **de·vo·tion** Ergebenheit *f*; Hingabe *f*; Frömmigkeit *f*, Andacht *f*

de·vour verschlingen

de·vout fromm; sehnlichst, innig

dew Tau *m*; **dew·y** taufeucht, taufrisch

dex·ter·i·ty Gewandtheit *f*

dex·ter·ous, dex·trous gewandt

di·a·bol·i·cal teuflisch

di·ag·nose diagnostizieren

di·ag·no·sis Diagnose *f*

di·ag·o·nal 1. diagonal; **2.** Diagonale *f*

di·a·gram Diagramm *n*, grafische Darstellung

di·al 1. Zifferblatt *n*; TEL Wählscheibe *f*; TECH Skala *f*; **2.** TEL wählen; **~ direct** durchwählen (*to* nach); **direct ~(l)ing** Durchwahl *f*

di·a·lect Dialekt *m*, Mundart *f*

di·al·ling code *Br* TEL Vorwahl(nummer) *f*

di·a·log, *Br* **di·a·logue** Dialog *m*, (Zwie)Gespräch *n*

di·am·e·ter Durchmesser *m*; **in ~** im Durchmesser

di·a·mond Diamant *m*; Raute *f*, Rhombus *m*; *cards*: Karo *n*

di·a·per Windel *f*

di·a·phragm ANAT Zwerchfell *n*; OPT Blende *f*; TEL Membran(e) *f*

di·ar·rh(o)e·a MED Durchfall *m*

di·a·ry Tagebuch *n*

dice 1. Würfel *m*; **2.** GASTR in Würfel schneiden; würfeln

dic·tate diktieren; *fig* vorschreiben

dic·ta·tion Diktat *n*

dic·ta·tor Diktator *m*

dic·ta·tor·ship Diktatur *f*

dic·tion Ausdrucksweise *f*, Stil *m*

dic·tion·a·ry Wörterbuch *n*

die¹ sterben; ZO eingehen, verenden; **~ of hunger** verhungern; **~ of thirst** verdursten; **~ away** sich legen (*wind*); verklingen (*sound*); **~ down** nachlassen; herunterbrennen; schwächer werden; ~ **out** aussterben (a. fig)

die² Würfel m

di·et 1. Diät f; Nahrung f; Kost f; **be on a ~** Diät leben; **put s.o. on a ~** j-m e-e Diät verordnen; 2. Diät leben

di·e·ti·cian Diätassistent(in)

dif·fer sich unterscheiden; anderer Meinung sein (**with**, **from** als); abweichen

dif·fe·rence Unterschied m; Differenz f; Meinungsverschiedenheit f

dif·fe·rent verschieden; andere(r, -s); anders (**from** als)

dif·fe·ren·ti·ate (sich) unterscheiden

dif·fi·cult schwierig

dif·fi·cul·ty Schwierigkeit f, pl Unannehmlichkeiten pl

dif·fi·dence Schüchternheit f

dif·fi·dent schüchtern

dif·fuse 1. fig verbreiten; 2. diffus; esp PHYS zerstreut; weitschweifig

dif·fu·sion CHEM, PHYS (Zer)Streuung f

dig 1. graben; ~ (**up**) umgraben; ~ (**up** or **out**) ausgraben (a. fig); ~ **s.o. in the ribs** j-m e-n Rippenstoß geben; 2. F Puff m, Stoß m; Seitenhieb m (**at** auf acc)

di·gest 1. verdauen; ~ **well** leicht verdaulich sein; 2. Abriss m; Auslese f, Auswahl f; **di·gest·i·ble** verdaulich; **di·ges·tion** Verdauung f; **di·ges·tive** verdauungsfördernd; Verdauungs...

dig·ger (esp Gold)Gräber m

dig·it Ziffer f; **three-~ number** dreistellige Zahl

di·gi·tal digital, Digital...

dig·i·tal| **clock**, ~ **watch** Digitaluhr f

dig·ni·fied würdevoll, würdig

dig·ni·ta·ry Würdenträger(in)

dig·ni·ty Würde f

di·gress abschweifen

dike¹ 1. Deich m, Damm m; Graben m; 2. eindeichen, eindämmen

dike² sl Lesbe f

di·lap·i·dat·ed verfallen, baufällig, klapp(e)rig

di·late (sich) ausdehnen or (aus)weiten; **Augen** weit öffnen

dil·a·to·ry verzögernd, hinhaltend; langsam

dil·i·gence Fleiß m

dil·i·gent fleißig, emsig

di·lute 1. verdünnen; fig verwässern; 2. verdünnt; fig verwässert

dim 1. (halb)dunkel, düster; undeutlich, verschwommen; schwach, trüb(e) (**light**); 2. (sich) verdunkeln or verdüstern; (sich) trüben; undeutlich werden; ~ **one's headlights** MOT abblenden

dime Zehncentstück n

di·men·sion Dimension f, Maß n, Abmessung f, pl a. Ausmaß n

di·min·ish (sich) vermindern or verringern

di·min·u·tive klein, winzig

dim·ple Grübchen n

din Getöse n, Lärm m

dine essen, speisen; ~ **in** zu Hause essen; ~ **out** auswärts essen, essen gehen

din·er Speisende m, f; Gast m; Speiselokal n; RAIL Speisewagen m

din·ghy MAR Jolle f; Dingi n; Beiboot n; Schlauchboot n

din·gy schmutzig, schmudd(e)lig

din·ing car RAIL Speisewagen m

din·ing room Ess-, Speisezimmer n

din·ner (Mittag-, Abend)Essen n; Diner n, Festessen n; ~ **jack·et** Smoking m; ~ **par·ty** Dinnerparty f, Abendgesellschaft f; ~ **ser·vice**, ~ **set** Speiseservice n, Tafelgeschirr n

din·ner·time Essens-, Tischzeit f

di·no F → **dinosaur**

di·no·saur ZO Dinosaurier m

dip 1. v/t (ein)tauchen; senken; schöpfen; ~ **one's headlights** Br MOT abblenden; v/i (unter)tauchen; sinken; sich neigen, sich senken; 2. (Ein-, Unter-)Tauchen n; F kurzes Bad; Senkung f, Neigung f, Gefälle n; GASTR Dip m

diph·the·ri·a MED Diphtherie f

di·plo·ma Diplom n

di·plo·ma·cy Diplomatie f

dip·lo·mat Diplomat m

dip·lo·mat·ic diplomatisch

dip·per Schöpfkelle f

dire schrecklich; höchste(r, -s), äußerste (r, -s)

di·rect 1. adj direkt; gerade; unmittelbar; offen, aufrichtig; 2. adv direkt, unmittelbar; 3. richten; lenken, steuern; leiten; anordnen; j-n anweisen; j-m den Weg zeigen; **Brief** adressieren; Regie führen bei; ~ **cur·rent** ELECTR Gleichstrom m; ~ **train** durchgehender Zug

di·rec·tion Richtung f; Leitung f, Führung f; film etc: Regie f; mst pl Anweisung f, Anleitung f; **~s for use** Gebrauchsanweisung f; **sense of ~** Ortssinn m; **~ in·di·ca·tor** MOT Fahrtrichtungsanzeiger m, Blinker m

di·rec·tive Anweisung f

di·rect·ly **1.** adv sofort; **2.** cj F sobald, sowie

di·rec·tor Direktor m; film etc: Regisseur(in)

di·rec·to·ry Adressbuch n

di·rect speech LING wörtliche Rede

dirt Schmutz m; (lockere) Erde

dirt cheap F spottbillig

dirt·y **1.** schmutzig (a. fig); **2.** v/t beschmutzen; v/i schmutzig werden, schmutzen

dis·a·bil·i·ty Unfähigkeit f

dis·a·bled **1.** arbeitsunfähig, erwerbsunfähig, invalid(e); MIL kriegsversehrt; körperlich or geistig behindert; **2. the ~** die Behinderten pl

dis·ad·van·tage Nachteil m; Schaden m; **dis·ad·van·ta·geous** nachteilig, ungünstig

dis·a·gree nicht übereinstimmen, uneinig sein; nicht bekommen (**with s.o.** j-m); **dis·a·gree·a·ble** unangenehm; **dis·a·gree·ment** Verschiedenheit f, Unstimmigkeit f, Uneinigkeit f; Meinungsverschiedenheit f

dis·ap·pear verschwinden

dis·ap·pear·ance Verschwinden n

dis·ap·point j-n enttäuschen; Hoffnungen etc zunichte machen

dis·ap·point·ing enttäuschend

dis·ap·point·ment Enttäuschung f

dis·ap·prov·al Missbilligung f

dis·ap·prove missbilligen; dagegen sein

dis·arm v/t entwaffnen (a. fig); v/i MIL, POL abrüsten; **dis·ar·ma·ment** Entwaffnung f; MIL, POL Abrüstung f

dis·ar·range in Unordnung bringen

dis·ar·ray Unordnung f

di·sas·ter Unglück n, Unglücksfall m, Katastrophe f; **~ ar·e·a** Katastrophen-, Notstandsgebiet n; **~ con·trol** Katastrophenschutz m

di·sas·trous katastrophal, verheerend

dis·be·lief Unglaube m; Zweifel m (**in** an dat); **dis·be·lieve** et. bezweifeln, nicht glauben

disc Br → **disk**

dis·card Karten ablegen, Kleidung etc a.

ausrangieren; Freund etc fallen lassen

di·scern wahrnehmen, erkennen

di·scern·ing kritisch, scharfsichtig

di·scern·ment Scharfblick m

dis·charge **1.** v/t entladen, ausladen; j-n befreien, entbinden; j-n entlassen; Gewehr etc abfeuern; von sich geben, ausströmen, -senden, -stoßen; MED absondern; Pflicht etc erfüllen; Zorn etc auslassen (**on** an dat); v/i ELECTR sich entladen; sich ergießen, münden (river); MED eitern; **2.** MAR Entladung f; MIL Abfeuern n; Ausströmen n; MED Absonderung f, Ausfluss m; ELECTR Entladung f; Entlassung f; Erfüllung f (e-r Pflicht)

di·sci·ple Schüler m; Jünger m

dis·ci·pline **1.** Disziplin f; **2.** disziplinieren; **well ~d** diszipliniert; **badly ~d** disziplinlos, undiszipliniert

dis·claim abstreiten, bestreiten; Verantwortung ablehnen; JUR verzichten auf (acc)

dis·close bekannt geben or machen; enthüllen, aufdecken

dis·clo·sure Enthüllung f

dis·co Disko f

dis·col·o·(u)r (sich) verfärben

dis·com·fort **1.** Unbehagen n; Unannehmlichkeit f; **2.** j-m Unbehagen verursachen

dis·con·cert aus der Fassung bringen

dis·con·nect trennen (a. ELECTR); TECH auskuppeln; ELECTR Gerät abschalten; Gas, Strom, Telefon abstellen; TEL Gespräch unterbrechen

dis·con·nect·ed zusammenhang(s)los

dis·con·so·late untröstlich

dis·con·tent Unzufriedenheit f

dis·con·tent·ed unzufrieden

dis·con·tin·ue aufgeben, aufhören mit; unterbrechen

dis·cord Uneinigkeit f, Zwietracht f, Zwist m; MUS Missklang m

dis·cord·ant nicht übereinstimmend; MUS unharmonisch, misstönend

dis·co·theque Diskothek f

dis·count ECON Diskont m; Preisnachlass m, Rabatt m, Skonto m, n

dis·cour·age entmutigen; abschrecken, abhalten, j-m abraten (**from** von)

dis·cour·age·ment Entmutigung f; Abschreckung f

dis·course **1.** Unterhaltung f, Gespräch

n; Vortrag *m*; **2.** e-n Vortrag halten (**on** über *acc*)

dis·cour·te·ous unhöflich

dis·cour·te·sy Unhöflichkeit *f*

dis·cov·er entdecken; ausfindig machen, (heraus)finden

dis·cov·e·ry Entdeckung *f*

dis·cred·it 1. Zweifel *m*; Misskredit *m*, schlechter Ruf; **bring ~ (up)on** in Verruf bringen; **2.** nicht glauben; in Misskredit bringen

di·screet besonnen, vorsichtig; diskret, verschwiegen

di·screp·an·cy Diskrepanz *f*, Widerspruch *m*

di·scre·tion Ermessen *n*, Gutdünken *n*; Diskretion *f*, Verschwiegenheit *f*

di·scrim·i·nate unterscheiden; **~ against** benachteiligen, diskriminieren; **di·scrim·i·nat·ing** kritisch, urteilsfähig; **di·scrim·i·na·tion** unterschiedliche (*esp* nachteilige) Behandlung; Diskriminierung *f*, Benachteiligung *f*; Urteilsfähigkeit *f*

dis·cus SPORT Diskus *m*

di·scuss diskutieren, erörtern, besprechen; **di·scus·sion** Diskussion *f*, Besprechung *f*

dis·cus| throw SPORT Diskuswerfen *n*; **~ throw·er** SPORT Diskuswerfer(in)

dis·ease Krankheit *f*

dis·eased erkrankt

dis·em·bark von Bord gehen (lassen); MAR Waren ausladen

dis·en·chant·ed: be ~ with sich keine Illusionen mehr machen über (*acc*)

dis·en·gage (sich) freimachen; losmachen; TECH auskuppeln, loskuppeln

dis·en·tan·gle entwirren; (sich) befreien

dis·fa·vo(u)r Missfallen *n*; Ungnade *f*

dis·fig·ure entstellen

dis·grace 1. Schande *f*; Ungnade *f*; **2.** Schande bringen über (*acc*), j-m Schande bereiten

dis·grace·ful schändlich; skandalös

dis·guise 1. verkleiden (**as** als); *Stimme etc* verstellen; *et.* verbergen, verschleiern; **2.** Verkleidung *f*; Verstellung *f*; Verschleierung *f*; *in ~* maskiert, verkleidet; *fig* verkappt; *in the ~ of* verkleidet als

dis·gust 1. Ekel *m*, Abscheu *m*; **2.** (an-) ekeln; empören, entrüsten

dish 1. flache Schüssel; (Servier)Platte *f*; GASTR Gericht *n*, Speise *f*; **the ~es** das Geschirr; **wash** or **do the ~es** abspülen, abwaschen; **2. ~ out** F austeilen; *often* **~ up** Speisen anrichten, auftragen; F *Geschichte etc* auftischen

dish·cloth Geschirrtuch *n*

dis·heart·en entmutigen

di·shev·el(l)ed zerzaust

dis·hon·est unehrlich, unredlich

dis·hon·est·y Unehrlichkeit *f*; Unredlichkeit *f*

dis·hon·o(u)r 1. Schande *f*; **2.** Schande bringen über (*acc*); ECON *Wechsel* nicht honorieren or einlösen

dis·hon·o(u)·ra·ble schändlich, unehrenhaft

dish·wash·er Tellerwäscher *m*, Spüler (-in); TECH Geschirrspülmaschine *f*, Geschirrspüler *m*

dish·wa·ter Spülwasser *n*

dis·il·lu·sion 1. Ernüchterung *f*, Desillusion *f*; **2.** ernüchtern, desillusionieren; **be ~ed with** sich keine Illusionen mehr machen über (*acc*)

dis·in·clined abgeneigt

dis·in·fect MED desinfizieren

dis·in·fec·tant Desinfektionsmittel *n*

dis·in·her·it JUR enterben

dis·in·te·grate (sich) auflösen; verfallen, zerfallen

dis·in·terest·ed uneigennützig, selbstlos; objektiv, unvoreingenommen

disk Scheibe *f*; (Schall)Platte *f*; Parkscheibe *f*; EDP Diskette *f*; ANAT Bandscheibe *f*; **slipped ~** MED Bandscheibenvorfall *m*

disk drive EDP Diskettenlaufwerk *n*

disk·ette EDP Floppy *f*, Diskette *f*

disk jock·ey Diskjockey *m*

disk park·ing MOT Parken *n* mit Parkscheibe

dis·like 1. Abneigung *f*, Widerwille *m* (**of**, **for** gegen); **take a ~ to s.o.** gegen j-n e-e Abneigung fassen; **2.** nicht leiden können, nicht mögen

dis·lo·cate MED sich *den Arm etc* verrenken or ausrenken

dis·loy·al treulos, untreu

dis·mal trüb(e), trostlos, elend

dis·man·tle TECH demontieren

dis·may 1. Schreck(en) *m*, Bestürzung *f*; **in ~, with ~** bestürzt; **to my ~** zu m-r

Bestürzung; **2.** v/t erschrecken, bestürzen

dis·miss v/t entlassen; wegschicken; ablehnen; *Thema etc* fallen lassen; JUR abweisen; **dis·miss·al** Entlassung f; Aufgabe f; JUR Abweisung f

dis·mount v/i absteigen, absitzen (*from* von); v/t demontieren; TECH auseinander nehmen

dis·o·be·di·ence Ungehorsam m

dis·o·be·di·ent ungehorsam

dis·o·bey nicht gehorchen, ungehorsam sein (gegen)

dis·or·der Unordnung f; Aufruhr m; MED Störung f

dis·or·der·ly unordentlich; ordnungswidrig; unruhig; aufrührerisch

dis·or·gan·ize durcheinander bringen; desorganisieren

dis·own nicht anerkennen; *Kind* verstoßen; ablehnen

di·spar·age verächtlich machen, herabsetzen; gering schätzen

di·spar·i·ty Ungleichheit f; *~ of or in age* Altersunterschied m

dis·pas·sion·ate leidenschaftslos; objektiv

di·spatch 1. schnelle Erledigung; (Ab-)Sendung f; Abfertigung f; Eile f; (Eil-)Botschaft f; Bericht m; **2.** schnell erledigen; absenden, abschicken, *Telegramm* aufgeben, abfertigen

di·spel *Menge etc* zerstreuen (*a. fig*), *Nebel* zerteilen

di·spen·sa·ble entbehrlich

di·spen·sa·ry Werks-, Krankenhaus-, Schul-, MIL Lazarettapotheke f

dis·pen·sa·tion Austeilung f; Befreiung f; Dispens m; *göttliche* Fügung f

di·spense austeilen; *Recht* sprechen; *Arzneien* zubereiten und abgeben; *~ with* auskommen ohne; überflüssig machen; **di·spens·er** Spender m, a. Abroller m (*for adhesive tape etc*), (*Briefmarken- etc*)Automat m

di·sperse verstreuen; (sich) zerstreuen

di·spir·it·ed entmutigt

dis·place verschieben; ablösen, entlassen; *j-n* verschleppen; ersetzen; verdrängen

dis·play 1. Entfaltung f; (Her)Zeigen n; (protzige) Zurschaustellung; EDP Display n, Bildschirm m, Datenanzeige f; ECON Display n, Auslage f; *be on* ~ ausgestellt sein; **2.** entfalten; zur Schau stellen; zeigen

dis·please *j-m* missfallen

dis·pleased ungehalten

dis·plea·sure Missfallen n

dis·pos·a·ble Einweg...; Wegwerf...

dis·pos·al Beseitigung f, Entsorgung f; Endlagerung f; Verfügung(srecht n) f; *be (put) at s.o.'s* ~ j-m zur Verfügung stehen (stellen)

dis·pose v/t (an)ordnen, einrichten; geneigt machen, bewegen; v/i: *~ of* verfügen über (*acc*); erledigen; loswerden; wegschaffen, beseitigen; *Abfall, a. Atommüll etc* entsorgen

dis·posed geneigt; ...gesinnt

dis·po·si·tion Veranlagung f

dis·pos·sess enteignen, vertreiben; berauben (*of gen*)

dis·pro·por·tion·ate(·ly) unverhältnismäßig

dis·prove widerlegen

di·spute 1. Disput m, Kontroverse f; Streit m; Auseinandersetzung f; **2.** streiten (über *acc*); bezweifeln

dis·qual·i·fy unfähig *or* untauglich machen; für untauglich erklären; SPORT disqualifizieren

dis·re·gard 1. Nichtbeachtung f; Missachtung f; **2.** nicht beachten

dis·rep·u·ta·ble übel; verrufen

dis·re·pute schlechter Ruf

dis·re·spect Respektlosigkeit f; Unhöflichkeit f

dis·re·spect·ful respektlos; unhöflich

dis·rupt unterbrechen

dis·sat·is·fac·tion Unzufriedenheit f

dis·sat·is·fied unzufrieden (*with* mit)

dis·sect MED sezieren, zerlegen, zergliedern (*a. fig*)

dis·sen·sion Meinungsverschiedenheit (en *pl*) f, Differenz(en *pl*) f; Uneinigkeit f

dis·sent 1. abweichende Meinung; **2.** anderer Meinung sein (*from* als)

dis·sent·er Andersdenkende m, f

dis·si·dent Andersdenkende m, f; POL Dissident(in), Regime-, Systemkritiker (-in)

dis·sim·i·lar (*to*) unähnlich (*dat*); verschieden (von)

dis·sim·u·la·tion Verstellung f

dis·si·pate (sich) zerstreuen; verschwinden

dis·si·pat·ed ausschweifend, zügellos

dis·so·ci·ate trennen; ~ *o.s.* sich distanzieren (*from* von)

dis·so·lute → *dissipated*

dis·so·lu·tion Auflösung f

dis·solve (sich) auflösen

dis·suade *j-m* abraten (*from* von)

dis·tance 1. Abstand m; Entfernung f; Ferne f; Strecke f; fig Distanz f, Zurückhaltung f; *at a* ~ von weitem; in einiger Entfernung; *keep s.o. at a* ~ j-m gegenüber reserviert sein; 2. hinter sich lassen; ~ *race* SPORT Langstreckenlauf m; ~ *run·ner* SPORT Langstreckenläufer(in), Langstreckler(in)

dis·tant entfernt; fern, Fern...; distanziert

dis·taste Widerwille m, Abneigung f

dis·taste·ful Ekel erregend; unangenehm; *be* ~ *to s.o.* j-m zuwider sein

dis·tem·per VET Staupe f

dis·tend (sich) (aus)dehnen; (auf)blähen; sich weiten

dis·til(l) destillieren

dis·tinct verschieden; deutlich, klar

dis·tinc·tion Unterscheidung f; Unterschied m; Auszeichnung f; Rang m

dis·tinc·tive unterscheidend; kennzeichnend, bezeichnend

dis·tin·guish unterscheiden; auszeichnen; ~ *o.s.* sich auszeichnen

dis·tin·guished berühmt; ausgezeichnet; vornehm

dis·tort verdrehen; verzerren

dis·tract ablenken; dis·tract·ed beunruhigt, besorgt; (*by, with* vor dat) außer sich, wahnsinnig; dis·trac·tion Ablenkung f; Zerstreuung f; Wahnsinn m; *drive s.o. to* ~ j-n wahnsinnig machen

dis·traught → *distracted*

dis·tress 1. Leid n, Kummer m, Sorge f; Not(lage) f; 2. beunruhigen, mit Sorge erfüllen

dis·tressed Not leidend; ~ *ar·e·a* Notstandsgebiet n

dis·tress·ing Besorgnis erregend

dis·trib·ute ver-, aus-, zuteilen; ECON *Waren* vertreiben, absetzen; *Filme* verleihen; dis·tri·bu·tion Ver-, Aus-, Zuteilung f, ECON Vertrieb m; Absatz m; *film*: Verleih m

dis·trict Bezirk m; Gegend f

dis·trust 1. Misstrauen n; 2. misstrauen (dat); dis·trust·ful misstrauisch

dis·turb stören; beunruhigen

dis·turb·ance Störung f; Unruhe f; ~ *of the peace* JUR Störung f der öffentlichen Sicherheit und Ordnung; *cause a* ~ für Unruhe sorgen; ruhestörenden Lärm machen

dis·turbed geistig gestört; verhaltensgestört

dis·used nicht mehr benutzt (*machinery etc*), stillgelegt (*colliery etc*)

ditch Graben m

di·van Diwan m; ~ *bed* Bettcouch f

dive 1. (unter)tauchen; *vom Sprungbrett* springen; e-n Hecht- or Kopfsprung machen; hechten (*for* nach); e-n Sturzflug machen; 2. *swimming*: Springen n; Kopfsprung m, Hechtsprung m; *soccer*: Schwalbe f; AVIAT Sturzflug m; F Spelunke f; div·er Taucher(in); SPORT Wasserspringer(in)

di·verge auseinander laufen; abweichen; di·ver·gence Abweichung f; di·ver·gent abweichend

di·verse verschieden; mannigfaltig

di·ver·si·fy verschieden(artig) *or* abwechslungsreich gestalten

di·ver·sion Ablenkung f; Zeitvertreib m; *Br* MOT Umleitung f

di·ver·si·ty Verschiedenheit f; Mannigfaltigkeit f

di·vert ablenken; *j-n* zerstreuen, unterhalten; *Br Verkehr* umleiten

di·vide 1. *v/t* teilen; ver-, aus-, aufteilen; trennen; MATH dividieren, teilen (*by* durch); *v/i* sich teilen; sich aufteilen; MATH sich dividieren *or* teilen lassen (*by* durch); 2. GEOGR Wasserscheide f

di·vid·ed geteilt; ~ *highway* Schnellstraße f

div·i·dend ECON Dividende f

di·vid·ers (*a pair of* ~ ein) Stechzirkel m

di·vine göttlich

di·vine ser·vice REL Gottesdienst m

div·ing 1. Tauchen n; SPORT Wasserspringen n; 2. Taucher...

div·ing·board Sprungbrett n

div·ing·suit Taucheranzug m

di·vin·i·ty Gottheit f; Göttlichkeit f; Theologie f

di·vis·i·ble teilbar

di·vi·sion Teilung f; Trennung f; Abteilung f; MIL, MATH Division f

di·vorce 1. (Ehe)Scheidung f; *get a* ~ sich scheiden lassen (*from* von); 2. JUR *j-n*, *Ehe* scheiden; **get** **~d** sich scheiden lassen; **di•vor•cee** Geschiedene *m, f*

DIY ABBR → **do-it-yourself**

DIY store Baumarkt *m*

diz•zy schwind(e)lig

do *v/t* tun, machen; (zu)bereiten; *Zimmer* aufräumen; *Geschirr* abwaschen; *Wegstrecke* zurücklegen, schaffen; **~ you know him?** *no, I don't* kennst du ihn? nein; **what can I ~ for you?** was kann ich für Sie tun?, womit kann ich (Ihnen) dienen?; **~ London** F London besichtigen; **have one's hair done** sich die Haare machen *or* frisieren lassen; **have done reading** fertig sein mit Lesen; *v/i* tun, handeln; sich befinden; genügen; **that will ~** das genügt; **how ~ you ~?** guten Tag!; **~ be quick** beeil dich doch; **~ you like New York? I ~** gefällt Ihnen New York? ja; **she works hard, doesn't she?** sie arbeitet viel, nicht wahr?; **~ well** s-e Sache gut machen; gute Geschäfte machen; **~ away with** beseitigen, weg-, abschaffen; **do s.o. in** F j-n umlegen; **I'm done in** F ich bin geschafft; **~ up** *Kleid etc* zumachen; *Haus etc* instand setzen; *Päckchen* zurechtmachen; **~ o.s. up** sich zurechtmachen; **I could ~ with ...** ich könnte ... brauchen *or* vertragen; **~ without** auskommen *or* sich behelfen ohne

doc F → **doctor**

do•cile gelehrig; fügsam

dock[1] stutzen, kupieren

dock[2] **1.** MAR Dock *n*; Kai *m*, Pier *m*; JUR Anklagebank *f*; **2.** *v/t* MAR (ein)docken; *Raumschiff* koppeln; *v/i* MAR anlegen; andocken, ankoppeln (*Raumschiff*)

dock•er Dock-, Hafenarbeiter *m*

dock•ing Docking *n*, Ankopp(e)lung *f*

dock•yard MAR Werft *f*

doc•tor Doktor *m* (*a.* UNIV), Arzt *m*, Ärztin *f*

doc•tor•al: ~ thesis UNIV Doktorarbeit *f*

doc•trine Doktrin *f*, Lehre *f*

doc•u•ment 1. Urkunde *f*; **2.** (urkundlich) belegen; **doc•u•men•ta•ry 1.** urkundlich; *film etc*: Dokumentar...; **2.** Dokumentarfilm *m*

dodge (rasch) zur Seite springen, ausweichen; F sich drücken (vor *dat*)

dodg•er Drückeberger *m*

doe ZO (Reh)Geiß *f*, Ricke *f*

dog 1. ZO Hund *m*; **2.** *j-n* beharrlich verfolgen

dog-eared mit Eselsohren (*book*)

dog•ged verbissen, hartnäckig

dog•ma Dogma *n*; Glaubenssatz *m*

dog•mat•ic dogmatisch

do-it-your•self 1. Heimwerken *n*; **2.** Heimwerker...

do-it-your•self•er Heimwerker *m*

dole 1. milde Gabe; *Br* F Stempelgeld *n*; **go** *or* **be on the ~** *Br* F stempeln gehen; **2. ~ out** sparsam ver- *or* austeilen

dole•ful traurig, trübselig

doll Puppe *f*

dol•lar Dollar *m*

dol•phin ZO Delphin *m*

dome Kuppel *f*

do•mes•tic 1. häuslich; inländisch, einheimisch; zahm; **2.** Hausangestellte *m, f*, **~ an•i•mal** Haustier *n*

do•mes•ti•cate *Tier* zähmen

do•mes•tic| flight AVIAT Inlandsflug *m*; **~ mar•ket** ECON Binnenmarkt *m*; **~ trade** ECON Binnenhandel *m*; **~ vi•olence** häusliche Gewalt

dom•i•cile Wohnsitz *m*

dom•i•nant dominierend, (vor)herrschend

dom•i•nate beherrschen; dominieren

dom•i•na•tion (Vor)Herrschaft *f*

dom•i•neer•ing herrisch, tyrannisch

do•nate schenken; stiften; spenden (*a.* MED); **do•na•tion** Schenkung *f*

done getan; erledigt; fertig; GASTR gar

don•key ZO Esel *m*

do•nor Spender(in) (*a.* MED)

do-noth•ing F Nichtstuer *m*

doom 1. Schicksal *n*, Verhängnis *n*; **2.** verurteilen, verdammen

Dooms•day der Jüngste Tag

door Tür *f*; Tor *n*; **next ~** nebenan

door•bell Türklingel *f*

door han•dle Türklinke *f*

door•keep•er Pförtner *m*

door•knob Türknauf *m*

door•mat (Fuß)Abtreter *m*

door•step Türstufe *f*

door•way Türöffnung *f*

dope 1. F Stoff *m* (*Rauschgift*); Betäubungsmittel *n*; SPORT Dopingmittel *n*; *sl* Trottel *m*; **2.** SPORT *j-m* Stoff geben; SPORT dopen; **~ test** SPORT Dopingkontrolle *f*

dor•mant schlafend, ruhend; untätig

dor·mi·to·ry Schlafsaal *m*; Studenten-wohnheim *n*

dor·mo·bile® Campingbus *m*, Wohn-mobil *n*

dor·mouse ZO Haselmaus *f*

dose 1. Dosis *f*; **2.** *j-m* e-e Medizin ge-ben

dot 1. Punkt *m*; Fleck *m*; **on the ~** F auf die Sekunde pünktlich; **2.** punktieren; tüpfeln; *fig* sprenkeln; **~ted line** punk-tierte Linie

dote: ~ on vernarrt sein in (*acc*)

dot·ing vernarrt

doub·le 1. doppelt; Doppel...; zweifach; **2.** Doppelte *n*; Doppelgänger(in); *film, TV* Double *n*; **3.** (sich) verdoppeln; *film, TV j-n* doubeln; *a.* **~ up** falten; *Decke* zusammenlegen; **~ back** kehrtmachen; **~ up with** sich krümmen vor (*dat*)

dou·ble-breast·ed zweireihig

dou·ble-check genau nachprüfen

dou·ble chin Doppelkinn *n*

dou·ble-cross ein doppeltes *or* fal-sches Spiel treiben mit

dou·ble-deal·ing 1. betrügerisch; **2.** Betrug *m*

dou·ble-deck·er Doppeldecker *m*

dou·ble-edged zweischneidig (*a. fig*); zweideutig

dou·ble fea·ture *film:* Doppelpro-gramm *n*

dou·ble-park MOT in zweiter Reihe parken

dou·bles *esp tennis:* Doppel *n*; **men's ~** Herrendoppel *n*; **women's ~** Damen-doppel *n*

dou·ble-sid·ed EDP zweiseitig

doubt 1. *v/i* zweifeln; *v/t* bezweifeln; misstrauen (*dat*); **2.** Zweifel *m*; **be in ~ about** Zweifel haben an (*dat*); **no ~** ohne Zweifel

doubt·ful zweifelhaft

doubt·less ohne Zweifel

douche 1. Spülung *f* (*a.* MED); Spülap-parat *m*; **2.** spülen (*a.* MED)

dough Teig *m*

dough·nut *appr* Krapfen *m*, Berliner Pfannkuchen, Schmalzkringel *m*

dove ZO Taube *f*

dow·dy unelegant; unmodern

dow·el TECH Dübel *m*

down[1] Daunen *pl*; Flaum *m*

down[2] **1.** *adv* nach unten, herunter, hi-nunter, herab, hinab, abwärts; unten;

2. *prp* herab, hinab, herunter, hinunter; **~ the river** flussabwärts; **3.** *adj* nach un-ten gerichtet; deprimiert; niederge-schlagen; **~ platform** Abfahrtsbahn-steig *m* (*in London*); **~ train** Zug *m* (von London fort); **4.** *v/t* niederschla-gen; *Flugzeug* abschießen; F *Getränk* runterkippen; **~ tools** die Arbeit nie-derlegen, in den Streik treten

down·cast niedergeschlagen

down·fall Platzregen *m*; *fig* Sturz *m*

down·heart·ed niedergeschlagen

down·hill 1. *adv* bergab; **2.** *adj* abschüs-sig; *skiing:* Abfahrts...; **3.** Abhang *m*; *skiing:* Abfahrt *f*

down pay·ment ECON Anzahlung *f*

down·pour Regenguss *m*, Platzregen *m*

down·right 1. *adv* völlig, ganz und gar, ausgesprochen; **2.** *adj* glatt (*lie etc*); ausgesprochen

downs Hügelland *n*

down·stairs die Treppe herunter *or* hinunter; (nach) unten

down·stream stromabwärts

down-to-earth realistisch

down·town 1. *adv* im *or* ins Geschäfts-viertel; **2.** *adj* im Geschäftsviertel (ge-legen *or* tätig); **3.** Geschäftsviertel *n*, Innenstadt *f*, City *f*

down·ward(s) abwärts, nach unten

down·y flaumig

dow·ry Mitgift *f*

doze 1. dösen, ein Nickerchen machen; **2.** Nickerchen *n*

doz·en Dutzend *n*

drab trist; düster; eintönig

draft 1. Entwurf *m*; (Luft)Zug *m*; Zug-luft *f*; Zug *m*, Schluck *m*; MAR Tiefgang *m*; ECON Tratte *f*, Wechsel *m*; MIL Ein-berufung *f*; *Bier* vom **~**, **~ beer** Bier *n* vom Fass, Fassbier *n*; **2.** entwerfen; *Brief etc* aufsetzen; MIL einberufen

draft·ee MIL Wehr(dienst)pflichtige *m*

drafts·man TECH Zeichner *m*

drafts·wom·an TECH Zeichnerin *f*

draft·y zugig

drag 1. Schleppen *n*, Zerren *n*; *fig* Hemmschuh *m*; F *et.* Langweiliges *n*; **2.** schleppen, zerren, ziehen, schleifen; *a.* **~ behind** zurückbleiben, nachhin-ken; **~ on** weiterschleppen; *fig* sich da-hinschleppen; *fig* sich in die Länge zie-hen

drag lift Schlepplift *m*

drag·on MYTH Drache *m*

drag·on-fly ZO Libelle *f*

drain 1. Abfluss(kanal) *m*, Abflussrohr *n*; Entwässerungsgraben *m*; **2.** *v/t* abfließen lassen; entwässern; austrinken, leeren; *v/i:* **~ off**, **~ away** abfließen, ablaufen; **drain·age** Abfließen *n*, Ablaufen *n*, Entwässerung *f*; Entwässerungsanlage *f*, -system *n*

drain·pipe Abflussrohr *n*

drake ZO Enterich *m*, Erpel *m*

dram Schluck *m*

dra·ma Drama *n*; **dra·mat·ic** dramatisch; **dram·a·tist** Dramatiker *m*; **dram·a·tize** dramatisieren

drape 1. drapieren; in Falten legen; **2.** *mst* **~s** Vorhänge *pl*

drap·er·y *Br* Textilien *pl*

dras·tic drastisch, durchgreifend

draught *Br* → **draft**

draughts *Br* Damespiel *n*

draughts·man *etc* → **draftsman** *etc*

draugh·ty *Br* → **drafty**

draw 1. *v/t* ziehen; *Vorhänge* auf-, zuziehen; *Atem* holen; *Tee* ziehen lassen; *fig Menge* anziehen; *Interesse* auf sich ziehen; zeichnen; *Geld* abheben; *Scheck* ausstellen; *v/i* ziehen; SPORT unentschieden spielen; **~ back** zurückweichen; **~ near** sich nähern; **~ out** *Geld* abheben; *fig* in die Länge ziehen; **~ up** *Schriftstück* aufsetzen; MOT (an)halten; vorfahren; **2.** Ziehen *n*; *lottery:* Ziehung *f*; SPORT Unentschieden *n*; Attraktion *f*, Zugnummer *f*

draw·back Nachteil *m*, Hindernis *n*

draw·bridge Zugbrücke *f*

draw·er[1] Schublade *f*, Schubfach *n*

draw·er[2] Zeichner(in); ECON Aussteller (-in)

draw·ing Zeichnen *n*; Zeichnung *f*; **~ board** Reißbrett *n*; **~ pin** *Br* Reißzwecke *f*, Reißnagel *m*, Heftzwecke *f*; **~ room** → **living room**; Salon *m*

drawl gedehnt sprechen

drawn abgespannt; SPORT unentschieden

dread 1. (große) Angst, Furcht *f*; **2.** (sich) fürchten

dread·ful schrecklich, furchtbar

dream 1. Traum *m*; **2.** träumen

dream·er Träumer(in)

dream·y träumerisch, verträumt

drear·y trübselig; trüb(e); langweilig

dredge 1. (Schwimm)Bagger *m*; **2.** (aus)baggern

dredg·er (Schwimm)Bagger *m*

dregs Bodensatz *m*; *fig* Abschaum *m*

drench durchnässen

dress 1. Kleidung *f*; Kleid *n*; **2.** (sich) ankleiden *or* anziehen; schmücken, dekorieren; zurechtmachen; GASTR zubereiten, *Salat* anmachen; MED *Wunde* verbinden; *Haare* frisieren; **get ~ed** sich anziehen; **~ s.o. down** F j-m e-e Standpauke halten; **~ up** (sich) fein machen; sich kostümieren *or* verkleiden

dress cir·cle THEA erster Rang

dress de·sign·er Modezeichner(in)

dress·er Anrichte *f*; Toilettentisch *m*

dress·ing An-, Zurichten *n*; Ankleiden *n*; MED Verband *m*; GASTR Dressing *n*, Füllung *f*

dressing-down F Standpauke *f*

dress·ing| gown *esp Br* Morgenrock *m*, -mantel *m*; SPORT Bademantel *m*; **~ room** THEA *etc* (Künstler)Garderobe *f*; SPORT (Umkleide)Kabine *f*; **~ ta·ble** Toilettentisch *m*

dress·mak·er (Damen)Schneider(in)

dress re·hears·al THEA *etc* Generalprobe *f*

drib·ble tröpfeln (lassen); sabbern, geifern; *soccer:* dribbeln

dried getrocknet, Dörr...

dri·er → **dryer**

drift 1. (Dahin)Treiben *n*; (Schnee)Verwehung *f*; Schnee-, Sandwehe *f*; *fig* Tendenz *f*; **2.** (dahin)treiben; wehen; sich häufen

drill 1. TECH Bohrer *m*; MIL Drill *m* (*a. fig*), Exerzieren *n*; **2.** bohren; MIL drillen (*a. fig*); **drill·ing site** TECH Bohrgelände *n*, Bohrstelle *f*

drink 1. Getränk *n*; **2.** trinken; **~ to s.o.** j-m zuprosten *or* zutrinken

drink-driv·ing *Br* Trunkenheit *f* am Steuer

drink·er Trinker(in)

drinks ma·chine Getränkeautomat *m*

drip 1. Tröpfeln *n*; MED Tropf *m*; **2.** tropfen *or* tröpfeln (lassen); triefen

drip-dry bügelfrei

drip·ping Bratenfett *n*

drive 1. Fahrt *f*; Aus-, Spazierfahrt *f*; Zufahrt(sstraße) *f*; (private) Auffahrt; TECH Antrieb *m*; EDP Laufwerk *n*; MOT (*Links- etc*)Steuerung *f*; PSYCH

Trieb m; fig Kampagne f; fig Schwung m, Elan m, Dynamik f; **2.** v/t treiben; *Auto etc* fahren, lenken, steuern; (im Auto etc) fahren; TECH (an)treiben; a. ~ **off** vertreiben; v/i treiben; (Auto) fahren; ~ **off** wegfahren; **what are you driving at?** F worauf wollen Sie hinaus?

drive-in 1. Auto...; ~ **cinema** Br, ~ **motion-picture theater** Autokino n; **2.** Autokino n; Drive-in-Restaurant n; Autoschalter m, Drive-in-Schalter m

driv·el 1. faseln; **2.** Geschwätz n, Gefasel n

driv·er MOT Fahrer(in); (Lokomotiv-)Führer m

driv·er's li·cense Führerschein m

driv·ing (an)treibend; TECH Antriebs..., Treib..., Trieb...; MOT Fahr...

driv·ing force fig Triebkraft f

driv·ing li·cence Br Führerschein m

driv·ing test Fahrprüfung f

driz·zle 1. Sprühregen m; **2.** sprühen, nieseln

drone 1. ZO Drohne f (a. fig); **2.** summen; dröhnen

droop (schlaff) herabhängen

drop 1. Tropfen m; Fallen n, Fall m; fig Fall m, Sturz m; Bonbon m, n; **fruit ~s** Drops pl; **2.** v/t tropfen (lassen); fallen lassen(a. fig); Brief einwerfen; Fahrgast absetzen; senken; ~ **s.o. a few lines** j-m ein paar Zeilen schreiben; v/i tropfen; herab-, herunterfallen; umsinken, fallen; ~ **in** (kurz) hereinschauen; ~ **off** abfallen; zurückgehen, nachlassen; F einnicken; ~ **out** herausfallen; aussteigen (**of** aus); a. ~ **out of school** (**university**) die Schule (das Studium) abbrechen

drop·out Drop-out m, Aussteiger m; (Schul-, Studien)Abbrecher m

drought Trockenheit f, Dürre f

drown v/t ertränken; überschwemmen; fig übertönen; v/i ertrinken

drow·sy schläfrig; einschläfernd

drudge sich (ab)placken, schuften, sich schinden; **drudg·er·y** (stumpfsinnige) Plackerei f, Schinderei or Schufterei f

drug 1. Arzneimittel n, Medikament n; Droge f, Rauschgift n; **be on ~s** drogenabhängig or drogensüchtig sein; **be off ~s** clean sein; **2.** j-m Medikamente geben; j-n unter Drogen setzen;

ein Betäubungsmittel beimischen (dat); betäuben (a. fig); ~ **a·buse** Drogenmissbrauch m; Medikamentenmissbrauch m; ~ **ad·dict** Drogenabhängige m, f, Drogensüchtige m, f; **be a ~** drogenabhängig or drogensüchtig sein

drug·gist Apotheker(in); Inhaber(in) e-s Drugstores

drug·store Apotheke f; Drugstore m

drug vic·tim Drogentote m, f

drum 1. MUS Trommel f; ANAT Trommelfell n; pl MUS Schlagzeug n; **2.** trommeln; **drum·mer** MUS Trommler m; Schlagzeuger m

drunk 1. adj betrunken; **get ~** sich betrinken; **2.** Betrunkene m, f; → **drunkard**

drunk·ard Trinker(in), Säufer(in)

drunk driv·ing Trunkenheit f am Steuer

drunk·en betrunken; ~ **driv·ing** Br Trunkenheit f am Steuer

dry 1. trocken, GASTR a. herb; F durstig; **2.** trocknen; dörren; ~ **out** trocknen; e-e Entziehungskur machen, F trocken werden; ~ **up** austrocknen; versiegen

dry-clean chemisch reinigen

dry clean·er's chemische Reinigung f

dry·er TECH Trockner m

dry goods Textilien pl

du·al doppelt, Doppel...; ~ **car·riage·way** Br Schnellstraße f

dub Film synchronisieren

du·bi·ous zweifelhaft

duch·ess Herzogin f

duck 1. ZO Ente f; Ducken n; F Schatz m; **2.** (unter)tauchen; (sich) ducken

duck·ling ZO Entchen n

due 1. zustehend; gebührend; angemessen; ECON fällig; ~ **to** wegen (gen); **be ~ to** zurückzuführen sein auf (acc); **2.** adv direkt, genau (nach Osten etc)

du·el Duell n

dues Gebühren pl; Beitrag m

du·et MUS Duett n

duke Herzog m

dull 1. dumm; träge, schwerfällig; stumpf; matt (eyes etc); schwach (hearing); langweilig; abgestumpft, teilnahmslos; dumpf; trüb(e); ECON flau; **2.** stumpf machen or werden; (sich) trüben; mildern, dämpfen; Schmerz betäuben; fig abstumpfen

du·ly ordnungsgemäß; gebührend; rechtzeitig

dumb stumm; sprachlos; F doof, dumm, blöd

dum(b)·found·ed verblüfft, sprachlos

dum·my Attrappe *f*; Kleider-, Schaufensterpuppe *f*; MOT Dummy *m*, Puppe *f*; *Br* Schnuller *m*

dump 1. *v/t* (hin)plumpsen *or* (hin)fallen lassen; auskippen; *Schutt etc* abladen; *Schadstoffe in e-n Fluss etc* einleiten, *im Meer* verklappen (**into** in); ECON *Waren* zu Dumpingpreisen verkaufen; **2.** Plumps *m*; Schuttabladeplatz *m*, Müllkippe *f*, Müllhalde *f*, (Müll)Deponie *f*; **dump·ing** ECON Dumping *n*, Ausfuhr *f* zu Schleuderpreisen

dune Düne *f*

dung AGR **1.** Dung *m*; **2.** düngen

dun·geon (Burg)Verlies *n*

dupe betrügen, täuschen

du·plex 1. doppelt, Doppel...; **2.** *a.* **~ apartment** Maisonette *f*, Maisonettewohnung *f*; *a.* **~ house** Doppel-, Zweifamilienhaus *n*

du·pli·cate 1. doppelt; **~ key** Zweit-, Nachschlüssel *m*; **2.** Duplikat *n*; Zweit-, Nachschlüssel *m*; **3.** doppelt ausfertigen; kopieren, vervielfältigen

du·plic·i·ty Doppelzüngigkeit *f*

dur·a·ble haltbar; dauerhaft

du·ra·tion Dauer *f*

du·ress Zwang *m*

dur·ing während

dusk (Abend)Dämmerung *f*

dusk·y dämmerig, düster (*a. fig*); schwärzlich

dust 1. Staub *m*; **2.** *v/t* abstauben; (be-)streuen; *v/i* Staub wischen, abstauben

dust·bin *Br* Abfall-, Mülleimer *m*; Abfall-, Mülltonne *f*; **~ lin·er** *Br* Müllbeutel *m*

dust·cart *Br* Müllwagen *m*

dust·er Staubtuch *n*

dust cov·er, dust jack·et Schutzumschlag *m*

dust·man *Br* Müllmann *m*

dust·pan Kehrichtschaufel *f*

dust·y staubig

Dutch 1. *adj* holländisch, niederländisch; **2.** *adv:* **go ~** getrennte Kasse machen; **3.** LING Holländisch *n*, Niederländisch *n*; **the ~** die Holländer *pl*, die Niederländer *pl*

Dutch·man Holländer *m*, Niederländer *m*; **Dutch·wom·an** Holländerin *f*, Niederländerin *f*

du·ti·a·ble ECON zollpflichtig

du·ty Pflicht *f*; Ehrerbietung *f*; ECON Abgabe *f*; Zoll *m*; Dienst *m*; **on ~** Dienst habend; **be on ~** Dienst haben; **be off ~** dienstfrei haben; **du·ty-free** zollfrei

dwarf 1. Zwerg(in); **2.** verkleinern, klein erscheinen lassen

dwell wohnen; *fig* verweilen (**on** bei)

dwell·ing Wohnung *f*

dwin·dle (dahin)schwinden, abnehmen

dye 1. Farbe *f*, **of the deepest ~** *fig* von der übelsten Sorte; **2.** färben

dy·ing 1. sterbend; Sterbe...; **2.** Sterben *n*; **~ of forests** Waldsterben *n*

dyke → **dike**[1,2]

dy·nam·ic dynamisch, kraftgeladen

dy·nam·ics Dynamik *f*

dy·na·mite 1. Dynamit *n*; **2.** (mit Dynamit) sprengen

dys·en·te·ry MED Ruhr *f*

dys·pep·si·a MED Verdauungsstörung *f*

E

E, e E, e *n*

each jede(r, -s); **~ other** einander, sich; **je**, pro Person, pro Stück

ea·ger begierig; eifrig

ea·ger·ness Begierde *f*; Eifer *m*

ea·gle ZO Adler *m*; HIST Zehndollarstück *n*; **ea·gle-eyed** scharfsichtig

ear BOT Ähre *f*; ANAT Ohr *n*; Öhr *n*; Henkel *m*; **keep an ~ to the ground** die Ohren offen halten

ear·ache Ohrenschmerzen *pl*

ear·drum ANAT Trommelfell *n*

earl *englischer* Graf

ear·lobe ANAT Ohrläppchen *n*

ear·ly früh; Früh...; Anfangs..., erste(r, -s); bald(ig); **as ~ as May** schon im Mai; **as ~ as possible** so bald wie möglich; **~ on** schon früh, frühzeitig

ear·ly bird Frühaufsteher(in)

ear·ly warn·ing sys·tem MIL Frühwarnsystem *n*

ear·mark 1. Kennzeichen *n*; Merkmal *n*; **2.** kennzeichnen; zurücklegen (**for** für)

earn verdienen; einbringen

ear·nest 1. ernst, ernstlich, ernsthaft; ernst gemeint; **2.** Ernst *m*; **in ~** im Ernst; ernsthaft

earn·ings Einkommen *n*

ear·phones Ohrhörer *pl*; Kopfhörer *pl*

ear·piece TEL Hörmuschel *f*

ear·ring Ohrring *m*

ear·shot: within (out of) ~ in (außer) Hörweite

earth 1. Erde *f*; Land *n*; **2.** *v/t* ELECTR erden

earth·en irden

earth·en·ware Steingut(geschirr) *n*

earth·ly irdisch, weltlich; F denkbar

earth·quake Erdbeben *n*

earth·worm ZO Regenwurm *m*

ease 1. Bequemlichkeit *f*; (Gemüts)Ruhe *f*; Sorglosigkeit *f*; Leichtigkeit *f*; **at (one's) ~** ruhig, entspannt; unbefangen; **be** *or* **feel ill at ~** sich (in s-r Haut) nicht wohl fühlen; **2.** *v/t* erleichtern; beruhigen; *Schmerzen* lindern; *v/i mst* **~ off, ~ up** nachlassen; sich entspannen (*situation etc*)

ea·sel Staffelei *f*

east 1. Ost, Osten *m*; **2.** *adj* östlich,

Ost...; **3.** *adv* nach Osten, ostwärts

Eas·ter Ostern *n*; Oster...; **~ bun·ny** Osterhase *m*; **~ egg** Osterei *n*

eas·ter·ly östlich, Ost...

east·ern östlich, Ost...

east·ward(s) östlich, nach Osten

eas·y leicht; einfach; bequem; gemächlich, gemütlich; ungezwungen; **go ~ on** schonen, sparsam umgehen mit; **go ~, take it ~** sich Zeit lassen; **take it ~!** immer mit der Ruhe!

eas·y chair Sessel *m*

eas·y-go·ing gelassen; ungezwungen

eat essen; (zer)fressen; **~ out** essen gehen; **~ up** aufessen

eat·a·ble essbar, genießbar

eat·er Esser(in)

eaves Dachrinne *f*, Traufe *f*

eaves·drop (heimlich) lauschen *or* horchen; **~ on** belauschen

ebb 1. Ebbe *f*; **2.** zurückgehen; **~ away** abnehmen; **~ tide** Ebbe *f*

eb·o·ny Ebenholz *n*

ec ABBR *of* **Eurocheque** *Br* Eurocheque *m*

ec·cen·tric 1. exzentrisch; **2.** Exzentriker *m*, Sonderling *m*

ec·cle·si·as·tic, ec·cle·si·as·ti·cal geistlich, kirchlich

echo 1. Echo *n*; **2.** widerhallen; *fig* echoen, nachsprechen

e·clipse ASTR (*Sonnen-, Mond*)Finsternis *f*; *fig* Niedergang *m*

e·co·cide Umweltzerstörung *f*

e·co·log·i·cal ökologisch, Umwelt...

e·col·o·gist Ökologe *m*

e·col·o·gy Ökologie *f*

ec·o·nom·ic Wirtschafts..., wirtschaftlich; **~ growth** Wirtschaftswachstum *n*

e·co·nom·i·cal wirtschaftlich, sparsam

e·co·nom·ics Volkswirtschaft(slehre) *f*

e·con·o·mist Volkswirt *m*

e·con·o·mize sparsam wirtschaften (mit)

e·con·o·my 1. Wirtschaft *f*; Wirtschaftlichkeit *f*, Sparsamkeit *f*; Einsparung *f*; **2.** Spar...

e·co·sys·tem Ökosystem *n*

ec·sta·sy Ekstase *f*, Verzückung *f*

ec·stat·ic verzückt

ed·dy 1. Wirbel *m*; **2.** wirbeln

edge 1. Schneide *f*; Rand *m*; Kante *f*; Schärfe *f*; **be on ~** nervös *or* gereizt sein; **2.** schärfen; (um)säumen; (sich) drängen

edge·ways, edge·wise seitlich, von der Seite

edg·ing Einfassung *f*; Rand *m*

edg·y scharf(kantig); F nervös; F gereizt

ed·i·ble essbar, genießbar

e·dict Edikt *n*

ed·i·fice Gebäude *n*

ed·it *Text* herausgeben, redigieren; EDP editieren; *Zeitung* als Herausgeber leiten; **e·di·tion** (*Buch*)Ausgabe *f*; Auflage *f*; **ed·i·tor** Herausgeber(in); Redakteur(in); **ed·i·to·ri·al 1.** Leitartikel *m*; **2.** Redaktions...

EDP ABBR *of electronic data processing* EDV, elektronische Datenverarbeitung

ed·u·cate erziehen; unterrichten

ed·u·cat·ed gebildet

ed·u·ca·tion Erziehung *f*; (Aus)Bildung *f*; Bildungs-, Schulwesen *n*; *Ministry of Education* appr Unterrichtsministerium

ed·u·ca·tion·al erzieherisch, pädagogisch, Erziehungs...; Bildungs...

ed·u·ca·tion·(al·)ist Pädagoge *m*

eel ZO Aal *m*

ef·fect (Aus)Wirkung *f*; Effekt *m*, Eindruck *m*; *pl* ECON Effekten *pl*; **be in ~** in Kraft sein; **in ~** in Wirklichkeit; *take ~* in Kraft treten; **ef·fec·tive** wirksam; eindrucksvoll; tatsächlich

ef·fem·i·nate verweichlicht; weibisch

ef·fer·vesce brausen, sprudeln

ef·fer·ves·cent sprudelnd, schäumend

ef·fi·cien·cy Leistung *f*; Leistungsfähigkeit *f*; **~ measure** ECON Rationalisierungsmaßnahme *f*; **ef·fi·cient** wirksam; leistungsfähig, tüchtig

ef·flu·ent Abwasser *n*, Abwässer *pl*

ef·fort Anstrengung *f*, Bemühung *f* (*at* um); Mühe *f*; *without ~* → **ef·fort·less** mühelos, ohne Anstrengung

ef·fron·te·ry Frechheit *f*

ef·fu·sive überschwänglich

egg¹ Ei *n*; *put all one's ~s in one basket* alles auf eine Karte setzen

egg²: *~ on* anstacheln

egg co·sy *Br* Eierwärmer *m*

egg·cup Eierbecher *m*

egg·head F Eierkopf *m*

egg·plant BOT Aubergine *f*

egg·shell Eierschale *f*

egg tim·er Eieruhr *f*

e·go·is·m Egoismus *m*, Selbstsucht *f*

e·go·ist Egoist(in)

E·gypt Ägypten *n*; **E·gyp·tian 1.** ägyptisch; **2.** Ägypter(in)

ei·der·down Eiderdaunen *pl*; Daunendecke *f*

eight 1. acht; **2.** Acht *f*

eigh·teen 1. achtzehn; **2.** Achtzehn *f*

eigh·teenth achtzehnte(r, -s)

eight·fold achtfach

eighth 1. achte(r, -s); **2.** Achtel *n*

eighth·ly achtens

eigh·ti·eth achtzigste(r, -s)

eigh·ty 1. achtzig; *the eighties* die Achtzigerjahre; **2.** Achtzig *f*

ei·ther jede(r, -s) (*von zweien*): eine(r, -s) (*von zweien*); beides; **~ ... or** entweder ... oder; *not ~* auch nicht

e·jac·u·late *v/t Samen* ausstoßen; *v/i* ejakulieren, e-n Samenerguss haben

e·jac·u·la·tion Samenerguss *m*

e·ject *j-n* hinauswerfen; TECH ausstoßen, auswerfen

eke: *~ out Vorräte etc* strecken; *Einkommen* aufbessern; *~ out a living* sich (mühsam) durchschlagen

e·lab·o·rate 1. sorgfältig (aus)gearbeitet; kompliziert; **2.** sorgfältig ausarbeiten

e·lapse verfließen, verstreichen

e·las·tic 1. elastisch, dehnbar; *~ band Br* → **2.** Gummiring *m*, Gummiband *n*

e·las·ti·ci·ty Elastizität *f*

e·lat·ed begeistert (*at, by* von)

el·bow 1. Ellbogen *m*; (scharfe) Biegung; TECH Knie *n*; *at one's ~* bei der Hand; **2.** mit dem Ellbogen (weg)stoßen; *~ one's way through* sich (mit den Ellbogen) e-n Weg bahnen durch

el·der¹ 1. ältere(r, -s); **2.** der, die Ältere; (Kirchen)Älteste(r) *m*

el·der² BOT Holunder *m*

el·der·ly ältlich, ältere(r, -s)

el·dest älteste(r, -s)

e·lect 1. gewählt; **2.** (aus-, er)wählen

e·lec·tion Wahl *f*; *~ vic·to·ry* POL Wahlsieg *m*; *~ win·ner* POL Wahlsieger *m*

e·lec·tor Wähler(in); POL Wahlmann *m*; HIST Kurfürst *m*; **e·lec·to·ral** Wähler..., Wahl...; *~ college* POL Wahlmän-

ner *pl*; **~ district** POL Wahlkreis *m*;
elec·to·rate POL Wähler(schaft *f*) *pl*

e·lec·tric elektrisch, Elektro...

e·lec·tri·cal elektrisch; Elektro...; **~ en·gi·neer** Elektroingenieur *m*, Elektrotechniker *m*; **~ en·gi·neer·ing** Eletrotechnik *f*

e·lec·tric chair elektrischer Stuhl

e·lec·tri·cian Elektriker *m*

e·lec·tri·ci·ty Elektrizität *f*

e·lec·tric ra·zor Elektrorasierer *m*

e·lec·tri·fy elektrifizieren; elektrisieren (*a. fig*)

e·lec·tro·cute auf dem elektrischen Stuhl hinrichten; durch elektrischen Strom töten

e·lec·tron Elektron *n*

e·lec·tron·ic elektronisch, Elektronen...; **~ da·ta pro·cess·ing** elektronische Datenverarbeitung

e·lec·tron·ics Elektronik *f*

e·le·gance Eleganz *f*; **el·e·gant** elegant; geschmackvoll; erstklassig

e·le·ment CHEM Element *n*; Urstoff *m*; (Grund)Bestandteil *m*; *pl* Anfangsgründe *pl*, Grundlage(n *pl*) *f*; Elemente *pl*, Naturkräfte *pl*

e·le·men·tal elementar; wesentlich

e·le·men·ta·ry elementar; Anfangs...; **~ school** Grundschule *f*

e·le·phant ZO Elefant *m*

e·le·vate erhöhen; *fig* erheben

e·le·vat·ed erhöht; *fig* gehoben, erhaben

e·le·va·tion Erhebung *f*; Erhöhung *f*; Höhe *f*; Erhabenheit *f*

e·le·va·tor TECH Lift *m*, Fahrstuhl *m*, Aufzug *m*

e·lev·en **1.** elf; **2.** Elf *f*

e·leventh **1.** elfte(r, -s); **2.** Elftel *n*

elf ZO Elch *m*; Elfe *f*; Kobold *m*

e·li·cit *et.* entlocken (*from dat*); ans (Tages)Licht bringen

el·i·gi·ble infrage kommend, geeignet; annehmbar, akzeptabel

e·lim·i·nate entfernen, beseitigen; ausscheiden; **e·lim·i·na·tion** Entfernung *f*, Beseitigung *f*; Ausscheidung *f*

é·lite Elite *f*; Auslese *f*

elk ZO Elch *m*; Wapitihirsch *m*

el·lipse MATH Ellipse *f*

elm BOT Ulme *f*

e·lon·gate verlängern

e·lope (mit s-m *or* s-r Geliebten) ausreißen *or* durchbrennen

el·o·quent redegewandt, beredt

else sonst, weiter; andere(r, -s)

else·where anderswo(hin)

e·lude geschickt entgehen, ausweichen, sich entziehen (*all: dat*); *fig* nicht einfallen (*dat*)

e·lu·sive schwer fassbar

e·ma·ci·ated abgezehrt, ausgemergelt

em·a·nate ausströmen; ausgehen (**from** von); **em·a·na·tion** Ausströmen *n*; *fig* Ausstrahlung *f*

e·man·ci·pate emanzipieren

e·man·ci·pa·tion Emanzipation *f*

em·balm (ein)balsamieren

em·bank·ment (Bahn-, Straßen-) Damm *m*; (Erd)Damm *m*; Uferstraße *f*

em·bar·go ECON Embargo *n*, (Hafen-, Handels)Sperre *f*

em·bark AVIAT, MAR an Bord nehmen *or* gehen, MAR *a.* (sich) einschiffen; *Waren* verladen; **~ on** *et.* anfangen, *et.* beginnen

em·bar·rass in Verlegenheit bringen, verlegen machen, in e-e peinliche Lage bringen; **em·bar·rass·ing** unangenehm, peinlich; verfänglich

em·bar·rass·ment Verlegenheit *f*

em·bas·sy POL Botschaft *f*

em·bed (ein)betten, (ein)lagern

em·bel·lish verschönern; *fig* ausschmücken, beschönigen

em·bers Glut *f*

em·bez·zle unterschlagen

em·bez·zle·ment Unterschlagung *f*

em·bit·ter verbittern

em·blem Sinnbild *n*; Wahrzeichen *n*

em·bod·y verkörpern; enthalten

em·bo·lis·m MED Embolie *f*

em·brace **1.** (sich) umarmen; einschließen; **2.** Umarmung *f*

em·broi·der (be)sticken; *fig* ausschmücken; **em·broi·der·y** Stickerei *f*; *fig* Ausschmückung *f*

em·broil verwickeln (**in** in *acc*)

e·mend *Texte* verbessern, korrigieren

em·er·ald **1.** Smaragd *m*; **2.** smaragdgrün

e·merge auftauchen; sich herausstellen *or* ergeben

e·mer·gen·cy **1.** Not *f*, Notlage *f*, Notfall *m*, Notstand *m*; *state of* **~** POL Ausnahmezustand *m*; **2.** Not...; **~ brake** Notbremse *f*; **~ call** Notruf *m*; **~ ex·it**

Notausgang *m*; ~ **land·ing** AVIAT Notlandung *f*; ~ **num·ber** Notruf(nummer *f*) *m*; ~ **room** MED Notaufnahme *f*

em·i·grant Auswanderer *m*, *esp* POL Emigrant(in)

em·i·grate auswandern, *esp* POL emigrieren

em·i·gra·tion Auswanderung *f*, *esp* POL Emigration *f*

em·i·nence Berühmtheit *f*, Bedeutung *f*; *Eminence* REL Eminenz *f*

em·i·nent hervorragend, berühmt; bedeutend; **~ly** ganz besonders, äußerst

e·mis·sion Ausstoß *m*, Ausstrahlung *f*, Ausströmen *n*; **~-free** abgasfrei

e·mit aussenden, ausstoßen, ausstrahlen, ausströmen; von sich geben

e·mo·tion (Gemüts)Bewegung *f*, Gefühl *n*, Gefühlsregung *f*; Rührung *f*

e·mo·tion·al emotional; gefühlsmäßig; gefühlsbetont

e·mo·tion·al·ly emotional, gefühlsmäßig; ~ *disturbed* seelisch gestört

e·mo·tion·less gefühllos

e·mo·tive word PSYCH Reizwort *n*

em·pe·ror Kaiser *m*

em·pha·sis Gewicht *n*; Nachdruck *m*

em·pha·size nachdrücklich betonen

em·phat·ic nachdrücklich; deutlich; bestimmt

em·pire Reich *n*, Imperium *n*; Kaiserreich *n*

em·pir·i·cal erfahrungsgemäß

em·ploy 1. beschäftigen, anstellen; an-, verwenden, gebrauchen; 2. Beschäftigung *f*, *in the ~ of* angestellt bei;

em·ploy·ee Angestellte *m*, *f*, Arbeitnehmer(in)

em·ploy·er Arbeitgeber(in)

em·ploy·ment Beschäftigung *f*, Arbeit *f*; ~ **ad** Stellenanzeige *f*; ~ **of·fice** Arbeitsamt *n*

em·pow·er ermächtigen; befähigen

em·press Kaiserin *f*

emp·ti·ness Leere *f* (*a. fig*)

emp·ty 1. leer (*a. fig*); 2. leeren, ausleeren, entleeren; sich leeren

em·u·late wetteifern mit; nacheifern (*dat*); es gleichtun (*dat*)

e·mul·sion Emulsion *f*

en·a·ble befähigen, es *j-m* ermöglichen; ermächtigen

en·act *Gesetz* erlassen; verfügen

e·nam·el 1. Email *n*, Emaille *f*; ANAT

(Zahn)Schmelz *m*; Glasur *f*, Lack *m*; Nagellack *m*; 2. emaillieren; glasieren; lackieren

en·am·o(u)red: ~ *of* verliebt in (*acc*)

en·camp·ment *esp* MIL (Feld)Lager *n*

en·cased: ~ *in* gehüllt in (*acc*)

en·chant bezaubern; **en·chant·ing** bezaubernd; **en·chant·ment** Bezauberung *f*; Zauber *m*

en·cir·cle einkreisen, umzingeln; umfassen, umschlingen

en·close einschließen, umgeben; beilegen, beifügen

en·clo·sure Einzäunung *f*; Anlage *f*

en·code verschlüsseln, chiffrieren; kodieren

en·com·pass umgeben

en·coun·ter 1. Begegnung *f*; Gefecht *n*; 2. begegnen (*dat*); auf *Schwierigkeiten etc* stoßen; mit *j-m feindlich* zusammenstoßen

en·cour·age ermutigen; fördern

en·cour·age·ment Ermutigung *f*; Anfeuerung *f*; Unterstützung *f*

en·cour·ag·ing ermutigend

en·croach (*on*) eingreifen (in *j-s Recht etc*), eindringen (in *acc*); über Gebühr in Anspruch nehmen (*acc*)

en·croach·ment Ein-, Übergriff *m*

en·cum·ber belasten; (be)hindern

en·cum·brance Belastung *f*

en·cy·clo·p(a)e·di·a Enzyklopädie *f*

end 1. Ende *n*; Ziel *n*, Zweck *m*; *no ~ of* unendlich viel(e), unzählige; *at the ~ of May* Ende Mai; *in the ~* am Ende, schließlich; *on ~* aufrecht; *stand on ~* zu Berge stehen (*hair*); *to no ~* vergebens; *go off the deep ~* F *fig* in die Luft gehen; *make* (*both*) *~s meet* durchkommen, finanziell über die Runden kommen; 2. enden; beend(ig)en (*-ig*)en

en·dan·ger gefährden

en·dear beliebt machen (*to s.o.* bei j-m); **en·dear·ing** gewinnend; liebenswert; **en·dear·ment:** *words of ~*, *~s* zärtliche Worte *pl*

en·deav·o(u)r 1. Bestreben *n*, Bemühung *f*; 2. sich bemühen

end·ing Ende *n*; Schluss *m*; LING Endung *f*

en·dive BOT Endivie *f*

end·less endlos, unendlich; TECH ohne Ende

enter

en·dorse ECON *Scheck etc* indossieren; *et.* vermerken (**on** auf der Rückseite); billigen; **en·dorse·ment** Vermerk *m*; ECON Indossament *n*, Giro *m*

en·dow *fig* ausstatten; *~ s.o. with s.th.* j-m et. stiften; **en·dow·ment** Stiftung *f*; *mst pl* Begabung *f*, Talent *n*

en·dur·ance Ausdauer *f*; *beyond ~, past ~* unerträglich; **en·dure** ertragen

end us·er Endverbraucher *m*

en·e·my 1. Feind *m*; 2. feindlich

en·er·get·ic energisch; tatkräftig

en·er·gy Energie *f*

en·er·gy cri·sis Energiekrise *f*

en·er·gy-sav·ing energiesparend

en·er·gy sup·ply Energieversorgung *f*

en·fold einhüllen; umfassen

en·force (mit Nachdruck, *a.* gerichtlich) geltend machen; *Gesetz etc* durchführen; durchsetzen, erzwingen; **en·force·ment** ECON, JUR Geltendmachung *f*; Durchsetzung *f*, Erzwingung *f*

en·fran·chise *j-m* das Wahlrecht verleihen

en·gage *v/t j-s Aufmerksamkeit* auf sich ziehen; TECH einrasten lassen; MOT *e-n Gang* einlegen; *j-n* einstellen, anstellen, *Künstler* engagieren; *v/i* TECH einrasten, greifen; *~ in* sich einlassen auf (*acc*) *or* in (*acc*); sich beschäftigen mit

en·gaged verlobt (**to** mit); beschäftigt (**in, on** mit); besetzt (*a.* TEL); *~ tone or signal Br* TEL Besetztzeichen *n*

en·gage·ment Verlobung *f*; Verabredung *f*; MIL Gefecht *n*

en·gag·ing einnehmend; gewinnend

en·gine Maschine *f*; Motor *m*; RAIL Lokomotive *f*; *~ driv·er Br* RAIL Lokomotivführer *m*

en·gi·neer 1. Ingenieur *m*, Techniker *m*, Mechaniker *m*; RAIL Lokomotivführer *m*; MIL Pionier *m*; 2. bauen; *fig* (geschickt) in die Wege leiten

en·gi·neer·ing Technik *f*, Ingenieurwesen *n*, Maschinen- und Gerätebau *m*

En·gland England *n*

En·glish 1. englisch; 2. LING Englisch *n*; *the ~* die Engländer *pl*; *in plain ~ fig* unverblümt

Eng·lish·man Engländer *m*

Eng·lish·wom·an Engländerin *f*

en·grave (ein)gravieren, (ein)meißeln, (ein)schnitzen; *fig* einprägen

en·grav·er Graveur *m*

en·grav·ing (Kupfer-, Stahl)Stich *m*; Holzschnitt *m*

en·grossed: *~ in* (voll) in Anspruch genommen von, vertieft *or* versunken in (*acc*)

en·hance erhöhen, verstärken, steigern

e·nig·ma Rätsel *n*

e·nig·mat·ic rätselhaft

en·joy sich erfreuen an (*dat*); genießen; *did you ~ it?* hat es Ihnen gefallen?; *~ o.s.* sich amüsieren, sich gut unterhalten; *~ yourself!* viel Spaß!; *I ~ my dinner* es schmeckt mir; **en·joy·a·ble** angenehm, erfreulich; **en·joy·ment** Vergnügen *n*, Freude *f*; Genuss *m*

en·large (sich) vergrößern *or* erweitern, ausdehnen; PHOT vergrößern; sich verbreiten *or* auslassen (**on** über *acc*)

en·large·ment Erweiterung *f*; Vergrößerung *f* (*a.* PHOT)

en·light·en aufklären, belehren

en·light·en·ment Aufklärung *f*

en·list MIL *v/t* anwerben; *v/i* sich freiwillig melden; *~ed men* Unteroffiziere *pl* und Mannschaften *pl*

en·liv·en beleben

en·mi·ty Feindschaft *f*

en·no·ble adeln; veredeln

e·nor·mi·ty Ungeheuerlichkeit *f*

e·nor·mous ungeheuer

e·nough genug

en·quire, en·qui·ry → *inquire, inquiry*

en·rage wütend machen

en·raged wütend (**at** über *acc*)

en·rap·ture entzücken, hinreißen

en·rap·tured entzückt, hingerissen

en·rich bereichern; anreichern

en·rol(l) (sich) einschreiben *or* eintragen; UNIV (sich) immatrikulieren

en·sign MAR *esp* (National)Flagge *f*; MIL Leutnant *m* zur See

en·sue (darauf-, nach)folgen

en·sure sichern

en·tail mit sich bringen, zur Folge haben

en·tan·gle verwickeln

en·ter *v/t* hinein-, hereingehen, -kommen, -treten in (*acc*), eintreten, einsteigen in (*acc*), betreten; einreisen in (*acc*); MAR, RAIL einlaufen, einfahren in (*acc*); eindringen in (*acc*); *Namen etc* eintragen, einschreiben; SPORT melden, nennen (**for** für); *fig* eintreten in (*acc*), beitreten (*dat*); EDP eingeben; *v/i* eintreten, herein-, hineinkommen, herein-, hineingehen; THEA auftreten; sich einschreiben *or* anmelden (**for** für); SPORT melden, nennen (**for** für)

en·ter key EDP Eingabetaste *f*

en·ter·prise Unternehmen *n* (*a.* ECON); ECON Unternehmertum *n*; Unternehmungsgeist *m*; **en·ter·pris·ing** unternehmungslustig; wagemutig; kühn

en·ter·tain unterhalten; bewirten

en·ter·tain·er Entertainer(in), Unterhaltungskünstler(in)

en·ter·tain·ment Unterhaltung *f*; Entertainment *n*; Bewirtung *f*

en·thral(l) fesseln, bezaubern

en·throne inthronisieren

en·thu·si·asm Begeisterung *f*, Enthusiasmus *m*; **en·thu·si·ast** Enthusiast(in); **en·thu·si·as·tic** begeistert, enthusiastisch

en·tice (ver)locken

en·tice·ment Verlockung *f*, Reiz *m*

en·tire ganz, vollständig; ungeteilt

en·tire·ly völlig; ausschließlich

en·ti·tle betiteln; berechtigen (**to** zu)

en·ti·ty Einheit *f*

en·trails ANAT Eingeweide *pl*

en·trance Eintreten *n*, Eintritt *m*; Eingang *m*, Zugang *m*; Zufahrt *f*; Einlass *m*, Eintritt *m*, Zutritt *m*

en·trance / ex·am(·i·na·tion) Aufnahmeprüfung *f*; **~ fee** Eintritt *m*, Eintrittsgeld *n*; Aufnahmegebühr *f*

en·treat inständig bitten, anflehen

en·trea·ty dringende *or* inständige Bitte

en·trench MIL verschanzen (*a. fig*)

en·tre·pre·neur ECON Unternehmer(in); **en·tre·pre·neu·ri·al** ECON unternehmerisch

en·trust anvertrauen (**s.th. to s.o.** j-m et.); *j-n* betrauen (**with** mit)

en·try Eintreten *n*, Eintritt *m*; Einreise *f*; Beitritt *m*; Einlass *m*, Zutritt *m*; Zugang *m*, Eingang *m*, Einfahrt *f*; Eintrag(ung *f*) *m*; Stichwort *n*; SPORT Nennung *f*, Meldung *f*; **no ~!** Zutritt verboten!, MOT keine Einfahrt!

en·try per·mit Einreiseerlaubnis *f*, -genehmigung *f*

en·try·phone Türsprechanlage *f*

en·try vi·sa Einreisevisum *n*

en·twine ineinander schlingen

e·nu·me·rate aufzählen

en·vel·op (ein)hüllen, einwickeln

en·ve·lope Briefumschlag *m*

en·vi·a·ble beneidenswert

en·vi·ous neidisch

en·vi·ron·ment Umgebung *f, a.* Milieu *n*; Umwelt *f*; **en·vi·ron·men·tal** Milieu...; Umwelt...; **en·vi·ron·mental·ist** Umweltschützer(in)

en·vi·ron·men·tal law Umweltschutzgesetz *n*; **~ pol·lu·tion** Umweltverschmutzung *f*

en·vi·ron·ment friend·ly umweltfreundlich

en·vi·rons Umgebung *f*

en·vis·age sich *et.* vorstellen

en·voy Gesandte *m*, Gesandtin *f*

en·vy Neid *m*; **2.** beneiden

ep·ic 1. episch; **2.** Epos *n*

ep·i·dem·ic MED **1.** seuchenartig; **~ dis·ease** → **2.** Epidemie *f*, Seuche *f*

ep·i·der·mis ANAT Oberhaut *f*

ep·i·lep·sy MED Epilepsie *f*

ep·i·log, *Br* **ep·i·logue** Epilog *m*, Nachwort *n*

e·pis·co·pal REL bischöflich

ep·i·sode Episode *f*

ep·i·taph Grabinschrift *f*

e·poch Epoche *f*, Zeitalter *n*

eq·ua·ble ausgeglichen (*a.* METEOR)

e·qual 1. gleich; gleichmäßig; **~ to** *fig* gewachsen (*dat*); **~ opportunities** Chancengleichheit *f*; **~ rights for women** Gleichberechtigung *f* der Frau; **2.** Gleiche *m, f*; **3.** gleichen (*dat*)

e·qual·i·ty Gleichheit *f*

e·qual·i·za·tion Gleichstellung *f*; Ausgleich *m*; **e·qual·ize** gleichmachen, gleichstellen, angleichen; SPORT ausgleichen; **e·qual·iz·er** SPORT Ausgleich *m*, Ausgleichstor *n*, -treffer *m*

eq·ua·nim·i·ty Gleichmut *m*

e·qua·tion MATH Gleichung *f*

e·qua·tor Äquator *m*

e·qui·lib·ri·um Gleichgewicht *n*

e·quip ausrüsten

e·quip·ment Ausrüstung *f*, Ausstattung *f*; TECH Einrichtung *f*; *fig* Rüstzeug *n*

e·quiv·a·lent 1. gleichwertig, äquivalent; gleichbedeutend (**to** mit); **2.** Äquivalent *n*, Gegenwert *m*

e·ra Zeitrechnung *f*; Zeitalter *n*

e·rad·i·cate ausrotten

e·rase ausradieren, ausstreichen, löschen (*a.* EDP); *fig* auslöschen

e·ras·er Radiergummi *m*

e·rect 1. aufrecht; **2.** aufrichten; *Denkmal etc* errichten; aufstellen

e·rec·tion Errichtung *f*; MED Erektion *f*

er·mine zo Hermelin *n*

e·rode GEOL erodieren

e·ro·sion GEOL Erosion *f*

e·rot·ic erotisch

err (sich) irren

er·rand Botengang *m*, Besorgung *f*; *go on an ~, run an ~* e-e Besorgung machen; *~ boy* Laufbursche *m*

er·rat·ic sprunghaft, unstet, unberechenbar

er·ro·ne·ous irrig

er·ror Irrtum *m*, Fehler *m* (*a.* EDP); *in ~* irrtümlicherweise; *~ of judg(e)ment* Fehleinschätzung *f*; *~s excepted* ECON Irrtümer vorbehalten; *~ mes·sage* EDP Fehlermeldung *f*

e·rupt ausbrechen (*volcano etc*); durchbrechen (*teeth*); **e·rup·tion** (*Vulkan-*) Ausbruch *m*; MED Ausschlag *m*

ESA ABBR *of* **European Space Agency** Europäische Weltraumbehörde

es·ca·late eskalieren; ECON steigen, in die Höhe gehen

es·ca·la·tion Eskalation *f*

es·ca·la·tor Rolltreppe *f*

es·ca·lope GASTR (*esp* Wiener) Schnitzel *n*

es·cape 1. entgehen (*dat*); entkommen, entrinnen (*both dat*); entweichen; *j-m* entfallen; **2.** Entrinnen *n*; Entweichen *n*, Flucht *f*; *have a narrow ~* mit knapper Not davonkommen

es·cape chute AVIAT Notrutsche *f*

es·cape key EDP Escape-Taste *f*

es·cort 1. MIL Eskorte *f*; Geleit(schutz *m*) *n*; **2.** MIL eskortieren; AVIAT, MAR Geleit(schutz) geben; geleiten

es·cutch·eon Wappenschild *m, n*

es·pe·cial besondere(r, -s);

es·pe·cial·ly besonders

es·pi·o·nage Spionage *f*

es·pla·nade (*esp* Strand)Promenade *f*

es·say Aufsatz *m*, kurze Abhandlung, Essay *m, n*

es·sence Wesen *n*; Essenz *f*; Extrakt *m*

es·sen·tial 1. wesentlich; unentbehrlich; **2.** *mst pl das* Wesentliche

es·sen·tial·ly im Wesentlichen, in der Hauptsache

es·tab·lish einrichten, errichten; *~ o.s.* sich etablieren *or* niederlassen; beweisen, nachweisen; **es·tab·lish·ment** Einrichtung *f*, Errichtung *f*; ECON Unternehmen *n*, Firma *f*; *the Establishment* das Establishment, die etablierte Macht, die herrschende Schicht

es·tate (großes) Grundstück, Landsitz *m*, Gut *n*; JUR Besitz *m*, (Erb)Masse *f*, Nachlass *m*; *housing ~* (Wohn)Siedlung *f*; *industrial ~* Industriegebiet *n*; *real ~* Liegenschaften *pl*; *~ agent Br* Grundstücks-, Immobilienmakler *m*; *~ car Br* MOT Kombiwagen *m*

es·teem 1. Achtung *f*, Ansehen *n* (*with* bei); **2.** achten, (hoch) schätzen

es·thet·ic ästhetisch

es·thet·ics Ästhetik *f*

es·ti·mate 1. (ab-, ein)schätzen; veranschlagen; **2.** Schätzung *f*, (Kosten)Voranschlag *m*; **es·ti·ma·tion** Meinung *f*; Achtung *f*, Wertschätzung *f*

es·tranged entfremdet

es·trange·ment Entfremdung *f*

es·tu·a·ry weite Flussmündung

etch ätzen; radieren

etch·ing Radierung *f*; Kupferstich *m*

e·ter·nal ewig

e·ter·ni·ty Ewigkeit *f*

e·ther Äther *m*

e·the·re·al ätherisch (*a. fig*)

eth·i·cal sittlich, ethisch

eth·ics Sittenlehre *f*, Ethik *f*

eu·ro Euro *m*

Eu·ro·cheque *Br* Eurocheque *m*

Eu·rope Europa *n*

Eu·ro·pe·an 1. europäisch; **2.** Europäer (in); *~ Com·mu·ni·ty* (ABBR *EC*) Europäische Gemeinschaft (ABBR EG)

e·vac·u·ate entleeren; evakuieren; *Haus etc* räumen

e·vade (geschickt) ausweichen (*dat*); umgehen

e·val·u·ate schätzen; abschätzen, bewerten, beurteilen

e·vap·o·rate verdunsten, verdampfen (lassen); *~d milk* Kondensmilch *f*

e·vap·o·ra·tion Verdunstung *f*, Verdampfung *f*

e·va·sion Umgehung *f*, Vermeidung *f*; (*Steuer*)Hinterziehung *f*; Ausflucht *f*

e·va·sive ausweichend; *be ~* ausweichen

eve Vorabend *m*; Vortag *m*; *on the ~ of*

unmittelbar vor (*dat*), am Vorabend (*gen*)

e·ven 1. *adj* eben, gleich; gleichmäßig; ausgeglichen; glatt; gerade (*Zahl*); **get ~ with s.o.** es j-m heimzahlen; **2.** *adv* selbst, sogar, auch; **not ~** nicht einmal; **~ though, ~ if** wenn auch; **3. ~ out** sich einpendeln; sich ausgleichen

eve·ning Abend *m*; **in the ~** am Abend, abends; **~ class·es** Abendkurs *m*, Abendunterricht *m*; **~ dress** Gesellschaftsanzug *m*; Frack *m*, Smoking *m*; Abendkleid *n*

e·ven·song REL Abendgottesdienst *m*

e·vent Ereignis *n*; Fall *m*; SPORT Disziplin *f*; SPORT Wettbewerb *m*; **at all ~s** auf alle Fälle; **in the ~ of** im Falle (*gen*)

e·vent·ful ereignisreich

ev·er·tu·al·(·ly) schließlich

ev·er immer (wieder); je(mals); **~ after, ~ since** seitdem; **~ so** F sehr, noch so; **for ~** für immer, auf ewig; **Yours ~, ...,** **Every ours, ...** Viele Grüße, dein(e) or Ihr(e), ...; **have you ~ been to Boston?** bist du schon einmal in Boston gewesen?

ev·er·green 1. immergrün; unverwüstlich, *esp* immer wieder gern gehört; **2.** immergrüne Pflanze; MUS Evergreen *m*, *n*

ev·er·last·ing ewig

ev·er·more: **(for) ~** für immer

ev·ery jede(r, -s); alle(r, -s); **~ now and then** von Zeit zu Zeit, dann und wann; **~ one of them** jeder von ihnen; **~ other day** jeden zweiten Tag, alle zwei Tage

ev·ery·bod·y jeder(mann)

ev·ery·day Alltags...

ev·ery·one jeder(mann)

ev·ery·thing alles

ev·ery·where überall(hin)

e·vict JUR zur Räumung zwingen; *j-n* gewaltsam vertreiben

ev·i·dence Beweis(material *n*) *m*, Beweise *pl*; (Zeugen)Aussage *f*; **give ~** (als Zeuge) aussagen; **ev·i·dent** augenscheinlich, offensichtlich

e·vil 1. übel, schlimm, böse; **2.** Übel *n*; das Böse; **e·vil-mind·ed** bösartig

e·voke (herauf)beschwören; *Erinnerungen* wachrufen

ev·o·lu·tion Entwicklung *f*; BIOL Evolution *f*

e·volve (sich) entwickeln

ewe ZO Mutterschaf *n*

ex *prp* ECON ab; **~ works** ab Werk

ex... Ex..., ehemalig

ex·act 1. exakt, genau; **2.** fordern, verlangen; **ex·act·ing** streng, genau; aufreibend, anstrengend; **ex·act·ly** exakt, genau; **~! ganz recht!**, genau!

ex·act·ness Genauigkeit *f*

ex·ag·ge·rate übertreiben

ex·ag·ge·ra·tion Übertreibung *f*

ex·am F Examen *n*

ex·am·i·na·tion Examen *n*, Prüfung *f*; Untersuchung *f*, JUR Vernehmung *f*, Verhör *n*; **ex·am·ine** untersuchen; JUR vernehmen, verhören; JUR PED *etc* prüfen (**in** in *dat*; **on** über *acc*)

ex·am·ple Beispiel *n*; Vorbild *n*, Muster *n*; **for ~** zum Beispiel

ex·as·pe·rate wütend machen

ex·as·pe·rat·ing ärgerlich

ex·ca·vate ausgraben, ausheben, ausschachten

ex·ceed überschreiten; übertreffen

ex·ceed·ing übermäßig

ex·ceed·ing·ly außerordentlich, überaus

ex·cel *v/t* übertreffen; *v/i* sich auszeichnen

ex·cel·lence ausgezeichnete Qualität

Ex·cel·len·cy Exzellenz *f*

ex·cel·lent ausgezeichnet, hervorragend

ex·cept 1. ausnehmen, ausschließen; **2.** *prp* ausgenommen, außer; **~ for** abgesehen von, bis auf (*acc*)

ex·cept·ing *prp* ausgenommen

ex·cep·tion Ausnahme *f*; Einwand *m* (**to** gegen); **make an ~** e-e Ausnahme machen; **take ~ to** Anstoß nehmen an (*dat*); **without ~** ohne Ausnahme, ausnahmslos; **ex·cep·tion·al** außergewöhnlich; **ex·cep·tion·al·ly** ungewöhnlich, außergewöhnlich

ex·cerpt Auszug *m*

ex·cess 1. Übermaß *n*; Überschuss *m*; Ausschweifung *f*; **2.** Mehr...; **~ baggage** AVIAT Übergepäck *n*; **~ fare** (Fahrpreis)Zuschlag *m*

ex·ces·sive übermäßig, übertrieben

ex·cess| lug·gage → excess baggage; **~ post·age** Nachgebühr *f*

ex·change 1. (aus-, ein-, um)tauschen (**for** gegen); wechseln; **2.** (Aus-, Um-) Tausch *m*; (*esp* Geld)Wechsel *m*; ECON *a.* **bill of ~** Wechsel *m;* Börse *f;* Wechselstube *f;* TEL Fernsprechamt *n;* ECON **foreign ~(s)** Devisen *pl;* **rate of ~** → **exchange rate; ~ of·fice** Wechselstube *f;* **~ rate** Wechselkurs *m;* **~ student** Austauschschüler(in), Austauschstudent(in)

Ex·cheq·uer: Chancellor of the ~ *Br* Finanzminister *m*

ex·cise Verbrauchssteuer *f*

ex·ci·ta·ble reizbar, (leicht) erregbar

ex·cite erregen, anregen; reizen

ex·cit·ed erregt, aufgeregt

ex·cite·ment Aufregung *f,* Erregung *f*

ex·cit·ing erregend, aufregend, spannend

ex·claim (aus)rufen

ex·cla·ma·tion Ausruf *m,* (Auf)Schrei *m;* **~ mark** *Br,* **~ point** Ausrufe-, Ausrufungszeichen *n*

ex·clude ausschließen

ex·clu·sion Ausschließung *f,* Ausschluss *m;* **ex·clu·sive** ausschließlich; exklusiv; Exklusiv...; **~ of** abgesehen von, ohne

ex·com·mu·ni·cate REL exkommunizieren; **ex·com·mu·ni·ca·tion** REL Exkommunikation *f*

ex·cre·ment Kot *m*

ex·crete MED ausscheiden

ex·cur·sion Ausflug *m*

ex·cu·sa·ble entschuldbar

ex·cuse 1. entschuldigen; **~ me** entschuldige(n Sie); **2.** Entschuldigung *f*

ex·di·rec·to·ry num·ber *Br* TEL Geheimnummer *f*

ex·e·cute ausführen; vollziehen; MUS vortragen; hinrichten; JUR *Testament* vollstrecken; **ex·e·cu·tion** Ausführung *f,* Vollziehung *f,* JUR (Zwangs-) Vollstreckung *f,* Hinrichtung *f,* MUS Vortrag *m;* **put** *or* **carry a plan into ~** e-n Plan ausführen *or* verwirklichen

ex·e·cu·tion·er JUR Henker *m,* Scharfrichter *m*

ex·ec·u·tive 1. vollziehend, ausübend, POL Exekutiv...; ECON leitend; **2.** POL Exekutive *f,* vollziehende Gewalt; ECON *der, die* leitende Angestellte

ex·em·pla·ry vorbildlich

ex·em·pli·fy veranschaulichen

ex·empt 1. befreit, frei; **2.** ausnehmen, befreien

ex·er·cise 1. Übung *f;* Ausübung *f;* PED Übung(sarbeit) *f,* Schulaufgabe *f;* MIL Manöver *n;* (körperliche) Bewegung *f;* **do one's ~s** Gymnastik machen; **take ~** sich Bewegung machen; **2.** üben; ausüben; (sich) bewegen; sich Bewegung machen; MIL exerzieren

ex·er·cise book Schul-, Schreibheft *n*

ex·ert *Einfluss etc* ausüben; **~ o.s.** sich anstrengen *or* bemühen; **ex·er·tion** Ausübung *f,* Anstrengung *f,* Strapaze *f*

ex·hale ausatmen; *Gas, Geruch etc* verströmen; *Rauch* ausstoßen

ex·haust 1. erschöpfen; *Vorräte* ver-, aufbrauchen; **2.** TECH Auspuff *m; a.* **~ fumes** TECH Auspuff-, Abgase *pl*

ex·haust·ed erschöpft, aufgebraucht (*supplies*), vergriffen (*book*)

ex·haus·tion Erschöpfung *f*

ex·haus·tive erschöpfend

ex·haust pipe TECH Auspuffrohr *n*

ex·hib·it 1. ausstellen; vorzeigen; *fig* zeigen, zur Schau stellen; **2.** Ausstellungsstück *n;* JUR Beweisstück *n*

ex·hi·bi·tion Ausstellung *f;* Zurschaustellung *f*

ex·hil·a·rat·ing erregend, berauschend

ex·hort ermahnen

ex·ile 1. Exil *n;* im Exil Lebende *m, f,* **2.** ins Exil schicken

ex·ist existieren; vorhanden sein; leben; bestehen; **ex·ist·ence** Existenz *f;* Vorhandensein *n,* Vorkommen *n;* Leben *n,* Dasein *n;* **ex·ist·ent** vorhanden

ex·it 1. Abgang *m;* Ausgang *m;* (Autobahn)Ausfahrt *f;* Ausreise *f;* **2.** *v/i* verlassen; EDP (das Programm) beenden; **~ Macbeth** THEA Macbeth (geht) ab

ex·o·dus Auszug *m;* Abwanderung *f;* **general ~** allgemeiner Aufbruch

ex·on·e·rate entlasten, entbinden, befreien

ex·or·bi·tant übertrieben, maßlos; unverschämt (*price etc*)

ex·or·cize *böse Geister* beschwören, austreiben (**from** aus); befreien (**of** von)

ex·ot·ic exotisch; fremd(artig)

ex·pand ausbreiten; (sich) ausdehnen *or* erweitern; ECON *a.* expandieren

ex·panse weite Fläche, Weite *f*

ex·pan·sion Ausbreitung *f;* Ausdehnung *f,* Erweiterung *f*

ex·pan·sive mitteilsam

E

expatriate

ex·pat·ri·ate *j-n* ausbürgern, *j-m* die Staatsangehörigkeit aberkennen

ex·pect erwarten; F annehmen; *be ~ing* in anderen Umständen sein

ex·pec·tant erwartungsvoll; *~ mother* werdende Mutter

ex·pec·ta·tion Erwartung *f*; Hoffnung *f*, Aussicht *f*

ex·pe·di·ent 1. zweckdienlich, zweckmäßig; ratsam; **2.** (Hilfs)Mittel *n*, (Not)Behelf *m*

ex·pe·di·tion Expedition *f*, (Forschungs)Reise *f*

ex·pe·di·tious schnell

ex·pel (*from*) vertreiben (aus); ausweisen (aus); ausschließen (von, aus)

ex·pen·di·ture Ausgaben *pl*, (Kosten-)Aufwand *m*

ex·pense Ausgaben *pl*; *pl* ECON Unkosten *pl*, Spesen *pl*, Auslagen *pl*; *at the ~ of* auf Kosten (*gen*)

ex·pen·sive kostspielig, teuer

ex·pe·ri·ence 1. Erfahrung *f*; (Lebens)Praxis *f*; Erlebnis *n*; **2.** erfahren, erleben; **ex·pe·ri·enced** erfahren

ex·per·i·ment 1. Versuch *m*; *~ with animals* MED Tierversuch *m*; **2.** experimentieren; **ex·per·i·men·tal** Versuchs...

ex·pert 1. erfahren, geschickt; fachmännisch; **2.** Fachmann *m*; Sachverständige *m, f*

ex·pi·ra·tion Ablauf *m*, Ende *n*; Verfall *m*

ex·pire ablaufen, erlöschen; verfallen

ex·plain erklären

ex·pla·na·tion Erklärung *f*

ex·pli·cit ausdrücklich; ausführlich; offen, deutlich; (*sexually*) *~* freizügig (*film etc*)

ex·plode *v/t* zur Explosion bringen; *v/i* explodieren; *fig* ausbrechen (*with in acc*), platzen (*with* vor); *fig* sprunghaft ansteigen

ex·ploit 1. (Helden)Tat *f*; **2.** ausbeuten; *fig* ausnutzen

ex·ploi·ta·tion Ausbeutung *f*, Auswertung *f*, Verwertung *f*, Abbau *m*

ex·plo·ra·tion Erforschung *f*

ex·plore erforschen

ex·plor·er Forscher(in); Forschungsreisende *m, f*

ex·plo·sion Explosion *f*; *fig* Ausbruch *m*; *fig* sprunghafter Anstieg

ex·plo·sive 1. explosiv; *fig* aufbrausend; *fig* sprunghaft ansteigend; **2.** Sprengstoff *m*

ex·po·nent MATH Exponent *m*, Hochzahl *f*; Vertreter(in), Verfechter(in)

ex·port ECON **1.** exportieren, ausführen; **2.** Export *m*, Ausfuhr *f*; *mst pl* Export-, Ausfuhrartikel *m*

ex·por·ta·tion ECON Ausfuhr *f*

ex·port·er ECON Exporteur *m*

ex·pose aussetzen; PHOT belichten; *Waren* ausstellen; *j-n* entlarven, bloßstellen, *et.* aufdecken

ex·po·si·tion Ausstellung *f*

ex·po·sure Aussetzen *n*, Ausgesetztsein *n* (*to dat*); *fig* Bloßstellung *f*, Aufdeckung *f*, Enthüllung *f*, Entlarvung *f*; PHOT Belichtung *f*; PHOT Aufnahme *f*; *die of ~* an Unterkühlung sterben; *~ me·ter* PHOT Belichtungsmesser *m*

ex·press 1. ausdrücklich, deutlich; Express..., Eil...; **2.** Eilbote *m*; Schnellzug *m*; *by ~* → **3.** *adv* durch Eilboten; als Eilgut; **4.** äußern, ausdrücken

ex·pres·sion Ausdruck *m*

ex·pres·sion·less ausdruckslos

ex·pres·sive ausdrucksvoll; *be ~ of et.* ausdrücken

ex·press let·ter *Br* Eilbrief *m*

ex·press·ly ausdrücklich, eigens

ex·press train Schnellzug *m*

ex·press·way Schnellstraße *f*

ex·pro·pri·ate JUR enteignen

ex·pul·sion (*from*) Vertreibung *f* (aus); Ausweisung *f* (aus)

ex·pur·gate reinigen

ex·qui·site erlesen; fein

ex·tant noch vorhanden

ex·tem·po·re aus dem Stegreif

ex·tem·po·rize aus dem Stegreif sprechen *or* spielen

ex·tend (aus)dehnen, (aus)weiten; *Hand etc* ausstrecken; *Betrieb etc* vergrößern, ausbauen; *Frist, Pass etc* verlängern; sich ausdehnen *or* erstrecken

ex·tend·ed fam·i·ly Großfamilie *f*

ex·ten·sion Ausdehnung *f*, Vergrößerung *f*, Erweiterung *f*; (Frist)Verlängerung *f*; ARCH Erweiterung *f*, Anbau *m*; TEL Nebenanschluss *m*, (-)Apparat *m*; *a. ~ cord* (*Br* **lead**) ELECTR Verlängerungskabel *n*, -schnur *f*

ex·ten·sive ausgedehnt, umfassend

ex·tent Ausdehnung *f*; Umfang *m*,

(Aus)**Maß** n, Grad m; **to some ~, to a certain ~** bis zu e-m gewissen Grade; **to such an ~ that** so sehr, dass

ex·ten·u·ate abschwächen, mildern; beschönigen; **extenuating circumstances** JUR mildernde Umstände pl

ex·te·ri·or 1. äußerlich, äußere(r, -s), Außen...; **2.** das Äußere; Außenseite f; äußere Erscheinung

ex·ter·mi·nate ausrotten (a. fig), vernichten, Ungeziefer, Unkraut a. vertilgen

ex·ter·nal äußere(r, -s), äußerlich, Außen...

ex·tinct erloschen; ausgestorben

ex·tinc·tion Erlöschen n; Aussterben n, Untergang m; Vernichtung f, Zerstörung f

ex·tin·guish (aus)löschen; vernichten

ex·tin·guish·er (Feuer)Löscher m

ex·tort erpressen (**from** von)

ex·tra 1. adj zusätzlich, Extra..., Sonder...; **be ~** gesondert berechnet werden; **2.** adv extra, besonders; **charge ~ for** et. gesondert berechnen; **3.** Sonderleistung f; esp MOT Extra n; Zuschlag m; Extrablatt n; THEA, film: Statist(in)

ex·tract 1. Auszug m; **2.** (heraus)ziehen; herauslocken; ableiten, herleiten

ex·trac·tion (Heraus)Ziehen n; Herkunft f

ex·tra·dite ausliefern; j-s Auslieferung erwirken;

ex·tra·di·tion Auslieferung f

extra·or·di·na·ry außerordentlich; ungewöhnlich; Sonder...

ex·tra pay Zulage f

ex·tra·ter·res·tri·al außerirdisch

ex·tra time SPORT (Spiel)Verlängerung f

ex·trav·a·gance Übertriebenheit f; Verschwendung f; Extravaganz f

ex·trav·a·gant übertrieben, über-

spannt; verschwenderisch; extravagant

ex·treme 1. äußerste(r, -s), größte(r, -s), höchste(r, -s); außergewöhnlich; **~ right** POL rechtsextrem(istisch); **~ right wing** POL rechtsradikal; **2.** das Äußerste; Extrem n; höchster Grad

ex·treme·ly äußerst, höchst

ex·trem·ism POL Extremismus m

ex·trem·ist POL Extremist(in)

ex·trem·i·ties Gliedmaßen pl, Extremitäten pl

ex·trem·i·ty das Äußerste; höchste Not; äußerste Maßnahme

ex·tri·cate herauswinden, herausziehen, befreien

ex·tro·vert Extrovertierte m, f

ex·u·be·rance Fülle f; Überschwang m;

ex·u·be·rant reichlich, üppig; überschwänglich; ausgelassen

ex·ult frohlocken, jubeln

eye 1. ANAT Auge n; Blick m; Öhr n; Öse f; **see ~ to ~ with s.o.** mit j-m völlig übereinstimmen; **be up to the ~s in work** bis über die Ohren in Arbeit stecken; **with an ~ to s.th.** im Hinblick auf et.; **2.** ansehen; mustern

eye·ball ANAT Augapfel m

eye·brow ANAT Augenbraue f

eye·catch·ing ins Auge fallend, auffallend

eye doc·tor F Augenarzt m, -ärztin f

eye·glass·es a. **pair of ~** Brille f

eye·lash ANAT Augenwimper f

eye·lid ANAT Augenlid n

eye·lin·er Eyeliner m

eye·o·pen·er: that was an ~ to me das hat mir die Augen geöffnet

eye shad·ow Lidschatten m

eye·sight Augen(licht n) pl, Sehkraft f

eye·sore F Schandfleck m

eye spe·cial·ist Augenarzt m, -ärztin f

eye·strain Ermüdung f or Überanstrengung f der Augen

eye·wit·ness Augenzeuge m, -zeugin f

E

F

F, f F, f *n*

fa·ble Fabel *f*; Sage *f*

fab·ric Gewebe *n*, Stoff *m*; Struktur *f*

fab·ri·cate fabrizieren (*mst fig*)

fab·u·lous sagenhaft, der Sage angehörend; fabelhaft

fa·cade, **fa·çade** ARCH Fassade *f*

face 1. Gesicht *n*; Gesichtsausdruck *m*, Miene *f*; (Ober)Fläche *f*; Vorderseite *f*; Zifferblatt *n*; **~ to ~** Auge in Auge mit; **save (lose) one's ~** das Gesicht wahren (verlieren); **on the ~ of it** auf den ersten Blick; **pull a long ~** ein langes Gesicht machen; **have the ~ to do s.th.** die Stirn haben, et. zu tun; **2.** *v/t* ansehen; gegenüberstehen (*dat*); (hinaus)gehen auf (*acc*); die Stirn bieten (*dat*); einfassen; ARCH bekleiden; *v/i*: **~ about** sich umdrehen

face·cloth, *Br* **face flan·nel** Waschlappen *m*

face·lift Facelifting *n*, Gesichtsstraffung *f*; *fig* Renovierung *f*, Verschönerung *f*

fa·ce·tious witzig

fa·cial 1. Gesichts...; **2.** Gesichtsbehandlung *f*

fa·cile leicht; oberflächlich

fa·cil·i·tate erleichtern

fa·cil·i·ty Leichtigkeit *f*; Oberflächlichkeit *f*, *mst pl* Erleichterung(en *pl*) *f*; Einrichtung(en *pl*) *f*, Anlage(n *pl*) *f*

fac·ing TECH Verkleidung *f*; *pl* Besatz *m*

fact Tatsache *f*, Wirklichkeit *f*, Wahrheit *f*; Tat *f*, *pl* Daten *pl*; **in ~** in der Tat, tatsächlich

fac·tion *esp* POL Splittergruppe *f*; Zwietracht *f*

fac·ti·tious künstlich

fac·tor Faktor *m*

fac·to·ry Fabrik *f*

fac·ul·ty Fähigkeit *f*; Kraft *f*; *fig* Gabe *f*; UNIV Fakultät *f*; Lehrkörper *m*

fad Mode *f*, Modeerscheinung *f*, -torheit *f*; (vorübergehende) Laune

fade (ver)welken (lassen); verschießen, verblassen (*color*); schwinden; immer schwächer werden (*person*); *film*, *radio*, TV **~ in** auf- *or* eingeblendet werden; auf- *or* einblenden; **~ out** aus- *or* abgeblendet werden; aus- *or* abblen-

den; **~d jeans** ausgewaschene Jeans *pl*

fail 1. *v/i* versagen; misslingen, fehlschlagen; versiegen; nachlassen; durchfallen (*candidate*); *v/t* im Stich lassen; j-n in e-r Prüfung durchfallen lassen; **2. without ~** mit Sicherheit, ganz bestimmt; **fail·ure** Versagen *n*; Fehlschlag *m*, Misserfolg *m*; Versäumnis *n*; Versager *m*, F Niete *f*

faint 1. schwach, matt; **2.** ohnmächtig werden, in Ohnmacht fallen (**with** vor); **3.** Ohnmacht *f*

faint-heart·ed verzagt

fair¹ gerecht, ehrlich, anständig, fair; recht gut, ansehnlich; schön (*weather*); klar (*sky*); blond (*hair*); hell (*skin*); **play ~** fair spielen; *fig* sich an die Spielregeln halten

fair² (Jahr)Markt *m*; Volksfest *n*; Ausstellung *f*, Messe *f*

fair game *fig* Freiwild *n*

fair-ground Rummelplatz *m*

fair·ly gerecht; ziemlich

fair·ness Gerechtigkeit *f*, Fairness *f*

fair play SPORT *and fig* Fair Play *n*, Fairness *f*

fai·ry Fee *f*; Zauberin *f*; Elf *m*, Elfe *f*

fai·ry·land Feen-, Märchenland *n*

fai·ry| sto·ry, **~ tale** Märchen *n* (*a. fig*)

faith Glaube *m*; Vertrauen *n*; **faith·ful** treu (**to** *dat*); **Yours ~ly** Hochachtungsvoll (*letter*); **faith·less** treulos

fake 1. Schwindel *m*; Fälschung *f*; Schwindler *m*; **2.** fälschen; imitieren, nachmachen; vortäuschen, simulieren; **3.** gefälscht; fingiert

fal·con ZO Falke *m*

fall 1. Fallen *n*, Fall *m*; Sturz *m*; Verfall *m*; Einsturz *m*; Herbst *m*, ECON Sinken *n* (*of prices etc*); Gefälle *n*; *mst pl* Wasserfall *m*; **2.** fallen, stürzen; ab-, einfallen; sinken; sich legen (*wind*); **in e-n Zustand verfallen; ~ ill, ~ sick** krank werden; **~ in love with** sich verlieben in (*acc*); **~ short of** den Erwartungen *etc* nicht entsprechen; **~ back** zurückweichen; **~ back on** *fig* zurückgreifen auf (*acc*); **~ for** hereinfallen auf (*acc*); F sich in j-n verknallen; **~ off** zurückgehen (*business*, *demand etc*), nachlassen; **~ on** herfallen über (acc); **~ out** sich streiten (**with** mit); **~ through** durchfallen (a. fig); **~ to** reinhauen, tüchtig zugreifen

fal·la·cious trügerisch

fal·la·cy Trugschluss m

fall guy F der Lackierte, der Dumme

fal·li·ble fehlbar

fall·ing star Sternschnuppe f

fall·out Fall-out m, radioaktiver Niederschlag

fal·low ZO falb; AGR brach(liegend)

false falsch

false·hood, false·ness Falschheit f; Unwahrheit f

false start Fehlstart m

fal·si·fi·ca·tion (Ver)Fälschung f

fal·si·fy (ver)fälschen

fal·si·ty Falschheit f, Unwahrheit f

fal·ter schwanken; stocken (voice); stammeln; fig zaudern

fame Ruf m, Ruhm m

famed berühmt (**for** wegen)

fa·mil·i·ar 1. vertraut; gewohnt; familiär; 2. Vertraute m, f

fa·mil·i·ar·i·ty Vertrautheit f; (plumpe) Vertraulichkeit f

fa·mil·i·ar·ize vertraut machen

fam·i·ly 1. Familie f; 2. Familien..., Haus...; **be in the ~ way** F in anderen Umständen sein; **~ al·low·ance** / **child benefit**; **~ doc·tor** Hausarzt m; **~ name** Familien-, Nachname m; **~ plan·ning** Familienplanung f; **~ tree** Stammbaum m

fam·ine Hungersnot f; Knappheit f (**of** an dat)

fam·ished verhungert; **be ~** F am Verhungern sein

fa·mous berühmt

fan¹ 1. Fächer m; Ventilator m; 2. (zu-)fächeln; anfachen; fig entfachen

fan² (Sport- etc)Fan m

fa·nat·ic Fanatiker(in)

fa·nat·i·cal fanatisch

fan belt TECH Keilriemen m

fan·ci·er BOT, ZO Liebhaber(in), Züchter(in)

fan·ci·ful fantastisch

fan club Fanklub m

fan·cy 1. Fantasie f; Einbildung f; plötzlicher Einfall, Idee f; Laune f; Vorliebe f, Neigung f; 2. ausgefallen; Fantasie...; 3. sich vorstellen; sich einbilden; ~

that! stell dir vor!, denk nur!; sieh mal einer an!

fan·cy| ball Kostümfest n, Maskenball m; **~ dress** (Masken)Kostüm n

fan·cy-free → footloose

fan·cy goods Modeartikel pl, -waren pl

fan mail Fanpost f, Verehrerpost f

fan·tas·tic fantastisch

fan·ta·sy Fantasie f

far 1. adj fern, entfernt, weit; 2. adv fern; weit; (sehr) viel; **as ~ as** bis; **in so ~ as** insofern als

far·a·way weit entfernt

fare Fahrgeld n; Fahrgast m; Verpflegung f, Kost f; 2. gut leben; **he ~d well** es (er)ging ihm gut

fare dodg·er Schwarzfahrer(in)

fare·well 1. int lebe(n Sie) wohl!; 2. Abschied m, Lebewohl n

far-fetched fig weit hergeholt, gesucht

farm 1. Bauernhof m, Gut n, Gehöft n, Farm f; 2. Land, Hof bewirtschaften

farm·er Bauer m, Landwirt m, Farmer m

farm·hand Landarbeiter(in)

farm·house Bauernhaus n

farm·ing 1. Acker..., landwirtschaftlich; 2. Landwirtschaft f

farm·stead Bauernhof m, Gehöft n

farm·yard Wirtschaftshof m

far-off entfernt, fern

far right POL rechtsgerichtet

far·sight·ed weitsichtig, fig a. weitblickend

fas·ci·nate faszinieren

fas·ci·nat·ing faszinierend

fas·ci·na·tion Zauber m, Reiz m, Faszination f

fas·cism POL Faschismus m

fas·cist POL 1. Faschist m; 2. faschistisch

fash·ion Mode f; Art f und Weise f; **be in ~** in Mode sein; **out of ~** unmodern; 2. formen, gestalten; **fash·ion·a·ble** modisch, elegant; in Mode

fash·ion| pa·rade, ~ show Mode(n)-schau f

fast¹ 1. Fasten n; 2. fasten

fast² schnell; fest; treu; echt, beständig (color); flott; **be ~** vorgehen (watch)

fast·back MOT (Wagen m mit) Fließheck n

fast breed·er (re·ac·tor) PHYS schneller Brüter

fas·ten befestigen, festmachen, anheften, anschnallen, anbinden, zuknöpfen, zu-, verschnüren; *Blick etc* richten (**on** auf *acc*); sich festmachen *or* schließen lassen; **fas·ten·er** Verschluss *m*

fast food Schnellgericht(e *pl*) *n*

fast-food res·tau·rant Schnellimbiss *m*, Schnellgaststätte *f*

fas·tid·i·ous anspruchsvoll, heikel, wählerisch, verwöhnt

fast lane MOT Überholspur *f*

fat 1. dick; fett; fettig, fetthaltig; **2.** Fett *n*; *be low in ~* fettarm sein

fa·tal tödlich; verhängnisvoll, fatal (**to** für); **fa·tal·i·ty** Verhängnis *n*; tödlicher Unfall; (Todes)Opfer *n*

fate Schicksal *n*; Verhängnis *n*

fa·ther Vater *m*

Fa·ther Christ·mas *esp Br* der Weihnachtsmann, der Nikolaus

fa·ther·hood Vaterschaft *f*

fa·ther-in-law Schwiegervater *m*

fa·ther·less vaterlos

fa·ther·ly väterlich

fath·om 1. MAR Faden *m*; **2.** MAR loten; *fig* ergründen

fath·om·less unergründlich

fa·tigue 1. Ermüdung *f*; Strapaze *f*; **2.** ermüden

fat·ten dick *or contp* fett machen *or* werden; mästen; **fat·ty** fett; fettig

fau·cet TECH (Wasser)Hahn *m*

fault Fehler *m*; Defekt *m*; Schuld *f*; *find ~ with* et. auszusetzen haben an (*dat*); *be at ~* Schuld haben

fault·less fehlerfrei, fehlerlos

fault·y fehlerhaft, TECH *a.* defekt

fa·vo(u)r 1. Gunst *f*, Gefallen *m*; Begünstigung *f*; *in ~ of* zu Gunsten von (*or gen*); *do s.o. a ~* j-m e-n Gefallen tun; **2.** begünstigen; bevorzugen, vorziehen; wohlwollend gegenüberstehen; SPORT favorisieren; **fa·vo(u)r·a·ble** günstig; **fa·vo(u)r·ite 1.** Liebling *m*; SPORT Favorit *m*; **2.** Lieblings...

fawn 1. ZO (Reh)Kitz *n*; Rehbraun *n*; **2.** rehbraun

fax 1. Fax *n*; **2.** faxen; *~ s.th. (through) to s.o.* j-m et. faxen

fax (ma·chine) Faxgerät *n*

fear 1. Furcht *f* (**of** vor *dat*); Befürchtung

f; Angst *f*; **2.** (be)fürchten; sich fürchten vor (*dat*)

fear·ful furchtsam; furchtbar

fear·less furchtlos

fea·si·ble durchführbar

feast 1. REL Fest *n*, Feiertag *m*; Festessen *n*; *fig* Fest *n*, (Hoch)Genuss *m*; **2.** *v/t* festlich bewirten; *v/i* sich gütlich tun (**on** an *dat*), schlemmen

feat große Leistung; (Helden)Tat *f*

feath·er 1. Feder *f*, *pl* Gefieder *n*; *birds of a ~* Leute vom gleichen Schlag; *birds of a ~ flock together* Gleich und Gleich gesellt sich gern; *that is a ~ in his cap* darauf kann er stolz sein; **2.** mit Federn polstern *or* schmücken; *Pfeil* fiedern

feath·er·bed verhätscheln

feath·er·brained F hohlköpfig

feath·ered ZO gefiedert

feath·er·weight SPORT Federgewicht *n*, Federgewichtler *m*; Leichtgewicht *n* (*person*)

feath·er·y gefiedert; federleicht

fea·ture 1. (Gesichts)Zug *m*; (charakteristisches) Merkmal; *radio*, TV *etc* Feature *n*; Haupt-, Spielfilm *m*; **2.** groß herausbringen; *film:* in der Hauptrolle zeigen; *~ film* Haupt-, Spielfilm *m*

Feb ABBR *of February* Febr., Februar *m*

Feb·ru·a·ry (ABBR *Feb*) Februar *m*

fed·e·ral POL Bundes...

Fed·e·ral Re·pub·lic of Ger·man·y *die* Bundesrepublik Deutschland (ABBR *BRD*)

fed·e·ra·tion POL Bundesstaat *m*; Föderation *f*, Staatenbund *m*; ECON, SPORT *etc* (Dach)Verband *m*

fee Gebühr *f*; Honorar *n*; (Mitglieds-)Beitrag *m*; Eintrittsgeld *n*

fee·ble schwach

feed 1. Futter *n*; Nahrung *f*; Fütterung *f*; TECH Zuführung *f*, Speisung *f*; **2.** *v/t* füttern; ernähren, TECH *Maschine* speisen; EDP eingeben; AGR weiden lassen; *be fed up with s.o. (s.th.)* j-n (et.) satt haben; *well fed* wohlgenährt; *v/i* (fr)essen; sich ernähren; weiden

feed·back ELECTR Feed-back *n*, Rückkoppelung *f*, radio, TV Reaktion *f*

feed·er Esser *m*

feed·er road Zubringer(straße *f*) *m*

feed·ing bot·tle (Saug)Flasche *f*

feel 1. (sich) fühlen; befühlen; empfinden; sich anfühlen; **~ sorry for s.o.** j-n bedauern *or* bemitleiden; **2.** Gefühl *n*; Empfindung *f*; **feel·er** ZO Fühler *m*; **feel·ing** Gefühl *n*

feign *Interesse etc* vortäuschen, *Krankheit a.* simulieren

feint Finte *f*

fell niederschlagen; fällen

fel·low 1. Gefährte *m*, Gefährtin *f*, Kamerad(in); Gegenstück *n*; F Kerl *m*; **old ~** F alter Knabe; **the ~ of a glove** der andere Handschuh; **2.** Mit...; **~ be·ing** Mitmensch *m*; **~ cit·i·zen** Mitbürger *m*; **~ coun·try·man** Landsmann *m*

fel·low·ship Gemeinschaft *f*; Kameradschaft *f*

fel·low trav·el·(l)er Mitreisende *m*, *f*, Reisegefährte *m*, -gefährtin *f*; POL Mitläufer(in)

fel·on JUR Schwerverbrecher *m*

fel·o·ny JUR (schweres) Verbrechen, Kapitalverbrechen *n*

felt Filz *m*; **~ pen**, **~ tip**, **~-tip(ped) pen** Filzstift *m*, Filzschreiber *m*

fe·male 1. weiblich; **2.** *contp* Weib *n*, Weibsbild *n*; ZO Weibchen *n*

fem·i·nine weiblich, Frauen...; feminin

fem·i·nism Feminismus *m*

fem·i·nist 1. Feminist(in); **2.** feministisch

fen Fenn *n*, Sumpf-, Marschland *n*

fence 1. Zaun *m*; *sl* Hehler *m*; **2.** *v/t* **~ in** einzäunen, umzäunen; einsperren; **~ off** abzäunen; *v/i* SPORT fechten; **fenc·er** SPORT Fechter *m*; **fenc·ing** *f*. Einfriedung *f*; SPORT Fechten *m*; **2.** Fecht...

fend: ~ off abwehren; **~ for o.s.** für sich selbst sorgen

fend·er Schutzvorrichtung *f*; Schutzblech *n*; MOT Kotflügel *m*; Kamingitter *n*, Kaminvorsetzer *m*

fen·nel BOT Fenchel *m*

fer·ment 1. Ferment *n*; Gärung *f*; **2.** gären (lassen)

fer·men·ta·tion Gärung *f*

fern BOT Farn(kraut *n*) *m*

fe·ro·cious wild; grausam

fe·roc·i·ty Wildheit *f*

fer·ret 1. ZO Frettchen *n*; *fig* Spürhund *m*; **2.** herumstöbern; **~ out** aufspüren, aufstöbern

fer·ry 1. Fähre *f*; **2.** übersetzen

fer·ry·boat Fährboot *n*, Fähre *f*

fer·ry·man Fährmann *m*

fer·tile fruchtbar; reich (**of, in** an *dat*)

fer·til·i·ty Fruchtbarkeit *f*

fer·ti·lize fruchtbar machen; befruchten; AGR düngen; **fer·ti·liz·er** AGR (*esp* Kunst)Dünger *m*, Düngemittel *n*

fer·vent glühend, leidenschaftlich

fer·vo(u)r Glut *f*; Inbrunst *f*

fes·ter MED eitern

fes·ti·val Fest *n*; Festival *n*, Festspiele *pl*

fes·tive festlich

fes·tiv·i·ty Festlichkeit *f*

fes·toon Girlande *f*

fetch holen; *Preis* erzielen; *Seufzer* ausstoßen; **fetch·ing** F reizend

fete, fête 1. Fest *n*; **village ~** Dorffest *n*; **2.** feiern

fet·id stinkend

fet·ter 1. Fessel *f*; **2.** fesseln

feud Fehde *f*

feu·dal Feudal..., Lehns...

feu·dal·ism Feudalismus *m*, Feudal-, Lehnssystem *n*

fe·ver MED Fieber *n*; **fe·ver·ish** MED fieb(e)rig, fieberhaft (*a. fig*)

few wenige; **a ~** ein paar, einige; **no fewer than** nicht weniger als; **quite a ~, a good ~** e-e ganze Menge

fi·an·cé Verlobte *m*

fi·an·cée Verlobte *f*

fi·as·co Fiasko *n*

fib F Flunkerei *f*, Schwindelei *f*; **2.** schwindeln, flunkern

fi·ber, *Br* **fi·bre** Faser *f*

fi·ber·glass TECH Fiberglas *n*, Glasfaser *f*

fi·brous faserig

fick·le wankelmütig; unbeständig

fic·tion Erfindung *f*; Prosaliteratur *f*, Belletristik *f*; Romane *pl*

fic·tion·al erdichtet; Roman...

fic·ti·tious erfunden, fiktiv

fid·dle 1. Fiedel *f*, Geige *f*; **play first (second) ~** *esp fig* die erste (zweite) Geige spielen; **(as) fit as a ~** kerngesund; **2.** MUS fiedeln; *a.* **~ about** *or* **around (with)** herumfingern (an *dat*), spielen (mit)

fid·dler Geiger(in)

fi·del·i·ty Treue *f*; Genauigkeit *f*

fid·get F nervös machen; (herum)zappeln; **fid·get·y** zapp(e)lig, nervös

field Feld *n*; SPORT Spielfeld *n*; Arbeitsfeld *n*; Gebiet *n*; Bereich *m*; **~ of vision**

OPT Gesichtsfeld n; ~ **e·vents** SPORT Sprung- und Wurfdisziplinen pl; ~ **glass·es** a. **pair of** ~ Feldstecher m, Fernglas n; ~ **mar·shal** MIL Feldmarschall m

field·work praktische (wissenschaftliche) Arbeit, a. Arbeit f im Gelände; ECON Feldarbeit f

fiend Satan m, Teufel m; F (Frischluftetc)Fanatiker(in)

fiend·ish teuflisch, boshaft

fierce wild; scharf; heftig; **fierce·ness** Wildheit f, Schärfe f; Heftigkeit f

fi·er·y feurig; hitzig

fif·teen 1. fünfzehn; 2. Fünfzehn f

fif·teenth fünfzehnte(r, -s)

fifth 1. fünfte(r, -s); 2. Fünftel n

fifth·ly fünftens

fif·ti·eth fünfzigste(r, -s)

fif·ty 1. fünfzig; 2. Fünfzig f

fif·ty·fif·ty F halbe-halbe

fig BOT Feige f

fight 1. Kampf m; MIL Gefecht n; Schlägerei f; boxing: Kampf m, Fight m; 2. v/t bekämpfen; kämpfen gegen or mit, SPORT a. boxen gegen; v/i kämpfen, sich schlagen; SPORT boxen

fight·er Kämpfer m; SPORT Boxer m, Fighter m; a. **~ plane** MIL Jagdflugzeug n

fight·ing Kampf m

fig·u·ra·tive bildlich

fig·ure 1. Figur f, Gestalt f; Zahl f, Ziffer f; Preis m; **be good at ~s** ein guter Rechner sein; 2. v/t abbilden, darstellen; F meinen, glauben; sich et. vorstellen; **~ out** Problem lösen, F rauskriegen; verstehen; **~ up** zusammenzählen; v/i erscheinen, vorkommen; **~ on** rechnen mit; **~ skat·er** Eiskunstläufer(in); **~ skat·ing** Eiskunstlauf m

fil·a·ment ELECTR Glühfaden m

filch F klauen, stibitzen

file[1] 1. Ordner m; Karteikasten m; Akte f, Akten pl; Ablage f; EDP Datei f; Reihe f; MIL Rotte f; **on ~** bei den Akten; 2. v/t Briefe etc ablegen, zu den Akten nehmen, einordnen; Antrag einreichen, Berufung einlegen; v/i hintereinander marschieren

file[2] TECH 1. Feile f; 2. feilen

file| man·age·ment EDP Dateiverwaltung f; **~ pro·tec·tion** EDP Schreibschutz m

fil·et GASTR Filet n

fi·li·al kindlich, Kindes...

fil·ing Ablegen n

fil·ing cab·i·net Aktenschrank m

fill 1. (sich) füllen; an-, aus-, erfüllen, voll füllen; Pfeife stopfen; Zahn füllen, plombieren; **~ in** einsetzen; **~ out** (Br **in**) Formular ausfüllen; **~ up** voll füllen; sich füllen; **~ her up!** F MOT voll tanken, bitte!; 2. Füllung f; **eat one's ~** sich satt essen

fil·let → filet

fill·ing Füllung f; MED (Zahn)Füllung f, Plombe f; **~ sta·tion** Tankstelle f

fil·ly ZO Stutenfohlen n

film 1. Häutchen n; Membran(e) f; Film m (a. PHOT); **take** or **shoot a** ~ e-n Film drehen; 2. (ver)filmen; sich verfilmen lassen; **~ star** esp Br Filmstar m

fil·ter 1. Filter m; 2. filtern

fil·ter tip Filter m; Filterzigarette f

fil·ter-tipped: ~ cigarette Filterzigarette f

filth Schmutz m

filth·y schmutzig; fig unflätig

fin ZO Flosse f; SPORT Schwimmflosse f

fi·nal 1. letzte(r, -s); End..., Schluss...; endgültig; 2. SPORT Finale n; mst pl Schlussexamen n, -prüfung f

fi·nal dis·pos·al Endlagerung f

fi·nal·ist SPORT Finalist(in)

fi·nal·ly endlich, schließlich; endgültig

fi·nal whis·tle SPORT Schlusspfiff m, Abpfiff m

fi·nance 1. Finanzwesen n; pl Finanzen pl; 2. finanzieren

fi·nan·cial finanziell

fi·nan·cier Finanzier m

finch ZO Fink m

find 1. finden; (an)treffen; herausfinden; JUR j-n für (nicht) schuldig erklären; beschaffen, besorgen; **~ out** v/t et. herausfinden; v/i es herausfinden; 2. Fund m, Entdeckung f; **find·ings** Befund m; JUR Feststellung f, Spruch m

fine[1] 1. adj fein; schön; ausgezeichnet; großartig; **I'm ~** mir geht es gut; 2. adv F sehr gut, bestens

fine[2] 1. Geldstrafe f, Bußgeld n; 2. zu e-r Geldstrafe verurteilen

fin·ger 1. ANAT Finger m; **→ cross** 3; 2. betasten, (herum)fingern an (dat)

fin·ger·nail ANAT Fingernagel m

fin·ger·print Fingerabdruck m

fin·ger·tip Fingerspitze *f*

fin·i·cky pedantisch; wählerisch

fin·ish 1. (be)enden, aufhören (mit); *a. ~ off* vollenden, zu Ende führen, erledigen, *Buch etc* auslesen; *a. ~ off, ~ up* aufessen, austrinken; 2. Ende *n*, Schluss *m*; SPORT Endspurt *m*, Finish *n*; Ziel *n*; Vollendung *f*, letzter Schliff

fin·ish·ing line SPORT Ziellinie *f*

Fin·land Finnland *n*

Finn Finne *m*, Finnin *f*

Finn·ish 1. finnisch; 2. LING Finnisch *n*

fir *a. ~ tree* BOT Tanne *f*

fir cone BOT Tannenzapfen *m*

fire 1. Feuer *n*; *be on ~* in Flammen stehen, brennen; *catch ~* Feuer fangen, in Brand geraten; *set on ~, set ~ to* anzünden; *v/t* anzünden, entzünden; *fig* anfeuern; abfeuern; *Ziegel etc* brennen; F *j-n* rausschmeißen; heizen; *v/i* Feuer fangen (*a. fig*); feuern

fire a·larm Feueralarm *m*; Feuermelder *m*

fire·arms Schusswaffen *pl*

fire bri·gade *Br* Feuerwehr *f*

fire·bug F Feuerteufel *m*

fire·crack·er Knallfrosch *m*; Knallbonbon *m, n*

fire de·part·ment Feuerwehr *f*

fire en·gine *Br* Löschfahrzeug *n*

fire es·cape Feuerleiter *f*, -treppe *f*

fire ex·tin·guish·er Feuerlöscher *m*

fire fight·er Feuerwehrmann *m*

fire·guard *Br* Kamingitter *n*

fire hy·drant Br Hydrant *m*

fire·man Feuerwehrmann *m*; Heizer *m*

fire·place (offener) Kamin

fire·plug Hydrant *m*

fire·proof feuerfest

fire·rais·ing *Br* Brandstiftung *f*

fire·screen Kamingitter *n*

fire ser·vice *Br* Feuerwehr *f*

fire·side (offener) Kamin

fire sta·tion Feuerwache *f*

fire truck Löschfahrzeug *n*

fire·wood Brennholz *n*

fire·works Feuerwerk *n*

fir·ing squad MIL Exekutionskommando *n*

firm[1] fest; hart; standhaft

firm[2] Firma *f*

first 1. *adj* erste(r, -s); beste(r, -s); 2. *adv* erstens; zuerst; *~ of all* an erster Stelle; zu allererst; 3. Erste(r, -s); *at ~* zuerst,

anfangs; *from the ~* von Anfang an

first aid MED erste Hilfe; *~ box, ~ kit* Verband(s)kasten *m*

first-born erstgeborene(r, -s), älteste(r, -s)

first class RAIL *etc* 1. Klasse

first-class erstklassig

first floor Erdgeschoss *n*, *Br* erster Stock; → *second floor*

first·hand aus erster Hand

first leg SPORT Hinspiel *n*

first·ly erstens

first name Vorname *m*

first-rate erstklassig

firth Förde *f*, Meeresarm *m*

fish 1. ZO Fisch *m*; 2. fischen, angeln

fish·bone Gräte *f*

fish·er·man Fischer *m*

fish·e·ry Fischerei *f*

fish fin·ger *Br* GASTR Fischstäbchen *n*

fish·hook Angelhaken *m*

fish·ing Fischen *n*, Angeln *n*; *~ line* Angelschnur *f*; *~ rod* Angelrute *f*; *~ tack·le* Angelgerät *n*

fish·mon·ger *esp Br* Fischhändler *m*

fish stick GASTR Fischstäbchen *n*

fish·y Fisch...; F verdächtig

fis·sion PHYS Spaltung *f*

fis·sure GEOL Spalt *m*, Riss *m*

fist Faust *f*

fit[1] 1. geeignet, passend; tauglich; SPORT fit, (gut) in Form; *keep ~* sich fit halten; 2. *v/t* passend machen (*for* für), anpassen; TECH einpassen, einbauen; anbringen; *~ in j-m* e-n Termin geben, *j-n, et.* einschieben; *a. ~ on* anprobieren; *a. ~ out* ausrüsten, ausstatten, einrichten (*with* mit); *a. ~ up* einrichten (*with* mit); montieren, installieren; *v/i* passen, sitzen (*dress etc*); 3. Sitz *m*

fit[2] MED Anfall *m*; *give s.o. a ~* F j-n auf die Palme bringen; *j-m* e-n Schock versetzen

fit·ful unruhig (*sleep etc*)

fit·ness Tauglichkeit *f*, *esp* SPORT Fitness *f*, (gute) Form; *~ cen·ter* (*Br* cen·tre) Fitnesscenter *n*

fit·ted zugeschnitten; *~ carpet* Spannteppich *m*, Teppichboden *m*; *~ kitchen* Einbauküche *f*

fit·ter Monteur *m*; Installateur *m*

fit·ting 1. passend; schicklich; 2. Montage *f*, Installation *f*; *pl* Ausstattung *f*; Armaturen *pl*

five 1. fünf; **2.** Fünf f

fix 1. befestigen, anbringen (**to** an *dat*); *Preis* festsetzen; fixieren; *Blick etc* richten (**on** auf *acc*); *Aufmerksamkeit etc* fesseln; reparieren, in Ordnung bringen (*a. fig*); *Essen* zubereiten; **2.** F Klemme f; sl Fix m

fixed fest; starr

fix·ings GASTR Beilagen pl

fix·ture Inventarstück n; **lighting ~** Beleuchtungskörper m

fizz zischen, sprudeln

flab·ber·gast F verblüffen; **be ~ed** F platt sein

flab·by schlaff

flac·cid schlaff, schlapp

flag[1] **1.** Fahne f, Flagge f; **2.** beflaggen

flag[2] **1.** (Stein)Platte f, Fliese f; **2.** mit (Stein)Platten *or* Fliesen belegen, fliesen

flag[3] nachlassen, erlahmen

flag·pole, flag·staff Fahnenstange f

flag·stone (Stein)Platte f, Fliese f

flake 1. Flocke f; Schuppe f; **2.** *mst* **~ off** abblättern; F **~ out** schlappmachen

flak·y flockig; blätt(e)rig

flak·y pas·try GASTR Blätterteig m

flame 1. Flamme f (*a. fig*); **be in ~s** in Flammen stehen; **2.** flammen, lodern

flam·ma·ble TECH brennbar, leicht entzündlich, feuergefährlich

flan GASTR Obst-, Käsekuchen m

flank 1. Flanke f; **2.** flankieren

flan·nel Flanell m; *Br* Waschlappen m; *pl Br* Flanellhose f

flap 1. Flattern n, (Flügel)Schlag m; Klappe f; **2.** mit *den Flügeln etc* schlagen; flattern

flare 1. flackern; sich weiten; **~ up** aufflammen; *fig* aufbrausen. **2.** Lichtsignal n

flash 1. Aufblitzen n, Aufleuchten n, Blitz m; *radio etc* Kurzmeldung f; PHOT F BLITZ m; F Taschenlampe f; **like a ~** wie der Blitz; **in a ~** im Nu; **a ~ of light·ning** ein Blitz; **2.** (auf)blitzen *or* aufleuchten (lassen); zucken; rasen, flitzen

flash·back *film*: Rückblende f

flash freeze GASTR schnell einfrieren

flash·light PHOT Blitzlicht n; Taschenlampe f

flash·y protzig; auffallend

flask Taschenflasche f

flat[1] **1.** flach, eben, platt; schal; ECON flau; MOT platt (*tire*); **2.** *adv* **fall ~** danebengehen; **sing ~** zu tief singen; **3.** Fläche f, Ebene f; flache Seite f; Flachland n, Niederung f; MOT Reifenpanne f

flat[2] *Br* Wohnung f

flat-foot·ed plattfüßig

flat·mate *Br* Mitbewohner(in)

flat·ten (ein)ebnen; abflachen; *a.* **~ out** flach(er) werden

flat·ter schmeicheln (*dat*)

flat·ter·er Schmeichler(in)

flat·ter·y Schmeichelei f

fla·vo(u)r 1. Geschmack m; Aroma n; Blume f; *fig* Beigeschmack m; Würze f; **2.** würzen

fla·vo(u)r·ing Würze f, Aroma n

flaw Fehler m, TECH a. Defekt m

flaw·less einwandfrei, tadellos

flax BOT Flachs m

flea ZO Floh m

flea mar·ket Flohmarkt m

fleck Fleck(en) m; Tupfen m

fledged zo flügge

fledg(e)·ling ZO Jungvogel m; *fig* Grünschnabel m

flee fliehen; meiden

fleece 1. Vlies n, *esp* Schafsfell n; **2.** F *j-n* neppen

fleet MAR Flotte f

flesh Fleisch n; **flesh·y** fleischig; dick

flex[1] *esp* ANAT biegen

flex[2] *esp Br* ELECTR (Anschluss-, Verlängerungs)Kabel n, (-)Schnur f

flex·i·ble flexibel, biegsam; *fig* anpassungsfähig; **~ working hours** Gleitzeit f

flex·i·time *Br*, **flex·time** Gleitzeit f

flick schnippen; schnellen

flick·er 1. flackern; TV flimmern; **2.** Flackern n; TV Flimmern n

fli·er AVIAT Flieger m; Reklamezettel m

flight Flucht f; Flug m (*a. fig*); ZO Schwarm m; *a.* **~ of stairs** Treppe f; **put to ~** in die Flucht schlagen; **take (to) ~** die Flucht ergreifen; **~ at·tend·ant** AVIAT Flugbegleiter(in)

flight·less ZO flugunfähig

flight re·cord·er AVIAT Flugschreiber m

flight·y flatterhaft

flim·sy dünn; zart; *fig* fadenscheinig

flinch (zurück)zucken, zusammenfahren; zurückschrecken (**from** vor *dat*)

fling 1. werfen, schleudern; **~ o.s.** sich

stürzen; **~ open (to)** *Tür etc* aufreißen (zuschlagen); **2. have a ~** sich austoben; **have a ~ at** es versuchen *or* probieren mit

flint Feuerstein *m*

flip schnippen, schnipsen; *Münze* hochwerfen

flip·pant respektlos, F schnodd(e)rig

flip·per ZO Flosse *f*; Schwimmflosse *f*

flirt 1. flirten; **2. be a ~** gern flirten

flir·ta·tion Flirt *m*

flit flitzen, huschen

float 1. *v/i* (auf dem Wasser) schwimmen, (im Wasser) treiben; schweben; *a.* ECON in Umlauf sein; *v/t* schwimmen *or* treiben lassen; MAR flottmachen; ECON *Wertpapiere etc* in Umlauf bringen; *Währung* floaten, den Wechselkurs *(gen)* freigeben; **2.** Festwagen *m*

float·ing 1. schwimmend, treibend; ECON umlaufend; frei *(exchange rate)*; frei konvertierbar *(currency)*; **2.** ECON Floating *n*

float·ing vot·er POL Wechselwähler(in)

flock 1. ZO Herde *f (a.* REL); Menge *f*, Schar *f*; **2.** *fig* strömen

floe (treibende) Eisscholle *f*

flog prügeln, schlagen

flog·ging Tracht *f* Prügel

flood 1. *a.* **~ tide** Flut *f*; Überschwemmung *f*; **2.** überfluten, überschwemmen

flood·gate Schleusentor *n*

flood·lights ELECTR Flutlicht *n*

floor 1. Boden *m*; Stock *m*, Stockwerk *n*, Etage *f*; Tanzfläche *f*; → **first floor**, **second floor**, **take the ~** das Wort ergreifen; **2.** e-n (Fuß)Boden legen in; zu Boden schlagen; *fig* F *j-n* umhauen

floor·board (Fußboden)Diele *f*

floor cloth Putzlappen *m*

floor·ing (Fuß)Bodenbelag *m*

floor lamp Stehlampe *f*

floor lead·er PARL Fraktionsführer *m*

floor-length bodenlang

floor show Nachtklubvorstellung *f*

floor·walk·er Aufsicht *f*

flop 1. sich (hin)plumpsen lassen; F durchfallen, danebengehen, ein Reinfall sein; **2.** Plumps *m*; F Flop *m*, Reinfall *m*, Pleite *f*; Versager *m*

flop·py (disk) EDP Floppy Disk *f*, Diskette *f*

flor·id rot, gerötet

flor·ist Blumenhändler(in)

floun·der[1] ZO Flunder *f*

floun·der[2] zappeln; strampeln; *fig* sich verhaspeln

flour (feines) Mehl

flour·ish 1. Schnörkel *m*; MUS Tusch *m*; **2.** *v/i* blühen, gedeihen; *v/t* schwenken

flow 1. fließen, strömen; wallen; **2.** Fluß *m*, Strom *m (both a. fig)*

flow·er 1. Blume *f*; Blüte *f (a. fig)*; **2.** blühen

flow·er·bed Blumenbeet *n*

flow·er·pot Blumentopf *m*

fluc·tu·ate schwanken

fluc·tu·a·tion Schwankung *f*

flu F MED Grippe *f*

flue Rauchfang *m*, Esse *f*

flu·en·cy Flüssigkeit *f*; (Rede)Gewandtheit *f*; **flu·ent** flüssig; gewandt; **speak ~ French** fließend Französisch sprechen

fluff 1. Flaum *m*; Staubflocke *f*; **2.** ZO aufplustern; **fluff·y** flaumig

flu·id 1. flüssig; **2.** Flüssigkeit *f*

flunk F durchfallen (lassen)

flu·o·res·cent fluoreszierend

flu·o·ride CHEM Fluor *n*

flu·o·rine CHEM Fluor *n*

flur·ry Windstoß *m*; (Regen-, Schnee-) Schauer *m*; *fig* Aufregung *f*, Unruhe *f*

flush 1. (Wasser)Spülung *f*; Erröten *n*; Röte *f*; **2.** *v/i a.* **~ out** (aus)spülen; **~ down** hinunterspülen; **~ the toilet** spülen; *v/i* erröten, rot werden; spülen; **3. be ~** F gut bei Kasse sein

flus·ter 1. nervös machen *or* werden; **2.** Nervosität *f*

flute MUS **1.** Flöte *f*; **2.** (auf der) Flöte spielen

flut·ter 1. flattern; **2.** Flattern *n*; *fig* Erregung *f*

flux *fig* Fluss *m*

fly[1] ZO Fliege *f*

fly[2] Hosenschlitz *m*; Zeltklappe *f*

fly[3] fliegen (lassen); stürmen, stürzen; flattern, wehen; (ver)fliegen *(time)*; *Drachen* steigen lassen; **~ at s.o.** auf *j-n* losgehen; **~ into a passion** *or* **rage** in Wut geraten; **fly·er → flier**

fly·ing fliegend; Flug...; **~ sau·cer** fliegende Untertasse *f*; **~ squad** Überfallkommando *n*; **~ vis·it** F Stippvisite *f*

fly·o·ver *Br* (Straßen-, Eisenbahn-) Überführung *f*

fly-screen Fliegenfenster *n*

fly-weight *boxing*: Fliegengewicht *n*, Fliegengewichtler *m*

fly-wheel TECH Schwungrad *n*

foal ZO Fohlen *n*

foam 1. Schaum *m*; **2.** schäumen; **~ ex·tin·guish·er** Schaumlöscher *m*, -lösch-gerät *n*; **~ rub·ber** Schaumgummi *m*

foam·y schaumig

fo·cus 1. Brennpunkt *m*, *fig a.* Mittelpunkt *m*; OPT, PHOT Scharfeinstellung *f*; **2.** OPT, PHOT scharf einstellen; *fig* konzentrieren (**on** auf *acc*)

fod·der AGR (Trocken)Futter *n*

foe POET Feind *m*, Gegner *m*

fog (dichter) Nebel

fog·gy neb(e)lig; *fig* nebelhaft

foi·ble (kleine) Schwäche

foil¹ Folie *f*; *fig* Hintergrund *m*

foil² vereiteln

foil³ *fencing*: Florett *n*

fold¹ 1. Falte *f*; Falz *m*; **2.** ...fach, ...fältig; **3.** (sich) falten; falzen; *Arme* verschränken; einwickeln; *often* **~ up** zusammenfalten, -legen, -klappen

fold² AGR Schafhürde *f*, Pferch *m*; REL Herde *f*

fold·er Aktendeckel *m*; Schnellhefter *m*; Faltprospekt *m*, -blatt *n*, Broschüre *f*

fold·ing zusammenlegbar; Klapp...; **~ bed** Klappbett *n*; **~ bi·cy·cle** Klapprad *n*; **~ boat** Faltboot *n*; **~ chair** Klappstuhl *m*; **~ door(s)** Falttür *f*

fo·li·age BOT Laub *n*, Laubwerk *n*

folk 1. Leute *pl*; *pl* F *m-e etc* Leute *pl*; *2.* Volks-

folk·lore Volkskunde *f*; Volkssagen *pl*; Folklore *f*

folk mu·sic Volksmusik *f*

folk song Volkslied *n*; Folksong *m*

fol·low folgen (*dat*); folgen auf (*acc*); befolgen; verfolgen; *s-m Beruf etc* nachgehen; **~ through** *Plan etc* bis zum Ende durchführen; **~ up** *e-r Sache* nachgehen; *e-e Sache* weiterverfolgen; **as ~s** wie folgt; **fol·low·er** Nachfolger(in); Verfolger(in); Anhänger(in); **fol·low·ing 1.** Anhängerschaft *f*, Anhänger *pl*; Gefolge *n*; **the ~** das Folgende; die Folgenden *pl*; **2.** folgende(r, -s); **3.** im Anschluss an (*acc*)

fol·ly Torheit *f*

fond zärtlich; vernarrt (**of** in *acc*); **be ~ of** gern haben, lieben

fon·dle liebkosen; streicheln; (ver)hätscheln

fond·ness Zärtlichkeit *f*; Vorliebe *f*

font REL Taufstein *m*, Taufbecken *n*

food Nahrung *f*, Essen *n*; Nahrungs-, Lebensmittel *pl*; AGR Futter *n*

fool 1. Narr *m*, Närrin *f*, Dummkopf *m*; **make a ~ of s.o.** j-n zum Narren halten; **make a ~ of o.s.** sich lächerlich machen; **2.** zum Narren halten; betrügen (**out of** um); **~ about**, **~ around** herumtrödeln; Unsinn machen, herumalbern

fool·har·dy tollkühn

fool·ish dumm, töricht; unklug

fool·ish·ness Dummheit *f*

fool·proof kinderleicht; todsicher

foot 1. ANAT Fuß *m* (*a. linear measure = 30,48 cm*); Fußende *n*; **on ~** zu Fuß; **2.** F *Rechnung* bezahlen; **have to ~ the bill** die Zeche bezahlen müssen; **~ it** zu Fuß gehen

foot·ball Football(spiel *n*) *m*; *Br* Fußball(spiel *n*) *m*; Football-Ball *m*; **~** Fußball *m*

foot·bal·ler *Br* Fußballer *m*

foot·ball| hoo·li·gan *Br* Fußballrowdy *m*; **~ play·er** *Br* Fußballspieler *m*

foot·bridge Fußgängerbrücke *f*

foot·fall Tritt *m*, Schritt *m*

foot·hold fester Stand, Halt *m*

foot·ing Halt *m*, Stand *m*; *fig* Grundlage *f*, Basis *f*; **be on a friendly ~ with s.o.** ein gutes Verhältnis zu j-m haben; **lose one's ~** den Halt verlieren

foot·lights THEA Rampenlicht(er *pl*) *n*

foot·loose frei, unbeschwert; **~ and fancy-free** frei und ungebunden

foot·note Fußnote *f*

foot·path (Fuß)Pfad *m*, (Fuß)Weg *m*

foot·print Fußabdruck *m*, *pl a.* Fußspur (en *pl*) *f*

foot·sore: be ~ wunde Füße haben

foot·step Tritt *m*, Schritt *m*; Fußstapfe *f*

foot·wear Schuhwerk *n*, Schuhe *pl*

fop Geck *m*, F Fatzke *m*

for 1. *prp mst* für; *purpose, direction*: zu; nach; *warten, hoffen etc* auf (*acc*); *sich sehnen etc* nach; *cause*: aus, vor (*dat*), wegen; *time*: **~ three days** drei Tage (lang); seit drei Tagen; *distance*:

I walked ~ a mile ich ging eine Meile (weit); *exchange*: (an)statt; als; *I ~ one* ich zum Beispiel; *~ sure* sicher!, gewiss!; **2.** *cj* denn, weil

for·age *a.* *~ about* (herum)stöbern, (-)wühlen (*in* in *dat*; *for* nach)

for·ay MIL Einfall *m*, Überfall *m*; *fig* Ausflug *m* (*into politics* in *die* Politik)

for·bid verbieten; hindern

for·bid·ding abstoßend

force 1. Stärke *f*, Kraft *f*, Gewalt *f*, Wucht *f*; *the* (*police*) *~* die Polizei; (*armed*) *~s* MIL Streitkräfte *pl*; *by ~* mit Gewalt; *come or put into ~* in Kraft treten *or* setzen; **2.** *j-n* zwingen; *et.* erzwingen; zwängen; drängen; *Tempo* beschleunigen; *~ s.th. on s.o.* j-m et. aufzwingen *or* aufdrängen; *~ o.s. on s.o.* sich j-m aufdrängen; *~ open* aufbrechen

forced erzwungen; gezwungen, gequält; *~ land·ing* AVIAT Notlandung *f*

force·ful energisch, kraftvoll; eindrucksvoll, überzeugend

for·ceps MED Zange *f*

for·ci·ble gewaltsam; eindringlich

ford 1. Furt *f*; **2.** durchwaten

fore 1. vorder, Vorder...; vorn; **2.** Vorderteil *m*, Vorderseite *f*, Front *f*

fore·arm ANAT Unterarm *m*

fore·bear *mst pl* Vorfahren *pl*, Ahnen *pl*

fore·bod·ing (böses) Vorzeichen; (*böse*) (Vor)Ahnung *f*

fore·cast 1. voraussagen, vorhersehen; *Wetter* vorhersagen; **2.** Voraussage *f*; METEOR Vorhersage *f*

fore·fa·ther Vorfahr *m*

fore·fin·ger ANAT Zeigefinger *m*

fore·foot ZO Vorderfuß *m*

fore·gone con·clu·sion ausgemachte Sache; *be a ~* a. von vornherein feststehen

fore·ground Vordergrund *m*

fore·hand SPORT **1.** Vorhand *f*, Vorhandschlag *m*; **2.** Vorhand...

fore·head ANAT Stirn *f*

for·eign fremd, ausländisch, Außen..., Auslands...; *~ af·fairs* Außenpolitik *f*; *~ aid* Auslandshilfe *f*

for·eign·er Ausländer(in)

for·eign| lan·guage Fremdsprache *f*; *~ min·is·ter* POL Außenminister *m*

For·eign Of·fice *Br* POL Außenministerium *n*

for·eign pol·i·cy Außenpolitik *f*

For·eign Sec·re·ta·ry *Br* POL Außenminister *m*

for·eign trade ECON Außenhandel *m*

for·eign work·er Gastarbeiter(in)

fore·knowl·edge vorherige Kenntnis

fore·leg ZO Vorderbein *n*

fore·man TECH Vorarbeiter *m*, Polier *m*; Werkmeister *m*; JUR Sprecher *m*

fore·most vorderste(r, -s), erste(r, -s)

fore·name Vorname *m*

fo·ren·sic JUR Gerichts...; *~ me·dicine* Gerichtsmedizin *f*

fore·run·ner Vorläufer(in)

fore·see vorhersehen, voraussehen

fore·see·a·ble vorhersehbar

fore·shad·ow ahnen lassen, andeuten

fore·sight Weitblick *m*; (*weise*) Voraussicht

for·est Wald *m* (*a. fig*); Forst *m*

fore·stall *et.* vereiteln; *j-m* zuvorkommen

for·est·er Förster *m*

for·est·ry Forstwirtschaft *f*

fore·taste Vorgeschmack *m*

fore·tell vorhersagen

for·ev·er, for ev·er für immer

fore·wom·an TECH Vorarbeiterin *f*

fore·word Vorwort *n*

for·feit verwirken; einbüßen

forge 1. Schmiede *f*; **2.** fälschen; schmieden

forg·er Fälscher *m*

for·ge·ry Fälschen *n*; Fälschung *f*

for·ge·ry-proof fälschungssicher

for·get vergessen

for·get·ful vergesslich

for·get-me-not BOT Vergissmeinnicht *n*

for·give vergeben, verzeihen

for·give·ness Verzeihung *f*; Vergebung *f*

for·giv·ing versöhnlich; nachsichtig

fork 1. Gabel *f*; **2.** (sich) gabeln

fork-lift truck MOT Gabelstapler *m*

form 1. Form *f*; Gestalt *f*; Formular *n*, Vordruck *m*; *Br* (Schul)Klasse *f*; Formalität *f*; Kondition *f*, Verfassung *f*; *in great ~* gut in Form; **2.** (sich) formen, (sich) bilden, gestalten

for·mal förmlich; formell

for·mal dress Gesellschaftskleidung *f*

for·mal·i·ty Förmlichkeit *f*; Formalität *f*

for·mat 1. Aufmachung *f*; Format *n*; **2.** EDP formatieren for·ma·tion Bildung f

form·a·tive bildend; gestaltend; ~ *years* Entwicklungsjahre pl

for·mat·ting EDP Formatierung f

for·mer 1. früher; ehemalig; 2. *the* ~ der or die or das Erstere

for·mer·ly früher

for·mi·da·ble Furcht erregend; gewaltig, riesig, gefährlich, schwierig

form| mas·ter Br Klassenlehrer m, -leiter m; ~ mis·tress Br Klassenlehrerin f, -leiterin f; ~ teach·er Br Klassenlehrer(in), Klassenleiter(in)

for·mu·la Formel f; Rezept n

for·mu·late formulieren

for·sake aufgeben; verlassen

for·swear abschwören, entsagen (dat)

fort MIL Fort n, Festung f

forth weiter, fort; (her)vor; *and so ~* und so weiter

forth·com·ing bevorstehend, kommend; in Kürze erscheinend (book) or anlaufend (film)

for·ti·eth vierzigste(r, -s)

for·ti·fi·ca·tion Befestigung f

for·ti·fy MIL befestigen; fig (ver)stärken

for·ti·tude (innere) Kraft or Stärke

fort·night Br vierzehn Tage

for·tress MIL Festung f

for·tu·i·tous zufällig

for·tu·nate glücklich; *be ~* Glück haben; for·tu·nate·ly glücklicherweise

for·tune Vermögen n; (glücklicher) Zufall, Glück n; Schicksal n

for·tune·tell·er Wahrsager(in)

for·ty 1. vierzig; *have ~ winks* F ein Nickerchen machen; 2. Vierzig f

for·ward 1. adv nach vorn, vorwärts; 2. adj Vorwärts...; fortschrittlich; vorlaut, dreist; 3. soccer: Stürmer m; 4. befördern, (ver)senden, schicken; Brief etc nachsenden

for·ward·ing a·gent Spediteur m

fos·sil GEOL Fossil n (a. F), Versteinerung f

fos·ter·child Pflegekind n

fos·ter·par·ents Pflegeeltern pl

foul 1. stinkend, widerlich; verpestet, schlecht (air, water); GASTR verdorben, faul; schmutzig, verschmutzt; METEOR stürmisch, schlecht; SPORT regelwidrig; esp Br F mies; 2. SPORT Foul n, Regelverstoß m; *vicious ~* böses or übles Foul; 3. beschmutzen, verschmutzen; SPORT foulen

found¹ gründen; stiften

found² TECH gießen

foun·da·tion ARCH Grundmauer f, Fundament n; fig Gründung f, Errichtung f; (gemeinnützige) Stiftung; fig Grundlage f, Basis f

found·er¹ Gründer(in); Stifter(in)

foun·der² MAR sinken; fig scheitern

found·ling JUR Findelkind n

foun·dry TECH Gießerei f

foun·tain Springbrunnen m; (Wasser-) Strahl m; ~ pen Füllfederhalter m

four 1. vier; 2. Vier f, rowing: Vierer m; *on all ~s* auf allen vieren

four star Br F Super n

four-star pet·rol Br Superbenzin n

four-stroke en·gine Viertaktmotor m

four·teen 1. vierzehn; 2. Vierzehn f

four·teenth vierzehnte(r, -s)

fourth 1. vierte(r, -s); 2. Viertel n

fourth·ly viertens

four-wheel drive MOT Vierradantrieb m

fowl ZO Geflügel n

fox ZO Fuchs m

fox·glove BOT Fingerhut m

fox·y schlau, gerissen

frac·tion Bruchteil m; MATH Bruch m

frac·ture MED 1. (Knochen)Bruch m; 2. brechen

fra·gile zerbrechlich

frag·ment Bruchstück n

fra·grance Wohlgeruch m, Duft m

fra·grant wohlriechend, duftend

frail gebrechlich; zerbrechlich; zart, schwach; frail·ty Zartheit f, Gebrechlichkeit f, Schwäche f

frame 1. Rahmen m; (Brillen- etc)Gestell n; Körper(bau) m; ~ *of mind* (Gemüts)Verfassung f, (-)Zustand m; 2. (ein)rahmen; bilden, formen, bauen; *a. ~ up* F j-m et. anhängen

frame-up F abgekartetes Spiel; Intrige f

frame·work TECH Gerüst n; fig Struktur f, System f

franc Franc m; Franken m

France Frankreich n

fran·chise POL Wahlrecht n; ECON Konzession f

frank 1. frei(mütig), offen; *~ly (speaking)* offen gesagt; 2. Brief freistempeln

frank·fur·ter GASTR Frankfurter (Würstchen *n*) *f*

frank·ness Offenheit *f*

fran·tic hektisch; *be ~* außer sich sein

fra·ter·nal brüderlich

frat·er·nize sich verbrüdern

frat·er·ni·za·tion Verbrüderung *f*

fra·ter·ni·ty Brüderlichkeit *f*; Vereinigung *f*, Zunft *f*; UNIV Verbindung *f*

fraud Betrug *m*; F Schwindel *m*

fraud·u·lent betrügerisch

fray ausfransen, (sich) durchscheuern

freak 1. Missgeburt *f*; Laune *f*; *in cpds* F ...freak *m*, ...fanatiker *m*; Freak *m*, irrer Typ; *~ of nature* Laune *f* der Natur; 2. F *a. ~ out* durchdrehen, die Nerven verlieren

freck·le Sommersprosse *f*

freck·led sommersprossig

free 1. frei; ungehindert; ungebunden; kostenlos, zum Nulltarif; freigebig; *~ and easy* zwanglos; sorglos; *set ~* freilassen; 2. befreien; freilassen

free·dom Freiheit *f*

free fares Nulltarif *m*

free·lance frei, freiberuflich tätig, freischaffend

Free·ma·son Freimaurer *m*

free skat·ing Kür *f*

free·style SPORT Freistil *m*

free time Freizeit *f*

free trade ECON Freihandel *m*; *~ ar·e·a* ECON Freihandelszone *f*

free·way Schnellstraße *f*

free·wheel im Freilauf fahren

freeze 1. *v/i* (ge)frieren; erstarren; *v/t* gefrieren lassen; GASTR einfrieren (*a.* ECON), tiefkühlen; 2. Frost *m*, Kälte *f*; ECON, POL Einfrieren *n*; *wage ~*, *~ on wages* ECON Lohnstopp *m*

freeze-dried gefriergetrocknet

freeze-dry gefriertrocknen

freez·er Gefriertruhe *f*, Tiefkühl-, Gefriergerät *n*; Gefrierfach *n*

freez·ing eisig; Gefrier...; *~ com·part·ment* Gefrierfach *n*; *~ point* Gefrierpunkt *m*

freight 1. Fracht *f*; Frachtgebühr *f*; 2. Güter...; 3. beladen; verfrachten

freight car RAIL Güterwagen *m*

freight·er MAR Frachter *m*, Frachtschiff *n*; AVIAT Transportflugzeug *n*

freight train Güterzug *m*

French 1. französisch; 2. LING Franzö-

sisch *n*; *the ~* die Franzosen *pl*

French doors Terrassen-, Balkontür *f*

French fries GASTR Pommes frites *pl*

French·man Franzose *m*

French win·dows → *French doors*

French·wom·an Französin *f*

fren·zied wahnsinnig, rasend (*with* vor *dat*); hektisch; **fren·zy** Wahnsinn *m*; Ekstase *f*; Raserei *f*

fre·quen·cy Häufigkeit *f*; ELECTR Frequenz *f*

fre·quent 1. häufig; 2. (oft) besuchen

fresh frisch; neu; unerfahren; frech; *get ~ (with s.o.)* (j-m gegenüber) zudringlich werden; **fresh·en** auffrischen (*wind*); *~ (o.s.) up* sich frisch machen

fresh·man UNIV Student(in) im ersten Jahr

fresh·ness Frische *f*; Frechheit *f*

fresh wa·ter Süßwasser *n*

fresh·wa·ter Süßwasser...

fret sich Sorgen machen

fret·ful verärgert, gereizt; quengelig

FRG ABBR *of Federal Republic of Germany* Bundesrepublik *f* Deutschland

Fri ABBR *of Friday* Fr., Freitag *m*

fri·ar REL Mönch *m*

fric·tion TECH *etc* Reibung *f* (*a. fig*)

Fri·day (ABBR *Fri*) Freitag *m*; *on ~* (am) Freitag; *on ~s* freitags

fridge F Kühlschrank *m*

friend Freund(in); Bekannte *m*, *f*; *make ~s with* sich anfreunden mit, Freundschaft schließen mit

friend·ly 1. freund(schaft)lich; 2. *esp Br* SPORT Freundschaftsspiel *n*

friend·ship Freundschaft *f*

fries F GASTR Fritten *pl*

frig·ate MAR Fregatte *f*

fright Schreck(en) *m*; *look a ~* F verboten aussehen; **fright·en** erschrecken; *be ~ed* erschrecken (*at, by, of* vor *dat*); Angst haben (*of* vor *dat*)

fright·ful schrecklich, fürchterlich

fri·gid PSYCH frigid(e); kalt, frostig

frill Krause *f*, Rüsche *f*

fringe 1. Franse *f*; Rand *m*; Pony *m*; 2. mit Fransen besetzen; *~ ben·e·fits* ECON Gehalts-, Lohnnebenleistungen *pl*; *~ e·vent* Randveranstaltung *f*; *~ group* soziale Randgruppe *f*

frisk herumtollen; F *j-n* filzen, durchsuchen; **frisk·y** lebhaft, munter

frit·ter: ~ *away* Geld etc vertun, Zeit vertrödeln, Geld, Kräfte vergeuden
fri·vol·i·ty Frivolität f, Leichtfertigkeit f; **friv·o·lous** frivol, leichtfertig
friz·zle F GASTR verbrutzeln
frizz·y gekräuselt, kraus
fro: *to and* ~ hin und her
frock REL Kutte f
frog ZO Frosch m
frog·man Froschmann m, MIL a. Kampfschwimmer m
frol·ic herumtoben, herumtollen
from von; aus; von ... aus or her; von ... (an), seit; aus, vor (dat); ~ **9 to 5** (o'clock) von 9 bis 5 (Uhr)
front 1. Vorderseite f; Front f (a. MIL); *at the* ~, *in* ~ vorn; *in* ~ *of* vor; *be in* ~ in Führung sein; **2.** Vorder...; **3.** a. ~ *on*, ~ *to*(*wards*) gegenüberstehen, gegenüberliegen
front·age ARCH (Vorder)Front f
front cov·er Titelseite f
front door Haustür f, Vordertür f
front en·trance Vordereingang m
fron·tier 1. (Landes)Grenze f; HIST Grenzland n, Grenze f; **2.** Grenz...
front-page F wichtig, aktuell
front-wheel drive MOT Vorderradantrieb m
frost 1. Frost m; a. hoar ~, white ~ Reif m; **2.** mit Reif überziehen; Glas mattieren; GASTR glasieren; mit Zuckerguss überziehen; mit (Puder)Zucker bestreuen
frost·bite MED Erfrierung f
frost·bit·ten MED erfroren
frost·ed glass Matt-, Milchglas n
frost·y eisig, frostig (a. fig)
froth 1. Schaum m; **2.** schäumen; zu Schaum schlagen
froth·y schäumend; schaumig
frown 1. Stirnrunzeln n; *with a* ~ stirnrunzelnd; **2.** v/i die Stirn runzeln
fro·zen adj (eis)kalt; (ein-, zu)gefroren; Gefrier...
fro·zen foods Tiefkühlkost f
fru·gal sparsam; bescheiden; einfach
fruit Frucht f; Früchte pl; Obst n
fruit·er·er Obsthändler m
fruit·ful fruchtbar
fruit·less unfruchtbar; erfolglos
fruit juice Fruchtsaft m
fruit·y fruchtartig; fruchtig (wine)
frus·trate vereiteln; frustrieren

frus·tra·tion Vereitelung f; Frustration f
fry braten; *fried eggs* Spiegeleier pl; *fried potatoes* Bratkartoffeln pl
fry·ing pan Bratpfanne f
fuch·sia BOT Fuchsie f
fuck V ficken, vögeln; ~ *off!* verpiss dich!; *get* ~*ed!* der Teufel soll dich holen!; **fuck·ing** V Scheiß..., verflucht; ~ *hell!* verdammte Scheiße!
fudge GASTR Fondant m
fu·el 1. Brennstoff m; MOT Treib-, Kraftstoff m; **2.** MOT, AVIAT (auf)tanken
fu·el in·jec·tion en·gine MOT Einspritzmotor m
fu·gi·tive 1. flüchtig (a. fig); **2.** Flüchtling m
ful·fil Br, **ful·fill** erfüllen; vollziehen; **ful·fil·(l)ing** befriedigend; **ful·fil·(l)·ment** Erfüllung f, Ausführung f
full 1. voll; ganz; Voll...; ~ *of* voll von, voller; ~ (*up*) (voll) besetzt (bus etc); F voll, satt; *house* ~*!* THEA ausverkauft!; ~ *of o.s.* (ganz) von sich eingenommen; **2.** adv völlig, ganz; **3.** *in* ~ vollständig; ganz; *write out in* ~ Wort etc ausschreiben
full board Vollpension f
full dress Gesellschaftskleidung f
full-fledged ZO flügge; fig richtig
full-grown ausgewachsen
full-length in voller Größe; bodenlang; abendfüllend (film etc)
full moon Vollmond m
full stop LING Punkt m
full time SPORT Spielende n
full-time ganztägig, Ganztags...; ~ *job* Ganztagsbeschäftigung f
ful·ly voll, völlig, ganz
ful·ly-fledged Br → full-fledged
ful·ly-'grown Br → full-grown
fum·ble tasten; fummeln
fume wütend sein
fumes Dämpfe pl, Rauch m; Abgase pl
fum·ing wutschnaubend
fun Scherz m, Spaß m; *for* ~ aus or zum Spaß; *make* ~ *of* sich lustig machen über (acc), verspotten
func·tion 1. Funktion f; Aufgabe f; Veranstaltung f; **2.** funktionieren
func·tion·a·ry Funktionär m
func·tion key EDP Funktionstaste f
fund ECON Fonds m; Geld(mittel pl) n
fun·da·men·tal 1. Grund..., grundle-

gend; **2. ~s** Grundlage *f*, Grundbegriffe *pl*

fun·da·men·tal·ist Fundamentalist *m*

fu·ne·ral Begräbnis *n*, Beerdigung *f*; **~ march** MUS Trauermarsch *m*; **~ o·ration** Trauerrede *f*; **~ pro·ces·sion** Trauerzug *m*; **~ ser·vice** Trauerfeier *f*

fun·fair Rummelplatz *m*

fun·gus BOT Pilz *m*, Schwamm *m*

fu·nic·u·lar *a.* **~ railway** (Draht)Seilbahn *f*

funk·y F irre, schräg, schrill

fun·nel Trichter *m*; MAR, RAIL Schornstein *m*

fun·nies F Comics *pl*

fun·ny komisch, lustig, spaßig; sonderbar

fur Pelz *m*, Fell *n*; MED Belag *m*; TECH Kesselstein *m*

fu·ri·ous wütend

furl *Fahne, Segel* aufrollen, einrollen; *Schirm* zusammenrollen

fur·nace TECH Schmelzofen *m*, Hochofen *m*; (Heiz)Kessel *m*

fur·nish einrichten, möblieren; liefern; versorgen, ausrüsten, ausstatten (**with** mit)

fur·ni·ture Möbel *pl*; **sectional ~** Anbaumöbel *pl*

furred MED belegt, pelzig

fur·ri·er Kürschner *m*

fur·row 1. Furche *f*; **2.** furchen

fur·ry pelzig; flauschig

fur·ther 1. weiter; **2.** fördern, unterstützen; **~ ed·u·ca·tion** Br Fortbildung *f*, Weiterbildung *f*

fur·ther·more *fig* weiter, überdies

fur·ther·most entfernteste(r, -s), äußerste(r, -s)

fur·tive heimlich, verstohlen

fu·ry Wut *f*, Zorn *m*

fuse 1. Zünder *m*; ELECTR Sicherung *f*; Zündschnur *f*; **2.** schmelzen; ELECTR durchbrennen

fuse box ELECTR Sicherungskasten *m*

fu·se·lage (Flugzeug)Rumpf *m*

fu·sion Verschmelzung *f*, Fusion *f*; PHYS **nuclear ~** Kernfusion *f*

fuss 1. (unnötige) Aufregung; Wirbel *m*, F Theater *n*; **2.** sich (unnötig) aufregen; viel Aufhebens machen (**about** um, von); **fuss·y** aufgeregt, hektisch; kleinlich, pedantisch; heikel, wählerisch

fus·ty muffig; *fig* verstaubt

fu·tile nutzlos, zwecklos

fu·ture 1. (zu)künftig; **2.** Zukunft *f*; LING Futur *n*, Zukunft *f*; **in ~** in Zukunft, künftig

fuzz feiner Flaum

fuzz·y kraus, wuschelig; unscharf, verschwommen; flaumig, flauschig

G

G, g G, g *n*

gab F Geschwätz *n*; **have the gift of the ~** ein gutes Mundwerk haben

gab·ar·dine Gabardine *m*

gab·ble 1. Geschnatter *n*, Geschwätz *n*; **2.** schnattern, schwatzen

ga·ble ARCH Giebel *m*

gad: F **~ about** (viel) unterwegs sein (in *dat*), sich herumtreiben

gad·fly ZO Bremse *f*

gad·get TECH Apparat *m*, Gerät *n*, Vorrichtung *f*; *often contp* technische Spielerei

gag 1. Knebel *m* (*a. fig*); F Gag *m*; **2.** knebeln; *fig* mundtot machen

gage 1. Eichmaß *n*; TECH Messgerät *n*,

Lehre *f*; TECH Stärke *f*, Dicke *f*; RAIL Spur(weite) *f*; **2.** TECH eichen; (ab-, aus)messen

gai·e·ty Fröhlichkeit *f*

gain 1. gewinnen; erreichen, bekommen; zunehmen an (*dat*); vorgehen (um) (*watch*); **~ speed** schneller werden; **~ 5 pounds** 5 Pfund zunehmen; **~ in** zunehmen an (*dat*); **2.** Gewinn *m*; Zunahme *f*; **~ of time** Zeitgewinn *m*

gait Gang *m*, Gangart *f*; Schritt *m*

gai·ter Gamasche *f*

gal F Mädchen *n*

ga·la 1. Festlichkeit *f*; Gala(veranstaltung) *f*; **2.** Gala...

gal·ax·y ASTR Milchstraße *f*, Galaxis *f*

gale Sturm m

gall[1] Frechheit f

gall[2] **1.** wund geriebene Stelle; **2.** wund reiben or scheuern; *fig* (ver)ärgern

gal·lant tapfer; galant, höflich

gal·lan·try Tapferkeit f; Galanterie f

gall blad·der ANAT Gallenblase f

gal·le·ry Galerie f; Empore f

gal·ley MAR Galeere f; Kombüse f; a. ~ **proof** PRINT Fahne f, Fahnenabzug m

gal·lon Gallone f (3,79 l, Br 4,55 l)

gal·lop 1. Galopp m; **2.** galoppieren (lassen)

gal·lows Galgen m

gal·lows hu·mo(u)r Galgenhumor m

ga·lore in rauen Mengen

gam·ble 1. (um Geld) spielen; **2.** Glücksspiel n

gam·bler (Glücks)Spieler(in)

gam·bol 1. Luftsprung m; **2.** (herum)tanzen, (herum)hüpfen

game (Karten-, Ball- *etc*)Spiel n; (einzelnes) Spiel (a. *fig*); HUNT Wild n; Wildbret n; *pl* Spiele *pl*; PED Sport m

game·keep·er Wildhüter m

game park, ~ **re·serve** Wildpark m; Wildreservat n

gan·der ZO Gänserich m

gang 1. (Arbeiter)Trupp m; Gang f, Bande f; Clique f; Horde f; **2.** ~ **up** sich zusammentun, *contp* sich zusammenrotten

gan·gling schlaksig

gang·ster Gangster m

gang war, ~ **war·fare** Bandenkrieg m

gang·way Gang m; AVIAT, MAR Gangway f

gaol, **gaol·bird**, **gaol·er** Br → **jail** etc

gap Lücke f; Kluft f; Spalte f

gape gähnen; klaffen; gaffen

gar·age 1. Garage f; (Reparatur)Werkstatt f (und Tankstelle f); **2.** Auto in e-r Garage ab- or unterstellen; Auto in die Garage fahren

gar·bage Abfall m, Müll m; ~ **bag** Müllbeutel m; ~ **can** Abfalleimer m, Mülleimer m; Abfalltonne f, Mülltonne f; ~ **truck** Müllwagen m

gar·den Garten m

gar·den·er Gärtner(in)

gar·den·ing Gartenarbeit f

gar·gle gurgeln

gar·ish grell, auffallend

gar·land Girlande f

gar·lic BOT Knoblauch m

gar·ment Kleidungsstück n; Gewand n

gar·nish GASTR garnieren

gar·ret Dachkammer f

gar·ri·son MIL Garnison f

gar·ter Strumpfband n; Sockenhalter m; Strumpfhalter m, Straps m

gas Gas n; F Benzin n, Sprit m

gas·e·ous gasförmig

gash klaffende Wunde

gas·ket TECH Dichtung(sring m) f

gas me·ter Gasuhr f, Gaszähler m

gas·o·lene, **gas·o·line** Benzin n; ~ **pump** Zapfsäule f

gasp 1. keuchen, röcheln; ~ (*for breath*) nach Atem ringen, F nach Luft schnappen; **2.** Keuchen n, Röcheln n

gas sta·tion Tankstelle f

gas stove Gasofen m, Gasherd m

gas·works TECH Gaswerk n

gate Tor n; Pforte f; Schranke f, Sperre f; AVIAT Flugsteig m

gate·crash F uneingeladen kommen (zu); sich ohne zu bezahlen hineinschmuggeln (in *acc*)

gate·post Tor-, Türpfosten m

gate·way Tor(weg m) n; Einfahrt f

gate·way drug Einstiegsdroge f

gath·er *v/t* sammeln, *Informationen* einholen, einziehen; *Personen* versammeln; ernten, pflücken; zusammenziehen, kräuseln; *fig* folgern, schließen (*from sth*); ~ **speed** schneller werden; *v/i* sich (ver)sammeln; sich (an)sammeln; **gath·er·ing** Versammlung f; Zusammenkunft f

gau·dy auffällig, bunt, grell; protzig

gauge Br → **gage**

gaunt hager; ausgemergelt

gaunt·let Schutzhandschuh m

gauze Gaze f; MED Bandage f, Binde f

gav·el Hammer m

gaw·ky linkisch

gay 1. lustig, fröhlich; bunt, (farben)prächtig; F schwul; **2.** F Schwule m

gaze 1. (starrer) Blick; **2.** starren; ~ **at** starren auf (*acc*), anstarren

ga·zette Amtsblatt n

ga·zelle ZO Gazelle f

gear TECH Getriebe n; MOT Gang m; *mst in cpds* Vorrichtung f, Gerät n; F Kleidung f, Aufzug m; **shift** (*esp Br change*) ~(**s**) MOT schalten; **shift** (*esp*

Br **change) *into second* ~** MOT in den zweiten Gang schalten

gear·box MOT Getriebe *n*

gear le·ver *Br*, **gear shift, gear stick** *Br* MOT Schalthebel *m*

Gei·ger count·er PHYS Geigerzähler *m*

geld·ing ZO Wallach *m*

gem Edelstein *m*

Gem·i·ni ASTR Zwillinge *pl*; **he (she) is (a) ~** er (sie) ist (ein) Zwilling

gen·der LING Genus *n*, Geschlecht *n*

gene BIOL Gen *n*, Erbfaktor *m*

gen·e·ral 1. allgemein; Haupt..., General...; **2.** MIL General *m*; ***in ~*** im Allgemeinen; ~ **de·liv·er·y: (*in care of*)** ~ postlagernd; **~ e·lec·tion** *Br* POL Parlamentswahlen *pl*

gen·e·ral·ize verallgemeinern

gen·er·al·ly im Allgemeinen, allgemein

gen·er·al prac·ti·tion·er (ABBR **GP**) *appr* Arzt *m* or Ärztin *f* für Allgemeinmedizin

gen·e·rate erzeugen; **gen·e·ra·tion** Erzeugung *f*; Generation *f*

gen·e·ra·tor ELECTR Generator *m*; MOT Lichtmaschine *f*

gen·e·ros·i·ty Großzügigkeit *f*

gen·e·rous großzügig; reichlich

ge·net·ic genetisch; **~ code** BIOL Erbanlage *f*; **~ en·gi·neer·ing** Gentechnologie *f*; **~ fin·ger·print** genetischer Fingerabdruck

ge·net·ics BIOL Genetik *f*, Vererbungslehre *f*

ge·ni·al freundlich

gen·i·tive *a*. **~ case** LING Genitiv *m*, zweiter Fall

ge·ni·us Genie *n*

gen·o·cide Völkermord *m*

gent *Br esp Br* Herr *m*; **gents** *Br* F Herrenklo *n*

gen·tle sanft, zart, sacht; mild

gen·tle·man Gentleman *m*; Herr *m*

gen·tle·man·ly gentlemanlike, vornehm

gen·tle·ness Sanftheit *f*, Zartheit *f*; Milde *f*

gen·try *Br* niederer Adel; Oberschicht *f*

gen·u·ine echt; aufrichtig

ge·og·ra·phy Geografie *f*

ge·ol·o·gy Geologie *f*

ge·om·e·try Geometrie *f*

germ BIOL, BOT Keim *m*; MED Bazillus *m*, Bakterie *f*, (Krankheits)Erreger *m*

Ger·man 1. deutsch; **2.** Deutsche *m*, *f*; LING Deutsch *n*; **~ shep·herd** ZO Deutscher Schäferhund

Ger·man·y Deutschland *n*

ger·mi·nate BIOL, BOT keimen (lassen)

ger·und LING Gerundium *n*

ges·tic·u·late gestikulieren

ges·ture Geste *f*, Gebärde *f*

get *v/t* bekommen, erhalten; sich *et*. verschaffen *or* besorgen; erwerben, sich aneignen; holen; bringen; F erwischen; F kapieren, verstehen; *j-n* dazu bringen (*to do* zu tun); *with pp*: lassen; ~ *one's hair cut* sich die Haare schneiden lassen; ~ *going* in Gang bringen; ~ *s.th. by heart* et. auswendig lernen; ~ *s.th. ready* et. fertig machen; *have got* haben; *have got to* müssen; *v/i* kommen, gelangen; *with pp or adj*: werden; ~ *tired* müde werden, ermüden; ~ *going* in Gang kommen; *fig* in Schwung kommen; ~ *home* nach Hause kommen; ~ *ready* sich fertig machen; ~ *about* herumkommen; sich herumsprechen *or* verbreiten (*rumor etc*); ~ *ahead of* übertreffen (*acc*); ~ *along* vorwärts-, vorankommen; auskommen (*with* mit *j-m*); zurechtkommen (*with* mit *et*.); ~ *at* herankommen an (*acc*); *what is he getting at?* worauf will er hinaus?; ~ *away* loskommen; entkommen; ~ *away with* davonkommen mit; ~ *back* zurückkommen; *et*. zurückbekommen; ~ *in* hinein-, hereinkommen; einsteigen (in *acc*); ~ *off* aussteigen (aus); davonkommen (*with* mit); ~ *on* einsteigen (in *acc*); → *get along*; ~ *out* herausgehen, hinausgehen; aussteigen (*of* aus); *et*. herausbekommen; ~ *over s.th.* über et. hinwegkommen; ~ *to* kommen nach; ~ *together* zusammenkommen; ~ *up* aufstehen

get·a·way Flucht *f*; **~ car** Fluchtauto *n*

get·up Aufmachung *f*

gey·ser GEOL Geysir *m*; *Br* TECH Durchlauferhitzer *m*

ghast·ly grässlich; schrecklich; (toten-)bleich

gher·kin Gewürzgurke *f*

ghet·to Getto *n*

ghost Geist *m*, Gespenst *n*; *fig* Spur *f*

ghost·ly geisterhaft

gi·ant 1. Riese *m*; **2.** riesig

gib·ber·ish Kauderwelsch *n*

G

gib·bet Galgen *m*

gibe 1. spotten (*at* über *acc*); **2.** höhnische Bemerkung, Stichelei *f*

gib·lets GASTR Hühner-, Gänseklein *n*

gid·di·ness MED Schwindel(gefühl *n*) *m*; **gid·dy** Schwindel erregend; *I feel ~* mir ist schwind(e)lig

gift Geschenk *n*; Talent *n*

gift·ed begabt

gig F MUS Gig *m*, Auftritt *m*, Konzert *n*

gi·gan·tic gigantisch, riesenhaft, riesig, gewaltig

gig·gle 1. kichern; **2.** Gekicher *n*

gild vergolden

gill ZO Kieme *f*; BOT Lamelle *f*

gim·mick F Trick *m*; Spielerei *f*

gin Gin *m*

gin·ger 1. Ingwer *m*; **2.** rötlich *or* gelblich braun;

gin·ger·bread Lebkuchen *m*, Pfefferkuchen *m*

gin·ger·ly behutsam, vorsichtig

gip·sy *Br* → *gypsy*

gi·raffe ZO Giraffe *f*

gir·der TECH Tragbalken *m*

gir·dle Hüfthalter *m*, Hüftgürtel *m*

girl Mädchen *n*

girl·friend Freundin *f*

girl guide *Br* Pfadfinderin *f*

girl·hood Mädchenjahre *pl*, Jugend *f*, Jugendzeit *f*

girl·ish mädchenhaft; Mädchen...

girl scout Pfadfinderin *f*

gi·ro *Br* Postgirodienst *m*

gi·ro ac·count *Br* Postgirokonto *n*

gi·ro cheque *Br* Postscheck *m*

girth (Sattel)Gurt *m*; (*a.* Körper)Umfang *m*

gist *das* Wesentliche, Kern *m*

give hingeben; schenken; spenden; *Leben* hingeben, opfern; *Befehl etc* geben, erteilen; *Hilfe* leisten; *Schutz* bieten; *Grund etc* angeben; THEA *etc* geben, aufführen; *Vortrag* halten; *Schmerzen* bereiten, verursachen; *Grüße etc* übermitteln; *~ her my love* bestelle ihr herzliche Grüße von mir; *~ birth to* zur Welt bringen; *~ s.o. to understand that* j-m zu verstehen geben, dass; *~ way* nachgeben; *Br* MOT die Vorfahrt lassen (*dat*); *~ away* hergeben, weggeben, verschenken; *j-n, etc.* verraten; *~ back* zurückgeben; *~ in Gesuch etc* einreichen; *Prüfungsarbeit etc* abgeben; nachgeben; aufgeben; *~ off* Geruch verbreiten; ausstoßen; ausströmen, verströmen; *~ on(to)* führen auf *or* nach, gehen nach; *~ out* aus-, verteilen; *esp Br* bekannt geben; zu Ende gehen (*supplies, strength etc*); F versagen (*engine etc*); *~ up* aufgeben; aufhören mit; *j-n* ausliefern; *~ o.s. up* sich (freiwillig) stellen (*to the police* der Polizei)

give-and-take beiderseitiges Entgegenkommen, Kompromiss(bereitschaft *f*) *m*

giv·en: be ~ to neigen zu (*dat*)

giv·en name Vorname *m*

gla·cial eisig; Eis...

gla·ci·er Gletscher *m*

glad froh, erfreut; *be ~ of* sich freuen über (*acc*); **glad·ly** gern(e)

glam·o(u)r Zauber *m*, Glanz *m*

glam·o(u)r·ous bezaubernd, reizvoll

glance 1. (schneller *or* flüchtiger) Blick (*at* auf *acc*); *at a ~* auf e-n Blick; **2.** (schnell *or* flüchtig) blicken (*at* auf *acc*)

gland ANAT Drüse *f*

glare 1. grell scheinen *or* leuchten; wütend starren; *~ at s.o.* j-n wütend anstarren; **2.** greller Schein, grelles Leuchten; wütender Blick

glar·ing *fig* schreiend

glass 1. Glas *n*; (Trink)Glas *n*; Glas (-gefäß) *n*; (Fern-, Opern)Glas *n*; *Br* F Spiegel *m*; *Br* Barometer *n*; (*a pair of*) *~es* (e-e) Brille *f*; **2.** gläsern; Glas...; **3.** *~ in*, *~ up* verglasen

glass case Vitrine *f*; Schaukasten *m*

glass·ful *ein* Glas (voll)

glass·house Gewächs-, Treibhaus *n*

glass·ware Glaswaren *pl*

glass·y gläsern; glasig

glaze 1. *v/t* verglasen; glasieren; *v/i: a. ~ over* glasig werden (*eyes*); **2.** Glasur *f*

gla·zi·er Glaser *m*

gleam 1. schwacher Schein, Schimmer *m*; **2.** leuchten, schimmern

glean *v/t* sammeln; *v/i* Ähren lesen

glee Fröhlichkeit *f*

glee club Gesangverein *m*

glee·ful ausgelassen, fröhlich

glen enges Bergtal *n*

glib gewandt; schlagfertig

glide 1. gleiten; segeln; **2.** Gleiten *n*; AVIAT Gleitflug *m*; **glid·er** Segelflugzeug *n*; **glid·ing** Segelfliegen *n*

glim·mer 1. schimmern; **2.** Schimmer *m*

glimpse 1. (nur) flüchtig zu sehen bekommen; **2.** flüchtiger Blick

glint 1. glitzern, glänzen; **2.** Glitzern *n*, Glanz *m*

glis·ten glitzern, glänzen

glit·ter 1. glitzern, funkeln, glänzen; **2.** Glitzern *n*, Funkeln *n*, Glanz *m*

gloat: ~ *over* sich hämisch *or* diebisch freuen über (*acc*)

gloat·ing hämisch, schadenfroh

glo·bal Welt..., global, weltumspannend; umfassend; ~ **warm·ing** Erwärmung *f* der Erdatmosphäre

globe (Erd)Kugel *f*; Globus *m*

gloom Düsterkeit *f*; Dunkelheit *f*; düstere *or* gedrückte Stimmung

gloom·y düster; hoffnungslos; niedergeschlagen; trübsinnig, trübselig

glo·ri·fi·ca·tion Verherrlichung *f*

glo·ri·fy verherrlichen

glo·ri·ous ruhmreich, glorreich; herrlich, prächtig

glo·ry Ruhm *m*; Herrlichkeit *f*, Pracht *f*

gloss 1. Glanz *m*; LING Glosse *f*; **2.** ~ *over* beschönigen, vertuschen

glos·sa·ry Glossar *n*

gloss·y glänzend

glove Handschuh *m*; ~ **com·part·ment** MOT Handschuhfach *n*

glow 1. glühen; **2.** Glühen *n*; Glut *f*

glow·er finster blicken

glow-worm ZO Glühwürmchen *n*

glu·cose Traubenzucker *m*

glue 1. Leim *m*; **2.** kleben

glum bedrückt

glut·ton *fig* Vielfraß *m*

glut·ton·ous gefräßig, unersättlich

gnarled knorrig; knotig (*hands etc*)

gnash knirschen (mit)

gnat ZO (Stech)Mücke *f*

gnaw (zer)nagen; (zer)fressen

gnome Gnom *m*; Gartenzwerg *m*

go 1. gehen, fahren, reisen (*to* nach); (fort)gehen; gehen, führen (*to* nach) (*road etc*); sich erstrecken, gehen (*to* bis zu); verkehren, fahren (*bus etc*); TECH gehen, laufen, funktionieren; vergehen (*time*); harmonieren, passen (*with* zu); ausgehen, ablaufen, ausfallen; werden (~ *mad*; ~ *blind*); *be ~ing to inf* im Begriff sein zu *inf*, *tun* wollen; *tun* werden; ~ *shares* teilen; ~ *swimming* schwim-

men gehen; *it is ~ing to rain* es gibt Regen; *I must be ~ing* ich muss gehen; ~ *for a walk* e-n Spaziergang machen, spazieren gehen; ~ *to bed* ins Bett gehen; ~ *to school* zur Schule gehen; ~ *to see* besuchen; *let* ~ loslassen; ~ *after* nachlaufen (*dat*); sich bemühen um; ~ *ahead* vorangehen; vorausgehen, vorausfahren; ~ *ahead with* beginnen mit; fortfahren mit; ~ *at* losgehen auf (*acc*); ~ *away* weggehen; ~ *between* vermitteln zwischen (*dat*); ~ *by* vorbeigehen, vorbeifahren; vergehen (*time*); *fig* sich halten an (*acc*), sich richten nach; ~ *down* untergehen (*sun*); ~ *for* holen; ~ *in* hineingehen; ~ *in for an examination* e-e Prüfung machen; ~ *off* fortgehen, weggehen; losgehen (*gun etc*); ~ *on* weitergehen, weiterfahren; *fig* fortfahren (*doing* zu tun); *fig* vor sich gehen, vorgehen; ~ *out* hinausgehen; ausgehen (*with* mit); ausgehen (*light etc*); ~ *through* durchgehen, durchnehmen; durchmachen; ~ *up* steigen; hinaufgehen, -steigen; ~ *without* sich behelfen ohne, auskommen ohne; **2.** F Schwung *m*, Schmiss *m*; *esp Br* F Versuch *m*; *it's my* ~ *esp Br* F ich bin dran *or* an der Reihe; *it's a* ~*!* F abgemacht!; *have a* ~ *at s.th. Br* F et. probieren; *be all the* ~ *Br* F große Mode sein

goad *fig* anstacheln

go-a·head[1]: *get the* ~ grünes Licht bekommen; *give s.o. the* ~ j-m grünes Licht geben

go-a·head[2] *Br* zielstrebig; unternehmungslustig

goal Ziel *n* (*a. fig*); SPORT Tor *n*; *keep* ~ im Tor stehen; *score a* ~ ein Tor schießen *or* erzielen; *consolation* ~ Ehrentreffer *m*; *own* ~ Eigentor *n*, Eigentreffer *m*; *shot at* ~ Torschuss *m*

goal·ie, **goal·keep·er** SPORT Torwart *m*, Torhüter *m*

goal kick *soccer.* Abstoß *m*

goal line SPORT Torlinie *f*

goal·mouth SPORT Torraum *m*

goal·post SPORT Torpfosten *m*

goat ZO Ziege *f*, Geiß *f*

gob·ble schlingen; *mst* ~ *up* verschlingen (*a. fig*)

go-be·tween Vermittler(in), Mittelsmann *m*

gob·lin Kobold m
god REL *God* Gott m; *fig* Abgott m
god·child Patenkind n
god·dess Göttin f
god·fa·ther Pate m (a. fig), Taufpate m
god·for·sak·en contp gottverlassen
god·head Gottheit f
god·less gottlos
god·like gottähnlich; göttlich
god·moth·er (Tauf)Patin f
god·pa·rent (Tauf)Pate, (Tauf)Patin f
god·send Geschenk n des Himmels
gog·gle glotzen
gog·gle box Br F TV Glotze f
gog·gles Schutzbrille f
go·ings-on F Treiben n, Vorgänge pl
gold 1. Gold n; **2.** golden
gold·en mst fig golden, goldgelb
gold·finch ZO Stieglitz m
gold·fish ZO Goldfisch m
gold·smith Goldschmied m
golf 1. Golf(spiel) n; **2.** Golf spielen
golf club Golfschläger m; Golfklub m
golf course, golf links Golfplatz m
gon·do·la Gondel f
gone adj verf; F futsch; vergangen; tot; F hoffnungslos
good 1. gut; artig; gütig; gründlich; **~ at** geschickt or gut in (dat); *real ~* F echt gut; **2.** Nutzen m, Wert m; *das Gute; do (no) ~* (nichts) nützen; *for ~* für immer; F *what ~ is ...?* was nützt ...?
good·by(e) 1. *wish s.o. ~, say ~ to s.o.* j-m Auf Wiedersehen sagen; **2.** int (auf) Wiedersehen!
Good Fri·day REL Karfreitag m
good-hu·mo(u)red gut gelaunt; gutmütig
good-look·ing gut aussehend
good-na·tured gutmütig
good·ness Güte f; *thank ~!* Gott sei Dank!; *(my) ~!, ~ gracious!* du meine Güte!, du lieber Himmel!; *for ~' sake* um Himmels willen!; *~ knows* weiß der Himmel
goods ECON Waren pl, Güter pl
good·will gute Absicht, guter Wille; ECON Firmenwert m
good·y F Bonbon m, n
goose ZO Gans f
goose·ber·ry BOT Stachelbeere f
goose·flesh, goose pim·ples fig Gänsehaut f
go·pher ZO Taschenratte f; Ziesel m

gore durchbohren, aufspießen
gorge 1. ANAT Kehle f, Schlund m; GEOGR enge (Fels)Schlucht; **2.** verschlingen; schlingen, (sich) voll stopfen
gor·geous prächtig
go·ril·la ZO Gorilla m
gor·y F blutrünstig
gosh int F Mensch!, Mann!
gos·ling ZO junge Gans
go-slow Br ECON Bummelstreik m
Gos·pel REL Evangelium n
gos·sa·mer Altweibersommer m
gos·sip 1. Klatsch m, Tratsch m; Klatschbase f; **2.** klatschen, tratschen
gos·sip·y geschwätzig; voller Klatsch und Tratsch (letter etc)
Goth·ic ARCH **1.** gotisch; *~ novel* Schauerroman m; **2.** Gotik f
gourd BOT Kürbis m
gout MED Gicht f
gov·ern v/t regieren; lenken, leiten; v/i herrschen
gov·ern·ess Erzieherin f
gov·ern·ment Regierung f, Staat m
gov·er·nor Gouverneur m; Direktor m, Leiter m; F Alte m
gown Kleid n; Robe f, Talar m
grab 1. packen, (hastig or gierig) ergreifen, fassen; **2.** (hastiger or gieriger) Griff; TECH Greifer m
grace 1. Anmut f, Grazie f; Anstand m; ECON Frist f, Aufschub m; Gnade f; REL Tischgebet n; **2.** zieren, schmücken
grace·ful anmutig
grace·less ungraziös
gra·cious gnädig
gra·da·tion Abstufung f
grade 1. Grad m, Rang m; Stufe f; ECON Qualität f; RAIL etc Steigung f, Gefälle n; PED Klasse f, Note f, Zensur f; **2.** sortieren, einteilen; abstufen
grade cross·ing RAIL schienengleicher Bahnübergang
grade school Grundschule f
gra·di·ent Br RAIL etc Steigung f, Gefälle n
grad·u·al stufenweise, allmählich
grad·u·al·ly nach und nach; allmählich
grad·u·ate 1. UNIV Hochschulabsolvent (in), Akademiker(in); Graduierte m, f; PED Schulabgänger(in); **2.** abstufen, staffeln; UNIV graduieren; PED die Abschlussprüfung bestehen

grad·u·a·tion Abstufung f, Staffelung f; UNIV Graduierung f; PED Absolvieren n (**from** gen)

graf·fi·ti Graffiti pl, Wandschmierereien pl

graft 1. MED Transplantat n; AGR Pfropfreis n; **2.** MED Gewebe verpflanzen, transplantieren; AGR pfropfen

grain (Samen-, esp Getreide)Korn n; Getreide n; (Sand- etc)Körnchen n, (-)Korn n; Maserung f; **go against the ~ for s.o.** fig j-m gegen den Strich gehen

gram Gramm n

gram·mar Grammatik f

gram·mar school Grundschule f; Br appr (humanistisches) Gymnasium

gram·mat·i·cal grammatisch, Grammatik...

gramme → **gram**

gra·na·ry Kornspeicher m

grand 1. fig großartig; erhaben; groß; Groß..., Haupt...; **2.** F Riese m (1000 dollars or pounds)

grand·child Enkel m, Enkelin f

grand·daugh·ter Enkelin f

gran·deur Größe f, Erhabenheit f; Großartigkeit f

grand·fa·ther Großvater m

gran·di·ose großartig

grand·moth·er Großmutter f

grand·par·ents Großeltern pl

grand·son Enkel m

grand·stand SPORT Haupttribüne f

gran·ny F Oma f

grant 1. bewilligen, gewähren; Erlaubnis etc geben; Bitte etc erfüllen; et. zugeben; **take s.th. for ~ed** et. als selbstverständlich betrachten or hinnehmen; **2.** Stipendium n; Bewilligung f, Unterstützung f

gran·u·lat·ed körnig, granuliert; **~ sugar** Kristallzucker m

gran·ule Körnchen n

grape BOT Weinbeere f, Weintraube f

grape·fruit BOT Grapefruit f, Pampelmuse f

grape·vine BOT Weinstock m

graph grafische Darstellung

graph·ic grafisch; anschaulich; **~ arts** Grafik f; **graph·ics** EDP Grafik f

grap·ple: ~ with kämpfen mit, fig a. sich herumschlagen mit

grasp 1. (er)greifen, packen; fig verstehen, begreifen; **2.** Griff m; Reichweite f (a. fig); fig Verständnis n

grass Gras n; Rasen m; Weide(land n) f; sl. Grass n (marijuana)

grass·hop·per ZO Heuschrecke f

grass roots POL Basis f

grass wid·ow Strohwitwe f

grass wid·ow·er Strohwitwer m

gras·sy grasbedeckt, Gras...

grate 1. (Kamin)Gitter n; (Feuer)Rost m; **2.** reiben, raspeln; knirschen (mit); **~ on s.o.'s nerves** an j-s Nerven zerren

grate·ful dankbar

grat·er Reibe f

grat·i·fi·ca·tion Befriedigung f; Freude f; **grat·i·fy** erfreuen; befriedigen

grat·ing¹ kratzend, knirschend, quietschend; schrill; unangenehm

grat·ing² Gitter(werk) n

grat·i·tude Dankbarkeit f

gra·tu·i·tous unentgeltlich; freiwillig

gra·tu·i·ty Abfindung f; Gratifikation f; Trinkgeld n

grave¹ ernst; (ge)wichtig; gemessen

grave² Grab n

grave·dig·ger Totengräber m

grav·el 1. Kies m; **2.** mit Kies bestreuen

grave·stone Grabstein m

grave·yard Friedhof m

grav·i·ta·tion PHYS Gravitation f, Schwerkraft f

grav·i·ty PHYS Schwerkraft f; Ernst m

gra·vy Bratensaft m; Bratensoße f

gray 1. grau; **2.** Grau n; **3.** grau machen or werden

gray·hound ZO Windhund m

graze¹ Vieh weiden (lassen); (ab)weiden; (ab)grasen

graze² 1. streifen; schrammen; Haut (ab-, auf)schürfen, (auf)schrammen; **2.** Abschürfung f, Schramme f; Streifschuss m

grease 1. Fett n; TECH Schmierfett n, Schmiere f; **2.** (ein)fetten; TECH schmieren; **greas·y** fett(ig), ölig; speckig; schmierig

great groß; Ur(groß)...; F großartig, super

Great Brit·ain Großbritannien n

great-grand·child Urenkel(in)

great-grand·par·ents Urgroßeltern pl

great·ly sehr

great·ness Größe f

Greece Griechenland *n*

greed Gier *f*; **greed·y** gierig (**for** auf *acc*, nach); habgierig; gefräßig

Greek 1. griechisch; **2.** Grieche *m*, Griechin *f*; LING Griechisch *n*

green 1. grün; *fig* grün, unerfahren; **2.** Grün *n*; Grünfläche *f*, Rasen *m*; *pl* grünes Gemüse, Blattgemüse *n*

green·back F Dollar *m*

green belt Grüngürtel *m*

green card Arbeitserlaubnis *f*

green·gro·cer *esp Br* Obst- und Gemüsehändler(in)

green·horn F Greenhorn *n*, Grünschnabel *m*

green·house Gewächs-, Treibhaus *n*; **~ ef·fect** Treibhauseffekt *m*

green·ish grünlich

greet grüßen; **greet·ing** Begrüßung *f*, Gruß *m*; *pl* Grüße *pl*

gre·nade MIL Granate *f*

grey *Br* → **gray**

grid Gitter *n*; ELECTR *etc* Versorgungsnetz *n*; Gitter(netz) *n* (*map etc*)

grid·i·ron Bratrost *m*

grief Kummer *m*

griev·ance (Grund *m* zur) Beschwerde *f*; Missstand *m*

grieve *v/t* betrüben, bekümmern; *v/i* bekümmert sein; **~ for** trauern um

griev·ous schwer, schlimm

grill 1. grillen; **2.** Grill *m*; Bratrost *m*; GASTR *das* Gegrillte *n*

grim grimmig; schrecklich; erbittert; F schlimm

gri·mace 1. Fratze *f*, Grimasse *f*; **2.** Grimassen schneiden

grime Schmutz *m*; Ruß *m*

grim·y schmutzig; rußig

grin 1. Grinsen *n*; **2.** grinsen

grind *v/t* (zer)mahlen, zerreiben, zerkleinern; *Messer etc* schleifen; *Fleisch* durchdrehen; **~ one's teeth** mit den Zähnen knirschen; *v/i* F schuften; pauken, büffeln; **2.** Schinderei *f*, F Schufterei *f*; **the daily ~** das tägliche Einerlei

grind·er (*Messer- etc*)Schleifer *m*; TECH Schleifmaschine *f*; TECH Mühle *f*

grind·stone Schleifstein *m*

grip 1. packen (*a. fig*); **2.** Griff *m*; *fig* Gewalt *f*; Herrschaft *f*; Reisetasche *f*

grip·ping spannend

gris·ly grässlich, schrecklich

gris·tle GASTR Knorpel *m*

grit 1. Kies *m*, (grober) Sand; *fig* Mut *m*; **2.** streuen; **~ one's teeth** die Zähne zusammenbeißen

griz·zly (bear) ZO Grislibär *m*, Graubär *m*

groan 1. stöhnen, ächzen; **2.** Stöhnen *n*, Ächzen *n*

gro·cer Lebensmittelhändler *m*

gro·cer·ies Lebensmittel *pl*

gro·cer·y Lebensmittelgeschäft *n*

grog·gy F groggy, schwach *or* wackelig (auf den Beinen)

groin ANAT Leiste *f*, Leistengegend *f*

groom 1. Pferdepfleger *m*, Stallbursche *m*; Bräutigam *m*; **2.** *Pferde* versorgen, striegeln; pflegen

groove Rinne *f*, Furche *f*, Rille *f*, Nut *f*

grope tasten; F *Mädchen* befummeln

gross 1. dick, feist; grob, derb; ECON Brutto...; **2.** Gros *n*

gro·tesque grotesk

ground¹ gemahlen (*coffee etc*); **~ meat** Hackfleisch *n*

ground² **1.** (Erd)Boden *m*, Erde *f*; Boden *m*, Gebiet *n*; SPORT (*Spiel*)Platz *m*; ELECTR Erdung *f*; (Boden)Satz *m*; *fig* Beweggrund *m*; *pl* Grundstück *n*, Park *m*, Gartenanlage *f*; **on the ~(s) of** aufgrund (*gen*); **hold** *or* **stand one's ~** sich behaupten; **2.** MAR auflaufen; ELECTR erden; *fig* gründen, stützen; **~ crew** AVIAT Bodenpersonal *n*; **~ floor** *esp Br* Erdgeschoss *n*; **~ forc·es** MIL Bodentruppen *pl*, Landstreitkräfte *pl*

ground·hog ZO Amer. Waldmurmeltier *n*

ground·ing ELECTR Erdung *f*; Grundlagen *pl*, Grundkenntnisse *pl*

ground·keep·er SPORT Platzwart *m*

ground·less grundlos

ground·nut BOT Erdnuss *f*

grounds·man *Br* SPORT Platzwart *m*

ground| staff *Br* AVIAT Bodenpersonal *n*; **~ sta·tion** Bodenstation *f*

ground·work *fig* Grundlage *f*, Fundament *n*

group 1. Gruppe *f*; **2.** (sich) gruppieren

group·ie F Groupie *n*

group·ing Gruppierung *f*

grove Wäldchen *n*, Gehölz *n*

grov·el (am Boden) kriechen

grow *v/i* wachsen; (allmählich) werden; **~ up** aufwachsen, heranwachsen; *v/t* BOT anpflanzen, anbauen, züchten; **~**

a beard sich e-n Bart wachsen lassen

grow·er Züchter *m*, Erzeuger *m*

growl knurren, brummen

grown-up 1. erwachsen; **2.** Erwachsene *m, f*

growth Wachsen *n*; Wachstum *n*; Wuchs *m*, Größe *f*; *fig* Zunahme *f*, Anwachsen *n*; MED Gewächs *n*, Wucherung *f*

grub 1. ZO Larve *f*, Made *f*; F Futter *n*; **2.** graben

grub·by schmudd(e)lig

grudge 1. missgönnen (*s.o. s.th.* j-m et.); **2.** Groll *m*

grudg·ing·ly widerwillig

gru·el Haferschleim *m*

gruff grob, schroff, barsch, unwirsch

grum·ble murren, F meckern (*über acc* about, at); *~ at* schimpfen über (*acc*)

grump·y F schlecht gelaunt, mürrisch, missmutig, verdrießlich, verdrossen

grun·gy F schmudd(e)lig-schlampig; MUS schlecht und laut

grunt 1. grunzen; brummen; stöhnen; **2.** Grunzen *n*; Stöhnen *n*

guar·an·tee 1. Garantie *f*; Kaution *f*, Sicherheit *f*; **2.** (sich ver)bürgen für; garantieren

guar·an·tor JUR Bürge *m*, Bürgin *f*

guar·an·ty JUR Garantie *f*, Sicherheit *f*

guard 1. Wache *f*, (Wacht)Posten *m*, Wächter *m*; Wärter *m*, Aufseher *m*; Wache *f*, Bewachung *f*; *Br* Zugbegleiter *m*; Schutz(vorrichtung *f*) *m*; Garde *f*; *be on ~* Wache stehen; *be on (off) one's ~* (nicht) auf der Hut sein; **2.** *v/t* bewachen, (be)schützen (*from* vor *dat*); *v/i* sich hüten *or* in Acht nehmen *or* schützen (*against* vor *dat*)

guard·ed vorsichtig, zurückhaltend

guard·i·an 1. JUR Vormund *m*; **2.** Schutz...

guard·i·an·ship JUR Vormundschaft *f*

gue(r)·ril·la MIL Guerilla *m*

gue(r)·ril·la war·fare Guerillakrieg *m*

guess 1. (er)raten; vermuten; schätzen; glauben, meinen; **2.** Vermutung *f*

guess·work (reine) Vermutung(en *pl*)

guest Gast *m*

guest·house (Hotel)Pension *f*, Fremdenheim *n*

guest-room Gäste-, Fremdenzimmer *n*

guf·faw 1. schallendes Gelächter; **2.** schallend lachen

guid·ance Führung *f*; (An)Leitung *f*

guide 1. (Reise-, Fremden)Führer(in); (Reise- *etc*)Führer *m* (*book*); Handbuch (*to gen*); *a ~ to London* ein London-Führer; **2.** leiten; führen; lenken

guide·book (Reise- *etc*)Führer *m*

guid·ed tour Führung *f*

guide·lines Richtlinien *pl* (*on gen*)

guild HIST Gilde *f*, Zunft *f*

guile·less arglos

guilt Schuld *f*

guilt·less schuldlos, unschuldig (*of* an *dat*)

guilt·y schuldig (*of gen*); schuldbewusst

guin·ea pig ZO Meerschweinchen *n*; *fig* Versuchsperson *f*, *f* Versuchskaninchen *n*

guise *fig* Gestalt *f*, Maske *f*

gui·tar MUS Gitarre *f*

gulch GEOGR tiefe Schlucht, Klamm *f*

gulf GEOGR Golf *m*; *fig* Kluft *f*

gull ZO Möwe *f*

gul·let ANAT Speiseröhre *f*; Gurgel *f*, Kehle *f*

gulp 1. (großer) Schluck; **2.** *often ~ down* Getränk hinunterstürzen, *Speise* hinunterschlingen

gum[1] ANAT *mst pl* Zahnfleisch *n*

gum[2] **1.** Gummi *m, n*; Klebstoff *m*; Kaugummi *m*; (Frucht)Gummi *m*; **2.** kleben

gump·tion F Grips *m*; Schneid *m*

gun 1. Gewehr *n*; Pistole *f*, Revolver *m*; Geschütz *n*, Kanone *f*; **2.** *~ down* niederschießen

gun·fight Feuergefecht *n*, Schießerei *f*

gun·fire Schüsse *pl*; MIL Geschützfeuer *n*

gun li·cence *Br*, **gun li·cense** Waffenschein *m*

gun·man Bewaffnete *m*

gun·point: *at ~* mit vorgehaltener Waffe, mit Waffengewalt

gun·pow·der Schießpulver *n*

gun·run·ner Waffenschmuggler *m*

gun·run·ning Waffenschmuggel *m*

gun·shot Schuss *m*; *within (out of) ~* in (außer) Schussweite

gur·gle 1. gurgeln, gluckern, glucksen; **2.** Gurgeln *n*, Gluckern *n*, Glucksen *n*

gush 1. strömen, schießen (*from* aus); **2.** Schwall *m*, Strom *m* (*a. fig*)

gust Windstoß *m*, Bö *f*

gust F Eingeweide *pl*; Schneid *m*, Mumm *m*

gut·ter Gosse *f (a. fig)*, Rinnstein *m*; Dachrinne *f*

guy F Kerl *m*, Typ *m*

guz·zle F saufen; fressen

gym F Fitnesscenter *n*; → **gymnasium**; → **gymnastics**

gym·na·si·um Turn-, Sporthalle *f*

gym·nast Turner(in)

gym·nas·tics Turnen *n*, Gymnastik *f*

gym shirt Turnhemd *n*

gym shorts Turnhose *f*

gy·n(a)e·col·o·gist Gynäkologe *m*, Gynäkologin *f*, Frauenarzt *m*, -ärztin *f*

gy·n(a)e·col·o·gy Gynäkologie *f*, Frauenheilkunde *f*

gyp·sy Zigeuner *m*, Zigeunerin *f*

gy·rate kreisen, sich (im Kreis) drehen, (herum)wirbeln

H

H, h H, h *n*

hab·it (An)Gewohnheit *f*; *esp* (Ordens-)Tracht *f*; **get into (out of) the ~ of smoking** sich das Rauchen angewöhnen (abgewöhnen); **ha·bit·u·al** gewohnheitsmäßig, Gewohnheits...

hack¹ hacken

hack² *contp* Schreiberling *m*

hack³ *contp* Klepper *m*

hack·er EDP Hacker *m*

hack·neyed abgedroschen

had·dock ZO Schellfisch *m*

h(a)e·mor·rhage MED Blutung *f*

hag hässliches altes Weib, Hexe *f*

hag·gard abgespannt; verhärmt, abgehärmt; hager

hag·gle feilschen, handeln

hail 1. Hagel *m*; 2. hageln

hail·stone Hagelkorn *n*

hail·storm Hagelschauer *m*

hair *einzelnes* Haar; *coll* Haar *n*, Haare *pl*; **let one's ~ down** F aus sich herausgehen; **without turning a ~** ohne mit der Wimper zu zucken

hair-breadth → **hair's breadth**

hair·brush Haarbürste *f*

hair·cut Haarschnitt *m*

hair·do F Frisur *f*

hair·dress·er Friseur(in)

hair·dri·er, hair·dry·er Trockenhaube *f*; Haartrockner *m*, Föhn *m*

hair·grip *Br* Haarklammer *f*, Haarklemme *f*

hair·less ohne Haare, kahl

hair·pin Haarnadel *f*; **~ bend** MOT Haarnadelkurve *f*

hair-rais·ing haarsträubend

hair's breadth: **by a ~** um Haaresbreite

hair slide *Br* Haarspange *f*

hair-split·ting Haarspalterei *f*

hair·spray Haarspray *m, n*

hair·style Frisur *f*

hair styl·ist Hair-Stylist *m*, Damenfriseur *m*

hair·y behaart, haarig

half 1. Hälfte *f*; **go halves** halbe-halbe machen, teilen; 2. halb; **~ an hour** e-e halbe Stunde; **~ a pound** ein halbes Pfund; **~ past ten** halb elf (Uhr); **~ way up** auf halber Höhe

half-breed Halbblut *n*

half-broth·er Halbbruder *m*

half-caste *esp contp* Mischling *m*

half-heart·ed halbherzig

half time SPORT Halbzeit *f*; **~ score** SPORT Halbzeitstand *m*

half·way halb; auf halbem Weg, in der Mitte; **~ line** soccer: Mittellinie *f*

half-wit·ted schwachsinnig

hal·i·but ZO Heilbutt *m*

hall Halle *f*, Saal *m*; Flur *m*, Diele *f*; *esp Br* Herrenhaus *n*; *Br* UNIV Speisesaal *m*; *Br* **~ of residence** Studentenheim *n*

hall·mark *fig* Kennzeichen *n*

Hal·low·e'en Abend *m* vor Allerheiligen

hal·lu·ci·na·tion Halluzination *f*

hall·way Halle *f*, Diele *f*; Korridor *m*

ha·lo ASTR Hof *m*; Heiligenschein *m*

halt 1. Halt *m*; 2. (an)halten

hal·ter Halfter *m, n*

halt·ing zögernd, stockend

halve halbieren

ham Schinken *m*; **~ and eggs** Schinken mit (Spiegel)Ei

ham·burg·er GASTR Hamburger *m*; Rinderhack *n*

ham·let Weiler *m*

ham·mer 1. Hammer *m*; **2.** hämmern

ham·mock Hängematte *f*

ham·per[1] (Deckel)Korb *m*; Präsentkorb *m*; Wäschekorb *m*

ham·per[2] (be)hindern

ham·ster ZO Hamster *m*

hand 1. Hand *f* (*a. fig*); Handschrift *f*; (Uhr)Zeiger *m*; *often in cpds* Arbeiter *m*; Fachmann *m*; *card game*: Blatt *n*, Karten *pl*; *~ in glove* ein Herz und eine Seele; *change ~s* den Besitzer wechseln; *give or lend a ~* mit zugreifen, *j-m* helfen (*with* by); *shake ~s with j-m* die Hand schütteln or geben; *at ~* in Reichweite; nahe; bei der or zur Hand; *at first ~* aus erster Hand; *by ~* mit der Hand; *on the one ~* einerseits; *on the other ~* andererseits; *on the right ~* rechts; *~s off!* Hände weg!; *~s up!* Hände hoch!; **2.** aushändigen, (über)geben, (über)reichen; *~ around* herumreichen; *~ down* weitergeben, überliefern; *in Prüfungsarbeit etc* abgeben; *Bericht, Gesuch etc* einreichen; *~ on* weiterreichen, weitergeben; überliefern; *~ out* austeilen, verteilen; *~ over* übergeben, aushändigen (*to dat*); *~ up* hinauf-, heraufreichen

hand·bag Handtasche *f*

hand bag·gage Handgepäck *n*

hand·ball SPORT Handball *m*; *soccer*: Handspiel *n*

hand·book Handbuch *n*

hand·bill Handzettel *m*, Flugblatt *n*

hand·brake TECH Handbremse *f*

hand·cart Handwagen *m*

hand·cuffs Handschellen *pl*

hand·ful Hand voll *f*; F Plage *f*

hand gre·nade MIL Handgranate *f*

hand·i·cap 1. Handikap *n*, MED *a.* Behinderung *f*, SPORT *a.* Vorgabe *f*; → *mental handicap, physical handicap*; **2.** behindern, benachteiligen

hand·i·capped 1. gehandikapt, behindert, benachteiligt; → *mental, physical*; **2.** *the* ~ MED die Behinderten *pl*

hand·ker·chief Taschentuch *n*

han·dle 1. Griff *m*; Stiel *m*; Henkel *m*; Klinke *f*; *fly off the* ~ F wütend werden; **2.** anfassen, berühren; hantieren or umgehen mit; behandeln

han·dle·bar(s) Lenkstange *f*

hand lug·gage Handgepäck *n*

hand·made handgearbeitet

hand·out Almosen *n*; Handzettel *m*; Hand-out *n*, Informationsmaterial *n*

hand·rail Geländer *n*

hand·shake Händedruck *m*

hand·some gut aussehend; *fig* ansehnlich, beträchtlich (*sum etc*)

hands-on praktisch

hand·spring Handstandüberschlag *m*

hand·stand Handstand *m*

hand·writ·ing Handschrift *f*

hand·writ·ten handgeschrieben

hand·y zur Hand; geschickt; handlich, praktisch; nützlich; *come in* ~ sich als nützlich erweisen; (sehr) gelegen kommen; **hand·y·man** Handwerker *m*; *be a* ~ *a.* handwerklich geschickt sein

hang (auf-, be-, ein)hängen; *Tapete* ankleben; *j-n* (auf)hängen; ~ *o.s.* sich erhängen; ~ *about*, ~ *around* herumlungern; ~ *on* sich klammern (*to an acc*) (*a. fig*), festhalten (*to acc*); TEL am Apparat bleiben; ~ *up* TEL einhängen, auflegen; *she hung up on me* sie legte einfach auf

han·gar Hangar *m*, Flugzeughalle *f*

hang·er Kleiderbügel *m*

hang glid·er SPORT (Flug)Drachen *m*; Drachenflieger(in)

hang glid·ing SPORT Drachenfliegen *n*

hang·ing 1. Hänge...; **2.** (Er)Hängen *n*

hang·ings Tapete *f*, Wandbehang *m*, Vorhang *m*

hang·man Henker *m*

hang·nail MED Niednagel *m*

hang·o·ver Katzenjammer *m*, Kater *m*

han·ker F sich sehnen (*after, for* nach)

han·kie, han·ky F Taschentuch *n*

hap·haz·ard willkürlich, planlos, wahllos

hap·pen (zufällig) geschehen; sich ereignen, passieren, vorkommen

hap·pen·ing Ereignis *n*, Vorkommnis *n*; Happening *n*

hap·pi·ly glücklich(erweise)

hap·pi·ness Glück *n*

hap·py glücklich; erfreut

hap·py-go-luck·y unbekümmert, sorglos

ha·rangue 1. (Straf)Predigt *f*; **2.** *v/t j-m* e-e Strafpredigt halten

har·ass ständig belästigen; schikanie-

ren; aufreiben, zermürben
har·ass·ment ständige Belästigung; Schikane(n *pl*) *f*; → **sexual harassment**
har·bo(u)r 1. Hafen *m*; Zufluchtsort *m*; **2.** *j-m* Zuflucht *or* Unterschlupf gewähren; Groll etc hegen
hard hart (*a. fig*); fest; schwer, schwierig; heftig, stark; streng (*a. winter*); *fig* nüchtern (*facts etc*); **give s.o. a ~ time** j-m das Leben schwer machen; **~ of hearing** schwerhörig; **be ~ on s.th.** et. strapazieren; **~ up** F in (Geld)Schwierigkeiten, knapp bei Kasse; F **the ~ stuff** die harten Sachen (*alcohol, drugs*)
hard·back gebundene Ausgabe
hard-boiled GASTR hart (gekocht); F *fig* hart, unsentimental, nüchtern
hard cash Bargeld *n*; klingende Münze
hard core harter Kern; **hard-core** zum harten Kern gehörend; hart
hard court *tennis:* Hartplatz *m*
hard cov·er 1. gebunden; **2.** Hard Cover *n*, gebundene Ausgabe
hard cur·ren·cy ECON harte Währung
hard disk EDP Festplatte *f*
hard·en härten; hart machen *or* werden; (sich) abhärten
hard hat Schutzhelm *m*
hard-head·ed nüchtern, praktisch; starrköpfig, dickköpfig
hard-heart·ed hartherzig
hard la·bo(u)r JUR Zwangsarbeit *f*
hard line *esp* POL harter Kurs
hard-line *esp* POL hart, kompromisslos
hard·ly kaum
hard·ness Härte *f*; Schwierigkeit *f*
hard·ship Not *f*; Härte *f*; Strapaze *f*
hard shoul·der *Br* MOT Standspur *f*
hard·top MOT Hardtop *n, m*
hard·ware Eisenwaren *pl*; Haushaltswaren *pl*; EDP Hardware *f*
hard-wear·ing strapazierfähig
har·dy zäh, robust, abgehärtet; BOT winterhart, winterfest
hare ZO Hase *m*
hare·bell BOT Glockenblume *f*
hare·brained verrückt
hare·lip MED Hasenscharte *f*
harm 1. Schaden *m*; **2.** verletzen; schaden (*dat*)
harm·ful schädlich
harm·less harmlos

har·mo·ni·ous harmonisch
har·mo·nize harmonieren; in Einklang sein *or* bringen
har·mo·ny Harmonie *f*
har·ness 1. (*Pferde- etc*)Geschirr *n*; **die in ~** *fig* in den Sielen sterben; **2.** anschirren; anspannen (**to** an *acc*)
harp 1. MUS Harfe *f*; **2.** MUS Harfe spielen; F **~ on** (*about*) herumreiten auf (*dat*)
har·poon 1. Harpune *f*; **2.** harpunieren
har·row AGR **1.** Egge *f*; **2.** eggen
har·row·ing quälend, qualvoll, erschütternd
harsh rau; grell; streng; schroff, barsch
hart ZO Hirsch *m*
har·vest 1. Ernte(zeit) *f*; (Ernte)Ertrag *m*; **2.** ernten
har·vest·er MOT Mähdrescher *m*
hash¹ GASTR Haschee *n*; F **make a ~ of s.th.** et. verpfuschen
hash² F Hasch *n*
hash browns GASTR Brat-, Röstkartoffeln *pl*
hash·ish Haschisch *n*
hasp TECH Haspe *f*
haste Eile *f*, Hast *f*
has·ten *j-n* antreiben; (sich be)einlen; *et.* beschleunigen
hast·y eilig, hastig, überstürzt; voreilig
hat Hut *m*
hatch¹: *a.* **~ out** ZO ausbrüten; ausschlüpfen
hatch² Durchreiche *f*; AVIAT, MAR Luke *f*
hatch·back MOT (Wagen *m* mit) Hecktür *f*
hatch·et Beil *n*; **bury the ~** das Kriegsbeil begraben
hate 1. Hass *m*; **2.** hassen
hate·ful verhasst; abscheulich
ha·tred Hass *m*
haugh·ty hochmütig, überheblich
haul 1. ziehen, zerren; schleppen; befördern, transportieren; **2.** Ziehen *n*; Fischzug *m*, *fig* F *a.* Fang *m*; Beförderung *f*, Transport *m*; Transportweg *m*
haul·age Beförderung *f*, Transport *m*
haul·er, *Br* **haul·i·er** Transportunternehmer *m*
haunch ANAT Hüfte *f*, Hüftpartie *f*, Hinterbacke *f*; GASTR Keule *f*
haunt 1. spuken in (*dat*); häufig besuchen; *fig* verfolgen, quälen; **2.** häufig besuchter Ort; Schlupfwinkel *m*

haunt·ing quälend; unvergesslich, eindringlich

have *v/t* haben; erhalten, bekommen; essen, trinken; **~ breakfast** frühstücken; **~ a cup of tea** e-n Tee trinken); *with inf*: müssen (*I ~ to go now* ich muss jetzt gehen); *with object and pp*: lassen (*I had my hair cut* ich ließ mir die Haare schneiden); **~ back** zurückbekommen; **~ on** *Kleidungsstück* anhaben, *Hut* aufhaben; *v/aux* haben; *v/i* often sein; *I ~ come* ich bin gekommen

ha·ven Hafen *m* (*mst fig*)

hav·oc Verwüstung *f*, Zerstörung *f*; **play ~ with** verwüsten, zerstören; *fig* verheerend wirken auf (*acc*)

hawk¹ ZO Habicht *m*, Falke *m*

hawk² hausieren mit; auf der Straße verkaufen; **hawk·er** Hausierer(in); Straßenhändler(in); Drücker(in)

haw·thorn BOT Weißdorn *m*

hay Heu *n*

hay fe·ver MED Heuschnupfen *m*

hay·loft Heuboden *m*

hay·stack Heuhaufen *m*

haz·ard Gefahr *f*, Risiko *n*

haz·ard·ous gewagt, gefährlich, riskant; **~ waste** Sonder-, Giftmüll *m*

haze Dunst(schleier) *m*

ha·zel 1. BOT Hasel(nuss)strauch *m*; **2.** (hasel)nussbraun

ha·zel·nut BOT Haselnuss *f*

haz·y dunstig, diesig; *fig* unklar, verschwommen

H-bomb H-Bombe *f*, Wasserstoffbombe *f*

he 1. er; **2.** Er *m*; ZO Männchen *n*; **~-goat** Ziegenbock *m*

head 1. Kopf *m*; (Ober)Haupt *n*; Chef *m*; (An)Führer(in), Leiter(in); Spitze *f*; Kopf(ende *n*) *m*; Kopf *m* (*of a page, nail etc*); Vorderseite *f*; Überschrift *f*; **20 dollars a ~** *or per* ~ zwanzig Dollar pro Kopf *or* Person; **40 ~** (*of cattle*) 50 Stück (Vieh); **~s or tails?** Kopf oder Zahl?; **at the ~ of** an der Spitze (*gen*); **~ over heels** kopfüber; bis über beide Ohren (*verliebt sein*); **bury one's ~ in the sand** den Kopf in den Sand stecken; **get it into one's ~ that ...** es sich in den Kopf setzen, dass; **lose one's ~** den Kopf *or* die Nerven verlieren; **2.** Ober..., Haupt..., Chef..., oberste(r, -s), erste(r, -s); **3.** *v/t* anführen, an der

Spitze stehen von (*or gen*); voran-, vorausgehen (*dat*); (an)führen, leiten; *soccer*: köpfen; *v/i* (**for**) gehen, fahren (nach); lossteuern, losgehen (auf *acc*); MAR Kurs halten (auf *acc*)

head·ache Kopfweh *n*

head·band Stirnband *n*

head·dress Kopfschmuck *m*

head·er Kopfsprung *m*; *soccer*: Kopfball *m*

head·first kopfuber, mit dem Kopf voran; *fig* ungestüm, stürmisch

head·gear Kopfbedeckung *f*

head·ing Überschrift *f*, Titel(zeile *f*) *m*

head·land Landspitze *f*, Landzunge *f*

head·light MOT Scheinwerfer *m*

head·line Schlagzeile *f*; **news ~s** *radio*, TV *das* Wichtigste in Schlagzeilen

head·long kopfüber; *fig* ungestüm

head·mas·ter *Br* PED Direktor *m*, Rektor *m*

head·mis·tress *Br* PED Direktorin *f*, Rektorin *f*

head-on frontal, Frontal...; **~ collision** MOT Frontalzusammenstoß *m*

head·phones Kopfhörer *pl*

head·quar·ters (ABBR **HQ**) MIL Hauptquartier *n*; Zentrale *f*

head·rest Kopfstütze *f*

head·set Kopfhörer *pl*

head start SPORT Vorgabe *f*, Vorsprung *m* (*a. fig*)

head·strong halsstarrig

head teach·er → **headmaster**, **headmistress**, **principal**

head·wa·ters GEOGR Quellgebiet *n*

head·way Fortschritt(e *pl*) *m*; **make ~** (gut) vorankommen

head·word Stichwort *n*

head·y zu Kopfe steigend, berauschend

heal heilen; **~ over, ~ up** (zu)heilen

heal·ing Heilung *f*; **~ power** Heilkraft *f*

health Gesundheit *f*; **~ cer·ti·fi·cate** Gesundheitszeugnis *n*; **~ club** Fitnessklub *m*, Fitnesscenter *n*; **~ food** Reform-, Biokost *f*; **~ food shop** *Br*, **~ food store** Reformhaus *n*, Bioladen *m*

health·ful gesund; heilsam

health in·su·rance Krankenversicherung *f*; **~ re·sort** Kurort *m*; **~ service** Gesundheitsdienst *m*

health·y gesund

heap 1. Haufe(n) *m*; **2.** *a.* **~ up** aufhäufen, *fig a.* anhäufen

hear hören; anhören; *j-m* zuhören; *Zeugen* vernehmen; *Lektion* abhören

hear·er (Zu)Hörer(in)

hear·ing Gehör *n*; Hören *n*; JUR Verhandlung *f*; JUR Vernehmung *f*, *esp* POL Hearing *n*, Anhörung *f*; **within (out of)** **~** in (außer) Hörweite

hear·ing aid Hörgerät *n*

hear·say Gerede *n*; **by ~** vom Hörensagen *n*

hearse Leichenwagen *m*

heart ANAT Herz *n* (*a. fig*); Kern *m*; *card games*: Herz(karte *f* *n*, *a. pl* Herz *n*; **lose** **~** den Mut verlieren; **take ~** sich ein Herz fassen; **take s.th. to ~** sich et. zu Herzen nehmen; **with a heavy ~** schweren Herzens

heart·ache Kummer *m*

heart at·tack MED Herzanfall *m*; Herzinfarkt *m*

heart·beat Herzschlag *m*

heart·break Leid *n*, großer Kummer

heart·break·ing herzzerreißend

heart·bro·ken gebrochen, verzweifelt

heart·burn MED Sodbrennen *n*

heart·en ermutigen

heart fail·ure MED Herzversagen *n*

heart·felt innig, tief empfunden

hearth Kamin *m*

heart·less herzlos

heart·rend·ing herzzerreißend

heart trans·plant MED Herzverpflanzung *f*, Herztransplantation *f*

heart·y herzlich; gesund; herzhaft

heat 1. Hitze *f*; PHYS Wärme *f*; Eifer *m*; ZO Läufigkeit *f*; SPORT (Einzel)Lauf *m*; **preliminary ~** Vorlauf *m*; 2. *v/t* heizen; *a.* **~ up** erhitzen, aufwärmen; *v/i* sich erhitzen (*a. fig*); **heat·ed** geheizt; heizbar; erhitzt, *fig a.* erregt

heat·er Heizgerät *n*, Heizkörper *m*

heath Heide *f*, Heideland *n*

hea·then REL 1. Heide *m*, Heidin *f*; 2. heidnisch

heath·er BOT Heidekraut *n*; Erika *f*

heat·ing 1. Heizung *f*; 2. Heiz...

heat·proof hitzebeständig

heat shield Hitzeschild *m*

heat·stroke MED Hitzschlag *m*

heat wave Hitzewelle *f*

heave *v/t* (hoch)stemmen, (hoch)hieven; *Anker* lichten; *Seufzer* ausstoßen; *v/i* sich heben und senken, wogen

heav·en Himmel *m*

heav·en·ly himmlisch

heav·y schwer; stark (*rain, smoker, drinker, traffic etc*); hoch (*fine, taxes etc*); schwer (verdaulich); drückend, lastend; Schwer...

heav·y cur·rent ELECTR Starkstrom *m*

heav·y-du·ty TECH Hochleistungs...; strapazierfähig

heav·y-hand·ed ungeschickt

heav·y·weight *boxing*: Schwergewicht *n*, Schwergewichtler *m*

He·brew 1. hebräisch; 2. Hebräer(in); LING Hebräisch *n*

heck·le *Redner* durch Zwischenrufe *or* Zwischenfragen stören; **heck·ler** Zwischenrufer *m*; **heck·ling** Zwischenrufe

hec·tic hektisch

hedge 1. Hecke *f*; 2. *v/t*: *a.* **~ in** mit e-r Hecke einfassen; *v/i fig* ausweichen

hedge·hog ZO Stachelschwein *n*; *Br* Igel *m*

hedge·row Hecke *f*

heed 1. beachten, Beachtung schenken (*dat*); 2. **give** *or* **pay ~ to**, **take ~ of** → 1

heed·less: be ~ of nicht beachten, *Warnung etc* in den Wind schlagen

heel 1. ANAT Ferse *f*; Absatz *m*; **down at ~ *fig*** abgerissen; heruntergekommen; 2. Absätze machen auf (*acc*)

hef·ty kräftig, stämmig; mächtig (*blow etc*), gewaltig; F saftig (*prices, fine etc*)

heif·er ZO Färse *f*, junge Kuh

height Höhe *f*; (Körper)Größe *f*; Anhöhe *f*; *fig* Höhe(punkt *m*) *f*

height·en erhöhen; vergrößern

heir Erbe *m*; **~ to the throne** Thronerbe *m*, Thronfolger *m*

heir·ess Erbin *f*

heir·loom Erbstück *n*

hel·i·cop·ter AVIAT Hubschrauber *m*, Helikopter *m*

hel·i·port AVIAT Hubschrauberlandeplatz *m*

hell 1. Hölle *f*; **a ~ of a noise** F ein Höllenlärm; **what the ~ ...?** F was zum Teufel ...?; **raise ~** F e-n Mordskrach schlagen; 2. Höllen...; 3. *int* F verdammt!, verflucht!; **hell·ish** F höllisch

hel·lo *int* hallo!

helm MAR Ruder *n*, Steuer *n*

hel·met Helm *m*

helms·man MAR Steuermann *m*

help 1. Hilfe *f*; Hausangestellte *f*; **a call** *or* **cry for ~** ein Hilferuf, ein Hilfeschrei; 2. helfen; ~ *o.s.* sich bedienen, zulangen; *I cannot ~ it* ich kann es nicht ändern; *I could not ~ laughing* ich musste einfach lachen

help·er Helfer(in)
help·ful hilfreich; nützlich
help·ing Portion f
help·less hilflos
help·less·ness Hilflosigkeit f
help men·u EDP Hilfemenü n
hel·ter-skel·ter 1. *adv* holterdiepolter, Hals über Kopf; 2. *adj* überstürzt
helve Stiel m, Griff m
Hel·ve·tian Schweizer ...
hem 1. Saum m; 2. säumen; ~ *in* einschließen
hem·i·sphere GEOGR Halbkugel f, Hemisphäre f
hem·line Saum m
hem·lock BOT Schierling m
hemp BOT Hanf m
hem·stitch Hohlsaum m
hen ZO Henne f, Huhn n; Weibchen n
hence daher; *a week ~* in e-r Woche
hence·forth von nun an
hen house Hühnerstall m
hen-pecked hus·band Pantoffelheld m
her sie; ihr; ihr(e); sich
her·ald 1. HIST Herold m; 2. ankündigen
her·ald·ry Wappenkunde f, Heraldik f
herb BOT Kraut n; Heilkraut n
her·ba·ceous BOT krautartig; ~ *plant* Staudengewächs n
herb·al BOT Kräuter..., Pflanzen...
her·bi·vore ZO Pflanzenfresser m
herd 1. Herde f (a. fig), Rudel n; 2. v/t Vieh hüten; v/i: a. ~ *together* in e-r Herde leben; sich zusammendrängen
herds·man Hirt m
here hier; hierher; ~ *you are* hier (bitte); ~*'s to you!* auf dein Wohl!
here·a·bout(s) hier herum, in dieser Gegend
here·af·ter 1. künftig; 2. *das* Jenseits
here·by hiermit
he·red·i·ta·ry BIOL erblich, Erb...
he·red·i·ty BIOL Erblichkeit f; ererbte Anlagen pl, Erbmasse f
here·in hierin
here·of hiervon
her·e·sy REL Ketzerei f
her·e·tic REL Ketzer(in)
here·up·on hierauf, darauf(hin)

here·with hiermit
her·i·tage Erbe n
her·maph·ro·dite BIOL Zwitter m
her·met·ic TECH hermetisch
her·mit Einsiedler m
he·ro Held m
he·ro·ic heroisch, heldenhaft, Helden...
her·o·in Heroin n
her·o·ine Heldin f
her·o·is·m Heldentum n
her·on ZO Reiher m
her·ring ZO Hering m
hers ihrs, ihre(r, -s)
her·self sie selbst, ihr selbst; sich (selbst); *by ~* von selbst, allein, ohne Hilfe
hes·i·tant zögernd, zaudernd, unschlüssig; **hes·i·tate** zögern, zaudern, unschlüssig sein, Bedenken haben; **hes·i·ta·tion** Zögern n, Zaudern n, Unschlüssigkeit f; *without ~* ohne zu zögern, bedenkenlos
hew hauen, hacken; ~ *down* fällen, umhauen
hey int F he!, heda!
hey·day Höhepunkt m, Gipfel m; Blüte (-zeit) f
hi inf F hallo!
hi·ber·nate ZO Winterschlaf halten
hic·cough, hic·cup 1. Schluckauf m; 2. den Schluckauf haben
hide¹ (sich) verbergen, verstecken; verheimlichen
hide² Haut f, Fell n
hide-and-seek Versteckspiel n
hide·a·way F Versteck n
hid·e·ous abscheulich, scheußlich
hide·out Versteck n
hid·ing¹ F Tracht f Prügel
hid·ing²: *be in ~* sich versteckt halten; *go into ~* untertauchen
hid·ing place Versteck n
hi-fi Hi-Fi n, Hi-Fi-Gerät n, -Anlage f
high 1. hoch; groß (hopes etc); GASTR angegangen; F blau; F high; *be in ~ spirits* in Hochstimmung sein; ausgelassen or übermütig sein; 2. METEOR Hoch n; Höchststand m; High School f
high·brow F 1. Intellektuelle m, f; 2. (betont) intellektuell
high-cal·o·rie kalorienreich
high-class erstklassig
high·er ed·u·ca·tion Hochschulausbildung f

high fi·del·i·ty High Fidelity f
high-grade hochwertig; erstklassig
high-hand·ed anmaßend, eigenmächtig
high-heeled hochhackig
high jump SPORT Hochsprung m
high jump·er SPORT Hochspringer(in)
high·land Hochland n
high·light 1. Höhe-, Glanzpunkt m; 2. hervorheben
high·ly fig hoch; **think ~ of** viel halten von; **high·ly-strung** reizbar, nervös
high·ness mst fig Höhe f; **Highness** Hoheit f (title)
high-pitched schrill; steil (roof)
high-pow·ered TECH Hochleistungs...; fig dynamisch
high-pres·sure METEOR, TECH Hochdruck...
high-rank·ing hochrangig
high rise Hochhaus n
high road esp Br Hauptstraße f
high school High School f
high sea·son Hochsaison f
high so·ci·e·ty High Society f
high-spir·it·ed übermütig, ausgelassen
high street Br Hauptstraße f
high tea Br frühes Abendessen
high tech·nol·o·gy Hochtechnologie f
high ten·sion ELECTR Hochspannung f
high tide Flut f
high time: **it is ~** es ist höchste Zeit
high wa·ter Hochwasser n
high·way Highway m, Haupt(verkehrs)straße f (belegt oder überliefert); **High·way Code** Br Straßenverkehrsordnung f
hi·jack 1. Flugzeug entführen; j-n, Geldtransport etc überfallen; 2. (Flugzeug-)Entführung f; Überfall m
hi·jack·er Räuber m; (Flugzeug)Entführer(in)
hike 1. wandern; 2. Wanderung f
hik·er Wanderer m, Wanderin f
hik·ing Wandern n
hi·lar·i·ous ausgelassen
hi·lar·i·ty Ausgelassenheit f
hill Hügel m, Anhöhe f
hill·bil·ly contp Hinterwäldler m
hill·ock kleiner Hügel
hill·side (Ab)Hang m
hill·top Hügelspitze f
hill·y hügelig
hilt Heft n, Griff m
him ihn; ihm; F er; sich

him·self er or ihm or ihn selbst; sich; sich (selbst); **by ~** von selbst, allein, ohne Hilfe
hind¹ ZO Hirschkuh f
hind² Hinter...
hin·der hindern (**from** an dat); hemmen
hind·most hinterste(r, -s), letzte(r, -s)
hin·drance Hindernis n
Hin·du Hindu m
Hin·du·ism Hinduismus m
hinge 1. TECH (Tür)Angel f, Scharnier n; 2. ~ **on** fig abhängen von
hint 1. Wink m, Andeutung f; Tipp m; Anspielung f; **take a ~** e-n Wink verstehen; 2. andeuten; anspielen (**at** auf acc)
hip¹ ANAT Hüfte f
hip² BOT Hagebutte f
hip·po F → **hip·po·pot·a·mus** ZO Flusspferd n, Nilpferd n
hire 1. Br Auto etc mieten, Flugzeug etc chartern; j-n anstellen; j-n engagieren, anheuern; ~ **out** Br vermieten; 2. Miete f; Lohn m; **for ~** zu vermieten; frei
hire car Br Leih-, Mietwagen m
hire pur·chase: **on ~** Br ECON auf Abzahlung, auf Raten
his sein(e); seins, seine(r, -s)
hiss 1. zischen; fauchen (cat); auszischen; 2. Zischen n; Fauchen n
his·to·ri·an Historiker(in)
his·tor·ic historisch, geschichtlich (bedeutsam); **his·tor·i·cal** historisch, geschichtlich (belegt oder überliefert); Geschichts...; ~ **novel** historischer Roman
his·to·ry Geschichte f; ~ **of civilization** Kulturgeschichte f; **contemporary ~** Zeitgeschichte f
hit 1. schlagen; treffen (a. fig); MOT etc j-n, et. anfahren, et. rammen; F ~ **it off (with s.o.)** sich (mit j-m) gut vertragen; ~ **on** (zufällig) auf et. stoßen, et. finden; 2. Schlag m; fig (Seiten)Hieb m; (Glücks)Treffer m; Hit m
hit-and-run: ~ **driver** (unfall)flüchtiger Fahrer; ~ **offense** (Br **offence**) Fahrerflucht f
hitch 1. befestigen, festmachen, festhaken, anbinden, ankoppeln (**to** an acc); ~ **up** hochziehen; ~ **a ride** or **lift** im Auto mitgenommen werden; 2. Ruck m, Zug m; Schwierigkeit f, Haken m; **without a ~** glatt, reibungslos
hitch·hike per Anhalter fahren, trampen

pen; **hitch·hik·er** Anhalter(in), Tramper(in)

hi-tech → **high tech**

HIV: ~ carrier HIV-Positive m, f; **~ negative** HIV-negativ; **~ positive** HIV- -positiv

hive Bienenstock m; Bienenschwarm m

hoard 1. Vorrat m, Schatz m; 2. a. ~ **up** horten, hamstern; **hoard·ing** Bauzaun m; Br Reklametafel f

hoar·frost (Rau)Reif m

hoarse heiser, rau

hoax 1. Falschmeldung f; (übler) Scherz; 2. j-n hereinlegen

hob·ble humpeln, hinken

hob·by Hobby n, Steckenpferd n

hob·by·horse Steckenpferd n (a. fig)

hob·gob·lin Kobold m

ho·bo F Landstreicher m

hock[1] weißer Rheinwein

hock[2] zo Sprunggelenk n

hock·ey SPORT Eishockey n; esp Br Hockey n

hodge·podge Mischmasch m

hoe AGR 1. Hacke f; 2. hacken

hog zo (Haus-, Schlacht)Schwein n

hoist 1. hochziehen; hissen; 2. TECH Winde f, (Lasten)Aufzug m

hold 1. halten; festhalten; Gewicht etc tragen, aushalten; zurück-, abhalten (**from** von); Wahlen, Versammlung etc abhalten; Stellung halten; SPORT Meisterschaft etc austragen; Aktien, Rechte etc besitzen; Amt bekleiden; Platz einnehmen; Rekord halten; fassen, enthalten; Platz bieten für; der Ansicht sein (**that** dass); halten für; fig fesseln, in Spannung halten; (sich) festhalten; anhalten, andauern (a. fig); **~ one's ground, ~ one's own** sich behaupten; **~ the line** TEL am Apparat bleiben; **~ responsible** verantwortlich machen; ~ **still** still halten; **~ s.th. against s.o.** j-m et. vorhalten or vorwerfen; j-m et. übel nehmen or nachtragen; **~ back** (sich) zurückhalten; fig zurückhalten mit; **~ on** (sich) festhalten (**to** an dat); aus-, durchhalten; andauern; TEL am Apparat bleiben; **~ out** aus-, durchhalten; reichen (supplies etc); **~ up** hochheben; hochhalten; hinstellen (**as** als); aufhalten, verzögern; j-n, Bank etc überfallen; 2. Griff m, Halt m; Stütze f; Gewalt f, Macht f, Einfluss m; MAR Lade-

raum m, Frachtraum m; **catch** (**get, take**) **~ of s.th.** et. ergreifen, et. zu fassen bekommen

hold·er TECH Halter m; esp ECON Inhaber(in)

hold·ing Besitz m; **~ com·pa·ny** ECON Holding-, Dachgesellschaft f

hold·up (Verkehrs)Stockung f; (bewaffneter) (Raub)Überfall

hole 1. Loch n; Höhle f, Bau m; fig F Klemme f; 2. durchlöchern

hol·i·day Feiertag m; freier Tag; esp Br mst pl Ferien pl, Urlaub m; **be on ~** im Urlaub sein, Urlaub machen; **~ home** Ferienhaus n, Ferienwohnung f

hol·i·day·mak·er Urlauber(in)

hol·i·ness Heiligkeit f; **His Holiness** Seine Heiligkeit

hol·ler F schreien

hol·low 1. hohl; 2. Hohlraum m, (Aus-) Höhlung f; Mulde f, Vertiefung f; 3. **~ out** aushöhlen

hol·ly BOT Stechpalme f

hol·o·caust Massenvernichtung f, Massensterben n, (esp Brand)Katastrophe f; **the Holocaust** HIST der Holocaust

hol·ster (Pistolen)Halfter m, f

ho·ly heilig

ho·ly wa·ter REL Weihwasser n

Ho·ly Week REL Karwoche f

home 1. Heim n; Haus n; Wohnung f; Zuhause n; Heimat f; **at ~** zu Hause; **make oneself at ~** es sich bequem machen; **at ~ and abroad** im In- und Ausland; 2. adj häuslich, Heim... (a. SPORT); inländisch, Inlands...; Heimat...; 3. adv heim, nach Hause; zu Hause; daheim; fig ins Ziel, ins Schwarze; **return ~** heimkehren; **strike ~** sitzen, treffen

home ad·dress Privatanschrift f

home com·put·er Heimcomputer m

home·less heimatlos; obdachlos; **~ person** Obdachlose m, f; **shelter for the ~** Obdachlosenasyl n

home·ly einfach; unscheinbar, reizlos

home·made selbst gemacht, Hausmacher...

home mar·ket ECON Binnenmarkt m

Home│Of·fice Br POL Innenministerium n; **~ Sec·re·ta·ry** Br POL Innenminister m

home·sick: be ~ Heimweh haben

home·sick·ness Heimweh n

home team SPORT Gastgeber pl

H

home·ward *adj* Heim..., Rück...
home·ward(s) *adv* nach Hause
home·work Hausaufgabe(n *pl*) *f*; **do one's ~** s-e Hausaufgaben machen (*a. fig*)
hom·i·cide JUR Mord *m*; Totschlag *m*; Mörder(in)
hom·i·cide squad Mordkommission *f*
ho·mo·ge·ne·ous homogen, gleichartig
ho·mo·sex·u·al 1. homosexuell; **2.** Homosexuelle *m*, *f*
hone TECH fein schleifen
hon·est ehrlich, rechtschaffen; aufrichtig; **hon·es·ty** Ehrlichkeit *f*, Rechtschaffenheit *f*; Aufrichtigkeit *f*
hon·ey Honig *m*; Liebling *m*, Schatz *m*
hon·ey·comb (Honig)Wabe *f*
hon·eyed *fig* honigsüß
hon·ey·moon 1. Flitterwochen *pl*, Hochzeitsreise *f*; **2. be ~ing** auf Hochzeitsreise sein
hon·ey·suck·le BOT Geißblatt *n*
honk MOT hupen
hon·or·ar·y Ehren...; ehrenamtlich
hon·o(u)r 1. Ehre *f*; Ehrung *f*, Ehre(n *pl*) *f*, *pl* besondere Auszeichnung(en *pl*); **Your Hono(u)r** JUR Euer Ehren; **2.** ehren; auszeichnen; ECON *Scheck etc* honorieren, einlösen
hon·o(u)r·a·ble ehrenvoll, ehrenhaft; ehrenwert
hood Kapuze *f*; MOT Verdeck *n*; (Motor)Haube *f*; TECH (Schutz)Haube *f*
hood·lum F Rowdy *m*; Ganove *m*
hood·wink *j-n* hinters Licht führen
hoof ZO Huf *m*
hook 1. Haken *m*; Angelhaken *m*; **by ~ or by crook** F mit allen Mitteln; **2.** an-, ein-, fest-, zuhaken; angeln (*a. fig*)
hooked krumm, Haken...; F süchtig (**on** nach) (*a. fig*); **~ on heroin** (*television*) heroinsüchtig (fernsehsüchtig)
hook·er F Nutte *f*
hook·y: play ~ F (die Schule) schwänzen
hoo·li·gan Rowdy *m*
hoo·li·gan·ism Rowdytum *n*
hoop Reif(en) *m*
hoot 1. Schrei *m* (*a. fig*); MOT Hupen *n*; **2.** *v/i* heulen; johlen; ZO schreien; MOT hupen; *v/t* auspfeifen, auszischen
Hoo·ver® *Br* **1.** Staubsauger *m*; **2.** *mst* **hoover** (staub)saugen

hop¹ 1. hüpfen, hopsen; hüpfen über (*acc*); **be ~ping mad** F e-e Stinkwut haben; **2.** Sprung *m*
hop² BOT Hopfen *m*
hope 1. Hoffnung *f* (**of** auf *acc*); **2.** hoffen (**for** auf *acc*); **~ for the best** das Beste hoffen; **I ~ so, let's ~ so** hoffentlich
hope·ful: be ~ that hoffen, dass
hope·ful·ly hoffnungsvoll; hoffentlich
hope·less hoffnungslos; verzweifelt
horde Horde *f* (*often contp*)
ho·ri·zon Horizont *m*
hor·i·zon·tal horizontal, waag(e)recht
hor·mone BIOL Hormon *n*
horn ZO Horn *n*, *pl* Geweih *n*; MOT Hupe *f*
hor·net ZO Hornisse *f*
horn·y schwielig; V geil
hor·o·scope Horoskop *n*
hor·ri·ble schrecklich, furchtbar, scheußlich
hor·rid *esp Br* grässlich, abscheulich; schrecklich
hor·rif·ic schrecklich, entsetzlich
hor·ri·fy entsetzen
hor·ror Entsetzen *n*; Abscheu *m*, Horror *m*; F Gräuel *m*
horse ZO Pferd *n*; Bock *m*, Gestell *n*; **wild ~s couldn't drag me there** keine zehn Pferde bringen mich dort hin
horse·back: on ~ zu Pferde, beritten
horse chest·nut BOT Rosskastanie *f*
horse·hair Rosshaar *n*
horse·man (geübter) Reiter
horse·pow·er TECH Pferdestärke *f*
horse race Pferderennen *n*
horse rac·ing Pferderennen *n or pl*
horse·rad·ish BOT Meerrettich *m*
horse·shoe Hufeisen *n*
horse·wom·an (geübte) Reiterin
hor·ti·cul·ture Gartenbau *m*
hose¹ Schlauch *m*
hose² Strümpfe *pl*, Strumpfwaren *pl*
ho·sier·y Strumpfwaren *pl*
hos·pice Sterbeklinik *f*
hos·pi·ta·ble gastfreundlich
hos·pi·tal Krankenhaus *n*, Klinik *f*; **in the ~** im Krankenhaus
hos·pi·tal·i·ty Gastfreundschaft *f*
hos·pi·tal·ize ins Krankenhaus einliefern *or* einweisen
host¹ 1. Gastgeber *m*; BIOL Wirt *m*; *radio*, TV Talkmaster *m*, Showmaster *m*, Moderator(in); **your ~ was ...** durch

die Sendung führte Sie ...; **2.** *radio*, TV F *Sendung* moderieren

host² Menge *f*, Masse *f*

host³ REL *often* **Host** Hostie *f*

hos·tage Geisel *m*, *f*; **take s.o.** ~ j-n als Geisel nehmen

hos·tel *esp Br* UNIV (Wohn)Heim *n*; *mst* **youth** ~ Jugendherberge *f*

host·ess Gastgeberin *f*; Hostess *f* (*a.* AVIAT); AVIAT Stewardess *f*

hos·tile feindlich; feindselig (**to** gegen); ~ **to foreigners** ausländerfeindlich

hos·til·i·ty Feindseligkeit *f* (**to** gegen); ~ **to foreigners** Ausländerfeindlichkeit *f*

hot heiß (*a. fig and sl*); GASTR scharf; warm (*meal*); *fig* hitzig, heftig; ganz neu *or* frisch (*news etc*); **I am** *or* **feel** ~ mir ist heiß

hot·bed Mistbeet *n*; *fig* Brutstätte *f*

hotch·potch *Br* → **hodgepodge**

hot dog GASTR Hot Dog *n*, *m*

ho·tel Hotel *n*

hot·head Hitzkopf *m*

hot·house Treib-, Gewächshaus *n*

hot line POL heißer Draht; TEL Hotline *f*

hot·plate Kochplatte *f*

hot spot *esp* POL Unruhe-, Krisenherd *m*

hot spring Thermalquelle *f*

hot-tem·pered jähzornig

hot-wa·ter bot·tle Wärmflasche *f*

hound ZO Jagdhund *m*

hour Stunde *f*; *pl* (*Arbeits*)Zeit *f*, (*Geschäfts*)Stunden *pl*; **hour·ly** stündlich

house **1.** Haus *n*; **2.** unterbringen

house·bound ans Haus gefesselt

house·break·ing Einbruch *m*

house·hold **1.** Haushalt *m*; **2.** Haushalts...

house hus·band Hausmann *m*

house·keep·er Haushälterin *f*

house·keep·ing Haushaltung *f*, Haushaltsführung *f*

house·maid Hausangestellte *f*, Hausmädchen *n*

house·man *Br* MED Assistenzarzt *m*, -ärztin *f*

House of Lords *Br* PARL Oberhaus *n*

house plant Zimmerpflanze *f*

house-warm·ing Hauseinweihung *f*, Einzugsparty *f*

house·wife Hausfrau *f*

house·work Hausarbeit *f*

hous·ing Wohnung *f*; ~ **de·vel·op-**

ment, *Br* ~ **es·tate** Wohnsiedlung *f*

hov·er schweben; herumlungern; *fig* schwanken

hov·er·craft Hovercraft *n*, Luftkissenfahrzeug *n*

how wie; ~ **are you?** wie geht es dir?; ~ **about ...?** wie steht's mit ...?, wie wäre es mit ...?; ~ **do you do?** guten Tag!; ~ **much?** wie viel?; ~ **many** wie viele?

how·ev·er **1.** *adv* wie auch (immer); **2.** *cj* jedoch

howl **1.** heulen; brüllen, schreien; **2.** Heulen *n*; **howl·er** *F* grober Schnitzer

hub TECH (Rad)Nabe *f*; *fig* Mittelpunkt *m*, Angelpunkt *m*

hub·bub Stimmengewirr *n*; Tumult *m*

hub·by F (Ehe)Mann *m*

huck·le·ber·ry BOT amerikanische Heidelbeere

hud·dle: ~ **together** (sich) zusammendrängen; ~ *d* **up** zusammengekauert

hue¹ Farbe *f*; (Farb)Ton *m*

hue²: ~ **and cry** *fig* großes Geschrei, heftiger Protest

huff: *in a* ~ verärgert, verstimmt

hug **1.** (sich) umarmen; an sich drücken; **2.** Umarmung *f*

huge riesig, riesengroß

hulk F Koloss *m*; sperriges Ding; *a ~ of a* **man** ein ungeschlachter Kerl

hull **1.** BOT Schale *f*, Hülse *f*; MAR Rumpf *m*; **2.** enthülsen, schälen

hul·la·ba·loo Lärm *m*, Getöse *n*

hul·lo *int* hallo!

hum summen; brummen

hu·man **1.** menschlich, Menschen...; **2.** *a.* ~ **being** Mensch *m*

hu·mane human, menschlich

hu·man·i·tar·i·an humanitär, menschenfreundlich

hu·man·i·ty die Menschheit, die Menschen *pl*; Humanität *f*, Menschlichkeit *f*; *pl* Geisteswissenschaften *pl*; Altphilologie *f*

hu·man·ly: ~ **possible** menschenmöglich

hu·man rights Menschenrechte *pl*

hum·ble **1.** demütig; bescheiden; **2.** demütigen; **hum·ble·ness** Demut *f*

hum·drum eintönig, langweilig

hu·mid feucht, nass

hu·mid·i·ty Feuchtigkeit *f*

hu·mil·i·ate demütigen, erniedrigen

H

hu·mil·i·a·tion Demütigung f, Erniedrigung f

hu·mil·i·ty Demut f

hum·ming·bird ZO Kolibri m

hu·mor·ous humorvoll, komisch

hu·mo(u)r 1. Humor m; Komik f; **2.** j-m s-n Willen lassen; eingehen auf (acc)

hump ZO Höcker m; MED Buckel m

hump·back(ed) → **hunchback(ed)**

hunch 1. → **hump**; dickes Stück; (Vor-) Ahnung f; **2.** a. ~ **up** krümmen; ~ **one's shoulders** die Schultern hochziehen

hunch·back Buckel m; Bucklige m, f

hunch·backed buck(e)lig

hun·dred 1. hundert; **2.** Hundert f

hun·dredth 1. hundertste(r, -s); **2.** Hundertstel n

hun·dred·weight appr Zentner m (= 50,8 kg)

Hun·ga·ri·an 1. ungarisch; **2.** Ungar(in); LING Ungarisch n

Hun·ga·ry Ungarn n

hun·ger 1. Hunger m (a. fig **for** nach); **2.** fig hungern (**for**, **after** nach)

hun·ger strike Hungerstreik m

hun·gry hungrig

hunk dickes or großes Stück

hunt 1. jagen; Jagd machen auf (acc); verfolgen; suchen (**for**, **after** nach); ~ **down** zur Strecke bringen; ~ **for** Jagd machen auf (acc); **2.** Jagd f (a. fig); Verfolgung f; Suche f (**for**, **after** nach)

hunt·er Jäger m; Jagdpferd n

hunt·ing 1. Jagen n; **2.** Jagd...

hunt·ing ground Jagdrevier n

hur·dle SPORT Hürde f (a. fig)

hur·dler SPORT Hürdenläufer(in)

hur·dle race SPORT Hürdenrennen n

hurl schleudern; ~ **abuse at s.o.** j-m Beleidigungen ins Gesicht schleudern

hur·rah, hur·ray int hurra!

hur·ri·cane Hurrikan m, Wirbelsturm m; Orkan m

hur·ried eilig, hastig, übereilt

hur·ry 1. v/t schnell or eilig befördern or bringen; often ~ **up** j-n antreiben, hetzen; et. beschleunigen; v/i eilen, hasten; ~ **(up)** sich beeilen; ~ **up!** (mach) schnell!; **2.** (große) Eile, Hast f; **be in a** ~ es eilig haben

hurt verletzen, verwunden (a. fig); schmerzen, wehtun; schaden (dat)

hurt·ful verletzend

hus·band (Ehe)Mann m

hush 1. int still!; **2.** Stille f; **3.** zum Schweigen bringen; ~ **up** vertuschen, totschweigen

hush mon·ey Schweigegeld n

husk BOT **1.** Hülse f, Schote f, Schale f; **2.** enthülsen, schälen

hus·tle 1. (in aller Eile) wohin bringen or schicken; hasten, hetzen; sich beeilen; **2.** ~ **and bustle** Gedränge n; Gehetze n; Betrieb m, Wirbel m

hut Hütte f

hutch Stall m

hy·a·cinth BOT Hyazinthe f

hy·(a)e·na ZO Hyäne f

hy·brid BIOL Mischling m, Kreuzung f

hy·drant Hydrant m

hy·drau·lic hydraulisch

hy·drau·lics Hydraulik f

hy·dro... Wasser...

hy·dro·car·bon CHEM Kohlenwasserstoff m

hy·dro·chlor·ic ac·id CHEM Salzsäure f

hy·dro·foil MAR Tragflächenboot n, Tragflügelboot n

hy·dro·gen CHEM Wasserstoff m; ~ **bomb** Wasserstoffbombe

hy·dro·plane AVIAT Wasserflugzeug n; MAR Gleitboot n

hy·dro·plan·ing MOT Aquaplaning n

hy·e·na ZO Hyäne f

hy·giene Hygiene f

hy·gien·ic hygienisch

hymn Kirchenlied n, Choral m

hype F **1.** a. ~ **up** (übersteigerte) Publicity machen für; **2.** (übersteigerte) Publicity; **media** ~ Medienrummel m

hy·per... hyper..., übermäßig

hy·per·mar·ket Br Groß-, Verbrauchermarkt m

hy·per·sen·si·tive überempfindlich (**to** gegen)

hy·phen Bindestrich m

hy·phen·ate mit Bindestrich schreiben

hyp·no·tize hypnotisieren

hy·po·chon·dri·ac Hypochonder m

hy·poc·ri·sy Heuchelei f

hyp·o·crite Heuchler(in); **hyp·o·crit·i·cal** heuchlerisch, scheinheilig

hy·poth·e·sis Hypothese f

hys·te·ri·a MED Hysterie f

hys·ter·i·cal hysterisch

hys·ter·ics hysterischer Anfall; **go into** ~ hysterisch werden

I

I, i I, i *n*

I ich; *it is* ~ ich bin es

ice 1. Eis *n*; **2.** *Getränke etc* mit *or* in Eis kühlen; GASTR glasieren, mit Zuckerguss überziehen; *~d over* zugefroren (*lake etc*); *~d up* vereist (*road*)

ice age Eiszeit *f*

ice-berg Eisberg *m* (*a. fig*)

ice-bound eingefroren

ice cream (Speise)Eis *n*

ice-cream par·lo(u)r Eisdiele *f*

ice cube Eiswürfel *m*

iced eisgekühlt

ice floe Eisscholle *f*

ice hock·ey SPORT Eishockey *n*

ice lol·ly *Br* Eis *n* am Stiel

ice rink (Kunst)Eisbahn *f*

ice skate Schlittschuh *m*

ice-skate Schlittschuh laufen

ice show Eisrevue *f*

i·ci·cle Eiszapfen *m*

ic·ing GASTR Glasur *f*, Zuckerguss *m*; *the ~ on the cake* das Tüpfelchen auf dem i

i·con REL Ikone *f*; EDP Ikone *f*, (Bild-) Symbol *n*

i·cy eisig; vereist

ID ABBR *of identity* Identität *f*; *ID card* (Personal)Ausweis *m*

i·dea Idee *f*, Vorstellung *f*, Begriff *m*; Gedanke *m*, Idee *f*; *have no ~* keine Ahnung haben

i·deal 1. ideal; **2.** Ideal *n*

i·deal·ism Idealismus *m*

i·deal·ize idealisieren

i·den·ti·cal identisch (*to, with* mit); ~ *twins* eineiige Zwillinge *pl*

i·den·ti·fi·ca·tion Identifizierung *f*; ~ *(pa·pers)* Ausweis(papiere *pl*) *m*

i·den·ti·fy identifizieren; ~ *o.s.* sich ausweisen

i·den·ti·kit® pic·ture *Br* JUR Phantombild *n*

i·den·ti·ty Identität *f*; ~ *card* (Personal)Ausweis *m*

i·de·o·log·i·cal ideologisch

i·de·ol·o·gy Ideologie *f*

id·i·om Idiom *n*, idiomatischer Ausdruck, Redewendung *f*

id·i·o·mat·ic idiomatisch

id·i·ot MED Idiot(in), *contp a.* Trottel *m*

id·i·ot·ic MED idiotisch, F *a.* blödsinnig, schwachsinnig

i·dle 1. untätig; faul, träge; nutzlos; leer, hohl (*talk*); TECH stillstehend, außer Betrieb; MOT leer laufend, im Leerlauf; **2.** faulenzen; MOT leer laufen; *mst ~ away* Zeit vertrödeln

i·dol Idol *n* (*a. fig*); Götzenbild *n*

i·dol·ize abgöttisch verehren, vergöttern

i·dyl·lic idyllisch

if wenn, falls; ob; ~ *I were you* wenn ich du wäre

ig·loo Iglu *m*, *n*

ig·nite anzünden, (sich) entzünden; MOT zünden; *ig·ni·tion* MOT Zündung *f*

ig·ni·tion key MOT Zündschlüssel *m*

ig·no·rance Unkenntnis *f*, Unwissenheit *f*; *ig·no·rant: be ~ of s.th.* et. nicht wissen *or* kennen, nichts wissen von et.

ig·nore ignorieren, nicht beachten

ill krank; schlimm, schlecht; *fall ~, be taken ~* krank werden, erkranken

ill-ad·vised schlecht beraten; unklug

ill-bred schlecht erzogen; ungezogen

il·le·gal verboten; JUR illegal, ungesetzlich; ~ *parking* Falschparken *n*

il·le·gi·ble unleserlich

il·le·git·i·mate unehelich; unrechtmäßig

ill feel·ing Verstimmung *f*; *cause ~* böses Blut machen

ill-hu·mo(u)red schlecht gelaunt

il·lic·it unerlaubt, verboten

il·lit·e·rate ungebildet

ill-man·nered ungehobelt, ungezogen

ill-na·tured boshaft, bösartig

ill·ness Krankheit *f*

ill-tem·pered schlecht gelaunt

ill-timed ungelegen, unpassend

ill-treat misshandeln

il·lu·mi·nate beleuchten

il·lu·mi·nat·ing aufschlussreich

il·lu·mi·na·tion Beleuchtung *f*; *pl* Illumination *f*, Festbeleuchtung *f*

il·lu·sion Illusion *f*, Täuschung *f*

il·lu·sive, il·lu·so·ry illusorisch, trügerisch

il·lus·trate illustrieren; bebildern;

illustration 464

erläutern, veranschaulichen
il·lus·tra·tion Erläuterung *f*; Illustration *f*; Bild *n*, Abbildung *f*
il·lus·tra·tive erläuternd
il·lus·tri·ous berühmt
ill will Feindschaft *f*
im·age Bild *n*; Ebenbild *n*; Image *n*; bildlicher Ausdruck, Metapher *f*
im·age·ry Bildersprache *f*, Metaphorik *f*
i·ma·gi·na·ble vorstellbar, denkbar
i·ma·gi·na·ry eingebildet, imaginär
i·ma·gi·na·tion Einbildung(skraft) *f*; Vorstellungskraft *f*, -vermögen *n*
i·ma·gi·na·tive ideenreich, einfallsreich; fantasievoll
i·ma·gine sich *j-n or et.* vorstellen; sich *et.* einbilden
im·bal·ance Unausgewogenheit *f*; POL *etc* Ungleichgewicht *n*
im·be·cile Idiot *m*, Trottel *m*
im·i·tate nachahmen, nachmachen, imitieren; **im·i·ta·tion 1.** Nachahmung *f*, Imitation *f*; **2.** nachgemacht, unecht, künstlich, Kunst...
im·mac·u·late unbefleckt, makellos; tadellos, fehlerlos
im·ma·te·ri·al unwesentlich, unerheblich (**to** für)
im·ma·ture unreif
im·mea·su·ra·ble unermesslich
im·me·di·ate unmittelbar; sofortig, umgehend; nächste(r, -s) (*family*)
im·me·di·ate·ly unmittelbar; sofort
im·mense riesig, *fig a.* enorm, immens
im·merse (ein)tauchen; **~ o.s. in** sich vertiefen in (*acc*)
im·mer·sion Eintauchen *n*
im·mer·sion heat·er Tauchsieder *m*
im·mi·grant Einwanderer *m*, Einwanderin *f*, Immigrant(in); **im·mi·grate** einwandern, immigrieren (**into** in *dat*); **im·mi·gra·tion** Einwanderung *f*, Immigration *f*
im·mi·nent nahe bevorstehend; **~ danger** drohende Gefahr
im·mo·bile unbeweglich
im·mod·e·rate maßlos
im·mod·est unbescheiden; schamlos, unanständig
im·mor·al unmoralisch
im·mor·tal 1. unsterblich; **2.** Unsterbliche *m*, *f*
im·mor·tal·i·ty Unsterblichkeit *f*

im·mo·va·ble unbeweglich; *fig* unerschütterlich; hart, unnachgiebig
im·mune MED immun (**to** gegen); geschützt (**from** vor, gegen); **~ sys·tem** MED Immunsystem *n*
im·mu·ni·ty MED Immunität *f*
im·mu·nize MED immunisieren, immun machen (**against** gegen)
imp Kobold *m*; F Racker *m*
im·pact Zusammenprall *m*, Anprall *m*; Aufprall *m*; Wucht *f*; *fig* (Ein)Wirkung *f*, (starker) Einfluss (**on** auf *acc*)
im·pair beeinträchtigen
im·part (**to** *dat*) mitteilen; vermitteln
im·par·tial unparteiisch, unvoreingenommen; **im·par·ti·al·i·ty** Unparteilichkeit *f*, Objektivität *f*
im·pass·a·ble unpassierbar
im·passe *fig* Sackgasse *f*; **reach an ~** in e-e Sackgasse geraten
im·pas·sioned leidenschaftlich
im·pas·sive teilnahmslos; ungerührt; gelassen
im·pa·tience Ungeduld *f*
im·pa·tient ungeduldig
im·peach JUR anklagen (**for, of, with** *gen*); JUR anfechten; infrage stellen, in Zweifel ziehen
im·pec·ca·ble untadelig, einwandfrei
im·pede (be)hindern
im·ped·i·ment Hindernis *n* (**to** für); Behinderung *f*
im·pel antreiben; zwingen
im·pend·ing nahe bevorstehend, drohend
im·pen·e·tra·ble undurchdringlich; *fig* unergründlich
im·per·a·tive 1. unumgänglich, unbedingt erforderlich; gebieterisch; LING Imperativ...; **2. a. ~ mood** LING Imperativ *m*, Befehlsform *f*
im·per·cep·ti·ble nicht wahrnehmbar, unmerklich
im·per·fect 1. unvollkommen; mangelhaft; **2. a. ~ tense** LING Imperfekt *n*, 1. Vergangenheit
im·pe·ri·al·ism POL Imperialismus *m*
im·pe·ri·al·ist POL Imperialist *m*
im·per·il gefährden
im·pe·ri·ous herrisch, gebieterisch
im·per·me·a·ble undurchlässig
im·per·son·al unpersönlich
im·per·so·nate *j-n* imitieren, nachahmen; verkörpern, THEA *etc* darstellen

im·per·ti·nence Unverschämtheit *f*, Frechheit *f*

im·per·ti·nent unverschämt, frech

im·per·tur·ba·ble unerschütterlich, gelassen

im·per·vi·ous undurchlässig; *fig* unzugänglich (**to** für)

im·pe·tu·ous ungestüm, heftig; impulsiv; vorschnell

im·pe·tus TECH Antrieb *m*, Impuls *m*

im·pi·e·ty Gottlosigkeit *f*; Pietätlosigkeit *f*, Respektlosigkeit *f* (**to** gegenüber)

im·pinge: **~ on** sich auswirken auf (*acc*), beeinflussen (*acc*)

im·pi·ous gottlos; pietätlos, respektlos (**to** gegenüber)

im·pla·ca·ble unversöhnlich

im·plant *med* implantieren, einpflanzen; *fig* einprägen

im·plau·si·ble unglaubwürdig

im·ple·ment 1. Werkzeug *n*, Gerät *n*; 2. ausführen

im·pli·cate *j-n* verwickeln, hineinziehen (*in* in *acc*); im·pli·ca·tion Verwicklung *f*; Folge *f*; Andeutung *f*

im·pli·cit vorbehaltlos, bedingungslos; impliziert, (stillschweigend *or* mit) inbegriffen

im·plore *j-n* anflehen; *et.* erflehen

im·ply implizieren, einbeziehen, mit enthalten; andeuten; bedeuten

im·po·lite unhöflich

im·pol·i·tic unklug

im·port ECON 1. importieren, einführen; 2. Import *m*, Einfuhr *f*

im·por·tance Wichtigkeit *f*, Bedeutung *f*; im·por·tant wichtig, bedeutend

im·por·ta·tion → **import** 2

im·port du·ty ECON Einfuhrzoll *m*

im·port·er ECON Importeur *m*

im·pose auferlegen, aufbürden (**on** *dat*); *Strafe* verhängen (**on** gegen); *et.* aufdrängen, aufzwingen (**on** *dat*); **~ o.s. on s.o.** sich j-m aufdrängen

im·pos·ing imponierend, eindrucksvoll, imposant

im·pos·si·bil·i·ty Unmöglichkeit *f*

im·pos·si·ble unmöglich

im·pos·ter, *Br* im·pos·tor Betrüger(in), *esp* Hochstapler(in)

im·po·tence Unvermögen *n*, Unfähigkeit *f*; Hilflosigkeit *f*; *med* Impotenz *f*

im·po·tent unfähig; hilflos; *med* impotent

im·pov·e·rish arm machen; **be ~ed** verarmen; verarmt sein

im·prac·ti·ca·ble undurchführbar; unpassierbar

im·prac·ti·cal unpraktisch; undurchführbar

im·preg·na·ble uneinnehmbar

im·preg·nate imprägnieren, tränken; *BIOL* schwängern

im·press aufdrücken, einprägen (*a. fig*); *j-n* beeindrucken; **be ~ed with** beeindruckt sein von

im·pres·sion Eindruck *m*; Abdruck *m*; **under the ~ that** in der Annahme, dass

im·pres·sive eindrucksvoll

im·print 1. (auf)drücken (**on** auf *acc*); **~ s.th. on s.o.'s memory** j-m et. ins Gedächtnis einprägen; 2. Abdruck *m*, Eindruck *m*; *PRINT* Impressum *n*

im·pris·on *JUR* inhaftieren

im·pris·on·ment Freiheitsstrafe *f*, Gefängnis(strafe *f*) *n*, Haft *f*

im·prob·a·ble unwahrscheinlich

im·prop·er ungeeignet, unpassend; unanständig, unschicklich; unrichtig

im·pro·pri·e·ty Unschicklichkeit *f*

im·prove *v/t* verbessern; *Wert etc* erhöhen, steigern; **~ on** übertreffen; *v/i* sich (ver)bessern, besser werden, sich erholen; im·prove·ment (Ver)Bess(e)rung *f*; Steigerung *f*; Fortschritt *m* (**on** gegenüber *dat*)

im·pro·vise improvisieren

im·pru·dent unklug

im·pu·dence Unverschämtheit *f*

im·pu·dent unverschämt

im·pulse Impuls *m* (*a. fig*); Anstoß *m*, Anreiz *m*; im·pul·sive impulsiv

im·pu·ni·ty: **with ~** straflos, ungestraft

im·pure unrein (*a.* REL), schmutzig; *fig* schlecht, unmoralisch

im·pu·ri·ty Unreinheit *f*

im·pute: **~ s.th. to s.o.** j-n e-r Sache beschuldigen; j-m et. unterstellen

in 1. *prp place*: in (*dat or acc*), an (*dat*), auf (*dat*): **~ New York** in New York; **~ the street** auf der Straße; **put it ~ your pocket** steck es in deine Tasche; *time*: in (*dat*), an (*dat*): **~ 1999** 1999; **~ two hours** in zwei Stunden; **~ the morning** am Morgen; *state, manner*: in (*dat*), auf (*acc*), mit; **~ English** auf Englisch; *ac-*

tivity: in (*dat*), bei, auf (*dat*): **~ *crossing the road*** beim Überqueren der Straße; *author*: bei: **~ *Shakespeare*** bei Shakespeare; *direction*: in (*acc, dat*), auf (*acc*), zu: **have confidence ~** Vertrauen haben zu; *purpose*: in (*dat*), zu, als: **~ defense of** zur Verteidigung *or* zum Schutz von; *material*: in (*dat*), aus, mit: **dressed ~ blue** in Blau (gekleidet); *amount etc*: in, von, aus, zu: **three ~ all** insgesamt *or* im Ganzen drei; **one ~ ten** eine(r, -s) von zehn; nach, gemäß: **~ my opinion** m-r Meinung nach; **2.** *adv* innen, drinnen; hinein, herein; da, (an)gekommen; da, zu Hause; **3.** *adj* F in (Mode)

in·a·bil·i·ty Unfähigkeit *f*

in·ac·ces·si·ble unzugänglich, unerreichbar (**to** für *or dat*)

in·ac·cu·rate ungenau

in·ac·tive untätig

in·ac·tiv·i·ty Untätigkeit *f*

in·ad·e·quate unangemessen; unzulänglich, ungenügend

in·ad·mis·si·ble unzulässig, unstatthaft

in·ad·ver·tent unbeabsichtigt, versehentlich; **~ly** *a.* aus Versehen

in·an·i·mate leblos; langweilig

in·ap·pro·pri·ate unpassend, ungeeignet (**for, to** für)

in·apt ungeeignet, unpassend

in·ar·tic·u·late unartikuliert, undeutlich (ausgesprochen), unverständlich; unfähig(, deutlich) zu sprechen

in·at·ten·tive unaufmerksam

in·au·di·ble unhörbar

in·au·gu·ral **1.** Eröffnungs..., Antritts...; **~ speech → 2.** Antrittsrede *f*

in·au·gu·rate *j-n* (feierlich) (in sein Amt) einführen; einweihen, eröffnen; einleiten; **in·au·gu·ra·tion** Amtseinführung *f*; Einweihung *f*, Eröffnung *f*; Beginn *m*; **Inauguration Day** Tag *m* der Amtseinführung des neu gewählten Präsidenten der USA

in·born angeboren

in·cal·cu·la·ble unberechenbar; unermesslich

in·can·des·cent (weiß) glühend

in·ca·pa·ble unfähig (**of** zu *inf or gen*), nicht imstande (**of doing** zu tun)

in·ca·pac·i·tate untauglich *or* untauglich machen; **in·ca·pac·i·ty** Unfähigkeit *f*, Untauglichkeit *f*

in·car·nate leibhaftig; personifiziert

in·cau·tious unvorsichtig

in·cen·di·a·ry Brand...; *fig* aufwiegelnd, aufhetzend

in·cense¹ REL Weihrauch *m*

in·cense² in Wut bringen, erbosen

in·cen·tive Ansporn *m*, Anreiz *m*

in·ces·sant ständig, unaufhörlich

in·cest Inzest *m*, Blutschande *f*

inch **1.** Inch *m* (*2,54 cm*), Zoll *m* (*a. fig*); **by ~es, ~ by ~** allmählich; **every ~** durch und durch; **2.** (sich) zentimeterweise *or* sehr langsam bewegen

in·ci·dence Vorkommen *n*

in·ci·dent Vorfall *m*, Ereignis *n*; POL Zwischenfall *m*

in·ci·den·tal nebensächlich, Neben...; beiläufig; **in·ci·den·tal·ly** nebenbei bemerkt, übrigens

in·cin·e·rate verbrennen

in·cin·e·ra·tor TECH Verbrennungsofen *m*; Verbrennungsanlage *f*

in·cise einschneiden; aufschneiden; einritzen, einschnitzen

in·ci·sion (Ein)Schnitt *m*

in·ci·sive schneidend, scharf; *fig* treffend

in·ci·sor ANAT Schneidezahn *m*

in·cite anstiften; aufwiegeln, aufhetzen

in·cite·ment Anstiftung *f*; Aufhetzung *f*, Aufwieg(e)lung *f*

in·clem·ent rau

in·cli·na·tion Neigung *f* (*a. fig*)

in·cline **1.** *v/i* sich neigen (**to, towards** nach); *fig* neigen (**to, towards** zu); *v/t* neigen; *fig* veranlassen; **2.** Gefälle *n*; (Ab)Hang *m*

in·close, in·clos·ure → **enclose, enclosure**

in·clude einschließen, enthalten; aufnehmen (**in** in *e-e* Liste etc); **the group ~d several ...** zu der Gruppe gehörten einige ...; **tax ~d** inklusive Steuer

in·clud·ing einschließlich

in·clu·sion Einschluss *m*, Einbeziehung *f*; **in·clu·sive** einschließlich, inklusive (**of** *gen*); **be ~ of** einschließen (*acc*)

in·co·her·ent unzusammenhängend, unklar, unverständlich

in·come ECON Einkommen *n*, Einkünfte *pl*; **~ tax** ECON Einkommensteuer *f*

in·com·ing hereinkommend; ankommend; nachfolgend, neu; **~ mail** Posteingang *m*

in·com·mu·ni·ca·tive verschlossen

in·com·pa·ra·ble unvergleichlich; unvergleichbar

in·com·pat·i·ble unvereinbar; unverträglich; inkompatibel

in·com·pe·tence Unfähigkeit *f*; Inkompetenz *f*; **in·com·pe·tent** unfähig; nicht fachkundig *or* sachkundig; unzuständig, inkompetent

in·com·plete unvollständig; unvollendet

in·com·pre·hen·si·ble unbegreiflich, unfassbar

in·com·pre·hen·sion Unverständnis *n*

in·con·cei·va·ble unbegreiflich, unfassbar; undenkbar

in·con·clu·sive nicht überzeugend; ergebnislos, erfolglos

in·con·gru·ous nicht übereinstimmend; unvereinbar

in·con·se·quen·tial unbedeutend

in·con·sid·e·ra·ble unbedeutend

in·con·sid·er·ate unüberlegt; rücksichtslos

in·con·sis·tent unvereinbar; widersprüchlich; inkonsequent

in·con·so·la·ble untröstlich

in·con·spic·u·ous unauffällig

in·con·stant unbeständig, wankelmütig

in·con·test·a·ble unanfechtbar

in·con·ti·nent MED inkontinent

in·con·ve·ni·ence 1. Unbequemlichkeit *f*; Unannehmlichkeit *f*, Ungelegenheit *f*; **2.** *j-m* lästig sein; *j-m* Umstände machen; **in·con·ve·ni·ent** unbequem; ungelegen, lästig

in·cor·po·rate (sich) vereinigen *or* zusammenschließen; (mit) einbeziehen; enthalten; eingliedern; *Ort* eingemeinden; ECON, JUR als Aktiengesellschaft eintragen (lassen)

in·cor·po·rat·ed com·pa·ny ECON Aktiengesellschaft *f*

in·cor·po·ra·tion Vereinigung *f*, Zusammenschluss *m*; Eingliederung *f*; Eingemeindung *f*; ECON, JUR Eintragung *f* als Aktiengesellschaft

in·cor·rect unrichtig, falsch; inkorrekt

in·cor·ri·gi·ble unverbesserlich

in·cor·rup·ti·ble unbestechlich

in·crease 1. zunehmen, (an)wachsen; steigen; vergrößern, vermehren, erhöhen; **2.** Vergrößerung *f*, Erhöhung *f*, Zunahme *f*, Zuwachs *m*, (An)Wachsen *n*, Steigerung *f*; **in·creas·ing·ly** immer mehr; **~ difficult** immer schwieriger

in·cred·i·ble unglaublich

in·cre·du·li·ty Ungläubigkeit *f*

in·cred·u·lous ungläubig, skeptisch

in·crim·i·nate *j-n* belasten

in·cu·bate ausbrüten; **in·cu·ba·tor** Brutapparat *m*; MED Brutkasten *m*

in·cur sich *et.* zuziehen, auf sich laden; *Schulden* machen; *Verluste* erleiden

in·cu·ra·ble unheilbar

in·cu·ri·ous nicht neugierig, gleichgültig, uninteressiert

in·cur·sion (feindlicher) Einfall; Eindringen *n*

in·debt·ed (zu Dank) verpflichtet; ECON verschuldet

in·de·cent unanständig, anstößig; JUR unsittlich, unzüchtig; **~ assault** JUR Sittlichkeitsverbrechen *n*

in·de·ci·sion Unentschlossenheit *f*

in·de·ci·sive unentschlossen; unentschieden; unbestimmt, ungewiss

in·deed 1. *adv* in der Tat, tatsächlich, wirklich; allerdings; **thank you very much ~!** vielen herzlichen Dank!; **2.** *int* ach wirklich?

in·de·fat·i·ga·ble unermüdlich

in·de·fen·si·ble unhaltbar

in·de·fi·na·ble undefinierbar, unbestimmbar

in·def·i·nite unbestimmt; unbegrenzt

in·def·i·nite·ly auf unbestimmte Zeit

in·del·i·ble unauslöschlich (*a. fig*); **~ pencil** Tintenstift *m*

in·del·i·cate taktlos; unfein, anstößig

in·dem·ni·fy *j-n* entschädigen, *j-m* Schadenersatz leisten (**for** für)

in·dem·ni·ty Entschädigung *f*

in·dent (ein)kerben, auszacken; PRINT *Zeile* einrücken

in·de·pen·dence Unabhängigkeit *f*; Selbstständigkeit *f*; **Independence Day** Unabhängigkeitstag *m*

in·de·pen·dent unabhängig; selbstständig

in·de·scri·ba·ble unbeschreiblich

in·de·struc·ti·ble unzerstörbar; unverwüstlich

in·de·ter·mi·nate unbestimmt; unklar, vage

in·dex Index *m*, (Inhalts-, Namens-, Stichwort)Verzeichnis *n*, (Sach)Register *n*; (An)Zeichen *n*; *cost of living* ~ Lebenshaltungsindex *m*

in·dex card Karteikarte *f*

in·dex fin·ger ANAT Zeigefinger *m*

In·di·a Indien *n*

In·di·an 1. indisch; *neg!* indianisch, Indianer...; **2.** Inder(in); *American* ~ Indianer(in); **~ corn** BOT Mais *m*; **file:** *in* ~ im Gänsemarsch; **~ sum·mer** Altweibersommer *m*, Nachsommer *m*

in·di·a rub·ber Gummi *n*, *m*; Radiergummi *m*

in·di·cate deuten *or* zeigen auf (*acc*); TECH anzeigen; MOT blinken; *fig* hinweisen *or* hindeuten auf (*acc*); andeuten; **in·di·ca·tion** (An)Zeichen *n*, Hinweis *m*, Andeutung *f*, Indiz *n*

in·dic·a·tive *a*. **~ mood** LING Indikativ *m*

in·di·ca·tor TECH Anzeiger *m*; MOT Richtungsanzeiger *m*, Blinker *m*

in·dict JUR anklagen (*for* wegen)

in·dict·ment JUR Anklage *f*

in·dif·fer·ence Gleichgültigkeit *f*

in·dif·fer·ent gleichgültig (*to* gegen); mittelmäßig

in·di·gent arm

in·di·ges·ti·ble unverdaulich

in·di·ges·tion MED Verdauungsstörung *f*, Magenverstimmung *f*

in·dig·nant entrüstet, empört, ungehalten (*about*, *at*, *over* über *acc*)

in·dig·na·tion Entrüstung *f*, Empörung *f* (*about*, *at*, *over* über *acc*)

in·dig·ni·ty Demütigung *f*, unwürdige Behandlung

in·di·rect indirekt; *by* ~ *means* *fig* auf Umwegen

in·dis·creet unbesonnen, unbedacht; indiskret; **in·dis·cre·tion** Unbesonnenheit *f*, Indiskretion *f*

in·dis·crim·i·nate kritiklos; wahllos

in·dis·pen·sa·ble unentbehrlich, unerlässlich

in·dis·posed indisponiert, unpässlich; abgeneigt; **in·dis·po·si·tion** Unpässlichkeit *f*; Abneigung *f* (*to do* zu tun)

in·dis·pu·ta·ble unbestreitbar, unstreitig

in·dis·tinct undeutlich; unklar, verschwommen

in·dis·tin·guish·a·ble nicht zu unterscheiden(d) (*from* von)

in·di·vid·u·al 1. individuell, einzeln, Einzel...; persönlich; **2.** Individuum *n*, Einzelne *m*, *f*

in·di·vid·u·al·ism Individualismus *m*

in·di·vid·u·al·ist Individualist(in)

in·di·vid·u·al·i·ty Individualität *f*, (persönliche) Note

in·di·vid·u·al·ly einzeln, jede(r, -s) für sich; individuell

in·di·vis·i·ble unteilbar

in·dom·i·ta·ble unbezähmbar, nicht unterzukriegen(d)

in·door Haus..., Zimmer..., Innen..., SPORT Hallen...

in·doors im Haus, drinnen; ins Haus (hinein); SPORT in der Halle

in·dorse → *endorse* etc

in·duce *j-n* veranlassen; verursachen, bewirken; **in·duce·ment** Anreiz *m*

in·duct einführen, -setzen; **in·duc·tion** Herbeiführung *f*; Einführung *f*, Einsetzung *f*; ELECTR Induktion *f*

in·dulge nachsichtig sein gegen; *e-r Neigung etc* nachgeben; ~ *in s.th.* sich et. gönnen *or* leisten; **in·dul·gence** Nachsicht *f*; Luxus *m*; REL Ablass *m*

in·dul·gent nachsichtig, nachgiebig

in·dus·tri·al industriell, Industrie..., Gewerbe..., Betriebs...

in·dus·tri·al ar·e·a Industriegebiet *n*

in·dus·tri·al·ist Industrielle *m*, *f*

in·dus·tri·al·ize industrialisieren

in·dus·tri·ous fleißig

in·dus·try Industrie(zweig *m*) *f*; Gewerbe(zweig *m*) *n*; Fleiß *m*

in·ed·i·ble ungenießbar, nicht essbar

in·ef·fec·tive, **in·ef·fec·tu·al** unwirksam, wirkungslos; unfähig, untauglich

in·ef·fi·cient ineffizient; unfähig, untauglich; unrationell, unwirtschaftlich

in·el·e·gant unelegant

in·el·i·gi·ble nicht berechtigt

in·ept unpassend; ungeschickt; albern, töricht

in·e·qual·i·ty Ungleichheit *f*

in·ert PHYS träge (*a. fig*); inaktiv

in·er·tia PHYS Trägheit *f* (*a. fig*)

in·es·cap·a·ble unvermeidlich

in·es·sen·tial unwesentlich, unwichtig (*to* für)

in·es·ti·ma·ble unschätzbar

in·ev·i·ta·ble unvermeidlich

in·ev·i·ta·bly zwangsläufig

in·ex·act ungenau

in·ex·cu·sa·ble unverzeihlich, unentschuldbar

in·ex·haus·ti·ble unerschöpflich; unermüdlich

in·ex·o·ra·ble unerbittlich

in·ex·pe·di·ent unzweckmäßig; nicht ratsam

in·ex·pen·sive billig, preiswert

in·ex·pe·ri·ence Unerfahrenheit *f*

in·ex·pe·ri·enced unerfahren

in·ex·pert unerfahren; ungeschickt

in·ex·plic·a·ble unerklärlich

in·ex·pres·si·ble unaussprechlich, unbeschreiblich

in·ex·pres·sive ausdruckslos

in·ex·tri·ca·ble unentwirrbar

in·fal·li·ble unfehlbar

in·fa·mous berüchtigt; schändlich, niederträchtig; **in·fa·my** Ehrlosigkeit *f*; Schande *f*; Niedertracht *f*

in·fan·cy frühe Kindheit; **be in its ~** *fig* in den Kinderschuhen stecken

in·fant Säugling *m*; kleines Kind, Kleinkind *n*; **in·fan·tile** kindlich; Kindes..., Kinder...; infantil, kindisch

in·fan·try MIL Infanterie *f*

in·fat·u·at·ed vernarrt (**with** in *acc*)

in·fect MED *j-n*, *et.* infizieren, *j-n* anstecken (*a. fig*); versuchen, verunreinigen; **in·fec·tion** MED Infektion *f*, Ansteckung *f* (*a. fig*); **in·fec·tious** MED infektiös, ansteckend (*a. fig*)

in·fer folgern, schließen (**from** aus)

in·fer·ence (Schluss)Folgerung *f*, (Rück)Schluss *m*

in·fe·ri·or 1. untergeordnet (**to** *dat*); niedriger (**to** als); weniger wert (**to** als); minderwertig; **be ~ to s.o.** *j-m* untergeordnet sein; *j-m* unterlegen sein; **2.** Untergebene *m*, *f*

in·fe·ri·or·i·ty Unterlegenheit *f*; Minderwertigkeit *f*; **~ com·plex** PSYCH Minderwertigkeitskomplex *m*

in·fer·nal höllisch, Höllen...

in·fer·no Inferno *n*, Hölle *f*

in·fer·tile unfruchtbar

in·fest verseuchen, befallen (**with** mit); *fig* überschwemmen (**with** mit)

in·fi·del·i·ty (*esp* eheliche) Untreue *f*

in·fil·trate einsickern in (*acc*); einschleusen (**into** *acc*); POL unterwandern

in·fi·nite unendlich

in·fin·i·tive *a.* **~ mood** LING Infinitiv *m*, Nennform *f*

in·fin·i·ty Unendlichkeit *f*

in·firm schwach, gebrechlich

in·fir·ma·ry Krankenhaus *n*; PED *etc* Krankenzimmer *n*

in·fir·mi·ty Schwäche *f*, Gebrechlichkeit *f*

in·flame entflammen (*mst fig*); erregen; **become ~d** MED sich entzünden

in·flam·ma·ble brennbar, leicht entzündlich; feuergefährlich

in·flam·ma·tion MED Entzündung *f*

in·flam·ma·to·ry MED entzündlich; *fig* aufrührerisch, Hetz...

in·flate aufpumpen, aufblasen, aufblähen (*a. fig*); ECON *Preise etc* in die Höhe treiben

in·fla·tion ECON Inflation *f*

in·flect LING flektieren, beugen

in·flec·tion LING Flexion *f*, Beugung *f*

in·flex·i·ble unbiegsam, starr (*a. fig*); *fig* inflexibel, unbeweglich, unbeugsam

in·flex·ion *Br* → **inflection**

in·flict (**on**) *Leid, Schaden etc* zufügen (*dat*); *Wunde etc* beibringen (*dat*); *Strafe* auferlegen (*dat*), verhängen (über *acc*); aufbürden, aufdrängen (*dat*)

in·flic·tion Zufügung *f*; Verhängung *f*; Plage *f*

in·flu·ence 1. Einfluss *m*; **2.** beeinflussen; **in·flu·en·tial** einflussreich

in·flux Zustrom *m*, Zufluss *m*, (*Waren*-)Zufuhr *f*

in·form benachrichtigen, unterrichten (**of** von), informieren (**of** über *acc*); **~ against** *or* **on s.o.** *j-n* anzeigen; *j-n* denunzieren

in·for·mal formlos, zwanglos

in·for·mal·i·ty Formlosigkeit *f*; Ungezwungenheit *f*

in·for·ma·tion Auskunft *f*, Information *f*; Nachricht *f*; **~ (su·per·)highway** EDP Datenautobahn *f*

in·for·ma·tive informativ; lehrreich; mitteilsam

in·form·er Denunziant(in); Spitzel *m*

in·fra·struc·ture Infrastruktur *f*

in·fre·quent selten

in·fringe: ~ on *Rechte, Vertrag etc* verletzen, verstoßen gegen

in·fu·ri·ate wütend machen

in·fuse *Tee* aufgießen

in·fu·sion Aufguss *m*; MED Infusion *f*

in·ge·ni·ous genial; einfallsreich; raffiniert; **in·ge·nu·i·ty** Genialität *f*; Einfallsreichtum *m*

in·gen·u·ous offen, aufrichtig; naiv

in·got (*Gold- etc*)Barren *m*

in·gra·ti·ate: ~ *o.s. with s.o.* sich bei j-m beliebt machen

in·grat·i·tude Undankbarkeit *f*

in·gre·di·ent Bestandteil *m*; GASTR Zutat *f*

in·hab·it bewohnen, leben in (*dat*)

in·hab·it·a·ble bewohnbar

in·hab·i·tant Bewohner(in); Einwohner (-in)

in·hale einatmen, MED *a.* inhalieren

in·her·ent innewohnend, eigen (*in dat*)

in·her·it erben; **in·her·i·tance** Erbe *n*

in·hib·it hemmen (*a.* PSYCH), (ver)hindern; **in·hib·it·ed** PSYCH gehemmt; **in·hi·bi·tion** PSYCH Hemmung *f*

in·hos·pi·ta·ble ungastlich; unwirtlich (*region etc*)

in·hu·man unmenschlich

in·hu·mane inhuman, menschenunwürdig

in·im·i·cal feindselig (**to** gegen); nachteilig (**to** für)

in·im·i·ta·ble unnachahmlich

i·ni·tial **1.** *adj* anfänglich, Anfangs...; **2.** Initiale *f*, (großer) Anfangsbuchstabe

i·ni·tial·ly am *or* zu Anfang, anfänglich

i·ni·ti·ate in die Wege leiten, ins Leben rufen; einführen

i·ni·ti·a·tion Einführung *f*

i·ni·tia·tive Initiative *f*, erster Schritt; **take the** ~ die Initiative ergreifen; **on one's own** ~ aus eigenem Antrieb

in·ject MED injizieren, einspritzen

in·jec·tion MED Injektion *f*, Spritze *f*

in·ju·di·cious unklug, unüberlegt

in·junc·tion JUR gerichtliche Verfügung

in·jure verletzen, verwunden; schaden (*dat*); kränken; **in·jured 1.** verletzt; **2. the** ~ die Verletzten *pl*

in·ju·ri·ous schädlich; **be** ~ **to** schaden (*dat*); ~ **to health** gesundheitsschädlich

in·ju·ry MED Verletzung *f*; Kränkung *f*; ~ **time** *Br esp soccer:* Nachspielzeit *f*

in·jus·tice Ungerechtigkeit *f*, Unrecht *n*; **do s.o. an** ~ j-m unrecht tun

ink Tinte *f*

ink·ling Andeutung *f*; dunkle *or* leise Ahnung

ink pad Stempelkissen *n*

ink·y Tinten...; tinten-, pechschwarz

in·laid eingelegt, Einlege...; ~ **work** Einlegearbeit *f*

in·land **1.** *adj* inländisch, einheimisch; ECON Binnen...; **2.** *adv* landeinwärts

In·land Rev·e·nue *Br* Finanzamt *n*

in·lay Einlegearbeit *f*; MED (Zahn)Füllung *f*, Plombe *f*

in·let GEOGR schmale Bucht; TECH Eingang *m*, Einlass *m*

in-line skate Inliner *m*, Inline Skate *m*

in·mate Insasse *m*, Insassin *f*; Mitbewohner(in)

in·most innerste(r, -s) (*a. fig*)

inn Gasthaus *n*, Wirtshaus *n*

in·nate angeboren

in·ner innere(r, -s); Innen...; verborgen

in·ner·most → **inmost**

in·nings *cricket, baseball:* Spielzeit *f*

inn·keep·er Gastwirt(in)

in·no·cence Unschuld *f*; Harmlosigkeit *f*; Naivität *f*; **in·no·cent** unschuldig; harmlos; arglos, naiv

in·noc·u·ous harmlos

in·no·va·tion Neuerung *f*

in·nu·en·do (versteckte) Andeutung *f*

in·nu·me·ra·ble unzählig, zahllos

i·noc·u·late MED impfen

i·noc·u·la·tion MED Impfung *f*

in·of·fen·sive harmlos

in·op·e·ra·ble MED inoperabel, nicht operierbar; undurchführbar (*plan etc*)

in·op·por·tune inopportun, unangebracht, ungelegen

in·or·di·nate unmäßig

in·pa·tient MED stationärer Patient, stationäre Patientin

in·put Input *m, n*, EDP *a.* (Daten)Eingabe *f*, ELECTR *a.* Eingangsleistung *f*

in·quest JUR gerichtliche Untersuchung

in·quire fragen *or* sich erkundigen (nach); ~ **into** *et.* untersuchen, prüfen

in·quir·ing forschend; wissbegierig

in·quir·y Erkundigung *f*, Nachfrage *f*; Untersuchung *f*; Ermittlung *f*; **make inquiries** Erkundigungen einziehen

in·qui·si·tion (amtliche) Untersuchung; Verhör *n*; **Inquisition** REL HIST Inquisition *f*

in·quis·i·tive neugierig, wissbegierig

in·roads (**in[to]**, **on**) Eingriff *m* (in *acc*), Übergriff *m* (auf *acc*)

in·sane geisteskrank, wahnsinnig

in·san·i·ta·ry unhygienisch

in·san·i·ty Geisteskrankheit *f*, Wahnsinn *m*

in·sa·tia·ble unersättlich

in·scrip·tion Inschrift *f*, Aufschrift *f*; Widmung *f*

in·scru·ta·ble unerforschlich, unergründlich

in·sect ZO Insekt *n*; **in·sec·ti·cide** Insektenvertilgungsmittel *n*, Insektizid *n*

in·se·cure unsicher; nicht sicher *or* fest

in·sen·si·ble unempfindlich (**to** gegen); bewusstlos; unempfänglich (**of**, **to** für), gleichgültig (**of**, **to** gegen); unmerklich

in·sen·si·tive unempfindlich (**to** gegen); unempfänglich (**of**, **to** für), gleichgültig (**of**, **to** gegen)

in·sep·a·ra·ble untrennbar; unzertrennlich

in·sert 1. einfügen, einsetzen, einführen, (hinein)stecken, *Münze* einwerfen; inserieren; **2.** (Zeitungs)Beilage *f*, (Buch)Einlage *f*

in·ser·tion Einfügen *n*, Einsetzen *n*, Einführen *n*, Hineinstecken *n*; Einfügung *f*; Einwurf *m*; Anzeige *f*, Inserat *n*

in·sert key EDP Einfügetaste *f*

in·shore an *or* nahe der Küste; Küsten...

in·side 1. Innenseite *f*; *das* Innere; **turn ~ out** umkrempeln; auf den Kopf stellen; **2.** *adj* innere(r, -s), Innen...; Insider...; **3.** *adv* im Inner(e)n, innen, drinnen; **~ of** F innerhalb (*gen*); **4.** *prp* innerhalb, im Inner(e)n

in·sid·er Insider(in) F, Eingeweihte *m*, *f*

in·sid·i·ous heimtückisch

in·sight Einsicht *f*, Einblick *m*; Verständnis *n*

in·sig·ni·a Insignien *pl*; Abzeichen *pl*

in·sig·nif·i·cant bedeutungslos; unbedeutend

in·sin·cere unaufrichtig

in·sin·u·ate andeuten, anspielen auf (*acc*); unterstellen; **~ that s.o. ...** j-m unterstellen, dass er ...

in·sin·u·a·tion Anspielung *f*, Andeutung *f*, Unterstellung *f*

in·sip·id geschmacklos, fad

in·sist bestehen, beharren (**on** auf *dat*)

in·sis·tence Bestehen *n*, Beharren *n*; Beharrlichkeit *f*

in·sis·tent beharrlich, hartnäckig

in·sole Einlegesohle *f*; Brandsohle *f*

in·so·lent unverschämt

in·sol·u·ble unlöslich (*substance etc*); unlösbar (*problem etc*)

in·sol·vent ECON zahlungsunfähig, insolvent

in·som·ni·a Schlaflosigkeit *f*

in·spect untersuchen, prüfen, nachsehen; besichtigen, inspizieren

in·spec·tion Prüfung *f*, Untersuchung *f*, Kontrolle *f*, Inspektion *f*

in·spec·tor Aufsichtsbeamte *m*, Inspektor *m*; (Polizei)Inspektor *m*, (Polizei)Kommissar *m*

in·spi·ra·tion Inspiration *f*, (plötzlicher) Einfall; **in·spire** inspirieren, anregen; *Gefühl etc* auslösen

in·stall TECH installieren, einrichten, aufstellen, einbauen, *Leitung* legen; *j-n in ein Amt* einsetzen

in·stal·la·tion TECH Installation *f*, Einrichtung *f*, Einbau *m*; TECH *fertige* Anlage *f*; *fig* Einsetzung *f*, Einführung *f*

in·stall·ment, **in·stal·ment** *Br* ECON Rate *f*; (Teil)Lieferung *f*; Fortsetzung *f*; *radio*, TV Folge *f*

in·stall·ment plan: buy on the ~ ECON auf Abzahlung *or* Raten kaufen

in·stance Beispiel *n*; (besonderer) Fall; JUR Instanz *f*; **for ~** zum Beispiel

in·stant 1. Moment *m*, Augenblick *m*; **2.** sofortig, augenblicklich

in·stan·ta·ne·ous sofortig, augenblicklich; **death was ~** der Tod trat sofort ein

in·stant| cam·e·ra PHOT Sofortbildkamera *f*; **~ cof·fee** GASTR Pulver-, Instantkaffee *m*

in·stant·ly sofort, augenblicklich

in·stead stattdessen, dafür; **~ of** anstelle von, (an)statt

in·step ANAT Spann *m*, Rist *m*

in·sti·gate anstiften; aufhetzen; veranlassen; **in·sti·ga·tor** Anstifter(in); (Auf)Hetzer(in)

in·still *Br*, **in·still** beibringen, einflößen (**into** *dat*)

in·stinct Instinkt *m*

in·stinc·tive instinktiv

in·sti·tute Institut *n*

in·sti·tu·tion Institution *f*, Einrichtung

f; Institut n; Anstalt f

in·struct unterrichten, -weisen; ausbilden, schulen; informieren; anweisen

in·struc·tion Unterricht m; Ausbildung f, Schulung f, Unterweisung f; Anweisung f, Instruktion f; EDP Befehl m; **~s for use** Gebrauchsanweisung f; **operating ~s** Bedienungsanleitung f

in·struc·tive instruktiv, lehrreich

in·struc·tor Lehrer m; Ausbilder m

in·struc·tress Lehrerin f; Ausbilderin f

in·stru·ment Instrument n (a. MUS); Werkzeug n (a. fig)

in·stru·men·tal MUS Instrumental...; behilflich; **be ~ in** beitragen zu

in·sub·or·di·nate aufsässig

in·sub·or·di·na·tion Auflehnung f, Aufsässigkeit f

in·suf·fe·ra·ble unerträglich, unausstehlich

in·suf·fi·cient unzulänglich, ungenügend

in·su·lar Insel...; fig engstirnig

in·su·late isolieren; **in·su·la·tion** Isolierung f; Isoliermaterial n

in·sult Beleidigung f; **2.** beleidigen

in·sur·ance Versicherung f; Versicherungssumme f; Absicherung f (**against** gegen); **~ com·pa·ny** Versicherungsgesellschaft f; **~ pol·i·cy** Versicherungspolice f

in·sure versichern (**against** gegen)

in·sured: the ~ der or die Versicherte

in·sur·gent 1. aufständisch; **2.** Aufständische m, f

in·sur·moun·ta·ble fig unüberwindlich

in·sur·rec·tion Aufstand m

in·tact unversehrt, unverletzt, unbeschädigt, ganz

in·take (Nahrungs- etc)Aufnahme f; (Neu)Aufnahme(n pl) f, (Neu)Zugänge pl; TECH Einlass(öffnung f) m

in·te·gral ganz, vollständig; wesentlich

in·te·grate (sich) integrieren; zusammenschließen; eingliedern, einbeziehen; **~d circuit** ELECTR integrierter Schaltkreis

in·te·gra·tion Integration f

in·teg·ri·ty Integrität f; Vollständigkeit f; Einheit f

in·tel·lect Intellekt m, Verstand m

in·tel·lec·tual 1. intellektuell, Verstandes..., geistig; **2.** Intellektuelle m, f

in·tel·li·gence Intelligenz f; nachrich-

tendienstliche Informationen pl

in·tel·li·gent intelligent, klug

in·tel·li·gi·ble verständlich (**to** für)

in·tem·per·ate unmäßig

in·tend beabsichtigen, vorhaben, planen; **~ed for** bestimmt für or zu

in·tense intensiv, stark, heftig

in·ten·si·fy intensivieren; (sich) verstärken

in·ten·si·ty Intensität f

in·ten·sive intensiv, gründlich; **~ care u·nit** MED Intensivstation f

in·tent 1. gespannt, aufmerksam; **~ on** fest entschlossen zu (dat); konzentriert auf (acc); **2.** Absicht f, Vorhaben n

in·ten·tion Absicht f; JUR Vorsatz m

in·ten·tion·al absichtlich, vorsätzlich

in·ter bestatten

in·ter... zwischen, Zwischen...; gegenseitig, einander

in·ter·act aufeinander (ein)wirken, sich gegenseitig beeinflussen

in·ter·ac·tion Wechselwirkung f

in·ter·cede vermitteln, sich einsetzen (**with** bei; **for** für)

in·ter·cept abfangen

in·ter·ces·sion Fürsprache f

in·ter·change 1. austauschen; **2.** Austausch m; MOT Autobahnkreuz n

in·ter·com Sprechanlage f

in·ter·course Verkehr m; a. **sexual ~** (Geschlechts)Verkehr m

in·terest 1. Interesse n (**in** an dat, für); Wichtigkeit f, Bedeutung f; Vorteil m, Nutzen m; ECON Anteil m, Beteiligung f; ECON Zins(en pl) m; **take an ~ in** sich interessieren für; **2.** interessieren (**in** für et); **in·terest·ed** interessiert (**in** an dat); **be ~ in** sich interessieren für

in·terest·ing interessant

in·terest rate ECON Zinssatz m

in·ter·face EDP Schnittstelle f

in·ter·fere sich einmischen (**with** in acc); stören; **in·ter·fer·ence** Einmischung f; Störung f

in·te·ri·or 1. innere(r, -s), Innen...; Binnen...; Inlands...; **2.** das Innere; Interieur n; POL innere Angelegenheiten pl; → **Department of the Interior**, **~ dec·o·ra·tor** Innenarchitekt(in)

in·ter·ject Bemerkung einwerfen

in·ter·jec·tion Einwurf m; Ausruf m; LING Interjektion f in·ter·lace (sich) (ineinander) verflechten

in·ter·lop·er Eindringling *m*

in·ter·lude Zwischenspiel *n*; Pause *f*; **~s of bright weather** zeitweilig schön

in·ter·me·di·a·ry Vermittler(in), Mittelsmann *m*

in·ter·me·di·ate in der Mitte liegend, Mittel..., Zwischen...; PED für fortgeschrittene Anfänger

in·ter·ment Beerdigung *f*, Bestattung *f*

in·ter·mis·sion Unterbrechung *f*; THEA *etc* Pause *f*

in·ter·mit·tent mit Unterbrechungen, periodisch (auftretend); **~ fever** MED Wechselfieber *n*

in·tern¹ internieren

in·tern² Assistenzarzt *m*, -ärztin *f*

in·ter·nal innere(r, -s); einheimisch, Inlands...

in·ter·nal-com·bus·tion en·gine Verbrennungsmotor *m*

in·ter·na·tion·al **1.** international; Auslands...; **2.** SPORT Internationale *m*, *f*, Nationalspieler(in); internationaler Wettkampf; Länderspiel *n*; **~ call** TEL Auslandsgespräch *n*; **~ law** JUR Völkerrecht *n*

in·tern·ist MED Internist *m*

in·ter·per·son·al zwischenmenschlich

in·ter·pret interpretieren, auslegen, erklären; dolmetschen

in·ter·pre·ta·tion Interpretation *f*, Auslegung *f*

in·ter·pret·er Dolmetscher(in)

in·ter·ro·gate verhören, vernehmen; (be)fragen; **in·ter·ro·ga·tion** Verhör *n*, Vernehmung *f*; Frage *f*

in·ter·rog·a·tive LING Interrogativ..., Frage...

in·ter·rupt unterbrechen

in·ter·rup·tion Unterbrechung *f*

in·ter·sect (durch)schneiden; sich schneiden *or* kreuzen; **in·ter·sec·tion** Schnittpunkt *m*; (Straßen)Kreuzung *f*

in·ter·sperse einstreuen, hier und da einfügen

in·ter·state **1.** zwischenstaatlich; **2.** *a.* **~ highway** Autobahn *f*

in·ter·twine (sich ineinander) verschlingen, sich verflechten

in·ter·val Intervall *n* (*a.* MUS), Abstand *m*; *Br* Pause *f* (*a.* THEA *etc*); **at regular ~s** in regelmäßigen Abständen

in·ter·vene eingreifen, einschreiten, intervenieren; dazwischenkommen

in·ter·ven·tion Eingreifen *n*, Einschreiten *n*, Intervention *f*

in·ter·view **1.** Interview *n*; Einstellungsgespräch *n*; **2.** interviewen; ein Einstellungsgespräch führen mit

in·ter·view·ee Interviewte *m*, *f*

in·ter·view·er Interviewer(in)

in·ter·weave (miteinander) verweben *or* verflechten

in·tes·tate: **die ~** JUR ohne Hinterlassung e-s Testaments sterben

in·tes·tine ANAT Darm *m*; *pl* Eingeweide *pl*; **large ~** Dickdarm *m*; **small ~** Dünndarm *m*

in·ti·ma·cy Intimität *f*, Vertrautheit *f*; (*a. plumpe*) Vertraulichkeit; intime (*sexuelle*) Beziehungen *pl*

in·ti·mate **1.** intim (*a. sexually*); vertraut, eng (*friends etc*); (*a. plump*)vertraulich; innerste(r, -s); gründlich, genau (*knowledge etc*); **2.** Vertraute *m*, *f*

in·tim·i·date einschüchtern

in·tim·i·da·tion Einschüchterung *f*

in·to in (*acc*), in (*acc*) ... hinein; gegen (*acc*); MATH in (*acc*); **4 ~ 20 goes five times** 4 geht fünfmal in 20

in·tol·e·ra·ble unerträglich

in·tol·e·rance Intoleranz *f*, Unduldsamkeit (*of* gegen)

in·tol·e·rant intolerant, unduldsam (*of* gegen)

in·to·na·tion MUS Intonation *f*, LING *a.* Tonfall *m*

in·tox·i·cat·ed berauscht, betrunken

in·tox·i·ca·tion Rausch *m* (*a. fig*)

in·trac·ta·ble eigensinnig; schwer zu handhaben(d)

in·tran·si·tive LING intransitiv

in·tra·ve·nous MED intravenös

in tray: **in the ~** im Posteingang *etc*

in·trep·id unerschrocken

in·tri·cate verwickelt, kompliziert

in·trigue **1.** Intrige *f*; **2.** faszinieren, interessieren; intrigieren

in·tro·duce vorstellen (**to** *dat*), *j*-n bekannt machen (**to** mit); einführen

in·tro·duc·tion Vorstellung *f*; Einführung *f*, Einleitung *f*, Vorwort *n*; **letter of ~** Empfehlungsschreiben *n*

in·tro·duc·to·ry Einführungs...; einleitend, Einleitungs...

in·tro·spec·tion Selbstbeobachtung f

in·tro·vert PSYCH introvertierter Mensch; **in·tro·vert·ed** PSYCH introvertiert, in sich gekehrt

in·trude (sich) aufdrängen; stören; *am I intruding?* störe ich?; **in·trud·er** Eindringling m, Störenfried m

in·tru·sion Störung f

in·tru·sive aufdringlich

in·tu·i·tion Intuition f

in·tu·i·tive intuitiv

In·u·it a. *Innuit* Inuit m, Eskimo m

in·un·date überschwemmen, überfluten (a. fig)

in·vade eindringen in (acc), einfallen in (acc), MIL a. einmarschieren in (acc); fig überlaufen, überschwemmen

in·vad·er Eindringling m

in·va·lid¹ **1.** krank; invalid(e); **2.** Kranke m; f; Invalide m, f

in·val·id² (rechts)ungültig

in·val·i·date JUR für ungültig erkären

in·val·u·a·ble fig unschätzbar, unbezahlbar

in·var·i·a·ble unveränderlich

in·var·i·a·bly ausnahmslos

in·va·sion Invasion f (a. MIL), Einfall m, MIL a. Einmarsch m; fig Eingriff m, Verletzung f

in·vec·tive Schmähung(en pl) f, Beschimpfung(en pl) f

in·vent erfinden

in·ven·tion Erfindung f

in·ven·tive erfinderisch; einfallsreich

in·ven·tor Erfinder(in)

in·ven·to·ry Inventar n, Bestand m; Bestandsliste f; Inventur f

in·verse **1.** umgekehrt; **2.** Umkehrung f, Gegenteil n; **in·ver·sion** Umkehrung f, LING Inversion f; **in·vert** umkehren

in·ver·te·brate ZO **1.** wirbellos; **2.** wirbelloses Tier

in·vert·ed com·mas LING Anführungszeichen pl

in·vest ECON investieren, anlegen

in·ves·ti·gate untersuchen; überprüfen; Untersuchungen or Ermittlungen anstellen (*into* über acc), nachforschen

in·ves·ti·ga·tion Untersuchung f; Ermittlung f, Nachforschung f

in·ves·ti·ga·tor: *private* ~ Privatdetektiv m

in·vest·ment ECON Investition f, (Kapital)Anlage f

in·ves·tor ECON Anleger m

in·vet·e·rate unverbesserlich; hartnäckig

in·vid·i·ous gehässig, boshaft, gemein

in·vig·o·rate stärken, beleben

in·vin·ci·ble unbesiegbar; unüberwindlich

in·vi·o·la·ble unantastbar

in·vis·i·ble unsichtbar

in·vi·ta·tion Einladung f; Aufforderung f

in·vite einladen; auffordern; *Gefahr etc* herausfordern; ~ *s.o. in* j-n hereinbitten; **in·vit·ing** einladend, verlockend

in·voice ECON **1.** (Waren)Rechnung f; **2.** in Rechnung stellen, berechnen

in·voke flehen um; *Gott etc* anrufen; beschwören

in·vol·un·ta·ry unfreiwillig; unabsichtlich; unwillkürlich

in·volve verwickeln, hineinziehen (*in* in acc); j-n, et. angehen, betreffen; zur Folge haben, mit sich bringen

in·volved kompliziert, verworren

in·volve·ment Verwicklung f; Beteiligung f

in·vul·ne·ra·ble unverwundbar; fig unanfechtbar

in·ward **1.** adj innere(r, -s), innerlich; **2.** adv mst ~*s* einwärts, nach innen

i·o·dine CHEM Jod n

i·on PHYS Ion n

IOU (= *I owe you*) Schuldschein m

IQ ABBR of *intelligence quotient* IQ, Intelligenzquotient m

I·ran Iran m; **I·ra·ni·an 1.** iranisch; **2.** Iraner(in); LING Iranisch n

I·raq Irak m; **I·ra·qi 1.** irakisch; **2.** Iraker(in); LING Irakisch n

i·ras·ci·ble jähzornig

i·rate zornig, wütend

Ire·land Irland n

ir·i·des·cent schillernd

i·ris ANAT Regenbogenhaut f, Iris f; BOT Schwertlilie f, Iris f

I·rish **1.** irisch; **2.** LING Irisch n; *the* ~ die Iren pl

I·rish·man Ire m

I·rish·wom·an Irin f

i·ron **1.** Eisen n; Bügeleisen n; *strike while the* ~ *is hot* fig das Eisen schmieden, solange es heiß ist; **2.** eisern (a. fig), Eisen..., aus Eisen; **3.** bügeln; ~ *out* ausbügeln

I·ron Cur·tain POL HIST Eiserner Vorhang

i·ron·ic, i·ron·i·cal ironisch, spöttisch

i·ron·ing board Bügelbrett n

i·ron·mon·ger Br Eisenwarenhändler m

i·ron·works TECH Eisenhütte f

i·ron·y Ironie f

ir·ra·tion·al irrational, unvernünftig

ir·rec·on·ci·la·ble unversöhnlich; unvereinbar

ir·re·cov·er·a·ble unersetzlich; unwiederbringlich

ir·re·fut·a·ble unwiderlegbar

ir·reg·u·lar unregelmäßig; ungleichmäßig; regelwidrig, vorschriftswidrig

ir·rel·e·vant irrelevant, unerheblich, belanglos (**to** für)

ir·rep·a·ra·ble irreparabel, nicht wieder gutzumachen(d)

ir·re·place·a·ble unersetzlich

ir·re·pres·si·ble nicht zu unterdrücken(d); unbezähmbar

ir·re·proach·a·ble einwandfrei, untadelig

ir·re·sist·i·ble unwiderstehlich

ir·res·o·lute unentschlossen

ir·re·spec·tive: **~ of** ohne Rücksicht auf (acc); unabhängig von

ir·re·spon·si·ble unverantwortlich; verantwortungslos

ir·re·trie·va·ble unwiederbringlich, unersetzlich

ir·rev·e·rent respektlos

ir·rev·o·ca·ble unwiderruflich, endgültig

ir·ri·gate bewässern

ir·ri·ga·tion Bewässerung f

ir·ri·ta·ble reizbar

ir·ri·tant Reizmittel n

ir·ri·tate reizen; (ver)ärgern

ir·ri·tat·ing ärgerlich

ir·ri·ta·tion Reizung f; Verärgerung f; Ärger m (**at** über acc)

is er, sie, es ist

Is·lam der Islam

is·land Insel f; a. **traffic ~** Verkehrsinsel f; **is·land·er** Inselbewohner(in)

isle POET Insel f

i·so·late absondern; isolieren

i·so·lat·ed isoliert, abgeschieden; einzeln; **become ~** vereinsamen

i·so·la·tion Isolierung f, Absonderung f; **~ ward** MED Isolierstation f

Is·rael Israel n

Is·rae·li 1. israelisch; **2.** Israeli m, f

is·sue 1. Streitfrage f, Streitpunkt m; Ausgabe f; Erscheinen n; JUR Nachkommen(schaft f) pl; fig Ausgang m, Ergebnis n; **be at ~** zur Debatte stehen; **point at ~** strittiger Punkt; **die without ~** kinderlos sterben; **2.** v/t Zeitung etc herausgeben; Banknoten etc ausgeben; Dokument etc ausstellen; v/i herauskommen, hervorkommen; herausfließen, herausströmen

it es; s.th. previously mentioned: es, er, ihn, sie

I·tal·i·an 1. italienisch; **2.** Italiener(in); LING Italienisch n

i·tal·ics PRINT Kursivschrift f

It·a·ly Italien n

itch 1. Jucken n, Juckreiz m; **2.** jucken, kratzen; **I ~ all over** es juckt mich überall; **be ~ing for s.th.** F et. unbedingt (haben) wollen; **be ~ing to** inf F darauf brennen zu inf

itch·y juckend; kratzend

i·tem Punkt m (on the agenda etc), Posten m (on a list); Artikel m, Gegenstand m; (Presse-, Zeitungs)Notiz f, (a. radio, TV) Nachricht f, Meldung f

i·tem·ize einzeln angeben or aufführen

i·tin·e·ra·ry Reiseweg m, Reiseroute f; Reiseplan m

its sein(e), ihr(e)

it·self sich; sich selbst; selbst; **by ~** (für sich) allein; von selbst; **in ~** an sich

i·vo·ry Elfenbein n

i·vy BOT Efeu m

J

J, j J, j *n*

jab 1. (hinein)stechen, (hinein)stoßen; **2.** Stich *m*, Stoß *m*

jab·ber F (daher)plappern

jack 1. TECH Hebevorrichtung *f*; MOT Wagenheber *m*; *cards*: Bube *m*; **2.** ~ **up** *Auto* aufbocken

jack·al ZO Schakal *m*

jack·ass ZO Esel *m* (*a. fig*)

jack·daw ZO Dohle *f*

jack·et Jacke *f*, Jackett *n*; TECH Mantel *m*; (Schutz)Umschlag *m*; (*Platten-*) Hülle *f*; **~ potatoes, potatoes** (**boiled**) **in their ~s** Pellkartoffeln *pl*

jack knife 1. Klappmesser *n*; **2.** zusammenklappen, -knicken

jack-of-all-trades Hansdampf *m* in allen Gassen

jack·pot Jackpot *m*, Haupttreffer *m*; **hit the ~** F den Jackpot gewinnen; *fig* das große Los ziehen

jade MIN Jade *m, f*; Jadegrün *n*

jag Zacken *m*

jag·ged gezackt, zackig; scharfig

jag·u·ar ZO Jaguar *m*

jail 1. Gefängnis *n*; **2.** einsperren

jail·bird F Knastbruder *m*

jail·er Gefängnisaufseher *m*

jail·house Gefängnis *n*

jam¹ Konfitüre *f*, Marmelade *f*

jam² 1. *v/t* (hinein)pressen, (hinein)-quetschen, (hinein)zwängen, *Menschen a.* (hinein)pferchen; (ein)klemmen, (ein)quetschen; *a.* ~ **up** blockieren, verstopfen; *Funkempfang* stören; ~ **on the brakes** MOT voll auf die Bremse treten; *v/i* sich (hinein)drängen *or* (hinein-) quetschen; TECH sich verklemmen; *brake*: blockieren; **2.** Gedränge *n*; TECH Blockierung *f*; Stauung *f*, Stockung *f*; **traffic ~** Verkehrsstau *m*; **be in a ~** F in der Klemme stecken

jamb (Tür-, Fenster)Pfosten *m*

jam·bo·ree Jamboree *n*, Pfadfindertreffen *n*; Fest *n*

Jan ABBR *of **January*** Jan., Januar *m*

jan·gle klimpern *or* klirren (mit)

jan·i·tor Hausmeister *m*

Jan·u·a·ry (ABBR *of **Jan***) Januar *m*

Ja·pan Japan *n*; **Jap·a·nese 1.** japa-

nisch; **2.** Japaner(in); LING Japanisch *n*; **the ~** die Japaner *pl*

jar¹ 1. Gefäß *n*, Krug *m*; (Marmelade-*etc*)Glas *n*

jar²: ~ **on** wehtun (*dat*)

jar·gon Jargon *m*, Fachsprache *f*

jaun·dice MED Gelbsucht *f*

jaunt 1. Ausflug *m*, MOT Spritztour *f*; **2.** e-n Ausflug *or* e-e Spritztour machen

jaun·ty unbeschwert, unbekümmert; flott

jav·e·lin SPORT Speer *m*; ~ (**throw**), **throwing the ~** SPORT Speerwerfen *n*

jav·e·lin throw·er SPORT Speerwerfer(in)

jaw ANAT Kiefer *m*; *pl* ZO Rachen *m*, Maul *n*; TECH Backen *pl*; **lower ~** ANAT Unterkiefer *m*; **upper ~** ANAT Oberkiefer; **jaw·bone** ANAT Kieferknochen *m*

jay ZO Eichelhäher *m*

jay·walk·er unachtsamer Fußgänger

jazz MUS Jazz *m*

jazz·y F poppig

jeal·ous eifersüchtig (*of* auf *acc*); neidisch; **jeal·ous·y** Eifersucht *f*; Neid *m*

jeans Jeans *pl*

jeer 1. (*at*) höhnische Bemerkung(en) machen (über *acc*); höhnisch lachen (über *acc*); ~ (*at*) verhöhnen; **2.** höhnische Bemerkung; Hohngelächter *n*

jel·lied GASTR in Aspik, in Sülze

jel·ly Gallert(e *f*) *n*; GASTR Gelee *n*; Aspik *m, n*, Sülze *f*; Götterspeise *f*; ~ **ba·by** *Br* Gummibärchen *n*; ~ **bean** Gummi-, Geleebonbon *m, n*

jel·ly·fish ZO Qualle *f*

jeop·ar·dize gefährden

jerk 1. ruckartig ziehen *an* (*dat*); (zusammen)zucken; sich ruckartig bewegen; **2.** (plötzlicher) Ruck, Sprung *m*, Satz *m*; MED Zuckung *f*

jerk·y ruckartig; holprig; rüttelnd

jer·sey Pullover *m*

jest 1. Scherz *m*, Spaß *m*; **2.** scherzen, spaßen; **jest·er** HIST (Hof)Narr *m*

jet 1. (Wasser-, Gas- *etc*)Strahl *m*; TECH Düse *f*; AVIAT Jet *m*; **2.** (heraus-, hervor)schießen (*from* aus); AVIAT F jetten; ~ **en·gine** AVIAT Düsen-, Strahltriebwerk *n*; **~ plane** AVIAT Düsenflugzeug *n*, Jet *m*

jet-pro·pelled AVIAT mit Düsenantrieb, Düsen...

jet pro·pul·sion AVIAT Düsen-, Strahlantrieb *m*

jet·ty MAR (Hafen)Mole *f*

Jew Jude *m*, Jüdin *f*

jew·el Juwel *n*, *m*, Edelstein *m*

jew·el·er, *Br* **jew·el·ler** Juwelier *m*

jew·el·lery *Br*, **jew·el·ry** Juwelen *pl*; Schmuck *m*

Jew·ess Jüdin *f*

Jew·ish jüdisch

jif·fy: F *in a ~* im Nu, sofort

jig·saw Laubsäge *f*; → **jig·saw puz·zle** Puzzle(spiel) *n*

jilt *Mädchen* sitzen lassen; *e-m Liebhaber* den Laufpass geben

jin·gle 1. klimpern (mit), bimmeln (lassen); **2.** Klimpern *n*, Bimmeln *n*; Werbesong *m*, Werbespruch *m*

jit·ters: F *the ~* Bammel *m*, e-e Heidenangst; **jit·ter·y** F nervös; ängstlich

job 1. (*einzelne*) Arbeit; Beruf *m*, Beschäftigung *f*, Stellung *f*, Stelle *f*, Arbeit *f*, Job *m* (*a.* EDP); Arbeitsplatz *m*; Aufgabe *f*, Sache *f*, Angelegenheit *f*; *a.* ~ **work** Akkordarbeit *f*; **by the ~** im Akkord; *out of a ~* arbeitslos; **2.** ~ **around** jobben; ~ **ad**, ~ **ad·ver·tise·ment** Stellenanzeige *f*

job·ber *Br* ECON Börsenspekulant *m*

job cen·tre *Br* Arbeitsamt *n*

job hop·ping häufiger Arbeitsplatzwechsel

job·hunt·ing Arbeitssuche *f*; *be ~* auf Arbeitssuche sein

job·less arbeitslos

jock·ey Jockei *m*

jog 1. stoßen an (*acc*) *or* gegen, *j-n* anstoßen; *mst* ~ **along**, ~ **on** dahintrotten, dahinzuckeln; SPORT joggen; **2.** (*leichter*) Stoß, Stups *m*; Trott *m*; SPORT Trimmtrab *m*

jog·ger SPORT Jogger(in)

jog·ging SPORT Joggen *n*, Jogging *n*

join 1. *v/t* verbinden, vereinigen, zusammenfügen; sich anschließen (*dat or an acc*), sich gesellen zu; eintreten in (*acc*), beitreten; teilnehmen *or* sich beteiligen an (*dat*), mitmachen bei; ~ **in** einstimmen in; *v/i* sich vereinigen *or* verbinden; ~ **in** teilnehmen *or* sich be-

teiligen (an *dat*), mitmachen (bei); **2.** Verbindungsstelle *f*, Naht *f*

join·er Tischler *m*, Schreiner *m*

joint 1. Verbindungs-, Nahtstelle *f*; ANAT, TECH Gelenk *n*; BOT Knoten *m*; *Br* GASTR Braten *m*; F Laden *m*; Bude *f*, Spelunke *f*; *sl* Joint *m*; *out of ~* MED ausgerenkt; *fig* aus den Fugen; **2.** gemeinsam, gemeinschaftlich; Mit...

joint·ed gegliedert; Glieder...

joint-stock com·pa·ny *Br* ECON Kapital- *or* Aktiengesellschaft *f*

joint ven·ture ECON Gemeinschaftsunternehmen *n*

joke 1. Witz *m*; Scherz *m*, Spaß *m*; *practical ~* Streich *m*; **play a ~ on s.o.** j-m e-n Streich spielen; **2.** scherzen, Witze machen; **jok·er** Spaßvogel *m*, Witzbold *m*; *cards*: Joker *m*

jol·ly 1. *adj* lustig, fröhlich, vergnügt; **2.** *adv Br* F ganz schön; ~ **good** prima

jolt 1. e-n Ruck *or* Stoß geben; durchrütteln, durchschütteln; rütteln, holpern (*vehicle*); *fig* aufrütteln; **2.** Ruck *m*, Stoß *m*; *fig* Schock *m*

joss stick Räucherstäbchen *n*

jos·tle (an)rempeln; dränge(l)n

jot 1. *not a ~* keine Spur; **2.** ~ **down** sich schnell *et.* notieren

joule PHYS Joule *n*

jour·nal Journal *n*; (Fach)Zeitschrift *f*; Tagebuch *n*

jour·nal·ism Journalismus *m*

jour·nal·ist Journalist(in)

jour·ney 1. Reise *f*; **2.** reisen

jour·ney·man Geselle *m*

joy Freude *f*; *for ~* vor Freude

joy·ful freudig; erfreut

joy·less freudlos, traurig

joy·stick AVIAT Steuerknüppel *m*; EDP Joystick *m*

jub·i·lant jubelnd, überglücklich

ju·bi·lee Jubiläum *n*

judge 1. JUR Richter(in); SPORT Kampf-, Schieds-, Preisrichter(in); *fig* Kenner(in); **2.** JUR *Fall* verhandeln; urteilen, ein Urteil fällen; beurteilen, einschätzen

judg·ment JUR Urteil *n*; Urteilsvermögen *n*; Meinung *f*, Ansicht *f*; göttliches (Straf)Gericht; *the Last Judgment* REL das Jüngste Gericht

Judgment Day, *a. Day of Judgment*

J

REL Tag *m* des Jüngsten Gerichts, Jüngster Tag

ju·di·cial JUR gerichtlich, Justiz...; richterlich

ju·di·cia·ry JUR Richter *pl*

ju·di·cious klug, weise

ju·do SPORT Judo *n*

jug Krug *m*; Kanne *f*, Kännchen *n*

jug·gle jonglieren (mit); ECON *Bücher etc* frisieren; **jug·gler** Jongleur *m*

juice Saft *m*; MOT F Sprit *m*

juic·y saftig; F pikant (*story etc*); F gepfeffert (*price etc*)

juke·box Musikbox *f*, Musikautomat *m*

Jul ABBR *of* **July** Juli *m*

Ju·ly (ABBR **Jul**) Juli *m*

jum·ble 1. *a.* **~ together**, **~ up** durcheinander bringen *or* werfen; **2.** Durcheinander *n*; **~ sale** *Br* Wohltätigkeitsbasar *m*

jum·bo 1. riesig, Riesen...; **2.** AVIAT F Jumbo *m*; **~ jet** AVIAT Jumbo-Jet *m*

jum·bo-sized riesig

jump 1. *v/i* springen; hüpfen; zusammenzucken, -fahren, hochfahren (**at** bei); **~ at the chance** mit beiden Händen zugreifen; **~ to conclusions** voreilige Schlüsse ziehen; *v/t* (hinweg)springen über (*acc*); überspringen; **~ the queue** *Br* sich vordränge(l)n; **~ the lights** bei Rot über die Kreuzung fahren; **2.** Sprung *m*

jump·er[1] SPORT (*Hoch- etc*) Springer(in)

jump·er[2] Trägerrock *m*, Trägerkleid *n*; *Br* Pullover *m*

jump·ing jack Hampelmann *m*

jump·y nervös

Jun ABBR *of* **June** Juni *m*

junc·tion (Straßen)Kreuzung *f*; RAIL Knotenpunkt *m*

junc·ture: **at this ~** zu diesem Zeitpunkt

June (ABBR **Jun**) Juni *m*

jun·gle Dschungel *m*

ju·ni·or 1. junior; jüngere(r, -s); untergeordnet; SPORT Junioren..., Jugend...; **2.** Jüngere *m*, *f*; **~ school** *Br* Grundschule *f* (*for children aged 7 to 11*)

junk[1] MAR Dschunke *f*

junk[2] F Trödel *m*; Schrott *m*; Abfall *m*; *sl* Stoff *m*

junk food F Junk-Food *n*

junk·ie, **junk·y** *sl* Junkie *m*, Fixer(in)

junk·yard Schuttabladeplatz *m*; Schrottplatz *m*; **auto ~** Autofriedhof *m*

ju·ris·dic·tion JUR Gerichtsbarkeit *f*; Zuständigkeit(sbereich *m*) *f*

ju·ris·pru·dence Rechtswissenschaft *f*

ju·ror JUR Geschworene *m*, *f*

ju·ry JUR *die* Geschworenen *pl*; SPORT *etc* Jury *f*, Preisrichter *pl*

ju·ry·man JUR Geschworene *m*

ju·ry·wom·an JUR Geschworene *f*

just 1. *adj* gerecht; berechtigt; angemessen; **2.** *adv* gerade, (so)eben; genau, eben; gerade (noch), ganz knapp; nur, bloß; **~ about** ungefähr, etwa; **~ like that** einfach so; **~ now** gerade (jetzt), (so)eben

jus·tice Gerechtigkeit *f*; JUR Richter *m*; **Justice of the Peace** Friedensrichter *m*; **court of ~** Gericht *n*, Gerichtshof *m*

jus·ti·fi·ca·tion Rechtfertigung *f*

jus·ti·fy rechtfertigen

just·ly mit *or* zu Recht

jut: **~ out** vorspringen, herausragen

ju·ve·nile 1. jugendlich; Jugend...; **2.** Jugendliche *m*, *f*; **~ court** JUR Jugendgericht *n*; **~ de·lin·quen·cy** JUR Jugendkriminalität *f*; **~ de·lin·quent** JUR straffälliger Jugendlicher, jugendlicher Straftäter

K

K, k K, k *n*

kan·ga·roo ZO Känguru *n*

ka·ra·te SPORT Karate *n*

keel MAR 1. Kiel *m*; 2. ~ *over* umschlagen, kentern

keen scharf (*a. fig*); schneidend (*cold*); heftig, stark; lebhaft (*interest*); groß (*appetite*); begeistert, leidenschaftlich; ~ *on* versessen *or* scharf auf (*acc*)

keep 1. *v/t* (auf-, fest-, zurück)halten; (bei)behalten, bewahren; *Gesetze etc* einhalten, befolgen; *Ware* führen; *Geheimnis* für sich behalten; *Versprechen, Wort* halten; ECON *Buch* führen; aufheben, aufbewahren; abhalten, hindern (*from* von); *Tiere* halten; *Bett* hüten; ernähren, erhalten, unterhalten; ~ *early hours* früh zu Bett gehen; ~ *one's head* die Ruhe bewahren; ~ *one's temper* sich beherrschen; ~ *s.o. company* j-m Gesellschaft leisten; ~ *s.th. from s.o.* j-m et. vorenthalten *or* verschweigen *or* verheimlichen; ~ *time* richtig gehen (*watch*); MUS Takt halten; *v/i* bleiben; sich halten; ~ *going* weitergehen; ~ *smiling* immer nur lächeln!; ~ (*on*) *talking* weitersprechen; ~ (*on*) *trying* es weiterversuchen, es immer wieder versuchen; ~ *s.o. waiting* j-n warten lassen; ~ *away* (sich) fern halten (*from* von); ~ *back* zurückhalten (*a. fig*); ~ *from doing s.th.* et. nicht tun; ~ *off* (sich) fern halten; ~ *off!* Betreten verboten!; ~ *on* *Kleidungsstück* anbehalten, anlassen, *Hut* aufbehalten; *Licht* brennen lassen; *keep on doing* fortfahren zu tun; ~ *out* nicht hinein- *or* hereinlassen; ~ *out!* Zutritt verboten!; ~ *to* sich halten an (*acc*); ~ *up fig* aufrechterhalten; *Mut* nicht sinken lassen; fortfahren mit, weitermachen; ~ *s.o. up* j-n nicht schlafen lassen; ~ *it up* so weitermachen; ~ *up with* Schritt halten mit; ~ *up with the Joneses* nicht hinter den Nachbarn zurückstehen (wollen); **2.** (Lebens)Unterhalt *m*; *for* ~*s* F für immer

keep·er Wärter(in), Wächter(in), Aufseher(in); *mst in cpds*: Inhaber(in), Besitzer(in); **keep·ing** Verwahrung *f*; Obhut *f*; *be in* (*out of*) ~ *with ...* (nicht) übereinstimmen mit ...

keep·sake Andenken *n*

keg Fässchen *n*, kleines Fass

ken·nel Hundehütte *f*; ~*s* Hundezwinger *m*; Hundepension *f*

kerb Br → **curb**

ker·chief (Hals-, Kopf)Tuch *n*

ker·nel BOT Kern *m* (*a. fig*)

ker·o·sene Petroleum *n*

ket·tle Kessel *m*

ket·tle·drum MUS (Kessel)Pauke *f*

key 1. Schlüssel *m* (*a. fig*); (Schreibmaschinen-, Klavier- *etc*)Taste *f*; MUS Tonart *f*; **2.** Schlüssel...; **3.** anpassen (*to* an *acc*); ~ *in* EDP Daten eingeben; ~*ed up* nervös, aufgeregt, überdreht

key·board Tastatur *f*

key·hole Schlüsselloch *n*

key·note MUS Grundton *m*; *fig* Grundgedanke *m*, Tenor *m*

key ring Schlüsselring *m*

key·stone ARCH Schlussstein *m*; *fig* Grundpfeiler *m*

key·word Schlüssel-, Stichwort *n*

kick 1. (mit dem Fuß) stoßen, treten, e-n Tritt geben *or* versetzen (*dat*); *soccer*: schießen, treten, kicken; strampeln; ausschlagen (*horse*); ~ *off* von sich schleudern; *soccer*: anstoßen; ~ *out* F rausschmeißen; ~ *up* hochschleudern; ~ *up a fuss or row* F Krach schlagen; **2.** (Fuß)Tritt *m*; Stoß *m*; *soccer*: Schuss *m*; *free* ~ Freistoß *m*; *for* ~*s* F zum Spaß; *they get a* ~ *out of it* es macht ihnen e-n Riesenspaß

kick·off *soccer*: Anstoß *m*

kick·out *soccer*: Abschlag *m*

kid¹ ZO Zicklein *n*, Kitz *n*; Ziegenleder *n*; F Kind *n*; ~ *brother* F kleiner Bruder

kid² *v/t* j-n auf den Arm nehmen; ~ *s.o.* j-m et. vormachen; *v/i* Spaß machen; *he is only* ~*ding* er macht ja nur Spaß; *no* ~*ding!* im Ernst!

kid gloves Glacéhandschuhe *pl* (*a. fig*)

kid·nap entführen, kidnappen

kid·nap·(p)er Entführer(in), Kidnapper(in)

kid·nap·(p)ing Entführung f, Kidnapping n

kid·ney ANAT Niere f; **~ bean** BOT Kidneybohne f, rote Bohne; **~ ma·chine** MED künstliche Niere

kill töten (a. fig), umbringen, ermorden; vernichten; ZO schlachten; HUNT erlegen, schießen; **be ~ed in an accident** tödlich verunglücken; **~ time** die Zeit totschlagen; **kill·er** Mörder(in), Killer (in); **kill·ing** mörderisch, tödlich

kill·joy Spielverderber m

kiln TECH Brennofen m

ki·lo F Kilo n

kil·o·gram(me) Kilogramm n

kil·o·me·ter, Br **kil·o·me·tre** Kilometer m

kilt Kilt m, Schottenrock m

kin Verwandtschaft f, Verwandte pl; **next of ~** der, die nächste Verwandte, die nächsten Angehörigen pl

kind¹ freundlich, liebenswürdig, nett; herzlich

kind² Art f, Sorte f; Wesen n; **all ~s of** alle möglichen, allerlei; **nothing of the ~** nichts dergleichen; **~ of** F ein bisschen

kin·der·gar·ten Kindergarten m

kind-heart·ed gütig

kin·dle anzünden, (sich) entzünden; Interesse etc wecken

kind·ly 1. adj freundlich, liebenswürdig, nett; **2.** adv → 1; freundlicherweise, liebenswürdigerweise, netterweise

kind·ness Freundlichkeit f, Liebenswürdigkeit f; Gefälligkeit f

kin·dred verwandt; **~ spirits** Gleichgesinnte pl

king König m

king·dom Königreich n; REL Reich n Gottes; fig Reich n; **animal ~** Tierreich n; **vegetable ~** Pflanzenreich n

king·ly königlich

king-size(d) Riesen...

kink Knick m, fig Tick m, Spleen m

kink·y spleenig; pervers

ki·osk Kiosk m; Br Telefonzelle f

kip·per GASTR Räucherhering m

kiss 1. Kuss m; **2.** (sich) küssen

kit Ausrüstung f; Arbeitsgerät n, Werkzeug(e pl) n; Werkzeugtasche f, -kasten m; Bastelsatz m; **kit bag** Seesack m

kitch·en 1. Küche f; **2.** Küchen...

kitch·en·ette Kleinküche f, Kochnische f

kitch·en gar·den Küchen-, Gemüsegarten m

kite Drachen m; ZO Milan m; **fly a ~** e-n Drachen steigen lassen

kit·ten ZO Kätzchen n

knack Kniff m, Trick m, F Dreh m; Geschick n, Talent n

knave card games: Bube m, Unter m

knead kneten; massieren

knee ANAT Knie n; TECH Knie(stück) n

knee·cap ANAT Kniescheibe f

knee-deep knietief, bis an die Knie (reichend)

knee joint ANAT Kniegelenk n (a. TECH)

kneel knien (**to** vor dat)

knee-length knielang

knell Totenglocke f

knick·er·bock·ers Knickerbocker pl, Kniehosen pl

knick·ers Br F (Damen)Schlüpfer m

knick-knack Nippsache f

knife 1. Messer n; **2.** mit e-m Messer stechen or verletzen; erstechen

knight 1. Ritter m; chess: Springer m; **2.** zum Ritter schlagen

knight·hood Ritterwürde f, -stand m

knit v/t stricken; a. **~ together** zusammenfügen, verbinden; **~ one's brows** die Stirn runzeln; v/i stricken; MED zusammenwachsen

knit·ting Stricken n; Strickzeug n; **2.** Strick...; **~ nee·dle** Stricknadel f

knit·wear Strickwaren pl

knob Knopf m, Knauf m, runder Griff; GASTR Stück(chen) n

knock 1. schlagen, stoßen; pochen, klopfen; **~ at the door** an die Tür klopfen; **~ about**, **~ around** herumstoßen; F sich herumtreiben; F herumliegen; **~ down** Gebäude etc abreißen; umstoßen, umwerfen; niederschlagen; anfahren, umfahren; überfahren; mit dem Preis heruntergehen; auction: et. zuschlagen (**to s.o.** j-m); **be ~ed down** überfahren werden; **~ off** herunter-, abschlagen; F et. hinhauen; F aufhören (mit); F Feierabend or Schluss machen; **~ out** herausschlagen, -klopfen, Pfeife ausklopfen; j-n bewusstlos schlagen; boxing: k.o. schlagen; fig betäuben (drug etc); fig F umhauen, schocken; **~ over** umwerfen, umstoßen; überfah-

ren; **be ~ed over** überfahren werden;
2. Schlag *m*, Stoß *m*; Klopfen *n*; **there
is a ~ (on** [*Br* **at**] **the door)** es klopft
knock·er Türklopfer *m*
knock-kneed x-beinig
knock·out *boxing:* K.o. *m*
knoll Hügel *m*
knot 1. Knoten *m*; BOT Astknoten *m*;
MAR Knoten *m*, Seemeile *f*; **2.** (ver-)
knoten, (ver)knüpfen; **knot·ty** knotig;
knorrig; *fig* verwickelt, kompliziert
know wissen; können; kennen; erfahren, erleben; (wieder) erkennen; verstehen; **~ French** Französisch können;
~ one's way around sich auskennen in
(*a place etc*); **~ all about it** genau Bescheid wissen; **get to ~** kennen lernen;
~ one's business, **~ the ropes**, **~ a**

thing or two, **~ what's what** F sich auskennen, Erfahrung haben; **you ~** wissen Sie
know-how Know-how *n*, (Sach-,
Spezial)Kenntnis(se *pl*) *f*
know·ing klug, gescheit; schlau; verständnisvoll; **know·ing·ly** wissend;
wissentlich, absichtlich, bewusst
knowl·edge Kenntnis(se *pl*) *f*; Wissen
n; **to my ~** meines Wissens; **have a
good ~ of** viel verstehen von, sich gut
auskennen in (*dat*)
knowl·edge·a·ble: be very ~ about
viel verstehen von
knuck·le 1. ANAT (Finger)Knöchel *m*; **2.
~ down to work** sich an die Arbeit machen
Krem·lin: POL **the ~** der Kreml

L

L, l L, l *n*
L ABBR *of* **large** (**size**) groß
lab F Labor *n*
la·bel 1. Etikett *n*, (Klebe- *etc*)Zettel *m*,
(-)Schild(chen) *n*; (Schall)Plattenfirma
f; **2.** etikettieren, beschriften; *fig* abstempeln als
la·bor 1. (schwere) Arbeit; Mühe *f*; Arbeiter *pl*, Arbeitskräfte *pl*; MED Wehen
pl; **2.** (schwer) arbeiten; sich bemühen,
sich abmühen, sich anstrengen
la·bor·a·to·ry Labor(atorium) *n*; **~
assis·tant** Laborant(in)
la·bored schwerfällig (*style etc*); mühsam (*breathing etc*)
la·bor·er (*esp* Hilfs)Arbeiter *m*
la·bo·ri·ous mühsam; schwerfällig
la·bor u·ni·on Gewerkschaft *f*
la·bour *Br* → **labor**
Labour *Br* POL die Labour Party
la·boured, la·bour·er *Br* → **labored,
laborer**
La·bour Par·ty *Br* POL Labour Party *f*
lace 1. Spitze *f*; Borte *f*; Schnürsenkel *m*;
2. ~ up (zu-, zusammen)schnüren;
Schuh zubinden; **~d with brandy** mit
e-m Schuss Weinbrand
la·ce·rate zerschneiden, zerkratzen,
aufreißen; *j-s Gefühle* verletzen

lack 1. (*of*) Fehlen *n* (von), Mangel *m*
(an *dat*); **2.** *v/t* nicht haben; **he ~s
money** es fehlt ihm an Geld; *v/i* **be
~ing** fehlen; **he is ~ing in courage** ihm
fehlt der Mut
lack·lus·ter, *Br* **lack·lus·tre** glanzlos,
matt
lac·quer 1. Lack *m*; Haarspray *m*, *n*; **2.**
lackieren
lad Bursche *m*, Junge *m*
lad·der Leiter *f*; *Br* Laufmasche *f*
lad·der-proof (lauf)maschenfest
la·den (schwer) beladen
la·dle 1. (Schöpf-, Suppen)Kelle *f*,
Schöpflöffel *m*; **2. ~ out** *Suppe* austeilen
la·dy Dame *f*; **Lady** Lady *f*; **~ doctor**
Ärztin *f*; **Ladies' room**, *Br* **Ladies(')**
Damentoilette *f*
la·dy·bird ZO Marienkäfer *m*
la·dy·like damenhaft
lag 1. *mst* **~ behind** zurückbleiben; **2.** →
time lag
la·ger Lagerbier *n*
la·goon Lagune *f*
lair ZO Lager *n*, Höhle *f*, Bau *m*
la·i·ty Laien *pl*
lake See *m*

lamb ZO **1.** Lamm *n*; **2.** lammen
lame 1. lahm (*a. fig*); **2.** lähmen
la·ment 1. jammern, (weh)klagen; trauern; **2.** Jammer *m*, (Weh)Klage *f*
lam·en·ta·ble beklagenswert; kläglich
lam·en·ta·tion (Weh)Klage *f*
lam·i·nat·ed laminiert, geschichtet, beschichtet; **~ glass** Verbundglas *n*
lamp Lampe *f*; Laterne *f*
lamp·post Laternenpfahl *m*
lamp·shade Lampenschirm *m*
lance Lanze *f*
land 1. Land *n*, AGR **a.** Boden *m*, POL **a.** Staat *m*; **by~** auf dem Landweg; **2.** landen, MAR **a.** anlegen; *Güter* ausladen, MAR **a.** löschen
land a·gent AGR Gutsverwalter *m*
land·ed Erdrutsch *m* (*a. POL*)...; **~ gentry** Landadel *m*; **~ property** Grundbesitz *m*
land·ing AVIAT Landung *f*, Landen *n*, MAR **a.** Anlegen *n*; Treppenabsatz *m*; **~ field** AVIAT Landeplatz *m*; **~ gear** AVIAT Fahrgestell *n*; **~ stage** MAR Landungsbrücke *f*, -steg *m*; **~ strip** AVIAT Landeplatz *m*
land·la·dy Vermieterin *f*; Wirtin *f*
land·lord Vermieter *m*; Wirt *m*; Grundbesitzer *m*
land·lub·ber MAR *contp* Landratte *f*
land·mark Wahrzeichen *n*; *fig* Meilenstein *m*
land·own·er Grundbesitzer(in)
land·scape Landschaft *f* (*a. paint*)
land·slide Erdrutsch *m* (*a. POL*); **a ~ victory** POL ein überwältigender Wahlsieg
land·slip (kleiner) Erdrutsch *m*
lane (Feld)Weg *m*; Gasse *f*, Sträßchen *n*; MAR Fahrrinne *f*; AVIAT Flugschneise *f*; SPORT (*einzelne*) Bahn; MOT (Fahr-)Spur *f*; **change ~s** MOT die Spur wechseln; **get in ~** MOT sich einordnen
lan·guage Sprache *f*; **~ la·bor·a·to·ry** Sprachlabor *n*
lan·guid matt; träg(e)
lank glatt
lank·y schlaksig
lan·tern Laterne *f*
lap¹ Schoß *m*
lap² SPORT **1.** Runde *f*; **~ of hono(u)r** Ehrenrunde *f*; **2.** *Gegner* überrunden; e-e Runde zurücklegen

lap³ *v/t*. **~ up** auflecken, aufschlecken; *v/i* plätschern
la·pel Revers *n*, *m*, Aufschlag *m*
lapse 1. Versehen *n*, (kleiner) Fehler *or* Irrtum; Vergehen *n*; Zeitspanne *f*; JUR Verfall *m*; **~ of memory**, **memory ~** Gedächtnislücke *f*; **2.** verfallen; JUR verfallen, erlöschen
lar·ce·ny JUR Diebstahl *m*
larch BOT Lärche *f*
lard 1. Schweinefett *n*, Schweineschmalz *n*; **2.** *Fleisch* spicken
lar·der Speisekammer *f*, -schrank *m*
large groß; beträchtlich, reichlich; umfassend, weitgehend; **at ~** in Freiheit, auf freiem Fuß; *fig* (sehr) ausführlich; in der Gesamtheit
large·ly großenteils, größtenteils
large-mind·ed aufgeschlossen, tolerant
large·ness Größe *f*
lar·i·at Lasso *m*, *n*
lark¹ ZO Lerche *f*
lark² F Jux *m*, Spaß *m*
lark·spur BOT Rittersporn *m*
lar·va ZO Larve *f*
lar·yn·gi·tis MED Kehlkopfentzündung *f*; **lar·ynx** ANAT Kehlkopf *m*
las·civ·i·ous geil, lüstern
la·ser PHYS Laser *m*; **~ beam** PHYS Laserstrahl *m*; **~ print·er** EDP Laserdrucker *m*; **~ tech·nol·o·gy** Lasertechnik *f*
lash 1. Peitschenschnur *f*; (Peitschen-)Hieb *m*; Wimper *f*; **2.** peitschen (mit); (fest)binden; schlagen; **~ out** (wild) um sich schlagen
las·so Lasso *n*, *m*
last¹ 1. *adj* letzte(r, -s), vorige(r, -s); **~ but one** vorletzte(r, -s); **~ night** gestern Abend; letzte Nacht; **2.** *adv* zuletzt, an letzter Stelle; **~ but not least** nicht zu letzt, nicht zu vergessen; **3.** *der, die, das* Letzte; **at ~** endlich; **to the ~** bis zum Schluss
last² (an-, fort)dauern; (sich) halten; (aus)reichen
last³ (Schuhmacher)Leisten *m*
last·ing dauerhaft; beständig
last·ly zuletzt, zum Schluss
latch 1. Schnappriegel *m*; Schnappschloss *n*; **2.** einklinken, zuklinken
latch·key Haus-, Wohnungsschlüssel *m*
late spät; jüngste(r, -s), letzte(r, -s), frühere(r, -s), ehemalig; verstorben;

be ~ zu spät kommen, sich verspäten; RAIL *etc* Verspätung haben; **as** ~ **as** noch, erst; **of** ~ kürzlich; **later on** später

late·ly kürzlich

lath Latte *f*, Leiste *f*

lathe TECH Drehbank *f*

la·ther 1. (Seifen)Schaum *m*; **2.** *v/t* einseifen; *v/i* schäumen

Lat·in LING **1.** lateinisch; südländisch; **2.** Latein(isch) *n*; ~ **A·mer·i·ca** Lateinamerika *n*; ~ **A·mer·i·can 1.** lateinamerikanisch; **2.** Lateinamerikaner(in)

lat·i·tude GEOGR Breite *f*

lat·ter Letztere(r, -s)

lat·tice Gitter(werk) *n*

lau·da·ble lobenswert

laugh 1. lachen (**at** über *acc*); ~ **at s.o.** *a.* j-n auslachen; **2.** Lachen *n*, Gelächter *n*

laugh·a·ble lächerlich, lachhaft

laugh·ter Lachen *n*, Gelächter *n*

launch[1] **1.** MAR vom Stapel lassen; MIL abschießen, *Rakete a.* starten; *fig Projekt etc* in Gang setzen, starten; **2.** MAR Stapellauf *m*; MIL Abschuss *m*, Start *m*

launch[2] MAR Barkasse *f*

launch pad → *launching pad*

launch·ing → *launch*[1] 2; ~ **pad** Abschussrampe *f*; ~ **site** Abschussbasis *f*

laun·der Wäsche waschen (und bügeln); F *esp* Geld waschen

laun·der·ette, **laun·drette** *esp Br*, **laun·dro·mat®** Waschsalon *m*

laun·dry Wäscherei *f*; Wäsche *f*

lau·rel BOT Lorbeer *m* (*a. fig*)

la·va GEOL Lava *f*

lav·a·to·ry Toilette *f*, Klosett *n*; *public* ~ Bedürfnisanstalt *f*

lav·en·der BOT Lavendel *m*

lav·ish 1. sehr freigebig, verschwenderisch; **2.** ~ *s.th.* **on s.o.** j-n mit et. überhäufen *or* überschütten

law Gesetz(e *pl*) *n*; Recht *n*, Rechtssystem *n*; Rechtswissenschaft *f*, Jura; F Bullen *pl* (*police*); F Bulle *m* (*policeman*); Gesetz *n*, Vorschrift *f*; ~ **and order** Recht *or* Ruhe und Ordnung

law-a·bid·ing gesetzestreu

law·court Gericht *n*, Gerichtshof *m*

law·ful gesetzlich, rechtmäßig, legitim; rechtsgültig

law·less gesetzlos; gesetzwidrig; zügellos

lawn Rasen *m*

lawn·mow·er Rasenmäher *m*

law·suit JUR Prozess *m*

law·yer JUR (Rechts)Anwalt *m*, (Rechts)Anwältin *f*

lax locker, schlaff; lax, lasch

lax·a·tive MED **1.** abführend; **2.** Abführmittel *n*

lay[1] REL weltlich; Laien...

lay[2] *v/t* legen; *Teppich* verlegen; belegen, auslegen (**with** mit); *Tisch* decken; ZO *Eier* legen; vorlegen (**before** *dat*); bringen (**before** vor *acc*); *Schuld etc* zuschreiben, zur Last legen (*dat*); *v/i* ZO (Eier) legen; ~ **aside** beiseite legen, zurücklegen; ~ **off** *Arbeiter* (*esp* vorübergehend) entlassen; *Arbeit* einstellen; ~ **open** offenlegen; ~ **out** ausbreiten, auslegen; *Garten etc* anlegen; entwerfen, planen; PRINT das Layout (*gen*) machen; ~ **up** anhäufen, (an)sammeln; **be laid up** das Bett hüten müssen

lay-by *Br* MOT Parkbucht *f*, Parkstreifen *m*; Parkplatz *m*, Rastplatz *m*

lay·er Lage *f*, Schicht *f*; BOT Ableger *m*

lay·man Laie *m*

lay-off ECON (*esp* vorübergehende) Entlassung

lay·out Grundriss *m*, Lageplan *m*; PRINT Layout *n*, Gestaltung *f*

la·zy faul, träg(e)

LCD ABBR *of* **liquid crystal display** Flüssigkristallanzeige *f*

lead[1] **1.** *v/t* führen; (an)führen, leiten; dazu bringen, veranlassen (**to do** zu tun); *v/i* führen; vorangehen; SPORT an der Spitze *or* in Führung liegen; ~ **off** anfangen, beginnen; ~ **on** j-m et. vormachen *or* weismachen; ~ **to** *fig* führen zu; ~ **up to** *fig* (allmählich) führen zu; **2.** Führung *f*; Leitung *f*; Spitzenposition *f*; Vorbild *n*, Beispiel *n*; THEA Hauptrolle *f*; Hauptdarsteller(in); (Hunde-) Leine *f*; Hinweis *m*, Tipp *m*, Anhaltspunkt *m*; SPORT *and fig* Führung *f*, Vorsprung *m*; **be in the** ~ in Führung sein; **take the** ~ in Führung gehen, die Führung übernehmen

lead[2] CHEM Blei *n*; MAR Lot *n*

lead·ed verbleit, bleihaltig

lead·en bleiern (*a. fig*), Blei...

lead·er (An)Führer(in), Leiter(in); Erste *m, f*; *Br* Leitartikel *m*

lead·er·ship Führung *f*, Leitung *f*

lead-free bleifrei

L

lead·ing leitend; führend; Haupt...

leaf 1. BOT, PRINT Blatt n; (Tür- etc)Flügel m; (Tisch)Klappe f, Ausziehplatte f; 2. ~ through durchblättern

leaf·let Hand-, Reklamezettel m; Prospekt m

league POL Bund m; SPORT Liga f

leak 1. lecken, leck sein; tropfen; ~ out auslaufen; fig durchsickern; 2. Leck n, undichte Stelle (a. fig)

leak·age Auslaufen n

leak·y leck, undicht

lean¹ (sich) lehnen; (sich) neigen; ~ on sich verlassen auf (acc)

lean² 1. mager (a. fig); 2. GASTR das Magere; ~ man·age·ment ECON schlanke Unternehmensstruktur

leap 1. springen; ~ at fig sich stürzen auf (acc); 2. Sprung m

leap·frog Bockspringen n

leap year Schaltjahr n

learn (er)lernen; erfahren, hören

learn·ed gelehrt

learn·er Anfänger(in); Lernende m, f; ~ driver Br MOT Fahrschüler(in)

learn·ing Gelehrsamkeit f

lease 1. Pacht f, Miete f; Pacht-, Mietvertrag m; 2. pachten, mieten, leasen; ~ out verpachten, vermieten

leash (Hunde)Leine f

least 1. adj geringste(r, -s), mindeste(r, -s), wenigste(r, -s); 2. adv am wenigsten; ~ of all am allerwenigsten; 3. das Mindeste, das wenigste; at ~ wenigstens; to say the ~ gelinde gesagt

leath·er 1. Leder n; 2. ledern; Leder...

leave 1. v/t (hinter-, über-, ver-, zurück-)lassen, übrig lassen; liegen or stehen lassen, vergessen; vermachen, vererben; be left übrig bleiben, übrig sein; v/i (fort-, weg)gehen, abreisen, abfahren, abfliegen; ~ alone allein lassen; j-n, et. in Ruhe lassen; ~ behind zurücklassen; ~ on anlassen; ~ out draußen lassen; auslassen, weglassen; 2. Erlaubnis f; Urlaub m; Abschied m; on ~ auf Urlaub

leav·en Sauerteig m

leaves BOT Laub n

leav·ings Überreste pl

lech·er·ous geil, lüstern

lec·ture 1. UNIV Vorlesung f (über acc on); Vortrag m; Strafpredigt f; 2. v/i UNIV e-e Vorlesung or Vorlesungen halten (über acc on; vor dat to); e-n Vortrag or Vorträge halten; v/t j-m e-e Strafpredigt halten

lec·tur·er UNIV Dozent(in); Redner(in)

ledge Leiste f, Sims m, n

leech ZO Blutegel m

leek BOT Lauch m, Porree m

leer 1. anzüglicher or lüsterner Seitenblick; 2. anzüglich or lüstern blicken or schielen (at nach)

left 1. adj linke(r, -s), Links...; 2. adv links; turn ~ (sich) nach links wenden; MOT links abbiegen; 3. die Linke (a. POL, boxing), linke Seite; on the ~ links, auf der linken Seite; to the ~ (nach) links; keep to the ~ sich links halten; links fahren

left-hand linke(r, -s)

left-hand drive MOT Linkssteuerung f

left-hand·ed linkshändig; für Linkshänder; be ~ Linkshänder(in) sein

left lug·gage of·fice Br RAIL Gepäckaufbewahrung f

left-o·vers (Speise)Reste pl

left-wing POL dem linken Flügel angehörend, links..., Links...

leg ANAT Bein n; GASTR Keule f; MATH Schenkel m; pull s.o.'s ~ F j-n auf den Arm nehmen; stretch one's ~ sich die Beine vertreten

leg·a·cy fig Vermächtnis n, Erbe n

le·gal legal, gesetzmäßig; gesetzlich, rechtlich; juristisch, Rechts...

le·gal·ize legalisieren

le·gal·i·za·tion Legalisierung f

le·gal pro·tec·tion Rechtsschutz m

le·ga·tion POL Gesandtschaft f

le·gend Legende f, Sage f

le·gen·da·ry legendär

le·gi·ble leserlich

leg·is·la·tion Gesetzgebung f

le·gis·la·tive POL 1. gesetzgebend, legislativ; 2. Legislative f, gesetzgebende Gewalt

le·gis·la·tor POL Gesetzgeber m

le·git·i·mate legitim; gesetzmäßig, rechtmäßig; ehelich

lei·sure freie Zeit; Muße f; at ~ ohne Hast; ~ cen·tre Br Freizeitzentrum n

lei·sure·ly gemächlich

lei·sure time Freizeit f

lei·sure-time ac·tiv·i·ties Freizeitbeschäftigung f, -gestaltung f

lei·sure·wear Freizeitkleidung f

lem·on BOT **1.** Zitrone *f*; **2.** Zitronen...
lem·on·ade Zitronenlimonade *f*
lend *j-m et.* (ver-, aus)leihen
length Länge *f*; Strecke *f*; (Zeit)Dauer *f*; **at** ~ ausführlich
length·en verlängern, länger machen; länger werden
length·ways, length·wise der Länge nach
length·y sehr lang
le·ni·ent mild(e), nachsichtig
lens ANAT, PHOT, PHYS Linse *f*; PHOT Objektiv *n*
Lent REL Fastenzeit *f*
len·til BOT Linse *f*
Le·o ASTR Löwe *m*; **he (she) is (a)** ~ er (sie) ist (ein) Löwe
leop·ard ZO Leopard *m*
le·o·tard (Tänzer)Trikot *n*
lep·ro·sy MED Lepra *f*
les·bi·an 1. lesbisch; **2.** Lesbierin *f*, Lesbe *f*
less 1. *adj and adv* kleiner, geringer, weniger; **2.** *prp* weniger, minus, abzüglich
less·en (sich) vermindern *or* verringern; abnehmen; herabsetzen
less·er kleiner, geringer
les·son Lektion *f*; (Unterrichts)Stunde *f*; *fig* Lehre *f*; *pl* Unterricht *m*
let lassen; *esp Br* vermieten, verpachten; ~ **alone** *j-n, et.* in Ruhe lassen; geschweige denn; ~ **down** hinunterlassen, herunterlassen; *Kleider* verlängern; *j-n* im Stich lassen, F *j-n* sitzen lassen; enttäuschen; ~ **go** loslassen; ~ **o.s. go** sich gehen lassen; ~**'s go** gehen wir!; ~ **in** (her)einlassen; ~ **o.s. in for s.th.** sich et. einbrocken, sich auf et. einlassen
le·thal tödlich; Todes...
leth·ar·gy Lethargie *f*
let·ter Buchstabe *m*; PRINT Type *f*; Brief *m*
let·ter·box *esp Br* Briefkasten *m*
let·ter car·ri·er Briefträger *m*
let·tuce BOT (*esp* Kopf)Salat *m*
leu·k(a)e·mia MED Leukämie *f*
lev·el 1. *adj* eben; gleich (*a. fig*); ausgeglichen; **my** ~ **with** auf gleicher Höhe sein mit; **my** ~ **best** F mein Möglichstes; **2.** Ebene *f* (*a. fig*), ebene Fläche *f*; Höhe *f* (*a.* GEOGR), (*Wasser- etc*)Spiegel *m*, (-)Stand *m*, (-)Pegel *m*; Wasserwaage *f*; *fig* Niveau *n*, Stufe *f*; **sea** ~ Mee-

resspiegel *m*; **on the** ~ F ehrlich, aufrichtig; **3.** (ein)ebnen, planieren; dem Erdboden gleichmachen; ~ **at** *Waffe* richten auf (*acc*); *Beschuldigungen* erheben gegen (*acc*); **4.** *adv*: ~ **with** in Höhe (*gen*)
lev·el cross·ing *Br* schienengleicher Bahnübergang
lev·el-head·ed vernünftig, nüchtern
le·ver Hebel *m*
lev·y 1. Steuer *f*, Abgabe *f*; **2.** *Steuern* erheben
lewd geil, lüstern; unanständig, obszön
li·a·bil·i·ty ECON, JUR Verpflichtung *f*, Verbindlichkeit *f*; ECON, JUR Haftung *f*, Haftpflicht *f*; Neigung *f* (**to** zu), Anfälligkeit *f* (**to** für); **li·a·ble** ECON, JUR haftbar, haftpflichtig; **be** ~ **for** haften für; **be** ~ **to** neigen zu, anfällig sein für
li·ar Lügner(in)
li·bel JUR **1.** (*schriftliche*) Verleumdung *or* Beleidigung; **2.** (*schriftlich*) verleumden *or* beleidigen
lib·e·ral 1. liberal (*a.* POL), aufgeschlossen; großzügig; reichlich; **2.** Liberale *m*, *f* (*a.* POL)
lib·e·rate befreien; **lib·e·ra·tion** Befreiung *f*; **lib·e·ra·tor** Befreier *m*
lib·er·ty Freiheit *f*; **take liberties with** sich Freiheiten gegen *j-n* herausnehmen; willkürlich mit *et.* umgehen; **be at** ~ frei sein
Li·bra ASTR Waage *f*; **he (she) is (a)** ~ er (sie) ist (eine) Waage
li·brar·i·an Bibliothekar(in)
li·bra·ry Bibliothek *f*; Bücherei *f*
li·cence 1. *Br* → **license** 1; **2.** e-e Lizenz *or* Konzession erteilen (*dat*); *behördlich* genehmigen
li·cense 1. Lizenz *f*, Konzession *f*; (*Führer-, Jagd-, Waffen- etc*)Schein *m*; **2.** *Br* → **licence** 2
li·cense plate MOT Nummernschild *n*
li·chen BOT Flechte *f*
lick 1. Lecken *n*; Salzlecke *f*; **2.** *v/t* ab-, auflecken; F verdreschen, verprügeln; F schlagen, besiegen; *v/i* lecken; züngeln (*flames*)
lic·o·rice Lakritze *f*
lid Deckel *m*; ANAT (Augen)Lid *n*
lie¹ 1. lügen; ~ **to s.o.** *j-n* belügen, *j-n* anlügen; **2.** Lüge *f*; **tell** ~**s, tell a** ~ lügen; **give the** ~ **to** *j-n et.* Lügen strafen
lie² 1. liegen; **let sleeping dogs** schla-

fende Hunde soll man nicht wecken; **~ behind** *fig* dahinter stecken; **~ down** sich hinlegen; **2.** Lage *f* (*a. fig*)

lie-down *Br* F Nickerchen *n*

lie-in: have a ~ *esp Br* F sich gründlich ausschlafen

lieu: in ~ of anstelle von (*or gen*)

lieu·ten·ant MIL Leutnant *m*

life Leben *n*; JUR lebenslängliche Freiheitsstrafe; **all her ~** ihr ganzes Leben lang; **for ~** fürs (ganze) Leben; *esp* JUR lebenslänglich

life as·sur·ance *Br* → **life insurance**

life belt Rettungsgürtel *m*

life·boat Rettungsboot *n*

life·guard Bademeister *m*; Rettungsschwimmer *m*

life im·pris·on·ment JUR lebenslängliche Freiheitsstrafe

life in·sur·ance Lebensversicherung *f*

life jack·et Schwimmweste *f*

life·less leblos; matt, schwung-, lustlos

life·like lebensecht

life·long lebenslang

life pre·serv·er Schwimmweste *f*; Rettungsgürtel *m*

life sen·tence JUR lebenslängliche Freiheitsstrafe

life·time Lebenszeit *f*

lift 1. *v/t* (hoch-, auf)heben; erheben; *Verbot etc* aufheben; *Gesicht etc* liften, straffen; F klauen; *v/i* sich heben, steigen (*a. fog*); **~ off** starten (*rocket*), AVIAT abheben; **2.** (Hoch-, Auf)Heben *n*; PHYS, AVIAT Auftrieb *m*; *Br* Lift *m*, Aufzug *m*, Fahrstuhl *m*; **give s.o. a ~** j-n (im Auto) mitnehmen; F j-n aufmuntern, j-m Auftrieb geben

lift-off Start *m*, Abheben *n*

lig·a·ment ANAT Band *n*

light¹ 1. Licht *n* (*a. fig*); Beleuchtung *f*; Schein *m*; Feuer *n*; *fig* Aspekt *m*; *Br mst pl* (Verkehrs)Ampel *f*; **do you have (*Br* have you got) a ~?** haben Sie Feuer?; **2.** *v/t* beleuchten, erleuchten; *a.* **~ up** anzünden; *v/i* sich entzünden; **~ up** *fig* aufleuchten; **3.** hell, licht

light² leicht (*a, fig*); **make ~ of s.th.** et. leicht nehmen; et. bagatellisieren

light·en¹ *v/t* erhellen; erleuchten; *v/i* hell (er) werden, sich aufhellen

light·en² leichter machen *or* werden; erleichtern

light·er Anzünder *m*; Feuerzeug *n*

light-head·ed (leicht) benommen; leichtfertig, töricht

light-heart·ed fröhlich, unbeschwert

light·house Leuchtturm *m*

light·ing Beleuchtung *f*

light·ness Leichtheit *f*; Leichtigkeit *f*

light·ning Blitz *m*; **like ~** wie der Blitz; **(as) quick as ~** blitzschnell

light·ning| con·duc·tor *Br*, **~ rod** ELECTR Blitzableiter *m*

light·weight SPORT Leichtgewicht *n*, Leichtgewichtler *m*

like¹ 1. *v/t* gern haben, mögen; **I ~ it** es gefällt mir; **I ~ her** ich kann sie gut leiden; **how do you ~ it?** wie gefällt es dir?, wie findest du es?; **I ~ that!** iro das hab ich gern!; **I should** *or* **would ~ to know** ich möchte gern wissen; *v/i* wollen; **(just) as you ~** (ganz) wie du willst; **if you ~** wenn du willst; **2. ~s and dislikes** Neigungen und Abneigungen *pl*

like² 1. gleich; wie; ähnlich; **~ that** so; **feel ~** Lust haben auf (*acc*) *or* zu; **what is he ~?** wie ist er?; **that is just ~ him!** das sieht ihm ähnlich!; **2.** *der, die, das* Gleiche; **his ~** seinesgleichen; **the ~** dergleichen; **the ~s of you** Leute wie du

like·li·hood Wahrscheinlichkeit *f*

like·ly 1. *adj* wahrscheinlich; geeignet; **2.** *adv* wahrscheinlich; **not ~!** F bestimmt nicht!

like·ness Ähnlichkeit *f*; Abbild *n*

like·wise ebenso

lik·ing Vorliebe *f*

li·lac 1. lila; **2.** BOT Flieder *m*

lil·y BOT Lilie *f*

lil·y of the val·ley BOT Maiglöckchen *n*

limb ANAT (*Körper*)Glied *n*; BOT Ast *m*

lime¹ Kalk *m*

lime² BOT Linde *f*; Limone *f*

lime·light *fig* Rampenlicht *n*

lim·it 1. Limit *n*, Grenze *f*; **within ~s** in Grenzen; **off ~s** Zutritt verboten (**to** für); **that is the ~!** F das ist der Gipfel!, das ist (doch) die Höhe!; **go to the ~** bis zum Äußersten gehen; **2.** beschränken (**to** auf *acc*)

lim·i·ta·tion Beschränkung *f*; *fig* Grenze *f*; JUR Verjährung *f*

lim·it·ed beschränkt, begrenzt; **~ (lia·bility) company** *Br* ECON Gesellschaft *f* mit beschränkter Haftung

lim·it·less grenzenlos
limp[1] **1.** hinken, humpeln; **2.** Hinken *n*, Humpeln *n*
limp[2] schlaff, schlapp, F lappig
line[1] **1.** Linie *f*, Strich *m*; Zeile *f*; Falte *f*, Runzel *f*; Reihe *f*; (Menschen-, *a.* Auto)Schlange *f*; (Abstammungs)Linie *f*; (Verkehrs-, *Eisenbahn- etc*)Linie *f*, Strecke *f*; (*Flug- etc*)Gesellschaft *f*; *esp* TEL Leitung *f*; MIL Linie *f*; Fach *n*, Gebiet *n*, Branche *f*; SPORT (*Ziel- etc*)Linie *f*; Leine *f*; Schnur *f*; Linie *f*, Richtung *f*; *fig* Grenze *f*; *pl* THEA Rolle *f*, Text *m*; **the** ~ der Äquator; **draw the** ~ Halt machen, die Grenze ziehen (**at** bei); **the** ~ **is busy** *or* **engaged** TEL die Leitung ist besetzt; **hold the** ~ TEL bleiben Sie am Apparat; **stand in** ~ anstehen, Schlange stehen (**for** um, nach); **2.** lin(i)ieren; *Gesicht* zeichnen, (zer)furchen; *Straße etc* säumen; ~ **up** (sich) in e-r Reihe *or* Linie aufstellen, SPORT sich aufstellen; sich anstellen (**for** um, nach)
line[2] *Kleid etc* füttern; TECH auskleiden, ausschlagen; MOT *Bremsen etc* belegen
lin·e·ar linear; Längen...
lin·en 1. Leinen *n*; (*Bett-, Tisch- etc* -)Wäsche *f*; **2.** leinen, Leinen...
lin·en| clos·et, *Br* → **cup·board** Wäscheschrank *m*
lin·er MAR Linienschiff *n*; AVIAT Verkehrsflugzeug *n*
lines·man SPORT Linienrichter *m*
lines·wom·an SPORT Linienrichterin *f*
line-up SPORT Aufstellung *f*; Gegenüberstellung *f* (zur Identifizierung)
lin·ger verweilen, sich aufhalten; *a.* ~ **on** dahinsiechen; ~ **on** noch dableiben; *fig* fortleben
lin·ge·rie Damenunterwäsche *f*
lin·ing Futter(stoff *m*) *n*; TECH Auskleidung *f*; MOT (*Brems- etc*)Belag *m*
link 1. (Ketten)Glied *n*; Manschettenknopf *m*; *fig* (Binde)Glied *n*, Verbindung *f*; **2.** *a.* ~ **up** (sich) verbinden
links → **golf links**
link-up Verbindung *f*
lin·seed BOT Leinsamen *m*
lin·seed oil Leinöl *n*
li·on ZO Löwe *m*
li·on·ess ZO Löwin *f*
lip ANAT Lippe *f*; (*Tassen- etc*)Rand *m*; F Unverschämtheit *f*

lip·stick Lippenstift *m*
liq·ue·fy (sich) verflüssigen
liq·uid 1. Flüssigkeit *f*; **2.** flüssig
liq·ui·date liquidieren (*a.* ECON); *Schulden* tilgen
liq·uid·ize zerkleinern, pürieren
liq·uid·iz·er Mixgerät *n*, Mixer *m*
liq·uor *Br* alkoholische Getränke *pl*, Alkohol *m*; Schnaps *m*, Spirituosen *pl*
liq·uo·rice *Br* → **licorice**
lisp 1. Lispeln; **2.** Lispeln *n*
list 1. Liste *f*, Verzeichnis *n*; MAR Schlagseite *f*; **2.** (in e-e Liste) eintragen, erfassen; MAR Schlagseite haben
lis·ten hören; ~ **in** Radio hören; ~ **in to** *et.* im Radio (an)hören; ~ **in on** *Telefongespräch etc* abhören *or* mithören; ~ **to** anhören (*acc*), zuhören (*dat*); hören auf (*acc*)
lis·ten·er Zuhörer(in); (Rundfunk-)Hörer(in)
list·less teilnahmslos, lustlos
li·ter Liter *m*, *n*
lit·e·ral (wort)wörtlich; genau; prosaisch
lit·e·ra·ry literarisch, Literatur...
lit·e·ra·ture Literatur *f*
lithe geschmeidig, gelenkig
lit·ter 1. (*esp Papier*)Abfall *m*; AGR Streu *f*; ZO Wurf *m*; Trage *f*; Sänfte *f*; **2.** *et.* herumliegen lassen in (*dat*) *or* auf (*dat*); **be** ~**ed with** übersät sein mit
lit·ter| bas·ket, ~ **bin** Abfallkorb *m*
lit·tle 1. *adj* klein; wenig; **the** ~ **ones** die Kleinen *pl*; **2.** *adv* wenig, kaum; **3.** Kleinigkeit *f*; *a* ~ ein wenig, ein bisschen; ~ **by** ~ (ganz) allmählich, nach und nach; *not a* ~ nicht wenig
live[1] leben; wohnen (**with** bei); ~ **to see** erleben; ~ **on** leben von; weiterleben; ~ **up to** *s-n Grundsätzen etc* gemäß leben; *Erwartungen etc* entsprechen; ~ **with** mit *j-m* zusammenleben; mit *et.* leben
live[2] **1.** *adj* lebend, lebendig; richtig, echt; ELECTR Strom führend; *radio,* TV Direkt..., Live-...; **2.** *adv* direkt, original, live
live·li·hood (Lebens)Unterhalt *m*
live·li·ness Lebhaftigkeit *f*
live·ly lebhaft, lebendig; aufregend
liv·er ANAT Leber *f* (*a.* GASTR)
liv·e·ry Livree *f*

live·stock Vieh *n*, Viehbestand *m*

liv·id bläulich; F fuchsteufelswild

liv·ing 1. lebend; *the ~ image of* das genaue Ebenbild (*gen*); **2.** Leben *n*, Lebensweise *f*; Lebensunterhalt *m*; *the ~* die Lebenden *pl*; *standard of ~* Lebensstandard *m*; *earn or make a ~* (sich) s-n Lebensunterhalt verdienen

liv·ing room Wohnzimmer *n*

liz·ard ZO Eidechse *f*

load 1. Last *f* (*a. fig*); Ladung *f*; Belastung *f*; **2.** *j-n* überhäufen (*with* mit); *Schusswaffe* laden; *~ a camera* e-n Film einlegen; *a. ~ up* (auf-, be-, ein)laden

loaf¹ Laib *m* (Brot); Brot *n*

loaf² *a. ~ about, ~ around* F herumlungern

loaf·er Müßiggänger(in)

loam Lehm *m*; **loam·y** lehmig

loan 1. (Ver)Leihen *n*, ECON Kredit *m*, Darlehen *n*; Leihgabe *f*; *on ~* leihweise; **2.** *~ s.o. s.th., ~ s.th. to s.o.* j-m et. (aus)leihen; et. an j-n verleihen

loan shark ECON Kredithai *m*

loath: *be ~ to do s.th.* et. nur (sehr) ungern tun

loathe verabscheuen, hassen

loath·ing Abscheu *m*

lob *esp tennis*: Lob *m*

lob·by 1. Vorhalle *f*; THEA, *film*: Foyer *n*; Wandelhalle *f*; POL Lobby *f*, Interessengruppe *f*; **2.** POL *Abgeordnete etc* beeinflussen

lobe ANAT, BOT Lappen *m*

lob·ster ZO Hummer *m*

lo·cal 1. örtlich, Orts..., lokal, Lokal...; **2.** Ortsansässige *m*, *f*, Einheimische *m*, *f*; *Br* F Stammkneipe *f*; *~ call* TEL Ortsgespräch *n*; *~ e·lec·tions* POL Kommunalwahlen *pl*; *~ gov·ern·ment* Gemeindeverwaltung *f*; *~ time* Ortszeit *f*; *~ traf·fic* Orts-, Nahverkehr *m*

lo·cate ausfindig machen; orten; *be ~d* gelegen sein, liegen, sich befinden

lo·ca·tion Lage *f*, Standort *m*; Platz *m* (*for* für); *film*, TV Gelände *n* für Außenaufnahmen; *on ~* auf Außenaufnahme

lock¹ **1.** (*Tür-, Gewehr- etc*)Schloss *n*; Schleuse(nkammer) *f*; Verschluss *m*; Sperrvorrichtung *f*; **2.** *v/t* zu-, verschließen, zu-, versperren (*a. ~ up*); umschlingen, umfassen; TECH sperren;

v/i schließen; abschließbar *or* verschließbar sein; MOT *etc* blockieren; *~ away* wegschließen; *~ in* einschließen, einsperren; *~ out* aussperren; *~ up* abschließen; einsperren

lock² (*Haar*)Locke *f*

lock·er Spind *m*, Schrank *m*; Schließfach *n*; *~ room* SPORT Umkleidekabine *f*, Umkleideraum *f*

lock·et Medaillon *n*

lock·out ECON Aussperrung *f*

lock·smith Schlosser *m*

lock·up Arrestzelle *f*

lo·cust ZO Heuschrecke *f*

lodge 1. Portier-, Pförtnerloge *f*; (*Jagd-, Ski- etc*)Hütte *f*; Sommer-, Gartenhaus *n*; (*Freimaurer*)Loge *f*; **2.** *v/i* logieren, (*esp* vorübergehend *or* in Untermiete) wohnen; stecken (bleiben) (*bullet etc*); *v/t* aufnehmen, beherbergen, (für die Nacht) unterbringen; *Beschwerde etc* einreichen; *Berufung, Protest* einlegen

lodg·er Untermieter(in); **lodg·ing** Unterkunft *f*; *pl esp* möbliertes Zimmer

loft (*Dach*)Boden *m*; Heuboden *m*; Empore *f*; (*converted*) *~* Loft *m*, Fabriketage *f*

loft·y hoch; erhaben; stolz, hochmütig

log (*Holz*)Klotz *m*; (*gefällter*) Baumstamm; (*Holz*)Scheit *n*; → **log·book** MAR Logbuch *n*; AVIAT Bordbuch *n*; MOT Fahrtenbuch *n*

log cab·in Blockhaus *n*, Blockhütte *f*

log·ger·heads: *be at ~* sich streiten, sich in den Haaren liegen (*with* mit)

lo·gic Logik *f*; **lo·gic·al** logisch

loin GASTR Lende(nstück *n*) *f*; *pl* ANAT Lende *f*

loi·ter trödeln; herumlungern

loll hängen (*head*), heraushängen (*tongue*); *~ around or about* F sich rekeln *or* lümmeln

lol·li·pop GASTR Lutscher *m*; *esp Br* Eis *n* am Stiel; *~ man Br* Schülerlotse *m*; *~ woman, ~ lady Br* Schülerlotsin *f*

lol·ly GASTR F Lutscher *m*; *ice ~* Eis *n* am Stiel

lone·li·ness Einsamkeit *f*

lone·ly einsam; *become ~* vereinsamen

lone·some einsam

long¹ **1.** *adj* lang; weit; langfristig; **2.** *adv* lang(e); *as or so ~ as* solange wie; vorausgesetzt, dass; *~ ago* vor langer

Zeit; **so ~!** F bis dann!, tschüs(s)!; **3.** (e-e) lange Zeit; **for ~** lange; **take ~** lange brauchen *or* dauern

long² sich sehnen (**for** nach)

long-dis·tance MIL Fern..., Langstrecken...; **~ call** TEL Ferngespräch *n*; **~ run·ner** SPORT Langstreckenläufer(in)

long-hand Schreibschrift *f*

long·ing 1. sehnsüchtig; **2.** Sehnsucht *f*, Verlangen *n*

lon·gi·tude GEOGR Länge *f*

long johns lange Unterhose

long jump SPORT Weitsprung *m*

long-life milk *esp Br* H-Milch *f*

long-play·er, long-play·ing rec·ord Langspielplatte *f*

long-range MIL, AVIAT Fern..., Langstrecken...; langfristig

long·shore·man Dock-, Hafenarbeiter *m*

long-sight·ed *esp Br* weitsichtig, *fig a.* weitblickend

long-stand·ing seit langer Zeit bestehend; alt

long-term langfristig, auf lange Sicht

long wave ELECTR Langwelle *f*

long-wear·ing strapazierfähig

long-wind·ed langatmig

look 1. sehen, blicken, schauen (**at, on** auf *acc*, nach); nachschauen, nachsehen; **krank etc** aussehen; nach *e-r Richtung* liegen, gehen (**window etc**); **~ here!** schau mal (her); hör mal (zu)!; **~ like** aussehen wie; **it ~s as if** es sieht (so) aus, als ob; **~ after** aufpassen auf (*acc*); sich kümmern um, sorgen für, **den Haushalt** etc versehen; **~ ahead** nach vorne sehen; *fig* vorausschauen; **~ around** sich umsehen; **~ at** ansehen; **~ back** sich umsehen; *fig* zurückblicken; **~ down** herab-, runtersehen (*a. fig* **on s.o.** auf j-n); **~ for** suchen; **~ forward to** sich freuen auf (*acc*); **~ in** F hereinschauen (**on** bei); **~ into** untersuchen, prüfen; **~ on** zusehen, zuschauen (*dat*); betrachten, ansehen (**as** als); **~ onto** liegen zu, (hinaus)gehen auf (*acc*) (**window** etc); **~ out** hinaus-, heraussehen; aufpassen, sich vorsehen; ausschauen *or* Ausschau halten (**for** nach); **~ over** *et.* durchsehen; j-n mustern; **~ round** sich umsehen; **~ through** *et.* durchsehen; **~ up** aufblicken, aufsehen; *et.* nachschla-

gen; *j-n* aufsuchen; **2.** Blick *m*; Miene *f*, (Gesichts)Ausdruck *m*; (**good**) **~s** gutes Aussehen; **have a ~ at s.th.** sich et. ansehen; **I don't like the ~ of it** es gefällt mir nicht

look·ing glass Spiegel *m*

look·out Ausguck *m*; Ausschau *f*; *fig* F Aussicht(en *pl*) *f*; **be on the ~ for** Ausschau halten nach; **that's his own ~** das ist allein seine Sache

loom¹ Webstuhl *m*

loom² *a.* **~ up** undeutlich sichtbar werden *or* auftauchen

loop 1. Schlinge *f*, Schleife *f*; Schlaufe *f*; Öse *f*; AVIAT Looping *m, n*; EDP Schleife *f*; **2.** (sich) schlingen

loop·hole MIL Schießscharte *f*, *fig* Hintertürchen *n*; **a ~ in the law** e-e Gesetzeslücke

loose 1. los(e); locker; weit; frei; **let ~** loslassen; freilassen; **2. be on the ~** frei herumlaufen

loos·en (sich) lösen *or* lockern; **~ up** SPORT Lockerungsübungen machen

loot 1. Beute *f*; **2.** plündern

lop *Baum* beschneiden, stutzen; **~ off** abhauen, abhacken

lop·sid·ed schief; *fig* einseitig

lord Herr *m*, Gebieter *m*; *Br* Lord *m*; **the Lord** REL Gott *m* (der Herr); **the Lord's Prayer** REL das Vaterunser; **the Lord's Supper** REL das (heilige) Abendmahl; **House of Lords** *Br* POL Oberhaus *n*

Lord May·or *Br* Oberbürgermeister *m*

lor·ry *Br* MOT Last(kraft)wagen *m*, Lastauto *n*, Laster *m*

lose verlieren; verpassen, versäumen; nachgehen (**watch**); **~ o.s.** sich verirren; sich verlieren; **los·er** Verlierer(in); **loss** Verlust *m*; Schaden *m*; **at a ~** ECON mit Verlust; **be at a ~** in Verlegenheit sein (**for** um); **lost** verloren; **be ~** sich verirrt haben, sich nicht mehr zurechtfinden (*a. fig*); **be ~ in thought** in Gedanken versunken sein; **get ~** sich verirren; **get ~!** *sl* hau ab!

lost-and-found (of·fice), *Br* **lost prop·er·ty of·fice** Fundbüro *n*

lot Los *n*; Parzelle *f*; Grundstück *n*; ECON Partie *f*, Posten *m*; Gruppe *f*, Gesellschaft *f*; Menge *f*, Haufen *m*; Los *n*, Schicksal *n*; **the ~** alles, das Ganze; **a ~ of F, ~s of F** viel, e-e Menge; **a**

L

bad ~ F ein übler Kerl; **cast** or **draw ~s** losen

loth → loath

lo·tion Lotion f

lot·te·ry Lotterie f

loud laut; *fig* schreiend, grell

loud·mouth *contp* Schwätzer m

loud·speak·er Lautsprecher m

lounge 1. Wohnzimmer n; Aufenthaltsraum m, Lounge f (a. AVIAT); Wartehalle f; **2.** F *contp* sich flegeln; **~ about**, **~ around** herumlungern

louse ZO Laus f

lou·sy verlaust; F miserabel, saumäßig

lout Flegel m, Lümmel m, Rüpel m

lov·a·ble liebenswert; reizend

love 1. Liebe f (**of, for, to, towards** zu); Liebling m, Schatz m; *tennis:* null; **be in ~ with s.o.** in j-n verliebt sein; **fall in ~ with s.o.** sich in j-n verlieben; **make ~** sich lieben, miteinander schlafen; **give my ~ to her** grüße sie herzlich von mir; **send one's ~ to** j-n grüßen lassen; **~ from ...** herzliche Grüße von ...; **2.** lieben; gern mögen

love af·fair Liebesaffäre f

love·ly (wunder)schön; nett, reizend; F prima

lov·er Liebhaber m, Geliebte m, f, (*Musik- etc*) Liebhaber(in), (-)Freund(in); *pl* Liebende pl, Liebespaar n

lov·ing liebevoll, liebend

low 1. *adj* niedrig (*a. fig*); tief (*a. fig*); knapp (*supplies etc*); gedämpft, schwach (*light*); tief (*sound*); leise (*sound, voice*); *fig* gering(schätzig); ordinär; niedergeschlagen, deprimiert; **2.** *adv* niedrig; tief (*a. fig*); leise **3.** METEOR Tief(druckgebiet) n; *fig* Tief(punkt) n

low·brow F **1.** geistig Anspruchslose m, f, Unbedarfte m, f; **2.** geistig anspruchslos, unbedarft

low-cal·o·rie kalorienarm, -reduziert

low-e·mis·sion schadstoffarm

low·er 1. niedriger; tiefer; untere(r, -s), Unter...; **2.** niedriger machen; herab-, herunterlassen; *Augen, Stimme, Preis etc* senken; *Standard* herabsetzen; *fig* erniedrigen

low-fat fettarm

low-fly·ing plane AVIAT Tiefflieger m

low·land Tief-, Flachland n

low·ly niedrig

low-necked (tief) ausgeschnitten

low-pitched MUS tief

low-pres·sure METEOR Tiefdruck...; TECH Niederdruck...

low-rise ARCH niedrig (gebaut)

low-spir·it·ed niedergeschlagen

low tide Ebbe f

low wa·ter Niedrigwasser n

loy·al loyal, treu

loy·al·ty Loyalität f, Treue f

loz·enge MATH Raute f, Rhombus m; GASTR Pastille f

lu·bri·cant TECH Schmiermittel n

lu·bri·cate TECH schmieren, ölen

lu·bri·ca·tion TECH Schmieren n, Ölen n

lu·cid klar

luck Schicksal n; Glück n; **bad ~, hard ~, ill ~** Unglück n, Pech n; **good ~** Glück n; **good ~!** viel Glück!; **be in (out of) ~** (kein) Glück haben

luck·i·ly glücklicherweise, zum Glück

luck·y glücklich, Glücks...; **be ~** Glück haben; **~ day** Glückstag m; **~ fellow** Glückspilz m

lu·cra·tive einträglich, lukrativ

lu·di·crous lächerlich

lug zerren, schleppen

luge SPORT Rennrodeln n; Rennrodel m, Rennschlitten m

lug·gage *esp Br* (Reise)Gepäck n; **~ rack** *esp Br* RAIL *etc* Gepäcknetz n, Gepäckablage f; **~ van** *Br* RAIL Gepäckwagen m

luke·warm lau(warm); *fig* lau, mäßig, halbherzig

lull 1. beruhigen; sich legen (*storm*); *mst* **~ to sleep** einlullen; **2.** Pause f; MAR Flaute f (*a. fig*)

lul·la·by Wiegenlied n

lum·ba·go MED Hexenschuss m

lum·ber¹ schwerfällig gehen; (dahin-) rumpeln (*vehicle*)

lum·ber² 1. Bau-, Nutzholz n; *esp Br* Gerümpel n; **2.** *v/t* **~ s.o. with s.th.** *Br* F j-m et. aufhalsen

lum·ber·jack Holzfäller m, -arbeiter m

lum·ber mill Sägewerk n

lum·ber room *esp Br* Rumpelkammer f

lum·ber·yard Holzplatz m, Holzlager n

lu·mi·na·ry *fig* Leuchte f, Koryphäe f

lu·mi·nous leuchtend, Leucht...

lu·mi·nous dis·play Leuchtanzeige f

lu·mi·nous paint Leuchtfarbe f

lump 1. Klumpen *m*; Schwellung *f*, Beule *f*; MED Geschwulst *f*, Knoten *m*; GASTR Stück *n*; **in the ~** in Bausch und Bogen, pauschal; **2.** *v/t*: **~ together** *fig* zusammenwerfen; in e-n Topf werfen; *v/i* Klumpen bilden, klumpen

lump sug·ar Würfelzucker *m*

lump sum Pauschalsumme *f*

lump·y klumpig

lu·na·cy Wahnsinn *m*

lu·nar ASTR Mond...

lu·nar mod·ule Mond(lande)fähre *f*

lu·na·tic *fig* **1.** wahnsinnig, verrückt; **2.** Wahnsinnige *m*, *f*, Verrückte *m*, *f*

lunch, *formal* **lun·cheon 1.** Lunch *m*, Mittagessen *n*; **2.** zu Mittag essen

lunch hour, lunch time Mittagszeit *f*, Mittagspause *f*

lung ANAT Lungenflügel *m*; *pl* die Lunge

lunge sich stürzen (**at** auf *acc*)

lurch 1. taumeln, torkeln; **2. leave s.o. in the ~** j-n im Stich lassen, F j-n sitzen lassen

lure 1. Köder *m*; *fig* Lockung *f*; **2.** ködern, (an)locken

lu·rid grell; grässlich, schauerlich

lurk lauern; **~ about, ~ around** herumschleichen

lus·cious köstlich, lecker; üppig; F knackig

lush saftig, üppig

lust 1. sinnliche Begierde, Lust *f*; Gier *f*; **2. ~ after, ~ for** begehren; gierig sein nach

lus·ter, *Br* **lus·tre** Glanz *m*, Schimmer *m*; **lus·trous** glänzend, schimmernd

lust·y kräftig, robust, vital

lute MUS Laute *f*

Lu·ther·an REL lutherisch

lux·u·ri·ant üppig

lux·u·ri·ate schwelgen (**in** in *dat*)

lux·u·ri·ous luxuriös, Luxus...

lux·u·ry 1. Luxus *m*; Komfort *m*; Luxusartikel *m*; **2.** Luxus...

lye Lauge *f*

ly·ing lügnerisch, verlogen

lymph MED Lymphe *f*

lynch lynchen; **~ law** Lynchjustiz *f*

lynx ZO Luchs *m*

lyr·ic 1. lyrisch; **2.** lyrisches Gedicht; *pl* Lyrik *f*; (Lied)Text *m*

lyr·i·cal lyrisch, gefühlvoll; schwärmerisch

M

M

M, m M, m *n*

M ABBR *of* **medium (size)** mittelgroß

ma F Mama *f*, Mutti *f*

ma'am → **madam**

ma·cad·am Asphalt *m*

mac·a·ro·ni Makkaroni *pl*

ma·chine 1. Maschine *f*; **2.** maschinell herstellen

ma·chine-gun Maschinengewehr *n*

ma·chine-read·a·ble EDP maschinenlesbar

ma·chin·e·ry Maschinen *pl*; Maschinerie *f*

ma·chin·ist TECH Maschinist *m*

mach·o *contp* Macho *m*

mack·e·rel ZO Makrele *f*

mac·ro... Makro..., (sehr) groß

mad wahnsinnig, verrückt; VET tollwütig; F wütend; *fig* **be ~ about** wild *or* versessen sein auf (*acc*), verrückt sein

nach; **drive s.o. ~** j-n verrückt machen; **go ~** verrückt werden; **like ~** wie verrückt

mad·am gnädige Frau

mad·cap verrückt

mad cow dis·ease VET Rinderwahn (-sinn) *m*

mad·den verrückt *or* rasend machen

mad·den·ing unerträglich; verrückt *or* rasend machend

made: ~ of gold aus Gold

made-to-meas·ure maßgeschneidert

made-up geschminkt; erfunden

mad·house *fig* F Irrenhaus *n*

mad·ly wie verrückt; F wahnsinnig, schrecklich

mad·man Verrückte *m*

mad·ness Wahnsinn

mad·wom·an Verrückte *f*

mag·a·zine Magazin *n* (*a.* PHOT, MIL),

Zeitschrift f; Lagerhaus n

mag·got ZO Made f

Ma·gi: *the* (*three*) ~ die (drei) Weisen aus dem Morgenland, die Heiligen Drei Könige

ma·gic 1. Magie f, Zauberei f; Zauber m; *fig* Wunder n; **2.** *a.* **magical** magisch, Zauber...

ma·gi·cian Magier m, Zauberer m; Zauberkünstler m

ma·gis·trate (Friedens)Richter(in)

mag·na·nim·i·ty Großmut f

mag·nan·i·mous großmütig

mag·net Magnet m

mag·net·ic magnetisch, Magnet...

mag·nif·i·cent großartig, prächtig

mag·ni·fy vergrößern

mag·ni·fy·ing glass Vergrößerungsglas n, Lupe f

mag·ni·tude Größe f; Wichtigkeit f

mag·pie ZO Elster f

ma·hog·a·ny Mahagoni(holz) n

maid (Dienst)Mädchen n, Hausangestellte f; ~ *of all work esp fig* Mädchen n für alles; ~ *of hono(u)r* Hofdame f; (erste) Brautjungfer

maid·en Jungfern..., Erstlings...

maid·en name Mädchenname m

mail 1. Post(sendung) f; *by* ~ mit der Post; **2.** mit der Post (zu)schicken, aufgeben, *Brief* einwerfen

mail·bag Postsack m; Posttasche f

mail·box Briefkasten m

mail car·ri·er, mail·man Briefträger m, Postbote m

mail or·der Bestellung f bei e-m Versandhaus

mail-or·der| firm, ~ house Versandhaus n

maim verstümmeln

main 1. Haupt..., wichtigste(r, -s); hauptsächlich; *by* ~ *force* mit äußerster Kraft; **2.** *mst pl* Hauptleitung f, Hauptgas-, Hauptwasser-, Hauptstromleitung f; (Strom)Netz n; *in the* ~ in der Hauptsache, im Wesentlichen

main·frame EDP Großrechner m

main·land Festland n

main·ly hauptsächlich

main mem·o·ry EDP Hauptspeicher m; Arbeitsspeicher m

main men·u EDP Hauptmenü n

main road Haupt(verkehrs)straße f

main·spring TECH Hauptfeder f; *fig* (Haupt)Triebfeder f

main·stay *fig* Hauptstütze f

main street Hauptstraße f

main·tain (aufrecht)erhalten, beibehalten; instand halten, pflegen, TECH *a.* warten; *Familie etc* unterhalten, versorgen; *et.* behaupten

main·te·nance (Aufrecht)Erhaltung f; Instandhaltung f, Pflege f, TECH *a.* Wartung f; Unterhalt m

maize Br BOT Mais m

ma·jes·tic majestätisch

ma·jes·ty Majestät f; *His* (*Her, Your*) *Majesty* Seine (Ihre, Eure) Majestät

ma·jor 1. größere(r, -s), *fig a.* bedeutend, wichtig; JUR volljährig; *C* ~ MUS C-Dur n; **2.** MIL Major m; JUR Volljährige m, f; UNIV Hauptfach n; MUS Dur n; ~ **gen·e·ral** MIL Generalmajor m

ma·jor·i·ty Mehrheit f, Mehrzahl f; JUR Volljährigkeit f

ma·jor league *baseball*: oberste Spielklasse

ma·jor road Haupt(verkehrs)straße f

make 1. machen; anfertigen, herstellen, erzeugen; (zu)bereiten; (er)schaffen; ergeben; bilden; machen zu; ernennen zu; *Geld* verdienen; sich erweisen als, abgeben (*person*); schätzen auf (*acc*); *Geschwindigkeit* erreichen; *Fehler* machen; *Frieden* etc schließen; *e-e Rede* halten; *F Strecke* zurücklegen; mit *inf*: *j-n* lassen, veranlassen zu, bringen zu, zwingen zu; ~ *it* es schaffen; *do with s.th.* mit et. auskommen, sich mit et. behelfen; *do you* ~ *one of us?* machen Sie mit?; *what do you* ~ *of it?* was halten Sie davon?; ~ *believe* vorgeben; ~ *friends with* sich anfreunden mit; ~ *good* wieder gutmachen; *Versprechen etc* halten; ~ *haste* sich beeilen; ~ *way* Platz machen; ~ *for* zugehen auf (*acc*); sich aufmachen nach; ~ *into* verarbeiten zu; ~ *off* sich davonmachen, sich aus dem Staub machen; ~ *out Rechnung, Scheck* etc ausstellen; ausmachen, erkennen; aus *j-m, e-r Sache* klug werden; ~ *over Eigentum* übertragen; ~ *up* et. zusammenstellen; sich et. ausdenken, et. erfinden; (sich) zurechtmachen *or* schminken; ~ *it up* sich versöhnen *or* wieder vertragen (*with* mit); ~ *up one's mind* sich schließen; *be made up of* bestehen aus, sich zusammensetzen aus; **~ up for** nachholen, aufholen; für *et.* entschädigen; **2.** Machart *f*, Bauart *f*; Fabrikat *n*, Marke *f*

make-be·lieve Schein *m*, Fantasie *f*

mak·er Hersteller *m*; **Maker** REL Schöpfer *m*

make·shift 1. Notbehelf *m*; **2.** behelfsmäßig, Behelfs...

make-up Make-up *n*, Schminke *f*; Aufmachung *f*; Zusammensetzung *f*

mak·ing Erzeugung *f*, Herstellung *f*, Fabrikation *f*; **be in the ~** noch in Arbeit sein; **have the ~s of** das Zeug haben zu

mal·ad·just·ed nicht angepasst, verhaltensgestört, milieugestört

mal·ad·min·i·stra·tion schlechte Verwaltung; POL Misswirtschaft *f*

mal·con·tent 1. unzufrieden; **2.** Unzufriedene *m*, *f*

male 1. männlich; **2.** Mann *m*; ZO Männchen *n*

male nurse (Kranken)Pfleger *m*

mal·for·ma·tion Missbildung *f*

mal·ice Bosheit *f*, Groll *m*; JUR böse Absicht, Vorsatz *m*

ma·li·cious boshaft; böswillig

ma·lign verleumden

ma·lig·nant bösartig (*a.* MED); boshaft

mall Einkaufszentrum *n*

mal·le·a·ble TECH verformbar; *fig* formbar

mal·let Holzhammer *m*; (Krocket-, Polo)Schläger *m*

mal·nu·tri·tion Unterernährung *f*; Fehlernährung *f*

mal·o·dor·ous übel riechend

mal·prac·tice Vernachlässigung *f* der beruflichen Sorgfalt; MED falsche Behandlung, (ärztlicher) Kunstfehler

malt Malz *n*

mal·treat schlecht behandeln; misshandeln

mam·mal ZO Säugetier *n*

mam·moth 1. ZO Mammut *n*; **2.** Mammut..., Riesen..., riesig

mam·my F Mami *f*

man 1. Mann *m*; Mensch(en *pl*) *m*; Menschheit *f*; F (Ehe)Mann *m*; F Geliebte *m*; (Schach)Figur *f*, (Dame)Stein *m*; **the ~ on** (*Br* **in**) **the street** der Mann auf der Straße; **2.** (*Raum*)Schiff *etc* bemannen; *Büro etc* besetzen

man·age *v/t Betrieb etc* leiten, führen; *Künstler, Sportler etc* managen; *et.* zustande bringen; es fertig bringen (**to do** zu tun); umgehen (können) mit; mit *j-m, et.* fertig werden; *Arbeit, Essen etc* bewältigen, schaffen; *v/i* auskommen (**with** mit; **without** ohne); F es schaffen, zurechtkommen; F es einrichten, es ermöglichen

man·age·a·ble handlich; lenksam

man·age·ment Verwaltung *f*; ECON Management *n*, Unternehmensführung *f*; Geschäftsleitung *f*, Direktion *f*

man·ag·er Verwalter *m*; ECON Manager *m* (*a.* THEA *etc*); Geschäftsführer *m*, Leiter *m*, Direktor *m*; SPORT (Chef-) Trainer *m*; **be a good ~** gut *or* sparsam wirtschaften können

man·a·ge·ri·al ECON geschäftsführend, leitend; **~ position** leitende Stellung; **~ staff** leitende Angestellte *pl*

man·ag·ing ECON geschäftsführend, leitend; **~ di·rec·tor** Generaldirektor *m*, leitender Direktor

man·date Mandat *n*; Auftrag *m*; Vollmacht *f*

man·da·to·ry obligatorisch, zwingend

mane ZO Mähne *f* (*a.* F)

ma·neu·ver *a. fig* **1.** Manöver *n*; **2.** manövrieren

mange VET Räude *f*

man·ger AGR Krippe *f*

man·gle 1. (Wäsche)Mangel *f*; **2.** mangeln; *j-n* übel zurichten, zerfleischen; *fig* Text verstümmeln

mang·y VET räudig; *fig* schäbig

man·hood Mannesalter *n*; Männlichkeit *f*

ma·ni·a Wahnsinn *m*; *fig* (**for**) Sucht *f* (nach), Leidenschaft *f* (für), Manie *f*, Fimmel *m*; **ma·ni·ac** F Wahnsinnige *m*, *f*, Verrückte *m*, *f*; *fig* Fanatiker(in)

man·i·cure Maniküre *f*, Handpflege *f*

man·i·fest 1. offenkundig; **2.** *v/t* offenbaren, manifestieren

man·i·fold mannigfaltig, vielfältig

ma·nip·u·late manipulieren; (geschickt) handhaben

ma·nip·u·la·tion Manipulation *f*

man·kind die Menschheit, die Menschen *pl*

man·ly männlich

man-made vom Menschen geschaffen, künstlich; **~ fiber** Kunstfaser *f*

man·ner Art *f* (und Weise *f*); Betragen *n*, Auftreten *n*; *pl* Benehmen *n*, Umgangsformen *pl*, Manieren *pl*; Sitten *pl*

ma·noeu·vre *Br* → **maneuver**

man·or *Br* (Land)Gut *n*; → **man·or house** Herrenhaus *n*

man·pow·er menschliche Arbeitskraft; Arbeitskräfte *pl*

man·sion (herrschaftliches) Wohnhaus *n*

man·slaugh·ter JUR Totschlag *m*, fahrlässige Tötung

man·tel·piece, man·tel·shelf Kaminsims *m*

man·u·al 1. Hand...; mit der Hand (gemacht); 2. Handbuch *n*

man·u·fac·ture 1. erzeugen, herstellen; 2. Herstellung *f*, Fertigung *f*; Erzeugnis *n*, Fabrikat *n*

man·u·fac·tur·er Hersteller *m*, Erzeuger *m*

man·u·fac·tur·ing Herstellungs...

ma·nure AGR 1. Dünger *m*, Mist *m*, Dung *m*; 2. düngen

man·u·script Manuskript *n*

man·y 1. viel(e); ~ **a** manche(r, -s), manch eine(r, -s); ~ **times** oft; **as** ~ ebenso viel(e); 2. viele; **a good** ~ ziemlich viel(e); **a great** ~ sehr viele

map 1. (Land- *etc*)Karte *f*; (Stadt- *etc*) Plan *m*; 2. e-e Karte machen von; auf e-r Karte eintragen; ~ **out** *fig* (bis in die Einzelheiten) (voraus)planen

ma·ple BOT Ahorn *m*

mar beeinträchtigen; verderben

Mar ABBR *of* **March** März *m*

mar·a·thon SPORT 1. *a.* ~ **race** Marathonlauf *m*; 2. Marathon... (*a. fig*)

ma·raud plündern

mar·ble 1. Marmor *m*; Murmel *f*; 2. marmorn

march 1. marschieren; *fig* fortschreiten; 2. Marsch *m*; *fig* (Fort)Gang *m*; **the** ~ **of events** der Lauf der Dinge

March (ABBR *Mar*) März *m*

mare ZO Stute *f*

mar·ga·rine, *Br* F **marge** Margarine *f*

mar·gin Rand *m* (*a. fig*); Grenze *f* (*a. fig*); *fig* Spielraum *m*; (Gewinn-, Verdienst)Spanne *f*; **by a wide** ~ mit großem Vorsprung; **mar·gin·al** Rand...; ~ **note** Randbemerkung *f*

mar·i·hua·na, mar·i·jua·na Marihuana *n*

ma·ri·na Boots-, Jachthafen *m*

ma·rine Marine *f*; MIL Marineinfanterist *m*

mar·i·ner Seemann *m*

mar·i·tal ehelich, Ehe...

mar·i·tal sta·tus Familienstand *m*

mar·i·time See...; Küsten...; Schifffahrts...

mark¹ (Deutsche) Mark *f*

mark² 1. Marke *f*, Markierung *f*; (Kenn)Zeichen *n*, Merkmal *n*; (Körper)Mal *n*; Ziel *n* (*a. fig*); (Körper)Mal *n*; (*Fabrik-, Waren*)Zeichen *n*, (*Schutz-, Handels*)Marke *f*; ECON Preisangabe *f*; PED Note *f*, Zensur *f*, Punkt *m*; SPORT Startlinie *f*; *fig* Zeichen *n*; *fig* Norm *f*; **be up to the** ~ den Anforderungen gewachsen sein (*person*) *or* genügen (*performance etc*); *gesundheitlich* auf der Höhe sein; **be wide of the** ~ weit danebenschießen; *fig* sich gewaltig irren; weit danebenliegen (*estimate etc*); **hit the** ~ (das Ziel) treffen; *fig* ins Schwarze treffen; **miss the** ~ danebenschießen, das Ziel verfehlen (*a. fig*); 2. markieren, anzeichnen; anzeigen; kennzeichnen; *Waren* auszeichnen; *Preis* festsetzen; Spuren hinterlassen auf (*dat*); Flecken machen auf (*dat*); PED benoten, zensieren; SPORT *Gegenspieler* decken, markieren; ~ **my words** denk an m-e Worte; **to** ~ **the occasion** zur Feier des Tages; ~ **time** auf der Stelle treten (*a. fig*); ~ **down** notieren, vermerken; *im Preis* herabsetzen; ~ **off** abgrenzen; *auf e-r Liste* abhaken; ~ **out** durch Striche *etc* markieren; bestimmen (**for** für); ~ **up** im Preis heraufsetzen

marked deutlich, ausgeprägt

mark·er Markierstift *m*; Lesezeichen *n*; SPORT Bewacher(in)

mar·ket 1. Markt *m*; Marktplatz *m*; (Lebensmittel)Geschäft *n*, Laden *m*; ECON Absatz *m*; (**for**) Nachfrage *f* (nach), Bedarf *m* (an *dat*); **on the** ~ auf dem Markt *or* im Handel; **put on the** ~ auf den Markt *or* in den Handel bringen; (zum Verkauf) anbieten; 2. *v/t* auf den Markt *or* in den Handel bringen; verkaufen, vertreiben

mar·ket·a·ble ECON marktgängig

mar·ket gar·den *Br* Gemüse- und Obstgärtnerei *f*

mar·ket·ing ECON Marketing *n*

mark·ing Markierung f; zo Zeichnung f; SPORT Deckung f; **man-to-man** ~ Manndeckung f

marks·man guter Schütze

mar·ma·lade esp Orangenmarmelade f

mar·mot zo Murmeltier n

ma·roon v/t 1. kastanienbraun; 2. auf e-r einsamen Insel aussetzen; 3. Leuchtrakete f

mar·quee Festzelt n

mar·quis Marquis m

mar·riage Heirat f, Hochzeit f (**to** mit); Ehe f; **civil** ~ standesamtliche Trauung

mar·ria·ge·a·ble heiratsfähig

mar·riage cer·tif·i·cate Trauschein m, Heiratsurkunde f

mar·ried verheiratet; ehelich, Ehe...; ~ **couple** Ehepaar n; ~ **life** Ehe(leben n) f

mar·row ANAT (Knochen)Mark n; fig Kern m, das Wesentliche

mar·ry v/t heiraten; Paar trauen; **be married** verheiratet sein (**to** mit); **get married** heiraten; sich verheiraten (**to** mit); v/i heiraten

marsh Sumpf(land n) m, Marsch f

mar·shal 1. MIL Marschall m; Bezirkspolizeichef m; **2.** ordnen; führen

marsh·y sumpfig

mar·ten zo Marder m

mar·tial kriegerisch; Kriegs..., Militär...; ~ **arts** asiatische Kampfsportarten pl; ~ **law** Kriegsrecht n

mar·tyr REL Märtyrer(in) (a. fig)

mar·vel 1. Wunder n; **2.** sich wundern, staunen; **mar·vel·(l)ous** wunderbar; fabelhaft, fantastisch

mar·zi·pan Marzipan n, m

mas·ca·ra Wimperntusche f

mas·cot Maskottchen n

mas·cu·line männlich; Männer...; maskulin (a. LING)

mash zerdrücken, zerquetschen

mashed po·ta·toes Kartoffelbrei m

mask 1. Maske f (a. EDP); **2.** maskieren; fig verbergen, verschleiern

masked maskiert; ~ **ball** Maskenball m

ma·son Steinmetz m; mst **Mason** Freimaurer m; **ma·son·ry** Mauerwerk n

masque THEA HIST Maskenspiel n

mas·que·rade 1. Maskerade f (a. fig); Verkleidung f; **2.** sich ausgeben (**as** als, für)

mass 1. Masse f; Menge f; Mehrzahl f;

the ~**es** die (breite) Masse; **2.** (sich) (an)sammeln or (an)häufen; **3.** Massen...

Mass REL Messe f

mas·sa·cre 1. Massaker n; **2.** niedermetzeln

mas·sage 1. Massage f; **2.** massieren

mas·seur Masseur m

mas·seuse Masseurin f, Masseuse f

mas·sif (Gebirgs)Massiv n

mas·sive massiv; groß, gewaltig

mass me·di·a Massenmedien pl

mass-pro·duce serienmäßig herstellen

mass pro·duc·tion Massen-, Serienproduktion f

mast MAR Mast m; Br ELECTR Sendemast m

mas·ter 1. Meister m (a. PAINT); Herr m; esp Br Lehrer m; Original(kopie f) n; UNIV Magister m; **Master of Arts** (ABBR **MA**) Magister m Artium; ~ **of ceremonies** Conférencier m; **2.** Meister...; Haupt...; ~ **copy** Originalkopie f; ~ **tape** TECH Mastertape n, Originaltonband n; **3.** Herr sein über (acc); Sprache etc beherrschen; Aufgabe etc meistern

mas·ter key Hauptschlüssel m

mas·ter·ly meisterhaft, virtuos

mas·ter·piece Meisterstück n, -werk n

mas·ter·y Herrschaft f; Oberhand f; Beherrschung f

mas·tur·bate masturbieren, onanieren

mat¹ 1. Matte f; Untersetzer m; **2.** sich verfilzen

mat² mattiert, matt

match¹ Streichholz n, Zündholz n

match² 1. der, die, das Gleiche; (dazu) passende Sache or Person, Gegenstück n; (Fußball- etc)Spiel n, (Box- etc -) Kampf m, (Tennis- etc)Match n, m; Heirat f; gute etc Partie (person); **be a** (**no**) ~ **for s.o.** j-m (nicht) gewachsen sein; **find** or **meet one's** ~ s-n Meister finden; **2.** v/t j-m, e-r Sache ebenbürtig or gewachsen sein, gleichkommen; j-m, e-r Sache entsprechen, passen zu; v/i zusammenpassen, übereinstimmen, entsprechen; **gloves to** ~ dazu passende Handschuhe

match·box Streichholz-, Zündholzschachtel f

match·less unvergleichlich, einzigartig

match·mak·er Ehestifter(in)

M

match point *tennis etc*: Matchball *m*
mate¹ → **checkmate**
mate² **1.** (Arbeits)Kamerad *m*, (-)Kollege *m*; ZO Männchen *n*, Weibchen *n*; MAR Maat *m*; **2.** ZO (sich) paaren
ma·te·ri·al **1.** Material *n*, Stoff *m*; *writing ~s* Schreibmaterial(ien *pl*) *n*; **2.** materiell; leiblich; wesentlich
ma·ter·nal mütterlich, Mutter...; mütterlicherseits
ma·ter·ni·ty **1.** Mutterschaft *f*; **2.** Schwangerschafts..., Umstands...
ma·ter·ni·ty| leave Mutterschaftsurlaub *m*; **~ ward** Entbindungsstation *f*
math F Mathe *f*
math·e·ma·ti·cian Mathematiker *m*
math·e·mat·ics Mathematik *f*
maths *Br* F Mathe *f*
mat·i·née THEA *etc* Nachmittagsvorstellung *f*
ma·tric·u·late (sich) immatrikulieren
mat·ri·mo·ni·al ehelich, Ehe...
mat·ri·mo·ny Ehe *f*, Ehestand *m*
ma·trix TECH Matrize *f*
ma·tron *Br* MED Oberschwester *f*; Hausmutter *f*; Matrone *f*
mat·ter **1.** Materie *f*, Material *n*, Substanz *f*, Stoff *m*; MED Eiter *m*; Sache *f*, Angelegenheit *f*; *printed ~* Drucksache *f*; *what's the ~ (with you)?* was ist los (mit dir)?; *no ~ who* gleichgültig, wer; *for that ~* was das betrifft; *a ~ of course* e-e Selbstverständlichkeit; *a ~ of fact* e-e Tatsache; *as a ~ of fact* tatsächlich, eigentlich; *a ~ of form* e-e Formsache *f*; *a ~ of time* e-e Frage der Zeit; **2.** von Bedeutung sein (*to* für); *it doesn't ~* es macht nichts
mat·ter-of-fact sachlich, nüchtern
mat·tress Matratze *f*
ma·ture **1.** reif (*a. fig*); **2.** (heran)reifen, reif werden
ma·tu·ri·ty Reife *f* (*a. fig*)
maud·lin rührselig
maul übel zurichten; *fig* verreißen
Maun·dy Thurs·day Gründonnerstag *m*
mauve malvenfarbig, mauve
mawk·ish rührselig
max·i F Maxi..., riesig, Riesen...
max·im Grundsatz *m*
max·i·mum **1.** Maximum *n*; **2.** maximal, Maximal..., Höchst...
May Mai *m*

may *v/aux ich* kann/mag/darf *etc*, *du* kannst/magst/darfst *etc*
may·be vielleicht
may·bug ZO Maikäfer *m*
May Day der 1. Mai
may·on·naise Mayonnaise *f*
mayor Bürgermeister *m*
may·pole Maibaum *m*
maze Irrgarten *m*, Labyrinth *n* (*a. fig*)
me mich; mir; F ich
mead·ow Wiese *f*, Weide *f*
mea·ger, *Br* **mea·gre** mager (*a. fig*), dürr; dürftig
meal¹ Mahl(zeit *f*) *n*; Essen *n*
meal² Schrotmehl *n*
mean¹ gemein, niederträchtig; geizig, knauserig; schäbig
mean² meinen; sagen wollen; bedeuten; beabsichtigen, vorhaben; *be meant for* bestimmt sein für; *~ well (ill)* es gut (schlecht) meinen
mean³ **1.** Mitte *f*, Mittel *n*, Durchschnitt *m*; **2.** mittlere(r, -s), Mittel..., durchschnittlich, Durchschnitts...
mean·ing **1.** Sinn *m*, Bedeutung *f*; **2.** bedeutungsvoll, bedeutsam
mean·ing·ful bedeutungsvoll; sinnvoll
mean·ing·less sinnlos
means Mittel *n or pl*, Weg *m*; ECON Mittel *pl*, Vermögen *n*; *by all ~s* auf alle Fälle, unbedingt; *by no ~s* keineswegs, auf keinen Fall; *by ~s of* durch, mit
mean·time **1.** inzwischen; **2.** *in the ~* inzwischen
mean·while inzwischen
mea·sles MED Masern *pl*
mea·sur·a·ble messbar
mea·sure **1.** Maß *n* (*a. fig*); TECH Messgerät *n*; MUS Takt *m*; *fig* Maßnahme *f*; *beyond ~* über alle Maßen; *in a great ~* großenteils; *take ~s* Maßnahmen treffen *or* ergreifen; **2.** (ab-, aus-, ver-)messen; *j-m* Maß nehmen; *~ up to* den Ansprüchen (*gen*) genügen; *measured* gemessen; wohl überlegt; maßvoll
mea·sure·ment (Ver)Messung *f*; Maß *n*; *~ of ca·pac·i·ty* Hohlmaß *n*
mea·sur·ing tape → **tape measure**
meat GASTR Fleisch *n*; *cold ~* kalter Braten
meat·ball GASTR Fleischklößchen *n*
me·chan·ic Mechaniker *m*

me·chan·i·cal mechanisch; Maschinen...

me·chan·ics PHYS Mechanik f

mech·a·nism Mechanismus m

mech·a·nize mechanisieren

med·al Medaille f; Orden m

med·al·(l)ist SPORT Medaillengewinner (-in)

med·dle sich einmischen (**with**, **in** in acc); **med·dle·some** aufdringlich

me·di·a Medien pl

med·i·ae·val → **medieval**

me·di·an a. ~ **strip** MOT Mittelstreifen m

me·di·ate vermitteln

me·di·a·tion Vermittlung f

me·di·a·tor Vermittler m

med·ic MIL Sanitäter m

med·i·cal 1. medizinisch, ärztlich; **2.** ärztliche Untersuchung

med·i·cal cer·tif·i·cate ärztliches Attest

med·i·cated medizinisch

med·i·ci·nal medizinisch, heilkräftig, Heil...

medi·cine Medizin f, a. Arznei f, a. Heilkunde f

med·i·e·val mittelalterlich

me·di·o·cre mittelmäßig

med·i·tate v/i (**on**) nachdenken (über acc); meditieren (über acc); v/t erwägen

med·i·ta·tion Nachdenken n; Meditation f

med·i·ta·tive nachdenklich

Med·i·ter·ra·ne·an Mittelmeer...

me·di·um 1. Mitte f; Mittel n; Medium n; **2.** mittlere(r, -s), Mittel..., a. mittelmäßig; GASTR medium, halb gar

med·ley Gemisch n; MUS Medley n, Potpourri n

meek sanft(mütig), bescheiden

meet v/t treffen, sich treffen mit; begegnen (dat); j-n kennen lernen; j-n abholen; zusammentreffen mit, stoßen or treffen auf (acc); Wünschen entgegenkommen, entsprechen; e-r Forderung, Verpflichtung nachkommen; v/i zusammenkommen, -treten; sich begegnen, sich treffen; (feindlich) zusammenstoßen; SPORT aufeinander treffen; sich kennen lernen; ~ **with** sich zusammentreffen mit; sich treffen mit; stoßen auf (Schwierigkeiten etc); erleben, erleiden

meet·ing Begegnung f, (Zusammen-)Treffen n; Versammlung f, Konferenz f, Tagung f; ~ **place** Tagungs-, Versammlungsort m; Treffpunkt m

mel·an·chol·y 1. Melancholie f, Schwermut f, Trübsinn m; **2.** melancholisch, traurig, trübsinnig, wehmütig

mel·low 1. reif, weich; sanft, mild (light), zart (colors); fig gereift (person); **2.** reifen (lassen) (a. fig); weich or sanft werden

me·lo·di·ous melodisch

mel·o·dra·mat·ic melodramatisch

mel·o·dy MUS Melodie f

mel·on BOT Melone f

melt (zer)schmelzen; ~ **down** einschmelzen

mem·ber Mitglied n, Angehörige m, f; ANAT Glied n, Gliedmaße f; (männliches) Glied; **Member of Parliament** Br Mitglied n des Unterhauses, Unterhausabgeordnete m, f; **mem·ber·ship** Mitgliedschaft f; Mitgliederzahl f

mem·brane Membran(e) f

mem·o Memo n

mem·oirs Memoiren pl

mem·o·ra·ble denkwürdig

me·mo·ri·al Denkmal n, Ehrenmal n, Gedenkstätte f (**to** für); Gedenkfeier f (**to** für)

mem·o·rize auswendig lernen, sich et. einprägen

mem·o·ry Gedächtnis n; Erinnerung f; Andenken n; EDP Speicher m; **in ~ of** zum Andenken an (acc); ~ **ca·pac·i·ty** EDP Speicherkapazität f

men·ace 1. (be)drohen; **2.** (Be)Drohung f

mend 1. v/t (ver)bessern; ausbessern, reparieren, flicken; ~ **one's ways** sich bessern; v/i sich bessern; **2.** ausgebesserte Stelle; **on the ~** auf dem Wege der Bess(e)rung

men·di·cant REL Bettelmönch m

me·ni·al niedrig, untergeordnet

men·in·gi·tis MED Meningitis f, Hirnhautentzündung f

men·o·pause MED Wechseljahre pl

men·stru·ate menstruieren

men·stru·a·tion Menstruation f

men·tal geistig, Geistes...; seelisch, psychisch; ~ **a·rith·me·tic** Kopfrechnen n; ~ **hand·i·cap** geistige Behinderung; ~ **hos·pi·tal** psychiatrische Klinik

men·tal·i·ty Mentalität f

M

mentally

men·tal·ly: ~ *handicapped* geistig behindert; ~ *ill* geisteskrank

men·tion 1. erwähnen; *don't ~ it!* keine Ursache!; **2.** Erwähnung *f*

men·u Speise(n)karte *f*; EDP Menü *n*

me·ow ZO miauen

mer·can·tile Handels...

mer·ce·na·ry 1. geldgierig; **2.** MIL Söldner *m*

mer·chan·dise 1. Ware(n *pl*) *f*; **2.** vermarkten

mer·chan·dis·ing Vermarktung *f*

mer·chant 1. (Groß)Händler *m*, (Groß-)Kaufmann *m*; **2.** Handels...

mer·ci·ful barmherzig, gnädig

mer·ci·less unbarmherzig, erbarmungslos

mer·cu·ry CHEM Quecksilber *n*

mer·cy Barmherzigkeit *f*, Erbarmen *n*, Gnade *f*

mere, mere·ly bloß, nur

merge verschmelzen (*into, with* mit); ECON fusionieren

merg·er ECON Fusion *f*

me·rid·i·an GEOGR Meridian *m*; *fig* Gipfel *m*, Höhepunkt *m*

mer·it 1. Verdienst *n*; Wert *m*; Vorzug *m*; **2.** verdienen

mer·maid Meerjungfrau *f*, Nixe *f*

mer·ri·ment Fröhlichkeit *f*; Gelächter *n*, Heiterkeit *f*

mer·ry lustig, fröhlich, ausgelassen; *Merry Christmas!* fröhliche *or* frohe Weihnachten

mer·ry-go-round Karussell *n*

mesh 1. Masche *f*; *fig often pl* Netz *n*, Schlingen *pl*; *be in* ~ TECH (ineinander) greifen; **2.** TECH (ineinander) greifen; *fig* passen (*with* zu), zusammenpassen

mess 1. Unordnung *f*, Durcheinander *n*; Schmutz *m*, F Schweinerei *f*; F Patsche *f*, Klemme *f*; MIL Messe *f*, Kasino *n*; *make a ~ of* F *fig* verpfuschen, ruinieren, *Pläne etc* über den Haufen werfen; **2.** ~ *about*, ~ *around* F herumspielen, herumbasteln (*with* an *dat*); herumgammeln; ~ *up* in Unordnung bringen, durcheinander bringen; *fig* F verpfuschen, ruinieren, *Pläne etc* über den Haufen werfen

mes·sage Mitteilung *f*, Nachricht *f*; Anliegen *n*, Aussage *f*; *can I take a ~?* kann ich etwas ausrichten?; *get*

the ~ F kapieren; **mes·sen·ger** Bote *m*

mess·y unordentlich; unsauber, schmutzig

me·tab·o·lis·m MED Stoffwechsel *m*

met·al Metall *n*

me·tal·lic metallisch; Metall...

met·a·mor·pho·sis Metamorphose *f*, Verwandlung *f*

met·a·phor Metapher *f*

me·tas·ta·sis MED Metastase *f*

me·te·or Meteor *m*

me·te·or·o·log·i·cal meteorologisch, Wetter..., Witterungs...; ~ *of·fice* Wetteramt *n*

me·te·o·rol·o·gy Meteorologie *f*, Wetterkunde *f*

me·ter¹ TECH Messgerät *n*, Zähler *m*

me·ter² Meter *m*, *n*; Versmaß *n*

meth·od Methode *f*, Verfahren *n*; System *n*; **me·thod·i·cal** methodisch, systematisch, planmäßig

me·tic·u·lous peinlich genau, übergenau

me·tre *Br* → *meter²*

met·ric metrisch; ~ *sys·tem* metrisches (Maß- und Gewichts)System

met·ro·pol·i·tan ... der Hauptstadt

me·trop·o·lis Weltstadt *f*

met·tle Eifer *m*, Mut *m*, Feuer *n*

mew ZO miauen

Mex·i·can 1. mexikanisch; **2.** Mexikaner(in)

Mex·i·co Mexiko *n*

mi·aow ZO miauen

mi·cro... Mikro..., (sehr) klein

mi·cro·chip Mikrochip *m*

mi·cro·e·lec·tron·ics Mikroelektronik *f*

mi·cro·film Mikrofilm *m*

mi·cro·or·gan·ism BIOL Mikroorganismus *m*

mi·cro·phone Mikrofon *n*

mi·cro·pro·ces·sor Mikroprozessor *m*

mi·cro·scope Mikroskop *n*

mi·cro·scop·ic mikroskopisch

mi·cro·wave Mikrowelle *f*; ~ *ov·en* Mikrowellenherd *m*

mid mittlere(r, -s), Mitt(el)...

mid·air: *in* ~ in der Luft

mid·day 1. Mittag *m*; **2.** mittägig, Mittag(s)...

mid·dle 1. mittlere(r, -s), Mittel...; **2.** Mitte *f*

mid·dle-aged mittleren Alters

Mid·dle Ag·es HIST Mittelalter *n*
mid·dle class(·es) Mittelstand *m*
mid·dle·man ECON Zwischenhändler
m; Mittelsmann *m*
mid·dle name zweiter Vorname *m*
mid·dle-sized mittelgroß
mid·dle-weight *boxing*: Mittelgewicht
n, Mittelgewichtler *m*
mid·dling F mittelmäßig, Mittel...; leidlich
mid·field *esp soccer*: Mittelfeld *n*
mid·field·er, mid·field play·er *esp
soccer*: Mittelfeldspieler *m*
midge ZO Mücke *f*
midg·et Zwerg *m*, Knirps *m*
mid·night Mitternacht *f*; **at ~** um Mitternacht
midst: in the ~ of mitten in (*dat*)
mid·sum·mer Hochsommer *m*; ASTR
Sommersonnenwende *f*
mid·way auf halbem Wege
mid·wife Hebamme *f*
mid·win·ter Mitte *f* des Winters; ASTR
Wintersonnenwende *f*; **in ~** mitten im
Winter
might Macht *f*, Gewalt *f*; Kraft *f*
might·y mächtig, gewaltig
mi·grate (aus)wandern, (fort)ziehen (*a.*
ZO)
mi·gra·tion Wanderung *f* (*a.* ZO)
mi·gra·to·ry Wander...; ZO Zug...
mike F Mikrofon *n*
mild mild, sanft, leicht
mil·dew BOT Mehltau *m*
mild·ness Milde *f*
mile Meile *f* (*1,6 km*)
mile·age zurückgelegte Meilenzahl *or*
Fahrtstrecke; Meilenstand *m*; *a.* ~ **allowance** Meilengeld *n*, *appr* Kilome-
tergeld *n*
mile·stone Meilenstein *m* (*a. fig*)
mil·i·tant militant; streitbar, kriegerisch
mil·i·ta·ry 1. militärisch, Militär...; **2.
the ~** das Militär; **~ gov·ern·ment** Mi-
litärregierung *f*; **~ po·lice** (ABBR *MP*)
Militärpolizei *f*
mi·li·tia Miliz *f*, Bürgerwehr *f*
milk 1. Milch *f*; **it's no use crying over
spilt ~** geschehen ist geschehen; **2.** *v/t*
melken; *v/i* Milch geben; **~ choc·o·late**
Vollmilchschokolade *f*
milk·man Milchmann *m*
milk pow·der Milchpulver *n*, Trocken-
milch *f*

milk shake Milchmixgetränk *n*
milk tooth ANAT Milchzahn *m*
milk·y milchig; Milch...
Milky Way ASTR Milchstraße *f*
mill 1. Mühle *f*; Fabrik *f*; **2.** *Korn etc*
mahlen; *Metall* verarbeiten; *Münze*
rändeln
mil·le·pede → *millipede*
mill·er Müller *m*
mil·let BOT Hirse *f*
mil·li·ner Hutmacherin *f*, Putzmacherin
f, Modistin *f*
mil·lion Million *f*
mil·lion·aire Millionär(in)
mil·lionth 1. millionste(r, -s); **2.** Mil-
lionstel *n*
mil·li·pede ZO Tausendfüß(l)er *m*
mill·stone Mühlstein *m*; **be a ~ round
s.o.'s neck** *fig* j-m ein Klotz am Bein
sein
milt ZO Milch *f*
mime 1. Pantomime *f*; Pantomime *m*; **2.**
(panto)mimisch darstellen; **mim·ic 1.**
mimisch; Schein...; **2.** Imitator *m*; **3.**
nachahmen; nachäffen; **mim·ic·ry**
Nachahmung *f*; ZO Mimikry *f*
mince 1. *v/t* zerhacken, (zer)schneiden;
he does not ~ matters *or* **his words** er
nimmt kein Blatt vor den Mund; *v/i*
tänzeln, trippeln; **2.** *a.* ~d **meat** Hackfleisch *n*; **minc·er** Fleischwolf *m*
mind 1. Sinn *m*, Gemüt *n*, Herz *n*; Verstand *m*, Geist *m*; Ansicht *f*, Meinung *f*;
Absicht *f*, Neigung *f*, Lust *f*; Erinnerung *f*, Gedächtnis *n*; **be out of one's
~** nicht (recht) bei Sinnen sein; **bear** *or*
keep in ~ (immer) denken an (*acc*), *et.*
nicht vergessen; **change one's ~** es
sich anders überlegen, s-e Meinung ändern; **enter s.o.'s ~** j-m in den Sinn
kommen; **give s.o. a piece of one's
~** j-m gründlich die Meinung sagen;
have (half) a ~ to *inf* (nicht übel) Lust
haben zu *inf*; **lose one's ~** den Verstand verlieren; **make up one's ~** sich
entschließen, e-n Entschluss fassen; **to
my ~** meiner Ansicht nach; **2.** *v/t* Acht
geben auf (*acc*); sehen nach, aufpassen
auf (*acc*); et. haben gegen; **the ~ the step!**
Vorsicht, Stufe!; **~ your own busi-
ness!** kümmere dich um deine eigenen Angelegenheiten!; **do you ~ if I
smoke?**, **do you ~ my smoking?** haben Sie et. dagegen *or* stört es Sie,

wenn ich rauche?; *would you ~ open-ing the window?* würden Sie bitte das Fenster öffnen?; *would you ~ coming* würden Sie bitte kommen?; *v/i* aufpassen; et. dagegen haben; *~ (you)* wohlgemerkt, allerdings; *never ~!* macht nichts!, ist schon gut!; *I don't ~* meinetwegen, von mir aus

mind·less gedankenlos, blind; unbekümmert (*of* um), ohne Rücksicht (*of* auf *acc*)

mine[1] meins; *that's ~* das gehört mir

mine[2] **1.** Bergwerk *n*, Mine *f*, Zeche *f*, Grube *f*; MIL Mine *f*; *fig* Fundgrube *f*; **2.** *v/i* schürfen, graben (*for* nach); *v/t* Erz, *Kohle* abbauen; MIL verminen

min·er Bergmann *m*, Kumpel *m*

min·e·ral 1. Mineral *n*; *pl Br* Mineralwasser *n*; **2.** Mineral...; *~ oil* Mineralöl *n*; *~ wa·ter* Mineralwasser *n*

min·gle *v/t* (ver)mischen; *v/i* sich mischen *or* mengen (*with* unter)

min·i... Mini..., Klein(st)...; → *miniskirt*

min·i·a·ture 1. Miniatur(gemälde *n*) *f*; **2.** Miniatur...; Klein...; *~ cam·e·ra* Kleinbildkamera *f*

min·i·mize auf ein Mindestmaß herabsetzen; herunterspielen, bagatellisieren

min·i·mum 1. Minimum *n*, Mindestmaß *n*; **2.** minimal, Mindest...

min·ing 1. Bergbau *m*; **2.** Berg(bau)..., Bergwerks...; Gruben...

min·i·skirt Minirock *m*

min·is·ter POL Minister(in); Gesandte *m*; REL Geistliche *m*; **min·is·try** POL Ministerium *n*; REL geistliches Amt

mink ZO Nerz *m*

mi·nor 1. kleinere(r, -s), *fig a.* unbedeutend, geringfügig; JUR minderjährig; *A ~* MUS a-Moll *n*; *~ key* MUS Moll(tonart *f*) *n*; **2.** JUR Minderjährige *m, f*; UNIV Nebenfach *n*; MUS Moll *n*; **mi·nor·i·ty** Minderheit *f*; JUR Minderjährigkeit *f*

min·ster *Br* Münster *n*

mint[1] **1.** Münze *f*, Münzanstalt *f*; **2.** prägen

mint[2] BOT Minze *f*

min·u·et MUS Menuett *n*

mi·nus 1. *prp* minus, weniger; F ohne; **2.** *adj* Minus...; **3.** Minus *n*, *fig a.* Nachteil *m*

min·ute[1] Minute *f*; Augenblick *m*; *in a ~* sofort; *just a ~!* Moment mal!

mi·nute[2] winzig; sehr genau

min·utes Protokoll *n*; *take* (*or* keep) *the ~* (das) Protokoll führen

mir·a·cle Wunder *n*

mi·rac·u·lous wunderbar

mi·rac·u·lous·ly wie durch ein Wunder

mi·rage Luftspiegelung *f*, Fata Morgana *f*

mire Schlamm *m*; *drag through the ~* *fig* in den Schmutz ziehen

mir·ror 1. Spiegel *m*; **2.** (wider)spiegeln (*a. fig*)

mis... miss..., falsch, schlecht

mis·ad·ven·ture Missgeschick *n*; Unglück *n*, Unglücksfall *m*

mis·an·thrope, **mis·an·thro·pist** Menschenfeind(in)

mis·ap·ply falsch an- *or* verwenden

mis·ap·pre·hend missverstehen

mis·ap·pro·pri·ate unterschlagen, veruntreuen

mis·be·have sich schlecht benehmen

mis·cal·cu·late falsch berechnen; sich verrechnen (in *dat*)

mis·car·riage MED Fehlgeburt *f*; Misslingen *n*, Fehlschlag(en *n*) *m*; *~ of jus-tice* JUR Fehlurteil *n*

mis·car·ry MED e-e Fehlgeburt haben; misslingen, scheitern

mis·cel·la·ne·ous gemischt, vermischt; verschiedenartig

mis·cel·la·ny Gemisch *n*; Sammelband *m*

mis·chief Schaden *m*; Unfug *m*; Übermut *m*; *~-mak·er* Unruhestifter(in)

mis·chie·vous boshaft, mutwillig; schelmisch

mis·con·ceive falsch auffassen, missverstehen

mis·con·duct schlechtes Benehmen; schlechte Führung; Verfehlung *f*

mis·con·strue falsch auslegen, missdeuten

mis·de·mea·no(u)r JUR Vergehen *n*

mis·di·rect fehlleiten, irreleiten; *Brief etc* falsch adressieren

mise-en-scène THEA Inszenierung *f*

mi·ser Geizhals *m*

mis·e·ra·ble erbärmlich, kläglich, elend; unglücklich

mi·ser·ly geizig, F knick(e)rig

mis·e·ry Elend *n*, Not *f*

mis·fire versagen (*gun*); MOT fehlzünden, aussetzen; *fig* danebengehen

mock

mis·fit Außenseiter(in)

mis·for·tune Unglück n, Unglücksfall m; Missgeschick n

mis·giv·ing Befürchtung f, Zweifel m

mis·guid·ed irregeleitet, irrig, unangebracht

mis·hap Unglück n; Missgeschick n; **without ~** ohne Zwischenfälle

mis·in·form falsch unterrichten

mis·in·ter·pret missdeuten, falsch auffassen or auslegen

mis·lay et. verlegen

mis·lead irreführen, täuschen; verleiten

mis·man·age schlecht verwalten or führen or handhaben

mis·place et. an e-e falsche Stelle legen or setzen; et. verlegen; **~d** fig unangebracht, deplatziert

mis·print 1. verdrucken; 2. Druckfehler m

mis·read falsch lesen; falsch deuten, missdeuten

mis·rep·re·sent falsch darstellen; entstellen, verdrehen

miss 1. v/t verpassen, versäumen, verfehlen; übersehen, nicht bemerken; überhören; nicht verstehen or begreifen; vermissen; a. **~ out** auslassen, übergehen, überspringen; v/i nicht treffen; missglücken; **~ out on** et. verpassen; 2. Fehlschuss m, Fehlstoß m, Fehlwurf m etc; Verpassen n, Verfehlen n

Miss Fräulein n

mis·shap·en missgebildet

mis·sile 1. Geschoss n; Rakete f; 2. Raketen...

miss·ing fehlend; **be ~** fehlen, verschwunden or weg sein; (MIL a. **~ in action**) vermisst; **be ~** MIL vermisst sein or werden

mis·sion (Militär- etc)Mission f; esp POL Auftrag m, Mission f (a. REL); MIL, AVIAT Einsatz m

mis·sion·a·ry REL Missionar m

mis·spell falsch buchstabieren or schreiben

mis·spend falsch verwenden; vergeuden

mist 1. (feiner or leichter) Nebel; 2. **~ over** sich trüben; **~ up** (sich) beschlagen

mis·take 1. verwechseln (**for** mit); verkennen, sich irren in (dat); falsch verstehen, missverstehen; 2. Irrtum m, Versehen n, Fehler m; **by ~** aus Versehen, irrtümlich; **mis·tak·en** irrig, falsch (verstanden); **be ~** sich irren

mis·tle·toe BOT Mistel f

mis·tress Herrin f; esp Br Lehrerin f; Geliebte f

mis·trust 1. misstrauen (dat); 2. Misstrauen n (**of** gegen)

mis·trust·ful misstrauisch

mist·y (leicht) neb(e)lig; fig unklar, verschwommen

mis·un·der·stand missverstehen; j-n nicht verstehen; **mis·un·der·standing** Missverständnis n

mis·use 1. missbrauchen; falsch gebrauchen; 2. Missbrauch m

mite ZO Milbe f; kleines Ding, Würmchen n; **a ~** F ein bisschen

mi·ter, Br mi·tre REL Mitra f, Bischofsmütze f

mitt baseball: Fanghandschuh m; → **mit·ten** Fausthandschuh m

mix 1. (ver)mischen, vermengen; Getränke mixen; sich (ver)mischen; sich mischen lassen; verkehren (**with** mit); **~ well** kontaktfreudig sein; **~ up** zusammenmischen, durcheinander mischen; (völlig) durcheinander bringen; verwechseln (**with** mit); **be ~ed up** verwickelt sein or werden (**in** in acc); (geistig) ganz durcheinander sein; 2. Mischung f

mixed gemischt (a. fig); vermischt, Misch...

mix·er Mixer m; TECH Mischmaschine f; radio, TV etc: Mischpult n

mix·ture Mischung f; Gemisch n

mix-up F Verwechs(e)lung f

moan 1. Stöhnen n; 2. stöhnen

moat (Burg-, Stadt)Graben m

mob 1. Mob m, Pöbel m; 2. herfallen über (acc); j-n bedrängen, belagern

mo·bile 1. beweglich; MIL mobil, motorisiert; fig lebhaft; 2. → **mobile phone** or **telephone**; **~ home** Wohnwagen m; **~ phone**, **~ tel·e·phone** Mobiltelefon n, Handy n

mo·bil·ize mobilisieren, MIL a. mobil machen

moc·ca·sin Mokassin m

mock 1. v/t verspotten; nachäffen; v/i sich lustig machen, spotten (**at** über acc); 2. nachgemacht, Schein...

M

mock·e·ry Spott *m*, Hohn *m*; Gespött *n*

mock·ing·bird ZO Spottdrossel *f*

mode (Art *f* und) Weise *f*; EDP Modus *m*, Betriebsart *f*

mod·el Modell *n*; Muster *n*; Vorbild *n*; Mannequin *n*; Model *n*, (Foto)Modell *n*; TECH Modell *n*, Typ *m*; *male ~* Dressman *m*; **2.** Modell..., Muster...; **3.** *v/t* modellieren, *a. fig* formen; *Kleider etc* vorführen; *v/i* Modell stehen *or* sitzen; als Mannequin *or* (Foto)Modell *or* Dressman arbeiten

mo·dem EDP Modem *m, n*

mod·e·rate 1. (mittel)mäßig; gemäßigt; vernünftig, angemessen; **2.** (sich) mäßigen

mod·e·ra·tion Mäßigung *f*

mod·ern modern, neu

mod·ern·ize modernisieren

mod·est bescheiden

mod·es·ty Bescheidenheit *f*

mod·i·fi·ca·tion (Ab-, Ver)Änderung *f*

mod·i·fy (ab-, ver)ändern

mod·u·late modulieren

mod·ule TECH Modul *n*, ELECTR *a.* Baustein *m*; (*Kommando- etc*)Kapsel *f*

moist feucht

moist·en *v/t* anfeuchten, befeuchten; *v/i* feucht werden

mois·ture Feuchtigkeit *f*

mo·lar ANAT Backenzahn *m*

mo·las·ses Sirup *m*

mold¹ Schimmel *m*; Moder *m*; Humus (boden) *m*

mold² TECH **1.** (Gieß-, Guss-, Press-) Form *f*; **2.** gießen; formen

mol·der *a. ~ away* vermodern; zerfallen

mold·y verschimmelt, schimm(e)lig; mod(e)rig

mole¹ ZO Maulwurf *m*

mole² Muttermal *n*, Leberfleck *m*

mole³ Mole *f*, Hafendamm *m*

mol·e·cule Molekül *n*

mole·hill Maulwurfshügel *m*; *make a mountain out of a ~* aus e-r Mücke e-n Elefanten machen

mo·lest belästigen

mol·li·fy besänftigen, beschwichtigen

mol·lusc *Br*, **mol·lusk** ZO Weichtier *n*

mol·ly·cod·dle F verhätscheln, verzärteln

molt (sich) mausern; *Haare* verlieren

mol·ten geschmolzen

mom F Mami *f*, Mutti *f*

mom-and-pop store Tante-Emma-Laden *m*

mo·ment Moment *m*, Augenblick *m*; Bedeutung *f*; PHYS Moment *n*

mo·men·ta·ry momentan, augenblicklich

mo·men·tous bedeutsam, folgenschwer

mo·men·tum PHYS Moment *n*; Schwung *m*

Mon ABBR *of Monday* Mo., Montag *m*

mon·arch Monarch(in), Herrscher(in)

mon·ar·chy Monarchie *f*

mon·as·tery REL (Mönchs)Kloster *n*

Mon·day (ABBR *Mon*) Montag *m*; *on ~* (am) Montag; *on ~s* montags

mon·e·ta·ry ECON Währungs...; Geld...

mon·ey Geld *n*

mon·ey·box *Br* Sparbüchse *f*

mon·ey·chang·er (Geld)Wechsler *m*; TECH Wechselautomat *m*

mon·ey or·der Post- *or* Zahlungsanweisung *f*

mon·grel ZO Bastard *m*, *esp* Promenadenmischung *f*

mon·i·tor 1. Monitor *m*; Kontrollgerät *n*, -schirm *m*; **2.** abhören; überwachen

monk REL Mönch *m*

mon·key 1. ZO Affe *m*; F (kleiner) Schlingel; *make a ~ (out) of s.o.* j-n zum Deppen machen; **2.** *~ about*, *~ around* F (herum)albern; *~ about or around with* F herumspielen mit *or* an (*dat*) herummurksen an (*dat*); *~ wrench* TECH Engländer *m*, Franzose *m*; *throw a ~ into s.th.* F et. behindern

mon·o 1. Mono *n*; F Monogerät *n*; F Monoschallplatte *f*; **2.** Mono...

mon·o... ein..., mono...

mon·o·log, *esp Br* **mon·o·logue** Monolog *m*

mo·nop·o·lize monopolisieren; *fig* an sich reißen

mo·nop·o·ly Monopol *n* (*of* auf *acc*)

mo·not·o·nous monoton, eintönig

mo·not·o·ny Monotonie *f*

mon·soon Monsun *m*

mon·ster 1. Monster *n*, Ungeheuer *n* (*a. fig*); Monstrum *n*; **2.** Riesen...

mon·stros·i·ty Ungeheuerlichkeit *f*; Monstrum *n*; **mon·strous** ungeheuer; *mst contp* ungeheuerlich; scheußlich

month Monat *m*; **month·ly 1.** monatlich, Monats...; **2.** Monatsschrift *f*

mon·u·ment Monument *n*, Denkmal *n*

mon·u·ment·al monumental; F kolossal, Riesen...; Gedenk...

moo ZO muhen

mooch F schnorren

mood Stimmung *f*, Laune *f*; *be in a good (bad)* ~ gute (schlechte) Laune haben, gut (schlecht) aufgelegt sein

mood·y launisch; schlecht gelaunt

moon 1. ASTR Mond *m*; 2. ~ *about*, ~ *around* F herumtrödeln; F ziellos herumstreichen

moon·light Mondlicht *n*, -schein *m*

moon·lit mondhell

moor[1] (Hoch)Moor *n*

moor[2] MAR vertäuen, festmachen

moor·ings MAR Vertäuung *f*; Liegeplatz *m*

moose ZO nordamerikanischer Elch

mop 1. Mopp *m*; F (Haar)Wust *m*; 2. wischen; ~ *up* aufwischen

mope Trübsal blasen

mo·ped *Br* MOT Moped *n*

mor·al 1. moralisch; Moral..., Sitten...; 2. Moral *f*, Lehre *f*; *pl* Moral *f*, Sitten *pl*

mo·rale Moral *f*, Stimmung *f*

mor·al·ize moralisieren (*about, on* über *acc*)

mor·bid morbid, krankhaft

more 1. *adj* mehr; noch (mehr); *some* ~ *tea* noch etwas Tee; 2. *adv* mehr; noch; ~ *and* ~ immer mehr; ~ *or less* mehr oder weniger; *once* ~ noch einmal; *the* ~ *so because* umso mehr, da; ~ *important* wichtiger; ~ *often* öfter; 3. Mehr *n* (*of* an *dat*); *a little* ~ etwas mehr

mo·rel BOT Morchel *f*

more·o·ver außerdem, weiter, ferner

morgue Leichenschauhaus *n*; F (Zeitungs)Archiv *n*

morn·ing Morgen *m*; Vormittag *m*; *good* ~*!* guten Morgen!; *in the* ~ morgens, am Morgen; vormittags, am Vormittag; *tomorrow* ~ morgen früh *or* Vormittag

mo·rose mürrisch, verdrießlich

mor·phi·a, **mor·phine** PHARM Morphium *n*

mor·sel Bissen *m*, Happen *m*; *a* ~ *of* ein bisschen

mor·tal 1. sterblich; tödlich; Tod(es)...; 2. Sterbliche *m*, *f*

mor·tal·i·ty Sterblichkeit *f*

mor·tar[1] Mörtel *m*

mor·tar[2] Mörser *m*

mort·gage 1. Hypothek *f*; 2. mit e-r Hypothek belasten; e-e Hypothek aufnehmen auf (*acc*)

mor·ti·cian Leichenbestatter *m*

mor·ti·fi·ca·tion Kränkung *f*; Ärger *m*, Verdruss *m*

mor·ti·fy kränken; ärgern, verdrießen

mor·tu·a·ry Leichenhalle *f*

mo·sa·ic Mosaik *n*

Mos·lem → *Muslim*

mosque Moschee *f*

mos·qui·to ZO Moskito *m*; Stechmücke *f*

moss BOT Moos *n*

moss·y BOT moosig, bemoost

most 1. *adj* meiste(r, -s), größte(r, -s); die meisten; ~ *people* die meisten Leute; 2. *adv* am meisten; ~ *of all* am allermeisten; *before adj*: höchst, äußerst; *the* ~ *important point* der wichtigste Punkt; 3. *das* meiste, *das* Höchste; das meiste, der größte Teil; die meisten *pl*; *at (the)* ~ höchstens; *make the* ~ *of et.* nach Kräften ausnutzen, das Beste herausholen aus

most·ly hauptsächlich, meist(ens)

mo·tel Motel *n*

moth ZO Motte *f*

moth-eat·en mottenzerfressen

moth·er 1. Mutter *f*; 2. bemuttern

moth·er coun·try Vaterland *n*, Heimatland *n*; Mutterland *n*

moth·er·hood Mutterschaft *f*

moth·er-in-law Schwiegermutter *f*

moth·er·ly mütterlich

moth·er-of-pearl Perlmutter *f*, *n*, Perlmutt *n*

moth·er tongue Muttersprache *f*

mo·tif Motiv *n*

mo·tion 1. Bewegung *f*; PARL Antrag *m*; *in quick* ~ *film*: im Zeitraffer; *in slow* ~ *film*: in Zeitlupe; *put or set in* ~ in Gang bringen (*a. fig*), in Bewegung setzen; 2. *v/t* j-n durch e-n Wink auffordern, j-m ein Zeichen geben; *v/i* winken

mo·tion·less bewegungslos, unbeweglich

mo·tion pic·ture Film *m*

mo·ti·vate motivieren, anspornen

mo·ti·va·tion Motivation *f*, Ansporn *m*

M

mo·tive 1. Motiv n, Beweggrund m; **2.** treibend (a. fig)

mot·ley bunt

mo·to·cross SPORT Motocross n

mo·tor 1. Motor m, fig a. treibende Kraft; **2.** Motor...

mo·tor·bike Moped n; Br F Motorrad n

mo·tor·boat Motorboot n

mo·tor·cade Auto-, Wagenkolonne f

mo·tor·car Br Kraftfahrzeug n

mo·tor car·a·van Br Wohnmobil n

mo·tor·cy·cle Motorrad n

mo·tor·cy·clist Motorradfahrer(in)

mo·tor home Wohnmobil n

mo·tor·ing Autofahren n; **school of ~** Fahrschule f

mo·tor·ist Autofahrer(in)

mo·tor·ize motorisieren

mo·tor launch Motorbarkasse f

mo·tor·way Br Autobahn f

mot·tled gefleckt, gesprenkelt

mould[1] Br → **mold**[1]

mould[2] Br → **mold**[2]

moul·der Br → **molder**

mould·y Br → **moldy**

moult Br → **molt**

mound Erdhügel m, Erdwall m

mount 1. v/t Pferd etc besteigen, steigen auf (acc); montieren; anbringen, befestigen; Bild etc aufziehen, aufkleben; Edelstein etc fassen; **~ed police** berittene Polizei; v/i aufsitzen (rider); steigen, fig a. (an)wachsen; **~ up to** sich belaufen auf (acc); **2.** Gestell n; Fassung f; Reittier n, Reitpferd n

moun·tain 1. Berg m, pl a. Gebirge n; **2.** Berg..., Gebirgs...

moun·tain bike Mountainbike n

moun·tain·eer Bergsteiger(in)

moun·tain·eer·ing Bergsteigen n

moun·tain·ous bergig, gebirgig

mourn v/i trauern (**for**, **over** um); v/t betrauern, trauern um

mourn·er Trauernde m, f

mourn·ful traurig

mourn·ing Trauer f; Trauerkleidung f

mouse ZO Maus f (a. EDP)

mous·tache → **mustache**

mouth Mund m; ZO Maul n, Schnauze f; GEOGR Mündung f; Öffnung f

mouth·ful ein Mund voll; Bissen m

mouth or·gan F Mundharmonika f

mouth·piece Mundstück n; fig Sprachrohr n

mouth·wash Mundwasser n

mo·va·ble beweglich

move 1. v/t (weg)rücken; transportieren; bewegen, rühren (both a. fig); chess etc: e-n Zug machen mit; PARL beantragen; **~ house** umziehen; **heaven and earth** Himmel und Hölle in Bewegung setzen; v/i sich (fort)bewegen; sich rühren; umziehen (**to** nach); chess etc: e-n Zug machen; **~ away** weg-, fortziehen; **~ in** einziehen; **~ off** sich in Bewegung setzen; **~ on** weitergehen; **~ out** ausziehen; **2.** Bewegung f; Umzug m; chess etc: Zug m; fig Schritt m; **on the ~** in Bewegung; auf den Beinen; **get a ~ on!** F Tempo!, mach(t) schon!, los!

move·a·ble → **movable**

move·ment Bewegung f (a. fig); MUS Satz m; TECH Werk n

mov·ie 1. Film m; Kino n; **2.** Film..., Kino...; **~ cam·e·ra** Filmkamera f; **~ star** Filmstar m; **~ thea·ter** Kino n

mov·ing sich bewegend, beweglich; fig rührend; **~ stair·case** Rolltreppe f; **~ van** Möbelwagen m

mow mähen

mow·er Mähmaschine f, esp Rasenmäher m

Mr. ABBR of **Mister** Herr m

Mrs. Frau f

Ms. Frau f

much 1. adj viel; **2.** adv sehr; viel; **~ better** viel besser; **very ~** sehr; **I thought as ~** das habe ich mir gedacht; **3.** große Sache; **nothing ~** nichts Besonderes; **make ~ of** viel Wesens machen von; **think ~ of** viel halten von; **I am not ~ of a dancer** F ich bin kein großer Tänzer

muck F Br AGR Mist m, Dung m; fig Dreck m, Schmutz m; F contp Fraß m

mu·cus (Nasen)Schleim m

mud Schlamm m, Matsch m; Schmutz m (a. fig)

mud·dle 1. Durcheinander n; **be in a ~** durcheinander sein; **2.** a. **~ up** durcheinander bringen; **~ through** F sich durchwursteln

mud·dy schlammig, trüb; schmutzig; fig wirr

mud·guard Kotflügel m; Schutzblech n

mues·li Müsli n

muff Muff m

muf·fle *Ton etc* dämpfen; *often ~ up* einhüllen, einwickeln

muf·fler (dicker) Schal; MOT Auspufftopf *m*

mug[1] Krug *m*; Becher *m*; große Tasse; F Visage *f*; V Fresse *f*

mug[2] F überfallen und ausrauben

mug·ger F (Straßen)Räuber *m*

mug·ging F Raubüberfall *m*, *esp* Straßenraub *m*

mug·gy schwül

mul·ber·ry BOT Maulbeerbaum *m*; Maulbeere *f*

mule ZO Maultier *n*; Maulesel *m*

mulled: *~ wine* Glühwein *m*

mul·li·on ARCH Mittelpfosten *m*

mul·ti... viel..., mehr..., Mehrfach..., Multi...

mul·ti·cul·tur·al multikulturell

mul·ti·far·i·ous mannigfaltig, vielfältig

mul·ti·lat·er·al vielseitig; POL multilateral, mehrseitig

mul·ti·me·di·a multimedial

mul·ti·na·tion·al ECON multinationaler Konzern, F Multi *m*

mul·ti·ple 1. vielfach, mehrfach; **2.** MATH Vielfache *n*

mul·ti·pli·ca·tion Vermehrung *f*; MATH Multiplikation *f*; *~ table* Einmaleins *n*

mul·ti·plic·i·ty Vielfalt *f*; Vielzahl *f*

mul·ti·ply (sich) vermehren, (sich) vervielfachen; MATH multiplizieren, malnehmen (*by* mit)

mul·ti·pur·pose Mehrzweck...

mul·ti·sto·rey Br mehrstöckig; *~ car park* Br Park(hoch)haus *n*

mul·ti·tude Vielzahl *f*

mul·ti·tu·di·nous zahlreich

mum[1] Br F Mami *f*, Mutti *f*

mum[2] **1.** *int*: *~'s the word* Mund halten!, kein Wort darüber!; **2.** *adj*: *keep ~* nichts verraten, den Mund halten

mum·ble murmeln, F nuscheln; mümmeln

mum·mi·fy mumifizieren

mum·my[1] Mumie *f*

mum·my[2] Br F Mami *f*, Mutti *f*

mumps MED Ziegenpeter *m*, Mumps *m*

munch mampfen

mun·dane alltäglich; weltlich

mu·ni·ci·pal städtisch, Stadt..., kommunal, Gemeinde...; *~ council* Stadt-, Gemeinderat *m*

mu·ni·ci·pal·i·ty Kommunalbehörde *f*; Stadtverwaltung *f*

mu·ral Wandgemälde *n*

mur·der 1. Mord *m*, Ermordung *f*; **2.** Mord...; **3.** ermorden; F verschandeln

mur·der·er Mörder *m*

mur·der·ess Mörderin *f*

mur·der·ous mörderisch

murk·y dunkel, finster

mur·mur 1. Murmeln *n*; Gemurmel *n*; Murren *n*; **2.** murmeln; murren

mus·cle Muskel *m*

mus·cu·lar Muskel...; muskulös

muse[1] (nach)sinnen, (nach)grübeln (*on, over* über *acc*)

muse[2] *a. Muse* Muse *f*

mu·se·um Museum *n*

mush Brei *m*, Mus *n*; Maisbrei *m*

mush·room 1. BOT Pilz *m*, *esp* Champignon *m*; **2.** rasch wachsen; *~ up fig* (wie Pilze) aus dem Boden schießen

mu·sic Musik *f*; Noten *pl*; *put* or *set to ~* vertonen

mu·si·cal 1. musikalisch; Musik...; **2.** Musical *m*; *~ box esp* Br Spieldose *f*; *~ in·stru·ment* Musikinstrument *n*

mu·sic| box Spieldose *f*; *~ cen·ter* (Br *cen·tre*) Kompaktanlage *f*; *~ hall* Br Varieté(theater) *n*

mu·si·cian Musiker(in)

mu·sic stand Notenständer *m*

musk Moschus *m*

musk·rat ZO Bisamratte *f*; Bisampelz *m*

Mus·lim 1. Muslim *m*, Moslem *m*; **2.** muslimisch, moslemisch

mus·sel ZO (Mies)Muschel *f*

must[1] *v/aux* ich muss; *du musst etc*; *you ~ not* (F *mustn't*) du darfst nicht; **2.** Muss *n*

must[2] Most *m*

mus·tache Schnurrbart *m*

mus·tard Senf *m*

mus·ter 1. *~ up s-e* Kraft *etc* aufbieten; *s-n Mut* zusammennehmen; **2.** *pass ~ fig* Zustimmung finden (*with* bei); den Anforderungen genügen

must·y mod(e)rig, muffig

mu·ta·tion Veränderung *f*; BIOL Mutation *f*

mute 1. stumm; **2.** Stumme *m, f*; MUS Dämpfer *m*

mu·ti·late verstümmeln

mu·ti·la·tion Verstümmelung *f*

mu·ti·neer Meuterer *m*
mu·ti·nous meuternd; rebellisch
mu·ti·ny **1.** Meuterei *f*; **2.** meutern
mut·ter **1.** murmeln; murren; **2.** Murmeln *n*; Murren *n*
mut·ton GASTR Hammel-, Schaffleisch *n*; *leg of ~* Hammelkeule *f*
mut·ton chop GASTR Hammelkotelett *n*
mu·tu·al gegenseitig; gemeinsam
muz·zle **1.** ZO Maul *n*, Schnauze *f*; Mündung *f* (*of a gun*); Maulkorb *m*; **2.** e-n Maulkorb anlegen (*dat*); *fig a.* j-n mundtot machen
my mein(e)

myrrh BOT Myrrhe *f*
myr·tle BOT Myrte *f*
my·self ich, mich *or* mir selbst; mich; mich (selbst); *by ~* allein
mys·te·ri·ous rätselhaft, unerklärlich; geheimnisvoll, mysteriös
mys·te·ry Geheimnis *n*, Rätsel *n*; REL Mysterium *n*; *~ tour* Fahrt *f* ins Blaue
mys·tic **1.** Mystiker(in); **2.** → **mystic·al**
mys·ti·cal mystisch
mys·ti·fy verwirren, vor ein Rätsel stellen; *be mystified* vor e-m Rätsel stehen
myth Mythos *m*, Sage *f*
my·thol·o·gy Mythologie *f*

N

N, n N, n *n*
nab F schnappen, erwischen
na·dir ASTR Nadir *m*; *fig* Tiefpunkt *m*
nag¹ **1.** nörgeln; *~ (at)* herumnörgeln an (*dat*); **2.** Nörgler(in)
nag² F Gaul *m*, Klepper *m*
nail **1.** ANAT, TECH Nagel *m*; **2.** (an-) nageln (*to* an *acc*); *~ pol·ish* Nagellack *m*; *~ scis·sors* Nagelschere *f*; *~ varnish* Br Nagellack *m*
na·ive, na·ïve naiv (*a. art*)
na·ked nackt, bloß; kahl; *fig* ungeschminkt; *nak·ed·ness* Nacktheit *f*
name **1.** Name *m*; Ruf *m*; *by ~* mit Namen, namentlich; *by the ~ of ...* namens ...; *what's your ~?* wie heißen Sie?; *call s.o. ~s* j-n beschimpfen; **2.** (be)nennen; erwähnen; ernennen zu
name·less namenlos; unbekannt
name·ly nämlich
name·plate Namens-, Tür-, Firmenschild *n*
name·sake Namensvetter *m*, Namensschwester *f*
name tag Namensschild *n*
nan·ny Kindermädchen *n*
nan·ny goat ZO Geiß *f*, Ziege *f*
nap **1.** Schläfchen *n*; *have or take a ~* → **2.** ein Nickerchen machen
nape *mst ~ of the neck* ANAT Genick *n*, Nacken *m*

nap·kin Serviette *f*
nap·py Br Windel *f*
nar·co·sis MED Narkose *f*
nar·cot·ic **1.** narkotisch, betäubend, einschläfernd; Rauschgift...; *~ addiction* Rauschgiftsucht *f*; **2.** Narkotikum *n*, Betäubungsmittel *n*; *often pl* Rauschgift *n*; *~s squad* Rauschgiftdezernat *n*
nar·rate erzählen; berichten, schildern
nar·ra·tion Erzählung *f*
nar·ra·tive **1.** Erzählung *f*; Bericht *m*, Schilderung *f*; **2.** erzählend
nar·ra·tor Erzähler(in)
nar·row **1.** eng, schmal; beschränkt; knapp; **2.** enger *or* schmäler werden *or* machen, (sich) verengen; beschränken, einschränken; *nar·row·ly* mit knapper Not; *nar·row-mind·ed* engstirnig, beschränkt; *nar·row·ness* Enge *f*; Beschränktheit *f*
na·sal nasal; Nasen...
nas·ty ekelhaft, eklig, widerlich (*smell, sight etc*); abscheulich (*weather etc*); böse, schlimm (*accident etc*); hässlich (*character, behavior etc*); gemein, fies; schmutzig, zotig (*language*)
na·tal Geburts...
na·tion Nation *f*, Volk *n*
na·tion·al **1.** national, National..., Landes..., Volks...; **2.** Staatsangehörige *m*, *f*; *~ an·them* Nationalhymne *f*

na·tion·al·i·ty Nationalität f, Staatsangehörigkeit f

na·tion·al·ize ECON verstaatlichen

na·tion·al‖ park Nationalpark m; **~ so·cial·ism** HIST POL Nationalsozialismus m; **~ so·cial·ist** HIST POL Nationalsozialist m; **~ team** SPORT Nationalmannschaft f

na·tion·wide landesweit

na·tive 1. einheimisch, Landes...; heimatlich, Heimat...; eingeboren, Eingeborenen...; angeboren; **2.** Eingeborene m, f; Einheimische m, f; **~ lan·guage** Muttersprache f; **~ speak·er** Muttersprachler(in)

Na·tiv·i·ty REL die Geburt Christi

nat·ty F schick, *Austrian* fesch

nat·u·ral natürlich; angeboren; Natur...; **~ gas** Erdgas n

nat·u·ral·ize naturalisieren, einbürgern

nat·u·ral·ly natürlich; von Natur (aus)

nat·u·ral‖ re·sourc·es Boden- u. Naturschätze pl; **~ sci·ence** Naturwissenschaft f

na·ture Natur f; **~ con·ser·va·tion** Naturschutz m; **~ re·serve** Naturschutzgebiet n; **~ trail** Naturlehrpfad m

naugh·ty unartig; unanständig

nau·se·a Übelkeit f, Brechreiz m

nau·se·ate: **~ s.o.** j-m Übelkeit verursachen; fig j-n anwidern

nau·se·at·ing Ekel erregend, widerlich

nau·ti·cal nautisch, See...

na·val MIL Flotten..., Marine...; See...; **~ base** MIL Flottenstützpunkt m; **~ of·fi·cer** MIL Marineoffizier m; **~ pow·er** MIL Seemacht f

nave ARCH Mittel-, Hauptschiff n

na·vel ANAT Nabel m (a. fig)

nav·i·ga·ble schiffbar

nav·i·gate MAR befahren; AVIAT, MAR steuern, lenken

nav·i·ga·tion Schifffahrt f; AVIAT, MAR Navigation f

nav·i·ga·tor AVIAT, MAR Navigator m

na·vy (Kriegs)Marine f; Kriegsflotte f

na·vy blue Marineblau n

nay PARL Gegen-, Neinstimme f

Na·zi HIST POL contp Nazi m

Na·zism HIST POL contp Nazismus m

near 1. adj nahe; kurz; nahe (verwandt); **in the ~ future** in naher Zukunft; **be a ~ miss** knapp scheitern; **2.** adv nahe, in der Nähe (a. **~ at hand**); nahe

(bevorstehend) (a. **~ at hand**); beinahe, fast; **~ the station** etc in der Nähe des Bahnhofs etc; **~ you** in deiner Nähe; **3.** prp nahe (dat), in der Nähe von (or gen); **4.** sich nähern, näher kommen (dat)

near·by 1. adj nahe (gelegen); **2.** adv in der Nähe

near·ly beinahe, fast; annähernd

near·sight·ed kurzsichtig

neat ordentlich; sauber; gepflegt; pur (whisky etc)

neb·u·lous verschwommen

ne·ces·sar·i·ly notwendigerweise; **not ~** nicht unbedingt

ne·ces·sa·ry notwendig, nötig; unvermeidlich

ne·ces·si·tate et. erfordern, verlangen

ne·ces·si·ty Notwendigkeit f; (dringendes) Bedürfnis; Not f

neck 1. ANAT Hals m (a. of bottle etc); Genick n, Nacken m; **be ~ and ~** F Kopf an Kopf liegen (a. fig); **be up to one's ~ in debt** F bis zum Hals in Schulden stecken; **2.** F knutschen, schmusen

neck·er·chief Halstuch n

neck·lace Halskette f

neck·let Halskettchen n

neck·line Ausschnitt m

neck·tie Krawatte f, Schlips m

née: **~ Smith** geborene Smith

need 1. (of, for) (dringendes) Bedürfnis (nach), Bedarf m (an dat); Notwendigkeit f; Mangel m (of, for an dat); Not f; **be in ~ of s.th.** et. dringend brauchen; **in ~** in Not; **in ~ of help** hilfs-, hilfebedürftig; **2.** v/t benötigen, brauchen; v/aux brauchen, müssen

nee·dle 1. Nadel f (a. BOT, MED); Zeiger m; **2.** F j-n aufziehen, hänseln

need·less unnötig, überflüssig

nee·dle·wom·an Näherin f

nee·dle·work Handarbeit f

need·y bedürftig, arm

ne·ga·tion Verneinung f

neg·a·tive 1. negativ; verneinend; **2.** Verneinung f; PHOT Negativ n; **answer in the ~** verneinen

ne·glect 1. vernachlässigen; es versäumen (doing, to do zu tun); **2.** Vernachlässigung f; Nachlässigkeit f

neg·li·gence Nachlässigkeit f, Unachtsamkeit f; **neg·li·gent** nachlässig, unachtsam; lässig, salopp

neg·li·gi·ble unbedeutend

ne·go·ti·ate verhandeln (über *acc*)

ne·go·ti·a·tion Verhandlung *f*

ne·go·ti·a·tor Unterhändler(in)

neigh ZO **1.** wiehern; **2.** Wiehern *n*

neigh·bo(u)r Nachbar(in)

neigh·bo(u)r·hood Nachbarschaft *f*, Umgebung *f*

neigh·bo(u)r·ing benachbart, Nachbar..., angrenzend

neigh·bo(u)r·ly (gut)nachbarlich

nei·ther 1. *adj and pron* keine(r, -s) (von beiden); **2.** *cj* ~ ... *nor* weder ... noch

ne·on CHEM Neon *n*; ~ **lamp** Neonlampe *f*; ~ **sign** Neon-, Leuchtreklame *f*

neph·ew Neffe *m*

nep·o·tism *contp* Vetternwirtschaft *f*

nerd F Trottel *m*; Computerfreak *m*

nerve Nerv *m*; Mut *m*, Stärke *f*, Selbstbeherrschung *f*; F Frechheit *f*; **get on s.o.'s ~s** j-m auf die Nerven gehen *or* fallen; **lose one's ~** den Mut *or* die Nerven verlieren; **you've got a ~!** F Sie haben Nerven!; **nerve·less** kraftlos; mutlos; ohne Nerven, kaltblütig

ner·vous nervös; Nerven...

ner·vous·ness Nervosität *f*

nest 1. Nest *n*; **2.** nisten

nes·tle (sich) schmiegen *or* kuscheln (**against, on** an *acc*); *a.* ~ **down** sich behaglich niederlassen, es sich bequem machen (**in** in *dat*)

net[1] Netz *n*; ~ **curtain** Store *m*; **2.** mit e-m Netz fangen *or* abdecken

net[2] **1.** netto, Netto..., Rein...; **2.** netto einbringen

Neth·er·lands die Niederlande *pl*

net·tle 1. BOT Nessel *f*; **2.** F *j-n* ärgern

net·work Netz *n* (*a.* EDP), Netzwerk *n*; (*Straßen- etc*)Netz *n*; *radio*, TV Sendernetz *n*; **be in the ~** EDP am Netz sein

neu·ro·sis MED Neurose *f*; **neu·rot·ic** MED **1.** neurotisch; **2.** Neurotiker(in)

neu·ter 1. LING sächlich; geschlechtslos; **2.** LING Neutrum *n*

neu·tral 1. neutral; **2.** Neutrale *m*, *f*; *a.* ~ **gear** MOT Leerlauf(stellung *f*) *m*

neu·tral·i·ty Neutralität *f*

neu·tral·ize neutralisieren

neu·tron PHYS Neutron *n*

nev·er nie, niemals; **nev·er-end·ing** endlos, nicht enden wollend, unendlich

nev·er·the·less nichtsdestoweniger, dennoch, trotzdem

new neu; frisch; unerfahren; **nothing ~** nichts Neues

new-born neugeboren

new·com·er Neuankömmling *m*; Neuling *m*

new·ly kürzlich; neu

news Neuigkeit(en *pl*) *f*, Nachricht(en *pl*) *f*

news·a·gent Zeitungshändler(in)

news·boy Zeitungsjunge *m*, Zeitungsausträger *m*

news bul·le·tin Kurznachricht(en *pl*) *f*

news·cast *radio*, TV Nachrichtensendung *f*; **news·cast·er** *radio*, TV Nachrichtensprecher(in)

news deal·er Zeitungshändler(in)

news·flash *radio*, TV Kurzmeldung *f*

news·let·ter Rundschreiben *n*

news·pa·per Zeitung *f*

news·print Zeitungspapier *n*

news·read·er *esp Br* → **newscaster**

news·reel *film*: Wochenschau *f*

news·room Nachrichtenredaktion *f*

news·stand Zeitungskiosk *m*, -stand *m*

news·ven·dor *esp Br* Zeitungsverkäufer(in)

new year Neujahr *n*, *das neue Jahr*; **New Year's Day** Neujahrstag *m*; **New Year's Eve** Silvester(abend *m*) *m*, *n*

next 1. *adj* nächste(r, -s); (**the**) ~ **day** am nächsten Tag; ~ **door** nebenan; ~ **but one** übernächste(r, -s); ~ **to** gleich neben *or* nach; beinahe, fast *unmöglich etc*; **2.** *adv* als Nächste(r, -s); demnächst, das nächste Mal; **3.** *der, die, das Nächste*; → **kin**

next-door (von) nebenan

nib·ble *v/i* knabbern (**at** an *dat*); *v/t Loch etc* nagen, knabbern (**in** in *acc*)

nice nett, freundlich; hübsch, schön; *fig* fein (*detail etc*)

nice·ly gut, fein; genau, sorgfältig

ni·ce·ty Feinheit *f*; Genauigkeit *f*

niche Nische *f*

nick 1. Kerbe *f*; **in the ~ of time** gerade noch rechtzeitig, im letzten Moment; **2.** (ein)kerben; *j-n* streifen (*bullet*); *Br* F *et.* klauen; *Br* F *j-n* schnappen

nick·el 1. MIN Nickel *n*; Fünfcentstück *n*; **2.** TECH vernickeln

nick·el-plate TECH vernickeln

nick-nack → **knick-knack**

nick-name **1.** Spitzname m; **2.** j-m den Spitznamen ... geben

niece Nichte f

nig-gard Geizhals m

nig-gard-ly geizig, knaus(e)rig; schäbig, kümmerlich

night Nacht f; Abend m; **at ~, by ~, in the ~** in der Nacht, nachts

night-cap Schlummertrunk m

night-club Nachtklub m, Nachtlokal n

night-dress (Damen-, Kinder)Nachthemd n

night-fall: **at ~** bei Einbruch der Dunkelheit

night-gown → **nightdress**

night-ie F → **nightdress**

nigh-tin-gale ZO Nachtigall f

night-ly (all)nächtlich; (all)abendlich; jede Nacht; jeden Abend

night-mare Albtraum m (a. fig)

night school Abendschule f

night shift Nachtschicht f

night-shirt (Herren)Nachthemd n

night-time: **in the ~, at ~** nachts

night watch-man Nachtwächter m

night-y F → **nightdress**

nil Nichts n, Null f; **our team won two to ~** or **by two goals to ~ (2-0)** unsere Mannschaft gewann zwei zu null (2:0)

nim-ble flink, gewandt; geistig beweglich

nine **1.** neun; **~ to five** normale Dienststunden (von 9-5); **a ~-to-five job** e-e (An)Stellung mit geregelter Arbeitszeit; **2.** Neun f

nine-pins Kegeln n

nine-teen **1.** neunzehn; **2.** Neunzehn f

nine-teenth neunzehnte(r, -s)

nine-ti-eth neunzigste(r, -s)

nine-ty **1.** neunzig; **2.** Neunzig f

ninth **1.** neunte(r, -s); **2.** Neuntel n

ninth-ly neuntens

nip¹ **1.** kneifen, zwicken; F flitzen, sausen; **~ off** F abknipsen; **~ in the bud** fig im Keim ersticken; **2.** Kneifen n, Zwicken n; **it was ~ and tuck** F es war ganz knapp; **there's a ~ in the air today** heute ist es ganz schön kalt

nip² Schlückchen n (of brandy etc)

nip-per: **(a pair of) ~s** (e-e) (Kneif)Zange f

nip-ple ANAT Brustwarze f; (Gummi-) Sauger m; TECH Nippel m

ni-ter, Br ni-tre CHEM Salpeter m

ni-tro-gen CHEM Stickstoff m

no **1.** adv nein; nicht; **2.** adj kein(e); **~ one** keiner, niemand; **in ~ time** im Nu, im Handumdrehen; **3.** Nein n

no-bil-i-ty (Hoch)Adel m; fig Adel m

no-ble adlig; edel, nobel; prächtig

no-ble-man Adlige m

no-ble-wom-an Adlige f

no-bod-y **1.** niemand, keiner; **2.** fig Niemand m, Null f

no-cal-o-rie di-et Nulldiät f

noc-tur-nal nächtlich, Nacht...

nod **1.** nicken (mit); **~ off** einnicken; **have a ~ding acquaintance with s.o.** j-n flüchtig kennen; **2.** Nicken n

node BOT, MED Knoten m

noise **1.** Krach m, Lärm m; Geräusch n; **2. ~ about (abroad, around)** Gerücht etc verbreiten; **noise-less** geräuschlos; **nois-y** laut, geräuschvoll

no-mad Nomade m, Nomadin f

nom-i-nal nominell; **~ value** ECON Nennwert m

nom-i-nate ernennen; nominieren, (zur Wahl) vorschlagen; **nom-i-na-tion** Ernennung f; Nominierung f

nom-i-na-tive a. **~ case** LING Nominativ m, erster Fall

nom-i-nee Kandidat(in)

non... nicht..., Nicht..., un...

non-al-co-hol-ic alkoholfrei

non-a-ligned POL blockfrei

non-com-mis-sioned of-fi-cer MIL Unteroffizier m

non-com-mit-tal unverbindlich

non-con-duc-tor ELECTR Nichtleiter m

non-de-script nichts sagend; unauffällig

none **1.** pron keine(r, -s), niemand; **2.** adv in keiner Weise, keineswegs

none-the-less nichtsdestoweniger, dennoch, trotzdem

non-ex-ist-ence Nichtvorhandensein n, Fehlen n

non-ex-ist-ent nicht existieren

non-fic-tion Sachbücher pl

non-flam-ma-ble, non-in-flam-ma-ble nicht brennbar

non-in-ter-fer-ence, non-in-ter-ven-tion POL Nichteinmischung f

non-i-ron bügelfrei

no-non-sense nüchtern, sachlich

N

non·par·ti·san POL überparteilich; unparteiisch

non·pay·ment ECON Nicht(be)zahlung *f*

non·plus verblüffen

non·pol·lut·ing umweltfreundlich

non·prof·it, *Br* **non-prof·it-mak·ing** gemeinnützig

non·res·i·dent 1. nicht (orts)ansässig; nicht im Hause wohnend; 2. Nichtansässige *m, f*; nicht im Hause Wohnende *m, f*

non·re·turn·a·ble Einweg...; **~ bot·tle** Einwegflasche *f*

non·sense Unsinn *m*, dummes Zeug

non·skid rutschfest, rutschsicher

non·smok·er Nichtraucher(in)

non·smok·ing Nichtraucher...

non·stick mit Antihaftbeschichtung

non·stop nonstop, ohne Unterbrechung; RAIL durchgehend; AVIAT ohne Zwischenlandung; **~ flight** *a.* Non-Stop-Flug *m*

non·u·nion nicht (gewerkschaftlich) organisiert

non·vi·o·lence (Politik *f* der) Gewaltlosigkeit *f*

non·vi·o·lent gewaltlos

noo·dle Nudel *f*

nook Ecke *f*, Winkel *m*

noon Mittag(szeit *f*) *m*; **at ~** um 12 Uhr (mittags)

noose Schlinge *f*

nope F ne(e), nein

nor → **neither** 2; auch nicht

norm Norm *f*

nor·mal normal

nor·mal·ize (sich) normalisieren

north 1. Nord, Norden *m*; 2. *adj* nördlich, Nord...; 3. *adv* nach Norden, nordwärts

north·east 1. Nordost, Nordosten *m*; 2. *a.* **northeastern** nordöstlich

nor·ther·ly, nor·thern Nord..., nördlich

North Pole Nordpol *m*

north·ward(s) *adv* nördlich, nach Norden

north·west 1. Nordwest, Nordwesten *m*; 2. *a.* **northwestern** nordwestlich

Nor·way Norwegen *n*

Nor·we·gian 1. norwegisch; 2. Norweger(in); LING Norwegisch *n*

nose 1. Nase *f*; ZO Schnauze *f*; *fig* Gespür *n*; 2. *Auto etc* vorsichtig fahren; *a.* **~ about**, **~ around** *fig* F herumschnüffeln (in *dat*) (**for** nach)

nose·bleed Nasenbluten *n*; **have a ~** Nasenbluten haben

nose·dive AVIAT Sturzflug *m*

nos·ey → **nosy**

nos·tal·gia Nostalgie *f*

nos·tril ANAT Nasenloch *n*, *esp* ZO Nüster *f*

nos·y F neugierig

not nicht; **~ a** kein(e)

no·ta·ble bemerkenswert; beachtlich

no·ta·ry *mst* **~ public** Notar *m*

notch 1. Kerbe *f*; GEOL Engpass *m*; 2. (ein)kerben

note (*mst pl*) Notiz *f*, Aufzeichnung *f*; Anmerkung *f*; Vermerk *m*; Briefchen *n*, Zettel *m*; (diplomatische) Note; Banknote *f*, Geldschein *m*; MUS Note *f*; *fig* Ton *m*; **take ~s** sich Notizen machen (über *acc*); **note·book** Notizbuch *n*; EDP Notebook *n*

not·ed bekannt, berühmt (**for** wegen)

note·pa·per Briefpapier *n*

note·wor·thy bemerkenswert

noth·ing nichts; **~ but** nichts als, nur; **~ much** F nicht viel; **for ~** umsonst; **to say ~ of** ganz zu schweigen von; **there is ~ like** es geht nichts über (*acc*)

no·tice 1. Ankündigung *f*, Bekanntgabe *f*, Mitteilung *f*, Anzeige *f*; Kündigung(sfrist) *f*; Beachtung *f*; **give or hand in one's ~** kündigen (**to** bei); **give s.o. ~** j-m kündigen; **give s.o. ~ to quit** j-m kündigen; **at six months' ~** mit halbjährlicher Kündigungsfrist; **take (no) ~ of** (keine) Notiz nehmen von, (nicht) beachten; **at short ~** kurzfristig; **until further ~** bis auf weiteres; **without ~** fristlos; 2. (es) bemerken; (besonders) beachten *or* achten auf (*acc*)

no·tice·a·ble erkennbar, wahrnehmbar; bemerkenswert

no·tice·board *Br* schwarzes Brett

no·ti·fy *et.* anzeigen, melden, mitteilen; *j-n* benachrichtigen

no·tion Begriff *m*, Vorstellung *f*; Idee *f*

no·tions Kurzwaren *pl*

no·to·ri·ous berüchtigt (**for** für)

not·with·stand·ing trotz (*gen*)

nought *Br*: **0.4** (**~ point four**) 0,4

noun LING Substantiv *n*, Hauptwort *n*

nour·ish (er)nähren; *fig* hegen

nour·ish·ing nahrhaft
nour·ish·ment Ernährung *f*; Nahrung *f*
Nov ABBR *of November* Nov., November *m*
nov·el 1. Roman *m*; **2.** (ganz) neu(artig)
nov·el·ist Romanschriftsteller(in)
no·vel·la Novelle *f*
nov·el·ty Neuheit *f*
No·vem·ber (ABBR *Nov*) November *m*
nov·ice Anfänger(in), Neuling *m*; REL Novize *m*, Novizin *f*
now 1. *adv* nun, jetzt; **~ and again**, **(every) ~ and then** von Zeit zu Zeit, dann und wann; **by ~** inzwischen; **from ~ (on)** von jetzt an; **just ~** gerade eben; **2.** *cj a.* **~ that** nun da; **now·a·days** heutzutage
no·where nirgends
nox·ious schädlich
noz·zle TECH Schnauze *f*; Stutzen *m*; Düse *f*; Zapfpistole *f*
nu·ance Nuance *f*
nub springender Punkt
nu·cle·ar Kern..., Atom..., atomar, nuklear, Nuklear...; **~ en·er·gy** PHYS Atomenergie *f*, Kernenergie *f*; **~ fam·i·ly** Kern-, Kleinfamilie *f*; **~ fis·sion** PHYS Kernspaltung *f*
nu·cle·ar-free atomwaffenfrei
nu·cle·ar| fu·sion PHYS Kernfusion *f*; **phys·ics** Kernphysik *f*; **~ pow·er** PHYS Atomkraft *f*, Kernkraft *f*
nu·cle·ar-pow·ered atomgetrieben
nu·cle·ar| pow·er plant ELECTR Atomkraftwerk *n*, Kernkraftwerk *n*; **~ re·ac·tor** PHYS Atomreaktor *m*, Kernreaktor *m*; **~ war** Atomkrieg *m*; **~ war·head** MIL Atomsprengkopf *m*; **~ waste** Atommüll *m*; **~ weap·ons** MIL Atomwaffen *pl*, Kernwaffen *pl*
nu·cle·us BIOL, PHYS Kern *m* (*a. fig*)
nude 1. nackt; **2.** *art:* Akt *m*
nudge 1. *j-n* anstoßen, (an)stupsen; **2.** Stups(er) *m*
nug·get (*esp* Gold)Klumpen *m*
nui·sance Plage *f*, Ärgernis *n*; Nervensäge *f*, Quälgeist *m*; **what a ~!** wie ärgerlich!; **be a ~ to s.o.** *j-m* lästig fallen, F *j-n* nerven; **make a ~ of o.s.** den Leu-

ten auf die Nerven gehen *or* fallen
nukes F Atom-, Kernwaffen *pl*
null: **~ and void** *esp* JUR null und nichtig
numb 1. starr (**with** vor), taub; *fig* wie betäubt (**with** vor); **2.** starr *or* taub machen
num·ber 1. Zahl *f*, Ziffer *f*; Nummer *f*; (An)Zahl *f*; Ausgabe *f*; (*Bus- etc*)Linie *f*; **sorry**, **wrong ~** TEL falsch verbunden!; **2.** nummerieren; zählen; sich belaufen auf (*acc*)
num·ber·less zahllos
num·ber·plate *esp* Br MOT Nummernschild *n*
nu·me·ral Ziffer *f*; LING Zahlwort *n*
nu·me·ra·tor MATH Zähler *m*
nu·me·rous zahlreich
nun REL Nonne *f*
nun·ne·ry REL Nonnenkloster *n*
nurse 1. (Kranken-, Säuglings)Schwester *f*; Kindermädchen *n*; (Kranken-)Pflegerin *f*; → **male nurse**; *a.* **wet ~** Amme *f*; **2.** stillen; pflegen; hegen; als Krankenschwester *or* -pfleger arbeiten; **~ s.o. back to health** *j-n* gesund pflegen
nur·se·ry Tagesheim *n*, Tagesstätte *f*; Baum-, Pflanzschule *f*; **~ rhyme** Kinderlied *n*, Kinderreim *m*; **~ school** Br Vorschule *f*; **~ slope** *skiing:* F Idiotenhügel *m*
nurs·ing Stillen *n*; (Kranken)Pflege *f*; **bot·tle** (Saug)Flasche *f*; **~ home** Pflegeheim *n*
nut BOT Nuss *f*; TECH (Schrauben)Mutter *f*; F verrückter Kerl; F Birne *f* (*head*); **be off one's ~** F spinnen
nut·crack·er(s) Nussknacker *m*
nut·meg BOT Muskatnuss *f*
nu·tri·ent 1. Nährstoff *m*; **2.** nahrhaft
nu·tri·tion Ernährung *f*
nu·tri·tious, **nu·tri·tive** nahrhaft
nut·shell Nussschale *f*; (**to put it**) **in a ~** F kurz gesagt, mit e-m Wort
nut·ty voller Nüsse; Nuss...; F verrückt
ny·lon Nylon *n*; **~ stock·ings** Nylonstrümpfe *pl*
nymph Nymphe *f*

N

O

O, o O, o *n*

o Null *f*

oaf Lümmel *m*, Flegel *m*

oak BOT Eiche *f*

oar Ruder *n*

oars·man SPORT Ruderer *m*

oars·wom·an SPORT Ruderin *f*

o·a·sis Oase *f* (*a. fig*)

oath Eid *m*, Schwur *m*; Fluch *m*; **take an ~** e-n Eid leisten *or* schwören; **be on** *or* **under ~** JUR unter Eid stehen; **take the ~** JUR schwören

oat·meal Hafermehl *n*, Hafergrütze *f*

oats BOT Hafer *m*; **sow one's wild ~** sich die Hörner abstoßen

o·be·di·ence Gehorsam *m*

o·be·di·ent gehorsam

o·bese fett, fettleibig

o·bes·i·ty Fettleibigkeit *f*

o·bey gehorchen (*dat*), folgen (*dat*); *Befehl etc* befolgen

o·bit·u·a·ry Nachruf *m*; *a.* **~ notice** Todesanzeige *f*

ob·ject 1. Objekt *n* (*a.* LING); Gegenstand *m*; Ziel *n*, Zweck *m*, Absicht *f*; 2. einwenden; et. dagegen haben

ob·jec·tion Einwand *m*, Einspruch *m* (*a.* JUR); **ob·jec·tion·a·ble** nicht einwandfrei; unangenehm; anstößig

ob·jec·tive 1. objektiv, sachlich; 2. Ziel *n*; **ob·jec·tive·ness** Objektivität *f*

ob·li·ga·tion Verpflichtung *f*; **be under an ~ to s.o.** j-m (*zu Dank*) verpflichtet sein; **be under an ~ to do** verpflichtet sein, et. zu tun; **ob·lig·a·to·ry** verpflichtend, verbindlich

o·blige nötigen, zwingen; (*zu Dank*) verpflichten; **~ s.o.** j-m e-n Gefallen tun; **much ~d** besten Dank

o·blig·ing entgegenkommend, gefällig

o·blique schief, schräg; *fig* indirekt

o·blit·er·ate auslöschen; vernichten, völlig zerstören; verdecken

o·bliv·i·on Vergessen(heit *f*) *n*; **fall into ~** in Vergessenheit geraten

o·bliv·i·ous: **be ~ of** *or* **to s.th.** sich e-r Sache nicht bewusst sein; et. nicht bemerken *or* wahrnehmen

ob·long rechteckig; länglich

ob·nox·ious widerlich

ob·scene obszön, unanständig

ob·scure 1. dunkel, *fig a.* unklar; unbekannt; 2. verdunkeln, verdecken

ob·scu·ri·ty Unbekanntheit *f*; Unklarheit *f*

ob·se·quies Trauerfeier(lichkeiten *pl*) *f*

ob·ser·va·ble wahrnehmbar, merklich; **ob·ser·vance** Beachtung *f*, Befolgung *f*; **ob·ser·vant** aufmerksam; **ob·ser·va·tion** Beobachtung *f*, Überwachung *f*; Bemerkung *f* (**on** über *acc*); **ob·ser·va·to·ry** Observatorium *n*, Sternwarte *f*; **ob·serve** beobachten; überwachen; *Vorschrift etc* beachten, befolgen, einhalten; bemerken, äußern; **ob·serv·er** Beobachter(in)

ob·sess: **be ~ed by** *or* **with** besessen sein von; **ob·ses·sion** Besessenheit *f*, fixe Idee, Zwangsvorstellung *f*; **ob·ses·sive** PSYCH zwanghaft

ob·so·lete veraltet

ob·sta·cle Hindernis *n*

ob·sti·na·cy Starrsinn *m*

ob·sti·nate hartnäckig; halsstarrig, eigensinnig, starrköpfig

ob·struct verstopfen, versperren; blockieren; behindern

ob·struc·tion Verstopfung *f*, Blockierung *f*; Behinderung *f*

ob·struc·tive blockierend; hinderlich

ob·tain erhalten, bekommen, sich et. beschaffen; **ob·tain·a·ble** erhältlich

ob·tru·sive aufdringlich

ob·tuse MATH stumpf; *fig* begriffsstutzig; **be ~** sich dumm stellen

ob·vi·ous offensichtlich, klar, einleuchtend

oc·ca·sion Gelegenheit *f*; Anlass *m*; Veranlassung *f*; (festliches) Ereignis; **on the ~ of** anlässlich (*gen*)

oc·ca·sion·al gelegentlich; vereinzelt

oc·ca·sion·al·ly gelegentlich, manchmal

Oc·ci·dent *der* Westen, *der* Okzident, *das* Abendland

oc·ci·den·tal abendländisch, westlich

oc·cu·pant Bewohner(in); Insasse *m*, Insassin *f*

oc·cu·pa·tion Beruf *m*; Beschäftigung

f; MIL, POL Besetzung *f*, Besatzung *f*, Okkupation *f*

oc·cu·py in Besitz nehmen; MIL, POL besetzen; *Raum* einnehmen; in Anspruch nehmen; beschäftigen; *be oc-cupied* bewohnt sein; besetzt sein (*seat*)

oc·cur sich ereignen; vorkommen; *it ~red to me that* es fiel mir ein *or* mir kam der Gedanke, dass

oc·cur·rence Vorkommen *n*; Ereignis *n*; Vorfall *m*

o·cean Ozean *m*, (Welt)Meer *n*

o'clock: (*at*) *five ~* (um) fünf Uhr

Oct ABBR *of October* Okt., Oktober *m*

Oc·to·ber (ABBR *Oct*) Oktober *m*

oc·u·lar Augen...

oc·u·list Augenarzt *m*, Augenärztin *f*

OD F *v/i*: *~ on heroin* an e-r Überdosis Heroin sterben

odd sonderbar, seltsam, merkwürdig; einzeln, Einzel...; ungerade (*number*); gelegentlich, Gelegenheits...; *~ jobs* Gelegenheitsarbeiten *pl*; F *30 ~* (et.) über 30, einige 30

odds (Gewinn)Chancen *pl*; *the ~ are 10 to 1* die Chancen stehen 10 zu 1; *the ~ are that* es ist sehr wahrscheinlich, dass; *against all ~* wider Erwarten, entgegen allen Erwartungen; *be at ~* uneins sein (*with* mit); *~ and ends* Krimskrams *m*; *odds-on* hoch, klar (*favorite*), aussichtsreichst (*candidate etc*); F *it's ~ that* es sieht ganz so aus, als ob ...

ode Ode *f*

o·do(u)r Geruch *m*

o·do(u)r·less geruchlos

of *prp* von; *origin*: von, aus; *material*: aus; um (*cheat s.o. ~ s.th.* j-n um et. betrügen); *cause*: an (*dat*) (*die ~* sterben an); aus (*~ charity* aus Nächstenliebe); vor (*dat*) (*be afraid ~* Angst haben vor); auf (*acc*) (*be proud ~* stolz sein auf); über (*acc*) (*be glad ~* sich freuen über); nach (*smell ~* riechen nach); von, über (*acc*) (*speak ~ s.th.* von *or* über et. sprechen); an (*acc*) (*think ~ s.th.* an et. denken); *the city ~ London* die Stadt London; *the works ~ Dickens* Dickens' Werke; *your letter ~ ...* Ihr Schreiben vom ...; *five minutes ~ twelve* fünf Minuten vor zwölf

off 1. *adv* fort(...), weg(...); ab(...), ab, abgegangen (*button etc*); weg, entfernt (*3 miles ~*); ELECTR aus(...), aus-, abgeschaltet; TECH zu; aus(gegangen), alle; aus, vorbei; verdorben (*food*); frei; *I must be ~* ich muss gehen *or* weg; *~ with you!* fort mit dir!; *be ~* ausfallen, nicht stattfinden; *10% ~* ECON 10% Nachlass; *~ and on* ab und zu, hin und wieder; *take a day ~* sich e-n Tag freinehmen; *be well (badly) ~* gut (schlecht) d(a)ran *or* gestellt *or* situiert sein; **2.** *prp* fort von, weg von, von (..., ab, weg, herunter); abseits von (*or gen*), von ... weg; MAR vor *der Küste etc*; *be ~ duty* nicht im Dienst sein, dienstfrei haben; *be ~ smoking* nicht mehr rauchen; **3.** *adj* frei, arbeits-, dienstfrei; *fig have an ~ day* e-n schlechten Tag haben

of·fal GASTR Innereien *pl*

off-col·o(u)r schlüpfrig, zweideutig

of·fence *Br* → *offense*

of·fend beleidigen, kränken; verstoßen (*against* gegen); **of·fend·er** (Übel-, Misse)Täter(in); *first ~* JUR nicht Vorbestrafte *m*, *f*, Ersttäter(in)

of·fense Vergehen *n*, Verstoß *m*; JUR Straftat *f*; Beleidigung *f*, Kränkung *f*; *take ~* Anstoß nehmen (*at* an *dat*)

of·fen·sive 1. beleidigend, anstößig; widerlich (*smell etc*); MIL Offensiv...; Angriffs...; **2.** MIL Offensive *f* (*a. fig*)

of·fer 1. *v/t* anbieten (*a.* ECON); *Preis, Möglichkeit etc* bieten; *Preis, Belohnung* aussetzen; sich bereit erklären (*to do* zu tun); *Widerstand* leisten; *v/i* es *or* sich anbieten; **2.** Angebot *n*

off·hand 1. *adj* lässig; Stegreif...; *be ~ with s.o.* F mit j-m kurz angebunden sein; **2.** *adv* auf Anhieb, so ohne weiteres

of·fice Büro *n*, Geschäftsstelle *f*, (Anwalts)Kanzlei *f*; (*esp* öffentliches) Amt, Posten *m*; *mst Office esp Br* Ministerium *n*; *~ block Br*, *~ build·ing* Bürohaus *n*; *~ hours* Dienstzeit *f*; Geschäfts-, Öffnungszeiten *pl*

of·fi·cer MIL Offizier *m*; (*Polizei- etc*) Beamte *m*, (-)Beamtin *f*

of·fi·cial 1. Beamte *m*, Beamtin *f*; **2.** offiziell, amtlich, dienstlich

of·fi·ci·ate amtieren

of·fi·cious übereifrig

O

off-licence *Br* Wein- und Spirituosen-handlung *f*

off-line EDP offline, Offline..., rechner-unabhängig

off-peak: **~ electricity** Nachtstrom *m*; **~ hours** verkehrsschwache Stunden *pl*

off sea·son Nebensaison *f*

off·set ECON ausgleichen; verrechnen (**against** mit)

off·shoot BOT Ableger *m*, Spross *m*

off·shore vor der Küste

off·side SPORT abseits; **~ position** Abseitsposition *f*, Abseitsstellung *f*; **~ trap** Abseitsfalle *f*

off·spring Nachkomme *m*, Nachkom-menschaft *f*

off-the-peg *Br*, **off-the-rack** Konfekti-ons..., ... von der Stange

off-the-rec·ord inoffiziell

of·ten oft(mals), häufig

oh *int* oh!

oil 1. Öl *n*; Erdöl *n*; **2.** (ein)ölen, schmieren (*a. fig*)

oil change MOT Ölwechsel *m*

oil·cloth Wachstuch *n*

oil·field Ölfeld *n*

oil paint·ing Ölmalerei *f*; Ölgemälde *n*

oil pan MOT Ölwanne *f*

oil plat·form → *oilrig*

oil pol·lu·tion Ölpest *f*

oil pro·duc·tion Ölförderung *f*

oil-pro·duc·ing coun·try Ölförder-land *n*

oil re·fin·e·ry Erdölraffinerie *f*

oil·rig (Öl)Bohrinsel *f*

oil·skins Ölzeug *n*

oil slick Ölteppich *m*

oil well Ölquelle *f*

oil·y ölig; *fig* schmierig, schleimig

oint·ment Salbe *f*

OK, o·kay F **1.** *adj and int* okay(!), o.k. (!), in Ordnung(!); **2.** genehmigen, *e-r Sache* zustimmen; **3.** Okay *n*, O.K. *n*, Genehmigung *f*, Zustimmung *f*

old 1. alt; **2. the ~** die Alten *pl*

old age (hohes) Alter; **~ pen·sion** Rente *f*, Pension *f*; **~ pen·sion·er** Rentner(in), Pensionär(in)

old-fash·ioned altmodisch

old·ish ältlich

old peo·ple's home Altersheim *n*, Al-tenheim *n*

ol·ive BOT Olive *f*; Olivgrün *n*

O·lym·pic Games SPORT Olympische Spiele *pl*

om·i·nous unheilvoll

o·mis·sion Auslassung *f*; Unterlassung *f*; Versäumnis *n*

o·mit auslassen, weglassen; unterlassen

om·nip·o·tent allmächtig

om·nis·ci·ent allwissend

on 1. *prp* auf (*acc or dat*) (**~ the table** auf dem *or* den Tisch); an (*dat*) (**~ the wall** an der Wand); in (*dat*) (**~ TV** im Fernsehen); *direction, target*: auf (*acc*) ... (hin), an (*acc*), nach (*dat*) ... (hin) (**march ~ London** nach London marschieren); *fig* auf (*acc*) ... (hin) (**~ demand** auf Anfrage); *time*: an (*dat*) (**~ Sunday** am Sonntag; **~ the 1st of April** am 1. April); (gleich) nach, bei (**~ his arrival**); *gehörig* zu, *beschäftigt bei* (**be ~ a committee** e-m Ausschuss angehören; **be ~ the "Daily Mail"** bei der „Daily Mail" be-schäftigt sein); *state*: in (*dat*), auf (*dat*) (**~ duty** im Dienst; **be ~** *fire* in Flam-men stehen); *subject*: über (*acc*) (**talk ~ a subject** über ein Thema sprechen); nach (*dat*) (**~ this model** nach diesem Modell); von (*dat*) (**live ~ s.th.** von et. leben); **~ the street** auf der Straße; **~ a train** in e-m Zug; **~ hearing it** als ich *etc* es hörte; **have you any money ~ you?** hast du Geld bei dir?; **2.** *adj and adv* an (geschaltet) (*light etc*), eingeschaltet (*radio etc*), auf (*faucet etc*); (dar)auf(le-legen, -schrauben *etc*); an(haben, -zie-hen) (**have a coat ~** e-n Mantel anha-ben); auf(*behalten*) (**keep one's hat ~** den Hut aufbehalten); weiter(*gehen, -sprechen etc*); **and so ~** und so weiter; **~ and ~** immer weiter; **from this day ~** von dem Tage an; **be ~** THEA gegeben werden; *film*: laufen; *radio*, TV gesen-det werden; **what's ~?** was ist los?

once 1. einmal; einst; **~ again**, **~ more** noch einmal; **~ in a while** ab und zu, hin und wieder; **~ and for all** ein für alle Mal; **not ~** kein einziges Mal, kein-mal; **at ~** sofort; auf einmal, gleichzei-tig; **all at ~** plötzlich; **for ~** diesmal, aus-nahmsweise; **this ~** dieses eine Mal; **~ upon a time there was ...** es war ein-mal ...; **2.** sobald

one ein(e); einzig; man; Eins *f*, eins; **~'s** sein(e); **~ day** eines Tages; **~ Smith** ein gewisser Smith; **~ another** sich (gegenseitig), einander; **~ by ~, ~ after another, ~ after the other** e-r nach dem andern; **I for ~** ich zum Beispiel; **the little ~s** die Kleinen pl

one-horse town F contp Nest n

one·self sich (selbst); sich selbst; **(all) by ~** ganz allein; **to ~** ganz für sich (allein)

one-sid·ed einseitig

one-time ehemalig, früher

one-track mind: have a ~ immer nur dasselbe im Kopf haben

one-two soccer: Doppelpass m

one-way Einbahn...; **~ street** Einbahnstraße f; **~ tick·et** RAIL etc einfache Fahrkarte, AVIAT einfaches Ticket; **~ traf·fic** MOT Einbahnverkehr m

on·ion BOT Zwiebel f

on·line EDP online, Online..., rechnerabhängig

on·look·er Zuschauer(in)

on·ly 1. adj einzige(r, -s); **2.** adv nur, bloß; erst; **~ yesterday** erst gestern; **3.** cj F nur, bloß

on·rush Ansturm m

on·set Beginn m; MED Ausbruch m

on·slaught (heftiger) Angriff (a. fig)

on·to auf (acc)

on·ward(s) adv vorwärts, weiter; **from now ~** von nun an

ooze v/i sickern; **~ away** fig schwinden; v/t absondern; fig ausstrahlen, verströmen

o·paque undurchsichtig; fig unverständlich

o·pen 1. offen, a. geöffnet, a. frei (country etc); öffentlich; fig offen, a. unentschieden, a. freimütig; fig zugänglich, aufgeschlossen (**to** für or dat); **~ all day** durchgehend geöffnet; **in the ~ air** im Freien; **2.** golf, tennis: offenes Turnier; **in the ~** im Freien; **come out into the ~** fig an die Öffentlichkeit treten; **3.** v/t öffnen, aufmachen, Buch etc a. aufschlagen; eröffnen; v/i sich öffnen, aufgehen; öffnen, aufmachen (store); anfangen, beginnen; **~ into** führen nach or in (acc); **~ onto** hinausgehen auf (acc)

o·pen-air im Freien

o·pen-end·ed zeitlich unbegrenzt

o·pen·er (Dosen- etc)Öffner m

o·pen-eyed mit großen Augen, staunend

o·pen-hand·ed freigebig, großzügig

o·pen-heart·ed offenherzig

o·pen·ing 1. Öffnung f; ECON freie Stelle; Eröffnung f, Erschließung f, Einstieg m; **2.** Eröffnungs...; Öffnungs...

o·pen-mind·ed aufgeschlossen

o·pen·ness Offenheit f

op·e·ra Oper f; **~ glass·es** Opernglas n; **~ house** Opernhaus n, Oper f

op·e·rate v/i wirksam sein or werden; TECH arbeiten, in Betrieb sein, laufen (machine etc); MED operieren (**on s.o.** j-n); v/t Maschine bedienen, Schalter etc betätigen; Unternehmen, Geschäft betreiben, führen

op·e·rat·ing| room MED Operationssaal m; **~ sys·tem** EDP Betriebssystem n; **~ thea·tre** Br MED Operationssaal m

op·e·ra·tion TECH Betrieb m, Lauf m; Bedienung f; ECON Tätigkeit f, Unternehmen n; MED, MIL Operation f; **in ~** TECH in Betrieb; **have an ~** MED operiert werden

op·e·ra·tive wirksam; MED operativ

op·e·ra·tor TECH Bedienungsperson f; EDP Operator m; TEL Vermittlung f

o·pin·ion Meinung f, Ansicht f; Gutachten n (**on** über acc); **in my ~** meines Erachtens

op·po·nent Gegner(in)

op·por·tune günstig, passend; rechtzeitig

op·por·tu·ni·ty (günstige) Gelegenheit

op·pose sich widersetzen (dat)

op·posed entgegengesetzt; **be ~ to** gegen ... sein

op·po·site 1. Gegenteil n, Gegensatz m; **2.** adj gegenüberliegend; entgegengesetzt; **3.** adv gegenüber (**to** dat); **4.** prp gegenüber (dat)

op·po·si·tion Widerstand m, Opposition f (a. PARL); Gegensatz m

op·press unterdrücken

op·pres·sion Unterdrückung f

op·pres·sive (be)drückend; hart, grausam; schwül (weather)

op·tic Augen..., Seh...; → **op·ti·cal** optisch; **op·ti·cian** Optiker(in)

op·ti·mism Optimismus m

op·ti·mist Optimist(in)

op·ti·mis·tic optimistisch

op·tion Wahl f; ECON Option f, Vorkaufsrecht n; MOT Extra n

op·tion·al freiwillig; Wahl...; **be an ~ ex-**

tra MOT gegen Aufpreis erhältlich sein; **~ sub·ject** PED *etc* Wahlfach *n*

or oder; **~ else** sonst

o·ral mündlich; Mund...

or·ange 1. BOT Orange *f*, Apfelsine *f*; **2.** orange(farben)

or·ange·ade Orangenlimonade *f*

o·ra·tion Rede *f*, Ansprache *f*

or·a·tor Redner(in)

or·bit 1. Kreisbahn *f*, Umlaufbahn *f*; **get** *or* **put into** ~ in e-e Umlaufbahn gelangen *or* bringen; **2.** *v/t die Erde etc* umkreisen; *v/i die Erde etc* umkreisen, sich auf e-r Umlaufbahn bewegen

or·chard Obstgarten *m*

or·ches·tra MUS Orchester *n*; THEA Parkett *n*

or·chid BOT Orchidee *f*

or·dain: ~ **s.o.** (**priest**) j-n zum Priester weihen

or·deal Qual *f*, Tortur *f*

or·der 1. Ordnung *f*; Reihenfolge *f*; Befehl *m*, Anordnung *f*; ECON Bestellung *f*, Auftrag *m*; PARL *etc* (Geschäfts)Ordnung *f*; REL *etc* Orden *m*; **to pay** ECON Zahlungsanweisung *f*; **in ~ to** *inf* um zu *inf*; **out of ~** TECH nicht in Ordnung, defekt; außer Betrieb; **make to ~** auf Bestellung *or* nach Maß anfertigen; **2.** *v/t j-m* befehlen (**to do** zu tun), *et.* befehlen, anordnen; *j-n* schicken, beordern; MED *j-m et.* verordnen; ECON bestellen; *fig* ordnen, in Ordnung bringen; *v/i* bestellen (*in restaurant*)

or·der·ly 1. ordentlich; *fig* gesittet, friedlich; **2.** MED Hilfspfleger *m*

or·di·nal *a.* ~ **number** MATH Ordnungszahl *f*

or·di·nary üblich, gewöhnlich, normal

ore MIN Erz *n*

or·gan ANAT Organ *n* (*a. fig*); MUS Orgel *f*; **~ do·nor** MED Organspender *m*; **~ grind·er** Leierkastenmann *m*; **~ recip·i·ent** MED Organempfänger *m*

or·gan·ic organisch

or·gan·ism Organismus *m*

or·gan·i·za·tion Organisation *f*

or·gan·ize organisieren; sich (gewerkschaftlich) organisieren

or·gan·iz·er Organisator(in)

or·gasm Orgasmus *m*

o·ri·ent 1. Orient der Osten, der Orient, das Morgenland; **2.** orientieren

o·ri·en·tal 1. orientalisch, östlich; **2. Ori-**

ental Orientale *m*, Orientalin *f*

o·ri·en·tate orientieren

or·i·gin Ursprung *m*, Abstammung *f*, Herkunft *f*

o·rig·i·nal 1. ursprünglich; Original...; originell; **2.** Original *n*

o·rig·i·nal·i·ty Originalität *f*

o·rig·i·nal·ly ursprünglich; originell

o·rig·i·nate *v/t* schaffen, ins Leben rufen; *v/i* zurückgehen (**from** auf *acc*), (her)stammen (**from** von, aus)

or·na·ment 1. Ornament (*a pl*) *n*, Verzierung(en *pl*) *f*, Schmuck *m*; *fig* Zier(de) *f* (**to** für *or* gen); **2.** verzieren, schmücken (**with** mit)

or·na·men·tal dekorativ, schmückend, Zier...

or·nate *fig* überladen

or·phan 1. Waise *f*, Waisenkind *n*; **2. be ~ed** Waise werden

or·phan·age Waisenhaus *n*

or·tho·dox orthodox

os·cil·late PHYS schwingen; *fig* schwanken (**between** zwischen *dat*)

os·prey ZO Fischadler *m*

os·ten·si·ble angeblich, vorgeblich

os·ten·ta·tion (protzige) Zurschaustellung; Protzerei *f*, Prahlerei *f*

os·ten·ta·tious protzend, prahlerisch

os·tra·cize ächten

os·trich ZO Strauß *m*

oth·er andere(r, -s); **the ~ day** neulich; **the ~ morning** neulich morgens; **every ~ day** jeden zweiten Tag, alle zwei Tage

oth·er·wise anders; sonst

ot·ter ZO Otter *m*

ought *v/aux* ich sollte, *du* solltest *etc*; **you ~ to have done it** Sie hätten es tun sollen

ounce Unze *f* (*28,35 g*)

our unser

ours unsere(r, -s)

our·selves wir *or* uns selbst; uns (selbst)

oust verdrängen, hinauswerfen (**from** aus); *j-n s-s Amtes* entheben

out 1. *adv, adj* aus; hinaus(*gehen, -werfen etc*); heraus(*kommen etc*); aus(*brechen etc*); draußen, im Freien; nicht zu Hause; SPORT aus, draußen; aus, vorbei; aus, erloschen; ausverkauft; F out, aus der Mode; **~ of** aus (... heraus); zu ... hinaus; außerhalb von (*or* gen); außer Reichweite *etc*; außer Atem, Übung *etc*; (hergestellt) aus; aus *Furcht etc*; *be ~ of bread* kein Brot mehr haben; *in nine ~ of ten cases* in neun von zehn Fällen; **2.** *prp* F aus (... heraus); zu ... hinaus; **3.** outen

out·bal·ance überwiegen
out·bid überbieten
out·board mo·tor Außenbordmotor *m*
out·break MED, MIL Ausbruch *m*
out·build·ing Nebengebäude *n*
out·burst fig Ausbruch *m*
out·cast 1. ausgestoßen; **2.** Ausgestoßene *m, f*, Verstoßene *m, f*
out·come Ergebnis *n*
out·cry Aufschrei *m*, Schrei *m* der Entrüstung
out·dat·ed überholt, veraltet
out·dis·tance hinter sich lassen
out·do übertreffen
out·door *adj* im Freien, draußen
out·doors *adv* draußen, im Freien
out·er äußere(r, -s)
out·er·most äußerste(r, -s)
out·er space Weltraum *m*
out·fit Ausrüstung *f*, Ausstattung *f*; Kleidung *f*; F (Arbeits)Gruppe *f*
out·fit·ter Ausstatter *m*; *men's ~* Herrenausstatter *m*
out·go·ing (aus dem Amt) scheidend
out·grow herauswachsen aus (*dat*); *Angewohnheit etc* ablegen; größer werden als
out·house Nebengebäude *n*
out·ing Ausflug *m*; Outing *n*
out·land·ish befremdlich, sonderbar
out·last überdauern, überleben
out·law HIST Geächtete *m, f*
out·lay (Geld)Auslagen *pl*, Ausgaben *pl*
out·let Abfluss *m*, Abzug *m*; fig Ventil *n*
out·line 1. Umriss *m*; Überblick *m*; **2.** umreißen, skizzieren
out·live überleben
out·look (Aus)Blick *m*, (Aus)Sicht *f*; Einstellung *f*, Auffassung *f*
out·ly·ing abgelegen, entlegen
out·num·ber in der Überzahl sein; *be ~ed by s.o.* j-m zahlenmäßig unterlegen sein
out-of-date veraltet, überholt
out-of-the-way abgelegen, entlegen; fig ungewöhnlich
out·pa·tient MED ambulanter Patient, ambulante Patientin

out·post Vorposten *m*
out·pour·ing (Gefühls)Erguss *m*
out·put ECON Output *m*, Produktion *f*, Ausstoß *m*, Ertrag *m*; EDP (Daten-)Ausgabe *f*
out·rage 1. Gewalttat *f*, Verbrechen *n*; Empörung *f*; **2.** grob verletzen; *j-n* empören; **out·ra·geous** abscheulich; empörend, unerhört
out·right 1. *adj* völlig, gänzlich, glatt (*lie etc*); **2.** *adv* auf der Stelle, sofort; ohne Umschweife
out·run schneller laufen als; fig übersteigen, übertreffen
out·set Anfang *m*, Beginn *m*
out·shine überstrahlen, fig a. in den Schatten stellen
out·side 1. Außenseite *f*; SPORT Außenstürmer(in); *at the (very) ~* (aller-)höchstens; *~ left (right)* SPORT Linksaußen (Rechtsaußen) *m*; **2.** *adj* äußere(r, -s), Außen...; **3.** *adv* draußen; heraus, hinaus; **4.** *prp* außerhalb
out·sid·er Außenseiter(in)
out·size 1. Übergröße *f*; **2.** übergroß
out·skirts Stadtrand *m*, Außenbezirke *pl*
out·spo·ken offen, freimütig
out·spread ausgestreckt, ausgebreitet
out·stand·ing hervorragend; ECON ausstehend; ungeklärt (*problem*); unerledigt (*work*)
out·stay länger bleiben als; → *welcome* 4
out·stretched ausgestreckt
out·strip überholen; fig übertreffen
out tray: *in the ~* im Postausgang *etc*
out·vote überstimmen
out·ward 1. äußere(r, -s); äußerlich; **2.** *adv mst* **outwards** auswärts, nach außen; **out·ward·ly** äußerlich
out·weigh fig überwiegen
out·wit überlisten, F reinlegen
out·worn veraltet, überholt
o·val 1. oval; **2.** Oval *n*
o·va·tion Ovation *f*; *give s.o. a standing ~* j-m stehende Ovationen bereiten, j-m stehend Beifall klatschen
ov·en Backofen *m*, Bratofen *m*
ov·en-read·y bratfertig
o·ver 1. *prp* über; über (*acc*), über (*acc*) ... (hin)weg; über (*dat*), auf der anderen Seite von (*or gen*); über (*acc*), mehr als; **2.** *adv* hinüber, herüber (*to* zu); drü-

ben; darüber, mehr; zu Ende, vorüber, vorbei; über..., um...: *et.* über(*geben etc*); über(*kochen etc*); um(*fallen, -werfen etc*); herum(*drehen etc*); von Anfang bis Ende, durch(*lesen etc*); (gründlich) über(*legen etc*); (*all*) **~** *again* noch einmal; *all* **~** ganz vorbei; **~** *and* (*again*) immer wieder; **~** *and above* obendrein, überdies

o·ver·age zu alt

o·ver·all **1.** gesamt, Gesamt...; allgemein; insgesamt; **2.** *Br* Arbeitsmantel *m*, Kittel *m*; (*Br* **~s**) Overall *m*, Arbeitsanzug *m*; Arbeitshose *f*

o·ver·awe einschüchtern

o·ver·bal·ance umstoßen, umkippen; das Gleichgewicht verlieren

o·ver·bear·ing anmaßend

o·ver·board MAR über Bord

o·ver·bur·den *fig* überladen

o·ver·cast bewölkt, bedeckt

o·ver·charge überlasten, ELECTR *a.* überladen; ECON *j-m* zu viel berechnen; *Betrag* zu viel verlangen

o·ver·coat Mantel *m*

o·ver·come überwinden, überwältigen; *be* **~** *with emotion* von s-n Gefühlen übermannt werden

o·ver·crowd·ed überfüllt; überlaufen

o·ver·do übertreiben; GASTR zu lange kochen *or* braten; *overdone a.* übergar

o·ver·dose Überdosis *f*

o·ver·draft ECON (Konto)Überziehung *f*; *a.* **~** *facility* ECON Überziehungskredit *m*

o·ver·draw ECON *Konto* überziehen (*by um*)

o·ver·dress (sich) zu fein anziehen; **~**ed overdressed, zu fein angezogen

o·ver·drive MOT Overdrive *m*, Schongang *m*

o·ver·due überfällig

o·ver·eat zu viel essen

o·ver·es·ti·mate zu hoch schätzen *or* veranschlagen; *fig* überschätzen

o·ver·ex·pose PHOT überbelichten

o·ver·feed überfüttern

o·ver·flow **1.** *v/t* überfluten, überschwemmen; *v/i* überlaufen, überfließen, überquellen (*with* von); **2.** TECH Überlauf *m*; Überlaufen *n*, -fließen *n*

o·ver·grown BOT überwachsen, überwuchert

o·ver·hang *v/t* über (*dat*) hängen; *v/i* überhängen

o·ver·haul *Maschine* überholen

o·ver·head **1.** *adv* oben, droben; **2.** *adj* Hoch..., Ober...; ECON **~** *expenses or costs* Gemeinkosten *pl*; SPORT Überkopf...; **~** *kick* soccer: Fallrückzieher *m*; **3.** ECON *esp Br a. pl* Gemeinkosten *pl*

o·ver·hear (zufällig) hören

o·ver·heat·ed überhitzt, überheizt; TECH heißgelaufen

o·ver·joyed überglücklich

o·ver·lap (sich) überlappen; sich überschneiden

o·ver·leaf umseitig, umstehend

o·ver·load überlasten (*a.* ELECTR), überladen

o·ver·look übersehen; **~** *ing the sea* mit Blick aufs Meer

o·ver·night **1.** über Nacht; *stay* **~** über Nacht bleiben, übernachten; **2.** Nacht..., Übernachtungs...; **~** *bag* Reisetasche *f*

o·ver·pass (Straßen-, Eisenbahn-) Überführung *f*

o·ver·pay zu viel (be)zahlen

o·ver·pop·u·lat·ed übervölkert

o·ver·pow·er überwältigen; **~**ing *fig* überwältigend

o·ver·rate überbewerten, überschätzen

o·ver·reach: **~** *o.s.* sich übernehmen

o·ver·re·act überreagieren, überzogen reagieren (*to* auf *acc*)

o·ver·re·ac·tion Überreaktion *f*, überzogene Reaktion

o·ver·ride sich hinwegsetzen über (*acc*)

o·ver·rule *Entscheidung etc* aufheben, *Einspruch etc* abweisen

o·ver·run länger dauern als vorgesehen; *Signal* überfahren; *be* **~** *with* wimmeln von

o·ver·seas **1.** *adj* überseeisch, Übersee...; **2.** *adv* in *or* nach Übersee

o·ver·see beaufsichtigen, überwachen

o·ver·shad·ow *fig* überschatten, in den Schatten stellen

o·ver·sight Versehen *n*

o·ver·size(d) übergroß, überdimensional, in Übergröße(n)

o·ver·sleep verschlafen

o·ver·staffed (personell) übersetzt

o·ver·state übertreiben

o·ver·state·ment Übertreibung f
o·ver·stay länger bleiben als; → **wel-come** 4
o·ver·step fig überschreiten
o·ver·take überholen; j-n überraschen
o·ver·tax zu hoch besteuern; fig überbe-anspruchen, überfordern
o·ver·throw 1. Regierung etc stürzen; 2. (Um)Sturz m
o·ver·time ECON Überstunden pl; SPORT (Spiel)Verlängerung f; **be on ~**, **do ~**, **work ~** Überstunden machen
o·ver·tired übermüdet
o·ver·ture MUS Ouvertüre f; Vorspiel n
o·ver·turn v/t umwerfen, umstoßen; Regierung etc stürzen; v/i umkippen, MAR kentern
o·ver·view fig Überblick m (of über acc)
o·ver·weight 1. Übergewicht n; 2. übergewichtig (person), zu schwer (by um); **be five pounds ~** fünf Pfund Übergewicht haben
o·ver·whelm überwältigen (a. fig)
o·ver·whelm·ing überwältigend
o·ver·work sich überarbeiten; überanstrengen

o·ver·wrought überreizt
o·ver·zeal·ous übereifrig
owe j-m et. schulden, schuldig sein; et. verdanken
ow·ing: **~ to** infolge, wegen
owl ZO Eule f
own 1. eigen; **my ~** mein Eigentum; (all) **on one's ~** allein; 2. besitzen; zugeben, (ein)gestehen
own·er Eigentümer(in), Besitzer(in)
own·er-oc·cu·pied esp Br eigengenutzt; **~ flat** Eigentumswohnung f
own·er·ship Besitz m; Eigentum n; Eigentumsrecht n
ox ZO Ochse m
ox·ide CHEM Oxid n, Oxyd n
ox·i·dize CHEM oxidieren
ox·y·gen CHEM Sauerstoff m; **~ ap·pa·ra·tus** MED Sauerstoffgerät n; **~ tent** MED Sauerstoffzelt n
oy·ster ZO Auster f
o·zone CHEM Ozon n
o·zone-friend·ly FCKW-frei, ohne Treibgas
o·zone| hole Ozonloch n; **~ lay·er** Ozonschicht f; **~ lev·els** Ozonwerte pl; **~ shield** Ozonschild m

P

P, p P, p n
pace 1. Tempo n, Geschwindigkeit f; Schritt m; Gangart f (of a horse); 2. v/t Zimmer etc durchschreiten; a. **~ out** abschreiten; v/i (einher)schreiten; **~ up and down** auf und ab gehen
pace·mak·er SPORT Schrittmacher(in); MED Herzschrittmacher m
pace·set·ter SPORT Schrittmacher(in)
Pa·cif·ic a. **~ Ocean** der Pazifik, der Pazifische or Stille Ozean
pac·i·fi·er Schnuller m
pac·i·fist Pazifist(in)
pac·i·fy beruhigen, besänftigen
pack 1. Pack(en) m, Paket n, Bündel n; Packung f, Schachtel f; ZO Meute f; Rudel n; contp Pack n, Bande f; MED etc Packung f; (Karten)Spiel n; **a ~ of lies** ein Haufen Lügen; 2. v/t ein-, zusammenpacken, abpacken, verpacken

(a. **~ up**); zusammenpferchen; voll stopfen; Koffer etc packen; **~ off** F fort-, wegschicken; v/i packen; (sich) drängen (**into** in acc); **~ up** zusammenpacken; **send s.o. ~ing** j-n fort- or wegjagen
pack·age Paket n; Packung f; **software ~** EDP Software-, Programmpaket n
pack·age| deal F Pauschalangebot n, -arrangement n; **~ hol·i·day** Br Pauschalurlaub m; **~ tour** Pauschalreise f
pack·et Päckchen n; Packung f, Schachtel f
pack·ing Packen n; Verpackung f
pact Pakt m, POL a. Vertrag m
pad 1. Polster n (Knie- etc)Schützer m; (Schreib- etc)Block m; (Stempel)Kissen n; ZO Ballen m; (Abschuss-)Rampe f; 2. (aus)polstern, wattieren
pad·ding Polsterung f, Wattierung f

pad·dle 1. Paddel n; MAR (Rad)Schaufel f; **2.** paddeln; plan(t)schen

pad·dock (Pferde)Koppel f

pad·lock Vorhängeschloss n

pa·gan 1. Heide m, Heidin f; **2.** heidnisch

page¹ **1.** Seite f; **2.** paginieren

page² **1.** (Hotel)Page m; **2.** j-n ausrufen (lassen)

pag·eant (a. historischer) Festzug

pa·gin·ate paginieren

pail Eimer m, Kübel m

pain 1. Schmerz(en pl) m; Kummer m; pl Mühe f, Bemühungen pl; **be in (great)** ~ (große) Schmerzen haben; **be a** ~ **(in the neck)** F e-m auf den Wecker gehen; **take** ~**s** sich Mühe geben; **2.** esp fig schmerzen; **pain·ful** schmerzhaft, schmerzend; fig schmerzlich; peinlich

pain·kill·er Schmerzmittel n

pain·less schmerzlos

pains·tak·ing sorgfältig, gewissenhaft

paint 1. Farbe f; Anstrich m; **2.** v/t anmalen, bemalen; (an)streichen; Auto etc lackieren; v/i malen

paint·box Malkasten m

paint·brush (Maler)Pinsel m

paint·er (a. Kunst)Maler(in), Anstreicher(in)

paint·ing Malerei f; Gemälde n, Bild n

pair 1. Paar n; **a** ~ **of** ... ein Paar ..., ein(e) ...; **a** ~ **of scissors** e-e Schere; **2.** v/i ZO sich paaren; a. ~ **off,** ~ **up** Paare bilden; v/t a. ~ **off,** ~ **up** paarweise anordnen; ~ **off** zwei Leute zusammenbringen, verkuppeln

pa·ja·ma(s) (a pair of) ~ (ein) Schlafanzug m, (ein) Pyjama m

pal Kamerad m, F Kumpel m, Spezi m

pal·ace Palast m, Schloss n

pal·a·ta·ble schmackhaft (a. fig)

pal·ate ANAT Gaumen m; fig Geschmack m

pale¹ **1.** blass, a. bleich, a. hell (color); **2.** blass or bleich werden

pale² Pfahl m; fig Grenzen pl

pale·ness Blässe f

Pal·es·tin·i·an 1. palästinensisch; **2.** Palästinenser(in)

pal·ings Lattenzaun m

pal·i·sade Palisade f; pl Steilufer n

pal·let TECH Palette f

pal·lid blass; **pal·lor** Blässe f

palm¹ a. ~ **tree** BOT Palme f

palm² **1.** ANAT Handfläche f; **2.** et. in der Hand verschwinden lassen; ~ **s.th. off on s.o.** F j-m et. andrehen

pal·pa·ble fühlbar, greifbar

pal·pi·tate MED klopfen, pochen

pal·pi·ta·tions MED Herzklopfen n

pal·sy MED Lähmung f

pal·try armselig

pam·per verwöhnen

pam·phlet Broschüre f

pan Pfanne f; Topf m

pan·a·ce·a Allheilmittel n

pan·cake Pfannkuchen m

pan·da ZO Panda m

pan·da car Br (Funk)Streifenwagen m

pan·de·mo·ni·um Hölle f, Höllenlärm m, Tumult m, Chaos n

pan·der Vorschub leisten (**to** dat)

pane (Fenster)Scheibe f

pan·el 1. (Tür)Füllung f, (Wand)Täfelung f; ELECTR, TECH Instrumentenbrett n, (Schalt-, Kontroll- etc)Tafel f; JUR Liste f der Geschworenen; Diskussionsteilnehmer pl, Diskussionsrunde f; Rateteam n; **2.** täfeln

pang stechender Schmerz; ~**s of hunger** nagender Hunger; ~**s of conscience** Gewissensbisse pl

pan·han·dle 1. Pfannenstiel m; GEOGR schmaler Fortsatz; **2.** F betteln

pan·ic 1. panisch; **2.** Panik f; **3.** in Panik versetzen or geraten

pan·ick·y: F **be** ~ in Panik sein

pan·ic-strick·en von Panik erfasst or erfüllt

pan·o·ra·ma Panorama n, Ausblick m

pan·sy BOT Stiefmütterchen n

pant keuchen, schnaufen, nach Luft schnappen

pan·ther ZO Panther m; Puma m; Jaguar m

pan·ties (Damen)Schlüpfer m, Slip m; Höschen n

pan·to·mime THEA Pantomime f; Br F Weihnachtsspiel n

pan·try Speisekammer f

pants Hose f; Br Unterhose f; Br Schlüpfer m

pant·suit Hosenanzug m

pan·ty·hose Strumpfhose f

pan·ty·lin·er Slipeinlage f

pap Brei m

pa·pal päpstlich

pa·per 1. Papier *n*; Zeitung *f*; (Prüfungs)Arbeit *f*; UNIV Klausur(arbeit) *f*; Aufsatz *m*; Referat *n*; Tapete *f*; *pl* (Ausweis)Papiere *pl*; **2.** tapezieren

pa·per·back Taschenbuch *n*, Paperback *n*

pa·per bag (Papier)Tüte *f*

pa·per·boy Zeitungsjunge *m*

pa·per clip Büro-, Heftklammer *f*

pa·per cup Pappbecher *m*

pa·per·hang·er Tapezierer *m*

pa·per knife *Br* Brieföffner *m*

pa·per mon·ey Papiergeld *n*

pa·per·weight Briefbeschwerer *m*

par: at ~ zum Nennwert; **be on a ~ with** gleich *or* ebenbürtig sein (*dat*)

par·a·ble Parabel *f*, Gleichnis *n*

par·a·chute Fallschirm *m*

par·a·chut·ist Fallschirmspringer(in)

pa·rade 1. Umzug *m*, *esp* MIL Parade *f*, *fig* Zurschaustellung *f*; **make a ~ of** *fig* zur Schau stellen; **2.** ziehen (**through** durch); MIL antreten (lassen), vorbeimarschieren (lassen); zur Schau stellen; **~ (through)** stolzieren durch

par·a·dise Paradies *n*

par·af·fin *Br* Petroleum *n*

par·a·glid·er SPORT Gleitschirm *m*; Gleitschirmflieger(in); **par·a·glid·ing** SPORT Gleitschirmfliegen *n*

par·a·gon Muster *n* (**of** an *dat*)

par·a·graph Absatz *m*, Abschnitt *m*; (Zeitungs)Notiz *f*

par·al·lel 1. parallel (**to, with** zu); **2.** MATH Parallele *f* (*a. fig*); **without ~** ohne Parallele, ohnegleichen; **3.** entsprechen (*dat*), gleichkommen (*dat*)

par·a·lyse *Br*, **par·a·lyze** MED lähmen, *fig a.* lahm legen, zum Erliegen bringen; **~d with** *fig* starr *or* wie gelähmt vor (*dat*)

pa·ral·y·sis MED Lähmung *f*, *fig a.* Lahmlegung *f*

par·a·med·ic MED Sanitäter *m*

par·a·mount größte(r, -s), übergeordnet; **~ importance** von (aller)größter Bedeutung *or* Wichtigkeit

par·a·pet Brüstung *f*

par·a·pher·na·li·a (persönliche) Sachen *pl*; Ausrüstung *f*; *esp Br* F Scherereien *pl*

par·a·phrase 1. umschreiben; **2.** Umschreibung *f*

par·a·site Parasit *m*, Schmarotzer *m*

par·a·troop·er MIL Fallschirmjäger *m*; *pl* Fallschirmjägertruppe *f*

par·boil halb gar kochen, ankochen

par·cel 1. Paket *n*; Parzelle *f*; **2. ~ out** aufteilen; **~ up** (als Paket) verpacken

parch ausdörren, austrocknen; vertrocknen

parch·ment Pergament *n*

par·don 1. JUR Begnadigung *f*; **I beg your ~** Entschuldigung!, Verzeihung!; erlauben Sie mal!, ich muss doch sehr bitten!; *a.* **~?** F (wie) bitte?; **2.** verzeihen; vergeben; JUR begnadigen; **~ me → I beg your pardon**; F (wie) bitte?

par·don·a·ble verzeihlich

pare sich *die Nägel* schneiden; *Apfel etc* schälen

par·ent Elternteil *m*, Vater *m*, Mutter *f*; *pl* Eltern *pl*; **par·ent·age** Abstammung *f*, Herkunft *f*; **pa·ren·tal** elterlich

pa·ren·the·ses (runde) Klammer

par·ents-in-law Schwiegereltern *pl*

par·ent-teach·er meet·ing PED Elternabend *m*

par·ings Schalen *pl*

par·ish REL Gemeinde *f*

par·ish church REL Pfarrkirche *f*

pa·rish·ion·er REL Gemeindemitglied *n*

park 1. Park *m*, (Grün)Anlage(n *pl*) *f*; **2.** MOT parken; **look for somewhere to ~ the car** e-n Parkplatz suchen

par·ka Parka *m*, *f*

park·ing MOT Parken *n*; **no ~** Parkverbot, Parken verboten; **~ disk** Parkscheibe *f*; **~ fee** Parkgebühr *f*; **~ garage** Park(hoch)haus *n*; **~ lot** Parkplatz *m*; **~ lot at·tend·ant** Parkplatzwächter *m*; **~ me·ter** Parkuhr *f*; **~ of·fend·er** Parksünder (in); **~ space** Parkplatz *m*, Parklücke *f*; **~ tick·et** Strafzettel *m*

par·ley *esp* MIL Verhandlung *f*

par·lia·ment Parlament *n*

par·lia·men·tar·i·an Parlamentarier(in)

par·lia·men·ta·ry parlamentarisch, Parlaments...

par·lo(u)r *mst in cpds* Salon *m*

pa·ro·chi·al REL Pfarr..., Gemeinde...; *fig* engstirnig, beschränkt

par·o·dy 1. Parodie *f*; **2.** parodieren

pa·role JUR **1.** Hafturlaub *m*; bedingte Haftentlassung; **he is out on ~** er hat Hafturlaub; er wurde bedingt entlassen; **2. ~ s.o.** j-m Hafturlaub gewähren; j-n bedingt entlassen

par·quet Parkett n (a. THEA)

par·quet floor Parkett(fuß)boden m

par·rot 1. ZO Papagei m (a. fig); **2.** et. (wie ein Papagei) nachplappern

par·ry abwehren, parieren

par·si·mo·ni·ous geizig

pars·ley BOT Petersilie f

par·son REL Pfarrer m

par·son·age REL Pfarrhaus n

part 1. Teil m; TECH Teil n, Bau-, Ersatzteil n; Anteil m; Seite f, Partei f; THEA, fig Rolle f; MUS Stimme f, Partie f; GEOGR Gegend f, Teil m; (Haar)Scheitel m; **for my ~** was mich betrifft; **for the most ~** größtenteils; meistens; **in ~** teilweise, zum Teil; **on the ~ of** vonseiten, seitens (gen); **on my ~** von m-r Seite; **take ~ in s.th.** an e-r Sache teilnehmen; **take s.th. in good ~** et. nicht übel nehmen; **2.** v/t trennen; (ab-, zer-) teilen; einteilen; Haar scheiteln; **~ company** sich trennen (**with** von); v/i sich trennen (**with** von); **3.** adj Teil...; **4.** adv: **~ ..., ~** teils ..., teils

par·tial Teil..., teilweise; parteiisch, voreingenommen (**to** für)

par·ti·al·i·ty Parteilichkeit f, Voreingenommenheit f; Schwäche f, besondere Vorliebe (**for** für)

par·tial·ly teilweise, zum Teil

par·tic·i·pant Teilnehmer(in)

par·tic·i·pate teilnehmen, sich beteiligen (**both: in** an dat)

par·tic·i·pa·tion Teilnahme f, Beteiligung f

par·ti·ci·ple LING Partizip n, Mittelwort n

par·ti·cle Teilchen n

par·tic·u·lar 1. besondere(r, -s), speziell; genau, eigen, wählerisch; **2.** Einzelheit f, pl nähere Umstände pl or Angaben pl; Personalien pl; **in ~** insbesondere; **par·tic·u·lar·ly** besonders

part·ing 1. Trennung f, Abschied m; esp Br (Haar)Scheitel m; **2.** Abschieds...

par·ti·san 1. Parteigänger(in), MIL Partisan(in); **2.** parteiisch

par·ti·tion 1. Teilung f; Trennwand f; **2. ~ off** abteilen, abtrennen

part·ly teilweise, zum Teil

part·ner Partner(in), ECON a. Teilhaber(in); **part·ner·ship** Partnerschaft f,

ECON a. Teilhaberschaft f

part-own·er Miteigentümer(in)

par·tridge ZO Rebhuhn n

part-time 1. adj Teilzeit..., Halbtags...; **~ worker → part-timer; 2.** adv halbtags

part-tim·er F Teilzeitbeschäftigte m, f, Halbtagskraft f

par·ty Partei f (a. POL); (Arbeits-, Reise-) Gruppe f; (Rettungs- etc)Mannschaft f; MIL Kommando n, Trupp m; Party f; Gesellschaft f; Teilnehmer(in), Beteiligte m, f; **~ line** POL Parteilinie f; **~ pol·i·tics** Parteipolitik f

pass v/i vorbeigehen, -fahren, -kommen, -ziehen etc (**by** an dat); übergehen (**to** auf acc), fallen (**to** an acc); vergehen (pain etc, time); durchkommen, (die Prüfung) bestehen; gelten (**as, for** als), gehalten werden (**as, for** für); PARL Rechtskraft erlangen; unbeanstandet bleiben; SPORT (den Ball) abspielen or passen (**to** zu); card game: passen (a. fig); **let s.o. ~** j-n vorbeilassen; **let s.th. ~** et. durchgehen lassen; v/t vorbeigehen, -fahren, -fließen, -kommen, -ziehen etc an (dat); überholen; Prüfung bestehen; Prüfling durchkommen lassen; (mit der Hand) streichen (**over** über acc); j-m et. reichen, geben, et. weitergeben; SPORT Ball abspielen, passen (**to** zu); Zeit verbringen; PARL Gesetz verabschieden; Urteil abgeben, fällen, JUR a. sprechen (**on** über acc); fig hinausgehen über (acc), übersteigen, übertreffen; **~ away** sterben; **~ off** j-n, et. ausgeben (**as** als); gut etc verlaufen; **~ out** ohnmächtig werden; **2.** Passierschein m; Bestehen n (examination); SPORT Pass m, Zuspiel n; (Gebirgs)Pass m; Durchgang m; **free ~** Frei(fahr)-karte f; **things have come to such a ~ that** F die Dinge haben sich derart zugespitzt, dass; **make a ~ at** F Annäherungsversuche machen bei

pass·a·ble passierbar, befahrbar; passabel, leidlich

pas·sage Passage f, Korridor m, Gang m; Durchgang m; (See-, Flug)Reise f; Durchfahrt f, Durchreise f; Passage f (a. MUS), Stelle f; **bird of ~** Zugvogel m

pass·book ECON Sparbuch n

pas·sen·ger Passagier m, Fahrgast m, Fluggast m, Reisende m, f, MOT Insasse m, Insassin f

P

pass·er·by Passant(in)
pas·sion Leidenschaft f; Wut f, Zorn m; **Passion** REL Passion f; **~s ran high** die Erregung schlug hohe Wellen
pas·sion·ate leidenschaftlich
pas·sive passiv; LING passivisch
Pass·o·ver REL Passah(fest) n
pass·port (Reise)Pass m
pass·word Kennwort n (a. EDP), MIL a. Parole f, Losung f
past 1. adj vergangen; frühere(r, -s); **be ~ a.** vorüber sein; **for some time ~** seit einiger Zeit; **~ tense** LING Vergangenheit f, Präteritum n; **2.** adv vorüber, vorbei; **go ~** vorbeigehen; **3.** prp time: nach; über (acc); über ... (acc) hinaus; an ... (dat) vorbei; **half ~ two** halb drei; **~ hope** hoffnungslos; **4.** Vergangenheit f (a. LING)
pas·ta Teigwaren pl
paste 1. Paste f; Kleister m; Teig m; **2.** kleben (**to**, **on** an acc); **~ up** ankleben
paste·board Karton m, Pappe f
pas·tel Pastell(zeichnung f) n
pas·teur·ize pasteurisieren
pas·time Zeitvertreib m, Freizeitbeschäftigung f
pas·tor REL Pastor m, Pfarrer m, Seelsorger m; **pas·tor·al** REL seelsorgerisch, pastoral; **~ care** Seelsorge f
pas·try GASTR (Blätter-, Mürbe)Teig m; Feingebäck n; **~ cook** Konditor m
pas·ture 1. Weide(land n) f; **2.** v/t weiden lassen; v/i grasen, weiden
pas·ty¹ esp Br GASTR (Fleisch)Pastete f
past·y² blass, F käsig
pat 1. Klaps m; GASTR Portion f; **2.** tätscheln; klopfen
patch 1. Fleck m; Flicken m; kleines Stück Land; **in ~es** stellenweise; **2.** flicken
pa·tent 1. offenkundig; patentiert; Patent...; **2.** Patent n; **take out a ~ for s.th.** (sich) et. patentieren lassen; **3.** et. patentieren lassen
pa·tent·ee Patentinhaber(in)
pa·tent leath·er Lackleder n
pa·ter·nal väterlich; väterlicherseits
pa·ter·ni·ty JUR Vaterschaft f
path Pfad m; Weg m
pa·thet·ic Mitleid erregend; kläglich, miserabel
pa·tience Geduld f; esp Br Patience f
pa·tient¹ geduldig
pa·tient² MED Patient(in)
pat·i·o Terrasse f; Innenhof m, Patio m
pat·ri·ot Patriot(in)
pat·ri·ot·ic patriotisch
pa·trol 1. Patrouille f (a. MIL), Streife f, Runde f; **on ~** auf Patrouille, auf Streife; **2.** abpatrouillieren, auf Streife sein in (dat), s-e Runde machen in (dat)
pa·trol car (Funk)Streifenwagen m
pa·trol·man Streifenpolizist m; Br motorisierter Pannenhelfer
pa·tron Schirmherr m; Gönner m, Förderer m; (Stamm)Kunde m; Stammgast m; **pat·ron·age** Schirmherrschaft f; Förderung f; **pat·ron·ess** Schirmherrin f; Gönnerin f, Förderin f; **patron·ize** fördern; (Stamm)Kunde or Stammgast sein bei or in (dat); gönnerhaft or herablassend behandeln
pa·tron saint REL Schutzheilige m, f
pat·ter prasseln (rain); trappeln (feet)
pat·tern 1. Muster n (a. fig); Schema n; **2.** bilden, formen (**after**, **on** nach)
paunch (dicker) Bauch
pau·per Arme m, f
pause 1. Pause f; **2.** innehalten, e-e Pause machen
pave pflastern; **~ the way for** fig den Weg ebnen für
pave·ment Fahrbahn f; Belag m, Pflaster n; Br Bürgersteig m, Gehsteig m
pave·ment ca·fé Br Straßencafé n
paw 1. ZO Pfote f, Tatze f; **2.** v/t Boden scharren; scharren an (dat); F betatschen; v/i scharren (**at** an dat)
pawn¹ chess: Bauer m; fig Schachfigur f
pawn² 1. verpfänden, versetzen; **2. be in ~** verpfändet or versetzt sein
pawn·bro·ker Pfandleiher m
pawn·shop Leihhaus n, Pfandhaus n
pay 1. v/t et. (be)zahlen; j-n bezahlen; Aufmerksamkeit schenken; Besuch abstatten; Kompliment machen; **~ attention** Acht geben auf (acc); PED aufpassen; **~ cash** bar bezahlen; v/i zahlen; fig sich lohnen; **~ for** (für) et. bezahlen; fig büßen; **~ in** einzahlen; **~ into** einzahlen auf (acc); **~ off** et. ab(be)zahlen; j-n auszahlen; **2.** Bezahlung f, Gehalt n, Lohn m
pay·a·ble zahlbar, fällig
pay·day Zahltag m
pay·ee Zahlungsempfänger(in)
pay en·ve·lope Lohntüte f

P

pay·ing lohnend

pay·mas·ter MIL Zahlmeister *m*

pay·ment (Be)Zahlung *f*

pay pack·et *Br* Lohntüte *f*

pay phone *Br* Münzfernsprecher *m*

pay·roll Lohnliste *f*

pay·slip Lohn-, Gehaltsstreifen *m*

PC ABBR *of personal computer* PC *m*, Personalcomputer *m*; *PC user* PC-Benutzer *m*

pea BOT Erbse *f*

peace Friede(n) *m*; Ruhe *f*; JUR öffentliche Ruhe und Ordnung; *at* ~ in Frieden

peace·a·ble friedlich, friedfertig

peace·ful friedlich

peace·lov·ing friedliebend

peace move·ment Friedensbewegung *f*

peace·time Friedenszeiten *pl*

peach BOT Pfirsich(baum) *m*

pea·cock ZO Pfau *m*, Pfauhahn *m*

pea·hen ZO Pfauhenne *f*

peak Spitze *f*, Gipfel *m*; Schirm *m*; *fig* Höhepunkt *m*, Höchststand *m*

peaked cap Schirmmütze *f*

peak hours Hauptverkehrszeit *f*, Stoßzeit *f*; ELECTR Hauptbelastungszeit *f*

peak| time, ~ viewing hours *Br* TV Haupteinschaltzeit *f*, Hauptsendezeit *f*, beste Sendezeit

peal (Glocken)Läuten *n*; (Donner-) Schlag *m*; *~s of laughter* schallendes Gelächter; 2. *a*. ~ *out* läuten; krachen

pea·nut BOT Erdnuss *f*; *pl* F lächerliche Summe

pear BOT Birne *f*; Birnbaum *m*

pearl 1. Perle *f*; Perlmutter *f*, Perlmutt *n*; 2. Perlen...

pearl·y perlenartig, Perlen...

peas·ant Kleinbauer *m*

peat Torf *m*

peb·ble Kiesel(stein) *m*

peck picken, hacken; ~ *at one's food* im Essen herumstochern

pe·cu·li·ar eigen, eigentümlich, typisch; eigenartig, seltsam

pe·cu·li·ar·i·ty Eigenheit *f*; Eigentümlichkeit *f*

ped·a·go·gic pädagogisch

ped·al 1. Pedal *n*; 2. das Pedal treten; (mit dem Rad) fahren, strampeln

pe·dan·tic pedantisch

ped·dle hausieren (gehen) mit; ~ *drugs* mit Drogen handeln

ped·dler Hausierer(in)

ped·es·tal Sockel *m*

pe·des·tri·an 1. Fußgänger(in); 2. Fußgänger...; ~ *cross·ing* Fußgängerübergang *m*; ~ *mall*, *esp Br* ~ *pre·cinct* Fußgängerzone *f*

ped·i·cure Pediküre *f*

ped·i·gree Stammbaum *m* (*a.* ZO)

ped·lar *Br* → *peddler*

pee F 1. pinkeln; 2. *have* (*or go for*) *a* ~ pinkeln (gehen)

peek 1. kurz *or* verstohlen gucken (*at* auf *acc*); 2. *have or take a* ~ *at* e-n kurzen *or* verstohlenen Blick werfen auf (*acc*)

peel 1. *v/t* schälen; *a*. ~ *off* abschälen, Folie, Tapete etc abziehen, ablösen; Kleid abstreifen; *v/i a*. ~ *off* sich lösen (*wallpaper etc*), abblättern (*paint etc*), sich schälen (*skin*); 2. BOT Schale *f*

peep[1] 1. kurz *or* verstohlen gucken (*at* auf *acc*); *mst* ~ *out* (her)vorschauen; 2. *take a* ~ *at* e-n kurzen *or* verstohlenen Blick werfen auf (*acc*)

peep[2] 1. Piep(s)en *n*; F Piepser *m*; 2. piep(s)en

peep·hole Guckloch *n*; (Tür)Spion *m*

peer angestrengt schauen, spähen; ~ *at s.o.* j-n anstarren

peer·less unvergleichlich, einzigartig

peev·ish verdrießlich, gereizt

peg 1. (Holz)Stift *m*, Zapfen *m*, Pflock *m*; (Kleider)Haken *m*; *Br* (Wäsche-) Klammer *f*; (Zelt)Hering *m*; *take s.o. down a* ~ (*or two*) F j-m e-n Dämpfer aufsetzen; 2. anpflocken; *Wäsche* anklammern, festklammern

pel·i·can ZO Pelikan *m*; ~ *cross·ing Br* Ampelübergang *m*

pel·let Kügelchen *n*; Schrotkorn *n*

pelt[1] *v/t* bewerfen, *v/i*: *it's* ~*ing* (*down*), *esp Br it's* ~*ing with rain* es gießt in Strömen

pelt[2] ZO Fell *n*, Pelz *m*

pel·vis ANAT Becken *n*

pen[1] (Schreib)Feder *f*; Füller *m*; Kugelschreiber *m*

pen[2] 1. Pferch *m*, (Schaf)Hürde *f*; 2. ~ *in*, ~ *up* Tiere einpferchen, *Personen* zusammenpferchen

pe·nal JUR Straf...; strafbar

pe·nal code JUR Strafgesetzbuch *n*

pe·nal·ize bestrafen

pen·al·ty Strafe *f*, SPORT *a.* Strafpunkt *m*; soccer: Elfmeter *m*; **~ ar·e·a**, **~ box** F soccer: Strafraum *m*; **~ goal** soccer: Elfmetertor *n*; **~ kick** soccer: Elfmeter *m*, Strafstoß *m*; **~ shoot-out** soccer: Elfmeterschießen *n*; **~ spot** soccer: Elfmeterpunkt *m*

pen·ance REL Buße *f*

pen·cil 1. Bleistift *m*; **2.** (mit Bleistift) markieren or schreiben or zeichnen; *Augenbrauen* nachziehen

pen·cil case Federmäppchen *n*

pen·cil sharp·en·er Bleistiftspitzer *m*

pen·dant, pen·dent (Schmuck)Anhänger *m*

pend·ing 1. *prp* bis zu; **2.** *adj esp* JUR schwebend

pen·du·lum Pendel *n*

pen·e·trate *v/t* eindringen in (*acc*); dringen durch, durchdringen; *v/i* eindringen (**into** in *acc*); **pen·e·trat·ing** durchdringend; *fig* scharf; scharfsinnig; **pen·e·tra·tion** Durchdringen *n*, Eindringen *n*; *fig* Scharfsinn *m*

pen friend *Br* Brieffreund(in)

pen·guin ZO Pinguin *m*

pen·in·su·la Halbinsel *f*

pe·nis ANAT Penis *m*

pen·i·tence Buße *f*, Reue *f*

pen·i·tent 1. reuig, bußfertig; **2.** REL Büßer(in)

pen·i·ten·tia·ry (Staats)Gefängnis *n*, Strafanstalt *f*

pen·knife Taschenmesser *n*

pen name Schriftstellername *m*, Pseudonym *n*

pen·nant Wimpel *m*

pen·ni·less (völlig) mittellos

pen·ny *a.* **new ~** *Br* Penny *m*

pen pal Brieffreund(in)

pen·sion 1. Rente *f*, Pension *f*; **2. ~ off** pensionieren, in den Ruhestand versetzen

pen·sion·er Rentner(in), Pensionär(in)

pen·sive nachdenklich

pen·tath·lete SPORT Fünfkämpfer(in)

pen·tath·lon SPORT Fünfkampf *m*

Pen·te·cost REL Pfingsten *n*

pent·house Penthouse *n*, Penthaus *n*

pent-up auf-, angestaut (*emotions*)

pe·o·ny BOT Pfingstrose *f*

peo·ple 1. Volk *n*, Nation *f*; die Menschen *pl*, die Leute *pl*; Leute *pl*, Personen *pl*; man; **the ~** das (*gemeine*) Volk; **2.** besiedeln, bevölkern (**with** mit)

peo·ple's re·pub·lic Volksrepublik *f*

pep 1. Pep *m*, Schwung *m*; **2.** *mst* **~ up** *j-n or et.* in Schwung bringen, aufmöbeln

pep·per 1. Pfeffer *m*; BOT Paprikaschote *f*; **2.** pfeffern

pep·per cast·er Pfefferstreuer *m*

pep·per·mint BOT Pfefferminze *f*; Pfefferminz *n*

pep·per·y pfeff(e)rig; *fig* hitzig

pep pill F Aufputschpille *f*

per per, durch; pro, für, je

per·ceive (be)merken, wahrnehmen; erkennen

per cent, per·cent Prozent *n*

per·cen·tage Prozentsatz *m*; F Prozente *pl*, (An)Teil *m*

per·cep·ti·ble wahrnehmbar, merklich; **per·cep·tion** Wahrnehmung *f*; Auffassung *f*, Auffassungsgabe *f*

perch¹ 1. (Sitz)Stange *f*; **2.** (**on**) sich setzen (auf *acc*), sich niederlassen (auf *acc*, *dat*); F hocken (**on** auf *dat*); **~ o.s.** F sich hocken (**on** auf *acc*)

perch² ZO Barsch *m*

per·co·la·tor Kaffeemaschine *f*

per·cus·sion Schlag *m*; Erschütterung *f*; MUS Schlagzeug *n*; **~ drill** TECH Schlagbohrer *m*; **~ in·stru·ment** MUS Schlaginstrument *n*

pe·remp·to·ry herrisch

pe·ren·ni·al ewig, immer während; BOT mehrjährig

per·fect 1. perfekt, vollkommen, vollendet; gänzlich, völlig; **2.** vervollkommnen; **3.** *a.* **~ tense** LING Perfekt *n*; **per·fec·tion** Vollendung *f*; Vollkommenheit *f*, Perfektion *f*

per·fo·rate durchbohren, -löchern

per·form *v/t* verrichten, durchführen, tun; *Pflicht etc* erfüllen; THEA, MUS aufführen, spielen, vortragen; *v/i* THEA *etc* e-e Vorstellung geben, auftreten, spielen; **per·form·ance** Verrichtung *f*, Durchführung *f*; Leistung *f*; THEA, MUS Aufführung *f*, Vorstellung *f*, Vortrag *m*; **per·form·er** THEA, MUS Darsteller(in), Künstler(in)

per·fume 1. Duft *m*; Parfüm *n*; **2.** parfümieren; **per·fum·er·y** Parfümerie *f*

per·haps vielleicht

per·il Gefahr *f*; **per·il·ous** gefährlich

P

pe·ri·od Periode *f*, Zeit *f*, Zeitdauer *f*, Zeitraum *m*, Zeitspanne *f*; (Unterrichts)Stunde *f*; MED Periode *f*; LING Punkt *m*; **~ fur·ni·ture** Stilmöbel *pl*

pe·ri·od·ic periodisch

pe·ri·od·i·cal 1. periodisch; **2.** Zeitschrift *f*

pe·riph·e·ral EDP Peripheriegerät *n*; **~ e·quip·ment** EDP Peripheriegeräte *pl*

pe·riph·e·ry Peripherie *f*, Rand *m*

per·ish umkommen; GASTR schlecht werden, verderben; TECH verschleißen

per·ish·a·ble leicht verderblich

per·ish·a·bles leicht verderbliche Lebensmittel

per·jure: ~ o.s. JUR e-n Meineid leisten

per·ju·ry JUR Meineid *m*; *commit* ~ e-n Meineid leisten

perk: ~ up *v/i* aufleben, munter werden; *v/t j-n* munter machen, F aufmöbeln

perk·y F munter, lebhaft; keck, selbstbewusst

perm 1. Dauerwelle *f*; *get a* ~ → **2. get one's hair ~ed** sich e-e Dauerwelle machen lassen

per·ma·nent 1. (be)ständig, dauerhaft, Dauer...; **2. a. ~ wave** Dauerwelle *f*

per·me·a·ble durchlässig (*to* für)

per·me·ate durchdringen; dringen (*into* in *acc*; *through* durch)

per·mis·si·ble zulässig, erlaubt

per·mis·sion Erlaubnis *f*

per·mis·sive liberal; (sexuell) freizügig; **~ so·ci·e·ty** tabufreie Gesellschaft

per·mit 1. erlauben, gestatten; **2.** Genehmigung *f*

per·pen·dic·u·lar senkrecht; rechtwink(e)lig (*to* zu)

per·pet·u·al fortwährend, ständig, ewig

per·plex verwirren

per·plex·i·ty Verwirrung *f*

per·se·cute verfolgen

per·se·cu·tion Verfolgung *f*

per·se·cu·tor Verfolger(in)

per·se·ver·ance Ausdauer *f*, Beharrlichkeit *f*

per·se·vere beharrlich weitermachen

per·sist beharren (*in* auf *dat*); anhalten

per·sis·tence Beharrlichkeit *f*

per·sis·tent beharrlich; anhaltend

per·son Person *f* (*a.* LING)

per·son·al persönlich (*a.* LING); Personal...; Privat...; **~ com·pu·ter** (ABBR

PC) Personalcomputer *m*; **~ da·ta** Personalien *pl*

per·son·al·i·ty Persönlichkeit *f*; *pl* anzügliche *or* persönliche Bemerkungen *pl*

per·son·al| or·ga·ni·zer Notizbuch *n*, Adressbuch *n* und Taschenkalender *m etc* (*in einem*); **~ pro·noun** LING Personalpronomen *n*; **~ ster·e·o** Walkman® *m*

per·son·i·fy personifizieren, verkörpern

per·son·nel Personal *n*, Belegschaft *f*; die Personalabteilung; **~ de·part·ment** Personalabteilung *f*; **~ man·ager** Personalchef *m*

per·spec·tive Perspektive *f*; Fernsicht *f*

per·spi·ra·tion Transpirieren *n*, Schwitzen *n*; Schweiß *m*

per·spire transpirieren, schwitzen

per·suade überreden; überzeugen

per·sua·sion Überredung(skunst) *f*; Überzeugung *f*

per·sua·sive überzeugend

pert keck, kess; schnippisch

per·tain: ~ to s.th. et. betreffen

per·ti·nent sachdienlich, relevant, zur Sache gehörig

per·turb beunruhigen

per·vade durchdringen, erfüllen

per·verse pervers; eigensinnig

per·ver·sion Verdrehung *f*; Perversion *f*

per·ver·si·ty Perversität *f*; Eigensinn *m*

per·vert 1. pervertieren; verdrehen; **2.** perverser Mensch

pes·sa·ry MED Pessar *n*

pes·si·mism Pessimismus *m*

pes·si·mist Pessimist(in)

pes·si·mis·tic pessimistisch

pest ZO Schädling *m*; F Nervensäge *f*; Plage *f*; **~ con·trol** Schädlingsbekämpfung *f*

pes·ter F *j-n* belästigen, *j-m* keine Ruhe lassen

pes·ti·cide Pestizid *n*, Schädlingsbekämpfungsmittel *n*

pet 1. (zahmes) (Haus)Tier; *often contp* Liebling *m*; **2.** Lieblings...; Tier...; **3.** streicheln; F Petting machen

pet·al BOT Blütenblatt *n*

pet food Tiernahrung *f*

pe·ti·tion 1. Eingabe *f*, Gesuch *n*, (schriftlicher) Antrag; **2.** ersuchen; ein

Gesuch einreichen (**for** um), e-n Antrag stellen (**for** auf *acc*)

pet name Kosename *m*

pet·ri·fy versteinern

pet·rol *Br* Benzin *n*

pe·tro·le·um Erdöl *n*, Mineralöl *n*

pet·rol pump *Br* Zapfsäule *f*; **~ station** *Br* Tankstelle *f*

pet shop Tierhandlung *f*, Zoogeschäft *n*

pet·ti·coat Unterrock *m*

pet·ting F Petting *n*

pet·tish launisch, gereizt

pet·ty belanglos, unbedeutend, JUR *a.* geringfügig; engstirnig; **~ cash** Portokasse *f*; **~ lar·ce·ny** JUR einfacher Diebstahl

pet·u·lant launisch, gereizt

pew (Kirchen)Bank *f*

pew·ter Zinn *n*; *a.* **~ ware** Zinn (-geschirr) *n*

phan·tom Phantom *n*; Geist *m*

phar·ma·cist Apotheker(in)

phar·ma·cy Apotheke *f*

phase Phase *f*

pheas·ant ZO Fasan *m*

phe·nom·e·non Phänomen *n*, Erscheinung *f*

phi·lan·thro·pist Philanthrop(in), Menschenfreund(in)

phil·is·tine F *contp* **1.** Spießer *m*; **2.** spießig

phi·lol·o·gist Philologe *m*, Philologin *f*

phi·lol·o·gy Philologie *f*

phi·los·o·pher Philosoph(in)

phi·los·o·phy Philosophie *f*

phlegm MED Schleim *m*

phone MED Telefon *n*; **answer the ~** ans Telefon gehen; **by ~** telefonisch; **on the ~** am Telefon; **be on the ~** Telefon haben; am Telefon sein; **2.** telefonieren, anrufen; **~ book** Telefonbuch *n*; **~ booth**, *Br* **~ box** Telefonzelle *f*; **~ call** Anruf *m*, Gespräch *n*

phone·card Telefonkarte *f*

phone-in *radio*, TV Sendung *f* mit telefonischer Zuhörer- *or* Zuschauerbeteiligung

phone num·ber Telefonnummer *f*

pho·net·ics Phonetik *f*

pho·n(e)y F **1.** Fälschung *f*; Schwindler(in); **2.** falsch, gefälscht, unecht; Schein...

phos·pho·rus CHEM Phosphor *m*

pho·to F Foto *n*, Bild *n*; **in the ~** auf dem Foto; **take a ~** ein Foto machen (**of** von)

pho·to·cop·i·er Fotokopiergerät *n*

pho·to·cop·y 1. Fotokopie *f*; **2.** fotokopieren

pho·to·graph 1. Fotografie *f*; **2.** fotografieren

pho·tog·ra·pher Fotograf(in)

pho·tog·ra·phy Fotografie *f*

phras·al verb LING Verb *n* mit Adverb (und Präposition)

phrase 1. (Rede)Wendung *f*, Redensart *f*, idiomatischer Ausdruck; **2.** ausdrücken; **phrase·book** Sprachführer *m*

phys·i·cal 1. physisch, körperlich; physikalisch; **~ly handicapped** körperbehindert; **2.** ärztliche Untersuchung; **~ ed·u·ca·tion** Leibeserziehung *f*, Sport *m*; **~ ex·am·i·na·tion** ärztliche Untersuchung; **~ hand·i·cap** Körperbehinderung *f*; **~ train·ing** Leibeserziehung *f*, Sport *m*

phy·si·cian Arzt *m*, Ärztin *f*

phys·i·cist Physiker(in)

phys·ics Physik *f*

phy·sique Körper(bau) *m*, Statur *f*

pi·a·nist Pianist(in)

pi·an·o MUS Klavier *n*

pick 1. (auf)hacken; (auf)picken; auflesen, aufnehmen; pflücken; *Knochen* abnagen; bohren *or* stochern in (*dat*); F *Schloss* knacken; aussuchen, auswählen; **~ one's nose** in der Nase bohren; **~ one's teeth** in den Zähnen (herum)stochern; **~ s.o.'s pocket** j-n bestehlen; **have a bone to ~ with s.o.** mit j-m ein Hühnchen zu rupfen haben; **~ out** (sich) *et.* auswählen; ausmachen, erkennen; **~ up** aufheben, auflesen, aufnehmen; aufpicken; *Spur* aufnehmen; *j-n* abholen; *Anhalter* mitnehmen; F *Mädchen* aufreißen; *Kenntnisse, Informationen etc* aufschnappen; sich *e-e Krankheit etc* holen; *a.* **~ up speed** MOT schneller werden; **2.** (Spitz)Hacke *f*, Pickel *m*; (Aus)Wahl *f*; **take your ~** suchen Sie sich etwas aus

pick-a-back huckepack

pick·ax, *Br* **pick·axe** (Spitz)Hacke *f*, Pickel *m*

pick·et 1. Pfahl *m*; Streikposten *m*; **2.** Streikposten aufstellen vor (*dat*), mit Streikposten besetzen; Streikposten stehen; **~ fence** Lattenzaun *m*; **~ line** Streikpostenkette *f*

pick·le GASTR **1.** Salzlake *f*; Essigsoße *f*; Essig-, Gewürzgurke *f*; *mst pl esp Br* Pickles *pl*; **be in a (pretty)** ~ (ganz schön) in der Patsche sitzen *or* sein *or* stecken; **2.** einlegen

pick·lock Einbrecher *m*; TECH Dietrich *m*

pick·pock·et Taschendieb(in)

pick·up Tonabnehmer *m*; Kleintransporter *m*; F (Zufalls)Bekanntschaft *f*

pick·y F wählerisch (**in** *dat* about)

pic·nic **1.** Picknick *n*; **2.** ein Picknick machen, picknicken

pic·ture **1.** Bild *n*; Gemälde *n*; PHOT Aufnahme *f*; Film *m*; *pl esp Br* Kino *n*; **2.** darstellen, malen; fig sich j-n, et. vorstellen; **~ book** Bilderbuch *n*; **~ post·card** Ansichtskarte *f*

pic·tur·esque malerisch

pie (*Fleisch- etc*)Pastete *f*; (*mst gedeckter*) (*Apfel- etc*)Kuchen

piece **1.** Stück *n*; Teil *n* (*of a machine etc*); Teil *m* (*of a set etc*); *chess:* Figur *f*; *board game:* Stein *m*; (Zeitungs)Artikel *m*, (-)Notiz *f*; **by the ~** stückweise; **a ~ of advice** ein Rat; **a ~ of news** e-e Neuigkeit; **give s.o. a ~ of one's mind** j-m gründlich die Meinung sagen; **go to ~s** F zusammenbrechen; **take to ~s** auseinander nehmen; **2.** **~ together** zusammensetzen, -stückeln; *fig* zusammenfügen

piece·meal schrittweise

piece·work Akkordarbeit *f*; **do** ~ im Akkord arbeiten

pier MAR Pier *m*, Landungsbrücke *f*; TECH Pfeiler *m*

pierce durchbohren, durchstechen, durchstoßen; durchdringen

pierc·ing durchdringend, (*Kälte etc a.*) schneidend, (*Schrei a.*) gellend, (*Blick, Schmerz etc a.*) stechend

pi·e·ty Frömmigkeit *f*

pig ZO Schwein *n* (*a.* F); F Ferkel *n*; *sl contp* Bulle *m*

pi·geon ZO Taube *f*

pi·geon·hole **1.** Fach *n*; **2.** ablegen

pig·gy F Schweinchen *n*

pig·gy·back huckepack

pig·gy bank Sparschwein(chen) *n*

pig·head·ed dickköpfig, stur

pig·let ZO Ferkel *n*

pig·sty Schweinestall *m*, F *contp* Saustall *m*

pig·tail Zopf *m*

pike¹ ZO Hecht *m*

pike² → **turnpike**

pile¹ **1.** Stapel *m*, Stoß *m*; F Haufen *m*, Menge *f*; (**atomic**) ~ Atommeiler *m*; **2.** ~ **up** (an-, auf)häufen, (auf)stapeln, aufschichten; sich anhäufen; MOT aufeinander auffahren

pile² Flor *m*

pile³ Pfahl *m*

piles *Br* F MED Hämorrhoiden *pl*

pile-up MOT Massenkarambolage *f*

pil·fer stehlen, klauen

pil·grim Pilger(in)

pil·grim·age Pilgerfahrt *f*, Wallfahrt *f*

pill PHARM Pille *f*; **the ~** F die (Antibaby)Pille; **be on the ~** die Pille nehmen

pil·lar Pfeiler *m*; Säule *f*

pil·li·on MOT Soziussitz *m*

pil·lo·ry **1.** HIST Pranger *m*; **2.** *fig* anprangern

pil·low (Kopf)Kissen *n*

pil·low·case, pil·low slip (Kopf)Kissenbezug *m*

pi·lot **1.** AVIAT Pilot *m*; MAR Lotse *m*; **2.** Versuchs..., Pilot...; **3.** lotsen; steuern; **~ film** TV Pilotfilm *m*; **~ scheme** Versuchs-, Pilotprojekt *n*

pimp Zuhälter *m*

pim·ple MED Pickel *m*, Pustel *f*

pin **1.** (Steck)Nadel *f*; (*Haar-, Krawatten- etc*)Nadel *f*; Brosche *f*; TECH Bolzen *m*, Stift *m*; *bowling:* Kegel *m*; Pin *m*; (*Wäsche*)Klammer *f*; *Br* (*Reiß*-)Nagel *m*, (-)Zwecke *f*; **2.** (an)heften, anstecken (**to** an *acc*), befestigen (**to** an *dat*); pressen, drücken (**against, to** gegen, an *acc*)

PIN *a.* ~ **number** ABBR of **personal identification number** PIN, persönliche Geheimzahl

pin·a·fore Schürze *f*

pin·ball Flippern *n*; **play** ~ flippern

pin·ball ma·chine Flipper(automat) *m*

pin·cers: (a pair of ~ e-e) (Kneif)Zange *f*

pinch **1.** *v/t* kneifen, zwicken; F klauen; *v/i* drücken; **2.** Kneifen *n*, Zwicken *n*; Prise *f*; *fig* Not(lage) *f*

pin·cush·ion Nadelkissen *n*

pine¹ BOT Kiefer *f*, Föhre *f*

pine² sich sehnen (**for** nach)

pine·ap·ple BOT Ananas *f*

pine cone BOT Kiefernzapfen *m*
pine·tree BOT Kiefer *f*, Föhre *f*
pin·ion ZO Schwungfeder *f*
pink 1. rosa(farben); **2.** Rosa *n*; BOT Nelke *f*
pint Pint *n (0,47 l, Br 0,57 l)*; *Br* F Halbe *f*
pi·o·neer 1. Pionier *m*; **2.** den Weg bahnen (für)
pi·ous fromm, religiös
pip[1] *Br* (Apfel-, Orangen- etc)Kern *m*
pip[2] (Piep)Ton *m*
pip[3] *on cards etc*: Auge *n*, Punkt *m*
pipe 1. TECH Rohr *n*, Röhre *f*; (Tabaks)Pfeife *f*; MUS (Orgel)Pfeife *f*; *pl Br* F Dudelsack *m*; **2.** (durch Rohre) leiten
pipe·line Rohrleitung *f*; Pipeline *f*
pip·er MUS Dudelsackpfeifer *m*
pip·ing 1. Rohrleitung *f*, Rohrnetz *n*; **2.** ~ *hot* kochend heiß, siedend heiß
pi·quant pikant *(a. fig)*
pique 1. *in a fit of* ~ gekränkt, verletzt, pikiert; **2.** kränken, verletzen; *be* ~*d* *a.* pikiert sein
pi·rate 1. Pirat *m*, Seeräuber *m*; **2.** unerlaubt kopieren *or* nachdrucken *or* nachpressen
pi·rate ra·di·o Piratensender *m or pl*
Pis·ces ASTR Fische *pl*; *he (she) is (a)* ~ er (sie) ist (ein) Fisch
piss V **1.** Pisse *f*; *take the* ~ *out of s.o.* j-n verarschen; **2.** pissen; ~ *off!* verpiss dich!
pis·tol Pistole *f*
pis·ton TECH Kolben *m*
pit[1] **1.** Grube *f (a. ANAT)*, MIN *a.* Zeche *f*; *esp Br* THEA Parkett *n*; *a.* ***orchestra*** ~ THEA Orchestergraben *m*; MED (esp Pocken)Narbe *f*; *car racing*: Box *f*; ~ *stop* Boxenstopp *m*; **2.** mit Narben bedecken
pit[2] **1.** BOT Kern *m*, Stein *m*; **2.** entkernen, entsteinen
pitch[1] **1.** *v/t* Zelt, Lager aufschlagen; werfen, schleudern; MUS (an)stimmen; *v/i* stürzen, fallen; MAR stampfen; sich neigen (roof etc); ~ *in* F sich ins Zeug legen; kräftig zulangen; **2.** *esp Br* SPORT (Spiel)Feld *n*; MUS Tonhöhe *f*; *fig* Grad *m*, Stufe *f*; *esp Br* Stand(platz) *m*; MAR Stampfen *n*; Neigung *f* (of a roof etc)
pitch[2] Pech *n*

pitch-black, pitch-dark pechschwarz; stockdunkel
pitch·er[1] Krug *m*
pitch·er[2] *baseball*: Werfer *m*
pitch·fork Heugabel *f*, Mistgabel *f*
pit·e·ous kläglich
pit·fall Fallgrube *f*; *fig* Falle *f*
pith BOT Mark *n*; weiße innere Haut; *fig* Kern *m*; **pith·y** markig, prägnant
pit·i·a·ble → *pitiful*
pit·i·ful Mitleid erregend, bemitleidenswert; erbärmlich, jämmerlich
pit·i·less unbarmherzig, erbarmungslos
pit·ta bread Fladenbrot *n*
pit·y 1. Mitleid *n* (*on* mit); *it is a (great)* ~ es ist (sehr) schade; *what a* ~*!* wie schade!; **2.** bemitleiden, bedauern
piv·ot 1. TECH Drehzapfen *m*; *fig* Dreh- und Angelpunkt *m*; **2.** sich drehen; ~ *on fig* abhängen von
pix·el EDP Pixel *m*
piz·za Pizza *f*
plac·ard 1. Plakat *n*; Transparent *n*; **2.** mit Plakaten bekleben
place 1. Platz *m*, Ort *m*, Stelle *f*; Stätte *f*; Haus *n*, Wohnung *f*; Wohnort *m*; (Arbeits-, Lehr)Stelle *f*; *in the first* ~ erstens; *in third* ~ SPORT *etc* auf dem dritten Platz; *in* ~ *of* anstelle von (or gen); *out of* ~ fehl am Platz; *take* ~ stattfinden; *take s.o.'s* ~ j-s Stelle einnehmen; **2.** stellen, legen, setzen; *Auftrag* erteilen (*with* dat), *Bestellung* aufgeben (*with* bei); *be* ~*d* SPORT sich platzieren (*second* an zweiter Stelle)
place mat Platzdeckchen *n*, Set *n*, *m*
place·ment test Einstufungsprüfung *f*
place name Ortsname *m*
plac·id ruhig; gelassen
pla·gia·rize plagiieren
plague 1. Seuche *f*; Pest *f*; Plage *f*; **2.** plagen
plaice ZO Scholle *f*
plaid Plaid *n or m*
plain 1. *adj* einfach schlicht; klar (und deutlich); offen (und ehrlich); unscheinbar, wenig anziehend; rein, völlig (nonsense etc); **2.** *adv* F (ganz) einfach; **3.** Ebene *f*, Flachland *n*
plain choc·o·late *Br* (zart)bittere Schokolade
plain-clothes ... in Zivil
plain·tiff JUR Kläger(in)
plain·tive traurig, klagend

plait *esp Br* **1.** Zopf *m*; **2.** flechten

plan 1. Plan *m*; **2.** planen; beabsichtigen

plane[1] Flugzeug *n*; **by ~** mit dem Flugzeug; **go by ~** fliegen

plane[2] **1.** flach, eben; **2.** MATH Ebene *f*; *fig* Stufe *f*, Niveau *n*

plane[3] **1.** Hobel *m*; **2.** hobeln; **~ down** abhobeln

plan·et ASTR Planet *m*

plank Planke *f*, Bohle *f*; **~ bed** Pritsche *f*

plank·ing Planken *pl*

plant 1. BOT Pflanze *f*; ECON Werk *n*, Betrieb *m*, Fabrik *f*; **2.** (an-, ein)pflanzen; bepflanzen; *Garten etc* anlegen; aufstellen, postieren; **~ s.th. on s.o** F j-m et. (*Belastendes*) unterschieben

plan·ta·tion Plantage *f*, Pflanzung *f*; Schonung *f*

plant·er Plantagenbesitzer(in), Pflanzer (in); Pflanzmaschine *f*; Übertopf *m*

plaque Gedenktafel *f*; MED Zahnbelag *m*

plas·ter 1. MED Pflaster *n*; (Ver)Putz *m*; *a.* **~ of Paris** Gips *m*; **have one's leg in ~** MED das Bein in Gips haben; **2.** verputzen; bekleben; **~ cast** Gipsabguss *m*, Gipsmodell *n*; MED Gipsverband *m*

plas·tic 1. plastisch; Plastik...; **2.** Plastik *n*, Kunststoff *m*; **→ ~ mon·ey** F Plastikgeld *n*, Kreditkarten *pl*; **~ wrap** Frischhaltefolie *f*

plate 1. Teller *m*; Platte *f*; (*Namens-, Nummern- etc*)Schild *n*; (Bild)Tafel *f*; (Druck)Platte *f*; Gegenstände *pl* aus Edelmetall; Doublé *n*, Dublee *n*; **2.** **~d with gold, gold-plated** vergoldet

plat·form Plattform *f*; RAIL Bahnsteig *m*; (Redner)Tribüne *f*, Podium *n*; POL Plattform *f*; MOT Pritsche *f*; **party ~** POL Parteiprogramm *n*; **election ~** POL Wahlprogramm *n*

plat·i·num CHEM Platin *n*

pla·toon MIL Zug *m*

plat·ter (Servier)Platte *f*

plau·si·ble plausibel, glaubhaft

play 1. Spiel *n*; Schauspiel *n*, (Theater-) Stück *n*; TECH Spiel *n*; *fig* Spielraum *m*; **at ~** beim Spiel(en); **in ~** im Spiel (*ball*); **out of ~** im Aus (*ball*); **2.** *v/i* spielen (*a.* SPORT, THEA *etc*); *v/t Karten, Rolle, Stück etc* spielen, SPORT *Spiel* austragen; **~ s.o.** SPORT spielen gegen j-n; **~ the guitar** Gitarre spielen; **~ a trick on s.o.** j-m e-n Streich spielen; **~ back**

Ball zurückspielen (**to** zu); *Tonband* abspielen; **~ s.th. down** verharmlosen, herunterspielen; **~ off** *fig* ausspielen (**against** gegen); **~ on** *fig* j-s Schwächen ausnutzen

play·back Play-back *n*, Wiedergabe *f*, Abspielen *n*

play·boy Playboy *m*

play·er MUS, SPORT Spieler(in); TECH Plattenspieler *m*

play·fel·low *Br* → **playmate**

play·ful verspielt; scherzhaft

play·go·er Theaterbesucher(in)

play·ground Spielplatz *m* (*a. fig*); Schulhof *m*

play·group *Br* Spielgruppe *f*

play·house THEA Schauspielhaus *n*; Spielhaus *n* (*for children*)

play·ing card Spielkarte *f*

play·ing field Sportplatz *m*, Spielfeld *n*

play·mate Spielkamerad(in)

play·pen Laufgitter *n*, Laufstall *m*

play·thing Spielzeug *n*

play·wright Dramatiker(in)

plc, PLC *Br* ECON ABBR *of public limited company* AG, Aktiengesellschaft *f*

plea: enter a ~ of (not) guilty JUR sich schuldig bekennen (s-e Unschuld erklären)

plead *v/i* (dringend) bitten (**for** um); **~ (not) guilty** JUR sich schuldig bekennen (s-e Unschuld erklären); *v/t a.* JUR zu s-r Verteidigung *or* Entschuldigung anführen, geltend machen; **~ s.o.'s case** sich für j-n einsetzen; JUR j-n vertreten

pleas·ant angenehm, erfreulich; freundlich; sympathisch

please 1. *j-m* gefallen; *j-m* zusagen, *j-n* erfreuen; zufrieden stellen; **only to ~ you** nur dir zuliebe; **~ o.s.** tun, was man will; **~ yourself!** mach, was du willst! **2.** *int* bitte; (**yes,**) **~** (ja,) bitte; (oh ja,) gerne; **~ come in!** bitte, treten Sie ein!

pleased erfreut, zufrieden; **be ~ about** sich freuen über (*acc*); **be ~ with** zufrieden sein mit; **I am ~ with it** es gefällt mir; **be ~ to do s.th.** et. gern tun; **~ to meet you!** angenehm!

pleas·ing angenehm

plea·sure Vergnügen *n*; **at (one's) ~** nach Belieben

pleat (Plissee)Falte *f*

pleat·ed skirt Faltenrock *m*

pledge 1. Pfand *n*; *fig* Unterpfand *n*; Versprechen *n*; **2.** versprechen, zusichern

plen·ti·ful reichlich

plen·ty 1. Überfluss *m*; **in ~** im Überfluss, in Hülle und Fülle; **~ of** e-e Menge, viel(e), reichlich; **2.** F reichlich

pleu·ri·sy MED Brustfell-, Rippenfellentzündung *f*

pli·a·ble, pli·ant biegsam; *fig* flexibel; *fig* leicht beeinflussbar

pli·ers (**a pair of ~** e-e) Beißzange *f*

plight Not *f*, Notlage *f*

plim·soll *Br* Turnschuh *m*

plod *v/i.* **~ along** sich dahinschleppen; **~ away** sich abplagen (**at** mit), schuften

plop F **1.** Plumps *m*, Platsch *m*; **2.** plumpsen, (*ins Wasser*) platschen

plot 1. Stück *n* Land, Parzelle *f*, Grundstück *n*; THEA, *film etc*: Handlung *f*, Komplott *n*, Verschwörung *f*; EDP grafische Darstellung; **2.** *v/i* sich verschwören (**against** gegen); *v/t* planen; einzeichnen

plot·ter EDP Plotter *m*

plough *Br*, **plow** AGR **1.** Pflug *m*; **2.** (um)pflügen; **plough·share** *Br*, **plow·share** Pflugschar *f*

pluck 1. *v/t Geflügel* rupfen; *mst* **~ out** ausreißen, ausrupfen, auszupfen; MUS *Saiten* zupfen; **~ up (one's) courage** Mut *or* sich ein Herz fassen; *v/i* zupfen (**at** an *dat*); **2.** F Mut *m*, Schneid *m*

pluck·y F mutig

plug 1. Stöpsel *m*; ELECTR Stecker *m*, F Steckdose *f*; MOT (*Zünd*)Kerze *f*; **2.** *v/t* F für *et.* Schleichwerbung machen; *a.* **~ up** zustöpseln; zustopfen, verstopfen; **~ in** ELECTR anschließen, einstecken

plug·ging F Schleichwerbung *f*

plum BOT Pflaume *f*; Zwetsch(g)e *f*

plum·age Gefieder *n*

plumb 1. (Blei)Lot *n*; **2.** ausloten, *fig a.* ergründen; **~ in** *esp Br Waschmaschine etc* anschließen; **3.** *adj* lotrecht, senkrecht; **4.** *adv* F (haar)genau

plumb·er Klempner *m*, Installateur *m*

plumb·ing Klempner-, Installateurarbeit *f*; Rohre *pl*, Rohrleitungen *pl*

plume (Schmuck)Feder *f*; Federbusch *m*; (*Rauch*)Fahne *f*

plump 1. *adj* drall, mollig, rund(lich), F pumm(e)lig; **2.** **~ down** fallen *or* plumpsen (lassen)

plum pud·ding *Br* Plumpudding *m*

plun·der 1. plündern; **2.** Plünderung *f*; Beute *f*

plunge 1. (ein-, unter)tauchen; (sich) stürzen (**into** in *acc*); MAR stampfen; **2.** (Kopf)Sprung *m*; **take the ~** *fig* den entscheidenden Schritt wagen

plu·per·fect *a.* **~ tense** LING Plusquamperfekt *n*, Vorvergangenheit *f*

plu·ral LING Plural *m*, Mehrzahl *f*

plus 1. *prp* plus, und, *esp* ECON zuzüglich; **2.** *adj* Plus...; **~ sign** MATH Plus *n*, Pluszeichen *n*; **3.** MATH Plus *n* (*a.* F), Pluszeichen *n*; F Vorteil *m*

plush Plüsch *m*

ply[1] *regelmäßig* verkehren, fahren (**between** zwischen *dat*)

ply[2] *mst in cpds* TECH Lage *f*, Schicht *f*; **three-~** dreifach (*thread etc*); dreifach gewebt (*carpet*)

ply·wood Sperrholz *n*

pm, PM ABBR *of* **after noon** (*Latin post meridiem*) nachm., nachmittags, abends

pneu·mat·ic Luft..., pneumatisch; TECH Druck..., Pressluft...

pneu·mat·ic drill Pressluftbohrer *m*

pneu·mo·ni·a MED Lungenentzündung *f*

poach[1] GASTR pochieren; **~ed eggs** verlorene Eier *pl*

poach[2] wildern

poach·er Wilddieb *m*, Wilderer *m*

PO Box Postfach *n*; **write to ~ 225** schreiben Sie an Postfach 225

pock MED Pocke *f*, Blatter *f*

pock·et 1. (Hosen- *etc*)Tasche *f*; **2.** *adj* Taschen...; **3.** einstecken, in die Tasche stecken; *fig* in die eigene Tasche stecken; **pock·et·book** Notizbuch *n*; Brieftasche *f*

pock·et| cal·cu·la·tor Taschenrechner *m*; **~ knife** Taschenmesser *n*; **~ money** Taschengeld *n*

pod BOT Hülse *f*, Schote *f*

po·di·a·trist Fußpfleger(in)

po·em Gedicht *n*

po·et Dichter(in)

po·et·ic dichterisch

P

po·et·i·cal dichterisch

po·et·ic jus·tice *fig* ausgleichende Gerechtigkeit

po·et·ry Gedichte *pl*; Poesie *f* (*a. fig*), Dichtkunst *f*, Dichtung *f*

poi·gnant schmerzlich; ergreifend

point **1.** Spitze *f*; GEOGR Landspitze *f*; LING, MATH, PHYS, SPORT *etc* Punkt *m*; MATH (Dezimal)Punkt *m*; Grad *m*; MAR (*Kompass*)Strich *m*; *fig* Punkt *m*, Stelle *f*, Ort *m*; Zweck *m*; Ziel *n*, Absicht *f*; springender Punkt; Pointe *f*; *two ~ five* (*2.5*) 2,5; *~ of view* Stand-, Gesichtspunkt *m*; *be on the ~ of doing s.th.* im Begriff sein, et. zu tun; *to the ~* zur Sache gehörig; *off or beside the ~* nicht zur Sache gehörig; *come to the ~* zur Sache kommen; *that's not the ~* darum geht es nicht; *what's the ~?* wozu?; *win on ~s* SPORT nach Punkten gewinnen; *winner on ~s* SPORT Punktsieger *m*; **2.** *v/t* (zu)spitzen; *Waffe etc* richten (*at* auf *acc*); *~ one's finger at s.o.* (mit dem Finger) auf j-n zeigen; *~ out* zeigen; *fig* hinweisen *or* aufmerksam machen auf (*acc*); *v/i* (mit dem Finger) zeigen (*at, to* auf *acc*); *~ to* nach e-r Richtung weisen *or* liegen; *fig* hinweisen auf (*acc*)

point·ed spitz; Spitz...; *fig* scharf (*remark etc*); ostentativ

point·er Zeiger *m*; Zeigestock *m*; ZO Pointer *m*, Vorstehhund *m*

point·less sinnlos, zwecklos

points *Br* RAIL Weiche *f*

poise **1.** (Körper)Haltung *f*; *fig* Gelassenheit *f*; **2.** balancieren; *be ~d* schweben

poi·son **1.** Gift *n*; **2.** vergiften

poi·son·ous giftig (*a. fig*)

poke **1.** *v/t* stoßen; *Feuer* schüren; stecken; *v/i ~ about, ~ around* F (herum-)stöbern, (-)wühlen (*in* in *dat*); **2.** Stoß *m*

pok·er Schürhaken *m*

pok·y F eng; schäbig

Po·land Polen *n*

po·lar polar; *~ bear* ZO Eisbär *m*

pole¹ GEOGR Pol *m*

pole² Stange *f*; Mast *m*; Deichsel *f*; SPORT (Sprung)Stab *m*

Pole Pole *m*, Polin *f*

pole·cat ZO Iltis *m*; F Skunk *m*, Stinktier *n*

po·lem·ic, po·lem·i·cal polemisch

pole star ASTR Polarstern *m*

pole vault SPORT Stabhochsprung *m*, Stabhochspringen *n*

pole-vault SPORT stabhochspringen

pole vault·er SPORT Stabhochspringer(in)

po·lice **1.** Polizei *f*; **2.** überwachen

po·lice car Polizeiauto *n*

po·lice·man Polizist *m*

po·lice| of·fi·cer Polizeibeamte *m*, -beamtin *f*, Polizist(in); ~ **sta·tion** Polizeiwache *f*, Polizeirevier *n*

po·lice·wom·an Polizistin *f*

pol·i·cy Politik *f*; Taktik *f*; Klugheit *f*; (Versicherungs)Police *f*

po·li·o MED Polio *f*, Kinderlähmung *f*

pol·ish **1.** polieren; *Schuhe* putzen; ~ **up** aufpolieren (*a. fig*); **2.** Politur *f*; (*Schuh*)Creme *f*; *fig* Schliff *m*

Pol·ish **1.** polnisch; **2.** LING Polnisch *n*

po·lite höflich

po·lite·ness Höflichkeit *f*

po·lit·i·cal politisch

pol·i·ti·cian Politiker(in)

pol·i·tics Politik *f*

pol·ka MUS Polka *f*

pol·ka-dot gepunktet, getupft

poll **1.** (*Meinungs*)Umfrage *f*; Wahlbeteiligung *f*; *a. pl* Stimmabgabe *f*, Wahl *f*; **2.** befragen; *Stimmen* erhalten

pol·len BOT Pollen *m*, Blütenstaub *m*

poll·ing Stimmabgabe *f*; Wahlbeteiligung *f*; ~ **booth** *esp Br* Wahlkabine *f*; ~ **day** Wahltag *m*; ~ **place,** *esp Br* ~ **sta·tion** Wahllokal *n*

polls Wahl *f*; Wahllokal *n*

poll·ster Demoskop(in), Meinungsforscher(in)

pol·lut·ant Schadstoff *m*; **pol·lute** beschmutzen, verschmutzen; verunreinigen; **pol·lut·er** *a.* **environmental** ~ Umweltsünder(in); **pol·lu·tion** (*Luft-, Wasser- etc*)Verschmutzung *f*; Verunreinigung *f*

po·lo SPORT Polo *n*

po·lo neck *a.* ~ **sweater** *esp Br* Rollkragenpullover *m*

pol·yp ZO, MED Polyp *m*

pol·y·sty·rene Styropor® *n*

pom·mel (Sattel- *etc*)Knopf *m*

pomp Pomp *m*, Prunk *m*

pom·pous aufgeblasen, wichtigtuerisch; schwülstig (*speech*)

pond Teich *m*, Weiher *m*

pon·der *v/i* nachdenken (**on**, **over** über *acc*); *v/t* überlegen

pon·der·ous schwerfällig; schwer

pon·toon Ponton *m*

pon·toon bridge Pontonbrücke *f*

po·ny ZO Pony *n*

po·ny·tail Pferdeschwanz *m*

poo·dle ZO Pudel *m*

pool[1] Teich *m*, Tümpel *m*; Pfütze *f*, (*Blut- etc*)Lache *f*, (*Schwimm*)Becken *n*, (*Swimming*)Pool *m*

pool[2] **1.** (*Arbeits-, Fahr*)Gemeinschaft *f*; (*Mitarbeiter- etc*)Stab *m*; (*Fuhr*)Park *m*; (*Schreib*)Pool *m*; ECON Pool *m*, Kartell *n*; *card games*: Gesamteinsatz *m*; Poolbillard *n*; **2.** Geld, Unternehmen etc zusammenlegen; Kräfte etc vereinen

pool hall, **pool·room** Billardspielhalle *f*

pools *a.* **football ~** *Br* (Fußball)Toto *n*, *m*

poor 1. arm; dürftig, mangelhaft, schwach; **2. the ~** die Armen *pl*

poor·ly 1. *adj esp Br* F kränklich, unpässlich; **2.** *adv* ärmlich, dürftig, schlecht, schwach

pop[1] **1.** *v/t* zerknallen; F schnell tun *or* stecken; *v/i* knallen; (zer)platzen; **~ in** F auf e-n Sprung vorbeikommen; **~ off** F (plötzlich) den Löffel weglegen; **~ up** (plötzlich) auftauchen; **2.** Knall *m*; F Limo *f*

pop[2] MUS **1.** Pop *m*; **2.** Schlager...; Pop...

pop[3] F Paps *m*, Papa *m*

pop[4] ABBR *of* **population** Einw., Einwohner(zahl *f*) *pl*

pop con·cert MUS Popkonzert *n*

pop·corn Popcorn *n*, Puffmais *m*

Pope REL Papst *m*

pop-eyed glotzäugig

pop group MUS Popgruppe *f*

pop·lar BOT Pappel *f*

pop mu·sic Popmusik *f*

pop·py BOT Mohn *m*

pop·u·lar populär, beliebt; volkstümlich; allgemein

pop·u·lar·i·ty Popularität *f*, Beliebtheit *f*; Volkstümlichkeit *f*

pop·u·late bevölkern, besiedeln; bewohnen

pop·u·la·tion Bevölkerung *f*

pop·u·lous dicht besiedelt, dicht bevölkert

porce·lain Porzellan *n*

porch überdachter Vorbau; Portal *n*; Veranda *f*

por·cu·pine ZO Stachelschwein *n*

pore[1] Pore *f*

pore[2]: **~ over** vertieft sein in (*acc*), et. eifrig studieren

pork GASTR Schweinefleisch *n*

porn F → **porno**

por·no F **1.** Porno *m*; **2.** Porno...

por·nog·ra·phy Pornografie *f*

po·rous porös

por·poise ZO Tümmler *m*

por·ridge Porridge *m*, Haferbrei *m*

port[1] Hafen *m*; Hafenstadt *f*

port[2] AVIAT, MAR Backbord *n*

port[3] EDP Port *m*, Anschluss *m*

port[4] Portwein *m*

por·ta·ble tragbar

por·ter (Gepäck)Träger *m*; *esp Br* Pförtner *m*, Portier *m*; RAIL Schlafwagenschaffner *m*

port·hole MAR Bullauge *n*

por·tion 1. (An)Teil *m*; GASTR Portion *f*; **2. ~ out** aufteilen, verteilen (**among**, **between** unter *acc*)

port·ly korpulent

por·trait Porträt *n*, Bild *n*, Bildnis *n*

por·tray porträtieren; darstellen; schildern; **por·tray·al** THEA Verkörperung *f*, Darstellung *f*; Schilderung *f*

Por·tu·gal Portugal *n*

Por·tu·guese 1. portugiesisch; **2.** Portugiese *m*, Portugiesin *f*; LING Portugiesisch *n*; **the ~** die Portugiesen *pl*

pose 1. *v/t* aufstellen; Problem, Frage aufwerfen; Bedrohung, Gefahr etc darstellen; *v/i* Modell sitzen *or* stehen; **~ as** sich ausgeben als *or* für; **2.** Pose *f*

posh *esp Br* F schick, piekfein

po·si·tion 1. Position *f*, Lage *f*, Stellung *f* (*a. fig*); Stand *m*; *fig* Standpunkt *m*; **2.** (auf)stellen

pos·i·tive 1. positiv; bestimmt, sicher, eindeutig; greifbar, konkret; konstruktiv; **2.** PHOT Positiv *n*

pos·sess besitzen; *fig* beherrschen

pos·sessed *fig* besessen

pos·ses·sion Besitz *m*; *fig* Besessenheit *f*

pos·ses·sive besitzergreifend; LING possessiv, besitzanzeigend

pos·si·bil·i·ty Möglichkeit *f*

pos·si·ble möglich

P

pos·si·bly möglicherweise, vielleicht; *if I ~ can* wenn ich irgend kann; *I can't ~ do this* ich kann das unmöglich tun

post¹ (Tür-, Tor-, Ziel- etc)Pfosten m; Pfahl m; **2.** a. ~ **up** Plakat etc anschlagen, ankleben; *be ~ed missing* AVIAT, MAR als vermisst gemeldet werden

post² esp Br **1.** Post f; Postsendung f; *by ~* mit der Post; **2.** mit der Post (zu-)schicken, aufgeben, *Brief* einwerfen

post³ **1.** Stelle f, Job m; Posten m; **2.** aufstellen, postieren; *esp Br* versetzen, MIL abkommandieren (*to* nach)

post... nach..., Nach...

post·age Porto n; ~ **stamp** Postwertzeichen n, Briefmarke f

post·al postalisch, Post...; ~ **or·der** Br ECON Postanweisung f; ~ **vote** POL Briefwahl f

post·bag esp Br Postsack m

post·box esp Br Briefkasten m

post·card Postkarte f; a. **picture** ~ Ansichtskarte f

post·code Br Postleitzahl f

post·er Plakat n; Poster n, m

poste res·tante Br **1.** Abteilung f für postlagernde Sendungen; **2.** postlagernd

pos·te·ri·or HUMOR Hinterteil n

pos·ter·i·ty die Nachwelt f

post-free esp Br portofrei

post-hu·mous posthum; nach(h)um

post·man esp Br Briefträger m, Postbote m

post·mark **1.** Poststempel m; **2.** (ab-)stempeln

post·mas·ter Postamtsvorsteher m

post of·fice Post f; Postamt n, -filiale f

post of·fice box → **PO Box**

post-paid portofrei

post·pone verschieben, aufschieben

post·pone·ment Verschiebung f, Aufschub m

post·script Postskript(um) n, Nachschrift f

pos·ture **1.** (Körper)Haltung f; Stellung f; **2.** fig sich aufspielen

post·war Nachkriegs...

post·wom·an esp Br Briefträgerin f, Postbotin f

po·sy Sträußchen n

pot **1.** Topf m; Kanne f; Kännchen n (Tee etc); SPORT F Pokal m; **2.** Pflanze eintopfen

po·tas·si·um cy·a·nide CHEM Zyankali n

po·ta·to Kartoffel f; → **chips**, **crisps**

pot·bel·ly Schmerbauch m

po·ten·cy Stärke f, Wirksamkeit f, Wirkung f; MED Potenz f

po·tent PHARM stark; MED potent

po·ten·tial **1.** potenziell, möglich; **2.** Potenzial n, Leistungsfähigkeit f

pot·hole MOT Schlagloch n

po·tion Trank m

pot·ter¹ Br: ~ **about** herumwerkeln

pot·ter² Töpfer(in)

pot·ter·y Töpferei f; Töpferware(n pl) f

pouch Beutel m (a. ZO); ZO (Backen-)Tasche f

poul·tice MED (warmer) Umschlag m

poul·try Geflügel n

pounce **1.** sich stürzen (**on** auf acc); **2.** Satz m, Sprung m

pound¹ Pfund n (453,59 g); ~ (**sterling**) (ABBR **£**) Pfund n

pound² Tierheim n; Abstellplatz m für (polizeilich) abgeschleppte Fahrzeuge

pound³ v/t zerstoßen, zerstampfen; trommeln or hämmern auf (acc) or an (acc) or gegen; v/i hämmern (**with** vor dat)

pour v/t gießen, schütten; ~ **out** ausgießen, ausschütten; Getränk eingießen; v/i strömen (a. fig)

pout v/t Lippen schürzen; v/i e-n Schmollmund machen; schmollen

pov·er·ty Armut f

pow·der **1.** Pulver n; Puder m; **2.** pulverisieren; (sich) pudern; ~ **puff** Puderquaste f; ~ **room** (Damen)Toilette f

pow·er **1.** Kraft f; Macht f; Fähigkeit f, Vermögen n; Gewalt f; JUR Befugnis f, Vollmacht f; MATH Potenz f; ELECTR Strom m; *in* ~ POL an der Macht; **2.** TECH antreiben; ~ **cut** ELECTR Stromsperre f; ~ **fail·ure** ELECTR Stromausfall m, Netzausfall m

pow·er·ful stark, kräftig; mächtig

pow·er·less kraftlos; machtlos

pow·er| plant Elektrizitäts-, Kraftwerk n; ~ **pol·i·tics** Machtpolitik f; ~ **sta·tion** Br Elektrizitäts-, Kraftwerk n

prac·ti·ca·ble durchführbar

prac·ti·cal praktisch; ~ **joke** Streich m

prac·ti·cal·ly so gut wie

prac·tice **1.** Praxis f; Übung f; Gewohnheit f, Brauch m; **it is common ~** es ist allgemein üblich; **put into ~** in die Praxis umsetzen; **2.** v/t (ein)üben; **als Beruf** ausüben; **~ law (medicine)** als Anwalt (Arzt) praktizieren; v/i praktizieren; üben

prac·ticed geübt (**in** in dat)

prac·tise Br → **practice** 2

prac·tised → **practiced**

prac·ti·tion·er: general ~ praktischer Arzt

prai·rie Prärie f

prai·rie schoo·ner HIST Planwagen m

praise 1. loben, preisen; **2.** Lob n

praise·wor·thy lobenswert

pram Br Kinderwagen m

prance sich aufbäumen, steigen (horse); tänzeln (horse); stolzieren

prank Streich m

prat·tle: ~ on plappern (**about** von)

prawn ZO Garnele f

pray beten (**to** zu; **for** für, um)

prayer REL Gebet n; often pl Andacht f; **the Lord's Prayer** das Vaterunser

prayer book REL Gebetbuch n

preach predigen (**to** zu, vor dat)

preach·er Prediger(in)

pre·am·ble Einleitung f

pre·ar·range vorher vereinbaren

pre·car·i·ous prekär, unsicher; gefährlich

pre·cau·tion Vorsichtsmaßnahme f; **as a ~** vorsorglich; **take ~s** Vorsichtsmaßnahmen treffen; **pre·cau·tion·a·ry** vorbeugend; vorsorglich

pre·cede voraus-, vorangehen (dat)

pre·ce·dence Vorrang m

pre·ce·dent Präzedenzfall m

pre·cept Regel f, Richtlinie f

pre·cinct (Wahl)Bezirk m; (Polizei)Revier m; pl Gelände n; esp Br (Einkaufs)Viertel n; (Fußgänger)Zone f

pre·cious 1. adj kostbar, wertvoll; Edel... (stone etc); **2.** adv: **~ little** F herzlich wenig

pre·ci·pice Abgrund m

pre·cip·i·tate 1. v/t (hinunter-, herunter)schleudern; CHEM ausfällen; beschleunigen; stürzen (**into** in acc); v/i CHEM ausfallen; **2.** adj überstürzt; **3.** CHEM Niederschlag m

pre·cip·i·ta·tion CHEM Ausfällung f; METEOR Niederschlag m; Überstürzung f, Hast f

pre·cip·i·tous steil (abfallend); überstürzt

pré·cis Zusammenfassung f

pre·cise genau, präzis

pre·ci·sion Genauigkeit f; Präzision f

pre·clude ausschließen

pre·co·cious frühreif; altklug

pre·con·ceived vorgefasst

pre·con·cep·tion vorgefasste Meinung

pre·cur·sor Vorläufer(in)

pred·a·to·ry ZO Raub...

pre·de·ces·sor Vorgänger(in)

pre·des·ti·na·tion Vorherbestimmung f; **pre·des·tined** prädestiniert, vorherbestimmt (**to** für, zu)

pre·de·ter·mine vorherbestimmen; vorher vereinbaren

pre·dic·a·ment missliche Lage, Zwangslage f

pred·i·cate LING Prädikat n, Satzaussage f; **pre·dic·a·tive** LING prädikativ

pre·dict vorhersagen, voraussagen

pre·dic·tion Vorhersage f, Voraussage f; **computer ~** Hochrechnung f

pre·dis·pose geneigt machen, einnehmen (**in favor of** für); esp MED anfällig machen (**to** für)

pre·dis·po·si·tion: ~ to Neigung f zu, esp MED a. Anfälligkeit f für

pre·dom·i·nant (vor)herrschend, überwiegend

pre·dom·i·nate vorherrschen, überwiegen; die Oberhand haben

pre·em·i·nent hervorragend, überragend

pre·emp·tive ECON Vorkaufs...; MIL Präventiv...

preen ZO sich or das Gefieder putzen

pre·fab F Fertighaus n

pre·fab·ri·cate vorfabrizieren, vorfertigen; **~d house** Fertighaus n

pref·ace 1. Vorwort n (**to** zu); **2.** Buch, Rede etc einleiten (**with** mit)

pre·fect Br PED Aufsichts-, Vertrauensschüler(in)

pre·fer vorziehen (**to** dat), lieber mögen (**to** als), bevorzugen

pref·er·a·ble: be ~ (to) vorzuziehen sein (dat), besser sein (als)

pref·er·a·bly vorzugsweise, lieber, am liebsten

pref·er·ence Vorliebe f (**for** für); Vorzug m

pre·fix LING Präfix n, Vorsilbe f

P

preg·nan·cy MED Schwangerschaft f; ZO Trächtigkeit f

preg·nant MED schwanger; ZO trächtig

pre·heat *Backofen etc* vorheizen

pre·judge *j-n* vorverurteilen; vorschnell beurteilen

prej·u·dice 1. Vorurteil n, Voreingenommenheit f, Befangenheit f; **to the ~ of** zum Nachteil *or* Schaden (*gen*); **2.** einnehmen (**in favo[u]r of** für; **against** gegen); schaden (*dat*), beeinträchtigen

prej·u·diced (vor)eingenommen, befangen

pre·lim·i·na·ry 1. vorläufig, einleitend, Vor...; **2.** *pl* Vorbereitungen *pl*

prel·ude Vorspiel n (a. MUS)

pre·mar·i·tal vorehelich

pre·ma·ture vorzeitig, verfrüht; *fig* voreilig

pre·med·i·tat·ed JUR vorsätzlich

pre·med·i·ta·tion: with ~ JUR vorsätzlich

prem·i·er POL Premier(minister) m

prem·i·ere, prem·i·ère THEA *etc* Premiere f, Ur-, Erstaufführung f

prem·is·es Gelände n, Grundstück n, (*Geschäfts*)Räume *pl*; **on the ~** an Ort und Stelle, im Haus, im Lokal

pre·mi·um Prämie f, Bonus m

pre·mi·um (gas·o·line) MOT Super n, Superbenzin n

pre·mo·ni·tion (böse) Vorahnung

pre·oc·cu·pa·tion Beschäftigung f (**with** mit)

pre·oc·cu·pied gedankenverloren, geistesabwesend

pre·oc·cu·py (stark) beschäftigen

prep *Br* F PED Hausaufgabe(n *pl*) f

pre·packed, pre·pack·aged abgepackt

pre·paid *post* frankiert, freigemacht; **~ envelope** Freiumschlag m

prep·a·ra·tion Vorbereitung f (**for** auf *acc*, für); Zubereitung f; CHEM, MED Präparat n

pre·par·a·to·ry vorbereitend

pre·pare *v/t* vorbereiten; GASTR zubereiten; *v/i:* **~ for** sich vorbereiten auf (*acc*); Vorbereitungen treffen für; sich gefasst machen auf (*acc*)

pre·pared vorbereitet; bereit

prep·o·si·tion LING Präposition f, Verhältniswort n

pre·pos·sess·ing einnehmend, anziehend

pre·pos·ter·ous absurd; lächerlich, grotesk

pro·gram(me) vorprogrammieren

pre·req·ui·site Vorbedingung f, Voraussetzung f

pre·rog·a·tive Vorrecht n

pre·school Vorschule f

pre·scribe *et.* vorschreiben; MED *j-m et.* verschreiben; **pre·scrip·tion** Verordnung f, Vorschrift f; MED Rezept n

pres·ence Gegenwart f, Anwesenheit f; **~ of mind** Geistesgegenwart f

pres·ent¹ Geschenk n

pres·ent² präsentieren; (über)reichen, (über)bringen, (über)geben; schenken; vorbringen, vorlegen; zeigen, vorführen, THEA *etc* aufführen; schildern, darstellen; *j-n, Produkt etc* vorstellen; *Programm etc* moderieren

pres·ent³ 1. anwesend; vorhanden; gegenwärtig, jetzig; laufend; vorliegend (*case etc*); **~ tense** LING Präsens n, Gegenwart f; **2.** Gegenwart f, LING *a.* Präsens n; **at ~** gegenwärtig, zurzeit; **for the ~** vorerst, vorläufig

pre·sen·ta·tion Präsentation f; Überreichung f; Vorlage f; Vorführung f; THEA *etc* Aufführung f; Schilderung f, Darstellung f; Vorstellung f; radio, TV Moderation f

pres·ent-day heutig, gegenwärtig, modern

pre·sent·er *esp Br* radio, TV Moderator(in)

pre·sen·ti·ment (böse) Vorahnung

pres·ent·ly zurzeit, jetzt; *Br* bald

pres·er·va·tion Bewahrung f, Erhaltung f; GASTR Konservierung f

pre·ser·va·tive GASTR Konservierungsmittel n

pre·serve 1. bewahren, (be)schützen; erhalten; GASTR konservieren, *Obst etc* einmachen, einkochen; **2.** (*Jagd-*)Revier n; *fig* Ressort n, Reich n; *mst pl* GASTR das Eingemachte

pre·side den Vorsitz haben (**at, over** bei); **pres·i·den·cy** POL Präsidentschaft f; Amtszeit f; **pres·i·dent** Präsident m; ECON Generaldirektor m

press¹ *v/t* drücken, pressen; *Frucht* (aus)pressen; drücken auf (*acc*); bügeln; drängen; *j-n* (be)drängen; bestehen auf (dat); v/i drücken; drängen (time etc); (sich) drängen; ~ for dringen or drängen auf (acc); ~ on (zügig) weitermachen; 2. Druck m (a. fig); (Wein- etc)Presse f; Bügeln n; die Presse; a. printing ~ Druckerpresse f

press a·gen·cy Presseagentur f

press box Pressetribüne f

press con·fe·rence Pressekonferenz f

press of·fice Pressebüro n, Pressestelle f; **press of·fi·cer** Pressereferent(in)

press·ing dringend

press re·lease Pressemitteilung f

press stud Br Druckknopf m

press-up esp Br SPORT Liegestütz m

pres·sure PHYS, TECH etc Druck m (a. fig); ~ **cook·er** Dampfkochtopf m, Schnellkochtopf m

pres·tige Prestige n, Ansehen n

pre·su·ma·bly vermutlich

pre·sume v/t annehmen, vermuten; sich erdreisten or anmaßen (**to do** zu tun); v/i annehmen, vermuten; anmaßend sein; ~ **on** et. ausnützen, et. missbrauchen

pre·sump·tion Annahme f, Vermutung f, Anmaßung f

pre·sump·tu·ous anmaßend, vermessen

pre·sup·pose voraussetzen

pre·sup·po·si·tion Voraussetzung f

pre·tence Br → **pretense**; **pre·tend** vortäuschen, vorgeben; sich verstellen; Anspruch erheben (**to** auf acc); **she is only ~ing** sie tut nur so; **pre·tend·ed** vorgetäuscht, gespielt; **pre·tense** Verstellung f, Vortäuschung f; Anspruch m (**to** auf acc); **pre·ten·sion** Anspruch m (**to** auf acc); Anmaßung f

pre·ter·it(e) LING Präteritum n

pre·text Vorwand m

pret·ty 1. adj hübsch; **2.** adv ziemlich, ganz schön

pret·zel Brezel f

pre·vail vorherrschen, weit verbreitet sein; siegen (**over, against** über acc)

pre·vail·ing (vor)herrschend

pre·vent verhindern, verhüten, e-r Sache vorbeugen; j-n hindern (**from** an dat)

pre·ven·tion Verhinderung f, Verhütung f, Vorbeugung f

pre·ven·tive vorbeugend

pre·view film, TV Voraufführung f; Vor-

besichtigung f; film, TV etc: Vorschau f (**of** auf acc)

pre·vi·ous vorhergehend, vorausgehend, vorherig, vorig; ~ **to** bevor, vor (dat); ~ **knowledge** Vorkenntnisse pl

pre·vi·ous·ly vorher, früher

pre-war Vorkriegs...

prey 1. ZO Beute f, Opfer n (a. fig); **be easy ~ for** or **to** fig e-e leichte Beute sein für; **2.** ~ **on** ZO Jagd machen auf (acc); fig nagen an (dat); ~ **on s.o.'s mind** j-m keine Ruhe lassen

price 1. Preis m; **2.** den Preis festsetzen für; auszeichnen (**at** mit)

price·less unbezahlbar

price tag Preisschild n

prick 1. Stich m; V Schwanz m; ~**s of conscience** Gewissensbisse pl; **2.** v/t (auf-, durch)stechen, stechen in (acc); **her conscience ~ed her** sie hatte Gewissensbisse; ~ **up one's ears** die Ohren spitzen; v/i stechen

prick·le BOT, ZO Stachel m, Dorn m

prick·ly stach(e)lig; prickelnd, kribbelnd

pride 1. Stolz m; Hochmut m; **take (a) ~ in** stolz sein auf (acc); **2.** ~ **o.s. on** stolz sein auf (acc)

priest REL Priester m

prig Tugendbold m

prig·gish tugendhaft

prim steif; steif

pri·mae·val esp Br → **primeval**

pri·ma·ri·ly in erster Linie, vor allem

pri·ma·ry 1. wichtigste(r, -s), Haupt...; grundlegend, elementar, Grund...; Anfangs..., Ur...; **2.** POL Vorwahl f

pri·ma·ry school Br Grundschule f

prime 1. MATH Primzahl f; fig Blüte(zeit) f; **in the ~ of life** in der Blüte s-r Jahre; **be past one's ~** s-e besten Jahre hinter sich haben; **2.** adj erste(r, -s), wichtigste (r, -s), Haupt...; erstklassig; **3.** v/t TECH grundieren; j-n instruieren, vorbereiten; ~ **min·is·ter** (ABBR POL F **PM**) Premierminister(in), Ministerpräsident(in); ~ **num·ber** MATH Primzahl f

prim·er Fibel f, Elementarbuch n

prime time TV Haupteinschaltzeit f, Hauptsendezeit f, beste Sendezeit

pri·me·val urzeitlich, Ur...

prim·i·tive erste(r, -s), ursprünglich, Ur...; primitiv

prim·rose BOT Primel *f*, *esp* Schlüsselblume *f*

prince Fürst *m*; Prinz *m*

prin·cess Fürstin *f*; Prinzessin *f*

prin·ci·pal 1. wichtigste(r, -s), hauptsächlich, Haupt...; **2.** PED Direktor(in), Rektor(in); THEA Hauptdarsteller(in); MUS Solist(in)

prin·ci·pal·i·ty Fürstentum *n*

prin·ci·ple Prinzip *n*, Grundsatz *m*; **on ~** grundsätzlich, aus Prinzip

print 1. PRINT Druck *m* (*a. art*); Gedruckte *n*; (*Finger- etc*)Abdruck *m*; PHOT Abzug *m*; bedruckter Stoff; *in ~* gedruckt; *out of ~* vergriffen; **2.** *v/i* drucken; *v/t* (ab-, auf-, be)drucken; in Druckbuchstaben schreiben; *fig* einprägen (**on** *dat*); *a.* **~ off** PHOT abziehen; **~ out** EDP ausdrucken

print·ed mat·ter *post* Drucksache *f*

print·er Drucker *m* (*a.* TECH); **~'s error** Druckfehler *m*; **~'s ink** Druckerschwärze *f*; **print·ers** Druckerei *f*

print·ing Drucken *n*; Auflage *f*; **~ ink** Druckerschwärze *f*; **~ press** Druckerpresse *f*

print·out EDP Ausdruck *m*

pri·or frühere(r, -s); vorrangig

pri·or·i·ty Priorität *f*, Vorrang *m*; MOT Vorfahrt *f*; **give s.th. ~** et. vordringlich behandeln

prise *esp Br* → **prize²**

prism Prisma *n*

pris·on Gefängnis *n*, Strafanstalt *f*

pris·on·er Gefangene *m, f*, Häftling *m*; **hold ~**, **keep ~** gefangen halten; **take ~** gefangen nehmen

pri·va·cy Intim-, Privatsphäre *f*; Geheimhaltung *f*

pri·vate 1. privat, Privat...; vertraulich; geheim; **~ parts** Geschlechtsteile *pl*; **2.** MIL gemeiner Soldat; *in* **~** privat; unter vier Augen

pri·va·tion Entbehrung *f*

priv·i·lege Privileg *n*; Vorrecht *n*

priv·i·leged privilegiert

priv·y: *be* **~ to** eingeweiht sein in (*acc*)

prize¹ 1. (Sieger-, Sieges)Preis *m*, Prämie *f*, Auszeichnung *f*; (*Lotterie*)Gewinn *m*; **2.** preisgekrönt; Preis...; **3.** (hoch) schätzen

prize²: **~ open** aufbrechen, aufstemmen

prize·win·ner Preisträger(in)

pro¹ F Profi *m*

pro²: *the* **~s and cons** das Pro und Kontra, das Für und Wider

prob·a·bil·i·ty Wahrscheinlichkeit *f*; **in all ~** höchstwahrscheinlich

prob·a·ble *adj* wahrscheinlich

prob·a·bly *adv* wahrscheinlich

pro·ba·tion Probe *f*, Probezeit *f*; JUR Bewährung *f*, Bewährungsfrist *f*

pro·ba·tion of·fi·cer JUR Bewährungshelfer(in)

probe 1. MED, TECH Sonde *f*; *fig* Untersuchung *f* (**into** *gen*); **2.** sondieren; (gründlich) untersuchen

prob·lem Problem *n*, MATH *etc* Aufgabe *f*; **prob·lem·at·ic**, **prob·lem·at·i·cal** problematisch

pro·ce·dure Verfahren *n*, Verfahrensweise *f*, Vorgehen *n*

pro·ceed (weiter)gehen, (weiter)fahren; sich begeben (**to** nach, zu); *fig* weitergehen; *fig* fortfahren; *fig* vorgehen; **~ from** kommen *or* herrühren von; **~ to do s.th.** sich anschicken *or* daranmachen, et. zu tun

pro·ceed·ing Verfahren *n*, Vorgehen *n*

pro·ceed·ings Vorgänge *pl*, Geschehnisse *pl*; **start** *or* **take** (**legal**) **~ against** JUR (gerichtlich) vorgehen gegen

pro·ceeds ECON Erlös *m*, Ertrag *m*, Einnahmen *pl*

pro·cess 1. Prozess *m*, Verfahren *n*, Vorgang *m*; **in the ~** dabei; **be in ~** im Gange sein; **in ~ of construction** im Bau (befindlich); **2.** TECH *etc* bearbeiten, behandeln; EDP Daten verarbeiten; PHOT Film entwickeln

pro·ces·sion Prozession *f*

pro·ces·sor EDP Prozessor *m*; (*Wort-, Text*)Verarbeitungsgerät *n*

pro·claim proklamieren, ausrufen

proc·la·ma·tion Proklamation *f*, Bekanntmachung *f*

pro·cure (sich) et. beschaffen *or* besorgen; verkuppeln

prod 1. stoßen; *fig* anstacheln, anspornen (**into** zu); **2.** Stoß *m*

prod·i·gal 1. verschwenderisch; **2.** F Verschwender(in)

pro·di·gious erstaunlich, großartig

prod·i·gy Wunder *n*; **child ~** Wunderkind *n*

pro·duce¹ ECON produzieren (*a. film,* TV), herstellen, erzeugen (*a. fig*); hervorholen (**from** aus); *Ausweis etc* (vor)zeigen; *Beweise etc* vorlegen; *Zeugen etc* beibringen; *Gewinn etc* (er)bringen, abwerfen; THEA inszenieren; *fig* hervorrufen, *Wirkung* erzielen

prod·uce² *esp* (*Agrar*)Produkt(e *pl*) *n*, (*Agrar*)Erzeugnis(se *pl*) *n*

pro·duc·er Produzent(in) (*a. film*, TV), Hersteller(in); THEA Regisseur(in)

prod·uct Produkt *n*, Erzeugnis *n*

pro·duc·tion ECON Produktion *f* (*a. film*, TV), Erzeugung *f*, Herstellung *f*; Produkt *n*, Erzeugnis *n*; Hervorholen *n*; Vorzeigen *n*, Vorlegen *n*, Beibringung *f*; THEA Inszenierung *f*

pro·duc·tive produktiv (*a. fig*), ergiebig, rentabel; *fig* schöpferisch

pro·duc·tiv·i·ty Produktivität *f*

prof F Prof *m*

pro·fa·na·tion Entweihung *f*

pro·fane **1.** (gottes)lästerlich; profan, weltlich; **2.** entweihen

pro·fan·i·ty: profanities Flüche *pl*, Lästerungen *pl*

pro·fess vorgeben, vortäuschen; behaupten (**to be** zu sein); erklären

pro·fessed erklärt (*enemy etc*); angeblich

pro·fes·sion (*esp* akademischer) Beruf; Berufsstand *m*

pro·fes·sion·al **1.** Berufs..., beruflich; Fach..., fachlich; fachmännisch; professionell; **2.** Fachmann *m*, Profi *m*; Berufsspieler(in), -sportler(in), Profi *m*

pro·fes·sor Professor(in); Dozent(in)

pro·fi·cien·cy Können *n*, Tüchtigkeit *f*

pro·fi·cient tüchtig (*at, in* in *dat*)

pro·file Profil *n*; *keep a low ~* Zurückhaltung üben

prof·it 1. Gewinn *m*, Profit *m*; Vorteil *m*, Nutzen *m*; **2.** *~ by*, *~ from* Nutzen ziehen aus, profitieren von

prof·it·a·ble Gewinn bringend, einträglich; nützlich, vorteilhaft

prof·it·eer *contp* Profitmacher *m*, Schieber *m*

prof·it shar·ing ECON Gewinnbeteiligung *f*

prof·li·gate verschwenderisch

pro·found *fig* tief; tiefgründig; profund (*knowledge etc*)

pro·fuse (über)reich; verschwenderisch; **pro·fu·sion** Überfülle *f*; *in ~* in Hülle und Fülle

prog·e·ny Nachkommen(schaft *f*) *pl*

prog·no·sis MED Prognose *f*

pro·gram 1. Programm *n* (*a.* EDP); *radio*, TV *a.* Sendung *f*; **2.** (vor)programmieren; planen; EDP programmieren

pro·gram·er EDP Programmierer(in)

pro·gramme *Br* → **program**

ˈpro·gram·mer *Br* → **programer**

pro·gress 1. Fortschritt(e *pl*) *m*; *make slow ~* (nur) langsam vorankommen; *be in ~* im Gange sein; **2.** fortschreiten; Fortschritte machen

pro·gres·sive progressiv, fortschreitend; fortschrittlich

pro·hib·it verbieten; verhindern

pro·hi·bi·tion Verbot *n*

pro·hib·i·tive Schutz... (*Zoll etc*); unerschwinglich

proj·ect¹ Projekt *n*, Vorhaben *n*

pro·ject² *v/i* vorspringen, vorragen, vorstehen; *v/t* werfen, schleudern; planen; projizieren

pro·jec·tile Projektil *n*, Geschoss *n*

pro·jec·tion Vorsprung *m*, vorspringender Teil; Werfen *n*, Schleudern *n*; Planung *f*; *film:* Projektion *f*

pro·jec·tion·ist Filmvorführer *m*

pro·jec·tor *film:* Projektor *m*

pro·le·tar·i·an 1. proletarisch; **2.** Proletarier(in)

pro·lif·ic fruchtbar

pro·log, *esp Br* **pro·logue** Prolog *m*

pro·long verlängern

prom·e·nade 1. (Strand)Promenade *f*; **2.** promenieren

prom·i·nent vorspringend, vorstehend; *fig* prominent

pro·mis·cu·ous sexuell freizügig

prom·ise 1. Versprechen *n*; *fig* Aussicht *f*; **2.** versprechen

prom·is·ing viel versprechend

prom·on·to·ry GEOGR Vorgebirge *n*

pro·mote *j-n* befördern; *Schüler* versetzen; ECON werben für; *Boxkampf, Konzert etc* veranstalten; *et.* fördern; *be ~d* SPORT *esp Br* aufsteigen (*to* in *acc*)

pro·mot·er Promoter(in), Veranstalter(in); ECON Verkaufsförderer *m*

pro·mo·tion Beförderung *f*; PED Versetzung *f*; SPORT Aufstieg *m*; ECON Verkaufsförderung *f*, Werbung *f*

pro·mo·tion·al *film* Werbefilm *m*

prompt 1. *j-n* veranlassen (**to do** zu tun);

führen zu, *Gefühle etc* wecken; *j-m* vorsagen; THEA *j-m* soufflieren; **2.** prompt, umgehend, unverzüglich; pünktlich

prompt·er THEA Souffleur *m*, Souffleuse *f*

prone auf dem Bauch *or* mit dem Gesicht nach unten liegend; **be ~ to** *a.* MED neigen zu, anfällig sein für

prong Zinke *f*; (*Geweih*)Sprosse *f*

pro·noun LING Pronomen *n*, Fürwort *n*

pro·nounce aussprechen; erklären für; JUR *Urteil* verkünden

pro·nun·ci·a·tion Aussprache *f*

proof **1.** Beweis(e *pl*) *m*, Nachweis *m*; Probe *f*; PRINT Korrekturfahne *f*, *a.* PHOT Probeabzug *m*; **2.** *adj in cpds* ...fest, ...beständig, ...dicht, ...sicher; → **heatproof, soundproof, waterproof**; **be ~ against** geschützt sein vor (*dat*); **3.** imprägnieren

proof·read PRINT Korrektur lesen

proof·read·er PRINT Korrektor(in)

prop 1. Stütze *f* (*a. fig*); **2.** *a.* **~ up** stützen; *sich or et.* lehnen (**against** gegen)

prop·a·gate BIOL sich fortpflanzen *or* vermehren; verbreiten

prop·a·ga·tion Fortpflanzung *f*, Vermehrung *f*; Verbreitung *f*

pro·pel (an)treiben; **pro·pel·lant, pro·pel·lent** Treibstoff *m*; Treibgas *n*

pro·pel·ler AVIAT Propeller *m*, MAR *a.* Schraube *f*

pro·pel·ling pen·cil Drehbleistift *m*

pro·pen·si·ty *fig* Neigung *f*

prop·er richtig, passend, geeignet; anständig, schicklich; echt, wirklich, richtig; eigentlich; eigen(tümlich); *esp Br* F ordentlich, tüchtig, gehörig

prop·er| name, ~ noun Eigenname *m*

prop·er·ty Eigentum *n*, Besitz *m*; Landbesitz *m*, Grundbesitz *m*; Grundstück *n*; *fig* Eigenschaft *f*

proph·e·cy Prophezeiung *f*

proph·e·sy prophezeien

proph·et Prophet *m*

pro·por·tion 1. Verhältnis *n*; (An)Teil *m*; *pl* Größenverhältnisse *pl*, Proportionen *pl*; **in ~ to** im Verhältnis zu; **2.** (*to*) in das richtige Verhältnis bringen (mit, zu); anpassen (*dat*)

pro·por·tion·al proportional; → **proportionate**

pro·por·tion·ate (**to**) im richtigen Verhältnis (zu), entsprechend (*dat*)

pro·pos·al Vorschlag *m*; (Heirats)Antrag *m*; **pro·pose** *v/t* vorschlagen; beabsichtigen, vorhaben; *Toast* ausbringen (**to** auf *acc*); **~ s.o.'s health** auf j-s Gesundheit trinken; *v/i*: **~ to** *j-m* e-n (Heirats)Antrag machen

prop·o·si·tion Behauptung *f*; Vorschlag *m*, ECON *a.* Angebot *n*

pro·pri·e·ta·ry ECON gesetzlich *or* patentrechtlich geschützt; *fig* besitzergreifend

pro·pri·e·tor Eigentümer *m*, Besitzer *m*, Geschäftsinhaber *m*

pro·pri·e·tress Eigentümerin *f*, Besitzerin *f*, Geschäftsinhaberin *f*

pro·pri·e·ty Anstand *m*; Richtigkeit *f*

pro·pul·sion TECH Antrieb *m*

pro·sa·ic prosaisch, nüchtern, sachlich

prose Prosa *f*

pros·e·cute JUR strafrechtlich verfolgen, (gerichtlich) belangen (**for** wegen)

pros·e·cu·tion JUR strafrechtliche Verfolgung, Strafverfolgung *f*; **the ~** die Staatsanwaltschaft, die Anklage(behörde)

pros·e·cu·tor *a.* **public ~** JUR Staatsanwalt *m*, Staatsanwältin *f*

pros·pect 1. Aussicht *f* (*a. fig*); Interessent *m*, ECON möglicher Kunde, potenzieller Käufer; **2. ~ for** *mining:* schürfen nach; bohren nach

pro·spec·tive voraussichtlich

pro·spec·tus (Werbe)Prospekt *m*

pros·per gedeihen; ECON blühen, florieren; **pros·per·i·ty** Wohlstand *m*; **pros·per·ous** ECON erfolgreich, blühend, florierend; wohlhabend

pros·ti·tute Prostituierte *f*, Dirne *f*; **male ~** Strichjunge *m*

pros·trate 1. hingestreckt; *fig* am Boden liegend; erschöpft; **~ with grief** grambeugt; **2.** niederwerfen; *fig* erschöpfen; *fig* niederschmettern

pros·y langweilig; weitschweifig

pro·tag·o·nist Vorkämpfer(in); THEA Hauptfigur *f*, Held(in)

pro·tect (be)schützen (**from** vor *dat*, **against** gegen)

pro·tec·tion Schutz *m*; F Schutzgeld *n*; **~ of animals** Tierschutz *m*; **~ of endangered species** Artenschutz *m*; **~ money** F Schutzgeld *n*; **~ rack·et** Schutzgelderpressung *f*

pro·tec·tive (be)schützend; Schutz...; ~ **cloth·ing** Schutzkleidung f; ~ **cus·tody** JUR Schutzhaft f; ~ **du·ty**, ~ **tar·iff** ECON Schutzzoll m

pro·tec·tor Beschützer m; (Brust- etc -) Schutz m

pro·tec·to·rate POL Protektorat n

pro·test 1. Protest m; Einspruch m; **2.** v/i protestieren (**against** gegen); v/t protestieren gegen; beteuern

Prot·es·tant REL **1.** protestantisch; **2.** Protestant(in)

prot·es·ta·tion Beteuerung f; Protest m (**against** gegen)

pro·to·col Protokoll n

pro·to·type Prototyp m

pro·tract in die Länge ziehen, hinziehen

pro·trude herausragen, vorstehen (**from** aus); **pro·trud·ing** vorstehend (a. teeth), vorspringend (chin)

proud stolz (**of** auf acc)

prove v/t be-, er-, nachweisen; v/i: ~ (**to be**) sich herausstellen or erweisen als

prov·en bewährt

prov·erb Sprichwort n

pro·vide v/t versehen, versorgen, beliefern; zur Verfügung stellen, bereitstellen; JUR vorsehen, vorschreiben (**that** dass); v/i: ~ **against** Vorsorge treffen gegen; JUR verbieten; ~ **for** sorgen für; vorsorgen für; JUR et. vorsehen

pro·vid·ed: ~ (**that**) vorausgesetzt(, dass)

pro·vid·er Ernährer(in) f

prov·ince Provinz f; (Aufgaben-, Wissens)Gebiet n; **pro·vin·cial 1.** Provinz..., provinziell, contp provinzlerisch; **2.** contp Provinzler(in)

pro·vi·sion Bereitstellung f, Beschaffung f; Vorkehrung f, Vorsorge f; Bestimmung f, Vorschrift f; pl Proviant m, Verpflegung f; **with the ~ that** unter der Bedingung, dass

pro·vi·sion·al provisorisch, vorläufig

pro·vi·so Bedingung f, Vorbehalt m; **with the ~ that** unter der Bedingung, dass

prov·o·ca·tion Provokation f

pro·voc·a·tive provozierend, (a. sexually) aufreizend

pro·voke provozieren, reizen

prowl 1. v/i a. ~ **about**, ~ **around** herumschleichen, herumstreifen; v/t durchstreifen; **2.** Herumstreifen n

prowl car (Funk)Streifenwagen m

prox·im·i·ty Nähe f

prox·y (Handlungs)Vollmacht f; (Stell-) Vertreter(in), Bevollmächtigte m, f; **by** ~ durch e-n Bevollmächtigten

prude: be a ~ prüde sein

pru·dence Klugheit f, Vernunft f; Besonnenheit f

pru·dent klug, vernünftig; besonnen

prud·ish prüde

prune[1] BOT (be)schneiden

prune[2] Backpflaume f

prus·sic ac·id CHEM Blausäure f

pry[1] neugierig sein; ~ **about** herumschnüffeln; ~ **into** s-e Nase stecken in (acc)

pry[2] → **prize**[2]

psalm REL Psalm m

pseu·do·nym Pseudonym n, Deckname m

psy·chi·a·trist Psychiater(in)

psy·chi·a·try Psychiatrie f

psy·cho·a·nal·y·sis Psychoanalyse f

psy·cho·log·i·cal psychologisch

psy·chol·o·gist Psychologe m, Psychologin f

psy·chol·o·gy Psychologie f

psy·cho·so·mat·ic psychosomatisch

pub Br Pub n, m, Kneipe f

pu·ber·ty Pubertät f

pu·bic hair Schamhaare pl

pub·lic 1. öffentlich; allgemein bekannt; **make ~** bekannt machen, an die Öffentlichkeit bringen; **2.** die Öffentlichkeit, das Publikum; **in ~** öffentlich, in aller Öffentlichkeit

pub·li·ca·tion Bekanntgabe f, Bekanntmachung f; Publikation f, Veröffentlichung f

pub·lic con·ve·ni·ence Br öffentliche Bedürfnisanstalt; ~ **en·e·my** Staatsfeind m; ~ **health** öffentliches Gesundheitswesen; ~ **hol·i·day** gesetzlicher Feiertag

pub·lic·i·ty Publicity f, a. Bekanntheit f, ECON a. Reklame f, Werbung f; ~ **de·part·ment** Werbeabteilung f

pub·lic li·bra·ry Leihbücherei f; ~ **rela·tions** (ABBR **PR**) Public Relations pl, Öffentlichkeitsarbeit f; ~ **school** staatliche Schule; Br Public School f; ~ **trans·port** esp Br, ~ **trans·por·ta·tion** öffentliche Verkehrsmittel pl

pub·lish bekannt geben or machen;

P

publizieren, veröffentlichen; *Buch etc* verlegen, herausgeben

pub·lish·er Verleger(in), Herausgeber(in); Verlag *m*; Verlagshaus *n*

pub·lish·er's, pub·lish·ers, publishing house Verlag *m*, Verlagshaus *n*

puck·er *a.* ~ *up* (sich) verziehen, (sich) runzeln

pud·ding *Br* GASTR Nachspeise *f*, Nachtisch *m*; (*Reis- etc*)Auflauf *m*; (*Art*) Fleischpastete *f*; Pudding *m*

pud·dle Pfütze *f*

pu·er·ile infantil, kindisch

puff 1. *v/i* schnaufen, keuchen; *a.* ~ *away* paffen (*at* an *dat*); ~ *up* (an)schwellen; *v/t* Rauch blasen; ~ *out* Kerze etc ausblasen; *Rauch etc* ausstoßen; *Brust* herausdrücken; **2.** Zug *m*; (*Wind-*) Hauch *m*, (*Wind*)Stoß *m*; (*Puder*)Quaste *f*; F Puste *f*

puffed sleeve Puffärmel *m*

puff pas·try GASTR Blätterteig *m*

puff·y (an)geschwollen; aufgedunsen

pug ZO Mops *m*

puke F (aus)kotzen

pull 1. Ziehen *n*; Zug *m*, Ruck *m*; Anstieg *m*, Steigung *f*; Zuggriff *m*, Zugleine *f*; F Beziehungen *pl*; **2.** ziehen; ziehen an (*dat*); zerren, reißen; *Pflanze* ausreißen; *esp Br Bier* zapfen; *fig* anziehen; ~ *ahead of* vorbeiziehen an (*dat*, MOT überholen (*acc*); ~ *away* anfahren (*bus etc*); ~ *down Gebäude* abreißen; ~ *in* einfahren (*train*), anhalten; ~ *off* F *et.* zustande bringen, schaffen; ~ *out* herausziehen (*of* aus); *Tisch* ausziehen; RAIL abfahren; MOT ausscheren; *fig* sich zurückziehen, aussteigen (*of* aus); ~ *over* (s-n Wagen) an die *or* zur Seite fahren; ~ *round* MED durchbringen; durchkommen; ~ *through j-n* durchbringen; ~ *o.s. together* sich zusammennehmen, F sich zusammenreißen; ~ *up* MOT anhalten; (an)halten; ~ *up to*, ~ *up with* SPORT *j-n* einholen

pull date Mindesthaltbarkeitsdatum *n*

pul·ley TECH Flaschenzug *m*

pull-in *Br* F Raststätte *f*, Rasthaus *n*

pull·o·ver Pullover *m*

pull-up SPORT Klimmzug *m*; *do a* ~ e-n Klimmzug machen

pulp 1. Fruchtfleisch *n*; Brei *m*; **2.** Schund...; ~ *novel* Schundroman *m*

pul·pit Kanzel *f*

pulp·y breiig

pul·sate pulsieren, vibrieren

pulse Puls *m*; Pulsschlag *m*

pul·ver·ize pulverisieren

pu·ma ZO Puma *m*

pum·mel mit den Fäusten bearbeiten

pump 1. Pumpe *f*; (*Zapf*)Säule *f*; **2.** pumpen; F *j-n* aushorchen; ~ *up* aufpumpen; ~ *at·tend·ant* Tankwart *m*

pump·kin BOT Kürbis *m*

pun 1. Wortspiel *n*; **2.** Wortspiele *or* ein Wortspiel machen

punch[1] **1.** boxen, (mit der Faust) schlagen; **2.** (Faust)Schlag *m*

punch[2] **1.** lochen; *Loch* stanzen (*in* in *acc*); ~ *in* einstempeln; ~ *out* ausstempeln; **2.** Locher *m*; Lochzange *f*; Locheisen *n*

punch[3] Punsch *m*

Punch *appr* Kasper *m*, Kasperle *n*, *m*; *be as pleased or proud as* ~ sich freuen wie ein Schneekönig; ~ *and Ju·dy show* Kasperletheater *n*

punc·tu·al pünktlich

punc·tu·al·i·ty Pünktlichkeit *f*

punc·tu·ate interpunktieren

punc·tu·a·tion LING Interpunktion *f*; ~ *mark* LING Satzzeichen *n*

punc·ture 1. (Ein)Stich *m*, Loch *n*; MOT Reifenpanne *f*; **2.** durchstechen, durchbohren; ein Loch bekommen, platzen; MOT e-n Platten haben

pun·gent scharf, stechend, beißend (*smell, taste*); scharf, bissig (*remark etc*)

pun·ish *j-n* (be)strafen

pun·ish·a·ble strafbar

pun·ish·ment Strafe *f*; Bestrafung *f*

punk Punk *m* (*a.* MUS); Punk(er) *m*

pu·ny schwächlich

pup ZO Welpe *m*, junger Hund

pu·pa ZO Puppe *f*

pu·pil[1] Schüler(in)

pu·pil[2] ANAT Pupille *f*

pup·pet Handpuppe *f*; Marionette *f* (*a. fig*); ~ *show* Marionettentheater *n*, Puppenspiel *n*

pup·pe·teer Puppenspieler(in)

pup·py ZO Welpe *m*, junger Hund

pur·chase 1. kaufen; *fig* erkaufen; **2.** Kauf *m*; *make* ~*s* Einkäufe machen

pur·chas·er Käufer(in)

pure rein; pur

pure·bred ZO reinrassig

pur·ga·tive MED **1.** abführend; **2.** Abführmittel *n*

pur·ga·to·ry REL Fegefeuer *n*

purge 1. *Partei etc* säubern (**of** von); **2.** Säuberung *f*, Säuberungsaktion *f*

pu·ri·fy reinigen

pu·ri·tan (HIST **Puritan**) **1.** Puritaner(in); **2.** puritanisch

pu·ri·ty Reinheit *f*

purl 1. linke Masche; **2.** links stricken

pur·ple purpurn, purpurrot

pur·pose 1. Absicht *f*, Vorsatz *m*; Zweck *m*, Ziel *n*; Entschlossenheit *f*; **on ~** absichtlich; **to no ~** vergeblich; **2.** beabsichtigen, vorhaben

pur·pose·ful entschlossen, zielstrebig

pur·pose·less zwecklos; ziellos

pur·pose·ly absichtlich

purr ZO schnurren; MOT summen, surren

purse[1] Geldbeutel *m*, Geldbörse *f*, Portemonnaie *n*; Handtasche *f*; SPORT Siegprämie *f*; *boxing:* Börse *f*

purse[2]: **~ (up) one's lips** die Lippen schürzen

purs·er MAR Zahlmeister *m*

pur·su·ance: **in (the) ~ of his duty** in Ausübung s-r Pflicht

pur·sue verfolgen; *s-m Studium etc* nachgehen; *Absicht, Politik etc* verfolgen; *Angelegenheit etc* weiterführen

pur·su·er Verfolger(in)

pur·suit Verfolgung *f*, Weiterführung *f*

pur·vey *Lebensmittel etc* liefern

pur·vey·or Lieferant *m*

pus MED Eiter *m*

push 1. stoßen, F schubsen; schieben; *Taste etc* drücken; drängen; (an)treiben; F *Rauschgift* pushen; *fig j-n* drängen (**to do** zu tun); *fig* Reklame machen für; **~ one's way** sich drängen (**through** durch); **~ ahead with** *Plan etc* vorantreiben; **~ along** F sich auf die Socken machen; **~ around** F herumschubsen; **~ for** drängen auf (*acc*); **~ forward with → push ahead with**; **~ o.s. forward** *fig* sich in den Vordergrund drängen *or* schieben; **~ in** F sich vordrängeln; **~ off!** F hau ab!; **~ on with → push ahead with**; **~ out** *fig j-n* hinausdrängen; **~ through** *et.* durchsetzen; **~ up** *Preise etc* hochtreiben; **2.** Stoß *m*, F Schubs *m*; (Werbe)Kampagne *f*; F Durchsetzungsvermögen *n*, Energie *f*, Tatkraft *f*

push but·ton TECH Druckknopf *m*, Drucktaste *f*; **push-but·ton** TECH (Druck)Knopf..., (Druck)Tasten...; **~ (tele)phone** Tastentelefon *n*

push·chair Br Sportwagen *m*

push·er F *contp* Rauschgifthändler *m*

push·o·ver F Kinderspiel *n*

push-up SPORT Liegestütz *m*

puss F ZO Mieze *f*

pus·sy *a.* **~ cat** F Miezekatze *f*

pus·sy·foot: F **~ about**, **~ around** leisetreten, sich nicht festlegen wollen

put legen, setzen, stecken, stellen, tun; *j-n in e-e Lage etc, et. auf den Markt, in Ordnung etc* bringen; *et. in Kraft, in Umlauf etc* setzen; SPORT *Kugel* stoßen; unterwerfen, unterziehen (**to** *dat*); *et.* ausdrücken, *in Worte* fassen; übersetzen (**into German** ins Deutsche); *Schuld* geben (**on** *dat*); **~ right** in Ordnung bringen; **~ s.th. before s.o.** *fig* j-m et. vorlegen; **~ to bed** ins Bett bringen; **~ to school** zur Schule schicken; **~ about** *Gerüchte* verbreiten, in Umlauf setzen; **~ across** *et.* verständlich machen; **~ ahead** SPORT in Führung bringen; **~ aside** beiseite legen; *Ware* zurücklegen; *fig* beiseite schieben; **~ away** weglegen, wegtun; auf-, wegräumen; **~ back** zurücklegen, -stellen, -tun; *Uhr* zurückstellen (**by** um); **~ by** *Geld* zurücklegen; **~ down** *v/t* hinlegen, niederlegen, hinsetzen, hinstellen; *j-n* absetzen, aussteigen lassen; (auf-, nieder-) schreiben, eintragen; zuschreiben (**to** *dat*); *Aufstand* niederschlagen; (*a. v/i*) AVIAT landen; **~ forward** *Plan etc* vorlegen; *Uhr* vorstellen (**by** um); *fig* vorverlegen (**two days** um zwei Tage; **to** auf *acc*); **~ in** *v/t* hineinlegen, -stecken, -stellen, *Kassette etc* einlegen; installieren; *Gesuch etc* einreichen, *Forderung etc a.* geltend machen; *Antrag stellen*; *Arbeit, Zeit* verbringen (**on** mit); *Bemerkung* einwerfen; *v/i* MAR einlaufen (**at** in *acc*); **~ off** *et.* verschieben (**until** auf *acc*); *j-m* absagen; *j-n* hinhalten (**with** mit), *j-n* vertrösten; *j-n* aus dem Konzept bringen; **~ on** *Kleider etc* anziehen, *Hut, Brille* aufsetzen; *Licht, Radio etc* anmachen, einschalten; *Sonderzug* einsetzen; THEA *Stück etc* herausbringen; *et.* vortäuschen; F *j-n* auf den Arm nehmen; **~ on airs** sich aufspielen; **~ on weight** zunehmen; **~ out** v/t hinauslegen, -setzen, -stellen; *Hand etc* ausstrecken; *Feuer* löschen; *Licht, Radio etc* ausmachen (*a. cigarette*), ab-, ausschalten; veröffentlichen, herausgeben; *radio*, TV bringen, senden; *j-n* aus der Fassung bringen; *j-n* verärgern; *j-m* Ungelegenheiten bereiten; *j-m* Umstände machen; sich *den Arm etc* verrenken *or* ausrenken; v/i MAR auslaufen; **~ over → put across**; **~ through** TEL *j-n* verbinden (**to** mit); durch-, ausführen; **~ together** zusammenbauen, -setzen, -stellen; **~ up** v/t hinauflegen, -stellen; *Hand* (hoch)heben; *Zelt etc* aufstellen; *Gebäude* errichten; *Bild etc* aufhängen; *Plakat, Bekanntmachung etc* anschlagen; *Schirm* aufspannen; *zum Verkauf* anbieten; *Preis* erhöhen; *Widerstand* leisten; *Kampf* liefern; *j-n* unterbringen, (bei sich) aufneh-

men; v/i **~ up at** absteigen in (*dat*); **~ up with** sich gefallen lassen; sich abfinden mit

pu·tre·fy (ver)faulen, verwesen
pu·trid faul, verfault, verwest; F scheußlich, saumäßig
put·ty 1. Kitt *m*; **2.** kitten
put-up job F abgekartetes Spiel
puz·zle 1. Rätsel *n*; Geduld(s)spiel *n*; **2.** v/t *j-n* vor ein Rätsel stellen; verwirren; **be ~d** vor e-m Rätsel stehen; **~ out** herausfinden, herausbringen, F austüfteln; v/i sich den Kopf zerbrechen (**about, over** über *dat or acc*)
pyg·my 1. Pygmäe *m*, Pygmäin *f*; Zwerg (in); **2.** *esp* ZO Zwerg...
py·ja·mas *Br* → **pajamas**
py·lon TECH Hochspannungsmast *m*
pyr·a·mid Pyramide *f*
pyre Scheiterhaufen *m*
py·thon ZO Python(schlange) *f*
pyx REL Hostienbehälter *m*

Q

Q, q Q, q *n*
quack[1] ZO **1.** quaken; **2.** Quaken *n*
quack[2] *a.* **~ doctor** Quacksalber *m*, Kurpfuscher *m*; **quack·er·y** Quacksalberei *f*, Kurpfuscherei *f*
quad·ran·gle Viereck *n*
quad·ran·gu·lar viereckig
quad·ra·phon·ic quadrophon(isch)
quad·rat·ic MATH quadratisch
quad·ri·lat·er·al MATH **1.** vierseitig; **2.** Viereck *n*
quad·ro·phon·ic → quadraphonic
quad·ru·ped ZO Vierfüß(l)er *m*; Vierbeiner *m*
quad·ru·ple 1. vierfach; **2.** (sich) vervierfachen
quad·ru·plets Vierlinge *pl*
quads Vierlinge *pl*
quag·mire Morast *m*, Sumpf *m*
quail ZO Wachtel *f*
quaint idyllisch, malerisch
quake 1. zittern, beben (**with, for** vor *dat*; **at** bei); **2.** F Erdbeben *n*
Quak·er REL Quäker(in)
qual·i·fi·ca·tion Qualifikation *f*, Befä-

higung *f*, Eignung *f* (**for** für, zu); Voraussetzung *f*; Einschränkung *f*
qual·i·fied qualifiziert, geeignet, befähigt (**for** für); berechtigt; bedingt, eingeschränkt; **qual·i·fy** v/t qualifizieren, befähigen (**for** für, zu); berechtigen (**to do** zu tun); einschränken, abschwächen, mildern; v/i sich qualifizieren *or* eignen (**for** für; **as** als); SPORT sich qualifizieren (**for** für)
qual·i·ty Qualität *f*; Eigenschaft *f*
qualms Bedenken *pl*, Skrupel *pl*
quan·da·ry: be in a ~ about what to do nicht wissen, was man tun soll
quan·ti·ty Quantität *f*, Menge *f*
quan·tum PHYS **1.** Quant *n*; **2.** Quanten...
quar·an·tine 1. Quarantäne *f*; **2.** unter Quarantäne stellen
quar·rel 1. Streit *m*, Auseinandersetzung *f*; **2.** (sich) streiten
quar·rel·some streitsüchtig, zänkisch
quar·ry[1] Steinbruch *m*
quar·ry[2] HUNT Beute *f*, *a. fig* Opfer *n*

quart Quart n (ABBR **qt**) (0,95 l, Br 1,14 l)

quar·ter 1. Viertel n, vierter Teil; Quartal n, Vierteljahr n; Viertelpfund n; Vierteldollar m; SPORT (Spiel)Viertel n; (Himmels)Richtung f; Gegend f, Teil m; (Stadt)Viertel n; GASTR (esp Hinter)Viertel n; Gnade f, Pardon m; pl Quartier n, Unterkunft f (a. MIL); **a ~ of an hour** e-e Viertelstunde; **a ~ of** (Br **to**) **five** (ein) Viertel vor fünf (4.45); **a ~ after** (Br **past**) **five** (ein) Viertel nach fünf (5.15); **at close ~s** in or aus nächster Nähe; **from official ~s** von amtlicher Seite; **2.** vierteln; esp MIL einquartieren (**on** bei)

quar·ter·deck MAR Achterdeck n

quar·ter·fi·nals SPORT Viertelfinale n

quar·ter·ly 1. vierteljährlich; **2.** Vierteljahresschrift f

quar·tet(te) MUS Quartett n

quartz MIN Quarz m; **~ clock** Quarzuhr f; **~ watch** Quarz(armband)uhr f

qua·ver 1. v/i zittern; v/t et. mit zitternder Stimme sagen; **2.** Zittern n

quay MAR Kai m

quea·sy: **I feel ~** mir ist übel or F mulmig

queen Königin f; card game, chess: Dame f; F Schwule m, Homo m

queen bee ZO Bienenkönigin f

queen·ly wie e-e Königin, königlich

queer komisch, seltsam; F wunderlich; F schwul

quench Durst löschen, stillen

quer·u·lous nörglerisch

que·ry 1. Frage f; Zweifel m; **2.** infrage stellen, in Zweifel ziehen

quest 1. Suche f (**for** nach); **in ~ of** auf der Suche nach; **2.** suchen (**after, for** nach)

ques·tion 1. Frage f, a. Problem n, a. Sache f, a. Zweifel m; **only a ~ of time** nur e-e Frage der Zeit; **this is not the point in ~** darum geht es nicht; **there is no ~ that, it is beyond ~ that** es steht außer Frage, dass; **there is no ~ about this** daran besteht kein Zweifel; **be out of the ~** nicht infrage kommen; **2.** befragen (**about** über acc); JUR vernehmen, verhören (**about** zu); bezweifeln, in Zweifel ziehen, infrage stellen

ques·tion·a·ble fraglich, zweifelhaft; fragwürdig

ques·tion·er Fragesteller(in)

ques·tion| mark Fragezeichen n; **~ mas·ter** esp Br Quizmaster m

ques·tion·naire Fragebogen m

queue esp Br **1.** Schlange f; → **jump**; **2.** mst **~ up** Schlange stehen, anstehen, sich anstellen

quib·ble sich herumstreiten (**with** mit; **about, over** wegen)

quick 1. adj schnell, rasch; aufbrausend, hitzig (temper); **be ~!** mach schnell!, beeil dich!; **2.** adv schnell, rasch; **3.** **cut s.o. to the ~** fig j-n tief verletzen

quick·en (sich) beschleunigen

quick·sand Treibsand m

quick-tem·pered aufbrausend, hitzig

quick-wit·ted schlagfertig; geistesgegenwärtig

qui·et 1. ruhig, still; **~, please** Ruhe, bitte; **be ~!** sei still!; **2.** Ruhe f, Stille f; **on the ~** F heimlich; **3.** v/t a. **~ down** j-n beruhigen; v/i a. **~ down** sich beruhigen

qui·et·en Br → **quiet** 3

qui·et·ness Ruhe f, Stille f

quill ZO (Schwung-, Schwanz)Feder f; Stachel m

quilt Steppdecke f; **quilt·ed** Stepp...

quince BOT Quitte f

quin·ine PHARM Chinin n

quint F Fünfling m

quin·tes·sence Quintessenz f; Inbegriff m

quin·tet(te) MUS Quintett n

quin·tu·ple 1. fünffach; **2.** (sich) verfünffachen

quin·tu·plets Fünflinge pl

quip 1. geistreiche or witzige Bemerkung; **2.** witzeln, spötteln

quirk Eigenart f, Schrulle f; **by some ~ of fate** durch e-e Laune des Schicksals, durch e-n verrückten Zufall

quit F v/t aufhören mit; **~ one's job** kündigen; v/i aufhören; kündigen

quite ganz, völlig; ziemlich; **~ a few** ziemlich viele; **~ nice** ganz nett, recht nett; **~ (so)!** esp Br genau, ganz recht; **be ~ right** völlig Recht haben; **she's ~ a beauty** sie ist e-e wirkliche Schönheit

quits F quitt (**with** mit); **call it ~** es gut sein lassen

quit·ter F **be a ~** schnell aufgeben

quiv·er¹ zittern (**with** vor dat; **at** bei)

quiv·er² Köcher m

Q

quiz 1. Quiz n; Prüfung f, Test m; **2.** ausfragen (*about* über acc)

quiz·mas·ter Quizmaster m

quiz·zi·cal spöttisch-fragend

quo·ta Quote f, Kontingent n

quo·ta·tion Zitat n; ECON Notierung f; Kostenvoranschlag m; ~ **marks** LING Anführungszeichen pl

quote zitieren; *Beispiel etc* anführen; *Preis* nennen; **be ~d at** ECON notieren mit

quo·tient MATH Quotient m

R

R, r R, r n

rab·bi REL Rabbiner m

rab·bit ZO Kaninchen n

rab·ble Pöbel m, Mob m

rab·ble-rous·ing Hetz..., aufwiegle-risch

rab·id VET tollwütig; *fig* fanatisch

ra·bies VET Tollwut f

rac·coon ZO Waschbär m

race¹ Rasse f, Rassenzugehörigkeit f; (*Menschen*)Geschlecht n

race² 1. (Wett)Rennen n, (Wett)Lauf m; **2.** v/i an (e-m) Rennen teilnehmen; um die Wette laufen *or* fahren *etc*; rasen, rennen; MOT durchdrehen; v/t um die Wette laufen *or* fahren *etc* mit; rasen mit

race car MOT Rennwagen m

race·course Rennbahn f

race·horse Rennpferd n

rac·er Rennpferd n; Rennrad n, Rennwagen m

race ri·ots Rassenunruhen pl

race·track Rennbahn f

ra·cial rassisch, Rassen...

rac·ing 1. Rennsport m; **2.** Renn...

rac·ing car Br MOT Rennwagen m

rac·ism Rassismus m

rac·ist 1. Rassist(in); **2.** rassistisch

rack 1. Gestell n, (*Geschirr-, Zeitungs-etc*)Ständer m, RAIL (*Gepäck*)Netz n, MOT (*Dach*)Gepäckständer m; HIST Folter(bank) f; **2. be ~ed by** *or* **with** geplagt *or* gequält werden von; ~ **one's brains** sich das Hirn zermar-tern, sich den Kopf zerbrechen

rack·et¹ *tennis etc*: Schläger m

rack·et² F Krach m, Lärm m; Schwindel m, Gaunerei f; (*Drogen- etc*)Geschäft n; organisierte Erpressung

rack·et·eer Gauner m; Erpresser m

ra·coon → **raccoon**

rac·y spritzig, lebendig; gewagt (*joke*)

ra·dar TECH Radar m, n; ~ **screen** Radarschirm m; ~ **speed check** MOT Radarkontrolle f; ~ **sta·tion** Radar-station f; ~ **trap** MOT Radarkontrolle f

ra·di·al 1. radial, Radial..., strahlenför-mig; **2.** MOT Gürtelreifen m

ra·di·al| tire, Br **~ tyre** → **radial** 2

ra·di·ant strahlend, leuchtend (*a. fig* **with** *or dat*)

ra·di·ate ausstrahlen; strahlenförmig ausgehen (*from* von)

ra·di·a·tion Ausstrahlung f

ra·di·a·tor Heizkörper m; MOT Kühler m

rad·i·cal 1. radikal (*a.* POL); MATH Wur-zel...; **2.** POL Radikale m, f

ra·di·o 1. Radio(apparat m) n; Funk m; Funkgerät n; **by ~** über Funk; **on the ~** im Radio; **2.** funken

ra·di·o·ac·tive radioaktiv; ~ **waste** Atommüll m, radioaktiver Abfall

ra·di·o·ac·tiv·i·ty Radioaktivität f

ra·di·o| ham Funkamateur m; ~ **play** Hörspiel n; ~ **set** Radioapparat m; ~ **sta·tion** Funkstation f; Rundfunksen-der m, -station f; ~ **ther·a·py** MED Strahlentherapie f, Röntgentherapie f; ~ **tow·er** Funkturm m

rad·ish BOT Rettich m; Radieschen n

ra·di·us MATH Radius m

raf·fle 1. Tombola f; **2.** a. ~ **off** verlosen

raft Floß n

raf·ter (*Dach*)Sparren m

rag Lumpen m, Fetzen m; Lappen m; **in ~s** zerlumpt

rage 1. Wut f, Zorn m; **fly into a ~** wü-tend werden; **the latest ~** F der letzte Schrei; **be all the ~** F große Mode sein;

2. wettern (**against, at** gegen); wüten, toben

rag·ged zerlumpt; struppig; *fig* stümperhaft

raid 1. (on) Überfall *m* (auf *acc*), MIL *a.* Angriff *m* (gegen); Razzia *f* (in *dat*); **2.** überfallen, MIL *a.* angreifen; e-e Razzia machen in (*dat*)

rail 1. Geländer *n*; Stange *f*; (*Handtuch*)Halter *m*; (Eisen)Bahn *f*, RAIL Schiene *f*, *pl a.* Gleis *n*; **by ~** mit der Bahn; **2. ~ in** einzäunen; **~ off** abzäunen

rail·ing *often pl* (Gitter)Zaun *m*

rail·road Eisenbahn *f*; **~ line** Bahnlinie *f*; **~·man** Eisenbahner *m*; **~ sta·tion** Bahnhof *m*

rail·way *Br* → **railroad**

rain 1. Regen *m*, *pl* Regenfälle *pl*; the **~s** die Regenzeit; (**come**) **~ or shine** *fig* was immer auch geschieht; **2.** regnen; **it is ~ing cats and dogs** F es gießt in Strömen; **it never ~s but it pours** es kommt immer gleich knüppeldick, ein Unglück kommt selten allein

rain·bow Regenbogen *m*

rain·coat Regenmantel *m*

rain·fall Niederschlag(smenge *f*) *m*

rain for·est GEOGR Regenwald *m*

rain·proof regendicht, wasserdicht

rain·y regnerisch, verregnet, Regen...; **save s.th. for a ~ day** et. für schlechte Zeiten zurücklegen

raise 1. heben; hochziehen; erheben; *Denkmal etc* errichten; *Staub etc* aufwirbeln; *Gehalt, Miete etc* erhöhen; *Geld* zusammenbringen, beschaffen; *Kinder* aufziehen, großziehen; *Tiere* züchten; *Getreide etc* anbauen; *Frage* aufwerfen; et. zur Sprache bringen; *Blockade etc, a. Verbot* aufheben; **2.** Lohn- *or* Gehaltserhöhung *f*

rai·sin Rosine *f*

rake 1. Rechen *m*, Harke *f*; **2.** *v/t:* **~ (up)** (zusammen)rechen, (zusammen)harken; F **~ in** scheffeln; *v/i:* **~ about, ~ around** herumstöbern

rak·ish flott, keck, verwegen

ral·ly 1. (sich) (wieder) sammeln; sich erholen (**from** von) (*a.* ECON); **~ round** sich scharen um; **2.** Kundgebung *f*, (Massen)Versammlung *f*, MOT Rallye *f*; *tennis etc:* Ballwechsel *m*

ram 1. ZO Widder *m*, Schafbock *m*; TECH Ramme *f*; **2.** rammen

ram·ble 1. wandern, umherstreifen; abschweifen; **2.** Wanderung *f*; **ram·bler** Wanderer *m*; BOT Kletterrose *f*

ram·bling weitschweifig; weitläufig; **~ rose** BOT Kletterrose *f*

ramp Rampe *f*; MOT (Autobahn)Auffahrt *f*; (Autobahn)Ausfahrt *f*

ram·page 1. ~ through (wild *or* aufgeregt) trampeln durch (*elephant etc*); → **2. go on the ~ through** randalierend ziehen durch

ram·pant: be ~ wuchern (*plant*); grassieren (**in** in *dat*)

ram·shack·le baufällig (*building*); klapp(e)rig (*vehicle*)

ranch Ranch *f*; (*Geflügel- etc*)Farm *f*

ranch·er Rancher *m*; (*Geflügel- etc*) Züchter *m*

ran·cid ranzig

ran·co(u)r Groll *m*, Erbitterung *f*

ran·dom 1. *adj* ziellos, wahllos; zufällig, Zufalls...; **~ sample** Stichprobe *f*; **2. at ~** aufs Geratewohl

range 1. Reich-, Schuss-, Tragweite *f*; Entfernung *f*, *fig* Bereich *m*, *a.* Spielraum *m*, *a.* Gebiet *n*; (*Schieß*)Stand *m*, (-)Platz *m*; (*Berg*)Kette *f*; offenes Weidegebiet; ECON Kollektion *f*, Sortiment *n*; Küchenherd *m*; **at close ~** aus nächster Nähe; **within ~ of vision** in Sichtweite; **a wide ~ of ...** eine große Auswahl an ... (*dat*); **2.** *v/i:* **~ from ... to ..., ~ between ... and ...** sich zwischen ... und ... bewegen (*prices etc*); *v/t* aufstellen, anordnen

range find·er PHOT Entfernungsmesser *m*

rang·er Förster *m*; Ranger *m*

rank[1] 1. Rang *m* (*a.* MIL), (soziale) Stellung; Reihe *f*; (*Taxi*)Stand *m*; **of the first ~** *fig* erstklassig; **the ~ and file** *fig* die Basis; **the ~s** *fig* das Heer, die Masse; **2.** *v/t* rechnen, zählen (**among** zu); stellen (**above** über *acc*); *v/i* zählen, gehören (**among** zu); gelten (**as** als)

rank[2] BOT (üppig) wuchernd; übel riechend, übel schmeckend; *fig* krass (*outsider*), blutig (*beginner*)

ran·kle *fig* nagen, wehtun, F wurmen

ran·sack durchwühlen, durchsuchen; plündern

ran·som 1. Lösegeld *n*; **2.** freikaufen, auslösen

rant: ~ (on) about, ~ and rave about eifern gegen

rap 1. Klopfen *n*; Klaps *m*; **2.** klopfen (an *acc*, auf *acc*)

ra·pa·cious habgierig

rape[1] **1.** vergewaltigen; **2.** Vergewaltigung *f*

rape[2] BOT Raps *m*

rap·id schnell, rasch

ra·pid·i·ty Schnelligkeit *f*

rap·ids GEOGR Stromschnellen *pl*

rapt: with ~ attention mit gespannter Aufmerksamkeit

rap·ture Entzücken *n*, Verzückung *f*; **go into ~s** in Verzückung geraten

rare[1] selten, rar; dünn (*air*); F Mords...

rare[2] GASTR blutig (*steak*)

rar·e·fied dünn (*air*)

rar·i·ty Seltenheit *f*; Rarität *f*

ras·cal Schlingel *m*

rash[1] voreilig, vorschnell, unbesonnen

rash[2] MED (Haut)Ausschlag *m*

rash·er dünne Speckscheibe

rasp 1. raspeln; kratzen; **2.** Raspel *f*; Kratzen *n*

rasp·ber·ry BOT Himbeere *f*

rat ZO Ratte *f* (*a. contp*); F **smell a ~** Lunte *or* den Braten riechen

rate Quote *f*, Rate *f*, (*Geburten-, Sterbe*)Ziffer *f*; (*Steuer-, Zins- etc*)Satz *m*; (*Wechsel*)Kurs *m*; Geschwindigkeit *f*, Tempo *n*; **at any ~** auf jeden Fall; **2.** einschätzen, halten (**as** für); *Lob etc* verdienen; **be ~d as** gelten als

rate of ex·change ECON (Umrechnungs-, Wechsel)Kurs *m*

rate of in·terest ECON Zinssatz *m*

ra·ther ziemlich; eher, vielmehr, besser gesagt; **~! esp Br** F und ob!; **I would or had ~ go** ich möchte lieber gehen

rat·i·fy POL ratifizieren

rat·ing Einschätzung *f*; *radio*, TV Einschaltquote *f*

ra·ti·o MATH Verhältnis *n*

ra·tion 1. Ration *f*; **2.** *et.* rationieren; **~ out** zuteilen (**to** *dat*)

ra·tion·al rational; vernunftbegabt; vernünftig; verstandesmäßig

ra·tion·al·i·ty Vernunft *f*

ra·tion·al·ize rational erklären; ECON rationalisieren

rat race F endloser Konkurrenzkampf

rat·tle 1. klappern; rasseln *or* klimpern (mit); prasseln (**on** auf *acc*) (*rain etc*); rattern, knattern (*vehicle*); rütteln an (*dat*); F *j-n* verunsichern; ~ **at** rütteln an (*dat*); ~ **off** F *Gedicht etc* herunterrasseln; F ~ **on** quasseln (**about** über *acc*); F ~ **through** *Rede etc* herunterrasseln; **2.** Klappern *n* (*etc* → 1); Rassel *f*, Klapper *f*

rat·tle·snake ZO Klapperschlange *f*

rau·cous heiser, rau

rav·age verwüsten

rav·ag·es Verwüstungen *pl*, *a. fig* verheerende Auswirkungen *pl*

rave fantasieren, irrereden; toben; wettern (**against**, **at** gegen); schwärmen (**about** von)

rav·el (sich) verwickeln *or* verwirren

ra·ven ZO Rabe *m*

rav·e·nous ausgehungert, heißhungrig

ra·vine Schlucht *f*, Klamm *f*

rav·ing mad tobsüchtig

rav·ings irres Gerede, Delirien *pl*

rav·ish·ing *fig* hinreißend

raw GASTR roh, ECON, TECH *a.* Roh...; MED wund; METEOR nasskalt; *fig* unerfahren; ~ **vegetables and fruit** Rohkost *f*

raw-boned knochig, hager

raw·hide Rohleder *n*

raw ma·te·ri·al Rohstoff *m*

ray Strahl *m*; *fig* Schimmer *m*

ray·on Kunstseide *f*

ra·zor Rasiermesser *n*; Rasierapparat *m*; **electric ~** Elektrorasierer *m*

ra·zor blade Rasierklinge *f*

ra·zor('s) edge *fig* kritische Lage; **be on a ~** auf des Messers Schneide stehen

re... wieder, noch einmal, neu

reach 1. *v/t* erreichen; reichen *or* gehen bis an (*acc*) *or* zu; ~ **down** herunter-, hinunterreichen (**from** von); ~ **out** *Arm etc* ausstrecken; *v/i* reichen, gehen, sich erstrecken; *a.* ~ **out** greifen, langen (**for** nach); ~ **out** die Hand ausstrecken; **2.** Reichweite *f*; **within** (**out of**) ~ in (außer) Reichweite; **within easy ~** leicht erreichbar

re·act reagieren (**to** auf *acc*; CHEM **with** mit); **re·ac·tion** Reaktion *f* (*a.* CHEM)

re·ac·tor PHYS Reaktor *m*

read lesen; TECH (an)zeigen; *Zähler etc*

ablesen; UNIV studieren; deuten, verstehen (**as** als); sich *gut etc* lesen (lassen); lauten; **~ (s.th.) to s.o.** j-m (et.) vorlesen; **~ medicine** Medizin studieren

read·a·ble lesbar; leserlich; lesenswert

read·er Leser(in); Lektor(in); Lesebuch *n*

read·i·ly bereitwillig; gern; leicht; ohne weiteres

read·i·ness Bereitschaft *f*

read·ing 1. Lesen *n*; Lesung *f* (*a.* PARL); TECH Anzeige *f*, (*Thermometer- etc -*) Stand *m*; Auslegung *f*; **2.** Lese...; **~ matter** Lesestoff *m*

re·ad·just TECH nachstellen, korrigieren; **~ (o.s.) to** sich wieder anpassen (*dat*) *or* an (*acc*), sich wieder einstellen auf (*acc*)

read·y bereit; fertig; bereitwillig; im Begriff (**to do** zu tun); schnell, schlagfertig; *zur* gebrauchsfertig; **get ~** (sich) fertig machen

read·y cash → **ready money**

read·y-made Konfektions...

read·y meal Fertiggericht *n*

read·y mon·ey Bargeld *n*

real echt; wirklich; tatsächlich; real; F **for ~** echt, im Ernst

real es·tate Grundbesitz *m*, Immobilien *pl*; **~ a·gent** Grundstücks-, Immobilienmakler *m*

re·a·lism Realismus *m*

re·al·ist Realist(in)

re·al·is·tic realistisch

re·al·i·ty Realität *f*, Wirklichkeit *f*

re·a·li·za·tion Erkenntnis *f*; Realisierung *f* (*a.* ECON), Verwirklichung *f*

re·al·ize sich klarmachen, erkennen, begreifen, einsehen; realisieren (*a.* ECON), verwirklichen

real·ly wirklich, tatsächlich; **well, ~!** ich muss schon sagen!; **~?** im Ernst?

realm Königreich *n*; *fig* Reich *n*

real·tor Grundstücks-, Immobilienmakler *m*

reap *Getreide etc* schneiden; *Feld* abernten; *fig* ernten

re·ap·pear wieder erscheinen

rear 1. *v/t Kind, Tier* aufziehen, großziehen; *Kopf* heben; *v/i* sich aufbäumen (*horse*); **2.** Rückseite *f*, Hinterseite *f*, MOT Heck *n*; **in** (*Br* **at**) **the ~ of** hinter (*dat*); **bring up the ~** die Nach-

hut bilden; **3.** hinter, Hinter..., Rück..., MOT *a.* Heck...

rear-end col·li·sion MOT Auffahrunfall *m*

rear·guard MIL Nachhut *f*

rear light MOT Rücklicht *n*

re·arm MIL (wieder) aufrüsten

re·ar·ma·ment MIL (Wieder)Aufrüstung *f*

rear·most hinterste(r, -s)

rear·view mir·ror MOT Rückspiegel *m*

rear·ward 1. *adj* hintere(r, -s), rückwärtig; **2.** *adv a.* **rearwards** rückwärts

rear-wheel drive MOT Hinterradantrieb *m*

rear win·dow MOT Heckscheibe *f*

rea·son 1. Grund *m*; Verstand *m*; Vernunft *f*; **by ~ of** wegen; **for this ~** aus diesem Grund; **it stands to ~ that** es leuchtet ein, dass; **2.** *v/i* vernünftig *or* logisch denken; vernünftig reden (**with** mit); *v/t* folgern, schließen (**that** dass); **~ s.o. into** (**out of**) **s.th.** j-m et. einreden (ausreden); **rea·son·a·ble** vernünftig; günstig (*price*); ganz gut, nicht schlecht

re·as·sure beruhigen

re·bate ECON Rabatt *m*, (Preis)Nachlass *m*; Rückzahlung *f*

reb·el[1] 1. Rebell(in); Aufständische *m, f*; **2.** aufständisch

re·bel[2] rebellieren, sich auflehnen (**against** gegen)

re·bel·lion Rebellion *f*, Aufstand *m*

re·bel·lious rebellisch, aufständisch

re·birth Wiedergeburt *f*

re·bound 1. abprallen, zurückprallen (**from** von); *fig* zurückfallen (**on** auf *acc.*); **2.** SPORT Abpraller *m*

re·buff 1. schroffe Abweisung, Abfuhr *f*; **2.** schroff abweisen

re·build wieder aufbauen (*a. fig*)

re·buke 1. rügen, tadeln; **2.** Rüge *f*, Tadel *m*

re·call 1. zurückrufen, abberufen; MOT (in die Werkstatt) zurückrufen; sich erinnern an (*acc*); erinnern an (*acc*); **2.** Zurückrufung *f*, Abberufung *f*; Rückrufaktion *f*; **have total ~** das absolute Gedächtnis haben; **beyond ~, past ~** unwiederbringlich *or* unwiderruflich vorbei

re·ca·pit·u·late rekapitulieren, (kurz) zusammenfassen

R

re·cap·ture wieder einfangen (*a. fig*); *Häftling* wieder fassen; MIL zurückerobern

re·cast TECH umgießen; umformen, neu gestalten; THEA *etc* umbesetzen, neu besetzen

re·cede schwinden; *receding chin* fliehendes Kinn

re·ceipt *esp* ECON Empfang *m*, Eingang *m*; Quittung *f*; *pl* Einnahmen *pl*

re·ceive bekommen, erhalten; empfangen; *j-n* aufnehmen (*into* in *acc*); *radio*, TV empfangen; **re·ceiv·er** Empfänger (in); TEL Hörer *m*; JUR Hehler(in); *a.* **official ~** *Br* JUR Konkursverwalter *m*

re·cent neuere(r, -s); jüngste(r, -s)

re·cent·ly kürzlich, vor kurzem

re·cep·tion Empfang *m*; Aufnahme *f* (*into* in *acc*); *radio*, TV Empfang *m*; *a.* **~ desk** *hotel*: Rezeption *f*, Empfang *m*

re·cep·tion·ist Empfangsdame *f*, -chef *m*; MED Sprechstundenhilfe *f*

re·cep·tive aufnahmefähig; empfänglich (**to** für)

re·cess Unterbrechung *f*, (Schul)Pause *f*; PARL, JUR Ferien *pl*; Nische *f*

re·ces·sion ECON Rezession *f*

re·ci·pe (Koch)Rezept *n*

re·cip·i·ent Empfänger(in)

re·cip·ro·cal wechselseitig, gegenseitig

re·cip·ro·cate *v/i* TECH sich hin- und herbewegen; sich revanchieren; *v/t Einladung etc* erwidern

re·cit·al Vortrag *m*, (*Klavier- etc*)Konzert *n*, (*Lieder*)Abend *m*; Schilderung *f*; **re·ci·ta·tion** Aufsagen *n*, Hersagen *n*; Vortrag *m*; **re·cite** aufsagen, hersagen; vortragen; aufzählen

reck·less rücksichtslos

reck·on *v/t* (aus-, be)rechnen; glauben, schätzen; **~ up** zusammenrechnen; *v/i*: **~ on** rechnen mit; **~ with** rechnen mit; **~ without** nicht rechnen mit

reck·on·ing (Be)Rechnung *f*; *be out in one's* **~** sich verrechnet haben

re·claim zurückfordern; *Gepäck etc* abholen; *dem Meer etc Land* abgewinnen; TECH wiedergewinnen

re·cline sich zurücklehnen

re·cluse Einsiedler(in)

rec·og·ni·tion (Wieder)Erkennen *n*; Anerkennung *f*

rec·og·nize (wieder) erkennen; anerkennen; zugeben, eingestehen

re·coil 1. zurückschrecken (**from** vor *dat*); **2.** Rückstoß *m*

rec·ol·lect sich erinnern an (*acc*)

rec·ol·lec·tion Erinnerung *f* (**of** an *acc*)

rec·om·mend empfehlen (**as** als; **for** für)

rec·om·men·da·tion Empfehlung *f*

rec·om·pense 1. entschädigen (**for** für); **2.** Entschädigung *f*

rec·on·cile versöhnen, aussöhnen; in Einklang bringen (**with** mit)

rec·on·cil·i·a·tion Versöhnung *f*, Aussöhnung *f* (**between** zwischen *dat*; **with** mit)

re·con·di·tion TECH (general)überholen

re·con·nais·sance MIL Aufklärung *f*, Erkundung *f*

re·con·noi·ter, *Br* **re·con·noi·tre** MIL erkunden, auskundschaften

re·con·sid·er noch einmal überdenken

re·con·struct wieder aufbauen (*a. fig*); *Verbrechen etc* rekonstruieren

re·con·struc·tion Wiederaufbau *m*; Rekonstruktion *f*

rec·ord[1] Aufzeichnung *f*; JUR Protokoll *n*; Akte *f*; (Schall)Platte *f*; SPORT Rekord *m*; *off the* **~** inoffiziell; *have a criminal* **~** vorbestraft sein

re·cord[2] aufzeichnen, aufschreiben, schriftlich niederlegen; JUR protokollieren, zu Protokoll nehmen; *auf Schallplatte, Tonband etc* aufnehmen, *Sendung a.* aufzeichnen, mitschneiden

re·cord·er (*Kassetten*)Rekorder *m*; (*Tonband*)Gerät *n*; MUS Blockflöte *f*

re·cord·ing Aufnahme *f*, Aufzeichnung *f*, Mitschnitt *m*

rec·ord play·er Plattenspieler *m*

re·count erzählen

re·cov·er *v/t* wiedererlangen, wiederbekommen, wieder finden; *Kosten etc* wiedereinbringen; *Fahrzeug, Verunglückten etc* bergen; **~ consciousness** MED wieder zu sich kommen, das Bewusstsein wiedererlangen; *v/i* sich erholen (**from** von); **re·cov·er·y** Wiedererlangen *n*; Wiederfinden *n*; Bergung *f*; Genesung *f*; Erholung *f*

rec·re·a·tion Entspannung *f*, Unterhaltung *f*, Freizeitbeschäftigung *f*

re·cruit 1. MIL Rekrut *m*; Neue *m*, *f*, neues Mitglied; **2.** MIL rekrutieren; *Personal* einstellen; *Mitglieder* werben rec·tan·gle MATH Rechteck n

rec·tan·gu·lar rechteckig

rec·ti·fy ELECTR gleichrichten

rec·tor REL Pfarrer m

rec·to·ry REL Pfarrhaus n

re·cu·pe·rate sich erholen (**from** von) (a. fig)

re·cur wiederkehren, wieder auftreten

re·cur·rence Wiederkehr f

re·cur·rent wiederkehrend

re·cy·cla·ble TECH recycelbar, wieder verwertbar; **re·cy·cle** TECH Abfälle recyceln, wieder verwerten; **~d paper** Recyclingpapier n, Umwelt(schutz)papier n; **re·cy·cling** TECH Recycling n, Wiederverwertung f

red 1. rot; 2. Rot n; **be in the ~** ECON in den roten Zahlen sein

red·breast → robin

Red Cres·cent Roter Halbmond

Red Cross Rotes Kreuz

red·cur·rant BOT Rote Johannisbeere

red·den röten, rot färben; rot werden

red·dish rötlich

re·dec·o·rate Zimmer etc neu streichen or tapezieren

re·deem Pfand, Versprechen etc einlösen; REL erlösen

Re·deem·er REL Erlöser m, Heiland m

re·demp·tion Einlösung f; REL Erlösung f

re·de·vel·op Gebäude, Stadtteil sanieren

red-faced verlegen, mit rotem Kopf

red-hand·ed: **catch s.o. ~** j-n auf frischer Tat ertappen

red·head F Rotschopf m, Rothaarige f

red-head·ed rothaarig

red her·ring fig falsche Fährte or Spur

red-hot rot glühend; fig glühend; F brandaktuell (news etc)

Red In·di·an contp Indianer(in)

red-let·ter day Freuden-, Glückstag m

red·ness Röte f

re·dou·ble verdoppeln

red tape Bürokratismus m, F Amtsschimmel m

re·duce verkleinern; Geschwindigkeit, Risiko etc verringern, Steuern etc senken, Preis, Waren etc herabsetzen, reduzieren (**from ... to** von ... auf acc), Gehalt etc kürzen; verwandeln (**to** in acc), machen (**to** zu); reduzieren, zurückführen (**to** auf acc); **re·duc·tion**

Verkleinerung f; Verringerung f, Senkung f, Herabsetzung f, Reduzierung f, Kürzung f

re·dun·dant überflüssig

reed BOT Schilf(rohr) n

re·ed·u·cate umerziehen

re·ed·u·ca·tion Umerziehung f

reef (Felsen)Riff n

reek 1. Gestank m; 2. stinken (**of** nach)

reel[1] 1. Rolle f, Spule f; 2. **~ off** abrollen, abspulen; fig herunterrasseln

reel[2] sich drehen; (sch)wanken, taumeln, torkeln; **my head ~ed** mir drehte sich alles

re·e·lect wieder wählen

re·en·ter wieder eintreten in (acc), wieder betreten; **re·en·try** Wiedereintreten n, Wiedereintritt m

ref F SPORT Schiri m

re·fer: **~ to** verweisen or hinweisen auf (acc); j-n verweisen an (acc); sich beziehen auf (acc); anspielen auf (acc); erwähnen (acc); nachschlagen in (dat)

ref·er·ee SPORT Schiedsrichter m, Unparteiische m; boxing: Ringrichter m

ref·er·ence Verweis m, Hinweis m (**to** auf acc); Verweisstelle f; Referenz f, Empfehlung f, Zeugnis n; Bezugnahme f (**to** auf acc); Anspielung f (**to** auf acc); Erwähnung f (**to** gen); Nachschlagen n (**to** in dat); **list of ~s** Quellenangabe f; **~ book** Nachschlagewerk n; **~ li·bra·ry** Handbibliothek f; **~ num·ber** Aktenzeichen n

ref·e·ren·dum POL Referendum n, Volksentscheid m

re·fill 1. wieder füllen, nachfüllen, auffüllen; 2. (Ersatz)Mine f; (Ersatz)Patrone f

re·fine TECH raffinieren; fig verfeinern, kultivieren; **~ on** verbessern, verfeinern

re·fined TECH raffiniert; fig kultiviert, vornehm

re·fine·ment TECH Raffinierung f; fig Verbess(e)rung f, Verfeinerung f; Kultiviertheit f, Vornehmheit f

re·fin·er·y TECH Raffinerie f

re·flect v/t reflektieren, zurückwerfen, -strahlen, (wider)spiegeln; **be ~ed in** sich (wider)spiegeln in (dat) (a. fig); v/i nachdenken (**on** über acc); **~ (badly) on** sich nachteilig auswirken

re·flec·tion Reflexion f, Zurückwerfung f, -strahlung f, (Wider)Spiegelung f (a. fig); Spiegelbild n; Überlegung f; Betrachtung f; **on ~** nach einigem Nachdenken

re·flec·tive reflektierend; nachdenklich

re·flex Reflex m; **~ ac·tion** Reflexhandlung f; **~ cam·e·ra** PHOT Spiegelreflexkamera f

re·flex·ive LING reflexiv, rückbezüglich

re·form 1. reformieren, verbessern; sich bessern; **2.** Reform f (a. POL), Besserung f; **ref·or·ma·tion** Reformierung f; Besserung f; **the Reformation** REL die Reformation; **re·form·er** esp POL Reformer m; REL Reformator m

re·fract Strahlen etc brechen

re·frac·tion (Strahlen- etc)Brechung f

re·frain[1]: **~ from** sich enthalten (gen), unterlassen (acc)

re·frain[2] Kehrreim m, Refrain m

re·fresh (o.s. sich) erfrischen, stärken; Gedächtnis auffrischen

re·fresh·ing erfrischend (a. fig)

re·fresh·ment Erfrischung f

re·fri·ge·rate TECH kühlen

re·fri·ge·ra·tor Kühlschrank m

re·fu·el auftanken

ref·uge Zuflucht f, Zufluchtsstätte f; Br Verkehrsinsel f

ref·u·gee Flüchtling m

ref·u·gee camp Flüchtlingslager n

re·fund 1. Rückzahlung f, Rückerstattung f; **2.** Geld zurückzahlen, zurückerstatten; Auslagen ersetzen

re·fur·bish aufpolieren (a. fig); renovieren

re·fus·al Ablehnung f, Weigerung f; Verweigerung f

re·fuse[1] v/t ablehnen; verweigern; sich weigern, es ablehnen (**to do** zu tun); v/i ablehnen; sich weigern

ref·use[2] Abfall m, Abfälle pl, Müll m

ref·use dump Müllabladeplatz m

re·fute widerlegen

re·gain wieder-, zurückgewinnen

re·gale: ~ s.o. with s.th. j-n mit et. erfreuen or ergötzen

re·gard 1. Achtung f; Rücksicht f; pl Grüße pl; **in this ~** in dieser Hinsicht; **with ~ to** im Hinblick auf (acc); hinsichtlich (gen); **with kind ~s** mit

freundlichen Grüßen; **2.** betrachten (a. fig), ansehen; **~ as** betrachten als, halten für; **as ~s ...** was ... betrifft

re·gard·ing bezüglich, hinsichtlich (gen)

re·gard·less: ~ of ohne Rücksicht auf (acc), ungeachtet (gen)

regd ABBR of **registered** ECON eingetragen; post eingeschrieben

re·gen·e·rate (sich) erneuern or regenerieren

re·gent Regent(in)

re·gi·ment 1. MIL Regiment n, fig a. Schar f; **2.** reglementieren, bevormunden

re·gion Gegend f, Gebiet n, Region f

re·gion·al regional, örtlich, Orts...

re·gis·ter 1. Register n, Verzeichnis n, (Wähler- etc)Liste f; **2.** v/t registrieren, eintragen (lassen); Messwerte anzeigen; Brief etc einschreiben lassen; v/i sich eintragen (lassen)

re·gis·tered let·ter Einschreib(e)brief m, Einschreiben n

re·gis·tra·tion Registrierung f, Eintragung f; MOT Zulassung f; **~ fee** Anmeldegebühr f; **~ num·ber** MOT (polizeiliches) Kennzeichen

re·gis·try Registratur f

re·gis·try of·fice esp Br Standesamt n

re·gret bedauern; bereuen; **2.** Bedauern n; Reue f; **re·gret·ful** bedauernd; **re·gret·ta·ble** bedauerlich

reg·u·lar 1. regelmäßig; geregelt, geordnet; richtig; normal; MIL Berufs...; **~ gas** (Br **petrol**) MOT Normalbenzin n; **2.** F Stammkunde m, Stammkundin f; Stammgast m; SPORT Stammspieler (in); MIL Berufssoldat m; MOT Normal (-benzin) n

reg·u·lar·i·ty Regelmäßigkeit f

reg·u·late regeln, regulieren; TECH einstellen, regulieren

reg·u·la·tion Reg(e)lung f, Regulierung f; TECH Einstellung f; Vorschrift f

reg·u·la·tor TECH Regler m

re·hears·al MUS, THEA Probe f

re·hearse MUS, THEA proben

reign 1. Regierung f, a. fig Herrschaft f; **2.** herrschen, regieren

re·im·burse Auslagen erstatten, vergüten

rein 1. Zügel m; **2. ~ in** Pferd etc zügeln; fig bremsen

rein·deer ZO Ren *n*, Rentier *n*
re·in·force verstärken
re·in·force·ment Verstärkung *f*
re·in·state *j-n* wieder einstellen (*as* als; *in* in *dat*)
re·in·sure rückversichern
re·it·e·rate (ständig) wiederholen
re·ject *j-n, et.* ablehnen, *Bitte* abschlagen, *Plan etc* verwerfen; *j-n* ab-, zurückweisen; MED *Organ etc* abstoßen
re·jec·tion Ablehnung *f*; Verwerfung *f*; Zurückweisung *f*; MED Abstoßung *f*
re·joice sich freuen, jubeln (*at, over* über *acc*); **re·joic·ing(s)** Jubel *m*
re·join¹ wieder zusammenfügen; wieder zurückkehren zu
re·join² erwidern
re·ju·ve·nate verjüngen
re·kin·dle *Feuer* wieder anzünden; *fig* wieder entfachen
re·lapse 1. zurückfallen, wieder verfallen (*into* in *acc*); rückfällig werden; MED e-n Rückfall bekommen; **2.** Rückfall *m*
re·late *v/t* erzählen, berichten; in Verbindung *or* Zusammenhang bringen (*to* mit); *v/i* sich beziehen (*to* auf *acc*); zusammenhängen (*to* mit)
re·lat·ed verwandt (*to* mit)
re·la·tion Verwandte *m*, *f*; Beziehung *f* (*between* zwischen *dat*; *to* zu); *pl* diplomatische, geschäftliche Beziehungen *pl*; *in or with* ~ *to* in Bezug auf (*acc*)
re·la·tion·ship Verwandtschaft *f*; Beziehung *f*; Verhältnis *n*
rel·a·tive¹ Verwandte *m*, *f*
rel·a·tive² relativ, verhältnismäßig; bezüglich (*to gen*); LING Relativ..., bezüglich
rel·a·tive pro·noun LING Relativpronomen *n*, bezügliches Fürwort
re·lax *v/t* Muskeln *etc* entspannen; *Griff etc* lockern; *fig* nachlassen in (*dat*); *v/i* sich entspannen, *fig a.* ausspannen; sich lockern
re·lax·a·tion Entspannung *f*; Erholung *f*; Lockerung *f*
re·laxed entspannt, zwanglos
re·lay¹ 1. Ablösung *f*; SPORT Staffel *f*; *radio*, TV Übertragung *f*; ELECTR Relais *n*; **2.** *radio*, TV übertragen
re·lay² *Kabel, Teppich* neu verlegen
re·lay race SPORT Staffel *f*
re·lease 1. entlassen, freilassen; loslas-

sen; freigeben, herausbringen, veröffentlichen; MOT *Handbremse* lösen; *fig* befreien, erlösen; **2.** Entlassung *f*, Freilassung *f*; Befreiung *f*; Freigabe *f*; Veröffentlichung *f*; TECH, PHOT Auslöser *m*; *film: often first* ~ Uraufführung *f*
re·lent nachgeben; nachlassen
re·lent·less unbarmherzig; anhaltend
rel·e·vant relevant, erheblich, wichtig; sachdienlich, zutreffend
re·li·a·bil·i·ty Zuverlässigkeit *f*
re·li·a·ble zuverlässig
re·li·ance Vertrauen *n*; Abhängigkeit *f* (*on* von)
rel·ic Relikt *n*, Überrest *m*; REL Reliquie *f*
re·lief Erleichterung *f*; Unterstützung *f*, Hilfe *f*; Sozialhilfe *f*; Ablösung *f*; Relief *n*; ~ *map* GEOGR Reliefkarte *f*
re·lieve *Schmerz, Not* lindern, *j-n, Gewissen* erleichtern; *j-n* ablösen
re·li·gion Religion *f*
re·li·gious Religions...; religiös; gewissenhaft
rel·ish 1. *fig* Gefallen *m*, Geschmack *m* (*for* an *dat*); GASTR Würze *f*, Soße *f*; *with* ~ mit Genuss; **2.** genießen, sich *et.* schmecken lassen; Geschmack *or* Gefallen finden an (*dat*)
re·luc·tance Widerstreben *n*; *with* ~ widerwillig, ungern
re·luc·tant widerstrebend, widerwillig
re·ly: ~ *on* sich verlassen auf (*acc*)
re·main 1. (ver)bleiben; übrig bleiben; **2.** *pl* (Über)Reste *pl*
re·main·der Rest *m*; Restbetrag *m*
re·make 1. wieder *or* neu machen; **2.** Remake *n*, Neuverfilmung *f*
re·mand JUR **1.** *be* ~*ed in custody* in Untersuchungshaft bleiben; **2.** *be on* ~ in Untersuchungshaft sein; *prisoner on* ~ Untersuchungsgefangene *m*, *f*
re·mark 1. *v/t* bemerken, äußern; *v/i* sich äußern (*on* über *acc*, zu); **2.** Bemerkung *f*
re·mark·a·ble bemerkenswert; außergewöhnlich
rem·e·dy 1. (Heil-, Hilfs-, Gegen)Mittel *n*; (Ab)Hilfe *f*; **2.** *Schaden etc* beheben; *Missstand* abstellen; *Situation* bereinigen
re·mem·ber sich erinnern an (*acc*); den-

R

ken an (*acc*); **please ~ me to her** grüße sie bitte von mir

re·mem·brance Erinnerung *f*; **in ~ of** zur Erinnerung an (*acc*)

re·mind erinnern (**of** an *acc*)

re·mind·er Mahnung *f*

rem·i·nis·cences Erinnerungen *pl* (**of** an *acc*); **rem·i·nis·cent: be ~ of** erinnern an (*acc*)

re·mit *Schulden, Strafe* erlassen; *Sünden* vergeben; *Geld* überweisen (**to** *dat* or an *acc*); **re·mit·tance** ECON Überweisung *f* (**to** an *acc*)

rem·nant (Über)Rest *m*

re·mod·el umformen, umgestalten

re·morse Gewissensbisse *pl*, Reue *f* (**über** *acc* for)

re·morse·ful zerknirscht, reumütig

re·morse·less unbarmherzig

re·mote fern, entfernt; abgelegen, entlegen; **~ con·trol** TECH Fernlenkung *f*, Fernsteuerung *f*; Fernbedienung *f*

re·mov·al Entfernung *f*; Umzug *m*

re·mov·al van Möbelwagen *m*

re·move *v/t* entfernen (**from** von); *Hut, Deckel etc* abnehmen; *Kleidung* ablegen; beseitigen, aus dem Weg räumen; *v/i* (um)ziehen (**from** von; **to** nach)

re·mov·er (*Flecken- etc*)Entferner *m*

Re·nais·sance *die* Renaissance

ren·der berühmt, schwierig, möglich etc machen; *Dienst* erweisen; *Gedicht, Musikstück* vortragen; übersetzen; übertragen (**into** in *acc*); *mst* **~ down** *Fett* auslassen

ren·der·ing *esp Br* → **rendition**

ren·di·tion MUS *etc* Vortrag *m*; Übersetzung *f*, Übertragung *f*

re·new erneuern; *Gespräch etc* wieder aufnehmen; *Kraft etc* wiedererlangen; *Vertrag, Pass* verlängern (lassen)

re·new·al Erneuerung *f*; Verlängerung *f*

re·nounce verzichten auf (*acc*); *s-m Glauben etc* abschwören

ren·o·vate renovieren

re·nown Ruhm *m*; **re·nowned** berühmt (**as** als; **for** wegen, für)

rent¹ 1. Miete *f*; Pacht *f*; Leihgebühr *f*; **for ~** zu vermieten, zu verleihen; **2.** mieten, pachten (**from** von); *a.* **~ out** vermieten, verpachten (**to** an *acc*); **~ed car** Miet-, Leihwagen *m*

rent² Riss *m*

rent·al Miete *f*; Pacht *f*; Leihgebühr *f*;

~ car Miet-, Leihwagen *m*

re·nun·ci·a·tion Verzicht *m* (**of** auf *acc*); Abschwören *n*

re·pair 1. reparieren, ausbessern; *fig* wieder gutmachen; **2.** Reparatur *f*; Ausbesserung *f*, *pl* Instandsetzungsarbeiten *pl*; **beyond ~** nicht mehr zu reparieren; **in good** (**bad**) **~** in gutem (schlechtem) Zustand; **be under ~** in Reparatur sein; **the road is under ~** an der Straße wird gerade gearbeitet

rep·a·ra·tion Wiedergutmachung *f*; Entschädigung *f*; *pl* POL Reparationen *pl*

rep·ar·tee Schlagfertigkeit *f*, schlagfertige Antwort(en *pl*) *f*

re·pay *et.* zurückzahlen; *Besuch* erwidern; *et.* vergelten; *j-n* entschädigen

re·pay·ment Rückzahlung *f*

re·peal *Gesetz* aufheben

re·peat 1. *v/t* wiederholen; nachsprechen; **~ o.s.** sich wiederholen; *v/i* F aufstoßen (**on s.o.** j-m) (*food*); **2.** *radio, TV* Wiederholung *f*; **re·peat·ed** wiederholt; **re·peat·ed·ly** verschiedentlich

re·pel *Angriff, Feind* zurückschlagen; *Wasser etc*, *fig* j-n abstoßen

re·pel·lent abstoßend

re·pent bereuen

re·pent·ance Reue *f* (**for** über *acc*)

re·pen·tant reuig, reumütig

re·per·cus·sion *mst pl* Auswirkungen *pl* (**on** auf *acc*)

rep·er·toire THEA *etc* Repertoire *n*

rep·er·to·ry the·a·ter (*Br* **the·a·tre**) Repertoiretheater *n*

rep·e·ti·tion Wiederholung *f*

re·place an *j-s* Stelle treten, *j-n, et.* ersetzen; TECH austauschen, ersetzen

re·place·ment TECH Austausch *m*; Ersatz *m*

re·plant umpflanzen

re·play 1. SPORT *Spiel* wiederholen; *Tonband-, Videoaufname etc* abspielen; **2.** SPORT Wiederholung *f*

re·plen·ish (wieder) auffüllen

re·plete satt; angefüllt, ausgestattet (**with** mit)

rep·li·ca *art*: Originalkopie *f*; Kopie *f*, Nachbildung *f*

re·ply 1. antworten, erwidern (**to** auf *acc*); **2.** Antwort *f*, Erwiderung *f* (**to** auf *acc*); **in ~ to** (als Antwort) auf (*acc*)

re·ply cou·pon Rückantwortschein *m*

re·ply-paid en·ve·lope Freiumschlag *m*

re·port 1. Bericht *m*; Meldung *f*, Nachricht *f*; Gerücht *n*; Knall *m*; **~ card** PED Zeugnis *n*; **2.** berichten (über *acc*); (sich) melden; anzeigen; *it is ~ed that* es heißt, dass; *~ed speech* LING indirekte Rede; **re·port·er** Reporter(in), Berichterstatter(in)

re·pose Ruhe *f*; Gelassenheit *f*

re·pos·i·to·ry (Waren)Lager *n*; *fig* Fundgrube *f*, Quelle *f*

rep·re·sent *j-n, Wahlbezirk* vertreten; darstellen; hinstellen (*as, to be* als)

rep·re·sen·ta·tion Vertretung *f*; Darstellung *f*

rep·re·sen·ta·tive 1. repräsentativ (*a.* POL), typisch (*of* für); **2.** (Stell)Vertreter(in); ECON (Handels)Vertreter(in); PARL Abgeordnete *m, f*; *House of Representatives* Repräsentantenhaus *n*

re·press unterdrücken; PSYCH verdrängen; **re·pres·sion** Unterdrückung *f*; PSYCH Verdrängung *f*

re·prieve JUR **1.** *he was ~d* er wurde begnadigt; *s-e* Urteilsvollstreckung wurde ausgesetzt; **2.** Begnadigung *f*; Vollstreckungsaufschub *m*

rep·ri·mand 1. rügen, tadeln (*for* wegen); **2.** Rüge *f*, Tadel *m*, Verweis *m*

re·print 1. neu auflegen *or* drucken, nachdrucken; **2.** Neuauflage *f*, Nachdruck *m*

re·pri·sal Repressalie *f*, Vergeltungsmaßnahme *f*

re·proach 1. Vorwurf *m*; **2.** vorwerfen (*s.o. with s.th.* j-m et.); Vorwürfe machen; **re·proach·ful** vorwurfsvoll

rep·ro·bate verkommenes Subjekt

re·pro·cess NUCL wieder aufbereiten

re·pro·cess·ing TECH Wiederaufbereitung *f*; **~ plant** TECH Wiederaufbereitungsanlage *f*

re·pro·duce *v/t* Ton etc wiedergeben; *Bild etc* reproduzieren; *~ o.s.* → *v/i* BIOL sich fortpflanzen, sich vermehren

re·pro·duc·tion BIOL Fortpflanzung *f*; Reproduktion *f*; Wiedergabe *f*; PED Nacherzählung *f*

re·pro·duc·tive BIOL Fortpflanzungs...

re·proof Rüge *f*, Tadel *m*

re·prove rügen, tadeln (*for* wegen)

rep·tile ZO Reptil *n*

re·pub·lic Republik *f*

re·pub·li·can 1. republikanisch; **2.** Republikaner(in)

re·pug·nant widerlich, abstoßend

re·pulse 1. *j-n, Angebot etc* zurückweisen; MIL *Angriff* zurückschlagen; **2.** MIL Zurückschlagen *n*; Zurückweisung *f*

re·pul·sion Abscheu *m*, Widerwille *m*; PHYS Abstoßung *f*

re·pul·sive abstoßend, widerlich, widerwärtig; PHYS abstoßend

rep·u·ta·ble angesehen

rep·u·ta·tion (guter) Ruf, Ansehen *n*

re·pute (guter) Ruf

re·put·ed angeblich

re·quest 1. (*for*) Bitte *f* (um), Wunsch *m* (nach); *at the ~ of s.o., at s.o.'s ~* auf j-s Bitte hin; *on ~* auf Wunsch; **2.** um *et.* bitten *or* ersuchen; *j-n* bitten, ersuchen (*to do* zu tun)

re·quest stop *Br* Bedarfshaltestelle *f*

re·quire erfordern; benötigen, brauchen; verlangen; *if ~d* wenn nötig

re·quire·ment Erfordernis *n*, Bedürfnis *n*; Anforderung *f*

req·ui·site 1. erforderlich; **2.** *mst pl* Artikel *pl*; *toilet ~s* Toilettenartikel *pl*

req·ui·si·tion 1. Anforderung *f*; MIL Requisition *f*, Beschlagnahme *f*; *make a ~ for et.* anfordern; **2.** anfordern; MIL requirieren, beschlagnahmen

re·sale Wieder-, Weiterverkauf *m*

re·scind JUR *Gesetz, Urteil etc* aufheben

res·cue 1. retten (*from* aus, vor *dat*); **2.** Rettung *f*; Hilfe *f*; **3.** Rettungs...

re·search 1. Forschung *f*; **2.** forschen; *et.* erforschen

re·search·er Forscher(in)

re·sem·blance Ähnlichkeit *f* (*to* mit; *between* zwischen *dat*)

re·sem·ble ähnlich sein, ähneln (*both: dat*)

re·sent übel nehmen, sich ärgern über (*acc*); **re·sent·ful** ärgerlich (*of, at* über *acc*); **re·sent·ment** Ärger *m* (*against, at* über *acc*)

res·er·va·tion Reservierung *f*, Vorbestellung *f*; Vorbehalt *m*; (*Indianer*)Reservat(ion *f*) *n*; (*Wild*)Reservat *n*

re·serve 1. (sich) *et.* aufsparen (*for* für); sich vorbehalten; reservieren (lassen), vorbestellen; **2.** Reserve *f* (*a.* MIL); Vorrat *m*; (*Naturschutz-, Wild*)Reservat *n*; SPORT Reservespieler(in); Reserviert-

R

re·served zurückhaltend, reserviert
res·er·voir Reservoir n (a. fig of an dat)
re·set Uhr umstellen; Zeiger etc zu-rückstellen (**to** auf acc)
re·set·tle umsiedeln
re·side wohnen, ansässig sein, s-n Wohnsitz haben
res·i·dence Wohnsitz m, Wohnort m; Aufenthalt m; Residenz f; **official ~** Amtssitz m; **~ per·mit** Aufenthaltsge-nehmigung f, -erlaubnis f
res·i·dent 1. wohnhaft, ansässig; **2.** Bewohner(in), in a town etc a. Ein-wohner(in); (Hotel)Gast m; MOT An-lieger(in)
res·i·den·tial Wohn...; **~ ar·e·a** Wohn-gebiet n, Wohngegend f
re·sid·u·al übrig (geblieben), restlich, Rest...; **~ pol·lu·tion** Altlasten pl
res·i·due Rest m, CHEM A. Rückstand m
re·sign v/i zurücktreten (**from** von); v/t Amt etc niederlegen; aufgeben; ver-zichten auf (acc); **~ o.s. to** sich fügen in (acc), sich abfinden mit
res·ig·na·tion Rücktritt m; Resignati-on f
re·signed ergeben, resigniert
re·sil·i·ence Elastizität f; fig Zähigkeit f; **re·sil·i·ent** elastisch; fig zäh
res·in Harz n
re·sist widerstehen (dat); Widerstand leisten, sich widersetzen (both: dat)
re·sist·ance Widerstand m (a. ELECTR); MED Widerstandskraft f; (Hitze- etc -)Beständigkeit f, (Stoß- etc)Festigkeit f; **line of least ~** Weg m des geringsten Widerstands
re·sist·ant widerstandsfähig; (hitze-etc)beständig, (stoß- etc)fest
res·o·lute resolut, entschlossen
res·o·lu·tion Beschluss m, PARL etc a. Resolution f; Vorsatz m; Entschlossen-heit f; Lösung f
re·solve 1. beschließen; Problem etc lösen; (sich) auflösen; **~ on** sich ent-schließen zu; **2.** Vorsatz m; Entschlos-senheit f
res·o·nance Resonanz f; voller Klang
res·o·nant voll(tönend); widerhallend
re·sort 1. Erholungsort m, Urlaubsort m; **have ~ to** → **2.** ~ **to** Zuflucht neh-men zu

re·sound widerhallen (**with** von)
re·source Mittel n, Zuflucht f; Ausweg m; Einfallsreichtum m; pl Mittel pl; (natürliche) Reichtümer pl, (Boden-, Natur)Schätze pl
re·source·ful einfallsreich, findig
re·spect 1. Achtung f, Respekt m (both: **for** vor dat); Rücksicht f (**for** auf acc); Beziehung f, Hinsicht f; **with ~ to ...** was ... anbelangt or betrifft; **in this ~** in dieser Hinsicht; **give my ~s to ...** e-e Empfehlung an ... (acc); **2.** v/t res-pektieren, a. achten, a. berücksichti-gen, beachten
re·spect·a·ble ehrbar, anständig, ge-achtet; F ansehnlich, beachtlich
re·spect·ful respektvoll, ehrerbietig
re·spec·tive jeweilig; **we went to our ~ places** jeder ging zu seinem Platz
re·spec·tive·ly beziehungsweise
res·pi·ra·tion Atmung f
res·pi·ra·tor Atemschutzgerät n
re·spite Pause f; Aufschub m, Frist f; **without ~** ohne Unterbrechung
re·splen·dent glänzend, strahlend
re·spond antworten, erwidern (**to** auf acc; **that** dass); reagieren, MED a. ansprechen (**to** auf acc)
re·sponse Antwort f, Erwiderung f (**to** auf acc); fig Reaktion f (**to** auf acc)
re·spon·si·bil·i·ty Verantwortung f; **on one's own ~** auf eigene Verantwor-tung; **sense of ~** Verantwortungsge-fühl n; **take (full) ~ for** die (volle) Ver-antwortung übernehmen für
re·spon·si·ble verantwortlich; ver-antwortungsbewusst; verantwortungs-voll
rest¹ 1. Ruhe(pause) f; Erholung f; TECH Stütze f; (Telefon)Gabel f; **have or take a ~** sich ausruhen; **set s.o.'s mind at ~** j-n beruhigen; **2.** v/i ruhen; sich ausru-hen; lehnen (**against**, **on** an dat); **let s.th. ~** et. auf sich beruhen lassen; **~ on** ruhen auf (dat) (a. fig); fig beruhen auf (dat); v/t (aus)ruhen (lassen); lehnen (**against** gegen; **on** an acc)
rest² **Rest m; **all the ~ of them alle Übri-gen; **for the ~** im Übrigen
rest ar·e·a MOT Rastplatz m
res·tau·rant Restaurant n, Gaststätte f
rest·ful ruhig, erholsam
rest home Altenpflegeheim n; Erho-lungsheim n

res·ti·tu·tion ECON Rückgabe f, Rückerstattung f

res·tive unruhig, nervös

rest·less ruhelos, rastlos; unruhig

res·to·ra·tion Wiederherstellung f; Restaurierung f; Rückgabe f, Rückerstattung f; **re·store** wiederherstellen; restaurieren; zurückgeben, -erstatten; **be ~d (to health)** wieder gesund sein

re·strain (from) zurückhalten (von), hindern an (dat); **I had to ~ myself** ich musste mich beherrschen (**from doing s.th.** um nicht et. zu tun)

re·strained beherrscht; dezent (color)

re·straint Beherrschung f, Zurückhaltung f; ECON Be-, Einschränkung f

re·strict ECON beschränken (**to** auf acc), einschränken

re·stric·tion ECON Be-, Einschränkung f; **without ~s** uneingeschränkt

rest room Toilette f

re·struc·ture umstrukturieren

re·sult 1. Ergebnis n, Resultat n; Folge f; **as a ~ of** als Folge von (or gen); **without ~** ergebnislos; **2.** folgen, sich ergeben (**from** aus); **~ in** zur Folge haben (acc), führen zu

re·sume wieder aufnehmen; fortsetzen; Platz wieder einnehmen

re·sump·tion Wiederaufnahme f; Fortsetzung f

Res·ur·rec·tion REL Auferstehung f

re·sus·ci·tate MED wieder beleben

re·sus·ci·ta·tion MED Wiederbelebung f

re·tail ECON **1.** Einzelhandel m; **by ~** im Einzelhandel; **2.** Einzelhandels...; **3.** adv im Einzelhandel; **4.** v/t im Einzelhandel verkaufen (**at, for** für); v/i im Einzelhandel verkauft werden (**at, for** für); **re·tail·er** ECON Einzelhändler(in)

re·tain (be)halten, bewahren; Wasser, Wärme speichern

re·tal·i·ate Vergeltung üben, sich revanchieren; **re·tal·i·a·tion** Vergeltung f, Vergeltungsmaßnahmen pl

re·tard verzögern, aufhalten, hemmen; (**mentally**) **~ed** (geistig) zurückgeblieben

retch würgen

re·tell nacherzählen

re·think et. noch einmal überdenken

re·ti·cent schweigsam, zurückhaltend

ret·i·nue Gefolge n

re·tire v/i in Rente or Pension gehen, sich pensionieren lassen; sich zurückziehen; **~ from business** sich zur Ruhe setzen; v/t in den Ruhestand versetzen, pensionieren; **re·tired** pensioniert, im Ruhestand (lebend); **be ~** a. in Rente or Pension sein; **re·tire·ment** Pensionierung f, Ruhestand m

re·tir·ing zurückhaltend

re·tort 1. (scharf) entgegnen or erwidern; **2.** (scharfe) Entgegnung or Erwiderung

re·touch PHOT retuschieren

re·trace Tathergang etc rekonstruieren; **~ one's steps** denselben Weg zurückgehen

re·tract v/t Angebot zurückziehen; Behauptung zurücknehmen; Geständnis widerrufen; TECH, ZO einziehen; v/i TECH, ZO eingezogen werden

re·train umschulen

re·tread MOT **1.** Reifen runderneuern; **2.** runderneuerter Reifen

re·treat 1. MIL Rückzug m; Zufluchtsort m; **beat a (hasty)** ~ das Feld räumen, F abhauen; **2.** sich zurückziehen; zurückweichen (**from** vor dat)

ret·ri·bu·tion Vergeltung f

re·trieve zurückholen, wiederbekommen; Fehler, Verlust etc wieder gutmachen; HUNT apportieren

ret·ro·ac·tive JUR rückwirkend

ret·ro·grade rückschrittlich

ret·ro·spect: in ~ im Rückblick

ret·ro·spec·tive rückblickend; JUR rückwirkend

re·try JUR Fall erneut verhandeln; neu verhandeln gegen j-n

re·turn 1. v/i zurückkehren, zurückkommen; zurückgeben; **~ to** auf ein Thema etc zurückkommen; in e-e Gewohnheit etc zurückfallen; in e-n Zustand etc zurückkehren; v/t zurückgeben (**to** dat); zurückbringen (**to** dat); zurückschicken, -senden (**to** dat or an acc); zurücklegen, -stellen; erwidern; Gewinn etc abwerfen; → **verdict**; **2.** Rückkehr f; fig Wiederauftreten n; Rückgabe f; Zurückbringen n; Zurückschicken n, -senden n; Zurücklegen n, -stellen n; Erwiderung f; (Steuer)Erklärung f; tennis etc: Return m, Rückschlag m; ECON a. pl Gewinn m; Br → **return ticket**; Br

many happy ~s (of the day) herzlichen Glückwunsch zum Geburtstag; **by ~ (of post)** umgehend, postwendend; **in ~ for** (als Gegenleistung) für; **3.** adj Rück...

re·turn·a·ble in cpds Mehrweg...; **~ bottle** Pfandflasche f

re·turn| key EDP Eingabetaste f; **~ game, ~ match** SPORT Rückspiel n; **~ tick·et** Br RAIL Rückfahrkarte f; AVIAT Rückflugticket n

re·u·ni·fi·ca·tion POL Wiedervereinigung f

re·un·ion Treffen n, Wiedersehensfeier f; Wiedervereinigung f

re·us·a·ble wieder verwendbar

rev F MOT **1.** Umdrehung f; **~ counter** Drehzahlmesser m; **2.** a. **~ up** aufheulen (lassen)

re·val·ue ECON Währung aufwerten

re·veal den Blick freigeben auf (acc), zeigen; Geheimnis etc enthüllen, aufdecken; **re·veal·ing** aufschlussreich (remark etc); offenherzig (dress etc)

rev·el: ~ in schwelgen in (dat); sich weiden an (dat)

rev·e·la·tion Enthüllung f; REL Offenbarung f

re·venge 1. Rache f; esp SPORT Revanche f; **in ~ for** aus Rache für; **take ~ on s.o. for s.th.** sich an j-m für et. rächen; **2.** rächen; **re·venge·ful** rachsüchtig

rev·e·nue Staatseinkünfte pl, Staatseinnahmen pl

re·ver·be·rate nach-, widerhallen

re·vere (ver)ehren; **rev·e·rence** Verehrung f; Ehrfurcht f (**for** vor dat)

Rev·e·rend REL Hochwürden m

rev·e·rent ehrfürchtig, ehrfurchtsvoll

rev·er·ie (Tag)Träumerei f

re·vers·al Umkehrung f; Rückschlag m

re·verse 1. adj umgekehrt; **in ~ order** in umgekehrter Reihenfolge; **2.** Wagen im Rückwärtsgang or rückwärts fahren; Reihenfolge etc umkehren; Urteil etc aufheben; Entscheidung etc umstoßen; **3.** Gegenteil n; MOT Rückwärtsgang m; Rückseite f, Kehrseite f (of a coin); Rückschlag m; **~ gear** MOT Rückwärtsgang m; **~ side** linke (Stoff)Seite

re·vers·i·ble doppelseitig (tragbar)

re·vert: ~ to in e-n Zustand zurückkehren; in e-e Gewohnheit etc zurückfallen; auf ein Thema zurückkommen

re·view 1. Überprüfung f; Besprechung f, Kritik f, Rezension f; MIL Parade f; PED (Stoff)Wiederholung f (**for** für e-e Prüfung); **2.** überprüfen; besprechen, rezensieren; MIL besichtigen, inspizieren; PED Stoff wiederholen (**for** für e-e Prüfung)

re·view·er Kritiker(in), Rezensent(in)

re·vise revidieren, Ansicht ändern, Buch etc überarbeiten; Br PED Stoff wiederholen (**for** für e-e Prüfung)

re·vi·sion Revision f; Überarbeitung f; überarbeitete Ausgabe; Br PED (Stoff-)Wiederholung f (**for** für e-e Prüfung)

re·viv·al Wiederbelebung f; Wiederaufleben n

re·vive wieder beleben; wieder aufleben (lassen); Erinnerungen wachrufen; MED wieder zu sich kommen; sich erholen

re·voke widerrufen, zurücknehmen, rückgängig machen

re·volt 1. v/i sich auflehnen, revoltieren (**against** gegen); Abscheu empfinden, empört sein (**against, at, from** über acc); v/t mit Abscheu erfüllen, abstoßen; **2.** Revolte f, Aufstand m

re·volt·ing abscheulich, abstoßend

rev·o·lu·tion Revolution f, Umwälzung f; ASTR Umlauf m (**round** um); TECH Umdrehung f; **number of ~s** Drehzahl f; **~ counter** Drehzahlmesser m; **rev·o·lu·tion·a·ry; Re·volutions...; 2.** POL Revolutionär(in)

rev·o·lu·tion·ize revolutionieren

re·volve sich drehen (**on, round** um); **~ around** fig sich drehen um

re·volv·er Revolver m

re·volv·ing Dreh...; **~ door(s)** Drehtür f

re·vue THEA Revue f; Kabarett n

re·vul·sion Abscheu m

re·ward 1. Belohnung f; **2.** belohnen

re·ward·ing lohnend

re·write neu schreiben, umschreiben

rhap·so·dy MUS Rhapsodie f

rhe·to·ric Rhetorik f

rheu·ma·tism MED Rheumatismus m, F Rheuma n

rhi·no F, **rhi·no·ce·ros** ZO Rhinozeros n, Nashorn n

rhu·barb BOT Rhabarber m

rhyme 1. Reim m; Vers m; **without ~ or**

reason ohne Sinn und Verstand; **2.** (sich) reimen

rhyth·m Rhythmus *m*

rhyth·mic, rhyth·mi·cal rhythmisch

rib ANAT Rippe *f*

rib·bon (*a.* Farb-, Ordens)Band *n*; Streifen *m*; Fetzen *m*

rib cage ANAT Brustkorb *m*

rice BOT Reis *m*

rice pud·ding GASTR Milchreis *m*

rich 1. reich (*in an dat*); prächtig, kostbar; GASTR schwer; AGR fruchtbar, fett (*soil*); voll (*sound*); satt (*color*); ~ (*in calories*) kalorienreich; **2. the ~** die Reichen *pl*

rick (Stroh-, Heu)Schober *m*

rick·ets MED Rachitis *f*

rick·et·y F *fig* gebrechlich; wack(e)lig

rid befreien (*of* von); **get ~ of** loswerden

rid·dance: *good ~!* den (die, das) sind wir los Gott sei Dank los!

rid·den *in cpds* geplagt von

rid·dle¹ Rätsel *n*

rid·dle² 1. grobes Sieb, Schüttelsieb *n*; sieben; durchlöchern, durchsieben

ride 1. *v/i* reiten; fahren (**on** auf *e-m* Fahrrad etc; **on** or Br **in** in *e-m* Bus etc); *v/t* reiten (auf *dat*); Fahrrad, Motorrad fahren, fahren auf (*dat*); **2.** Ritt *m*; Fahrt *f*; **rid·er** Reiter(in); (Motorrad-, Rad)Fahrer(in)

ridge GEOGR (Gebirgs)Kamm *m*, Grat *m*; ARCH (Dach)First *m*

rid·i·cule Spott *m*; **2.** lächerlich machen, spotten über (*acc*), verspotten

ri·dic·u·lous lächerlich

rid·ing Reit...

riff-raff *contp* Gesindel *n*

ri·fle¹ Gewehr *n*

ri·fle² durchwühlen

rift Spalt *m*, Spalte *f*; *fig* Riss *m*

rig 1. Schiff auftakeln; ~ *out* j-n ausstaffieren; ~ *up* F (behelfsmäßig) zusammenbauen (*from* aus); **2.** MAR Takelage *f*; TECH Bohrinsel *f*; F Aufmachung *f*

rig·ging MAR Takelage *f*

right 1. *adj* recht; richtig; rechte(r, -s), Rechts...; *all ~!* in Ordnung!, gut!; *that's all ~!* das macht nichts!, schon gut!, bitte!; *that's ~!* richtig!, ganz recht!, stimmt!; *be ~* Recht haben; *put ~*, *set ~* in Ordnung bringen; berichtigen, korrigieren; **2.** *adv* (nach) rechts; richtig; recht; genau; gerade(wegs), direkt; ganz, völlig; ~ *away* sofort; ~ *now* im Moment; sofort; ~ *on* geradeaus; *turn ~* (sich) nach rechts wenden; MOT rechts abbiegen; **3.** Recht *n*; *die* Rechte (*a.* POL, *boxing*), rechte Seite; *on the ~* rechts, auf der rechten Seite; *to the ~* (nach) rechts; *keep to the ~* sich rechts halten; MOT rechts fahren; **4.** aufrichten; *et.* wieder gutmachen; in Ordnung bringen

right an·gle MATH rechter Winkel

right-an·gled MATH rechtwink(e)lig

right·eous gerecht (*anger etc*)

right·ful rechtmäßig

right-hand rechte(r, -s); ~ *drive* MOT Rechtssteuerung *f*

right-hand·ed rechtshändig; für Rechtshänder; *be ~* Rechtshänder(in) sein

right·ly richtig; mit Recht

right of way MOT Vorfahrt *f*, Vorfahrtsrecht *n*; Durchgangsrecht *n*

right-wing POL dem rechten Flügel angehörend, Rechts...

rig·id starr, steif; *fig* streng, strikt

rig·a·ma·role Geschwätz *n*; *fig* Theater *n*, Zirkus *m*

rig·or·ous streng; genau

rig·o(u)r Strenge *f*, Härte *f*

rile F ärgern, reizen

rim Rand *m*; TECH Felge *f*

rim·less randlos

rind (Zitronen- *etc*)Schale *f*; (Käse)Rinde *f*; (Speck)Schwarte *f*

ring¹ 1. Ring *m*; Kreis *m*; Manege *f*; (Box)Ring *m*; (Spionage- *etc*)Ring *m*; **2.** umringen, umstellen; *Vogel* beringen

ring² 1. läuten; klingeln; klingen (*a. fig*); *Br* TEL anrufen; *the bell is ~ing* es läutet *or* klingelt; ~ *the bell* läuten, klingeln; ~ *back Br* TEL zurückrufen; ~ *for* nach j-m, *et.* läuten; *Arzt etc* rufen; ~ *off Br* TEL (den Hörer) auflegen, Schluss machen; ~ *s.o.* (*up*) j-n *or* bei j-m anrufen; **2.** Läuten *n*, Klingeln *n*; *fig* Klang *m*; *Br* TEL Anruf *m*; F *give s.o. a ~* j-n anrufen

ring bind·er Ringbuch *n*

ring fin·ger Ringfinger *m*

ring·lead·er Rädelsführer(in)

ring·let (Ringel)Löckchen *n*

ring road *Br* Umgehungsstraße *f*; Ringstraße *f*

R

ring·side: at the ~ boxing: am Ring

rink (Kunst)Eisbahn f; Rollschuhbahn f

rinse a. ~ out (aus)spülen

ri·ot 1. Aufruhr m; Krawall m; run ~ randalieren; run ~ through randalierend ziehen durch; 2. Krawall machen, randalieren; ri·ot·er Aufrührer(in); Randalierer(in); ri·ot·ous aufrührerisch; randalierend; ausgelassen, wild

rip 1. a. ~ up zerreißen; ~ open aufreißen; F ~ s.o. off j-n neppen; 2. Riss m

ripe reif; rip·en reifen (lassen)

rip-off F Nepp m

rip·ple 1. (sich) kräuseln; plätschern, rieseln; 2. kleine Welle; Kräuselung f; Plätschern n, Rieseln n

rise 1. aufstehen, sich erheben; REL auferstehen; aufsteigen (smoke etc); sich heben (curtain, spirits); ansteigen (road, river etc), anschwellen (river etc); (an)steigen (temperature etc), prices etc: a. anziehen; stärker werden (wind etc); aufgehen (sun etc, bread etc); entspringen (river etc); fig aufsteigen; fig entstehen (from, out of aus); a. ~ up sich erheben (against gegen); ~ to the occasion sich der Lage gewachsen zeigen; 2. (An)Steigen n; Steigung f; Anhöhe f; ASTR Aufgang m; Br Lohn- or Gehaltserhöhung f; fig Anstieg m; Aufstieg m; give ~ to verursachen, führen zu

ris·er: early ~ Frühaufsteher(in)

ris·ing 1. Aufstand m; 2. aufstrebend

risk 1. Gefahr f, Risiko n; at one's own ~ auf eigene Gefahr; at the ~ of doing s.th. auf die Gefahr hin, et. zu tun; be at ~ gefährdet sein; run the ~ of doing s.th. Gefahr laufen, et. zu tun; run a ~, take a ~ ein Risiko eingehen; 2. wagen, riskieren; risk·y riskant

rite Ritus m; Zeremonie f

rit·u·al 1. rituell; Ritual...; 2. Ritual n

ri·val 1. Rivale m, Rivalin f, Konkurrent (in); 2. Konkurrenz..., rivalisierend; 3. rivalisieren or konkurrieren mit; ri·val·ry Rivalität f; Konkurrenz f; Konkurrenzkampf m

riv·er Fluss m; Strom m; riv·er·side Flussufer n; by the ~ am Fluss

riv·et 1. TECH Niet m, n, Niete f; 2. TECH (ver)nieten; fig Aufmerksamkeit, Blick richten (on auf acc)

road (Auto-, Land)Straße f; fig Weg m; on the ~ auf der Straße; unterwegs; THEA auf Tournee

road ac·ci·dent Verkehrsunfall m

road·block Straßensperre f

road hog F Verkehrsrowdy m

road map Straßenkarte f

road safe·ty Verkehrssicherheit f

road·side Straßenrand m; at the ~, by the ~ am Straßenrand

road toll Straßenbenutzungsgebühr f

road·way Fahrbahn f

road works Straßenarbeiten pl

road·wor·thi·ness Verkehrssicherheit f; road·wor·thy verkehrssicher

roam v/i (umher)streifen, (-)wandern; v/t streifen or wandern durch

roar 1. Brüllen n, Gebrüll n; Brausen n, Krachen n, Donnern n; ~s of laughter brüllendes Gelächter; 2. brüllen; brausen; donnern (truck, gun etc)

roast GASTR 1. v/t braten (a. v/i); Kaffee etc rösten; 2. Braten m; 3. adj gebraten

roast beef GASTR Rinderbraten m

rob Bank etc überfallen; j-n berauben

rob·ber Räuber m

rob·ber·y Raubüberfall m, (Bank-) Raub m, (Bank)Überfall m

robe a. pl Robe f, Talar m

rob·in ZO Rotkehlchen n

ro·bot Roboter m

ro·bust robust, kräftig

rock¹ schaukeln, wiegen; erschüttern (a. fig)

rock² 1. Fels(en) m; Felsen pl; GEOL Gestein n; Felsbrocken m; Stein m; Br Zuckerstange f; pl Klippen pl; F on the ~s in ernsten Schwierigkeiten (business etc), kaputt (marriage etc); GASTR mit Eis

rock³ a. ~ music Rock(musik f) m; → rock 'n' roll

rock·er Kufe f; Schaukelstuhl m; Br Rocker m; off one's ~ F übergeschnappt

rock·et 1. Rakete f; 2. rasen, schießen; a. ~ up hochschnellen, in die Höhe schießen (prices)

rock·ing chair Schaukelstuhl m

rock·ing horse Schaukelpferd n

rock 'n' roll MUS Rock 'n' Roll m

rock·y felsig; steinhart

rod Rute f; TECH Stab m, Stange f

ro·dent ZO Nagetier n

ro·de·o Rodeo m, n

roe ZO a. **hard** ~ Rogen m; a. **soft** ~ Milch f

roe·buck ZO Rehbock m

roe deer ZO Reh n

rogue Schurke m, Gauner m; Schlingel m, Spitzbube m

ro·guish schelmisch, spitzbübisch

role THEA etc Rolle f (a. fig)

roll 1. v/i rollen; sich wälzen; fahren; MAR schlingern; (g)rollen (thunder); v/t et. rollen; auf-, zusammenrollen; Zigarette drehen; ~ **down** Ärmel herunterkrempeln; MOT Fenster herunterkurbeln; ~ **out** ausrollen; ~ **up** aufrollen; (sich) zusammenrollen; Ärmel hochkrempeln; MOT Fenster hochkurbeln; 2. Rolle f; GASTR Brötchen n, Semmel f; Namens-, Anwesenheitsliste f; (G)Rollen n (of thunder); (Trommel)Wirbel m; MAR Schlingern n

roll call Namensaufruf m

roll·er (Locken)Wickler m; TECH Rolle f, Walze f

roll·er coast·er Achterbahn f

roll·er skate Rollschuh m

roll·er-skate Rollschuh laufen

roll·er-skat·ing Rollschuhlaufen n

roll·er tow·el Rollhandtuch n

roll·ing pin Nudelholz n

roll-on Deoroller m

Ro·man 1. römisch; 2. Römer(in)

ro·mance Abenteuer-, Liebesroman m; Romanze f; Romantik f

Ro·mance LING romanisch

Ro·ma·ni·a Rumänien n

Ro·ma·ni·an 1. rumänisch; 2. Rumäne m, Rumänin f; LING Rumänisch n

ro·man·tic 1. romantisch; 2. Romantiker(in)

ro·man·ti·cism Romantik f

romp v/i: ~ **about**, ~ **around** herumtollen, herumtoben

romp·ers Spielanzug m

roof 1. Dach n; MOT Verdeck n; 2. mit e-m Dach versehen; ~ **in**, ~ **over** überdachen

roof·ing felt Dachpappe f

roof-rack MOT Dachgepäckträger m

rook[1] ZO Saatkrähe f

rook[2] chess: Turm m

rook[3] F j-n betrügen (of um)

room 1. Raum m, a. Zimmer n, a. Platz m; fig Spielraum m; 2. wohnen

room·er Untermieter(in)

room·ing-house Fremdenheim n, Pension f

room·mate Zimmergenosse m, -genossin f

room ser·vice Zimmerservice m

room·y geräumig

roost 1. (Hühner)Stange f; ZO Schlafplatz m; 2. auf der Stange etc sitzen or schlafen

roost·er ZO (Haus)Hahn m

root 1. Wurzel f; ~ **take** ~ Wurzeln schlagen (a. fig); 2. v/i Wurzeln schlagen; wühlen (**for** nach); ~ **about** herumwühlen (**among** in dat); v/t ~ **out** fig ausrotten; ~ **up** mit der Wurzel ausreißen

root·ed: **deeply** ~ fig tief verwurzelt; **stand** ~ **to the spot** wie angewurzelt dastehen

rope 1. Seil n; MAR Tau n; Strick m; (Perlen- etc)Schnur f; **give s.o. plenty of** ~ j-m viel Freiheit or Spielraum lassen; **know the** ~**s** F sich auskennen; **show s.o. the** ~**s** F j-n einarbeiten; 2. festbinden (**to** an dat or acc); ~ **off** (durch ein Seil) absperren or abgrenzen; ~ **lad·der** Strickleiter f

ro·sa·ry REL Rosenkranz m

rose 1. BOT Rose f; Brause f; 2. rosarot, rosenrot

ros·trum Redner-, Dirigentenpult n

ros·y rosig (a. fig)

rot 1. v/t (ver)faulen or verrotten lassen; v/i a. ~ **away** (ver)faulen, verrotten, morsch werden; 2. Fäulnis f

ro·ta·ry rotierend, sich drehend; Rotations..., Dreh...; **ro·tate** rotieren (lassen), (sich) drehen; turnusmäßig (aus-)wechseln; **ro·ta·tion** Rotation f, Drehung f; Wechsel m

ro·tor TECH Rotor m

rot·ten verfault, faul; verrottet, morsch; fig miserabel; gemein; **feel** ~ F sich mies fühlen

ro·tund rund und dick

rough 1. adj rau; uneben (road etc); stürmisch (sea, crossing, weather); grob; barsch; hart; grob, ungefähr (estimate etc); roh, Roh...; 2. adv **sleep** ~ im Freien übernachten; **play** ~ SPORT hart spielen; 3. golf: Rough n; **write it out in** ~ **first** zuerst ins Unreine schreiben; 4. ~ **it** F primitiv or anspruchslos leben; ~ **out** entwerfen,

R

skizzieren; **~ up** F j-n zusammenschlagen

rough·age MED Ballaststoffe pl

rough·cast ARCH Rauputz m

rough| cop·y Rohentwurf m, Konzept n; **~ draft** Rohfassung f

rough·en rau werden; rau machen, anrauen, aufrauen

rough·ly grob, fig a. ungefähr

rough·neck F Schläger m

rough·shod: ride **~ over** j-n rücksichtslos behandeln; sich rücksichtslos über et. hinwegsetzen

round 1. adj runden; **a ~ dozen** ein rundes Dutzend; **in ~ figures** aufgerundet, abgerundet, rund(e) ...; **2.** adv rund(her)um, rings(her)um; überall, auf or von or nach allen Seiten; **turn ~** sich umdrehen; **invite s.o. ~** j-n zu sich einladen; **~ about** F ungefähr; **all (the) year ~** das ganze Jahr hindurch or über; **the other way ~** umgekehrt; **3.** prp (rund) um, um (acc ~ herum); in or auf (dat) ... herum; **trip ~ the world** Weltreise f; **4.** Runde f, a. Rundgang m, MED Visite f, a. Lage f (beer etc); Schuss m; esp Br Scheibe f (bread etc); MUS Kanon m; **5.** rund machen, (ab)runden, Lippen spitzen; umfahren, fahren um, Kurve nehmen; **~ down** Zahl etc abrunden (**to** auf acc); **~ off** Essen etc abrunden, beschließen (**with** mit); Zahl etc auf- or abrunden (**to** acc); **~ up** Vieh zusammentreiben; Leute etc zusammentrommeln; Zahl etc aufrunden (**to** auf acc)

round·a·bout 1. Br MOT Kreisverkehr m; Br Karussell n; **2. take a ~ route** e-n Umweg machen; **in a ~ way** fig auf Umwegen

round trip Hin- und Rückfahrt f; Hin- und Rückflug m

round-trip tick·et Rückfahrkarte f; Rückflugticket n

round-up Razzia f

rouse j-n wecken; fig j-n aufrütteln, wachrütteln; j-n erzürnen, reizen

route Route f, Strecke f, Weg m, (Busetc)Linie f

rou·tine 1. Routine f; **the same old (daily) ~** das (tägliche) ewige Einerlei; **2.** üblich, routinemäßig, Routine...

rove (umher)streifen, (umher)wandern

row[1] Reihe f

row[2] **1.** rudern; **2.** Kahnfahrt f

row[3] Br F **1.** Krach m; (lauter) Streit; **2.** (sich) streiten

row·boat Ruderboot n

row·er Ruderer m, Ruderin f

row house Reihenhaus n

row·ing boat Br Ruderboot n

roy·al königlich, Königs...

roy·al·ty die königliche Familie; Tantieme f (**on** auf acc)

rub 1. v/t reiben; abreiben; polieren; **~ dry** trocken reiben; **~ it in** fig F darauf herumreiten; **~ shoulders with** F verkehren mit; v/i reiben, scheuern (**against, on** an dat); **~ down** abreiben, trocken reiben; abschmirgeln, abschleifen; **~ off** abreiben; abgehen (paint etc); **~ off on(to)** fig abfärben auf (acc); **~ out** Br ausradieren; **2. give s.th. a ~** et. abreiben or polieren

rub·ber Gummi n, m; esp Br Radiergummi m; Wischtuch n; F Gummi m

rub·ber band Gummiband n

rub·ber din·ghy Schlauchboot n

rub·ber·neck F **1.** neugierig gaffen; **2.** a. **rubbernecker** Gaffer(in), Schaulustige m, f

rub·ber·y gummiartig; zäh

rub·bish Br Abfall m, Abfälle pl, Müll m; F Schund m; Quatsch m, Blödsinn m; **~ bin** Br Mülleimer m; **~ chute** Br Müllschlucker m

rub·ble Schutt m; Trümmer pl

ru·by Rubin m; Rubinrot n

ruck·sack esp Br Rucksack m

rud·der AVIAT, MAR Ruder n

rud·dy frisch, gesund

rude unhöflich, grob; unanständig (joke etc); bös (shock etc)

ru·di·men·ta·ry elementar, Anfangs...; primitiv

ru·di·ments Anfangsgründe pl

rue·ful reuevoll, reumütig

ruff Halskrause f (a. ZO)

ruf·fle 1. kräuseln; Haar zerzausen; Federn sträuben; **~ s.o.'s composure** j-n aus der Fassung bringen; **2.** Rüsche f

rug Vorleger m, Brücke f; esp Br dicke Wolldecke

rug·by a. **~ football** SPORT Rugby n

rug·ged GEOGR zerklüftet, schroff; TECH robust, stabil; zerfurcht (face)

ru·in 1. Ruin m; mst pl Ruine(n pl) f, Trümmer pl; **2.** ruinieren, zerstören

ru·in·ous ruinös

rule 1. Regel *f;* Spielregel *f;* Vorschrift *f;* Herrschaft *f;* Lineal *n; **against the ~s*** regelwidrig; verboten; ***as a ~*** in der Regel; ***as a ~ of thumb*** als Faustregel; ***work to ~*** Dienst nach Vorschrift tun; **2.** *v/t* herrschen über (*acc*); *esp* JUR entscheiden; Papier lin(i)ieren; Linie ziehen; ***be ~d by*** fig sich leiten lassen von; beherrscht werden von; ***~ out*** et. ausschließen; *v/i* herrschen (**over** über *acc*); *esp* JUR entscheiden

rul·er Herrscher(in); Lineal *n*

rum Rum *m*

rum·ble rumpeln (*vehicle*); (g)rollen (*thunder*); knurren (*stomach*)

ru·mi·nant ZO Wiederkäuer *m*

ru·mi·nate ZO wiederkäuen

rum·mage F **1.** *a.* **~ about** herumstöbern, herumwühlen (**among, in, through** in *dat*); **2.** Ramsch *m;* **~ sale** Wohltätigkeitsbasar *m*

ru·mo(u)r 1. Gerücht *n; **~ has it that*** es geht das Gerücht, dass; **2. it is ~ed that** es geht das Gerücht, dass; **he is ~ed to be ...** man munkelt, er sei ...

rump F Hinterteil *n*

rum·ple zerknittern, zerknüllen, zerwühlen; *Haar* zerzausen

run 1. *v/i* laufen (*a.* SPORT), rennen; fahren, verkehren, gehen (*train, bus etc*); laufen, fließen; zerfließen, zerlaufen (*butter, paint etc*); TECH laufen (*engine*), in Betrieb *or* Gang sein; verlaufen (*road etc*); *esp* JUR gelten, laufen (**for one year** ein Jahr); THEA *etc* laufen (**for three months** drei Monate lang); lauten (*text*); gehen (*melody*); POL kandidieren (**for** für); **~ dry** austrocknen; **~ low** knapp werden; **~ short** knapp werden; **~ short of gas** (*Br petrol*) kein Benzin mehr haben; *v/t Strecke, Rennen* laufen; *Zug, Bus* fahren *or* verkehren lassen; *Wasser, Maschine etc* laufen lassen; *Geschäft, Hotel etc* führen; *Zeitungsartikel etc* abdrucken, bringen; → **s.o. home** F j-n nach Hause bringen *or* fahren; **be ~ning a temperature** erhöhte Temperatur *or* Fieber haben; → **errand;** **~ across** j-n zufällig treffen; stoßen auf (*acc*); **~ after** hinterherlaufen, nachlaufen (*dat*); **~ along!** F ab mit dir!; **~ away** davonlaufen (**from** vor *dat*); **~ away with** durchbrennen mit; durchgehen mit (*feelings etc*); **~ down** MOT anfahren, umfahren; F schlecht machen; ausfindig machen; ablaufen (*watch*); leer werden (*battery*); **~ in** *Wagen etc* einfahren; F *Verbrecher* schnappen; **~ into** laufen *or* fahren gegen; j-n zufällig treffen; *fig* geraten in (*acc*); *fig* sich belaufen auf (*acc*); **~ off with →** **run away with;** **~ on** weitergehen, sich hinziehen (*until* bis); F unaufhörlich reden (*about* über *acc,* von); **~ out** ablaufen (*time etc*); ausgehen, zu Ende gehen (*supplies etc*); **~ out of gas** (*Br petrol*) kein Benzin mehr haben; **~ over** MOT überfahren; überlaufen, überfließen; *fig* überfliegen, durchgehen, durchlesen; **~ through** *fig* durchbohren; **~ up** *Flagge* hissen; *hohe Rechnung, Schulden* machen; **~ up against** stoßen auf (*acc*); **2.** Lauf *m (a.* SPORT); Fahrt *f;* Spazierfahrt *f;* Ansturm *m,* ECON *a.* Run *m* (**on** auf *acc*); THEA *etc* Laufzeit *f;* Laufmasche *f;* Gehege *n;* Auslauf *m,* (*Hühner*)Hof *m;* SPORT (*Bob-, Rodel-*) Bahn *f;* (*Ski*)Hang *m;* **~ of good (bad) luck** Glückssträhne *f* (Pechsträhne *f*); **in the long ~** auf die Dauer; **in the short ~** zunächst; **on the ~** auf der Flucht

run·a·bout F MOT Stadt-, Kleinwagen *m*

run·a·way Ausreißer(in)

rung Sprosse *f*

run·ner SPORT Läufer(in); Rennpferd *n; mst in cpds* Schmuggler(in); (*Schlitten-, Schlittschuh-*)Kufe *f;* Tischläufer *m;* TECH (Gleit)Schiene *f;* BOT Ausläufer *m;* **~ bean** BOT grüne Bohne

run-up SPORT Zweite *m,* *f,* Vizemeister(in)

run·ning 1. Laufen *n,* Rennen *n;* Führung *f,* Leitung *f;* **2.** fließend; SPORT Lauf...; **two days ~** zwei Tage hintereinander; **~ costs** ECON Betriebskosten *pl,* laufende Kosten *pl*

run·ny F flüssig; laufend (*nose*), tränend (*eyes*)

run-off POL Stichwahl *f*

run·way AVIAT Start- und Landebahn *f,* Rollbahn *f,* Piste *f*

rup·ture 1. Bruch *m* (*a.* MED *and fig*), Riss *m;* **2.** bersten, platzen; (zer)reißen; **~ o.s.** MED sich e-n Bruch heben *or* zuziehen

ru·ral ländlich

ruse List *f*, Trick *m*

rush[1] **1.** *v/i* hasten, hetzen, stürmen, ra·sen; **~ at** losstürzen *or* sich stürzen auf (*acc*); **~ in** hineinstürzen, hineinstür·men, hereinstürzen, hereinstürmen; **~ into** *fig* sich stürzen in (*acc*); *et.* über·stürzen; *v/t* antreiben, drängen, hetzen; schnell bringen; *Essen* hinunterschlin·gen; losstürmen auf (*acc*); **don't ~ it** lass dir Zeit dabei; **2.** Ansturm *m*; Hast *f*, Hetze *f*; Hochbetrieb *m*; ECON stürmi·sche Nachfrage; **what's all the ~?** wo·zu diese Eile *or* Hetze?

rush[2] BOT Binse *f*

rush hour Rushhour *f*, Hauptverkehrs·zeit *f*, Stoßzeit *f*

rush-hour traf·fic Stoßverkehr *m*

rusk *esp Br* Zwieback *m*

Rus·sia Russland *n*

Rus·sian 1. russisch; **2.** Russe *m*, Russin *f*; LING Russisch *n*

rust 1. Rost *m*; **2.** *v/t* (ein-, ver)rosten lassen; *v/i* (ein-, ver)rosten

rus·tic ländlich, bäuerlich; rustikal

rus·tle 1. rascheln (mit), knistern; *Vieh* stehlen; **2.** Rascheln *n*

rust·proof rostfrei, nicht rostend

rust·y rostig; *fig* eingerostet

rut[1] **1.** (Rad)Spur *f*, Furche *f*; *fig* (alter) Trott; **the daily ~** das tägliche Einerlei; **2.** furchen; **rutted** ausgefahren

rut[2] ZO Brunft *f*, Brunst *f*

ruth·less unbarmherzig; rücksichtslos, skrupellos

rye BOT Roggen *m*

S

S, s S, s *n*

S ABBR *of* **small** (**size**) klein

sa·ber, *Br* **sa·bre** Säbel *m*

sa·ble ZO Zobel *m*; Zobelpelz *m*

sab·o·tage 1. Sabotage *f*; **2.** sabotie·ren

sack 1. Sack *m*; **get the ~** *Br* F rausge·schmissen werden; **give s.o. the ~** *Br* F j-n rausschmeißen; **hit the ~** F sich in die Falle *or* Klappe hauen; **2.** in Säcke füllen, einsacken; *Br* F j-n rausschmei·ßen

sack·cloth, sack·ing Sackleinen *n*

sac·ra·ment REL Sakrament *n*

sa·cred geistlich (*music etc*); heilig

sac·ri·fice 1. Opfer *n*; **2.** opfern

sac·ri·lege REL Sakrileg *n*; Frevel *m*

sac·ris·ty REL Sakristei *f*

sad traurig; schmerzlich; schlimm

sad·dle 1. Sattel *m*; **2.** satteln

sa·dism Sadismus *m*

sa·dist Sadist(in)

sa·dis·tic sadistisch

sad·ness Traurigkeit *f*

sa·fa·ri Safari *f*; **~ park** Safaripark *m*

safe 1. sicher; **2.** Safe *m, n*, Tresor *m*, Geldschrank *m*

safe con·duct freies Geleit

safe de·pos·it Tresor *m*

safe-de·pos·it box Schließfach *n*

safe·guard 1. Schutz *m* (**against** gegen, **vor** *dat*); **2.** schützen (**against, from** ge·gen, **vor** *dat*)

safe·keep·ing sichere Verwahrung

safe·ty 1. Sicherheit *f*; **2.** Sicherheits...; **~ belt → seat belt**; **~ is·land** Verkehrsin·sel *f*; **~ lock** Sicherheitsschloss *n*; **~ mea·sure** Sicherheitsmaßnahme *f*; **~ pin** Sicherheitsnadel *f*; **~ ra·zor** Rasier·apparat *m*

sag sich senken, absacken; durch·hängen; (herab)hängen (*shoulders*); *fig* sinken (*morale*); nachlassen (*in·terest etc*)

sa·ga·cious scharfsinnig

sa·ga·ci·ty Scharfsinn *m*

sage BOT Salbei *m, f*

Sa·git·tar·i·us ASTR Schütze *m*; **he** (**she**) **is** (**a**) **~** er (sie) ist (ein) Schütze

sail 1. Segel *n*; Segelfahrt *f*; (Windmüh·len)Flügel *m*; **set ~** auslaufen (**for** nach); **go for a ~** segeln gehen; **2.** *v/i* MAR segeln, fahren; auslaufen (**for** nach); gleiten, schweben; **go ~ing** se·geln gehen; *v/t* MAR befahren; *Schiff* steuern, *Boot* segeln

sail·board Surfbrett *n*

sail·boat Segelboot *n*

sapphire

sail·ing Segeln *n*; Segelsport *m*; **when is the next ~ to ...?** wann fährt das nächste Schiff nach ...?; **~ boat** *Br* Segelboot *n*; **~ ship** Segelschiff *n*

sail·or Seemann *m*, Matrose *m*; **be a good (bad) ~** (nicht) seefest sein

sail·plane Segelflugzeug *n*

saint Heilige *m, f*

saint·ly heilig, fromm

sake: **for the ~ of ...** um ... (*gen*) willen; **for my ~** meinetwegen; **for God's ~** F um Gottes willen

sal·a·ble verkäuflich

sal·ad Salat *m*; **~ dress·ing** Dressing *n*, Salatsoße *f*

sal·a·ried: **~ employee** Angestellte *m, f*, Gehaltsempfänger(in)

sal·a·ry Gehalt *n*

sale Verkauf *m*; Absatz *m*, Umsatz *m*; (Saison)Schlussverkauf *m*; Auktion *f*, Versteigerung *f*; **for ~** zu verkaufen; **not for ~** unverkäuflich; **be on ~** verkauft werden, erhältlich sein

sale·a·ble → **salable**

sales·clerk (Laden)Verkäufer(in)

sales·girl (Laden)Verkäuferin *f*

sales·man Verkäufer *m*; (Handels-)Vertreter *m*

sales rep·re·sen·ta·tive Handlungsreisende *m, f*; (Handels)Vertreter(in)

sales slip ECON Quittung *f*

sales tax ECON Umsatzsteuer *f*

sales·wom·an Verkäuferin *f*; (Handels)Vertreterin *f*

sa·line salzig, Salz...

sa·li·va Speichel *m*

sal·low gelblich

salm·on ZO Lachs *m*

sal·on (Schönheits- *etc*)Salon *m*

sa·loon *Br* MOT Limousine *f*; HIST Saloon *m*; MAR Salon *m*

sa·loon car *Br* MOT Limousine *f*

salt **1.** Salz *n*; **2.** salzen; (ein)pökeln, einsalzen (*a.* **~ down**); *Straße etc* mit Salz (be)streuen; **3.** Salz...; gepökelt; salzig, gesalzen

salt·cel·lar *Br* Salzstreuer *m*

salt·pe·ter, *esp Br* salt·pe·tre CHEM Salpeter *m*

salt shak·er Salzstreuer *m*

salt wa·ter Salzwasser *n*

salt·y salzig

sal·u·ta·tion Gruß *m*, Begrüßung *f*; Anrede *f*; **sa·lute 1.** MIL salutieren; (be-)

grüßen; **2.** Gruß *m*; MIL Ehrenbezeugung *f*; Salut *m*

sal·vage **1.** Bergung *f*; Bergungsgut *n*; **2.** bergen (**from** aus); retten (*a. fig*)

sal·va·tion Rettung *f*; REL Erlösung *f*; (Seelen)Heil *n*

Sal·va·tion Ar·my Heilsarmee *f*

salve (Heil)Salbe *f*

same: **the ~** derselbe, dieselbe, dasselbe; **all the ~** trotzdem; **it is all the ~ to me** es ist mir ganz egal

sam·ple **1.** Muster *n*, Probe *f*; **2.** kosten, probieren

san·a·to·ri·um Sanatorium *n*

sanc·ti·fy heiligen

sanc·tion **1.** Billigung *f*, Zustimmung *f*; *mst pl* Sanktionen *pl*; **2.** billigen, sanktionieren

sanc·ti·ty Heiligkeit *f*

sanc·tu·a·ry Zuflucht *f*, Asyl *n*; ZO Schutzgebiet *n*

sand **1.** Sand *m*; *pl* Sandfläche *f*; **2.** *Straße etc* mit Sand (be)streuen; TECH schmirgeln

san·dal Sandale *f*

sand·bag Sandsack *m*

sand·bank GEOGR Sandbank *f*

sand·box Sandkasten *m*

sand·cas·tle Sandburg *f*

sand·man Sandmännchen *n*

sand·pa·per Sand-, Schmirgelpapier *n*

sand·pip·er ZO Strandläufer *m*

sand·pit *Br* Sandkasten *m*; Sandgrube *f*

sand·stone GEOL Sandstein *m*

sand·storm Sandsturm *m*

sand·wich **1.** Sandwich *n*; **2. be ~ed between** eingekeilt sein zwischen (*dat*); **~ s.th. in between** *fig* et. einschieben zwischen (*acc or dat*)

sand·y sandig; rotblond

sane geistig gesund; JUR zurechnungsfähig; vernünftig

san·i·tar·i·um → **sanatorium**

san·i·ta·ry hygienisch; Gesundheits...; **~ nap·kin**, *Br* **~ tow·el** (Damen)Binde *f*

san·i·ta·tion sanitäre Einrichtungen *pl*; Kanalisation *f*

san·i·ty geistige Gesundheit *f*; JUR Zurechnungsfähigkeit *f*

San·ta Claus der Weihnachtsmann, der Nikolaus

sap¹ BOT Saft *m*

sap² schwächen

sap·phire Saphir *m*

sar·casm Sarkasmus *m*
sar·cas·tic sarkastisch
sar·dine ZO Sardine *f*
sash[1] Schärpe *f*
sash[2] Fensterrahmen *m*
sas·sy frech
Sat ABBR *of* ***Saturday*** Sa., Samstag *m*, Sonnabend *m*
Sa·tan der Satan
satch·el (Schul)Ranzen *m*; Schultasche *f*
sat·ed *fig* übersättigt
sat·el·lite 1. Satellit *m*; **by** *or* **via** ~ über Satellit; 2. Satelliten...; ~ **dish** F Satellitenschüssel *f*
sat·in Satin *m*
sat·ire Satire *f*
sat·ir·ic, **sat·ir·i·cal** satirisch
sat·i·rist Satiriker(in)
sat·i·rize verspotten
sat·is·fac·tion Befriedigung *f*; Genugtuung *f*, Zufriedenheit *f*
sat·is·fac·to·ry befriedigend, zufrieden stellend
sat·is·fy befriedigen, zufrieden stellen; überzeugen; **be satisfied that** davon überzeugt sein, dass
sat·u·rate (durch)tränken (**with** mit); CHEM sättigen (*a. fig*)
Sat·ur·day Sonnabend *m*, Samstag *m*; **on** ~ (am) Sonnabend *or* Samstag; **on** ~**s** sonnabends, samstags
sauce Soße *f*
sauce·pan Kochtopf *m*
sau·cer Untertasse *f*
sauc·y *Br* frech
saun·ter bummeln, schlendern
sau·sage Wurst *f*, *a.* **small** ~ Würstchen *n*
sav·age 1. wild; unzivilisiert; 2. Wilde *m*, *f*; **sav·ag·e·ry** Wildheit *f*; Rohheit *f*, Grausamkeit *f*
save 1. retten (**from** vor *dat*); *Geld, Zeit etc* (ein)sparen; *et.* aufheben, aufsparen (**for** für); *j-m et.* ersparen; EDP (ab)speichern, sichern; SPORT *Schuss* halten, parieren, *Tor* verhindern; 2. SPORT Parade *f*
sav·er Retter(in); ECON Sparer(in)
sav·ings ECON Ersparnisse *pl*; ~ **ac·count** Sparkonto *n*; ~ **bank** Sparkasse *f*; ~ **de·pos·it** Spareinlage *f*
sa·vio(u)r Retter(in); **the Savio(u)r**

REL der Erlöser, der Heiland
sa·vo(u)r mit Genuss essen *or* trinken; ~ **of** *fig* e-n Beigeschmack haben von
sa·vo(u)r·y schmackhaft
saw 1. Säge *f*; 2. sägen
saw·dust Sägemehl *n*, Sägespäne *pl*
saw·mill Sägewerk *n*
Sax·on 1. (Angel)Sachse *m*, (Angel-) Sächsin *f*; 2. (angel)sächsisch
say 1. sagen; aufsagen; *Gebet* sprechen, *Vaterunser* beten; ~ **grace** bei Tischgebet sprechen; **what does your watch** ~? wie spät ist es auf deiner Uhr?; **he is said to be ...** er soll ... sein; **it** ~**s** es lautet (*letter etc*); **it** ~**s here** hier heißt es; **it goes without** ~**ing** es versteht sich von selbst; **no sooner said than done** gesagt, getan; **that is to** ~ das heißt; **(and) that's** ~**ing s.th.** (und) das will was heißen; **you said it** du sagst es; **you can** ~ **that again!** das kannst du laut sagen!; **you don't** ~ **(so)!** was du nicht sagst!; **I** ~ sag(en Sie) mal!; ich muss schon sagen!; **I can't** ~ das kann ich nicht sagen; 2. Mitspracherecht *n* (**in** bei); **have one's** ~ s-e Meinung äußern, zu Wort kommen; **he always has to have his** ~ er muss immer mitreden
say·ing Sprichwort *n*, Redensart *f*; **as the** ~ **goes** wie man so (schön) sagt
scab MED, BOT Schorf *m*; *contp* Streikbrecher(in)
scaf·fold (Bau)Gerüst *n*; Schafott *n*
scaf·fold·ing (Bau)Gerüst *n*
scald 1. *sich die Zunge etc* verbrühen; *Milch* abkochen; ~**ing hot** kochend heiß; 2. MED Verbrühung *f*
scale[1] 1. Skala *f* (*a. fig*), Grad- *or* Maßeinteilung *f*; MATH, TECH Maßstab *m* (*a. fig*); Waage *f*; MUS Skala *f*, Tonleiter *f*; *fig* Ausmaß *n*, Umfang *m*; 2. erklettern; ~ **down** *fig* verringern; ~ **up** *fig* erhöhen
scale[2] Waagschale *f*; (**a pair of**) ~**s** (e-e) Waage
scale[3] 1. ZO Schuppe *f*; TECH Kesselstein *m*; **the** ~**s fell from my eyes** es fiel mir wie Schuppen von den Augen; 2. *Fisch* (ab)schuppen
scal·lop ZO Kammmuschel *f*
scalp 1. Kopfhaut *f*; Skalp *m*; 2. skalpieren
scal·y ZO schuppig (*a. fig*)

scamp F Schlingel *m*, (kleiner) Strolch

scam·per trippeln; huschen

scan 1. *et.* absuchen (**for** nach); *Zeitung etc* überfliegen; EDP, *radar*, TV abtasten, scannen; 2. MED *etc* Scanning *n*

scan·dal Skandal *m*; Klatsch *m*

scan·dal·ize: **be ~d at s.th.** über et. empört or entrüstet sein

scan·dal·ous skandalös; **be ~** *a.* ein Skandal sein (**that** dass)

Scan·di·na·vi·a Skandinavien *n*

Scan·di·na·vi·an 1. skandinavisch; 2. Skandinavier(in)

scan·ner TECH Scanner *m*

scant dürftig, gering

scant·y dürftig, kärglich, knapp

scape·goat Sündenbock *m*

scar MED 1. Narbe *f (a. fig)*; 2. e-e Narbe or Narben hinterlassen auf (*dat*) or *fig* bei *j-m*; ~ **over** vernarben

scarce knapp (*food etc*); selten; **be ~** Mangelware sein (*a. fig*); **scarce·ly** kaum; **scar·ci·ty** Mangel *m*, Knappheit *f* (**of** an *dat*)

scare 1. erschrecken; **be ~d** Angst haben (**of** vor *dat*); ~ **away**, ~ **off** verjagen, -scheuchen; 2. Schreck(en) *m*; Panik *f*

scare·crow Vogelscheuche *f (a. fig)*

scarf Schal *m*; Hals-, Kopf-, Schultertuch *n*

scar·let scharlachrot; ~ **fe·ver** MED Scharlach *m*

scarred narbig

scath·ing bissig (*remark etc*); vernichtend (*criticism etc*)

scat·ter (sich) zerstreuen (*crowd*); ausstreuen, verstreuen; auseinander stieben (*birds etc*)

scat·ter·brained F schusselig, schusslig

scat·tered verstreut; vereinzelt

scav·enge: ~ **on** ZO leben von; ~ **for** suchen (nach)

scene Szene *f*; Schauplatz *m*; *pl* THEA Kulissen *pl*

sce·ne·ry Landschaft *f*, Gegend *f*; THEA Bühnenbild *n*, Kulissen *pl*

scent 1. Duft *m*, Geruch *m*; *esp Br* Parfüm *m*; HUNT Witterung *f*; Fährte *f*, Spur *f (a. fig)*; 2. wittern; *esp Br* parfümieren; **scent·less** geruchlos

scep·ter, *Br* scep·tre Zepter *n*

scep·tic, scep·ti·cal *Br* → **skeptic** *etc*

sched·ule 1. Aufstellung *f*, Verzeichnis *n*; (*Arbeits-, Stunden-, Zeit- etc*)Plan *m*; Fahr-, Flugplan *m*; **ahead of ~** dem Zeitplan voraus, früher als vorgesehen; **be behind ~** Verspätung haben; im Verzug or Rückstand sein; **on ~** (fahr-) planmäßig, pünktlich; 2. **the meeting is ~d for Monday** die Sitzung ist für Montag angesetzt; **it is ~d to take place tomorrow** es soll morgen stattfinden

sched·uled| de·par·ture (fahr)planmäßige Abfahrt; ~ **flight** Linienflug *m*

scheme 1. *esp Br* Programm *n*, Projekt *n*; Schema *n*, System *n*; Intrige *f*, Machenschaft *f*; 2. intrigieren

schmaltz·y F schnulzig

schnit·zel GASTR Wiener Schnitzel *n*

schol·ar Gelehrte *m*, *f*; UNIV Stipendiat(in); schol·ar·ly gelehrt

schol·ar·ship Gelehrsamkeit *f*; UNIV Stipendium *n*

school[1] Schule *f (a. fig)*; UNIV Fakultät *f*; Hochschule *f*; **at ~** auf or in der Schule; **go to ~** in die or zur Schule gehen; 2. *j-n* schulen, unterrichten; *Tier* dressieren

school[2] ZO Schule *f*, Schwarm *m*

school·bag Schultasche *f*

school·boy Schüler *m*

school·child Schulkind *n*

school·fel·low → **schoolmate**

school·girl Schülerin *f*

school·ing (Schul)Ausbildung *f*

school·mate Mitschüler(in), Schulkamerad(in)

school·teach·er (Schul)Lehrer(in)

school·yard Schulhof *m*

schoo·ner MAR Schoner *m*

sci·ence Wissenschaft *f*; *a.* **natural ~** Naturwissenschaft(en *pl*) *f*; ~ **fic·tion** (ABBR **SF**) Sciencefiction *f*

sci·en·tif·ic (natur)wissenschaftlich; exakt, systematisch

sci·en·tist (Natur)Wissenschaftler(in)

sci-fi F Sciencefiction *f*

scis·sors: (**a pair of ~** e-e) Schere *f*

scoff 1. spotten (**at** über *acc*); 2. spöttische Bemerkung

scold schimpfen (mit)

scoop 1. Schöpfkelle *f*; (*Mehl- etc -*) Schaufel *f*; (*Eis- etc*)Portionierer *m*; Kugel *f (icecream)*; *newspaper, radio*, TV Exklusivmeldung *f*, F Knüller *m*;

2. schöpfen, schaufeln; **~ up** aufheben, hochheben

scoot·er (Kinder)Roller *m*; (*Motor-*)Roller *m*

scope Bereich *m*; Spielraum *m*

scorch *v/t* ansengen, versengen, verbrennen; ausdörren; *v/i Br* MOT F rasen

score 1. SPORT (Spiel)Stand *m*, (-)Ergebnis *n*; MUS Partitur *f*; Musik *f*; 20 (Stück); *a.* **~ mark** Kerbe *f*, Rille *f*; **what is the ~?** wie steht es *or* das Spiel?; **the ~ stood at** *or* **was 3-2** das Spiel stand 3:2; **keep (the) ~** anschreiben; **~s of** e-e Menge; **four ~ and ten** neunzig; **on that ~** deshalb, in dieser Hinsicht; **have a ~ to settle with s.o.** e-e alte Rechnung mit j-m zu begleichen haben; **2.** *v/t* SPORT Punkte, Treffer erzielen, Tor *a.* schießen; Erfolg, Sieg erringen; MUS instrumentieren; die Musik schreiben zu *or* für; einkerben; *v/i* SPORT e-n Treffer *etc* erzielen, ein Tor schießen; erfolgreich sein

score·board SPORT Anzeigetafel *f*

scor·er SPORT Torschütze *m*, Torschützin *f*; Anschreiber(in)

scorn Verachtung *f*

scorn·ful verächtlich

Scor·pi·o ASTR Skorpion *m*; **he (she) is (a) ~** er (sie) ist (ein) Skorpion

Scot Schotte *m*, Schottin *f*

Scotch 1. schottisch; **2.** Scotch *m*

scot-free: F **get off ~** ungeschoren davonkommen

Scot·land Schottland *n*

Scots schottisch; **Scotsman** Schotte *m*; **Scots·wom·an** Schottin *f*

Scot·tish schottisch

scoun·drel Schurke *m*

scour[1] scheuern, schrubben

scour[2] *Gegend* absuchen, durchkämmen (**for** nach)

scourge 1. Geißel *f* (*a. fig*); **2.** geißeln, *fig a.* heimsuchen

scout 1. *esp* MIL Kundschafter *m*; *Br* motorisierter Pannenhelfer; *a.* **boy ~** Pfadfinder *m*; *a.* **girl ~** Pfadfinderin *f*; *a.* **talent ~** Talentsucher(in); **2. ~ about**, **~ around** sich umsehen (**for** nach); *a.* **~ out** MIL auskundschaften

scowl 1. finsteres Gesicht; **2.** finster blicken; **~ at s.o.** j-n böse *or* finster anschauen

scram·ble 1. klettern; sich drängeln (**for** zu); **2.** Kletterei *f*; Drängelei *f*

scram·bled eggs Rührei(er *pl*) *n*

scrap[1] Stückchen *n*, Fetzen *m*; Altmaterial *n*; Schrott *m*; *pl* Abfall *m*, Speisereste *pl*; **2.** verschrotten; ausrangieren; *Plan etc* aufgeben, fallen lassen

scrap[2] F **1.** Streiterei *f*; Balgerei *f*; **2.** sich streiten; sich balgen

scrap·book Sammelalbum *n*

scrape 1. (ab)kratzen, (ab)schaben; sich *die Knie etc* aufschürfen; *Wagen etc* ankratzen; scheuern (**against** an *dat*); (entlang)streifen; scharren; **2.** Kratzen *n*; Kratzer *m*, Schramme *f*; *fig* Klemme *f*

scrap heap Schrotthaufen *m*

scrap met·al Altmetall *n*, Schrott *m*

scrap pa·per *esp Br* Schmierpapier *n*

scrap val·ue Schrottwert *m*

scrap·yard Schrottplatz *m*

scratch 1. (zer)kratzen; abkratzen; *s-n Namen etc* einkratzen; (sich) kratzen; scharren; **2.** Kratzer *m*, Schramme *f*; Gekratze *n*; Kratzen *n*; **from ~** F ganz von vorn; **3.** (bunt) zusammengewürfelt

scratch·pad Notiz-, Schmierblock *m*

scratch pa·per Schmierpapier *n*

scrawl 1. kritzeln; **2.** Gekritzel *n*

scraw·ny dürr

scream 1. schreien (**with** vor *dat*); *a.* **~ out** schreien; **~ with laughter** vor Lachen brüllen; **2.** Schrei *m*; **~s of laughter** brüllendes Gelächter; **be a ~** F zum Schreien (komisch) sein

screech 1. kreischen (*a. fig*), (gellend) schreien; **2.** Kreischen *n*; (gellender) Schrei

screen 1. Wand-, Ofen-, Schutzschirm *m*; *film*: Leinwand *f*; *radar*, TV, EDP Bildschirm *m*; Fliegengitter *n*, -gitter *n*; *fig* Tarnung *f*; **2.** abschirmen; *film* zeigen, *Fernsehprogramm a.* senden; *fig* j-n decken; *fig* j-n überprüfen; **~ off** abtrennen

screen·play Drehbuch *n*

screen sav·er EDP Bildschirmschoner *m*

screw 1. TECH Schraube *f*; **he has a ~ loose** F bei ihm ist e-e Schraube locker; **2.** (an)schrauben (**to** an *acc*); V bumsen, vögeln; **~ up** *Gesicht* verziehen; *Augen* zusammenkneifen; **~ up one's courage** sich ein Herz fassen

screw·ball F Spinner(in)

screw·driv·er Schraubenzieher m

screw top Schraubverschluss m

scrib·ble 1. (hin)kritzeln; **2.** Gekritzel n

scrimp: ~ *and save* jeden Pfennig zweimal umdrehen

script Manuskript n; film, TV Drehbuch n, Skript n; THEA Text m, Textbuch n; Schrift(zeichen pl) f; Br UNIV (schriftliche) Prüfungsarbeit

Scrip·ture a. *the* ~s REL die Heilige Schrift

scroll 1. Schriftrolle f; **2.** ~ *down* (*up*) EDP zurückrollen (vorrollen)

scro·tum ANAT Hodensack m

scrub[1] **1.** schrubben, scheuern; **2.** Schrubben n, Scheuern n

scrub[2] Gebüsch n, Gestrüpp n

scru·ple 1. Skrupel m, Zweifel m, Bedenken pl; **2.** Bedenken haben

scru·pu·lous gewissenhaft

scru·ti·nize genau prüfen; mustern

scru·ti·ny genaue Prüfung; prüfender Blick

scu·ba div·ing (Sport)Tauchen n

scuf·fle 1. Handgemenge n, Rauferei f; **2.** sich raufen

scull 1. Skull n; Skullboot n; **2.** rudern, skullen

sculp·tor Bildhauer m

sculp·ture 1. Bildhauerei f; Skulptur f, Plastik f; **2.** hauen, meißeln, formen

scum Schaum m; fig Abschaum m; *the* ~ *of the earth* fig der Abschaum der Menschheit

scurf (Kopf)Schuppen pl

scur·ri·lous beleidigend; verleumderisch

scur·ry huschen; trippeln

scur·vy MED Skorbut m

scut·tle: ~ *away*, ~ *off* davonlaufen

scythe Sense f

sea Meer n (a. fig), See f; *at* ~ auf See; *be all* or *completely at* ~ fig F völlig ratlos sein; *by* ~ auf dem Seeweg; *by the* ~ am Meer

sea·food GASTR Meeresfrüchte pl

sea·gull ZO Seemöwe f

seal[1] ZO Robbe f, Seehund m

seal[2] **1.** Siegel n; TECH Plombe f; TECH Dichtung f; **2.** (ver)siegeln; TECH plombieren; abdichten; fig besiegeln; ~ed *envelope* verschlossener Briefumschlag; ~ *off* Gegend etc abriegeln

sea lev·el: *above* (*below*) ~ über (unter) dem Meeresspiegel

seal·ing wax Siegellack m

seam Naht f; Fuge f; GEOL Flöz n

sea·man Seemann m

seam·stress Näherin f

sea·plane Wasserflugzeug n

sea·port Seehafen m; Hafenstadt f

sea pow·er Seemacht f

search 1. v/i suchen (*for* nach); ~ *through* durchsuchen; v/t j-n, et. durchsuchen (*for* nach); ~ *me!* F keine Ahnung!; **2.** Suche f (*for* nach); Fahndung f (*for* nach); Durchsuchung f; *in* ~ *of* auf der Suche nach; **search·ing** prüfend (*look*); eingehend (*examination*)

search·light (Such)Scheinwerfer m

search par·ty Suchmannschaft f

search war·rant JUR Haussuchungs-, Durchsuchungsbefehl m

sea·shore Meeresküste f

sea·sick seekrank

sea·side: *at* or *by the* ~ am Meer; *go to the* ~ ans Meer fahren

sea·side re·sort Seebad n

sea·son[1] Jahreszeit f; Saison f, THEA etc a. Spielzeit f, (Jagd-, Urlaubs- etc)Zeit f; *in* (*out of*) ~ in (außerhalb) der (Hoch)Saison; *cherries are now in* ~ jetzt ist Kirschenzeit; *Season's Greetings!* Frohe Weihnachten!; *with the compliments of the* ~ mit den besten Wünschen zum Fest

sea·son[2] Speise würzen (*with* mit); Holz ablagern

sea·son·al saisonbedingt, Saison...

sea·son·ing GASTR Gewürz n

sea·son tick·et RAIL etc Dauer-, Zeitkarte f; THEA Abonnement n

seat 1. Sitz(gelegenheit f) m; (Sitz)Platz m; Sitz(fläche f) m; Hosenboden m; Hinterteil n; (Geschäfts-, Regierungsetc)Sitz m; PARL Sitz m; *take a* ~ Platz nehmen; *take one's* ~ s-n Platz einnehmen; **2.** j-n setzen; Sitzplätze bieten für; *be* ~ed sitzen; *please be* ~ed bitte nehmen Sie Platz; *remain* ~ed sitzen bleiben

seat belt AVIAT, MOT Sicherheitsgurt m; *fasten one's* ~ sich anschnallen

sea ur·chin ZO Seeigel m

sea·ward(s) seewärts

sea·weed BOT (See)Tang m

S

sea·wor·thy seetüchtig

sec F Augenblick *m*, Sekunde *f*; *just a ~* Augenblick(, bitte)!

se·cede sich abspalten (**from** von)

se·ces·sion Abspaltung *f*, Sezession *f* (**from** von)

se·clud·ed abgelegen, abgeschieden (*place*); zurückgezogen (*life*)

se·clu·sion Abgeschiedenheit *f*; Zurückgezogenheit *f*

sec·ond¹ **1.** *adj* zweite(r, -s); *every ~ day* jeden zweiten Tag, alle zwei Tage; *~ to none* unerreicht, unübertroffen; *but on ~ thought* (*Br* thoughts) aber wenn ich es mir so überlege; **2.** *adv* als Zweite(r, -s); **3.** *der, die, das* Zweite; MOT zweiter Gang; Sekundant *m*; *pl* F ECON Waren *pl* zweiter Wahl; **4.** *Antrag etc* unterstützen

sec·ond² Sekunde *f*; *fig* Augenblick *m*, Sekunde *f*; *just a ~* Augenblick(, bitte)!

sec·ond·a·ry sekundär, zweitrangig; PED höher

sec·ond-best zweitbeste(r, -s)

sec·ond class RAIL *etc* zweiter Klasse

sec·ond-class zweitklassig

sec·ond floor erster (*Br* zweiter) Stock

sec·ond hand Sekundenzeiger *m*

sec·ond-hand aus zweiter Hand; gebraucht; antiquarisch

sec·ond·ly zweitens

sec·ond-rate zweitklassig

se·cre·cy Verschwiegenheit *f*; Geheimhaltung *f*

se·cret 1. geheim, Geheim...; heimlich; verschwiegen; **2.** Geheimnis *n*; *in ~* heimlich, im Geheimen; *keep s.th. a ~ et.* geheim halten (**from** vor *dat*); *can you keep a ~?* kannst du schweigen?

se·cret a·gent Geheimagent(in)

sec·re·ta·ry Sekretär(in); POL Minister(in)

Sec·re·ta·ry of State POL Außenminister(in); *Br* Minister(in)

se·crete MED absondern; **se·cre·tion** MED Sekret *n*; Absonderung *f*

se·cre·tive verschlossen

se·cret·ly heimlich

se·cret ser·vice Geheimdienst *m*

sec·tion Teil *m*; Abschnitt *m*; JUR Paragraf *m*; Abteilung *f*, MATH, TECH Schnitt *m*

sec·tor Sektor *m*, Bereich *m*

sec·u·lar weltlich

se·cure 1. sicher (**against, from** vor *dat*); **2.** Tür *etc* fest verschließen; *et.* sichern (**against, from** vor *dat*)

se·cu·ri·ty Sicherheit *f*; *pl* ECON Wertpapiere *pl*; *~* **check** Sicherheitskontrolle *f*; *~* **mea·sure** Sicherheitsmaßnahme *f*; *~* **risk** Sicherheitsrisiko *n*

se·dan MOT Limousine *f*

se·date ruhig, gelassen

sed·a·tive *mst* MED **1.** beruhigend; **2.** Beruhigungsmittel *n*

sed·i·ment (Boden)Satz *m*

se·duce verführen

se·duc·er Verführer(in)

se·duc·tion Verführung *f*

se·duc·tive verführerisch

see¹ *v/i* sehen; nachsehen; *I ~!* (ich) verstehe!, ach so!; *you ~* weißt du; *let me ~* warte mal, lass mich überlegen; *we'll ~* mal sehen; *v/t* sehen; besuchen; *j-n* aufsuchen; *j-n* konsultieren; *~* **s.o.** *home j-n* nach Hause bringen *or* begleiten; *~ you!* bis dann!, auf bald!; *~ about* sehen nach, sich kümmern um; *~ off j-n* verabschieden (*at* am *Bahnhof etc*); *~ out j-n* hinausbringen, hinausgeleiten; *~ through j-n, et.* durchschauen; *j-m* hinweghelfen über (*acc*); *~ to it that* dafür sorgen, dass

see² REL Bistum *n*, Diözese *f*; *Holy See der* Heilige Stuhl

seed 1. BOT Same(n) *m*; AGR Saat *f*, Saatgut *n*; (*Apfel- etc*)Kern *m*; SPORT gesetzter Spieler, gesetzte Spielerin; *go or run to ~* BOT schießen; *go to ~* F herunterkommen, verkommen; **2.** *v/t* besäen; entkernen; SPORT *Spieler* setzen; *v/i* BOT in Samen schießen

seed·less BOT kernlos

seed·y F heruntergekommen

seek Schutz, Wahrheit *etc* suchen

seem scheinen; **seem·ing** scheinbar

seep sickern

see·saw Wippe *f*, Wippschaukel *f*

seethe schäumen (*a. fig*); *fig* kochen

see-through durchsichtig

seg·ment Teil *m*, *n*; Stück *n*; Abschnitt *m*; Segment *n*

seg·re·gate trennen

seg·re·ga·tion Rassentrennung *f*

seize *j-n, et.* packen, ergreifen; *Macht etc* an sich reißen; *et.* beschlagnahmen; *et.* pfänden; **sei·zure** Beschlagnahme *f*;

Pfändung *f*; MED Anfall *m*

sel·dom *adv* selten

se·lect 1. (aus)wählen; **2.** ausgewählt; exklusiv; **se·lec·tion** (Aus)Wahl *f*; ECON Auswahl *f* (**of** an *dat*)

self Ich *n*, Selbst *n*

self-as·sured selbstbewusst, -sicher

self-cen·tered, *Br* **self-cen·tred** egozentrisch

self-col·o(u)red einfarbig

self-con·fi·dence Selbstbewusstsein *n*, Selbstvertrauen *n*

self-con·fi·dent selbstbewusst

self-con·scious befangen, gehemmt, unsicher

self-con·tained (in sich) abgeschlossen; *fig* verschlossen; **~ flat** *Br* abgeschlossene Wohnung

self-con·trol Selbstbeherrschung *f*

self-crit·i·cal selbstkritisch

self-de·fence *Br*, **self-de·fense** Selbstverteidigung *f*; **in ~** in or aus Notwehr

self-de·ter·mi·na·tion POL Selbstbestimmung *f*

self-em·ployed selbstständig

self-es·teem Selbstachtung *f*

self-ev·i·dent selbstverständlich; offensichtlich

self-gov·ern·ment POL Selbstverwaltung *f*

self-help Selbsthilfe *f*; **~ group** Selbsthilfegruppe *f*

self-im·por·tant überheblich

self-in·dul·gent nachgiebig gegen sich selbst; zügellos

self-in·terest Eigennutz *m*

self·ish selbstsüchtig, egoistisch

self-knowl·edge Selbsterkenntnis *f*

self-pit·y Selbstmitleid *n*

self-por·trait Selbstporträt *n*

self-pos·sessed selbstbeherrscht

self-re·li·ant selbstständig

self-re·spect Selbstachtung *f*

self-right·eous selbstgerecht

self-sat·is·fied selbstzufrieden

self-ser·vice 1. mit Selbstbedienung, Selbstbedienungs...; **2.** Selbstbedienung *f*

self-stud·y Selbststudium *n*

self-suf·fi·cient ECON autark

self-sup·port·ing finanziell unabhängig

self-willed eigensinnig, eigenwillig

sell *v/t* verkaufen; *v/i* verkauft werden

(**at**, **for** für); sich *gut etc* verkaufen (lassen), gehen; **~ by ...** mindestens haltbar bis ...; **~ off** (*esp* billig) abstoßen; **~ out** ausverkaufen; **be sold out** ausverkauft sein; **~ up** *esp Br sein Geschäft etc* verkaufen; **sell-by date** Mindesthaltbarkeitsdatum *n*; **sell·er** Verkäufer(in); **good ~** ECON gut gehender Artikel

sem·blance Anschein *m* (**of** von)

se·men MED Samen(flüssigkeit *f*) *m*, Sperma *n*

se·mes·ter UNIV Semester *n*

sem·i... halb..., Halb...

sem·i·cir·cle Halbkreis *m*

sem·i·co·lon LING Semikolon *n*, Strichpunkt *m*

sem·i·con·duc·tor ELECTR Halbleiter *m*

sem·i·de·tached (**house**) *Br* Doppelhaushälfte *f*

sem·i·fi·nals SPORT Semi-, Halbfinale *n*

sem·i·nar·y Priesterseminar *n*

sem·i·pre·cious: ~ stone Halbedelstein *m*

sem·i-skilled angelernt

sem·o·li·na Grieß *m*

sen·ate POL Senat *m*

sen·a·tor POL Senator *m*

send *et.*, *a.* Grüße, Hilfe etc senden, schicken (**to** dat or an acc); Ware etc versenden, verschicken (**to** an acc); *j-n* schicken (**to** ins Bett etc); *with adj or pp* machen: **~ s.o. mad** *j-n* wahnsinnig machen; **~ word to s.o.** *j-m* Nachricht geben; **~ away** fort-, wegschicken; *Brief etc* absenden, abschicken; **~ down** Preise etc fallen lassen; **~ for** nach *j-m* schicken, *j-n* kommen lassen; sich *et.* kommen lassen, *et.* anfordern; **~ in** einsenden, einschicken, einreichen; **~ off** fort-, wegschicken; *Brief etc* absenden, abschicken; SPORT *j-n* vom Platz stellen; **~ on** *Brief etc* nachsenden, nachschicken (**to** an acc); *Gepäck etc* vorausschicken; **~ out** hinausschicken; *Einladungen etc* verschicken; **~ up** *Preise etc* steigen lassen

send·er Absender(in)

se·nile senil; **se·nil·i·ty** Senilität *f*

se·ni·or 1. senior; älter (**to** als); dienstälter; rangälter; Ober...; **2.** Ältere *m*, *f*; UNIV Student(in) im letzten Jahr; **he is my ~ by a year** er ist ein Jahr älter

S

als ich; **~ cit·i·zens** ältere Mitbürger *pl*, Senioren *pl*

se·ni·or·i·ty (höheres) Alter; (höheres) Dienstalter; (höherer) Rang

se·ni·or part·ner ECON Seniorpartner *m*

sen·sa·tion Empfindung *f*; Gefühl *n*; Sensation *f*

sen·sa·tion·al F großartig, fantastisch; sensationell, Sensations...

sense 1. Sinn *m*; Verstand *m*; Vernunft *f*; Gefühl *n*; Bedeutung *f*; **bring s.o. to his ~s** j-n zur Besinnung *or* Vernunft bringen; **come to one's ~s** zur Besinnung *or* Vernunft kommen; **in a ~, in** gewisser Hinsicht; **make ~** e-n Sinn ergeben; vernünftig sein; **~ of duty** Pflichtgefühl *n*; **~ of security** Gefühl *n* der Sicherheit; **2.** fühlen, spüren

sense·less bewusstlos; sinnlos

sen·si·bil·i·ty Empfindlichkeit *f*; *a. pl* Empfindsamkeit *f*, Zartgefühl *n*

sen·si·ble vernünftig; spürbar, merklich; *esp Br* praktisch (*clothes etc*)

sen·si·tive empfindlich; sensibel, empfindsam, feinfühlig

sen·sor TECH Sensor *m*

sen·su·al sinnlich

sen·su·ous sinnlich

sen·tence 1. LING Satz *m*; JUR Strafe *f*, Urteil *n*; **pass** *or* **pronounce ~** das Urteil fällen (**on** über *acc*); **2.** JUR verurteilen (**to** zu)

sen·ti·ment Gefühle *pl*; Sentimentalität *f*; *a. pl* Ansicht *f*, Meinung *f*

sen·ti·men·tal sentimental; gefühlvoll

sen·ti·men·tal·i·ty Sentimentalität *f*

sen·try MIL Wache *f*, (Wach[t])Posten *m*

sep·a·ra·ble trennbar; **sep·a·rate 1.** (sich) trennen; (auf-, ein-, zer)teilen (**into** in *acc*); **2.** getrennt, separat; einzeln; **sep·a·ra·tion** Trennung *f*; (Auf-, Ein-, Zer)Teilung *f*

Sept ABBR *of* **September** Sept., September *m*

Sep·tem·ber September *m*

sep·tic MED vereitert, septisch

se·quel Nachfolgeroman *m*, -film *m*, Fortsetzung *f*; *fig* Folge *f*; Nachspiel *n*

se·quence (Aufeinander-, Reihen)Folge *f*; *film*, TV Sequenz *f*, Szene *f*; **~ of tenses** LING Zeitenfolge *f*

ser·e·nade MUS **1.** Serenade *f*, Ständ-

chen *n*; **2.** j-m ein Ständchen bringen

se·rene klar; heiter; gelassen

ser·geant MIL Feldwebel *m*; (Polizei-) Wachtmeister *m*

se·ri·al 1. Fortsetzungsroman *m*; (*Rundfunk-, Fernseh*)Serie *f*; **2.** serienmäßig, Serien..., Fortsetzungs...

se·ries Serie *f*, Reihe *f*, Folge *f*; (*Buch*)Reihe *f*; (*Rundfunk-, Fernseh*)Serie *f*, Sendereihe *f*

se·ri·ous ernst, ernsthaft; ernstlich; schwer (*illness, damage, crime etc*); **be ~** es ernst meinen (**about** mit)

se·ri·ous·ness Ernst *m*, Ernsthaftigkeit *f*, Schwere *f*

ser·mon REL Predigt *f*; F Moral-, Strafpredigt *f*

ser·pen·tine gewunden, kurvenreich

ser·rat·ed zackig, gezackt

se·rum MED Serum *n*

ser·vant Diener(in) (*a. fig*); Dienstmädchen *n*; → **civil servant**

serve 1. *v/t* s-m, s-m *Land etc* dienen; *Dienstzeit* (*a.* MIL) ableisten; *Amtszeit etc* durchlaufen; *j-n*, *et.* versorgen (**with** mit); *Essen* servieren; *Alkohol etc* ausschenken; *j-n* (*im Laden*) bedienen; JUR *Strafe* verbüßen; *e-m Zweck* dienen; *e-n Zweck* erfüllen; JUR *Vorladung etc* zustellen (**on s.o.** j-m); *tennis etc*: aufschlagen; **are you being ~d?** werden Sie schon bedient?; (**it**) **~s him right** F (das) geschieht ihm ganz recht; *v/i esp* MIL dienen; servieren; dienen (**as, for** als); *tennis etc*: aufschlagen; **XY to ~** *tennis etc*: Aufschlag XY; **~ on a committee** e-m Ausschuss angehören; **2.** *tennis etc*: Aufschlag *m*

serv·er *tennis etc*: Aufschläger(in); GASTR Servierlöffel *m*

ser·vice 1. Dienst *m* (**to** an *dat*); Dienstleistung *f*; (*Post-, Staats-, Telefon- etc*) Dienst *m*; (*Zug- etc*)Verkehr *m*; ECON Service *m*, Kundendienst *m*; Bedienung *f*, Betrieb *m*; REL Gottesdienst *m*; TECH Wartung *f*; *a.* Inspektion *f*; (*Tee- etc*)Service *n*; JUR Zustellung *f* (*e-r Vorladung*); *tennis etc*: Aufschlag *m*; *pl* MIL Streitkräfte *pl*; **2.** TECH warten

ser·vice·a·ble brauchbar; strapazierfähig

ser·vice| ar·e·a MOT (Autobahn)Raststätte *f*; **~ charge** Bedienung *f*, Bedienungszuschlag *m*; ~ **sta·tion** Tankstelle *f*; (Reparatur)Werkstatt *f*

ser·vi·ette *esp Br* Serviette *f*

ser·vile sklavisch (*a. fig*); servil, unterwürfig

serv·ing Portion *f*

ser·vi·tude Knechtschaft *f*; Sklaverei *f*

ses·sion Sitzung *f*; Sitzungsperiode *f*; *be in* ~ JUR, PARL tagen

set 1. *v/t* setzen, stellen, legen; *in e-n Zustand* versetzen; veranlassen (*doing* zu tun); TECH einstellen, *Uhr* stellen (*by* nach), *Wecker* stellen (*for auf acc*); *Tisch* decken; *Preis*, *Termin etc* festsetzen, festlegen; *Rekord* aufstellen; *Edelstein* fassen (*with* mit); *Ring etc* besetzen (*with* mit); *Flüssigkeit* erstarren lassen; *Haar* legen; *Knochen* einrenken, einrichten; MUS vertonen; PRINT absetzen; *Aufgabe*, *Frage* stellen; ~ *at ease* beruhigen; ~ *an example* ein Beispiel geben; ~ *s.o. free* freilassen; ~ *going* in Gang setzen; ~ *s.o. thinking* j-m zu denken geben; ~ *one's hopes on* s-e Hoffnung setzen auf (*acc*); ~ *s.o.'s mind at rest* j-n beruhigen; ~ *great* (*little*) *store by* großen (geringen) Wert legen auf (*acc*); *the novel is* ~ *in* der Roman spielt in (*dat*); *v/i* ASTR untergehen; fest werden, erstarren; HUNT vorstehen; ~ *about doing s.th.* sich daranmachen, et. zu tun; ~ *about s.o.* F über j-n herfallen; ~ *aside* beiseite legen; JUR *Urteil etc* aufheben; ~ *back* verzögern; j-n, et. zurückwerfen (*by two months* um zwei Monate); ~ *in* einsetzen; ~ *off* aufbrechen, sich aufmachen; hervorheben, betonen; *et.* auslösen; ~ *out* arrangieren, herrichten; aufbrechen, sich aufmachen; ~ *out to do s.th.* sich daranmachen, et. zu tun; ~ *up* errichten; *Gerät etc* aufbauen; *Firma etc* gründen; *et.* auslösen, verursachen; *j-n* versorgen (*with* mit); sich niederlassen; ~ *o.s. up as* sich ausgeben für; **2.** *adj* festgesetzt, festgelegt; F bereit, fertig; starr (*smile etc*); ~ *lunch or meal Br* Menü *n*; ~ *phrase* feststehender Ausdruck; *be* ~ *on doing s.th.* (fest) entschlossen sein, et. zu tun; *be all* ~ F startklar sein; **3.** Satz *m*; (*Möbel- etc*)Garnitur *f*, (*Tee- etc*)Service *n*; (*Fernseh-, Rundfunk-*)Apparat *m*, (-)Gerät *n*; THEA Bühnen-

bild *n*; *film*, TV Set *n*, *m*; *tennis etc*: Satz *m*; (Personen)Kreis *m*, Clique *f*; (*Kopf- etc*)Haltung *f*; *have a shampoo and* ~ sich die Haare waschen und legen lassen

set·back Rückschlag *m* (*to* für)

set·square *Br* Winkel *m*, Zeichendreieck *n*

set·tee Sofa *n*

set the·o·ry MATH Mengenlehre *f*

set·ting ASTR Untergang *m*; TECH Einstellung *f*; Umgebung *f*; *film etc*: Schauplatz *m*; (*Gold- etc*)Fassung *f*

set·ting lo·tion Haarfestiger *m*

set·tle *v/i* sich niederlassen (*on auf acc or dat*), sich setzen (*on auf acc*) (*a.* ~ *down*); sich niederlassen (*in in dat*); sich legen (*dust*); sich setzen (*coffee etc*); sich senken (*building etc*); sich beruhigen (*person, stomach etc*); sich legen (*a.* ~ *down*); sich einigen; *v/t* *j-n, Nerven etc* beruhigen; vereinbaren; *Frage etc* klären, entscheiden; *Streit etc* beilegen; *Land* besiedeln; *Leute* ansiedeln; *Rechnung* begleichen, bezahlen; *Konto* ausgleichen; *Schaden* regulieren; *s-e Angelegenheiten* in Ordnung bringen; ~ *o.s.* sich niederlassen (*on auf acc or dat*), sich setzen (*on auf acc*); *that* ~*s it* damit ist der Fall erledigt; *that's* ~*d then* das ist also klar; ~ *back* sich (gemütlich) zurücklehnen; ~ *down* → *v/i*; sesshaft werden; ~ *down to* sich widmen (*dat*); ~ *for* sich zufrieden geben *or* begnügen mit; ~ *in* sich einleben *or* eingewöhnen; ~ *on* sich einigen auf (*acc*); ~ *up* (be)zahlen; abrechnen (*with* mit)

set·tled fest (*ideas etc*); geregelt (*life*); beständig (*weather*)

set·tle·ment Vereinbarung *f*; Klärung *f*; Beilegung *f*; Einigung *f*; Siedlung *f*; Besiedlung *f*; Begleichung *f*; Bezahlung *f*; *reach a* ~ sich einigen

set·tler Siedler(in)

sev·en 1. sieben; **2.** Sieben *f*

sev·en·teen 1. siebzehn; **2.** Siebzehn *f*

sev·en·teenth siebzehnte(r, -s)

sev·enth 1. siebente, siebte(r, -s); **2.** Siebentel *n*, Siebtel *f*

sev·enth·ly siebentens, siebtens

sev·en·ti·eth siebzigste(r, -s)

sev·en·ty 1. siebzig; **2.** Siebzig *f*

sev·er durchtrennen; abtrennen; *Bezie-*

S

hungen abbrechen; (zer)reißen

sev·er·al mehrere

sev·er·al·ly einzeln, getrennt

se·vere schwer (*injuries, setback etc*); stark (*pain*); hart, streng (*winter*); streng (*person, discipline etc*); scharf (*criticism etc*); **se·ver·i·ty** Schwere *f*; Stärke *f*; Härte *f*; Strenge *f*; Schärfe *f*

sew nähen

sew·age Abwasser *n*

sew·age works Kläranlage *f*

sew·er Abwasserkanal *m*

sew·er·age Kanalisation *f*

sew·ing 1. Nähen *n*; Näharbeit *f*; **2.** Näh...; **~ ma·chine** Nähmaschine *f*

sex Geschlecht *n*; Sexualität *f*; Sex *m*; Geschlechtsverkehr *m*

sex·ism Sexismus *m*

sex·ist 1. sexistisch; **2.** Sexist(in)

sex·ton Küster *m* (und Totengräber *m*)

sex·u·al sexuell, Sexual..., geschlechtlich, Geschlechts...; **~ ha·rass·ment** sexuelle Belästigung *f*; **~ in·ter·course** Geschlechtsverkehr *m*

sex·u·al·i·ty Sexualität *f*

sex·y F sexy, aufreizend

shab·by schäbig

shack Hütte *f*, Bude *f*; F *contp* Schuppen *m*

shack·les Fesseln *pl*, Ketten *pl* (*both a. fig*)

shade 1. Schatten *m* (*a. fig*); (Lampen-) Schirm *m*; Schattierung *f*; Rouleau *n*; *fig* Nuance *f*; **a ~** *fig* ein kleines bisschen, e-e Spur; **2.** abschirmen (**from** gegen), schattieren; **~ off** allmählich übergehen (**into** in *acc*)

shad·ow 1. Schatten *m* (*a. fig*); **there's not a** *or* **the ~ of a doubt about it** daran besteht nicht der geringste Zweifel; **2.** *j-n* beschatten

shad·ow·y schattig, dunkel; verschwommen, vage, schemenhaft

shad·y schattig; Schatten spendend; F zwielichtig, fragwürdig

shaft (Pfeil- *etc*)Schaft *m*; (Hammer*etc*)Stiel *m*; TECH Welle *f*; (Aufzugs-, Bergwerks- *etc*)Schacht *m*; (Sonnen*etc*)Strahl *m*

shag·gy zottig, struppig

shake 1. *v/t* schütteln; rütteln an (*dat*); erschüttern; **~ hands** sich die Hand geben *or* schütteln; *v/i* zittern, beben, wackeln (**with** vor *dat*); **~ down** herun-

terschütteln; durchsuchen, F filzen; *Br* F kampieren; **~ off** abschütteln; *Erkältung etc* loswerden; **~ up** *Kissen etc* aufschütteln; *Flasche, Flüssigkeit* (durch-) schütteln; *fig* erschüttern; **2.** Schütteln *n*; F Milchshake *m*; **~ of the head** Kopfschütteln *n*

shake·down F Erpressung *f*; Durchsuchung *f*, Filzung *f*; *Br* (Not)Lager *n*

shak·en *a.* **~ up** erschüttert

shak·y wack(e)lig; zitt(e)rig

shall *v/aux future*: ich werde, wir werden; *in questions*: soll ich ...?, sollen wir ...?; **~ we go?** gehen wir?

shal·low seicht, flach, *fig a.* oberflächlich; **shal·lows** seichte *or* flache Stelle, Untiefe *f*

sham 1. Farce *f*; Heuchelei *f*; **2.** unecht, falsch; vorgetäuscht, geheuchelt; **3.** *v/t* *Mitgefühl etc* vortäuschen, heucheln; *Krankheit etc* simulieren; *v/i* sich verstellen, heucheln; **he's only ~ming** er tut nur so

sham·bles F Schlachtfeld *n*, wüstes Durcheinander, Chaos *n*

shame 1. Scham *f*, Schamgefühl *n*; Schande *f*; **~!** pfui!; **~ on you!** pfui!; schäm dich!; **put to ~** → **2.** beschämen; Schande machen (*dat*)

shame·faced betreten, verlegen

shame·ful beschämend; schändlich

shame·less schamlos

sham·poo 1. Shampoo *n*, Schampon *n*, Schampun *n*; Haarwäsche *f*; → **set** 3; **2.** *Haare* waschen; *j-m* die Haare waschen; *Teppich etc* schamponieren

shank TECH Schaft *m*; GASTR Hachse *f*

shan·ty[1] Hütte *f*, Bude *f*

shan·ty[2] Shanty *n*, Seemannslied *n*

shan·ty·town Elendsviertel *n*

shape 1. Form *f*, Gestalt *f*; Verfassung *f*, Zustand *m*; **in good (bad) ~** in gutem (schlechtem) Zustand; **(out of) ~** SPORT (nicht) gut in Form; **take ~** *fig* Gestalt annehmen; **2.** *v/t* formen; gestalten; *v/i a.* **~ up** sich *gut etc* machen

shape·less formlos; ausgebeult

shape·ly wohlgeformt

share 1. Anteil *m* (**in, of** an *dat*); *esp Br* ECON Aktie *f*; **go ~s** teilen; **have a (no) ~ in** (nicht) beteiligt sein an (*dat*); **2.** *v/t* (sich) *et.* teilen (**with** mit); *a.* **~ out** verteilen (**among, between** an *acc*, unter *acc*); *v/i* teilen; **~ in** sich teilen in (*acc*)

share·hold·er *esp Br* ECON Aktionär(in)

shark ZO Hai(fisch) *m*; → *loan shark*

sharp 1. *adj* scharf (*a. fig*); spitz; abrupt; schneidend (*wind, frost, command, voice, etc*); beißend (*cold, smell etc*); stechend, heftig (*pain*); gescheit; MUS (*um e-n Halbton*) erhöht; *C* **~** MUS Cis *n*; **2.** *adv* scharf, abrupt; MUS zu hoch; pünktlich, genau; *at eight o'clock* **~** Punkt 8 (Uhr); *look* **~** F sich beeilen; *look* **~**/F mach schnell!, Tempo!; F pass auf!, gib Acht!

sharp·en *Messer etc* schärfen, schleifen; *Bleistift etc* spitzen

sharp·en·er (*Messer- etc*)Schärfer *m*; (*Bleistift*)Spitzer *m*

sharp·ness Schärfe *f* (*a. fig*)

sharp·shoot·er Scharfschütze *m*

sharp·sight·ed scharfsichtig

sharp·wit·ted scharfsinnig

shat·ter *v/t* zerschmettern, zerschlagen; *Hoffnungen etc* zerstören; *v/i* zerspringen, zersplittern

shat·ter·ing vernichtend; erschütternd

shat·ter·proof splitterfrei

shave 1. (sich) rasieren; (glatt) hobeln; *j-n, et.* streifen; **2.** Rasur *f*; *have a* **~** sich rasieren; *that was a close* **~** das war knapp, das ist gerade noch einmal gut gegangen!; **shav·en** kahl geschoren

shav·er (*esp* elektrischer) Rasierapparat *m*

shav·ing 1. Rasieren *n*; **2.** Rasier...; **~ bag** Kulturbeutel *m*; **~ brush** Rasierpinsel *m*; **~ cream** Rasiercreme *f*

shav·ings Späne *pl*

shawl Umhängetuch *n*; Kopftuch *n*

she 1. *pron* sie; **2.** Sie *f*; ZO Weibchen *n*; **3.** *adj* in *cpds* ZO ...weibchen *n*; **~-bear** Bärin *f*

sheaf Bündel *n*; AGR Garbe *f*

shear 1. scheren; **2.** (*a pair of*) **~s** (e-e) große Schere

sheath (*Schwert- etc*)Scheide *f*; Hülle *f*; *Br* Kondom *n, m*; **sheathe** *Schwert etc* in die Scheide stecken; TECH umhüllen, verkleiden, ummanteln

shed¹ Schuppen *m*; Stall *m*

shed² *Tränen etc* vergießen; *Blätter etc* verlieren; *fig Hemmungen etc* ablegen; **~ its skin** sich häuten; **~ a few pounds**

ein paar Pfund abnehmen

sheen Glanz *m*

sheep ZO Schaf *n*

sheep·dog ZO Schäferhund *m*

sheep·ish verlegen

sheep·skin Schaffell *n*

sheer rein, bloß; steil, (fast) senkrecht; hauchdünn

sheet Betttuch *n*, (Bett)Laken *n*, Leintuch *n*; (*Glas-, Metall- etc*)Platte *f*; Blatt *n*, Bogen *m*; weite (*Eis- etc*)Fläche; *the rain was coming down in* **~s** es regnete in Strömen

sheet light·ning Wetterleuchten *n*

shelf (*Bücher-, Wand- etc*)Brett *n*, (-)Bord *n*; GEOGR Riff *n*; *pl* Regal *n*; *off the* **~** gleich zum Mitnehmen

shell 1. (*Austern-, Eier-, Nuss- etc*) Schale *f*; BOT (*Erbsen- etc*)Hülse *f*; ZO Muschel *f*; (*Schnecken*)Haus *n*; ZO Panzer *m*; MIL Granate *f*; (*Geschoss-, Patronen*)Hülse *f*; Patrone *f*; TECH Rumpf *m*, Gerippe *n*, ARCH *a.* Rohbau *m*; **2.** schälen, enthülsen; mit Granaten beschießen

shell·fish ZO Schal(en)tier *n*

shel·ter 1. Zuflucht *f*, Schutz *m*; Unterkunft *f*, Obdach *n*; MIL Unterstand *m*; *run for* **~** Schutz suchen; *take* **~** sich unterstellen (*under* unter *dat*); *bus* **~** Wartehäuschen *n*; **2.** *v/t* schützen (*from* vor *dat*); *v/i* sich unterstellen

shelve *v/t Bücher* in ein Regal stellen; *Plan etc* aufschieben, zurückstellen; *v/i* sanft abfallen (*garden etc*)

shep·herd 1. Schäfer *m*, Hirt *m*; **2.** *j-n* führen

sher·iff Sheriff *m*

shield 1. Schild *m*; **2.** *j-n* (be)schützen (*from* vor *dat*); *j-n* decken

shift 1. *v/t et.* bewegen, schieben, *Möbelstück a.* (ver)rücken; *Schuld etc* (ab-) schieben (*onto* auf *acc*); **~** *gear(s)* MOT schalten; *v/i* sich bewegen; umspringen (*wind*); *fig* sich verlagern *or* verschieben *or* wandeln; MOT schalten (*into, to* in *acc*); **~** *from one foot to the other* von e-m Fuß auf den anderen treten; **~** *on one's chair* auf s-m Stuhl *ungeduldig etc* hin und her rutschen; **2.** *fig* Verlagerung *f*, Verschiebung *f*, Wandel *m*; ECON Schicht *f*, *pl*; **~** *key* TECH Umschalttaste *f*; **~ work·er** Schichtarbeiter(in)

shift·y F verschlagen

shim·mer schimmern; flimmern

shin 1. *a.* ~ **bone** ANAT Schienbein *n*; **2.** ~ **up** hinaufklettern; ~ **down** herunterklettern

shine 1. *v/i* scheinen; leuchten; glänzen (*a. fig*); *v/t Schuhe etc* polieren; **2.** Glanz *m*

shin·gle¹ grober Strandkies

shin·gle² (Dach)Schindel *f*

shin·gles MED Gürtelrose *f*

shin·y blank, glänzend

ship 1. Schiff *n*; **2.** verschiffen; ECON verfrachten, versenden

ship·ment ECON Ladung *f*; Verschiffung *f*, Verfrachtung *f*, Versand *m*

ship·own·er Reeder *m*; Schiffseigner *m*

ship·ping Schifffahrt *f*; Schiffsbestand *m*; ECON Verschiffung *f*, Verfrachtung *f*, Versand *m*

ship·wreck Schiffbruch *m*

ship·wrecked 1. be ~ Schiffbruch erleiden; **2.** schiffbrüchig

ship·yard (Schiffs)Werft *f*

shirk sich drücken (vor *dat*)

shirk·er Drückeberger(in)

shirt Hemd *n*

shirt·sleeve 1. Hemdsärmel *m*; **in** (**one's**) ~**s** in Hemdsärmeln, hemdsärmelig; **2.** hemdsärmelig

shish ke·bab GASTR Schaschlik *m, n*

shit V **1.** Scheiße *f* (*a. fig*); *fig* Scheiß *m*; **2.** (voll)scheißen

shiv·er 1. zittern (**with** vor *dat*); **2.** Schauer *m*; *pl* MED F Schüttelfrost *m*; **the sight send** ~**s** (**up and**) **down my spine** bei dem Anblick überlief es mich eiskalt

shoal¹ Untiefe *f*; Sandbank *f*

shoal² ZO Schwarm *m*

shock¹ 1. Schock *m* (*a.* MED); Wucht *f*; ELECTR Schlag *m*, (*a.* MED Elektro-) Schock *m*; **be in** (**a state of**) ~ unter Schock stehen; **2.** schockieren, empören; *j-m* e-n Schock versetzen

shock² (~ **of hair** Haar)Schopf *m*

shock ab·sorb·er TECH Stoßdämpfer *m*

shock·ing schockierend, empörend, anstößig; F scheußlich

shod·dy minderwertig (*goods*); gemein, schäbig (*trick etc*)

shoe 1. Schuh *m*; Hufeisen *n*; **2.** *Pferd* beschlagen

shoe·horn Schuhanzieher *m*, -löffel *m*

shoe·lace Schnürsenkel *m*

shoe·mak·er Schuhmacher *m*, Schuster *m*

shoe·shine boy Schuhputzer *m*

shoe store (*Br* **shop**) Schuhgeschäft *n*

shoe·string Schnürsenkel *m*

shoot 1. *v/t* schießen, HUNT *a.* erlegen; abfeuern, abschießen; erschießen; *Riegel* vorschieben; *j-n* fotografieren, aufnehmen, *Film* drehen; *Heroin etc* spritzen; ~ **the lights** MOT bei Rot fahren; *v/i* schießen (**at** auf *acc*); jagen; *fig* schießen, rasen; *film,* TV drehen, filmen; BOT sprießen, treiben; **2.** BOT Trieb *m*; Jagd *f*; Jagdrevier *n*

shoot·er F Schießeisen *n*

shoot·ing 1. Schießen *n*; Schießerei *f*; Erschießung *f*; Anschlag *m*; Jagd *f*; *film,* TV Dreharbeiten *pl*, Aufnahmen *pl*; **2.** stechend (*pain*); ~ **gal·le·ry** Schießbude *f*; ~ **range** Schießstand *m*; ~ **star** ASTR Sternschnuppe *f*

shop 1. *Br* Laden *m*, Geschäft *n*; Werkstatt *f*; Betrieb *m*; **talk** ~ fachsimpeln; **2.** *mst* **go shopping** einkaufen gehen

shop as·sis·tant *Br* Verkäufer(in)

shop·keep·er *Br* Ladenbesitzer(in), Ladeninhaber(in)

shop·lift·er Ladendieb(in)

shop·lift·ing Ladendiebstahl *m*

shop·per Käufer(in)

shop·ping 1. Einkauf *m*, Einkaufen *n*; Einkäufe *pl* (*items bought*); **do one's** ~ *Br* einkaufen, (s-e) Einkäufe machen; **2.** Einkaufs...; ~ **bag** Einkaufsbeutel *m*, -tasche *f*; ~ **cart** Einkaufswagen *m*; ~ **cen·ter** (*Br* **cen·tre**) Einkaufszentrum *n*; ~ **list** Einkaufsliste *f*, -zettel *m*; ~ **mall** Einkaufszentrum *n*; ~ **pre·cinct** *Br* Fußgängerzone *f*; ~ **street** Geschäfts-, Ladenstraße *f*

shop stew·ard ECON gewerkschaftlicher Vertrauensmann

shop·walk·er *Br* Aufsicht(sperson) *f*

shop win·dow Schaufenster *n*

shore¹ Küste *f*; (*See*)Ufer *n*; **on** ~ an Land

shore²: ~ **up** (ab)stützen

short 1. *adj* kurz; klein (*person*); kurz angebunden, barsch, schroff (**with** zu); GASTR mürbe; **be** ~ **for** die Kurzform sein von; **be** ~ **of ...** nicht genügend ... haben; **2.** *adv* plötzlich, abrupt; ~

of außer; *cut* ~ plötzlich unterbrechen; *fall* ~ *et.* nicht erreichen; *stop* ~ plötzlich innehalten, stutzen; *stop* ~ *of or at* zurückschrecken vor (*dat*); → *run* 1; 3. F Kurzfilm *m*; ELECTR Kurze *m*; *called ... for* ~ kurz ... genannt; *in* ~ kurz(um)

short·age Knappheit *f*, Mangel *m* (*of an dat*)

short·com·ings Unzulänglichkeiten *pl*, Mängel *pl*, Fehler *pl*

short cut Abkürzung *f*; *take a* ~ (den Weg) abkürzen

short·en *v/t* (ab-, ver)kürzen; *v/i* kürzer werden

short·hand Kurzschrift *f*, Stenografie *f*; ~ *typ·ist* Stenotypistin *f*

short·ly bald; barsch, schroff; mit wenigen Worten

short·ness Kürze *f*; Schroffheit *f*

shorts *a*. **pair of** ~ Shorts *pl*; (Herren-) Unterhose *f*

short·sight·ed *esp Br* kurzsichtig (*a. fig*)

short sto·ry Kurzgeschichte *f*

short-tem·pered aufbrausend, hitzig

short-term ECON kurzfristig

short time ECON Kurzarbeit *f*

short wave ELECTR Kurzwelle *f*

short-wind·ed kurzatmig

shot Schuss *m*; Schrot(kugeln *pl*) *m*, *n*; SPORT Kugel *f*, *guter etc* Schütze *m*; *soccer etc*: Schuss *m*; *basketball etc*: Wurf *m*; *tennis, golf*: Schlag *m*; PHOT Schnappschuss *m*, Aufnahme *f*; *film*, TV Aufnahme *f*, Einstellung *f*; MED F Spritze *f*; F Schuss *m* (*of drugs*); *fig* F Versuch *m*; *a* ~ *of rum* ein Schluck Rum; *I'll have a* ~ *at it* ich probier's mal; *not by a long* ~ F noch lange nicht; ~ *big shot*

shot·gun Schrotflinte *f*

shot·gun wed·ding F Mussheirat *f*

shot put SPORT Kugelstoßen *n*

shot put·ter SPORT Kugelstoßer(in)

shoul·der 1. ANAT Schulter *f*; MOT Standspur *f*; 2. schultern; *Kosten, Verantwortung etc* übernehmen; (mit den Schulter) stoßen; ~ *bag* Schulter-, Umhängetasche *f*; ~ *blade* ANAT Schulterblatt *n*; ~ *strap* Träger *m*; Tragriemen *m*

shout 1. *v/i* rufen, schreien (*for* nach; *for help* um Hilfe); ~ *at s.o.* j-n anschrei-

en; *v/t* rufen, schreien; 2. Ruf *m*, Schrei *m*

shove 1. stoßen, F schubsen; *et.* schieben, stopfen; 2. Stoß *m*, F Schubs *m*

shov·el 1. Schaufel *f*; 2. schaufeln

show 1. *v/t* zeigen, vorzeigen, anzeigen; *j-n* bringen, führen (*to* zu); ausstellen; zeigen, *film etc a.* vorführen, TV *a.* bringen; *v/i* zu sehen sein; *be* ~*ing* gezeigt werden, laufen; ~ *around* herumführen; ~ *in* herein-, hineinführen, herein-, hineinbringen; ~ *off* angeben oder protzen (mit); vorteilhaft zur Geltung bringen; ~ *out* heraus-, hinausführen, heraus-, hinausbringen; ~ *round* herumführen; ~ *up* *v/t* herauf-, hinaufführen, herauf-, hinaufbringen; sichtbar machen; *j-n* entlarven, bloßstellen; *et.* aufdecken; *j-n* in Verlegenheit bringen; *v/i* zu sehen sein; F auftauchen; 2. THEA *etc* Vorstellung *f*, Show *f*; *radio*, TV Sendung *f*; Ausstellung *f*; Zurschaustellung *f*, Demonstration *f*; *fig leerer Schein*; *be on* ~ ausgestellt *or* zu besichtigen sein; *steal the* ~ *from s.o. fig* j-m die Schau stehlen; *make a* ~ *of Anteilnahme, Interesse etc* heucheln; *put up a poor* ~ F e-e schwache Leistung zeigen; *be in charge of the whole* ~ F den ganzen Laden schmeißen; 3. Muster...

show-biz F, **show busi·ness** Showbusiness *n*, Showgeschäft *n*, Unterhaltungsindustrie *f*

show·case Schaukasten *m*, Vitrine *f*

show·down Kraft-, Machtprobe *f*

show·er 1. (Regen- *etc*)Schauer *m*; (*Funken*)Regen *m*; (*Wasser-, Wort- etc*)Schwall *m*; Dusche *f*; (Geschenk-) Party *f*; *have or take a* ~ duschen; 2. *v/t j-n mit et.* überschütten *or* überhäufen; *v/i* duschen; ~ *down* niederprasseln

show jump·er SPORT Springreiter(in)

show jump·ing SPORT Springreiten *n*

show-off F Angeber(in)

show·room Ausstellungsraum *m*

show tri·al JUR Schauprozess *m*

show·y auffallend

shred 1. Fetzen *m*; 2. zerfetzen; in (schmale) Streifen schneiden, schnitzeln; in den Papier- *or* Reißwolf geben; **shred·der** Schnitzelmaschine *f*; Papier-, Reißwolf *m*

shrewd scharfsinnig; schlau
shriek 1. (gellend) aufschreien; **~ with laughter** vor Lachen kreischen; **2.** (schriller) Schrei
shrill schrill; *fig* heftig, scharf, lautstark
shrimp ZO Garnele *f*; *fig contp* Knirps *m*
shrine Schrein *m*
shrink 1. (ein-, zusammen)schrumpfen (lassen); einlaufen; *fig* abnehmen; **2.** F Klapsdoktor *m*
shrink·age Schrumpfung *f*; Einlaufen *n*; *fig* Abnahme *f*
shrink-wrap einschweißen
shriv·el schrumpfen (lassen); runz(e)lig werden (lassen)
shroud 1. Leichentuch *n*; **2.** *fig* hüllen
Shrove Tues·day Fastnachts-, Faschingsdienstag *m*
shrub Strauch *m*, Busch *m*
shrub·ber·ry BOT Strauch-, Buschwerk *n*, Gebüsch *n*
shrug 1. *a.* **~ one's shoulders** mit den Achseln *or* Schultern zucken; **2.** Achselzucken *n*, Schulterzucken *n*
shuck BOT **1.** Hülse *f*, Schote *f*; Schale *f*; **2.** enthülsen; schälen
shud·der 1. schaudern; **2.** Schauder *m*
shuf·fle 1. *v/t Karten* mischen; *Papiere etc* umordnen, hierhin oder dorthin legen; **~ one's feet** schlurfen; *v/i* schlurfen; *Karten* mischen; **2.** Schlurfen *n*, schlurfender Gang; Mischen *n*
shun *j-n, et.* meiden
shunt *Zug etc* rangieren, verschieben; *a.* **~ off** F *j-n* abschieben (**to** in *acc*, nach)
shut (sich) schließen; zumachen; **~ down** *Fabrik etc* schließen; **~ off** *Wasser, Gas, Maschine etc* abstellen; **~ up** einschließen; einsperren; *Geschäft* schließen; **~ up!** F halt die Klappe!
shut·ter Fensterladen *m*; PHOT Verschluss *m*
shut·tle 1. Pendelverkehr *m*; (Raum-)Fähre *f*, (-)Transporter *m*; TECH Schiffchen *n*; **2.** hin- und herbefördern
shut·tle·cock SPORT Federball *m*
shut·tle ser·vice Pendelverkehr *m*
shy 1. scheu; schüchtern; **2.** scheuen (**at** vor *dat*); **~ away from** *fig* zurückschrecken vor (*dat*)
shy·ness Scheu *f*; Schüchternheit *f*
sick 1. krank; **be ~** *esp Br* sich übergeben; **she was** *or* **felt ~** ihr war schlecht;

get ~ krank werden; **be off ~** krank (geschrieben) sein; **report ~** sich krank melden; **be ~ of s.th.** F et. satt haben; **it makes me ~** F mir wird schlecht davon, *a. fig* es ekelt *or* widert mich an; **2. the ~** die Kranken *pl*
sick·bed Krankenbett *n*
sick·en *v/t j-n* anekeln, anwidern; *v/i esp Br* krank werden
sick·le ['sɪkl] Sichel *f*
sick leave: be on ~ krank (geschrieben) sein, wegen Krankheit fehlen
sick·ly kränklich; ungesund; matt; widerlich (*smell etc*)
sick·ness Krankheit *f*; Übelkeit *f*; **~ ben·e·fit** *Br* Krankengeld *n*
side 1. Seite *f*; *esp Br* SPORT Mannschaft *f*; **~ by ~** nebeneinander; **take ~s** Partei ergreifen (**with** für; **against** gegen); **2.** Seiten...; Neben...; **3.** Partei ergreifen (**with** für; **against** gegen)
side·board Anrichte *f*, Sideboard *n*
side·car MOT Bei-, Seitenwagen *m*
side dish GASTR Beilage *f*
side·long seitlich; Seiten...; **~ glance** Seitenblick *m*
side street Nebenstraße *f*
side·swipe Seitenhieb *m*
side·track *j-n* ablenken; F et. abbiegen; RAIL *etc* rangieren, verschieben
side·walk Bürgersteig *m*, Gehsteig *m*
side·walk ca·fé Straßencafé *n*
side·ways seitlich; seitwärts, nach der *or* zur Seite
sid·ing RAIL Nebengleis *n*
si·dle: ~ up to s.o. sich an j-n heranschleichen
siege MIL Belagerung *f*; **lay ~ to** belagern (*a. fig*)
sieve 1. Sieb *n*; **2.** (durch)sieben
sift (durch)sieben; *a.* **~ through** *fig* sichten, durchsehen, prüfen
sigh 1. seufzen; **2.** Seufzer *m*
sight 1. Sehvermögen *n*, Sehkraft *f*, Augenlicht *n*; Anblick *m*; Sicht(weite) *f*; *pl* Visier *n*; Sehenswürdigkeiten *pl*; **at ~**, **on ~** sofort; **at the ~ of** beim Anblick von (*or gen*); **at first ~** auf den ersten Blick; **catch ~ of** erblicken; **know by ~** vom Sehen kennen; **lose ~ of** aus den Augen verlieren; **be (with)in ~** in Sicht sein (*a. fig*); **2.** sichten
sight-read MUS vom Blatt singen *or* spielen

sight·see·ing Sightseeing n, Besichtigung f von Sehenswürdigkeiten; **go ~** sich die Sehenswürdigkeiten anschauen; **~ tour** Sightseeingtour f, Besichtigungstour f, (Stadt)Rundfahrt f

sight·se·er Tourist(in)

sight test Sehtest m

sign 1. Zeichen n; (Hinweis-, Warn etc)Schild n; fig (An)Zeichen n; **2.** unterschreiben, unterzeichnen; Scheck ausstellen; **~ in** sich eintragen; **~ out** sich austragen

sig·nal 1. Signal n (a. fig); Zeichen n (a. fig); **2.** (ein) Zeichen geben; signalisieren

sig·na·to·ry Unterzeichner(in)

sig·na·ture Unterschrift f; Signatur f; **~ tune** radio, TV Kennmelodie f

sign·board (Aushänge)Schild n

sign·er Unterzeichnete m, f

sig·net Siegel n

sig·nif·i·cance Bedeutung f, Wichtigkeit f; **sig·nif·i·cant** bedeutend, bedeutsam, wichtig; bezeichnend

sig·ni·fy bedeuten; andeuten

sign·post Wegweiser m

si·lence 1. Stille f, Schweigen n; **~!** Ruhe!; **in ~** schweigend; **reduce to ~** → **2.** zum Schweigen bringen

si·lenc·er TECH Schalldämpfer m; Br MOT Auspufftopf m

si·lent still; schweigend; schweigsam; stumm; **~ part·ner** ECON stiller Teilhaber

sil·i·con CHEM Silizium n

sil·i·cone CHEM Silikon n

silk 1. Seide f; **2.** Seiden...

silk·worm ZO Seidenraupe f

silk·y seidig; samtig (voice)

sill (Fenster)Brett n

sil·ly 1. albern, töricht, dumm; **2.** F Dummerchen n

sil·ver 1. Silber n; **2.** silbern, Silber...; versilbern

sil·ver-plat·ed versilbert

sil·ver·ware Tafelsilber n

sil·ver·y silberglänzend; fig silberhell

sim·i·lar ähnlich (to dat)

sim·i·lar·i·ty Ähnlichkeit f

sim·i·le Gleichnis n, Vergleich m

sim·mer leicht kochen, köcheln; **~ with** fig kochen vor (rage etc), fiebern vor (excitement etc); **~ down** F sich beruhigen, F sich abregen

sim·per albern or affektiert lächeln

sim·ple einfach, schlicht; leicht; dumm, einfältig; naiv; **the ~ fact is that ...** es ist einfach e-e Tatsache, dass ...

sim·ple-mind·ed dumm; naiv

sim·pli·ci·ty Einfachheit f, Schlichtheit f; Dummheit f; Naivität f

sim·pli·fi·ca·tion Vereinfachung f

sim·pli·fy vereinfachen

sim·ply einfach; bloß, nur

sim·u·late vortäuschen; MIL, TECH simulieren

sim·ul·ta·ne·ous simultan, gleichzeitig

sin 1. Sünde f; **2.** sündigen

since 1. adv a. **ever ~** seitdem, seither; **2.** prp seit (dat); **3.** cj seit(dem); da

sin·cere aufrichtig, ehrlich, offen

sin·cer·i·ty Aufrichtigkeit f; Offenheit f

sin·ew ANAT Sehne f

sin·ew·y sehnig; fig kraftvoll

sin·ful sündig, sündhaft

sing singen; **~ s.th. to s.o.** j-m et. vorsingen

singe (sich et.) ansengen or versengen

sing·er Sänger(in)

sing·ing Singen n, Gesang m

sin·gle 1. einzig, einzeln, Einzel...; einfach; ledig, unverheiratet; **in ~ file** im Gänsemarsch; **2.** Br RAIL etc einfache Fahrkarte, AVIAT einfaches Ticket (both a. **~ ticket**); Single f; Single m, Unverheiratete m, f; **3. ~ out** sich herausgreifen

sin·gle-breast·ed einreihig

sin·gle-en·gined AVIAT einmotorig

sin·gle fam·i·ly home Einfamilienhaus n

sin·gle fa·ther allein erziehender Vater

sin·gle-hand·ed eigenhändig, allein

sin·gle-lane MOT einspurig

sin·gle-mind·ed zielstrebig, -bewusst

sin·gle moth·er allein erziehende Mutter

sin·gle pa·rent Alleinerziehende m, f

sin·gle room Einzelzimmer n

sin·gles esp tennis: Einzel n; **a ~ match** ein Einzel; **men's ~** Herreneinzel n; **women's ~** Dameneinzel n

sin·glet Br ärmelloses Unterhemd or Trikot

sin·gle-track eingleisig, einspurig

sin·gu·lar 1. einzigartig, einmalig; **2.** LING Singular m, Einzahl f

sin·is·ter finster, unheimlich

S

sink 1. *v/i* sinken, untergehen; sich senken; ~ *in* eindringen (*a. fig*); ~ *in* versenken; *Brunnen etc* bohren; *Zähne etc* vergraben (*into* in *acc*); **2.** Spülbecken *n*, Spüle *f*; Waschbecken *n*

sin·ner Sünder(in)

sip 1. Schlückchen *n*; **2.** *v/t* nippen an (*dat*) *or* von; schluckchenweise trinken; *v/i* nippen (*at* an *dat or* von)

sir mein Herr; *Dear Sir or Madam* Sehr geehrte Damen und Herren (*address in letters*)

sire zo Vater *m*, Vatertier *n*

si·ren Sirene *f*

sis·sy F Weichling *m*

sis·ter Schwester *f*; *Br* MED Oberschwester *f*; REL (Ordens)Schwester *f*

sis·ter·hood Schwesternschaft *f*

sis·ter-in-law Schwägerin *f*

sis·ter·ly schwesterlich

sit *v/i* sitzen; sich setzen; tagen; *v/t* j-n setzen; *esp Br Prüfung* ablegen, machen; ~ *down* sich setzen; ~ *for Br Prüfung* ablegen, machen; ~ *in* ein Sit-in veranstalten; an e-m Sit-in teilnehmen; ~ *in for* j-n vertreten; ~ *in on* als Zuhörer teilnehmen an (*dat*); ~ *on* sitzen auf (*dat*) (*a. fig*); ~ *on a committee* e-m Ausschuss angehören; ~ *out Tanz* auslassen; das Ende (*gen*) abwarten; *Krise etc* aussitzen; ~ *up* sich *or* j-n aufrichten *or* aufsetzen; aufrecht sitzen; aufbleiben

sit·com → *situation comedy*

sit-down *a.* ~ *strike* Sitzstreik *m*; *a.* ~ *demonstration or* F *demo* Sitzblockade *f*

site Platz *m*, Ort *m*, Stelle *f*; (*Ausgrabungs*)Stätte *f*; Baustelle *f*

sit-in Sit-in *n*, Sitzstreik *m*

sit·ting Sitzung *f*

sit·ting room *esp Br* Wohnzimmer *n*

sit·u·at·ed: *be* ~ liegen, gelegen sein

sit·u·a·tion Lage *f*, Situation *f*; ~ *com-e·dy* TV *etc* Situationskomödie *f*

six 1. sechs; **2.** Sechs *f*

six·teen 1. sechzehn; **2.** Sechzehn *f*

six·teenth sechzehnte(r, -s)

sixth 1. sechste(r, -s); **2.** Sechstel *n*

sixth·ly sechstens

six·ti·eth sechzigste(r, -s)

six·ty 1. sechzig; **2.** Sechzig *f*

size 1. Größe *f*, *fig a.* Ausmaß *n*, Umfang *m*; **2.** ~ *up* F abschätzen

siz(e)·a·ble beträchtlich

siz·zle brutzeln

skate 1. Schlittschuh *m*; Rollschuh *m*; **2.** Schlittschuh laufen, Eis laufen; Rollschuh laufen

skate·board Skateboard *n*

skat·er Eisläufer(in), Schlittschuhläufer(in); Rollschuhläufer(in)

skat·ing Eislaufen *n*, Schlittschuhlaufen *n*; Rollschuhlaufen *n*; *free* ~ Kür *f*, Kürlauf *m*; ~ *rink* (Kunst)Eisbahn *f*; Rollschuhbahn *f*

skel·e·ton Skelett *n*, Gerippe *n*

skep·tic Skeptiker(in)

skep·ti·cal skeptisch

sketch 1. Skizze *f*; THEA *etc* Sketch *m*; **2.** skizzieren

skew·er 1. (Brat)Spieß *m*; **2.** (auf)spießen

ski 1. Ski *m*; **2.** Ski...; **3.** Ski fahren *or* laufen

skid 1. MOT rutschen, schleudern; **2.** MOT Rutschen *n*, Schleudern *n*; TECH Kufe *f*

skid mark(s) MOT Bremsspur *f*

ski·er Skifahrer(in), Skiläufer(in)

ski·ing Skifahren *n*, Skilaufen *n*, Skisport *m*

ski jump (Sprung)Schanze *f*

ski jump·er Skispringer *m*

ski jump·ing Skispringen *n*

skil·ful *Br* → *skillful*

ski lift Skilift *m*

skill Geschicklichkeit *f*, Fertigkeit *f*

skilled geschickt (*at*, *in* in *dat*)

skilled work·er Facharbeiter(in)

skill·ful geschickt

skim *Fett etc* abschöpfen (*a.* ~ *off*); *Milch* entrahmen; (hin)gleiten über (*acc*); *a.* ~ *over*, ~ *through Bericht etc* überfliegen

skim(med) milk Magermilch *f*

skimp *a.* ~ *on* sparen an (*dat*)

skimp·y dürftig; knapp

skin 1. ANAT Haut *f*; ZO Fell *n*; BOT Schale *f*; **2.** *Tier* abhäuten; *Zwiebel etc* schälen; sich *das Knie etc* aufschürfen

skin-deep (nur) oberflächlich

skin div·ing Sporttauchen *n*

skin·flint Geizhals *m*

skin·ny F dürr, mager

skin·ny-dip F nackt baden

skip 1. *v/i* hüpfen, springen; seilhüpfen, seilspringen; *v/t et.* überspringen, auslassen; **2.** Hüpfer *m*

S

skip·per MAR, SPORT Kapitän m

skir·mish Geplänkel n

skirt 1. Rock m; 2. a. ~ (a)round umgeben; *Problem etc* umgehen

skirt·ing board Br Scheuerleiste f

ski‖ run Skipiste f; ~ tow Schlepplift m

skit·tle Kegel m

skulk sich herumdrücken, herumschleichen

skull ANAT Schädel m

skul(l)·dug·ge·ry F fauler Zauber

skunk ZO Skunk m, Stinktier n

sky a. skies Himmel m

sky·jack Flugzeug entführen

sky·jack·er Flugzeugentführer(in)

sky·lark ZO Feldlerche f

sky·light Dachfenster n

sky·line Skyline f, Silhouette f

sky·rock·et F hochschnellen, in die Höhe schießen

sky·scrap·er Wolkenkratzer m

slab (*Stein- etc*)Platte f; dickes Stück

slack 1. locker; ECON flau; *fig* lax, lasch, nachlässig; 2. bummeln; ~ off, ~ up *fig* nachlassen, (*person a.*) abbauen

slack·en v/t lockern; verringern; ~ speed langsamer werden; v/i locker werden; a. ~ off nachlassen

slacks F Hose f

slag TECH Schlacke f

sla·lom SPORT Slalom m

slam 1. a. ~ shut zuschlagen, F zuknallen; a. ~ down F et. knallen (on auf acc); ~ on the brakes F MOT auf die Bremse steigen; 2. Zuschlagen n; Knall m

slan·der 1. Verleumdung f; 2. verleumden; slan·der·ous verleumderisch

slang 1. Slang m; Jargon m; 2. esp Br F j-n wüst beschimpfen

slant 1. schräg legen or liegen; sich neigen; 2. schräge Fläche; Abhang m; *fig* Einstellung f; at or on a ~ schräg

slant·ing schräg

slap 1. Klaps m, Schlag m; 2. e-n Klaps geben (*dat*); schlagen; klatschen (down on auf acc; against gegen)

slap·stick THEA Slapstick m, Klamauk m; ~ com·e·dy Slapstickkomödie f

slash 1. auf-, zerschlitzen; *Preise* drastisch herabsetzen; *Ausgaben etc* drastisch kürzen; ~ at schlagen nach; 2. Hieb m; Schlitz m

slate 1. Schiefer m; Schiefertafel f; POL

Kandidatenliste f; 2. mit Schiefer decken; j-n vorschlagen (for, to be als); *et.* planen (for für)

slaugh·ter 1. Schlachten n; *fig* Blutbad n, Gemetzel n; 2. schlachten; *fig* niedermetzeln; slaugh·ter·house Schlachthaus n, Schlachthof m

Slav 1. Slawe m, Slawin f; 2. slawisch

slave 1. Sklave m, Sklavin f (a. *fig*); 2. a. ~ away sich abplagen, F schuften

slav·er geifern, sabbern

sla·ve·ry Sklaverei f

slav·ish sklavisch

sleaze unsaubere Machenschaften; Kumpanei f; F POL Filz m

slea·zy schäbig, heruntergekommen; anrüchig

sled 1. (a. Rodel)Schlitten m; 2. Schlitten fahren, rodeln

sledge Br → sled

sledge·ham·mer TECH Vorschlaghammer m

sleek 1. glatt, glänzend; geschmeidig; MOT schnittig; 2. glätten

sleep 1. Schlaf m; I couldn't get to ~ ich konnte nicht einschlafen; go to ~ einschlafen (F a. leg etc); put to ~ Tier einschläfern; 2. v/i schlafen; ~ late lang or länger schlafen; ~ on Problem etc überschlafen; ~ with s.o. mit j-m schlafen; v/t Schlafgelegenheit bieten für

sleep·er Schlafende m, f, Schläfer(in); Br RAIL Schwelle f; RAIL Schlafwagen m

sleep·ing bag Schlafsack m

Sleep·ing Beau·ty Dornröschen n

sleep·ing‖ car RAIL Schlafwagen m; ~ part·ner Br ECON stiller Teilhaber; ~ pill PHARM Schlaftablette f, -mittel n; ~ sick·ness MED Schlafkrankheit f

sleep·less schlaflos

sleep·walk·er Schlafwandler(in)

sleep·y schläfrig, müde; verschlafen

sleep·y·head F Schlafmütze f

sleet 1. Schneeregen m; Graupelschauer m; 2. it's ~ing es gibt Schneeregen; es graupelt

sleeve Ärmel m; TECH Manschette f, Muffe f; esp Br (Platten)Hülle f

sleeve·less ärmellos

sleigh (esp Pferde)Schlitten m

sleight of hand Fingerfertigkeit f; *fig* (Taschenspieler)Trick m

S

slen·der schlank; *fig* mager, dürftig; schwach (*hope etc*)

slice 1. Scheibe *f*, Stück *n*; *fig* Anteil *m* (*of* an *dat*); **2.** *a.* **~ up** in Scheiben *or* Stücke schneiden; **~ off** Stück abschneiden (*from* von)

slick 1. gekonnt; geschickt; raffiniert; glatt (*road etc*); **2.** F (*Öl*)Teppich *m*; **3. ~ down** Haar glätten, F anklatschen

slick·er Regenmantel *m*

slide 1. gleiten (lassen); rutschen; schlüpfen; schieben; *let things ~ fig* die Dinge schleifen lassen; **2.** Gleiten *n*, Rutschen *n*; Rutsche *f*, Rutschbahn *f*; TECH Schieber *m*; PHOT Dia *n*; Objektträger *m*; (*Erd- etc*)Rutsch *m*; *Br* (*Haar*)Spange *f*; **~ rule** Rechenschieber *m*; **~ tack·le** *soccer*: Grätsche *f*

slid·ing door Schiebetür *f*

slight 1. leicht, gering(fügig), unbedeutend; **2.** beleidigen, kränken; **3.** Beleidigung *f*, Kränkung *f*

slim 1. schlank; *fig* gering; **2.** *a.* **be slimming, be on a slimming diet** e-e Schlankheitskur machen, abnehmen

slime Schleim *m*

slim·y schleimig (*a. fig*)

sling 1. aufhängen; F schleudern; **2.** Schlinge *f*; Tragriemen *m*; Tragetuch *n*; Schleuder *f*

slip¹ 1. *v/i* rutschen, schlittern; ausgleiten, ausrutschen; schlüpfen; *v/t* sich losreißen von; **~ s.th. into s.o.'s hand** j-m et. in die Hand schieben; **~ s.o. s.th.** j-m et. zuschieben; **~ s.o.'s attention** j-m *or* j-s Aufmerksamkeit entgehen; **~ s.o.'s mind** j-m entfallen; **she has ~ped a disk** MED sie hat e-n Bandscheibenvorfall; **~ by, ~ past** verstreichen (*time*); **~ off, ~ out of** schlüpfen aus; **~ on** überstreifen, schlüpfen in (*acc*); **2.** Ausgleiten *n*, (Aus)Rutschen *n*; Versehen *n*; Unterrock *m*; (*Kissen*)Bezug *m*; **~ of the tongue** Versprecher *m*; **give s.o. the ~** F j-m entwischen

slip² *a.* **~ of paper** Zettel *m*

slip·case Schuber *m*

slip-on 1. *adj* **~ shoe → 2.** Slipper *m*

slipped disk MED Bandscheibenvorfall *m*

slip·per Hausschuh *m*, Pantoffel *m*

slip·per·y glatt, rutschig, glitschig

slip road *Br* MOT **→ ramp**

slip·shod schlampig

slit 1. Schlitz *m*; **2.** schlitzen; **~ open** aufschlitzen

slith·er gleiten, rutschen

sliv·er (*Glas- etc*)Splitter *m*

slob·ber sabbern

slo·gan Slogan *m*

sloop MAR Schaluppe *f*

slop 1. *v/t* verschütten; *v/i* überschwappen; schwappen (*over* über *acc*); **2.** *a. pl* schlabb(e)riges Zeug; (*Tee-, Kaffee-*)Rest(e *pl*) *m*; *esp Br* Schmutzwasser *n*

slope 1. (Ab)Hang *m*; Neigung *f*, Gefälle *n*; **2.** sich neigen, abfallen

slop·py schlampig; F gammelig; F rührselig

slot Schlitz *m*, (*Münz*)Einwurf *m*; EDP Steckplatz *m*

sloth ZO Faultier *n*

slot ma·chine (*Waren-, Spiel*)Automat *m*

slouch 1. krumme Haltung; F latschiger Gang; **2.** krumm dasitzen *or* dastehen; F latschen

slough¹: ~ off Haut abstreifen, ZO sich häuten

slough² Sumpf *m*, Sumpfloch *n*

Slo·vak 1. slowakisch; **2.** Slowake *m*, Slowakin *f*; LING Slowakisch *n*

Slo·va·ki·a Slowakei *f*

slov·en·ly schlampig

slow 1. *adj* langsam; begriffsstutzig; ECON schleppend; *be* (*ten minutes*) **~** (zehn Minuten) nachgehen; **2.** *adv* langsam; **3.** *v/t often* **~ down, ~ up** Geschwindigkeit verringern; *v/i often* **~ down, ~ up** langsamer fahren *or* gehen *or* werden

slow·coach *Br* **→ slowpoke**

slow·down ECON Bummelstreik *m*

slow lane MOT Kriechspur *f*

low mo·tion PHOT Zeitlupe *f*

slow-mov·ing kriechend (*traffic*)

slow·poke Langweiler(in)

slow·worm ZO Blindschleiche *f*

sludge Schlamm *m*

slug¹ ZO Nacktschnecke *f*

slug² F (*Gewehr- etc*)Kugel *f*; Schluck *m* (*whisky etc*)

slug³ *j-m* e-n Faustschlag versetzen

slug·gish träge; ECON schleppend

sluice TECH Schleuse *f*

slum *a. pl* Slums *pl*, Elendsviertel *n or pl*

slum·ber POET **1.** schlummern; **2.** *a. pl* Schlummer *m*

slump 1. ECON stürzen (*prices*), stark zurückgehen (*sales etc*); *sit ~ed over* zusammengesunken sitzen über (*dat*); *~ into a chair* sich in e-n Sessel fallen lassen; **2.** ECON starker Konjunkturrückgang; *~ in prices* Preissturz *m*

slur¹ 1. MUS Töne binden; *~ one's speech* undeutlich sprechen; lallen; **2.** undeutliche Aussprache

slur² 1. verleumden; **2.** *~ on s.o.'s reputation* Rufschädigung *f*

slurp F schlürfen

slush Schneematsch *m*; F Kitsch *m*

slush·y F kitschig

slut Schlampe *f*; Nutte *f*

sly gerissen, schlau, listig; *on the ~* heimlich

smack¹ 1. *j-m* e-n Klaps geben; *~ one's lips* sich (geräuschvoll) die Lippen lecken; *~ down* F *et.* hinklatschen; **2.** klatschendes Geräusch, Knall *m*; F Schmatz *m* (*kiss*); F Klaps *m*

smack²: *~ of fig* schmecken *or* riechen nach

small 1. *adj and adv* klein; *~ wonder* (*that*) kein Wunder, dass; *feel ~ fig* sich klein (und hässlich) vorkommen; **2.** *~ of the back* ANAT Kreuz *n*; *~ ad* Kleinanzeige *f*; *~ arms* Handfeuerwaffen *pl*; *~ change* Kleingeld *n*; *~ hours: in the ~* in den frühen Morgenstunden

small-mind·ed engstirnig; kleinlich

small·pox MED Pocken *pl*

small print *das* Kleingedruckte

small talk Small Talk *m*, *n*, oberflächliche Konversation; *make ~* plaudern

small-time F klein, unbedeutend; *in cpds* Schmalspur...

small town Kleinstadt *f*

smart 1. schick, fesch; smart, schlau, clever; **2.** wehtun; brennen; **3.** (brennender) Schmerz; *~ al·eck* F Besserwisser(in), Klugscheißer(in)

smart·ness Schick *m*; Schlauheit *f*, Cleverness *f*

smash 1. *v/t* zerschlagen (*a. ~ up*); schmettern (*a. tennis etc*); *Aufstand etc* niederschlagen, *Drogenring etc* zerschlagen; *~ up one's car* s-n Wagen zu Schrott fahren; *v/i* zerspringen; *~ into* prallen an (*acc*) *or* gegen, krachen ge-

gen; **2.** Schlag *m*; *tennis etc*: Schmetterball *m*; *→ smash hit, smash-up*

smash hit Hit *m*

smash-up MOT, RAIL schwerer Unfall

smat·ter·ing: *have a ~ of English* ein paar Brocken Englisch können

smear 1. Fleck *m*; MED Abstrich *m*; Verleumdung *f*; **2.** (ein-, ver)schmieren; (sich) verschmieren; verleumden

smell 1. *v/i* riechen (*at* an *dat*); duften; stinken; *v/t* riechen (an *dat*); **2.** Geruch *m*; Gestank *m*; Duft *m*

smell·y übel riechend, stinkend

smelt *Erz* schmelzen

smile 1. Lächeln *n*; **2.** lächeln; *~ at j-n* anlächeln; *j-m* zulächeln; *j-n*, *et.* belächeln, lächeln über (*acc*); *~ to o.s.* schmunzeln

smirk (selbstgefällig *or* schadenfroh) grinsen

smith Schmied *m*

smith·e·reens: *smash (in)to ~* F in tausend Stücke schlagen *or* zerspringen

smith·y Schmiede *f*

smit·ten verliebt, F verknallt (*with* in *acc*); *be ~ by or with fig* gepackt werden von

smock Kittel *m*

smog Smog *m*

smoke 1. Rauch *m*; *have a ~* eine rauchen; **2.** rauchen; räuchern

smok·er Rauchen *n*; RAIL Raucher *m*, Raucherabteil *n*

smoke·stack Schornstein *m*

smok·ing Rauchen *n*; *no ~* Rauchen verboten; *~ com·part·ment* RAIL Raucher *m*, Raucherabteil *n*

smok·y rauchig; verräuchert

smooch F schmusen

smooth 1. glatt (*a. fig*); ruhig (*a. journey etc*); mild (*wine*); *fig* (aal)glatt; **2.** *a. ~ out* glätten, glatt streichen; *~ away Falten etc* glätten; *Schwierigkeiten etc* aus dem Weg räumen; *~ down* glatt streichen

smoth·er ersticken

smo(u)l·der glimmen, schwelen

smudge 1. Schmutzfleck *m*; **2.** (be-, ver)schmieren; (sich) verwischen

smug selbstgefällig

smug·gle schmuggeln (*into* nach; in *acc*); **smug·gler** Schmuggler(in)

smut Rußflocke *f*; Schmutz *m* (*a. fig*)

smut·ty *fig* schmutzig

S

snack Snack *m*, Imbiss *m*; **have a ~** e-e Kleinigkeit essen

snack bar Snackbar *f*, Imbissstube *f*

snag 1. *fig* Haken *m*; 2. mit *et*. hängen bleiben (**on** an *dat*)

snail ZO Schnecke *f*

snake ZO Schlange *f*

snap 1. *v/i* (zer)brechen, (zer)reißen; *a*. **~ shut** zuschnappen; **~ at** schnappen nach; *j-n* anschnauzen; **~ out of it!** F Kopf hoch!, komm, komm!; **~ to it!** mach fix!; *v/t* zerbrechen; PHOT F knipsen; **~ one's fingers** mit den Fingern schnalzen; **~ one's fingers at** *fig* keinen Respekt haben vor (*dat*), sich hinwegsetzen über (*acc*); **~ off** abbrechen; **~ up** *et*. schnell entschlossen kaufen; **~ it up!** mach fix!; 2. Krachen *n*, Knacken *n*, Knall *m*; PHOT F Schnappschuss *m*; Druckknopf *m*; F Schwung *m*; **cold ~** Kälteeinbruch *m*

snap fas·ten·er Druckknopf *m*

snap·pish *fig* bissig

snap·py modisch, schick; **make it ~!** F mach fix!

snap·shot PHOT Schnappschuss *m*

snare 1. Schlinge *f*, Falle *f* (*a. fig*); 2. in der Schlinge fangen; F *et*. ergattern

snarl 1. knurren; **~ at s.o.** j-n anknurren; 2. Knurren *n*

snatch 1. *v/t et*. packen; *Gelegenheit* ergreifen; *ein paar Stunden Schlaf* etc ergattern; **~ s.o.'s handbag** j-m die Handtasche entreißen; *v/i* **~ at** (schnell) greifen nach; *Gelegenheit* ergreifen; 2. **make a ~ at** (schnell) greifen nach; **~ of conversation** Gesprächsfetzen *m*

sneak 1. *v/i* (sich) schleichen; *Br* F petzen; *v/t* F stibitzen; 2. *Br* F Petze *f*

sneak·er Turnschuh *m*

sneer 1. höhnisch *or* spöttisch grinsen (**at** über *acc*); spotten (**at** über *acc*); 2. höhnisches *or* spöttisches Grinsen; höhnische *or* spöttische Bemerkung

sneeze 1. niesen; 2. Niesen *n*

snick·er kichern (**at** über *acc*)

sniff 1. *v/i* schniefen; schnüffeln (**at** an *dat*); **~ at** *fig* die Nase rümpfen über (*acc*); *et*. *Klebstoff* etc schnüffeln, *Kokain* etc schnupfen; 2. Schniefen *n*

snif·fle 1. schniefen; 2. Schniefen *n*; **she's got the ~s** F ihr läuft dauernd die Nase

snig·ger *esp Br* → **snicker**

snip 1. Schnitt *m*; 2. durchschnippeln; **~ off** abschnippeln

snipe[1] ZO Schnepfe *f*

snipe[2] aus dem Hinterhalt schießen (**at** auf *acc*)

snip·er Heckenschütze *m*

sniv·el greinen, jammern

snob Snob *m*; **snob·bish** versnobt

snoop: **~ about**, **~ around** F herumschnüffeln

snoop·er F Schnüffler(in)

snooze F 1. ein Nickerchen machen; 2. Nickerchen *n*

snore 1. schnarchen; 2. Schnarchen *n*

snor·kel 1. Schnorchel *m*; 2. schnorcheln

snort 1. schnauben; 2. Schnauben *n*

snot·ty nose F Rotznase *f*

snout ZO Schnauze *f*, Rüssel *m*

snow 1. Schnee *m* (*a. sl cocaine*); 2. schneien; **be ~ed in** *or* **up** eingeschneit sein

snow·ball Schneeball *m*; **~ fight** Schneeballschlacht *f*

snow·bound eingeschneit

snow·capped schneebedeckt

snow·drift Schneewehe *f*

snow·drop BOT Schneeglöckchen *n*

snow·fall Schneefall *m*

snow·flake Schneeflocke *f*

snow line Schneegrenze *f*

snow·man Schneemann *m*

snow·mo·bile Schneemobil *n*

snow·plough *Br*, **snow·plow** Schneepflug *m*

snow·storm Schneesturm *m*

snow-white schneeweiß

Snow White Schneewittchen *n*

snow·y schneereich; verschneit

snub *j-n* brüskieren, *j-n* vor den Kopf stoßen

snub nose Stupsnase *f*

snuff[1] Schnupftabak *m*

snuff[2] *Kerze* ausdrücken, löschen; **~ out** *Leben* auslöschen

snuf·fle schnüffeln, schniefen

snug gemütlich, behaglich; *clothing*: gut sitzend; eng (anliegend)

snug·gle: **~ up to s.o.** sich an j-n kuscheln; **~ down in bed** sich ins Bett kuscheln

so so; deshalb; → **hope** 2, **think**; **is that ~?** wirklich?; **an hour or ~** etwa e-e

Stunde; *she is tired - ~ am I* sie ist müde - ich auch; *~ far* bisher

soak *v/t* einweichen (*in* in *dat*); durchnässen; *~ up* aufsaugen; *v/i* sickern

soak·ing *a*. *~ wet* völlig durchnässt, F klatschnass

soap 1. Seife *f*; F → *soap opera*; **2.** (sich) einseifen

soap op·e·ra *radio,* TV Seifenoper *f*

soap·y Seifen...; seifig; *fig* F schmeichlerisch

soar (hoch) aufsteigen; hochragen; ZO, AVIAT segeln, gleiten; *fig* in die Höhe schnellen (*prices etc*)

sob 1. schluchzen; **2.** Schluchzen *n*

so·ber 1. nüchtern (*a. fig*); **2.** ernüchtern; *~ up* nüchtern machen *or* werden

so-called so genannt

soc·cer Fußball *m*

soc·cer hoo·li·gan Fußballrowdy *m*

so·cia·ble gesellig

so·cial sozial, Sozial...; gesellschaftlich, Gesellschafts...; ZO gesellig; *~ dem·ocrat* POL Sozialdemokrat(in); *~ in·sur·ance* Sozialversicherung *f*

so·cial·ism Sozialismus *m*

so·cial·ist 1. Sozialist(in); **2.** sozialistisch

so·cial·ize *v/i* gesellschaftlich verkehren (*with* mit); *v/t* sozialisieren

so·cial| sci·ence Sozialwissenschaft *f*; *~ se·cu·ri·ty* *Br* Sozialhilfe *f*; *be on ~* Sozialhilfe beziehen; *~ ser·vic·es* *esp Br* Sozialeinrichtungen; *~ work* Sozialarbeit *f*; *~ work·er* Sozialarbeiter(in)

so·ci·e·ty Gesellschaft *f*; Verein *m*

so·ci·ol·o·gy Soziologie *f*

sock Socke *f*

sock·et ELECTR Steckdose *f*; Fassung *f*; (Anschluss)Buchse *f*; ANAT (*Augen*)Höhle *f*

so·da Soda(wasser) *n*; (*Orangen- etc*)Limonade *f*

sod·den aufgeweicht (*ground*); durchweicht (*clothes*)

so·fa Sofa *n*

soft weich; sanft; leise; gedämpft (*light etc*); F leicht, angenehm, ruhig (*job etc*); alkoholfrei (*drink*); F verweichlicht

soft drink Soft Drink *m*, alkoholfreies Getränk

soft·en *v/t* weich machen; *Wasser* enthärten; *Ton, Licht, Stimme etc* dämpfen; *~ up* F *j-n* weich machen; *v/i* weich(er) *or* sanft(er) *or* mild(er) werden

soft·heart·ed weichherzig

soft land·ing weiche Landung

soft·ware EDP Software *f*; *~ pack·age* EDP Softwarepaket *n*

soft·y F Softie *m*, Weichling *m*

sog·gy aufgeweicht, matschig

soil[1] Boden *m*, Erde *f*

soil[2] beschmutzen, schmutzig machen

so·lar Sonnen...; *~ en·er·gy* Solar-, Sonnenenergie *f*; *~ pan·el* Sonnenkollektor *m*; *~ sys·tem* Sonnensystem *n*

sol·der TECH (ver)löten

sol·dier Soldat *m*

sole[1] **1.** (Fuß-, Schuh)Sohle *f*; **2.** besohlen

sole[2] ZO Seezunge *f*

sole[3] einzig; alleinig, Allein...

sole·ly (einzig und) allein, ausschließlich

sol·emn feierlich; ernst

so·lic·it bitten um

so·lic·i·tous besorgt (*about, for* um)

sol·id 1. fest; stabil; massiv; MATH körperlich; gewichtig, triftig (*reason etc*), stichhaltig (*argument etc*); solid(e), gründlich (*work etc*); einmütig, geschlossen; *a ~ hour* F e-e geschlagene Stunde; **2.** MATH Körper *m*; *pl* feste Nahrung

sol·i·dar·i·ty Solidarität *f*

so·lid·i·fy fest werden (lassen); *fig* (sich) festigen

sol·il·o·quy Selbstgespräch *n*, *esp* THEA Monolog *m*

sol·i·taire Solitär *m*; Patience *f*

sol·i·ta·ry einsam, (*Leben a.*) zurückgezogen, (*Ort etc a.*) abgelegen; einzig; *~ con·fine·ment* JUR Einzelhaft *f*

so·lo MUS Solo *n*; AVIAT Alleinflug *m*

so·lo·ist MUS Solist(in)

sol·u·ble CHEM löslich; *fig* lösbar

so·lu·tion CHEM Lösung *f*; *fig* (Auf)Lösung *f*

solve *Fall etc* lösen

sol·vent 1. ECON zahlungsfähig; **2.** CHEM Lösungsmittel *n*

som·ber, *Br* **som·bre** düster, trüb(e); *fig* trübsinnig

some (irgend)ein; *pl* einige, ein paar; manche; etwas, ein wenig, ein bisschen; ungefähr; **~ 20 miles** etwa 20 Meilen; **~ more cake** noch ein Stück Kuchen; **to ~ extent** bis zu e-m gewissen Grade

some·bod·y jemand

some·day eines Tages

some·how irgendwie

some·one jemand

some·place irgendwo, irgendwohin

som·er·sault 1. Salto *m*; Purzelbaum *m*; **turn a ~ → 2.** e-n Salto machen; e-n Purzelbaum schlagen

some·thing etwas; **~ like** ungefähr

some·time irgendwann

some·times manchmal

some·what ein bisschen, ein wenig

some·where irgendwo(hin)

son Sohn *m*; **~ of a bitch** V Scheißkerl *m*

so·na·ta MUS Sonate *f*

song MUS Lied *n*; Gesang *m*; **for a ~** für ein Butterbrot

song·bird ZO Singvogel *m*

son·ic Schall...; **~ bang** *Br*, **~ boom** Überschallknall *m*

son-in-law Schwiegersohn *m*

son·net Sonett *n*

so·nor·ous sonor, volltönend

soon bald; **as ~ as** sobald; **as ~ as possible** so bald wie möglich

soon·er eher, früher; **~ or later** früher oder später; **the ~ the better** je eher, desto besser; **no ~ ... than** kaum ... als; **no ~ said than done** gesagt, getan

soot Ruß *m*

soothe beruhigen, beschwichtigen (*a.* **~ down**); *Schmerzen* lindern, mildern

sooth·ing beruhigend; lindernd

soot·y rußig

sop[1] Beschwichtigungsmittel *n* (**to** für)

sop[2]: **~ up** aufsaugen

so·phis·ti·cat·ed anspruchsvoll, kultiviert; intellektuell; TECH raffiniert, hoch entwickelt

soph·o·more Student(in) im zweiten Jahr

sop·o·rif·ic einschläfernd

sop·ping *a.* **~ wet** F klatschnass

sor·cer·er Zauberer *m*, Hexenmeister *m*, Hexer *m*

sor·cer·ess Zauberin *f*, Hexe *f*

sor·cer·y Zauberei *f*, Hexerei *f*

sor·did schmutzig; schäbig

sore 1. weh, wund (*a. fig*); entzündet; F *fig* sauer; **I'm ~ all over** mir tut alles

weh; **~ throat** Halsentzündung *f*; **have a ~ throat** *a.* Halsschmerzen haben; **2.** wunde Stelle, Wunde *f*

sor·rel[1] BOT Sauerampfer *m*

sor·rel[2] **1.** ZO Fuchs *m* (*horse*); **2.** rotbraun

sor·row Kummer *m*, Leid *n*, Schmerz *m*, Trauer *f*

sor·row·ful traurig, betrübt

sor·ry 1. *adj* traurig, jämmerlich; **be** *or* **feel ~ for s.o.** j-n bedauern *or* bemitleiden; **I'm ~ for her** sie tut mir leid; **I am ~ to say** ich muss leider sagen; **I'm ~ → 2.** *int* (es) tut mir leid!; Entschuldigung!, Verzeihung!; **~?** *esp Br* wie bitte?

sort 1. Sorte *f*, Art *f*; **~ of** F irgendwie; **of a ~**, **of ~s** F so etwas Ähnliches wie; **all ~s of things** alles Mögliche; **nothing of the ~** nichts dergleichen; **what ~ of (a) man is he?** wie ist er?; **be out of ~s** F nicht auf der Höhe *or* auf dem Damm sein; **be completely out of ~s** SPORT F völlig außer Form sein; **2.** sortieren; **~ out** aussortieren; *Problem etc* lösen, *Frage etc* klären

SOS SOS *n*; **send an ~** ein SOS funken; **~ call** *or* **message** SOS-Ruf *m*

soul Seele *f* (*a. fig*); MUS Soul *m*

sound[1] **1.** Geräusch *n*; Laut *m*; PHYS Schall *m*; *radio*, TV Ton *m*; MUS Klang *m*, Sound *m*; **2.** *v/i* (er)klingen, (er)tönen; sich *gut etc* anhören; *v/t* LING (aus)sprechen; MAR (aus)loten; MED abhorchen; **~ one's horn** MOT hupen

sound[2] gesund; intakt, in Ordnung; solid(e), stabil, sicher; klug, vernünftig (*person, advice etc*); gründlich (*training etc*); gehörig (*beating*); vernichtend (*defeat*); fest, tief (*sleep*)

sound bar·ri·er Schallgrenze *f*, Schallmauer *f*; **~ film** Tonfilm *m*

sound·less lautlos

sound·proof schalldicht

sound·track Filmmusik *f*; Tonspur *f*

sound wave Schallwelle *f*

soup 1. Suppe *f*; **2. ~ up** F Motor frisieren

sour 1. sauer; *fig* mürrisch; **2.** sauer werden (lassen); *fig* trüben, verbittern

source Quelle *f*, *fig a.* Ursache *f*, Ursprung *m*

south 1. Süd, Süden *m*; **2.** *adj* südlich,

Süd...; **3.** *adv* nach Süden, südwärts

south·east 1. Südost, Südosten *m*; **2.** *a.* **south·east·ern** südöstlich

south·er·ly, south·ern südlich, Süd...

south·ern·most südlichste(r, -s)

South Pole Südpol *m*

south·ward(s) südlich, nach Süden

south·west 1. Südwest, Südwesten *m*; **2.** *a.* **south·west·ern** südwestlich

sou·ve·nir Souvenir *n*, Andenken *n* (*of* an *acc*)

sove·reign 1. Monarch(in), Landesherr(in); **2.** POL souverän

sove·reign·ty Souveränität *f*

So·vi·et HIST POL sowjetisch, Sowjet...

sow¹ (aus)säen

sow² ZO Sau *f*

soy bean BOT Sojabohne *f*

spa (Heil)Bad *n*

space 1. Raum *m*, Platz *m*; (Welt-)Raum *m*; Zwischenraum *m*; Zeitraum *m*; **2.** *a.* **~ out** in Abständen anordnen; PRINT sperren

space age Weltraumzeitalter *n*

space bar TECH Leertaste *f*

space cap·sule Raumkapsel *f*

space cen·ter (*Br* **cen·tre**) Raumfahrtzentrum *n*

space·craft (Welt)Raumfahrzeug *n*

space flight (Welt)Raumflug *m*

space·lab Raumlabor *n*

space·man F Raumfahrer *m*; Außerirdische *m*

space probe (Welt)Raumsonde *f*

space re·search (Welt)Raumforschung *f*

space·ship Raumschiff *n*

space shut·tle Raumfähre *f*, Raumtransporter *m*

space sta·tion (Welt)Raumstation *f*

space·suit Raumanzug *m*

space walk Weltraumspaziergang *m*

space·wom·an F (Welt)Raumfahrerin *f*; Außerirdische *f*

spa·cious geräumig

spade Spaten *m*; *card game*: Pik *n*, Grün *n*; **king of ~s** Pikkönig *m*; **call a ~ a ~** das Kind beim (rechten) Namen nennen

Spain Spanien *n*

span 1. Spanne *f*; Spannweite *f*; **2.** *Fluss etc* überspannen; *fig* sich erstrecken über (*acc*)

span·gle 1. Flitter *m*, Paillette *f*; **2.** mit

Flitter *or* Pailletten besetzen; *fig* übersäen (**with** mit)

Span·iard Spanier(in)

span·iel ZO Spaniel *m*

Span·ish 1. spanisch; **2.** LING Spanisch *n*; **the ~** die Spanier *pl*

spank *j-m* den Hintern versohlen

spank·ing Tracht *f* Prügel

span·ner *esp Br* Schraubenschlüssel *m*; **put** *or* **throw a ~ in the works** F *j-m* in die Quere kommen

spar *boxing*: sparren (**with** mit); *fig* sich ein Wortgefecht liefern (**with** mit)

spare 1. *j-n, et.* entbehren; *Geld, Zeit etc* übrig haben; *keine Kosten, Mühen etc* scheuen; **~ s.o. s.th.** *j-m et.* ersparen; **2.** Ersatz..., Reserve...; überschüssig; **3.** MOT Ersatz-, Reservereifen *m*; *esp Br* → **~ part** TECH Ersatzteil *n, m*

spare room Gästezimmer *n*

spare time Freizeit *f*

spar·ing sparsam; *use* **~ ly** sparsam umgehen mit

spark 1. Funke(n) *m* (*a. fig*); **2.** Funken sprühen

spark·ing plug *Br* → **spark plug**

spar·kle 1. funkeln, blitzen (**with** vor *dat*); perlen (*drink*); **2.** Funkeln *n*, Blitzen *n*; **spar·kling** funkelnd, blitzend; (geist)sprühend, spritzig; **~ wine** Sekt *m*, Schaumwein *m*

spark plug MOT Zündkerze *f*

spar·row ZO Spatz *m*, Sperling *m*

spar·row·hawk ZO Sperber *m*

sparse spärlich, dünn

spasm MED Krampf *m*; Anfall *m*

spas·mod·ic MED krampfartig; *fig* sporadisch, unregelmäßig

spas·tic MED **1.** spastisch; **2.** Spastiker(in)

spa·tial räumlich

spat·ter (be)spritzen

spawn 1. ZO laichen; *fig* hervorbringen; **2.** ZO Laich *m*

speak *v/i* sprechen, reden (**to, with** mit; **about** über *acc*); sprechen (**to** *or* **about, on** über *acc*); **so to ~** sozusagen; **speaking!** TEL am Apparat!; **~ up** lauter sprechen; *v/t* sprechen, sagen; *Sprache* sprechen

speak·er Sprecher(in), Redner(in)

spear 1. Speer *m*; **2.** aufspießen; durchbohren

spear·head Speerspitze *f*; MIL Angriffs-

S

spitze *f*; SPORT (Sturm-, Angriffs)Spitze *f*

spear·mint BOT Grüne Minze

spe·cial 1. besondere(r, -s); speziell; Sonder-, Spezial...; **2.** Sonderbus *m*, Sonderzug *m*; *radio*, TV Sondersendung *f*; ECON F Sonderangebot *n*; *be on ~* ECON im Angebot sein

spe·cial·ist Spezialist(in), MED *a.* Facharzt *m*, Fachärztin *f* (*in* für)

spe·cial·i·ty *Br* → **specialty**

spe·cial·ize sich spezialisieren (*in* auf *acc*)

spe·cial·ty Spezialgebiet *n*; GASTR Spezialität *f*

spe·cies Art *f*, Spezies *f*

spe·cif·ic konkret, präzis; spezifisch, speziell, besondere(r, -s); eigen (*to* dat)

spe·ci·fy genau beschreiben *or* angeben *or* festlegen

spe·ci·men Exemplar *n*; Probe *f*, Muster *n*

speck kleiner Fleck, (Staub)Korn *n*; Punkt *m* (*on the horizon* am Horizont)

speck·led gefleckt, gesprenkelt

spec·ta·cle Schauspiel *n*; Anblick *m*; (*a pair of*) *~s* (e-e) Brille

spec·tac·u·lar 1. spektakulär; **2.** große (*Fernseh- etc*)Show

spec·ta·tor Zuschauer(in)

spec·ter (*fig a.* Schreck)Gespenst *n*

spec·tral geisterhaft, gespenstisch

spec·tre *Br* → **specter**

spec·u·late spekulieren, Vermutungen anstellen (*about, on* über *acc*); ECON spekulieren (*in* mit); **spec·u·la·tion** Spekulation *f* (*a.* ECON), Vermutung *f*; **spec·u·la·tive** spekulativ, ECON *a.* Spekulations...; **spec·u·la·tor** ECON Spekulant(in)

speech Sprache *f*, Rede *f*, Ansprache *f*; *make a ~* e-e Rede halten

speech day *Br* PED (Jahres)Schlussfeier *f*

speech·less sprachlos (*with* vor *dat*)

speed 1. Geschwindigkeit *f*, Tempo *n*, Schnelligkeit *f*; TECH Drehzahl *f*; PHOT Lichtempfindlichkeit *f*; *sl* Speed *n*; MOT *etc* Gang *m*; *five-speed gearbox* Fünfganggetriebe *n*; *at a ~ of* mit e-r Geschwindigkeit von; *at full or top ~* mit Höchstgeschwindigkeit; **2.** *v/i* rasen; *be ~ing* MOT zu schnell fahren; *~ up* be-

schleunigen, schneller werden; *v/t* rasch bringen *or* befördern; *~ up et.* beschleunigen

speed·boat Rennboot *n*

speed·ing MOT zu schnelles Fahren, Geschwindigkeitsüberschreitung *f*

speed lim·it MOT Geschwindigkeitsbegrenzung *f*, Tempolimit *n*

speed·om·e·ter MOT Tachometer *m*, *n*

speed trap MOT Radarfalle *f*

speed·y schnell, (*reply etc a.*) prompt

spell¹ *a. ~ out* buchstabieren; (*orthographisch* richtig) schreiben

spell² Weile *f*; (*Husten- etc*)Anfall *m*; *for a ~* e-e Zeit lang; *a ~ of fine weather* e-e Schönwetterperiode *f*; *hot ~* Hitzewelle *f*

spell³ Zauber *m* (*a. fig*)

spell·bound wie gebannt

spell·er EDP Speller *m*, Rechtschreibsystem *n*; *be a good* (*bad*) *~* in Rechtschreibung gut (schlecht) sein

spell·ing Buchstabieren *n*; Rechtschreibung *f*; Schreibung *f*, Schreibweise *f*; *~ mis·take* (Recht)Schreibfehler *m*

spend Geld ausgeben (*on* für); *Urlaub, Zeit* verbringen

spend·ing Ausgaben *pl*

spend·thrift Verschwender(in)

spent verbraucht

sperm BIOL Sperma *n*, Samen *m*

sphere Kugel *f*, *fig* (*Einfluss- etc*)Sphäre *f*, (*Einfluss- etc*)Bereich *m*, Gebiet *n*

spher·i·cal kugelförmig

spice 1. Gewürz *n*; *fig* Würze *f*; **2.** würzen

spick-and-span blitzsauber

spic·y gut gewürzt, würzig; *fig* pikant

spi·der ZO Spinne *f*

spike 1. Spitze *f*; Dorn *m*; Stachel *m*; SPORT Spike *m*, Dorn *m*; *pl* Spikes *pl*, Rennschuhe *pl*; **2.** aufspießen

spill 1. *v/t* ausschütten, verschütten; *~ the beans* F alles ausplaudern, singen; → *milk* 1; *v/i fig* strömen (*out of* aus); *~ over* überlaufen; *fig* übergreifen (*into* auf *acc*); **2.** F Sturz *m*

spin 1. *v/t* drehen; *Wäsche* schleudern; *Münze* hochwerfen; *Fäden, Wolle etc* spinnen; *~ out* Arbeit *etc* in die Länge ziehen; *Geld etc* strecken; *v/i* sich drehen; spinnen; *my head was ~ning* mir drehte sich alles; *~ along* MOT dahinra-

sporadic

sen; ~ *round* herumwirbeln; **2.** (schnelle) Drehung; SPORT Effet *m;* TECH Schleudern *n;* AVIAT Trudeln *n;* **be in a (flat)** ~ *esp Br* F am Rotieren sein; **go for a** ~ MOT F e-e Spritztour machen

spin·ach BOT Spinat *m*

spin·al ANAT Rückgrat...; ~ **col·umn** ANAT Wirbelsäule *f,* Rückgrat *n;* ~ **cord,** ~ **mar·row** ANAT Rückenmark *n*

spin·dle Spindel *f*

spin·dri·er (Wäsche)Schleuder *f*

spin-dry *Wäsche* schleudern

spin-dry·er → **spin-drier**

spine ANAT Wirbelsäule *f,* Rückgrat *n;* ZO Stachel *m,* BOT *a.* Dorn *m;* (*Buch-*)Rücken *m*

spin·ning| mill TECH Spinnerei *f;* ~ **top** Kreisel *m;* ~ **wheel** Spinnrad *n*

spin·ster ältere unverheiratete Frau, *contp* alte Jungfer, spätes Mädchen

spin·y ZO stach(e)lig, BOT *a.* dornig

spi·ral 1. spiralförmig, Spiral...; **2.** (*a.* ECON *Preis- etc*)Spirale *f*

spi·ral stair·case Wendeltreppe *f*

spire (*Kirch*)Turmspitze *f*

spir·it Geist *m;* Stimmung *f,* Einstellung *f;* Schwung *m;* Elan *m;* CHEM Spiritus *m; mst pl* Spirituosen *pl*

spir·it·ed energisch; erregt (*debate etc*)

spir·it·less temperamentlos; mutlos

spir·its Laune *f,* Stimmung *f;* **be in high** ~ in Hochstimmung sein; ausgelassen *or* übermütig sein; **be in low** ~ niedergeschlagen sein

spir·i·tu·al 1. geistig; geistlich; **2.** MUS Spiritual *n*

spit¹ 1. spucken; knistern (*fire*), brutzeln (*meat etc*); *a.* ~ **out** ausspucken; ~ **at s.o.** j-n anspucken; **it is ~ting (with rain)** es tröpfelt; **2.** Spucke *f*

spit² (*Brat*)Spieß *m;* GEOGR Landzunge *f*

spite 1. Bosheit *f,* Gehässigkeit *f;* **out of** *or* **from pure** ~ aus reiner Bosheit; **in** ~ **of** trotz (*gen*); **2.** j-n ärgern

spite·ful boshaft, gehässig

spit·ting im·age Ebenbild *n;* **she is the** ~ **of her mother** sie ist ihrer Mutter wie aus dem Gesicht geschnitten

spit·tle Speichel *m,* Spucke *f*

splash 1. (be)spritzen; klatschen; plan(t)schen; platschen; ~ **down** wassern; **2.** Klatschen *n,* Platschen *n;* Sprit-

zer *m,* Spritzfleck *m; esp Br* GASTR Spritzer *m,* Schuss *m*

splash·down Wasserung *f*

splay *a.* ~ **out** *Finger, Zehen* spreizen

spleen ANAT Milz *f*

splen·did großartig, herrlich, prächtig

splen·do(u)r Pracht *f*

splice miteinander verbinden, *Film etc* (zusammen)kleben

splint MED Schiene *f;* **put in a** ~, **put in** ~**s** schienen

splin·ter 1. Splitter *m;* **2.** (zer)splittern; ~ **off** absplittern; *fig* sich abspalten (**from** von)

split 1. *v/t* (zer)spalten; zerreißen; *a.* ~ **up** aufteilen (**between** unter *acc;* **into** in *acc*); sich *et.* teilen; ~ **hairs** Haarspalterei treiben; ~ **one's sides** F sich vor Lachen biegen; *v/i* sich spalten; zerreißen; sich teilen (**into** in *acc*); *a.* ~ **up (with)** Schluss machen (mit), sich trennen (von); **2.** Riss *m;* Spalt *m;* Aufteilung *f; fig* Bruch *m; fig* Spaltung *f*

split·ting heftig, rasend (*headache etc*)

splut·ter stottern (*a.* MOT); zischen

spoil 1. *v/t* verderben; ruinieren; j-n verwöhnen, *Kind a.* verziehen; *v/i* verderben, schlecht werden; **2.** *mst pl* Beute *f*

spoil·er MOT Spoiler *m*

spoil·sport F Spielverderber(in)

spoke TECH Sprecher *m*

spokes·man Sprecher *m*

spokes·wom·an Sprecherin *f*

sponge 1. Schwamm *m;* Schnorrer(in); *Br* → **sponge cake; 2.** *v/t a.* ~ **down** (mit e-m Schwamm) abwaschen; ~ **off** weg-, abwischen; ~ **(up)** aufsaugen, aufwischen (**from** von); *et.* schnorren (**from, off, on** von, bei); *v/i* schnorren (**from, off, on** bei)

sponge cake Biskuitkuchen *m*

spong·er Schnorrer(in)

spong·y schwammig; weich

spon·sor 1. Bürge *m,* Bürgin *f;* Sponsor(in), Geldgeber(in); Spender(in); **2.** bürgen für; sponsern

spon·ta·ne·ous spontan

spook F Geist *m*

spook·y F gespenstisch, unheimlich

spool Spule *f;* ~ **of thread** Garnrolle *f*

spoon 1. Löffel *m;* **2.** löffeln

spoon-feed *Kind etc* füttern

spoon·ful (*ein*) Löffel (*voll*)

spo·rad·ic sporadisch, gelegentlich

spore BOT Spore f

sport 1. Sport m; Sportart f; F feiner Kerl; pl Sport m; **2.** herumlaufen mit; protzen mit

sports com...; **~ car** MOT Sportwagen m; **~ cen·ter** (Br **cen·tre**) Sportzentrum n

sports·man Sportler m

sports·wear Sportkleidung f

sports·wom·an Sportlerin f

spot 1. Punkt m, Tupfen m; Fleck m; MED Pickel m; Ort m, Platz m, Stelle f; radio, TV (Werbe)Spot m; F Spot m; **a ~ of** Br F ein bisschen; **on the ~** auf der Stelle, sofort; zur Stelle; an Ort und Stelle, vor Ort; auf der Stelle; **be in a ~** F in Schwulitäten sein; **soft ~** fig Schwäche f (**for** für); **tender ~** empfindliche Stelle; **weak ~** schwacher Punkt; Schwäche f; **2.** entdecken, sehen

spot check Stichprobe f

spot·less tadellos sauber; fig untad(e)lig

spot·light Spotlight n, Scheinwerfer m; Scheinwerferlicht n

spot·ted getüpfelt; fleckig

spot·ter Beobachter m

spot·ty pick(e)lig

spouse Gatte m, Gattin f, Gemahl(in)

spout v/t Wasser etc (heraus)spritzen; v/i spritzen (**from** aus); **2.** Schnauze f, Tülle f; (Wasser- etc)Strahl m

sprain MED **1.** sich et. verstauchen; **2.** Verstauchung f

sprat ZO Sprotte f

sprawl ausgestreckt liegen or sitzen (a. **~ out**); sich ausbreiten

spray 1. (be)sprühen; spritzen; sich die Haare sprayen; Parfüm etc versprühen, zerstäuben; **2.** Sprühnebel m; Gischt m, f; Spray m, n; → **sprayer**

spray can → **spray·er** Sprüh-, Spraydose f, Zerstäuber m

spread 1. v/t ausbreiten, Arme a. ausstrecken, Finger etc spreizen (all a. **~ out**); Furcht, Krankheit, Nachricht etc verbreiten, Gerücht a. ausstreuen; Butter etc streichen (**with** mit); Brot etc (be)streichen (**with** mit); v/i sich ausbreiten (a. **~ out**); sich erstrecken (**over** über acc); sich verbreiten, übergreifen (**to** auf acc); sich streichen lassen (butter etc); **2.** Ausbreitung f,

Verbreitung f; Ausdehnung f; Spannweite f; GASTR Aufstrich m

spread·sheet EDP Tabellenkalkulation f, Tabellenkalkulationsprogramm n

spree: go (**out**) **on a ~** F e-e Sauftour machen; **go on a buying** (or **shopping, spending**) **~** wie verrückt einkaufen

sprig BOT kleiner Zweig

spright·ly lebhaft; rüstig

spring 1. v/i springen; **~ from** herrühren von; **~ up** aufkommen (wind); aus dem Boden schießen (building etc); v/t: **~ a leak** ein Leck bekommen; **~ a surprise on s.o.** j-n überraschen; **2.** Frühling m, Frühjahr n; Quelle f; TECH Feder f; Elastizität f; Federung f; Sprung m, Satz m; **in** (**the**) **~** im Frühling

spring·board Sprungbrett n

spring-clean gründlich putzen, Frühjahrsputz machen (in dat)

spring tide Springflut f

spring·time Frühling m, Frühlingszeit f, Frühjahr n

spring·y elastisch, federnd

sprin·kle 1. Wasser etc sprengen (**on** auf acc); Salz etc streuen (**on** auf acc); et. (be)sprengen or bestreuen (**with** mit); **it is sprinkling** es tröpfelt; **2.** Sprühregen m

sprin·kler (Rasen)Sprenger m; Sprinkler m, Berieselungsanlage f

sprin·kling: a ~ of ein bisschen, ein paar

sprint SPORT **1.** sprinten; spurten; **2.** Sprint m; Spurt m

sprint·er SPORT Sprinter(in)

sprite Kobold m

sprout BOT **1.** sprießen (a. fig), keimen; wachsen lassen; **2.** Spross m; (**Brussels**) **~s** Rosenkohl m

spruce[1] BOT Fichte f; Rottanne f

spruce[2] adrett

spry rüstig, lebhaft

spur 1. Sporn m (a. ZO); fig Ansporn m (**to** zu); **on the ~ of the moment** spontan; **2.** e-m Pferd die Sporen geben; often **~ on** fig anspornen (**to** zu)

spurt[1] spurten, sprinten; **2.** plötzliche Aktivität, (Arbeits)Anfall m; Spurt m, Sprint m

spurt[2] **1.** spritzen (**from** aus); **2.** (Wasser etc)Strahl m

sput·ter stottern (a. MOT); zischen

spy 1. Spion(in); **2.** spionieren, Spionage treiben (**for** für); ~ **into** fig herumspionieren in (dat); ~ **on** j-m nachspionieren

spy·hole (Tür)Spion m

squab·ble (sich) streiten (**about, over** um, wegen)

squad Mannschaft f, Trupp m; (Überfall- etc)Kommando n; Dezernat n

squad car (Funk)Streifenwagen m

squad·ron MIL, AVIAT Staffel f; MAR Geschwader n

squal·id schmutzig, verwahrlost, verkommen, armselig

squall Bö f

squan·der Geld, Zeit etc verschwenden, Chance vertun

square 1. Quadrat n; Viereck n; öffentlicher Platz; MATH Quadrat(zahl f) n; board game: Feld n; TECH Winkel(maß n) m; **2.** quadratisch, Quadrat...; viereckig; rechtwink(e)lig; eckig (shoulders etc); fig fair, gerecht; **be (all)** ~ quitt sein; **3.** quadratisch or rechtwink(e)lig machen (a. ~ **off** or **up**); in Quadrate einteilen (a. ~ **off**); MATH Zahl ins Quadrat erheben; Schultern straffen; Konto ausgleichen; Schulden begleichen; fig in Einklang bringen or stehen (**with** mit); ~ **up** F abrechnen; ~ **up to** sich j-m, e-m Problem etc stellen

square root MATH Quadratwurzel f

squash[1] 1. zerdrücken, zerquetschen; quetschen, zwängen (**into** in acc); ~ **flat** flach drücken, F platt walzen; **2.** Gedränge n; SPORT Squash n

squash[2] BOT Kürbis m

squat 1. hocken, kauern; leer stehendes Haus besetzen; ~ **down** sich (hin)kauern or (hin)hocken; **2.** gedrungen, untersetzt; **squat·ter** Hausbesetzer(in)

squaw Squaw f

squawk kreischen, schreien; F lautstark protestieren (**about** gegen)

squeak 1. piep(s)en (mouse etc); quietschen (door etc); **2.** Piep(s)en n; Piep(s) m; Quietschen n; **squeak·y** piepsig (voice); quietschend (door etc)

squeal 1. kreischen (**with** vor dat); ~ **on s.o.** fig F j-n verpfeifen; **2.** Kreischen n; Schrei m

squeam·ish empfindlich, zart besaitet

squeeze 1. drücken; auspressen, ausquetschen; (sich) quetschen or zwängen (**into** in acc); **2.** Druck m; GASTR Spritzer m; Gedränge n

squeez·er (Frucht)Presse f

squid ZO Tintenfisch m

squint schielen; blinzeln

squirm sich winden

squir·rel ZO Eichhörnchen n

squirt 1. (be)spritzen; **2.** Strahl m

stab 1. v/t niederstechen; **be ~bed in the arm** e-n Stich in den Arm bekommen; v/i stechen (**at** nach); **2.** Stich m

sta·bil·i·ty Stabilität f; fig Dauerhaftigkeit f; Ausgeglichenheit f

sta·bil·ize (sich) stabilisieren

sta·ble[1] stabil; fig dauerhaft; ausgeglichen

sta·ble[2] Stall m

stack 1. Stapel m, Stoß m; ~**s of, a ~ of** fig jede Menge Arbeit etc; **2.** stapeln; voll stapeln (**with** mit); ~ **up** aufstapeln

sta·di·um SPORT Stadion n

staff 1. Stab m; Mitarbeiter(stab m) pl; Personal n, Belegschaft f; Lehrkörper m; MIL Stab m; **2.** besetzen (**with** mit)

staff room Lehrerzimmer n

stag ZO Hirsch m

stage 1. THEA Bühne f (a. fig); Etappe f (a. fig), (Reise)Abschnitt m; Teilstrecke f, Fahrzone f (bus etc); fig Stufe f, Stadium n, Phase f; **2.** THEA inszenieren; veranstalten

stage·coach Postkutsche f

stage\| di·rec·tion THEA Regieanweisung f; ~ **fright** Lampenfieber n; ~ **man·ag·er** THEA Inspizient m

stag·ger 1. v/i (sch)wanken, taumeln, torkeln; v/t j-n sprachlos machen, F umhauen; Arbeitszeit etc staffeln; **2.** Wanken n, Schwanken n, Taumeln n

stag·nant stehend (water); esp ECON stagnierend

stag·nate esp ECON stagnieren

stain 1. v/t beflecken; (ein)färben; Holz beizen; Glas bemalen; v/i Flecken bekommen, schmutzen; **2.** Fleck m; TECH Färbemittel n; (Holz)Beize f; Makel m

stained glass Bunt-, Farbglas n

stain·less nicht rostend, rostfrei

stair (Treppen)Stufe f, pl Treppe f

stair·case, stair·way Treppe f; Treppenhaus n

stake[1] 1. Pfahl m, Pfosten m; HIST Marterpfahl m; **2.** ~ **off,** ~ **out** abstecken

S

stake² **1.** Anteil *m*, Beteiligung *f* (*in* an *dat*) (*a.* ECON); (Wett- *etc*)Einsatz *m*; *be at ~ fig* auf dem Spiel stehen; **2.** Geld *etc* setzen (*on* auf *acc*); Ruf *etc* riskieren, aufs Spiel setzen

stale alt(backen); abgestanden, *beer etc*: *a.* schal, *air etc*: *a.* verbraucht

stalk¹ BOT Stängel *m*, Stiel *m*, Halm *m*

stalk² *v/t* sich heranpirschen an (*acc*); verfolgen, hinter *j-m, et.* herschleichen; *v/i* stolzieren

stall¹ **1.** (*Obst- etc*)Stand *m*, (*Markt-*) Bude *f*; AGR Box *f*; *pl* REL Chorgestühl *n*; Br THEA Parkett *n*; **2.** *v/t* Motor abwürgen; *v/i* MOT absterben

stall² *v/i* Ausflüchte machen; Zeit schinden; *v/t j-n* hinhalten; *et.* hinauszögern

stal·li·on ZO (Zucht)Hengst *m*

stal·wart kräftig, robust; *esp* POL treu

stam·i·na Ausdauer *f*; Durchhaltevermögen *n*, Kondition *f*

stam·mer **1.** stottern, stammeln; **2.** Stottern *n*, Stammeln *n*

stamp **1.** *v/i* sta(m)pfen, trampeln; *v/t* Pass *etc* (ab)stempeln; Datum *etc* aufstempeln (*on* auf *acc*); Brief *etc* frankieren; *fig j-n* abstempeln (*as* als, zu); ~ *one's foot* aufstampfen; ~ *out* Feuer austreten; TECH ausstanzen; **2.** (Brief-) Marke *f*; (Steuer- *etc*)Marke *f*; Stempel *m*; *~ed addressed envelope* Freiumschlag *m*

stam·pede **1.** ZO wilde Flucht; wilder Ansturm, Massensturm *m* (*for* auf *acc*); **2.** *v/i* ZO durchgehen; *v/t* in Panik versetzen

stanch treu, zuverlässig

stand **1.** *v/i* stehen; aufstehen; *fig* festetc bleiben; ~ *still* still stehen; *v/t* stellen (*on* auf *acc*); aushalten, ertragen; *e-r* Prüfung *etc* standhalten; Probe bestehen; Chance haben; Drink *etc* spendieren; *I can't ~ him* (*or it*) ich kann ihn (*or* das) nicht ausstehen *or* leiden; ~ *around* herumstehen; ~ *back* zurücktreten; ~ *by* danebenstehen; *fig* zu *j-m* halten; zu *et.* stehen; ~ *idly by* tatenlos zusehen; ~ *down* verzichten; zurücktreten; JUR den Zeugenstand verlassen; ~ *for* stehen für, bedeuten; sich *et.* gefallen lassen, *et.* dulden; *esp* Br kandidieren für; ~ *in* einspringen (*for* für); ~ *in for s.o. a.* j-n vertreten; ~ *on* (*fig* be)stehen auf (*dat*); ~ *out* her-

vorstechen; sich abheben (*against* gegen, von); ~ *over* überwachen, aufpassen auf (*acc*); ~ *together* zusammenhalten, -stehen; ~ *up* aufstehen, sich erheben; ~ *up for* eintreten *or* sich einsetzen für; ~ *up to j-m* mutig gegenübertreten, *j-m* die Stirn bieten; **2.** (*Obst-, Messe- etc*)Stand *m*; (*Schirm-, Noten- etc*)Ständer *m*; SPORT *etc* Tribüne *f*; (*Taxi*)Stand(platz) *m*; JUR Zeugenstand *m*; *take a ~ fig* Position beziehen (*on* zu)

stan·dard¹ **1.** Norm *f*, Maßstab *m*; Standard *m*, Niveau *n*; ~ *of living, living ~* Lebensstandard *m*; **2.** normal, Normal...; durchschnittlich, Durchschnitts...; Standard...

stan·dard² Standarte *f*, MOT Stander *m*; HIST Banner *n*

stan·dard·ize vereinheitlichen, *esp* TECH standardisieren, normen

stand·ard lamp Br Stehlampe *f*

stand·by **1.** Reserve *f*, AVIAT Stand-by *n*; *be on ~* in Bereitschaft stehen; **2.** Reserve..., Not...; AVIAT Stand-by...

stand·in *film*, TV Double *n*; Ersatzmann *m*; Vertreter(in)

stand·ing **1.** stehend; *fig* ständig; → *ovation*; **2.** Rang *m*, Stellung *f*; Ansehen *n*, Ruf *m*; Dauer *f*; *of long ~* alt, seit langem bestehend; ~ *or·der* ECON Dauerauftrag *m*; ~ *room: ~ only* nur noch Stehplätze

stand·off·ish F (sehr) ablehnend, hochnäsig

stand·point *fig* Standpunkt *m*

stand·still Stillstand *m*; *be at a ~* stehen (*car etc*); ruhen (*production etc*); *bring to a ~* Auto *etc* zum Stehen bringen; Produktion *etc* zum Erliegen bringen

stand·up Steh...; → *fight* Schlägerei *f*

stan·za Strophe *f*

sta·ple¹ **1.** Hauptnahrungsmittel *n*; ECON Haupterzeugnis *n*; **2.** Haupt...; üblich

sta·ple² **1.** Heftklammer *f*; Krampe *f*; **2.** heften

sta·pler TECH (Draht)Hefter *m*

star **1.** ASTR Stern *m*; PRINT Sternchen *n*; THEA, SPORT *etc* Star *m*; **2.** *v/t* PRINT mit e-m Sternchen kennzeichnen; *~ring ...* in der Hauptrolle *or* in den Hauptrollen ...; *a film ~ring ...* ein Film mit ... in der Hauptrolle *or* den Hauptrollen ...; *v/i*

die *or* e-e Hauptrolle spielen (**in** in *dat*)
star·board AVIAT, MAR Steuerbord *n*
starch 1. (*Kartoffel- etc*)Stärke *f*; stärkereiches Nahrungsmittel; (*Wäsche-*)Stärke *f*; **2.** *Wäsche stärken*
stare 1. starren; **~** *at j-n* anstarren; **2.** (starrer) Blick, Starren *n*
stark 1. *adj fig* nackt; *be in* **~** *contrast to* in krassem Gegensatz stehen zu; **2.** *adv*: F **~** *naked* splitternackt; **~** *raving mad*, **~** *staring mad* total verrückt
star·light ASTR Sternenlicht *n*
star·ling ZO Star *m*
star·lit (*sternen*)klar
star·ry Stern..., Sternen...
star·ry-eyed F blauäugig, naiv
start 1. *v/i* anfangen, beginnen (*a.* **~** *off*); aufbrechen (**for** nach) (*a.* **~** *off*, **~** *out*); RAIL *etc* abfahren, MAR ablegen, AVIAT abfliegen, starten; MOT anspringen; TECH anlaufen; SPORT starten; zusammenfahren, -zucken (**at** bei); **to** **~** *with* anfangs, zunächst; erstens; **~** *from scratch* ganz von vorn anfangen; *v/t* anfangen, beginnen (*a.* **~** *off*); in Gang setzen *or* bringen, *Motor etc a.* anlassen, starten; **2.** Anfang *m*, Beginn *m*, (*esp* SPORT) Start *m*; Aufbruch *m*; Auffahren *n*, Aufschrecken *n*; *at the* **~** am Anfang; SPORT am Start; *for a* **~** erstens; *from* **~** *to finish* von Anfang bis Ende
start·er SPORT Starter(in); MOT Anlasser *m*, Starter *m*; *esp Br* GASTR F Vorspeise *f*; *for* **~***s* zunächst einmal
start·le erschrecken; überraschen, bestürzen
starv·a·tion Hungern *n*; *die of* **~** verhungern; **~** *diet* F Fasten-, Hungerkur *f*, Nulldiät *n*
starve hungern (lassen); **~** (*to death*) verhungern (lassen); *I'm starving!* Br F, *I'm* **~***d!* F ich komme um vor Hunger!
state 1. Zustand *m*; Stand *m*, Lage *f*; POL (*Bundes-, Einzel*)Staat *m*; *often* **State** POL Staat *m*; **2.** Staats-, staatlich?; **3.** angeben, nennen; erklären, JUR aussagen (*that* dass); festlegen, festsetzen
State De·part·ment POL Außenministerium *n*
state·ly gemessen, würdevoll; prächtig
state·ment Statement *n*, Erklärung *f*;

Angabe *f*; JUR Aussage *f*, ECON (*Bank-, Konto*)Auszug *m*; *make a* **~** e-e Erklärung abgeben
state-of-the-art TECH neuest, modernst
states·man POL Staatsmann *m*
stat·ic statisch
sta·tion 1. (*a. Bus-, U-*)Bahnhof *m*, Station *f*; (*Forschungs-, Rettungs- etc*)Station *f*; Tankstelle *f*; (*Feuer*)Wache *f*; (*Polizei*)Revier *n*; (*Wahl*)Lokal *n*; *radio*, TV Sender *m*, Station *f*; **2.** aufstellen, postieren; MIL stationieren
sta·tion·ar·y stehend
sta·tion·er Schreibwarenhändler(in); **sta·tion·er's** (*shop*) Schreibwarenhandlung *f*; **sta·tion·er·y** Schreibwaren *pl*; Briefpapier *n*
sta·tion·mas·ter RAIL Stations-, Bahnhofsvorsteher *m*
sta·tion wag·on MOT Kombiwagen *m*
sta·tis·ti·cal statistisch
stat·is·ti·cian Statistiker *m*
sta·tis·tics Statistik(en *pl*) *f*
stat·ue Statue *f*, Standbild *n*
sta·tus Status *m*, Rechtsstellung *f*; (*Familien*)Stand *m*; Stellung *f*, Rang *m*, Status *m*; **~** *line* EDP Statuszeile *f*
stat·ute Gesetz *n*; Statut *n*, Satzung *f*
stat·ute of lim·i·ta·tions Verjährungsfrist *f*; *come under the* **~** verjähren
staunch[1] *Br* → **stanch**
staunch[2] *Blutung* stillen
stay 1. bleiben (*with* s.o. bei j-m); wohnen (*at* in *dat*; *with* s.o. bei j-m); **~** *put* F sich nicht (vom Fleck) rühren; **~** *away* wegbleiben, sich fern halten (*from* von); **~** *up* aufbleiben; **2.** Aufenthalt *m*; JUR Aussetzung *f*, Aufschub *m*
stead·fast treu, zuverlässig; fest
stead·y 1. *adj* fest; stabil; ruhig (*hand*), gut (*nerves*); gleichmäßig; **2.** (sich) beruhigen; **3.** *int a.* **~** *on!* Br F Vorsicht!; **4.** *adv*: *go* **~** *with s.o.* (fest) mit j-m gehen; **5.** feste Freundin, fester Freund
steak GASTR Steak *n*; (*Fisch*)Filet *n*
steal stehlen (*a. fig*); sich stehlen, (sich) schleichen (*out of* aus)
stealth: *by* **~** heimlich, verstohlen
stealth·y heimlich, verstohlen
steam 1. Dampf *m*; Dunst *m*; *let off* **~** Dampf ablassen, *fig a.* sich Luft machen; **2.** Dampf...; **3.** *v/i* dampfen; **~**

S

***up** beschlagen (*mirror etc*); *v/t* GASTR dünsten, dämpfen

steam·boat Dampfboot *n*, Dampfer *m*

steam·er Dampfer *m*, Dampfschiff *n*; Dampf-, Schnellkochtopf *m*

steam·ship Dampfer *m*, Dampfschiff *n*

steel 1. Stahl *m*; **2. ~ o.s. for** sich wappnen gegen

steel·work·er Stahlarbeiter *m*

steel·works Stahlwerk *n*

steep¹ steil; *fig* stark (*rise etc*); F happig

steep² eintauchen (**in** in *acc*); *Wäsche* (ein)weichen

stee·ple Kirchturm *m*

stee·ple·chase *horse racing*: Hindernisrennen *n*; SPORT Hindernislauf *m*

steer¹ ZO (junger) Ochse

steer² steuern, lenken

steer·ing col·umn MOT Lenksäule *f*

steer·ing wheel MOT Lenkrad *n*, *a.* MAR Steuerrad *n*

stein Maßkrug *m*

stem 1. BOT Stiel *m* (*a. of a wine glass etc*), Stängel *m*; LING Stamm *m*; **2. ~ from** stammen *or* herrühren von

stench Gestank *m*

sten·cil Schablone *f*; PRINT Matrize *f*

ste·nog·ra·pher Stenotypistin *f*

step 1. Schritt *m* (*a. fig*); Stufe *f*; Sprosse *f*; (**a pair of**) **~s** (e-e) Tritt- *or* Stufenleiter; **mind the ~!** Vorsicht, Stufe!; **~ by ~** Schritt für Schritt; **take ~s** Schritte *or* et. unternehmen; **2.** gehen; treten (**in** in *acc*; **on** auf *acc*); **~ on it**, **~ on the gas** MOT F Gas geben, auf die Tube drücken; **~ aside** zur Seite treten; *fig* Platz machen; **~ down** *fig* Platz machen; **~ up** Produktion *etc* steigern

step-by-step *fig* schrittweise

step·fa·ther Stiefvater *m*

step·lad·der Tritt-, Stufenleiter *f*

step·moth·er Stiefmutter *f*

steppes GEOGR Steppe *f*

step·ping-stone *fig* Sprungbrett *n* (**to** für)

ster·e·o 1. Stereo *n*; Stereogerät *n*, Stereoanlage *f*; **2.** Stereo...; **~ sys·tem** MUS Kompaktanlage *f*

ster·ile steril (*a. fig*), *a.* unfruchtbar, MED *a.* keimfrei

ste·ril·i·ty Sterilität *f* (*a. fig*), Unfruchtbarkeit *f*

ster·il·ize MED sterilisieren

ster·ling das Pfund Sterling

stern¹ streng

stern² MAR Heck *n*

stew 1. *Fleisch, Gemüse* schmoren, *Obst* dünsten; **~ed apples** Apfelkompott *n*; **2.** Eintopf *m*; **be in a ~** in heller Aufregung sein

stew·ard Ordner *m*; AVIAT, MAR Steward *m*

stew·ard·ess AVIAT, MAR Stewardess *f*

stick¹ trockener Zweig; Stock *m*; ([*Eis*]*Hockey*)Schläger *m*; (*Besenetc-*) Stiel *m*; AVIAT (*Steuer*)Knüppel *m*; Stück *n*, Stange *f*, (*Lippen- etc*)Stift *m*, Stäbchen *n*

stick² *v/t* mit e-r *Nadel etc* stechen (**into** in *acc*); *et*. kleben (**on** auf, an *acc*); ankleben (**with** mit); stecken; F tun, stellen, setzen, legen; **I can't ~ him** (*or* **it**) F ich kann ihn (*or* das) nicht ausstehen *or* leiden; *v/i* kleben; kleben bleiben (**to** an *dat*); stecken bleiben; **~ at nothing** vor nichts zurückschrecken; **~ by** F bleiben bei; F zu j-m halten; **~ out** vorstehen; abstehen; *et*. ausstrecken *or* vorstrecken; **~ to** bleiben bei

stick·er Aufkleber *m*

stick·ing plas·ter *Br* Heftpflaster *n*

stick·y klebrig (**with** von); F heikel, unangenehm

stiff 1. *adj* steif; F stark (*drink etc*); schwer, hart (*task, penalty etc*); hartnäckig (*resistance*); F happig, gepfeffert, gesalzen (*price*); **keep a ~ upper lip** *fig* Haltung bewahren; **2.** *adv* äußerst; höchst; **be bored ~** F sich zu Tode langweilen; **be scared ~** e-e wahnsinnige Angst haben; **be worried ~** sich furchtbare Sorgen machen

stiff·en *v/t Wäsche* steifen; versteifen; verstärken; *v/i* steif werden; sich verhärten *or* versteifen

sti·fle ersticken; *fig* unterdrücken

stile Zauntritt *m*

sti·let·to Stilett *n*; **~ heel** Bleistift-, Pfennigabsatz *m*

still¹ 1. *adv* (immer) noch, noch immer; *with comparative*: noch; **2.** *cj* dennoch, trotzdem

still² 1. *adj* still; ruhig; GASTR ohne Kohlensäure; **2.** *film*, TV Standfoto *n*

still·born MED tot geboren

still life PAINT Stillleben *n*

stilt Stelze *f*; **stilt·ed** *fig* gestelzt

stim·u·lant MED Stimulans *n*, Anregungs-, Aufputschmittel *n*; *fig* Anreiz *m*, Ansporn *m* (**to** für)

stim·u·late MED stimulieren (*a. fig*), anregen, *fig a.* anspornen

stim·u·lus Reiz *m*; *fig* Anreiz *m*, Ansporn *m* (**to** für)

sting 1. stechen (*insect*); brennen (auf *or* in *dat*); **2.** Stachel *m*; Stich *m*; Brennen *n*, brennender Schmerz

stin·gy F knaus(e)rig, knick(e)rig (*person*); mick(e)rig (*meal etc*)

stink 1. stinken (**of** nach); ~ **up** (*Br* **out**) verpesten; **2.** Gestank *m*

stint: ~ **o.s.** (**of s.th.**) sich einschränken (mit et.); ~ (**on**) **s.th.** sparen mit et.

stip·u·late zur Bedingung machen; festsetzen, vereinbaren; **stip·u·la·tion** Bedingung *f*; Vereinbarung *f*

stir 1. (um)rühren; (sich) rühren *or* bewegen; *j-n* aufwühlen; ~ **up** Unruhe stiften; *Streit* entfachen; *Erinnerungen* wachrufen; **2. give s.th. a** ~ et. umrühren; *cause* (*or create*) **a** ~ für Aufsehen sorgen

stir·rup Steigbügel *m*

stitch 1. Stich *m*; Masche *f*; MED Seitenstechen *n*; **2.** zunähen, *Wunde* nähen (*a.* ~ **up**); heften

stock 1. Vorrat *m* (**of** an *dat*); GASTR Brühe *f*; *a.* **live-** Viehbestand *m*; (*Gewehr*)Schaft *m*; *fig* Abstammung *f*, Herkunft *f*; ECON Aktie(n *pl*) *f*; *pl* Aktien *pl*, Wertpapiere *pl*; **have s.th. in** ~ ECON et. vorrätig *or* auf Lager haben; *take* ~ ECON Inventur machen; *take* ~ *of* sich klar werden über (*acc*); **2.** ECON *Ware* vorrätig haben, führen; ~ **up** sich eindecken *or* versorgen (**on**, **with** mit); **3.** Serien...; Standard...; stereotyp

stock·breed·er AGR Viehzüchter *m*

stock·breed·ing AGR Viehzucht *f*

stock·brok·er ECON Börsenmakler *m*

stock ex·change ECON Börse *f*

stock·hold·er ECON Aktionär(in)

stock·ing Strumpf *m*

stock mar·ket ECON Börse *f*

stock·pile 1. Vorrat *m* (**of** an *dat*); **2.** e-n Vorrat anlegen an (*dat*)

stock-still regungslos

stock·tak·ing ECON Inventur *f*, *fig* Bestandsaufnahme *f*

stock·y stämmig, untersetzt

stol·id gleichmütig

stom·ach 1. ANAT Magen *m*; Bauch *m*; *fig* Appetit *m* (**for** auf *acc*); **2.** vertragen (*a. fig*)

stom·ach·ache MED Magenschmerzen *pl*, Bauchschmerzen *pl*, Bauchweh *n*

stom·ach up·set MED Magenverstimmung *f*

stone 1. Stein *m*, BOT *a.* Kern *m*; (*Hagel*)Korn *n*; **2.** mit Steinen bewerfen; steinigen; entkernen, entsteinen

stone·ma·son Steinmetz *m*

stone·ware Steingut *n*

ston·y steinig; steinern (*face etc*), eisig (*silence*)

stool Hocker *m*, Schemel *m*; MED Stuhl *m*, Stuhlgang *m*

stool·pi·geon F (Polizei)Spitzel *m*

stoop 1. *v/i* sich bücken (*a.* ~ **down**); gebeugt gehen; ~ **to** *fig* sich herablassen *or* hergeben zu; **2.** gebeugte Haltung

stop 1. *v/i* (an)halten, stehen bleiben (*a.* *watch etc*), stoppen; aufhören; *esp Br* bleiben; ~ **dead** plötzlich *or* abrupt stehen bleiben; ~ **at nothing** vor nichts zurückschrecken; ~ **short of** doing, ~ **short at** *s.th.* zurückschrecken vor (*dat*); *v/t* anhalten, stoppen; aufhören mit; ein Ende machen *or* setzen (*dat*); *Blutung* stillen; *Arbeiten, Verkehr etc* zum Erliegen bringen; et. verhindern; *j-n* abhalten (**from** von), hindern (**from** an *dat*); *Rohr etc* verstopfen (*a.* ~ **up**); *Zahn* füllen, plombieren; *Scheck* sperren (lassen); ~ **by** vorbeischauen; ~ **in** vorbeischauen (**at** bei); ~ **off** F kurz Halt machen; ~ **over** kurz Halt machen; Zwischenstation machen; **2.** Halt *m*; (*Bus*)Haltestelle *f*, PHOT Blende *f*; *mst* **full** ~ LING Punkt *m*

stop·gap Notbehelf *m*

stop·light MOT Bremslicht *n*; rotes Licht

stop·o·ver Zwischenstation *f*; AVIAT Zwischenlandung *f*

stop·page Unterbrechung *f*, Stopp *m*; Verstopfung *f*; Streik *m*; *Br* (Gehalts-, Lohn)Abzug *m*

stop·per Stöpsel *m*

stop sign MOT Stoppschild *n*

stop·watch Stoppuhr *f*

stor·age ECON Lagerung *f*, Lagergeld *n*; EDP Speicher *m*

store 1. (ein)lagern; *Energie* speichern;

S

EDP (ab)speichern, sichern; *a.* **~ up** sich e-n Vorrat anlegen an (*dat*); **2.** Vorrat *m*; Lager *n*, Lagerhalle *f*, Lagerhaus *n*; Laden *m*, Geschäft *n*, *esp Br* Kaufhaus *n*, Warenhaus *n*; **set great ~ by** großen Wert legen auf (*acc*)

store·house Lagerhaus *n*; *fig* Fundgrube *f*

store·keep·er Ladenbesitzer(in)

store·room Lagerraum *m*

sto·rey *Br* → **story²**

...sto·reyed *Br*, **...sto·ried** mit ... Stockwerken, ...stöckig

stork ZO Storch *m*

storm 1. Unwetter *n*; Gewitter *n*; Sturm *m*; **2.** *v/t* MIL *etc* stürmen; *v/i* stürmen, stürzen; **storm·y** stürmisch

sto·ry¹ Geschichte *f*; Märchen *n* (*a. fig*); Story *f, a.* Handlung *f, a.* Bericht *m* (**on** über *acc*)

sto·ry² Stock *m*, Stockwerk *n*, Etage *f*

stout korpulent, vollschlank; *fig* unerschrocken; entschieden

stove Ofen *m*, Herd *m*

stow *a.* **~ away** verstauen

stow·a·way AVIAT, MAR blinder Passagier

strad·dle rittlings sitzen auf (*dat*)

strag·gle verstreut liegen *or* stehen; BOT *etc* wuchern; **~ in** F einzeln eintrudeln

strag·gler Nachzügler(in)

strag·gly verstreut (*liegend*), BOT *etc* wuchernd; struppig (*mustache etc*)

straight 1. *adj* gerade; glatt (*hair*); pur (*whisky etc*); aufrichtig, offen, ehrlich; *sl* hetero(*sexuell*); *sl* clean, sauber; **put ~** in Ordnung bringen; **2.** *adv* gerade; genau, direkt; klar; ehrlich, anständig; **~ ahead** geradeaus; **~ off** F sofort; **~ on** geradeaus; **~ out** F offen, rundheraus; **3.** SPORT (*Gegen-, Ziel*)Gerade *f*

straight·en *v/t* gerade machen, (gerade) richten; **~ out** in Ordnung bringen; *v/i a.* **~ out** gerade werden; **~ up** sich aufrichten

straight·for·ward aufrichtig; einfach

strain 1. *v/t* Seil *etc* (an)spannen; sich, Augen *etc* überanstrengen; sich *im* Muskel *etc* zerren; Gemüse, Tee *etc* abgießen; *v/i* sich anstrengen; **~ at** zerren *or* ziehen an (*dat*); **2.** Spannung *f*, Anspannung *f*; Strapaze *f*; *fig* Belastung *f*; MED Zerrung *f*; **strained** MED gezerrt;

gezwungen (*smile etc*); gespannt (*relations*); **look ~** abgespannt aussehen

strain·er Sieb *n*

strait GEOGR Meerenge *f*, Straße *f*; *pl fig* Notlage *f*

strait·ened: live in ~ circumstances in beschränkten Verhältnissen leben

strand Strang *m*; Faden *m*; (*Kabel-*) Draht *m*; (*Haar*)Strähne *f*

strand·ed: be ~ MAR gestrandet sein; **be (left) ~** festsitzen (**in** in *dat*)

strange merkwürdig, seltsam, sonderbar; fremd; **strang·er** Fremde *m, f*

stran·gle erwürgen

strap 1. Riemen *m*, Gurt *m*; (*Uhr*)Armband *n*; Träger *m*; **2.** festschnallen; anschnallen

stra·te·gic strategisch

strat·e·gy Strategie *f*

stra·tum GEOL Schicht *f* (*a. fig*)

straw Stroh *n*; Strohhalm *m*

straw·ber·ry BOT Erdbeere *f*

stray 1. (herum)streunen; sich verirren; *fig* abschweifen (**from** von); **2.** verirrtes *or* streunendes Tier; **3.** verirrt (*bullet, dog etc*); streunend (*dog etc*); vereinzelt

streak 1. Streifen *m*; Strähne *f*; (*Charakter*)Zug *m*; **a ~ of lightning** ein Blitz; **lucky ~** Glückssträhne *f*; **2.** flitzen; streifen

streak·y streifig; GASTR durchwachsen

stream 1. Bach *m*; Strömung *f*; *fig* Strom *m*; **2.** strömen; flattern, wehen

stream·er Luft-, Papierschlange *f*; Wimpel *m*; EDP Streamer *m*

street 1. Straße *f*; **on** (*esp Br* **in**) **the ~** auf der Straße; **2.** Straßen...

street·car Straßenbahn(wagen *m*) *f*

street sweep·er Straßenkehrer *m*

strength Stärke *f*, Kraft *f*, Kräfte *pl*

strength·en *v/t* (ver)stärken; *v/i* stärker werden

stren·u·ous anstrengend, strapaziös; unermüdlich

stress 1. *fig* Stress *m*; PHYS, TECH Beanspruchung *f*, Belastung *f*, Druck *m*; LING Betonung *f*; *fig* Nachdruck *m*; **2.** betonen

stress·ful stressig, aufreibend

stretch 1. *v/t* strecken; (aus)weiten, dehnen; spannen; *fig* es nicht allzu genau nehmen mit; **~ out** ausstrecken; **be fully ~ed** *fig* richtig gefordert werden; voll ausgelastet sein; *v/i* sich dehnen, *a.*

länger *or* weiter werden; sich dehnen *or* recken *or* strecken; sich erstrecken; **~ out** sich ausstrecken; **2.** Dehnbarkeit *f*, Elastizität *f*; Strecke *f*; SPORT (*Gegen-, Ziel*)Gerade *f*; Zeit *f*, Zeitraum *m*, Zeitspanne *f*; **have a ~** sich dehnen *or* recken *or* strecken

stretch·er Trage *f*

strick·en schwer betroffen; **~ with** befallen *or* ergriffen von

strict streng, strikt; genau; **~ly (speaking)** genau genommen

strict·ness Strenge *f*

stride 1. schreiten, mit großen Schritten gehen; **2.** großer Schritt

strife Streit *m*

strike 1. *v/t* schlagen; treffen; einschlagen in (*acc*) (*lightning*); Streichholz anzünden; MAR auflaufen auf (*acc*); streichen (*from, off* aus *dat*, von); stoßen auf (*acc*); j-n beeindrucken; j-m einfallen, in den Sinn kommen; *Münze* prägen; *Saite etc* anschlagen; *Lager, Zelt* abbrechen; *Flagge, Segel* streichen; **~ out** (aus)streichen; **~ up** *Lied etc* anstimmen; *Freundschaft etc* schließen; *v/i* schlagen; einschlagen; ECON streiken; **~ (out) at s.o.** auf j-n einschlagen; **2.** ECON Streik *m*; (*Öl-etc*)Fund *m*; MIL Angriff *m*; *soccer:* Schuss *m*; **be on ~** streiken; **go on ~** streiken, in den Streik treten; **a lucky ~** ein Glückstreffer

strik·er ECON Streikende *m, f; soccer:* Stürmer(in)

strik·ing apart; auffallend

string 1. Schnur *f*, Bindfaden *m*; (*Schürzen-, Schuh- etc*)Band *n*; (*Puppenspiel-*) Faden *m*, Draht *m*; (*Perlenetc*)Schnur *f*; MUS, SPORT Saite *f*; (*Bogen*)Sehne *f*; BOT Faser *f*; EDP Zeichenfolge *f*, *fig* Reihe *f*, Serie *f*; **the ~s** MUS die Streichinstrumente *pl*, die Streicher *pl*; **pull a few ~s** *fig* ein paar Beziehungen spielen lassen; **with no ~s attached** *fig* ohne Bedingungen; **2.** *Perlen etc* aufreihen; *Gitarre etc* besaiten, *Tennisschläger etc* bespannen; *Bohnen* abziehen; **3.** MUS Streich…; **~ bean** BOT grüne Bohne

strin·gent streng

string·y fas(e)rig

strip 1. *v/i: a.* **~ off** sich ausziehen (**to** bis auf *acc*); *v/t* ausziehen; *Farbe etc* abkratzen, *Tapete etc* abreißen (**from, off** von); *a.* **~ down** TECH zerlegen, auseinander nehmen; **~ s.o. of s.th.** j-m et. rauben *or* wegnehmen; **2.** (*Land-, Papier- etc*)Streifen *m*; Strip *m*

stripe Streifen *m*; **striped** gestreift

strive: ~ for *or* **after** streben nach

stroke 1. streicheln; streichen über (*acc*); **2.** Schlag *m* (*a.* SPORT); MED Schlag(anfall) *m*; (*Pinsel-*)Strich *m*; *swimming:* Zug *m*; TECH Hub *m*; → **four-stroke engine; ~ of lightning** Blitzschlag *m*; **a ~ of luck** *fig* ein glücklicher Zufall, ein Glücksfall

stroll 1. bummeln, spazieren; **2.** Bummel *m*, Spaziergang *m*

stroll·er Bummler(in), Spaziergänger(in); Sportwagen *m*

strong stark (*a.* GASTR, PHARM); kräftig; mächtig; stabil; fest; robust

strong·box (Geld-, Stahl)Kassette *f*

strong·hold Festung *f*; Stützpunkt *m*; *fig* Hochburg *f*

strong-mind·ed willensstark

strong room Tresor(raum) *m*

struc·ture Struktur *f*; (Auf)Bau *m*, Gliederung *f*; Bau *m*, Konstruktion *f*

strug·gle 1. kämpfen, ringen (**with** mit; **for** um); sich abmühen; sich winden, zappeln; **~ against** sich sträuben gegen; **2.** Kampf *m*

strum klimpern auf (*dat*) (*or* **on** auf *dat*)

strut¹ stolzieren

strut² TECH Strebe *f*; Stütze *f*

stub 1. (*Bleistift-, Zigaretten- etc*)Stummel *m*; Kontrollabschnitt *m*; **2.** sich die Zehe anstoßen; **~ out** Zigarette ausdrücken

stub·ble Stoppeln *pl*

stub·bly stoppelig

stub·born eigensinnig, stur; hartnäckig

stub·born·ness Starrsinn *m*

stuck-up F hochnäsig

stud¹ 1. (*Kragen-, Manschetten*)Knopf *m; soccer:* Stollen *m*; Beschlagnagel *m*; Ziernagel *m*; *pl* MOT Spikes *pl*; **2. be ~ded with** besetzt sein mit; übersät sein mit; **~ded tires** Spikesreifen *pl*

stud² Gestüt *n*

stu·dent Student(in); Schüler(in)

stud farm Gestüt *n*

stud horse ZO Zuchthengst *m*

stud·ied wohl überlegt; gesucht

stu·di·o Studio *n*; Atelier *n*; *a.* **~ apart-**

ment, *Br* ~ **flat** Studio *n*, Einzimmer-appartement *n*; ~ **couch** Schlafcouch *f*

stu·di·ous fleißig

stud·y 1. Studium *n*; Studie *f*, Untersuchung *f*; Arbeitszimmer *n*; *pl* Studium *n*; **be in a brown** ~ in Gedanken versunken *or* geistesabwesend sein; **2.** studieren; lernen (**for** für)

stuff 1. Zeug *n*; **2.** (aus)stopfen, (voll) stopfen; füllen (*a.* GASTR.); ~ **o.s.** F sich voll stopfen; **stuff·ing** Füllung *f* (*a.* GASTR.)

stuff·y stickig; spießig; prüde

stum·ble 1. stolpern (**on**, **over**, *fig* **at**, **over** über *acc*); ~ **across**, ~ **on** stoßen auf (*acc*); **2.** Stolpern *n*

stump 1. Stumpf *m*; Stummel *m*; **2.** stampfen, stapfen

stump·y F kurz und dick

stun betäuben; *fig* sprachlos machen

stun·ning fantastisch; unglaublich

stunt¹ (*das Wachstum gen*) hemmen; ~**ed** BIOL verkümmert; **become** ~**ed** BIOL verkümmern

stunt² (*Film*)Stunt *m*; (*gefährliches*) Kunststück; (*Reklame*)Gag *m*

stunt| man *film*, TV Stuntman *m*, Double *m*; ~ **wom·an** *film*, TV Stuntwoman *f*, Double *n*

stu·pid dumm; F blöd

stu·pid·i·ty Dummheit *f*

stu·por Betäubung *f*; **in a drunken** ~ im Vollrausch

stur·dy kräftig, stämmig; *fig* entschlossen, hartnäckig

stut·ter 1. stottern (*a.* MOT); stammeln; **2.** Stottern *n*, Stammeln *n*

sty¹ → **pigsty**

sty², **stye** MED Gerstenkorn *n*

style 1. Stil *m*; Ausführung *f*; Mode *f*; **2.** entwerfen; gestalten

styl·ish stilvoll; modisch, elegant

styl·ist Stilist(in)

Sty·ro·foam® Styropor® *n*

suave verbindlich

sub·con·scious Unterbewusstsein *n*; ~**ly** im Unterbewusstsein

sub·di·vi·sion Unterteilung *f*, Unterabteilung *f*

sub·due unterwerfen; *Ärger etc* unterdrücken; **sub·dued** gedämpft (*light*, *voice etc*); ruhig, still (*person*)

sub·ject 1. Thema *n*; PED, UNIV Fach *n*; LING Subjekt *n*, Satzgegenstand *m*;

Untertan(in); Staatsangehörige *m*, *f*, -bürger(in); **2** *adj:* ~ **to** anfällig für; **be** ~ **to** *a.* neigen zu; **be** ~ **to** unterliegen (*dat*); abhängen von; **prices** ~ **to change** Preisänderungen vorbehalten; **3.** unterwerfen; ~ **to** e-m Test etc unterziehen; *der Kritik etc* aussetzen

sub·jec·tion Unterwerfung *f*; Abhängigkeit *f* (**to** von)

sub·ju·gate unterjochen, unterwerfen

sub·junc·tive LING *a.* ~ **mood** Konjunktiv *m*

sub·lease, **sub·let** untervermieten, weitervermieten

sub·lime großartig; *fig* total

sub·ma·chine gun Maschinenpistole *f*

sub·ma·rine 1. unterseeisch; **2.** Unterseeboot *n*, U-Boot *n*

sub·merge tauchen; (ein)tauchen (**in** *in acc*)

sub·mis·sion Einreichung *f*; *boxing etc*: Aufgabe *f*; Unterwerfung *f* (**to** unter); **sub·mis·sive** unterwürfig

sub·mit *Gesuch etc* einreichen (**to** *dat or* bei); sich fügen (**to** *dat or* in *acc*); *boxing etc*: aufgeben

sub·or·di·nate 1. untergeordnet (**to** *dat*); **2.** Untergebene *m*, *f*; **3.** ~ **to** unterordnen (*dat*), zurückstellen (hinter *acc*); ~ **clause** LING Nebensatz *m*

sub·scribe *v/t* Geld gegen, spenden (**to** für); *v/i:* ~ **to** *Zeitung etc* abonnieren; **sub·scrib·er** Abonnent(in); TEL Teilnehmer(in); **sub·scrip·tion** Abonnement *n*; (Mitglieds)Beitrag *m*

sub·se·quent später

sub·side sich senken (*building*, *road etc*); zurückgehen (*flood*, *demand etc*), sich legen (*storm*, *anger etc*)

sub·sid·i·a·ry 1. Neben...; ~ **question** Zusatzfrage *f*; **2.** ECON Tochtergesellschaft *f*

sub·si·dize subventionieren

sub·si·dy Subvention *f*

sub·sist leben, existieren (**on** von)

sub·sis·tence Existenz *f*

sub·stance Substanz *f* (*a. fig*), Stoff *m*; *das* Wesentliche, Kern *m*

sub·stan·dard minderwertig

sub·stan·tial solid (*furniture etc*); beträchtlich (*salary etc*), (*changes etc a.*) wesentlich; reichlich, kräftig (*meal*)

sub·stan·ti·ate beweisen

sub·stan·tive LING Substantiv *n*, Hauptwort *n*

sub·sti·tute 1. Ersatz *m*; Stellvertreter(in), Vertreter *f*; SPORT Auswechselspieler(in), Ersatzspieler(in); **2. ~ s.th. for s.th.** et. durch et. ersetzen, et. gegen et. austauschen *or* auswechseln; **~ for** einspringen für, *j-n* vertreten

sub·sti·tu·tion Ersatz *m*; SPORT Austausch *m*, Auswechslung *f*

sub·ter·fuge List *f*

sub·ter·ra·ne·an unterirdisch

sub·ti·tle Untertitel *m*

sub·tle fein (*differences etc*); raffiniert (*plan etc*); scharf (*mind*); scharfsinnig

sub·tract MATH abziehen, subtrahieren (*from* von); **sub·trac·tion** MATH Abziehen *n*, Subtraktion *f*

sub·trop·i·cal subtropisch

sub·urb Vorort *m*, Vorstadt *f*

sub·ur·ban Vorort..., vorstädtisch, Vorstadt...

sub·ver·sive umstürzlerisch, subversiv

sub·way Unterführung *f*; U-Bahn *f*

suc·ceed *v/i* Erfolg haben, erfolgreich sein, (*plan etc a.*) gelingen; **~ to** in e-m Amt nachfolgen; **~ to the throne** auf dem Thron folgen; *v/t:* **~ s.o. as** j-s Nachfolger werden als

suc·cess Erfolg *m*

suc·cess·ful erfolgreich

suc·ces·sion Folge *f*; Erb-, Nach-, Thronfolge *f*; **five times in** ~ fünfmal hintereinander; **in quick** ~ in rascher Folge; **suc·ces·sive** aufeinander folgend; **suc·ces·sor** Nachfolger(in); Thronfolger(in)

suc·cu·lent GASTR saftig

such solche(r, -s); derartige(r, -s); so; derart; **~ a** so ein(e)

suck 1. *v/t* saugen; lutschen (an *dat*); *v/i* saugen (*at* an *dat*); **2. have** *or* **take a ~ at** saugen *or* lutschen an (*dat*)

suck·er ZO Saugnapf *m*, Saugorgan *n*; TECH Saugfuß *m*; BOT Wurzelschössling *m*, Wurzelspross *m*; F Trottel *m*, Simpel *m*; Lutscher *m*

suck·le säugen, stillen

suc·tion (An)Saugen *n*; Saugwirkung *f*; **~ pump** TECH Saugpumpe *f*

sud·den plötzlich, unvermittelt; **all of a ~** F ganz plötzlich

sud·den·ly plötzlich

suds Seifenschaum *m*

sue JUR *j-n* verklagen (**for** auf *acc*, wegen); klagen (**for** auf *acc*)

suede, suède Wildleder *n*, Velours(-leder) *n*

su·et GASTR Nierenfett *n*, Talg *m*

suf·fer *v/i* leiden (**from** an *dat*, unter *dat*); darunter leiden; *v/t* erleiden; *Folgen* tragen; **suf·fer·er** Leidende *m*, *f*; **suf·fer·ing** Leiden *n*; Leid *n*

suf·fi·cient genügend, genug, ausreichend; **be** ~ genügen, (aus)reichen

suf·fix LING Suffix *n*, Nachsilbe *f*

suf·fo·cate ersticken

suf·frage POL Wahl-, Stimmrecht *n*

suf·fuse durchfluten (*light etc*); überziehen (*color etc*)

sug·ar 1. Zucker *m*; **2.** zuckern

sug·ar beet BOT Zuckerrübe *f*

sug·ar bowl Zuckerdose *f*

sug·ar·cane BOT Zuckerrohr *n*

sug·ar tongs Zuckerzange *f*

sug·ar·y süß; *fig* süßlich

sug·gest vorschlagen, anregen; hindeuten *or* hinweisen auf (*acc*), schließen lassen auf (*acc*); andeuten

sug·ges·tion Vorschlag *m*, Anregung *f*; Anflug *m*, Spur *f*; Andeutung *f*; PSYCH Suggestion *f*

sug·ges·tive zweideutig (*remark etc*), viel sagend (*look etc*)

su·i·cide Selbstmord *m*; Selbstmörder(in); **commit** ~ Selbstmord begehen

suit 1. Anzug *m*; Kostüm *n*; *card game:* Farbe *f*; JUR Prozess *m*; **follow** ~ *fig* dem Beispiel folgen, dasselbe tun; **2.** *v/t* *j-m* passen (*date etc*); *j-n* kleiden, *j-m* stehen; et. anpassen (**to** *dat*); **~ s.th., be ~ed to s.th.** geeignet sein *or* sich eignen für; **~ yourself!** mach, was du willst!

sui·ta·ble passend, geeignet (**for, to** für)

suit·case Koffer *m*

suite (*Möbel-, Sitz*)Garnitur *f*; Suite *f*; Zimmerflucht *f*; MUS Suite *f*; Gefolge *n*

sul·fur CHEM Schwefel *m*

sul·fu·ric ac·id CHEM Schwefelsäure *f*

sulk schmollen, F eingeschnappt sein

sulk·y schmollend, F eingeschnappt

sul·len mürrisch, verdrossen

sul·phur *Br* → **sulfur**

sul·phu·ric ac·id *Br* → **sulfuric acid**

sul·try schwül; aufreizend (*look etc*)

sum 1. Summe *f*; Betrag *m*; (einfache)

Rechenaufgabe; **do ~s** rechnen; **2. ~ up** zusammenfassen; *j-n, et* abschätzen

sum·mar·ize zusammenfassen

sum·ma·ry Zusammenfassung *f*, (kurze) Inhaltsangabe

sum·mer Sommer *m*; **in (the)** ~ im Sommer; **~ camp** Ferienlager *n*; **~ hol·i·days** *Br* Sommerferien *pl*; **~ resort** Sommerfrische *f*; **~ school** Ferienkurs *m*

sum·mer·time Sommer *m*, Sommerszeit *f*; **in (the)** ~ im Sommer

sum·mer| time *esp Br* Sommerzeit *f*; **~ va·ca·tion** Sommerferien *pl*

sum·mer·y sommerlich, Sommer...

sum·mit Gipfel *m* (*a.* ECON, POL, *fig*); **~ con·fe·rence** POL Gipfelkonferenz *f*; **~ meet·ing** POL Gipfeltreffen *n*

sum·mon auffordern; *Versammlung etc* einberufen; JUR vorladen; **~ up** Kraft, *Mut etc* zusammennehmen

sum·mons JUR Vorladung *f*

sump *Br* MOT Ölwanne *f*

sump·tu·ous luxuriös, aufwändig

sun 1. Sonne *f*; **2.** Sonnen...; **3. ~ o.s.** sich sonnen

Sun ABBR *of* **Sunday** So., Sonntag *m*

sun·bathe sich sonnen, ein Sonnenbad nehmen

sun·beam Sonnenstrahl *m*

sun·bed Sonnenbank *f*

sun·burn Sonnenbrand *m*

sun cream Sonnencreme *f*

sun·dae GASTR Eisbecher *m*

Sun·day (ABBR **Sun**) Sonntag *m*; **on** ~ (am) Sonntag; **on ~s** sonntags

sun·di·al Sonnenuhr *f*

sun·dries Diverses, Verschiedenes

sun·dry diverse, verschiedene

sun·glass·es (**a pair of** ~ e-e) Sonnenbrille *f*

sunk·en MAR gesunken, versunken; versenkt; tief liegend; eingefallen (*cheeks*), (*a.* eyes) eingesunken

sun·light Sonnenlicht *n*

sun·lit sonnenbeschienen

sun·ny sonnig

sun·rise Sonnenaufgang *m*; **at** ~ bei Sonnenaufgang

sun·roof Dachterrasse *f*; MOT Schiebedach *n*

sun·set Sonnenuntergang *m*; **at** ~ bei Sonnenuntergang

sun·shade Sonnenschirm *m*

sun·shine Sonnenschein *m*

sun·stroke MED Sonnenstich *m*

sun·tan (Sonnen)Bräune *f*; **~ lo·tion** Sonnenschutz *m*, Sonnencreme *f*; **~ oil** Sonnenöl *n*

su·per F super, spitze, klasse

su·per... Über..., über...

su·per·a·bun·dant überreichlich

su·per·an·nu·at·ed pensioniert, im Ruhestand

su·perb ausgezeichnet

su·per·charg·er MOT Kompressor *m*

su·per·cil·i·ous hochmütig, F hochnäsig

su·per·fi·cial oberflächlich

su·per·flu·ous überflüssig

su·per·hu·man übermenschlich

su·per·im·pose überlagern; *Bild etc* einblenden (**on** in *acc*)

su·per·in·tend die (Ober)Aufsicht haben über (*acc*), überwachen; leiten

su·per·in·tend·ent Aufsicht *f*, Aufsichtsbeamter *m*, -beamtin *f*; *Br* Kriminalrat *m*

su·pe·ri·or 1. ranghöher (**to** als); überlegen (**to** *dat*), besser (**to** als); ausgezeichnet, hervorragend; überheblich, überlegen; **Father Superior** REL Superior *m*; **Mother Superior** REL Oberin *f*; **2.** Vorgesetzte *m, f*; **su·pe·ri·or·i·ty** Überlegenheit *f* (**over** gegenüber)

su·per·la·tive 1. höchste(r, -s), überragend; **2.** *a.* **~ degree** LING Superlativ *m*

su·per·mar·ket Supermarkt *m*

su·per·nat·u·ral übernatürlich

su·per·nu·me·ra·ry zusätzlich

su·per·sede ablösen, ersetzen, verdrängen

su·per·son·ic AVIAT, PHYS Überschall...

su·per·sti·tion Aberglaube *m*

su·per·sti·tious abergläubisch

su·per·store Großmarkt *m*

su·per·vene dazwischenkommen

su·per·vise beaufsichtigen, überwachen; **su·per·vi·sion** Beaufsichtigung *f*, Überwachung *f*; **under s.o.'s** ~ unter j-s Aufsicht; **su·per·vi·sor** Aufseher(in), Aufsicht *f*

sup·per Abendessen *n*; **have** ~ zu Abend essen; → **lord**

sup·plant verdrängen

sup·ple gelenkig, geschmeidig, biegsam

sup·ple·ment 1. Ergänzung *f*; Nachtrag

m, Anhang *m*; Ergänzungsband *m*; (*Zeitungs- etc*)Beilage *f*; **2.** ergänzen; **sup·ple·men·ta·ry** ergänzend, zusätzlich

sup·pli·er ECON Lieferant(in), *a. pl* Lieferfirma *f*

sup·ply 1. liefern; stellen, sorgen für; *j-n, et.* versorgen, ECON beliefern (**with** mit); **2.** Lieferung *f* (**to** an *acc*); Versorgung *f*, ECON Angebot *n*; *mst pl* Vorrat *m* (**of** an *dat*), *a.* Proviant *m*, MIL Nachschub *m*; **~ and demand** ECON Angebot und Nachfrage

sup·port 1. (ab)stützen, *Gewicht etc* tragen; *Währung* stützen; unterstützen; unterhalten, sorgen für; **2.** Stütze *f*; TECH Träger *m*; *fig* Unterstützung *f*

sup·port·er Anhänger(in) (*a.* SPORT), Befürworter(in)

sup·pose 1. annehmen, vermuten; **be ~d to ...** sollen; **what is that ~d to mean?** was soll denn das?; *I ~ so* ich nehme es an, vermutlich; **2.** *cj* angenommen; wie wäre es, wenn

sup·posed angeblich, vermeintlich

sup·pos·ing → **suppose** 2

sup·po·si·tion Annahme *f*, Vermutung *f*

sup·pos·i·to·ry PHARM Zäpfchen *n*

sup·press unterdrücken

sup·pres·sion Unterdrückung *f*

sup·pu·rate MED eitern

su·prem·a·cy Vormachtstellung *f*

su·preme höchste(r, -s), oberste(r, -s), Ober...; größte(r, -s)

sur·charge 1. Nachporto *or* e-n Zuschlag erheben (**on** auf *acc*); **2.** Aufschlag *m*, Zuschlag *m* (**on** auf *acc*); Nach-, Strafporto *n* (**on** auf *acc*)

sure 1. *adj* sicher; *of o.s.* selbstsicher; **~ of winning** siegessicher; **~ thing!** F (aber) klar!; **be** *or* **feel ~** sicher sein; **be ~ to ...** vergiss nicht zu ...; **for ~** ganz sicher *or* bestimmt; **make ~ that** sich (davon) überzeugen, dass; **to be ~** sicher(lich); **2.** *adv* F sicher, klar; **~ enough** tatsächlich

sure·ly sicher(lich)

sure·ty JUR Bürge *m*, Bürgin *f*; Bürgschaft *f*, Sicherheit *f*; **stand ~ for s.o.** für j-n bürgen

surf 1. Brandung *f*; **2.** SPORT surfen

sur·face 1. Oberfläche *f*; (*Straßen*)Belag *m*; **2.** auftauchen; *Straße* mit e-m Belag

versehen; **3.** Oberflächen...; *fig* oberflächlich; **~ mail** gewöhnliche Post

surf·board Surfboard *n*, Surfbrett *n*

surf·er Surfer(in), Wellenreiter(in)

surf·ing Surfen *n*, Wellenreiten *n*

surge 1. *fig* Welle *f*, Woge *f*, (*Gefühls*)Aufwallung *f*; **2.** (vorwärts) drängen; **~ (up)** aufwallen

sur·geon MED Chirurg(in)

sur·ge·ry MED Chirurgie *f*; operativer Eingriff, Operation *f*; *Br* Sprechzimmer *n*; *Br* Sprechstunde *f*; *a.* **doctor's ~** Arztpraxis *f*; **~ hours** MED *Br* Sprechstunde(n) *pl*) *f*

sur·gi·cal MED chirurgisch

sur·ly mürrisch, unwirsch

sur·name Familienname *m*, Nachname *m*, Zuname *m*

sur·pass *Erwartungen etc* übertreffen

sur·plus 1. Überschuss *m* (**of** an *dat*); **2.** überschüssig

sur·prise 1. Überraschung *f*, Verwunderung *f*; **take s.o. by ~** j-n überraschen; **2.** überraschen; **be ~d at** *or* **by** überrascht sein über (*acc*)

sur·ren·der 1. *v/i* **~ to** MIL, *a. fig* sich ergeben (*dat*), kapitulieren vor (*dat*); **~ to the police** sich der Polizei stellen; *v/t et.* übergeben, ausliefern (*to dat*); aufgeben, verzichten auf (*acc*); **~ o.s. to the police** sich der Polizei stellen; **2.** MIL Kapitulation *f* (*a. fig*); Aufgabe *f*, Verzicht *m*

sur·ro·gate Ersatz *m*

sur·ro·gate moth·er Leihmutter *f*

sur·round umgeben; umstellen

sur·round·ing umliegend

sur·round·ings Umgebung *f*

sur·vey 1. (sich) *et.* betrachten (*a. fig*); *Haus etc* begutachten; *Land* vermessen; **2.** Umfrage *f*; Überblick *m* (**of** über *acc*); Begutachtung *f*; Vermessung *f*

sur·vey·or Gutachter *m*; Land(ver)messer *m*

sur·viv·al Überleben *n* (*a. fig*); Überbleibsel *n*; **~ in·stinct** Selbsterhaltungstrieb *m*; **~ kit** Überlebensausrüstung *f*; **~ train·ing** Überlebenstraining *n*

sur·vive überleben; *Feuer etc* überstehen; erhalten bleiben *or* sein

sur·vi·vor Überlebende *m, f* (**from, of** gen)

S

sus·cep·ti·ble empfänglich, anfällig (*both*: **to** für)

sus·pect 1. *v/t* *j-n* verdächtigen (*of* gen); *et.* vermuten; *et.* anzweifeln, *et.* bezweifeln; **2.** Verdächtige *m, f*; **3.** verdächtig, suspekt

sus·pend *Verkauf, Zahlungen etc* (vorübergehend) einstellen; JUR *Verfahren, Urteil* aussetzen; *Strafe* zur Bewährung aussetzen; *j-n* suspendieren; vorübergehend ausschließen (**from** aus); SPORT *j-n* sperren; (auf)hängen; **~ed** schweben; **sus·pend·er** *Br* Strumpfhalter *m*, Straps *m*; Sockenhalter *m*; (*a.* **a pair of**) **~s** Hosenträger *pl*

sus·pense Spannung *f*; **in ~** gespannt, voller Spannung

sus·pen·sion (vorübergehende) Einstellung; Suspendierung *f*; vorübergehender Ausschluss; SPORT Sperre *f*; MOT *etc* Aufhängung *f*; **~ bridge** Hängebrücke *f*; **~ rail·way** *esp Br* Schwebebahn *f*

sus·pi·cion Verdacht *m*; Verdächtigung *f*, Argwohn *m*, Misstrauen *n*; *fig* Hauch *m*, Spur *f*; **sus·pi·cious** verdächtig; argwöhnisch, misstrauisch; **become ~** Verdacht schöpfen

sus·tain *j-n* stärken; *Interesse etc* aufrechterhalten; *Schaden, Verlust* erleiden; JUR *e-m Einspruch etc* stattgeben

swab MED **1.** Tupfer *m*; Abstrich *m*; **2.** *Wunde* abtupfen

swad·dle *Baby* wickeln

swag·ger stolzieren

swal·low¹ 1. schlucken (*a.* F); hinunterschlucken; **~ up** *fig* schlucken, verschlingen; **2.** Schluck *m*

swal·low² ZO Schwalbe *f*

swamp 1. Sumpf *m*; **2.** überschwemmen; **be ~ed with** *fig* überschwemmt werden mit; **swamp·y** sumpfig

swan ZO Schwan *m*

swank 1. F *esp Br* angeben; **2.** F *esp Br* Angeber(in); Angabe *f*; **3.** F piekfein; **swank·y** F piekfein; *esp Br* angeberisch

swap F **1.** (ein)tauschen; **2.** Tausch *m*

swarm 1. ZO Schwarm *m* (*a. fig*); **2.** ZO schwärmen, *fig a.* strömen; *a. fig* wimmeln (**with** von)

swar·thy dunkel (*skin*), dunkelhäutig (*person*)

swas·ti·ka Hakenkreuz *n*

swat *Fliege etc* totschlagen

sway 1. *v/i* sich wiegen, schaukeln; **~ between** *fig* schwanken zwischen (*dat*); *v/t* hin- und herbewegen, schwenken, *s-n Körper* wiegen; beeinflussen; **2.** Schwanken *n*, Schaukeln *n*

swear fluchen; schwören; **~ at s.o.** *j-n* wüst beschimpfen; **~ by** *fig* F schwören auf (*acc*); **~ s.o. in** JUR *j-n* vereidigen

sweat 1. *v/i* schwitzen (**with** vor *dat*); *v/t*: **~ out** *Krankheit* ausschwitzen; **~ blood** F sich abrackern (**over** mit); **2.** Schweiß *m*; F Schufterei *f*; **get in(to) a ~** *fig* F ins Schwitzen geraten *or* kommen

sweat·er Pullover *m*

sweat·shirt Sweatshirt *n*

sweat·y schweißig, verschwitzt; nach Schweiß riechend, Schweiß...; schweißtreibend

Swede Schwede *m*, Schwedin *f*

Swe·den Schweden *n*

Swe·dish 1. schwedisch; **2.** LING Schwedisch *n*

sweep 1. *v/t* kehren, fegen; *fig* fegen über (*acc*) (*storm etc*); *Horizont etc* absuchen (**for** nach); *fig Land etc* überschwemmen; **~ along** mitreißen; *v/i* kehren, fegen; rauschen (*person*); **2.** Kehren *n*, Fegen *n*; Hieb *m*, Schlag *m*; F Schornsteinfeger *m*, Kaminkehrer *m*; **give the floor a good ~** den Boden gründlich kehren *or* fegen; **make a clean ~** gründlich aufräumen; SPORT gründlich abräumen

sweep·er (*Straßen*)Kehrer *m*; Kehrmaschine *f*; *soccer*: Libero *m*

sweep·ing durchgreifend (*changes etc*); pauschal, zu allgemein

sweep·ings Kehricht *m*

sweet 1. süß (*a. fig*); lieblich; lieb; **~ nothings** Zärtlichkeiten *pl*; **have a ~ tooth** gern naschen; **2.** *Br* Süßigkeit *f*, Bonbon *m*; *Br* Nachtisch *m*; **~ corn** *esp Br* BOT Zuckermais *m*

sweet·en süßen

sweet·heart Schatz *m*, Liebste *m, f*

sweet pea BOT Gartenwicke *f*

sweet shop *esp Br* Süßwarengeschäft *n*

swell 1. *v/i a.* **~ up** MED (an)schwellen; *a.* **~ out** sich blähen; *v/t fig Zahl etc* anwachsen lassen; *a.* **~ out** *Segel* blähen); **2.** MAR Dünung *f*; **3.** F klasse

swell·ing MED Schwellung *f*

swel·ter vor Hitze fast umkommen

swerve 1. schwenken (**to the left** nach

links; e-n Schwenk machen; *fig* abweichen (*from* von); **2.** Schwenk *m*, Schwenkung *f*, MOT *etc a.* Schlenker *m*

swift schnell

swim 1. *v/i* schwimmen; *fig* verschwimmen; *my head was ~ming* mir drehte sich alles; *v/t Strecke* schwimmen; *Fluss etc* durchschwimmen; **2.** Schwimmen *n*; *go for a ~* schwimmen gehen

swim·mer Schwimmer(in)

swim·ming Schwimmen *n*; **~ bath(s)** *Br* Schwimmbad *n*, *esp* Hallenbad *n*; **~ cap** Badekappe *f*, Bademütze *f*; **~ cos·tume** Badeanzug *m*; **~ pool** Swimmingpool *m*, Schwimmbecken *n*; **~ trunks** Badehose *f*

swim·suit Badeanzug *m*

swin·dle 1. *j-n* beschwindeln (*out of* um); **2.** Schwindel *m*

swine ZO Schwein *n* (*a.* F *fig*)

swing 1. *v/i* (hin- und her)schwingen; sich schwingen; einbiegen, -schwenken (*into* in *acc*); MUS schwungvoll spielen (*band etc*); Schwung haben (*music*); **~ round** sich ruckartig umdrehen; **~ shut** zuschlagen (*door etc*); *v/t* et., *die Arme etc* schwingen; **2.** Schwingen *n*; Schaukel *f*; *fig* Schwung *m*; *fig* Umschwung *m*; *in full ~* in vollem Gang

swing door Pendeltür *f*

swin·ish ekelhaft

swipe 1. Schlag *m*; **2.** schlagen (*at* nach)

swirl 1. wirbeln; **2.** Wirbel *m*

swish¹ 1. *v/i* sausen, zischen; rascheln (*silk etc*); *v/t* mit *dem Schwanz* schlagen; **2.** Sausen *n*, Zischen *n*; Rascheln *n*; Schlagen *n*

swish² *Br* feudal, schick

Swiss 1. schweizerisch, eidgenössisch, Schweizer...; **2.** Schweizer(in); *the ~* die Schweizer *pl*

switch 1. ELECTR, TECH Schalter *m*; RAIL Weiche *f*; Gerte *f*, Rute *f*; *fig* Umstellung *f*; **2.** ELECTR, TECH (um)schalten (*a. ~ over*) (*to* auf *acc*); RAIL rangieren; wechseln (*to* zu); **~ off** abschalten, ausschalten; **~ on** anschalten, einschalten

switch·board ELECTR Schalttafel *f*; (Telefon)Zentrale *f*

Swit·zer·land die Schweiz

swiv·el (sich) drehen

swiv·el chair Drehstuhl *m*

swoon in Ohnmacht fallen

swoop 1. *fig* F zuschlagen (*police etc*); *a.* **~ down** ZO herabstoßen (*on* auf *acc*); **~ on** F herfallen über (*acc*); **2.** Razzia *f*

swop F → **swap**

sword Schwert *n*

syc·a·more BOT Bergahorn *m*; Platane *f*

syl·la·ble Silbe *f*

syl·la·bus PED, UNIV Lehrplan *m*

sym·bol Symbol *n*

sym·bol·ic symbolisch

sym·bol·is·m Symbolik *f*

sym·bol·ize symbolisieren

sym·met·ri·cal symmetrisch

sym·me·try Symmetrie *f*

sym·pa·thet·ic mitfühlend; verständnisvoll; wohlwollend

sym·pa·thize mitfühlen; sympathisieren

sym·pa·thiz·er Sympathisant(in)

sym·pa·thy Mitgefühl *n*; Verständnis *n*

sym·pho·ny MUS Sinfonie *f*; **~ orches·tra** MUS Sinfonieorchester *n*

symp·tom Symptom *n*

syn·chro·nize *v/t* aufeinander abstimmen; *Uhren, Film* synchronisieren; *v/i* synchron gehen *or* sein

syn·o·nym Synonym *n*

sy·non·y·mous synonym; gleichbedeutend

syn·tax LING Syntax *f*, Satzlehre *f*

syn·the·sis Synthese *f*

syn·thet·ic CHEM synthetisch; **~ fi·ber** (*Br* **fi·bre**) Kunstfaser *f*

Syr·i·a Syrien *n*

sy·ringe MED Spritze *f*

syr·up Sirup *m*

sys·tem System *n*; (*Straßen- etc*)Netz *n*; Organismus *m*

sys·te·mat·ic systematisch

sys·tem er·ror EDP Systemfehler *m*

S

T

T, t T, t *n*

tab Aufhänger *m*, Schlaufe *f*; Lasche *f*; Etikett *n*, Schildchen *n*; Reiter *m*; F Rechnung *f*

ta·ble 1. Tisch *m*; (Tisch)Runde *f*; Tabelle *f*, Verzeichnis *n*; MATH Einmaleins *n*; **at** bei Tisch; **at the** am Tisch; **turn the ~s (on s.o.)** *fig* den Spieß umdrehen; 2. *fig* auf den Tisch legen; *esp fig* zurückstellen

ta·ble·cloth Tischdecke *f*, Tischtuch *n*

ta·ble·land GEOGR Tafelland *n*, Plateau *n*, Hochebene *f*

ta·ble lin·en Tischwäsche *f*

ta·ble·mat Untersetzer *m*

ta·ble·spoon Esslöffel *m*

tab·let PHARM Tablette *f*; Stück *n*; (Stein etc)Tafel *f*

ta·ble ten·nis SPORT Tischtennis *n*

ta·ble·top Tischplatte *f*

ta·ble·ware Geschirr *n* und Besteck *n*

tab·loid Boulevardblatt *n*, -zeitung *f*

tab·loid press Boulevardpresse *f*

ta·boo 1. tabu; 2. Tabu *n*

tab·u·lar tabellarisch

tab·u·late tabellarisch (an)ordnen

tab·u·la·tor Tabulator *m*

tach·o·graph MOT Fahrtenschreiber *m*

ta·chom·e·ter MOT Drehzahlmesser *m*

ta·cit stillschweigend

ta·ci·turn schweigsam, wortkarg

tack 1. Stift *m*, (Reiß)Zwecke *f*; Heftstich *m*; 2. heften (**to an** *acc*); **~ on** anfügen (**to** *dat*)

tack·le 1. *Problem etc* angehen; *soccer etc*: *ballführenden Gegner* angreifen; *j-n* zur Rede stellen (**about** wegen); 2. TECH Flaschenzug *m*; (*Angel*)Gerät (e *pl*) *n*; *soccer etc*: Angriff *m*

tack·y klebrig; F schäbig

tact Takt *m*, Feingefühl *n*

tact·ful taktvoll

tac·tics Taktik *f*

tact·less taktlos

tad·pole ZO Kaulquappe *f*

taf·fe·ta Taft *m*

taf·fy Sahnebonbon *m*, *n*, Toffee *n*

tag 1. Etikett *n*; (Namens-, Preis)Schild *n*; (Schnürsenkel)Stift *m*; stehende Redensart *f*; *a.* **question ~** LING Fragean-

hängsel *n*; 2. etikettieren; *Waren* auszeichnen; anhängen; **~ along** F mitgehen, mitkommen; **~ along behind s.o.** F hinter j-m hertrotten

tail 1. Schwanz *m*; Schweif *m*; hinterer Teil; F Schatten *m*, Beschatter(in); *pl* Rück-, Kehrseite *f*; Frack *m*; **put a ~ on** *j-n* beschatten lassen; **turn ~** *fig* sich auf dem Absatz umdrehen; **with one's ~ between one's legs** *fig* mit eingezogenem Schwanz; 2. F *j-n* beschatten; **~ back** *esp Br* MOT sich stauen (**to** bis zu); **~ off** schwächer werden, abnehmen, nachlassen

tail·back *esp Br* MOT Rückstau *m*

tail·coat Frack *m*

tail end Ende *n*, Schluss *m*

tail·light MOT Rücklicht *n*

tai·lor 1. Schneider *m*; 2. schneidern

tai·lor-made Maß...; maßgeschneidert (*a. fig*)

tail pipe TECH Auspuffrohr *n*

tail·wind Rückenwind *m*

taint·ed GASTR verdorben

take 1. *v/t* nehmen; (weg)nehmen; mitnehmen; bringen; MIL, MED einnehmen; *chess etc*: *Figur, Stein* schlagen; *Gefangene, Prüfung etc* machen; UNIV studieren; *Preis etc* erringen; *Scheck etc* (an)nehmen; *Rat* annehmen; *et.* hinnehmen; fassen, Platz bieten für; *et.* aushalten, ertragen; PHOT *et.* aufnehmen, *Aufnahme* machen; *Temperatur* messen; *Notiz* niederschreiben; *ein Bad, Zug, Bus, Weg etc* nehmen; *Gelegenheit, Maßnahmen* ergreifen; *Mut* fassen; *Zeit, Geduld etc* erfordern, brauchen; *Zeit* dauern; **it took her four hours** sie brauchte vier Stunden; **I ~ it that** ich nehme an, dass; **~ it or leave it** F mach, was du willst; **~n all in all** im Großen (und) Ganzen; **this seat is ~n** dieser Platz ist besetzt; **be ~n by** *or* **with** angetan sein von; **be ~n ill** *or* **sick** erkranken, krank werden; **~ to bits** *or* **pieces** *et.* auseinander nehmen, zerlegen; **~ the blame** die Schuld auf sich nehmen; **~ care** vorsichtig sein, aufpassen; **~ care!** F mach's gut!; → **care** 1; **~ hold of** ergrei-

fen; **~ part** teilnehmen (*in* an *dat*); →
part 1; **~ pity** on Mitleid haben mit;
~ a walk e-n Spaziergang machen; →
my word for it verlass dich drauf; →
advice, bath 1, **break** 1, **lead**¹ 2, **message, oath, offense, place** 1, **prisoner, risk** 1, **seat** 1, **step** 1, **trouble** 1,
turn 2, *etc*; *v/i* MED wirken, anschlagen;
~ after *j-m* nachschlagen, ähneln; **~
along** mitnehmen; **~ apart** auseinander nehmen (*a. fig* F), zerlegen; **~ away**
wegnehmen (**from** *s.o.* j-m); **... to ~
away** *Br* ... zum Mitnehmen; **~ back**
zurückbringen; zurücknehmen; bei
j-m Erinnerungen wachrufen; *j-n*
zurückversetzen (**to** in *acc*); **~ down**
herunternehmen, abnehmen; *Hose*
herunterlassen; auseinander nehmen,
zerlegen; (sich) *et.* aufschreiben *or* notieren; sich *Notizen* machen; **what do
you ~ me for?** wofür hältst du mich eigentlich?; **~ from** *j-m* et. wegnehmen;
MATH abziehen von; **~ in** *j-n* (bei sich)
aufnehmen; *fig* et. einschließen; *Kleidungsstück* enger machen; *et.* begreifen; *j-n* hereinlegen, F aufs Kreuz
legen; **be ~n in by** hereinfallen auf
(*acc*); **~ off** *Kleidungsstück* ablegen,
ausziehen, *Hut etc* abnehmen; *et.* ab-
wegnehmen; abziehen; AVIAT abheben;
SPORT abspringen; F sich davonmachen; **~ a day off** sich e-n Tag freinehmen; **~ on** *j-n* einstellen; *Arbeit etc* annehmen, übernehmen; *Farbe, Aus-
druck etc* annehmen; sich anlegen mit;
~ out herausnehmen, *Zahn* ziehen; *j-n*
ausführen, ausgehen mit *j-m*; *Versicherung* abschließen; *s-n Frust etc* F
auslassen (**on** an *dat*); **~ over** *Amt,
Macht, Verantwortung etc* übernehmen;
die *Macht* übernehmen; *die Macht übernehmen*; **~ to** Ge-
fallen finden an (*dat*); **~ to doing s.th.**
anfangen, et. zu tun; **~ up** *Vorschlag etc*
aufgreifen; *Zeit etc* in Anspruch nehmen, *Platz* einnehmen; *Erzählung etc*
aufnehmen; **~ up doing s.th.** anfangen, sich mit et. zu beschäftigen; **~
up with** sich einlassen mit; **2.** *film*, TV
Einstellung *f*; F Einnahmen *pl*

take·a·way *Br* **1.** Essen *n* zum Mitnehmen; **2.** Restaurant *n* mit Straßenver-
kauf
take·off AVIAT Abheben *n*, Start *m*;
SPORT Absprung *m*

tak·ings Einnahmen *pl*
tale Erzählung *f*; Geschichte *f*; Lüge *f*,
Lügengeschichte *f*, Märchen *n*; **tell
~s** petzen
tal·ent Talent *n*, Begabung *f*
tal·ent·ed talentiert, begabt
tal·is·man Talisman *m*
talk 1. *v/i* reden, sprechen, sich
unterhalten (**to, with** mit; **about** über
acc; **of** von); **~ about** *s.th.* a. et. besprechen; **s.o. to ~** to Ansprechpartner(in);
v/t Unsinn etc reden; reden *or* sprechen
or sich unterhalten über (*acc*); **~ s.o.
into s.th.** j-n zu et. überreden; **~ s.o.
out of s.th.** j-m et. ausreden; **~ s.th.
over** *Problem etc* besprechen (**with**
mit); **~ round** *j-n* herum-, umstimmen; **2.** Gespräch *n*, Unterhaltung
f (**with** mit; **about** über *acc*); Vortrag *m*;
Sprache *f*, Sprechweise *f*, Gerede *n*,
Geschwätz *n*; **give a ~** e-n Vortrag
halten (**to** vor *dat*; **about, on** über
acc); **be the ~ of the town** Stadtge-
spräch sein; **baby ~** Babysprache *f*,
kindliches Gebabbel; → **small talk**
talk·a·tive gesprächig, redselig
talk·er: be a good ~ gut reden können
talk·ing-to F Standpauke *f*; **give** *s.o.* **a ~**
j-m e-e Standpauke halten
talk show TV Talkshow *f*
talk-show host TV Talkmaster *m*
tall groß (*person*), hoch (*building etc*)
tal·low Talg *m*
tal·ly¹ SPORT *etc* Stand *m*; **keep a ~ of**
Buch führen über (*acc*)
tal·ly² übereinstimmen (**with** mit); *a.* **~
up** zusammenrechnen, -zählen
tal·on ZO Kralle *f*, Klaue *f*
tame 1. ZO zahm; *fig* fad(e), lahm; **2.** ZO
zähmen (*a. fig*)
tam·per: ~ with sich zu schaffen machen an (*dat*)
tam·pon MED Tampon *m*
tan 1. *Fell* gerben; bräunen; braun werden; **2.** Gelbbraun *n*; (Sonnen)Bräune
f, **3.** gelbbraun
tang (scharfer) Geruch *or* Geschmack
tan·gent MATH Tangente *f*; **fly** *or* **go off
at a ~** plötzlich (vom Thema) ab-
schweifen
tan·ge·rine BOT Mandarine *f*
tan·gi·ble greifbar, *fig a.* handfest, klar
tan·gle 1. (sich) verwirren *or* verhed-
dern, durcheinander bringen; durchei-

T

nander kommen; **2.** Gewirr *n*, *fig a.* Wirrwarr *m*, Durcheinander *n*

tank MOT *etc* Tank *m*; MIL Panzer *m*

tank·ard (Bier)Humpen *m*

tank·er MAR Tanker *m*, Tankschiff *n*; AVIAT Tankflugzeug *n*; MOT Tankwagen *m*

tan·ner Gerber *m*

tan·ne·ry Gerberei *f*

tan·ta·lize *j-n* aufreizen

tan·ta·liz·ing verlockend

tan·ta·mount: be ~ to gleichbedeutend sein mit, hinauslaufen auf (*acc*)

tan·trum Wut-, Tobsuchtsanfall *m*

tap¹ 1. TECH Hahn *m*; **beer on ~** Bier *n* vom Fass; **2.** *Naturschätze etc* erschließen; *Vorräte etc* angreifen; *Telefon(leitung)* abhören, F anzapfen; *Fass* anzapfen, anstechen

tap² 1. mit *den Fingern, Füßen* klopfen, mit *den Fingern* trommeln (**on** auf *acc*); antippen; **~ s.o. on the shoulder** j-m auf die Schulter klopfen; **~ on** (leicht) klopfen an (*acc*) *or* auf (*acc*) *or* gegen; **2.** (leichtes) Klopfen; Klaps *m*

tap dance Stepptanz *m*

tape 1. (schmales) Band; Kleb(e)streifen *m*; (Magnet-, Video-, Ton)Band *n*; (Video- *etc*)Kassette *f*; (Band)Aufnahme *f*; TV Aufzeichnung *f*; SPORT Zielband *n*; → **red tape; 2.** (auf Band) aufnehmen; TV aufzeichnen; *a.* **~ up** (mit Klebeband) zukleben

tape deck Tapedeck *n*

tape meas·ure Bandmaß *n*, Maßband *n*, Messband *n*

ta·per: a. ~ off spitz zulaufen, sich verjüngen; *fig* langsam nachlassen

tape re·cord·er Tonbandgerät *n*

tape re·cord·ing Tonbandaufnahme *f*

ta·pes·try Gobelin *m*, Wandteppich *m*

tape·worm ZO Bandwurm *m*

taps MIL Zapfenstreich *m*

tap wa·ter Leitungswasser *n*

tar 1. Teer *m*; **2.** teeren

tare ECON Tara *f*

tar·get (Schieß-, Ziel)Scheibe *f*; MIL Ziel *n* (*a. fig*), ECON *a.* Soll *n*; *fig* Zielscheibe *f*; **~ ar·e·a** MIL Zielbereich *m*; **~ group** Zielgruppe *f*

tar·iff ECON Zoll(tarif) *m*; *esp Br* Preisverzeichnis *n*

tar·mac Asphalt *m*; AVIAT Rollfeld *n*, Rollbahn *f*

tar·nish *v/i* anlaufen; *v/t Ansehen etc* beflecken

tart¹ *esp Br* Obstkuchen *m*; Obsttörtchen *n*; F Flittchen *n*, *sl* Nutte *f*

tart² herb, sauer; scharf (*a. fig*)

tar·tan Tartan *m*; Schottenstoff *m*; Schottenmuster *n*

tar·tar MED Zahnstein *m*; CHEM Weinstein *m*

task Aufgabe *f*; **take s.o. to ~** *fig* j-n zurechtweisen (**for** wegen); **~ force** MIL *etc* Sonder-, Spezialeinheit *f*

tas·sel Troddel *f*, Quaste *f*

taste 1. Geschmack *m* (*a. fig*), Geschmackssinn *m*; Kostprobe *f*; Vorliebe *f* (**for** für); **2.** *v/t* kosten, probieren; schmecken; *v/i* schmecken (**of** nach)

taste·ful *fig* geschmackvoll

taste·less geschmacklos (*a. fig*)

tast·y schmackhaft

tat·tered zerlumpt

tat·ters Fetzen *pl*; **in ~** zerfetzt, in Fetzen; *fig* ruiniert

tat·too¹ 1. Tätowierung *f*; **2.** (ein)tätowieren

tat·too² MIL Zapfenstreich *m*

taunt 1. verhöhnen, verspotten; **2.** höhnische *or* spöttische Bemerkung

Tau·rus ASTR Stier *m*; **he (she) is (a) ~** er (sie) ist (ein) Stier

taut straff; *fig* angespannt

taw·dry (billig und) geschmacklos

taw·ny gelbbraun

tax 1. Steuer *f* (**on** auf *acc*); **2.** besteuern; *j-s Geduld etc* strapazieren

tax·a·ble steuerpflichtig

tax·a·tion Besteuerung *f*

tax e·va·sion Steuerhinterziehung *f*

tax·i 1. Taxi *n*, Taxe *f*; **2.** AVIAT rollen

tax·i driv·er Taxifahrer(in)

tax·i rank, tax·i stand Taxistand *m*

tax of·fi·cer Finanzbeamte *m*

tax·pay·er Steuerzahler(in)

tax re·duc·tion Steuersenkung *f*

tax re·turn Steuererklärung *f*

T-bar Bügel *m*; *a.* **~ lift** Schlepplift *m*

tea Tee *m*; **have a cup of ~** e-n Tee trinken; **make some ~** e-n Tee machen *or* kochen

tea·bag Teebeutel *m*, Aufgussbeutel *m*

teach lehren, unterrichten (in *dat*); *j-m et.* beibringen; unterrichten (**at** an *dat*)

teach·er Lehrer(in)

tea co·sy Teewärmer *m*

tea·cup Teetasse *f*; *a storm in a ~ fig* ein Sturm im Wasserglas

team Team *n, a.* Arbeitsgruppe *f*, SPORT *a.* Mannschaft *f, soccer: a.* Elf *f*

team·ster MOT LKW-Fahrer *m*

team·work Zusammenarbeit *f*, Teamwork *n*; Zusammenspiel *n*

tea·pot Teekanne *f*

tear[1] Träne *f*; *in ~s* weinend, in Tränen (aufgelöst)

tear[2] **1.** *v/t* zerreißen; sich *et.* zerreißen (**on** an *dat*); weg-, losreißen (**from** von); *v/i* (zer)reißen; F rasen, sausen; **~ down** *Plakat etc* herunterreißen; *Haus etc* abreißen; **~ off** abreißen; sich *Kleidung* vom Leib reißen; **~ out** (her)ausreißen; **~ up** aufreißen; zerreißen; **2.** Riss *m*

tear·drop Träne *f*

tear·ful weinend; tränenreich

tear·jerk·er F Schnulze *f*

tea·room Teestube *f*

tease necken, hänseln; ärgern

tea·spoon Teelöffel *m*

teat ZO Zitze *f; Br* (Gummi)Sauger *m*

tech·ni·cal technisch; fachlich, Fach...

tech·ni·cal·i·ty technische Einzelheit; reine Formsache

tech·ni·cian Techniker(in)

tech·nique Technik *f*, Verfahren *n*

tech·nol·o·gy Technologie *f*; Technik *f*

ted·dy bear Teddybär *m*

te·di·ous langweilig, ermüdend

teem: **~ with** wimmeln von, strotzen von *or* vor (*dat*)

teen·age(d) im Teenageralter; für Teenager; **teen·ag·er** Teenager *m*

teens: *be in one's ~* im Teenageralter sein

tee·ny(-wee·ny) F klitzeklein, winzig

tee shirt → T-shirt

teethe zahnen

tee·to·tal·(l)er Abstinenzler(in)

tel·e·cast Fernsehsendung *f*

tel·e·com·mu·ni·ca·tions Telekommunikation *f*, Fernmeldewesen *n*

tel·e·gram Telegramm *n*

tel·e·graph **1.** *by ~* telegrafisch; **2.** telegrafieren

tel·e·graph·ic telegrafisch

te·leg·ra·phy Telegrafie *f*

tel·e·phone **1.** Telefon *n*; **2.** telefonieren; anrufen; **~ booth, ~ box** *Br* Telefonzelle *f*, Fernsprechzelle *f*; **~ call** Telefonanruf *m*, Telefongespräch *n*; **~ di·rec·to·ry → phone book; ~ exchange** Fernsprechamt *n*; **~ number** Telefonnummer *f*

te·leph·o·nist *esp Br* Telefonist(in)

tel·e·pho·to lens PHOT Teleobjektiv *n*

tel·e·print·er Fernschreiber *m*

tel·e·scope Teleskop *n*, Fernrohr *n*

tel·e·text Teletext *m*, Videotext *m*

tel·e·type·writ·er Fernschreiber *m*

tel·e·vise im Fernsehen übertragen *or* bringen; **tel·e·vi·sion** **1.** Fernsehen *n*; *a.* **~ set** Fernsehapparat *m*, -gerät *n*, F Fernseher *m*; **on ~** im Fernsehen; **watch ~** fernsehen; **2.** Fernseh...

tel·ex **1.** Telex *n*, Fernschreiben *n*; **2.** telexen (**to** an *acc*), ein Telex schicken (*dat*)

tell *v/t* sagen; erzählen; erkennen (**by** an *dat*); *Namen etc* nennen; *et.* anzeigen; *j-m* sagen, befehlen (**to do** zu tun); *I can't ~ one from the other*, *I can't ~ them apart* ich kann sie nicht auseinander halten; *v/i* sich auswirken (**on** bei, auf *acc*); sich bemerkbar machen; *who can ~?* wer weiß?; *you can never ~, you never can ~* man kann nie wissen; **~ against** sprechen gegen; von Nachteil sein für; **~ s.o. off** F mit j-m schimpfen (**for** wegen); **~ on s.o.** j-n verpetzen *or* verraten

tell·er Kassierer(in)

tell·ing aufschlussreich

tell·tale **1.** verräterisch; **2.** F Petze *f*

tel·ly *Br* F Fernseher *m*

te·mer·i·ty Frechheit *f*, Kühnheit *f*

tem·per **1.** Temperament *n*, Wesen *n*, Wesensart *f*; Laune *f*, Stimmung *f*; TECH Härte(grad *m*) *f*; *keep one's ~* sich beherrschen, ruhig bleiben; *lose one's ~* die Beherrschung verlieren; **2.** TECH *Stahl* härten

tem·per·a·ment Temperament *n*, Naturell *n*, Wesen *n*, Wesensart *f*

tem·per·a·men·tal launisch; von Natur aus

tem·per·ate gemäßigt (*climate, region*)

tem·per·a·ture Temperatur *f*; *have or be running a ~* MED erhöhte Temperatur *or* Fieber haben

tem·pest POET (heftiger) Sturm

tem·ple[1] Tempel *m*

tem·ple[2] ANAT Schläfe *f*

tem·po·ral weltlich; LING temporal, der Zeit

tem·po·ra·ry vorübergehend, zeitweilig

tempt *j-n* in Versuchung führen; *j-n* verführen (**to** zu); **temp·ta·tion** Versuchung *f*, Verführung *f*; **tempt·ing** verführerisch

ten 1. zehn; **2.** Zehn *f*

ten·a·ble *fig* haltbar

te·na·cious hartnäckig, zäh

ten·ant Pächter(in), Mieter(in)

tend neigen, tendieren (**to** zu); **~ up·wards** e-e steigende Tendenz haben

ten·den·cy Tendenz *f*; Neigung *f*

ten·der¹ empfindlich, *fig a.* heikel; GASTR zart, weich; sanft, zart, zärtlich

ten·der² RAIL, MAR Tender *m*

ten·der³ ECON **1.** Angebot *n*; *legal* **~** gesetzliches Zahlungsmittel; **2.** ein Angebot machen (**for** für)

ten·der·foot F Neuling *m*, Anfänger *m*

ten·der·loin GASTR zartes Lendenstück

ten·der·ness Zartheit *f*; Zärtlichkeit *f*

ten·don ANAT Sehne *f*

ten·dril BOT Ranke *f*

ten·e·ment Mietshaus *n*, *contp* Mietskaserne *f*

ten·nis Tennis *n*; **~ court** Tennisplatz *m*; **~ play·er** Tennisspieler(in)

ten·or MUS, JUR Tenor *m*, JUR *a.* Wortlaut *m*, Sinn *m*; Verlauf *m*

tense¹ LING Zeit(form) *f*, Tempus *n*

tense² gespannt, straff (*rope etc*), (an)gespannt (*a. fig*), (über)nervös, verkrampft (*person*)

ten·sion Spannung *f* (*a.* ELECTR)

tent Zelt *n*

ten·ta·cle ZO Tentakel *m, n*, Fangarm *m*

ten·ta·tive vorläufig; vorsichtig, zaghaft

ten·ter·hooks: be on ~ wie auf (glühenden) Kohlen sitzen

tenth 1. zehnte(r, -s); **2.** Zehntel *n*

tenth·ly zehntens

ten·u·ous *fig* lose (*link, relationship etc*)

ten·ure Besitz *m*, Besitzdauer *f*; **~ of office** Amtsdauer *f*, Dienstzeit *f*

tep·id lau(warm)

term 1. Zeit *f*, Zeitraum *m*, Dauer *f*; JUR Laufzeit *f*; PED, UNIV Semester *n*, *esp Br* Trimester *n*; Ausdruck *m*, Bezeichnung *f*; **~ of office** Amtsdauer *f*, Amtsperiode *f*, Amtszeit *f*; *pl* Bedingungen *pl*; **be on good (bad) ~s with** gut (schlecht) auskommen mit; **they are**

not on speaking ~s sie sprechen nicht (mehr) miteinander; **come to ~s** sich einigen (**with** mit); **2.** nennen, bezeichnen als

ter·mi·nal 1. End...; letzte(r, -s); MED unheilbar; im Endstadium; **~ly ill** unheilbar krank; **2.** RAIL *etc* Endstation *f*; Terminal *m*; ELECTR Pol *m*; EDP Terminal *n*, Datenendstation *f*

ter·mi·nate *v/t* beenden; *Vertrag* kündigen, lösen; MED *Schwangerschaft* unterbrechen; *v/i* enden; ablaufen (*contract*)

ter·mi·na·tion Beendigung *f*; Kündigung *f*, Lösung *f*; Ende *n*; Ablauf *m*

ter·mi·nus RAIL *etc* Endstation *f*

ter·race Terrasse *f*; Häuserreihe *f*; *mst pl esp Br* SPORT Ränge *pl*

ter·raced house *Br* Reihenhaus *n*

ter·res·tri·al irdisch; Erd...; *esp* BOT, ZO Land...

ter·ri·ble schrecklich

ter·rif·ic F toll, fantastisch; irre (*speed, heat etc*)

ter·ri·fy *j-m* schreckliche Angst einjagen

ter·ri·to·ri·al territorial, Gebiets...

ter·ri·to·ry Territorium *n*, (*a.* Hoheits-, Staats)Gebiet *n*

ter·ror Entsetzen *n*; Schrecken *m*; POL Terror *m*; F Landplage *f*; **in ~** in panischer Angst

ter·ror·is·m Terrorismus *m*

ter·ror·ist Terrorist(in)

ter·ror·ize terrorisieren

terse *fig* knapp, kurz (und bündig)

test 1. Test *m*, Prüfung *f*; Probe *f*; **2.** testen, prüfen; probieren; *j-s Geduld etc* auf e-e harte Probe stellen

tes·ta·ment: last will and ~ JUR letzter Wille, Testament *n*

test an·i·mal Versuchstier *n*

test card TV Testbild *n*

test drive MOT Probefahrt *f*

tes·ti·cle ANAT Hoden *m*

tes·ti·fy JUR aussagen

tes·ti·mo·ni·al Referenz *f*

tes·ti·mo·ny JUR Aussage *f*; Beweis *m*

test pi·lot AVIAT Testpilot *m*

test tube CHEM Reagenzglas *n*

tes·ty gereizt

tet·a·nus MED Tetanus *m*, Wundstarrkrampf *m*

teth·er 1. Strick *m*; Kette *f*; **at the end of**

one's ~ *fig* mit s-n Kräften *or* Nerven am Ende sein; **2.** *Tier* anbinden; anketten

text Text *m*

text·book Lehrbuch *n*

tex·tile 1. Stoff *m*, *pl* Textilien *pl*; **2.** Textil...

tex·ture Textur *f*, Gewebe *n*; Beschaffenheit *f*; Struktur *f*

than als

thank 1. *j-m* danken, sich bei *j-m* bedanken (**for** für); **~ you** danke; **~ you very much** vielen Dank; **no, ~ you** nein, danke; (**yes,**) **~ you** ja, bitte; **2. ~s** Dank *m*; **~s** danke (schön); **no, ~s** nein, danke; **~s to** dank (*gen*), wegen (*gen*)

thank·ful dankbar

thank·less undankbar

that 1. *pron and adj* das; jene(r, -s), der, die, das, derjenige, diejenige, dasjenige; **2.** *relative pron* der, die, das, welche(r, -s); **3.** *cj* dass; **4.** *adv* so, dermaßen; **it's ~ simple** so einfach ist das

thatch 1. mit Stroh *or* Reet decken; **2.** (Dach)Stroh *n*, Reet *n*; Strohdach *n*, Reetdach *n*

thaw 1. (auf)tauen; **2.** Tauwetter *n*; (Auf)Tauen *n*

the 1. der, die, das, *pl* die; **2.** *adv*: **~ ... ~ ...** je ... desto ...; **~ sooner ~ better** je eher, desto besser

the·a·ter Theater *n*; UNIV (*Hör*)Saal *m*; MIL (Kriegs)Schauplatz *m*

the·a·ter·go·er Theaterbesucher(in)

the·a·tre *Br* → **theater**, MED Operationssaal *m*

the·at·ri·cal Theater...; *fig* theatralisch

theft Diebstahl *m*

their ihr(e)

theirs der (die, das) ihrige *or* ihre

them sie (*acc pl*); ihnen (*dat*)

theme Thema *n*

them·selves sie (*acc pl*) selbst; sich (selbst)

then 1. *adv* dann; da; damals; **by ~** bis dahin; **from ~ on** von da an; → **every**, **now** 1, **there**; **2.** *adj* damalig

the·o·lo·gian Theologe *m*, Theologin *f*

the·ol·o·gy Theologie *f*

the·o·ret·i·cal theoretisch

the·o·rist Theoretiker *m*

the·o·ry Theorie *f*

ther·a·peu·tic therapeutisch; F wohltuend; gesund

ther·a·pist Therapeut(in)

ther·a·py Therapie *f*

there 1. da, dort; (da-, dort)hin; **~ is**, **~ are** es gibt, es ist, *pl* es sind; **~ and then** auf der Stelle; **~ you are** hier bitte; siehst du!, na also!; **2.** *int* so; siehst du!, na also!; **~, ~** ist ja gut!

there·a·bout(s) so ungefähr

there·af·ter danach

there·by dadurch

there·fore deshalb, daher; folglich

there·up·on darauf(hin)

ther·mal 1. thermisch, Thermo..., Wärme...; **2.** Thermik *f*

ther·mom·e·ter Thermometer *n*

ther·mos® Thermosflasch® *f*

the·sis These *f*; UNIV Dissertation *f*, Doktorarbeit *f*

they sie *pl*; man

thick 1. *adj* dick, (*fog etc a.*) dicht; F dumm; F dick befreundet; **be ~ with** wimmeln von; **~ with smoke** verräuchert; **that's a bit ~!** *esp Br* F das ist ein starkes Stück!; **2.** *adv* dick, dicht; **lay it on ~** F dick auftragen; **3. in the ~ of** mitten in (*dat*); **through ~ and thin** durch dick und dünn; **thick·en** dicker werden, (*fog etc a.*) dichter werden; GASTR eindicken, binden

thick·et Dickicht *n*

thick·head·ed F strohdumm

thick·ness Dicke *f*; Lage *f*, Schicht *f*

thick·set gedrungen, untersetzt

thick·skinned *fig* dickfellig

thief Dieb(in)

thigh ANAT (Ober)Schenkel *m*

thim·ble Fingerhut *m*

thin 1. *adj* dünn; dürr; spärlich, dürftig; schütter (*hair*); schwach, (*excuse etc a.*) fadenscheinig; **2.** *adv* dünn; **3.** verdünnen; dünner werden, (*fog, hair a.*) sich lichten

thing Ding *n*; Sache *f*; *pl* Sachen *pl*, Zeug *n*; *fig* Dinge *pl*, Lage *f*, Umstände *pl*; **I couldn't see a ~** ich konnte überhaupt nichts sehen; **another ~** et. anderes; **the right ~** das Richtige

thing·a·ma·jig F Dings(bums) *m*, *f*, *n*

think *v/i* denken (**of** an *acc*); nachdenken (**about** über *acc*); **I ~ so** ich glaube *or* denke schon; **I'll ~ about it** ich überlege es mir; **~ of** sich erinnern an (*acc*); **~**

of doing s.th. beabsichtigen *or* daran denken, et. zu tun; ***what do you ~ of or about ...?*** was halten Sie von ...?; *v/t* denken, glauben, meinen; *j-n, et.* halten für; *~ over* nachdenken über (*acc*), sich *et.* überlegen; *~ up* sich *et.* ausdenken

think tank Beraterstab *m*, Sachverständigenstab *m*, Denkfabrik *f*

third 1. dritte(r, -s); **2.** Drittel *n*

third·ly drittens

third·rate drittklassig

Third World Dritte Welt

thirst Durst *m*

thirst·y durstig; *be ~* Durst haben, durstig sein

thir·teen 1. dreizehn; **2.** Dreizehn *f*

thir·teenth dreizehnte(r, -s)

thir·ti·eth dreißigste(r, -s)

thir·ty 1. dreißig; **2.** Dreißig *f*

this diese(r, -s); *~ morning* heute Morgen; *~ is John speaking* TEL hier (spricht) John

this·tle BOT Distel *f*

thong (Leder)Riemen *m*

thorn Dorn *m*

thorn·y dornig; *fig* schwierig, heikel

thor·ough gründlich, genau; fürchterlich (*mess etc*)

thor·ough·bred ZO Vollblüter *m*

thor·ough·fare Hauptverkehrsstraße *f*; *no ~!* Durchfahrt verboten!

though 1. *cj* obwohl; (je)doch; *as ~* als ob; **2.** *adv* dennoch, trotzdem

thought Denken *n*; Gedanke *m* (*of an acc*); *on second ~* wenn ich es mir (recht) überlege

thought·ful nachdenklich; rücksichtsvoll, aufmerksam

thought·les gedankenlos; rücksichtslos

thou·sand 1. tausend; **2.** Tausend *n*

thou·sandth 1. tausendste(r, -s); **2.** Tausendstel *n*

thrash verdreschen, verprügeln; SPORT F *j-m* e-e Abfuhr erteilen; *~ about, ~ around* sich *im Bett etc* hin und her werfen; um sich schlagen; zappeln (*fish*); *~ out* Problem *etc* ausdiskutieren

thrash·ing Dresche *f*, Tracht *f* Prügel

thread 1. Faden *m* (*a. fig*); Garn *n*; TECH Gewinde *n*; **2.** Nadel einfädeln; *Perlen etc* auffädeln, aufreihen

thread·bare abgewetzt, abgetragen; *fig* abgedroschen

threat Drohung *f*; Bedrohung *f*, Gefahr *f* (**to** *gen or* für)

threat·en (be)drohen

threat·en·ing drohend

three 1. drei; **2.** Drei *f*

three·fold dreifach

three·ply → ply²

three·score sechzig

three·stage dreistufig

thresh AGR dreschen

thresh·ing ma·chine AGR Dreschmaschine *f*

thresh·old Schwelle *f*

thrift Sparsamkeit *f*

thrift·y sparsam

thrill 1. prickelndes Gefühl; Nervenkitzel *m*; aufregendes Erlebnis; **2.** *v/t be ~ed* (ganz) hingerissen sein (**at, about** von)

thrill·er Thriller *m*, F Reißer *m*

thrill·ing spannend, fesselnd, packend

thrive gedeihen; *fig* blühen, florieren

throat ANAT Kehle *f*, Gurgel *f*; Rachen *m*; Hals *m*; *clear one's ~* sich räuspern; *→ sore* 1

throb 1. hämmern (*machine*), (*heart etc a.*) pochen, schlagen; pulsieren (*pain*); **2.** Hämmern *n*, Pochen *n*, Schlagen *n*

throm·bo·sis MED Thrombose *f*

throne Thron *m*

throng 1. Schar *f*, Menschenmenge *f*; **2.** sich drängen (*in dat*)

throt·tle 1. erdrosseln; *~ down* MOT, TECH drosseln, Gas wegnehmen; **2.** TECH Drosselklappe *f*

through 1. *prp* durch (*acc*); bis (einschließlich); *Monday ~ Friday* von Montag bis Freitag; **2.** *adv* durch; *~ and ~* durch und durch; *put s.o. ~ to* TEL j-n verbinden mit; *wet ~* völlig durchnässt; **3.** *adj* durchgehend (*train etc*); Durchgangs...

through·out 1. *prp*: *~ the night* die ganze Nacht hindurch; *~ the country* im ganzen Land, überall im Land; **2.** *adv* ganz, überall; die ganze Zeit (hindurch)

through traf·fic Durchgangsverkehr *m*

through·way *Br → thruway*

throw 1. werfen; *Hebel etc* betätigen; *Reiter* abwerfen; *Party* geben, F schmeißen; *~ a four* e-e Vier würfeln;

~ off *Jacke etc* abwerfen; *Verfolger* abschütteln; *Krankheit* loswerden; **~ on** sich *e-e Jacke etc* (hastig) überwerfen; **~ out** hinauswerfen; wegwerfen; **~ up** *v/t* hochwerfen; F *Job etc* hinschmeißen; F (er)brechen; *v/i* F (sich er)brechen; **2.** Wurf *m*

throw·a·way Wegwerf..., Einweg...; **~ pack** Einwegpackung *f*

throw-in *soccer*: Einwurf *m*

thru F → **through**

thrum → **strum**

thrush zo Drossel *f*

thrust 1. *j-n, et.* stoßen (**into** in *acc*); *et.* stecken, schieben (**into** in *acc*); **~ at** stoßen nach; **~ s.th. upon s.o.** j-m et. aufdrängen; **2.** Stoß *m*; MIL Vorstoß *m*; PHYS Schub *m*, Schubkraft *f*

thru·way Schnellstraße *f*

thud 1. dumpfes Geräusch, Plumps *m*; **2.** plumpsen

thug Verbrecher *m*, Schläger *m*

thumb 1. ANAT Daumen *m*; **2. ~ a lift** *or* **ride** per Anhalter fahren, trampen (**to** nach); **~ through a book** ein Buch durchblättern; **well-thumbed** abgegriffen

thumb·tack Reißzwecke *f*, Reißnagel *m*, Heftzwecke *f*

thump 1. *v/t* j-m e-n Schlag versetzen; **~ out** *Melodie* herunterhämmern (**on the piano** auf dem Klavier); *v/i* (heftig) schlagen *or* hämmern *or* pochen (*d. heart*); plumpsen; trampeln; **2.** dumpfes Geräusch, Plumps *m*; Schlag *m*

thun·der 1. Donner *m*, Donnern *n*; **2.** donnern

thun·der·bolt Blitz *m* und Donner *m*

thun·der·clap Donnerschlag *m*

thun·der·cloud Gewitterwolke *f*

thun·der·ous donnernd (*applause*)

thun·der·storm Gewitter *n*, Unwetter *n*

thun·der·struck wie vom Donner gerührt

Thur(s) ABBR *of* **Thursday** Do., Donnerstag *m*

Thurs·day (ABBR **Thur, Thurs**) Donnerstag *m*; **on ~** (am) Donnerstag; **on ~s** donnerstags

thus so, auf diese Weise; folglich, somit; **~ far** bisher

thwart durchkreuzen, vereiteln

thyme BOT Thymian *m*

thy·roid (gland) ANAT Schilddrüse *f*

tick¹ 1. Ticken *n*; Haken *m*, Häkchen *n*; **2.** *v/i* ticken; *v/t mst* **~ off** ab-, anhaken

tick² zo Zecke *f*

tick³: on ~ *Br* F auf Pump

tick·er·tape pa·rade Konfettiparade *f*

tick·et 1. Fahrkarte *f*, Fahrschein *m*; Flugkarte *f*, Flugschein *m*, Ticket *n*; (Eintritts-, Theater- etc)Karte *f*; (Gepäck)Schein *m*; Etikett *n*, (Preis- etc -) Schild *n*; POL Wahl-, Kandidatenliste *f*; (*a.* **parking ~**) MOT Strafzettel *m*; **2.** etikettieren; bestimmen, vorsehen (**for** für)

tick·et-can·cel·(l)ing ma·chine (Fahrschein)Entwerter *m*

tick·et col·lec·tor (Bahnsteig)Schaffner(in); **~ machine** Fahrkartenautomat *m*; **~ of·fice** RAIL Fahrkartenschalter *m*

tick·ing Inlett *n*; Matratzenbezug *m*

tick·le kitzeln

tick·lish kitz(e)lig, *fig a.* heikel

tid·al wave Flutwelle *f*

tid·bit Leckerbissen *m*

tide 1. Gezeiten *pl*; Flut *f*; *fig* Strömung *f*, Trend *m*; **high ~** Flut *f*; **low ~** Ebbe *f*; **2. ~ over** *fig* j-m hinweghelfen über (*acc*); *j-n* über Wasser halten

ti·dy 1. sauber, ordentlich, aufgeräumt; F hübsch, beträchtlich (*Sum etc*); **2. a. ~ up** in Ordnung bringen, (*Zimmer a.*) aufräumen; **~ away** wegräumen, aufräumen

tie 1. Krawatte *f*, Schlips *m*; Band *n*; Schnur *f*; Stimmengleichheit *f*; SPORT Unentschieden *n*; (*Pokal*)Spiel *n*; RAIL Schwelle *f*; *mst pl fig* Bande *pl*; **2.** *v/t* an-, festbinden; (sich) *Krawatte etc* binden; *fig* verbinden; **the game was ~d** SPORT das Spiel ging unentschieden aus; *v/i*: **they ~d for second place** SPORT *etc* sie belegten gemeinsam den zweiten Platz; **~ down** *fig* (an)binden; *j-n* festlegen (**to** auf *acc*); **~ in with** übereinstimmen mit, passen zu; verbinden *or* koppeln mit; **~ up** *Paket etc* verschnüren; *et.* in Verbindung bringen (**with** mit); *Verkehr etc* lahm legen; **be ~d up** ECON fest angelegt sein (**in** in *dat*)

tie-break(·er) *tennis*: Tie-Break *m*, *n*

tie-in (enge) Verbindung, (enger) Zusammenhang; ECON Kopplungsgeschäft *n*; *a book movie* ~ *appr* das Buch von Film

tie-on Anhänge...

tie-pin Krawattennadel *f*

tier (Sitz)Reihe *f*, Lage *f*, Schicht *f*; *fig* Stufe *f*

tie-up (enge) Verbindung, (enger) Zusammenhang; ECON Fusion *f*

ti-ger ZO Tiger *m*

tight 1. *adj* fest (sitzend), fest angezogen; straff (*rope etc*); eng (*a. dress etc*); knapp (*a. fig*); F knick(e)rig; F blau; *be in a* ~ *corner* in der Klemme sein *or* sitzen *or* stecken; **2.** *adv* fest; F gut; *hold* ~ festhalten; *sleep* ~*!* F schlaf gut!

tight-en festziehen, anziehen; *Seil etc* straffen; ~ *one's belt* fig den Gürtel enger schnallen; ~ *up* (*on*) *Gesetz etc* verschärfen

tight-fist-ed F knick(e)rig

tights (*Tänzer-, Artisten*)Trikot *n*; *esp Br* Strumpfhose *f*

ti-gress ZO Tigerin *f*

tile 1. (Dach)Ziegel *m*; Fliese *f*, Kachel *f*; **2.** (mit Ziegeln) decken; fliesen, kacheln

til-er Dachdecker *m*; Fliesenleger *m*

till¹ → *until*

till² (Laden)Kasse *f*

tilt 1. kippen; sich neigen; **2.** Kippen *n*; *at a* ~ schief, schräg; (*at*) *full* ~ F mit Volldampf

tim-ber *Br* Bau-, Nutzholz *n*; Baumbestand *m*, Bäume *pl*; Balken *m*

time 1. Zeit *f*; Uhrzeit *f*; MUS Takt *m*; Mal *n*; ~ *after* ~, ~ *and again* immer wieder; *every* ~ *I* ... jedes Mal, wenn ich ...; *how many* ~*s?* wie oft?; *next* ~ nächstes Mal; *this* ~ diesmal; *three* ~ *s* dreimal; *three* ~*s four equals* *or is twelve* drei mal vier ist zwölf; *what's the* ~*?* wie spät ist es?; *what* ~*?* um wie viel Uhr?; *all the* ~ die ganze Zeit; *at all* ~*s, at any* ~ jederzeit; *at the* ~ damals; *at the same* ~ gleichzeitig; *at* ~*s* manchmal; *by the* ~ wenn; als; *for a* ~ e-e Zeit lang; *for the* ~ *being* vorläufig, fürs Erste; *from* ~ *to* ~ von Zeit zu Zeit; *have a good* ~ sich gut unterhalten *or* amüsieren; *in* ~ rechtzeitig; *in no* ~ (*at all*) im Nu; *on* ~ pünktlich; *some* ~ *ago* vor einiger Zeit; *to pass the* ~ zum Zeitver-

treib; *take one's* ~ sich Zeit lassen; **2.** *et.* timen (*a.* SPORT); (ab)stoppen; zeitlich abstimmen, den richtigen Zeitpunkt wählen *or* bestimmen für

time| card Stechkarte *f*; ~ **clock** Stechuhr *f*; ~ **lag** Zeitdifferenz *f*

time-lapse *film:* Zeitraffer...

time-less immer während, ewig; zeitlos

time lim-it Frist *f*

time-ly (recht)zeitig

time sheet Stechkarte *f*

time sig-nal *radio:* Zeitzeichen *n*

time-ta-ble *Br* Fahrplan *m*, Flugplan *m*; Stundenplan *m*; Zeitplan *m*

tim-id ängstlich, furchtsam, zaghaft

tim-ing Timing *n*

tin 1. Zinn *n*; *Br* (Blech-, Konserven)Dose *f*, (-)Büchse *f*; **2.** verzinnen; *Br* einmachen, eindosen

tinc-ture Tinktur *f*

tin-foil Stanniol(papier) *n*; Alufolie *f*

tinge 1. tönen; *be* ~*d with* fig e-n Anflug haben von; **2.** Tönung *f*; fig Anflug *m*, Spur *f* (*of* von)

tin-gle prickeln, kribbeln

tink-er herumpfuschen, herumbasteln (*at* an *dat*)

tin-kle bimmeln; klirren

tinned *Br* Dosen..., Büchsen...

tinned fruit *Br* Obstkonserven *pl*

tin o-pen-er *Br* Dosenöffner *m*, Büchsenöffner *m*

tin-sel Lametta *n*; Flitter *m*

tint 1. (Farb)Ton *m*, Tönung *f*; **2.** tönen

ti-ny winzig

tip¹ 1. Spitze *f*; Filter *m*; *it's on the* ~ *of my tongue* fig es liegt mir auf der Zunge; **2.** mit e-r Spitze versehen

tip² 1. *esp Br* (aus)kippen, schütten; kippen; ~ *over* umkippen; **2.** *esp Br* (*Schutt- etc*)Ablageplatz *m*, (-)Halde *f*; *Br* fig F Saustall *m*

tip³ 1. Trinkgeld *n*; **2.** j-m ein Trinkgeld geben

tip⁴ 1. Tipp *m*, Rat(schlag) *m*; **2.** tippen auf (*acc*) (*as* als); ~ *s.o. off* j-m e-n Tipp *or* Wink geben

tip-sy angeheitert

tip-toe 1. on ~ auf Zehenspitzen; **2.** auf Zehenspitzen gehen

tire¹ MOT Reifen *m*

tire² ermüden, müde machen *or* werden

tired müde; *be* ~ *of* j-n, *et.* satt haben

tire-less unermüdlich

tire·some ermüdend; lästig

tis·sue BIOL Gewebe n; Papier(taschen)tuch n; → **~ pa·per** Seidenpapier n

tit[1] F *contp* Titte f

tit[2] ZO Meise f

tit·bit *esp Br* → **tidbit**

tit·il·late *j-n* (*sexuell*) anregen

ti·tle Titel m; JUR (Rechts)Anspruch m (**to** *auf acc*)

ti·tle-hold·er SPORT Titelhalter(in)

ti·tle page Titelseite f

ti·tle role THEA *etc* Titelrolle f

tit·mouse ZO Meise f

tit·ter 1. kichern; 2. Kichern n

to 1. *prp* zu; an (*acc*), auf (*acc*), für, in (*acc*), in (*dat*); nach; (*im Verhältnis or im Vergleich*) zu, gegen(über); *extent, limit, degree*: bis, (bis) zu, (bis) an (*acc*); *time*: bis, bis zu, bis gegen, vor (*dat*); *from Monday ~ Friday* von Montag bis Freitag; *a quarter ~ one* (ein) Viertel vor eins, drei viertel eins; *go ~ Italy* nach Italien fahren; *go ~ school* in die *or zur* Schule gehen; *have you ever been ~ Rome?* bist du schon einmal in Rom gewesen?; ~ *me etc* mir *etc*; *here's ~ you!* auf Ihr Wohl!, prosit!; 2. *adv* zu; *pull ~* Tür *etc* zuziehen; *come ~* (wieder) zu sich kommen; ~ *and fro* hin und her, auf und ab; 3. *with infinitive*: zu; *intention, aim*: um zu; ~ *go* gehen; *easy ~ learn* leicht zu lernen; ... ~ *earn money* ... um Geld zu verdienen

toad ZO Kröte f, Unke f

toad·stool BOT ungenießbarer Pilz; Giftpilz m

toad·y 1. Kriecher(in); 2. ~ *to s.o. fig* vor j-m kriechen

toast[1] 1. Toast m; 2. toasten; rösten

toast[2] 1. Toast m, Trinkspruch m; 2. auf *j-n or j-s* Wohl trinken

toast·er TECH Toaster m

to·bac·co Tabak m; **to·bac·co·nist** Tabak(waren)händler(in)

to·bog·gan 1. (Rodel)Schlitten m; 2. Schlitten fahren, rodeln

to·day 1. *adv* heute; heutzutage; *a week ~, ~ week* heute in e-r Woche, heute in acht Tagen; 2. ~ *'s paper* die heutige Zeitung, die Zeitung von heute; *of ~, ~'s* von heute, heutig

tod·dle auf wack(e)ligen *or* unsicheren Beinen gehen

to-do F *fig* Theater n

toe ANAT Zehe f; Spitze f

toe·nail ANAT Zehennagel m

tof·fee, tof·fy Sahnebonbon m, n, Toffee n

to·geth·er zusammen; gleichzeitig

toi·let Toilette f; ~ **pa·per** Toilettenpapier n; ~ **roll** *esp Br* Rolle f Toilettenpapier

to·ken Zeichen n; *as a ~*, *in ~ of* als *or* zum Zeichen (*gen*); zum Andenken an (*acc*); ~ *strike* Warnstreik m

tol·e·ra·ble erträglich

tol·e·rance Toleranz f; Nachsicht f

tol·e·rant tolerant (*of, towards* gegenüber)

tol·e·rate tolerieren, dulden; ertragen

toll[1] Benutzungsgebühr f, Maut f; *heavy death* ~ große Zahl an Todesopfern; *take its ~* (*on*) *fig* s-n Tribut fordern (*von*); s-e Spuren hinterlassen (*bei*)

toll[2] läuten

toll-free TEL gebührenfrei

toll road gebührenpflichtige Straße, Mautstraße f

tom F → **tomcat**

to·ma·to BOT Tomate f

tomb Grab n; Grabmal n; Gruft f

tom·boy Wildfang m

tomb·stone Grabstein m

tom·cat ZO Kater m

tom·fool·e·ry Unsinn m

to·mor·row 1. *adv* morgen; *a week ~, ~ week* morgen in e-r Woche, morgen in acht Tagen; ~ *morning* morgen früh; ~ *night* morgen Abend; 2. *the day after* ~ übermorgen; *of ~, ~'s* von morgen

ton (ABBR **t, tn**) Tonne f

tone 1. Ton m; Klang m; (Farb)Ton m; MUS Note f; MED Tonus m; *fig* Niveau n; 2. ~ *down* abschwächen; ~ *up* Muskeln *etc* kräftigen

tongs (*a pair of* ~ e-e) Zange f

tongue ANAT, TECH Zunge f; (*Mutter*)Sprache f; Klöppel m (*e-r Glocke*); *hold one's* ~ den Mund halten

ton·ic Tonikum n, Stärkungsmittel n; Tonic n; MUS Grundton m

to·night heute Abend *or* Nacht

ton·sil ANAT Mandel f

ton·sil·li·tis MED Mandelentzündung f; Angina f

T

too zu; zu, sehr; auch (noch)

tool Werkzeug *n*, Gerät *n*; ~ **bag** Werkzeugtasche *f*; ~ **box** Werkzeugkasten *m*; ~ **kit** Werkzeug *n*

tool·mak·er Werkzeugmacher *m*

tool·shed Geräteschuppen *m*

toot *esp* MOT hupen

tooth Zahn *m*

tooth·ache Zahnschmerzen *pl*, Zahnweh *n*

tooth·brush Zahnbürste *f*

tooth·less zahnlos

tooth·paste Zahncreme *f*, Zahnpasta *f*

tooth·pick Zahnstocher *m*

top¹ **1.** oberer Teil; GEOGR Gipfel *m*, Spitze *f*, BOT Krone *f*, Wipfel *m*; Kopfende *n*, oberes Ende; Oberteil *n*; Oberfläche *f*; Deckel *m*; Verschluss *m*; MOT Verdeck *n*; MOT höchster Gang; **at the ~ of the page** oben auf der Seite; **at the ~ of one's voice** aus vollem Hals; **on ~** oben(auf); darauf, F drauf; **on ~ of** (oben) auf (*dat or acc*); über (*dat or acc*); **2.** oberste(r, -s); Höchst..., Spitzen..., Top...; **3.** bedecken (**with** mit); fig übersteigen, übertreffen; ~ **up** *Tank etc* auffüllen; F *j-m* nachschenken

top² Kreisel *m* (*toy*)

top hat Zylinder *m*

top·heav·y kopflastig (*a. fig*)

top·ic Thema *n*; **top·i·cal** aktuell

top·ple 1. *mst* ~ **over** umkippen; ~ **the government** die Regierung stürzen

top·sy·tur·vy in e-r heillosen Unordnung

torch *Br* Taschenlampe *f*; Fackel *f*

torch·light Fackelschein *m*; ~ **procession** Fackelzug *m*

tor·ment 1. Qual *f*; **2.** quälen, peinigen, plagen

tor·na·do Tornado *m*, Wirbelsturm *m*

tor·pe·do MIL **1.** Torpedo *m*; **2.** torpedieren (*a. fig*)

tor·rent reißender Strom; *fig* Schwall *m*

tor·ren·tial: ~ **rain** sintflutartige Regenfälle *pl*

tor·toise ZO Schildkröte *f*

tor·tu·ous gewunden

tor·ture 1. Folter *f*, Folterung *f*; *fig* Qual *f*, Tortur *f*; **2.** foltern; *fig* quälen

toss **1.** *v/t* werfen; *Münze* hochwerfen; GASTR schwenken; ~ **off** F *Bild etc* hinhauen; *v/i a.* ~ **about**, ~ **and turn** sich

im Schlaf hin und her werfen; *a.* ~ **up** e-e Münze hochwerfen; ~ **for s.th.** um et. losen; ~ **one's head** den Kopf zurückwerfen; **2.** Wurf *m*; Zurückwerfen *n*; Hochwerfen *n*

tot F Knirps *m*

to·tal 1. völlig, total; ganz, gesamt, Gesamt...; **2.** Gesamtbetrag *m*, -menge *f*; **3.** sich belaufen auf (*acc*); ~ **up** zusammenrechnen, -zählen

tot·ter schwanken, wanken

touch **1.** (sich) berühren; anfassen; *Essen etc* anrühren; *fig* herankommen an (*acc*); *fig* rühren; ~ **wood!** toi, toi, toi!; ~ **down** AVIAT niedergehen; ~ **up** ausbessern; PHOT retuschieren; **2.** Tastempfindung *f*; Berührung *f*, MUS *etc* Anschlag *m*; (*Pinsel- etc*)Strich *m*; GASTR Spur *f*; Verbindung *f*, Kontakt *m*; *fig* Note *f*; *fig* Anflug *m*; **a ~ of flu** e-e leichte Grippe; **get in ~ with s.o.** sich mit *j-m* in Verbindung setzen

touch-and-go F kritisch, riskant, prekär; **it was ~ whether** es stand auf des Messers Schneide, ob

touch·down AVIAT Aufsetzen *n*, Landung *f*

touched gerührt; F leicht verrückt

touch·ing rührend

touch·line *soccer:* Seitenlinie *f*

touch·stone Prüfstein *m* (**of** für)

touch·y empfindlich; heikel (*subject etc*)

tough zäh; widerstandsfähig; *fig* hart; schwierig (*problem, negotiations etc*)

tough·en *a.* ~ **up** hart or zäh machen or werden

tour **1.** Tour *f* (**of** durch), (Rund)Reise *f*, (Rund)Fahrt *f*; Ausflug *m*; Rundgang *m* (**of** durch); THEA Tournee *f* (*a. SPORT*); **go on** ~ auf Tournee gehen; → **conduct** 2; **2.** bereisen, reisen durch

tour·is·m Tourismus *m*, Fremdenverkehr *m*

tour·ist 1. Tourist(in); **2.** Touristen...; ~ **class** AVIAT, MAR Touristenklasse *f*; ~ **in·dus·try** Tourismusgeschäft *n*; ~ **in·for·ma·tion of·fice**, ~ **of·fice** Verkehrsverein *m*; ~ **sea·son** Reisesaison *f*, Reisezeit *f*

tour·na·ment Turnier *n*

tou·sled zerzaust

tow **1.** *Boot etc* schleppen, *Auto etc a.* abschleppen; **2.** **give s.o. a** ~ *j-n* abschleppen; *take in* ~ *Auto etc* abschleppen

to·ward, *esp Br* **to·wards** auf (*acc*) ... zu, (in) Richtung, zu; *time*: gegen; *fig* gegenüber

tow·el 1. Handtuch *n*, (*Bade- etc*)Tuch *n*; **2.** (mit e-m Handtuch) abtrocknen *or* abreiben

tow·er 1. Turm *m*; **2.** ~ *above*, ~ *over* überragen; ~ *block Br* Hochhaus *n*

tow·er·ing turmhoch; *fig* überragend; *in a* ~ *rage* rasend vor Zorn

town Stadt *f*; Kleinstadt *f*; *go into* ~ in die Stadt gehen; ~ *cen·tre Br* Innenstadt *f*, City *f*; ~ *coun·cil Br* Stadtrat *m*; ~ *coun·ci(l)·lor Br* Stadtrat *m*, Stadträtin *f*; ~ *hall* Rathaus *n*

town·ie F Städter(in), Stadtmensch *m*

town| plan·ner Stadtplaner(in); ~ *plan·ning* Stadtplanung *f*

towns·peo·ple Städter *pl*, Stadtbevölkerung *f*

tow-rope MOT Abschleppseil *n*

tox·ic toxisch, giftig; Gift...

tox·ic waste Giftmüll *m*

tox·ic waste dump Giftmülldeponie *f*

toy 1. Spielzeug *n*, *pl a.* Spielsachen *pl*, ECON Spielwaren *pl*; **2.** Spielzeug...; Miniatur...; Zwerg...; **3.** ~ *with* spielen mit (*a. fig*)

trace 1. (durch)pausen; *j-n, et.* ausfindig machen, aufspüren; *et.* finden; *a.* ~ *back et.* zurückverfolgen (*to* bis zu); ~ *s.th. to et.* zurückführen auf (*acc*); **2.** Spur *f* (*a. fig*)

track 1. Spur *f* (*a. fig*), Fährte *f*; Pfad *m*, Weg *m*; RAIL Gleis *n*, Geleise *n*; TECH Raupe *f*, Raupenkette *f*; SPORT (Renn-, Aschen-)Bahn *f*, (*Renn*)Strecke *f*; *tape etc*: Spur *f*; Nummer *f* (*on an LP etc*); **2.** verfolgen; ~ *down* aufspüren; auftreiben

track and field SPORT Leichtathletik *f*

track e·vent SPORT Laufdisziplin *f*

track·ing sta·tion Bodenstation *f*

track·suit Trainingsanzug *m*

tract Fläche *f*, Gebiet *n*; ANAT (*Verdauungs*)Trakt *m*, (*Atem*)Wege *pl*

trac·tion Ziehen *n*, Zug *m*

trac·tion en·gine Zugmaschine *f*

trac·tor Traktor *m*, Trecker *m*

trade 1. Handel *m*; Branche *f*, Gewerbe *n*; (*esp* Handwerks)Beruf *m*; **2.** Handel treiben, handeln; ~ *on* ausnutzen; ~

a·gree·ment Handelsabkommen *n*

trade·mark Warenzeichen *n*

trade name Markenname *m*, Handelsbezeichnung *f*

trade price Großhandelspreis *m*

trad·er Händler(in)

trades·man (Einzel)Händler *m*; Ladeninhaber *m*; Lieferant *m*

trade(s *Br*)| **u·nion** Gewerkschaft *f*; ~ **u·nion·ist** Gewerkschaftler(in)

tra·di·tion Tradition *f*; Überlieferung *f*

tra·di·tion·al traditionell

traf·fic 1. Verkehr *m*; (*esp* illegaler) Handel *m* (*in* mit); **2.** (*esp* illegal) handeln (*in* mit); ~ *cir·cle* MOT Kreisverkehr *m*; ~ *in·struc·tion* Verkehrsunterricht *m*; ~ *is·land* Verkehrsinsel *f*; ~ *jam* (Verkehrs)Stau *m*, Verkehrsstockung *f*; ~ *light(s)* Verkehrsampel *f*; ~ *of·fense* (*Br* -*fence*) Verkehrsdelikt *n*; ~ *of·fend·er* Verkehrssünder (in); ~ *reg·u·la·tions* Straßenverkehrsordnung *f*; ~ *sign* Verkehrszeichen *n*, -schild *n*; ~ *sig·nal* → *traffic light(s)*; ~ *war·den Br* Parküberwacher *m*, Politesse *f*

tra·ge·dy Tragödie *f*

tra·gic tragisch

trail 1. *v/t et.* nachschleifen lassen; verfolgen; SPORT zurückliegen hinter (*dat*) (*by* um); *v/i* sich schleppen; BOT kriechen; SPORT zurückliegen (*by 3-0* 0:3); ~ *(along) behind s.o.* hinter j-m herschleifen; **2.** Spur *f* (*a. fig*), Fährte *f*; Pfad *m*, Weg *m*; ~ *of blood* Blutspur *f*; ~ *of dust* Staubwolke *f*

trail·er MOT Anhänger *m*; Wohnwagen *m*, Caravan *m*; TV Trailer *m*, Vorschau *f*; ~ *park* Standplatz *m* für Wohnwagen

train 1. RAIL Zug *m*; Kolonne *f*, Schlange *f*; Schleppe *f*; *fig* Folge *f*, Kette *f*; *by* ~ mit der Bahn, mit dem Zug; ~ *of thought* Gedankengang *m*; **2.** *v/t j-n* ausbilden (*as* als, zum), schulen; SPORT trainieren; *Tier* abrichten, dressieren; *Kamera et.* richten (*on* auf *acc*); *v/i* ausgebildet werden (*as* als, zum); SPORT trainieren (*for* für)

train·ee Auszubildende *m, f*

train·er Ausbilder(in); ZO Abrichter(in), Dompteur *m*, Dompteuse *f*; SPORT Trainer(in); *Br* Turnschuh *m*

train·ing Ausbildung *f*, Schulung *f*; Abrichten n, Dressur f; SPORT Training n

trait (Charakter)Zug m

trai·tor Verräter m

tram Br Straßenbahn(wagen m) f

tram·car Br Straßenbahnwagen m

tramp 1. sta(m)pfen or trampeln (durch); 2. Tramp m, Landstreicher m, Vagabund m; Wanderung f; Flittchen n; **tram·ple** (zer)trampeln

trance Trance f

tran·quil ruhig, friedlich

tran·quil·(l)i·ty Ruhe f, Frieden m

tran·quil·(l)ize beruhigen

tran·quil·(l)iz·er PHARM Beruhigungsmittel n

trans·act Geschäft abwickeln, Handel abschließen

trans·ac·tion Abwicklung f, Abschluss m; Geschäft n, Transaktion f

trans·at·lan·tic transatlantisch, Transatlantik..., Übersee...

tran·scribe abschreiben, kopieren; Stenogramm etc übertragen

tran·script Abschrift f, Kopie f

tran·scrip·tion Umschreibung f, Umschrift f; Abschrift f, Kopie f

trans·fer 1. v/t (to) Betrieb etc verlegen (nach); j-n versetzen (nach); SPORT Spieler transferieren (zu), abgeben (an acc); Geld überweisen (an acc, auf acc); JUR Eigentum, Recht übertragen (auf acc); v/i SPORT wechseln (to zu); umsteigen (from ... to ... von ... auf ... acc); 2. Verlegung f; Versetzung f; SPORT Transfer m, Wechsel m; ECON Überweisung f; JUR Übertragung f; Umsteige(fahr)karte f

trans·fer·a·ble übertragbar

trans·fixed fig versteinert, starr

trans·form umwandeln, verwandeln

trans·for·ma·tion Umwandlung f, Verwandlung f

trans·form·er ELECTR Transformator m

trans·fu·sion Bluttransfusion f, Blutübertragung f

trans·gress verletzen, verstoßen gegen

tran·sient flüchtig, vergänglich

tran·sis·tor Transistor m

tran·sit Transit-, Durchgangsverkehr m; ECON Transport m; **in ~** unterwegs, auf dem Transport

tran·si·tion Übergang m

tran·si·tive LING transitiv

tran·si·to·ry → **transient**

trans·late übersetzen (**from English into German** aus dem Englischen ins Deutsche)

trans·la·tion Übersetzung f

trans·la·tor Übersetzer(in)

trans·lu·cent lichtdurchlässig

trans·mis·sion MED Übertragung f; radio, TV Sendung f; MOT Getriebe n

trans·mit Signale (aus)senden; radio, TV senden; PHYS Wärme etc leiten, Licht etc durchlassen; MED Krankheit übertragen

trans·mit·ter Sender m

trans·par·en·cy Durchsichtigkeit f (a. fig); fig Durchschaubarkeit f; Dia (-positiv) n; Folie f; **trans·par·ent** durchsichtig (a. fig); fig durchschaubar

tran·spire transpirieren, schwitzen; fig durchsickern; F passieren

trans·plant 1. umpflanzen, verpflanzen (a. MED); MED transplantieren; 2. MED Transplantation f, Verpflanzung f; Transplantat n

trans·port 1. Transport m, Beförderung f; Beförderungs-, Verkehrsmittel n or pl; MIL Transportschiff n, -flugzeug n, (Truppen)Transporter m; 2. transportieren, befördern

trans·port·a·ble transportabel, transportfähig

trans·por·ta·tion Transport m, Beförderung f

trap 1. Falle f (a. fig); **set a ~ for s.o.** j-m e-e Falle stellen; **shut one's ~, keep one's ~ shut** F die Schnauze halten; 2. (in or mit e-r Falle) fangen; fig in e-e Falle locken; **be ~ped** eingeschlossen sein

trap·door Falltür f; THEA Versenkung f

tra·peze Trapez n

trap·per Trapper m, Fallensteller m, Pelztierjäger m

trap·pings Rangabzeichen pl; fig Drum und Dran n

trash F Schund m; Quatsch m, Unsinn m; Abfall m, Abfälle pl, Müll m; Gesindel n

trash·can Abfall-, Mülleimer m; Abfall-, Mülltonne f

trash·y Schund...

trav·el 1. v/i reisen; fahren; TECH etc sich bewegen; fig sich verbreiten; fig schweifen, wandern; v/t bereisen; Strecke zurücklegen, fahren; 2. Reisen

n; pl (esp Auslands)Reisen pl; ~
a·gen·cy Reisebüro n; ~ **a·gent's**, ~ **bu·reau**
Reisebüroinhaber(in); Angestellte m, f in
e-m Reisebüro; ~ **a·gent's**, ~ **bu·reau**
Reisebüro n

trav·el·(l)er Reisende m, f
trav·el·(l)er's check (Br **cheque**) Reise-, Travellerscheck m
trav·el·(l)ing bag Reisetasche f; ~ **ex·pens·es** Reisekosten pl
trav·el sick·ness Reisekrankheit f
trav·es·ty Zerrbild n
trawl 1. Schleppnetz n; **2.** mit dem Schleppnetz fischen
trawl·er MAR Trawler m
tray Tablett n; Ablagekorb m
treach·er·ous verräterisch; tückisch
treach·er·y Verrat m
trea·cle esp Br Sirup m
tread 1. treten (**on** auf acc; in acc); Pfad etc treten; **2.** Gang m; Schritt(e pl) m; (Reifen)Profil n
tread·mill Tretmühle f (a. fig)
trea·son Landesverrat m
trea·sure 1. Schatz m; **2.** sehr schätzen; in Ehren halten
trea·sur·er Schatzmeister(in)
trea·sure trove Schatzfund m
Trea·su·ry Br, ~ **De·part·ment** Finanzministerium n
treat 1. j-n, et. umgehen mit; et. ansehen, betrachten (**as** als); MED j-n behandeln (**for** gegen); j-n einladen (**to** zu); ~ **s.o. to s.th.** a. j-m et. spendieren; ~ **o.s. to s.th.** sich et. leisten or gönnen; **be ~ed for** MED in ärztlicher Behandlung sein wegen; **2.** (besondere) Freude or Überraschung; **this is my ~** das geht auf meine Rechnung, ich lade dich etc ein
trea·tise Abhandlung f
treat·ment Behandlung f
treat·y Vertrag m
tre·ble¹ 1. dreifach; **2.** (sich) verdreifachen
tre·ble² MUS Knabensopran m; radio: (Ton)Höhe f
tree BOT Baum m
tre·foil BOT Klee m
trel·lis BOT Spalier n
trem·ble zittern (**with** vor dat)
tre·men·dous gewaltig, enorm; F klasse, toll
trem·or Zittern n; Beben n

trench Graben m; MIL Schützengraben m
trend Trend m, Entwicklung f, Tendenz f; Mode f
trend·y F **1.** modern, modisch; **be ~** als schick gelten, in sein; **2.** esp Br contp Schickimicki m
tres·pass 1. ~ **on** Grundstück etc unbefugt betreten; j-s Zeit etc über Gebühr in Anspruch nehmen; **no ~ing** Betreten verboten!; **2.** unbefugtes Betreten
tres·pass·er: ~**s will be prosecuted** Betreten bei Strafe verboten!
tres·tle Bock m, Gestell n
tri·al 1. JUR Prozess m, (Gerichts)Verhandlung f, (-)Verfahren n; Erprobung f, Probe f, Prüfung f, Test m; Plage f; **on** ~ auf or zur Probe; **be on** ~ erprobt or getestet werden; **be on** ~, **stand** ~ vor Gericht stehen (**for** wegen); **by way of** ~ versuchsweise; **2.** Versuchs..., Probe...
tri·an·gle Dreieck n; Winkel m, Zeichendreieck n
tri·an·gu·lar dreieckig
tri·ath·lon SPORT Triathlon m, Dreikampf m
trib·al Stammes...
tribe (Volks)Stamm m
tri·bu·nal JUR Gericht(shof m) n
trib·u·ta·ry GEOGR Nebenfluss m
trib·ute: **be a ~ to** j-m Ehre machen; **pay ~ to** j-m Anerkennung zollen
trick 1. Trick m; (Karten- etc)Kunststück n; Streich m; card game: Stich m; (merkwürdige) Angewohnheit, Eigenart f; **play a ~ on s.o.** j-m e-n Streich spielen; **2.** Trick...; ~ **question** Fangfrage f; **3.** überlisten, F reinlegen
trick·er·y Tricks pl
trick·le 1. tröpfeln; rieseln; **2.** Tröpfeln n; Rinnsal n
trick·ster Betrüger(in), Schwindler(in)
trick·y heikel, schwierig; durchtrieben, raffiniert
tri·cy·cle Dreirad n
tri·dent Dreizack m
tri·fle 1. Kleinigkeit f; Lappalie f; **a ~** ein bisschen, etwas; **2.** ~ **with** fig spielen mit; **he is not to be ~d with** er lässt nicht mit sich spaßen
tri·fling geringfügig, unbedeutend
trig·ger Abzug m; **pull the ~** abdrücken
trig·ger-hap·py F schießwütig

trill

618

trill 1. Triller *m*; **2.** trillern

trim 1. *Hecke etc* stutzen, beschneiden, sich *den Bart etc* stutzen; *Kleidungsstück* besetzen (**with** mit); **~med with fur** pelzbesetzt, mit Pelzbesatz; **~ off** abschneiden; **2. give s.th. a ~** et. stutzen, et. (be)schneiden; **be in good ~** F gut in Form sein; **3.** gepflegt

trim·mings Besatz *m*; GASTR Beilagen *pl*

Trin·i·ty REL Dreieinigkeit *f*

trin·ket (*esp* billiges) Schmuckstück

trip 1. *v/i* stolpern (**over** über *acc*); (e-n) Fehler machen; *v/t a.* **~ up** *j-m* ein Bein stellen (*a. fig*); **2.** (kurze) Reise; Ausflug *m*, Trip *m* (*a. sl*); Stolpern *n*, Fallen *n*

tripe GASTR Kaldaunen *pl*, Kutteln *pl*

trip·le 1. dreifach; **2.** verdreifachen

trip·le jump SPORT Dreisprung *m*

trip·lets Drillinge *pl*

trip·li·cate 1. dreifach; **2. in ~** in dreifacher Ausfertigung

tri·pod PHOT Stativ *n*

trip·per *esp Br* (*esp Tages*)Ausflügler(in)

trite abgedroschen, banal

tri·umph 1. Triumph *m*, *fig* Sieg *m* (**over** über *acc*); **2.** triumphieren (**over** über *acc*)

tri·um·phal Triumph...

tri·um·phant triumphierend

triv·i·al unbedeutend, bedeutungslos; trivial, alltäglich

trol·ley *esp Br* Einkaufswagen *m*; Gepäckwagen *m*, Kofferkuli *m*; (*Tee- etc*)Wagen *m*; (**supermarket**) **~** Einkaufswagen *m*; **shopping ~** Einkaufsroller *m*

trol·ley·bus Oberleitungsbus *m*, Obus *m*

trom·bone MUS Posaune *f*

troop 1. Schar *f*; *pl* MIL Truppen *pl*; **2.** (*herein- etc*)strömen; **~ the colour** *Br* MIL e-e Fahnenparade abhalten

troop·er MIL Kavallerist *m*; Panzerjäger *m*; Polizist *m*

tro·phy Trophäe *f*

trop·ic ASTR, GEOGR Wendekreis *m*; **the ~ of Cancer** der Wendekreis des Krebses; **the ~ of Capricorn** der Wendekreis des Steinbocks

trop·i·cal tropisch, Tropen...

trop·ics Tropen *pl*

trot 1. Trab *m*; Trott *m*; **2.** traben (las-sen); **~ along** F losziehen

trou·ble 1. Schwierigkeit *f*, Problem *n*, Ärger *m*; Mühe *f*; MED Beschwerden *pl*; *a. pl* POL Unruhen *pl*; *pl* Unannehmlichkeiten *pl*; **be in ~** in Schwierigkeiten sein; **get into ~** Schwierigkeiten *or* Ärger bekommen; *j-n* in Schwierigkeiten bringen; **get or run into ~** in Schwierigkeiten geraten; **have ~ with** Schwierigkeiten *or* Ärger haben mit; **put s.o. to ~** *j-m* Mühe *or* Umstände machen; **take the ~ to do s.th.** sich die Mühe machen, et. zu tun; **2.** *v/t j-n* beunruhigen; *j-m* Mühe *or* Umstände machen; *j-n* bemühen (**for** um), bitten (**for** um; **to do** zu tun); **be ~d by** geplagt werden von, leiden an (*dat*); *v/i* sich bemühen (**to do** zu tun), Umstände machen (**about** wegen)

trou·ble·mak·er Störenfried *m*, Unruhestifter(in)

trou·ble·some lästig

trou·ble spot *esp* POL Krisenherd *m*

trough Trog *m*; Wellental *n*

trounce SPORT haushoch besiegen

troupe THEA Truppe *f*

trou·ser: (**a pair of**) **~s** (e-e) Hose *f*

trou·ser suit *Br* Hosenanzug *m*

trous·seau Aussteuer *f*

trout ZO Forelle *f*

trow·el (Maurer)Kelle *f*

tru·ant Schulschwänzer(in); **play ~** *Br* (die Schule) schwänzen

truce MIL Waffenstillstand *m* (*a. fig*)

truck 1. MOT Lastwagen *m*; Fernlaster *m*; *Br* RAIL (offener) Güterwagen; Transportkarren *m*; **2.** auf *or* mit Lastwagen transportieren

truck driv·er, **truck·er** MOT Lastwagenfahrer *m*; Fernfahrer *m*

truck farm ECON Gemüse- und Obstgärtnerei *f*

trudge (mühsam) stapfen

true wahr; echt, wirklich; treu (**to** *dat*); **be ~** wahr sein, stimmen; **come ~** in Erfüllung gehen; wahr werden; **~ to life** lebensecht

tru·ly wahrheitsgemäß; wirklich, wahrhaft; aufrichtig

trump 1. Trumpf(karte *f*) *m*; *pl* Trumpf *m*; **2.** mit e-m Trumpf stechen; **~ up** erfinden

trum·pet 1. MUS Trompete *f*; **2.** trompeten; *fig* ausposaunen

trun·cheon (Gummi)Knüppel *m*, Schlagstock *m*

trun·dle *Karren etc* ziehen

trunk (Baum)Stamm *m*; Schrankkoffer *m*; ZO Rüssel *m*; ANAT Rumpf *m*; MOT Kofferraum *m*; **~ road** *Br* Fernstraße *f*

trunks (*a.* **a pair of ~** e-e) (Bade)Hose *f*; SPORT Shorts *pl*

truss 1. *a.* **~ up** *j-n* fesseln; GASTR *Geflügel etc* dressieren; **2.** MED Bruchband *n*

trust 1. Vertrauen *n* (**in** zu); JUR Treuhand *f*; ECON Trust *m*; Großkonzern *m*; **hold s.th. in ~** et. treuhänderisch verwalten (**for** für); **place s.th. in s.o.'s ~** *j-m* et. anvertrauen; **2.** *v/t* (ver)trauen (*dat*); sich verlassen auf (*acc*); (zuversichtlich) hoffen; **~ him!** das sieht ihm ähnlich!; *v/i:* **~ in** vertrauen auf (*acc*); **~ to** sich verlassen auf (*acc*)

trust·ee JUR Treuhänder(in); Sachverwalter(in)

trust·ful, **trust·ing** vertrauensvoll

trust·wor·thy vertrauenswürdig, zuverlässig

truth Wahrheit *f*

truth·ful wahr; wahrheitsliebend

try 1. *v/t* versuchen; *et.* (aus)probieren; JUR (über) *e-e Sache* verhandeln; *j-m* den Prozess machen (**for** wegen); *j-n*, *j-s* Geduld, Nerven *etc* auf die harte Probe stellen; **~ s.th. on** Kleid *etc* anprobieren; **~ s.th. out** et. ausprobieren; *v/i* versuchen; **~ for** *Br*, **~ out for** sich bemühen um; **2.** Versuch *m*; **give s.o.**, **s.th. a ~** es mit *j-m*, et. versuchen; **have a ~** es versuchen; **try·ing** anstrengend

tsar HIST Zar *m*

T-shirt T-Shirt *n*

tub Bottich *m*, Zuber *m*, Tonne *f*; Becher *m*; F (Bade)Wanne *f*

tub·by F pumm(e)lig

tube Röhre *f* (*a.* ANAT), Rohr *n*; Schlauch *m*; Tube *f*; *Br* F U-Bahn *f* (*in* London); F Röhre *f*, Glotze *f*

tube·less schlauchlos

tu·ber BOT Knolle *f*

tu·ber·cu·lo·sis MED Tuberkulose *f*

tu·bu·lar röhrenförmig

tuck 1. stecken; **~ away** F wegstecken; **~ in** *esp Br* F reinhauen, zulangen; **~ up** (**in bed**) *Kind* ins Bett packen; **2.** Biese *f*; Saum *m*; Abnäher *m*

Tue(s) ABBR *of* **Tuesday** Di., Dienstag *m*

Tues·day (ABBR **Tue**, **Tues**) Dienstag *m*; **on ~** (am) Dienstag; **on ~s** dienstags

tuft (*Gras-*, *Haar- etc*)Büschel *n*

tug 1. zerren *or* ziehen (**an** *dat or* **at** an *dat*); **2.** **give s.th. a ~** zerren *or* ziehen an (*dat*)

tug-of-war SPORT Tauziehen *n* (*a. fig*)

tu·i·tion Unterricht *m*; Unterrichtsgebühr(en *pl*) *f*

tu·lip BOT Tulpe *f*

tum·ble 1. fallen, stürzen; purzeln (*a. fig*); **2.** Fall *m*, Sturz *m*

tum·ble·down baufällig

tum·bler (Trink)Glas *n*

tu·mid MED geschwollen

tum·my F Bauch *m*, Bäuchlein *n*

tu·mo(u)r MED Tumor *m*

tu·mult Tumult *m*

tu·mul·tu·ous tumultartig, (*applause etc*) stürmisch

tu·na ZO Thunfisch *m*

tune 1. MUS Melodie *f*; **be out of ~** verstimmt sein; **2.** *v/t mst* **~ in** Radio *etc* einstellen (**to** auf *acc*); *a.* **~ up** MUS stimmen; *a.* **~ up** Motor tunen; *v/i:* **~ in** (das Radio *etc*) einschalten; **~ up** MUS (die Instrumente) stimmen

tune·ful melodisch

tune·less unmelodisch

tun·er radio, TV Tuner *m*

tun·nel 1. Tunnel *m*; **2.** Berg durchtunneln; Fluss *etc* untertunneln

tun·ny ZO Thunfisch *m*

tur·ban Turban *m*

tur·bid trüb (*water*); dick, dicht (*smoke etc*); *fig* verworren, wirr

tur·bine TECH Turbine *f*

tur·bo F, **tur·bo·charg·er** MOT Turbolader *m*

tur·bot ZO Steinbutt *m*

tur·bu·lent turbulent

tu·reen (Suppen)Terrine *f*

turf 1. Rasen *m*; Sode *f*, Rasenstück *n*; **the ~** die (Pferde)Rennbahn; der Pferderennsport; **2.** mit Rasen bedecken

tur·gid MED geschwollen

Turk Türke *m*, Türkin *f*

Tur·key die Türkei

tur·key ZO Truthahn *m*, Truthenne *f*, Pute *f*, Puter *m*; **talk ~** F offen *or* sachlich reden

Turk·ish 1. türkisch; **2.** LING Türkisch *n*

tur·moil Aufruhr *m*

turn 1. *v/t* drehen, herum-, umdrehen; (um)wenden; *Seite* umblättern; *Schlauch etc* richten (**on** auf *acc*); *Antenne* ausrichten (**toward[s]** auf *acc*); *Aufmerksamkeit* zuwenden (**to** *dat*); verwandeln (**into** in *acc*); *Laub etc* färben; *Milch* sauer werden lassen; TECH formen, drechseln; **~ the corner** um die Ecke biegen; **~ loose** los-, freilassen; **~ s.o.'s stomach** j-m den Magen umdrehen; → **inside** 1, **upside down, somersault** 1; *v/i* sich (um)drehen; abbiegen; einbiegen (**onto** auf *acc*; **into** in *acc*); MOT wenden; *blass, sauer etc* werden; sich verwandeln, *fig a.* umschlagen (**into, to** in *acc*); → **left** 2, **righ** 2; **~ against** j-n aufbringen *or* aufhetzen gegen; *fig* sich wenden gegen; **~ away** (sich) abwenden (**from** von); j-n abweisen, wegschicken; **~ back** umkehren; j-n zurückschicken; *Uhr* zurückstellen; **~ down** *Radio etc* leiser stellen; *Gas etc* klein(er) stellen; *Heizung etc* runterschalten; j-n, *Angebot etc* ablehnen; *Kragen* umschlagen; *Bettdecke* zurückschlagen; **~ in** *v/t* zurückgeben; *Gewinn etc* erzielen, machen; *Arbeit* einreichen, abgeben; **~ o.s. in** sich stellen; *v/i* F sich aufs Ohr legen; **~ off** *v/t Gas, Wasser etc* abdrehen; *Licht, Radio etc* ausmachen, ausschalten; *Motor* abstellen; F j-n anwidern; F j-m die Lust nehmen; *v/i* abbiegen; **~ on** *Gas, Wasser etc* aufdrehen; *Gerät* anstellen; *Licht, Radio etc* anmachen, an-, einschalten; F j-n antörnen; **~ out** *v/t Licht* ausmachen, ausschalten; j-n hinauswerfen; F *Waren* ausstoßen; *Tasche etc* (aus)leeren; *v/i* kommen (**for** zu); sich erweisen *or* herausstellen als; **~ over** (sich) umdrehen; *Seite* umblättern; wenden; *et.* umkippen; sich *et.* überlegen; j-n, *et.* übergeben (**to** *dat*); *Waren* umsetzen; **~ one's car round** sich umdrehen; **~ to** sich an j-n wenden; sich zuwenden (*dat*); **~ up** *Kragen* hochschlagen; *Ärmel, Saum etc* umschlagen; *Radio etc* lauter stellen; *Gas etc* aufdrehen; *fig* auftauchen; **2.** (Um)Drehung *f*, Biegung *f*, Kurve *f*, Kehre *f*; Abzweigung *f*; *fig* Wende *f*, Wendung *f*; **at every ~** auf Schritt und

Tritt; **by ~s** abwechselnd; **in ~** der Reihe nach; abwechselnd; **it is my ~** ich bin an der Reihe *or* F dran; **make a left ~** (nach) links abbiegen; **take ~s** sich abwechseln (**at** bei); **take a ~ for the better** (**worse**) sich bessern (sich verschlimmern); **do s.o. a good** (**bad**) **~** j-m e-n guten (schlechten) Dienst erweisen

turn·coat Abtrünnige *m, f,* Überläufer (in); (*political*) ~ F Wendehals *m*

turn·er Drechsler *m*; Dreher *m*

turn·ing *esp Br* Abzweigung *f*

turn·ing cir·cle MOT Wendekreis *m*

turn·ing point *fig* Wendepunkt *m*

tur·nip BOT Rübe *f*

turn-off Abzweigung *f*

turn·out Besucher(zahl *f*) *pl,* Beteiligung *f*; Wahlbeteiligung *f*; F Aufmachung *f*

turn·o·ver ECON Umsatz *m*; Personalwechsel *m,* Fluktuation *f*

turn·pike (**road**) gebührenpflichtige Schnellstraße

turn·stile Drehkreuz *n*

turn·ta·ble Plattenteller *m*

turn-up *Br* (Hosen)Aufschlag *m*

tur·pen·tine CHEM Terpentin *n*

tur·quoise MIN Türkis *m*

tur·ret ARCH Ecktürmchen *n*; MIL (Panzer)Turm *m*; MAR Gefechtsturm *m,* Geschützturm *m*

tur·tle ZO (See)Schildkröte *f*

tur·tle-dove ZO Turteltaube *f*

tur·tle-neck Rollkragen(pullover) *m*

tusk ZO Stoßzahn *m*; Hauer *m*

tus·sle F Gerangel *n*

tus·sock Grasbüschel *n*

tu·te·lage (An)Leitung *f*; JUR Vormundschaft *f*

tu·tor Privat-, Hauslehrer(in); *Br* UNIV Tutor(in), Studienleiter(in)

tu·to·ri·al *Br* UNIV Tutorenkurs *m*

tux·e·do Smoking *m*

TV 1. TV *n,* Fernsehen *n*; Fernsehgerät *n,* F Fernseher *m*; **on ~** im Fernsehen; **watch ~** fernsehen; **2.** Fernseh...

twang 1. Schwirren *n*; *mst* **nasal ~** näselnde Aussprache; **2.** schwirren (lassen)

tweak F zwicken, kneifen

tweet ZO piep(s)en

tweez·ers (*a pair of ~* e-e) Pinzette *f*

twelfth 1. zwölfte(r, -s); **2.** Zwölftel *n*

twelve 1. zwölf; **2.** Zwölf *f*
twen·ti·eth zwanzigste(r, -s)
twen·ty 1. zwanzig; **2.** Zwanzig *f*
twice zweimal
twid·dle (herum)spielen mit (*or* **with** mit); **~ one's thumbs** Däumchen drehen
twig BOT dünner Zweig, Ästchen *n*
twi·light (*esp* Abend)Dämmerung *f*; Zwielicht *n*, Dämmerlicht *n*
twin 1. Zwilling *m*; *pl* Zwillinge *pl*; **2.** Zwillings...; doppelt; **3. be ~ned with** die Partnerstadt sein von
twin-bed·ded room Zweibettzimmer *n*
twin beds zwei Einzelbetten
twin broth·er Zwillingsbruder *m*
twine 1. Bindfaden *m*, Schnur *f*; **2.** (sich) schlingen *or* winden (*round* um); *a.* **~ together** zusammendrehen
twin-en·gined AVIAT zweimotorig
twinge stechender Schmerz, Stechen *n*; **a ~ of conscience** Gewissensbisse *pl*
twin·kle 1. glitzern (*stars*), (*a.* *eyes*) funkeln (*with* vor *dat*); **2.** Glitzern *n*, Funkeln *n*; **with a ~ in one's eye** augenzwinkernd
twin sis·ter Zwillingsschwester *f*
twin town Partnerstadt *f*
twirl 1. (herum)wirbeln; wirbeln (*round* über *acc*); **2.** Wirbel *m*
twist 1. *v/t* drehen; wickeln (*round* um); *fig* verdrehen; **~ off** abdrehen, *Deckel* abschrauben; **~ one's ankle** (mit dem Fuß) umknicken, sich den Fuß vertreten; **her face was ~ed with pain** ihr Gesicht war schmerzverzerrt; *v/i* sich winden, (*river etc a.*) sich schlängeln; **2.** Drehung *f*; Biegung *f*; (*überraschende*) Wendung; MUS Twist *m*
twitch 1. *v/t* zucken (mit); *v/i* zucken (*with* vor); zupfen (*at* an *dat*); **2.** Zucken *n*; Zuckung *f*

twit·ter 1. zwitschern; **2.** Zwitschern *n*, Gezwitscher *n*; **be all of a ~** F ganz aufgeregt sein
two 1. zwei; *the ~ cars* die beiden Autos; *the ~ of us* wir beide; *in ~s* zu zweit, paarweise; *cut in ~* in zwei Teile schneiden; *put ~ and ~ together* zwei und zwei zusammenzählen; **2.** Zwei *f*
two-edged zweischneidig
two-faced falsch, heuchlerisch
two·fold zweifach
two·pence *Br* zwei Pence *pl*
two·pen·ny *Br* F für zwei Pence
two-piece zweiteilig; **~ dress** Jackenkleid *n*
two-seat·er AVIAT, MOT Zweisitzer *m*
two-sid·ed zweiseitig
two-sto·ried, *Br* **two-sto·rey** zweistöckig
two-way traf·fic MOT Gegenverkehr *m*
ty·coon (*Industrie- etc*)Magnat *m*
type 1. Art *f*, Sorte *f*; Typ *m*; PRINT Type *f*, Buchstabe *m*; **2.** *v/t et.* mit der Maschine schreiben, tippen; *v/i* Maschine schreiben, tippen
type·writ·er Schreibmaschine *f*
type·writ·ten maschine(n)geschrieben
ty·phoid (*fe·ver*) MED Typhus *m*
ty·phoon Taifun *m*
ty·phus MED Flecktyphus *m*, -fieber *n*
typ·i·cal typisch, bezeichnend (*of* für)
typ·i·fy typisch sein für, kennzeichnen; verkörpern
typ·ing er·ror Tippfehler *m*
typ·ing pool ECON Schreibzentrale *f*
typ·ist Schreibkraft *f*; Maschinenschreiber(in)
ty·ran·ni·cal tyrannisch
ty·ran·nize tyrannisieren
ty·ran·ny Tyrannei *f*
ty·rant Tyrann(in)
tyre *Br* → **tire**¹
tzar → **tsar**

T

U

U, u U, u *n*

ud·der zo Euter *n*

ug·ly hässlich (*a. fig*); bös(e), schlimm (*wound etc*)

ul·cer MED Geschwür *n*

ul·te·ri·or: ~ *motive* Hintergedanke *m*

ul·ti·mate letzte(r, -s), End...; höchste (r, -s)

ul·ti·mate·ly letztlich; schließlich

ul·ti·ma·tum Ultimatum *n*; *deliver an ~ to s.o.* j-m ein Ultimatum stellen

ul·tra·high fre·quen·cy ELECTR Ultrakurzwelle *f*

ul·tra·ma·rine ultramarin

ul·tra·son·ic Ultraschall...

ul·tra·sound PHYS Ultraschall *m*

ul·tra·vi·o·let ultraviolett

um·bil·i·cal cord ANAT Nabelschnur *f*

um·brel·la (Regen)Schirm *m*; *fig* Schutz *m*

um·pire SPORT 1. Schiedsrichter(in); 2. als Schiedsrichter(in) fungieren (bei)

un·a·bashed unverfroren

un·a·bat·ed unvermindert

un·a·ble unfähig, außerstande, nicht in der Lage

un·ac·cept·a·ble unzumutbar

un·ac·count·a·ble unerklärlich

un·ac·cus·tomed ungewohnt

un·ac·quaint·ed: *be ~ with s.th.* et. nicht kennen, mit e-r Sache nicht vertraut sein

un·ad·vised unbesonnen, unüberlegt

un·af·fect·ed natürlich, ungekünstelt; *be ~ by* nicht betroffen sein von

un·aid·ed ohne Unterstützung, (ganz) allein

un·al·ter·a·ble unabänderlich

un·an·i·mous einmütig; einstimmig

un·an·nounced unangemeldet

un·an·swer·a·ble unwiderlegbar; nicht zu beantworten(d)

un·ap·pe·tiz·ing unappetitlich

un·ap·proach·a·ble unnahbar

un·armed unbewaffnet

un·asked ungestellt (*question*); unaufgefordert, ungebeten (*guest etc*)

un·as·sist·ed ohne (fremde) Hilfe, (ganz) allein

un·as·sum·ing bescheiden

un·at·tached ungebunden, frei

un·at·tend·ed unbeaufsichtigt

un·at·trac·tive unattraktiv, wenig anziehend, reizlos

un·au·thor·ized unberechtigt, unbefugt

un·a·void·a·ble unvermeidlich

un·a·ware: *be ~ of s.th.* sich e-r Sache nicht bewusst sein, et. nicht bemerken

un·a·wares: *catch or take s.o. ~* j-n überraschen

un·bal·ance *j-n* aus dem (seelischen) Gleichgewicht bringen

un·bal·anced unausgeglichen, labil

un·bar aufriegeln, entriegeln

un·bear·a·ble unerträglich; *person:* unausstehlich

un·beat·a·ble unschlagbar

un·beat·en ungeschlagen, unbesiegt

un·be·com·ing unvorteilhaft

un·be·known(st): ~ *to s.o.* ohne j-s Wissen

un·be·liev·a·ble unglaublich

un·bend gerade biegen; sich aufrichten; *fig* aus sich herausgehen, auftauen

un·bend·ing unbeugsam

un·bi·as(s)ed unvoreingenommen; JUR unbefangen

un·bind losbinden

un·blem·ished makellos

un·born ungeboren

un·break·a·ble unzerbrechlich

un·bri·dled *fig* ungezügelt, zügellos; ~ *tongue* lose Zunge

un·bro·ken ununterbrochen; heil, unversehrt; nicht zugeritten (*horse*)

un·buck·le aufschnallen, losschnallen

un·bur·den: ~ *o.s. to s.o.* j-m sein Herz ausschütten

un·but·ton aufknöpfen

un·called-for ungerechtfertigt; unnötig; unpassend

un·can·ny unheimlich

un·cared-for vernachlässigt

un·ceas·ing unaufhörlich

un·cer·e·mo·ni·ous brüsk, unhöflich; überstürzt

un·cer·tain unsicher, ungewiss, unbestimmt; vage; METEOR unbeständig

un·cer·tain·ty Unsicherheit f, Ungewissheit f
un·chain losketten
un·changed unverändert
un·chang·ing unveränderlich
un·char·i·ta·ble unfair
un·checked ungehindert; ungeprüft
un·chris·tian unchristlich
un·civ·il unhöflich
un·civ·i·lized unzivilisiert
un·cle Onkel m
un·com·fort·a·ble unbequem; feel ~ sich unbehaglich fühlen
un·com·mon ungewöhnlich
un·com·mu·ni·ca·tive wortkarg, verschlossen
un·com·pre·hend·ing verständnislos
un·com·pro·mis·ing kompromisslos
un·con·cerned: be ~ about sich keine Gedanken or Sorgen machen über (acc); be ~ with uninteressiert sein an (dat)
un·con·di·tion·al bedingungslos
un·con·firmed unbestätigt
un·con·scious unbewusst; unbeabsichtigt; MED bewusstlos; be ~ of sich e-r Sache nicht bewusst sein, nicht bemerken; un·con·scious·ness MED Bewusstlosigkeit f
un·con·sti·tu·tion·al verfassungswidrig
un·con·trol·la·ble unkontrollierbar; nicht zu bändigen(d); unbändig (rage etc); un·con·trolled unkontrolliert
un·con·ven·tion·al unkonventionell
un·con·vinced: be ~ nicht überzeugt sein (about von)
un·con·vinc·ing nicht überzeugend
un·cooked ungekocht, roh
un·cork entkorken
un·count·a·ble unzählbar
un·coup·le abkoppeln
un·couth fig ungehobelt
un·cov·er aufdecken, fig a. enthüllen
un·crit·i·cal unkritisch; be ~ of s.th. e-r Sache unkritisch gegenüberstehen
unc·tion REL Salbung f
unc·tu·ous salbungsvoll
un·cut ungekürzt (film, novel etc); ungeschliffen (diamond etc)
un·dam·aged unbeschädigt, unversehrt, heil
un·dat·ed undatiert, ohne Datum
un·daunt·ed unerschrocken, furchtlos

un·de·cid·ed unentschieden, offen; unentschlossen
un·de·mon·stra·tive zurückhaltend, reserviert
un·de·ni·a·ble unbestreitbar
un·der 1. prp unter (dat or acc); 2. adv unten; darunter
un·der·age minderjährig
un·der·bid unterbieten
un·der·brush → undergrowth
un·der·car·riage AVIAT Fahrwerk n, Fahrgestell n
un·der·charge zu wenig berechnen; zu wenig verlangen
un·der·clothes, un·der·cloth·ing → underwear
un·der·coat Grundierung f
un·der·cov·er: ~ agent verdeckter Ermittler
un·der·cut j-n (im Preis) unterbieten
un·der·de·vel·oped unterentwickelt; ~ country Entwicklungsland n
un·der·dog Benachteiligte m, f
un·der·done nicht durchgebraten
un·der·es·ti·mate zu niedrig schätzen or veranschlagen; fig unterschätzen
un·der·ex·pose PHOT unterbelichten
un·der·fed unterernährt
un·der·go erleben, durchmachen; MED sich e-r Operation etc unterziehen
un·der·grad F, un·der·grad·u·ate Student(in)
un·der·ground 1. adv unterirdisch, unter der Erde; 2. adj unterirdisch; fig Untergrund...; 3. esp Br Untergrundbahn f, U-Bahn f; by ~ mit der U-Bahn
un·der·growth Unterholz n
un·der·hand, un·der·hand·ed heimlich; hinterhältig
un·der·line unterstreichen (a. fig)
un·der·ling contp Untergebene m, f
un·der·ly·ing zugrunde liegend
un·der·mine unterspülen; fig untergraben, unterminieren
un·der·neath 1. prp unter (dat or acc); 2. adv darunter
un·der·nour·ished unterernährt
un·der·pants Unterhose f
un·der·pass Unterführung f
un·der·pay j-m zu wenig bezahlen, j-n unterbezahlen
un·der·priv·i·leged unterprivilegiert, benachteiligt
un·der·rate unterbewerten, -schätzen

U

un·der·sec·re·ta·ry POL Staatssekretär m

un·der·sell ECON *Ware* verschleudern, unter Wert verkaufen; **~ o.s.** *fig* sich schlecht verkaufen

un·der·shirt Unterhemd n

un·der·side Unterseite f

un·der·signed: the ~ der or die Unterzeichnete, die Unterzeichneten pl

un·der·size(d) zu klein

un·der·staffed (personell) unterbesetzt

un·der·stand verstehen; erfahren or gehört haben (**that** dass); **make o.s. understood** sich verständlich machen; **am I to ~ that** soll das heißen, dass; **give s.o. to ~ that** j-m zu verstehen geben, dass

un·der·stand·a·ble verständlich

un·der·stand·ing 1. Verstand m; Verständnis n; Abmachung f; Verständigung f; **come to an ~** e-e Abmachung treffen (**with** mit); **on the ~ that** unter der Voraussetzung, dass; **2.** verständnisvoll

un·der·state untertreiben, untertrieben darstellen; **un·der·state·ment** Understatement n, Untertreibung f

un·der·take *et.* übernehmen; sich verpflichten (**to do** zu tun)

un·der·tak·er Leichenbestatter m; Beerdigungs-, Bestattungsinstitut n

un·der·tak·ing Unternehmen n; Zusicherung f

un·der·tone *fig* Unterton m; **in an ~** mit gedämpfter Stimme

un·der·val·ue unterbewerten

un·der·wa·ter 1. *adj* Unterwasser...; **2.** *adv* unter Wasser

un·der·wear Unterwäsche f

un·der·weight 1. Untergewicht n; **2.** untergewichtig, zu leicht (**by** um); **she is five pounds ~** sie hat fünf Pfund Untergewicht

un·der·world Unterwelt f

un·de·served unverdient

un·de·sir·a·ble unerwünscht

un·de·vel·oped unerschlossen (*area*); unentwickelt

un·dies F (Damen)Unterwäsche f

un·dig·ni·fied würdelos

un·di·min·ished unvermindert

un·dis·ci·plined undiszipliniert

un·dis·cov·ered unentdeckt

un·dis·guised unverhohlen

un·dis·put·ed unbestritten

un·dis·turbed ungestört

un·di·vid·ed ungeteilt

un·do aufmachen, öffnen; *fig* zunichte machen; **un·do·ing: be s.o.'s ~** j-s Ruin or Verderben sein; **un·done** unerledigt; offen; **come ~** aufgehen

un·doubt·ed unbestritten

un·doubt·ed·ly zweifellos, ohne (jeden) Zweifel

un·dreamed-of, un·dreamt-of ungeahnt

un·dress sich ausziehen; *j-n* ausziehen

un·due übermäßig

un·du·lat·ing sanft (*hills*)

un·dy·ing ewig

un·earned *fig* unverdient

un·earth ausgraben, *fig a.* ausfindig machen, aufstöbern

un·earth·ly überirdisch; unheimlich; **at an ~ hour** F zu e-r unchristlichen Zeit

un·eas·i·ness Unbehagen n

un·eas·y unruhig (*sleep*); unsicher (*peace*); **feel ~** sich unbehaglich fühlen; **I'm ~ about** mir ist nicht wohl bei

un·e·co·nom·ic unwirtschaftlich

un·ed·u·cat·ed ungebildet

un·e·mo·tion·al leidenschaftslos, kühl, beherrscht

un·em·ployed 1. arbeitslos; **2. the ~** die Arbeitslosen pl

un·em·ploy·ment Arbeitslosigkeit f; **~ ben·e·fit** Br, **~ com·pen·sa·tion** Arbeitslosengeld n

un·end·ing endlos

un·en·dur·a·ble unerträglich

un·en·vi·a·ble wenig beneidenswert

un·e·qual ungleich (*a. fig*), unterschiedlich; *fig* einseitig; **be ~ to** e-r Aufgabe *etc* nicht gewachsen sein

un·e·qual(l)ed unerreicht, unübertroffen

un·er·ring unfehlbar

un·e·ven uneben; ungleich(mäßig); ungerade (*number*)

un·e·vent·ful ereignislos

un·ex·am·pled beispiellos

un·ex·pec·ted unerwartet

un·ex·posed PHOT unbelichtet

un·fail·ing unerschöpflich; nie versagend

un·fair unfair, ungerecht

un·faith·ful untreu (**to** dat)

un·fa·mil·i·ar ungewohnt; unbekannt; nicht vertraut (**with** mit)

un·fas·ten aufmachen, öffnen; losbinden

un·fa·vo(u)r·a·ble ungünstig; unvorteilhaft (**for, to** für); negativ, ablehnend

un·feel·ing gefühllos, herzlos

un·fin·ished unvollendet; unfertig; unerledigt

un·fit nicht fit, nicht in Form; ungeeignet, untauglich; unfähig

un·flag·ging unermüdlich, unentwegt

un·flap·pa·ble F nicht aus der Ruhe zu bringen(d)

un·fold auffalten, auseinander falten; darlegen, enthüllen; sich entfalten

un·fore·seen unvorhergesehen, unerwartet

un·for·get·ta·ble unvergesslich

un·for·got·ten unvergessen

un·for·tu·nate unglücklich; unglückselig; bedauerlich

un·for·tu·nate·ly leider

un·found·ed unbegründet

un·friend·ly unfreundlich (**to, towards** zu)

un·furl *Fahne* aufrollen, entrollen, *Segel* losmachen

un·fur·nished unmöbliert

un·gain·ly linkisch, unbeholfen

un·god·ly gottlos; **at an ~ hour** F zu e-r unchristlichen Zeit

un·gra·cious ungnädig; unfreundlich

un·grate·ful undankbar

un·guard·ed unbewacht; unbedacht, überlegt

un·hap·pi·ly unglücklicherweise, leider; **un·hap·py** unglücklich

un·harmed unversehrt

un·health·y kränklich, nicht gesund; ungesund; *contp* krankhaft, unnatürlich

un·heard: **go ~** keine Beachtung finden, unbeachtet bleiben; **un·heard-of** noch nie da gewesen, beispiellos

un·hinge: **~ s.o.('s mind)** *fig* j-n völlig aus dem Gleichgewicht bringen

un·ho·ly F furchtbar, schrecklich

un·hoped-for unverhofft, unerwartet

un·hurt unverletzt

u·ni·corn Einhorn *n*

un·i·den·ti·fied unbekannt, nicht identifiziert

u·ni·fi·ca·tion Vereinigung *f*

u·ni·form 1. Uniform *f*; 2. gleichmäßig; einheitlich

u·ni·form·i·ty Einheitlichkeit *f*

u·ni·fy verein(ig)en; vereinheitlichen

u·ni·lat·e·ral *fig* einseitig

un·i·mag·in·a·ble unvorstellbar

un·i·mag·in·a·tive fantasielos, einfallslos

un·im·por·tant unwichtig

un·im·pressed: **remain ~** unbeeindruckt bleiben (**by** von)

un·in·formed nicht unterrichtet *or* eingeweiht

un·in·hab·it·a·ble unbewohnbar

un·in·hab·it·ed unbewohnt

un·in·jured unverletzt

un·in·tel·li·gi·ble unverständlich

un·in·ten·tion·al unabsichtlich, unbeabsichtigt

un·in·terest·ed uninteressiert (**in** an *dat*); **be ~ in** a. sich nicht interessieren für; **un·in·terest·ing** uninteressant

un·in·ter·rupt·ed ununterbrochen

u·nion Vereinigung *f*; Union *f*; Gewerkschaft *f*; **u·nion·ist** Gewerkschaftler(in); **u·nion·ize** (sich) gewerkschaftlich organisieren

u·nique einzigartig; einmalig

u·ni·son: **in ~** gemeinsam

u·nit Einheit *f*; PED Unit *f*, Lehreinheit *f*; MATH Einer *m*; TECH (Anbau)Element *n*, Teil *n*; **~ furniture** Anbaumöbel *pl*

u·nite verbinden, vereinigen; sich vereinigen *or* zusammentun

u·nit·ed vereinigt, vereint

U·nit·ed King·dom *das* Vereinigte Königreich (*England, Scotland, Wales and Northern Ireland*)

U·nit·ed States of A·mer·i·ca *die* Vereinigten Staaten von Amerika

u·ni·ty Einheit *f*; MATH Eins *f*

u·ni·ver·sal allgemein; universal, universell; Welt...

u·ni·verse Universum *n*, Weltall *n*

u·ni·ver·si·ty Universität *f*, Hochschule *f*; **~ grad·u·ate** Akademiker(in)

un·just ungerecht

un·kempt ungekämmt (*hair*); ungepflegt (*clothes etc*)

un·kind unfreundlich

un·known 1. unbekannt (**to** dat); 2. der, die, das Unbekannte; **~ quan·ti·ty**

MATH unbekannte Größe (*a. fig*), Unbekannte *f*

un·law·ful ungesetzlich, gesetzwidrig

un·lead·ed bleifrei

un·learn *Ansichten etc* ablegen, aufgeben

un·less wenn ... nicht, außer wenn ..., es sei denn ...

un·like *prp* im Gegensatz zu; *he is very ~ his father* er ist ganz anders als sein Vater; *that is very ~ him* das sieht ihm gar nicht ähnlich

un·like·ly unwahrscheinlich

un·lim·it·ed unbegrenzt

un·list·ed: *be ~* nicht im Telefonbuch stehen; *~* **num·ber** TEL Geheimnummer *f*

un·load entladen, abladen, ausladen; MAR *Ladung* löschen

un·lock aufschließen

un·loos·en losmachen; lockern; lösen

un·loved ungeliebt

un·luck·y unglücklich; *be ~* Pech haben

un·made ungemacht

un·manned unbemannt

un·marked nicht gekennzeichnet; SPORT ungedeckt, frei

un·mar·ried unverheiratet, ledig

un·mask *fig* entlarven

un·matched unübertroffen, unvergleichlich

un·men·tio·na·ble Tabu...; *be ~* tabu sein

un·mis·tak·a·ble unverkennbar, unverwechselbar, untrüglich

un·mo·lest·ed unbehelligt

un·moved ungerührt; *she remained ~ by it* es ließ sie kalt

un·mu·si·cal unmusikalisch

un·named ungenannt

un·nat·u·ral unnatürlich; widernatürlich

un·ne·ces·sa·ry unnötig

un·nerve entnerven

un·no·ticed unbemerkt

un·num·bered unnummeriert

un·ob·tru·sive unauffällig, unaufdringlich

un·oc·cu·pied leer (stehend), unbewohnt; unbeschäftigt

un·of·fi·cial inoffiziell

un·pack auspacken

un·paid unbezahlt; *post* unfrei

un·par·al·leled einmalig, beispiellos

un·par·don·a·ble unverzeihlich

un·per·turbed gelassen, ruhig

un·pick *Naht etc* auftrennen

un·placed: *be ~* SPORT sich nicht platzieren können

un·play·a·ble SPORT unbespielbar

un·pleas·ant unangenehm, unerfreulich; unfreundlich

un·plug den Stecker (*gen*) herausziehen

un·pol·ished unpoliert; *fig* ungehobelt

un·pol·lut·ed sauber, unverschmutzt

un·pop·u·lar unpopulär, unbeliebt

un·pop·u·lar·i·ty Unbeliebtheit *f*

un·prac·ti·cal unpraktisch

un·prac·ticed, *Br* **un·prac·tised** ungeübt

un·pre·ce·dent·ed beispiellos, noch nie da gewesen

un·pre·dict·a·ble unvorhersehbar; unberechenbar (*person*)

un·prej·u·diced unvoreingenommen; JUR unbefangen

un·pre·med·i·tat·ed nicht vorsätzlich; unüberlegt

un·pre·pared unvorbereitet

un·pre·ten·tious bescheiden, einfach, schlicht

un·prin·ci·pled skrupellos, gewissenlos

un·prin·ta·ble nicht druckfähig *or* druckreif

un·pro·duc·tive unproduktiv, unergiebig

un·pro·fes·sion·al unprofessionell; unfachmännisch

un·prof·it·a·ble unrentabel

un·pro·nounce·a·ble unaussprechbar

un·pro·tect·ed ungeschützt

un·proved, **un·prov·en** unbewiesen

un·pro·voked grundlos

un·pun·ished unbestraft, ungestraft; *go ~* straflos bleiben

un·qual·i·fied unqualifiziert, ungeeignet (*for* für); uneingeschränkt

un·ques·tion·a·ble unbestritten

un·ques·tion·ing bedingungslos

un·quote: *quote ... ~* Zitat ... Zitat Ende

un·rav·el (sich) auftrennen (*pullover etc*); entwirren

un·read·a·ble nicht lesenswert, unlesbar, *a.* unleserlich

un·re·al unwirklich

un·re·al·is·tic unrealistisch

un·rea·son·a·ble unvernünftig; übertrieben, unzumutbar

un·rec·og·niz·a·ble nicht wieder zu erkennen(d)

un·re·lat·ed: *be* ~ in keinem Zusammenhang stehen (*to* mit)

un·re·lent·ing unvermindert

un·re·li·a·ble unzuverlässig

un·re·lieved ununterbrochen, ständig

un·re·mit·ting unablässig, unaufhörlich

un·re·quit·ed: ~ *love* unerwiderte Liebe

un·re·served uneingeschränkt; nicht reserviert

un·rest POL *etc* Unruhen *pl*

un·re·strained hemmungslos, ungezügelt

un·re·strict·ed uneingeschränkt

un·ripe unreif

un·ri·val(l)ed unerreicht, unübertroffen, einzigartig

un·roll (sich) aufrollen *or* entrollen; sich entfalten

un·ruf·fled gelassen, ruhig

un·ru·ly ungebärdig, wild; widerspenstig (*hair*)

un·sad·dle *Pferd* absatteln; *Reiter* abwerfen

un·safe unsicher, nicht sicher

un·said unausgesprochen

un·sal(e)·a·ble unverkäuflich

un·salt·ed ungesalzen

un·san·i·tar·y unhygienisch

un·sat·is·fac·to·ry unbefriedigend

un·sat·u·rat·ed CHEM ungesättigt

un·sa·vo(u)r·y anrüchig, unerfreulich

un·scathed unversehrt, unverletzt

un·screw abschrauben, losschrauben

un·scru·pu·lous skrupellos, gewissenlos

un·seat *Reiter* abwerfen; *j-n* s-s Amtes entheben

un·seem·ly ungebührlich

un·self·ish selbstlos, uneigennützig

un·set·tle durcheinander bringen; beunruhigen; aufregen

un·set·tled ungeklärt, offen (*question etc*); unsicher (*situation etc*); METEOR unbeständig

un·shak(e)·a·ble unerschütterlich

un·shav·en unrasiert

un·shrink·a·ble nicht eingehend *or* einlaufend

un·sight·ly unansehnlich, hässlich

un·skilled: ~ *worker* ungelernter Arbeiter

un·so·cia·ble ungesellig

un·so·cial: *work* ~ *hours* außerhalb der normalen Arbeitszeit arbeiten

un·so·lic·it·ed unaufgefordert ein- *or* zugesandt, ECON *a.* unbestellt

un·solved ungelöst (*problem etc*)

un·so·phis·ti·cat·ed einfach, schlicht; TECH unkompliziert

un·sound nicht gesund; nicht in Ordnung; morsch; unsicher, schwach; nicht stichhaltig (*argument etc*); *of* ~ *mind* JUR unzurechnungsfähig

un·spar·ing großzügig, freigebig, verschwenderisch; schonungslos, unbarmherzig

un·speak·a·ble unbeschreiblich, entsetzlich

un·spoiled, un·spoilt unverdorben; nicht verwöhnt *or* verzogen

un·sta·ble instabil; unsicher, schwankend; labil (*person*)

un·stead·y wack(e)lig, schwankend, unsicher; unbeständig; ungleichmäßig, unregelmäßig

un·stop *Abfluss etc* freimachen; *Flasche* entstöpseln

un·stressed LING unbetont

un·stuck: *come* ~ abgehen, sich lösen; *fig* scheitern

un·stud·ied ungekünstelt, natürlich

un·suc·cess·ful erfolglos, ohne Erfolg; vergeblich

un·suit·a·ble unpassend, ungeeignet; unangemessen

un·sure unsicher; ~ *of o.s.* unsicher

un·sur·passed unübertroffen

un·sus·pect·ed unverdächtig; unvermutet; **un·sus·pect·ing** nichts ahnend, ahnungslos

un·sus·pi·cious arglos; unverdächtig, harmlos

un·sweet·ened ungesüßt

un·swerv·ing unbeirrbar, unerschütterlich

un·tan·gle entwirren (*a. fig*)

un·tapped unerschlossen (*resource etc*)

un·teach·a·ble unbelehrbar (*person*); nicht lehrbar

un·ten·a·ble unhaltbar (*theory etc*)

un·think·a·ble undenkbar, unvorstellbar; **un·think·ing** gedankenlos

un·ti·dy unordentlich

U

un·tie aufknoten, *Knoten etc* lösen; losbinden

un·til *prp, cj* bis; *not* ~ erst; erst wenn, nicht bevor

un·time·ly vorzeitig, verfrüht; unpassend, ungelegen

un·tir·ing unermüdlich

un·told *fig* unermesslich

un·touched unberührt, unangetastet

un·true unwahr, falsch

un·trust·wor·thy unzuverlässig, nicht vertrauenswürdig

un·used¹ unbenutzt, ungebraucht

un·used²: be ~ to s.th. an et. nicht gewöhnt sein, et. nicht gewohnt sein; **be ~ to doing s.th.** es nicht gewohnt sein, et. zu tun

un·u·su·al ungewöhnlich

un·var·nished *fig* ungeschminkt

un·var·y·ing unveränderlich, gleich bleibend

un·veil *Denkmal etc* enthüllen

un·versed unbewandert, unerfahren (*in* in *dat*)

un·voiced unausgesprochen

un·want·ed unerwünscht, ungewollt

un·war·rant·ed ungerechtfertigt

un·washed ungewaschen

un·wel·come unwillkommen

un·well: be or **feel ~** sich unwohl or nicht wohl fühlen

un·whole·some ungesund (*a. fig*)

un·wield·y unhandlich, sperrig

un·will·ing widerwillig; ungern; **be ~ to do s.th.** et. nicht tun wollen

un·wind (sich) abwickeln; F abschalten, sich entspannen

un·wise unklug

un·wit·ting unwissentlich; unbeabsichtigt

un·wor·thy unwürdig; **he (she) is ~ of it** er (sie) verdient es nicht, er (sie) ist es nicht wert

un·wrap auswickeln, auspacken

un·writ·ten ungeschrieben

un·yield·ing unnachgiebig

un·zip den Reißverschluss (*gen*) aufmachen

up 1. *adv* herauf, hinauf, aufwärts, nach oben, hoch, in die Höhe; oben; ~ *there* dort oben; **jump ~ and down** hüpfen; **walk ~ and down** auf und ab gehen, hin und her gehen; ~ *to* bis zu; **be ~ to s.th.** F et. vorhaben, et. im Schilde

führen; *not to be ~ to s.th.* e-r Sache nicht gewachsen sein; *it's ~ to you* das liegt bei dir; **2.** *prp* herauf, hinauf; oben auf (*dat*); ~ *the river* flussaufwärts; **3.** *adj* nach oben (gerichtet), Aufwärts...; ASTR aufgegangen; ECON gestiegen; *time:* abgelaufen, um; aufgestanden, F auf; *the ~ train* nach London; **be ~ and about** F wieder auf den Beinen sein; *what's ~?* F was ist los?; **4.** F *v/t Angebot, Preis etc* erhöhen; **5.** *the ~s and downs* F die Höhen und Tiefen *pl* (*of life* des Lebens)

up-and-com·ing aufstrebend, viel versprechend

up·bring·ing Erziehung *f*

up·com·ing bevorstehend

up·coun·try landeinwärts; im Landesinneren

up·date 1. auf den neuesten Stand bringen; aktualisieren; **2.** Lagebericht *m*

up·end hochkant stellen

up·grade *j-n* befördern

up·heav·al *fig* Umwälzung *f*

up·hill aufwärts, bergan; bergauf führend; *fig* mühsam

up·hold *Rechte etc* schützen, wahren; JUR *Urteil* bestätigen

up·hol·ster *Möbel* polstern

up·hol·ster·er Polsterer *m*

up·hol·ster·y Polsterung *f*; Bezug *m*; Polsterei *f*

up·keep Instandhaltung(skosten *pl*) *f*; Unterhalt(ungskosten *pl*) *m*

up·land *mst pl* Hochland *n*

up·lift 1. *j-n* aufrichten, *j-m* Auftrieb geben; **2.** Auftrieb *m*

up·on → **on, once** 1

up·per obere(r, -s), Ober...;

up·per·most 1. *adj* oberste(r, -s), größte (r, -s), höchste(r, -s); **be ~** oben sein; *fig* an erster Stelle stehen; **2.** *adv* nach oben

up·right aufrecht, *a.* gerade, *fig a.* rechtschaffen

up·ris·ing Aufstand *m*

up·roar Aufruhr *m*; **up·roar·i·ous** lärmend, laut; schallend (*laughter*)

up·root ausreißen, entwurzeln; *fig j-n* herausreißen (*from* aus)

up·set umkippen, umstoßen, umwerfen; *Pläne etc* durcheinander bringen, stören; *j-n* aus der Fassung bringen; *the fish has ~ me* or *my stomach* ich habe mir durch den Fisch den Magen verdorben; *be* ~ aufgeregt sein; aus der Fassung *or* durcheinander sein; gekränkt *or* verletzt sein

up·shot Ergebnis *n*

up·side down verkehrt herum; *fig* drunter und drüber; *turn* ~ umdrehen, *a. fig* auf den Kopf stellen

up·stairs 1. die Treppe herauf *or* hinauf, nach oben; oben; **2.** im oberen Stockwerk (gelegen), obere(r, -s)

up·start Emporkömmling *m*

up·state im Norden (e-s Bundesstaats)

up·stream fluss-, stromaufwärts

up·take: F *be quick (slow) on the* ~ schnell begreifen (schwer von Begriff sein)

up-to-date modern; aktuell, auf dem neuesten Stand

up·town in den Wohnvierteln; in die Wohnviertel

up·turn Aufschwung *m*

up·ward(s) aufwärts, nach oben

u·ra·ni·um CHEM Uran *n*

ur·ban städtisch, Stadt...

ur·ban·i·za·tion Verstädterung *f*

ur·chin Bengel *m*

urge 1. *j-n* drängen (*to do* zu tun); drängen auf (*acc*); *a.* ~ *on j-n* drängen, antreiben; **2.** Drang *m*, Verlangen *n*

ur·gen·cy Dringlichkeit *f*

ur·gent dringend; *be* ~ *a.* eilen

u·ri·nate urinieren; **u·rine** Urin *m*

urn Urne *f*; Großteemaschine *f*, Großkaffeemaschine *f*

us uns; *all of* ~ wir alle; *both of* ~ wir beide

us·age Sprachgebrauch *m*; Behandlung *f*; Verwendung *f*, Gebrauch *m*

use 1. *v/t* benutzen, gebrauchen, anwenden, verwenden; (ver)brauchen; ~ *up* auf-, verbrauchen; *v/i: I* ~*d to live here*

ich habe früher hier gewohnt; **2.** Benutzung *f*, Gebrauch *m*, Verwendung *f*; Nutzen *m*; *be of* ~ nützlich *or* von Nutzen sein (*to* für); *it's no* ~ *doing* es ist nutzlos *or* zwecklos *zu inf*; → *milk* 1

used¹: *be* ~ *to s.th.* an et. gewöhnt sein, et. gewohnt sein; *be* ~ *to doing s.th.* es gewohnt sein, et. zu tun

used² gebraucht; ~ *car* Gebrauchtwagen *m*; ~ *car deal·er* Gebrauchtwagenhändler(in)

use·ful nützlich

use·less nutzlos, zwecklos

us·er Benutzer(in); Verbraucher(in)

us·er-friend·ly benutzer- *or* verbraucherfreundlich

us·er in·ter·face EDP Benutzeroberfläche *f*

ush·er 1. Platzanweiser *m*; Gerichtsdiener *m*; **2.** *j-n* führen, geleiten (*into* in *acc*; *to* zu)

ush·er·ette Platzanweiserin *f*

u·su·al gewöhnlich, üblich

u·su·al·ly (für) gewöhnlich, normalerweise

u·sur·er Wucherer *m*

u·su·ry Wucher *m*

u·ten·sil Gerät *n*

u·te·rus ANAT Gebärmutter *f*

u·til·i·ty Nutzen *m*; *pl* Leistungen *pl* der öffentlichen Versorgungsbetriebe

u·til·ize nutzen

ut·most äußerste(r, -s), größte(r, -s), höchste(r, -s)

u·to·pi·an utopisch

ut·ter¹ total, völlig

ut·ter² äußern, *Seufzer etc* ausstoßen, *Wort* sagen

U-turn MOT Wende *f*; *fig* Kehrtwendung *f*

u·vu·la ANAT (Gaumen)Zäpfchen *n*

V

V, v V, v *n*

va·can·cy freie *or* offene Stelle; **vacancies** Zimmer frei; **no vacancies** belegt

va·cant leer stehend, unbewohnt; frei (*seat etc*); frei, offen (*job*); *fig* leer (*expression, stare etc*)

va·cate Hotelzimmer räumen; *Stelle etc* aufgeben

va·ca·tion 1. Ferien *pl*, Urlaub *m*; *esp Br* UNIV Semesterferien *pl*; JUR Gerichtsferien *pl*; **be on ~** im Urlaub sein, Urlaub machen; **2.** Urlaub machen, die Ferien verbringen

va·ca·tion·er, va·ca·tion·ist Urlauber(in)

vac·cin·ate MED impfen

vac·cin·a·tion MED (Schutz)Impfung *f*

vac·cine MED Impfstoff *m*

vac·il·late *fig* schwanken

vac·u·um 1. PHYS Vakuum *n*; **2.** F *Teppich, Zimmer etc* saugen; **~ bot·tle** Thermosflasche®; **~ clean·er** Staubsauger *m*; **~ flask** *Br* Thermosflasche® *f*; **~-packed** vakuumverpackt

vag·a·bond Vagabund *m*, Landstreicher(in)

va·ga·ry *mst pl* Laune *f*; wunderlicher Einfall

va·gi·na ANAT Vagina *f*, Scheide *f*

va·gi·nal ANAT vaginal, Scheiden...

va·grant Nichtsesshafte *m, f*, Landstreicher(in)

vague verschwommen; vage; unklar

vain eingebildet, eitel; vergeblich; **in ~** vergebens, vergeblich

val·en·tine Valentinskarte *f*

va·le·ri·an BOT, PHARM Baldrian *m*

val·et (Kammer)Diener *m*

val·id stichhaltig, triftig; gültig (**for two weeks** zwei Wochen); JUR rechtsgültig, rechtskräftig; **be ~** *a.* gelten

va·lid·i·ty (JUR Rechts)Gültigkeit *f*; Stichhaltigkeit *f*, Triftigkeit *f*

val·ley Tal *n*

val·u·a·ble 1. wertvoll; **2.** *pl* Wertgegenstände *pl*, Wertsachen *pl*

val·u·a·tion Schätzung *f*; Schätzwert *m* (**on** *gen*)

val·ue 1. Wert *m*; **be of ~** wertvoll sein

(**to** für); **get ~ for money** reell bedient werden; **2.** *Haus etc* schätzen (**at** auf *acc*); *j-n, j-s Rat etc* schätzen

val·ue-ad·ded tax *Br* ECON (ABBR **VAT**) Mehrwertsteuer *f*

val·ue·less wertlos

valve TECH, MUS Ventil *n*; ANAT (*Herz-etc*)Klappe *f*

vam·pire Vampir *m*

van MOT Lieferwagen *m*, Transporter *m*; *Br* RAIL (geschlossener) Güterwagen

van·dal Wandale *m*, Vandale *m*

van·dal·ism Wandalismus *m*, Vandalismus *m*

van·dal·ize mutwillig beschädigen *or* zerstören

vane TECH (*Propeller- etc*)Flügel *m*; (*Wetter*)Fahne *f*

va·nil·la Vanille *f*

van·ish verschwinden

van·i·ty Eitelkeit *f*; **~ bag** Kosmetiktäschchen *n*; **~ case** Kosmetikkoffer *m*

van·tage-point Aussichtspunkt *m*; **from my ~** *fig* aus m-r Sicht

va·por·ize verdampfen; verdunsten (lassen)

va·po(u)r Dampf *m*, Dunst *m*; **~ trail** AVIAT Kondensstreifen *m*

var·i·a·ble 1. variabel, veränderlich; unbeständig, wechselhaft; TECH einstellbar, regulierbar; **2.** MATH, PHYS Variable *f*, veränderliche Größe (*both a. fig*)

var·i·ance: be at ~ with im Gegensatz *or* Widerspruch stehen zu

var·i·ant 1. abweichend, verschieden; **2.** Variante *f*, **var·i·a·tion** Abweichung *f*; Schwankung *f*; MUS Variation *f*

var·i·cose veins MED Krampfadern *pl*

var·ied unterschiedlich; abwechslungsreich

va·ri·e·ty Abwechslung *f*; Vielfalt *f*; ECON Auswahl *f*, Sortiment *n* (**of** an *dat*); BOT, ZO Art *f*; Varietee *n*; **for a ~ of reasons** aus den verschiedensten Gründen; **~ show** Varieteevorstellung *f*; **~ thea·ter** (*Br* **thea·tre**) Varietee(theater) *n*

var·i·ous verschieden; mehrere, verschiedene

var·nish 1. Lack *m*; **2.** lackieren

var·si·ty team SPORT Universitäts-, College-, Schulmannschaft *f*

var·y *v/i* sich (ver)ändern; variieren, auseinander gehen (*opinions etc*) (**on** über *acc*); **~ in size** verschieden groß sein; *v/t* (ver)ändern; variieren

vase Vase *f*

vast gewaltig, riesig, (*area a.*) ausgedehnt, weit; **vast·ly** gewaltig, weitaus

vat (großes) Fass, Bottich *m*

VAT ABBR of *value-added tax* ECON Mehrwertsteuer *f*

vau·de·ville Varietee(theater) *n*

vault¹ ARCH Gewölbe *n*; *a. pl* Stahlkammer *f*, Tresorraum *m*; (Keller)Gewölbe *n*; Gruft *f*

vault² 1. ~ (over) springen über (*acc*); **2.** *esp* SPORT Sprung *m*

vault·ing| horse *gymnastics*: Pferd *n*; **~ pole** SPORT Sprungstab *m*

VCR ABBR of *video cassette recorder* Videorekorder *m*, Videogerät *n*

veal GASTR Kalbfleisch *n*; **~ chop** Kalbskotelett *n*; **~ cutlet** Kalbsschnitzel *n*; **~ roast · ~** Kalbsbraten *m*

veer (sich) drehen; MOT ausscheren; **~ to the right** das Steuer nach rechts reißen

veg·e·ta·ble 1. *mst pl* Gemüse *n*; **2.** Gemüse...; Pflanzen...

veg·e·tar·i·an 1. Vegetarier(in); **2.** vegetarisch

veg·e·tate (dahin)vegetieren

veg·e·ta·tion Vegetation *f*

ve·he·mence Vehemenz *f*, Heftigkeit *f*; **ve·he·ment** vehement, heftig

ve·hi·cle Fahrzeug *n*; *fig* Medium *n*

veil 1. Schleier *m*; **2.** verschleiern (*a. fig*)

vein ANAT Vene *f*, Ader *f* (*a.* BOT, GEOL, *fig*); *fig* (*Charakter*)Zug *m*; Stimmung *f*

ve·loc·i·ty TECH Geschwindigkeit *f*

ve·lour(s) Velours *m*

vel·vet Samt *m*; **vel·vet·y** samtig

vend·er → *vendor*

vend·ing ma·chine (Verkaufs-, Waren)Automat *m*

vend·or (*Straßen*)Händler(in), (*Zeitungs- etc*)Verkäufer(in)

ve·neer 1. Furnier *n*; *fig* Fassade *f*; **2.** furnieren

ven·e·ra·ble ehrwürdig

ven·e·rate verehren

ven·e·ra·tion Verehrung *f*

ve·no·re·al dis·ease MED Geschlechtskrankheit *f*

Ve·ne·tian 1. Venezianer(in); **2.** venezianisch; **~ blind** (Stab)Jalousie *f*

ven·geance Rache *f*; **take ~ on** sich rächen an (*dat*); **with a ~** mächtig, F wie verrückt

ve·ni·al entschuldbar, verzeihlich; REL lässlich

ven·i·son GASTR Wildbret *n*

ven·om ZO Gift *n*, *fig a.* Gehässigkeit *f*; **ven·om·ous** giftig, *fig a.* gehässig

ve·nous MED venös

vent 1. *v/t s-m* Zorn etc Luft machen, *s-e* Wut etc auslassen, abreagieren (**on** an *dat*); **2.** Schlitz *m* (*in a coat etc*); TECH (Abzugs)Öffnung *f*; **give ~ to** *s-m* Ärger etc Luft machen

ven·ti·late (be)lüften; *fig* äußern

ven·ti·la·tion (Be)Lüftung *f*, Ventilation *f*

ven·ti·la·tor Ventilator *m*

ven·tri·cle ANAT Herzkammer *f*

ven·tril·o·quist Bauchredner(in)

ven·ture 1. *esp* ECON Wagnis *n*, Risiko *n*; ECON Unternehmen *n*; → *joint venture*; **2.** sich wagen; riskieren

ven·ue SPORT Austragungsort *m*

verb LING Verb *n*, Zeitwort *n*

verb·al mündlich; wörtlich, Wort...

ver·dict JUR (Urteils)Spruch *m*; *fig* Urteil *n*; **bring in** or **return a ~ of** (**not**) **guilty** JUR auf (nicht) schuldig erkennen

ver·di·gris Grünspan *m*

verge 1. Rand *m* (*a. fig*); **be on the ~ of** kurz vor (*dat*) stehen; **be on the ~ of despair** (**tears**) der Verzweiflung (den Tränen) nahe sein; **2. ~ on** *fig* grenzen an (*acc*)

ver·i·fy bestätigen; nachweisen; (über-) prüfen

ver·i·ta·ble wahr

ver·mi·cel·li Fadennudeln *pl*

ver·mi·form ap·pen·dix ANAT Wurmfortsatz *m*, Blinddarm *m*

ver·mil·i·on 1. zinnoberrot; **2.** Zinnoberrot *n*

ver·min Ungeziefer *n*; Schädlinge *pl*; *fig* Gesindel *n*, Pack *n*

ver·min·ous voller Ungeziefer

ver·nac·u·lar Dialekt *m*, Mundart *f*; **in the ~** im Volksmund

ver·sa·tile vielseitig; vielseitig verwendbar

verse Verdichtung f; Vers m; Strophe f

versed: *be* (*well*) ~ *in* beschlagen or bewandert sein in (*dat*)

ver·sion Version f; TECH Ausführung f; Darstellung f (*of an event*); Fassung f (*of a film etc*); Übersetzung f

ver·sus (ABBR *v.*, *vs.*) SPORT, JUR gegen

ver·te·bra ANAT Wirbel m

ver·te·brate ZO Wirbeltier n

ver·ti·cal vertikal, senkrecht

ver·ti·go MED Schwindel m; *suffer from* ~ an or unter Schwindel leiden

verve Elan m, Schwung m

ver·y **1.** *adv* sehr; aller...; *I* ~ *much hope that* ich hoffe sehr, dass; *the* ~ *best* das Allerbeste; *for the* ~ *last time* zum allerletzten Mal; **2.** *adj the* ~ genau der or die or das; *the* ~ *opposite* genau das Gegenteil; *the* ~ *thing* genau das Richtige; *the* ~ *thought of* schon der or der bloße Gedanke an (*acc*)

ves·i·cle MED Bläschen n

ves·sel ANAT, BOT Gefäß n; Schiff n

vest Weste f; *Br* Unterhemd n; *kugelsichere* Weste

ves·ti·bule (Vor)Halle f

ves·tige Spur f

vest·ment Ornat n, Gewand n, Robe f

ves·try REL Sakristei f

vet¹ F Tierarzt m, Tierärztin f

vet² *esp Br* F überprüfen

vet³ MIL F Veteran m

vet·er·an **1.** MIL Veteran m (*a. fig*); **2.** altgedient; erfahren; ~ *car Br* Oldtimer m (*built before 1905*)

vet·er·i·nar·i·an Tierarzt m, -ärztin f

vet·er·i·na·ry tierärztlich; ~ *sur·geon Br* Tierarzt m, Tierärztin f

ve·to 1. Veto n; **2.** sein Veto einlegen gegen

vexed ques·tion leidige Frage

vi·a über (*acc*), via

vi·a·duct Viadukt m, n

vi·al (*esp Arznei*)Fläschchen n

vibes F Atmosphäre f

vi·brant kräftig (*color etc*); pulsierend (*city etc*)

vi·brate *v/i* vibrieren, zittern; flimmern; *fig* pulsieren; *v/t* in Schwingungen versetzen; **vi·bra·tion** Vibrieren n, Zittern n; *pl* F Atmosphäre f

vic·ar REL Pfarrer m

vic·ar·age Pfarrhaus n

vice¹ Laster n

vice² *esp Br* Schraubstock m

vice... Vize..., stellvertretend

vice squad Sittendezernat n, Sittenpolizei f; Rauschgiftdezernat n

vi·ce ver·sa: *and* ~ und umgekehrt

vi·cin·i·ty Nähe f; Nachbarschaft f

vi·cious brutal; bösartig

vi·cis·si·tudes *das* Auf und Ab, *die* Wechselfälle pl

vic·tim Opfer n

vic·tim·ize (ungerechterweise) bestrafen, ungerecht behandeln; schikanieren

vic·to·ri·ous siegreich

vic·to·ry Sieg m

vid·e·o 1. Video n; Videokassette f; F Videodram n; *esp Br* Videorekorder m, Videogerät n; *on* ~ auf Video; Video...; **3.** *esp Br* auf Video aufnehmen, aufzeichnen; ~ *cam·e·ra* Videokamera f; ~ *cas·sette* Videokassette f; ~ *cassette re·cord·er* → *video recorder*; ~ *clip* Videoclip m

vid·e·o·disk Bildplatte f

vid·e·o| game Videospiel n; ~ *li·brary* Videothek f; ~ *re·cord·er* Videorekorder m, Videogerät n; ~ *re·cord·ing* Videoaufnahme f, Videoaufzeichnung f; ~ *shop Br*, ~ *store* Videothek f

vid·e·o·tape 1. Videokassette f; Videoband n; **2.** auf Video aufnehmen, aufzeichnen

vid·e·o·text Bildschirmtext m

vie wetteifern (*with* mit; *for* um)

Vi·en·nese 1. Wiener(in); **2.** wienerisch, Wiener...

view 1. Sicht f (*of* auf *acc*); Aussicht f, (Aus)Blick m (*of* auf *acc*); Ansicht f (*a.* PHOT), Meinung f (*about, on* über *acc*); *fig* Überblick m (*of* über *acc*); *a room with a* ~ ein Zimmer mit schöner Aussicht; *be on* ~ ausgestellt or zu besichtigen sein; *be hidden from* ~ nicht zu sehen sein; *come into* ~ in Sicht kommen; *in full* ~ *of* direkt vor j-s Augen; *in* ~ *of fig* angesichts (*gen*); *in my* ~ m-r Ansicht nach; *keep in* ~ et. im Auge behalten; *with a* ~ *to fig* mit Blick auf (*acc*); **2.** *v/t* Haus etc besichtigen; *fig* betrachten (*as* als); *v/i* fernsehen

view·da·ta Bildschirmtext m

view·er Fernsehzuschauer(in), F Fernseher(in); TECH *(Dia)*Betrachter *m*

view·find·er PHOT Sucher *m*

view·point Gesichts-, Standpunkt *m*

vig·il (Nacht)Wache *f*

vig·i·lance Wachsamkeit *f*

vig·i·lant wachsam

vig·or·ous energisch; kräftig

vig·o(u)r Energie *f*

Vi·king 1. Wikinger *m*; **2.** Wikinger...

vile gemein, niederträchtig; F scheußlich

vil·lage Dorf *n*; **~ green** Dorfanger *m*

vil·lag·er Dorfbewohner(in)

vil·lain Bösewicht *m*, Schurke *m*; *Br* F Ganove *m*

vin·di·cate *j-n* rehabilitieren; *et.* rechtfertigen; *et.* Bestätigen

vin·dic·tive rachsüchtig, nachtragend

vine BOT (Wein)Rebe *f*; Kletterpflanze *f*

vin·e·gar Essig *m*

vine·grow·er Winzer *m*

vine·yard Weinberg *m*

vin·tage 1. Weinernte *f*, Weinlese *f*; GASTR Jahrgang *m*; **2.** GASTR Jahrgangs...; *fig* hervorragend, glänzend; *a* **1994** ~ ein 1994er Jahrgang *or* Wein

vin·tage car *esp Br* Oldtimer *m* (*built between 1919 and 1930*)

vi·o·la MUS Bratsche *f*

vi·o·late *Vertrag etc* verletzen, *a. Versprechen* brechen, *Gesetz etc* übertreten; *Ruhe etc* stören; *Grab etc* schänden; **vi·o·la·tion** Verletzung *f*, Bruch *m*, Übertretung *f*

vi·o·lence Gewalt *f*; Gewalttätigkeit *f*; Ausschreitungen *pl*; Heftigkeit *f*

vi·o·lent gewalttätig; gewaltsam; heftig

vi·o·let 1. BOT Veilchen *n*; **2.** violett

vi·o·lin MUS Geige *f*, Violine *f*

vi·o·lin·ist Geiger(in), Violinist(in)

VIP ABBR *of* **very important person** VIP *f*; **~ lounge** AVIAT *etc* VIP-Lounge *f*; SPORT Ehrentribüne *f*

vi·per ZO Viper *f*, Natter *f*

vir·gin 1. Jungfrau *f*; **2.** jungfräulich, unberührt (*both a. fig*)

Vir·go ASTR Jungfrau *f*; **he (she) is (a) ~** er (sie) ist Jungfrau

vir·ile männlich; potent

vi·ril·i·ty Männlichkeit *f*; Potenz *f*

vir·tu·al eigentlich, praktisch

vir·tu·al·ly praktisch, so gut wie

vir·tu·al re·al·i·ty EDP virtuelle Realität *f*

vir·tue Tugend *f*, Vorzug *m*, Vorteil *m*;

by *or* **in ~ of** aufgrund (*gen*), kraft (*gen*); **make a ~ of necessity** aus der Not e-e Tugend machen

vir·tu·ous tugendhaft

vir·u·lent MED (akut und) bösartig; schnell wirkend (*poison*); *fig* bösartig, gehässig

vi·rus MED Virus *m*, *n*

vi·sa Visum *n*, Sichtvermerk *m*

vis·cose Viskose *f*

vis·cous dickflüssig, zähflüssig

vise TECH Schraubstock *m*

vis·i·bil·i·ty Sicht *f*, Sichtverhältnisse *pl*, Sichtweite *f*

vis·i·ble sichtbar; (er)sichtlich

vi·sion Sehkraft *f*; Weitblick *m*; Vision *f*

vi·sion·a·ry 1. weitblickend; eingebildet, unwirklich; **2.** Fantast(in), Träumer(in); Seher(in)

vis·it 1. *v/t j-n* besuchen, *Schloss etc a.* besichtigen; *et.* inspizieren; *v/i*: **be ~ing** auf Besuch sein (**with** bei); **~ with** plaudern mit; **2.** Besuch *m*, Besichtigung *f* (**to** *gen*); Plauderei *f*, **for** *or* **on a ~** auf Besuch; **have a ~ from** Besuch haben von; **pay a ~ to** *j-n* besuchen, *j-m* e-n Besuch abstatten; *Arzt* aufsuchen

vis·it·ing hours MED Besuchszeit *f*

vis·it·or Besucher(in), Gast *m*

vi·sor Visier *n*; Schirm *m*; MOT (*Sonnen-*)Blende *f*

vis·u·al Seh...; visuell; **~ aids** PED Anschauungsmaterial *n*, Lehrmittel *pl*; **~ dis·play u·nit** EDP Bildschirmgerät *n*, Datensichtgerät *n*; **~ in·struc·tion** PED Anschauungsunterricht *m*

vis·u·al·ize sich *et.* vorstellen

vi·tal vital, Lebens...; lebenswichtig; unbedingt notwendig; **of ~ importance** von größter Wichtigkeit

vi·tal·i·ty Vitalität *f*

vit·a·min Vitamin *n*; **~ de·fi·cien·cy** Vitaminmangel *m*

vit·re·ous Glas...

vi·va·cious lebhaft, temperamentvoll

viv·id hell (*light*); kräftig, leuchtend (*color*); anschaulich (*description*); lebhaft (*imagination*)

vix·en ZO Füchsin *f*

V-neck V-Ausschnitt *m*

V-necked mit V-Ausschnitt

vo·cab·u·la·ry Vokabular *n*, Wortschatz *m*; Wörterverzeichnis *n*

vo·cal Stimm...; F lautstark; MUS Vo-

V

kal..., Gesang...; **~ cords** ANAT Stimmbänder *pl*

vo·cal·ist Sänger(in)

vo·ca·tion Begabung *f* (*for* für); Berufung *f*

vo·ca·tion·al Berufs...; **~ ed·u·ca·tion** Berufsausbildung *f*; **~ guid·ance** Berufsberatung *f*; **~ train·ing** Berufsausbildung *f*

vogue Mode *f*; *be in ~* Mode sein

voice 1. Stimme *f*; *active* **~** LING Aktiv *n*; *passive* **~** LING Passiv *n*; 2. zum Ausdruck bringen; LING (stimmhaft) aussprechen; **voiced** LING stimmhaft; **voice·less** LING stimmlos

void 1. leer; JUR ungültig; **~ of** ohne; 2. (Gefühl *n* der) Leere *f*

vol ABBR *of* **volume** Bd., Band *m*

vol·a·tile cholerisch (*person*); explosiv (*situation etc*); CHEM flüchtig

vol·ca·no Vulkan *m*

vol·ley 1. Salve *f*; (*Geschoss- etc*)Hagel *m* (*a. fig*); *tennis*: Volley *m*, Flugball *m*; *soccer*: Volleyschuss *m*; 2. Ball volley schießen

vol·ley·ball SPORT Volleyball *m*

volt ELECTR Volt *n*

volt·age ELECTR Spannung *f*

vol·u·ble redselig; wortreich

vol·ume Band *m*; Volumen *n*, Rauminhalt *m*; Umfang *m*, große Menge; Lautstärke *f*

vo·lu·mi·nous bauschig (*dress etc*); geräumig; umfangreich (*notes etc*)

vol·un·ta·ry freiwillig; unbezahlt

vol·un·teer 1. *v/i* sich freiwillig melden (*for* zu) (*a.* MIL); *v/t* Hilfe *etc* anbieten; *et.* von sich aus sagen, F herausrücken mit; 2. Freiwillige *m*, *f*; freiwilliger Helfer

vo·lup·tu·ous sinnlich (*lips etc*); aufreizend (*gesture etc*); üppig (*body etc*); kurvenreich (*woman*)

vom·it 1. *v/t* erbrechen; *v/i* (sich er)brechen, sich übergeben; 2. Erbrochene *n*

vo·ra·cious unersättlich (*appetite etc*)

vote 1. Abstimmung *f* (*about, on* über *acc*); (Wahl)Stimme *f*; Stimmzettel *m*; *a. pl* Wahlrecht *n*; **~ of no confidence** Misstrauensvotum *n*; *take a ~ on s.th.* über *et.* abstimmen; 2. *v/i* wählen; **~ for** (*against*) stimmen für (gegen); **~ on** abstimmen über (*acc*); *v/t* wählen; *et.* bewilligen; **~ out of office** abwählen

vot·er Wähler(in)

vot·ing booth Wahlkabine *f*

vouch: **~ for** (sich ver)bürgen für

vouch·er Gutschein *m*, Kupon *m*

vow 1. Gelöbnis *n*; Gelübde *n*; *take a ~*, *make a ~* ein Gelöbnis *or* Gelübde ablegen; 2. geloben, schwören (*to do* zu tun)

vow·el LING Vokal *m*, Selbstlaut *m*

voy·age (See)Reise *f*

vul·gar vulgär, ordinär; geschmacklos

vul·ne·ra·ble *fig* verletzbar, verwundbar; verletzlich; anfällig (*to* für)

vul·ture ZO Geier *m*

W

W, w W, w *n*

wad (*Watte- etc*)Bausch *m*; Bündel *n*; (*Papier- etc*)Knäuel *m*, *n*

wad·ding Einlage *f*, Füllmaterial *n*

wad·dle watscheln

wade *v/i* waten; **~ through** waten durch; F sich durchkämpfen durch, *et.* durchackern; *v/t* durchwaten

wa·fer (*esp* Eis)Waffel *f*; Oblate *f*, REL Hostie *f*

waf·fle¹ Waffel *f*

waf·fle² *Br* F schwafeln

waft *v/i* ziehen (*smell etc*); *v/t* wehen

wag 1. wedeln (mit); 2. *with a ~ of its tail* schwanzwedelnd

wage¹ *mst pl* (Arbeits)Lohn *m*

wage²: **~ (a) war against** *or* **on** MIL Krieg führen gegen; *fig* e-n Feldzug führen gegen

wage| earn·er Lohnempfänger(in); Verdiener(in); **~ freeze** Lohnstopp *m*; **~ ne·go·ti·a·tions** Tarifverhandlungen *pl*; **~ pack·et** Lohntüte *f*; **~ rise** Lohnerhöhung *f*

wa·ger Wette *f*

wag·gle F wackeln (mit)

wag·gon *Br* → **wag·on** Fuhrwerk *n*, Wagen *m*; *Br* RAIL (offener) Güterwagen; *(Tee- etc)* Wagen *m*

wag·tail ZO Bachstelze *f*

wail 1. jammern; heulen *(siren, wind)*; **2.** Jammern *n*; Heulen *n*

wain·scot (Wand)Täfelung *f*

waist Taille *f*

waist·coat *esp Br* Weste *f*

waist·line Taille *f*

wait 1. *v/i* warten *(for,* on auf *acc)*; **~** *for s.o. a.* j-n erwarten; *keep s.o. ~ing* j-n warten lassen; **~** *and see!* warte es ab!; **~** *on (Br at)* table bedienen, servieren; **~** *on s.o.* j-n bedienen; **~** *up* F aufbleiben *(for* wegen); *v/t:* **~** *one's chance* auf e-e günstige Gelegenheit warten *(to do* zu tun); **~** *one's turn* warten, bis man an der Reihe ist; **2.** Wartezeit *f*; *have a long ~* lange warten müssen; *lie in ~ for s.o.* j-m auflauern

wait·er Kellner *m*, Ober *m*; **~,** *the check (Br bill)*, *please!* (Herr) Ober, bitte zahlen!

wait·ing Warten *n*; *no ~* MOT Halt(e)verbot *n*; **~** *list* Warteliste *f*; **~** *room* MED *etc* Wartezimmer *n*; RAIL Wartesaal *m*

wait·ress Kellnerin *f*, Bedienung *f*; **~,** *the check (Br bill)*, *please!* Fräulein, bitte zahlen!

wake¹ *v/i a.* **~** *up* aufwachen, wach werden; *v/t a.* **~** *up* (auf)wecken; *fig* wachrufen, wecken

wake² MAR Kielwasser *n*; *follow in the ~ of fig* folgen auf *(acc)*

wake·ful schlaflos

wak·en *v/i a.* **~** *up* aufwachen, wach werden; *v/t a.* **~** *up* (auf)wecken

walk 1. *v/i* (zu Fuß) gehen, laufen; spazieren gehen; wandern; *v/t* Strecke gehen, laufen; j-n bringen *(to* zu; *home* nach Hause); *Hund* ausführen; *Pferd* im Schritt gehen lassen; **~** *away* → *walk off;* **~** *in* hineingehen, hereinkommen; **~** *off* fort-, weggehen; **~** *off with* F abhauen mit; F *Preis etc* locker gewinnen; **~** *out* hinausgehen; *(unter Protest)* den Saal *etc* verlassen; ECON streiken, in (den) Streik treten; **~** *out on s.o.* F j-n verlassen, j-n im Stich lassen; **~** *up* hinaufgehen, heraufkommen; **~** *up to s.o.* auf j-n zugehen; **~** *up!* treten

Sie näher!; **2.** Spaziergang *m*; Wanderung *f*; Spazier-, Wanderweg *m*; *go for a ~, take a ~* e-n Spaziergang machen, spazieren gehen; *an hour's ~* e-e Stunde Fußweg *or* zu Fuß; *from all ~s of life Leute* aus allen Berufen *or* Schichten

walk·a·way F Spaziergang *m*, leichter Sieg

walk·er Spaziergänger(in); Wanderer *m*, Wand(r)erin *f*; SPORT Geher(in); *be a good ~* gut zu Fuß sein

walk·ie-talk·ie Walkie-Talkie *n*, tragbares Funksprechgerät

walk·ing Gehen *n*, Laufen *n*; Spazierengehen *n*; Wandern *n*; **~** *pa·pers: get one's ~* F den Laufpass bekommen; **~** *shoes* Wanderschuhe *pl*; **~** *stick* Spazierstock *m*; **~** *tour* Wanderung *f*

Walk·man® Walkman® *m*

walk·out Auszug *m* (*by, of* e-r *Delegation etc)*; ECON Ausstand *m*, Streik *m*

walk·over → *walkaway*

walk·up F (Miets)Haus *n* ohne Fahrstuhl; Wohnung *f or* Büro *n etc* in e-m Haus ohne Fahrstuhl

wall 1. Wand *f*; Mauer *f*; **2.** *a.* **~** *in* mit e-r Mauer umgeben; **~** *up* zumauern

wall cal·en·dar Wandkalender *m*

wall·chart Wandkarte *f*

wal·let Brieftasche *f*

wall·flow·er F Mauerblümchen *n*

wal·lop F *j-m* ein Ding verpassen; SPORT *j-n* erledigen, vernichten *(at* in *dat)*

wal·low sich wälzen; *fig* schwelgen, sich baden *(in* in *dat)*

wall·pa·per 1. Tapete *f*; **2.** tapezieren

wall-to-wall: ~ *carpet(ing)* Spannteppich *m*, Teppichboden *m*

wal·nut BOT Walnuss(baum *m*) *f*

wal·rus ZO Walross *n*

waltz 1. Walzer *m*; **2.** Walzer tanzen

wand *(Zauber)*Stab *m*

wan·der (herum)wandern, herumlaufen, umherstreifen; *fig* abschweifen; fantasieren

wane 1. ASTR abnehmen; *fig* schwinden; **2.** *be on the ~ fig* im Schwinden begriffen sein

wan·gle F deichseln, hinkriegen; **~** *s.th. out of s.o.* j-m et. abluchsen; **~** *one's way out of* sich herauswinden aus

want 1. *v/t* et. wollen; j-n brauchen; j-n sprechen wollen; F et. brauchen, nötig haben; **be ~ed** (*polizeilich*) gesucht werden (*for* wegen); *v/i* wollen; *I don't ~ to* ich will nicht; *he does not ~ for anything* es fehlt ihm an nichts; **2.** Mangel *m* (*of* an *dat*); Bedürfnis *n*, Wunsch *m*; Not *f*; **~ ad** Kleinanzeige *f*

want·ed (*polizeilich*) gesucht

wan·ton mutwillig

war Krieg *m* (*a. fig*); *fig* Kampf *m* (*against* gegen)

war·ble ZO trillern

ward 1. MED Station *f*; *Br* POL Stadtbezirk *m*; JUR Mündel *n*; **2. ~ off** Schlag *etc* abwehren, *Gefahr etc* abwenden

war·den Aufseher(in); Heimleiter(in); (Gefängnis)Direktor(in)

ward·er *Br* Aufsichtsbeamte *m*, -beamtin *f*

war·drobe Kleiderschrank *m*; Garderobe *f*

ware·house Lager(haus) *n*

war·fare Krieg *m*; Kriegführung *f*

war·head MIL Spreng-, Gefechtskopf *m*

war·like kriegerisch; Kriegs...

warm 1. *adj* warm, *fig a.* herzlich; *I am ~, I feel ~* mir ist warm; **2.** *v/t a.* **~ up** wärmen, sich *die Hände etc* wärmen; *Motor* warm laufen lassen; *v/i a.* **~ up** warm *or* wärmer werden, sich erwärmen; **warmth** Wärme *f*

warm-up SPORT Aufwärmen *n*

warn warnen (*against*, *of* vor *dat*); *j-n* verständigen

warn·ing Warnung *f* (*of* vor *dat*); Verwarnung *f*; *without ~* ohne Vorwarnung; **~ sig·nal** Warnsignal *n*

warp sich verziehen *or* werfen

war·rant 1. JUR (Durchsuchungs-, Haft*etc*)Befehl *m*; **2.** *et.* rechtfertigen; **~ of ar·rest** Haftbefehl *m*

war·ran·ty ECON Garantie(erklärung) *f*; *it's still under ~* darauf ist noch Garantie

war·ri·or Krieger *m*

war·ship Kriegsschiff *n*

wart MED Warze *f*

war·y vorsichtig

was ich, er, sie, es war; *passive*: ich, er, sie, es wurde

wash 1. *v/t* waschen, sich *die Hände etc* waschen; *v/i* sich waschen; sich *gut etc* waschen (*lassen*); **~ up** *v/t Br* abwaschen, (das) Geschirr spülen; *v/t* anschwemmen, anspülen; **~ one's dirty**

linen schmutzige Wäsche waschen; **2.** Wäsche *f*; MOT Waschanlage *f*, Waschstraße *f*; *be in the ~* in der Wäsche sein; *give s.th. a ~* et. waschen; *have a ~* sich waschen

wash·a·ble (ab)waschbar

wash-and-wear bügelfrei; pflegeleicht

wash·ba·sin *Br*, **wash·bowl** Waschbecken *n*

wash·cloth Waschlappen *m*

wash·er Waschmaschine *f*; TECH Unterlegscheibe *f*

wash·ing 1. Wäsche *f*; **2.** Wasch...

wash·ing| ma·chine Waschmaschine *f*; **~ pow·der** Waschpulver *n*, -mittel *n*

washing-up *Br* Abwasch *m*; *do the ~* den Abwasch machen

wash·room Toilette *f*

wasp ZO Wespe *f*

waste 1. Verschwendung *f*; Abfall *m*; Müll *m*; **~ of time** Zeitverschwendung *f*, *hazardous ~, special toxic ~* Sondermüll *m*; *special ~ dump* Sondermülldeponie *f*; **2.** *v/t* verschwenden, vergeuden; *j-n* auszehren; *v/i* **~ away** immer schwächer werden (*person*); **3.** überschüssig; Abfall...; brachliegend, öde; *lay ~* verwüsten

waste dis·pos·al Abfall-, Müllbeseitigung *f*; Entsorgung *f*; **~ site** Deponie *f*

waste·ful verschwenderisch

waste| gas Abgas *n*; **~ pa·per** Abfallpapier *n*; Altpapier *n*

waste·pa·per bas·ket Papierkorb *m*

waste pipe Abflussrohr *n*

watch 1. *v/i* zuschauen; **~ for** warten auf (*acc*); **~ out!** pass auf!; Vorsicht!; **~ out for** Ausschau halten nach; sich in Acht nehmen vor (*dat*); *v/t* beobachten; zuschauen bei, sich *et.* ansehen; → *television*; **2.** (Armband-, Taschen)Uhr *f*; Wache *f*; *keep ~* Wache halten, wachen (*over* über *acc*); *be on the ~ for* Ausschau halten nach; auf der Hut sein vor (*dat*); *keep (a) careful or close ~ on* genau beobachten, scharf im Auge behalten

watch·dog Wachhund *m*

watch·ful wachsam

watch·mak·er Uhrmacher(in)

watch·man Wachmann *m*, Wächter *m*

watch·tow·er Wach(t)turm *m*

wa·ter 1. Wasser *n*; **2.** *v/t Blumen* gießen, *Rasen etc* sprengen; *Vieh* tränken; **~**

down verdünnen, verwässern; *fig* abschwächen; *v/i* tränen (*eyes*); **make s.o. 's mouth ~** j-m den Mund wässerig machen

wa·ter bird ZO Wasservogel *m*

wa·ter·col·o(u)r Wasser-, Aquarellfarbe *f*; Aquarellmalerei *f*; Aquarell *n*

wa·ter·course Wasserlauf *m*

wa·ter·cress BOT Brunnenkresse *f*

wa·ter·fall Wasserfall *m*

wa·ter·front Hafenviertel *n*; **along the ~** am Wasser entlang

wa·ter·hole Wasserloch *n*

wa·ter·ing can Gießkanne *f*

wa·ter jump SPORT Wassergraben *m*

wa·ter lev·el Wasserstand *m*

wa·ter lil·y BOT Seerose *f*

wa·ter·mark Wasserzeichen *n*

wa·ter·mel·on BOT Wassermelone *f*

wa·ter' pol·lu·tion Wasserverschmutzung *f*; **~ po·lo** SPORT Wasserball(spiel *n*) *m*

wa·ter·proof 1. wasserdicht; **2.** *Br* Regenmantel *m*; **3.** imprägnieren

wa·ters Gewässer *pl*; Wasser *pl*

wa·ter·shed GEOGR Wasserscheide *f*; *fig* Wendepunkt *m*

wa·ter·side Ufer *n*

wa·ter ski·ing SPORT Wasserskilaufen *n*

wa·ter·tight wasserdicht, *fig a.* hieb- und stichfest

wa·ter·way Wasserstraße *f*

wa·ter·works Wasserwerk *n*; **turn on the ~** F zu heulen anfangen

wa·ter·y wäss(e)rig

watt ELECTR Watt *n*

wave 1. *v/i* schwenken, winken mit; *Haar* wellen, in Wellen legen; **~ one's hand** winken; **~ s.o. aside** j-n beiseite winken; *v/i* winken; wehen (*flag etc*); sich wellen (*hair*); **~ at s.o., ~ to s.o.** j-m zuwinken; **2.** Welle *f* (*a. fig*); Winken *n*

wave·length PHYS Wellenlänge *f* (*a. fig*)

wa·ver flackern; schwanken

wav·y wellig, gewellt

wax¹ 1. Wachs *n*; (*Ohren*)Schmalz *n*; **2.** wachsen; bohnern

wax² ASTR zunehmen

wax·en wächsern

wax·works Wachsfigurenkabinett *n*

wax·y wächsern

way 1. Weg *m*; Richtung *f*, Seite *f*; Entfernung *f*, Strecke *f*; Art *f*, Weise *f*; **~s**

and means Mittel und Wege *pl*; **~ back** Rückweg *m*, Rückfahrt *f*; **~ home** Heimweg *m*; **~ in** Eingang *m*; **~ out** Ausgang *m*; **be on the ~ to, be on one's ~ to** unterwegs sein nach; **by ~ of** über (*acc*), via; *esp Br* statt; **by the ~** übrigens; **give ~** nachgeben; *Br* MOT die Vorfahrt lassen; **in a ~** in gewisser Hinsicht; **in no ~** in keiner Weise; **lead the ~** vorangehen; **let s.o. have his (own) ~** j-s-n Willen lassen; **lose one's ~** sich verlaufen or verirren; **make ~** Platz machen (**for** für); **no ~!** F kommt überhaupt nicht in Frage!; **out of the ~** ungewöhnlich; **this ~** hierher; hier entlang; **2.** *adv* weit

way·bill ECON Frachtbrief *m*

way·lay j-m auflauern; j-n abfangen, abpassen

way·ward eigensinnig, launisch

we wir *pl*

weak schwach (**at, in** in *dat*), GASTR *a.* dünn; **weak·en** *v/t* schwächen (*a. fig*); *v/i* schwächer werden; *fig* nachgeben; **weak·ling** Schwächling *m*, F Schlappschwanz *n*; **weak·ness** Schwäche *f*

weal Striemen *m*

wealth Reichtum *m*; *fig* Fülle *f* (**of** von)

wealth·y reich

wean entwöhnen; **~ s.o. from** or **off s.th.** j-n et. abgewöhnen

weap·on Waffe *f* (*a. fig*)

wear 1. *v/t* Bart, Brille, Schmuck etc tragen, Mantel etc a. anhaben, Hut etc a. aufhaben; abnutzen, abtragen; **~ the pants** (*Br* **trousers**) F die Hosen anhaben; **~ an angry expression** verärgert dreinschauen; *v/i* sich abnutzen, verschleißen; sich gut *etc* halten; **s.th. to ~** et. zum Anziehen; **~ away** (sich) abtragen or abschleifen; **~ down** (sich) abtreten (*stairs*), (sich) ablaufen (*heels*), (sich) abfahren (*tires*); abschleifen; j-n zermürben; **~ off** nachlassen (*pain etc*); **~ on** sich hinziehen (*all day* über den ganzen Tag); **~ out** (sich) abnutzen or abtragen; *fig* j-n erschöpfen; **2.** *often in cpds* Kleidung *f*; *a.* **~ and tear** Abnutzung *f*, Verschleiß *m*; **the worse for ~** abgenutzt, verschlissen; F lädiert

wear·i·some ermüdend; langweilig; lästig

wear·y erschöpft, müde; ermüdend, anstrengend; *be ~ of s.th.* F et. satt haben

wea·sel ZO Wiesel *n*

weath·er 1. Wetter *n*; Witterung *f*; **2.** *v/t* dem Wetter aussetzen; *fig* Krise etc überstehen; *v/i* verwittern

weath·er-beat·en verwittert

weath·er| chart METEOR Wetterkarte *f*; **~ fore·cast** METEOR Wettervorhersage *f*, Wetterbericht *m*

weath·er·man *radio*, TV Wetteransager *m*

weath·er·proof 1. wetterfest; **2.** wetterfest machen

weath·er| re·port METEOR Wetterbericht *m*; **~ sta·tion** METEOR Wetterwarte *f*; **~ vane** Wetterfahne *f*

weave weben; *Netz* flechten; **~ one's way through** sich schlängeln durch; **weav·er** Weber(in)

web Netz *n* (*a. fig*), Gewebe *n*; ZO Schwimmhaut *f*

wed heiraten

Wed(s) ABBR of *Wednesday* Mi., Mittwoch *m*

wed·ding 1. Hochzeit *f*; **2.** Hochzeits..., Braut..., Ehe..., Trau...

wed·ding ring Ehering *m*, Trauring *m*

wedge 1. Keil *m*; **2.** verkeilen, mit e-m Keil festklemmen; **~ in** einkeilen, einzwängen

wed·lock: born in (out of) ~ ehelich (unehelich) geboren

Wednes·day (ABBR *Wed*, *Weds*) Mittwoch *m*; **on ~** (am) Mittwoch; **on ~s** mittwochs

wee[1] F **1.** klein, winzig; **a ~ bit** ein (kleines) bisschen

wee[2] F **1.** Pipi machen; **2.** *do* or *have a ~* Pipi machen

weed 1. Unkraut *n*; **2.** jäten

weed·kill·er Unkrautvertilgungsmittel *n*

weed·y voll Unkraut; F schmächtig; F rückgratlos

week Woche *f*; **~ after ~** Woche um Woche; **a ~ today**, **today ~** heute in e-r Woche or in acht Tagen; **every other ~** jede zweite Woche; **for ~s** wochenlang; **three times a ~** viermal die Woche; **in a ~('s time)** in e-r Woche

week·day Wochentag *m*

week·end Wochenende *n*; **on (Br at) the ~** am Wochenende; **week·end·er** Wochenendausflügler(in)

week·ly 1. Wochen...; wöchentlich; **2.** Wochenblatt *n*, Wochen(zeit)schrift *f*, Wochenzeitung *f*

weep weinen (*for* um j-n; *over* über acc); MED nässen

weep·ing wil·low BOT Trauerweide *f*

weep·y F weinerlich; rührselig

wee-wee F → *wee*[2]

weigh *v/t* (ab)wiegen; *fig* abwägen (*against* gegen); **~ anchor** MAR den Anker lichten; *be ~ed down with fig* niedergedrückt werden von; *v/i* ... Kilo *etc* wiegen; **~ on** *fig* lasten auf (*dat*)

weight 1. Gewicht *n*; Last *f* (*a. fig*); *fig* Bedeutung *f*; **gain ~**, **put on ~** zunehmen; **lose ~** abnehmen; **2.** beschweren

weight·less schwerelos

weight·less·ness Schwerelosigkeit *f*

weight lift·er SPORT Gewichtheber *m*

weight lift·ing SPORT Gewichtheben *n*

weight·y schwer; *fig* schwerwiegend

weir Wehr *n*

weird unheimlich; F sonderbar, verrückt

wel·come 1. *int* **~ back!**, **~ home!** willkommen zu Hause!; **~ to England!** willkommen in England!; **2.** *v/t* begrüßen (*a. fig*), willkommen heißen; **3.** *adj* willkommen; **you are ~ to do it** Sie können es gerne tun; **you're ~!** nichts zu danken!, keine Ursache!, bitte sehr!; **4.** Empfang *m*, Willkommen *n*; **outstay** or **overstay one's ~** j-s Gastfreundschaft überstrapazieren or zu lange in Anspruch nehmen

weld TECH schweißen

wel·fare Wohl(ergehen) *n*; Sozialhilfe *f*; **be on ~** Sozialhilfe beziehen; **~ state** Wohlfahrtsstaat *m*; **~ work** Sozialarbeit *f*; **~ work·er** Sozialarbeiter(in)

well[1] **1.** *adv* gut; gründlich; **as ~** ebenso, auch; **as ~ as ...** sowohl ... als auch ...; nicht nur ..., sondern auch ...; **very ~** also gut, na gut; **~ done!** bravo!; **~ off** 1; **2.** *int* nun, also; **~**, **~!** na so was!; **3.** *adj* gesund; **feel ~** sich wohl fühlen

well[2] **1.** Brunnen *m*; (*Öl*)Quelle *f*; (*Aufzugs- etc*)Schacht *m*; **2.** *a. ~ out* quellen (*from* aus); **tears ~ed (up) in their eyes** die Tränen stiegen ihnen in die Augen

well-bal·anced ausgeglichen (*person*); ausgewogen (*diet*)

well-be·haved artig, gut erzogen

W

well-be·ing Wohl(befinden) n

well-dis·posed: *be ~ towards s.o.* j-m wohlgesinnt sein

well-done GASTR durchgebraten

well-earned wohlverdient

well-fed gut genährt

well-found·ed (wohl) begründet

well-in·formed gut unterrichtet; gebildet

well-known (wohl) bekannt

well-mean·ing wohlmeinend, gut gemeint; **well-meant** gut gemeint

well-off **1.** wohlhabend, vermögend, besser gestellt; *be ~ for* gut versorgt sein mit; **2.** *the ~* die Wohlhabenden *pl*

well-read belesen

well-timed (zeitlich) günstig, im richtigen Augenblick

well-to-do wohlhabend, reich

well-worn abgetragen; *fig* abgedroschen

Welsh **1.** walisisch; **2.** LING Walisisch *n*; *the ~* die Waliser *pl*

welt Striemen *m*

wel·ter Wirrwarr *m*, Durcheinander *n*

wel·ter·weight SPORT Weltergewicht *n*; Weltergewichtler *m*

were *du* warst, *Sie* waren, *wir, sie* waren, *ihr* wart

west **1.** West, Westen *m*; *the West* POL der Westen; die Weststaaten *pl*; **2.** *adj* westlich, West...; **3.** *adv* nach Westen, westwärts; **west·er·ly** West..., westlich; **west·ern 1.** westlich, West...; **2.** Western *m*; **west·ward(s)** westlich, nach Westen

wet **1.** nass, feucht; **2.** Nässe *f*; **3.** nass machen, anfeuchten

weth·er ZO Hammel *m*

wet nurse Amme *f*

whack (knallender) Schlag; F Anteil *m*

whacked F fertig, erledigt

whack·ing **1.** *Br* F Mords...; **2.** (Tracht *f*) Prügel *pl*

whale ZO Wal *m*

wharf Kai *m*

what **1.** *pron* was; *~ about ...?* wie wärs mit ...?; *~ for?* wozu?; *so ~?* na und?; *know ~'s ~* F wissen, was Sache ist; **2.** *adj* was für ein(e), welche(r, -s); alle, die; alles, was

what·cha·ma·call·it F → **whatsit**

what·ev·er **1.** *pron* was (auch immer); alles, was; egal, was; **2.** *adj* welche(r,

-s) ... auch (immer); *no ... ~* überhaupt kein(e) ...

whats·it F Dings(bums, -da) *m*, *f*, *n*

what·so·ev·er → **whatever**

wheat BOT Weizen *m*

whee·dle beschwatzen; *~ s.th. out of s.o.* j-m et. abschwatzen

wheel **1.** Rad *n*; MOT, MAR Steuer *n*; **2.** schieben, rollen; kreisen; *~ about, ~ (a)round* herumfahren, herumwirbeln

wheel·bar·row Schubkarre(n *m*) *f*

wheel·chair Rollstuhl *m*

wheel clamp MOT Parkkralle *f*

wheeled mit Rädern; fahrbar; *in cpds* ...räd(e)rig

wheeze keuchen, pfeifend atmen

whelp ZO Welpe *m*, Junge *n*

when wann; als; wenn; obwohl; *since ~?* seit wann?

when·ev·er wann auch (immer); jedes Mal, wenn

where wo; wohin; *~ ... (from)?* woher?; *~ ... (to)?* wohin?; **where·a·bouts 1.** *adv* wo etwa; **2.** Verbleib *m*; Aufenthalt *m*, Aufenthaltsort *m*

where·as während, wohingegen

where·by wodurch, womit; wonach

where·u·pon worauf, woraufhin

wher·ev·er wo auch immer (immer); ganz gleich wo *or* wohin

whet *Messer etc* schärfen; *fig Appetit* anregen

wheth·er ob

whey Molke *f*

which welche(r, -s); der, die, das; was; *~ of you?* wer von euch?

which·ev·er welche(r, -s) auch (immer); ganz gleich, welche(r, -s)

whiff Luftzug *m*; Hauch *m* (*a. fig of* von); Duft *m*, Duftwolke *f*

while **1.** Weile *f*; *for a ~* e-e Zeit lang; **2.** *cj* während; obwohl; **3.** *mst ~ away* sich *die Zeit* vertreiben (*by doing s.th.* mit et.)

whim Laune *f*

whim·per **1.** wimmern; ZO winseln; **2.** Wimmern *n*; ZO Winseln *n*

whim·si·cal wunderlich; launisch

whine **1.** ZO jaulen; jammern (*about* über *acc*); **2.** ZO Jaulen *n*; Gejammer *n*

whin·ny ZO **1.** wiehern; **2.** Wiehern *n*

whip **1.** Peitsche *f*; GASTR Creme *f*; **2.** *v/t* (aus)peitschen; GASTR schlagen; *v/i* sausen, flitzen, (*wind*) fegen

whipped| cream Schlagsahne *f*, Schlagrahm *m*; **~ eggs** Eischnee *m*

whip·ping (Tracht *f*) Prügel *pl*

whip·ping boy Prügelknabe *m*

whip·ping cream Schlagsahne *f*, Schlagrahm *m*

whir → **whirr**

whirl 1. wirbeln; *my head is ~ing* mir schwirrt der Kopf; **2.** Wirbeln *n*; Wirbel *m* (*a. fig*); *my head's in a ~* mir schwirrt der Kopf

whirl·pool Strudel *m*; Whirlpool *m*

whirl·wind Wirbelsturm *m*

whirr schwirren

whisk 1. schnelle Bewegung; Wedel *m*; GASTR Schneebesen *m*; **2.** GASTR schlagen; **~ its tail** ZO mit dem Schwanz schlagen; **~ away** Fliegen *etc* verscheuchen *or* wegscheuchen; *et.* schnell verschwinden lassen *or* wegnehmen

whis·ker ZO Schnurr- *or* Barthaar *n*; *pl* Backenbart *m*

whis·k(e)y Whisky *m*

whis·per 1. flüstern; **2.** Flüstern *n*; *say s.th. in a ~* et. im Flüsterton sagen

whis·tle 1. Pfeife *f*; Pfiff *m*; **2.** pfeifen

white 1. weiß; **2.** Weiß(e) *n*; Weiße *m*, *f*; Eiweiß *n*; **~ bread** Weißbrot *n*; **~ cof·fee** *Br* Milchkaffee *m*, Kaffee *m* mit Milch

white-col·lar work·er (Büro)Angestellte *m*, *f*

white lie Notlüge *f*

whit·en weiß machen *or* werden

white·wash 1. Tünche *f*; **2.** tünchen, anstreichen; weißen; *fig* beschönigen

whit·ish weißlich

Whit·sun Pfingstsonntag *m*; Pfingsten *n* *or* *pl*

Whit Sunday Pfingstsonntag *m*

Whit·sun·tide Pfingsten *n* *or* *pl*

whit·tle (zurecht)schnitzen; **~ away** Gewinn *etc* allmählich aufzehren; **~ down** *et.* reduzieren (**to** auf *acc*)

whiz(z) *F* **1.** **~ by**, **~ past** vorbeizischen, vorbeidüsen; **2.** Ass *n*, Kanone *f* (**at** in *dat*); **~ kid** *F* Senkrechtstarter(in)

who wer; wen; wem; welche(r, -s); der, die, das

who·dun·(n)it *F* Krimi *m*

who·ev·er wer *or* wen *or* wem auch (immer); egal, wer *or* wen *or* wem

whole 1. *adj* ganz; **2.** *das* Ganze; **the ~ of**

London ganz London; **on the ~** im Großen (und) Ganzen

whole-heart·ed ungeteilt (*attention*), voll (*support*), ernsthaft (*effort etc*)

whole-heart·ed·ly uneingeschränkt, voll und ganz

whole·meal Vollkorn...; **~ bread** Vollkornbrot *n*

whole·sale ECON **1.** Großhandel *m*; **2.** Großhandels...; **~ mar·ket** ECON Großmarkt *m*

whole·sal·er ECON Großhändler *m*

whole·some gesund

whole wheat → **wholemeal**

whol·ly gänzlich, völlig

whoop 1. schreien, *esp* jauchzen; **~ it up** *F* auf den Putz hauen; **2.** (*esp* Freuden)Schrei *m*

whoop·ee *F* **make ~** auf den Putz hauen

whoop·ing cough MED Keuchhusten *m*

whore Hure *f*

why warum, weshalb; *that's ~* deshalb

wick Docht *m*

wick·ed gemein, niederträchtig

wick·er·work Korbwaren *pl*

wick·et *cricket*: Tor *n*

wide 1. *adj* weit; offen, aufgerissen (*eyes*), *fig* umfangreich (*knowledge etc*), vielfältig (*interests etc*); **2.** *adv* weit; **go ~** danebengehen; **go ~ of the goal** SPORT am Tor vorbeigehen

wide-an·gle lens PHOT Weitwinkelobjektiv *n*

wide-a·wake hellwach; *fig* aufgeweckt, wach

wide-eyed mit großen *or* aufgerissenen Augen; naiv

wid·en verbreitern; breiter werden

wide-o·pen weit offen, aufgerissen (*eyes*)

wide·spread weit verbreitet

wid·ow Witwe *f*

wid·owed verwitwet; **be ~** verwitwet sein; Witwe(r) werden

wid·ow·er Witwer *m*

width Breite *f*; Bahn *f*

wield *Einfluss etc* ausüben

wife (Ehe)Frau *f*, Gattin *f*

wig Perücke *f*

wild 1. *adj* wild; stürmisch (*wind*, *applause etc*); außer sich (*with* vor *dat*); verrückt (*idea etc*); **make a ~ guess**

einfach drauflosraten; *be ~ about (ganz)* verrückt sein nach; **2.** *adv:* **go ~** ausflippen; *let one's children run ~* s-e Kinder machen lassen, was sie wollen; **3.** *in the ~* in freier Wildbahn; *the ~s* die Wildnis

wild·cat ZO Wildkatze *f*

wild·cat strike ECON wilder Streik

wil·der·ness Wildnis *f*

wild·fire: *spread like ~* sich wie ein Lauffeuer verbreiten

wild·life Tier- und Pflanzenwelt *f*

wil·ful *Br* → **willful**

will[1] *v/aux ich, du* will(st) *etc; ich werde ... etc*

will[2] Wille *m*; Testament *n*; *of one's own free ~* aus freien Stücken

will[3] durch Willenskraft erzwingen; JUR vermachen

will·ful eigensinnig; absichtlich, *esp* JUR vorsätzlich

will·ing bereit (*to do* zu tun); (be-reit)willig

will-o'-the-wisp Irrlicht *n*

wil·low BOT Weide *f*

wil·low·y *fig* gertenschlank

wil·pow·er Willenskraft *f*

wil·ly-nil·ly wohl oder übel

wilt verwelken, welk werden

wi·ly gerissen, raffiniert

wimp F Schlappschwanz *m*

win[1] *v/t* gewinnen; *~ s.o. over or round to* j-n gewinnen für; *v/i* gewinnen, siegen; *OK, you ~* okay, du hast gewonnen; **2.** *esp* SPORT Sieg *m*

wince zusammenzucken (*at* bei)

winch TECH Winde *f*

wind[1] **1.** Wind *m*; Atem *m*, Luft *f*; MED Blähungen *pl*; *the ~* MUS die Bläser *pl*; **2.** *j-m* den Atem nehmen *or* verschlagen; HUNT wittern

wind[2] **1.** *v/t* drehen (an *dat*); Uhr *etc* aufziehen; wickeln (*round* um); *v/i* sich winden *or* schlängeln; *~ back* Film *etc* zurückspulen; *~ down* Autofenster *etc* herunterdrehen, -kurbeln; *Produktion etc* reduzieren; sich entspannen; *~ forward* Film *etc* weiterspulen; *~ up v/t* Autofenster *etc* hochdrehen, -kurbeln; Uhr *etc* aufziehen; Versammlung *etc* schließen (*with* mit); Unternehmen liquidieren, auflösen; *v/i* F enden, landen; (*esp* s-e Rede) schließen (*by*

saying mit den Worten); **2.** Umdrehung *f*

wind·bag F Schwätzer(in)

wind·fall BOT Fallobst *n*; unverhofftes Geschenk; unverhoffter Gewinn

wind·ing gewunden

wind·ing stairs Wendeltreppe *f*

wind in·stru·ment MUS Blasinstrument *n*

wind·lass TECH Winde *f*

wind·mill Windmühle *f*

win·dow Fenster *n*; Schaufenster *n*; Schalter *m*; *~ clean·er* Fensterputzer *m*; *~ dress·er* Schaufensterdekorateur(in); *~ dress·ing* Schaufensterdekoration *f; fig* F Mache *f*

win·dow·pane Fensterscheibe *f*

win·dow seat Fensterplatz *m*

win·dow shade Rouleau *n*

win·dow-shop: *go window-shopping* e-n Schaufensterbummel machen

win·dow·sill Fensterbank *f*, -brett *n*

wind·pipe ANAT Luftröhre *f*

wind·screen *Br* MOT Windschutzscheibe *f; ~ wip·er Br* MOT Scheibenwischer *m*

wind·shield MOT Windschutzscheibe *f; ~ wip·er* MOT Scheibenwischer *m*

wind·surf·ing SPORT Windsurfing *n*, Windsurfen *n*

wind·y windig; MED blähend

wine Wein *m; ~ cel·lar* Weinkeller *m; ~ list* Weinkarte *f; ~ mer·chant* Weinhändler *m*

win·er·y Weinkellerei *f*

wine tast·ing Weinprobe *f*

wing ZO Flügel *m*, Schwinge *f; Br* MOT Kotflügel *m*; AVIAT Tragfläche *f;* AVIAT MIL Geschwader *n; pl* THEA Seitenkulisse *f*

wing·er SPORT Außenstürmer(in), Flügelstürmer(in)

wink 1. zwinkern; *~ at j-m* zuzwinkern; *et.* geflissentlich übersehen; *~ one's lights Br* MOT blinken; **2.** Zwinkern *n; I didn't get a ~ of sleep last night, I didn't sleep a ~ last night* ich habe letzte Nacht kein Auge zugetan; → **forty**[1]

win·ner Gewinner(in), *esp* SPORT Sieger(in)

win·ning 1. einnehmend, gewinnend; **2.** *pl* Gewinn *m*

win·ter 1. Winter *m; in (the) ~* im Win-

ter; **2.** überwintern; den Winter verbringen; **~ sports** Wintersport *m*
win·ter·time Winter *m*; Winterzeit *f*; *in*
(the) ~ im Winter
win·try winterlich; *fig* frostig
wipe *v/t* (ab-, auf)wischen; **~ off** ab-, wegwi-
schen; **~ out** auswischen; auslöschen;
ausrotten; **~ up** aufwischen
wip·er MOT *(Scheiben)*Wischer *m*
wire 1. Draht *m*; ELECTR Leitung *f*; Telegramm *n*; **2.** Leitungen verlegen in
(dat) (*a.* **~ up**); *j-m* ein Telegramm schicken; *j-m* et. telegrafieren
wire·less drahtlos, Funk...
wire net·ting Maschendraht *m*
wire-tap *j-n, j-s* Telefon abhören
wir·y *fig* drahtig
wis·dom Weisheit *f*, Klugheit *f*
wis·dom tooth Weisheitszahn *m*
wise weise, klug
wise·crack F **1.** Witzelei *f*; **2.** witzeln
wise guy F Klugscheißer *m*
wish 1. wünschen; wollen; ~ **s.o. well**
j-m alles Gute wünschen; *if you* ~ (*to*)
wenn du willst; ~ *for s.th.* sich et. wünschen; **2.** Wunsch *m* (*for* nach)
wish·ful think·ing Wunschdenken *n*
wish·y-wash·y F labb(e)rig, wäss(e)rig;
fig lasch (*person*); verschwommen
wisp *(Gras-, Haar)*Büschel *m*
wist·ful wehmütig
wit Geist *m*, Witz *m*; geistreicher
Mensch; *a. pl* Verstand *m*; *be at one's*
~s' end mit s-r Weisheit am Ende sein;
keep one's **~s about one** e-n klaren
Kopf behalten
witch Hexe *f*
witch·craft Hexerei *f*
with mit; bei; vor *(dat)*
with·draw *v/t* Geld abheben (*from* von);
Angebot *etc* zurückziehen, Anschuldigung *etc* zurücknehmen; MIL
Truppen zurückziehen, abziehen; *v/i*
sich zurückziehen; zurücktreten (*from*
von)
with·draw·al Rücknahme *f*; *esp* MIL
Abzug *m*, Rückzug *m*; Rücktritt *m*
(*from* von), Ausstieg *m* (*from* aus);
MED Entziehung *f*, Entzug *m*; *make*
a ~ Geld abheben (*from* von); ~ *cure*
MED Entziehungskur *f*; ~ *symp·toms*
MED Entzugserscheinungen *pl*
with·er eingehen *or* verdorren *or*
(ver)welken (lassen)

with·hold zurückhalten; ~ *s.th. from*
s.o. *j-m* et. vorenthalten
with·in innerhalb *(gen)*
with·out ohne *(acc)*
with·stand *e-m Angriff etc* standhalten;
Beanspruchung etc aushalten
wit·ness 1. Zeuge *m*, Zeugin *f*; ~ *for the*
defense (*Br* **defence**) JUR Entlastungszeuge *m*, -zeugin *f*; ~ *for the*
prosecution JUR Belastungszeuge *m*,
-zeugin *f*; **2.** Zeuge sein von *et.*; *et.* be-
zeugen, *Unterschrift* beglaubigen; ~
box *Br*, ~ **stand** JUR Zeugenstand *m*
wit·ti·cis·m geistreiche *or* witzige Bemerkung; **wit·ty** geistreich, witzig
wiz·ard Zauberer *m*; *fig* Genie *n* (*at* in
dat)
wiz·ened verhutzelt
wob·ble *v/i* wackeln, zittern (*a. voice*),
schwabbeln; *fig* schwan-
ken; *v/t* wackeln an *(dat)*
woe·ful traurig; bedauerlich
wolf 1. ZO Wolf *m*; *lone* ~ *fig* Einzel-
gänger(in); **2.** *a.* ~ *down* F *Essen* hinunterschlingen
wom·an Frau *f*; ~ **doc·tor** Ärztin *f*; ~
driv·er Frau *f* am Steuer
wom·an·ish weibisch
wom·an·ly fraulich; weiblich
womb ANAT Gebärmutter *f*
women's│ lib·ber F Emanze *f*; ~
move·ment Frauenbewegung *f*; ~
ref·uge *Br*, ~ **shel·ter** Frauenhaus *n*
won·der 1. neugierig *or* gespannt sein,
gern wissen mögen; sich fragen, überlegen; sich wundern, erstaunt sein
(*about* über *acc*); *I ~ if you could help*
me vielleicht können Sie mir helfen; **2.**
Staunen *n*, Verwunderung *f*; Wunder
n; *do or work* ~*s* wahre Wunder voll-
bringen, Wunder wirken (*for* bei)
won·der·ful wunderbar, wundervoll
wont 1. *be* ~ *to do s.th.* et. zu tun pflegen; **2.** *as was his* ~ wie es s-e Gewohnheit war
woo umwerben, werben um
wood Holz *n*; Holzfass *n*; *a. pl* Wald *m*,
Gehölz *n*; *touch* ~*!* unberufen!, toi, toi,
toi!; *he can't see the* ~ *for the trees* er
sieht den Wald vor lauter Bäumen
nicht
wood·cut Holzschnitt *m*
wood·cut·ter Holzfäller *m*
wood·ed bewaldet

wood·en hölzern (*a. fig*), aus Holz, Holz...

wood·peck·er ZO Specht *m*

wood·wind: *the* ~ MUS die Holzblasinstrumente *pl*, die Holzbläser *pl*; ~ *instrument* Holzblasinstrument *n*

wood·work Holzarbeit *f*

wood·y waldig; BOT holzig

wool Wolle *f*

wool·(l)en 1. wollen, Woll...; **2.** *pl* Wollsachen *pl*, Wollkleidung *f*

wool·(l)y 1. wollig; *fig* schwammig; **2.** *pl* F Wollsachen *pl*

word 1. Wort *n*; Nachricht *f*; Losung *f*, Losungswort *n*; Versprechen *n*; Befehl *m*; *pl* MUS *etc* Text *m*; *have a* ~ *or a few* ~*s with s.o.* mit j-m sprechen; **2.** *et.* ausdrücken; *Text* abfassen, formulieren; **word·ing** Wortlaut *m*

word| or·der *for* LING Wortstellung *f*; ~ **pro·cess·ing** EDP Textverarbeitung *f*; ~ **pro·ces·sor** EDP Textverarbeitungsgerät *n*

word·y wortreich, langatmig

work 1. Arbeit *f*; Werk *n*; *pl* TECH Werk *n*, Getriebe *n*; ECON Werk *n*, Fabrik *f*; *at* ~ bei der Arbeit; *be in* ~ Arbeit haben; *be out of* ~ arbeitslos sein; *go or set to* ~ an die Arbeit gehen; **2.** *v/i* arbeiten (*at, on* an *dat*); TECH funktionieren (*a. fig*); wirken; ~ *to rule* Dienst *m* nach Vorschrift tun; *v/t* j-n arbeiten lassen; *Maschine etc* bedienen, *et.* betätigen; *et.* bearbeiten; bewirken, herbeiführen; ~ *one's way* sich durcharbeiten *or* durchkämpfen; ~ *off Schulden* abarbeiten; *Wut etc* abreagieren; ~ *out v/t* ausrechnen; *Aufgabe* lösen; *Plan etc* ausarbeiten; *fig* sich *et.* zusammenreimen; *v/i* gut gehen, F klappen; aufgehen; F SPORT trainieren; ~ *up Zuhörer etc* aufpeitschen, aufwühlen; *et.* ausarbeiten (*into* zu); *be* ~*ed up* aufgeregt *or* nervös sein (*about* wegen)

work·a·ble formbar; *fig* durchführbar

work·a·day Alltags...

work·a·hol·ic F Arbeitssüchtige *m, f*

work·bench TECH Werkbank *f*

work·book PED Arbeitsheft *n*

work·day Arbeitstag *m*; Werktag *m*; *on* ~*s* werktags

work·er Arbeiter(in); Angestellte *m, f*

work ex·pe·ri·ence Erfahrung *f*

work·ing werktätig; Arbeits...; ~ *knowl-*

edge Grundkenntnisse *pl*; *in* ~ *order* in betriebsfähigem Zustand; ~ *class* Arbeiterklasse *f*; ~ *day* → *workday*; ~ *hours* Arbeitszeit *f*; *fewer* ~ Arbeitszeitverkürzung *f*; *reduced* ~ Kurzarbeit *f*

work·ings Arbeits-, Funktionsweise *f*

work·man Handwerker *m*

work·man·like fachmännisch

work·man·ship fachmännische Arbeit

work of art Kunstwerk *n*

work·out F SPORT Training *n*

work·place Arbeitsplatz *m*; *at the* ~ am Arbeitsplatz

works coun·cil Betriebsrat *m*

work·sheet PED *etc* Arbeitsblatt *n*

work·shop Werkstatt *f*; Workshop *m*

work·shy arbeitsscheu

work·sta·tion EDP Bildschirmarbeitsplatz *m*

work-to-rule *Br* Dienst *m* nach Vorschrift

world 1. Welt *f*; *all over the* ~ in der ganzen Welt; *bring into the* ~ auf die Welt bringen; *do s.o. a or the* ~ *of good* j-m unwahrscheinlich gut tun; *mean all the* ~ *to s.o.* j-m alles bedeuten; *they are* ~*s apart* zwischen ihnen liegen Welten; *think the* ~ *of* große Stücke halten von; *what in the* ~ ...? was um alles in der Welt ...?; **2.** Welt...; ~ **cham·pi·on** SPORT Weltmeister *m*; ~ **cham·pi·onship** SPORT Weltmeisterschaft *f*

World Cup Fußballweltmeisterschaft *f*; *skiing:* Weltcup *m*

world-fa·mous weltberühmt

world lit·er·a·ture Weltliteratur *f*

world·ly weltlich; irdisch

world·ly-wise weltklug

world| mar·ket ECON Weltmarkt *m*; ~ **pow·er** POL Weltmacht *f*; ~ **rec·ord** SPORT Weltrekord *m*; ~ **trip** Weltreise *f*; ~ **war** Weltkrieg *m*

world·wide weltweit; auf der ganzen Welt

worm 1. ZO Wurm *m*; **2.** *Hund etc* entwurmen; ~ *one's way through* sich schlängeln *or* zwängen durch; ~ *o.s. into s.o.'s confidence* sich in j-s Vertrauen einschleichen; ~ *s.th. out of s.o.* j-m et. entlocken

worm-eat·en wurmstichig

worm's-eye view Froschperspektive *f*

W

worn-out abgenutzt, abgetragen; *fig* erschöpft

wor·ried besorgt, beunruhigt

wor·ry 1. beunruhigen; (sich) Sorgen machen; *don't ~!* keine Angst!, keine Sorge!; **2.** Sorge *f*

worse schlechter, schlimmer; *~ still* was noch schlechter ist; *to make matters ~* zu allem Übel

wors·en schlechter machen *or* werden, (sich) verschlechtern

wor·ship 1. Verehrung *f*; Gottesdienst *m*; **2.** *v/t* anbeten, verehren; *v/i* den Gottesdienst besuchen

wor·ship·(p)er Anbeter(in), Verehrer(in); Kirchgänger(in)

worst 1. *adj* schlechteste(r, -s), schlimmste(r, -s); **2.** *adv* am schlechtesten, am schlimmsten; **3.** *der, die, das* Schlechteste *or* Schlimmste *m*; *at (the) ~* schlimmstenfalls

wor·sted Kammgarn *n*

worth 1. wert; *~ reading* lesenswert; **2.** Wert *m*; *worth·less* wertlos

worth·while lohnend; *be ~* sich lohnen

worth·y würdig

would-be Möchtegern...

wound 1. Wunde *f*, Verletzung *f*; **2.** verwunden, verletzen

wow *int* F wow!, Mensch!, toll!

wran·gle 1. (sich) streiten; **2.** Streit *m*

wrap 1. *v/t a. ~ up* (ein)packen, (ein)wickeln (*in* in *dat*); *et.* wickeln ([*a*]*round* um); *v/i: ~ up* sich warm anziehen; **2.** Umhang *m*

wrap·per (Schutz)Umschlag *m*

wrap·ping Verpackung *f*; *~ pa·per* Einwickel-, Pack-, Geschenkpapier *n*

wrath Zorn *m*

wreath Kranz *m*

wreck 1. MAR Wrack *n* (*a. fig*); **2.** *Pläne etc* zunichte machen; *be ~ed* MAR zerschellen; Schiffbruch erleiden

wreck·age Trümmer *pl* (*a. fig*), Wrackteile *pl*

wreck·er Abschleppwagen *m*

wreck·ing| com·pa·ny Abbruchfirma *f*; *~ ser·vice* MOT Abschleppdienst *m*

wren ZO Zaunkönig *m*

wrench 1. MED sich *das Knie etc* verrenken; *~ s.th. from or out of s.o.'s hands* j-m et. aus den Händen winden, j-m et. entwinden; *~ off* et. mit e-m Ruck abreißen *or* wegreißen; *~ open*

aufreißen; **2.** Ruck *m*; MED Verrenkung *f*; *Br* TECH Schraubenschlüssel *m*

wrest: *~ s.th. from or out of s.o.'s hands* j-m et. aus den Händen reißen, j-m et. entreißen *or* entwinden

wres·tle *v/i* SPORT ringen (*with* mit), *fig a.* kämpfen (*with* mit); *v/t* SPORT ringen gegen; **wres·tler** SPORT Ringer *m*; **wres·tling** SPORT Ringen *n*

wretch *often* HUMOR Schuft *m*, Wicht *m*; *a.* **poor ~** armer Teufel

wretch·ed elend; (tod)unglücklich; scheußlich; verdammt, verflixt

wrig·gle *v/i* sich winden; zappeln; *~ out of fig* F sich herauswinden aus; F sich drücken vor (*dat*); *v/t* mit *den Zehen* wackeln

wring *j-m die Hand* drücken; *die Hände* ringen; *den Hals* umdrehen; *~ out* *Wäsche etc* auswringen; *~ s.o.'s heart* j-m zu Herzen gehen

wrin·kle 1. Falte *f*, Runzel *f*; **2.** runzeln; *Nase* kraus ziehen, rümpfen; faltig *or* runz(e)lig werden

wrist ANAT Handgelenk *n*

wrist·band Bündchen *n*, (Hemd)Manschette *f*; Armband *n*

wrist·watch Armbanduhr *f*

writ JUR Befehl *m*, Verfügung *f*

write schreiben; *~ down* auf-, niederschreiben; *~ off* j-n, ECON et. abschreiben; *~ out* Namen etc ausschreiben; *Bericht etc* ausarbeiten; *j-m e-e Quittung etc* ausstellen; *~ pro·tec·tion* EDP Schreibschutz *m*

writ·er Schreiber(in), Verfasser(in), Autor(in); Schriftsteller(in)

writhe sich krümmen *or* winden (*in, with* vor *dat*)

writ·ing 1. Schreiben *n*; (Hand)Schrift *f*; Schriftstück *n*; *pl* Werke *pl*; schriftlich; **2.** Schreib...; *~ case* Schreibmappe *f*; *~ desk* Schreibtisch *m*; *~ pad* Schreibblock *m*; *~ pa·per* Briefpapier *n*, Schreibpapier *n*

writ·ten schriftlich

wrong 1. *adj* falsch; unrecht; *be ~* falsch sein, nicht stimmen; Unrecht haben; falsch gehen (*watch*); *be on the ~ side of forty* über 40 (Jahre alt) sein; *is any·thing ~?* ist et. nicht in Ordnung?; *what's ~ with her?* was ist los mit ihr?, was hat sie?; **2.** *adv* falsch; *get ~* j-n, et. falsch verstehen; *go ~* e-n Fehler ma-

chen; kaputtgehen; *fig* F schief gehen;
3. Unrecht *n*; *be in the ~* im Unrecht
sein; **4.** *j-m* unrecht tun
wrong•ful ungerechtfertigt; gesetzwidrig
wrong-way driv•er MOT F Geisterfah-
rer(in)
wrought i•ron Schmiedeeisen *n*
wrought-i•ron schmiedeeisern

wry süßsauer (*smile*); ironisch, sarkastisch (*humor etc*)
wt ABBR *of **weight*** Gew., Gewicht *n*
WWF ABBR *of **World Wide Fund for
Nature*** WWF *m*
WYSIWYG ABBR *of **what you see is
what you get*** EDP was du (*auf dem
Bildschirm*) siehst, bekommst du (*auch
ausgedruckt*)

X

X, x X, x *n*
xen•o•pho•bi•a Fremdenhass *m*; Ausländerfeindlichkeit *f*
XL ABBR *of **extra large (size)*** extra-
groß

X•mas F → ***Christmas***
X-ray MED **1.** röntgen; **2.** Röntgenstrahl
m; Röntgenaufnahme *f*, -bild *n*; Rönt-
genuntersuchung *f*
xy•lo•phone MUS Xylophon *n*

Y

Y, y Y, y *n*
yacht MAR **1.** (Segel)Boot *n*; Jacht *f*; **2.**
segeln; *go ~ing* segeln gehen
yacht club Segelklub *m*, Jachtklub *m*
yacht•ing Segeln *n*, Segelsport *m*
Yan•kee F Yankee *m*, Ami *m*
yap kläffen; F quasseln
yard[1] (ABBR **yd**) Yard *n* (91, 44 cm)
yard[2] Hof *m*; (*Bau-, Stapel- etc*)Platz *m*;
Garten *m*
yard•stick *fig* Maßstab *m*
yarn Garn *n*; *spin s.o. a ~ about* j-m e-e
abenteuerliche Geschichte *or* e-e Lügengeschichte erzählen von
yawn 1. gähnen; **2.** Gähnen *n*
yeah F ja
year Jahr *n*; *all the ~ round* das ganze
Jahr hindurch; *~ after ~* Jahr für Jahr; *~
in ~ out* jahraus, jahrein; *this ~* dieses
Jahr; *this ~ 's* diesjährige(r, -s)
year•ly jährlich
yearn sich sehnen (*for* nach; *to do* danach, zu tun); **yearn•ing 1.** Sehnsucht
f; **2.** sehnsüchtig
yeast Hefe *f*
yell 1. schreien, brüllen (*with* vor *dat*); *~*

at s.o. j-n anschreien *or* anbrüllen; *~
(out) et.* schreien, brüllen; **2.** Schrei *m*
yel•low 1. gelb; F feig(e); **2.** Gelb *n*; *at ~*
MOT bei Gelb; **3.** (sich) gelb färben;
gelb werden; vergilben
yel•low fe•ver MED Gelbfieber *n*
yel•low•ish gelblich
Yel•low Pag•es® TEL *die* Gelben Seiten
pl, Branchenverzeichnis *n*
yel•low press Sensationspresse *f*
yelp 1. (auf)jaulen; aufschreien; **2.**
(Auf)Jaulen *n*; Aufschrei *m*
yes 1. ja; doch; **2.** Ja *n*
yes•ter•day gestern; *~ morning (afternoon)* gestern Morgen (Nachmittag);
the day before ~ vorgestern
yet 1. *adv in questions:* schon; noch;
(doch) noch; doch, aber; *as ~* bis jetzt,
bisher; *not ~* noch nicht; **2.** *cj* aber,
doch
yew BOT Eibe *f*
yield 1. *v/t* Früchte tragen; Gewinn abwerfen; *Resultat etc* ergeben, liefern;
v/i nachgeben; *~ to* MOT *j-m* die Vorfahrt lassen; **2.** Ertrag *m*
yip•pee *int* F hurra!

V

yo·del 1. jodeln; **2.** Jodler *m*

yo·ga Joga *m, n*, Yoga *m, n*

yog·h(o)urt, yog·urt Jog(h)urt *m, n*

yoke Joch *n* (*a. fig*)

yolk (Ei)Dotter *m, n*, Eigelb *n*

you du, ihr, Sie; (*dat*) dir, euch, Ihnen; (*acc*) dich, euch, Sie; man

young 1. jung; **2.** ZO Junge *pl*; **with ~** ZO trächtig; **the ~** die jungen Leute *pl*, die Jugend

young·ster Junge *m*

your dein(e); *pl* euer, eure; Ihr(e) (*a. pl*)

yours deine(r, -s); *pl* euer eure(s); Ihre (r, -s) (*a. pl*); **a friend of ~** ein Freund von dir; **Yours, Bill** Dein Bill

your·self selbst; dir, dich, sich; **by ~** allein

youth Jugend *f*; Jugendliche *m*

youth club Jugendklub *m*

youth·ful jugendlich

youth hos·tel Jugendherberge *f*

yuck·y F *contp* scheußlich

Yu·go·slav 1. jugoslawisch; **2.** Jugoslawe *m*, Jugoslawin *f*; **Yu·go·sla·vi·a** Jugoslawien *n*

yup·pie, yup·py ABBR *of young upwardly-mobile or urban professional* junger, aufstrebender *or* städtischer Karrieremensch, Yuppie *m*

Z

Z, z Z, z *n*

zap F *esp computer game etc*: abknallen, fertig machen; MOT beschleunigen (**from ... to ...** von ... auf *acc* ...); jagen, hetzen; TV *Fernbedienung* bedienen; TV zappen, umschalten; **~ off** abzischen; **~ to** jagen *or* jagen *or* hetzen nach

zap·per TV F Fernbedienung *f*

zap·py *Br* F voller Pep, schmissig, fetzig

zeal Eifer *m*

zeal·ot Fanatiker(in), Eiferer *m*, Eiferin *f*; **zeal·ous** eifrig; **be ~ to do s.th.** eifrig darum bemüht sein, et. zu tun

ze·bra ZO Zebra *n*

ze·bra cross·ing *Br* Zebrastreifen *m*

zen·ith Zenit *m* (*a. fig*)

ze·ro 1. Null *f*; Nullpunkt *m*; **20 degrees below ~** 20 Grad unter Null; **2.** Null...; **~ growth** Nullwachstum *n*; **~ in·terest: have ~ in s.th.** F null Bock auf et. haben; **~ op·tion** POL Nulllösung *f*

zest *fig* Würze *f*; Begeisterung *f*; **~ for life** Lebensfreude *f*

zig·zag 1. Zickzack *m*; **2.** Zickzack...; **3.** im Zickzack fahren, laufen *etc*, zickzackförmig verlaufen

zinc CHEM Zink *n*

zip¹ 1. Reißverschluss *m*; **2. ~ the bag open** (**shut**) den Reißverschluss der Tasche aufmachen (zumachen); **~ s.o. up** j-m den Reißverschluss zumachen

zip² 1. Zischen *n*, Schwirren *n*; F Schwung *m*; **2.** zischen, schwirren; **~ by, ~ past** vorbeiflitzen

zip code Postleitzahl *f*

zip fas·ten·er *esp Br* → **zipper**

zip·per Reißverschluss *m*

zo·di·ac ASTR Tierkreis *m*; **signs of the ~** Tierkreiszeichen *pl*

zone Zone *f*

zoo Zoo *m*, Tierpark *m*

zo·o·log·i·cal zoologisch; **~ gar·dens** Tierpark *m*, zoologischer Garten

zo·ol·o·gist Zoologe *m*, Zoologin *f*

zo·ol·o·gy Zoologie *f*

zoom 1. surren; F sausen; F *fig* in die Höhe schnellen; PHOT zoomen; **~ by, ~ past** F vorbeisausen; **~ in on** PHOT et. heranholen; **2.** Surren *n*; *a.* **~ lens** PHOT Zoom *n*, Zoomobjektiv *n*

APPENDIX

States of the
Federal Republic of Germany

Baden-Württemberg ['ba:dən'vʏrtəm-
berk] Baden-Württemberg
Bayern ['baɪɐn] Bavaria
Berlin [bɛr'li:n] Berlin
Brandenburg ['brandənbʊrk] Branden-
burg
Bremen ['bre:mən] Bremen
Hamburg ['hambʊrk] Hamburg
Hessen ['hɛsən] Hesse
Mecklenburg-Vorpommern ['me:klən-
bʊrk'fo:ʁpɔmɐn] Mecklenburg-West-
ern Pomerania
Niedersachsen ['ni:dɐzaksən] Lower
Saxony
Nordrhein-Westfalen ['nɔrtraɪnvɛst-
'fa:lən] North Rhine-Westphalia
Rheinland-Pfalz ['raɪnlant'pfalts]
Rhineland-Palatinate
Saarland ['za:ɐlant]: *das* ~ the Saar-
land
Sachsen ['zaksən] Saxony
Sachsen-Anhalt ['zaksən'anhalt] Sax-
ony-Anhalt
Schleswig-Holstein ['ʃle:svɪç'hɔlʃtaɪn]
Schleswig-Holstein
Thüringen ['ty:rɪŋən] Thuringia

States of the Republic of Austria

Burgenland ['bʊrgənlant]: *das* ~ the
Burgenland
Kärnten ['kɛrntən] Carinthia
Niederösterreich ['ni:dɐʔø:stəraɪç]
Lower Austria
Oberösterreich ['o:bɐʔø:stəraɪç] Up-
per Austria
Salzburg ['zaltsbʊrk] Salzburg
Steiermark ['ʃtaɪɐmark]: *die* ~ Styria
Tirol [ti'ro:l] Tyrol
Vorarlberg ['fo:ɐʔarlbɛrk] Vorarlberg
Wien [vi:n] Vienna

Cantons of the Swiss Confederation

Aargau ['a:rgaʊ]: *der* ~ the Aargau
Appenzell [apən'tsɛl] Appenzell
Basel ['ba:zəl] Basel, Basle
Bern [bɛrn] Bern(e)
Freiburg ['fraɪbʊrk], *French* **Fribourg**
[fri'bu:r] Fribourg
Genf [gɛnf], *French* **Genève** [ʒə'nɛːv]
Geneva
Glarus ['gla:rʊs] Glarus
Graubünden [graʊ'bʏndən] Graubün-
den, Grisons
Jura ['ju:ra]: *der* ~ the Jura
Luzern [lu'tsɛrn] Lucerne
Neuenburg ['nɔʏənbʊrk], *French* **Neu-
châtel** [nøʃa'tɛl] Neuchâtel
St. Gallen [zaŋkt 'galən] St Gallen,
St Gall
Schaffhausen [ʃaf'haʊzən] Schaffhau-
sen
Schwyz [ʃviːts] Schwyz
Solothurn ['zo:loturn] Solothurn
Tessin [tɛ'si:n]: *der* ~ the Ticino, *Italian*
Ticino [ti'tʃi:no]: *das* ~ the Ticino
Thurgau ['tu:rgaʊ]: *der* ~ the Thur-
gau
Unterwalden ['ʊntɐvaldən] Unterwal-
den
Uri ['u:ri] Uri
Waadt [va(:)t], *French* **Vaud** [vo]
Vaud
Wallis ['valɪs], *French* **Valais** [va'lɛ]: *das*
~ the Valais, Wallis
Zug [tsu:k] Zug
Zürich ['tsy:rɪç] Zurich

German and European Currency

German Money
(valid till December 31, 2001)

1 DM = 100 Pfennig

coins

1 Pf (= Pfennig)
5 Pf
10 Pf
50 Pf
1 DM (= Deutsche Mark)
2 DM
5 DM

bills (*Br* bank notes)

5 DM (= Deutsche Mark)
10 DM
20 DM
50 DM
100 DM
1000 DM

Euro
(official European currency from January 1, 2002)

coins

1 Cent
2 Cent
5 Cent
10 Cent
20 Cent
50 Cent
1 Euro
2 Euro

bills (*Br* bank notes)

5 Euro
10 Euro
20 Euro
50 Euro
100 Euro
200 Euro
500 Euro

Numerals

Cardinal Numbers

0 null *nought, zero*		**41** einundvierzig *forty-one*
1 eins *one*		**50** fünfzig *fifty*
2 zwei *two*		**51** einundfünfzig *fifty-one*
3 drei *three*		**60** sechzig *sixty*
4 vier *four*		**61** einundsechzig *sixty-one*
5 fünf *five*		**70** siebzig *seventy*
6 sechs *six*		**71** einundsiebzig *seventy-one*
7 sieben *seven*		**80** achtzig *eighty*
8 acht *eight*		**81** einundachtzig *eighty-one*
9 neun *nine*		**90** neunzig *ninety*
10 zehn *ten*		**91** einundneunzig *ninety-one*
11 elf *eleven*		**100** hundert *a* or *one hundred*
12 zwölf *twelve*		**101** hunderteins *a hundred and one*
13 dreizehn *thirteen*		**200** zweihundert *two hundred*
14 vierzehn *fourteen*		**300** dreihundert *three hundred*
15 fünfzehn *fifteen*		**572** fünfhundertzweiundsiebzig *five hundred and seventy-two*
16 sechzehn *sixteen*		**1000** tausend *a* or *one thousand*
17 siebzehn *seventeen*		**1999** neunzehnhundertneunundneunzig *nineteen hundred and ninety-nine*
18 achtzehn *eighteen*		
19 neunzehn *nineteen*		**2000** zweitausend *two thousand*
20 zwanzig *twenty*		**5044** TEL fünfzig vierundvierzig *five O* (or *zero*) *double four*
21 einundzwanzig *twenty-one*		**1 000 000** eine Million *one million*
22 zweiundzwanzig *twenty-two*		**2 000 000** zwei Millionen *two million*
30 dreißig *thirty*		
31 einunddreißig *thirty-one*		
40 vierzig *forty*		

Ordinal Numbers

1. erste *first* (*1st*)		**17.** siebzehnte *seventeenth*
2. zweite *second* (*2nd*)		**18.** achtzehnte *eighteenth*
3. dritte *third* (*3rd*)		**19.** neunzehnte *nineteenth*
4. vierte *fourth* (*4th*)		**20.** zwanzigste *twentieth*
5. fünfte *fifth* (*5th*) *etc.*		**21.** einundzwanzigste *twenty-first*
6. sechste *sixth*		**22.** zweiundzwanzigste *twenty-second*
7. siebente *seventh*		**23.** dreiundzwanzigste *twenty-third*
8. achte *eighth*		**30.** dreißigste *thirtieth*
9. neunte *ninth*		**31.** einunddreißigste *thirty-first*
10. zehnte *tenth*		**40.** vierzigste *fortieth*
11. elfte *eleventh*		**41.** einundvierzigste *forty-first*
12. zwölfte *twelfth*		**50.** fünfzigste *fiftieth*
13. dreizehnte *thirteenth*		**51.** einundfünfzigste *fifty-first*
14. vierzehnte *fourteenth*		**60.** sechzigste *sixtieth*
15. fünfzehnte *fifteenth*		**61.** einundsechzigste *sixty-first*
16. sechzehnte *sixteenth*		**70.** siebzigste *seventieth*

71. einundsiebzigste *seventy-first*	**572.** fünfhundert(und)zweiundsieb-zigste *five hundred and seventy-second*
80. achtzigste *eightieth*	
81. einundachtzigste *eighty-first*	
90. neunzigste *ninetieth*	**1000.** tausendste *(one) thousandth*
100. hundertste *(one) hundredth*	**1970.** neunzehnhundert(und)siebzigste *nineteen hundred and seventieth*
101. hundert(und)erste *(one) hundred and first*	
200. zweihundertste *two hundredth*	**500 000.** fünfhunderttausendste *five hundred thousandth*
300. dreihundertste *three hundredth*	**1 000 000.** millionste *(one) millionth*

Fractional Numbers and other Numerical Values

$^1/_2$ halb *one* or *a half*
$^1/_2$ eine halbe Meile *half a mile*
$1^1/_2$ anderthalb *or* eineinhalb *one and a half*
$2^1/_2$ zweieinhalb *two and a half*
$^1/_3$ ein Drittel *one* or *a third*
$^2/_3$ zwei Drittel *two thirds*
$^1/_4$ ein Viertel *one* or *a fourth, one* or *a quarter*
$^3/_4$ drei Viertel *three fourths, three quarters*
$1^1/_4$ ein und eine viertel Stunde *one hour and a quarter*
$^1/_5$ ein Fünftel *one* or *a fifth*
$3^4/_5$ drei vier Fünftel *three and four fifths*
0,4 null Komma vier *point four (.4)*
2,5 zwei Komma fünf *two point five (2.5)*

einfach *single*
zweifach *double, twofold*
dreifach *threefold, treble, triple*
vierfach *fourfold, quadruple*
fünffach *fivefold, quintuple*

einmal *once*
zweimal *twice*
drei-, vier-, fünfmal *three* or *four* or *five times*
zweimal so viel (so viele) *twice as much (many)*

erstens, zweitens, drittens *first(ly), secondly, thirdly; in the first* or *second* or *third place*

$2 \times 3 = 6$ zwei mal drei ist sechs, zwei multipliziert mit drei ist sechs *two threes are six, two multiplied by three is six*

$7 + 8 = 15$ sieben plus acht ist fünfzehn *seven plus eight is fifteen*

$10 - 3 = 7$ zehn minus drei ist sieben *ten minus three is seven*

$20 : 5 = 4$ zwanzig (dividiert) durch fünf ist vier *twenty divided by five is four*

German Weights and Measures

I Linear Measure

1 mm   *Millimeter* millimeter, *Br* millimetre
= $^1/_{1000}$ meter (*Br* metre)
= 0.003 feet
= 0.039 inches

1 cm   *Zentimeter* centimeter, *Br* centimetre
= $^1/_{100}$ meter (*Br* metre)
= 0.39 inches

1 dm   *Dezimeter* decimeter, *Br* decimetre
= $^1/_{10}$ meter (*Br* metre)
= 3.94 inches

1 m   *Meter* meter, *Br* metre
= 1.094 yards
= 3.28 feet
= 39.37 inches

1 km   *Kilometer* kilometer, *Br* kilometre
= 1,000 meters (*Br* metres)
= 1,093.637 yards
= 0.621 (statute) miles

1 sm   *Seemeile* nautical mile
= 1,852 meters (*Br* metres)

II Square Measure

1 mm²   *Quadratmillimeter* square millimeter (*Br* millimetre)
= 0.0015 square inches

1 cm²   *Quadratzentimeter* square centimeter (*Br* centimetre)
= 0.155 square inches

1 m²   *Quadratmeter* square meter (*Br* metre)
= 1.195 square yards
= 10.76 square feet

1 a   *Ar* are
= 100 square meters (*Br* metres)
= 119.59 square yards
= 1,076.40 square feet

1 ha   *Hektar* hectare
= 100 ares
= 10,000 square meters (*Br* metres)
= 11,959.90 square yards
= 2.47 acres

1 km²   *Quadratkilometer* square kilometer (*Br* kilometre)
= 100 hectares
= 1,000,000 square meters (*Br* metres)
= 247.11 acres
= 0.386 square miles

III Cubic Measure

1 cm³   *Kubikzentimeter* cubic centimeter (*Br* centimetre)
= 1,000 cubic millimeters (*Br* millimetres)
= 0.061 cubic inches

1 dm³   *Kubikdezimeter* cubic decimeter (*Br* decimetre)
= 1,000 cubic centimeters (*Br* centimetres)
= 61.025 cubic inches

1 m³   *Kubikmeter*
1 rm   *Raummeter*   } cubic meter (*Br* metre)
1 fm   *Festmeter*
= 1,000 cubic decimeters (*Br* decimetres)
= 1.307 cubic yards
= 35.31 cubic feet

1 RT   *Registertonne* register ton
= 2.832 m³
= 100 cubic feet

IV Measure of Capacity

1 l   *Liter* liter, *Br* litre
- = 10 deciliters (*Br* decilitres)
- = 2.11 pints (*Am*)
- = 8.45 gills (*Am*)
- = 1.06 quarts (*Am*)
- = 0.26 gallons (*Am*)
- = 1.76 pints (*Br*)
- = 7.04 gills (*Br*)
- = 0.88 quarts (*Br*)
- = 0.22 gallons (*Br*)

1 hl   *Hektoliter* hectoliter, *Br* hectolitre
- = 100 liters (*Br* litres)
- = 26.42 gallons (*Am*)
- = 2.84 bushels (*Am*)
- = 22.009 gallons (*Br*)
- = 2.75 bushels (*Br*)

V Weight

1 mg   *Milligramm* milligram(me)
- = $^1/_{1000}$ gram(me)
- = 0.015 grains

1 g   *Gramm* gram(me)
- = $^1/_{1000}$ kilogram(me)
- = 15.43 grains

1 Pfd   *Pfund* pound (German)
- = $^1/_2$ kilogram(me)
- = 500 gram(me)
- = 1.102 pounds (1b)

1 kg   *Kilogramm*, *Kilo* kilogram(me)
- = 1,000 gram(me)s
- = 2.204 pounds (1b)

1 Ztr.   *Zentner* centner
- = 100 pounds (German)
- = 50 kilogram(me)s
- = 110.23 pounds (1b)
- = 1.102 US hundredweights
- = 0.98 British hundredweights

1 t   *Tonne* ton
- = 1,000 kilogram(me)s
- = 1.102 US tons
- = 0.984 British tons

Conversion Tables for Temperatures

°C (Celsius)	°F (Fahrenheit)
100	212
95	203
90	194
85	185
80	176
75	167
70	158
65	149
60	140
55	131
50	122
45	113
40	104
35	95
30	86
25	77
20	68
15	59
10	50
5	41
0	32
−5	23
−10	14
−15	5
−17.8	0
−20	−4
−25	−13
−30	−22
−35	−31
−40	−40
−45	−49
−50	−58

Clinical Thermometer

°C (Celsius)	°F (Fahrenheit)
42.0	107.6
41.8	107.2
41.6	106.9
41.4	106.5
41.2	106.2
41.0	105.8
40.8	105.4
40.6	105.1
40.4	104.7
40.2	104.4
40.0	104.0
39.8	103.6
39.6	103.3
39.4	102.9
39.2	102.6
39.0	102.2
38.8	101.8
38.6	101.5
38.4	101.1
38.2	100.8
38.0	100.4
37.8	100.0
37.6	99.7
37.4	99.3
37.2	99.0
37.0	98.6
36.8	98.2
36.6	97.9

Rules for Conversion

$$°F = \frac{9}{5}°C + 32$$

$$°C = (°F - 32)\frac{5}{9}$$

Alphabetical List of the German Irregular Verbs

Infinitive – Past Tense – Past Participle

backen – backte – gebacken
bedingen – bedang (bedingte) – bedungen (*conditional*: bedingt)
befehlen – befahl – befohlen
beginnen – begann – begonnen
beißen – biss – gebissen
bergen – barg – geborgen
bersten – barst – geborsten
bewegen – bewog – bewogen
biegen – bog – gebogen
bieten – bot – geboten
binden – band – gebunden
bitten – bat – gebeten
blasen – blies – geblasen
bleiben – blieb – geblieben
bleichen – blich – geblichen
braten – briet – gebraten
brauchen – brauchte – gebraucht (*v/aux* brauchen)
brechen – brach – gebrochen
brennen – brannte – gebrannt
bringen – brachte – gebracht
denken – dachte – gedacht
dreschen – drosch – gedroschen
dringen – drang – gedrungen
dürfen – durfte – gedurft (*v/aux* dürfen)
empfehlen – empfahl – empfohlen
erlöschen – erlosch – erloschen
erschrecken – erschrak – erschrocken
essen – aß – gegessen
fahren – fuhr – gefahren
fallen – fiel – gefallen
fangen – fing – gefangen
fechten – focht – gefochten
finden – fand – gefunden
flechten – flocht – geflochten
fliegen – flog – geflogen
fliehen – floh – geflohen
fließen – floss – geflossen
fressen – fraß – gefressen
frieren – fror – gefroren
gären – gor (*esp fig* gärte) – gegoren (*esp fig* gegärt)
gebären – gebar – geboren
geben – gab – gegeben
gedeihen – gedieh – gediehen
gehen – ging – gegangen
gelingen – gelang – gelungen
gelten – galt – gegolten
genesen – genas – genesen
genießen – genoss – genossen
geschehen – geschah – geschehen
gewinnen – gewann – gewonnen
gießen – goss – gegossen
gleichen – glich – geglichen
gleiten – glitt – geglitten
glimmen – glomm – geglommen
graben – grub – gegraben
greifen – griff – gegriffen
haben – hatte – gehabt
halten – hielt – gehalten
hängen – hing – gehangen
hauen – haute (hieb) – gehauen
heben – hob – gehoben
heißen – hieß – geheißen
helfen – half – geholfen
kennen – kannte – gekannt
klingen – klang – geklungen
kneifen – kniff – gekniffen
kommen – kam – gekommen
können – konnte – gekonnt (*v/aux* können)
kriechen – kroch – gekrochen
laden – lud – geladen
lassen – ließ – gelassen (*v/aux* lassen)
laufen – lief – gelaufen
leiden – litt – gelitten
leihen – lieh – geliehen
lesen – las – gelesen
liegen – lag – gelegen
lügen – log – gelogen
mahlen – mahlte – gemahlen
meiden – mied – gemieden
melken – melkte (molk) – gemolken (gemelkt)
messen – maß – gemessen
misslingen – misslang – misslungen
mögen – mochte – gemocht (*v/aux* mögen)
müssen – musste – gemusst (*v/aux* müssen)
nehmen – nahm – genommen
nennen – nannte – genannt

pfeifen – pfiff – gepfiffen
preisen – pries – gepriesen
quellen – quoll – gequollen
raten – riet – geraten
reiben – rieb – gerieben
reißen – riss – gerissen
reiten – ritt – geritten
rennen – rannte – gerannt
riechen – roch – gerochen
ringen – rang – gerungen
rinnen – rann – geronnen
rufen – rief – gerufen
salzen – salzte – gesalzen (gesalzt)
saufen – soff – gesoffen
saugen – sog – gesogen
schaffen – schuf – geschaffen
schallen – schallte (scholl) – geschallt
(*for* **erschallen** *a.* erschollen)
scheiden – schied – geschieden
scheinen – schien – geschienen
scheißen – schiss – geschissen
scheren – schor – geschoren
schieben – schob – geschoben
schießen – schoss – geschossen
schinden – schund – geschunden
schlafen – schlief – geschlafen
schlagen – schlug – geschlagen
schleichen – schlich – geschlichen
schleifen – schliff – geschliffen
schließen – schloss – geschlossen
schlingen – schlang – geschlungen
schmeißen – schmiss – geschmissen
schmelzen – schmolz – geschmolzen
schneiden – schnitt – geschnitten
schrecken – schrak – *rare* geschrocken
schreiben – schrieb – geschrieben
schreien – schrie – geschrie(e)n
schreiten – schritt – geschritten
schweigen – schwieg – geschwiegen
schwellen – schwoll – geschwollen
schwimmen – schwamm – geschwommen
schwinden – schwand – geschwunden
schwingen – schwang – geschwungen
schwören – schwor – geschworen
sehen – sah – gesehen
sein – war – gewesen
senden – sandte – gesandt
sieden – sott – gesotten
singen – sang – gesungen
sinken – sank – gesunken

sinnen – sann – gesonnen
sitzen – saß – gesessen
sollen – sollte – gesollt (*v/aux* sollen)
spalten – spaltete – gespalten (gespaltet)
speien – spie – gespie(e)n
spinnen – spann – gesponnen
sprechen – sprach – gesprochen
sprießen – spross – gesprossen
springen – sprang – gesprungen
stechen – stach – gestochen
stecken – steckte (stak) – gesteckt
stehen – stand – gestanden
stehlen – stahl – gestohlen
steigen – stieg – gestiegen
sterben – starb – gestorben
stinken – stank – gestunken
stoßen – stieß – gestoßen
streichen – strich – gestrichen
streiten – stritt – gestritten
tragen – trug – getragen
treffen – traf – getroffen
treiben – trieb – getrieben
treten – trat – getreten
trinken – trank – getrunken
trügen – trog – getrogen
tun – tat – getan
verderben – verdarb – verdorben
verdrießen – verdross – verdrossen
vergessen – vergaß – vergessen
verlieren – verlor – verloren
verschleißen – verschliss – verschlissen
verzeihen – verzieh – verziehen
wachsen – wuchs – gewachsen
wägen – wog (*rare* wägte) – gewogen (*rare* gewägt)
waschen – wusch – gewaschen
weben – wob – gewoben
weichen – wich – gewichen
weisen – wies – gewiesen
wenden – wandte – gewandt
werben – warb – geworben
werden – wurde – geworden (worden*)
werfen – warf – geworfen
wiegen – wog – gewogen
winden – wand – gewunden
wissen – wusste – gewusst
wollen – wollte – gewollt (*v/aux* wollen)
wringen – wrang – gewrungen
ziehen – zog – gezogen
zwingen – zwang – gezwungen

* only in connection with the past participles of other verbs, *e.g.* **er ist gesehen worden** he has been seen.

Alphabetical List of the English Irregular Verbs

Infinitive – Past Tense – Past Participle

arise – arose – arisen
awake – awoke – awoke*
be – was – been
bear – bore – *getragen*: borne – *geboren*: born
beat – beat – beaten, beat
become – became – become
beget – begot – begotten
begin – began – begun
bend – bent – bent
bereave – bereft* – bereft*
beseech – besought – besought
bet – bet * – bet*
bid – bade, bid – bidden, bid
bide – bode* – bided
bind – bound – bound
bite – bit – bitten
bleed – bled – bled
bless – blest* – blest*
blow – blew – blown
break – broke – broken
breed – bred – bred
bring – brought – brought
build – built – built
burn – burnt* – burnt*
burst – burst – burst
buy – bought – bought
cast – cast – cast
catch – caught – caught
choose – chose – chosen
cleave – cleft, clove* – cleft, cloven*
cling – clung – clung
clothe – clad* – clad*
come – came – come
cost – cost – cost
creep – crept – crept
crow – crew* – crowed
cut – cut – cut
deal – dealt – dealt
dig – dug – dug
dive – dived, *a.* dove – dived
do – did – done
draw – drew – drawn
dream – dreamt* – dreamt*
drink – drank – drunk
drive – drove – driven
dwell – dwelt* – dwelt*

eat – ate – eaten
fall – fell – fallen
feed – fed – fed
feel – felt – felt
fight – fought – fought
find – found – found
fit – fitted, *a.* fit – fitted, *a.* fit
flee – fled – fled
fling – flung – flung
fly – flew – flown
forbid – forbade – forbidden
forget – forgot – forgotten
forsake – forsook – forsaken
freeze – froze – frozen
get – got – got, *a.* gotten
give – gave – given
go – went – gone
grind – ground – ground
grow – grew – grown
hang – hung – hung
have – had – had
hear – heard – heard
heave – hove* – hove*
hew – hewed – hewn*
hide – hid – hidden
hit – hit – hit
hold – held – held
hurt – hurt – hurt
keep – kept – kept
kneel – knelt* – knelt*
knit – knit* – knit*
know – knew – known
lay – laid – laid
lead – led – led
lean – leant* – leant*
leap – leapt* – leapt*
learn – learnt* – learnt*
leave – left – left
lend – lent – lent
let – let – let
lie – lay – lain
light – lit* – lit*
lose – lost – lost
make – made – made
mean – meant – meant
meet – met – met
mow – mowed – mown*

pay – paid – paid
plead – pleaded, *a.* pled – pleaded, *a.* pled
put – put – put
read – read – read
rid – rid – rid
ride – rode – ridden
ring – rang – rung
rise – rose – risen
run – ran – run
saw – sawed – sawn*
say – said – said
see – saw – seen
seek – sought – sought
sell – sold – sold
send – sent – sent
set – set – set
sew – sewed – sewn*
shake – shook – shaken
shave – shaved – shaven*
shear – sheared – shorn*
shed – shed – shed
shine – shone – shone
shit – shit – shit
shoe – shod – shod
shoot – shot – shot
show – showed – shown*
shrink – shrank – shrunk
shut – shut – shut
sing – sang – sung
sink – sank – sunk
sit – sat – sat
slay – slew – slain
sleep – slept – slept
slide – slid – slid
sling – slung – slung
slink – slunk – slunk
slit – slit – slit
smell – smelt* – smelt*
sow – sowed – sown*
speak – spoke – spoken
speed – sped* – sped*
spell – spelt* – spelt*
spend – spent – spent

spill – spilt* – spilt*
spin – spun – spun
spit – spat – spat
split – split – split
spoil – spoilt* – spoilt*
spread – spread – spread
spring – sprang, *a.* sprung – sprung
stand – stood – stood
stave – stove* – stove*
steal – stole – stolen
stick – stuck – stuck
sting – stung – stung
stink – stank, stunk – stunk
strew – strewed – strewn*
stride – strode – stridden
strike – struck – struck
string – strung – strung
strive – strove – striven
swear – swore – sworn
sweat – sweat* – sweat*
sweep – swept – swept
swell – swelled – swollen
swim – swam – swum
swing – swung – swung
take – took – taken
teach – taught – taught
tear – tore – torn
tell – told – told
think – thought – thought
thrive – throve* – thriven*
throw – threw – thrown
thrust – thrust – thrust
tread – trod – trodden, trod
wake – woke* – woke(n)*
wear – wore – worn
weave – wove – woven
wed – wedded, wed – wedded, wed
weep – wept – wept
wet – wet* – wet*
win – won – won
wind – wound – wound
wring – wrung – wrung
write – wrote – written

Irregular forms marked with asterisks (*)
can be exchanged for the regular forms.

Examples of German Declension and Conjugation

A. Declension

Order of cases: *nom*, *gen*, *dat*, *acc*, *sg* and *pl*. – Compound nouns and adjectives (e.g. *Eisbär*, *Ausgang*, *abfällig* etc.) inflect like their last elements (*Bär*, *Gang*, *fällig*). *dem* = demonstrative, *imp* = imperative, *ind* = indicative, *perf* = perfect, *pres* = present, *pres p* = present participle, *rel* = relative, *su* = substantive.

I. Nouns

1 Bild   ~(e)s[1]   ~(e)   ~
Bilder[2]   ~   ~n   ~

[1] *es only*: Geist, Geistes.
[2] **a, o, u > ä, ö, ü**: Rand, Ränder; Haupt, Häupter; Dorf, Dörfer; Wurm, Würmer.

2 Reis*   ~es ['-zəs] ~(e)   ~
Reiser[1] ['-zɐ]   ~n   ~

[1] **a, o > ä, ö**: Glas, Gläser ['glɛːzɐ]; Haus, Häuser ['hɔYzɐ]; Fass, Fässer; Schloss, Schlösser.

* Fass, Fasse(s).

3 Arm   ~(e)s[1,2]   ~(e)[1]   ~
Arme[3]   ~   ~n   ~

[1] *without* e: Billard, Billard(s).
[2] *es only*: Maß, Maßes.
[3] **a, o, u > ä, ö, ü**: Gang, Gänge; Saal, Säle; Gebrauch, Gebräuche [gə'brɔYçə]; Sohn, Söhne; Hut, Hüte.

4 Greis[1]*   ~es ['-zəs] ~(e)   ~
Greise[2] ['-zə] ~   ~n   ~

[1] **s > ss**: Kürbis, Kürbisse(s).
[2] **a, o, u > ä, ö, ü**: Hals, Hälse; Bass, Bässe; Schoß, Schöße; Fuchs, Füchse; Schuss, Schüsse.

* Ross, Rosse(s).

5 Strahl   ~(e)s[1,2]   ~(e)[2]   ~
Strahlen[3] ~   ~   ~

[1] *es only*: Schmerz, Schmerzes.
[2] *without* e: Juwel, Juwel(s).
[3] Sporn, Sporen.

6 Lappen   ~s   ~   ~*
Lappen[1]   ~   ~   ~

[1] **a, o > ä, ö**: Graben, Gräben; Boden, Böden.

* *Infinitives used as nouns have no pl*: Geschehen, Befinden etc.

7 Maler   ~s   ~   ~
Maler[1]   ~   ~n   ~

[1] **a, o, u > ä, ö, ü**: Vater, Väter; Kloster, Klöster; Bruder, Brüder.

8 Untertan   ~s   ~   ~
Untertanen[1,2] ~   ~   ~

[1] *with change of accent*: Pro'fessor, Profes'soren [-'soːrən]; 'Dämon ['dɛːmɔn], Dä'monen [dɛ'moːnən].
[2] *pl* ien [-jən]: Kolleg, Kollegien [-'leːgjən]; Mineral, Mineralien.

9 Studium   ~s   ~   ~
Studien[1,2] ['-djən] ~   ~   ~

[1] **a** *and* **o(n) > en**: Drama, Dramen; Stadion, Stadien.
[2] **on** *and* **um > a**: Lexikon, Lexika; Neutrum, Neutra.

10 Auge ~s ~ ~
    Augen ~ ~ ~

11 Genie ~s[1]* ~ ~
    Genies[2]* ~ ~ ~
  [1] *without inflection:* Bouillon etc.
  [2] *pl* **s** *or* **ta:** Komma, Kommas *or* Kommata; *but:* 'Klima, Klimate [kli'maːtə] (3).
  * **s** *is pronounced:* [ʒe'niːs].

12 Bär* ~en[1] ~en[1] ~en[1]
    Bären ~ ~ ~
  [1] Herr, *sg mst* Herrn; Herz, *gen* Herzens, *acc* Herz.
  * ...'**log** *as well as* ... '**loge** (13), e.g. Biolog(e).

13 Knabe ~n[1] ~n ~n
    Knaben ~ ~ ~
  [1] **ns:** Name, Namens.

14 Trübsal ~ ~ ~
    Trübsale[1,2,3] ~ ~n ~
  [1] **a, o, u** > **ä, ö, ü:** Hand, Hände;

Braut, Bräute; Not, Nöte; Luft, Lüfte; Nuss, Nüsse; *without* **e:** Tochter, Töchter; Mutter, Mütter.
  [2] **s** > **ss:** Kenntnis, Kenntnisse; Nimbus, Nimbusse.
  [3] **is** *or* **us** > **e:** Kultus, Kulte; *with change of accent:* Di'akonus, Dia'kone [-'koːnə].

15 Blume ~ ~ ~
    Blumen ~ ~ ~
  ...**ee:** eː, *pl* eːən, e.g. I'dee, I'deen.
  ...**ie** { *stressed syllable:* iː, *pl* iːən, e.g. Batte'rie(n). *unstressed syllable:* jə, *pl* jən, e.g. Ar'terie(n).

16 Frau ~ ~ ~
    Frauen[1,2,3] ~ ~ ~
  [1] **in** > **innen:** Freundin, Freundinnen.
  [2] **a, is, os** *and* **us** > **en:** Firma, Firmen; Krisis, Krisen; Epos, Epen; Genius, Genien; *with change of accent:* 'Heros, He'roen [he'roːən]; Di'akonus, Dia'konen [-'koːnən].
  [3] **s** > **ss:** Kirmes, Kirmessen.

II. Proper nouns

17 *In general proper nouns have no pl.*

The following form the gen sg with **s:**

1. *Proper nouns without a definite article:* Friedrichs, Paulas, (Friedrich von) Schillers, Deutschlands, Berlins;

2. *Proper nouns, masculine and neuter* (*except the names of countries*) *with a definite article and an adjective:* des braven Friedrichs Bruder, des jungen Deutschlands (Söhne).

  After **s, sch, ß, tz, x,** *and* **z** *the gen sg ends in* -**ens** *or* ' (*instead of* ' *it is*

more advisable to use the definite article or von), e.g. die Werke des [*or* von] Sokrates, Voß *or* Sokrates', Voß' [*not* Sokratessens, *seldom* Vossens] Werke; *but:* die Umgebung von Mainz.
  Feminine names ending in a consonant or the vowel e *form the gen sg with* (en)s *or* (n)s; *in the dat and acc sg such names may end in* (e)n (*pl* = a).

  If a proper noun is followed by a title, only the following forms are inflected:

1. *the title when used* with *a definite article:*
    der Kaiser Karl   (der Große)
    des ~s ~   (des ~n)
    etc.

2. *the (last) name when used* with- | Kaiser Karl   (der Große)
out *an article:* | ~   ~**s** (des   ~**n**) etc.
| (*but:* Herrn Lehmanns Brief).

III. Adjectives and participles
(also used as nouns*), pronouns, etc.

18

	m	f	n	pl	
a) gut	er[1,2]	~e	~es	~e°	*without article, after prepositions,*
	en**	~er	~en**	~er	*personal pronouns, and invariables*
	em	~er	~em	~en	
	en	~e	~es	~e	

	m	f	n	pl	
b) gut	e[1,2]	~e	~e	~en	*with definite article* (22) *or with pro-*
	en	~en	~en	~en	*noun* (21)
	en	~en	~en	~en	
	en	~e	~e	~en	

	m	f	n	pl	
c) gut	er[1,2]	~e	~es	~en	*with indefinite article or with pronoun*
	en	~en	~en	~en	(20)
	en	~en	~en	~en	
	en	~e	~es	~en	

[1] krass, krasse(r, ~s, ~st etc.).

[2] **a, o, u > ä, ö, ü** *when forming the* comp *and* sup: alt, älter(e, ~es etc.), ältest (der ~e, am ~en); grob, gröber(e, ~es etc.), gröbst (der ~e, am ~en); kurz, kürzer(e, ~es etc.), kürzest (der ~e, am ~en).

* e.g. Böse(r) su: der (die, eine) Böse, ein Böser; Böse(s) n: das Böse, **without**

article Böses; *in the same way* Abgesandte(r) su, Angestellte(r) su etc.; *in some cases the use varies.*

** *Sometimes the* gen sg *ends in* ~es *instead of* ~**en:** gutes (*or* guten) Mutes sein.

° *In* böse, böse(r, ~s, ~st etc.) one e *is dropped.*

The Grades of Comparison

The endings of the comparative *and* superlative *are:*

	reich	schön	*inflected according to* (18[2]).
comp	reicher	schöner	
sup	reichst	schönst	

After vowels (except e [18°]) *and after* d, s, sch, ß, st, t, tz, x, y, z *the* sup *ends in* ~**est,** *but in unstressed syllables after* d, sch *and* t *generally in* ~**st:** blau, 'blau**est**; rund, 'rund**est**; rasch, 'rasch**est** etc.; *but:* 'dringend, 'dringend**st**; 'närrisch, 'närrisch**st**; ge'eignet, ge'eignet**st**.

Note. – The adjectives ending in ~**el,** ~**en** *(except* ~**nen**) *and* ~**er** *(e.g.* dunkel, eben, heiter), *and also the possessive adjectives* unser *and* euer *generally drop* e.

Inflection:	~e	~em*	~en	~er	~es, and
~el >	~le	~lem*	~len*	~ler	~les
~en >	~(e)ne	~(e)nem	~(e)nen	~(e)ner°	~(e)nes
~er >	~(e)re	~rem*	~ren*	~(e)rer°	~(e)res

* or ~elm, ~eln, ~erm, ~ern; e.g. dunk|el: ~le, ~lem (or ~elm), ~len (or ~eln), ~ler, ~les; eb|en: ~(e)ne, ~(e)nem etc.; heit|er: ~(e)re, ~rem (or ~erm) etc.

° The inflected comp ends in ~ner and ~rer only: eben, ebnere(r, ~s etc.); heiter, heitrere(r, ~s etc.); but sup ebenst, heiterst.

19

		1st pers.	2nd pers.	3rd pers.		
		m, f, n	m, f, n	m	f	n
sg	⎧	ich	du	er	sie	es
	⎪	meiner*	deiner*	seiner*	ihrer	seiner*
	⎨	mir	dir	ihm	ihr	ihm°
	⎩	mich	dich	ihn	sie	es°
pl	⎧	wir	ihr	sie	(Sie)	
	⎪	unser	euer	ihrer	(Ihrer)	
	⎨	uns	euch	ihnen	(Ihnen)°	
	⎩	uns	euch	sie	(Sie)°	

* In poetry sometimes without inflection: gedenke mein!; also es instead of seiner n (= e-r Sache): ich bin es überdrüssig.
° Reflexive form: sich.

20

	m		f	n	pl
mein			~e	~	~e*
dein	⎰	es	~er	~es	~er
sein	⎱	em	~er	~em	~en
(k)ein	⎰	en	~e	~	~e

* The indefinite article ein has no pl. – In poetry mein, dein and sein may stand behind the su without inflection: die Mutter (Kinder) mein, or as predicate: der Hut [die Tasche, das Buch] ist mein; without su: meiner m, meine f, mein(e)s n, meine pl etc.: wem gehört der Hut [die Tasche, das Buch]? es ist meiner (meine, mein[e]s); or with definite article: der (die, das) meine, pl die meinen (18b). Regarding unser and euer see note (18).

¹ welche(r, s) as rel pron: gen sg dessen, deren, gen pl deren, dat pl denen (23).

* Used as su, dies is preferable to dieses.

** manch, solch, welch frequently are uninflected:

manch ⎫	guter (ein guter) Mann	
solch ⎬	~en (~es ~en)	~es
welch ⎭	~em (~em ~en)	~e
	etc. (18)	

Similarly all:

all der (dieser, mein) Schmerz		
~ des (~es, ~es)	~es	

21

	m		f	n	pl
dies	⎧	er	~e	~es*	~e**
jen	⎪	es	~er	~es	~er
manch	⎨	em	~er	~em	~en¹
welch	⎩	en	~e	~es*	~e

22

	m	f	n	pl	
der	die	das	die¹	⎫	
des	der	des	der	⎬	definite article
dem	der	dem	den	⎪	
den	die	das	die	⎭	

¹ derjenige, derselbe – desjenigen, demjenigen, desselben, demselben etc. (18b).

¹ **also** derer, **when used as** *dem pron*

* **also** des.

---

23 *Relative pronoun*

m	f	n	pl
der	die	das	die
dessen*	deren	dessen*	deren¹
dem	der	dem	denen
den	die	das	die

24

wer	was	jemand, niemand
wessen*	wessen	~(e)s
wem	–	~(em°)
wen	was	~(en°)

* **also** wes.

° **preferably without inflection.**

B. Conjugation

In the conjugation tables (25–30) only the simple verbs may be found; in the alphabetical list of the German irregular verbs compound verbs are only included when no simple verb exists (e.g. **beginnen;** *ginnen* does not exist). In order to find the conjugation of any compound verb (with separable or inseparable prefix, regular or irregular) look up the respective simple verb.

Verbs with separable and stressed prefixes such as **'ab-, 'an-, 'auf-, 'aus-, 'bei-, be'vor-, 'dar-, 'ein-, em'por-, ent'gegen-, 'fort-, 'her-, he'rab-** etc. and also *'klar-*[legen], *'los-*[schießen], *'sitzen* [bleiben], *über'hand* [nehmen] etc. (but not the verbs derived from compound nouns as *be'antragen* or *be'ratschlagen* from *Antrag* and *Ratschlag* etc.) take the preposition **zu** (in the *inf* and the *pres p*) and the syllable **ge** (in the *pp* and in the passive voice) between the stressed prefix and their root.

Verbs with inseparable and unstressed prefixes such as **be-, emp-, ent-, er-, ge-, ver-, zer-** and generally **miss-** (in spite of its being stressed) take the preposition **zu** before the prefix and drop the syllable **ge** in the *pp* and in the passive voice. The prefixes **durch-, hinter-, über-, um-, unter-, voll-,**

wi(e)der- are separable when stressed and inseparable when unstressed, e.g.

geben: *zu geben, zu gebend; gegeben; ich gebe, du gibst* etc.;

'abgeben: *'abzugeben, 'abzugebend; 'abgegeben; ich gebe (du gibst etc.) ab;*

ver'geben: *zu ver'geben, zu ver'gebend; ver'geben; ich ver'gebe, du ver'gibst* etc.;

'umgehen: *'umzugehen, 'umzugehend; 'umgegangen; ich gehe (du gehst etc.) um;*

um'gehen: *zu um'gehen, zu um'gehend; um'gangen; ich um'gehe, du um'gehst* etc.

The same rules apply to verbs with two prefixes, e.g.

zu'rückbehalten [see *halten*]: *zu'rückzubehalten, zu'rückzubehaltend; zu'rückbehalten; ich behalte (du behältst etc.) zurück;*

wieder 'aufheben [see *heben*]: *wieder 'aufzuheben, wieder 'aufzuhebend; wieder 'aufgehoben; ich hebe (du hebst etc.) wieder auf.*

The forms in parentheses ( ) follow the same rules.

a) 'Weak' Conjugation

25   loben

| *pres ind* | { lobe | lobst | lobt |
| | loben | lobt | loben |

| *pres subj* | { lobe | lobest | lobe |
| | loben | lobet | loben |

| *pret ind* | { lobte | lobtest | lobte |
| and *subj* | lobten | lobtet | lobten |

imp sg lob(e), *pl* lob(e)t, loben Sie;
inf pres loben; *inf perf* gelobt haben;
pres p lobend; *pp* gelobt (18; 29**).

26   reden

| *pres ind* | { rede | redest | redet |
| | reden | redet | reden |

| *pres subj* | { rede | redest | rede |
| | reden | redet | reden |

| *pret ind* | { redete | redetest | redete |
| and *subj* | redeten | redetet | redeten |

imp sg rede, *pl* redet, reden Sie;
inf pres reden; *inf perf* geredet haben;
pres p redend; *pp* geredet (18; 29**).

27   reisen

| *pres ind* | { reise | rei(se)st* | reist |
| | reisen | reist | reisen |

| *pres subj* | { reise | reisest | reise |
| | reisen | reiset | reisen |

| *pret ind* | { reiste | reistest | reisten |
| and *subj* | reisten | reistet | reisten |

imp sg reise, *pl* reist, reisen Sie;
inf pres reisen; *inf perf* gereist sein *or now
rare* haben; *pres p* reisend; *pp* gereist
(18; 29**).

  * **sch:** naschen, nasch(e)st; **ß:** spaßen, spaßt (spaßest); **tz:** ritzen, ritzt (rit-
zest); **x:** hexen, hext (hexest); **z:** reizen,
reizt (reizest); faulenzen, faulenzt (fau-
lenzest).

28   fassen

| *pres ind* | { fasse | fasst (fassest)fasst |
| | fassen | fasst | fassen |

| *pres subj* | { fasse | fassest | fasse |
| | fassen | fasst | fassen |

| *pret ind* | { fasste | fasstest | fasste |
| and *subj* | fassten | fasstet | fassten |

imp sg fasse (fass), *pl* fasst, fassen Sie;
inf pres fassen; *inf perf* gefasst haben;
pres p fassend; *pp* gefasst (18; 29**).

29   handeln

pres ind

| handle* | handelst | handelt |
| handeln | handelt | handeln |

pres subj

| handle* | handelst | handle* |
| handeln | handelt | handeln |

pret ind and *subj*

| handelte | handeltest | handelte |
| handelten | handeltet | handelten |

imp sg handle, *pl* handelt, handeln Sie;
inf pres handeln; *inf perf* gehandelt haben; *pres p* handelnd; *pp* gehandelt (18).

  * **Also** handele; wandern, wand(e)re;
bessern, bessere (bessre); donnern, don-
nere.

  ** **Without ge, when the first syllable
is unstressed,** e.g. be'grüßen, be'grüßt;
ent'stehen, ent'standen; stu'dieren,
studiert (**not** gestudiert); trom'peten,
trom'petet (**also when preceded by a
stressed prefix:** 'austrompeten, 'aus-
trompetet, **not** 'ausgetrompetet). **In
some weak verbs the pp ends in en instead of t,** e.g. mahlen, gemahlen. **With
the verbs** brauchen, dürfen, heißen, helfen, hören, können, lassen, lehren, lernen, machen, mögen, müssen, sehen, sollen, wollen **the pp is replaced by inf
(without ge), when used in connection
with another inf,** e.g. ich habe ihn singen
hören, du hättest es tun können, er hat gehen müssen, ich hätte ihn laufen lassen
sollen.

b) 'Strong' Conjugation

30   **fahren**

pres ind	{	fahre	fährst	fährt	*pres subj*	{	führe	führest	führe
		fahren	fahrt	fahren			führen	führet	führen

pres subj	{	fahre	fahrest	fahre
		fahren	fahret	fahren

imp sg fahr(e), *pl* fahr(e)t, fahren Sie;
inf pres fahren; *inf perf* gefahren haben **or** sein;

pret ind	{	fuhr	fuhr(e)st	fuhr
		fuhren	fuhrt	fuhren

pres p fahrend; *pp* gefahren (18; 29**).

Proper Names

Aachen ['a:xən] Aachen, Aix-la-Chapelle
Adler ['a:dlɐ] *Austrian psychologist*
Adria ['a:dria]: *die* ~ the Adriatic (Sea)
Afrika ['a:frika] Africa
Ägäis[ɛ'gɛ:ɪs]: *die* ~ the Aegean (Sea)
Ägypten [ɛ'gʏptən] Egypt
Albanien [al'ba:njən] Albania
Algerien [al'ge:rjən] Algeria
Algier ['alʒi:ɐ] Algiers
Allgäu ['algɔʏ]: *das* ~ the Al(l)gäu (*region of Bavaria, Germany*)
Alpen ['alpən]: *die* ~ *pl* the Alps
Amerika [a'me:rika] America
Anden ['andən]: *die* ~ *pl* the Andes
Antillen [an'tɪlən]: *die* ~ *pl* the Antilles
Antwerpen [ant'vɛrpən] Antwerp
Apenninen [ape'ni:nən]: *die* ~ *pl* the Apennines
Argentinien [argɛn'ti:njən] Argentina, the Argentine
Ärmelkanal ['ɛrməlkana:l]: *der* ~ the English Channel, the Channel
Asien ['a:zjən] Asia
Athen [a'te:n] Athens
Äthiopien [ɛ'tjo:pjən] Ethiopia
Atlantik [at'lantɪk]: *der* ~ the Atlantic (Ocean)
Australien [aʊs'tra:ljən] Australia

Bach [bax] *German composer*
Barlach ['barlax] *German sculptor*
Basel ['ba:zəl] Basel, Basle
Bayern ['baɪɐn] Bavaria
Beethoven ['be:tho:fən] *German composer*
Belgien ['bɛlgjən] Belgium
Belgrad ['bɛlgra:t] Belgrade
Berlin [bɛr'li:n] *German city*
Bern [bɛrn] Bern(e)
Bloch [blɔx] *German philosopher*
Böcklin ['bœkli:n] *German painter*
Bodensee ['bo:dənze:]: *der* ~ Lake Constance
Böhm [bø:m] *Austrian conductor*
Böhmen ['bø:mən] HIST Bohemia
Böll [bœl] *German author*

Bonn [bɔn] *German city*
Brahms [bra:ms] *German composer*
Brasilien [bra'zi:ljən] Brazil
Braunschweig ['braʊnʃvaɪk] Braunschweig, Brunswick
Brecht [brɛçt] *German dramatist*
Bremen ['bre:mən] *German city*
Bruckner ['brʊknɐ] *Austrian composer*
Brüssel ['brʏsəl] Brussels
Budapest ['bu:dapɛst] *Hungarian city*
Bukarest ['bu:karɛst] Bucharest
Bulgarien [bʊl'ga:rjən] Bulgaria

Calais [ka'lɛ:]: *die Straße von* ~ the Straits of Dover
Calvin [kal'vi:n] *Swiss religious reformer*
Chile ['tʃi:le] Chile
China ['çi:na] China

Daimler ['daɪmlɐ] *German inventor*
Dänemark ['dɛ:nəmark] Denmark
Deutschland ['dɔʏtʃlant] Germany
Diesel ['di:zəl] *German inventor*
Döblin ['dø:bli:n] *German author*
Dolomiten [dolo'mi:tən]: *die* ~ *pl* the Dolomites
Donau ['do:naʊ]: *die* ~ the Danube
Dortmund ['dɔrtmʊnt] *German city*
Dresden ['dre:sdən] *German city*
Dünkirchen ['dʏ:nkɪrçən] Dunkirk
Dürer ['dy:rɐ] *German painter*
Dürrenmatt ['dʏrənmat] *Swiss dramatist*
Düsseldorf ['dʏsəldɔrf] *German city*

Egk [ɛk] *German composer*
Eichendorff ['aɪçəndɔrf] *German poet*
Eiger ['aɪgɐ] *Swiss mountain*
Einstein ['aɪnʃtaɪn] *German physicist*
Elbe ['ɛlbə]: *die* ~ (*German river*)
Elsass ['ɛlzas]: *das* ~Alsace
England ['ɛŋlant] England
Essen ['ɛsən] *German city*
Europa [ɔʏ'ro:pa] Europe

Finnland ['fɪnlant] Finland
Florenz [flo'rɛnts] Florence

668

Fontane [fɔn'taːnə] *German author*
Franken ['fraŋkən] Franconia
Frankfurt am Main ['fraŋkfʊrt am 'maɪn] Frankfurt on the Main
Frankfurt an der Oder ['fraŋkfʊrt an deːɐ 'oːdɐ] Frankfurt on the Oder
Frankreich ['fraŋkraɪç] France
Freud [frɔyt] *Austrian psychologist*
Frisch [frɪʃ] *Swiss author*

Garmisch ['garmɪʃ] *health resort in Bavaria, Germany*
Genf [gɛnf] Geneva; **~er See** Lake Geneva
Genua ['geːnua] Genoa
Goethe ['gøːtə] *German poet*
Grass [gras] *German author*
Griechenland ['griːçənlant] Greece
Grillparzer ['grɪlpartsɐ] *Austrian dramatist*
Grönland ['grøːnlant] Greenland
Gropius ['groːpjʊs] *German architect*
Großbritannien [groːsbri'tanjən] (Great) Britain
Großglockner ['groːsglɔknɐ]: **der ~** (*Austrian mountain*)
Grünewald ['gryːnəvalt] *German painter*

Haag [haːk]: **Den ~** The Hague
Hahn [haːn] *German chemist*
Hamburg ['hambʊrk] *German city*
Händel ['hɛndəl] Handel (*German composer*)
Hannover [ha'noːfɐ] Hanover
Harz [haːrts]: **der ~** the Harz (Mountains)
Hauptmann ['haʊptman] *German dramatist*
Haydn ['haɪdən] *Austrian composer*
Hegel ['heːgəl] *German philosopher*
Heidegger ['haɪdɛgɐ] *German philosopher*
Heidelberg ['haɪdəlbɛrk] *German city*
Heine ['haɪnə] *German poet*
Heisenberg ['haɪzənbɛrk] *German physicist*
Heißenbüttel ['haɪsənbʏtəl] *German poet*
Helgoland ['hɛlgolant] Hel(i)goland
Helsinki ['hɛlzɪŋki] *Finnish city*
Hesse ['hɛsə] *German poet*
Hindemith ['hɪndəmɪt] *German composer*

Hölderlin ['hœldɛliːn] *German poet*
Holland ['hɔlant] Holland

Indien ['ɪndjən] India
Inn [ɪn]: **der ~** (*affluent of the Danube*)
Innsbruck ['ɪnsbrʊk] *Austrian city*
Irak [i'raːk]: **der ~** Iraq
Iran [i'raːn]: **der ~** Iran
Irland ['ɪrlant] Ireland
Island ['iːslant] Iceland
Israel ['ɪsraɛl] Israel
Italien [i'taːljən] Italy

Japan ['jaːpan] Japan
Jaspers ['jaspɛs] *German philosopher*
Jordanien [jɔr'daːnjən] Jordan
Jugoslawien [jugo'slaːvjən] Yugoslavia
Jung [jʊŋ] *Swiss psychologist*
Jungfrau ['jʊŋfraʊ]: **die ~** (*Swiss mountain*)

Kafka ['kafka] *Czech author*
Kanada ['kanada] Canada
Kant [kant] *German philosopher*
Karlsruhe ['karlsruːə] *German city*
Kärnten ['kɛrntən] Carinthia
Kästner ['kɛstnɐ] *German author*
Kiel [kiːl] *German city*
Klee [kleː] *Swiss-born painter*
Kleist [klaɪst] *German poet*
Koblenz ['koːblɛnts] Koblenz, Coblenz
Kokoschka [ko'kɔʃka] *Austrian painter*
Köln [kœln] Cologne
Kolumbien [ko'lʊmbjən] Colombia
Kolumbus [ko'lʊmbʊs] Columbus
Konstanz ['kɔnstants] Constance
Kopenhagen [koːpən'haːgən] Copenhagen
Kordilleren [kɔrdɪl'jeːrən]: **die ~** *pl* the Cordilleras
Kreml ['kreːməl]: **der ~** the Kremlin

Leibniz ['laɪbnɪts] *German philosopher*
Leipzig ['laɪptsɪç] Leipzig, Leipsic
Lessing ['lɛsɪŋ] *German poet*
Libanon ['liːbanɔn]: **der ~** (the) Lebanon
Liebig ['liːbɪç] *German chemist*
Lissabon ['lɪsabɔn] Lisbon
London ['lɔndən] London
Lothringen ['loːtrɪŋən] Lorraine
Lübeck ['lyːbɛk] *German city*
Luther ['lʊtɐ] *German religious reformer*

Luxemburg ['lʊksəmbʊrk] Luxem-b(o)urg
Luzern [lu'tsɛrn] Lucerne

Maas [maːs]: *die* ~ the Meuse, the Maas
Madrid [ma'drɪt] Madrid
Mahler ['maːlɐ] *Austrian composer*
Mailand ['maɪlant] Milan
Main [maɪn]: *der* ~ *(German river)*
Mainz [maɪnts] *German city*
Mann [man] *name of three German authors*
Marokko [ma'rɔko] Morocco
Matterhorn ['matɐhɔrn]: *das* ~ *(Swiss mountain)*
Meißen ['maɪsən] Meissen
Memel ['meːməl]: *die* ~ *(frontier river in East Prussia)*
Menzel ['mɛntsəl] *German painter*
Mexiko ['mɛksiko] Mexico
Mies van der Rohe ['miːs fan deːɐ 'roːə] *German architect*
Mittelmeer ['mɪtəlmeːɐ]: *das* ~ the Mediterranean (Sea)
Moldau ['mɔldaʊ]: *die* ~ the Vltava; HIST the Moldau *(Bohemian river)*
Mörike ['møːrɪkə] *German poet*
Mosel ['moːzəl]: *die* ~ the Moselle
Mössbauer ['mœsbaʊɐ] *German physicist*
Moskau ['mɔskaʊ] Moscow
Mozart ['moːtsart] *Austrian composer*
München ['mʏnçən] Munich

Neapel [ne'aːpəl] Naples
Neiße ['naɪsə]: *die* ~ *(German river)*
Neufundland [nɔy'fʊntlant] Newfoundland
Neuseeland [nɔy'zeːlant] New Zealand
Niederlande ['niːdɐlandə]: *die* ~ *pl* the Netherlands
Nietzsche ['niːtʃə] *German philosopher*
Nil [niːl]: *der* ~ the Nile
Nordamerika ['nɔrt'ʔa'meːrika] North America
Nordsee ['nɔrtzeː]: *die* ~ the North Sea
Normandie [nɔrman'diː]: *die* ~ Normandy
Norwegen ['nɔrveːgən] Norway
Nürnberg ['nʏrnbɛrk] Nuremberg

Oder ['oːdɐ]: *die* ~ *(German river)*
Orff [ɔrf] *German composer*

Oslo ['ɔslo] Oslo
Ostende [ɔst'ʔɛndə] Ostend
Österreich ['øːstəraɪç] Austria
Ostsee ['ɔstzeː]: *die* ~ the Baltic (Sea)

Palästina [palɛs'tiːna] Palestine
Paris [pa'riːs] Paris
Pfalz [pfalts]: *die* ~ the Palatinate
Philippinen [fɪlɪ'piːnən]: *die* ~ *pl* the Philippines
Planck [plaŋk] *German physicist*
Polen ['poːlən] Poland
Porsche ['pɔrʃə] *German inventor*
Portugal ['pɔrtugal] Portugal
Prag [praːk] Prague
Preußen ['prɔysən] HIST Prussia
Pyrenäen [pyre'nɛːən]: *die* ~ *pl* the Pyrenees

Rhein [raɪn]: *der* ~ the Rhine
Rilke ['rɪlkə] *Austrian poet*
Rom [roːm] Rome
Röntgen ['rœntgən] *German physicist*
Ruhr [ruːr]: *die* ~ *(German river)*; **Ruhrgebiet** ['ruːrgəbiːt]: *das* ~ *(industrial center of Germany)*
Rumänien [ru'mɛːnjən] Rumania, Ro(u)mania
Russland ['rʊslant] Russia

Saale ['zaːlə]: *die* ~ *(German river)*
Saar [zaːr]: *die* ~ *(affluent of the Moselle)*
Salzburg ['zaltsbʊrk] *Austrian city*
Schiller ['ʃɪlɐ] *German poet*
Schönberg ['ʃøːnbɛrk] *Austrian composer*
Schottland ['ʃɔtlant] Scotland
Schubert ['ʃuːbɐt] *Austrian composer*
Schumann ['ʃuːman] *German composer*
Schwaben ['ʃvaːbən] Swabia
Schwarzwald ['ʃvartsvalt]: *der* ~ the Black Forest
Schweden ['ʃveːdən] Sweden
Schweiz [ʃvaɪts]: *die* ~ Switzerland
Sibirien [zi'biːrjən] Siberia
Siemens ['ziːməns] *German inventor*
Sizilien [zi'tsiːljən] Sicily
Skandinavien [skandi'naːvjən] Scandinavia
Slowakei [slova'kaɪ]: *die* ~ Slovakia
Sofia ['zɔfja] Sofia
Spanien ['ʃpaːnjən] Spain
Spitzweg ['ʃpɪtsveːk] *German painter*

Spranger [ˈʃpraŋɐ] *German philosopher*
Stifter [ˈʃtɪftɐ] *Austrian author*
Stockholm [ˈʃtɔkhɔlm] Stockholm
Storm [ʃtɔrm] *German poet*
Straßburg [ˈʃtraːsbʊrk] Strasbourg
Strauß [ʃtraʊs] *Austrian composer*
Strauss [ʃtraʊs] *German composer*
Südamerika [ˈzyːtʔaˈmeːrika] South America
Syrien [ˈzyːrjən] Syria

Themse [ˈtɛmzə]: *die* ~ the Thames
Tirol [tiˈroːl] (the) Tyrol
Tschechien [ˈtʃɛçjən] Czech Republic
Türkei [tʏrˈkaɪ]: *die* ~ Turkey

Ungarn [ˈʊŋgarn] Hungary
Ural [uˈraːl]: *der* ~ the Urals

Venedig [veˈneːdɪç] Venice
Vereinigte Staaten (von Amerika)
[fɛrˈʔaɪnɪçtə ˈʃtaːtən (fɔn aˈmeːrika)]: *die Vereinigten Staaten (von Amerika)* the United States (of America)
Vierwaldstätter See [fiːɐˈvaltʃtɛtɐ ˈzeː]: *der* ~ Lake Lucerne

Wagner [ˈvaːgnɐ] *German composer*
Wankel [ˈvaŋkəl] *German inventor*
Warschau [ˈvarʃaʊ] Warsaw
Weichsel [ˈvaɪksəl]: *die* ~ the Vistula
Weiß [vaɪs] *German dramatist*
Werfel [ˈvɛrfəl] *Austrian author*
Weser [ˈveːzɐ]: *die* ~ (*German river*)
Wien [viːn] Vienna
Wiesbaden [ˈviːsbaːdən] German city

Zuckmayer [ˈtsʊkmaɪɐ] *German dramatist*
Zweig [tsvaɪk] *Austrian author*
Zürich [ˈtsyːrɪç] Zurich
Zypern [ˈtsyːpɐn] Cyprus

German Abbreviations

Abb. *Abbildung* illustration
Abf. *Abfahrt* departure, ABBR dep.
Abt. *Abteilung* department, ABBR dept.
a. D. *außer Dienst* retired
ADAC *Allgemeiner Deutscher Automobil-Club* General German Automobile Association
AG *Aktiengesellschaft* (stock) corporation, joint-stock company
allg. *allgemein* general
Ank. *Ankunft* arrival
atü *Atmosphärenüberdruck* atmospheric excess pressure

Bd. *Band* volume, ABBR vol.; **Bde.** *Bände* volumes, ABBR vols.
Betr. *Betreff, betrifft letter* : subject, re
BRD *Bundesrepublik Deutschland* Federal Republic of Germany

CDU *Christlich-Demokratische Union* Christian Democratic Union
CSU *Christlich-Soziale Union* Christian Social Union

DB *Deutsche Bundesbahn* German Federal Railway
DDR HIST *Deutsche Demokratische Republik* German Democratic Republic
DGB *Deutscher Gewerkschaftsbund* Federation of German Trade Unions
d. h. *das heißt* that is, ABBR i. e.
DIN *Deutsche Industrie-Norm(en)* German Industrial Standards
DM *Deutsche Mark* German Mark(s)
dpa *Deutsche Presse-Agentur* German Press Agency
Dr. *Doktor* Doctor, ABBR Dr.
DRK *Deutsches Rotes Kreuz* German Red Cross

EDV *Elektronische Datenverarbeitung* electronic data processing, ABBR EDP
EG *Europäische Gemeinschaft* European Community, ABBR EC

EM *Europameisterschaft* European championship(s)
e. V. *eingetragener Verein* registered association, incorporated, ABBR inc.

FDP *Freie Demokratische Partei* Liberal Democratic Party
Forts. *Fortsetzung* continuation

geb. *geboren* born; *geborene ...* née; *gebunden* bound
Ges. *Gesellschaft* association, company; society
gez. *gezeichnet* signed, ABBR sgd
GmbH *Gesellschaft mit beschränkter Haftung* private limited liability company

h. c. *honoris causa* = ehrenhalber; *academic title* : honorary
Hrsg. *Herausgeber* editor, ABBR ed.

i. A. *im Auftrage* for, by order, under instruction
Ing. *Ingenieur* engineer
Inh. *Inhaber* proprietor
inkl. *inklusive, einschließlich* inclusive
'Interpol *Internationale Kriminalpolizeiliche Organisation* International Criminal Police Commission
IOK *Internationales Olympisches Komitee* International Olympic Committee, ABBR IOC
ISBN *Internationale Standardbuchnummer* international standard book number, ABBR ISBN
i. V. *in Vertretung* by proxy, as a substitute

jr., jun. *junior, der Jüngere* junior ABBR jr, jun.

Kat *Katalysator* catalytic converter, catalyst, ABBR cat.
Kfm. *Kaufmann* merchant
Kfz. *Kraftfahrzeug* motor vehicle

KG *Kommanditgesellschaft* limited partnership

Kl. *Klasse* class; *school:* form

'Kripo *Kriminalpolizei* Criminal Investigation Department, ABBR CID

Kto. *Konto* account, ABBR a/c

lfd. *laufend* current, running

Lfg., Lfrg. *Lieferung* delivery; instal(l)-ment, part

Lit *Literatur* literature

Lkw, LKW *Lastkraftwagen* truck, lorry

lt. *laut* according to

MdB *Mitglied des Bundestages* Member of the Bundestag

MEZ *mitteleuropäische Zeit* Central European Time

MS, Ms. *Manuskript* manuscript, ABBR MS, ms.

mtl. *monatlich* monthly

n. Chr. *nach Christus* after Christ, ABBR AD

No., Nr. *Numero, Nummer* number, ABBR No., no

NS *Nachschrift* postscript, ABBR PS

o. B. *ohne Befund* MED without findings

OEZ *osteuropäische Zeit* Eastern European Time, ABBR EET

PDS *Partei des Demokratischen Sozialismus* Party of Democratic Socialism

Pf *Pfennig* *German coin :* pfennig

Pfd. *Pfund* *German weight :* pound

PKW, Pkw *Personenkraftwagen* car

PLZ *Postleitzahl* zip code, *Br* postcode

Prof. *Professor* professor

PS *Pferdestärke(n)* horse-power, ABBR HP, h.p.; *postscriptum, Nachschrift* postscript, ABBR PS

Rel. *Religion* religion

S. *Seite* page

s. *siehe* see, ABBR v., vid. (= vide)

Sa. *Summa, Summe* sum, total

sen. *senior, der Ältere* senior

s. o. *siehe oben* see above

sog. *so genannt* so-called

SPD *Sozialdemokratische Partei Deutschlands* Social Democratic Party of Germany

St. *Stück* piece; *Sankt* Saint

Std. *Stunde* hour, ABBR h

Str. *Straße* street, ABBR St.

StVO *Straßenverkehrsordnung* (road) traffic regulations, *in GB :* Highway Code

s. u. *siehe unten* see below

tägl. *täglich* daily, per day

Tel. *Telefon* telephone; *Telegramm* wire, cable

TH *Technische Hochschule* college *or* institute of technology

TU *Technische Universität* technical university; college *or* institute of technology

TÜV *Technischer Überwachungs-Verein* safety standards authority

u. a. *und andere(s)* and others; *unter anderem or anderen* among other things, inter alia

UKW *Ultrakurzwelle* ultra-short wave, very high frequency, ABBR VHF

V *Volt* volt; *Volumen* volume

v. Chr. *vor Christus* before Christ, ABBR BC

vgl. *vergleiche* confer, ABBR cf.

v. H. *vom Hundert* per cent

v. T. *vom Tausend* per thousand

VW *Volkswagen* Volkswagen, People's Car

WAA *Wiederaufbereitungsanlage* reprocessing plant

WEZ *westeuropäische Zeit* Greenwich Mean Time, ABBR GMT

WG *Wohngemeinschaft* flat share, flat sharing (community)

WM *Weltmeisterschaft* world championship(s); *soccer:* World Cup

z. B. *zum Beispiel* for instance, ABBR e.g.

z. H(d). *zu Händen* attention of, to be delivered to, care of, ABBR c/o

z. T. *zum Teil* partly

zus. *zusammen* together

z. Z(t). *zur Zeit* at the time, at present, for the time being

am Mittwoch um
8 uhr in der Therese
Paulo .